WORLD ENCYCLOPEDIA OF POLITICAL SYSTEMS & PARTIES

Second Edition

Volume II

Madagascar—Zimbabwe

and Smaller Countries and Microstates

WORLD ENCYCLOPEDIA OF POLITICAL SYSTEMS & PARTIES

Second Edition

Volume II

Madagascar—Zimbabwe

and Smaller Countries and Microstates

Edited by

George E. Delury

Second Edition Supervised by
Marc Aronson

Facts On File Publications
New York, New York • Oxford, England

World Encyclopedia of
Political Systems & Parties
Second Edition

by George E. Delury

Published by Facts On File, Inc. 460 Park Avenue South, New York, N.Y. 10016 and Facts On File, Ltd., Collins Street, Oxford, England 0X4 1XJ

Library of Congress Cataloging-in-Publication Data

World Encyclopedia of political systems & parties.

Includes bibliographies and index.
Contents: v. 1. Afghanistan-Luxembourg

1. Political parties—Handbooks, manuals, etc.
2. Comparative government—Handbooks, manuals, etc.
I. Delury, George E.   II. Facts on File, Inc.
JF2011.w67 1987   324.2'02'02   86-29097
ISBN 0-8160-1539-2 (set)
ISBN 0-8160-1564-3 (v. 1)
ISBN 0-8160-1565-1 (v. 2)

WORLD ENCYCLOPEDIA OF POLITICAL SYSTEMS & PARTIES

Second Edition

Volume II

Madagascar—Zimbabwe

and Smaller Countries and Microstates

DEMOCRATIC REPUBLIC OF MADAGASCAR
(République Démocratique de Madagascar [French]; Repoblika Demokratika Madagasikara [Malagasy])

by Philip M. Allen, Ph.D.

The System of Government

Madagascar, a sparsely populated island country of nearly ten million people in the western Indian Ocean, has a strong presidential system which relies on informal compromises and accommodations among ethnic, economic, and bureaucratic interests. These interests are largely represented by several parties which make their influence felt more in the bureaucracy and state corporations than in the legislature.

The French conquest of the island in 1895 imposed a regime of mercantile exploitation on what had been a relatively well-developed centralized monarchy dominated by the Merina aristocracy of the island's central plateau. As the Malagasy Republic, the island became autonomous within the French Community in 1958. Under the independent First Republic, led by President Philibert Tsiranana from 1960 to 1972, the Merina continued to control intellectual and professional life, the civil service, and those sectors of commerce not monopolized by French companies and their resident Indian and Chinese partners. Both the French and Tsiranana, however, favored the various coastal ethnic groups in a divide-and-rule policy designed to deprive the Merina of significant political power.

In 1972, popular unrest forced Tsiranana to turn over the government to his army commander in chief who supported a relatively peaceful but revolutionary nationalist resurgence, hitherto associated with the Merina middle class. The complex French colonial fabric of banking, plantation agriculture, oligopolist trade, and controlled industrial projects was gradually abolished; the French military presence on the island was ended; and the country adopted a conscientiously nonaligned foreign policy.

While the break with France was never as complete as rhetoric made it seem, Madagascar began to develop a bureaucratic structure of state corporations and interlocking political institutions dominated by a congeries of Malagasy elites who agreed with one another only on the nationalist purpose of the program. By mid-1983, the national system had evolved into a centralized socialist state which controlled 70 percent of the economy and which adopted ideological cues from the Soviet Union and North Korea. This socialist orientation has since been substantially weakened as the system responds to market liberalization principles urged by the International Monetary Fund, the World Bank, and Madagascar's Western creditors, all of them seeking to stabilize a debt-ridden, virtually paralyzed economy.

Executive

Following a three-year transition in which three military chiefs of state sought to implement the revolutionary idea of 1972 without sacrificing continuity, the Second Republic took shape in a new constitution submitted to referendum on December 21, 1975. An executive president, elected by direct universal suffrage for a seven-year term, governs through a Supreme Council of the Revolution (CSR); two-thirds of the twenty-one Council members are appointed by the president, who chairs its sessions and approves the list of remaining members submitted to him by the legislature. The president also appoints his prime minister and endorses the list of government ministers who carry out CSR policy.

Having served the first three years of the revolution as foreign minister and leader of its so-called radical wing, Didier Ratsiraka, a navy captain, was named chief of state by the CSR on June 15, 1975, and was subsequently confirmed by 92 percent of the voters in a referendum.

Ratsiraka was reelected to a seven-year term in November 1982. He has since been promoted to Admiral of the Fleet, although Madagascar has virtually no navy, and has used his office, his command of ideology, and his claims to international status to personalize presidential authority.

Ratsiraka does not have a popular power base. His political position depends in part on his capacity to manipulate a fractious coalition of elites called the National Front for the Defense of the Revolution (FNDR). He reshuffles his CSR and cabinet constantly, sometimes for ideological purposes, more often, as he put it in February 1985, as a "dribbling" tactic, going left or right to get what he wants. Policy formation consists of compromises between the practical and ideological requirements of nationalist interests and the interests of bureaucratic and business classes still tied to French and other international arrangements, many of them necessary. France remains Madagascar's principal trade partner and source of capital. Japan, a Western consortium of lenders and donors, Algeria, and the socialist powers provide capital, technology, and other complementary assets.

Secluded in his fortified residence and protected by security agencies and their secret police, the president regularly denounces domestic and foreign conspiracies against him. In January 1982, true to the typical Malagasy blend of fact, reticence, and imagination, the president's brother-in-law, commander of one of the presidential security services, reported the discovery and abortion of a plot against Ratsiraka that allegedly involved foreign mercenaries, local politicians, and a Catholic priest. Close Malagasy affinities with the Seychelles archipelago suggested to the government that the plot was somehow related to the commando team that had failed to overthrow the Seychelles government the previous November. At the same time, Ratsiraka is responsible for Madagascar's assertion of its African and Indian Ocean affinities and has developed openings to the Soviet Union, North Korea, Cuba, and other socialist states without entirely sacrificing French interests in the island.

Legislature

The 137-seat National People's Assembly (ANP) is renewed every five years by direct suffrage, although the most recent elections were postponed from June 1982 until August 1983 on financial pretexts that served to shield the difficult 1982 presidential reelection from the recriminations of candidates in a concurrent legislative campaign. Only parties sanctioned for ideological compatibility with the president may present candidates, and Ratsiraka's AREMA party holds 115 of the seats. The legislature has limited powers, meeting for only four months in the year, and requiring a two-thirds majority to overturn a government budgetary or other proposal. Although the body is relegated to an essentially rhetorical utility in the complex Malagasy system, its debates have occasionally dramatized national problems and executive deficiencies. In June 1981 and May 1982, parliamentary leaders called general attention to inefficiencies and corruption in public services, managing even to penetrate the otherwise suffocated national press.

Judiciary

Civil and criminal procedures in Madagascar conform largely to French legal codes and jurisprudence; the High Constitutional Court determines the constitutionality of laws, electoral disputes, and conflicts between central and local authorities. High Constitutional Court judges are elected by the National Assembly, but most appeals to the court must first be approved by the president. A parallel system of courts, which makes its own rules, handles political and security cases, using the several intelligence agencies and the gendarmerie for enforcement. Madagascar has encountered steady criticism in international human rights forums for its lengthy detention periods, the torpor of its military-trial system, verdicts apparently issued for reasons of expediency rather than justice, and alleged torture of political prisoners.

Regional & Local Government

Coordination between the central authority and local populations has eluded all regimes in this large island of relatively isolated and autonomous regions linked only by extraordinarily deficient road, rail, air, and radio ties. The First Republic had sought to knit the provinces to the capital, Antananarivo, by a dominant political party network that permitted mandarinates for local leaders in alliance with overseas French and local Chinese and Indian entrepreneurs. The inefficacy of this structure became increasingly apparent through the 1960s, inviting a dramatic peasant revolt in

1971 and the alliance of urban intellectuals and labor which brought down the Tsiranana government a year later.

Even before the accession of Ratsiraka in 1975, the revolutionary solution for Madagascar's structural incoherence took the form of a revival of the *fokonolona* (village council) system implemented by the Merina monarchy of the nineteenth century. Genuine powers of taxation, public borrowing, rural production and marketing control, police and public services are bestowed on 11,400 village and urban-district councils (*fokontany*) of directly elected officials. The councils are grouped into a hierarchical structure of representative bodies—*firaisana* or cantons, *fivondrono* which correspond to prefectures, and six *faritany* or provinces. In theory, this decentralized system replaces the old apparatus of appointed prefects and sub-prefects who supervised elected communal officials. In actuality, the president's AREMA party, holds 89.5 percent of the 73,000 electoral positions at the several levels of local government, and central policies are conveyed from national party headquarters through these channels to the putatively autonomous local apparatus. Central government technical expertise, attached to the local economic committees (*vatoeka*), also enforces a Malagasy version of "democratic centralism."

Marketing inefficiencies, profiteering, and black market operations have contaminated the division of national and local responsibilities and diminished popular participation. In early January 1982, voters in Antsiranana province (formerly Diego-Suarez) voted to recall the *faritany* chief and seven of nine *fivondrono* presidents because of corruption and malfeasance. Refusal by the Interior Ministry to honor this constitutional recourse led to violent confrontations between police and rioting citizens in several northern towns.

The Electoral System

Political participation revived in 1976 after four years of transitional military rule. Respecting the vast diversity of Malagasy loyalties—regional, ethnic, and class—Ratsiraka restricted participation only by requiring overt acceptance of his generally socialist and anti-imperialist program. Elections for legislative and local government representation took place serially during 1983 and 1984, with the traditionally acquiescent electorate (universally en-franchised at eighteen years of age) supporting candidates proposed by central authority. Participation ranges from 72 percent to the government's claim of 88 percent of a generally apathetic electorate. With 60 percent illiteracy, the electorate chooses ballots marked by party symbols and colors.

The Party System

Malagasy parties first appeared in preparation for the 1958 elections. Most were formed as affiliates of mother parties in France. Chief among these was the *Parti Social Démocrate* (PSD) of Philibert Tsiranana, the first president of Madagascar. The primary Malagasy party without immediate ties to France was the Congress Party for the Independence of Madagascar (AKFM), a coalition of several pro-independence groups.

In 1976, authorized political parties were grouped for purposes of national unity into a loose National Front for the Defense of the Revolution (FNDR). Each party may share power within the CSR and other institutions of state. In practice, however, the vast divergence between interests and personalities has tended to neutralize the FNDR as a genuine political body. These conflicts have also blocked Ratsiraka's avowed effort to establish a one-party state. Two parties (National Movement for the Independence of Madagascar and Militants for Power to the People) have entered and left the Front on several occasions, and Ratsiraka has usually had to govern through his own coterie of loyal Advance Guard of the Malagasy Revolution adherents.

Advance Guard of the Malagasy Revolution
(*Avant-Garde de la Révolution Malagasy;* AREMA)

AREMA holds 115 of the 137 National Assembly seats and almost 90 percent of local elected offices. A personal creation of President Ratsiraka, AREMA is far from a monolithic power bloc. It includes a strong militant wing, cutting across age and geographical lines, with ideological influence from North Korea and other socialist models. However, the party also contains prominent representatives of the Merina bourgeoisie and other more "pragmatic" (albeit nationalistic) interests, as well as sheer opportunists and unreconstructed Social Democrats from the Tsiranana First Republic. Champions of each faction shuttle in and out of government, as determined by the president's fluctuating needs to maintain personal control, to satisfy his international patrons, and to alternate ideological with "pragmatic" expedients. The party maintains affiliates in youth and women's groups and in labor affairs.

Congress Party for the Independence of Madagascar
(Antokon'ny Kongresy ho'any Fahaleovantenan'i Madagasikara; AKFM)

The AKFM was formed in 1958 to campaign for outright independence, rather than the French Community solution proposed in General De Gaulle's Fifth Republic constitution. It lost that vote, but remained as the principal opposition party in the First Republic, usually holding three seats in the old National Assembly, as well as the city administration of the capital, Antananarivo. Its leader since 1958, Pastor Richard Andriamanjato, has been repeatedly reelected as mayor of the capital. Still limited primarily to the Merina intellectual and professional elite of the city, the AKFM nevertheless defines itself as a "scientific socialist" party of Soviet inspiration, which earns the antagonism of large numbers of the population opposed to the Merina or the Soviet features. Where it has appeal, the party is well organized, and its veteran secretary general, Gisèle Rabesahala, has been minister of culture for over a decade. However, its ANP representation fell from 16 in the 1977 to nine in the 1983 elections (with 8.8 percent of the vote).

Militants for Power to the People
((Mpitolona ho an'ny Fanjakan'ny Madinika; MFM)

The MFM formed as a coalition of labor, unemployed urban workers, students, and intellectuals in the aftermath of the anti-Tsiranana street revolts of 1972. The party's influence remains restricted to the capital, but it was accused of successful manipulation in the Antsiranana recall vote in early 1982.

The MFM hesitated to join the FNDR, but having done so in 1977 it continues to oppose the dominance of the AREMA and its tendency to favor the elites of both the coast and the Merina. Alleging discrimination in earlier local balloting, the MFM refused to contest the 1977 elections. Its leader, sociologist Manandafy Rakotonirina, spent periods of 1973 and 1976 in prison for his disputes with the prevailing power.

National Movement for the Independence of Madagascar
(Mouvement National pour l'Indépendence de Madagascar; MONIMA)

MONIMA has been a regional-based advocate for the interests of the rural south since the late 1950s and has added strength in Antananarivo. Its leader, Monja Jaona, has been an outspoken critic of both republics and has suffered persecution from both sources of authority. The aged (eighty-three years or more) but charismatic Monja, who is held responsible for the peasant jacqueries of 1971, broke from the FNDR in 1977 and boycotted the elections of that year. It rejoined the FNDR in 1981, but quarrelled again with Ratsiraka in mid-1982 over government control of agricultural production and marketing. Monja thereupon opposed Ratsiraka in the 1982 presidential reelection, winning over 20 percent of the national vote (with 50 percent in the capital), and was re-arrested for calling the elections fraudulent. His party then split into factions loyal to each of the two leaders. Even so, in 1983 Monja managed to win one of the two ANP seats captured by his party in its first legislative contest.

People's Movement for National Unity
(Vonjy Iray Tsy Mivaky)

Vonjy grew out of the old Tsiranana PSD, which had survived the 1972 revolution as the Malagasy Socialist Union, headed until 1976 by Tsiranana's former vice president, André Resampa. The Vonjy held seven seats in both the 1977 and 1983 Assemblies. It appeals to the more conservative cultural traditions of the island's west coast. Its leader, Dr. Marojaima (Jerome) Razanabahiny, and its affiliated press are under constant official scrutiny for their dissent.

Union of Christian Democrats (*Union des Démocrates-Chrétiens;* UDECMA)

UDECMA is a tiny party of the Catholic proletariat along the east coast. It held two ANP seats after 1977, but lost them in 1983. UDECMA is led by Norbert Randriamorasata.

Other Political Forces

Military

The army and gendarmerie have been politicized and given important roles in national policymaking. A Military Development Committee of 55 members acts as a watchdog agency of the CSR, and the enlarged, well-trained army (19,555, including 8,000 gendarmes and 1,000 presidential guards) serves in development projects. Internal security outside Antananarivo is the responsibility of the gendarmerie, which has clashed with citizens' groups on a number of occasions, most recently in a tragic "massacre" of over a hundred villagers in the south who had been mistaken for cattle rustlers. Soviets, North Koreans, East Germans, and Cubans "advise" the armed forces closely, but Ratsiraka denied United States press reports in 1984 of 3,000 Soviet advisors. He is said to be seeking French replacements for some of the Socialist mentors.

Students and Youth Groups

The number of university students quadrupled to 15,000 in the decade after 1972, and student restiveness remains troublesome for the regime. Student-led riots in February 1981 touched off demonstrations by unemployed and other discontents, threatening a repetition of the movement that toppled Tsiranana's regime in 1972. Leaders of the riots were imprisoned until late June of 1982. Even more violent were street combats in December 1984 and August

1985, pitting organized gangs (some of them, outlawed in 1984, identified as enthusiasts of Kung Fu) against security forces and the *Tanora Tonga Saina* (Youth Meeting Responsibilities, TTS), an AREMA-inspired militia of commandos reminiscent of Haiti's *tonton macoutes.* In a major purge of the national security apparatus following the December 1984 riots in which at least fifty died, one of the distinguished heads to fall was that of Col. Bienaimé Ravelison Mahasampa, the president's brother-in-law and once one of the most powerful, if shadowy, figures of his regime.

Ethnic Groups

Madagascar's ethnic groups do not differ greatly in either language or culture. They are distinguished rather by strong clan loyalties and relative isolation from each other. The Merina, nearly twice as numerous as any of the other groups, are dominant both culturally and economically, a position that makes them suspect in the eyes of the rest of the population. The Merina intellectuals tend to support the MFM, while the business and landholding elite support the AKFM. The Betsileo, the most Indonesian of all the remaining groups, live on the plateau south of the Merina and do not favor one party. Among the more African groups, the Betsimisaraka, who live in the Tamatave area, support AREMA and the UDECMA, while the Tsimihety of the northwest support both *Vonjy* and AREMA. The Sakalawa of the west coast support MONIMA and AREMA, and the Antandroy in the far south support MONIMA. These and the other ethnic groups play some role as such in the political system, but class and economic interests as well as party loyalties cut across ethnic group lines. Reopening part of the economy to market competition since 1983 has helped restore pre-revolutionary status enjoyed by entrepreneurial Chinese and Indian Muslim communities as well as middle-class Merina.

Opposition and Criticism

Remnants of the former regime and some of their dispossessed French sympathizers have gathered around the figure of André Resampa in exile. Resampa and other social democrats had been arrested for implication in the assassination of former president Richard Ratsimandrava in February 1975, but were subsequently acquitted and allowed to go to France. The Roman Catholic hierarchy, always politicized in Madagascar, has been the most outspoken domestic critic of the regime since 1981, mainly through pastoral letters denouncing electoral fraud, repression of opponents, personal monopoly of power, censorship, mendacity, false praise and state exploitation of people whom it exists to serve. Ratsiraka, himself a practicing Catholic, publicly "confessed" in January 1985 that he had been unable thus far to convert the Malagasy personality to the values of socialism.

National Prospects

For the time being, Ratsiraka seeks to balance his revolutionary strategy and nonaligned foreign policy against urgent needs for balance of payments support and for productive capital, which has not appeared in the domestic economy. He will probably neutralize the challenge to his leadership from the right. Nevertheless, failure to increase production, assure orderly distribution of goods and services, and knit the sprawling social fabric into harmony has encouraged rebelliousness in the population. Urban vandalism expands frequently into mortal riot; peasant discontent expresses itself in criminal truculence and resistance to production exhortations; and corruption and mismanagement are notorious in a swollen, inert bureaucracy, despite tight security controls and press censorship.

Further Reading

(to appear): Allen, Philip M., *Madagascar*. Nations of Contemporary Africa series. Boulder, Colorado: Westview Press, scheduled 1987.

DeBarrin, Jacques. "Madagascar: la révolution en panne," series in *Le Monde*, 21, 22, 23 March 1985.

Deschamps, Hubert.*Madagascar. Que sais-je?* No. 529. Paris: Presses Universitaires de France, 1976.

Heseltine, Nigel. *Madagascar*. New York: Praeger, 1971.

Legum, Colin, ed. *Africa Contemporary Record*. London and New York: Holmes and Meier, annual.

Leymarie, Philippe. "Madagascar: la course de vitesse des socialistes." *Le Monde Diplomatique*, No. 340, July 1982.

REPUBLIC OF MALAWI

by Timothy Dunmore, Ph.D. revised by Peter 'Molotsi, Ph.D.

The System of Government

Malawi, a country of some six million people, is a single-party republic and a unitary state. It was formerly the British protectorate of Nyasaland. In 1953 Malawi became part of the British-ruled Federation of Rhodesia (the present Zimbabwe and Zambia) and Nyasaland. After a period of active native opposition to both the federation and the colonial power, the former was dissolved in December 1963. Six months later the independent state of Malawi was created.

In 1966, Malawi became a republic under a constitution that remains in effect. The first and current president of Malawi is Dr. Hastings Kamuzu Banda. Both constitutionally and in practice the political system is dominated by Banda and his Malawi Congress Party (MCP).

Executive

The executive branch consists of a president and a cabinet. The president is both head of state and head of the government. He appoints all the members of the cabinet, and they are responsible directly to him rather than to the legislature. In 1985, Banda was also minister of external affairs, agriculture and natural resources, justice, and works and supplies. He appoints senior civil servants and leading officers in the armed forces. The cabinet, the civil service, and the army do not present any real challenge to President Banda's position. He dominates the legislature through the MCP of which he is president. In addition, the president has an unlimited right to declare a state of emergency.

In spite of his advanced age (eighty) and his consequently increased reliance on his senior advisers, the president still determines the basic lines of Malawi government policy, particularly with regard to its most powerful neighbor, South Africa. The only active opposition to Banda comes from political organizations in exile.

According to the constitution, the president is directly elected every five years. However, in 1971 Banda was elected president for life by the people of Malawi. On his death, he is to be succeeded by a three-man Presidential Council chaired by the head of the ruling Malawi Congress Party and staffed by two members of the cabinet.

Legislature

The National Assembly is a single chamber consisting of up to 124 members, every member belongs to the Malawi Congress Party. One hundred and one members are elected from approximately equal electoral districts. In addition to the elected members, the constitution allows the president to nominate up to fifteen people to the Assembly. Furthermore, he can participate in Assembly debates whenever he wishes. The president can also veto any bill passed by the Assembly. In the unlikely event of the legislature repassing the same bill within a six-month period, the president is supposed to call new elections. Both constitutionally and in view of the party system, the legislature is dominated by the executive in Malawi. Its real powers are consultative and advisory rather than legislative.

The normal parliamentary term is five years, although the president may dissolve the Assembly before that time, as he did in 1978 after only a two-year term.

Judiciary

Formally, the highest court in Malawi is the Supreme Court of Appeal which hears appeals against decisions of the High Court. It is the High Court, however, that makes the most important judicial decisions in all civil and criminal matters. It is headed by the chief justice, who is a presidential appointee. It does not challenge the executive's powers or decisions. Traditional courts were established in 1970 and are presided over by chiefs.

Regional & Local Government

Malawi is divided into three major areas, the Southern, the Central, and the Northern regions. Each is represented in the national cabinet by an appointed regional minister. The regions in turn are divided into a total of twenty-four districts, the cities of Blantyre and Lilongue, and six towns. While local councils are elected, all are supervised by the Ministry of Local Government, which also controls the allocations of money to all levels.

The Electoral System

Deputies to the National Assembly are directly elected in single-member districts. The ballot is secret, although a high level of illiteracy requires voters to show their preferences by placing voting slips in a separate box for each candidate.

The 1971 and 1976 elections were uncontested, but in 1978 forty-seven of the eighty-seven electoral districts were contested by two or three candidates; candidates in the other forty were returned unopposed. All candidates were from the MCP, and all were personally approved by the president. Candidates were not allowed to campaign or to spend any money for political purposes. In contested constituencies, all the candidates were presented to the voters at the same mass meeting. The only speeches were made by Banda himself.

No less than thirty-one sitting MPs were defeated, including two cabinet ministers. However, President Banda had previously announced that he would use the elections to reshuffle his cabinet and expressed himself content at the defeat of so many MPs. Malawi's first experiment at single-party electoral competition was skeptically regarded by Western journalists at the time, but it did provide Malawi citizens with something of a choice among personalities, although not among policies.

General elections were held in June 1983, proceeding calmly despite political confusion surrounding the mysterious death of four cabinet ministers. Banda retained the four key posts in the cabinet, thereby reaffirming his power. As in 1978, the elections were open only to MCP candidates, all of whom were approved by the president. Of the 101 elective seats, seventy-five were contested by up to five candidates

each, while twenty-one candidates were elected unopposed.

Five seats remained unfilled, officially because none of the candidates for these seats could pass the required English language proficiency test. Banda appointed a number of additional members to the National Assembly in 1983 and 1984, briging its total membership to 124 in 1984. The five vacant seats were to remain empty until by-elections were held.

Malawi Congress Party (MCP)

History

The MCP was established in 1959 under Banda's leadership to fight for the end of the federation with Rhodesia and for independence from British colonial rule. The party's position benefited from Banda's personal success in securing independence and from his successful program of economic development. Since 1965, the only opposition to the MCP has come from small minorities within the country and from former cabinet ministers in exile.

Organization

The party is more of an organization for promoting support for the regime than a forum for debating policy issues. Officially, party policy is made by the annual party convention which is composed of party officials from national, regional, and district levels; members of Parliament; some traditional chiefs; chairmen of the district councils; and representatives of other organizations, such as the League of Malawi Youth and the League of Malawi Women. In practice, the convention's role is at best advisory and at worst merely ceremonial. In fact, the party is organized along democratic-centralist lines, with all appointments and elections controlled by Banda.

Policy

The policy of the MCP is basically that of Banda. In foreign affairs, Malawi is distinguished from other black African states by its willingness to remain on good terms with South Africa. Only in 1975, when a black government came to power in Mozambique, did Banda temporarily modify his friendship with Pretoria.

Even then, the modification lasted less than two years.

MCP policy toward South Africa is based primarily on economic necessity. The Malawi economy relies heavily on the earnings of its citizens—more than 100,000—who work in South Africa. Malawi's army also depends heavily on South Africa for its arms. Opposition to Malawi's economic and military reliance on South Africa has come mainly from outside rather than inside Malawi.

Malawi joined the Southern Africa Development Co-ordination Conference (SADCC) in 1980. This grouping is intended to lessen the members' economic dependence on South Africa.

Internally, Banda has sought to encourage the growth of private industry, especially agriculture, by providing state financing and advice to farmers and industrialists through the Malawi Development Corporation.

Membership

All Malawi adults are members of the MCP, but few take an active part in it.

Financing

Much of the party's income appears to come from the government itself.

Leadership

Dick Tennyson Matenje became secretary general of the party in January 1982, replacing Elson Bakili Muluzi, who had been regarded as Banda's most likely successor. Officially, Muluzi resigned for "personal reasons." Banda (born 1906) is president of the party, but takes little direct part in running it.

In 1983, Matenje was reported to be locked in a power struggle for succession with John Tembo, governor of the Reserve Bank. However, on May 19, 1983 Matenje, together with three other senior politicians, was reported killed in a car accident. Robson W. Chirwa, no relation of Orton Chirwa, was appointed a caretaker administrative secretary. He also serves as a minister without portfolio. He has no power and very little influence in both the government and the MCP.

In early April 1985, Banda dissolved his cabinet and temporarily took over all the posts himself, giving no explanation for his action. His new cabinet largely consisted of the same politicians appointed to new posts. The most important change in the new cabinet was the appointment of Chakakala Chaziya (previously the finance minister) as governor of the Reserve Bank, replacing Tembo. It was initially thought that Tembo would be appointed to the key post of MCP secretary-general, thus strengthening his position as possible successor to President Banda. Although Tembo retains his post as a member of the executive committee of MCP, the unfilled post of secretary general of the party clearly indicates that Banda does not intend to allow any other political leader to acquire more power in the country.

Opposition

There are three opposition parties in exile, two based in Tanzania and one in Mozambique. They all claim to be socialist and are encouraged by the governments of Tanzania and Mozambique, which dislike Malawi's ties with South Africa.

The Congress for the Second Republic is based in Dar es Salaam, Tanzania, and is led by Kanyama Chiume, a former prime minister. The Malawi Freedom Movement (MAFREMO) is led by another former cabinet minister, Orton Chirwa; its policies are perhaps more populist than socialist. Orton Chirwa, his wife Vera, and their son were allegedly kidnapped from Zambia on December 24, 1981. He and his wife were put on trial for treason. On May 5, 1983, they were sentenced to death by a Blantyre traditional court. The president, bowing to international pressure and protest, commuted the sentence to life imprisonment in June 1984. The most left wing of these parties is the Socialist League of Malawi (LESOMA) led by Dr. Attati Mpakati. It has the support of the Cuban and Russian governments, and in 1980 established a military organization, the Peoples' Liberation Army of Malawi (PLAM), to overthrow the Banda regime.

The LESOMA suffered a serious setback in March 1983 when its leader was assassinated in Harare.

In May 1983 Malawi exiles in Lusaka launched the Save Malawi Committee (SAMACO) to "unite all the forces against the Malawi government." Their efforts at uniting the opposition forces have up to now met with little success.

Other Political Forces

Military

Malawi's army has no great history of political involvement, although it did suppress the rebellion of Harry Chipembere in 1965. Its leaders are appointed by the president, and its direct ties with the South African Armed Forces isolate it from any links with opposition groups.

Organized Labor

The Malawi Trades Union Congress unites three unions which in 1981 had a total membership of 6,500. The only other labor organization is the Teachers' Union. These unions are not politically active. In any case, the vast majority of the population is not unionized. Most work in agriculture or abroad.

Ethnic Groups

The vast majority of the population is African. Since Banda values their role in his country's economic development, the small European minority is well treated. As in Kenya and Uganda, however, the Asian minority has been subjected to repression. They have been driven out of their positions as traders in the villages, but there is no firm indication that they are to be expelled from the country. The Africans come from many different tribes including the Chewa, the Ngoni, and the Yao.

After many years of preparation, the capital of Malawi was moved in 1975 from Zombe in the Southern Region to Lilongwe in the Central Region. Banda announced that this move would promote the development of the Central Region, but it caused some resentment among the ethnic groups in the more developed and prosperous Southern Region, notably the Nyanja. They viewed the decision as showing bias towards particularly the Chewa people, who are more concentrated in the Central Region and whose language has become dominant in the country.

Religious Groups

About half the population is Christian, one fourth Hindu, one fifth Muslim. Jehovah's Witnesses are officially proscribed because of their refusal to acknowledge the government's authority.

National Prospects

In spite of the claims of its opponents, the Banda regime is generally accepted within Malawi. There are now few, if any, political prisoners. The competitive element was introduced into the 1978 elections partly because of the stability of the regime. This stability, however, depends heavily on continuing good relations with South Africa and a continuing economic success. Any change in the political climate to the south could endanger Malawi's economy and its political system, especially if it coincided with Banda's death. It seems unlikely that any accommodation will be reached with the opposition groups in exile until the president's demise.

Further Reading

McMaster, Carolyn. *Malawi: Foreign Policy and Development.* London: Julian Freedman, 1974.

Pachai, B. *Malawi: The History of a Nation.* London: Longman, 1973.

Pike, John G. *Malawi: A Political and Economic History.* London: Pall Mall Press, 1968.

Rotberg, Robert I. *The Rise of Nationalism in Central Africa.* London: Oxford University Press, 1966.

Short, Philip. *Banda.* London: Routledge and Kegan Paul, 1974.

Williams, T. David. *Malawi: The Politics of Despair.* Ithaca, N. Y.: Cornell University Press, 1978.

MALAYSIA

by Peter Dawson

The System of Government

Malaysia is a parliamentary federation comprising the eleven states of the Malay peninsula together with the federal territory of Kuala Lumpur, the capital, which comprise West Malaysia, and the states of Sabah and Sarawak on the island of Borneo, which comprise East Malaysia. The country has a population of nearly 14.5 million people of whom about 47 percent are Malay, 32 percent Chinese, and 9 percent Indian. It achieved independence from British colonial rule on August 31, 1957, as the Malayan Federation, then consisting of the states of the peninsula only. In September 1963, Sabah, Sarawak, and Singapore joined the federation, but Singapore seceded on August 9, 1965. The federal territory of Kuala Lumpur was created in 1974. The present constitution has been effective from 1957, with only limited subsequent alterations. It provides for a parliamentary and cabinet system closely modeled on that of the United Kingdom.

Executive

The head of state is the *Yang di-Pertuan Agong* (or king) who serves for a term of five years. The office rotates according to precedence among the royal rulers of nine of the thirteen states of the federation, but accession to the office is confirmed by election among these nine rulers. The office thus constitutes a unique combination of monarchic, rotational, and elective principles. Although formally the head of government, the king is in practice a constitutional monarch with only very limited discretionary powers. The effective head of government is the *Perdana Mentri* (prime minister), working with and through the *Juma'ah Mentri* (cabinet). The king appoints as prime minister the member of the *Dewan Ra'ayat* (House of Representatives) likely to command the confidence of a majority in the House, normally the leader of the majority party. Members of the cabinet are appointed by the king from either of the two houses of Parliament on the advice of the prime minister. The cabinet is required by the constitution to be collectively responsible to the parliament.

Legislature

The legislature consists of the king and the two *majlis* (councils): the *Dewan Negara* (Senate) and the *Dewan Ra'ayat* (House of Representatives). The king, however, takes no active part in the proceedings of Parliament.

The Senate, which is the less powerful of the two houses, has sixty-eight members. Two members are elected by each of the thirteen state legislatures, while the king, acting on advice from the prime minister, appoints an additional forty-two, including two to represent the federal territory. Senators serve for three years, their term being unaffected by a dissolution of the House of Representatives. Senators tend to be prominent older figures in public life, representative of occupational and ethnic groupings, although in recent years Senate seats have sometimes been used to groom younger, rising politicians. Despite the minority group of territorial representatives, the Senate has never been active in promoting states' rights against those of the federation.

The House of Representatives currently has 154 members (176 from the next election) directly elected from single-member constituencies by simple majorities. The minimum qualifying age for membership is twenty-one. Dual membership of the two federal houses is forbidden as is simultaneous representation of two federal constituencies, but several federal legislators also hold seats or office in their state assemblies. The maximum life of the House of Representatives is five years, but it may be dissolved at any time by the king acting upon the request of the prime minister. The king does have the power, never used so far, to refuse such a request. In recent years, Parliament has met for about eleven weeks in each year.

A simple majority in both houses is sufficient to carry legislation. The Senate has a delaying power of one month over money bills and of one year over other bills. Most constitutional amendments require a two-thirds majority while certain articles of the constitution cannot be amended without the consent of the *Majlis Raja Raja*.

The *Majlis Raja Raja* (Conference of Rulers), which meets three or four times a year, comprises the thirteen rulers of the states of the federation including the nine hereditary royal rulers and the governors of Penang, Malacca, Sabah, and Sarawak. It acts as a third house of the Parliament on amendments to certain sections of the constitution (especially Article 153 which protects the position of Malays), the extension of Islamic religious practices, the making of certain major state appointments (such as judges of the Supreme Court), as well as on legislation affecting the position of rulers and the boundaries of states. The nine royal rulers, sitting within the Conference of Rulers, are responsible also for the election of the king and his deputy.

Since independence the government coalition, dominated by the United Malays National Organization, has always held an absolute majority of the seats in the House of Representatives. In the 1982 general election, the Democratic Action Party (DAP) was able to win seats in the federal territory and in only four states including Sabah and Sarawak. The Pan-Malaysian Islamic Party (PAS) won seats in only two states, while the independents were all elected in Sabah and Sarawak. The dominance of the National Front and the very limited territorial base of the opposition parties was confirmed by the results of the elections to state assemblies which were held at the same time.

Judiciary

The Supreme Court is the highest judicial authority in Malaysia with the power to interpret the constitution and to adjudicate in disputes between states or between any state and the federal government. It is also the highest court of appeal in criminal cases for the federation. Beneath the Federal Court are two High Courts, one for West and one for East Malaysia, which have original jurisdiction in their areas in both civil and criminal cases as well as appeal from subordinate courts. The lord president, who heads the Supreme Court, is appointed by

HOUSE OF REPRESENTATIVES ELECTION RESULTS (1982)		
National Front		
United Malays National Organization (UMNO)	70	(69)
Malayan Chinese Association (MCA)	24	(17)
Berjaya	10	(9)
United Bumiputra Party (PPBB)	8	(8)
Sarawak National Party (SNAP)	6	(9)
Sarawak United People's Party (SUPP)	5	(6)
Gerakan	5	(4)
Malayan Indian Congress (MIC)	4	(3)
Others	—	(6)
	132	(131)
Opposition Parties		
Democratic Action Party (DAP)	9	(16)
Pan-Malaysian Islamic Party (PAS)	5	(5)
Independents	8	(—)
Others	—	(2)
	22	(23)
Total Seats		154

* Figures for 1978 in parentheses.

the king who must act on the advice of the prime minister after consulting the Conference of Rulers. Other senior judges are similarly appointed with the lord president also being consulted. The independence of the judiciary is maintained by this means as well as by the stipulation of legal qualifications, a high security of tenure and remuneration, and restrictions on discussion of judicial conduct in the legislatures. In numerous cases, the judiciary have displayed a very high standard of independence from political influence.

Regional & Local Government

Each state is governed by a *Mentri Besar* (chief minister) who is responsible to a unicameral legislative assembly whose members are directly elected, except in Sabah which retains a limited number of nominated members. The relations among the state ruler or governor, the chief minister, and the assembly are broadly similar to those which prevail at federal level among the king, prime minister, and the Parliament. But the powers of states are limited, being confined principally to land and natural-resource management and the oversight of local government. Sabah and Sarawak, however, enjoy some powers not available to the states of West Malaysia. The federal government is the main taxing authority and controls the borrowing powers of states so that apart from land revenue, states enjoy no significant sources of income. Since state legislatures are now dominated by political parties that are members of the governing coalition at federal level, a further degree of state and federal harmonization is achieved.

The Electoral System

All members of the House of Representatives are directly elected by a simple majority within each of the 154 single-member constituencies. Twenty-six of the sixty-eight members of the Senate are elected by their state legislatures. All citizens over the age of twenty-one (other than those detained as being of "unsound mind" or serving a prison sentence or who have been sentenced to death or imprisonment of more than twelve months) are eligible to vote by secret ballot in elections for the House of Representatives or legislative assemblies. The Election Commission conducts elections and prepares and annually revises electoral rolls. It is also responsible every eight to ten years for reviewing and recommending changes to the boundaries of state and national constituencies. Registration of voters is neither automatic nor compulsory. The ballot paper in each constituency lists all the candidates and their party symbols; voters indicate their choice by marking an X. Votes are counted centrally within each constituency in the presence of candidates and their agents. Turnout is high, usually above 70 percent. The system is in the main fair and equitable, although various technical factors relating to voter registration and constituency delimitation together with the effects of the simple-majority method have produced in all national elections a highly disproportionate number of seats for the governing coalition in relation to the number of votes.

The Party System

Origins of the Parties

The most distinctive feature of Malaysian political parties is that they are all communally based, but a second major feature is a tendency towards consociation and coalition. The communal divisions are not only racial, but are also reinforced by language, religion, culture, and to a considerable extent, economic role. With Malays constituting approximately half of the total population, Chinese approximately one-third, and people of Indian descent one-tenth, parties which represent the interests of these groups are assured of substantial support. The three major parties (UMNO, MCA, and MIC) all came into existence in the late 1940s specifically to defend their respective ethnic communities against threats perceived in the various constitutional proposals advanced by the colonial government. Well before independence in 1957, they had formed a coalition which was formally registered as the Alliance Party in 1958. The Alliance collapsed in the wake of communal rioting after the 1969 election, which had shown a growth in support for non-Alliance parties and thus an erosion of the claim by the Alliance to represent a national interest.

After a period of emergency rule, during which electoral and parliamentary activity were suspended, the coalition was reconstituted in 1971 as the National Front (*Barisan Nasional*). At the same time, it was broadened to include several smaller parties, previously in opposition, so that the Malay and Chinese communities were now represented by more than one party within the Front. The United Malays National Organization (UMNO) has always been the dominant participant. With intercommunal harmony the overriding aim of government throughout Malaysia's history, the National Front has achieved this aim by private interparty compromise. However, resentment among some sections of the population against this process of elite adjustment has sustained support for several opposition parties.

The Parties in Law

The constitution makes no reference to political parties, but under separate legislation (the Societies Act 1966) all organizations seeking to contest elections must be formally registered. On a few occasions, the refusal of registration has effectively suppressed the activities of some smaller opposition parties. A 1981 amendment to the Societies Act requires all clubs, societies, and associations to register as either political or nonpolitical. This has been seen as limiting the capacity of pressure groups to campaign and lobby to secure changes in government policy.

From time to time, security and sedition laws have been used to detain members of opposition parties either because of suspected communist links or because their activities were deemed to be subversive. Parties receive no direct, formal state support. Any qualified election candidate whose nomination has been properly made can be included on the ballot whether or not he is a representative of a political party.

Party Organization

Malaysian parties are too numerous, too different in size, and in several cases too limited to particular regions for many substantial generalizations to be possible. The parties are permanent associations sustained by membership dues and private donations. Most maintain a three-tiered organization at constituency, state, and national level. They are identifiable principally by communal characteristics, although different parties drawing their membership from the same community may be distinguished by socioeconomic and, to a limited degree, ideological differences. The major support for the DAP, for example, comes from the poorer stratum of Chinese, while the MCA is more substantially supported by the better off.

The participation of the major parties in the National Front and the dependence of all on that membership, except UMNO, for access to cabinet office and the consequent benefits to their communities necessitates the maintenance of close central control over subordinate levels. A major instrument of this control for parties within the National Front is the patronage exercised by the chief ministers of states. Although the principal parties hold annual conferences at which major policy issues are determined and national officers are chosen, these processes are usually closely and sucessfully regulated. Nevertheless, despite this consistent pattern of central and elite domination, some opportunity remains for local leaders to develop local support. For the wealthier, especially within Chinese communities, contributions to community projects, such as schools and places of worship, may generate prestige and power. For all aspirants to party office or candidacy, the role of broker—representing constituents' interests within the multiple and many-layered processes of governmental bureaucracy—is universally expected. Thus, education and experience of working within bureaucracies are im-portant factors determining election at the local level.

Campaigning

Fear of threats to public order have led the government, in recent elections, to ban large public rallies by any party. The preferred method of campaigning has been to hold meetings within private houses at which a largely invited audience participates in a process akin to a seminar, with an address by a speaker followed by questions and discussion. This method, where it is used, permits issues to be presented in a way which is specific to particular areas or occupational groups. In addition, door-to-door canvassing occurs, and pamphlets and posters are widely distributed and displayed although their influence, if any, is difficult to assess. The press has an important role. Seven newspapers, published in English as well as the vernacular languages, have an influence that is generally felt to be substantial, their effect being usually to enhance support for candidates representing the ruling National Front.

It is difficult to determine accurately the full expenditure of parties during election campaigns. Local party branches are in all cases dependent on central party funds derived either from voluntary contributions or from levies on holders of well-paid posts which have been secured by party intervention. The larger parties, most of which are in the National Front, are by far the richer and can thus readily afford the costs of publicity, transport for party workers, and other necessary expenses.

There is usually not any close national party control of local campaigns. With the larger parties, pre-existing party cohesion encourages a uniformity of approach, although the fact that state assembly elections are held at the same time as those for the national legislature will often ensure that wholly local issues may be promoted in a manner which conflicts with the national party's line.

Independent Voters

The existence of the National Front as an electoral, as well as a governing, coalition may present some voters with a dilemma when the NF-endorsed candidate is not from their own ethnic community. In that event, if a candidate from their own community is standing for an opposition party a conflict arises between the desire to vote for the coalition—which almost inevitably enjoys a national majority and which is regarded as the source of many material benefits—and the wish to assert communal solidarity. There has been some evidence of differential voting for national and for state assemblymen.

National Front
(*Barisan Nasional*)

Although registered for legal purposes as a political party, the Front is an electoral and governing coalition comprising eleven parties and has no organizational structure of its own. Its constituent parties (each of which has a separate entry) are UMNO, Berjasa, Berjaya, MCA, MIC, Gerakan, PPBB, PPP, SNAP, SUPP, and PBDS.

United Malays National Organization (UMNO;
Pertubohan Kebangsaan Melayu Bersatu)

History

The UMNO was founded in May 1946, with Dato Onn bin Jaafar as its first president, in order to resist the introduction, by the British colonial administration, of a unitary form of government throughout Peninsular Malaya. This was seen by Malays and especially by their hereditary rulers as detrimental to Malay interests. The UMNO was not formally registered as a political party until April 1950. Throughout Malaysia's history, it has been the largest national party and the dominant party of government. All four of Malaysia's prime ministers since 1957 have been the leaders of UMNO. Data Onn's attempts in 1950 to widen UMNO membership to include non-Malays and to introduce other reforms were strongly opposed and led to his resignation and replacement as party president in 1951 by Tunku Abdul Rahman. An ad hoc coalition between UMNO and the MCA to fight the Kuala Lumpur municipal elections in 1952 led to the establishment a year later of the Alliance coalition which also included the MIC. Tunku Abdul Rahman became

prime minister following the first general election in 1955 and led his country to independence in 1957. Throughout the 1960s, his attempts to hold the Alliance together and placate ultranationalist Malays in his own party weakened his position. The decline in support both for UMNO and the Alliance which was revealed by the 1969 election results and the communal rioting which followed led to his resignation, both as prime minister and as party president, and his replacement by Tun Abdul Razak.

After a period of emergency rule during which Parliament was suspended, Razak was able to put together a wider governing coalition of nine parties, including some which had previously been in opposition. This National Front was registered as a political party on June 1, 1974. In the parliamentary elections which followed the Front won 135 out of the 154 seats.

Other major measures taken during the emergency period were the introduction of the New Economic Policy (NEP) which sought to promote substantially the economic advancement of the Malay population and the passing of a constitutional amendment which declared seditious any questioning of Malay privileges, the status of Malay as the national language, and as such issues as citizenship and the position of traditional rulers. Important controversies were thus barred from public debate, even in Parliament, and the grounds on which opposition parties might base their criticisms were denied to them.

The death of Tun Abdul Razak in 1976 and the succession of Datuk Hussein Onn was followed by a brief period of factional fighting within UMNO. In part, the conflict was between older members of the party who had been associates of Tunku Abdul Rahman and younger men, technocratically inclined, who had been brought to prominence by Tun Abdul Razak. The outcome involved the arrest of several of the latter group for alleged communist activities, although much of the evidence, including their confessions, appeared fragile. At the same time others of Razak's protegés, untainted by any communist association, survived. Of this group, Dr. Mahatir bin Mohamad, who in 1970 had been expelled from the party's supreme council, was appointed to the deputy premiership over the heads of more senior men. A major casualty of this period was Datuk Harun, the chief minister of Selangor. His control over the massive patronage of his state and his support in the youth wing of the party constituted a threat to the leadership of Razak and then of Datuk Hussein Onn. He was charged with corruption in late 1975. Over the next two years, he was successively stripped of office, expelled from the party, and tried and sentenced to a term of imprisonment, thus demonstrating Hussein Onn's gathering control of the party. But in August 1982 he was granted a royal pardon and has since resumed party activity.

In July 1981, Hussein Onn was succeeded as prime minister by Dr. Mahatir Mohamad who, within a year, led his party into a general election, the results of which reemphasized UMNO's continuing dominance in the political life of Malaysia. The 1984 UMNO general assembly returned him for three more years as party president.

Organization

The UMNO is a cadre party, exclusively Malay in membership, which has succeeded through its extensive organization in every state and penetration to village level in uniting Malay interests across region and class. As an exclusively Malay party, UMNO enjoys a high degree of homogeneity. It is distinguished also by being the only party with branches throughout the federation, including Sabah and Sarawak. It is relatively highly structured with a president, deputy president, and five vice presidents. The heads of the party's youth wing and its women's wing (*Wanita* UMNO) are automatically vice presidents, the remaining three being elected by the party's general assembly. Together with other appointed and elected members, including a secretary-general, treasurer, and publicity chief, they constitute the principal power center of the party. The dual roles of party president and prime minister have been employed in a mutually enhancing manner by all four incumbents, whose positions have usually been supported by the senior party officers who are also cabinet ministers.

The youth and women's wings enjoy a semiautonomous status, at times acting as pressure groups within the party. They have both performed vitally important functions during elections in organizing campaigns at the local level.

Policy

The principal objectives of UMNO policy have consistently been UMNO dominance and Malay unity. The one is seen as reinforcing the other. These aims are secured by maintaining tight central control of the party while securing the widest possible electoral and governing coalition with Malay and non-Malay parties. These two strategies have at times been felt to conflict, leading to strains within the party, notably in 1969. Over the past decade, the party has promoted the New Economic Policy (NEP), which uses active discriminatory measures to advance the material well being of Malays. This policy has coincided with a more strident assertion of economic nationalism which has led the government to buy its way into many of the large expatriate corporations, especially in the mining and plantation industries. Determinedly anticommunist both at home and abroad the party's and government's foreign policy has been characterized by active membership in the Association of South East Asian Nations, an increasing concern to promote cooperation among Islamic countries, very cautious relations with China, and of late, the assertion of ostensibly anti-British sentiment coupled with a more markedly amenable attitude toward Japan.

Membership & Constituency

No information is available on the size of the membership of UMNO. The party's supporters include most of the Malays of West Malaysia and many in Sabah and Sarawak. Only those Malays whose political views are most influenced by their Islamic faith support other parties in any appreciable number.

Financing

No information is available on details of UMNO financial sources or expenditures.

Leadership

Dr. Mahatir bin Mohamad (born 1925) is in firm control of the party. He is the first prime minister to have been educated locally (in medicine), and unlike his predecessors, he is not a member of a Malay royal house. Once identified with the radical right, he is thought by many observers to retain an inclination in that direction.

Prospects

While the party's leadership remains acutely sensitive to any threat to its hegemony, especially from rival Malay parties, it is extremely difficult to envisage UMNO being displaced as the governing party.

Malayan Chinese Association (MCA)

The MCA was founded in 1949 to protect the interests of the Chinese people, approximately one-third of the population, in the face of what were regarded as markedly pro-Malay policies of the British colonial government. Officially registered as a party in 1952, the MCA cooperated with UMNO at an electoral level and, in 1953, became a member, together with the MIC, of the Alliance coalition. The MCA was again a member of the Front, but the inclusion in the Front of Gerakan, a rival Chinese party, has reduced the MCA's standing, since it can no longer claim to be the sole representative of Chinese interests in the government. While it has a widespread organization throughout Malaysia, it does not control any state assembly, unlike Gerakan which controls Penang. Although from its inception it attempted to be a mass membership party, it is seen as representing the interests of the better off among the Chinese community and is vulnerable to the more populist appeal of some of the opposition parties among the poorer Chinese. These difficulties were reflected in a sharp factional struggle through the 1970s between some of the older founding members of the party and younger and more radical elements. With twenty-four seats in the federal Parliament, it is the second-largest coalition partner, but its freedom to formulate policy is powerfully circumscribed by its membership in the Front. In order to protect its position and that of its members it must acquiesce in policies, especially with regard to Malay advancement, which cannot always be regarded as being in the immediate interest of its members.

Organizationally, the MCA is very similar to UMNO, with a powerful central committee comprising members elected by a general assembly or nominated by the party president. It has a strong state-level organization with subordinate levels down to ward branches. During the past two years the party has been riven by major internal disputes, with evidence of fraudulent inflation of branch membership numbers, the expulsion and counter expulsion of senior office holders and the threat that unless the party can resolve its quarrels it will be expelled from the National Front.

Gerakan
(Parti Gerakan Rakyat Malaysia)

The party is universally known as Gerakan, but its full name can be loosely translated as Malaysian People's Movement. It was founded in 1968 by Dr. Lim Chong Eu and pledged to a program of noncommunalism, moderate socialism, and democracy. Despite the presence of Malays on the party committee it is still seen as a Chinese party. Its power base is in Penang, where it controls the state government with the patronage which that entails, but it also has a few branches elsewhere. It entered the Front in 1972.

Malayan Indian Congress (MIC)

From its inception in 1946, the MIC has been faced by the difficulty of sustaining unity in the face of divisions within the Indian community, which constitutes less than 10 percent of the population and which is clustered in geographically scattered locations or thinly spread in urban centers. Although a member of the Alliance and subsequently of the National Front, it is the weakest partner with only four seats in the federal Parliament. Since the Indian population nowhere comprises more than 25 percent of the voters in any constituency, without the constituencies and seats allocated to it by the Front it could not hope to survive as a significant group.

Sabah People's Union
(Bersatu Rakyat Jelata Sabah; Berjaya)

Berjaya was founded in 1975 and from 1976 till its defeat in 1985 held an overwhelming majority of seats in the state assembly. It still holds ten of the sixteen Sabah seats in the federal assembly. It was regarded as one of the few mult-communal parties in Malaysia, but its 1985 defeat was largely the result of the belief, on the part of the majority Christian, Kadazan population, that it had become more markedly proMuslim in its policies.

United People Party
(*Parti Pesaka Bumiputra Bersaut;* PPBB)

The PPBB is a Sarawak-based party established in 1973 within the Front. It obtained eight of the twenty-four Sarawak seats in the 1982 federal election. Its appeal is to the Malay population of that state.

Sarawak Dayak Party
(*Parti Bansa Dayak Sarawak;* PBDS)

Formed in July 1983 by federal MPs who had broken away from SNAP it has yet to contest an election. Its major object is to represent the interests of the indigenous Dayak community.

Sarawak United People's Party
(SUPP)

The oldest Sarawak party in the Front was founded in 1959. Its support is predominantly from the Chinese population. It has five seats in the federal Parliament.

Sarawak National Party (SNAP)

Founded in 1961 this Sarawak-based party, whose support came mainly from the indigenous peoples of the state, came into the National Front in 1976. In 1982, it won six of the twenty-four federal parliamentary seats in Sarawak and together with its Front allies, the PPBB and the SUPP, sought to secure that territory's interests within the NF. In July 1983, three of its federal members resigned from the party. Together with three independent members they formed a new party, the PBDS, specifically to represent the interests of the Dayak community.

People's Progressive Party of Malaysia (PPP)

Originally founded in 1953 as the Perak Progressive Party, it changed to its present name in 1956. Its appeal is restricted mainly to non-Malays in the Ipoh area. It survives as a party within the Perak state assembly where its appeal to poorer Chinese offsets some of the advantage which might otherwise accrue to the DAP, one of the two opposition parties in that state.

Berjasa
(*Barisan Jama'ah Islamiah Semalaysia*)

Most commonly known by its Malay acronym, Berjasa, the party's name could be translated as the Malaysian Islamic People's Front. It was formed in 1977 as a splinter group from the PAS and has served to weaken that party's electoral support within the state of Kelantan in which both are based. A more assertively Islamic party than UMNO, it holds no seats in the federal Parliament, but is represented in the Kelantan state assembly.

Opposition Parties

Democratic Action Party (DAP)

Founded in 1966 in the wake of Singapore's secession from the federation, the DAP was the Malayan version of the People's Action Party, Lee Kuan Yew's Singapore-based party. DAP's objective was and is to establish a democratic and socialist society in Malaysia. It analyzes Malaysian society in class rather than communal terms, and while its support comes mainly from urban, working-class Chinese, it retains an appeal for many disaffected non-Malays including some of the intelligentsia. Although efficiently organized, the competition from rival Chinese parties, MCA and Gerakan, and its inability to secure any substantial support in rural areas have denied it control of any state assembly and thus substantially limited its capacity to secure federal parliamentary seats. The party chairman is Chen Man Hin (born 1924 in

China), who was educated at the University of Malaya in Singapore and has worked as a medical practitioner.

Hamim (*Parti Hisbul Muslimin Malaysia*; (Muslim Front)

Formed in 1983 by Datuk Haji Mohamed Asri bin Haji Muda when he resigned from PAS. The simultaneous defection of four of his former party's five federal MPs, coupled with his own substantial political experience makes Hamim a significant grouping, but one which will have difficulty in straddling the divide between the fundamentalist Muslim appeal of PAS and the more avowedly modernistic stance of UMNO.

Pan Malaysian Islamic Party (*Partai Islam Se Malaysia;* PAS)

Known variously by its English (PMIP) or Malay/Arabic acronyms, PAS originated in the early 1950s as an Islamic promotional group within UMNO. In 1955, alienated by UMNO concessions to non-Malays, it was established as a separate party. A Malay nationalist party, its primary appeal is to poorer, especially rural, Malays. It seeks to combine Islamic traditions with a modernizing thrust and some elements of socialism. Islam is regarded as a force for national unity. Religious teachers are active in its campaigning and religious themes are interwoven with political assertions. PAS may represent the only significant potential threat to UMNO's dominance, partly because the rural poor as a whole have derived the least benefit from the substantial economic changes since independence, partly because PAS is least ready to accommodate the interests of other racial groups, and partly because its appeal echoes the success of radical Islamic movements elsewhere. For a short period between 1973 and 1977, PAS was a member of the National Front, but since then its power in Kelantan, the one state where it was dominant, has been eroded. In 1982, it won only five seats in the federal Parliament, four of them in Kelantan, and only eighteen state assembly seats. The ten seats in the Kelantan assembly were insufficient to secure a majority. Since 1982 the role of the Islamic "theocratic" element in the party has been greatly strengthened. Attacks by fundamentalist elements on the party's president led to his resignation in 1983. Four of the five federal MPs resigned with him to form a new party—Hamim.

Minor Parties

There are a number of very minor parties, most of which are active only in state assembly elections.

Other Political Forces

Formal groups other than political parties are not of significance in Malaysian politics. The principal parties are capable of articulating within themselves and within the governing coalition many of the demands and pressures which would elsewhere find separate institutional expression. Traditional social structures within the main communal groups provide a further channel for meeting demands, while extensive networks of patronage and clientalism within and outside the public sector perform the same function. Another important factor inhibiting the rise of other political organizations has been the 1981 amendment to the Societies Act, which forbids political activity to groups not registered as political. This has severely inhibited overt political activities on the part of all nonparty groups.

Organized Labor

Trade unions provide only a very limited exception to these generalizations. Their membership is drawn principally from the Chinese and Indian communities. Subject to strict government control, not affiliated with any political party, and with the joint holding of union and political party office forbidden, their role is restricted to localized place-of-work bargaining with employers. They have no impact on national political activity.

Ethnic occupational groups also exist, such as the Chinese Chambers of Commerce or the United Chinese School Teachers' Association, but a largely overlapping membership with the MCA ensures that collective interests are promoted within and through the party.

Briefly, during the early to mid 1970s, student organizations, notably the University of Malaya Students Union, were active in making political assertions especially on behalf of poor peasant communities, but separate legislation making political activity on university campuses a punishable offense and the more general restraints referred to above have served to preempt any further student role in national or local parties.

National Prospects

Malaysia's political system is remarkably stable and relatively peaceful, even though it is based on Malay dominance and Chinese acquiescence. The government and the unique political arrangement of the National Front will continue to maintain communal peace by any means necessary. The most serious threat to that peace remains the ideals of ultranationalist and fervently Islamic Malays who object to the declining but still major role the Chinese continue to play in the economy and what they perceive to be the un-Islamic policies of UMNO.

A separate but possibly associated threat could arise among poor, especially rural, Malays, many of whom see the benefits of the New Economic Policy accruing to a relatively small and mainly urban middle class. Were they able to make common cause with the poor Chinese, who are mostly to be found in rural areas, the National Front would be faced with a more serious challenge than that which culminated in violence in 1969.

Further Reading

Crouch, Harold; Lee Kam Hing; and Ong, Michael, eds. *Malaysian Politics and the 1978 Election.* Oxford and New York: Oxford University Press, 1980.

Funston, N. J. *Malay Politics in Malaysia: a Study of the United Malays National Organisation and Party Islam.* Kuala Lumpur: Heinemann Educational Books, 1983.

Kassim, Ismail. *Race, Politics and Moderation: A Study of the Malaysian Electoral Process.* Singapore: Times Books International, 1979.

Mauzy, Diane K. *Barisan Nasional: Coalition Government in Malaysia* Selangor: Marican, 1983.

Means, Gordon P. *Malaysian Politics.* 2nd. ed. London: Hodder & Stoughton, 1976.

Milne, R. S., and Mauzy, Diane K. *Politics and Government in Malaysia.* Singapore: Federal Publications, 1978.

Milne, R. S., and Ratnam, K. J. *Malaysia—New States in a New Nation. Political Development of Sarawak and Sabah in Malaysia.* London and Portland, Ore.: Frank Cass, 1974.

Sheridan, L. A., and Groves, Harry E. *The Constitution of Malaysia.* 3rd ed. Singapore: Malayan Law Journal (Pte) Ltd., 1979.

Suffian, Tun Mohamed; Lee, H. P.; and Trindade, F. A. *The Constitution of Malaysia. Its development: 1957–1977.* Oxford and New York: Oxford University Press, 1978.

Von Vorys, Karl. *Democracy Without Consensus: Communalism and Political Stability in Malaysia.* Princeton, N. J.: Princeton University Press, 1975.

REPUBLIC OF MALI
(République du Mali)
by Andrew Norton

The System of Government

Mali, a country of seven million people in the heart of west Africa, is a one-party unitary state with a mixed military-civilian government. The present government came to power in 1968 in a bloodless military coup led by then-lieutenant Moussa Traoré, who ousted the one-party leftist civilian regime of Modibo Keita. The country's present constitution was approved by referendum in 1974.

Executive

Brigadier General Moussa Traoré is head of state, head of government, and minister of defense. He presides over a cabinet composed largely of civilians, but in which army officers control the key ministries of agriculture, planning, interior, and defense. Traoré was elected president in June 1979 without opposition and soon thereafter dissolved the Military Committee of National Liberation (*Comité Militaire de Libération Nationale;* CMLN) which had previously exercised all executive and legislative powers. Presidential elections were held again in June 1985. The official results claimed a statistically improbable 99.97 percent turnout, and a 99.4 percent vote for President Traoré, who was the sole candidate. A clause in the 1974 constitution that limited the national president to one bid for reelection was abolished in March 1985, and there is now no constitutional obstacle to General Traoré's continuing as president indefinitely.

Legislature

Elections to the eighty-two member National Assembly were held in June 1979, 1982 and 1985. The Assembly rarely meets and does little, while the single party's national congress functions as a legislature, approving and disapproving Traoré's proposals. The congress is composed of close to 400 delegates selected by local and regional party organizations. Since the public appears to be extremely apathetic toward the party, it is unclear how representative the congress delegates may be of the country's populace.

Judiciary

The nineteen-member Supreme Court supervises a judicial system consisting of the Court of Appeal and lower courts. Supreme Court justices are appointed to five-year terms by the president. Few signs of judicial independence have been observed.

Regional & Local Government

Mali is divided into seven administrative districts governed by appointees of the president. The capital district of Bamako is administered directly by the central government. The regions are further divided into *cercles* and *arrondissements*. Larger towns and cities have elected councils with some ability to administer local affairs and influence the regional administration. Regional governors have apparently found their authority undercut by regional leaders of the government party. To improve their position, they have been made ex officio members of the party's National Council.

The Electoral System

Candidates for the National Assembly are supposed to be selected by local committees of the party. No details of the electoral system have been reported in available sources.

The Party System

Political parties first appeared in Mali in the pre-independence period. The anticolonial, leftist Sudanese Union (*Union Soudanaise-Rassemblement Démocratique Africain;* US-RDA) was founded by Modibo Keita in the late 1940s. It was opposed by the Sudanese Progressive Party (*Parti Soudanais Progressiste;* PSP), which was supported by merchants in towns along the Niger, veterans of the French colonial army, and the nomad chieftans of the semiarid north. The PSP was banned in the early 1960s when Keita turned Mali into a one-party state. The radical socialist and anti-French policies of the US-RDA had disastrous effects on the Malian economy, and, in 1967, Keita sought a reapproachment with France. Radical elements in his own party opposed this move, and Keita was forced to rely on a private militia to suppress opposition. The 1968 coup ended all overt political activity in the country.

Democratic Union of the Malian People (*Union Démocratique du Peuple Malien;* UDPM)

History

The UDPM was officially chartered as Mali's only party in the constitution of 1974. The party was not actually organized on the grass-roots level, however, until 1978 when local branches were organized in preparation for the 1979 elections. The party has not been a success. Set up as part of a five-year transition to civilian rule, its initial leadership was predominantly military. Hampered by apathy, factionalism, and poor organization, it has had no grass-roots appeal. Despite periodic attempts to increase membership and widen participation popular enthusiasm for the party remains low. By the end of 1985, the party probably consisted of no more than its national and regional leaders and their clients.

Organization

Although the UDPM is organized along Marxist-Leninist lines, it is not a Marxist party. At the top is the Central Executive Bureau (*Bureau Exécutif Central;* BEC) of some nineteen members. Most BEC members are now civilians. The BEC, equivalent to a communist party politburo, is elected by the party congress, which consists of some 400 delegates selected by regional and local committees. Between congresses, party affairs are in the hands of the elected National Council of over 125 people. With the exception of the BEC and the congress, which Traoré has increasingly relied upon to generate support for his policies and enthusiasm for the party, most party organs appear to be moribund, coming to life only to select delegates to the congress. Local and regional party organs are probably little more than the personal political vehicles of local notables. The discipline usually associated with this form of party and state is absent in Mali.

Policy

Under Traoré's leadership, party and government policy is pragmatic.

Through its first decade in power, his government continued the policies of the Keita era, including a high degree of state intervention in the economy through trading monopolies and state-owned enterprises. Since about 1981 a new line in economic policy has become increasingly evident, reportedly as a result of pressure from the main aid donors. The principal measures taken have been aimed at liberalising the internal grain market and reducing employment in the state sector by trimming the civil service and shedding state-run enterprises. Despite these initiatives the Malian economy remains chronically weak, partly because of two severe droughts over the last fifteen years. At the end of 1985 the agricultural and livestock production on which the country's economy depends was still in the early stages of recovery from the effects of the most recent drought which had, by the middle of that year, rendered around 100,000 rural Malians destitute. By 1983, well before this crisis had reached its peak, the public debt had reached $880 million, and Mali remains strongly dependent on various kinds of foreign aid from sources that include the IMF, France, West Germany, the World Bank and the United States.

In foreign policy Mali has been heavily reliant on the Soviet Union for arms, though there are signs that France will play an increasingly prominant role in military aid. The government is nonaligned and seeks assistance from any quarter. After a long period of delay, Mali rejoined the West African Monetary Union, the UMOA, in June 1984, replacing the Malian franc with the CFA franc at a rate of Mfr2 = CFAfr1. Mali had originally left this union in 1962 as part of the US-RDA's policy of seeking greater independence from France. It rejoined the franc zone (meaning the area where currencies can be converted to the French franc by arrangement with the French Treasury), but not the UMOA, in 1968. The change of currencies caused substantial inflation in Mali, and this had led to considerable popular discontent.

Negotiations over Mali's entry into UMOA had been persistently held back by the failure to resolve a border dispute with neighbouring Burkina Faso (formerly Upper Volta), over a twenty kilometer-wide band of territory known as the Agacher Strip in north-eastern Mali. At the International Court of Justice at The Hague, a solution was worked out that allowed Mali to rejoin the union. On Christmas Day 1985, however, the dispute flared up into war, as Mali launched air and ground assaults on Burkina, claiming that Burkinase attempts to conduct a census in the disputed zone amounted to illegal annexation. Hostilities lasted for five days before an effective ceasefire was arranged, and the process of arbitration is theoretically supposed to continue.

Membership & Constituency

No figures are available on UDPM membership. Given the general public apathy toward the party, it is likely that it consists of only a small number of paid functionaries and opportunists.

Financing

Information on UDPM finances does not exist. At an extraordinary session of the party's first congress in late 1980, Traoré was able to persuade the members of the National Council to forgo their expense accounts, which suggests that the party is not well financed and relies on state subsidies for its work.

Leadership

Moussa Traoré's tenure of the party presidency means that it is difficult for opposition to his government, or even open political debate, to surface through the UDPM. The BEC, once mostly made up of military officers, is now mostly civilian. The outstanding exception is Colonel Ahmadou Baba Diarra, one of the few members of the original Traoré group to remain in politics. He also holds the influential post of planning minister in Traoré's cabinet.

Other Political Forces

Military

Little is known of the factions within the army. Nearly all the officers formerly in government have returned to the barracks or settled into comfortable roles in the bureaucracy. Promotion in the army is slow and has tended to occur only after failed coups, when rebellious officers are cashiered. Traoré has survived various attempts by army factions to overthrow his government, the most serious being an attempt by hardline opponents of moves towards civilian rule in 1978 and an attempted coup by some junior officers in 1980.

Bureaucracy

Policies involving considerable expansion of the state sector after independence have left Mali with a civil service that is hugely overmanned in most areas. State departments, such as public works, frequently lack the resources to undertake work of any kind, and thus large numbers of state employees suffer from long periods of enforced idleness. One major element in reforms sought by foreign aid donors has been a reduction of employment in the state sector, particularly through reorganization of the thirty state companies which have been a major drain on the country's finances because of poor productivity, lax management and chronic deficits. These companies employ over 20,000 people and constitute a source of patronage for an even larger number, so the issue is sensitive politically. The current program of privatization is expected to lead to some 3,000 layoffs.

Organized Labor

Trade unions are federated in the National Union of Malian Workers (*Union Nationale des Travailleurs Maliens;* UNTM) which is supposed to be controlled by the ruling party. Nevertheless, the union's official publication, *Barakela* (The Worker), is often critical of the government and Traoré. In the second half of 1985, Malian unions became increasingly vocal in criticising current economic policies, especially the program of reorganizing state enterprises. There is considerable unrest in the public sector, where salaries are often two to three months in arrears and steep inflation associated with the entry into UMOA has dramatically reduced their value. In December 1985, the largest component of the UNTM, the National Union of Education and Culture (SNEC), went on strike. Following the end of the border war with Burkina Faso, President Traoré made the very serious allegation that the SNEC was being funded by Burkina to promote internal unrest aimed at the overthrow of his government. It was widely expected at the end of 1985 that this would be used as a pretext to crack down on the more militant elements in the union leadership.

Students

The party controls the National Union of Mali Youth (*Union Nationale de la Jeunesse Malien;* UNJM), but a breakaway faction sparked major demonstrations against the government in 1979 and 1980. The dissident organization, the National Union of Students and Pupils (*Union Nationale des Étudiants et des Élèves Maliens;* UNEEM) protested against the severity of examinations, the inflexibility of the educational system, poor teaching, and lack of student grants. They also demanded that corrupt officials be brought to trial and that the country return to Keita's socialist policies. Schools were closed for several months after students fought with police and soldiers in the streets. Hundreds of students were arrested and the UNEEM leader was killed in prison. The sharp repression of the students was seen as the responsibility of the BEC and further alienated youth from the party. Since this time, however, the students have been far more docile. The government has been able to introduce measures which demonstrate the current weakness of the students as a political force. In 1983, for example, competitive entry examinations were introduced for the civil service for the first time, thereby ending the policy of automatically recruiting all graduates for public employment. In January 1985, a period of two years national service was introduced as a response to the problem of youth unemployment created by the earlier measure, a solution which is unpopular

with the students, who are currently unable to launch effective opposition.

Ethnic Groups

Although Mali has several different ethnic groups, there is little ethnic rivalry. About three-quarters of the population is Muslim, and less than 1 percent is Christian. The remainder practice traditional religions. About 80 percent speak a common language, Bambara. Only the nomadic Taureg in the north are not fully integrated into the society. Both Libya and Algeria have encouraged Taureg distrust of the central government.

National Prospects

At the end of 1985, Mali's predominantly agricultural economy began emerging from the second major crisis of drought and famine within fifteen years. Agriculture will need a long respite from the poor rainfall of recent years if the country is to stand any chance of recovering, and becoming self-sufficient in basic foodstuffs once again. Moussa Traoré's government has proved relatively flexible in the face of pressure for change from the major aid donors and the period since 1981 has seen a substantial shift in government policy. This has included attempts to trim down the overweight state sector and a policy of liberalizing grain markets that is supposed to stimulate agricultural production by giving the peasant farmer the incentive of higher prices for his crops. The prolonged drought has made it difficult to gauge the beneficial impact of these policies. Foreign investment in mineral-resource development is a continuing feature of the economy, but this has yet to produce any substantial result, and it seems likely that the country will continue to rely on agriculture and livestock as the basis of its economy for many years to come.

Moussa Traoré's government currently faces considerable public discontent from various sections of the population. Public sector employees have seen the value of their salaries consistently eroded by inflation, and have borne the brunt of austerity imposed by current economic policies. In rural areas, the administration's apparent impotence in the face of current problems has been highlighted by the fact that most food aid distribution during the recent drought was conducted through an assortment of independent foreign organizations rather than through state channels. President Traoré has, however, shown considerable staying power in the face of problems such as these, and there is as yet little sign that public discontent is likely to lead to effective opposition to his rule. Given Mali's dependence on foreign assistance, it is debatable whether it would be possible for any government to depart radically from the policies currently being pursued.

Further Reading

Harrison Church, R. J. *West Africa* 7th ed. London: Longman, 1974.

Imperato, Pascal James. *Historical Dictionary of Mali.* Metuchen, N. J.: Scarecrow Press, 1977.

"Mali." In *Africa Contemporary Record, Annual Survey and Documents,* Harrison Church, R. J., et al., eds. New York and London: Africana Publishing Co., 1981.

MALTA
(Repubblika ta' Malta)

by Charles R. Foster, Ph.D. revised by Kenneth E. Bauzon, Ph.D.

The System of Government

Malta, an island nation of 380,000 people south of Sicily, Italy, has a two-party parliamentary system. The republic gained its independence from Great Britain in September 1964. Until 1974, the monarch of England was titular head of state, represented in Malta by a governor general. In that year, Malta became a republic within the Commonwealth.

Executive

The head of state is a president elected to a five-year term by the legislature. Miss Agatha Barbara became president on February 15, 1983. The head of government and chief executive officer is the prime minister, a post filled by Dr. Karmenu Mifsud Bonnici since 1981. The prime minister, as leader of the majority party in the legislature, determines legislative policy and names his own cabinet, which is formally appointed by the president.

Legislature

Malta's unicameral legislature, the House of Representatives, consists of sixty-five members, elected to five-year terms by universal suffrage. In 1976, the Malta Labour Party won 51.2 percent of the vote and thirty-four seats; in 1981, it won only 49.1 percent of the vote, but retained its thirty-four seats. The opposition Nationalist Party won 48.8 percent of the vote in 1976 and 50.9 percent of the vote in 1981, but won only 31 seats each year. Charging that the Labour Party had skillfully readjusted the boundaries of constituencies to deprive the Nationalists of their rightful majority in the House, the Nationalists boycotted the new legislative session in February 1982. In April, the speaker of the House announced that the Nationalist seats had been formally vacated under a rule that forbids a member to be absent more than two months. The government now operates with the approval of a legislature consisting solely of the thirty-four Labour Party members. In March 1983, the political impasse appeared to have been resolved with the prime minister's assurance that talks on election reforms would take place. By mid-year discussions were suspended when violent anti-government activities intensified and the Nationalist Party accused the government of undermining the parliamentary system.

Judiciary

As originally constituted, Malta's judicial branch was independent of the executive. Nine judges, appointed by the president on the advice of the prime minister, served in the superior courts. A constitutional court of three judges was supposed to review laws and executive acts. All judges are entitled to serve until age sixty-five. In 1980, however, after four private persons filed suit against the government over the closure of a private hospital, the government suspended the superior judges and announced the resignation of the chief judge. In early 1981, the courts resumed their work under a new law which barred the courts from ruling on the validity of government actions or of "any person holding public office." The legislation set up a five-member panel to supervise the administration of justice. The panel was to consist of two members of the Labour Party, and one of the Nationalist Party, one representative of organized labor, and one representative of the bar. The bar representative and the Nationalist boycotted the new panel.

Regional & Local Government

Malta has no local government and few regional branches of the central government. The country is administered as a unit from the capital, Valletta.

The Electoral System

Malta use the single transferable vote system of proportional representation. Candidates run in multimember districts. Their names appear on the ballot in alphabetical order with their party affiliations noted. The voter is required to rank the candidates in order of preference. To be elected, a candidate must reach a quota of votes—the total votes in the district divided by the number of seats to be filled, plus one additional vote. Votes in excess of the quota are distributed to candidates ranked second on the ballots for first-ranked winners. If a voter's first choice does not reach the necessary quota, his or her vote goes to the highest-ranked candidate who can achieve the quota. While this system does not guarantee proportionality, it is calculated to provide the broadest representation of parties and beliefs.

Citizens age eighteen and over are eligible to vote, and turnout is very high. In the last three elections, it has exceeded 90 percent.

The Party System

Political activity in Malta is based upon strong mass-based organizations, such as clubs and teams, which are affiliated with one political party or another. The first Maltese political groups were born out of a controversy over language which followed the publication of a British government report on education in 1880. The report recommended that English replace Italian in the primary schools. The pro-English faction ultimately evolved into the present Malta Labour Party, while the more conservative Italian faction later became the Nationalist Party. By 1930, the language issue had become irrelevant as English and the native Maltese (a Semitic language) came to predominate, but the liberal versus conservative tendencies sharpened in the dispute continue to mark the two parties.

Malta Labour Party (MLP)

History

The Labour Party was founded officially in 1921 by Dr. Paul Boffa. It came to power for the first time in 1955. After a period out of power, it returned to government in 1971 and has remained in power since then.

Organization

The MLP is organized at the national, district, and village level; virtually every village has its own MLP committee, which is elected annually by the local dues-paying members. Every local committee elects one member to sit on the district committee, which acts as a clearing house for party propaganda and campaign work. At the apex of the pyramid is the National Executive composed of representatives of the district committees and of the Labor League of Youth, party members in the legislature, and additional members elected by the annual National Conference. Conference delegates are representatives of the local committees of each village and town. While the party is highly democratic, the leadership is cohesive and there are no signs of serious party divisions or factions.

Policy

The MLP intends to transform Malta into a socialist state and has gone far toward achieving this aim. Important sectors of the economy, including commercial banks, have been nationalized, taxation is high and wealth disparities are low. The party has long been anticlerical and, in 1974, pushed through a constitutional amendment which prohibited the Roman Catholic Church from speaking out on political issues.

In foreign policy, the party has adopted a neutralist stance and the Labour government is seeking international recognition of Malta as a formally neutral state. That neutrality has been recognized by Italy, France, Saudi Arabia, Algeria, Iraq, the United Arab Emirates, and the Soviet Union. The government permits NATO forces to use Maltese facilities, but it also provides supply and repair services to Soviet ships. The party also pursues a variety of economic and trade policies aimed at making Malta as economically independent as possible.

Membership & Constituency

No reliable data is available on party membership, but the party draws its members and electoral support from nonprofessionals and the working class. It also draws much of its support from anticlericals in the villages who see themselves engaged in a daily struggle against the conservative social teachings of the Roman Catholic Church.

Financing

The party is largely financed by membership dues and other personal contributions.

Leadership

Dominic Mintoff (born 1916) has been the dominant figure in the party since the late 1940s. An energetic and self-assertive man, Mintoff presents himself as the embodiment of the proudly independent and often beleaguered Maltese. He was succeeded as party president in 1981 by Alfred Sant, a management expert educated at Harvard.

Prospects

With the exclusion of the Opposition MPs from their parliamentary seats, Malta has virtually, although not officially, become a one-party state. The MLP has been able to keep control through access to government institutions and resources and by the growing resort to coercion as opposition grew. In the long run, however, it will have to reckon with the power of the Church, the apparent strength of the opposition NP, and growing defiance at the grassroots level of its manipulation of the government to undercut the strength and effectiveness of the opposition.

Nationalist Party
(*Partit Nazzjonalista*)

History

During the dispute over language, the conservative faction was led by Dr. Fortunato Mizzi and later by his son, Dr. Enrico Mizzi, who was a founder of the Nationalist Party in the 1920s. In 1950 Dr. Giorgio Borg Olivier became party leader and was prime minister until 1955, and from 1962 to 1971. The Nationalists were in power in 1964 when independence from Great Britain was negotiated and led the government

until 1971. Olivier retired in 1976 and was succeeded by Dr. Edward Fenech-Adami.

Organization

The Nationalists are less formally organized than the MLP. The primary elements of the party are the personal organizations of the party's candidates and members in the House, most of whom are local notables. A party executive group selected by local party leaders serves as a policy- and strategy-making body. There are no permanently organized village committees or party clubs, although some do exist at the township and district level.

Policy

The Nationalist Party subscribes to a modern liberal and free-enterprise policy. While it does not reject the socialist measures taken by the Labour Party, it wants to ease trade-restriction policies imposed by the Mintoff government to enhance Malta's economic independence. The Nationalists are prepared to rely on the economic and political support of the West, call for rapid formal association with the European Economic Community, and support the NATO military alliance. The party is also supportive of the Roman Catholic Church's role in education and hospital operation.

Membership & Constituency

Support for the party comes primarily from devout churchgoers in the villages, businessmen and small entrepreneurs, and white-collar professionals.

Financing

Funds come mainly from membership dues and private voluntary contributions.

Leadership

Dr. Edward Fenech-Adami (born 1934) is the party leader. He is noted for a quiet urbane manner and for his tactful negotiating skills. Guido de Marco is deputy leader and Louis Golea general secretary.

Prospects

Claiming that it has been cheated out of its victory in the 1981 elections, the NP has consistently challenged the government's legitimacy. It is likely to continue its civil disobedience campaign unless the government resumes talks on electoral reforms. With Mintoff fading into the background and the government's resort to dictatorial methods indicating its growing isolation, the NP may yet recapture power.

National Prospects

In the short run, Malta will continue to be dominated by the MLP supported by the government's authoritarian strictures. Given the persistent challenge of the NP, discontent at home and criticism from abroad, the MLP might have to share power with the opposition. Affected by world recession, the country's exports have declined, but the economy appears to have recovered thanks to the government's restrictions on tight imports, which have kept the balance of payments deficit under control. The government's grip on the economy can be expected to tighten as it works to make the country self-reliant. The imposition of industrial peace to attract foreign investments is a step in this direction, along with the intensified search for oil in the Mediterranean seabed. Despite the recent conflict with Libya, Malta will continue to seek friends among the Arabs. It will reaffirm its neutral position and emphasize its role as a "bridge of peace" in the Mediterranean. Thus it will continue to solicit international recognition for this position, which may have little practical value in preventing international conflicts in the region but which, nevertheless, has domestic political and emotional appeal.

Further Reading
Austin, Dennis. *Malta and the End of Empire.* London: F. Cass Co., 1971.
Blouet, Brian. *The Story of Malta.* London: Faber & Faber, 1972.
Boissevain, Jeremy. *Saints and Fireworks: Religion and Politics in Rural Malta.* London: University of London, 1965.
Dobie, Edith. *Malta's Road to Independence.* Norman, OK: University of Oklahoma, 1967.
"Malta: Backing Away from Helsinki." *The World Today*, V. 40. August-September, 1984.
Owen, Charles. *The Maltese Islands.* New York: Praeger, 1969.

ISLAMIC REPUBLIC OF MAURITANIA
(République Islamique de Mauritanie; Joumhouriyyat al-Ishamiyya Mouritania)
by Isla MacLean

The System of Government

Mauritania, a country of nearly two million people in northwest Africa, has been ruled by a military committee since the July 1978 coup that toppled the one-party regime led by Mokhtar Ould Daddah, president since the country gained independence from France in 1960. The immediate cause of the coup was military and popular dissatisfaction with a crippling war with the Polisario guerrillas in the Western Sahara, annexed by Mauritania in 1976. A cease-fire was signed with the Polisario in 1979. Mauritania recognized Western Sahara's independence and proclaimed its neutrality in the continuing war between the Polisario and Morocco. The country continues to be divided between pro- and anti-Polisario forces and by ethnic, tribal, and regional divisions.

Executive

Full executive and legislative powers are vested in the Military Committee for National Salvation (*Comité Militaire de Salut National;* CMSN), led by Colonel Maouiya Ould Sid'Ahmed Taya, who became chairman of the CMSN and head of state in December 1984. (The committee had had three other leaders between the time of the coup and Taya's appointment). The CMSN is assisted by a cabinet of over twenty members of whom the great majority are now civilian.

In December 1980, a civilian prime minister was appointed to head a transitional government and a draft parliamentary constitution was published. It provided for a multiparty state with a presidential system of government. Three months later, however, the constitution was suspended and army officers returned to key government posts following an attempt to overthrow the government of Lieutenant Colonel Mohamed Khouna Ould Haidallah, Taya's predecessor.

Legislature

Mauritania has been without a legislature since the National Assembly was dissolved in the wake of the 1978 coup.

Judiciary

In 1980, Islamic law (shari'ah) was introduced and the Islamic Court of Justice was founded to try crimes against people and property and adjudicate in family matters. The first application of the shari'ah (a public execution and three hand amputations) was in September of that year. In June 1983, it was decided to apply the shari'ah in all domains. The Special (Military) Court of Justice was set up in 1980 to investigate and try cases which threaten the security of the government and state. In 1985, the court was reorganized to include civilian magistrates and the right of appeal in civilian and commercial cases. The Supreme Court, appointed by the CMSN, is the last court of appeal.

Regional and Local Government

Mauritania is divided into twelve regions administered by appointees of the central government. Nouakchott, the capital, is administered directly by the central government. More traditional administrative structures (emirates) have all but disappeared. During Ould Daddah's presidency, it was decided that when an emir died his title would die with him. In early 1986, only the emir of Trarza survives.

Since 1978, it has been CMSN policy to decentralize regional government, but progress has been slow. In June 1985, a conference on territorial administration was held to speed up the process.

In December 1985, Colonel Ould Taya announced plans to hold elections for mayors in the twelve regional capitals and the district of Nouakchott in the second half of 1986.

The Party System

Political parties have been illegal since the 1978 coup. The CMSN is pledged to restore democracy. It rejects the one-party rule that was exercised by Ould Daddah's Mauritanian People's Party (*Parti du Peuple Mauritanien*; *PPM*) from 1964 until the coup. The draft parliamentary constitution of 1980 guaranteed free political association and a multiparty system. It was suspended, however, in the wake of the March 1981 coup attempt.

The coup attempt highlighted political divisions within the government and army over policy on the Western Sahara. Fearing that the creation of political parties would make formal political, ethnic, and tribal divisions within the country, the CMSN suspended introduction of a multiparty system. Since 1982, it has set up a new organization, Structures for the Education of the Masses (*Structures d'Education des Masses*), that is intended to overcome these divisions and remove the influence of other countries. The CMSN has given repeated assurances that a return to civilian rule and to free elections has not been deferred indefinitely.

Structures for the Education of the Masses (*Structures d'Education des Masses*: SEM)

These popular committees are based on the family unit. Ten families make a cell, ten cells a district, and ten to fifteen districts a zone. Delegates are then mandated to departmental, regional, and national level, although no national conference has been held by early 1986. The SEM are directed and controlled by the CMSN. Their triple aim is to strengthen national unity through collective responsibility, promote economic development, and improve social conditions. Their work is based on community activities such as holding adult literacy classes; building roads, mosques, and classrooms; clearing sand from buildings; market gardening and tree planting. The SEM have been relatively successful in Nouakchott where many former

members of the PPM and other banned movements have taken part in their work, but their influence has been less marked in rural areas.

The 10th of July Movement (*Le Mouvement du 10 Juillet*)

This faction within the CMSN takes its name from the date in 1978 when a group of army officers ousted the Ould Daddah regime. It has three aims: withdrawal from the war with the Polisario (and neutrality in the continuing conflict between the Polisario and Morocco); economic recovery; and restoration of democracy. Failure to achieve or respect these goals was the downfall of three military leaders. Colonel Mustapha Ould Mohamed Salek was unable to extricate Mauritania from the war or to quell social unrest. Lieutenant Colonel Mohamed Mahmoud Ould Ahmed Louli, who took over in June 1979, was little more than a figurehead for his prime minister, Lieutenant Colonel Mohamed Khouna Ould Haidallah, who replaced him in January 1980.

Architect of the peace treaty with the Polisario in 1979, Haidallah then abandoned neutrality for a pro-Polisario stand. Diplomatic relations with Morocco were severed for its involvement in the 1981 coup attempt, a friendship treaty was signed with Algeria (the Polisario's main backer), and Mauritania recognized the Polisario's Sahrawi Arab Democratic Republic (SADR) in 1984. Meanwhile, Mauritania's economic crisis deepened. In December 1984, Colonel Ould Taya took over. Within four months, agreement was reached with the International Monetary Fund, which eased the economic crisis, and neutrality was restored with the resumption of diplomatic relations with Morocco.

National Democratic Movement (*Mouvement National Démocratique*; MND)

Begun as a leftist student movement, the MND became a major, albeit partly clandestine, political force in the 1970s. It advocated racial harmony and a more open and democratic system. But it suffered serious setbacks when prominent members joined the PPM in the mid-1970s, then others joined the government and administration after the 1978 coup. In 1982, it called for the formation of a united national front with the participation of all the political movements. The call was rejected by the CMSN as it would have meant acknowledgment of the existence of the various factions. Since the creation of the SEM, the MND, in common with the other factions, has virtually ceased to exist.

Ba'athists

The largest and most active Arab nationalist faction, this group has close ties with the Iraqi Ba'ath Party. It favors the full arabization of Mauritania. Its extremist views are considered racist and provocative by the CMSN, given the country's ethnic composition. Scores of activists were arrested by security forces during Ould Haidallah's presidency. The Ba'athists' position on the Western Sahara is unclear but is assumed to be against the existence of the Polisario's SADR, given its belief in one Arab nation.

Nasserites

This pan-Arab group also favors the arabization of Mauritania. Its position differs from that of the pro-Iraqi Ba'athist faction in that it views arabization from a cultural rather than a racist standpoint. Its position on the Western Sahara is unclear.

Muslim Brotherhood

The smallest Arab nationalist faction, this group is composed mainly of middle-aged businessmen. Given their position in society, this group is essentially a conservative force. It favors the strict application of the shari'ah.

Strict Nationalists (*Nationalistes Etroites*)

This group of black Mauritanians, advocates the creation of a more secular state and greater freedom for blacks. It opposed the war to annex the Western Sahara.

Free Man (*El Hor*)

El Hor is an organization of the Harratine, former slaves of the Moorish upper class. Set up in the late 1970s, the group opposed the continued existence of slavery in the country. (Under the Ould Daddah regime, slaves theoretically were free to leave their masters, but the institution remained untouched.) *El Hor's* activities hastened the abolition of slavery, by

CMSN decree, in July 1980. The movement now opposes discrimination against former slaves. *El Hor* is led by educated ex-slaves who now hold high positions in the army, government and trade unions.

Opposition

The ban on political activity curbs organized civilian opposition to military rule within the country. The most powerful opposition movement to emerge abroad was the Alliance for a Democratic Mauritania (*Alliance pour Une Mauritanie Démocratique*; AMD). Established by a group of conservative businessmen and members of the banned PPM, the AMD was the vehicle by which Ould Daddah hoped to return to power. Based in Paris, but with support from Morocco and Senegal, the AMD sponsored the unsuccessful coup attempt against Haidallah in March 1981. Thereafter, it suffered serious setbacks: Senegal expelled known AMD activists, the major AMD military leaders captured in Mauritania were executed, and Ould Daddah apparently gave up the leadership. Since Haidallah's removal from power, the AMD has virtually ceased to exist and most prominent members, including former chairman Cheikh Ould Jiddou, have returned home from exile.

Other Political Forces

Military

The loyalty of senior army officers to the 10th of July Movement has been questioned on occasion. This has led to frequent changes being made in the top military personnel and membership of the CMSN. Two officers dismissed from the CMSN by Haidallah, Lieutenant Colonels Ahmed Salem Ould Sidi and Mohamed Ould Bah Ould Abdel-Qader, led a band of renegade soldiers across the border with Senegal in the 1981 coup attempt. They failed to rally the support of the 8,500-man armed forces and were captured, tried, and executed. Several plots to remove Haidallah from the presidency were reported. One such plot involved the first military head of state, Salek, and former civilian prime minister Sid'Ahmed Ould B'Neijara; they were sentenced to ten years' hard labor in 1982, but granted amnesty when Taya became head of state in 1984.

Ethnic Groups

About 60 percent of Mauritanians are Arabic-speaking Moors of mixed Arab, Berber, and black African stock. They are divided into numerous tribal groups and into the "white" Moors, the dominant class, and "black" Moors, the ex-slaves, or Harratine. Some 40 percent of the population is black African and belongs to the Peul, Toucouleur, Soninké, and Wolof ethnic groups. Their society is also highly stratified and traditionally permitted the ownership of slaves. The black Africans were traditionally settled farmers in the Senegal River basin on the southern border, while the Moors were traditionally nomadic pastoralists.

The dominant position occupied by "white" Moors in the past is being eroded. "Black" Moors now constitute a sizable portion of the free labor force and urban shantytown dwellers. The black African population is growing at a faster rate than the Moorish population. (The actual balance of numbers is disputed.) Black demands for greater representation and protests at the arabization of education have erupted periodically into violence. A concession was made on education reform with agreement to permit teaching in the ethnic languages from the 1985 to 1986 school year. Periodically, organizations have been formed in the south to seek an independent black state.

The fragile unity of the country is maintained through a common adherence to Islam and, more importantly, an intricate power-balancing process. The government includes representatives of the various ethnic groups, although "white" Moors still predominate.

Organized Labor

The Mauritanian Workers' Union (Union des Travailleurs Mauritaniens; UTM) is the only organized force in the country outside of the army. Union militancy reached its height in the late 1960s and early 1970s. A series of strikes in support of nationalist demands forced the government's hand on revision of the cooperation agreement with France, creation of a national currency, and nationalization of the iron ore mines. The UTM was brought under the control of the PPM and government in 1973 and the leadership remained in the hands of Ould Daddah appointees until 1981.

Since then, the work of the UTM has been hampered by disagreement within the executive over the political role the trade union should play. Its secretary-general, El Kory Ould M'Heitty, was imprisoned for pro-Libyan activities during Haidallah's presidency, but released under the general amnesty of December 1984.

Bureaucracy

Corruption is a serious problem. Many army officers, government figures, and heads of state companies, display obvious signs of new wealth. Haidallah's failure to tackle growing corruption, particularly among his associates and family, was a major issue leading to his removal from the leadership in 1984. Since taking over as head of state, Taya has launched an anticorruption drive.

Religious Leaders

All Mauritanian nationals are Muslim, although not all practice their religion. The traditional religious figures, the marabouts, gain their position partly by inheritance and partly by their reputations for wisdom and piety. Most Mauritanians, black and Moor, are followers of one or another marabout and frequently consult that marabout on all matters. Given their dominant role in society, the marabouts are essentially a conservative political force. They favored introduction of the shar'iah and many opposed the abolition of slavery on the grounds that the practice is sanctioned in the Koran.

National Prospects

The first elections to be held since the 1978 military coup are due to take place at the end of 1986. Mauritanians in the regional capitals and Nouakchott will be given the opportunity to elect their mayors. Elections to other local government posts have been promised for 1987. But, for the moment, the ban on political parties remains in force. And no target date has been set by the CMSN for a return to barracks. As a result, an early return to civilian rule is unlikely.

Another indication that the CMSN intends to retain control in the medium-term is its desire to see through the three-year economic recovery program (1985–1988). The program involves austerity measures and the restructuring and rehabilitation of key sectors of the economy. For Mauritanians, the reform measures mean wage freezes, job losses in the state sector, higher energy and utility charges, and inflation (linked to devaluation and the phasing out of subsidies). The CMSN and government have admitted that these measures will cause social hardship but have said that they are committed to the recovery program.

The social difficulties caused by the austerity measures and the continuing process of urbanization are potential destabilizing factors. But, the primary threat to the stability of the leadership in the future is likely to be disunity within the CMSN. In the six years of military rule (1978–1984), there were four military heads of state and frequent changes of personnel within the ruling military committee. Prospects for long-term stability of leadership are not encouraging.

Further Reading

Gerteiny, A.G. *Mauritania.* London: Pall Mall, 1967; and New York: Praeger, 1967.

Gerteiny, A.G. *Historical Dictionary of Mauritania,* African Historical Dictionaries, No. 31, The Scarecrow Press, Inc., Metuchen, N.J. & London.

"Mauritania." In *Africa Contemporary Record. Annual Survey and Documents,* R.J. Harrison Church et al., eds Vol. 12, 1979-80. New York and London: Africana Publishing Co., 1981.

UNITED MEXICAN STATES
(Estados Unidos Mexicanos)
by Marvin Alisky, Ph.D. revised by Dale Story, Ph.D.

The System of Government

Mexico's constitution officially designates this nation as the "United Mexican States," indicating a federal republic in form. However, in practice Mexico remains a centralized or unitary republic with token states' rights. For example, while a governor is popularly elected within each of the thirty-one states, the dominant Institutional Revolutionary Party (*Partido Institucional Revolucionario;* PRI) has always won in every state. The president of Mexico unofficially selects all PRI gubernatorial candidates on the basis of their loyalty to his cabinet ministers, whose directives they must carry out. The constitution reserves for the federal government all authority over commerce, banking, land use, public health, labor laws, corporations, and licensing of professionals.

Any understanding of Mexican public life must begin with the concept of the Revolution, always spelled with a capital *R* to distinguish this ongoing struggle for social justice from the various revolts for political power which preceded it.

Prior to the Revolution General Porfirio Díaz had ruled Mexico as a repressive dictator from 1876 to 1911. The army and police maintained order through force. Díaz took land from political opponents and peasant villages, concentrating large farm-ranch-plantations (called *haciendas*) among a ruling elite. A few hundred *hacienda* owners controlled half of the nation's arable area. Some 90 percent of the rural population spent their lives working on the *haciendas* at marginal pay, perennially in debt to their employers, virtually under feudal conditions.

The military phase of the Revolution began in November 1910; during the ten years of civil war one million lives, out of a population of fifteen million, were lost. With the federal constitution of 1917 in force, the Revolution became a program of continuing social and economic re-

forms to redress the inequities of centuries. Intellectual Francisco Madero, the first Revolutionary president (1911–13), provided the political theme: "Effective suffrage, no reelection." Peasant leader Emiliano Zapata provided the social theme: "Land, bread, and justice." Zapata's goals have been translated into welfare benefits in a mixed public-private economy.

The "no reelection" protection against extended dictatorship limits the president and the governments to one six-year term, with no second term ever, and prohibits members of Congress, state legislatures, and municipal councils from serving two consecutive terms. After an intervening term, these lesser officials can run again for the same office. Thus the Mexican political structure is a "musical chairs" system under which PRI leaders rotate horizontally as well as vertically from one government position to another.

With its population reaching seventy million, by 1985 Mexico had experienced sixty-five years of relatively nonviolent government headed by a self-replenishing leadership that uses the PRI to win major elections. A dominant coalition of government, party, industrial, labor, and agrarian leaders has contributed to this political stability.

Executive

Executive power is vested in a president as head of government and head of state. The president must be a native-born Mexican of native-born parents, indicating the nationalism in the constitution, and at least thirty-five years of age.

Unofficially, he must have had experience as a cabinet minister, be physically vigorous, and able to mediate between the left and right wings of the dominant PRI. Since its founding, the PRI has always elected its presidential candidate. Its inner circle chooses the nominee, with the incumbent president having the most influential vote in picking the cabinet minister most likely to hold together the Revolutionary coalition. During the last year of his six-year term, the incumbent strives to inculcate in his successor his personal concept of the ongoing Revolutionary goals. From 1913 to 1946, presidents had been army generals as well as civilian administrators; since 1946 every president has been a civilian.

There is no vice president. In the event of the death or resignation of the president, the federal Congress elects an interim president.

Presidential powers are extensive and allow the chief executive to dominate the legislative branch. The president can introduce bills directly into both houses of Congress and can assign legislative priorities. The president can veto legislation; he has never had to do so, however, as no law opposed by him has ever been enacted.

The president appoints the cabinet ministers, diplomats, high-ranking officers of the armed forces, and all federal judges, with Senate confirmation. One-party dominance assures approval of his choices. The president can pardon anyone convicted of any felony, and chief executives have used this right freely in political matters to co-opt former opponents.

The constitution allows the chief executive to issue decree laws in most areas of public life. For example, the income tax was created by presidential decree, followed years later by congressional action. Presidential decrees have created cabinet ministries, government corporations, major public-works projects, significant budget changes, and public policies ranging from family planning to nuclear energy, followed later by congressional legislation.

The senior cabinet officer is the *Secretario de Gobernación* (minister of internal affairs), who controls federal-state-municipal relations, liaison with Congress, elections, voter and party registration, immigration and emigration, motion picture production and theaters, television and radio noncommercial air time, the federal police, and federal prisons.

The next most important members of the cabinet are the ministers of planning and budget, finance and public credit, commerce and industrial promotion, and public enterprises. These four help the president formulate economic and other domestic policies. Ranking next is the minister of foreign relations, who helps the president conduct foreign policy in conjunction with the aforementioned four ministers.

Presidents Lázaro Cárdenas (1934–40) and Manuel Avila Camacho (1940–46) had been minister of defense. Presidents Miguel Alemán (1946–52), Adolfo Ruiz Cortines (1952–58), Gustavo Díaz Ordaz (1964–70), and Luis Echeverría (1970–76) had been *Secretario de Gobernación*. President Adolfo López Mateos (1958–64) had been minister of labor, and President José López Portillo (1976–82), minister of finance. President Miguel de la Madrid (1982–88) was minister of planning and budget.

Legislature

The federal Congress consists of a Senate and a Chamber of Deputies. There are sixty-four senators, two from each of the thirty-one states and two from the Federal District surrounding the national capital, Mexico City. A senator's term runs six years and coincides with the presidential term. The PRI has always won every Senate seat except one, in 1976, which went to a candidate of the opposition Popular Socialist Party (*Partido Popular Socialista;* PPS) from the state of Oaxaca.

The Chamber of Deputies has 400 members, of which 300 are elected from congressional districts based on population. In each congressional district, the candidate with the most votes, plurality or majority, wins the seat. In 1979, the PRI won 296 district seats, and the PAN won the other four. In 1982, the PRI won 299 of the seats, while PAN kept only one. In 1985, the PRI gained only 290 seats, the PAN winning eight and the PARM the remaining two.

The remaining 100 seats are for the six minority parties, chosen on the basis of proportional representation. A deputy's term runs three years, every other election coinciding with the presidential election.

MINORITY-PARTY DEPUTIES		
	1982	1985
PAN	50	32
PCM	17	12
PPS	10	11
PARM	0	9
PST	11	12
PDM	12	12
PMT	0	6
PRT	0	6

The PRI dominates Congress regardless of slight shifts in the number of minority-party deputy seats. Since the legislative branch debates the form rather than the substance of new laws, changes in bills received from the executive branch are cosmetic rather than substantive. Both houses put legislation in final form in committee hearings which follow the guidelines set down by the appropriate cabinet ministry. Floor debate serves as an escape valve for frustration, but has little effect on legislation. The bandwagon journalism of the pro-establishment media filters congressional criticism of the government, making it appear more moderate than it really is.

Sessions run from September 1 to December 31 annually. Each year, the president calls Congress into special sessions for two months or more sometime during a period in January to August. When Congress is not in session, each chamber furnishes half of the thirty members of the Congressional Commission (*Gran Comisión*), which functions in place of Congress, including the confirmation of presidential appointments.

Without consecutive terms, senators and deputies cannot acquire seniority in Congress. Committee, subcommittee, and chamber leaders are chosen instead on the basis of party seniority.

Judiciary

Mexico's federal court system has exclusive authority for all important civil litigation, leaving to the court system of each state civil jurisdiction over minor sums of money and divorce cases. Suits involving contracts, finance and banking, labor-management relations, corporations, and interstate and intrastate commerce are handled by federal courts.

In criminal law, federal courts handle bank robberies, kidnappings, and most major felonies. Murder cases, however, are heard in state courts.

The one major restraint on presidential power is judicial, the writ of *amparo* (relief), which can be issued by any federal judge on behalf of a citizen claiming his constitutional rights have been violated by a government official. The *amparo* can be directed against a government official at any level, but can be obtained only from a federal court.

This writ stays the disputed governmental action until an appeal can be heard by the federal Supreme Court. The *amparo* combines some of the judicial powers found in the Anglo-Saxon writs of injunction, mandamus, and habeas corpus. It may halt official action, compel officials to carry out constitutional obligations, or force judges to tell a defendant the specific charges against him in a criminal case. Political disputes over elections and campaigns are excluded from the authority of *amparos*.

From 1917 to 1980, some 5,500 writs of *amparo* involved the president and his cabinet ministers as defendants. In one-third of these cases, private citizens or groups won their Supreme Court appeal over presidential action.

The federal Supreme Court has twenty-six members: a chief justice and twenty-five justices who divide into five divisions (*salas* or chambers) of five members each. The *salas* consider penal, civil, labor, administrative, and *amparo* appeals cases, respectively.

Supreme Court justices must be native-born Mexicans and be at least thirty-five years old. The president appoints them with Senate confirmation. A justice must retire at age sixty-five or at any time after age sixty if he has completed ten years of service. Since 1929 every justice has been a member of the dominant party, the PRI.

The intermediate federal judicial level is circuit courts of appeal, which there are six. The Supreme Court selects appellate judges from among Federal District Court judges to serve four-year terms. The president can grant an appellate judge tenure until age sixty-five.

Each of the thirty-one states has a state supreme court (*Supremo Tribunal de Justicia*), ranging in size from three to eight justices. The governor selects these justices for six-year terms.

Regional & Local Government

In each of the thirty-one states, a governor is popularly elected for a six-year term and can never serve a second term. Since 1929, every governor has been a member of the PRI. Despite the formality of state party conventions, the dominant party's inner circle in Mexico City preselects the candidate most likely to carry out the national administration's wishes. Except in six states, gubernatorial terms do not coincide with the presidential term. Thus, each incoming president "inherits" twenty-five governors who were selected by his predecessor, albeit unofficially.

Under Article 76 of the constitution, the president can have the Senate remove the governor of any state in which law and order cannot be maintained. The chief executive then designates an interim governor to finish the term. From 1917 to 1964, presidents have removed an average of one governor per year. Since 1964, presidents have averaged only one removal per presidential term. However, each chief executive has pressured one to three other governors to voluntarily resign when political crises got out of control.

Each state has a one-chamber legislature, with members elected for three-year terms, every other election coinciding with the election of the governor. State constitutions reserve most of the powers for the governor, making the legislature a rubber-stamp committee formalizing details of his programs. Legislatures vary from nine to twenty-five members.

In each state the legislature must approve all municipal budgets, which the governor's finance director coordinates.

Mexico has 2,359 municipalities (*municipios*), which are like counties in the United States. Every town and city within the *municipio* is governed by the municipal council (*ayuntamiento*). Councils range in size from five to eleven members who serve three-year terms. Mayors (*presidente municipal*) have the constitutional powers to dominate the councils. About fifty local governments are controlled by minority parties, the remainder being held by the PRI.

The Electoral System

Elections at all levels of government are popular and direct and provide representation by a simple majority winner, except for the 100 seats in the federal Chamber of Deputies which are reserved for minority parties on the basis of proportional representation. Federal Chamber of Deputies districts and state legislative districts each have a single representative. Two Senators are elected statewide from each state. For each senator and deputy, as well as state legislators and municipal council members, a substitute is also elected. This allows each party to reward its workers with nominations as substitutes. In the event of a vacancy between elections, the substitute immediately fills the post, obviating the need for a by-election.

For purposes of determining minority-party winners by proportional representation, Mexico is divided into five regions. Each minority party prepares lists of candidates for the proportional-representation ballot of each electoral district. All voters receive two ballots, one with congressional-district candidates and one with minority-party candidates. Each voter may choose one party on the ballot listing the minority-party candidates. After the count, each minority party's vote in the five regions is totaled and proportional representation of each party in each region is determined. If it is determined that a minority party is entitled to five seats, for example, in one of the regions, the top five vote getters of that party in that region will get those seats.

Voting is secret in booths. Each voter gets a separate ballot for local, state, and federal races should these occur simultaneously. Voters cannot split their ballot but must choose an entire party slate. When given the paper ballot, the voter has his or her thumb coated with indelible yellow ink, which will not wear off for twenty-four hours, thereby preventing voting twice. All Mexican federal elections must be held on the first Sunday in July, and all state and local elections must be on Sunday.

With the PRI dominant, voter indifference characterizes most elections. Half of the eligible voters do not go to the polls in presidential elections; in congressional or municipal races with strong minority-party candidates, the turnout may reach 70 percent of the registered voters. PRI leaders encourage PRI voter turnout with promises of continuing welfare programs and patronage.

The Federal Electoral Commission protects PRI interests in tabulating disputed congressional elections. Opposition charges of fraudulent vote counting arise in fifteen to twenty-five congressional districts every three years and in several municipalities each year.

The Party System

Origins of the Parties

After Mexico achieved independence from Spain in 1821, its party system consisted of several small parties, each a personalistic group following a strong leader. The real impetus for the institutionalization of parties and the end of purely personalistic movements was the formal uniting of the Agrarian, Labor, and Peasant parties in March 1929 as the National Revolutionary Party (*Partido Nacional Revolucionario;* PNR), now the PRI.

The Parties in Law

The federal Law of Political Organizations and Electoral Processes (*Ley Federal de Organizaciones Politicas y Procesos Electorales* or LOPPE) gives Congress the authority to set requirements for a party to qualify for a place on the ballot.

The 1977 LOPPE requires a party to have at least 65,000 members, with at least 3,000 in each of half of the states. While a new party is awarded temporary recognition for the next federal election, it must win 1.5 percent of the total national vote to retain its legal status. In the 1985 congressional elections, eight minority parties participated as registered parties. A new party must be active for four years before it can petition the Federal Electoral Commission for recognition. To get on the ballot for any office, a candidate must have a party affiliation.

Party Organization

The LOPPE requires each party to maintain a permanent national headquarters and a national executive committee. At least six months before an election, a party must hold a national convention to publicly announce its candidates for all offices it intends to contest. In practice, each party's inner circle chooses its candidates.

National officers of each party dominate state and local committees. The only party with active municipal committees throughout the republic is the dominant PRI, which maintains them with government patronage and informal, extralegal use of contingency funds from federal and state budgets.

Campaigning

The Federal Electoral Commission awards each party free postage and telegraph service proportional to the party's percentage of the total vote in the previous election. The government furnishes each party with an equal number of political posters; in 1979, each of the six minority parties got one million posters, the same number the PRI received.

The ministry of internal affairs requires television and radio networks and stations to give free air time to be shared equally by all recognized parties in congressional races. No additional air time can be purchased, and no air time is allotted to state and local contests. All parties must share four hours of television and four hours of radio time per month for three months preceding elections. In 1979, the seven parties equally divided that time. Campaign broadcasts must deal with issues and policies and not individual candidates.

Independent Voters

Independent voters constitute less than 10 percent of the registered voters.

Authentic Party of the Mexican Revolution
(*Partido Auténtico de la Revolución Mexicana;* PARM)

History

The PARM was founded in 1954 by General Jacinto B. Trevino, former minister of industry. PARM elected its first two deputies to the federal Congress in 1958; adding seats each three years thereafter, it elected twelve deputies in 1979. PARM usually wins from 2 to 2.5 percent of the total congressional vote in each federal election, but in 1982 did so poorly (1.36 percent) that it won no seats and lost its status as a recognized party. It regained conditional registration in 1985 and even won two of the 300 congressional district seats along with nine minority-party seats. Besides deputy seats, its only other officeholders have run six municipal governments since 1958.

Organization

PARM organization is rudimentary. It is primarily a loose association of retired generals who manage the party from Mexico City. There is very little local organization.

National headquarters are at Edison 11, Colonia Revolución, Mexico, D.F.

Policy

This party calls for a moderate approach to the ongoing social Revolution, with protection of private property and welfare programs. It wants increased government aid to small farmers.

Membership & Constituency

PARM claims a membership of 200,000, most of whom are middle-aged, middle-class men. Its strength centers in Mexico City and the states of Nuevo León, Jalisco, and Tamaulipas.

Financing

PARM's financing comes from dues, contributions from conservative retired generals, and from government subsidies. In return for subsidies, PARM always supports the PRI presidential candidate.

Leadership

Retired general Antonio Gómez Velasco (born 1920) was PARM president from 1976 to 1982. He directed physical education for the Education Ministry in the 1970s.

The present PARM president, Jesús Guzmán Rubio (born 1940), is a retired army general with a law degree. He was a deputy in the federal Congress from 1973 to 1976 and 1979 to 1982.

Carlos Enrique Cantú Rosas (born 1922), PARM secretary general, is a former mayor of Nuevo Laredo and was a deputy in the federal Congress from 1973 to 1976.

Prospects

PARM's resurrection as a party in 1985 was primarily due to the PRI's desire to have another surrogate party. It remains weak at the national level.

Communist Party of Mexico (*Partido Comunista de México;* PCM); or Unified Socialist Party of Mexico (*Partido Socialista Unificado de México;* PSUM)

History

Francisco Cervantes López—publisher of a weekly socialist newspaper, and Manabendra N. Roy, a Marxist from India—founded the PCM at a Mexico City socialist conference in September 1919. Roy became PCM secretary general and José C. Valadés, head of the Politburo.

In 1920, the PCM began publishing its official organ, *Vida Nueva,* twice a month. In 1921, the party launched its Communist Youth of Mexico group, sent delegates to the Third Comintern Congress in Moscow, and held its own First Party Congress.

In 1922, the famous painters Diego Rivera and David Siqueiros joined the PCM and began its magazine, *El Machete.* From 1930 to 1935, the party was outlawed for its violence against the government. The Hitler-Stalin nonaggression pact in 1939 cost the PCM 1,000 of its 30,000 members. In 1940, the PCM helped French Stalinist Jacques Mornard assassinate Soviet dissident Leon Trotsky in Mexico City. In the 1950s, the PCM lost members to the Popular Socialist Party. In 1978 the PCM applied for conditional registration after thirty years of being denied legal status. It gained full legal registration after the 1979 elections.

Organization

The PCM's Central Committee has sixty-five members. In 1976, the eleven-member Executive Committee replaced the Politburo. A party congress is held every two to three years. Arnoldo Martínez Verdugo has been PCM secretary general since 1964 and dominates the party. The Central Committee publishes a weekly, *Oposición.*

An auxiliary, Communist Youth of Mexico, (*Juventud Comunista de México;* JCM) is active on all Mexican university campuses. Since 1978, the PCM has publicly disavowed its former support for the 23rd of September Communist League guerrillas, whose bombings and kidnappings in the states of Guerrero, Morelos, and Jalisco provoked military counterinsurgency. The guerrillas were suppressed in all three states and are no longer active.

PCM controls the Socialist Revolutionary Party, the Mexican People's Party, and the Socialist Action and Unity Movement, none of which have legal status on the ballot. In November 1981, the PCM adopted the name Unified Socialist Party of Mexico (*Partido Socialista Unificado de México;* PSUM) for the 1982 elections so that its candidates and those of its unregistered satellite groups could run as a coalition on the ballot. The party's JCM controls the Student Federation of the National Autonomous University of Mexico.

Party headquarters are at Montery No. 159, Colonia Roma, Mexico, D.F.

Policy

PCM's domestic policy calls for expropriation of all privately owned businesses, industries, and services under a Marxist government; party ownership of all media; and abolition of nonsocialist schools. Its foreign policy is anti-United States and pro-Soviet Union. PCM supports Cuba, the Sandinista government in Nicaragua, and the Democratic Revolutionary Front in El Salvador.

Membership & Constituency

PCM claims a membership of 120,000. However, not until the 1979 congressional elections—when it got 703,068 votes or 5.2 percent of the total vote, winning eighteen deputy seats in Congress—did it qualify for the ballot. It lost one of those seats in 1982 and won only twelve seats in 1985.

Financing

The party collects dues from members. In addition, it receives grants from the Communist Party of the Soviet Union, the Cuban Women's Federation, the government of Libya, the Palestine News Agency, and other unspecified foreign sources. The PCM owns and rents out office buildings in Mexico City, Tepic, and Veracruz.

Leadership

Secretary General Arnoldo Martínez Verdugo was born in 1925 in Sinaloa state and was a clerk in the Sinaloa state government from 1940 to 1955. He was head of the JCM from 1945 to 1949. He has been a member of the Central Committee since 1955. Valentín Campa, PCM political secretary, and Alejo Méndez García, another prominent leader, were born in 1930 in Mexico City.

Prospects

PCM will continue to be the largest party on the Mexican left. The party hopes that high unemployment and inflation will discredit the PRI to the advantage of the PCM. Depending on its future success, the PCM may remain permanently the PSUM. It remains hampered by divisions in the Mexican left and PRI dominance of labor unions.

Institutional Revolutionary Party (*Partido Revolucionario Institucional;* PRI)

History

With the institutionalizing of the social Revolution under the constitution of 1917, the Agrarian, Labor, and Peasant parties clustered in an alliance under presidents Alvaro Obregón from 1920 to 1924 and Plutarco Calles from 1924 to 1928.

The dominant party of Mexico, the PRI, was founded as the National Revolutionary Party (*Partido Nacional Revolucionario;* PNR) by former Mexican president Plutarco Calles on March 4, 1929, in Querétaro. The PNR brought together regional and national leaders from the agrarian, labor, bureaucratic, and military sectors.

In 1933, the PNR established the practice of putting forward six-year plans for the country; each subsequent president has adopted the existing plan as the program of his government. The party's national assembly changed the name to the Institutional Revolutionary Party in 1946 to emphasize the continuing social and economic reforms to which it is committed.

President Manuel Avila Camacho in 1943 created the National Federation of Popular Organizations (*Confederación Nacional de Organizaciones Populares;* CNOP) as the sector for bureaucrats, professionals, housewives, merchants, and others of the growing middle class. CNOP subsequently became a dominant force in the party, overshadowing the labor and agrarian sectors in policymaking.

In 1963, the party created an Institute of Political, Economic, and Social Studies (*Instituto de Estudios Politicos, Economicos, y Sociales;* IEPES) to research national needs and policy priorities. The IEPES coordinates PRI and government policy formulation.

In 1964, the PRI elected as its president attorney Carlos Madrazo, former governor of Tabasco. He convinced the PRI to adopt a policy of party primaries to open nominations for state and local offices to those not tied to political cliques. Madrazo arranged party primaries in two states, Baja California Norte and Chihuahua. However, since its 1929 founding, the PRI has relied on an elite inner circle to select nominees. The inner circle, therefore, got the party's National Executive Committee to cancel the policy of primaries and forced Madrazo to resign. Since 1966, the Revolutionary coalition elite have continued to choose nominees privately.

In the 1982 elections, the PRI won 69.3 percent of the total vote for the 300 congressional districts, taking 299 of the seats, plus all the seats in the Senate. The PRI won 68 percent of the vote in the presidential race, electing Miguel de la Madrid for the 1982–88 term. Inasmuch as the PPS and the PARM also listed him as their candidate, de la Madrid got 71 percent of the presidential vote. In its lowest vote total ever, the PRI gathered 65 percent of the vote for the congressional district seats in 1985, winning 290 districts.

Organization

At the apex of the PRI's organization is the National Executive Committee (*Comité Ejecutivo Nacional;* CEN). The "inner circle" of the CEN includes the party president; the secretary general; secretaries for agrarian, labor, and popular action; and two secretaries of political action (always one federal deputy and one senator). The CEN has thirteen additional secretaries, who are designated by the inner circle.

The next level is the National Council, which has at least sixty representatives from each of the agrarian, labor, and popular sectors, plus the heads of the state committees from the thirty-one states and the Federal District. The CEN dominates the Council. The Council guides state and municipal PRI assemblies and reports on them to four staff officers of the CEN: the director of administrative services, the director of adjudication, the director of electoral action, and the director of social activities.

The lowest nationwide entity is the National Assembly, in which about 2,000 representatives chosen from both the sectoral and regional divisions of the party represent the general PRI membership. National assemblies meet every three or four years and merely ratify CEN policies. In addition, the PRI convenes a national convention every six years to formally ratify the presidential candidate which the CEN already has announced.

The agrarian sector is dominated by the National Confederation of Peasants (*Confederación Nacional de Campesinos*). The labor sector includes eight confederations, seven federations, and nineteen independent unions, all under the umbrella of the Congress of Labor. The largest of these labor groups is the Mexican Confederation of Labor (*Confederación de Trabajadores de Mexico*). The popular sector is headed by the National Confederation of Popular Organizations (CNOP), with government employees being the dominant force.

PRI publishes a monthly magazine, *La República*, which circulates to party municipal committees, federal and state government agencies, and public libraries. PRI publishes a semimonthly journal, *Proyección Politica*, for party leaders at every level. The party owns jointly with the federal government the Mexico City daily newspaper, *El Nacional*. Every six years the CEN appoints its publisher.

The party's women's group is the Revolutionary Feminine Association (*Asociación Nacional Femenina Revolucionaria;* ANFER). The PRI's youth group is the National Movement of Revolutionary Youth (*Movimiento Nacional de la Juventud Revolucionaria;* MNJR). The ANFER and MNJR directors attend CEN meetings.

National headquarters are at Insurgents Nte. 59, Z.P.3, Mexico, D.F.

Policy

PRI's domestic policy stresses "no reelection," a Revolutionary ban on continuation in one office. The party supports the right to strike, even for those working for the government in essential services (except for the military). Minimum wages for all trades and for unskilled labor, social security, basic health care for the poor, public housing for workers, communal or individual farms for peasants, and profit sharing for private-sector workers are PRI policies.

PRI's foreign policy stresses Mexico's independence from the United States, the Soviet Union, and Europe. It favors cooperation with the Organization of American States to promote Latin American regional common markets. The party favors left-of-center Latin American governments.

Membership & Constituency

PRI members hold all executive government posts from minister down through middle-level bureaucrats, all federal judgeships, all governorships, all Senate seats, and 290 of the 300 congressional district deputy seats. Before the 1982 elections, it also held 478 of the 483 seats in state legislatures and controlled 2,341 of the 2,359 municipal governments. PRI members hold 99 percent of all federal, state, and local executive-branch jobs and all diplomatic appointments.

Civil service merit systems are only token, with the PRI's political patronage being the rule in public life. Government jobs are filled on the basis of the political clique (*camarilla*) system. A successful PRI politician's entourage is horizontal among peers who were classmates in school and vertical among rising administrators and their trusted assistants. Since a *camarilla* is based on close friendships, as a *camarilla* leader rises in the PRI and in government, he has his associates promoted into higher-level offices.

Among rank-and-file PRI members, extended family relationships form clusters within the party, based on lifelong friendships within each age group, class, and community.

Financing

Bureaucrats pay party dues equal to three days' pay a year. Other members pay token dues or are given credit for dues by performing various services for the party. Prominent politicians fund banquets and entertainment within their own cities and states. At every level of government, unaudited government contingency funds are used for PRI activities.

Leadership

The current PRI president is Adolfo Lugo Verduzco. He was born in Huichapan, Hidalgo, and received a law degree from the National University. He has served in the Ministry of Planning and Budget and presently is a federal senator representing Hidalgo. The PRI secretary general is Irma Cue de Duarte, a former federal deputy from the state of Veracruz.

Miguel de la Madrid (born 1934 in Colima), the president of Mexico, is the real leader of the party. De la Madrid has a law degree from the National University and a degree in public ad-

ministration from Harvard University. He has been assistant director of finance for the national oil company (PEMEX), the Mexican envoy to several international economic conferences, and a director of the National Bank for Foreign Trade. He was minister of planning and budget from May 1979 to September 1981.

Prospects

The PRI has run the government since 1929 and dominates most facets of public life. Opposition minority parties receive substantial, although slanted, media coverage as they challenge PRI legislation in Congress and government daily operations, but the policy changes they occasionally coax the PRI to adopt have been more cosmetic than substantive.

In the 1960s and the 1970s, communist guerrilla kidnappings and killings did selective damage to the PRI in a few cities. The most serious challenge to the PRI came during July–October 1968 when student demonstrators protested political repression, hoping to force the government to cancel the Olympics. Such a cancellation might have discredited the PRI enough to drive it from power, but the demonstrators were repressed violently by the government.

Even with the pressures of inflation, high unemployment, massive foreign debt, and a declining currency, the government of the PRI continues to command the support of a majority of citizens and likely will remain in power for the foreseeable future.

Mexican Democrat Party
(*Partido Demócrata Mexicano;* PDM)

History

In the city of Irapuato on May 23, 1971, Juan Aguilera Aspeitia founded the right-wing PDM. Aguilera, a business executive in the state of Guanajuato, is head of the Sinarquista National Union (*Union Nacional Sinarquista;* UNS), a fascist group which began in Guanajuato in 1937. In addition to UNS members, he assembled other rightists who wanted parochial education to replace public schools.

Organization

PDM's National Executive Committee and its twenty-three regional committees include secretaries for finance, membership, public relations, and campaigns. Each committee has representatives of artisans, proprietors of small businesses, and peasants. PDM publishes a party monthly magazine, *El Demócrata*, distributed to members throughout the republic.

Party headquarters are at Edison No. 89, Colonia Revolucion, Mexico, D.F.

Policy

PDM's domestic policy calls for a reduction of state-owned enterprises, reduction of welfare programs, an end to PRI cronyism in government, and a "union of Church and State." Its foreign policy favors alliances with anticommunist nations.

Membership & Constituency

PDM's membership of 100,000 in twenty-two states and the Federal District includes many middle-class religiously oriented urbanites. On the ballot for the first time in the 1979 congressional elections, the PDM won ten deputy seats. In the 1982 elections, PDM won 2.3 percent of the proportional representation congressional vote, sufficient for it to add two more seats. It retained its twelve seats with 2.7 percent of the vote in the 1985 elections.

Financing

PDM does not make public its party financing.

Leadership

From 1978 until 1984 a business executive from Irapuato, Gumersindo Magaña Negrete, was PDM president. The current PDM president is Ignacio González Gollaz, a business executive in San Luis Potosi and PDM presidential candidate in 1982.

Prospects

PDM's chances for growth are almost nil. Catholic lay leaders favor the National Action Party. Its major power base is the state of Guanajuato, where it controls the town of Guanajuato.

National Action Party (*Partido de Accion Nacional;* PAN)

History

The PAN was founded on September 14, 1939, by Manuel Gómez Morín, on a platform of Catholic social principles within the framework of the institutionalized Revolution. Gómez Morín (1897–1972) was dean of the law school of the National University of Mexico and University president.

PAN's roots went back to the National Catholic Party, which was active in Congress from 1911 to 1913. When PAN got on the ballot in 1940, it was the first time since 1914 that a conservative party could fully participate in Revolutionary Mexico.

In 1946, PAN won four deputy seats in Congress and its first two municipal governments. In 1947, PAN won its first seat in a state legislature in Michoacan.

Organization

The party president and secretary general direct the National Executive Committee, which has secretaries for political action, public relations, finance, recruitment, and campaigning. The Committee guides state and municipal chairmen.

In 1958, PAN presidential candidate Luis H. Alvarez introduced into Mexico the first open party convention; an obvious contrast to the PRI's inner-circle selection of candidates. PAN's subsequent conventions also have been open contests. In 1976, the necessary 80 percent of delegates could not agree to nominate Pablo Emilio Madero, nephew of the father of the 1910 Revolution Francisco Madero. The party then voted not to offer a 1976 presidential candidate.

PAN publishes a monthly magazine, *La Nación.* The daily newspapers *El Heraldo* in Mexico City and *El Norte* in Monterrey editorially support it. PAN has a youth sector and a women's association.

Party headquarters are at Serapio Rendon 8, Mexico, D.F.

Policy

Its domestic policy calls for multiparty policy formulation in the government, less government investment in industrial and commercial corporations, and effective suffrage by ending fraudulent vote tabulations favoring the PRI in some congressional districts. Its foreign policy calls for a strong anticommunist stance.

Membership & Constituency

PAN has 500,000 members, a majority being from the middle class and upper class. In percentage of total presidential votes, PAN improved from 7.9 percent in 1952 to 13.9 percnt in 1970, when it got two million votes. In the 1964 and 1970 presidential elections, PAN got 31 percent of the vote in Mexico City.

In the 1979 congressional elections, PAN won four districts plus thirty-eight minority-party seats, for a total of forty-two deputies, getting 11.4 percent of the total vote.

In the 1982 congressional elections, PAN won 18 percent of the total vote, getting fifty of the 100 minority party seats. It won only one of the 300 congressional district seats. PAN candidate Emilio Madero won 15.7 percent of the total presidential vote, getting 3.7 million votes to 16.7 million for PRI candidate De la Madrid. With fifteen percent of the vote in 1985, it won eight district seats but only 32 minority-party seats.

Since 1946, PAN has won twenty-nine of the mayor's races and seats in thirty-seven Municipal Councils. Key victories came in 1967 when PAN took over local government in two state capitals, Hermosillo in Sonora and Mérida in Yucatan. Today it controls the mayor's office in the state capitals of Chihuahua, Durango, and Hermosillo and in the fourth largest city in Mexico, Cuidad Juárez. Up to 1979, PAN had won seats in seven state legislatures.

Financing

Three-fourths of the members pay voluntary, locally set dues. Catholic Action groups make contributions. The party holds fund-raising raffles, dances, and concerts.

Leadership

National Committee members include José Angel Conchello, an attorney from Monterrey and a deputy in Congress; Manuel González Hinojoa, 1976–78 PAN president; and Abel Vincencio Tovar, 1978-84 PAN president. The current PAN president is Pablo Emilio Madero, its presidential candidate in 1982. Madero is a conservative Monterrey entrepreneur and a nephew of Francisco Madero. Protesting the rightward drift of the party, a number of former leaders have left the PAN since 1976.

Prospects

Because of longtime Church-state conflicts in Mexico, PAN will not affiliate with Christian Democratic parties of Europe, but accepts Catholic social reforms, especially papal encyclicals calling for increased social justice. If fraud were removed from congressional districts in which the PRI barely wins, PAN could win twenty-five or more deputy seats over its current total. It cannot win the presidency, although its candidate is the principal opponent of the PRI candidate.

Popular Socialist Party (*Partido Popular Socialista;* PPS)

History

On September 25, 1947, labor leader Vicente Lombardo Toledano founded the Popular Party. In 1948, he added "Socialist" to its name, trying to unite Marxists and noncommunist leftists.

A union organizer, Lombardo Toledano was ousted as head of the Mexican Federation of Labor in 1940 because he organized the communist-oriented Latin American Workers Federation. He was the unsuccessful PPS presidential candidate in 1952 and a PPS deputy in Congress from 1964 to 1967. He died in 1968.

Since 1958 the PPS has supported the PRI presidential candidate, but fields its own candidates for Congress and for state and local office.

Organization

PPS has a National Executive Committee and state and municipal committees. It publishes a monthly magazine, *Nueva Democracia,* and a weekly newspaper, *El Combatiente.* Its auxiliaries are the National Socialist Youth and the Socialist Women's Association.

Party headquarters are at Alvaro Obregón No. 185, Colonia Roma, Mexico, D.F.

Policy

PPS advocates a payment moratorium on Mexico's enormous international debt. Its foreign policy supports all leftist and Marxist developing nations and is strongly anti-imperialist.

Membership & Constituency

PPS claims 300,000 members. Its strongholds are the states of Oaxaca, Nayarit, and the Federal District. Most members pay voluntary dues, and it receives grants from European Socialist parties.

In 1968 Jorge Cruickshank, without opposition in the state of Oaxaca, became the first PPS senator, breaking the thirty-nine-year PRI monopoly on senate seats. Every three years from 1964 through 1976, PPS won from five to ten deputy seats in Congress. In 1979 it won 2.9 percent of the total congressional vote and eleven deputy seats. In 1982 and 1985, its share of the vote was consistent at 1.9 percent and it won ten and eleven seats, respectively. Since 1948 PPS has won ten municipal governments.

Financing

The PPS owns office buildings which it rents, and a printing company which accepts non-political business. Profits go into the party treasury. PPS does not make public the status of its income from contributions.

Leadership

The head of the party is the secretary general, a post filled by Jorge Cruickshank since 1968. Born in 1915 in Oaxaca, he was a mechanical engineer and taught at the National Polytechnic Institute. From 1943 to 1951, he led the National Union of Education Workers. He was a deputy in Congress from 1964 to 1967 and 1970 to 1973 and a senator from 1976 to 1982.

Prospects

PPS's influence on government remains indirect, through its ties to the leftists within the dominant PRI. As a result of poor electoral showings in 1982 and 1985, that influence seems to have diminished.

Socialist Workers Party (*Partido Socialista de los Trabajadores;* PST)

History

This Marxist party was founded in July 1973. In the 1979 elections, it got 2.3 percent of the congressional vote, winning ten of the minority-party seats in Congress. In 1982, it won only 1.8 percent of the vote and eleven seats. Its share of the vote increased in 1985 to 2.5 percent and it gained twelve seats.

Organization

The PST is well organized, directed from the center, and highly disciplined. Headquarters are at Avenida Mexico No. 199, Colonia Condesa, Mexico, D.F.

Policy

The PST calls for government expropriation of all industries and businesses, with each enterprise to be headed by a workers committee. Municipal governments would operate all utilities.

Membership & Constituency

The PST claims 110,000 members, primarily working class, including some Indians.

Financing

The party does not report any financial information.

Leadership

The PST was founded and is still led by Rafael Aguilar Talamantes. Born in 1940 in Baja California Sur, he studied economics at the National University from 1958 to 1964. He was in prison for six years (1964–70) for leading riots which resulted in student deaths.

Prospects

The party's main chance for survival and expansion depends on its organizational efforts among groups of Indians, especially the Maya, Aztec, Zapotec, and Tarascan, to which the PST devotes more energy than any other party.

Revolutionary Party of the Workers (*Partido Revolucionario de los Trabajadores*; PRT)

History

The PRT was founded in September 1976 as the first Trotskyite party in Mexico. It received conditional registration in 1981 and full registration with the election of 1982.

Organization

The PRT is governed by a collective body, with some six to ten individuals participating in the decision-making process.

Policy

The PRT declares itself to be in "service to the proletariat" and committed to the socialist revolution to construct a socialist democracy.

Membership and Constituency

The PRT has become significant as a tool for protesting political repression, especially after the selection of Rosario Ibarra de Piedra as its 1982 presidential candidate. As the first woman candidate in Mexican history, mother of a political prisoner, and well-known leader of a human rights group, her campaign attracted considerable attention. Though the PRT won no federal deputies in 1982, Ibarra de Piedra polled 1.76 percent of the presidential vote and thus the party gained its full registration. In 1985 the PRT received 1.25 percent of the vote and six minority-party deputies.

Financing

The party does not report any financial information.

Leadership

As mentioned, the leadership is a collective body. The most well-known individual in the party is Ibarra de Piedra.

Prospects

The PRT has a future not so much as a Trotskyite party but as a vehicle for protesting political repression in Mexico.

Mexican Workers' Party (*Partido Mexicano de los Trabajadores*; PMT)

History

The PMT was established in September 1974 by a distinguished group of Mexican leftists who had been involved in the railroad strike of 1959 and the student protests of 1968. The PMT chose not to participate in elections prior to 1985, because it believed they were not fair or democratic. It finally gained conditional registration in 1984 and fielded its first candidates in 1985.

Organization

The PMT is governed by a National Assembly, a National Plenary, and a National Committee. The National Committee really directs the party. It is composed of a party president and eleven secretariats.

Party headquarters are at Bucareli 20, Mexico, D.F.

Policy

The PMT proposes to socialize the means of production and to produce a just and egalitarian society without discrimination or privileges.

Membership and Constituency

Its popular strength is difficult to determine, since it had not run in elections before 1985. In those elections, the PMT won 1.53 percent of the total vote and gained six minority-party deputies.

Financing

The party does not report any financial information.

Leadership

The dominant force in organizing the party is Heberto Castillo, who was born in the state of Veracruz and is a civil engineer by profession. He was a private secretary to Lázaro Cárdenas and participated in various leftist movements in the 1960s. He was jailed after the 1968 student protests and upon his release became one of the most respected opponents of the Echeverría and López Portillo administrations. He now serves as president of the PMT.

Prospects

Partially due to its late start in the electoral game, the PMT is not expected to rival the PCM/PSUM as the leading party on the left. Its degree of success is primarily due to the fame of Castillo.

Other Political Forces

Organized Management

Under a 1941 law, every retail store or commercial company must join the local chamber of commerce. These chambers in turn must unite in the Confederation of National Chambers of Commerce (*Confederación de Cámaras Nacionales de Comercio;* CONCANACO). It has an executive council, annual general assemblies, and assesses dues on a scale based on annual sales.

Under that 1941 law, every manufacturer, wholesaler, and distributor within a nationwide industry must belong to that industry's national chamber. For example, every shoe manufacturer must belong to the National Chamber of the Shoe Industry; every radio and television station must belong to the National Chamber of Broadcasters. These industrywide chambers in turn must unite in the Confederation of Industrial Chambers (*Confederación de Cámaras Industriales;* CONCAMIN). It, too, has an executive council, an annual general assembly, and assesses dues on a scale based on annual sales.

Neither CONCANACO nor CONCAMIN are part of the PRI, but individual business and industrial executives may join the PRI. CONCAMIN and CONCANACO have full-time staffs of economists, lawyers, and other specialists who draft suggested policies, regulations, and procedures. They then lobby directly with the highest appropriate level of government concerned, such as the ministers of commerce, labor, finance, or foreign relations.

Organized Bureaucracy

All federal government employees below the top five levels of administrators belong to unions. Thirty-one unions have members throughout the agencies and departments of the executive branch and among staff employees of the judicial and legislative branches. Since 1936, these unions have been united in the Federation of Unions of Workers in the Service of the State (*Federación de Sindicatos de los Trabajadores en el Servicio del Estado;* FSTSE). It has one million members.

The FSTSE dominates the popular sector of the PRI and helps formulate major government policies. Its well-disciplined members turn out for political rallies, campaign speeches, and elections. The FSTSE has its own Social Security Institute, which provides better pensions and health services than the social security system for workers in the private sector.

Following the lead of the FSTSE in political activities is the separate National Union of Employees in Service to State and Municipal Governments.

Organized Labor

The largest group of unions is the Mexican Federation of Labor (*Confederación de Trabajadores de México;* CTM), which helps formulate labor policy for the PRI and the government.

Other federations less politically powerful are the Revolutionary Federation of Workers and Peasants (*Confederación Revolucionario de Obreros y Campesinos;* CROC) and the National Workers Federation (*Confederación Nacional de Trabajadores;* CNT).

The Railroad Workers, Petroleum Workers, and Telephone Workers Unions are semiautonomous, having loose links to the CTM but operating independently. All federations and autonomous unions meet annually in the Congress of Labor, whose key committees articulate organized labor's needs and goals.

National Prospects

Mexico's political prospects during the six-year term of President Miguel de la Madrid are linked to the economic condition of the republic. For twenty-two years (1954–76), during steady economic growth, the peso remained at 12.5 to the dollar. Since 1978, Mexico has been the fourth-largest petroleum exporter in the world; however, most oil profits have gone to service a huge foreign debt rather than to elevate living standards.

In 1982 the peso slipped from 48 to the dollar to more than 100 and by 1986 had devalued to almost 500 to the dollar. In August 1982 the government for the first time used currency controls, preventing dollars from leaving the country except for vital payments. Inasmuch as the government had periodically promised not to use such controls, their imposition engendered discernible political cynicism.

The International Monetary Fund, private United States and European banks, and foreign governments renegotiated Mexico's loans on condition that the government adopt austerity measures, including reduction of subsidies for food and fuel purchased by Mexicans. With the largest foreign debt of any developing nation in the world, over $90 billion, Mexico had to finally adopt measures to reduce deficit spending, a move which was politically unpopular among most Mexicans. The alternative was national bankruptcy, so the severe standards which the government imposed were accepted, with disgruntlement, by a majority of citizens. Economic conditions in 1985 worsened as government revenues declined due to lower oil prices. Nevertheless, political stability likely will continue during the 1980s.

Further Reading

Alisky, Marvin. "Mexico's Population and Migration Problems." *Current History*, Vol. 80, No. 469, November 1981.

———. *Latin American Media: Guidance and Censorship.* Ames, Iowa: Iowa State University Press, 1981.

Briggs, Donald C. and Alisky, Marvin. *Historical Dictionary of Mexico.* Metuchen, N. J.: Scarecrow Press, 1981.

Camp, Roderic A. *Mexico's Leaders: Their Education and Recruitment.* Tuscon, Ariz.: University of Arizona Press, 1980.

Cornelius, Wayne A. *Politics and Migrant Poor in Mexico City.* Stanford, Calif.: Stanford University Press, 1975.

Grindle, Merilee S. *Bureaucrats, Politicians, and Peasants in Mexico.* Berkeley: University of California Press, 1977.

Hansen, Roger D. *The Politics of Mexican Development.* Baltimore: Johns Hopkins Press, 1971.

Johnson, Kenneth F. *Mexican Democracy: A Critical View.* 2nd ed. New York: Praeger, 1978.

Levy, Daniel and Székely, Gabriel. *Mexico: Paradoxes of Stability and Change.* Boulder, Colorado; Westview Press, 1983.

Meyer, Michael C., and Sherman, William L. *The Course of Mexican History.* New York: Oxford University Press, 1979.

Needler, Martin C. *Mexican Politics: The Containment of Conflict.* New York; Praeger, 1982.

Padgett, L. Vincent. *The Mexican Political System.* 2nd ed. Boston: Houghton Mifflin, 1976.

Ross, Stanley R., ed. *Is the Mexican Revolution Dead?* 2nd ed. Philadelphia: Temple University Press, 1975.

Story, Dale. *The Mexican Ruling Party: Stability and Authority.* New York; Praeger, 1986.

Wilkie, James W. *The Mexican Revolution: Federal Expenditure and Social Change Since 1910.* 2nd ed. Berkeley: University of California Press, 1970.

MONGOLIAN PEOPLE'S REPUBLIC
(Bugd Nairamdakh Mongol Ard Uls)
by Paul Hyer, Ph.D.

The System of Government

The Mongolian People's Republic, a nation of nearly two million people, is a communist state politically patterned after the Soviet Union. It is generally characterized as a satellite of the Soviet Union; indeed, it was the prototype of the satellite system that later emerged in the Soviet bloc in Eastern Europe.

Mongolia had been under Chinese control from 1691 to 1911, when the Mongolian nobility declared it an independent monarchy under a "reincarnated" Buddhist lama. In 1921, Outer Mongolia was the scene of the first communist revolution in Asia when it revolted against renewed Chinese domination. With Soviet aid, it became an independent republic in 1924. Most, although not all, Mongols continue to believe that their independence from China requires a strong link to the Soviet Union.

The constitution of 1960 theoretically places government in the hands of the people acting through representatives elected to the Great National Khural (*soviet* or assembly). In fact, government is in the hands of a Presidium and Council of Ministers, whose election by the Khural is assured by direct or indirect manipulation by the Central Committee of the single party, the Mongolian People's Revolutionary Party (MPRP) which monopolizes power and administers it through the party Politburo.

Executive

The highest executive body of government through which party policies are implemented is the Council of Ministers which directs the work of the ministries, guides the planned economy, directs foreign affairs, supervises the state monopoly of foreign trade, directs the national defense, and maintains public order through the police. The chairman of this council functions as a premier. In 1984, a Presidium was set up in this council to enhance efficiency.

Legislature

The People's Great Khural is a single house with members elected for a term of four years. By last count it had 354 deputies, of which 328 were party members. The Khural meets annually for about one week to rubber stamp party policy and decisions. When the Khural is not in session, the nine-member Presidium rules in its name. The president of the Presidium, Jambyn Batmonh, is head of state; he is also the party secretary.

Judiciary

Supreme Court justices are elected for terms of four years by the Khural. In courts of province, town, and district levels, lay assistants, usually party members, sit with professional judges to hear cases. The 1960 constitution is the basic law. There is no provision for judicial review of legislation. The legal system is a blend of Mongolian, Russian, and Chinese elements.

Regional & Local Government

The administrative system consists of eighteen provinces, with over 350 districts, and twenty separate municipalities. The boundaries of the districts and the agricultural collectives are the same. Each subdivision is nominally administered by People's Deputies Khurals which, in fact, are controlled by local party secretaries.

The Electoral System

The party controls elections to the Khurals by creating single-candidate election lists. To indicate approval, a voter simply places an unmarked ballot in the box. The only other option is to cross out names. Suffrage is universal for those eighteen years of age and over. In the national election in 1980, 99 percent of the electorate was reported to have turned out to give their near-unanimous approval to the party's candidates.

Mongolian People's Party
(*Mongol Ardyn Nam*)

History

Mongolian politics were traditionally characterized by fragmented political power in the hands of a hereditary nobility which was paralleled and complemented by a powerful monastic clergy of lamaist Buddhism. Politics were dominated by these elites and the people had no active role.

The declaration of independence in 1911 was followed by a decade of nationalistic fervor and continued political turbulence. Radical Mongolian nationalists, encouraged by the victory of the Bolsheviks in Russia, organized the vanguard of the MPRP in January 1920. The party itself emerged in 1921 with the rise of a small group of procommunist leaders who looked to the Soviet Union for direction and institutions to revolutionize the nation. Their success was insured by Moscow's decision in 1921 to set up a satellite government in Ulan Bator. Support from the Red Army and the introduction of Soviet political directors consolidated the party's power. During the 1920s there were great internal divisions between left-wing radicals and right-wing moderates and conservatives. The late 1920s and the 1930s saw violent purges and a forced collectivizing of the countryside. The nobility and clergy were neutralized, but covert competition for personal power continued within the party for many years.

Finally, Khorlain Choibalsan emerged as the strong man in 1939 and the institutions of the party and government were firmly established in, more or less, in their present form. A dominating personality not unlike Stalin, Choibalsan ran the government with virtually no consultation with formal government bodies. Only two party congresses were convened between 1939 and 1952, the year when Choibalsan died. He was succeeded by Yumjhagiin Tsedenbal, whose administrative style was much more moderate and conventional and whose leadership lasted forty-four years, until 1984. Jambyn

Batmonh has continued Tsedenbal's moderate approach to government since he succeeded him in 1984.

Organization

The party's structure follows the conventional communist model. A party congress nominally appoints the Central Committee to handle the day-to-day affairs of the party. This pattern is duplicated in the eighteen provincial administrative jurisdictions, called *aimaks*. The party secretary, Batmonh, is also president, thus combining the top party and state posts. (This represents more personal concentration of power than is usually found in Moscow.) Batmonh is unrivaled, but he shares power with the party's Politburo, the leading collective decision-making group in the system. A nine-man body, the Politburo effectively controls the party's Central Committee.

There is a system-wide tendency for party members to simultaneously hold government jobs. By one recent count, almost half the full membership of the Central Committee also held government posts, a pattern repeated at each lower level. At the same time, there appears to be little participation of lower-level party members in higher party councils; few regional party leaders or officials are represented on the Central Committee.

Jambyn Batmonh assumed leadership of the party in August 1984, in a smooth transition of power, and offered much praise for his predecessor, Tsedenbal. By last count, the congress included 708 delegates and forty-four alternates. Selected by various organizations to represent them, roughly 50 percent of the delegates are from party and state organs; 25 percent from the combined areas of industry, construction, and communications; and 25 percent from the livestock and agricultural sector.

The party congress, if not the elite, generally reflects the ethnic divisions of the country. About 80 percent of the delegates are from the Khalka Mongolian ethnic group which makes up about 76 percent of the population. Most of the rest of the congress comes from two other Mongolian ethnic groups, about 13 percent of the population. Kazakhs are the largest single minority in the country, but they comprise only 2 percent of the population and are not a source of friction. They are represented in the party congress. Chinese are a tiny urban minority, and unlike their unassimilated counterparts in

Southeast Asia, have little impact on policy and no power to disrupt.

Two satellite associations of the party are the association of labor unions with well over 100,000 members, and the party's youth organization, the *Revsomols*, with 80,000 to 100,000 members. The youth organization was once a major independent force within the party, but has now become thoroughly subordinate to party leadership.

Policy

Dependence on the USSR is crucial in internal politics and also in foreign policy, which has been anti-Chinese but is moderating. Top party leadership pushes for solid integration of the country into the Council for Mutual Economic Assistance, the other members of which are the USSR and the Eastern European countries. (Mongolia is not a member of the Warsaw Pact organization, but Soviet troops are stationed within the country along its border with China.) Soviet Union party decisions are invariably echoed in Ulan Bator.

Intraparty disputes continue over such problems as overdependence on the Soviet Union, support for particular Soviet policies, and relations with China. The 1984 dismissal of Yumjhagiin Tsedenbal, ostensibly for poor health, may have been related to the USSR's move to improve relations. A narrow nationalist element, anathema to Moscow has been a worry to party leadership.

Recent purges have not led to the execution of the opposition figures, but only to their removal from office. In fact, in recent years the party has had considerable stability in its structure, dynamics, and personnel, and there has been a fair amount of intraparty mobility or "changing of the guard."

Membership & Constituency

Total party membership probably exceeds 70,000, about 4 percent of the population. Some 50 percent of the membership consists of the "intelligentsia" and government employees, another 30 percent is made up of urban workers, and the remaining 20 percent consists of *arats*, members of the livestock cooperatives. Projections indicate that the relative number of workers is increasing and that of the *arats* decreasing. The word "intelligentsia" is commonly used in Mongolia to refer to the so-called "working intelligentsia" which includes many poorly educated and inarticulate persons. The party elite are virtually all true intelligentsia— bureaucrats, officials, and professionals.

Financing

No information is available on party finances. Presumably, membership dues and state support cover party expenses.

Leadership

The leadership is relatively young. For example, Jambyn Batmonh, the head of government, was born in 1926. Young leadership indicates a lack of education among older Mongolians, which in turn partly explains why party power has been so narrowly concentrated.

The personality cult that marked the reign of earlier leaders has not been continued, but personality and personal differences still appear to be of as much importance in the alignments of the elite as policy and ideology.

Many of the elite have been educated in the Soviet Union and have personal as well as political ties there. Soviet-educated economists predominate at the top levels of the party. Among other leaders, one is the author of a widely used book on livestock finances, one is a planning specialist, and a third is a financial expert. Apart from the group of economists, a group of party officials who specialize in foreign affairs has remained especially strong.

A third group of leaders is composed of military men, although professional soldiers do not seem to have great influence in the party outside of the area of their immediate expertise. Nevertheless, the army is generally regarded as a key element in both the integration and indoctrination of a once-fragmented society. It has also played a major role in the spread of literacy. The structure and dynamics of the internal-security apparatus, the Ministry of State Security, is modeled closely on that of the Soviet Union, but it is not important as a separate leadership group.

Opposition

There is some evidence of irritation among artists and teachers over party controls and censorship, but there are no signs of consistent or organized dissent. Religion, long under a shadow, has shown continued vitality.

National Prospects

The political system of Mongolia is totalitarian in intent, but less so in fact and effectiveness. The majority of the people are less than a generation removed from an almost completely nomadic society, and while the change to an industrial and agricultural society has proceeded rapidly, it is by no means complete. The nomadic spirit of free-wheeling independence is still alive in Mongolia. The slow development of education, communications, and transportation also make the classic formula for communist control difficult to apply effectively. Bureaucratic incompetence and inefficiency are endemic: party policy is often not carried out, not because of deliberate opposition, but because of the ineptitude and lethargy of those who must deal directly with the people and the problems.

At the same time, the last quarter of a century has seen a major increase in the percentage of the population involved in the political life of the country. It is the consensus of specialists that a higher percentage of the Mongolian people are represented in the power structure of Mongolia than is the case in any other communist nation, or indeed of most other Asian nations. This is due in part to the sparse and relatively homogeneous population; but it also reflects the growth of education, communication and transportation—developments which are essential to the communist recipe for totalitarian control.

Further Reading

Bawden, Charles R. *The Modern History of Mongolia.* New York: Praeger, 1968.

Friters, Gerard M. *Outer Mongolia and Its International Position.* New York: Octagon Books, 1978.

Ginsburg, George. "Local Government in the Mongolian People's Republic 1940–1960." *Journal of Asian Studies,* Vol. 20, No. 4, August 1961.

Jagchid, Sechin and Hyer, Paul. *Mongolia's Culture and Society.* Boulder, Colo.: Westview Press, 1980.

Shirendev, B. and Sanjdorj, M. *History of the Mongolian People's Republic.* Translated and annotated by William A. Brown and Urgunge Onon. Cambridge, Mass.: Harvard University Press, 1977.

Lattimore, Owen. *Nomads and Commissars; Mongolia Revisited.* New York and London: Oxford University Press, 1962.

——— "Satellite Politics: The Mongolian Prototype." *Western Political Quarterly,* Vol. 9 (1956).

Rupen, Robert A. *How Mongolia Is Really Ruled.* Stanford, Calif.: Hoover Institution Press, Stanford University, 1979.

——— *Mongols of the Twentieth Century.* 2 Vols. Bloomington, Ind: Indiana University Press, 1964.

KINGDOM OF MOROCCO
(Al-Mamlaka al-Maghrebia)
by David Seddon, Ph.D.

The System of Government

The Kingdom of Morocco, with a population of nearly 20.5 million, is a traditional monarchy. Although there is a constitution, the reigning Alawite dynasty is not a "constitutional monarchy" in so far as all three of Morocco's postindependence constitutions (adopted in 1962, 1970, and 1972) have enhanced rather than limited the king's power.

The Monarchy

The pivotal role of the monarch is spelled out in the 1972 constitution: "The King is the Commander of the Faithful, the Supreme Representative of the Nation, the Symbol of her Unity and the Guarantor of her existence and continuity. He is the Defender of the Faith and the Guardian of respect for the Constitution."

The constitutional powers of the king are wide-ranging: he appoints and dismisses the prime minister and the other ministers; he has the right to address the Chamber of Representatives and "the content of his address shall be above comment"; he is commander-in-chief of the armed forces and appoints the senior military officers; and he controls the judiciary by virtue of his powers to appoint the judges and preside over the Higher Judicial Council.

The king has the right to dissolve the Chamber of Representatives by decree and exercise its legislative powers until new elections, which must be held within three months. However, by virtue of Article 35 of the constitution, the king may declare a state of exception under which he may rule by decree for an indefinite period. This right was first invoked by Hassan II in 1965. The state of exception lasted almost five years, until the promulgation of the 1970 constitution. Hassan II was able once again to rule by decree without any elected legislative body between 1972 and 1977 simply by refusing to call general elections after the adoption of the 1972 constitution.

Constitutional revision, which can be initiated by the king without reference to the Chamber of Representatives, requires approval in a referendum, but the consitution specifies that "the monarchical system, and provisions relating to Islam, shall not be subject to revision."

The king claims a divine right to rule, as *Amir al-Muminin*, or Commander of the Faithful; and it is this presumption to both the spiritual and temporal leadership of his subjects which sanctions his claim to ultimate control over the nation's political life.

A rule of primogeniture is established in the constitution. If the king dies or abdicates before his successor reaches the age of sixteen, the king's powers are exercised by a regency council, composed primarily of royal appointees. Until the heir reaches his twentieth birthday, it acts as a consultative body.

Executive powers are delegated by the king to the Council of Ministers, which is headed by the prime minister. Since the last general elections, in 1983, the government has been a coalition of proroyalist "independents," the *Istiqlal* (Independence) party, the Popular Movement (*Mouvement Populaire*; MP), the Socialist Union of Popular Forces (*Union Socialiste des Forces Populaires*; USFP) and nonparty technocrats. Since November 1983, the premier has been Mohamed Karim Lamrani, who has no party affiliation.

Although its influence on the process of decision making is considerable, the Council of Ministers is subordinate and responsible to the king, who personally makes the most important policy decisions. The king is advised by a small, influential royal cabinet, a group of four or five royal counselors headed by a director-general, who are among the king's most trusted political allies.

Legislature

Since 1977, when the first parliamentary elections were held under the 1972 constitution, Morocco has had a unicameral legislature, known as the Chamber of Representatives. Two-thirds of its seats are elected directly, and the remaining third by provincial and prefectoral assemblies and by corporate groups representing commerce, industry, agriculture, crafts, and labor. Originally, representatives were to serve four-year terms, but a constitutional amendment, approved by referendum in May 1980, extended the life of the Chamber to six years, thereby postponing the elections due in 1981. In June 1983, the representatives adopted a proposal to modify the composition of the Chamber of Representatives to provide for 306 members instead of 267; of these, 204 would be elected directly. This implies a redefinition of constituencies and creates five seats for candidates elected by Moroccans living abroad. General elections to the legislature took place in September 1984, fifteen months after the local elections in June 1983.

The Chamber's legislative competence is relatively narrow. The consitution bars the Chamber from adopting bills or amendments which reduce the state's revenue or raise public expenditure. If, by December 31, the Chamber has not approved the following year's budget, the government can simply proceed as if the budget had been approved. The deputies have the right to vote on the development plan but cannot amend it. With regard to the broad objectives of economic, social, and cultural policy, the Chamber can pass *lois cadres* (framework laws), but the details of such laws and all other subjects not specified as falling within the Chamber's competence are considered to come under the government's administrative authority. The government is entitled to reject any legislative proposal passed by the Chamber which it deems to be outside its legislative competence. In the event of a disagreement between the Chamber and the government in such a case, a ruling is made by the constitutional chamber of the Supreme Court.

In fact, the Chamber has engaged in very little legislative activity since 1977, and there has been a high rate of absenteeism on the part of the deputies, possibly because of the Chamber's relative lack of importance in the political system.

Judiciary

Although formally independent of the executive and the legislature, the judiciary is under the strong influence of the king, who appoints the judges and presides over the Higher Judicial Council, which supervises the judicial system. In political trials, sentences often appear to be predetermined by the Ministry of Justice; and Amnesty International has claimed that political prisoners frequently are not given a fair trial, often subjected to torture, and may be held incommunicado for months or years.

The court system includes communal and district courts for minor offenses, thirty tribunals of first instance, nine appeal courts, a Supreme Court (with criminal, civil, administrative, social, and constitutional chambers), social courts for labor cases, the High Court for crimes committed by ministers in the exercise of their public functions, the Special Court of Justice for crimes committed by civil servants, and the Court of Justice which judges serious state security and political cases.

Regional & Local Government

At the local level, Morocco is divided into several hundred rural and municipal communes, which are administered by state officials known as *caids* in the rural areas and *pashas* in the municipalities. They are appointed by and responsible to the Ministry of the Interior. The communal councils, which have between nine and fifty-one members each, directly elected with a six-year mandate, have neither the funds nor the authority to be more than "rubber stamp" bodies for the decisions of the local *caid* or *pasha* and his administration. Several communes comprise a *cercle*, which is headed by a *supercaid*.

The highest unit of of subnational administration is the province or, in large conurbations, the prefecture. They are administered by governors, appointed by the king, and responsible to the Ministry of the Interior. Each province and prefecture has an indirectly elected assembly of eleven to thirty-three members selected by the communal councillors. Like the communal councils, the provincial assemblies have little real power, their decisions being subject to the approval of the governor.

The Electoral System

The Chamber of Representatives has 306 seats, 204 of which were filled at the last general elections in 1984 by direct election (199 from constituencies in Morocco and the occupied territories of the Western Sahara, and five from constituencies in western Europe and the Middle East). Suffrage is universal for Moroccan citizens age twenty-one and over. The remaining 102 seats are elected directly. Of these, sixty are elected by the provincial and prefectoral assemblies, which are in turn elected by the municipal and rural communal councils; roughly equivalent numbers are elected by the chambers of Agriculture, Commerce and Industry, Crafts and by representatives of salaried employees.

The largely urban opposition parties are generally at a disadvantage to the overtly proroyalist forces in this system. First, rural voters still greatly outnumber urban voters. Second, the antimonarchical parties generally have failed to penetrate the countryside, partly because the king's religious prestige is greater there than in the cities, but also because the Ministry of the Interior, through its network of *caids*, effectively bars the more radical urban parties from campaigning in many rural areas. Certainly the results of the 1983 local elections demonstrate the continuing strength of the socalled "independents" or royalists in Moroccan local politics; the official "independents," combined with the National Assembly of Independents (*Rassemblement National des Independents*; RNI) and the other essentially conservative, loyalist parties—the Popular Movement (*Mouvement Populaire*; MP), the National Democratic Party (*Parti National Democrate*; PND), and the newly formed Constitutional Union (*Union Constitutionnelle*; UC), together accounted for 78 per cent of the seats and for 84 per cent of the rural and municipal commune presidents. In the national elections, these conservative, loyalist groupings provided 69 percent of seats obtained through direct election; overall, they commanded 70 percent of all seats in the Chamber of Representatives after the 1984 elections.

The apparent decline in support for the traditional opposition party, the Istiqlal, since the 1977 elections was striking; in 1977 it won nearly 20 percent of the seats in the Chamber (with fifty-one out of 264) and constituted the largest single party in the Chamber (after the independents), but in the 1984 elections it was able to acquire only forty-three seats out of 306

(14 percent). By contrast, the strength of the USFP increased substantially, to give it a total of thirty-nine seats (nearly 13 percent) in 1984, in comparison with 1977 when it had only fifteen (less than 6 percent).

1983 LOCAL ELECTIONS

Party	Seats	Affiliation of communal presidents
Independents	3,451	194
UC	2,731	187
RNI	2,211	135
Istiqlal	2,605	124
MP	1,896	102
PND	1,839	99
USFP	508	9
MPDC	94	5
PPS	19	–
Others	69	3
TOTAL	15,423	858

1984 NATIONAL ELECTIONS DIRECT ELECTIONS

	Morocco & the Western Sahara			Foreign Constituencies Seats
	Votes	Seats	% seats	
UC	24.8	55	27.6	1
RNI	17.2	38	19.1	1
Istiqlal	15.3	23	11.5	1
MP	15.6	31	15.6	—
PND	8.9	15	7.5	—
USFP	12.4	34	17.1	1
MPDC	1.6	—	—	—
PPS	2.3	2	1.0	—
OADP	0.7	1	0.5	—
Others	1.1	—	—	1
TOTAL		199		5

Accusations of election-rigging frequently have been levelled against the government by opposition parties. The official returns for referenda held to legitimize successive constitutions and constitutional amendments in particular have been viewed skeptically by independent observers. It hardly seems credible, for example, that 96.7 percent of the votes cast in the May 1980 referendum supported the constitutional amendment extending the life of a parliament from four to six years despite the vigorous opposition of the two main opposition parties, the USFP and the Party of Progress and Socialism (*Parti du Progrès et du Socialisme;* PPS).

1984 NATIONAL ELECTIONS INDIRECT ELECTIONS		
	Provincial/ prefectorial assemblies seats	Chambers seats
UC	18	9
RNI	11	11
Istiqlal	11	8
MP	12	4
PND	7	2
USFP	1	3
UMT	—	5
Others	—	—
TOTAL	60	42

The King

Hassan II (born 1929) has displayed remarkable skill in defending the monarchy's grip on power, which he codified when he finally drew up the country's first constitution in 1962.

Like his father, he tried to undermine the UNFP and the Istiqlal Party (which was forced to leave the government in 1963) by building up rival ultraroyalist movements, like the MP and a royalist coalition, the Front for the Defense of Constitutional Institutions (*Front pour la Défense des Institutions Constitutionelles; FDIC*) which was formed to contest the first general elections, in 1963. Although the FDIC itself was short-lived, royal support for such loyalist movements has been a constant theme of Hassan II's political strategy. Thus, it was the MP and the "independents" who received the palace's support in the 1977 elections. In the 1983 and 1984 elections, the newly formed Constitutional Union (*Union Constitutionnelle*; UC), which held its founding congress in April 1983, clearly had the support of the palace in its objective of creating a new conservative "center" for Moroccan politics.

It has been in the countryside, where the king still enjoys considerable religious prestige and the Ministry of the Interior's *caids* can prevent effective penetration by the opposition parties, that the king has been able to rely on solid electoral support for these loyalist movements.

Hassan's control of state resources, including radio and television, is an important political advantage of which he makes full use. Press circulations rarely exceed 50,000, but there are 1.7 million radios and 465,000 television sets (1977),

and the king commands an audience whenever he makes a speech, which he does frequently. The educational system is also used to inculcate loyalty to the monarchy, which is portrayed in textbooks as the country's bastion against foreign rule.

The king also uses his powers of appointment and patronage to buy support and placate critics. Indeed, favoritism and corruption are an integral part of his strategy of rule. He is also a renowned master of creating and exploiting divisiveness; a political juggler who has successfully orchestrated the political system by playing up the rivalries and mutual suspicions of the country's main factions—political parties, trade unions, and the armed forces—and so diminished the threat to the throne from each.

Additionally, he has been careful to include "safety valves" in the political system—outlets for the expression of grievances and protest which, although circumscribed, discourage most opposition politicians from dropping out of the established system altogether and engaging in more radical forms of opposition. Thus, within certain bounds, political parties are allowed to exist legally, publish newspapers, and, from time to time, contest elections and express their views in Parliament.

This does not, however, prevent the king from repressing his political opponents or curbing civil liberties when he finds it opportune or necessary to defend his rule. In July 1963, for example, his government announced the discovery of a "plot" against the monarchy, arrested 130 members of the UNFP, including twenty-one of its twenty-eight deputies, and sentenced ten party members, among them its exiled leader, Mehdi Ben Barka, to death. In October 1965, Ben Barka was murdered in mysterious circumstances in Paris. The previous March, hundreds of slum-dwellers were killed in Casablanca when the army suppressed antigovernment riots. The riots, and the factional squabbling with the FDIC, prompted Hassan to declare a state of exception in June 1965 and to rule by decree for the next five years. Opposition newspapers frequently have been censored or suppressed; opposition parties have sometimes been banned (a fate suffered at times by both the communists and the socialists); and over the years thousands of oppositionists have been detained, sometimes to be tortured and occasionally executed.

An additional weapon in the king's armory is his populism. After narrowly thwarting two military coups in 1971 and 1972, for example, he rallied popular support by ordering the Moroccanization of the remaining French land-holdings, sending troops to fight in the October 1973 Middle East war and, above all, launching his great campaign to annex Spanish-ruled Western Sahara. Spain's cession of its desert colony in 1976 allowed the king to recoup his lost popularity, neutralize the opposition parties, and so permit a relative liberalization, which culminated in the calling of the 1977 general elections.

However, as the enthusiasm generated by the "recovery" of Western Sahara gave way to renewed mass agitation over the country's chronic domestic problems, the king resorted once again to the stick. In June 1981, the king ordered the army to suppress riots in Casablanca sparked by huge rises in food prices. More than 600 are believed to have been killed and 2,000 arrested. More than 200 leaders of the USFP and its trade unions received jail terms in a series of political trials, and the party's newspapers were shut down. In January 1984, after the introduction of austerity measures—including a reduction in the subsidies on basic foodstuffs in the second half of the previous year—riots in Marrakesh and in several towns in the north of the country were subdued with violence by the state security forces. As many as 400 may have died during the two weeks of disturbances. Only when Hassan appeared on television to announce the restoration of subsidies did the demonstrations cease.

During his two decades of rule, King Hassan generally has aligned his foreign policy with the West. He has maintained especially close relations with France and the United States. While condemning Zionism, he has tended to favor detente between Israel and the Arab world and met with the prime minister of Israel in 1986. He has allied with the most pro-Western regimes in Africa and sent troops to help crush the Shaba uprisings in Zaire in 1977 and 1978. In the Maghreb (North Africa, excluding Egypt), he abandoned Morocco's traditional claims to Mauritania and the Algerian Sahara in 1969 to 1972, but maintained the claim to Western Sahara. Since 1975, the war against the Western Saharan nationalist guerrillas of the Polisario Front has been his major preoccupation. Domestically, he favors retaining an important place for private business and foreign investment in the economy, though many large industries, including the key phosphate mines, are in public hands. A pragmatic and flexible politician, King Hassan is, above all, committed to the maintenance of his rule and the survival of his dynasty.

The fate of many monarchies in the Third World suggests that eventually the Alawite dynasty will be overturned. The progressive urbanization and modernization of Moroccan society bring greater questioning of the monarch's claim to a divine right to rule. His religious prestige is lowest in the urban areas, where 44 percent of Moroccans now live (compared to only 14 percent at the time of independence).

The Party System

Parties first emerged in Morocco as a consequence of the nationalist struggle against French and Spanish rule, which began under the leadership of French-educated intellectuals and religious reformists (*Salafis*) and reached a mass scale in the late 1930s. In 1943, Ahmed Balafrej and other nationalists founded the Istiqlal Party, which was to spearhead the struggle for independence under the leadership of Allal el-Fassi.

The Istiqlal Party formed a close alliance with Sultan Mohammed V, whose Alawite dynasty had been forced to accept a Franco-Spanish "protectorate" in 1912. After about 1946, he refused to cooperate with the French authorities, who retaliated by exiling him to Madagascar in 1953. This step only fanned the flames of nationalist revolt. An Army of Liberation began guerrilla attacks in 1955, and France, which was already facing a rebellion in Algeria, decided to come to terms with the Moroccan nationalists. Mohammed V returned to Morocco as a national hero and, in 1956, France and Spain ended their protectorate.

In granting Morocco independence, France and Spain returned full sovereignty to the sultan, who acquired the title of king. A struggle for primacy then ensued between the monarch and the more radical factions of the nationalist movement. The king retained all legislative powers and refused to hold elections or allow a constitution to be drafted. He also encouraged the emergence of royalist political movements. The king's enormous prestige stood him in good stead in this contest, as did the practical support of France, which helped to build up the king's Royal Armed Forces (*Forces Armées Royales;* FAR) and provided many of his government's civil servants for serval years. Between

1956 and 1959, the irregulars of the Army of Liberation were gradually forced to hand over their arms, join the FAR, or disband. Though the Istiqlal Party was included in the postindependence government, the king tried to weaken it by giving cabinet posts to royalist independents and the small Democratic Independence Party (*Parti Démocratique de l'Indépendance;* PDI) and by encouraging the Berber-based MP after its creation in 1957. As little more than a loose alliance of factions united in support of independence, the Istiqlal Party was unable to check Mohammed V's tightening grip on power; and in 1959 the party split, the more radical nationalists setting up the National Union of Popular Forces (*Union Nationale des Forces Populaires;* UNFP). By the time of Hassan II's ascent to the throne, in 1961, upon Mohammed V's death, the monarchy was well entrenched in power.

Istiqlal (Independence) Party

History

Founded in 1943, the Istiqlal Party led the struggle for independence, in close alliance with Sultan Mohammed V. As a broad alliance united in pursuit of independence, it enjoyed overwhelming popular support, but it had no agreed program of policies for independent Morocco. It was unable to offer effective resistance to the consolidation of political power in the hands of the monarch. The party was greatly weakened by the split with the UNFP in 1959, as well as by the palace's encouragement of ultraloyalist factions. In 1963 it was forced out of the government, in which it had participated since 1956, and it remained in opposition until 1977, when it reentered the government with eight cabinet posts. It continued to maintain an important involvement in government after November 1983 when the new cabinet was formed, although its strength has been somewhat reduced.

Organization

Between party congresses, which are held every two or three years, with over 5,000 delegates attending, the party is headed by a 510-member National Council. Day-to-day leadership is provided by the much smaller Executive Commit-

tee. The party publishes two daily newspapers, *Al-Alam* in Arabic and *L'Opinion* in French.

Policy

Party policy is strongly nationalist. In the immediate postindependence years, it championed the idea of "Greater Morocco"—the incorporation into Morocco of Western Sahara, Ifni, Mauritania, the Algerian Sahara, and northwestern Mali. The party objected strongly to King Hassan's recognition of Mauritania and to the de facto border with Algeria in 1969 to 1972. Istiqlal would be the most resistant to concessions to the Polisario Front in Western Sahara. The party is noted for supporting full Arabization of education, strict adherence to Islamic principles, rejection of birth control, and denigration of "foreign ideologies" like Marxism. It accepts royal primacy, despite irritation at the king's refusal to share real power. Since 1977, it has loyally backed government policies and so muted its support for such causes as rapid Arabization and the nationalization of banks.

Membership & Constituency

The party is primarily urban and middle class and enjoys the support of much of the country's religious officialdom. It is weak among students and unionized workers, though it has a very small student organization and a labor organization.

Financing

Istiglal's funding traditionally has come from prominent bourgeois families. This support, however, has declined significantly since the early 1960s.

Leadership

Since Allal el-Fassi's death in 1974, M'hammed Boucetta (born 1925 in Marrakesh) has been Secretary General. He has been foreign minister since 1977.

Prospects

Because of its association with unpopular government policies, the party is likely to continue losing support to forces on its left, in particular the USFP, and perhaps also to Islamic fundamentalist groups.

National Assembly of Independents (*Rassemblement National des Indépendants;* RNI)

History

Founded in October 1978, the RNI was initially a loose coalition of the royalist "independents" who won the 1977 general elections. It had much in common with the earlier FDIC, the bloc of proroyalist forces which held half the seats in the 1963–65 Parliament, although, unlike the FDIC, it did not include the MP. Like the FDIC, the RNI was soon beset by internal squabbles. Two rival factions emerged in 1980; and, in April 1981, fifty-nine of the RNI's deputies announced that they were forming a new parliamentary group, known as the Democrat Independents (*Indépendants Démocrates;* ID). The RNI rump then suffered a serious setback when its six members in the government lost their ministerial posts in a cabinet reshuffle in November 1981. The cabinet formed in November 1983, however, once again contained RNI ministers.

Organization

The RNI remains a loosely structured bloc of royalists. It has two daily newspapers—*Al-Mihttaq* in Arabic and *Al-Maghrib* in French.

Policy

The RNI is strongly proroyalist. It is supportive of private business, strongly antisocialist, and pro-Western in foreign policy.

Membership & Constituency

The party's top leaders come mainly from the wealthiest strata of Moroccan society. Many have important commercial or industrial interests or have served as senior technocrats in successive governments. The party enjoys support from members of the chambers of commerce and industry and such bodies as the employer's General Economic Confederation of Morocco (*Confederation Generale Economique du Maroc;* CGEM). Its electoral support is primarily rural.

Financing

The RNI is supported by the personal funds of its leading members.

Leadership

Ahmed Osman (born 1930 in Oujda) is the RNI's president. He is a brother-in-law of King Hassan and was prime minister from 1973 to 1979.

Prospects

Despite continuing difficulties, the party continues to have a presence in the government and to command considerable support among the electors; it remains the second largest group in the Chamber of Representatives.

National Democratic Party (*Parti National Démocrate;* PND)

History

Registered as a parliamentary group in April 1981 and as a political party a few weeks later, the National Democratic Party is a breakaway from the RNI. In the November 1981 cabinet reshuffle, its increased its number of ministerial posts from three to five, while the RNI rump left the government. In the cabinet of November 1983 its number of ministerial posts was back to three, while the RNI also obtained a ministerial presence. The PND continues to attract electoral support, although to a significantly lesser extent than does the RNI; it has twenty-four seats in the Chamber of Representatives.

Organization

Organization remains rudimentary and consists primarily of the parliamentary bloc and the network of patron-client relationships of its rural leaders. Nevertheless it has made efforts to develop a more coherent organization, and in 1983 formed a student union, the National Union of Democratic Students (*Union Nationale des Etudiants Democrates;* UNED); it has also made efforts to organize among women and young people.

Policy

Like the RNI, the PND is strongly proroyalist. It is antisocialist, proWestern in foreign policy, and supportive of private business. But, whereas the RNI rump tends to represent the interests of industry and commerce, the PND is supported by many of the large landowners and therefore supports policies favourable to the development of large-scale commercial farming. Nevertheless, it presents itself as the defender of the interests of the small farmer and peasant, claims to be progressive; and condemns those political tendencies and ideologies which encourage the division into left and right.

Membership & Constituency

The leaders of the PND are generally wealthy and are often large landowners. Their electoral base is overwhelmingly rural.

Financing

The financial support of its wealthy constituency covers ID expenses.

Leadership

Arsalane el-Jadidi (minister of labor), Khalihenna Ould Rachid (secretary of state for Saharan affairs), Moussa Saadi (minister of energy and mines), and Abdelhamid Kassimi are the principal leaders of the PND.

Prospects

Although for a while, between 1981 and 1983, it seemed as though the PND would emerge as the favoured conservative, loyalist grouping, its position has been seriously undermined by the formation of the Constitutional Union (*Union Constitutionnelle*; UC). It is probable that its strongly rural base will weaken its claim to be a broad and unifying party.

Constitutional Union
(*Union Constitutionnelle*; UC)

History

This party was founded in April 1983 under the leadership of the former prime minister M. Maati Bouabid after extensive preparation during the preceding three months. Between January and April 1983, M. Bouabid toured the country and held innumerable meetings with local officials, dignitaries, and other influential persons, with a view to constructing a broad-based popular yet conservative and loyalist political alliance. The new alliance received support from the palace and was able to command very considerable electoral support both in the local elections of June 1983 and the national elections of September–October 1984. In electoral terms it was the most popular party of all—in all stages of the elections—garnering more seats, both in the rural and municipal commune councils and in the Chamber of Representatives, than any other party.

Organization

Relatively well-organized as a national (rural and urban) party, the UC is formally headed by an executive bureau and administrative committee under the presidency of M. Maati Bouabid. It also has four advisory committees on social, political, economic, and organizational issues. These make recommendations to the party congress. The party congress elects the members of the executive bureau and the administrative committee; it also elects the president. The UC publishes a weekly paper in Arabic, *Rissalat Al Oumma*.

Policy

The UC declares that it is faithful to the country's constitutional traditions and to the monarchy. It seeks to mobilize a new alliance centered around a program "quite distinct from the demagogy of imported ideologies and destructive forces." Its major stated concern is to move beyond the politics of the immediate postindependence period and to develop a new "centrist" grouping. Essentially a party of national unity, it hopes to draw support away from the Istiqlal, the RNI, the PND, and the MP, on the one hand, and from the USFP and the PPS, on the other; but its ideological continuity with the RNI is evident. It is weak on specific economic and social policy.

Membership and Constituency

Party members are drawn generally from the wealthy and middle classes, both urban and rural; landowners, industrialists, and businessmen are represented, as are the professional middle classes. The electoral base is predominantly, but by no means exclusively, rural.

Financing

The financial support of its broad constituency covers the UC expenses. It may also have support from the palace.

Leadership

The president is Maati Bouabid, former prime minister. Both he and one other member of the executive bureau, M. Abdellatif Semlali, were appointed as ministers in the November 1983 cabinet.

Prospects

As the major conservative, loyalist political grouping, with evident electoral support and the approval of the palace, the UC seems likely to maintain its importance in the short term. As the strains within Moroccan economy and society increase, however, the capacity of such an alliance of national unity to hold together and maintain its early broad-based support will come increasingly into question.

Party of Progress and Socialism
(*Parti du Progrès et du Socialisme;* PPS)

History

Founded in 1974, the PPS is the direct successor of two previous Communist parties—the Moroccan Communist Party, which was founded in 1943 and banned in 1952 and 1959, and the Party of Liberation and Socialism, which was founded in 1968 and banned in 1969.

The pro-Moscow communists were allowed by the king to reorganize as the PPS in 1974 as a result of the relative liberalization that accompanied the campaign to annex Western Sahara. Since then, the party has managed to retain its legality. In contrast to the USFP, it did not face severe repression after the June 1981 Casablanca riots, apparently because of the moderation of its leadership, the party's small size, and its relatively limited audience.

Organization

The party is tightly knit and headed by a central committee and political bureau. It publishes two daily newspapers, one in French, the other in Arabic, both titled *Al-Bayane.* They were banned for four weeks after the June 1981 riots. Since 1974, the party has been able to consolidate organizationally and extend the circulation of its press.

Policy

The PPS faithfully toes the Moscow line on major international issues, with the single important exception of the Western Saharan question, on which the USSR is a supporter of Saharawi self-determination, while the PPS defends Morocco's annexation of the territory and supports the war against the Polisario Front. For defensive reasons, the party avoids overt criticism of the monarchy. With Stalinist orthodoxy, it adheres to the notion of revolution by stages, i.e., before the socialist revolution there must first be a "national democratic revolution" carried out by a broad alliance of classes to achieve land reform, democratization, and the end of imperialist domination.

Membership & Constituency

The PPS is an urban-based party; most of its members are students, teachers, and other intellectuals. It has some working-class electoral support and is active in the unions affiliated with the Moroccan Union of Labor (*Union Marocaine du Travail;* UMT). It decries the other major labor confederation as divisive. The party is represented in the leadership of the National Union of Moroccan Students (*Union Nationale des Etudiants Marocains;* UNEM).

Financing

Membership dues and sales of its publications may cover some of PPS's needs. Nothing is known about its finances.

Leadership

Ali Yata, who was secretary general of the earlier communist parties, has been secretary general of the PPS since its founding.

Prospects

Though Morocco's economic and social crises might increase the party's audience, popular discontent is more likely to benefit the larger USFP. Moreover, the party faces competition from other Marxist groups to its left. In the event of a military coup or a shift in the palace's political strategy, the party could be banned again.

Popular Movement
(*Mouvement Populaire;* MP)

Created in 1957 and legalized in 1959, the MP exploited local rural grievances that lay behind rural rebellions in 1957 to 1959. It presented itself in the Berber-populated mountainous regions as an alternative to the Arab-dominated, urban-based Istiqlal Party. It received encouragement from the palace, which saw the movement as a useful counterweight to the urban parties. It gave loyal support to the king and joined the FDIC in the sixties. It received four posts in the government after the 1977 elections. It continues to have a ministerial presence in the cabinet.

The MP's distinctive features are its royalism and Berberism. It has no prospect of extending its popular appeal beyond the Berber rural regions, although these features were sufficient for it to obtain forty-seven seats in the Chamber of Representatives in the 1984 election, relegating the nationalist Intiqlal party into fourth place. The party is very loosely organized and publishes only a weekly newspaper, *Al-Haraka*, in Arabic. The secretary general is Mahjoubi Aherdane (born 1921), the founder of the party and minister of cooperation in the current government.

Socialist Union of Popular Forces
(*Union Socialiste des Forces Populaires;* USFP)

History

Founded in 1974, the USFP emerged from a split in the UNFP in 1972. The UNFP had itself split from the Istiqlal Party in 1959. Led by the more radical Istiqlal leaders, among them Mehdi Ben Barka, the UNFP was immediately harrassed by the palace—first by its expulsion from the government in 1960, then by the mass trial of UNFP leaders in 1963. Two years later, Ben Barka was assassinated. Although originally backed in its breakaway from the Istiqlal Party by the UMT, the party was further weakened by the UMT's refusal to back its political initiatives in the mid-sixties.

The loss of the party's most radical leaders led to the emergence of a more compromise-prone leadership, while the uneasy relations between the UNFP and UMT leaders led to a party split in 1972. One faction, led by Abderrahim Bouabid, broke ranks with a rival faction led by Abdallah Irbahim and the UMT's leader, Mahjoub Ben Seddik. Bouabid's "Rabat wing" of the UNFP was briefly banned in 1973 and 1974, but was relegalized as a result of the liberalization initiated by the king in 1974, changing its name to the *Union Socialiste des Forces Populaires* the same year. The party accused the government of fixing many of the results in the 1977 elections and has since remained in opposition. It was severely repressed after the June 1981 Casablanca riots and massacre. Its newspapers were immediately suppressed and had still not been allowed to restart publication a year later. Some 200 leaders of the party and its allied Democratic Labor Confederation (*Confederation Démocratique du Travail;* CDT) were jailed. Abderrahim Bouabid and two other members of the party's political bureau were imprisoned between September 1981 and March 1982. In May 1983, the king pardoned twenty-two of the imprisoned of USFP and CDT members, and the USFP decided to participate in the local and national elections. In November 1983, Abderrahman Bouabid, leader of the party, was included in the government as a minister of state. During and after the 'bread riots' of January 1984, many USFP militants were arrested.

Organization

The USFP has held a national congress about once every two to three years. Its leadership consists of a thirty-five–member national administrative commission and a nine-member political bureau. Until the repression unleashed against the party in June 1981, it published two newspapers—an Arabic-language daily, *Al-Moharrir,* and a French-language weekly, *Liberation.* It has a youth wing known as the *Jeunesse Ittihadia* (United Youth) and has close relations with the Socialist International. The party is politically heterogeneous and includes a revolutionary socialist tendency known by the name of its clandestine newspaper, *Alikhtier Athaouri* (Revolutionary Option), inspired by one of the UNFP's historic leaders, Mohammed Basri, who has lived in exile in Paris since the early sixties.

Policy

The USFP's political outlook is, broadly speaking, social democratic. It advocates reform of the constitution, civil liberties, and the liberation of political prisoners. It calls for the nationalization of the principal means of production, transport, exchange, and credit; land reform on the basis of "land to the tiller"; large-scale housing programs and the control of urban rents and property speculation; anticorruption measures; and wage increases. Strongly nationalist, it supports the war against the Polisario Front and, like the PPS, tends to criticize the government for alleged weakness in prosecuting the war effort.

Membership & Constituency

Primarily urban-based, the USFP draws most of its members from the educated middle class. It is particularly strong among students, teachers, and lower-level civil servants, but it also recruits through the trade unions affiliated with the CDT, which it controls. In elections, it enjoys wide support in the cities from workers, the unemployed poor, students and the middle class. It has a majority on several municipal councils, including Rabat.

Financing

The USFP has been liberally supported by its wealthier adherents.

Leadership

Abderrahim Bouabid (born 1920) is the party's first secretary. Since November 1983, he has been a member of the government.

Prospects

As the major left-wing party, the USFP could be expected to be the principal beneficiary of the widespread discontent in the cities. However, the repression it has suffered since June 1981 has seriously handicapped the party and prevented it from capitalizing effectively on its political opportunities. Nevertheless, its growing strength is attested to by its results in the 1983 and 1984 elections. It remains to be seen whether the incorporation of its leader in the king's national unity government will affect the party's ability to maintain its left-wing stance and its credibility as a party.

Minor Parties

Action Party (*Parti de l'Action;* PA)

Founded in 1977 and led by Abdallah Senhaji, the PA is Berber based, proroyalist, and conservative.

Forward (*Ilal-Amam*)

Founded in 1970 in a split from the PPS's predecessor, the Party of Liberation and Socialism, this group supports self-determination in Western Sahara and the Polisario Front. It is outlawed and many members, including its principal leader, Abraham Serfaty, are in jail.

March 23 (*23 Mars*)

Founded in 1970 in a split from the UNFP, March 23 is led by Mohammed Ben Said. It is Marxist-Leninist. In 1978 and 1979, it split over attitudes towards the USFP and the Western Saharan war: one faction joined the USFP; other factions remained outlawed, with some members in jail. It is active and influential in the UNEM.

Organization of Democratic and Popular Action (*Organisation de l'Action Démocratique et Populaire*; OADP)

Formed in January 1983, the OADP is, in effect, a recreation of the March 23 movement and is led by Mohamed Ben Said. It was unable to put forward candidates for the local elections in 1983 because its official recognition as a party preceded the closing date for submission of candidates' names by only eleven days. In the national elections it gained one seat.

National Union of Popular Forces (*Union Nationale des Forces Populaires*; (UNFP)

The rump of UNFP since the split by forces which founded the USFP in 1974, this group is led by Abdallah Ibrahim. It favors radical change as a basis for the construction of socialism and has close links with the UMT. It boycotted the 1977 parliamentary elections. It also refused to participate in the 1983–1984 elections.

Popular Democratic and Constitutional Movement (*Mouvement Populaire Démocratique et Constitutionel;* MPDC)

Founded in 1967 in a split from the MP, this royalist group is led by Abdelkrim Khatib.

Other Political Forces

Military

The Royal Armed Forces (*Forces Armées Royales;* FAR) were formed in 1956, primarily with Moroccan troops that had served in the French and Spanish armies. Crown Prince Hassan, who became chief of staff in 1957, used these troops to put down several localized rural rebellions in 1957 to 1959 and to disband and partially absorb the irregular forces of the Army of Liberation. Hassan integrated the officers into the royal patronage system, using his position as chief of staff to determine promotions. The FAR came to be seen as one of the pillars of the monarchical regime.

In 1971 a group of senior military officers, angered by corruption, attempted a coup. It failed, but the attempt revealed that the armed forces

could no longer be considered a secure bastion of royal power. In August 1972, there was a second unsuccessful coup attempt, this time by air force officers.

The king's reaction to these challenges was diverse. The officer corps was purged. The post of defense minister was abolished, and the king again became chief of staff of the armed forces. Part of the army was dispatched to the Middle East in 1973, while most of the rest was virtually disarmed until the outbreak of the war in Western Sahara.

Since 1972 there has been no centralized command structure between the king and the army battalion and brigade commanders and the chiefs of the air force and the navy. This, the king hopes, will make the planning of another coup much more difficult. A military inspectorate keeps the king directly informed of the FAR's activities, as do such parallel security forces as the *Forces Auxiliaires*, the *Gendarmerie Royale,* and the *Sûreté Nationale.*

Traditionally, most of the FAR's officers and men were Berbers from the Atlas and Rif mountains, which had been the main recruiting grounds for the French and Spanish armies in Morocco. However, the composition of the officer corps was transformed by the events of 1971 and 1972. Most senior postindependence officers have been recruited from Arab urban bourgeois families. The composition of the ranks has been changed by the introduction of selective conscription in 1967, though voluntary enlistment by rural Berbers remains important.

The political importance of the war in the Sahara and the commitment of a large proportion of the FAR to the maintenance of security in the Moroccan–occupied territory of the Western Sahara mean that the army has a crucial strategic significance in Moroccan politics today. The "accidental" death of the commander of the Moroccan armed forces in the Sahara, General Dlimi on January 25, 1983 may have been linked to undercover attempts to negotiate with the Polisario on the basis of a settlement of the conflict.

Organized Labor

Though French unions had had affiliates in Morocco for some years, the first Moroccan labor federation, the Moroccan Union of Labor (*Union Marocaine du Travail;* UMT) was founded in 1955 by supporters of the Istiqlal Party. Under Mahjoub Ben Seddik, the federation supported the UNFP's split from the party in 1959; but, from 1962, relations between the UMT and the UNFP were strained. The UMT, which was subsidized by the government, was generally unwilling to back the UNFP's political campaigns and concentrated on narrow trade-union matters. After the split in the UNFP in 1972, Ben Seddik retained links with the rump led by Abdallah Ibrahim. In consequence, the larger faction, which sent on to form the USFP in 1974, set about building a rival trade-union movement. From the beginning it had the support of the National Education Union (*Syndicat National de l'Enseignement;* SNE) which had been independent of the UMT since its creation in 1965, and the postal workers' union, which had split from the UMT in 1963. In 1978, eight USFP-led unions, representing teachers, phosphate workers, postal workers, health employees, sugar and tea workers, water and electricity workers, petroleum and gas workers, and some railwaymen, founded the Democratic Labor Confederation (*Confédération Démocratique du Travail;* CDT). By 1979 there were three more affiliates, representing workers in the tobacco industry, agriculture, and municipal administration; and, although the UMT retained some of its traditional strength in basic industries, notably the railway and the electricity-generating industry, the CDT had become the more powerful of the two federations by 1981. Both the UMT and the CDT called general strikes in June 1981 to protest the massive increases in food prices decreed by the government; and it was the CDT's strike, on June 20, which ended in widespread rioting and the army's bloody intervention. Almost all the CDT's top leaders, including its secretary general, Noubir el-Amaoui, were jailed. A year later most remained in jail, and Noubir el-Amaoui was still awaiting his trial. During the January 1984 "bread riots," by contrast, the labor unions were not involved until after the event.

Student Movements

Since the founding of the National Union of Moroccan Students (*Union Nationale des Etudiants Marocaines;* UNEM) in 1955, the student movement has been one of the most radicalized sectors of Moroccan society. In 1970 to 1973, student protest reached a peak, with many universities almost permanently on strike; and, at UNEM's fifteenth congress in

1972, Marxist-Leninist *frontistes* from the March 23 movement and Ilal-Amam displaced the UNFP leadership which had headed the union since the 1950s. The government reacted by banning UNEM in January 1973 and jailing many of its leaders. Some remain in jail to this day. The government relegalized UNEM in November 1978, but ensured that it would be reconstituted by "responsible" socialists of the USFP and the PPS. However, UNEM has resumed its tradition of militant opposition to government policies, mainly over specific student grievances such as grants, university entrance requirements, and Arabization, and on the charged issue of political prisoners. At the seventeenth congress in August 1981, the UNFP withdrew from UNEM's executive commission, leaving the leadership in the hands of the PPS, the March 23 movement, and the *Groupe des Martyrs* faction. Strikes became frequent in 1981; and in December three of the union's executive members were detained. Student activists were heavily involved in the street demonstrations of January 1984, and it was significant that the "bread riots" were preceded by student protests over increased fees and other costs. Ilal-Amam was most certainly involved, both in the student protests and in the subsequent upsurge of popular discontent.

National Prospects

Much of the educated elite in the universities, the state administration, the officer corps of the armed forces, and the political parties is alienated by the corruption and favoritism of the patronage system, the failure to provide reward based on merit, and the king's unwillingness to allow a real dispersal of decision-making power. The scale of Morocco's economic and social problems—the oil-import bill, fluctuating prices for phosphate ore (the main export), soaring food imports and agricultural failings, the ongoing rural exodus into the cities, and the swelling unemployment and shantytowns—suggests that discontent with the established order will grow. It is doubtful that any of the political parties could overthrow the monarchy. The one organized force that would be capable of doing so is the army, and its political ambitions may hinge on the outcome of the war in Western Sahara which, in 1985, its tenth year, still showed few signs of coming to an end.

Further Reading

Amnesty International Briefing: Morocco. London: Amnesty International, 1985.

Gellner, Ernest, and Micaud, Charles, ed. *Arabs and Berbers, From Tribe to Nation in North Africa.* Lexington, Mass: Lexington Books, D.C. Heath, 1972.

Knapp, Wilfrid. *North West Africa, A Political and Economic Survey.* 3rd ed. New York: Oxford University Press, 1977.

Nelson, Harold D., ed. *Morocco, A Country Study.* Foreign Area Studies. Washington, D.C.: American University, 1978.

Parker, R.B., *North Africa: Regional Tensions and Strategic Concerns,* New York: Praeger, 1984.

Seddon, D., "Winter of Discontent: Economic Crisis in Tunisia and Morocco," *Middle East Research & Information Project (MERIP)*, Report no. 127, October 1984.

Waterbury, John. *The Commander of the Faithful: The Moroccan Political Elite, A Study in Segmented Politics.* New York: Columbia University Press, 1970.

———. "Corruption, Political Stability, and Development: Comparative Evidence from Egypt and Morocco." *Government and Opposition* (London), VII, Autumn 1976.

Zartman, William, ed. *Man, State and Society in the Contemporary Maghrib.* New York: Praeger, 1973.

SAHARAN ARAB DEMOCRATIC REPUBLIC
(República Árabe Saharaui Democrática)
by Tony Hodges revised by David Seddon, Ph.D.

The System of Government

The former Spanish colony of Western Sahara has been disputed territory since 1975–76 when, upon Spain's withdrawal, it was annexed and partitioned by Morocco and Mauritania. An indigenous nationalist movement, the Polisario Front, with support from Algeria, put up strong resistance to the annexation and finally forced Mauritania to withdraw in 1979. Since then, the Polisario Front has continued its war against Morocco; by 1982 its forces controlled approximately nine-tenths of the territory, though Morocco retained the main centers near the coast, and about half the area's total population of some 80,000. Between 1981 and 1985, the Moroccans constructed a series of defensive walls to enclose a substantial proportion of the northern part of the territory and began work on a 600 kilometre structure designed to enclose much of the southern part of the territory. The Polisario Front is able, however, to mount effective assaults on the Moroccan defences, and the war continues. A large part of the population lives under Polisario administration in refugee camps in southwestern Algeria.

In February 1976, a pro-Polisario assembly of notables, the Provisional Saharawi National Council, proclaimed the founding of the Saharan Arab Democratic Republic (SADR). By 1982, the new state had been recognized by fifty foreign governments and admitted to the Organization of African Unity (OAU). Morocco's claim to sovereignty in Western Sahara has not been recognized by any nation.

The government is, in reality, synonymous with the political movement, the Polisario Front, which inspired its creation. Under the constitution, which was adopted in August 1976, the Front's leaders automatically fill the main executive posts in the government.

Executive

The Council for the Command of the Revolution (CCR) is "the supreme organ of executive power of the SADR." It is constituted, for the duration of the war, by the Polisario Front's Executive Committee. It has nine members and is presided over by the Polisario Front's secretary general, who is therefore head of state. The Council of Ministers, which had eleven members in 1982, is designated by the CCR, headed by a prime minister who must be a member of the CCR, and carries out the CCR's "directives."

Legislature

The Saharawi National Council has "legislative and consultative power," according to the constitution. However, it appears to have little real power, since the CCR has wide-ranging legislative as well as executive powers. Of its forty-one members, twenty-one are ex officio by virtue of their membership in the Polisario Front's political bureau. The remaining twenty members are elected by "popular base congresses." The council has three commissions, responsible for political and social affairs, foreign relations, and military matters, respectively.

Judiciary

Primary tribunals, an appeals court, and a people's supreme court, whose judges are appointed by a Judicial Council, presided over by the minister of justice comprise the judiciary. There is also a special State Security Court, designated by the CCR.

Regional & Local Government

The SADR is divided into three *wilayat* (sing., *wilaya*), which are administered by wilaya people's councils. Each council is headed by a *wali*, or governor, and is comprised of the officials who head the people's councils of the lower administrative units, the *dairat* (sing., *daira*), whose members are elected by the popular-base congresses. In current practice, this administrative structure exists only in the Saharawi refugee camps in southwestern Algeria.

The Electoral System

Elections are "nonparty" in character. The members of the Daira People's Councils are elected directly in the *dairat*, that is to say in the refugee camps at present, but the higher wilaya people's councils are elected indirectly. Of the forty-one members of the theoretical legislature, the Saharawi National Council, only twenty are elected directly, from the *dairat*, as noted above. The others are ex officio, as members of the Polisario Front's Political Bureau.

Popular Front for the Liberation of Saguia el-Hamra and Río de Oro (Polisario Front) (*Frente Popular para la Liberación de Saguia el Hamra y Río de Oro; Frente Polisario*)

History

The Polisario Front was founded in May 1973 and began a guerrilla war against Spain the same month. At its second congress, in August 1974, it officially adopted the goal of independence. After Spain's withdrawal in 1975–76, it fought a guerrilla war against Morocco and (until 1979) Mauritania.

Organization

The Front's highest decision-making body is the congress, which has been held six times between 1973 and 1985. Between congresses, the top leadership body is the nine-member Executive Committee, which is elected by the congress and headed by the secretary general. A subordinate body, also elected by the congress, is the Political Bureau, whose twenty-one members include the SADR's three *walis* and the secretaries general of auxilliary movements for women, students, and workers: the National Union of Saharawi Women (*Unión Nacional de Mujeres Saharauis;* UNMS), the General Union of Saharawi Workers (*Unión General de Trabajadores Saharauis;* UGTS), and the General Union of Students of Saguia el Hamra and Río de Oro (*Unión General de los Estudiantes de Saguia el Hamra y Río de Oro;* UGESARIO). In the Polisario-run refugee camps, all adult Saharawi refugees belong to eleven-member cells headed by an *arifa* (pl., *arifat*) who is responsible to the *wilaya's* Department of Training and Orientation.

The Polisario Front publishes a fortnightly newspaper, *Sahara Libre,* and a monthly magazine, *20 de Mayo,* in Spanish, Arabic, and French editions.

Policy

The Front's overriding and unifying objective is the achievement of full independence. It supports the holding of a referendum on self-determination under United Nations or Organization of African Unity auspices, and it calls on Morocco to hold bilateral peace talks. The Front officially embraces socialism, Islam, Arabization, the unification of the Arab world, and the improvement of the status of women. After the war, a Polisario Front government would be likely to pursue a pragmatic, nonaligned foreign policy and would probably cooperate with foreign companies to exploit the country's phosphates and other mineral wealth.

Membership & Constituency

The Front is not a "vanguard party." Rather it is a mass movement of which all Saharawis, except those who have allied with Morocco, are members. Hence, the entire adult refugee population is enrolled in the Front's cells.

Financing

The Algerian and Libyan governments are presumed to be the main sources of funds, as well as armaments.

Leadership

Mohammed Abdelaziz (born c. 1947) is secretary general of the Polisario Front. He comes from the territory's largest gabila (tribe), the Reguibat, and was educated in Morocco. A founder-member of the Front, he was elected secretary general at the third congress, in August 1976. As such, he is also president of the CCR and so head of state of the SADR.

Bachir Mustapha Sayed (born c. 1950–52), also a member of the Reguibat, was educated in Morocco and was elected deputy secretary general at the third congress in August 1976. He is a member of the Front's executive committee and of the SADR's CCR.

Mohammed Lamine Ould Ahmed is prime minister of the SADR. Born c. 1947, he is a member of a small tribe, the Taoubalt. He was educated at Mohammed V University in Rabat, Morocco. He was appointed prime minister in March 1976. He is a member of the Front's executive committee and of the SADR's CCR.

Other Political Forces

A small minority of Saharawis have declared support for Western Sahara's integration into Morocco. These are mainly traders who have sided with Morocco to preserve their business interests in the Moroccan-controlled towns. A number of Saharawis have joined Moroccan political parties—notably the Istiqlal Party , the proroyalist "independents," and the *Mouvement Populaire*—and some have been elected to the communal councils and provincial assemblies in the Moroccan-controlled areas and to the Moroccan Chamber of Representatives.

National Prospects

In 1982, Morocco controlled about one-tenth of the land area of Western Sahara—notably a zone in the northwest known as the "useful triangle" because it includes the old Spanish colonial capital, El-Ayoun; the important phosphate mines at Bou-Craa; and the country's only precolonial city, Smara. The SADR's forces, the Saharawi People's Liberation Army (SPLA), controlled the rest of the territory, but seemed unlikely to have the military means to evict the Moroccan army from the heavily defended enclaves it controlled near the coast. Since 1982, the Moroccan forces have been able to construct an extensive system of defensive walls enclosing the greater portion of the northern part of the territory, thus substantially increasing the area under occupation. A total Moroccan withdrawal seems unlikely in the absence of far-reaching political change in Morocco, since King Hassan II has effectively staked his prestige and credibility as a ruler on the annexation of the territory. However, Morocco is under very powerful military, diplomatic, and economic pressures to resolve the conflict. These pressures may ultimately be sufficient to force a complete Moroccan withdrawal. Hence the Polisario Front and its main external ally, Algeria, are likely to continue what is, in essence, a war of attrition.

Further Reading
Barbier, Maurice. *Le Conflit du Sahara Occidental*. Paris: Editions L'Harmattan, 1982.
———. *Historical Dictionary of Western Sahara*. Metuchen, N. J.: Scarecrow Press, 1982.
———. "Whither Western Sahara?" *Africa Research Bulletin*, Political Series, Vol. 19, No. 2, 15 March 1982.
———. *Western Sahara: the Roots of a Desert War*, Westport, Connecticut;: Lawrence Hill & Co., 1983.

————. "The Western Sahara File", *Third World Quarterly*, 6,1, 1984.

————. *The Western Saharans*, Minority Rights Group, Report No. 40, London: The Minority Rights Group, 1984.

Mercer, John. *Spanish Sahara*. London: George Allen and Unwin, 1976.

PEOPLE'S REPUBLIC OF MOZAMBIQUE
(Republica Popular de Mozambique)

by Denise Jackson, M.A.

The System of Government

Mozambique, whose population was officially estimated at 12,615,200 in 1981, is a socialist state with a one-party presidential political system. The country became independent on June 25, 1975, following more than a decade of guerrilla war against the Portuguese colonial rule. The colonial war was waged by the Front for the Liberation of Mozambique (*Frente de Liberacão de Mozambique*; FRELIMO) which had headquarters in Dar es Salaam, Tanzania. FRELIMO signed a cease-fire with the Portuguese on September 7, 1974. Until June 25, 1975, when Mozambique became officially independent, it was ruled by a transitional government led by a prime minister, Joaquim Chissano, and composed of Portuguese officers and representatives of FRELIMO. After independence, it adopted a presidential system with Samora Machel as president and Chissano as foreign minister. The country was proclaimed a people's republic, with Marxism–Leninism as its official ideology and FRELIMO as the only legal party.

Executive

Samora Machel has been president of Mozambique since 1975. The president is head of state, commander-in-chief of the armed forces, and president of the party. Over the years he has also assumed ministerial responsibilities such as defense. Policy is implemented by twenty ministries which cover all areas of economic and social services. The ministers are appointed by and responsible to the president himself.

Legislative

The National People's Assembly is the legislative organ of the government. It has 226 members whose names were proposed by the Central Committee and approved by the Provincial Assemblies from September to December 1977. The National Assembly meets regularly twice a year and has a Permanent Commission of fifteen members, which is responsible for business in the interim. Legislative initiative belongs to the Central Committee, the Politburo, the president, the government, the Assembly's Permanent Commission, and committees.

The composition of the Assembly elected in 1977 is as follows: 31 percent workers, 28 percent peasants, 11 percent state workers, 15 percent military, 5 percent representatives of mass organizations.

Judiciary

After independence, FRELIMO faced the task of restructuring the archaic Portuguese system. Because of the lack of legally trained personnel and the difficulty involved in writing a new code, the dynamizing groups *grupos dinamisadores*), which had been established by the party at all local levels, were made responsible temporarily for a system of informal justice. Dynamizing groups were voluntary village, factory, or neighborhood units that focused on teaching Marxism–Leninism. In 1978, the Ministry of Justice created a national court system at the local, district, and provincial levels. More serious crimes carrying greater penalties were heard by the higher courts. Each court includes professional and lay judges who are elected by the people, and at the local levels the tribunals are composed entirely of lay judges elected by the local assembly or community-at-large. There are still many problems in implementing this system. For example, presiding, legally-trained judges usually have de facto authority over their lay counterparts, and in 1980 over two-thirds of the 3,800 accused detained in jails were still awaiting trial.

---

* Machel was killed in a helicopter crash Oct. 19, 1986.

Regional and Local Government

The president appoints the governor for each of the ten provinces. There are administrative organs at the local, urban, rural, and district levels. In addition, in 1977 local-level assemblies were created with the responsibility of controlling and supporting state structures.

Electoral System

Mozambique has an indirect system for the election of the popular assemblies, involving mass meetings throughout the country to select members for the lower tier of representative power, the local people's assemblies. The last elections were held in 1977, and the government has announced its intent to carry out new elections in 1986, despite threats posed by the MNR (Mozambican National Resistance).

Between September and December of 1977, 22,000 men and women were chosen as deputies for the 892 local assemblies. Lists of candidates were proposed by the dynamizing groups, and each candidate's qualifications were debated in open meetings. By the end of the electoral process, 2,200 candidates had been rejected in wake of accusations ranging from collaboration with the Portuguese police to robbery or sexual misconduct.

Front for the Liberation of Mozambique
(*Frente de Liberacao de Mozambique*; FRELIMO)

FRELIMO was created on June 25, 1962 when Dr. Eduardo Mondlane unified three different movements headquartered in Dar es Salaam: UDENAMO (National Democratic Union of Mozambique), MANU (Mozambican-Makonde Union), and UNAMI (National African Union of Independent Mozambique). He was then chosen as president of the umbrella group FRELIMO.

However, within FRELIMO debate on the objectives and strategies of the liberation movement continued. One faction favored a reformist conciliatory approach; the more militant elements advocated force to gain independence. The latter faction prevailed in wake of the intransigence of the Portuguese regime and its appeal for NATO assistance to repress nationalist movements. On September 25, 1964, FRELIMO initiated its first attack against the Portuguese regime at the administrative post of Chai in Cabo Delgado. By 1968, FRELIMO had secured a liberated zone in the north that extended as far south as the Lurio river, and it had established a new front in the central province of Tete.

In the liberated zones, yet another split within the movement appeared. Disagreement centered on the necessity of planning beyond the limited objective of national independence from Portugal to create a real socioeconomic transformation of Mozambique. Experiences in the liberated zones strengthened the argument to transform completely the colonial Portuguese structure. A mass-mobilization strategy was advocated instead of the more limited focus on urban guerrilla strategies; thus, objectives were defined in terms of class rather than racial divisions. As a result, traditional rulers, richer peasants, and even FRELIMO members who sought personal gain became enemies in the ongoing liberation struggle.

On February 3, 1969, President Mondlane was killed in Dar es Salaam by a letter bomb. Vice President Simango, who had clashed with the Central Committee was expelled in November 1969. Samora Machel was immediately installed as president of FRELIMO with Marcelino dos Santos vice-president.

The liberated zones became models for a future national government. Their administration was based on a system of weekly meetings in which all the inhabitants of a village or farm would participate in the decision-making. Different kinds of cooperatives were established, based on the wishes of the local inhabitants.

Despite Portuguese efforts to extinguish the nationalist movement, FRELIMO continued to gain ground. Portugal's inability to break the prevailing stalemate in its war against three colonies—Guinea-Bissau, Angola, and Mozambique—finally led its military to overthrow the Salazar–Caetano regime which had controlled the country since 1926. The April Revolution of 1974 led to an independence settlement on September 7 that transferred all power to FRELIMO after a one-year period of a mixed Portuguese–FRELIMO transitional government.

Since achieving independence, FRELIMO has shifted its focus onto Mozambique's pressing economic and social problems. The Third Party Congress in 1977 adopted a program for a war on underdevelopment within a strictly

Marxist framework. The party called for the martialing of political, ideological, scientific, technical, and material resources toward that end.

FRELIMO's efforts to improve the nation's economy were made more difficult by its support for nationalist movements in Rhodesia. In 1976, Mozambique closed its borders with Rhodesia in response to the international boycott of the Ian Smith regime. This boycott was extremely costly to Mozambique. The United Nations estimated that between 1976 and 1980 Mozambique lost 550 million dollars in trade. In addition, the Rhodesians had trained and financed a counterrevolutionary movement, the MNR (Mozambican National Resistance).

To expand its organization to the areas which had been more isolated from the liberation war, FRELIMO created dynamizing groups at the grass-root level. In 1977, the Third Party Congress transformed the broad liberation coalition into a vanguard party, which adopted a Marxist–Leninist ideology and stated that its long-term goal was to make Mozambique a socialist state. In 1980, Machel initiated a series of surprise visits to factories, farms, and bureaucracies, finding widespread inefficiency, corruption, and mismanagement. This led to a two-phase offensive: punishing those who obstructed party goals by incompetence, corruption, and sabotage; and solving problems encountered in the implementation of annual plans. The emerging policy sought to strengthen leadership, respect for the hierarchy and for discipline in work. As a result, there was a purge of party officials, creation of workers' councils, and a strengthened chain of command within the hierarchies. This offensive highlighted an important division within FRELIMO: the tension between the hierarchical structures necessary to increase productivity and the party's doctrine of popular participation at all levels.

In 1980 Mozambique faced two major problems: a serious drought, which extended from Ethiopia to South Africa, and increased tension within South Africa. After independence, FRELIMO was left with an economy that had been almost completely destroyed by the war and attendant loss of the middle class. Also, the Mozambican economy was still dependent on the income from migrant workers in South Africa and fees from South African goods exported from the Mozambican ports of Maputo and Beira. It is only when placed in this context that the devastation of the drought can be fully understood. Second, rising conflict within South Africa led it to increase support for guerrilla groups in bordering countries. The MNR, which had lost its foreign support with the fall of the Rhodesian Smith regime, began to receive aid from South Africa and waged a campaign of economic destruction, kidnapping, and killing of the civilian population.

In April 1983, FRELIMO held its Fourth Party Congress. This Congress criticized the government's performance, singling out deskbound bureaucrats. As a result, three ministers were reshuffled, four were reassigned, and five new deputy ministries and one new ministry were created. To win increased foreign aid and support for Mozambique, President Machel toured six European countries before the end of 1983. Revitalizing the economy became the major aim of the regime.

Problems with South Africa persisted throughout 1984. MNR activities had increasingly escalated since 1980. No longer able to sustain the economic and human losses, Machel reached an agreement with South Africa; on March 16, 1984, the Nkomati Accords were signed by both countries. The Accords were a nonagression treaty in which Mozambique agreed to bar the ANC (African National Congress) from its territory and South Africa agreed to end its support for the MNR. The Nkomati Accords were controversial. In June, three major government officials were dismissed from their positions because of their hard-line stance against them. The treaty was widely criticized as a concession to the white South African government. Machel's optimism about Mozambique's ability to make accomodations with South Africa proved to be ill-founded. By December 1984, ANC operations were no longer conducted from Mozambique, but MNR operations had, in fact, increased and were receiving support from South African army personnel. In October 1985, Mozambique conducted a joint military operation with Zimbabwe against the MNR, which involved 7,000 men. The government was able to capture the rebel headquarters in Gorongosa National Park and several lesser camps. By September, even South Africa's foreign minister admitted that there was continuous contact between Pretoria and the MNR. MNR operations have continued and its base headquarters was recovered by the rebels at the end of 1985.

Organization

In 1978, FRELIMO began to create party cells in all regions and work places. Candidates for the party cells were presented at meetings of the full local population and their abilities assessed. These party cells replaced the dynamizing groups at the grass-roots level.

The Party Congress, which convenes about every five years, selects the members of the Central Committee. The Central Committee convenes twice a year and selects the members of the Central Committee's Secretariat that conducts business in the interim, with party secretariats responsible for most socioeconomic activities. The Central Committee also selects the eleven-member Politburo, which is the supreme organ of the party.

Policy

Immediately after independence, 200,000 Portuguese fled the country and left the remaining infrastructure in shambles. This situation, along with FRELIMO's Marxist ideology, led to nationalization of most of the economy. The rural sector is divided between state farms, cooperatives, and family plots. While some progress has been achieved in the development of state farms and cooperatives, some 80 percent of agricultural production comes from privately-owned farms. Nationalized industry has workers' councils to ensure their participation in decision-making.

Although Mozambique has had close ties to the Soviet Union due to its Marxist orientation and because the Soviets supported FRELIMO during the war of independence, it has never been able to get from the Soviets needed financial and technical assistance. Therefore, since 1983 Mozambique has initiated a rapprochment with the West. Machel's 1983 trip to Europe was followed by visits to Mozambique by such prominent western financiers as David Rockefeller and Machel's United States visit in September 1985.

Mozambique has become a member of the Lome Convention, the World Bank, and the IMF. These moves are part of an attempt to attract badly needed foreign investment and were accompanied by increased incentives to the country's private sector.

Leadership

Samora Moises Machel was born in 1933 in Gaza province, the son of a local chief. He had only four years of formal education. Until 1963, when he joined FRELIMO, he worked as an orderly at a Maputo hospital. He underwent military training in Algeria and, in 1964, led the first FRELIMO raid inside Mozambique. Machel became the movement's secretary for defense in 1966 and commander-in-chief in 1968. In 1971, Machel received the Lenin Centenary Award in Moscow.

Marcelino dos Santos was born in 1931 in Maputo. He studied at the universities of Lisbon and Paris. In April 1961, he became secretary of the umbrella organization of the anti-Portuguese groups in Portugal's African colonies, the Conference of Nationalist Organizations of the Portuguese Colonies (*Conferencia des Organizações Nacionalistas des Colonias Portuguesas*; CONCP) and the following year became one of FRELIMO's founders.

In 1965, dos Santos became responsible for FRELIMO's foreign affairs. Since May 1970, he has been FRELIMO's vice-president. Between 1975 and 1979, he was planning minister, and thereafter secretary for economic affairs and the Politburo's second-ranking member. Of all FRELIMO leaders, he is certainly the closest to the Soviets and to the Portuguese Communist Party, with which he was formally associated in the late 1950s.

Joaquin Chissano was born in 1939 in Gaza province and studied in Mozambique and Portugal. Between 1964 and 1974, he was FRELIMO's representative in Tanzania and minister of defense. Between September 20, 1974, and June 25, 1975, Chissano was prime minister of the transitional government of Mozambique and since then has remained the third-ranking Politburo member and foreign affairs minister.

Opposition

The only opposition movement within Mozambique is the MNR (Mozambican National Resistance) also called RENAMO (*Movimento Nacional da Resistencia de Mozambique*). The MNR was founded by Ian Smith's secret service in Rhodesia shortly after Mozambique's independence. After the independence of Zimbabwe, financing and support were taken over by the South Africans, enabling MNR's activities to escalate in Mozambique. However, both Rhodesia and South Africa have recruited MNR members from disaffected groups within Mozambique. Among these are Portuguese settlers who left the country, former colonial army officers, and FRELIMO outcasts.

Orlando Cristina was one of MNR's most prominent leaders. A member of the Portuguese secret police (PIDE), Cristina infiltrated FRELIMO, worked for Jeorge Jardim, the most prominent separatist settler, and then formed and commanded the dreaded special African units within the Portuguese army (GEPs and Flechas).

From the time of MNR's inception, Cristina played a powerful role. He was the main contact first with the Rhodesians and then the South Africans. After Cristina was shot on his farm near Pretoria, in April 1983, the MNR was left in disarray. Operations have increased, but the organization lacks firm leadership.

National Prospects

Mozambique faces grave problems. In 1985, the tenth anniversary of its independence, exports had declined 22 percent from the previous year and industrial production was down by 25 percent. In order to improve its economy, Mozambique needs foreign investment and technology. Obtaining these may necessitate alterations in the country's socialist orientation and its efforts to promote self-reliance. At the same time, the pressure to improve efficiency has led to the creation of hierarchical structures which conflict with FRELIMO's ideal of popular participation in the government and the economy. Such shifts may exacerbate divisions within FRELIMO and lead to factional conflicts.

Given the potentially volatile political environment of the region, and Mozambique's profound economic and social problems, FRELIMO will be under great stress. While it is likely to remain in power, regional and global forces will have a large role to play in its future development.

Further Readings

Egero, Bertil. "Mozambique Before the Second Phase of Socialist Development." *Review of African Political Economy*, Vols. 23-25, 1982.

Fauvet, Paul. "Roots of Counter Revolution: the Mozambique National Resistance." *Review of African Political Economy*, Vol. 29, 1984.

Isaacman, Allan and Barbara. *Mozambique: From Colonialism to Revolution, 1900-1982.* Colorado: Westview Press, 1983.

Luke, Timothy W. "angola and Mozambique: Institutionalizing social Revolution." *Review of Politics*, Vol. 44 1982.

Meyns, Peter. "Liberation Ideology and National Development Strategy in Mozambique." *Review of African Political Economy.* Vols. 20-22, 1981.

KINGDOM OF NEPAL
(Nepal Adhirajya)
by Kanak Mani Dixit, M.A. revised by N. Koirala

The System of Government

Nepal, a nation of nearly fifteen million people in the Himalaya mountains north of India, has been a monarchy since the present king's tenth ancestor unified the country two centuries ago. There have been extended periods when the king was merely a figurehead while the country was ruled by various oligarchs, the last of whom was ousted in 1951. King Mahendra initiated a brief experiment in parliamentary democracy in 1959, but terminated it in December 1960. Since then, Nepal has remained an absolute monarchy in which all executive, legislative, and judicial powers are vested in the crown. While there is a stirring towards more open politics in the country today, there has been no real break from the past.

In 1961, King Mahendra developed the *panchayat* system of guided "partyless democracy" to facilitate his direct involvement in national politics. The *panchayat* system was based on the king's vehement objections to party politics. Parties were said to foster factionalism and their internecine feuds were thought to distract the national consciousness from the tasks of development. The *panchayat* system was initially a four-tiered structure (later reduced to three) leading up from village assemblies to a national legislature of indirectly elected and appointed members representing localities, the king, and class and professional organizations (of women, peasants, exservicemen, etc.). Party alignments of any form were prohibited. In 1975 the system was further restricted when the class and professional organizations were disbanded and all candidates for the national legislature were selected by a government body.

In May 1979, King Birendra, King Mahendra's son, who ascended the throne in 1972, announced a national plebiscite that gave the people a choice between a "suitably reformed" *panchayat* system and a multiparty system of government. The announcement followed large-scale agitation in Katmandu, the capital, and in other towns. In 1980, the majority (54.7 percent) of the six million eligible voters opted for the *panchayat* system. The monarchy's close association with the *panchayat* system to a large extent explains the outcome of the plebiscite. Despite his bold step in announcing the exercise, King Birendra failed to disassociate himself from the issues. As a result, the "multiparty" proponents were pitted not only against the *panchayat* status quo, but also against kingship.

Executive

King Birendra Bir Bikram Shah Dev (born 1945) introduced policies intended to decentralize some of the powers that were centralized over the years during his father's rule (1955–1972). Under the latest constitutional amendment, the prime minister is elected by the legislature rather than appointed by the king. But the royal family's affairs and defense matters remain outside the jurisdiction of the cabinet and legislature; furthermore, all bills can be vetoed by the king. The long years of direct palace rule have taken the initiative from the cabinet, which constantly turns to the king and his palace secretariat for guidance and advice. The secretariat still makes the policy decisions, while the ministers serve as mere implementing bodies. It remains to be seen whether King Birendra can succeed in restoring sufficient confidence in the cabinet to enable it to practice the authority and powers that the constitution has granted it in theory.

Legislature

The 1980 plebiscite on the *panchayat* system was followed by a constitutional change which established a 140-seat legislature (*Rastriya Panchayat*). The king appointed only twenty-eight members; the remaining 112 were elected by direct adult suffrage. The legislature was empowered to recommend a prime-ministerial candidate who could gain the support of 60 percent of the members. The prime minister would be responsible to the legislature, rather than to the king, but the king retained the right to dismiss the prime minister. Party alignments and the formation of an official opposition in the legislature are still banned.

The present legislature recommended Lokendra Bahadur Chand for prime minister, and the king assented to this choice. Prior to this appointment, the Surya Bahadur Thapa government was overthrown by a no-confidence motion in the assembly. Thapa was the king's appointed prime minister in 1965 and again in 1968 and 1980. He had shown initiative in trying to assume some policy-making functions previously exercised by the palace secretariat alone.

In the absence of political parties in the legislature, loyalties of the Rastriya-Panchayat members revolve around individuals. A gradual evolution of party politics, as distinct from the present group politics, seems inevitable.

Judiciary

A uniform judicial system was established in 1956. At its top is the Supreme Court consisting of a chief justice and up to six associate justices. The king appoints all judges.

Regional & Local Government

Nepal is divided into fourteen zones and subdivided into seventy-five districts. Zonal commissioners are appointed by the king and serve as executive heads within the zones. Individual districts are handled by central district officers, who are assigned from the Home Ministry of Katmandu. Nepal has also been divided into four development regions, but this division has yet to take practical effect.

The Electoral System

Under the new constitutional amendments, elections to the national legislature are now directed and based on universal adult (age twenty-one) suffrage. Of 7.8 million registered voters, 52.2 percent turned out in 1981 to vote for candidates running in multimember districts on individual platforms. Simple pluralities determined the winners.

The Party System

Political parties made their debut in the late 1940s and early 1950s and were strongly influenced in policy and structure by the parties of neighboring India, which gained independence from the British in 1947. While the India parties were preoccupied with shedding colonialism, the Nepali parties were engaged in ousting the Rana family, whose oligarchy finally collapsed in 1951.

Prior to the royal coup of 1960, there was a host of minor parties which existed primarily as personal vehicles for ambitious individuals. With the banning of parties, these groups disappeared as the leaders began to bargain individually with the king for ministerial positions. The exceptions were the Congress Party and the Communist Party, which continued to maintain a shadowy existence as their leaders either went underground or into exile in India.

Party alignments continued as pervasive undercurrents under the partyless *panchayat* system, and party ideologies emerged whenever free elections were allowed. For example, student union voting and elections for the graduate constituency and the various class and professional organizations were consistently marked by party rhetoric and positions. The graduate constituency consisted of four seats in the legislature reserved for university graduates, predominantly from Nepal's only university. This group of legislators proved consistently irksome to the political elite, so the second amendment of the Nepali constitution abolished this constituency and with it the special representation of the other class organizations.

In the 1981 elections, the main party units, still smarting under the plebiscite defeat, refused to take part, though some independent candidates did gain grudging support from the organizations. Some communists also ran as independents. Subsequent events seemed to have pushed the parties into the background.

Congress Party

The Congress Party originated in the late 1940s as a movement against the fuedalistic Rana oligarchs in Nepal. The party won an absolute majority in the first general elections of 1959. With the dissolution of parliamentary democracy in December 1960, Congress activists were prosecuted under the Panchayat system as they provided the most potent threat to the newly established Panchayat regime.

The party weathered two-and-a-half decades underground or in exile, and the defection and the co-option of some of its leaders, to emerge as a still-viable entity. It abandonned its confrontationist policy with the king when its leader B. P. Koirala called for national reconciliation and returned to Nepal from exile in India. Although constitutionally banned, the party has been allowed to function in a semilegal fashion. The party has, so far, refrained from participation in the Panchayat elections and demands more liberalization—primarily the legalization of its status—as a precondition to participation. With Koirala's death in July 1982, the leadership role has returned to old stalwarts like Krishna Prasad Bhattrai, Ganesh Man Singh and Koirala's younger brother Girija Prasad Koirala.

The younger generation of party leaders, who were student activists of the 1960s and the 1970s and spent long years of imprisonment during that period, seems to be following the line of national reconciliation so far. But if their demands for participation in the national political mainstream are not met, they might turn to more radical politics. The King may attempt to co-opt some of them into the system; either alternative would undermine the evolution of a healthy democratic system in the country.

Communist Party

The Communist Party, whose beginnings were similar to that of the Congress Party, is today crippled by a variety of schisms. The major split is between the Russian-backed and well-funded conservative Communists under Keshar Jung Rayamajhi, and the Maoists, who are themselves split further into personalistic factions. While the Muscovites do not have a strong following, Maoist leaders Mohan Bickram Gharti and Mana Mohan Adhikari each have a relatively strong base, especially among students. However, their power will remain limited until the communists find a way to smooth over their ideological differences.

National Prospects

The political system remains extremely fluid in Nepal, and it is difficult to predict what formal system might finally emerge. Violent revolution or definitive demands for change seem to have been diffused by the 1980 plebiscite and once again by the 1981 elections. However, demand for more open and representative politics continues on all sides, and a slow evolution of the *panchayat* system can be envisaged.

The king will be tempted to retain the absolute authority of old. Likewise, his private secretaries, the royal family, military commanders (all of the warrior caste and loyalty monarchist), and many political leaders have strong incentives to retain the status quo. However, if the king shows restraint and the people's representatives are allowed free play, it is doubtful that the system will remain partyless for long. Political dynamics probably would soon convert the system into a parliamentary democracy with openly competing parties. Ultimately, the future will depend on how freely the new cabinet arrangement is allowed to operate, and whether the parties will join the system and work from within or opt instead for agitation.

Further Reading

Blaike, Piers; Cameron, John; Seddon, David. *Nepal in Crisis*, London: Oxford University Press, 1980.

Gaige, Frederick. *Regionalism and National Unity in Nepal*. Berkeley: University of California Press, 1975.

Gurung, Harka. "The Sociology of Elections in Nepal, 1959–1981." *Asian Survey*, Vol. 22, No. 3, March 1982.

Joshi, Bhuwan Lal, and Rose, Leo E. *Democratic Innovations in Nepal: A Case Study of Political Acculturation*. Berkeley: University of California Press, 1966.

Rose, Leo E., and Fisher, Margaret W. *The Politics of Nepal: Persistence and Change in an Asian Monarchy*. Ithaca, N. Y.: Cornell University Press, 1970.

Shaha, Hrishikesh. *Nepalese Politics, Retrospect and Prospect*. Delhi: Oxford University Press, 1978.

KINGDOM OF THE NETHERLANDS
(Koninkrijk der Nederlanden)
by Gordon Smith, Ph.D. revised by William G. Andrews, Ph. D.

The System of Government

The modern state of the Netherlands (now with a population of about 14.4 million) dates from 1815 when William of Orange-Nassau was created monarch of the north and south Netherlands. The fragile union was broken when the south seceded and became the independent state of Belgium in 1831. The king ruled as a constitutional monarch, but the system was not substantially democratized until 1849 when the structure of representation through the estates was abolished in favor of direct suffrage, although at the outset the franchise was very limited. The modern political system dates from the period after 1849.

Executive

The House of Orange is an hereditary monarchy, and until 1849 the king took a dominant executive role. Following the Napoleonic tradition of strong central administration, the Netherlands—as a unitary state—has maintained an emphasis on executive authority. From 1849 onwards, however, the principle of government responsibility was recognized, and increasingly the scope for active intervention by the monarch diminished. Effective executive authority now resides with the prime minister and cabinet.

The prime minister and his cabinet are responsible to the bicameral States General (*Staten-Generaal*), although in practice the executive is responsible to the directly elected lower house, the Second Chamber. Once a government is formed, it becomes a distinct entity from the legislature. There is a tradition of dualism between the executive and the States General, and that is exemplified by an incompatibility rule by which government ministers have to relinquish their seats in the States General on appointment. The separation also means that government ministers need not be recruited from the legislature—they could be nonpolitical experts or public officials; but over the years parliamentary recruitment has become paramount.

After an election, the monarch appoints an *informateur* who has the task of finding which combination of parties can provide the basis for a governing majority in the Second Chamber. In recent years, the problem of finding a "coalition formula" has become difficult and intense; negotiations leading to the establishment of a new executive normally take several months.

Between 1973 and the elections of May 1986, the Netherlands had five governments: from 1973 to 1977, the Labor Party (PvdA) led a coalition which included the Christian Democrats (CDA) and Democrats '66 (D'66); from 1977 to 1981, the CDA led a coalition with the People's Party (VVD); in 1981, the CDA, PvdA, and D'66 coalition returned, this time led by the CDA; from May to November 1982, a CDA-led minority caretaker coalition with D'66; and from then until the May 1986 elections, a CDA-VVD coalition. In May 1986, the CDA-VVD coalition was returned to office with a slight shift in seats toward the CDA.

Legislature

Legislative power is shared between the First and Second chambers, but the popularly elected Second Chamber with 150 members has primary authority. The First Chamber, indirectly elected through the provincial assemblies of the eleven provinces, has a general power of veto, but it is unable to propose amendments to legislation.

Most legislation is proposed by the government, but prior to consideration by the States General it is submitted to an independent administrative body, the Council of State, which scrutinizes the draft laws for consistency and compatibility with existing law. Constitutional changes follow a special procedure: before their adoption, new elections must be held for the Second Chamber, and then the proposed changes require a two-thirds majority in both houses.

In theory, there is a possibility of conflict between the two chambers of the States General, but in practice this does not occur often because their party composition is much the same. The First Chamber is elected by proportional representation in the provincial assemblies and therefore mirrors the national distribution of party support. There may be some disproportion between the two chambers, since the members of the First Chamber are elected for six-year terms, one half retiring every three years, while the Second Chamber is elected for four years.

ELECTIONS TO THE SECOND CHAMBER OF THE STATES GENERAL

Party	1977 %	1981 %	1982 %	Seats
Christian Democratic Appeal (CDA)*	31.9	30.8	29.3	45
Labor Party (PvdA)	33.8	29.3	30.4	47
People's Party for Freedom & Democracy (VVD)	18.0	17.3	23.1	36
Radical Political Party (PPR)	1.7	2.0	1.7	2
Communist Party of the Netherlands (CPN)	1.7	2.0	1.8	3
Democrats '66 (D'66)	5.4	11.0	4.3	6
Democratic Socialists '70 (DS'70)	0.7	0.6	0.4	—
State Reform Party (SGP)	2.1	2.3	1.9	3
Farmers' Party (BP)	0.8	0.2	0.3	—
Reformed Political Union (GPV)	1.0	0.8	0.3	1
Pacifist Socialist Party (PSP)	1.0	2.1	2.3	3
Reformatoric Political Federation (RPF)	—	1.2	1.5	2
Others	1.5	1.6	2.3	2

* The CDA was not formed until 1977. For the 1972 election, the share of the vote won by the three parties that later formed the CDA has been aggregated.

Judiciary

The Supreme Court of the Netherlands, with twenty judges appointed for life (in practice, retirement age is seventy), is the ultimate court of appeal from the lower courts. The Supreme Court has a restricted function of judicial interpretation, but none of judicial review: it cannot consider whether a particular law is contrary to the constitution, and that applies also to foreign treaties. This limitation places the onus for protecting basic rights on the States General and the government, with the judiciary concerned solely with correct application of the law.

Regional & Local Government

Dutch local government consists of two tiers: the eleven provinces and 842 municipalities. Both the provinces and the municipalities have elected councils serving four-year terms. Both types of council also elect executive committees, but they are led by an appointed official from the central government: a royal commissioner in the case of the province and a burgomaster in the case of the municipality. This degree of central government involvement and control is exceptional in Western Europe, and it underlies the strength of executive authority in the Netherlands.

The appointment of the burgomaster merits special attention. He is a career official and, once in office, he remains on a more or less permanent basis. However, the central government in selecting a candidate will pay due attention to the wishes of the elected council, with local factors—especially religious and party-political considerations—given proper weight. At the local level, party cooperation is fairly high, for it is rare that any one party will have an absolute majority on a council, so that the executive committee may be composed of several parties. Moreover, the fact that the burgomaster himself will have no formal political attachment helps to ensure that executive proceedings and policies will be nonpartisan.

The Electoral System

The Netherlands provides one of the best examples of "pure" proportional representation, since there is very little distortion between the number of votes a party obtains and the seats it receives in the Second Chamber. In consequence, all elections result in the representation of minute splinter parties, so that the Dutch party system gives the appearance of entrenched multipartism.

The exactness of proportionality is achieved by treating the whole country as a *single* constituency, with the result that a party's representation depends entirely on its aggregated national vote. The electoral quotient, the number of votes needed to win a seat, is arrived at by totalling all the votes cast in the election and dividing this figure by the number of seats in the Second Chamber. The present size of the Chamber is fixed at 150 seats, so it is only necessary for a party to win about 0.67 percent of the national vote in order to qualify for a seat. Many countries with proportional representation systems impose an arbitrary barrier or threshold (usually between 2 and 5 percent), but there is no such imposition under the Dutch electoral law.

Voting is entirely by means of party lists, although candidates' names are given and voters may change the presented order. The country is divided into eighteen electoral districts, and a party is free to present lists in as many districts as it chooses and to present different lists in the individual districts. However, any such variations do not vitiate the principle of national proportionality. Seats are first allocated on a district level and a final allocation is made nationally. Any seats which are unallocated after the first distribution are then allotted on the basis of the "highest average," that is, to the party or parties with the highest average of votes to seats already won.

One consequence of the Dutch electoral system is that there is no tradition that an elected deputy represents the interests of a particular constituency. That is difficult to establish with a party-list system in any case, but in the Netherlands the emphasis is on the deputies representing the nation at large, rather than being attached to regional or local interests.

Interest in elections is considerable, with a turnout of over 85 percent, although this shows a decline from earlier years, before compulsory voting was abolished in 1970.

The Party System

Origins of the Parties

Prior to the period of the extension of the franchise between 1887 and 1918, parties were very loosely organized, and the modern party system did not begin to emerge until the 1880s. Until the widening of suffrage in 1887, the vote was restricted to about 3 percent of the population, and political power was in the hands of the Conservatives and Liberals. Subsequently, parties took shape around the complex cleavages of Dutch society, especially those relating to religion. The division between Protestants (Calvinists) and Roman Catholics represented one line of cleavage, but there was also a line separating the religious forces in society from the secular ones; the latter in turn were split between the anticlerical, bourgeois liberals and the organized working-class movement.

Various factors helped to prevent the system fragmenting. One was the fact that organized religion was not identified with a single state church, so that religious pluralism fostered political pluralism as well. A second reason was that a fundamental compromise was reached (in 1917) on the "schools issue": denominational schools were thereafter to receive state subsidies, removing a contentious issue for the religious parties. A third reason relates to the balance of political forces: no one grouping by itself constituted a majority, so that alliances and accommodation were essential. This conciliatory impulse has remained a hallmark of Dutch political life.

Five parties were dominant in the interwar years and remained so until the recent past, providing the pattern of governing coalitions and accounting for up to 90 percent of the popular vote. Three of the five were religious parties, the other two were the Liberals (later to become the People's Party for Freedom and Democracy) and the Social Democrats (which became the Labor Party). Despite the proliferation of parties—no fewer than fifty-four parties contested the 1933 election—the inherent stability of Dutch parliamentary democracy was never in doubt.

Two changes have become evident since the 1960s. One is the long-term decline of the religious parties, a development which led to the amalgamation of the three major ones in the late 1970s. A second and possibly related change has been the growth in support for parties which are opposed to the lack of electoral influence on the formation of the government. The direction of voting frequently has little influence on the composition of the governing coalition which ultimately results. Thus, after the 1971 election, four parties which had *lost* seats became members of the new government.

The Parties in Law

As is evident, there is very little restriction on the free formation and operation of parties in the Netherlands. The main regulation is achieved through the operation of the electoral law. In this respect, there is a barrier against very small parties: those that fail to win 75 percent of the electoral quotient within any of the eighteen electoral districts lose their deposits in those districts, so that a party failing in all eighteen districts will stand to forfeit a substantial sum. There is no provision for direct state subsidies to the parties, but they receive substantial indirect help: at elections they benefit from access to the public broadcasting media; the parliamentary blocs in the States General receive assistance for their parliamentary work; and party research institutes are also partly financed from state funds. The executive also has an important restrictive power at its disposal in that parties can be declared extremist and banned without involving the Supreme Court. A well-known case involved the extreme right-wing Dutch People's Union which won 0.4 percent of the vote in 1977. A parliamentary majority was in favor of the party being banned, but in April 1979 it was officially declared to be a legal party.

Party Organization

The coexistence of several large and many very small parties means that there are considerable differences in organization and wide variations in the size of membership. All the major parties have complete coverage at the local level, with district associations which are active for local, provincial, and parliamentary elections. Typically, an annual delegate congress is the supreme party organ to which an executive committee is responsible, but there is also a party "council" which exercises the authority of the congress when the latter is not in session.

Dutch parties are membership parties, but there has been a general decline in membership since the mid-1960s. The larger ones have a membership of 100,000 or more, while the smaller ones represented in the States General have around 10,000, although the Dutch Communist Party is nearly three times that size. On average, the ratio of members to voters is rather low and declining—about five members per 100 voters, with the PdvA as few as 3.9 per 100. However, it is important to take into account the contribution to the vitality of the parties made by a political "infrastructure" of social organizations: the churches, church-related organizations, and the trade unions.

Party membership is important as a source of finance, and the majority of parties rely heavily on membership dues. Except for the Liberals, the parties receive over 90 percent of their budgetary expenditure from members' contributions. Taken together, the three largest parties have an annual outlay of around 10 million guilders (about $4 million) which is a rather modest expenditure, although it does not include the cost of running national election campaigns, nor does it take account of the indirect state support already mentioned. The effect of declining membership has inevitably given the parties major financial problems.

Campaigning

Election campaigns in the Netherlands are relatively short, since polling takes place forty-three days after the nomination of candidates. There is a heavy reliance on television and radio broadcasting, and the leaders of the larger parties loom as the major contestants. Campaign expenditure is not very high: the total for all parties in 1977 amounted to about 3,300,000 guilders ($1.35 million). Most parties can also rely on the support of at least one national daily newspaper, although official party publications, with the exception of the Communist Party, are weeklies or magazines and journals.

Campaigning concentrates on mobilizing support among adherents, since structural and historical factors determine party loyalties, and these are not weakened in the course of a single campaign. Moreover, as already indicated, elections are primarily about the choice of parties rather than a choice of government. As a result, party leaders are regarded primarily as party representatives rather than as potential national leaders. This emphasis may be changing, since even if recent elections have been indeterminate in their outcome, increasingly the parties have been forced to spell out their coalition preferences during the course of the election campaign.

Independent Voters

The best single predictor of voting behaviour remains religion, and practicing members of the Protestant and Catholic churches will tend to support one or other of the religious parties. But the scale of the decline of the three main confessional parties—from about 50 percent of the vote in the 1950s to 30 percent in the 1970s and 1980s—indicates that party identification has weakened considerably. Nor is it safe to rely on social-class variables, since parties tend to be interclass in their appeal. Thus, while the Dutch Labor Party attracts about a half of the working-class vote, the Christian Democratic Appeal takes about a third. A third variable, that based on urban-rural differences, also reveals less than might be supposed, for although the religious parties tend to fare better in rural communities and the Liberals and Labor in the cities and suburbs, all the major parties are strongly competitive in all types of communities.

These factors all point to a considerable flux in electoral behavior now that the formerly strong segmentation of Dutch society with its "spiritual families" is in decay. Evidence of the growing volatility is seen in the rise of "protest" parties, the most important of which is Democrats '66. They are particularly attractive to younger voters and draw support from all sections of the electorate.

Christian Democratic Appeal (*Christen Democratisch Appèl*; CDA)

History

The CDA was formed as a unified party in 1980. It is an amalgamation of the three main religious parties—the Catholic People's Party (KVP) and two Protestant groups, the Anti-Revolutionary Party (ARP) and the Christian-Historical Union (CHU). The ARP, founded in 1879, was the oldest Dutch party; the CHU was formed in 1908; and the Catholic party was based on the League of Roman Catholic Voters' Clubs established in 1904. The KVP, the largest of the three, was formed in 1946 as the successor to the more exclusive Roman Catholic State Party (founded in 1926). It was consistently the strongest single party in the States General until the 1970s, when the three parties all experienced a downturn in membership and in their electoral appeal. The first moves to create the CDA began in the early 1970s, and the three parties fought the 1977 election as a loose federation.

Organization

Since the full merger took place in 1980, the constituent parties have harmonized their structures, but the CDA is not yet a unitary party. The old parties are still distinct entities within the CDA and membership remains largely indirect. Nevertheless, the decisions of the CDA central organs (congress and executive) are binding on the subgroupings, party income goes to a common fund, and the apportionment of candidates on CDA lists is determined by the central leadership, not the subgroups.

Party headquarters are at Dr. Kuyperstraat 3,2514 BA The Hague.

Policy

Of the three constituent groups, the ARP was the most conservative; it was founded to oppose the spirit and ideas of the French Revolution. It was, nevertheless, flexible in practice. The CHU, smallest of the three, was less populist than the ARP, but in some ways more progressive. The KVP, moderate and centrist, was the essential party in any coalition and able to join with the conservatives on the right or with the Labor Party to form a government. The CDA is a center party, advocating the application of Christian principles in political life. On a secular level, the party favors orthodox financial and economic management. Disagreement on economic policy led to the break up of the CDA-Labor coalition after only eight months in May 1982. The CDA supports NATO and provided the leadership in the negotiations that led to the acceptance of the deployment of forty-eight Cruise missiles. Also, the CDA was the leader in the development of the economic austerity policies of the government in the mid-1980s.

Membership & Constituency

With a reported membership of 144,000 the CDA is the largest party in the Netherlands. Its most faithful supporters are likely to be professed Christians who are independent tradesmen and farmers, but it draws nearly equal support from all social classes. The CDA is particularly strong in smaller towns and rural areas.

Financing

The party depends on membership dues for 90 percent of its income. Annual expenditures probably do not exceed $1.5 million, not counting campaign expenses.

Leadership

Ruud Lubbers (born 1939), millionaire businessman and economist, has been CDA leader and prime minister since 1982. Previously, he had been parliamentary leader since 1977 and minister of economics. He succeeded Andries Van Agt (born 1931), prime minister 1977-1982, who retired from the leadership, but remained active in politics. Party president is P. Bukman, parliamentary leader is Dr. Bert de Vries (born 1938), and general secretary is M. Smits. Because the Catholic wing is the largest element in the CDA, the leader is normally of that faith.

Prospects

Lubbers' dynamic leadership has reinvigorated the CDA and made him much the most popular politician in the country. Combined with the party's solid organization and basis of support in the religious communities, the future of the CDA seems well-assured, despite the declining intensity of religious commitment in the Dutch population. Lubbers' skillful handling of the problems of economic austerity and Cruise missile deployment have reinforced his party's position as a nearly essential member of all governmental coalitions.

Democrats '66
(Democraten '66; D'66)

History

The D'66 originated in 1966 as a party demanding constitutional reform. After initial successes the party lost momentum, recovered slightly in 1981, when it became the fourth-strongest party in the States General, and seems to have stabilized as the largest of the minor parties, but far short of the big three.

Organization

The D'66 is predominantly an urban party with a strong base in Amsterdam. The structure of the party is very open and democratic. Until 1977, all ordinary members had the right to vote at the annual policymaking congress.

Party headquarters are at Bezuidenhoutsweg 195, The Hague.

Policy

A liberal-radical party, D'66 finds a natural ally in the PvdA. The party argues that the political system fails to alter governments to reflect the wishes of the voters. It advocates the abolition of proportional representation and the direct election of the prime minister. It also wants the parties to set forth their coalition commitments in advance of the elections so that the voters will have a clear choice between potential governments. The party also actively promotes an environmental-protection program. The party's social policies are progressive, but its economic policies are more in line with those of the CDA rather than with the Labor party.

Membership & Constituency

Membership is only about 10,000. Its staunchest supporters tend to be younger than average, upwardly mobile, and relatively well-educated urbanites.

Financing

With its small membership, D'66 is financially hard pressed and depends more on small contributions and volunteer effort than most other parties.

Leadership

The party's founder was Jan Terlouw (born 1931), deputy premier and economics minister 1981-1982. He resigned when D'66 lost eleven of its seventeen seats in the 1982 elections and was replaced by Laurens Brinkhorst. Present leaders are president J. Kohnstamm, parliamentary leader M. B. Engwirda (born 1943), and general secretary J. Michiel ten Brink.

Prospects

The D'66 has now become an eligible "party of government" and has served in coalitions with both the PdvA and the religious parties. It has so far failed to secure any of the constitutional reforms it wants and is unlikely to be more successful in the future. The party may yet succeed in its aim of creating a two-bloc party system and thus give voters a clear choice between alternative government formations, because its pivotal place on the political spectrum and its status as largest of the minor parties may enable it to arbitrate among its larger rivals in a way that maximizes its influence.

Labor Party
(*Partij ven de Arbeid;* PvdA)

History

The PvdA was founded in 1946, but was largely based on the old Social Democratic Workers' Party which dated from 1894 and was orthodox Marxist in its origins. The experience of World War II led to the organization of a more broadly based movement to include progressive Christians and members of various resistance groups. The PvdA served in various coalitions, always with the KVP, until 1973 when the party was successful in providing its first prime minister, Joop Den Uyl, who led a broad center-left coalition until 1977. The PvdA benefited from the gradual weakening of the religious parties, becoming the largest single party in the Second Chamber for the first time in 1971. Elections since then have given the party approximate parity with the CDA.

Organization

The PvdA is the best organized of Dutch parties, with over 800 district organizations and the full panoply of regional and national organizations. The annual congress decides policy and formulates the party's election platform. The National Executive brings together all competing streams in the party.

Party headquarters are at Nicolaas Witsenkade 30, POB 1310, 1017 2T, Amsterdam.

Policy

With the organization of the party in 1946, the Marxist emphasis was replaced by a "personal socialism" which allowed for religious and humanist commitments to socialism, as well as that based on Marxist philosophy. Despite this nondogmatic brand of socialism, the PvdA is firmly to the left in the party spectrum. This was confirmed in the late 1960s when the New Left took over the party leadership and some of the moderate old guard left to form the Democratic Socialists in 1970. The party strongly supports European integration. It tends toward a pacifist outlook in foreign policy and was the principal opponent of the Cruise missile deployment. Also, it was the main critic of the government's economic austerity programs of the 1980s.

Membership & Constituency

The move to the left did not harm the party membership or electoral strength. With about 120,000 members, the PvdA is the second-largest party. Its supporters come from all sectors of the population, but its most faithful members are likely to be urban working-class people without religious ties, and middle-class professionals. It also draws heavily on white-collar workers. Support for the party is fairly evenly spread through all age groups.

Financing

The party is considerably better financed than any of the others. Most of the party's income derives from membership dues. Expenditures probably exceed $1.5 million, not counting campaign costs.

Leadership

Joop Den Uyl (born 1919) continues to lead the party. He enjoys considerable authority and was the party's first prime minister (1973–77). Since the party has taken a more leftist course, leadership tensions have been overcome. The question of succession has not yet arisen, but there are several prominent figures in the party who have had government experience. Max van den Berg is party president and Wim van Velzen is general secretary.

Prospects

The PvdA is at a disadvantage in comparison with other European socialist parties in that the structure of Dutch politics and parties, particularly the religious ones, operates against a purely class-based party, so that the PvdA lags in growth despite the decline of the Communist Party. At the same time, the party, with its natural alliance partners, D'66 and the Radical Catholics (PPR), does not produce a parliamentary majority. Therefore, the PvdA can only come to office in coalition with the CDA, a combination not likely to produce the legislation the PvdA would most like to see enacted. Nevertheless, the party's solid organization and membership base is likely to ensure that it will continue to claim nearly a third of the vote and will remain a major force in Parliament.

People's Party for Freedom and Democracy
(*Volkspartij voor Vrijheid en Democratie;* VVD)

History

The Dutch Liberals were historically a dominant force until the extension of the franchise and the adoption of proportional representation in 1917. Thereafter, the Liberals went into partial eclipse. In its origins, the Liberal Party was decidedly anticlerical and insisted on the separation of church and state. In 1948, the party took its present name and has gradually emerged again as one of the most important parties, shedding its anticlerical image and adopting a more progressive program while still maintaining its middle-class outlook.

Organization

The VVD is a fairly decentralized party, especially in the question of candidate selection, over which the party congress itself has some say. The party is also notable for limiting the influence of parliamentary deputies on the party executive. Otherwise, the VVD's organization is similar to that of the other parties. The congress is the supreme authority, but the smaller council elected by the congress has more practical day-to-day influence on the party executive.

Party headquarters are at Koninginnegracht 57, 2514 AE The Hague.

Policy

On many counts, the VVD has to be regarded as an orthodox conservative party, since on most domestic issues it stands well to the right of the others, including the CDA. However, it supports the social security programs and advocates worker participation in profits and management. The VVD represents a moderately polarizing force in the Dutch context, particularly in its attachment to free enterprise and to a restrictive view of government economic intervention. Its secular orientation has not prevented the VVD from cooperating with the religious parties in governing coalitions. The party strongly supports the European Economic Community and NATO, including the deployment of the Cruise missiles.

Membership & Constituency

The VVD doubled its membership in the 1970s. With more than 100,000 members, the VVD is now the third-largest party and it consistently draws the third-largest share of the vote. Its primary appeal is to the upper and middle classes, but it also draws support from white-collar workers. Like the PvdA, the party attracts the support of those with no religious attachment.

Financing

To a greater extent than any other party the VVD can depend on substantial contributions from business and industry, and therefore it does not rely as much on membership dues. Annual expenditures, not counting campaign costs, run in the neighborhood of $1.3 million.

Leadership

The party leader is energetic, impulsive Ed Nijpels (born 1950). Other prominent leaders are Gijs van Aardenne, deputy premier; party president J. Kamminga; and general secretary W. J. A. van den Berg.

Prospects

The decline of the religious parties over the years has probably been a contributory factor in the VVD's success. That trend will continue, though perhaps at a slower pace than in the recent past. The party's conservative policies make it unacceptable as a coalition partner to the parties on the left, and the CDA takes an ambivalent attitude toward it. Van Agt favored it as a coalition partner, but Lubbers is less enthusiastic. Nevertheless, its electoral strength will give it a continuing role in all but leftist Dutch governments.

Minor Parties

Farmers Party (*Boerenpartij;* BP)

The BP was founded in 1958 and first entered the States General in 1963. Its title was to some extent a misnomer, since the BP was much more of an antisystem, protest party which expressed dissatisfaction with personal taxes, bureaucracy, and big business, but it was also strongly antisocialist and against big government in general. After reaching a peak vote of 4.8 percent in 1967, it declined rapidly and won no seats in the 1981, 1982 or 1986 Parliaments.

Headquarters: 18 Bovenweg, Bennekom.

Communist Party of the Netherlands (*Communistische Partij van Nederland;* CPM)

The CPN was formed in 1918 as a breakaway from the Social Democratic Workers' Party . It has never participated in government, and the party has usually been isolated and weak. Its best post-1945 result was 10.6 percent in 1946; thereafter the CPN declined until the 1960s, with a modest recovery in 1972. The CPN broke with Soviets in 1964, and gradually adopted a Eurocommunist line. It has called for a coalition of all "progressive" parties. The CPN emphasizes its "proletarian" nature as against the predominance of "intellectuals" in the other left-wing parties, but it has to compete with the PvdA as well as with the Radicals (PPR) and the Pacifist Socialist Party (PSP). Party membership (at 27,000) is relatively high in comparison with other Dutch parties.

Headquarters: Postbus 19563, 1000 GN Amsterdam.

Democratic Socialists 1970 (*Democratische Socialisten 1970;* DS'70)

As a reaction to the leftward drift of the PvdA in the late 1960s, DS'70 represented a right-wing movement against the influence of the New Left in the party. It was especially insistent on the need to produce balanced budgets and a retrenchment of public expenditure. After an initial success in the 1971 election (5.3 percent) and service in a nonsocialist coalition, DS'70 rapidly faded into insignificance.

Headquarters: Postbus 3889, 1001 AR, Amsterdam.

Pacifist Socialist Party (*Pacifistisch Socialistische Partij;* PSP)

The PSP, formed in 1957, is one of the minor "splinter" parties on the left (with a best performance of 3 percent in 1963). In spite of its small size, its outlook—especially its opposition to NATO, nuclear weapons, etc.—corresponds to a large section of Dutch public opinion, so that the PSP's place in the party system appears assured. It acts as a pressure group on the policies of the PvdA, but it has never participated in government. It won three parliamentary seats in both the 1981 and 1982 elections and claims 10,000 members.

Headquarters: Nieuwe Looiersstraat 45, Postbus 700, 1000 AS Amsterdam.

Radical Political Party (*Politieke Partij Radikalen;* PPR)

The rather "traditional," although not conservative, outlook of the former Catholic People's Party (KVP) led to the disaffection of many younger, activist Catholics who formed the new Catholic PPR in 1968. The PPR is a left-wing party with a socialist program; it is strongly opposed to the use of nuclear energy and to nuclear armament. The party won 4.8 percent of the vote in 1972 and supported the center-left coalition government between 1973 and 1977. It won three seats in the 1981 parliamentary elections, two in 1982, and claims about 13,000 members.

Headquarters: Singel 277, 1012 WG Amsterdam.

Reformatoric Political Federation (*Reformatorische Politieke Federatie;* RPF)

The RPF is the newest of the three very small Calvinist parties represented in the States General. It was formed in 1975 largely as a splinter off the Anti-Revolutionary Party , arguing that Calvinist teachings should be more directly applied to political and social problems. It won two seats in both the 1981 and 1982 elections and claims 10,000 members.

Headquarters: POB 302, 8070 AH Nunspeet.

Reformed Political Association (*Gereformeerd Politiek Verbond;* GPV)

The GPV, founded in 1948, is a fundamentalist religious party which looks back to the national Calvinism of the seventeenth century for its political doctrine, holding that the Anti-Revolutionary Party diluted these ideas with liberalism and socialism. The GPV has a small but consistent following and is usually represented in the Second chamber with a single seat. It claims 13,000 members.

Headquarters: POB 439, 3800 AK Amersfoort.

State Reform Party (*Staatkundig Gereformeerde Partij;* SGP)

The State Reform Party (SGP) is the oldest and largest of the small Calvinist parties, and like the others was a split (in 1918) from the Anti-Revolutionary Party. The SGP is conservative in outlook, drawing its support mainly from members of the Dutch Reformed Church. The party over the years has consistently won about 2 percent of the vote and three seats in Parliament. It claims 20,000 members.

Headquarters: Laan van Meerdervoort 165, 2517 AZ, The Hague.

Two other small parties have appeared on the political scene in recent years. The Center Party is a right-wing, antiimmigrant organization. It won 0.8 percent of the vote and one seat in 1982, but lost it again in 1986. It claims about 4,000 members. The Evangelical People's Party is the newest addition to the ranks of the confessional parties. It claims 3,000 members and won 0.7 percent and one seat in 1982.

National Prospects

The Dutch party and political systems can best be described as being "in transition." At one time, the Netherlands was held to be a "pillarized" society, in which the various pillars—secular and lay—each with its own sector of support, coexisted with the others. Over the past two decades, there have been fundamental changes in Dutch politics as illustrated by the waning of the religious factor. At the same time, the idea of a "governing club" is still evident,

especially in the atmosphere surrounding the formation of governments. However, the fact that D'66 has been taken into the government suggests that the "club" is open to new members if hard pressed.

At the electoral level, on the other hand, there are signs of polarization between left and right. The disjunction between voting shifts and eventual makeup of coalition governments is clearly shown in the difficulties surrounding coalition building in the last five elections (1972, 1977, 1981, 1982 and 1986). In each case, the results gave no clear guide to the coalition outcome and interparty negotiations took several months—after the 1977 election nine months were needed to form a new government. Although such an impasse is serious, it also serves to underline the stability of Dutch politics: in spite of serious problems with government cohesion, a high degree of tolerance and social consensus holds the system together and diffuses political tension.

Two specific problems have dominated the Dutch political scene in recent years. One is the general economic situation, especially the persistent unemployment. Successive governments have remained intact only with the greatest difficulty, mainly because of their inability to agree on how strong a dose of austerity they should administer. The other was the long debate over the NATO decision to deploy Cruise missiles. That controversy seems to have been settled by the coalitions' unexpected success in the 1986 elections.

Further Reading
Daalder, H. "The Netherlands." In *Political Parties in the European Community,* S. Henig, ed. London: George Allen & Unwin, 1979.
———. "Extreme Proportional Representation: The Dutch Experience." In *Adversary Politics and Electoral Reform,* S. E. Finer, ed. London: Anthony Wigram, 1975.
Day, A. J. and Degenhardt, H. W. eds. *Political Parties of the World.* Harlow, Essex: Longman, 1980.
Irving, R. E. M. *The Christian Democratic Parties of Western Europe.* London: George Allen & Unwin, 1979.
Irwin, G. A. "The Netherlands." In *Western European Party Systems: Trends and Prospects,* P. H. Merkl, ed. New York: The Free Press, 1980.
Lijphart, A. *The Politics of Accommodation: Pluralism and Democracy in the Netherlands.*

Berkeley: University of California Press, 1975.

MacMullen, A. L. "The Netherlands." In *Government and Administration in Western Europe*, F. F. Ridley, ed. Oxford: Martin Robertson, 1979.

Weil, G. L. *The Benelux Nations: The Politics of Small-Country Democracies*. New York: Holt, Rinehart and Winston, 1970.

Wolinetz, S. B. "The Dutch Labour Party: A Social Democratic Party in Transition." In *Social Democratic Parties in Western Europe*, W. E. Paterson and A. H. Thomas, eds. London: Croom Helm, 1977.

NEW ZEALAND

by Lois Fenichell revised by Bruce Dixon, M.A.

The System of Government

New Zealand, a parliamentary democracy, has had a unitary government since the abolition of the federated provinces in 1876. Its constitutional framework is not a written document but a collection of acts of Parliament, British precedents, and accepted conventions. The country was a British colony from 1841 to 1907, when it was granted dominion status, and achieved complete autonomy in 1947. New Zealand with some three and a half million people, is a member of the British Commonwealth of Nations.

Executive

Executive power resides in a cabinet headed by the prime minister, who is leader of the majority party in Parliament. Only elected members of Parliament may hold portfolios in the twenty-member cabinet. The head of state is the reigning sovereign of Great Britain, represented by a governor-general appointed for a five-year term. The governor-general invariably accepts ministerial advice and his assent to legislation is a formality. He attends meetings of the Executive Council, whose membership is identical with that of the cabinet, and performs ceremonial functions. He formally appoints judges and cabinet ministers, including the prime minister. His latent power to dissolve Parliament and call a general election has never been exercised. The present governor-general, whose term began in November 1980, is His Excellency the Honorable David Stuart Beattie.

Legislature

Legislative power is vested in a ninety-two-member unicameral Parliament, the House of Representatives, elected triennially. An appointed upper house, the Legislative Council, was abolished in 1950. Constitutionally, Parliament is a bipartite body; cabinet and House share in the legislative process. The presiding officer is the speaker, elected from the M.P.s of the majority party, but expected to be nonpartisan. Legislative sessions have been getting longer in recent years, averaging about 120 sitting days annually.

All revenue and expenditure bills must be introduced by the government. In practice, cabinet members introduce most legislation through a complicated committee and caucus system. All bills are referred to the appropriate committee in order to allow interested members of the public to present their views. After passing through three readings, the second consisting of clause-by-clause debate, a bill with its amendments may be passed in final form and sent to the governor-general for the Royal Assent.

Private members may introduce bills, but these may be choked off in their early stages by the majority party. Local bills and private bills, designed to secure benefits to a locality, group, or individual, may also be introduced. Parliament accepts petitions from the public if the subject matter is justiciable and all other legal and equitable remedies have been exhausted.

Real power in the legislature resides in the government, and power within that body has centralized so that New Zealand's system is frequently called prime-ministerial government.

ELECTION RESULTS (1984)				
	Total Vote	Percent	Change from 1981	Seats
Labour	755,551	42.87	+19.1	56
National	633,564	35.95	− 0.8	37
Social Credit	136,774	7.76	−59.1	2
New Zealand Party	216,436	12.28	n.a.*	—
All others	19,969	1.13	−24.8	—

*this was the first election for the New Zealand Party.

Judiciary

The judicial branch is independent of both the government and Parliament. Judges are appointd by the governor-general. Above the district (formerly called magistrate's) court, which has both civil and criminal jurisdiction, is the High (formerly Superior) Court, which deals with serious crimes and civil cases involving large sums. The highest court is the Court of Appeals. Final appeal is to the Judicial Committee of the Privy Council in the United Kingdom. District judges may be removed by the governor-general for inability or misbehavior; High Court judges, who must retire at seventy-two, may be removed only by the sovereign, upon a recommendation by the House of Representatives.

Ombudsman

New Zealand was the first non-Scandinavian country to establish this office, in 1962. The ombudsman investigates individual complaints against administrative decisions and is not concerned with official policy. Responsible to Parliament, the ombudsman does not serve as a constitutional check on government.

Regional & Local Government

New Zealand is organized territorially into different classes of local authority depending on the concentration of population: 98 counties (rural); 132 boroughs (urban); four communities (urban areas in rural districts); and four districts (neither wholly urban nor wholly rural). Each of these territorial units has a council elected triennially. County and a few borough councils are elected by district; other councils are elected on an at-large basis.

In addition to the territorially based councils, New Zealand's local units have special-purpose councils, also triennially elected, with responsibilities for hospitals, harbors, electric power, pest control, and the like. Almost any elector can stand for councillor, since residence and financial requirements are minimal. Local councils tend to be nonpartisan, and most councillors represent conservative citizens' groups. The turnout in local elections is low, less than half that of national elections, and even lower for the special-purpose boards.

Under its powers to alter the structure of local bodies, Parliament in 1974 passed a law consolidating local government legislation into a single act. The law established regional councils, which added still another level of representation, but its intent was to reduce the number of overlapping functions of local bodies. New Zealanders' participation in local government developed out of a long tradition of community voluntarism, and they have tended to resist attempts at consolidated government. Nevertheless, the changes are slowly being put into place.

The Electoral System

The structure of the electoral system is not part of the constitution. It is prescribed by statute alone and may be amended by Parliament. Amendment of certain basic provisions, like the life of Parliament and the minimum voting age, requires a vote of 75 percent of the membership of Parliament or a simple majority in a national referendum.

Each of New Zealand's ninety-two electoral districts, or electorates (eighty-eight general, formerly called European; and four reserved for the Maoris, the aboriginal population), is represented by one member in the House of Representatives. Based on population, the general electorates are closer to numerical equality than any in the world, each having about 35,000 people. Redistricting takes place every five years, after the census, and since the 1950s it has been the subject of increasing interparty dissension and charges of gerrymandering. Critics of the electoral system say that the Representation Commission, which conducts the redistricting, pays more attention to the fetish of numerical equality than to the distortions arising from it. The electoral law itself has been frequently amended in recent years, as each party seeks to shape the law to its own advantage.

Elections in New Zealand are uncomplicated. Electors vote for one candidate by crossing off the names of the others, and the candidate with the most votes wins. With a few minor exceptions, all persons aged eighteen or over are required to register after living in the district for three months. A general reregistration takes place every five years. A $20 fine for nonregistration is not enforced.

The prime minister selects the election date, usually the last Saturday in November. The establishment of polling places at shopping centers, race tracks, and other public places encourages people to vote. Absentee ballots are provided for those overseas, hospitalized, or religiously opposed to voting on Saturday. Voter turnout averages around 90 percent. In recent years, charges of inaccurate rolls and fraudulent voting have grown more common, along with growing dismay that the "first past the post" (simple plurality) system does not accurately reflect voter opinion. A system of proportional representation has been suggested.

The Party System

Origins of the Parties

Since the late nineteenth century, the major political issues in New Zealand have been its long tradition of government intervention in the economy and the desirable extent of social legislation, in which the country has always played a pioneering role. The approach to these questions by both the leftist parties and their conservative opposition has generally been pragmatic rather than ideological.

New Zealand has maintained its two-party system through several realignments, the most recent in the 1930s when the Labour and National parties developed out of issues related to the world depression. Minor parties include the Social Credit Political League, a party of rural protest and monetary reform; the environmentalist Values Party; and the Soviet-oriented Socialist Unity Party. Appearing for the first time in the 1981 election was Mana Motuhake, a party devoted to the advancement of Maori interests.

The Parties in Law

New Zealand's political tradition is British, and as in Britain the parties originated within Parliament. Parties are not banned because of extremist beliefs. Securing a place on the ballot is easy, since legally any citizen who is a registered elector may be nominated by any two other registered electors. A deposit of $100 is required of each candidate, which is refunded to the winner and to any candidate who polls 25 percent of the winner's vote.

Party Organization

New Zealand's political organizations combine elements of the mass-based and the cadre-based type of party. Party members, as distinct from mere supporters, pay dues to the party, and it is from their ranks that candidates are chosen by selection committees whose meetings are open only to enrolled members. Candidates need not reside in the districts they seek to represent.

The parties draw up their own constitutions. Policies are formed through a consultative process between regional and local branches and the central leadership, ratified at national conferences, and issued to the public at election time in the form of manifestoes. Party leaders are chosen by and from the caucus of the party's M.P.s.

The relationship between local, or branch, parties and their central organizations is different in the two major parties. Labour's local units serve largely as constituencies for delegates to the national conference, while local autonomy is both a structural feature of the National Party and one of its major tenets. National's candidate-selection committees are composed entirely of members of the branch, or local, party organizations, while Labour uses a combination of central and local members. Nevertheless, the Aukland division of both parties tends to be dominant and to lead the parties toward those policies which will appeal to the greatest number of voters.

Between elections, the parliamentary parties and the local and national extraparliamentary parties, each with a complex internal structure, go their separate ways. This often places a strain on individual M.P.s, who find the parliamentary demands of loyalty and teamwork at odds with the roads-and-bridges concerns of their local branches.

Campaigning

Intensive campaigning is limited to three of four weeks and receives much attention in the media. Government-owned radio and television provide free broadcast time as well as regular news coverage. A legal limit of $4,000 is placed on the expenditures of individual candidates, but the parties themselves have no legal financial limits or disclosure requirements. Since the 1960s, candidates have increasingly adopted what New Zealanders call the presidential style of campaign, resembling campaigns in the United States.

Independent Voters

Traditional party loyalties have been declining since the 1950s. Since ticket splitting is not possible in voting for Parliament and local councils are largely nonpartisan, diminishing party loyalty is illustrated more by crossover voting than by support given to independent candidates. In the 1978 election, fifty-three candidates stood for Parliament on a total of twenty-eight splinter-party and independent labels. They polled only 1.3 percent of the total vote, and 80 percent of this was in five electorates where special circumstances prevailed.

Labour Party

History

The Labour Party was founded in 1916 and entered its first general election in 1919. The party's growth in the 1920s and 1930s was aided by New Zealand's growing urbanization, the party's demonstrated concern for farmers, and the incumbent Reform Party's inability to deal with the worsening depression. Coming to power in 1935 with Michael Savage as prime minister, Labour established programs of direct relief and social-welfare legislation culminating in a comprehensive socialized-medicine scheme in 1941. Under the leadership of Prime Minister Peter Fraser, Labour dominated the wartime coalition, but lost to National in 1949. The second Labour government (1957–60), facing a severe balance-of-payments crisis, was doomed by the "Black Budget" (as National promptly labeled it) of 1958, which in spite of many social and economic merits, raised taxes on such working-class luxuries as cigarettes and beer. The third Labour government (1972–75), voted into power in the hope that it could solve the problems of the world oil crisis and a declining economy, was perceived by voters as insufficiently decisive, and lost to National at the next election. But in the 1984 elections, the Labour Party, led by David Lange, was voted back into power.

Organization

Both in theory and pratice Labour has traditionally been a centralized party. Its branches elect 400 to 500 delegates to the annual party conference, "the supreme governing body of the party," as its constitution says, where the party platform is drawn up by a policy committee and ratified by the conference. The party manifesto embodying these policies is binding on all candidates. The party is dominated by its parliamentary branch and its affiliated unions, whose leaders are granted bloc votes at the conference in return for their affiliation fees. In recent years the unions' role has declined, and since World War II the party has been undergoing a continuous process of reorganization punctuated by periodic membership drives. Nevertheless, the postwar decline of Labour is demonstrated by every quantifiable indicator of organizational activity. Between 1938 and 1968, branch party membership dropped from 51,174 in 630 branches in eighty constituencies to 13,476 in 307 branches in eighty-four constituencies. The financial membership (dues payers) dropped from 9,304 to 3,024. The average annual number of branch party meetings fell from seventeen in 1938 to six in 1970; average attendance at these meetings fell from twenty-three in 1947 to eleven in 1970.

To offset this loss and as the result of pressure from the professional and intellectual reformist elements in the party, Labour has finally accepted a plan for restructuring the party in regional councils equipped with professional headquarters staffs. This plan is seen as the best way to coordinate and articulate grass-roots activity and opinion, countering the party's historic tendencies toward centralism and oligarchy.

The address of Labour Party headquarters is: P. O. Box 6146, Te Aro, Wellington, N.Z.

Policy

Even before World War II, Labour began to modify its original socialist objective. The 1950 manifesto deleted any avowal of traditional socialist aims and substituted the phrase "to promote and protect the freedom of the people and their political, social, economic and cultural welfare." In 1974, phrases were added committing the party "to educate the people in the principles of democratic socialism and economic and social cooperation," and "to insure the just distribution of the production and services of New Zealand for the benefit of all the people."

Labour follows a moderate social democratic line, emphasizing social welfare plans and favoring nationalization of some sectors of the economy. Labour envisions a generally more activist role for government than the National

Party. Labour's current recipe for economic growth includes fundamental tax reform and the development of small, labor-intensive industries. Labour policies on the advancement of women and Maoris are more activist than those of National. In foreign policy, Labour is more internationalist, regionalist, and supportive of détente than National, and less enthusiastic about the American alliance. When in power, Labour has excluded American nuclear vessels from New Zealand ports and still advocates a "nuclear-free Pacific."

Membership & Constituency

Despite vigorous organizing activity, membership in the Labour Party has declined since World War II: in absolute terms from 235,000 in 1938 to 198,000 in 1978; in proportion to the total population from 14.5 percent in 1940 to 6.4 percent in 1976; in proportion to Labour supporters who are party members from 46 percent in 1940 to 31 percent in 1975. The party's traditional bases of support were eroded by fading memories of the Depression and by such postwar societal changes as the smaller percentage of the work force engaged in industry, the destruction of working-class neighborhoods by urban renewal, and the larger proportion of New Zealanders who identify themselves as middle class. Other supporters, including several unions, were alienated by Labour's acquiescence in Cold War measures, higher taxes and budget cuts, and its comparatively hard line in labor disputes.

The composition of Labour's support has altered with changing conditions. In the 1960s the number of agricultural workers dropped from 19 percent to 12 percent; mining and manufacturing stayed at around 25 percent; and service, administrative, and professional workers rose sharply. Trade-union support of the party also declined, and although postwar leaders Norman Kirk and Norman Douglas made partially successful attempts to strengthen it, the historic pattern of union withdrawal reasserted itself with the rise to power in 1970 of Wallace (Bill) Rowling, a future prime minister, who opposed strong union influence on the party. In the mid-1970s, several powerful unions seceded over anti-union legislation by the Labour government. But by 1980, the National government's Industrial Reform Bill, which placed labor disputes under criminal law, its arrests of picketers, and its interference in wage negotia-

tions had driven the unions back to the Labour camp.

Financing

New Zealand law does not require the disclosure of party campaign expenditures or other financial details, and these are a closely guarded secret. It is clear, though, that the sources of campaign funds have changed. Both individual dues and union affiliation fees are down, and branch party contributions—partly from local dues, but mostly from raffles and other fundraisers—in recent years have had little impact on the party's ability to wage a national campaign. Labour increasingly depends on contributions from unions, business, and individuals.

Leadership

The Labour Party's president is Margaret Wilson, who replaced Jim Anderton in 1984. The party and parliamentary leader is David Lange, born 1942; Lange is both prime minister and foreign minister under the current government. The leader of the house is Geoffrey Palmer, born 1943, and the speaker is Basil Arthur.

Prospects

The major tensions in the Labour Party are, first, between an aging leadership, cautious and defensive in attitude, and the young, left-leaning liberals who are beginning to assume positions of power; and second, between the trade unionists and the middle-class intellectuals and professionals who regard the unions as essentially a pressure group operating outside and against the best interests of the party. The increasing prominence of this attitude, and the party's stance on social issues particularly dear to intellectuals, tend to alienate the skilled and maritime workers who have been the party's backbone. The previous two Labour governments were in power for only one term; but as long as it can manage the many economic problems now facing the country and as long as the National Party remains divided, sharing the conservative vote with the Social Credit and New Zealand parties, Labour has a good chance of remaining in power.

National Party

History

The National Party developed during the Great Depression as a unifying movement among various anti-Labour parties: the Reform Party, in power during the 1920s; the United Party, which formed a Depression coalition with Labour but forfeited support because of its harsh retrenchment measures; and the Democratic Party, whose hasty formation created further confusion among anti-Labour voters and helped to produce Labour's smashing victory in 1935. The leadership of the federated Reform and United parties, seeing the formation of unified financial and candidate-selection procedures as their paramount task, thereupon called a convention to organize the National Party as an effective weapon against Labour.

Until 1972, National was led by former Reform M.P.s Adam Hamilton, Sidney Holland, and Keith Holyoake. Coming to power in 1949, National saw its success confirmed in a 1951 election prematurely called to secure ratification of the government's action in breaking a dock strike. With the exception of the 1957–60, 1972–75 and 1984 to the present, National has been in power continuously. From 1974-1984, the party leader and prime minister was Robert D. Muldoon, who has dominated New Zealand politics more than any other politician in the twentieth century. However, after his party's defeat, Muldoon was replaced by Jim McClay, born 1945.

Organization

From the beginning, structure has been as important to the National Party as program or ideology. The party's underlying principles emphasize independently financed, permanent organizations at local, regional, and national levels, free of control by the parliamentary party; the grouping of rural electorates around the cities; local selection of candidates from as wide a membership as possible, with the successful ones being left free to get on with their parliamentary duties; and frequent policy consultations between party leaders and the membership. Under these guidelines, National developed into more of a mass party than Labour. Members are not, as in Labour, required to subscribe to the party principles. They make a donation, instead of paying an enrollment fee, and in return they get a receipt, not a membership card.

The basic unit of National is the branch party, and the keystone is the division. In early policy discussions, the chairmen and professional staffs of the five numerically unequal divisions constitute the significant link between the leadership and the rank and file. At regional conferences and the annual dominion conference, further policy discussions are held and remits, or resolutions from local groups, are adopted. The Central Executive makes the party rules and is the liaison between the membership and the National M.P.s. The governing body of the party is the Dominion Council, which rejects or approves the recommendations of the rules committee and appoints the party's headquarters staff. The Dominion Council of about fifty members and the Dominion Executive of about twelve are elected annually by divisions, on the basis of one councillor for every four electorates in the division. Ex officio members of the council include some M.P.s; the division chairmen; the women's vice-president and other party officers; and the chairman and deputy chairman of the Young Nationals, the party's active youth movement, which runs its own conferences and sends delegates to the major party conferences.

This complex structure provides ample and satisfying opportunities for a large number of the party faithful, and it is an important element of National's strength that its officers have generally been content to remain organization men rather than to follow Labour's example of using their offices as springboards to parliamentary candidacy.

The address of party headquarters is: Customhouse Quay and Hunter Street, Wellington, N.Z.

Policy

National is a moderately conservative party, stressing free enterprise, individual initiative, and limited government intervention in the economy. In practice, however, National's anti-statist, anti-union, and antiwelfare policies have been considerably modified by the party's and Muldoon's pragmatism. In 1981, National's chief economic plank was government encouragement of large, energy-based industries—the so-called "Think Big" strategy. In foreign policy, the party is less internationalist than Labour, more inclined to favor a large defense establishment, and wholeheartedly in favor of the American alliance. National's belief that class and special-interest divisions should be minimized in the good society and that local government especially should be kept "out of politics" is reflected in the party's habitual abstention from contesting local council posts.

Membership & Constituency

From its beginnings, National has been an alliance between rural interests and wealthy urban and business groups, backed by a broad middle-class following. Since its founding, National has appealed to the apolitical, and under Robert Muldoon's leadership, the party grew increasingly populist. The flocking of isolationist, lower-middle-class conservatives (called "little New Zealanders") to his banner tested the allegiance of the propertied classes severely.

Financing

The party's Dominion Council levies quotas on each of the five divisions, which in turn levy quotas on the electorates. Other money comes from membership subscriptions, local fundraisers, and, most significantly, donations from business and from wealthy supporters. National's budget for its 1978 campaign was reputedly about $400,000.

Leadership

Following its defeat in 1984, the National Party removed Robert Muldoon as its leader. Muldoon had been parliamentary leader between 1974 and 1984, after rising from poverty to be a successful accountant, and entered the cabinet as finance minister. The party's current leader is Jim McClay, a protégé of his predecessor Muldoon and deputy leader and justice minister during the previous government. Jim Bolger, born 1935, was named deputy leader of the party at the same time. The president of the party is Sue Wood.

Prospects

The prospects of the National Party are closely tied to the political fortunes of Prime Minister Muldoon. His combative style has wide appeal, but the drop in National's vote in 1978 and 1981 and its ultimate defeat in 1984

are attributable partly to voter desire for less abrasive and divisive leadership. Muldoon has also been under pressure from ambitious younger politicians, particularly those on the right, who regard his pragmatic social policies as excessively liberal and his style of leadership overbearing. Another source of tension is the increasingly populist composition of the party under Muldoon, which is distasteful to the conservative propertied interests that have traditionally been the backbone of the party. These are the factors that led to the party's dismal showing in the most recent elections and created the conditions for Muldoon's removal as party leader a few months later. However, his influence over the policies and prospects of the party remains strong; Muldoon has announced that he alone is capable of leading the party back into power in the next elections in 1987.

Minor Parties

Mana Motuhake

The name of this new party, which first entered the lists in the 1981 election, means "self-determination" in Maori. It marks an attempt by the aboriginal people to alter what they charge is Labour's habit of taking the four Maori seats for granted. During Labour's 1972–75 term, the government established several programs favorable to the Maoris, recognized certain of their land claims, and moved to end discrimination in education and employment. But according to Mana Motuhake's leaders, National has allowed these programs to fall into disrepair, and Labour, in opposition, has been insufficiently zealous in standing up for Maori rights. The 1981 election saw a 20 percent swing against Labour in the Maori electorates, ample encouragement for the party to increase its efforts in the next campaign. However, the party's vote was cut in half in the 1984 elections.

The party leader is Matiu Rata, born 1934, a former Labour M.P. and minister of Maori affairs, who resigned his parliamentary seat in 1980 to take charge of the new party. Party headquarters are in Auckland, which has the largest Maori population.

Social Credit Political League

Founded as a party in 1954, Social Credit developed during the 1930s out of the ideas of a former British army engineer, Major Clifford Hugh Douglas, who proposed a government system of "national dividends" and "just price" payments as compensation for what he considered the insufficient purchasing power of workers. This mildly socialist remedy, posing little threat to individualism or private property, influenced many Labour M.P.s and some legislation during the Depression, but its consistent appeal has been to small farmers; until the late 1970s, Social Credit was accurately characterized as a party of rural protest. Deploring big government, Social Credit advocates equal rights to acquire property, decentralization of political power, and Christian morality. Members and supporters include blue-collar workers, small businessmen, and the self-employed, many of them labeled by pollsters as apolitical.

In the 1954 election, Social Credit polled 16 percent of the vote and stayed at about that level until a sharp drop in 1972. Since then, younger members have been able to push the party into mainstream politics. Social Credit is now committed to a social-conscience approach to health, welfare, and environmental questions; a willingness to experiment with cooperativism; and a belief in small-unit decision making.

In recent years, as both political and economic discontent have increased, Social Credit has become a viable alternative for disaffected Labour and National voters. The party won its first seat in a 1977 by-election and held it in 1978 while winning 16 percent of the total vote. In 1981, Social Credit won almost 21 percent of the total and two seats, which gave the party a balance of power between National and Labour. It retained its two seats in the 1984 elections, but its support among voters was cut by almost two-thirds, as the protest vote swung to the New Zealand Party.

The party leader is Bruce Beetham, born 1936. The president is Stephan Lupa. The address of party headquarters is 170 Cuba Street, Wellington, N.Z.

Values Party

New Zealand's concern with environmental questions resulted in the founding of the Values Party in 1972. A national TV program on the party manifesto, which was inspired by the Club of Rome study, *Limits to Growth*, elicited support. Forty-two candidates stood on the Values ticket in the 1972 election. The party won 2 percent of the vote and ousted Social Credit from third place in nine electorates. The 1978 Values manifesto proposed a program of taxing wealth and land instead of income and government encouragement of cooperatives. The share of the total vote rose to only 2.4 percent in 1978, and most of that was lost in 1981, when Values fielded fewer than fifteen candidates. In 1984, the party received fewer votes over 29 seats than it had over 15 in 1981.

The prospects for Values are dim because many of its supporters consider it essentially an educational movement rather than a party and are not really interested in national power; moreover, the major parties have adopted some of their ideas. A schism over party leadership in 1979 resulted in the appointment of joint leaders from different regions: Janet Roborgh (New Plymouth), John Mayson (Tauranga), and Alan Wilkinson (Christchurch). The address of party headquarters is P.O. Box 1987, Auckland, N.Z.

New Zealand Party

The recently founded New Zealand Party was established to provide an alternative for conservative voters who had been alienated by the pragmatic policies and abrasive leadership associated with the National Party's Robert Muldoon. Its strong showing was an indication that a large number of New Zealanders were ready for an alternative to the more established parties. Following the election, it was widely suggested that National should merge with the New Zealand Party as a way of regaining voter support that had been shrinking over the past decade. Having succeeded in shifting some of the policies of the National and Labour parties, the New Zealand Party disbanded in 1986.

The leader of the New Zealand Party was Bob Jones. Malcolm McDonald was president and Charles Bogg was director-general.

National Prospects

Many observers predicted that the 1981 election would be the most significant since National's 1949 victory, would offer voters a clear choice between the government's proposed "think big" economic-development policies and the New Zealander's traditional "small" approach to the economy, and would point the way to a major realignment of parties. The returns, however, were so close that it was not clear until all absentee and overseas ballots had been counted and one recount was held whether National would retain a working majority. The final result showed National with only forty-six working votes since one National M.P. must serve as speaker. Insofar as the results were anything but inconclusive, they indicated a further decline in voting and in party allegiance and a continuing rise in the protest vote. At the same time, some hints of future realignment could be detected in the shift by both parties away from their postwar centrism.

The 1981 election and other indicators demonstrate New Zealanders' perception of their country's declining position in the world economy and its ambiguous position in world affairs, as well as a general feeling that New Zealand should do better.

New Zealand has for years been suffering from a combination of inflation and of unemployment mitigated only by heavy emigration. Productivity and the rate of economic growth have declined and the balance-of-payments deficit has grown. New Zealand needs assurances from both the United States and the European Economic Community regarding prices and marketing of its agricultural products. The country needs to develop more marketing expertise to improve its poor export performance and must capitalize on the tourist industry, potentially one of its greatest assets. Although National was voted out of office in large part over its policies of rapid economic growth, the Labour government has not reversed those policies to the extent expected.

New Zealand's role in world affairs, another issue on which its citizens are deeply divided, is bound up with its growing sense of national identity and independence since World War II and with the emergence of many newly independent nations in the Pacific. Under Prime Minister David Lange, New Zealand's military alliance with the United States and Australia has been strained to the breaking point over Labour's policy not to allow ships into its waters unless they certify that they do not carry nuclear weapons and are not nuclear powered. The United States has refused to comply with this stipulation.

Nor is any major change in the country's political structure, seen by many commentators as New Zealand's only hope of "getting back on the rails," any more likely. Opposition to local-government reform may be nourished by National's traditional sensitivity to parochial concerns; but cries for parliamentary reform, proportional representation, and the like will be ignored as long as neither major party is committed to basic changes. No real change of any kind is forseeable until one party achieves a decisive majority in Parliament.

Further Reading

Bush, Graham. *Local Government and Politics in New Zealand.* Allen Unwin, 1980.

Jackson, Keith. *New Zealand.* New York: Walker, 1969.

King, Frank P. *Oceana and Beyond: Essays in the Pacific Since 1945.* Westport, Conn.: Greenwood Press, 1976.

Levine, Stephen. *The New Zealand Political System.* Sydney and Boston: George Allen and Unwin, 1979.

———. *New Zealand Politics: A Reader.* Melborne: Cheshire, 1975.

———. *Politics in New Zealand: A Reader.* Sydney and London: George Allen and Unwin, 1978.

———. *The New Zealand Political System: Politics in a Small Country.* Allen Unwin, 1979.

———, ed. *Politics in New Zealand.* Allen Unwin, 1978.

Mulgan, Richard. *Democracy and Power in New Zealand: A Study in New Zealand Politics.* Oxford University Press, 1984.

Oliver, W.H., ed. *The Oxford History of New Zealand.* Oxford University Press, 1981.

Sinclair, Keith. *New Zealand.* Baltimore: Penguin Books, 1979.

REPUBLIC OF NICARAGUA
(República de Nicaragua)
by John A. Booth, Ph.D.

The System of Government

The Republic of Nicaragua, a nation of nearly three million people, is a revolutionary political system under the leadership of the Sandinista National Liberation Front (*Frente Sandinista de Liberación Nacional;* FSLN). The present system of government originated with the July 19, 1979, overthrow of Anastasio Somoza Debayle's regime following a two-year popular insurrection. The Somoza dynasty had ruled Nicaragua since 1936 through the National Guard and the Liberal Nationalist Party . The insurrection against the Somoza regime involved a broad coalition of opposition groups led by FSLN guerrilla forces. The FSLN consolidated its dominant role in the revolutionary government within the first six months following Somoza's ouster. Since then the nine-member FSLN National Directorate has established basic policy guidelines for the Nicaraguan state.

The revolutionary government of the Republic of Nicaragua has sought to promote recovery from the economic devastation wrought by the 1977–79 insurrection, to improve the well-being of the lower classes through redistributive and developmental economic and social policies, and to increase lower-class influence over public policy and economic decisions. The revolutionaries are also laying the groundwork for an eventual transition to socialism by expanding public-sector ownership of key means of production, including enterprises once belonging to the Somoza family and its collaborators. The revolutionary government, however, has sought to encourage growth of the remaining private sector (which produced about 60 percent of GNP in 1981) in order to rebuild the economy. In 1984 certain interim governing institutions were replaced through national elections. A new constitution was being drafted in 1985–1986 and was expected to be concluded by early 1987.

Executive

The Governing Junta of National Reconstruction (*Junta de Gobierno de Reconstruccion Nacional*) replaced the pre-1979 presidency. The three-member junta, chosen by the FSLN National Directorate and chaired by Directorate member Daniel Ortega Saavedra, held formal executive authority until replaced by an elected president in January 1985. The Governing Junta extensively employed its decree power, declared a state of emergency that suspended civil liberties from March 1982 through August 1984, allegedly because of the war with the U.S.-backed counterrevolutionary forces, and substantially reworked government structures and laws. Despite Sandinista dominance over public policy, representatives of other political parties which took part in the insurrection have been included in the junta, the cabinet, and the national bureaucracy.

In the November 1984 elections, the FSLN's Daniel Ortega Saavedra was elected president and Sergio Ramírez Mercado vice-president. Since then the presidency has been organized into a ministry providing support services, advisory councils, and links with other government agencies. According to the government, the continued war with counterrevolutionary (*contra*) forces led to the reimposition of the state of emergency in early 1986. The government also attributes the suspension of certain civil liberties and President Ortega's expanded power to legislate by decree to the exigencies of the war. These powers, to be defined further by the new constitution expected in 1987, included extensive authority over administration, fiscal policy, and international affairs, and the right to curtail the legislative power of the National Assembly under a state of emergency. Such centralization is common among new governments, but may also reflect both needed planning-budgetary reforms and the regime's Marxist-Leninist ideology.

President Daniel Ortega, 38 years of age when inaugurated in January 1985, led the Governing Junta until 1984. He provided continuity of executive leadership and represented a moderate faction within the FSLN's Marxist-oriented leadership. Ortega was expected to follow the policy guidance of the FSLN's National Directorate, but his power within both the government and party leadership has been substantially enhanced by his election as president and by the institutionalization of the presidency. Other FSLN Directorate members retained their key cabinet portfolios in defense, agrarian reform, and interior. This will serve as a restraint on Daniel Ortega's ability to alter the distribution of power within the regime.

Legislature

The Council of State (*Consejo de Estado*) was a consultative representative assembly with "colegislative" authority (shared with the junta). It replaced the pre-1979 bicameral Congress from 1980 through 1984. The Council reviewed junta-drafted law and recommended modifications, and initiated legislation. The old Congress had geographical electoral districts for each house, with seats divided between the Somozas' Liberal Nationalists (60 percent) and the Conservatives (40 percent). Representation in the Council of State was corporatist, rather than geographic, including representatives of groups in the anti-Somoza coalition.

Great controversy ensued in 1980 when the FSLN Directorate and the Junta added seats for several pro-Sandinista groups to the Council of State, giving the FSLN a working majority. An opposition and a pro-FSLN coalition developed within the Council by 1981. Although always a minority, the opposition won important changes in key legislation involving elections and political parties.

In January 1985, the unicameral National Assembly (*Asamblea Nacional*) replaced the Council of State. Ninety of the Assembly's seats were apportioned geographically by administrative region in proportion to population and to the parties' vote in the November 1984 Assembly election. The remaining six seats went to the losing presidential candidates of the six parties that contested the presidency with the FSLN (see Table 1). Although it has greater formal powers than the Council of State, under FSLN leadership in 1985–1986 the Assembly has deferred much of its legislative role to the

presidency and has opted to emphasize its constituent function until a new fundamental document is adopted.

The National Assembly's major functions are to legislate and to draft a new Nicaraguan constitution to replace the Fundamental Statute (*Estatuto Fundamental*), the interim revolutionary governing document in effect after the 1979 overthrow of the Somoza regime. Organization of the Assembly resembles that of the Council of State; specialized committees with members from all parties study and draft legislation for debate in plenary sessions. Carlos Núñez Téllez of the FLSN Directorate was elected president of the Assembly in 1985 (see Table 1).

With sixty-one members out of ninety-six (64 percent) in the first Assembly, the FSLN's solid majority permitted it to dominate the organization. A 60 percent rule for adoption of constitutional provisions gave the Sandinista delegation effective control of drafting the constitution, but the opposition has influenced key provisions of the draft documents. Public hearings and consultation on a draft constitution were underway in 1986. The constitution was expected to provide for a three-way separation of powers but still retain a strong presidency (similar to other Latin American constitutions), to provide for restrictions upon the rights of property ownership and to give a broad economic role for the state.

Judiciary

Because of the widespread judicial corruption of the Somoza era, the revolutionary government quickly replaced virtually all judges in the national court system. The Supreme Court of Justice (*Tribunal Supremo de Justicia*) and even some lower courts have exercised a certain independence from the regime. On occasion, the courts have ruled against the government, which has generally complied. For example, the Ministry of Interior obeyed habeas corpus rulings for the release of former Somoza associates despite clamorous popular opposition. In 1980 the courts received the power to order redress of administrative excess or error through a writ of *amparo*. For example, in August 1982, the Supreme Court of Justice awarded *amparo* relief to owners of three large agricultural holdings confiscated in 1979 because of their owners' alleged ties to the Somozas. Following the court's ruling, the *Junta de Gobierno* ordered the Min-

Table 1.
Nicaraguan National Assembly (1985–1989).

A. Distribution of seats by party

Party	Number of seats	Percent of seats
Frente Sandinista (FSLN)	61	64
Democratic Conservative (PCD)	14	15
Independent Liberals (PLI)	9	9
Popular Social Christian (PPSC)	6	6
Communist (PCdeN)	2	2
Socialist (PSN)	2	2
Marxist-Leninist Popular Action Movement (MAP-ML)	2	2

B. National Assembly Executive Committee
President: Carlos Núñez Téllez (FSLN)

Vice Presidents	Secretaries
First: Leticia Herrera (FSLN)	First: Rafael Solís (FSLN)
Second: Clemente Guido (PCD)	Domingo Sánchez (PSN)
Third: Mauricio Díaz (PPSC)	Constantino Pereira (PLI)

Sources: *Barricada Internacional*, January 17, 1985, pp. 4–5; Consejo Supremo Electoral, Managua; Latin American Studies Association, *The Electoral Process in Nicaragua*, (Austin, Texas: November 1984), Table 3.

istry of Agricultural Development and Agrarian Reform to return these properties to their original owners. The right to seek *amparo* in economic matters was suspended temporarily in late 1981. *Amparo* in general was suspended in 1982 under the war-related state of emergency, restored for most matters in August 1984, then again suspended in early 1986.

The regime also set up Special Courts (*Tribunales Especiales*) to try captured personnel of the National Guard for alleged war crimes and human rights violations.

The Special Tribunals, which convicted about 4,200 persons of such crimes and acquitted or dismissed charges against another 2,000 defendants, were disbanded in 1981.

In 1983, the regime created two Popular Anti-Somocista Tribunals (*Tribunales Populares Anti-Somocistas;* TPAs) to try persons accused of crimes against national security. Although the judges of both the TPAs (one a trial court, the other for appeals) are appointed by the Supreme Court, the courts are outside the regular judiciary and are highly politicized. The accused parties do have right to counsel, but the fairness of their proceedings is flawed by political bias and by procedural flaws. A 1980 decree established police courts with authority to impose prison sentences of up to two years for minor nonpolitical offenses. Critics claim these courts operate outside judicial review, lack due process, and are sometimes used against political dissidents.

Under the Fundamental Statute the regular judiciary, headed by a Supreme Court, was guaranteed independence from the government. The judiciary has often exercised this independence by overruling the government, which has often, but not always, complied with judicial orders. The Special Tribunals, TPAs, and agrarian reform tribunals have been established to advance revolutionary policy outside judicial review. In 1983, the nation's jury courts were reformed to alleviate crowded dockets; modernization and reforms of criminal law were undertaken by various decrees between 1979 and 1984.

The restoration of public order after July 19, 1979, proved difficult because the National Guard's collapse required building a wholly new public security system out of young guerrilla soldiers. Hundreds of new police officers were trained in 1981–82.

Several hundred Sandinista Police have been dismissed or tried for abuse of authority since the establishment of an internal review system in 1980. Military authorities have established a credible, although not wholly consistent, record of investigating and punishing Sandinista Popular Army elements who abuse human rights.

The Sandinista government's human rights record has been controversial. It established a governmental commission, the National Commission for the Promotion and Protection of Human Rights (*Comisión Nacional de Promoción y Protección de los Derechos Humanos*) to promote investigation and discussion of human rights abuses. However, the private and independent Permanent Commission On Human Rights (*Comisión Permante de Derechos Humanos*) has been sharply critical of the government's human rights record and has encountered strong opposition from the Sandinistas.

Regional & Local Government

Nicaragua was formerly divided into sixteen departments, which were largely administrative units of the national government. A 1982 administrative reform reorganized the departmental structure. Departments of the populous western half of the nation were combined into six regions, and the immense eastern Zelaya department was split into three special zones. Several ministries (including Agrarian Reform, Public Works, Internal Commerce, Education, and Health) appointed delegates to Regional Revolutionary Councils with mass organization, military, and municipal government representation. The councils were to facilitate regional development and administration. While the new structures did decentralize some authority and create avenues for citizen and interest group influence over programs and policy, the overall success of the regional councils was mixed. Local government consisted of traditional municipalities (*municipios*) with limited legislative, executive, and judicial powers. Since 1979 the municipalities have been run by councils appointed by the FSLN and its allies and will be so administered until elections are resumed.

The Electoral System

Elections under the Somoza regime were consistently manipulated and fraudulent. In 1980, the revolutionary government promised to hold elections by 1985. Under growing criticism and military pressure from United States-backed counterrevolutionary forces, the regime set national elections for November 4, 1984. The Sandinista government hoped that the election would enhance its legitimacy and thus deter a feared U.S. intervention. (Municipal elections would be deferred to a later date to be set by the new National Assembly.) A Political Parties Law (1983) and an Electoral Law (1984) to establish the election system were debated, amended, and passed by the Council of State. The Electoral Law established a Supreme Electoral Council (*Consejo Supremo Electoral*; CSE) to register voters and administer elections. With extensive international aid and advice (especially from Swedish electoral officials), the CSE developed a system to ensure procedural honesty, ballot secrecy, and an accurate count, and to prevent any intimidation of voters. In a July 1984 registration drive, the CSE enrolled an estimated 94 percent of the voting-age populace.

Electoral laws provided for a presidential–vice presidential slate to be chosen by simple majority from among the contending parties on one ballot. On a separate ballot, ninety delegates to the National Assembly would be elected from among contending party lists from multimember geographical districts (the new

administrative regions). Each party's share of these 90 delegate seats would be apportioned according to its percentage of valid Assembly votes. An additional seat would be apportioned to the presidential candidate of each of the parties losing the presidential race.

FSLN presidential–vice presidential candidates Daniel Ortega Saavedra and Sergio Ramírez Mercado won 67 percent of the valid votes cast. The FSLN slate also won 64 percent of the National Assembly's seats.

Table 2.
Results of the 1984 Nicaraguan Presidential Election.

A. Turnout

Registered	Voted	Turnout	Null ballots
1,560,580	1,170,142	75%	71,209 (6%)

B. Presidential election

Party	Candidates	Valid Vote	Percent
FSLN	Daniel Ortega	735,967	67
Democratic Conservative	Clemente Guido	154,327	14
Independent Liberal	Virgilio Godoy	195,560	10

Source: Consejo Supremo Electoral, Managua; Latin American Studies Association, *The Electoral Process in Nicaragua*, (Austin, Texas: November 1984) Table 3.

The Party System

Origins of the Parties

The contemporary party system originated in economic and regional factions dating back to the late Spanish colonial era. Independence from Spain (1821) and Nicaragua's inclusion into the Central America Republic (1823) brought the Liberal and Conservative factions into clear focus and pitted them in a nearly continuous and often violent struggle for power which hardened regional and clan-based partisan identification and established a tradition of violent political conflict. By the early twentieth century, most of the Liberal and Conservative parties' ideological differences had vanished, and both had become clan-dominated factions with a popular base linked to the plantation work forces of the parties' landholding elites.

The United States intervened heavily in Nicaraguan politics after 1909 in order to protect its trans-isthmian canal monopoly in Panama. United States Marines were in Nicaragua for most of the period from 1909 until 1925 in support of Conservative governments. A Liberal revolt against the Conservatives in 1926 led to another U.S. occupation of Nicaragua and an arranged truce between the combatants. One populist Liberal general, anti-interventionist Augusto César Sandino, refused the truce and waged a six-year guerrilla struggle against the large United States occupation force and the U.S.-trained Nicaraguan National Guard. Without defeating Sandino, the United States withdrew its troops in 1933.

The legacy of U.S. occupation included badly weakened Nicaraguan political institutions, a strong anti-American resentment among the people, and the powerful National Guard. The director in chief of the National Guard, Liberal Anastasio Somoza García, had Sandino assassinated in 1933 and in 1936 seized control of the government. Somoza García then took over the Liberal Party and transformed it into the Liberal Nationalist Party, a personal vehicle for control of the government and for the distribution of graft. From 1948 until 1979, major Conservative leaders usually collaborated with the Somozas in exchange for a share of public offices and their spoils. Most of the parties that survived the ouster of the Somoza regime arose as reactions against Somocista Nationalist Liberalism or collaborationist Conservatism. Both the Liberal Nationalist and Conservative parties, however, disappeared with the old regime.

The Parties in Law

Because of the revolutionary nature of the political system, the legal standing of parties was at first unclear. The dominant FSLN did affirm its commitment to anti-Somocista parties' right to exist, proselytize, and participate in governing. The Political Parties Law (1983), later amended, defined parties as contenders for political power, established a National Council of Political Parties (*Consejo Nacional de Partidos Políticos*) that named two members to the Supreme Electoral Council, and guaranteed that all political parties participating in the 1984 elections would retain their legal status regardless of how poor their showing. Opposition

parties also were covered by the numerous provisions of the 1984 Electoral Law (1984). They were entitled to state subsidy of a portion of campaign costs, National Assembly seats for losing presidential candidates, free broadcast time on state television and radio for the 1984 campaign, extensions of candidate registration deadlines, poll-watching provisions, a system for CSE investigation and evaluation of complaints about irregularities, and provisions to protect their supporters from post-election reprisals.

Party Organization

Dramatic organizational differences exist between the FSLN and the other parties. The FSLN is a mass-based, ideological, revolutionary party with an elaborate bureaucratic structure and numerous ancillary organizations. The other parties tend to be small, cadre parties with either an ideological focus (e.g., the Socialists, Social Christians, and Independent Liberals), interest-group support (Nicaraguan Democratic Movement), or personalistic in nature (Democratic Conservative Party). All parties are strongly centralized with the national leaders and organizations dominant. Some personalism marks all parties, including the FSLN, but it tends to be more pronounced in the smaller groups.

Campaigning

The pre-1979 election campaigns were largely ritualistic; the regime always manipulated the results so that campaigns had no real effect on the outcomes. When occasional opposition coalition movements developed an active campaign, the National Guard normally responded by disrupting (sometimes violently) opposition activities.

Campaigning for the 1984 national election was limited to a period from August 1 through November 2, 1984 and was open only to parties and coalitions registered to contend. The campaign was monitored by a large group of outside observers, which included journalists, lawyers, and scholars. While their conclusions about the overall conduct of the elections were diverse, their general consensus was that by the standards of the region the conduct of the campaign was essentially fair. Government-inspired groups called *turbas* disrupted some rallies of the Democratic Coordinating Committee coalition (*Coordinadora Democrática;* CD), which was supported by the United States and many exiles, but which had chosen not to register as an official party. On the other hand, candidates run by a variety of parties did campaign, appear on government-run television, and win office.

Sandinista National Liberation Front (*Frente Sandinista de Liberación Nacional;* FSLN)

History

The FSLN was founded in 1961 to pursue a guerrilla struggle against the Somoza regime by Carlos Fonseca Amador. A Marxist-Leninist, he resigned from the Nicaraguan Socialist (pro-Soviet Communist) Party in 1959 because of its rejection of armed struggle. Fonseca's cofounders were Tomás Borge Martínez, a former Independent Liberal activist, and Silvio Mayorga (both also Marxists). All three men had attended the public high school in Matagalpa (a region of strong loyalty to the 1927–33 Sandino movement), had been student activists at the National University, and had suffered imprisonment for their antiregime efforts.

From 1962 until the mid-1970s, the FSLN grew very slowly, beginning as a single tiny guerrilla band in the mountainous northern jungles. Cuba provided some limited training and other assistance during this period. Urban operations and university support groups developed in the 1960s, but despite such gains, the FSLN suffered serious defeats by the National Guard in 1963 and 1967 and grew fastest when it limited its military engagements with the regime.

In the mid- and late 1970s, the enlarging opposition to the Somoza regime evoked an increasingly repressive government response. This lead in turn, to greater popular support for the FSLN, the only organization mounting sustained armed resistance to the regime. The Sandinista movement suffered an internal schism in the mid-1970s, splitting into three factions with different strategies. This split was resolved, however, when widespread spontaneous popular uprisings (August to October 1978) reduced the importance of the strategic dispute. The FSLN grew rapidly in late 1978 and 1979, reaching a maximum of some 5,000 troops for the final offensive that defeated the National Guard. Because of its military leadership and its role in organizing the final opposition coalition, the FSLN was the major voice in the new government which took power on July 19, 1979.

Organization

The FSLN has a highly elaborated, nationwide structure, with numerous specialized divisions or support organizations. The major decision-making organ is the nine-member National Directorate (*Directorio Nacional*), consisting mainly of top military commanders from the insurrection. The Directorate has made policy both for the FSLN and for the Governing Junta, acting as the guiding force in the revolutionary transformation of Nicaraguan society. The Directorate's members and other top Sandinistas also hold key posts in the government. The FSLN is also fused with key security institutions—the police and the armed forces.

In 1985, the FSLN's National Directorate was reorganized with the establishment of a five-person Executive Commission that included President Daniel Ortega, his brother Defense Minister Humberto Ortega, Interior Minister Tomás Borge, Agrarian Reform Minister Jaime Wheelock, and Bayardo Arce. This shift may portend a concentration of National Directorate power and influence among the new commission's members, as well as an increase in the power of Daniel Ortega over the FLSN and its policies.

Policy

The FSLN's leaders consider the party the vanguard of the revolution, entitled to a leadership role through its eighteen-year armed struggle. The party's goals, embodied in the public policy of the new regime, may be summarized as populist, Marxist-Leninist, and pragmatic. Among key aspects of the party's policies are the improvement of popular living standards, increasing the role of lower classes in both economic and political decision making, a progressive socialization of the economy in order to reduce the influence of upper-class interests, the abolition of the political system of the old regime, and the implementation of popular (but not necessarily liberal-constitutional) democracy. Avenues for participation in the workplace, neighborhood, and policymaking areas have been established. The FSLN, while officially tolerant of other anti-Somocista parties, subjects its competitors to a fierce ideological criticism.

On international issues, the FSLN has frequently been critical or even hostile toward the foreign policy goals of the United States, from whence Nicaragua has experienced its most serious foreign interventions. The FSLN formally favors nonalignment and has particularly curried favor and relations with European social democratic parties. Whether the Sandinista movement's further shift toward Moscow stems from U.S. interventions and economic sanctions or its inherent political orientation is an open question.

Membership & Constituency

The fusion of the FSLN with the armed forces and police and its large number of auxiliary organizations make the organization's size difficult to judge. Estimated broadly and including members of FSLN-affiliated labor unions, peasant organizations, the armed forces, and other support organizations (for women, students, etc.), membership ranges between 300,000 and 400,000. Defined more narrowly as the armed forces and the FSLN's organizational leadership and cadres, the FSLN has from 50,000 to 60,000 members. FSLN support comes disproportionately from the urban poor, peasants in the west and north, and middle-class groups. Middle-class elements predominate among the leadership, but persons of upper-class background are not unknown.

Financing

During the insurrection, most of the FLSN's funding came from urban support groups and other sympathetic donors. External support (both money and arms) was limited until the final months of the insurrection. Since it came to power, the FSLN's financial support comes from member and affiliate group contributions. Public officials who are FSLN members and party officials contribute a share of their salaries to the party.

Leadership

Major Sandinista leaders come primarily from middle-class backgrounds, most having entered the anti-Somoza struggle through university student opposition. Many recruits to the leadership cadre came from families with ties to the Liberal and Conservative parties. When families refused to participate in or even countenance the corruption of the Somoza regime, they were usually excluded from any participation in the mixed process of government and business. Often, family members suffered severe personal consequences, including imprisonment, for refusing to participate in the regime's corrupt largesse. Some members from such families sought redress with the Sandinistas. In the case of the Conservative party, its consistent alliance with the Somoza regime deeply alienated some of the more principled Conservatives and led some of them to join the Sandinistas or to form splinter parties. Through prior conviction or by intensive contact with socialists, most Sandinista leaders adopted Marxist views, an ideological trend which now predominates in the top ranks and in official party programs. Sandinista Marxism, however, seems undogmatic and strongly pragmatic. Although no women serve on the National Directorate, women do hold numerous top party posts. The Directorate and the FSLN officially eschew personalism; public responsibilities and visibility are carefully shared among top Sandinistas.

The members of the FSLN National Directorate are:

Bayardo Arce Castaño (born 1950 in Managua) is the youngest on the Directorate. He is of middle-class background and was a journalist before going underground with FSLN. He heads the FSLN Secretariat for Propaganda and Political Education.

Thomás Borge Martínez (born 1930 in Matagalpa) is the oldest member of the Directorate and a cofounder of the FSLN. Borge is of middle-class background. He studied law and owned a small bookstore before taking up arms with Fonseca about 1960. His family had an Independent Liberal Party background, and while in high school and at university he was militantly against the Somozas. Since 1979, he has been minister of interior and in charge of police and prisons. Borge was twice imprisoned and tortured under the Somozas, and the National Guard killed his wife, Yelba, in 1979. He and his ministry received much credit for limiting human rights violations prior to 1984, but the state security police and police courts have been blamed for the deteriorating human rights situation since then. Borge, regarded by observers as a hardline Marxist-Leninist and as one of the most influential members of the National Directorate, became a member of its new Executive Commission in 1985. He is also an army Commander of the Revolution.

Luis Carrión Cruz (born 1948 in Managua) is of upper-class background and an intellectual. Although he is vice minister of defense, he had little military experience.

Carlos Núñez Téllez (born 1951 in León) served as president of the Council of State (1981–1984) and, as head of the FSLN delegation, became president of the new National Assembly in 1985. After joining the FSLN in 1971, Núñez saw extensive combat experience during the insurrection. He is known for his diplomatic skills, holds the military rank of Commander of the Revolution, and coordinates mass organizations for the FSLN.

Daniel Ortega Saavedra (born 1945 in La Libertad, municipality of Chontales), was elected president of Nicaragua in November 1984 at the head of the FSLN ticket. He had interrupted his university studies to join the FSLN in 1963, acquired extensive combat experience during the insurrection, was captured in 1967, and spent seven years in prison. When released in a hostage trade in 1974, he became a National Directorate member. In 1979, the Directorate named him to the Governing Junta, and he served as its liaison with the Directorate. He chaired the junta from 1981 until his inauguration as president in January 1985. A member of the Directorate's Executive Commission since it formed in 1985, Daniel Ortega is generally regarded by observers as a pragmatist on policy issues and as an ideological moderate among the FSLN's Marxist leadership. He is a Commander of the Revolution.

Humberto Ortega Saavedra (born in 1947), the brother of Daniel, was an early FSLN recruit. During his guerrilla combat experience, he lost his right hand. A student of Nicaraguan politics and theorist of guerrilla warfare, he became the principal strategist of the insurrection. He has served as a member of the Directorate and commander in chief of the Sandinista Popular Army since 1979, and as minister of defense since 1980. A leader within the FSLN National Directorate, Humberto Ortega became a member of its Executive Commission in 1985. He is the architect of Nicaragua's military development since 1980.

Henry Ruíz Hernández (from Jinotepe) studied at Patrice Lumumba University in Moscow in the 1960s and trained with Palestinians. He joined the FSLN in 1967 and gained renown for his bravery during ten years of combat experience. He became a Directorate member in 1969

and for years commanded a major guerrilla column. Since 1980, he has been a Commander of the Revolution. In 1980, he became minister of planning; in the wake of the 1985 government reorganization, he left that post to become minister of external cooperation. Observers view Ruíz as one of the Directorate's more radical and pro-Soviet members.

Victor Tirado López (born 1934 in Mexico) was an early recruit to the FSLN, and became a Nicaraguan citizen only after the triumph of the insurrection. He is a doctrinaire Marxist who makes few public appearances. He handles FSLN labor matters.

Jaime Wheelock Román (born 1946 in Managua) is an intellectual, a theorist, and author of two books on the effects of imperialism on the Nicaraguan socioeconomic system. The Minister of Agricultural Development and Agrarian Reform, he comes from an upper-class background and had no known combat experience. Wheelock studied in Chile and Europe before joining the FSLN in 1975. He is a Commander of the Revolution. Once viewed as a doctrinaire Marxist, Wheelock has proven to be an economic pragmatist; he has been the major designer of the agrarian reform programs and the mixed economy.

Satellite Organizations

The Luisa Amanda Espinosa Nicaraguan Women's Association (*Asociación de Mujeres Nicaragüenses Luisa Amanda Espinosa;* AMNLAE) mobilized protest demonstrations over human rights during the insurrection and now mobilizes women into the revolutionary effort, promoting improvement of the status of women in the national culture.

The July 19th Sandinista Youth (*Juventud Sandinista 19 de julio;* JS19) coordinates FSLN student organizational activity. During the insurrection era, it united the pro-FSLN secondary and university student groups.

The Sandinista Workers Central (*Central Sandinista de Trabajadores;* CST) has won affiliates from previously extant unions, but is made up primarily of new unions formed since July 19, 1979. It supports the government's call for austerity in wages, promoting FSLN support within the labor movement.

The Association of Rural Workers (*Asociación de Trabajadores del Campo;* ATC) originated as a union of commercial agricultural day laborers in 1977; the ATC was formed by Jesuit rural development workers and the FSLN. It now mobilizes peasant support for the revolution.

The National Union of Farmers and Ranchers (*Unión Nacional de Agricultores y Ganaderos;* UNAG) spun off from the ATC in 1981 to represent small farmers whose interests diverged too widely from those of the ATC's other main constituency, rural wage laborers. UNAG has exerted great influence upon agrarian reform, shifting its emphasis away from state farms and collectives and toward the redistribution of land as private property to individuals and cooperatives.

Sandinista Defense Committees (*Comités de Defensa Sandinista;* CDSs) are neighborhood committees, many formed during the insurrection, supporting the FSLN. Since July 19, 1979, they have mobilized mass support for the party and assisted the government in public health, education, and security programs. By the mid-1980s less than a third of the original CDSs continued to function.

Prospects

The FSLN won great popularity by providing military and political leadership for the insurrection against the hated Somoza dynasty, and has steadily consolidated its power and influence within the government and security forces. Several years of revolutionary policies that shifted public services and program benefits in health, education, and agrarian reform toward Nicaragua's poor majority contributed substantially to assuring the FSLN's popularity. In 1984, the party won almost two-thirds of the vote for president and National Assembly. These facts suggest that the FSLN's prospects for continued dominance within the Nicaraguan political system are good for the middle-run future.

Potential threats to the Sandinistas' rule come from several sources. First has been increasing domestic discontent due to deteriorating economic circumstances, tough economic austerity programs, and war mobilization. A combination of inherited debt, heavy new borrowing to operate the government, declining terms of trade, a United States credit and trade embargo, and escalating defense spending along with economic damage caused by the war reversed Nicaragua's 1979–1983 economic recovery and sharply lowered living conditions after 1984. Opposition parties, critics of the un-

popular draft, private sector organizations, and the hierarchy of the Catholic Church emerged as key critics of and mobilizers against the Sandinista regime. However, it appears very unlikely that, in the near future, these forces could topple the regime in face of the FSLN's superior organization, persistent popular support, and large reserve of coercive potential.

Another problem has been the armed external opponents of the regime, counterrevolutionary forces known as *contras,* who have been fighting the Sandinista government with U.S. support since 1981. Originally formed from remnants of the Somoza National Guard, the *contras* recruited former allies of the FSLN who had broken with the regime, conservative northern peasants, and angry Miskito Indians. Heavy U.S. aid (over $100 million between 1981 and 1985) and U.S. Central Intelligence Agency advice and training helped build the *contras* to a peak of some 15,000 men by 1984. The Sandinista Popular Army and Militia's buildup and military effectiveness, the severe internal factionalism among various anti-Sandinista rebel groups, and a lack of popular support within Nicaragua combined to frustrate the *contras'* efforts to topple the FSLN from power. By 1984, the counterrevolutionaries had adopted tactics of economic attrition and terrorism to discredit the regime. The government won key battles with the rebels in 1985, and, by 1986, *contra* ranks had dwindled to some 10,000 to 12,000 troops, most of whom had retreated into Honduras and Costa Rica. Most Miskito fighters reconciled with the regime in 1985 and 1986, and the southern flank rebel elements effectively collapsed. By the mid-1980s, military experts concurred that the rebels could never oust the FSLN from power without direct U.S. armed intervention on their behalf.

The United States' Reagan administration has been the major threat to the regime. Beginning in 1981, the United States applied escalating economic pressures (aid, credit, and trade embargos), employed diplomatic pressure, and furnished support for the anti-Sandinista rebels in an effort to weaken or oust the Sandinistas. Nicaraguan leaders have long expected the United States to escalate its hostility, possibly by a full-scale invasion with U.S. troops, and have prepared for that contingency. Prospects for such an action, however, appeared to dwindle after 1985 as President Ronald Reagan encountered increasing resistance to his Nicaraguan policies within the U.S. Congress and as the

Sandinistas showed no serious signs of internal weakness.

Other Parties

Several other parties have conducted activities or taken part in the government since July 19, 1979. Most of them are independent anti-Somoza parties with followings that precede the events of 1979; most joined at least one of the opposition coalitions that formed in the 1978–79 period. Several parties held one seat apiece in the Council of State between 1980 and 1984. Six parties ran in the 1984 national elections and won seats in the National Assembly. Given the FSLN's strong nationwide electoral showing in 1984, none of the minor parties appears to have strong prospects for more than National Assembly or municipal government representation for some time to come.

Democratic Conservative Party (*Partido Conservador Democrático;* PDC)

Independent, anti-Somoza Conservative splinter, the PDC was led by Rafaél Córdoba Rivas, a member of the Governing Junta until 1984. The party ran Clemente Guido for president in 1984, advocating negotiations with the *contras,* an end to the state of emergency, and a separation of the FSLN party from the state. The PDC captured 14 percent of the vote nationwide and ran best in the southwestern and central departments.

Independent Liberal Party (*Partido Liberal Independiente;* PLI)

A Liberal splinter established in 1944, the PLI has a history of struggle against the Somozas. Its ideology is social democratic.

Virgilio Godoy, labor minister from 1979 to 1984, headed the PLI ticket in 1984. He tried to withdraw from the race two weeks before the election, but was opposed in this by much of the PLI legislative slate and was not allowed to be removed from the ballot by election authorities. Godoy and the PLI won about 10 percent of the national vote, running strongest in the northern quarter of the country.

Marxist-Leninist Popular Action Movement (*Movimiento de Acción Popular-Marxista Leninista;* MAP-ML)

A radical Trotskyite splinter party, the MAP-ML denounced the FSLN as bourgeois and called for an atheist state and accelerated revolution. Isidoro Téllez was the presidential nominee. The party ran dead last, gaining 1 percent of the 1984 vote and capturing two seats in the National Assembly.

Nicaraguan Communist Party (*Partido Comunista de Nicaragua;* PCdeN)

Headed by presidential candidate Allan Zambrana Salmerón, the PCdeN is a pro-Soviet splinter from the PSN. The PCdeN accused the FSLN of petty-bourgeois reformism and opposed the 1984 elections as a concession to the United States and the Nicaraguan right. Zambrana won 1.3 percent of the vote and the party captured two Assembly seats.

Nicaraguan Democratic Movement (*Movimiento Democrático Nicaragüense;* MDN)

Formed by Alfonso Robelo Callejas as an opposition organization during the last year of the insurrection against the Somoza regime, the MDN drew support from professionals and middle-sized business interests. Robelo became a member of the Governing Junta in 1979. In 1980, the MDN changed itself into a political party headed by Robelo and adopted a social democratic platform. When Alfonso Robelo resigned from the Junta (1980) and then went into exile to join forces with anti-Sandinista rebel groups in Costa Rica (1981), the MDN collapsed as a domestic political force.

Democratic Coordinating Committee (*Coordinadora Democrática "Ramiro Sacasa";* CD)

This coalition of opposition parties and other groups arose in the Council of State during the early 1980s and consisted of representatives of several parties (MDN, PSCN) and business organizations. In 1984, the CD coalition (including the PSCN and the tiny Liberal Constitutionalist, Social Democratic, and Nicaraguan Conservative parties) chose former Governing

Junta member and former Nicaraguan ambassador to Washington Arturo Cruz Porras as its presidential nominee. Strongly backed by the United States as the only legitimate opposition to the FSLN, the CD held several rallies in Nicaragua and negotiated with the regime over terms for participating in the elections. It finally chose not to run and subsequently sought to discredit the election.

Nicaraguan Socialist Party (*Partido Socialista Nicaragüense;* PSN)

The PSN has been pro-Soviet since its founding in the 1940s. It collaborated with Somoza García from 1944 to 1948, but was later proscribed constitutionally. It has close ties to the CGT labor federation. Opposed to the FSLN's armed struggle until the last months of the insurrection, it has had no more influence on the Sandinista regime than any other minor party. The PSN ran longtime trade union leader Domingo Sánchez for president in 1984. The party captured 1.5 percent of the national vote and two National Assembly seats.

Popular Social Christian Party (*Partido Popular Social Cristiano;* PPSC)

The PPSC is a left-leaning mid-1970s spinoff of the Social Christian Party. The PPSC supported the FSLN in the Council of State, but broke its legislative alliance with the FSLN and ran Mauricio Diaz Dávila for president in 1984. Although generally in accord with the regime's economic programs, the PPSC strongly criticized the FSLN for its closeness to the Soviet Union and its bad relations with the Catholic Church. The PPSC won almost 6 percent of the 1984 vote and captured six National Assembly seats.

Social Christian Party of Nicaragua (*Partido Social Cristiano Nicaragüense;* PSCN)

Founded in 1957, the PSCN led the 1960s electoral movement against the Somoza dynasty. It established a Christian labor-union movement and took a leadership role in university student politics in 1960s. The PSCN supported the opposition CD coalition in the Council of State and joined the CD electoral coalition in 1984 only to sit out the election.

Other Political Forces

Military

Under the Somozas, the National Guard (*Guardia Nacional*) was the key to the family's political control. It consisted not only of the police and armed forces, but included all mail and telegraph personnel, tax collectors, health inspectors, and customs officers. Its massive human rights violations during the 1970s became a major catalyst for the popular insurrection against the regime. The Guard disbanded completely after its defeat by the FSLN in July 1979.

The FSLN guerrilla army replaced the National Guard as the Nicaraguan security force, transforming itself into regular military services, which included the Sandinista Popular Army (*Ejército Popular Sandinista;* EPS), Sandinista Air Force (*Fuerza Aérea Sandinista;* FAS), and a Sandinista Popular Militia (*Milicias Populares Sandinistas;* MPS), all under the Ministry of Defense headed by Humberto Ortega Saavedra. Another FSLN segment became the Sandinista Police (*Policia Sandinista*), under Tomás Borge Martínez's Ministry of Interior. These security services of the government also constitute a part of the FSLN party itself.

The EPS and MPS had grown to roughly 60,000 regulars by 1985, apparently in response to fears of possible aggression from the United States and to the very real *contra* war. The militia's reserve strength was about 30,000. Troops receive ideological training and are assumed to be highly loyal and disciplined although the draft may have eroded loyalty.

Organized Labor

Freed from Somocista repression, the labor movement expanded greatly after 1979. The union movement consists of some 1,100 unions grouped in several federations, although the new, FSLN-affiliated Sandinista Workers Central (*Central Sandinista de Trabajadores;* CST) has become by far the largest. The CST follows the FSLN's policy of wage restraint as an inflation curb, the unpopularity of which with some unions has helped sustain the independent confederations. Among the independents are the Independent Central Confederation of Workers (*Confederación General de Trabajadores-Independiente;* CGTI); the Social Christian Nicaraguan Confederation of Workers (*Confederación de Trabajadores de Nicaragua;* CTN); and the Council for Union Action and Unity (*Consejo de Acción y Unidad Sindical;* CAUS). In 1980, the CST, CGTI, and CAUS formed a National Interunion Council to promote labor unity. In mid-1981, the government suspended the right to strike, citing the continuing postwar economic emergency. Austerity programs and devaluations have eroded real wages since 1984. When restrictions on strikes were lifted in 1985, the resultant outbreak of strikes led to a new strike ban.

Business Groups

Private-sector interests find expression through several national chambers (commerce, industry, construction, agriculture), through the Nicaraguan Development Institute (*Instituto Nicaragüense de Desarrollo;* INDE), and the Superior Council of Private Enterprise (*Consejo Superior de la Empresa Privada;* COSEP). INDE and COSEP took part in the opposition coalitions of 1977 to 1979 and have represented the entrepreneurial community within the revolutionary government. Several private-sector groups held seats in the Council of State, but lost formal corporate representation in the new National Assembly. Organized business interests broke with the government by 1981 and joined the CD opposition coalition. COSEP and business leaders such as Enrique Bolaños Geyer played a major role in the CD's decision to boycott the 1984 elections. Business groups castigate the revolutionary government for its domestic and foreign policies.

Counter-revolutionary Rebel Groups

Several organizations make up the anti-Sandinista rebel forces that began receiving U.S. aid in 1981 and rapidly escalated their military activity in 1983. Honduran-based groups are as follows: the Nicaraguan Democratic Forces (*Fuerzas Democráticas Nicaragüenses;* FDN), led by Aldofo Calero and militarily dominated by ex-National Guard officers; Nicaraguan Revolutionary Armed Forces (*Fuerzas Armadas Revolucionarias Nicaragüenses;* FARN), led by Fernando Chamorro and Conservative Party interests; and MISURA, a Miskito group led by ex-Somoza agent Steadman Fagoth. At their peak in 1984–1985, Honduran-based groups had some

15,000 troops. Costa Rican-based groups are as follows: the Revolutionary Democratic Alliance (*Alianza Revolucionaria Democrática;* ARDE), including Alfonso Robelo's MDN and former Sandinista leader Edén Pastora's Sandinista Revolutionary Front (*Frente Revolucionaria Sandinista;* FRS); and MISURASATA, the Miskito group led by Baptist minister Brooklyn Rivera. At its peak in 1984–1985 Costa Rican-based *contra* forces had some 4,000 troops.

U.S. Central Intelligence Agency efforts to unify the badly divided *contras* and reduce the role of ex-National Guard elements have been only partly successful. An umbrella organization, the United Nicaraguan Opposition (*Unión Opositora Nicaragüense*) was formed but could not win Edén Pastora's support. Political figureheads have defected and openly manifested dissension. Honduras and Costa Rica have permitted sanctuary for *contra* camps and groups, but both nations have also arrested *contra* leaders, interfered with U.S. aid, and tolerated the Nicaraguan army's pursuit of the rebels. The U.S. Congress cut off military aid to the rebels in 1984, but the White House marshaled compensatory private assistance until Congress restored nonlethal aid in 1985. *Contra* troop strength peaked in early 1985 and began to decline in wake of Nicaraguan army counterinsurgency successes. By 1986, Pastora's FRS had collapsed, both Miskito groups had diminished in size, most *contras* had withdrawn from Nicaragua, and total rebel troop strength had fallen to no more than 12,000. Human rights organizations have verified allegations of severe and widespread *contra* human rights abuses.

Atlantic Coastal Zone & Ethnic Minorities

Along the Atlantic coast, a heterogeneous population of Indians (Miskito, Sumu, and Rama) and English-speaking blacks (about 10 percent of Nicaragua's population) have long suffered isolation from the rest of the nation and distrusted any government in Managua. Attempts by Hispanic governments in Managua and by occasional rebel groups, also Hispanic, to use the Atlantic coast populations for their own purposes seldom resulted in any material benefit for the blacks and Indians. Private businesses in the region and the teachings of the predominant Protestant sect (Moravian) also supported a consistent anticommunist view among the coastal population. The new Sandinista regime nationalized many of the coastal businesses and at the same time encouraged the workers to form unions. When black and Indian workers with pent-up grievances presented their demands to their new employers, the Sandinista regime, the negative response intensified their suspicion and resentment toward Managua and the new government.

The government's efforts to integrate the coastal-zone populations into the nation have caused tension in the region. There were anti-Sandinista disturbances and demonstrations in Atlantic zone towns in 1980–81. Atlantic-zone groups have taken part in a plot to assassinate FSLN leaders.

Religious Groups

The Roman Catholic Church hierarchy opposed the Somoza regime during the 1970s, but also opposed the FSLN's coming to power and worked against it. In contrast, many rank-and-file clergy and laity, influenced by the Second Vatican Council and the 1968 Latin American Bishops Council at Medellín, became active in community religious organizations that were politicized by Somoza's repression in the mid-1970s. Many Catholics entered the opposition to Somoza, joining forces with the FSLN; some actively took part in the insurrection. Numerous clergy hold positions of influence in the revolutionary government, but the Catholic hierarchy increasingly has criticized and openly opposed the regime. The Church blames the government for harassing and embarrassing a top archdiocesan official, for disrupting Pope John Paul II's 1982 Managua public mass, for censoring Cardinal Obando's homilies and Catholic Radio, for interfering with church schools, and for expelling several foreign priests. The government accuses the Church of resisting reasonable regulation of education, supporting *contra* military attacks on Nicaragua, and overtly using religious activities to mobilize political opposition to the government. The government has oscillated between criticizing the Catholic Church and seeking to mollify it by readmitting some of the expelled foreign clergy and by shelving proposed birth control programs and family law reforms.

Within the small Protestant community, numerous clergy and laity also joined the Sandinist insurrection. Hundreds of Protestant missionaries have been admitted to proselytize since 1979, but a handful were expelled in 1982 for antigovernment activity. Support for the Sandinista regime varies among Protestant sects at the present, with Atlantic-zone groups more likely to oppose it.

Religious freedom and practice have generally grown as a consequence of the insurrection and revolution. Regime tolerance does not extend, however, to the promotion of anti-Sandinista political activity by religious organizations. Tensions with the Catholic hierarchy remain grave. The regime expelled a bishop and closed Catholic Radio in 1986.

National Prospects

Nicaragua's mid-range economic future appears good in the areas of agrarian reform, a movement toward "appropriate technology," agricultural production, diversified foreign markets, and minimal popular living standards. Prospects are much bleaker for the capacity of the state to finance its extensive programs with taxes instead of foreign loans and for the needs for continued or increased investment, control of inflation, job creation, and domestic private investment. Nicaragua's economic performance for 1980–1985 was the best in Central America: its gross domestic product (GDP) increased by 4.4 percent despite a sharp 1984–1985 downturn; its GDP per capita for 1980–1985, however, declined 11.6 percent overall. Economic performance was hampered by several factors: worsening terms of trade, war damage to the economy, administrative errors, U.S. embargoes on bilateral credit and trade (beginning in 1981 and 1984, respectively), shrinking multilateral credit because of U.S. pressure on international lenders, an exodus of technicians and managers in search of higher salaries, private investor reluctance, and increased military spending. Several external economic factors beyond Nicaragua's control could markedly better the country's economic recovery prospects: improved coffee and cotton prices, decreased political and economic antagonism by the United States, and a general recovery of the depressed international economy.

In the political realm, there are strong anti-Sandinista sentiments among certain groups and many criticisms of regime policy and performance even among those who favor the revolution. However, the regime remains popular among the lower classes, who have benefited from its reforms, and its consolidation and survival appear likely even without a strong economic recovery. The likelihood of broader regime support from middle-class and entrepreneurial sectors appeared vitually nil by the mid-1980s. Opposition parties seemed too weak to capture power through elections, and the *contra* rebels far too weak to defeat the regime. Moreover, the Sandinista government's election-enhanced legitimacy, strong rural and organizational backing, and considerable military power had strengthened its position.

U.S. antagonism could still escalate to direct military intervention on behalf of the failing anti-Sandanista forces, but uncertain congressional backing for and firm U.S. public opposition to such intervention seemed to diminish that prospect by the mid-1980's. Moreover, Latin American nations under the auspices of the Cantadora Group (Mexico, Venezuela, Columbia, and Panama) were actively seeking to negotiate a settlement of Central American intraregional conflicts and to reduce foreign military involvement in the region. Success of the Contadora process would virtually assure the survival of the Sandinista revolution in Nicaragua.

Further Reading

Anderson, Thomas P. *Politics in Central America: Guatemala, El Salvador, Honduras, and Nicaragua.* New York: Praeger Publishers, 1982.

Booth, John A. *The End and the Beginning: The Nicaraguan Revolution.* Boulder, Colo.: Westview Press, 1985 ed.

Inter-American Commission on Human Rights. *Report on the Situation of Human Rights in Nicaragua.* Washington, D.C.: Organization of American States, 1978.

Latin American Studies Association. *The Electoral Process in Nicaragua: Domestic and International Influences,* Report of the Latin American Studies Association Delegation to the Nicaraguan General Election of November 4, 1984. Austin, Texas: November 19, 1984.

Lawyers Committee for International Human Rights. *Nicaragua: Revolutionary Justice,* A Report on Human Rights and the Judicial System. New York: April 1985.

Millett, Richard. *The Guardians of the Dynasty: A History of the U.S.-Created Guardia Nacional de Nicaragua and the Somoza Family.* Maryknoll, N. Y.: Orbis Books, 1977.

Nolan, David. *The Ideology of the Sandinistas and the Nicaraguan Revolution.* Coral Gables, Fl.: Institute of Interamerican Studies, University of Miami, 1984.

Rudolph, James D., ed. *Nicaragua: A Country Study.* Washington, D.C.: U.S. Government Printing Office for Foreign Area Studies, American University, 1982.

Somoza, Anastasio, and Cox, Jack. *Nicaragua Betrayed.* Belmont, Mass.: Western Islands, 1980.

————, ed. *Nicaragua: The First Five Years.* New York: Praeger Publishers, 1985.

United States Department of State. "*Revolution Beyond Our Borders*": Sandinista Intervention in Central America, Special Report No. 132. Washington, D.C.: September 1985.

Walker, Thomas W., ed. *Nicaragua in Revolution.* New York: Praeger Publishers, 1981.

————. *Nicaragua: Land of Sandino.* Boulder, Colo.: Westview Press, 1981.

Woodward, Ralph Lee, Jr. *Central America: A Nation Divided.* New York: Oxford University Press, 1976.

REPUBLIC OF NIGER
(République du Niger)
by Richard Vengroff, Ph.D.

The System of Government

Niger, a central west African nation whose five and a half million people have lived under military rule since 1974, is slowly approaching a return to civilian rule. The government of Lieutenant Colonel Seyni Kountché, the chief of state for the last twelve years, had until the disastrous drought of 1984 and the precipitous drop in world prices for uranium done remarkably well in providing moderate improvements in living conditions in one of the world's poorest nations (GNP per capita equals U.S. $240).

Executive

The regime is run by the Supreme Military Council (*Conseil Militaire Supreme*) and a council of ministers, the majority of whom are civilians.

Widely regarded as one of Black Africa's few successful military chiefs of state, Colonel Seyni Kountché (born 1931) has established a reputation of being extremely hard-working and completely intolerant of corruption. He began service with the French colonial army in 1949. After completing officer-training school (1957–59), he was commissioned and rapidly rose to the rank of major (1968) and army chief of staff in 1973. He has not built up a broad base of support, but his directness, honesty, and severity in dealing with opponents have helped maintain him in office. Present reform efforts center around the stated goal of creating a "development society" (*la société de developpement*) based on massive participation by those at the base of the system: the young in the rural areas represented by the *samariyas* (traditional youth organizations) and farmers represented by cooperatives. The form which the government of the future "development society" will take remains unclear in light of the continued civilian-military mix and the pressure from the IMF and the major donors to diminish the role of the state in managing the economy.

Legislature

The National Assembly, which consisted of sixty members elected for five-year terms, ceased to function with the suspension of the constitution in 1974. The National Development Council (*Counseil National de Developpement*) was established shortly thereafter, but only as an advisory body.

The Commission for the Establishment of the Development Society, a national body, was charged in 1979 with the task of creating "authentically" Nigerien institutions for development. The process of establishing a constituent assembly has already begun. Although the exact role to be played by this assembly is not yet clear, it is designed to provide strong representation to rural interests. Half of the seats will be allocated to members of the *samariyas* and agricultural cooperatives. The constituent assembly, which began functioning in 1983, drew up the country's new constitution.

Judiciary

The Supreme Court was suspended after the 1974 *coup d'etat* and replaced with a Court of State Security, a military tribunal. There is a civilian Court of Appeals and district courts.

Regional & Local Government

For administrative purposes, Niger is divided into seven departments which are further divided into thirty-five *arrondissements*. In an effort to build the new "development society" from the bottom up, village-level development councils have been established. Although the council representatives are elected, 50 percent must be drawn from the *samariyas* and rural cooperatives. Recent studies indicate that these local councils have not yet penetrated the consciousness of the peasants and do not have the status of popular institutions.

The Party System

Between World War II and 1959, Niger had many political parties. In 1959, it officially became a one-party state, and only the ruling Niger Progressive Party (PPN) was legally allowed to exist. All political parties in Niger were officially suspended in 1974. The regime has been trying to fill the void with its so-called development society which incorporates many of the organizational elements of the banned PPN. Whether this new quasiparty can effectively mobilize popular support and mass participation by all sectors of Nigerian society remains to be seen.

In 1985, the remnants of only two of Niger's banned parties, the PPN and Sawaba, were of any significance.

Niger Progressive Party (*Parti Progressiste Nigérien;* PPN)

The first political party in Niger, the PPN was affiliated with the regional *Rassemblement Democratique Africain* (RDA) led by Félix Houphouet-Boigny of the Ivory Coast. Although the PPN was dominated by the minority Djerma tribe, it gained the support of the chiefs of the majority Hausa (about 55 percent) when it supported continued association with France in a referendum in 1958. It became the majority party shortly thereafter and was responsible for suppressing all opposition. The party's leader, Hamani Diori, the first president of Niger, was overthrown in 1974 over charges of corruption during the Sahelian drought. Diori was released from detention in April 1980, but is forbidden to resume any political activity. He was again placed under house arrest in 1985 after the Libyan-sponsored attack in Northern Niger.

Sawaba (*Freedom*)

This party represents the left wing of the PPN which split with the main body of the party in 1951. In alliance with Hausa Traditionalists, it won the territorial elections of 1957. When the party's leader, Djibo Bakary, campaigned against continued association with France in the 1958 referendum, his coalition disintegrated and the party was badly defeated. After the Sawaba party was outlawed by the PNN in 1959, it waged a brief guerrilla struggle against the regime. When the military ousted Diori in 1974, Bakary returned from exile, only to be imprisoned for plotting against the military. He, too, has been released from prison and forbidden to participate in political activity.

Other Political Forces

Military

The 2,000-man army and 200-man air force are mostly officered by men trained in the French colonial army. Many officers have received further training in France. The officer corps has several factions which appear to be based more on personalities than on ideologies or ethnic affiliations.

Since the unsuccessful coup attempt in 1983, the military has seen civilians increasing their role in the government; in fact a civilian prime minister has been named. This trend has been at least partially reversed since the cabinet reshuffle of 1985, due to pressures to enforce strict economic policies.

Ethnic Groups

The Hausa is the largest ethnic group in Niger, comprising about 50 percent of the population. The Djerma, about 20 percent of the population, because of their residence along the Niger River and early alliance with the French during the colonial period, has been the dominant group politically. Ethnic rivalry was important in the early period of party formation but appears to be much less so today. The Toureg (about 10 percent of the population) have long felt isolated from the government and its development efforts which have been concentrated in the south. Libyan efforts to destabilize the regime center around the organization of Toureg opposition in the *Front Populaire de Libération de Niger* (FPLN), which, in May 1985, launched a commando raid on a government outpost in the north. The Kountche regime has responded by bringing more Touregs into the government. In addition to the prime minister, Hamid Algabid, the ministries of agriculture and interior have been given to Touregs.

National Prospects

Niger is currently experiencing major difficulties resulting from the so-called "conjoncture," consisting of the combination of the 1984 drought, the decline in the demand for uranium, and IMF pressures for a program of national austerity. The dismantling of several parastatals, the dismissal of a large number of civil servants, declines in agricultural productivity, and the collapse of the rural credit system have all placed tremendous pressure on the regime. Increasing pressure for a complete return to civilian rule is likely, especially with the rising tide of unemployed youth in the urban areas.

Continuing efforts to create a development society based on broad mass participation may be productive, but only if local development efforts can be backed up by national resources. With world-market prices for Niger's minerals in a state of decline, the regime may find it necessary to place limits on the participation it is trying to stimulate.

Finally, the regime sees the country as under some threat from its northern neighbor, Libya. While Libyan leader Muammar al-Qaddafi might like to control Niger's uranium, he is unlikely to risk war with France, the major buyer, over it. He may be expected, however, to try to embarrass and destabilize the government of Niger through continuing support for opposition groups, particularly the northern Toureg.

Further Reading

Baier, Stephen. *An Economic History of Central Niger.* Oxford: Clarendon Press, 1980.

Charlick, Robert and Thompson, James. *Niger.* Boulder, Colo. Westview Press, 1986.

Decalo, Samuel. *Historical Dictionary of Niger.* Metuchen, N. J.: The Scarecrow Press, 1979.

Higgott, Richard and Fuglestad, Finn. "The 1974 Coup d'Etat in Niger: Towards an Explanation." *Journal of Modern African Studies,* Vol. 13, No. 3, 1975.

FEDERAL REPUBLIC OF NIGERIA

by Naomi Chazan, Ph.D.

The System of Government

Nigeria, a country of perhaps as many as 100 million people, is presently governed by a military junta composed of twenty-eight officers called the Armed Forces Ruling Council (AFRC). The AFRC is headed by the president and commander-in-chief of the armed forces, Major-General Ibrahim Babangida. A federal state with a multiparty, presidential system of government based in part on the United States model, Nigeria obtained its independence from Great Britain on October 1, 1960.

The "Richards" constitution of 1946 provided Nigeria with its first federal administrative framework, dividing the country into Northern, Eastern, and Western Regions (the last two both in the south of the country), each with an elected House of Assembly and a degree of autonomy. Under the 1951 "Macpherson" constitution, with the establishment of a Nigerian central government and the appointment of Nigerian ministers, Nigerians enjoyed a slightly greater say in policymaking. By that time, the tension between regional autonomy and national unity was already well rooted, as the three regions were each dominated by different powerful ethnic groups: the Hausa-Fulani in the north and the Yoruba and Ibo in the Western and Eastern regions, respectively. A 1954 constitution prepared the way for Nigerian independence. The Eastern and Western Regions became self-governing in 1957; the Northern Region in 1959. With independence Abubakar Tafawa Balewa (a Northerner) became prime minister and Nnamdi Azikiwe (an Easterner) became governor-general under a British style parliamentary system of government.

Independence intensified the campaign by many Nigerians, particularly among the country's minority ethnic groups, for greater autonomy. The campaign had its first success in 1963 with the carving of the Mid-Western Region out of Western Region. In that year, Nigeria became a republic; Azikiwe became president, replacing the British monarch as formal head of state. Given the strong centrifugal forces in Nigeria and the lack of experience in a politics of compromise and accommodation, the country was expected to have problems, but no one was prepared for the rapid succession of political crises which followed—treason trials; a severe controversy over the 1963 national census; an election crisis; and a party system characterized by relatively rigid ethnicity on the one hand and shifting, opportunistic political alliances on the other.

On January 15, 1966, the Nigerian military took over the government, ending the First Republic. Most Nigerians welcomed the demise of a regime hopelessly compromised by corruption, rampant patronage, sectionalism, factionalism, and election fraud. On May 24, the Federal Military Government (FMG) abolished the regions and introduced a unitary state. Because the leader of the FMG was an Ibo, the move was not seen as a step toward national unity, but as a device to break the powerful grip of the Northerners on the country. Violent protests in the north resulted in great loss of life and property, primarily among Ibos settled there. On July 26, after another military coup, the new leadership restored the *status quo ante*, which satisfied few. On May 27, 1967, the FMG divided the country into twelve states. Nevertheless, three days later, the former Eastern Region, renamed Biafra, seceded. A bitter thirty-month-long civil war followed, with some 600,000 military and civilian deaths. The defeat of Biafra and the exile of its leader, Lieutenant Colonel Odumegwu Ojukwu, reaffirmed the continuation of a federal system rather than the confederal one Ojukwu had proposed.

The FMG leader, Lieutenant Colonel Yakubu Gowon, who had pursued the war against secession and presided over the relatively enlightened reintegration of the Ibo people into Nigeria, nevertheless failed to prepare to return the nation to civilian rule. He was overthrown on July 29, 1975, by Brigadier Murtala Muhammed. By October, Muhammed had appointed the fifty-member Constitution Drafting Committee to prepare a constitution to be submitted to a constituent assembly for debate, amendment, and approval before October 1978. Four months later Muhammed decreed the creation of seven new states, raising the total to nineteen. He also introduced a plan to move the capital from Lagos, a Yoruba stronghold, to a federal capital territory in the ethnically mixed center of the country, and he proposed a uniform local government plan which would do away with the remains of the colonial system of centralized control.

Muhammed was assassinated in February 1976, but his timetable was carried out by his replacement, Lieutenant Colonel Olusegun Obasanjo. The draft constitution was submitted to the Constituent Assembly, most of whose 232 members were elected, some directly, some indirectly. After a year of debate, the much-amended constitution was promulgated as an FMG decree to take effect October 1, 1979. On that date, the Second Republic came into being under civilians elected during the previous summer. It succumbed to a coup on the last day of 1983, which brought into power a mixed military-civilian government headed by Major-General Muhamadu Buhari. His repressive regime was toppled by Ibrahim Babangida on August 27, 1985.

Executive and Legislature

The highest decision-making body of the Babangida government is the Armed Forces Ruling Council which, unlike its predecessor, the Supreme Military Council (SMC), is composed exclusively of senior military men. It includes the commanders of major army, navy, and air force divisions, as well as the inspector general of the police. Approximately half of the twenty-eight members of the first AFRC also served on the SMC, although the Babangida government has made an effort to dissociate itself from the Buhari regime. To this end the new chief of general staff, Commodore Ebitu Ukiwe, was put in charge only of political affairs, and almost all final decision-making powers related to military as well as political matters have been placed in the hands of the president.

The AFRC has been assisted by several other public bodies. The National Council of Ministers (NCM) includes heads of the various government ministries, many of whom are civil-

ians. The NCM, like its predecessor, the Federal Executive Council, is responsible for the day-to-day operation of the federal government. The National Council of State is primarily a civilian organ with consultative status. A secretariat was established in the fall of 1985 to serve these two advisory councils, and another permanent secretariat was set up for the National Security and Defense Council.

Upon its accession to office, the Babangida government took certain measures to rectify the arbitrary image of military rule which began to emerge during the Buhari period. It immediately repealed Decrees No. Two and Four, which had muzzled the press and led to the incarceration of journalists and political dissidents. It also reshuffled thirteen of the nineteen military governors, and took steps to hasten the trial of various members of previous governments. Babangida also lifted the ban imposed by Buhari on the Nigerian Medical Association (NMA) and the National Association of Nigerian Students (NANS), thus establishing a more open political climate in the country.

The structure of the Babangida regime continued the pattern of executive government which commenced with the military administration of Yakubu Gowon and continued through the establishment of a presidential system under the constitution of the Second Republic. Ibrahim Babangida has formalized this trend by being the first of Nigeria's six military leaders to assume the title of president.

Judiciary

The Supreme Court is the highest court in the land. Heretofore the chief justice has been appointed by the president at his discretion, while the other judges on the Supreme Court, no more than fifteen, are appointed by the president on the advice of the Judicial Service Commission. The Supreme Court is the final court of appeal and has original jurisdiction in disputes between the federal government and a state or between states. The Supreme Court is duly constituted by five judges in most cases, but requires seven judges in cases which require constitutional interpretation or involve questions of civil or human rights.

The Federal Court of Appeal, consisting of not less than fifteen judges, is headed by a president appointed by the president of the republic on advice of the Judicial Service Commission. The other members of the court are appointed by the president of the republic on the recommendation of the Commission. The Court of Appeal is duly constituted by three judges. In cases of appeals from state sharia (Islamic law) courts or state customary law courts, the Court of Appeal judges must be experts in those fields.

State courts consist of a high court with appellate and supervisory functions as well as original jurisdiction. States that require them also have sharia courts of appeal and/or customary courts of appeal. These courts deal with appeals from lower sharia and customary courts, which handle personal and family matters on the basis of Islamic or traditional law. Judges may be removed only for disability or misconduct.

Regional & Local Government

The structure of state government has usually paralleled that of the federal government. During the Second Republic each state has a governor and vice governor of the same party elected statewide to a four-year term and a state legislature. Under military rule the states are administered by military governors who have powers at a state level similar to those of the president at the federal level.

Considerable pressure exists in most states to create new states, and all the parties have made promises to support many of these demands. The push for additional states reflects the desire of minority ethnic groups for greater autonomy and, during periods of civilian rule, it also expresses a wish to create more political offices and more government jobs. Since the 1976 redivision of the country into nineteen states, however, no new states have been established.

The only unit of government below that of the state is local government. Elections for local government councils were last held in December 1976. Since then, many posts have been filled by appointment, enabling leaders to use these offices as a means of patronage.

A hotly debated issue in Nigerian politics is that of revenue allocation from the federal to the state and local governments. During the Second Republic, after months of debate over the amount to go to the state governments and whether the allocation to local governments should go directly to them or through state offices, the National Assembly finally agreed in 1982 that the federal government would keep 55 percent of the revenues, distribute 35 percent to the states, and pass 10 percent directly to the local governments. The amount of the shares of each state and local government also causes great controversy. A few states, particularly the oil-rich ones of Bendel, Rivers, and Cross River, produce large amounts of federal revenue compared to most of the others, while some poorer states have greater needs and/or population. Furthermore, since there has been no generally accepted census since 1963, and even that was heavily criticized, there is great uncertainty as to a fair allocation of revenue even on the simple basis of population. There is also the fear that if the northern states have more than half the country's population, as they claim, the allocation to them of more than half the nonfederal share of revenue will simply increase their power, which the southern states perceive as already too great.

The Electoral System

With the suspension of the civilian constitution, Nigeria lacks a formal electoral system. The electoral register consists of all Nigerians eighteen years of age and over. Prior to the 1979 elections, nearly fifty million voters were registered in a house-to-house campaign, but voter turnout was very low (ranging from about 26 percent in the senatorial elections to 35.5 percent in the presidential elections).

In December 1985, General Babangida appointed a seventeen-person Political Bureau charged with preparing the country for a return to civilian rule, and set October 1, 1990 as the deadline for the transfer of power.

The Party System

Origins of the Parties

Political activity by Africans appeared in the south, especially in Lagos, as early as the 1880s. It was largely a consequence of the spread of European-style education brought by Christian missionaries, as well as a natural continuation of southern Nigerian patterns of participation in government. In the north, where the British indirectly ruled a feudal society from which missionaries were banned, popular political activity was rare until the 1950s.

The first political parties were formed to contest very limited indirect elections to a southern advisory legislative council in 1922. Herbert Macauly, of Yoruba–Sierra Leonean descent, founded the Nigerian National Democratic

Party (NNDP) in Lagos prior to those elections. The NNDP dominated southern politics until 1934, when students founded the Nigerian Youth Movement (NYM). Although based in Lagos and largely Yoruba in membership, the NYM made efforts to be a national party. It replaced the NNDP as the dominant party in 1938.

As World War II drew to a close, political activity became more intense. In 1944, Nnamdi Azikiwe, popularly known as Zik, founded the National Council of Nigeria and the Cameroons (NCNC). An American-educated Ibo, Azikiwe aimed at national unity in spite of the fact that the NCNC was largely Ibo in membership. In 1951, Chief Obafemi Awolowo, popularly known as Awo, founded the Action Group as an outgrowth of a Yoruba cultural preservation society. Awolowo argued that the sharp ethnic divisions in Nigeria made it unrealistic to expect the populace to suddenly abandon their ethnic identifications and adopt a vague national one. Instead, he advocated that ethnic identities be protected and enhanced as the first step in a process of developing a pluralistic national polity. Also in 1951, the Northern People's Congress (NPC) was founded by Ahmadu Bello, the Sardauna of Sokoto, heir apparent to the Fulani Sultan of Sokoto, the most important political and religious position in the north.

The first government of independent Nigeria in 1960 was a coalition between the NPC and the NCNC (which in 1961 changed its name to the National Convention of Nigerian Citizens). The Action Group was the formal opposition party. Awolowo and Azikiwe shifted their focus to the national level, with Azikiwe becoming the governor-general and later president. The Sardauna, on the contrary, concentrated his efforts on the Northern Region, of which he became premier. His representative in Lagos was Abubakar Tafawa Balewa, who became prime minister.

In 1962, a splinter of the Action Group formed the Nigerian National Democratic Party under the leadership of S. L. Akintola. Shortly thereafter, Awolowo and many other Action Group leaders were arrested and tried on charges of conspiracy to overthrow the government. Their conviction remains highly controversial. They were sentenced to various terms; most, including Awolowo, were released in 1966 in the aftermath of the military takeover.

The NCNC and the Action Group boycotted the elections of 1964, won overwhelmingly by an NPC-NNDP alliance. Azikiwe, as president, tried to force new national elections, but failed. New elections were held in the Western Region in October 1965, and after a particularly violent campaign, the NNDP won openly rigged elections and Akintola became premier of the region.

When the army took over in January 1966, the constitution was suspended, regional governments were dissolved, and political-party activity was banned. The coup was particularly bloody: Akintola and the Sardauna were killed, as were Balewa and some other politicians. Ten senior army officers, most of them Northerners, were also killed.

When political parties were allowed to reform in 1978, most of them could trace their roots directly to the precoup parties. Azikiwe and Awolowo, now quite elderly, reappeared as the major leaders in the south and the northern leader, Shagari, was again a Fulani from Sokoto.

The Parties in Law

Party activity has been banned under all Nigerian military governments, including the AFRC. No party political activity is permitted in the country at this time.

Party Organization

Nigerian political parties varied widely in organization, ranging from the extremely well-structured and professionally organized UPN to the more localized and fractious PRP. Most parties in Nigerian history have had a strong base in one of the three major ethnic groups although they have varied somewhat in terms of ideological position and class composition and appeal. Because of the need of parties in the past to attract people of other ethnic groups and to make alliances across ethnic lines, they generally avoided sharp ideological and policy distinctions. Thus, during the Second Republic, with the marginal exception of the UPN and the PRP, all parties adopted broadly centrist positions. Party disputes were generally over personalities, patronage distribution, and attitudes toward alliances with other parties, not over ideology.

National Party of Nigeria (NPN)

The NPN led by Shehu Shagari, was formed in 1978 as a coalition of a variety of political groups and major figures from all the pre-1966 parties, particularly the NPC and the NNDP. Referred to often as the "party of heavyweights" (or, among the opposition, "deadweights"), the NPN included a remarkable number of Nigeria's richest and most notable personalities. The party's wealth and multi-ethnic base gave it an overwhelming advantage in the 1979 elections. Shagari won absolute majorities in seven states, and the party elected governors and assembly majorities in those same states, as well as an assembly majority in an eighth. It won federal House seats in all but three Yoruba-dominated states, Senate seats in all but seven states, and state assembly seats in all but two, thus qualifying as the only national party.

The predominance of the NPN was further underscored in the 1983 elections, although the incumbent party was charged with misusing its position, especially in the Yoruba-speaking states, to maintain its electoral plurality. The NPN reclaimed the presidency with a decisive first ballot victory, increased its governorships to thirteen, and took two-thirds of the seats in the National Assembly.

Nigerian People's Party (NPP)

The NPP began as a coalition of smaller groups, among them, the National Union Council for Understanding led by Alhaji Waziri Ibrahim; Club 19, a Constituent Assembly group which had successfully opposed the establishment of a separate federal sharia court of appeal and included at least one member from every state; the Committee for National Unity, a group of former NCNC personalities led by Chief Adeniran Ogunsanya, who had supported Azikiwe during the First Republic; and the Progressive Front led by Alhaji Lateef Olufemi Okunnu, another Azikiwe backer.

The party's first convention in November 1978 ended in disaster. The southern members, led by Ogunsanya, refused to make Waziri both the chairman and the presidential candidate, prompting Waziri to quit the party and form his own GNPP. The Progressive Front split when Okunnu shifted his allegiance to the NPN. At a hastily assembled second convention, the new party elected Chief Olu Akinfosile, a former NCNC member, national chairman, and chose Azikiwe, who had previously announced that he would not reenter politics, as the NPP presidential candidate.

The NPP's birth pangs delayed its nationwide organization, and the party fared poorly in the elections, winning governorships and legislative majorities in only three states: Anambra and Imo, both primarily Ibo, and Plateau, with its mixed and minority ethnic groups. Azikiwe won resounding majorities in Anambra and Imo, but fell just short of winning half the vote in Plateau.

Although the NPP won only eleven federal House seats outside of the three states where its major strength lay, the party's total of seventy-eight was enough to make it an attractive coalition partner to the NPN. Several NPP leaders joined Shagari's cabinet, chief among them Ishaya Audu, a Hausa Christian, who became foreign minister. Soon after the coalition broke up in 1981, the party authorized its three governors to join the "progressive" governors group. In 1983 the NPP, much as the UPN, suffered greatly from the NPN sweep of state governors and federal legislative institutions.

Unity Party of Nigeria (UPN)

The UPN, formed prior to the 1979 elections, was virtually a direct outgrowth of the Action Group. It grew out of the National Committee of Friends, which consisted mostly of former Action Group elements and was led by Chief Obafemi Awolowo.

The national appeal of the UPN was weakened by a severe lack of support in the north and by suspicions among Ibos that it was merely a Yoruba nationalist party.

In the 1979 elections the UPN won solidly in the four Yoruba states and in neighboring Bendel state, which is largely populated by the Edo ethnic group. The party was completely closed out of eight states, and put up only moderate showings in Gongola, Cross River, and in Kwara, which has a large Yoruba population. In the 1983 elections, in a heavily disputed contest, it lost its majority in several states, including Ondo, a major Yoruba stronghold.

Minor Parties

Prior to 1983 several other parties were formed, the most important being the Great

Nigeria People's Party (GNPP) of Alhaji Waziri Ibrahim, which drew its strength from the minority areas of the north (especially Bornu and Gongola); and the People's Redemption Party (PRP), headed by the late Alhaji Aminu Kano, a northern aristocrat who had nevertheless opposed the traditional power structure for many years. The PRP won two gubernatorial elections in 1979. It became, however, heavily divided after the elections, and in 1982 some of the original founders resigned from the party. Although considered the most ideological of the parties of the Second Republic, the PRP suffered continuously from internal strife during its short history.

Other Political Forces

Military

The Nigerian military numbered close to 250,000 soldiers throughout the 1970s and early 1980s. Although the Nigerian armed forces are the largest in sub-Saharan Africa, their size is nevertheless small in comparison to the population. During the past few years, efforts have been made to streamline the armed forces, causing a certain amount of discontent in the ranks.

The officer corps is largely Hausa-Fulani and Yoruba, roughly in proportion to these groups' representation in the general population. The Ibo, as a result of losses in the civil war, have been underrepresented in the officer corps and hence in successive military governments.

Ethnic Groups

Depending on the definitions used, there are between 250 and 350 distinct ethnic groups in Nigeria with different customs, social structures, and languages or dialects. Aside from the three major groups, most of these groups are very small, and most are in the "middle belt," an uneven swath that stretches across the country from Kwara state in the west to Gongola state in the east.

North of the "middle belt," the Hausa-Fulani dominate, although Fulani concentrations can be found in the eastern section of the "belt" in Plateau and Gongola states. Conservative and strictly Islamic, the Fulani are descended from nomadic peoples, partly of Berber origin; some Fulani still lead a semi-nomadic life in the far north. Settled Fulani are the aristocrats of the north, leaders of a stratified feudal society whose emirs wield great political and social authority. That society includes the Hausa, who had established several city states and the feudal system in the north before the founding of the Sokoto state by the militantly Islamic Fulani in the early nineteenth century. Hausa is the *lingua franca* of the north. Another major people of the north, the Kanuri of Borno state, were once the center of a series of kingdoms that dominated the center of the Sudan for a thousand years until about 1600. Nearly all the peoples of the north are Muslim and together make up at least half of Nigeria's population.

The Yoruba of the southeast are probably the largest single ethnic group. Yoruba society is structured in communal groups based on large extended families. After the fourteenth century, the Yorubas formed several sizable monarchies based on divine kingship, but with considerable delegation of power and limitations on monarchical authority. Today the *Oni* of Ife remains a primary politico religious authority even though Yorubas, in nearly equal numbers, also profess Islam and Protestant Christianity. The *Obas*, or chiefs, continue to exercise effective social, and often political control, and the *Alafin* of Oyo is still the preeminent traditional political ruler.

The Ibos of the southeast are known over much of Africa for their individualism, energy, and personal enterprise. They never developed any central political organization and are unusual in their egalitarian and democratic approach to social arrangements. They are largely Roman Catholic with few vestiges of traditional religion.

Among the minority ethnic groups, the Tiv are perhaps the most numerous. Concentrated in the east of Benue state, their social system is decentralized and relatively individualistic. The Nupe, most of whom are Muslim, are concentrated in the south of Kwara state and have a hierarchic society. The Edo, who predominate in Bendel state, have much in common with the Yoruba, while the Ibibio in Cross River state have been influenced by Ibo culture. The Ijaw of Rivers state are probably of mixed origin, a product of the social disruptions caused by the former slave trade.

Organized Labor

Union-registration laws under the first military government were so liberal that a group as small as five could form a union. By 1975, there were 1,870 registered unions, most of them linked to one of four trade-union alliances: the United Labor Congress, the largest and affiliated to the International Confederation of Free Trade Unions based in Brussels; the Nigerian Trade Union Congress, the next largest group and affiliated with the Soviet-dominated World Federation of Trade Unions; the Nigerian Workers' Council; and the Labor Unity Front. In December 1975, the government decreed that foreign trade-union organizations were barred from operating in Nigeria; ties between the Nigerian unions and the international organizations in Europe were broken off.

In February 1978, the unions united in the Nigerian Labor Congress (NLC), and in August the new organization was recognized by the government and given a one-time grant of nearly $700,000 to get started. At the same time, the NLC and its leaders were barred from engaging in partisan political activity, a restriction that became a part of the NLC constitution. At its beginning, the NLC consisted of fifty-five industrial unions, with twenty-three more in the planning stage.

The union represents a potential political force of sizable power. Its organizations cut across ethnic and regional lines; it concentrates on basic issues of workers' welfare such as minimum wages, fringe benefits, and a variety of special subsidies; and it is the major champion of the demands of government employees, a sizable part of the 25 percent of the labor force which is not engaged in agriculture. The NLC also has representatives sitting on various national and state committees dealing with economic and labor issues. While there are some signs of ideological factionalism within the NLC, it is basically a unified and well-organized body with relatively democratic procedures for selecting leadership at all levels.

Moves to change the labor law to end the automatic dues check-off system and to permit individual workers to opt out of NLC organizations are seen by some labor leaders as an attempt to destroy the unity of the trade-union movement and the NLC. Some NLC leaders have talked of nationwide strikes if these measures are passed.

Students and Professional Associations

The expansion of Nigeria's system of higher education during the 1970s, which brought a university to every state in the federation, increased the political importance of the students, who have consistently been an invaluable indicator of public opinion in the country. During the Shagari and Buhari administrations, students were vociferous in opposition to the government. Buhari also aroused the wrath of professionals, journalists, and intellectuals, who have come to speak for a broad array of public interests. As educational institutions expanded, these forces have become important factors on the Nigerian political, economic, and social scene.

National Prospects

Sharply increased oil output and prices were partly responsible for the social peace and growing prosperity of Nigeria in the 1970s, when the country began to depend on oil for nearly all its foreign exchange and government revenue. The first years of the 1980s saw oil prices drop, and production fell off by well over 50 percent. Foreign debt increased and the inflation rate climbed to 25 percent annually. As a consequence, the government has had to impose austerity measures, which hit the poor masses the hardest. Economic disparities and inefficiencies continue to plague the economy, which also suffered severely from a drop in agricultural production during the past decade.

Since 1984 successive governments undertook self-imposed austerity measures, which included the retrenchment of employees in the civil service, the floating of the national currency, the naira, and, most recently, the divestment or closure of a large number of state corporations and agricultural marketing boards. Both Buhari and Babangida, however, refused to abide by IMF preconditions for the opening of credit facilities, and attempted, instead, to design their own program for economic resuscitation. The heady days of massive development projects and ostentatious infrastructural development projects funded by oil revenues appear to be over. Even if the agricultural sector can be revived and the sources of revenue diversified— a task that will undoubtedly take several years—the pace of economic change in the country will probably slow down substantially.

Economic prescriptions are closely related in Nigeria to changes in other aspects of the political economy as well. The issue of corruption and mismanagement still looms large, despite the "War Against Indiscipline" launched by Buhari and continued by Babangida. The absence of a code of public conduct and a recognized system of public accountability has hindered the smooth implementation of policy and created an atmosphere of mistrust and frequent disorder.

Until 1983, the military had a reputation for governing the country with relative discipline and effectiveness. The experience of the Buhari tenure somewhat dispelled this image. Nigeria is, therefore, presently at both a political and economic crossroads. The challenges of restructuring the public arena, establishing a strong leadership, and creating effective channels of participation are central to the governability of this large and potentially prosperous country. The steps toward economic stabilization are hence tied to political reforms, which in all probability will undergo a certain amount of experimentation (albeit not a return of the old guard politicians) in the latter part of the present decade.

Further Reading

Awolowo, Obafegmi. *The Strategy and Tactics of the People's Republic of Nigeria.* London: Macmillan, 1970.

————. *Thoughts on the Nigerian Constitution.* Ibadan and London: Oxford University Press, 1966.

Coleman, James S. *Nigeria: Background to Nationalism.* Los Angeles: University of California Press, 1958.

Dudley, B. J. *Instability and Political Order: Politics and Crisis in Nigeria.* Ibadan: Ibadan University Press, 1973.

————. *Nigerian Government and Politics.* London: MacMillan, 1982.

Graf, William D. *Elections, 1979.* Lagos: Daily Times Publications, 1979.

Herskovits, Jean. *Nigeria: Power and Democracy in Africa.* Headline Series No. 257. New York: Foreign Policy Association, 1982.

Kirk-Greene, A. M. H. *Nigeria Since 1970: A Political and Economic Outline.* London: Hedder and Stoughton, 1981.

Mackintosh, John P. *Nigerian Government and Politics.* London: Allen and Unwin, 1966.

Nnoli, Okwudiba. *Ethnic Politics in Nigeria.* Enugu, Nigeria: Fourth Dimension Press, 1978.

Ojiako, James O. *Thirteen Years of Military Rule.* Lagos: Daily Times Publications, 1980.

Schwartz, Frederick, and Otto, August. *Nigeria: The Tribes, the Nation, or the Race; The Politics of Independence.* London: Cambridge University Press, 1965.

KINGDOM OF NORWAY
(Kongeriket Norge)
by John T. S. Madeley, Ph.D.

The System of Government

The kingdom of Norway, a nation of just over four million people, is a parliamentary democracy with a unitary system of government. The constitution was introduced in 1814 at a time when a group of national leaders attempted to seize independence from the Danish crown which had ruled the country for some 400 years. While the constitution, much amended, has remained in force since then—making it the oldest written constitution still in force in Europe—the country remained subject to the Swedish crown (by cession from Denmark) from 1814 to 1905. When independence was finally secured in 1905, it was decided by referendum to reintroduce the ancient Norwegian monarchy.

Executive

Executive power is formally vested in the crown which is hereditary in the male line. The king in council appoints all officials and authorizes all legislative and administrative acts. He is commander-in-chief of the country's armed forces and head of the Church of Norway to which he must belong. Since the introduction of parliamentarism in 1884, the monarch's performance of all these functions is in fact subject to the decision of the elected government, which is in turn answerable to the national assembly, the *Storting*. The functions of the monarchy are now almost entirely ceremonial, although in the event of an inconclusive election the king would be called upon to decide, with the advice of the president of the *Storting*, which party leader should be requested to form a government. The present king, Olav V (born 1903), acceded to the throne in 1957.

Legislature

Primary legislative and budgetary authority rests with the *Storting*, the crown's suspensive veto having fallen into disuse. The *Storting* consists of 157 members elected from the nineteen county constituencies into which the country is divided. Elections occur at regular four-year intervals, there being no provision for dissolution of the Parliament. There are no by-elections since a system of alternates (deputy representatives) ensures immediate replacement if a member is unable to perform his or her duties through death or other causes.

The *Storting* is elected as a single body. Once constituted, it elects one quarter (thirty-nine) of its members to form the *Lagting* or upper division, the remaining three-quarters forming the *Odelsting*, or lower division. Many matters are considered by the *Storting* as a whole, but most general legislation requires separate consideration by both divisions. The balance of strength between the parties is mirrored as closely as possible in the membership of both divisions, but if a conflict between the houses does arise, the outcome is decided by the whole *Storting*, a two-thirds majority being required for a measure to pass. Constitutional amendments always require a two-thirds majority of the *Storting* in order to pass. In addition, a general election must be held before a proposed constitutional amendment can be enacted.

The *Storting*, *Lagting*, and *Odelsting* each elect their own officers who collectively constitute a presidium with the president of the *Storting* as chairman. The members of the presidium sit with the chairmen of the *Storting* committees as a steering committee responsible for the ordering of business and such other arrangements as are necessary to the smooth working of the legislature. Twelve standing committees, which correspond to the government ministries, perform many of the legislative, budgetary, and controlling functions within the political system. Decisions about policy and about the membership of the presidium and the committees are controlled by the caucuses of the political parties represented in the *Storting*. A system of tight internal party discipline and regular interparty relations effectively controls the operation of the legislature to such a degree that it is the electorate which has the final say not only in the composition of governments after an election, but also in the implementation of policy in the subsequent four-year term of a *Storting*. It is

very rare for a government to be defeated on a motion of no confidence. It happened last in 1963 when a minority Labor government was felled by the withdrawal of parliamentary support by two Socialist People's Party representatives.

STORTING ELECTION RESULTS (1973-85)

	1973		1977		1981		1985	
	Vote %	Seats	Vote %	Seats	Vote %	Seats	Vote %	Seats
Labor	35.3	62	42.4	76	37.3	65*	40.8	71
Conservative	17.4	29	24.7	41	31.6	54*	30.4	50
Christian People's	12.2	20	12.1	22	9.3	15	8.3	16
Center	11.0	21	8.6	12	6.7	11	6.6	12
Progress	5.0	4	1.9	—	4.5	4	3.7	2
Liberal	3.5	2	3.2	2	3.9	2	3.1	0
Liberal People's	3.4	1	1.7	—	0.6	—	0.5	0
Socialist Left	11.2	16	4.1	2	4.9	4	5.5	6
Red Electoral Alliance	—	—	0.6	—	0.7	—	0.6	0
Communist	—	—	0.4	—	0.3	—	0.2	0
Others	0.9	—	0.9	—	0.1	—	0.4	0
TOTAL	99.9	155	100.0	155	99.9	155	100.1	157
Turnout	80.2%		82.9%		81.0%		80.2%	

* After disputes about the local results, reelections were held in two constituencies, resulting in a loss of one seat by the Conservatives to Labor. In the 1981 *Storting*, these parties, therefore, held fifty-three and sixty-six seats respectively. The voting figures in the table do not incorporate these changes.

Judiciary

The highest ordinary court is called the Supreme Court of Justice (*Hoiesterett*). Its members are appointed by the king in council and can only be removed after due process. Among the court's duties is the protection of the constitution, however, government or *Storting* actions have rarely been found to be at variance with the constitution. Impeachment trials are held before a specially constituted High Court of the Realm, the membership of which is drawn from the Supreme Court (one-third) and the *Lagting* (two-thirds). As elsewhere, however, impeachment trials are extremely rare.

Regional & Local Government

The country is divided into nineteen counties (*fylker*) which vary considerably in size: the smallest in area, Oslo, has the largest population (almost half a million) while the largest in area, Finnmark in the far north, has the smallest population (under 100,000). The counties have only the powers granted to them in national legislation, forming the administrative

units between the central state and the lowest level of administration, the municipality. The principal functions of the county tier concern health, education, roads, and electricity supply. The chief executive officer is the *fylkesmann*, who is appointed by the central government. Since 1975 he has been responsible to county councils directly elected every four years in conjunction with municipal elections.

There are approximately 450 municipalities, of which about fifty are urban, while the rest are rural. Each is governed by a popularly elected municipal council which in turn elects a mayor and an executive board. County and municipal council elections are now almost entirely fought on national party lines. Since these are held every four years midway through the term of the *Storting*, they constitute important electoral tests for the relative strength of government and opposition parties.

The Electoral System

The 157 members of the *Storting* are chosen by direct election in multimember constituencies. Eligible to vote are all citizens who have reached or will reach the age of eighteen before the end of the year in which the election is held. Voter registration is the responsibility of officials who draw up the electoral register in the summer months immediately preceding an election. The representation of the nineteen constituencies varies from Oslo (fifteen members) to Finnmark and Aust-Agder (four members each). In each constituency voters choose between party lists containing at least as many candidates as the constituency has seats. Voters may strike out individual names from one party's list and replace them with names from other lists or none, but this has never had any but the most marginal effect on electoral outcomes. A proportional system (modified St. Laguë) is employed to translate the party list votes into seats. The system does not give complete proportionality of representation, but proposals to introduce a number of national seats to ensure greater proportionality have not been adopted. One aspect of the present disproportionality is that relatively small losses of electoral support can result in very large losses of *Storting* representation if a party has a significant number of vulnerable seats (i.e., the last seats allotted by the proportional system). Thus in 1977, the Centre Party's percentage of the total popular vote declined 2.4 percent (from 11 percent in 1973 to 8.6 percent in 1974, or less than 25 percent), but it suffered the much greater loss of nine *Storting* seats (almost one-half of its 1973 total). In 1985, a minor reform of the system allowed parties to avoid this effect by entering into agreements to pool the votes for different lists in particular constituencies. The number of seats in the *Storting* was increased from 155 to 157 at the same time.

Voting turnout has steadily increased over the last fifty years. Over the last five elections it has averaged in excess of 82 percent for *Storting* elections and approximately 10 percent less for local elections.

The Party System

Origins of the Parties

The Norwegian party system is almost exactly 100 years old. The first national (as opposed to purely parliamentary) parties, the Conservatives and Liberals, were organized as such in the early 1880s at the climax of the constitutional struggle which resulted in the "breakthr-

ough to parliamentarism" (1884). With the extension of the suffrage in the years before 1914, the Labor Party emerged as a major electoral force; it was joined shortly after the First World War by the Agrarian Party when proportional representation was introduced. The successful founding of the Christian People's Party in the 1930s completed the basic framework of the system of "established" parties. To the left of these parties the Communist Party has led a fitful existence since the early 1920s. In 1960, the Socialist People's Party became the main representative of the left-socialist tradition and in 1973 joined with communists and others to form the basis for the Socialist Left Party. Also in 1973, the maverick right-wing grouping that later took the name of the Progress Party emerged.

The Labor, Conservative, and Agrarian/Center parties are each closely associated with a basic economic interest, representing worker, business, and farming interests, respectively. With the partial exception of Labor, the parties adopt a formal position of neutrality with respect to the interest-group organizations concerned with these particular economic constituencies, but analyses of voting behavior clearly demonstrate the parties' alignment with the socioeconomic structure.

In ideological terms, the parties hold standard positions along the political left-right spectrum: Labor to the left, Conservatives to the right, Agrarian/Centrists in the middle. Since 1945 the principal division on this spectrum has been between the socialist and nonsocialist (or bourgeois, *borgerlig*) party blocs; this is reflected in a fairly strict alternation of governments between the two blocs.

Other divisions are also important factors in structuring the party system and the vote. In particular, center-periphery, urban-rural and cultural divisions cut across the left-right one. All parties have been affected by the existence of these cleavages, but they have been particularly important in the development of the Christian People's and Liberal parties, whose respective constituencies cannot be identified by economic or class interest, even though these parties are generally regarded, along with the Agrarians, as centrist. Despite a high degree of consensus on central economic and social policy from 1945 until recently, all parties retain more or less distinct ideological profiles which are reflected in their programs. Highly articulated systems of party discipline ensure that these ideological differences are translated into action by the party representatives in the *Storting*.

The Parties in Law

Although there are no obstacles in Norwegian law to the formation of new parties, legislation does lay down standard procedures for the nomination of candidates for elective office. Parties wishing to receive public subsidies are required to abide by these procedures, thereby reinforcing further the structural similarity of all the main parties. Any group, however, even those which do not wish to adopt the standard nomination procedures, may present lists of candidates for election, if they have properly registered an official party name with the Department of Justice.

Since the early 1970s a system of public subsidies calculated in terms of the parties' respective electoral strength has led to a situation where about 50 percent of the income of most parties is now derived from public funds. A portion of these subsidies is tied to the parties' educational activities—courses, evening classes, and study groups—which have been characteristic of Norwegian (and Scandinavian) parties.

Party Organization

All parties are of the mass-branch type with relatively high levels of dues-paying membership. Overall the proportion of members to voters for the different parties has been something under 20 percent, with the Agrarian and Labor parties, in that order, having rather higher proportions. The Labor Party is unusual in allowing collective membership, by local trade-union branches. This exception does not affect the basic fact that all Norwegian parties share the same type of structure; their party constitutions resemble each other to a remarkable degree.

The basic unit in all parties is the local association which includes all dues-paying members in a particular locality. Associations are joined together at municipal, county (i.e., *Storting* constituency), and national levels. An important feature is that the municipal and county party organizations have complete power to nominate candidates for elective office.

This means, in particular, that central party organs have no formal power to affect the composition of party lists, even at the level of the *Storting*. This decentralized structure of power in the matter of nominations is reinforced by the existence of residential qualifications for *Storting* candidates. The nominating conventions of the constituency organizations usually take pains to include on the party list representatives of a range of groups (whether by locality, sex, or interest group) in order to attract the widest possible support consistent with the (local) party's political line.

The highest governing body in each party is the national conference, usually held every two years. Delegates to the conference are elected by constituency organizations, but also include government ministers (where a party has any), members of the *Storting*, and representatives of the party's women's and youth organizations. The principal business of a conference is usually the discussion and adoption of the party program on the basis of a draft circulated to and debated by local parties in advance. In addition, the conference elects party leaders and rules on general matters of organization and discipline. The principal party leader is generally the national chairman, who in most cases is also the leader of the party in the *Storting*.

The national chairman presides over the national committee, which is elected by the conference and includes members from all constituent organizations. The national chairman also presides over the executive committee, which is in charge of the day-to-day activities of the party. The national committee, which meets much less frequently than the executive committee, possesses the highest authority in the party between conferences. The chairman is assisted by the party general secretary who heads the party's administrative apparatus.

At the municipal, county, and national level, the party's elected office holders (*Storting* deputies and county or municipal council members) frequently meet in caucus with the appropriate level of party leaders. These caucuses ensure a high degree of internal party agreement and discipline. The national or local party membership organizations, through their representatives in conference are accorded final authority in the party constitutions, but conflicts between them on the one hand and the caucuses of elected representatives are rare.

Campaigning

Election campaigns are rarely colorful or exciting affairs because the electoral system ensures that the decisive contest lies between disciplined party organizations rather than between individual candidates. Much of the press is bound to particular parties and few newspapers in the country can be considered nonpartisan, so voters are generally presented with news and views which only confirm their initial predispositions. Since 1960, however, television has tended to supersede the press as the citizens' principal source of information, and the press and party rallies have become less important. Although the electronic media generally have exposed the public to a wider spectrum of political debate and have doubtless contributed to the recent increase in electoral volatility, this new element of drama has been restricted by the absence of political commercials (there is no commercial advertising on radio or television) and the rule that all parties receive equal exposure.

Independent Voters

Party identification in Norway has been an important factor underpinning the remarkable stability of the electorate until recent years. Over the twenty years after 1945, a substantial majority of voters regularly identified with one of the major parties. Until the 1970s the reflection of social and economic cleavages in the party system further reinforced this stability. However, since the issue of Norway's membership in the European Economic Community (EEC) became a major concern, the country has experienced a wave of electoral volatility unprecedented since the 1930s. During the stable years, it was unusual for individual parties to vary by as much as 3 percent in electoral support from one election to another. Since the post-EEC referendum election of 1973, however, a substantial floating vote, perhaps as high as 25 percent of voters, has made its impact felt in marked changes of electoral strength. These changes, however, have occurred principally among parties which comprise the socialist and nonsocialist blocs, respectively, rather than between the blocs themselves. Overall, the last twenty years have seen a distinct electoral shift toward the nonsocialist parties.

Center Party
(*Senterpartiet;* SP)

History

The Center Party was founded in 1920 as the Agrarian League. The following year it changed its name to Farmers' Party; the Center Party name was adopted in 1959. From the start it was an agrarian-interest party closely associated with the farmers' organizations. In the postwar period, it has joined in government coalitions with non–socialist parties in 1963, 1965 to 1971, and 1972–73, and since 1983.

Organization

The Center Party shares the mass-branch structure described above. It maintains auxiliary organizations for women and youth and conducts a variety of educational programs, particularly in rural areas. Its primary publication is *Informasjon* (Information), a quarterly journal of opinion, but it also receives important support from the daily newspaper *Nationen* (The Nation). The party's national headquarters are at Arbeidergate 4, Egertorget, Oslo 1.

Policy

The Center's principal aim has been to promote the interests of those engaged in agriculture by securing favorable credit, marketing, and pricing arrangements. Despite this advocacy of government intervention and support in agriculture, the party is firmly nonsocialist.

The party changed its name in 1959 in an attempt to make up for the decline of the agricultural sector by appealing to all centrist voters, regardless of their occupation or residence. This attempt has largely failed, even though the party has adopted a range of environmental and decentralist policies, which have modified its traditional political stance.

In foreign policy, the party was firmly opposed to Norway's membership in the EEC, a policy that placed it in sharp conflict with the other nonsocialist parties and was largely responsible for the collapse of the center-right coalition in 1971. In other respects, the party's foreign policy is orthodox—pro-West, pro-NATO—and favors a strong defense establishment.

Membership & Constituency

The Center reported a membership of 60,000 in 1980, approximately 40 percent of its electoral strength in 1981. A great majority of the membership also belongs to the various agrarian-interest associations. By and large, the party draws more support from the larger landowners than from small farmers. Regionally, the party's greatest strength is in the Trondelag.

Financing

As is the case with all Norwegian parties, the exact breakdown of sources of finance is not publicly known. While the government subsidy is almost certainly the largest single source of funds, important contributions are received from the agricultural organizations while membership dues make up the balance.

Leadership

In the late 1970s, the party underwent something of a leadership crisis. In early 1977, the party chairman, who had supported close cooperation with the Conservatives, resigned; his replacement, a clergyman, signally failed to provide the kind of strong leadership which might have avoided electoral defeat later that year. He was replaced in early 1979 by the current chairman, Johan J. Jacobsen, a young man in the mainstream of the party, who has managed with only moderate success to unite the divergent tendencies within the membership.

Prospects

The party's recent decline (from a postwar high of 11 percent of the vote and 21 *Storting* seats in 1973) is partly a result of the leadership conflict, but more a result of the resurgent appeal of the Conservatives. The Center was initially extremely wary of entering a coalition with the Conservatives for fear of losing its identity and influence. In 1983, however, it joined the Conservative and Christian People's Parties in government and at the 1985 election managed to arrest its declining electoral fortunes.

Christian People's Party
(*Kristelig Folkeparti;* KrF)

History

The party was founded in 1933 by a group of religious temperance activists after one of their main leaders was dropped from the Liberal Party list for the *Storting* election that year. It emerged as a national party in 1945 and since then has advanced to become the third-largest party in the system. It attracts support principally from religious activists both within and outside the state church, in particular from those who are members of the numerous organizations for home and foreign missions. It joined government coalitions with the other nonsocialist parties in 1963, 1965 to 1971, and 1972–73, (when it also provided the prime minister, Lars Korvald) and 1983.

Organization

The Christians share the mass-branch structure described above and also maintain auxiliary organizations for women and youth. Unlike the other major parties, they receive no direct support from a major national newspaper although two nonpartisan Christian papers give them a generally sympathetic press. The party's own principal organs are *Folkets Framtid* (The People's Future), published twice weekly, and *Ide* (Idea), a quarterly journal. National headquarters are at Rosenkrantzgt. 13, Oslo 1.

Policy

From its inception the party has been committed to the promotion and defense of fundamentalist Christian values, including temperance. The party has distinguished itself from all others through its stands on moral and religious issues. Since the late 1960s the most controversial of these stands has been the party's strong opposition to the liberal abortion law espoused and then introduced by the Labor Party. The party's inability in recent years to persuade the Conservative Party to adopt an equally strong position led directly to the failure of attempts to form a majority nonsocialist coalition after the 1981 election. When it finally joined the Conservative and Center parties in government in 1983, it firmly reserved its position on this issue.

In economic policy, the party is nonsocialist, although in the area of social welfare it has often been closer to Labor than the other nonsocialist parties. In foreign affairs, it is strongly pro-NATO, but the EEC question in the early 1970s caused severe internal divisions.

Membership & Constituency

The party has for most of the postwar period had a relatively weak membership base. This is compensated for by its ability to borrow strength from the religious and temperance organizations, despite the fact that the party has no formal connections with them. Its principal stronghold is still in those areas, particularly in the south and west of the country, where these organizations maintain an important, if declining, strength. In 1980 the party reported a membership of 60,000, which amounts to approximated 30 percent of its 1981 vote.

Financing

Unlike the other major parties, the Christian People's Party does not receive support from the major economic-interest organizations. Nor does it receive funds from the politically neutral religious organizations. Consequently, membership dues, private contributions, and the government subsidy account for almost all of the party's finances.

Leadership

The party has been led since the 1981 party conference by Kaare Kristiansen, chairman, and Kjell Magne Bondevik, parliamentary leader. For most of the 1970s the main leader was Lars Korvald, who was opposed to EEC entry and strongly against any compromise on the abortion issue. On both these issues, he was generally regarded as disagreeing with the current chairman. Bondevik, the nephew of a former leading figure in the party, is widely looked to for dynamic leadership in the future.

Prospects

Having reached a peak of popular support in 1977 with 12.4 percent of the vote, the party suffered a reverse in 1981, as the Conservatives attracted votes from among the Christians' traditional religious constituency, not least in the south and west. A majority of the party's supporters were known to favor the formation of a majority nonsocialist government despite the inability to agree on the repeal of the existing abortion law.

In 1983, after a special party conference, KrF finally joined the Conservative and Center Parties in government. The 1985 election saw a further decline in popular support although the changed electoral law compensated for the loss. The results of the last two elections and the countinuing decline of the religious and temperance organizations do not augur well for the party's future prospects.

Conservative Party
(*Hoyre* [literally, "The Right"])

History

The party was founded in 1884 to oppose Liberals' demands that the royal veto should be defied and the rules of parliamentarism be adopted. For most of this century it has aspired to be the principal national party of all those opposed to socialism. While in most of the post-1945 period it has been the largest of the nonsocialist parties, on the other hand, it has usually taken only about 18 percent of the votes. It constituted a major element in the nonsocialist coalitions of 1963 and 1965 to 1971. Since 1973, it has enjoyed a remarkable growth of support, in 1981 taking 31.6 percent of the popular vote and far outdistancing the other nonsocialist parties. After that election the party formed a minority government that was broadened in 1983 into a majority coalition with the inclusion of the Christian People's and Center Parties. At the 1985 election, this government narrowly lost its overall majority but continued in office.

Organization

Like the other major parties, the Conservatives have a mass-branch type of organization with women's and youth wings. In the 1970s the organization was reformed and greatly expanded after a successful membership recruitment drive. The party receives indirect support from a number of important national and regional daily newspapers. National headquarters are at Hoyres Hus, Stortingsgate 20, Oslo 1.

Policy

The party's opposition to socialism has been associated with the championship of private enterprise and initiative in the context of a free market. Like the other nonsocialist parties, however, it has come to accept the most central aspects of the country's highly developed welfare state. In recent years it has called for the deregulation of the economy and the reduction of taxes, claiming that such a strategy would generate new economic growth and so leave the welfare state intact.

In foreign policy the Conservatives have been strongly pro-NATO and pro-EEC. Its support for the EEC in the early 1970s, when the country voted by referendum not to join, led to a relative decline in the party's fortunes. Since then, with EEC membership no longer an issue, it has attracted growing support for its economic program.

Membership & Constituency

Around the turn of the century, the party changed from being the party of the old class of officials, which had administered the state for centuries, to become the party of the rising class of businessmen and higher professionals. Because of the survival of the other nonsocialist parties, the party failed to become a national party appealing to all classes and regions, remaining instead a largely urban-based party of high-income earners. Its recent membership drive has broadened this base somewhat. Membership in 1982 stood at almost 170,000, a figure more than 50 percent greater than that of a decade ago.

Financing

The party receives large contributions from private business organizations, although, as in the case of the other parties, exact figures are unknown. The party claims that membership subscriptions and the government subsidy nonetheless account for the lion's share of party finances.

Leadership

Since the early 1970s the party has benefited from the services of an able and generally harmonious leadership. The main political figure has been Kare Willoch (born 1928), the current prime minister. A young and dynamic general secretary and chairman from the north of the country was primarily responsible for the organizational rejuvenation of the party in the

1970s. The current parliamentary leader of the Conservatives is Jan P. Syse.

Prospects

The party's recent successes in the regional strongholds of the centrist parties and among the young and the better-paid (and more highly taxed) workers support its claim to have become at last the "progressive, liberal-conservative, and moderate" party of the country—and the worthy counterpart and opponent of the long-dominant Labor Party. In 1985, it lost ground slightly even though the continuing bipolarization between it and Labor helped to maintain its dominance among the nonsocialists. The weakness of the other nonsocialist parties seems likely to reinforce this dominance in the future but might also deny the Conservatives the prospects of government office since they are unlikely to take a majority of *Storting* seats in their own right.

Norwegian Labor Party (*Det Norske Arbeiderparti;* DNA)

History

Founded in 1887, the party did not become an important electoral force until after the introduction of manhood suffrage in 1898. It was from the first closely associated with trade unions, which experienced considerable membership growth in the industrial take-off period immediately before the First World War. In 1918 the party was taken over by a radical new leadership which shortly after brought the party into the Communist International, thereby precipitating a number of splits. When the party was reunited in the late 1920s, it immediately established itself as the largest electoral force in the system, a status it has been able to maintain with ease until the most recent election. In 1935 Labor began a term of office which was to last for thirty years, interrupted only by the German occupation and the two-month nonsocialist coalition of 1963. From 1945 to 1961 it enjoyed an absolute majority in the *Storting*. In 1971 the party again formed a minority government committed to negotiating Norwegian entry into the EEC. When this policy was rejected in the September 1972 referendum, the government resigned. In the 1973 election, the party suffered its heaviest loss of votes since 1930 but was able to form a minority government by relying on the support of the Socialist Electoral League (see under *Socialist Left Party* below). For eight years thereafter it clung to office on the strength of a single-seat majority for the parties of the socialist bloc, but was finally defeated in the election of 1981.

Organization

Like the other major parties, Labor has a mass-branch type of organization with important women's and youth sections. Its close association with the trade unions is institutionalized in a system of collective membership; i.e., trade-union locals are members of the party at the local level. This feature lends the party organization great depth and penetration. The party is involved in the management of the main national daily newspaper of the labor movement, *Arbeiderbladet* (Workers' Paper), and of some forty other regional and local newspapers.

Party headquarters are at Youngstorgt 2, Oslo 1.

Policy

As the natural party of government since the mid-1930s, Labor has abandoned its early policies of radical social and economic change, opting instead for policies of gradual reform aimed at maintaining full employment and the development of a welfare state in a mixed economy. In contrast to the nonsocialist parties, it is committed to a relatively high degree of government planning and intervention in the economy.

In foreign policy, the party adopted a firmly pro-NATO position in the late 1940s. It has generally maintained this stance ever since, but it is opposed to stationing of foreign troops and installation of nuclear weapons in Norway in peacetime. It has recently committed itself to the introduction of a nuclear-free zone in the Nordic area. From the early 1960s, the party was for a decade also strongly pro-EEC, but the defeat of this policy in the 1972 referendum led it to abandon this commitment.

Membership & Constituency

The party has traditionally been supported by the industrial working class, which is highly unionized, but also by workers in primary industry and smallholders in agriculture. It is the urban-rural basis of support which accounts for the party's historic strength. Membership in 1980 was reported to be 160,000, of which more than half comes from collective trade-union affiliation.

Financing

Substantial financial support is received from the trade unions, but membership dues and the government subsidy still account for a major proportion of party finance.

Leadership

Labor's electoral fortunes were undermined in the mid-1970s by tensions between the party's radical and moderate wings. It attempted to accommodate the two sides by dividing the leadership between a moderate prime minister and a more radical chairman. The experiment failed to resolve the tensions and in early 1981 the two functions were reunited in the person of Gro Harlem Brundtland (born 1939), the country's first woman prime minister. Younger and more radical elements in the party continued to present problems for the leadership, however, and despite Mrs. Brundtland's personal popularity she was unable to restore the party's electoral appeal to its former level.

Prospects

Labor's 1981 electoral performance, although not as bad as that of 1973 when it suffered a hemorrhage of support to its left, was approximately 10 percent below its average vote in the 1950s and 1960s. This was doubtless partly due to the party's incumbency at a time of world recession, domestic inflation, and problems arising from economic distortions associated with the development of North Sea oil. In 1985, after five years of Conservative-led governments, it enjoyed a resurgence of support as it campaigned successfully on social welfare issues. The resurgence was insufficient to return it to office, however, even with the increased support for the Socialist Left Party; and the continuing loss of support among the young and the higher-paid workers in the more prosperous parts of the country remained as warning signs for the future.

Minor Parties

Communist Party of Norway (*Norges Kommunistiske Parti;* NKP)

The party was founded by left-wing members of the Labor Party when it disaffiliated from the Third (Communist) International in 1923 after a short period of membership. In the interwar period it declined to the status of an insignificant political sect, but enjoyed a strong revival (taking almost 12 percent of the vote) in 1945 after a period of active involvement in the resistance to the German occupation. From that high point it again declined, losing its last *Storting* representative in 1961. In 1973 it joined the Socialist Electoral League (see under *Socialist Left Party* below) and shared in the success of that organization as it capitalized on the strong wave of mobilization against the EEC. Two years later, however, die-hard elements refused to go along with the decision to merge with other left-socialist elements in the new Socialist Left Party.

In the years after 1945 the party purged itself of "bourgeois-nationalist," "Trotskyite," and "Titoist" elements and reverted to being a strict Stalinist, Moscow-aligned party. With the exception of the EEC referendum episode, it has largely remained within this mold and is now again a party of almost no electoral importance.

Liberal Party (*Venstre;* literally "The Left")

Founded in the early 1880s on the basis of a coalition of peasants and urban intellectuals committed to the introduction of parliamentarism, the Liberal Party's history since then has been very checkered. Until the First World War it remained the predominant party of government despite two serious splits on the right. In the period since then, however, it was first overtaken by Labor as the principal party of social reform and then lost support to the Agrarian and Christian People's Parties in the center of the political spectrum. Its remaining support was based on an uneasy alliance of diverse groups: temperance, religious, and language activists; secularist libertarians; and low-salaried workers. Unlike other parties it had no single social or economic constituency and was sustained by little more than a common commitment to rather vague liberal ideas and the party's historic traditions. As such it joined the other nonsocialist parties in the 1963 and

1965–71 coalitions. The EEC issue found the party badly divided, however, and it split into two soon after, the faction opposed to the EEC retaining the old party label. The Liberal Party since the 1973 election has not been able to take more than two seats in the *Storting*. In 1985, it declared its willingness to lend support to a socialist government in exchange for the adoption of its environmentalist policies, but at the election it failed to gain any representation for the first time in its long history. Its hopes of returning to the *Storting* would seem to rely on the uncertain prospects of new electoral reform, unless it can rejoin what is left of the Liberal People's Party.

Liberal People's Party (*Det Liberale Folkepartiet;* DLF)

When the Liberal Party split in 1972, the pro-EEC faction, which included nine of the thirteen members of the old Liberal *Storting* group, broke away to form the New People's Party. In the 1973 election it fared even worse than the remaining Liberals, taking only a single seat, which it lost in 1977 and was unable to regain in 1981. With less than 1 percent of the vote the party is clearly moribund with little or no prospect of resuscitation.

Progress Party (*Fremskrittspartiet*)

The party was founded in 1973 under the name Anders Lange's Party for Substantial Reduction in Taxes, Duties, and Governmental Interference. Anders Lange was a well-known political maverick. In 1973 the party took 5 percent of the vote and four seats. After Lange's death a year later the party was torn by internal strife, for which it payed in 1977 with the loss of its *Storting* representation, despite the shift to its present name. At the 1981 election it rode the conservative wave of popular resentment against high taxes and returned to the *Storting* with four members. In 1985, although its representation was halved, it was placed in the position of holding the balance of power. Since both government and opposition are pledged not to negotiate with it, the party seems unlikely to be able to exert much leverage. It has, instead, cast itself in the role of watchdog for the right, alert to any slips or sellouts on the part of, in particular, the Conservative Party.

Socialist Left Party (*Sosialistisk Venstreparti;* SV)

In 1961, a Socialist People's Party was founded by a group of anti-NATO activists who had been expelled from the Labor Party. In the election of the same year they deprived Labor of its overall *Storting* majority by taking two seats, which they managed to hold for eight years, to 1969. With the success of the anti-EEC referendum campaign in 1972, the party enjoyed a revival which was strengthened by cooperation with other anti-EEC and anti-NATO groups (including the Communist Party and a further splinter from Labor known as the Workers' Information Office) in the Socialist Electoral League. In the 1973 election, it took 11.2 percent of the vote and sixteen seats. Two years later, the League was converted into the Socialist Left Party. The process was attended by considerable internal disagreement; the Communist Party die-hards eventually refused to merge into the new party. In the two most recent elections, SV failed to sustain the 1973 level of support for its radical socialist and neutralist policies. With the Labor Party in opposition there is the danger it might shift leftwards and undercut the Socialist Left Party, but nuclear deployment issues and Labor's continued support for NATO are likely to leave adequate space for the party at the far left of the party spectrum.

Red Electoral Alliance (*Rod Valgallianse;* RV)

In 1973 a Maoist party was formed by the merger of a number of extreme left splinter groups, the largest of which had split in 1968 from the Socialist People's Party's youth section. The party took the name Workers' Communist Party Marxist-Leninist (*Arbeidernes Kommunist parti Marxist-Leninistene;* AKP-ML). Since 1971, the party fought the *Storting* elections under the name Red Electoral Alliance, failing to gain representation. Despite internal problems connected with attitudes toward China, the party will doubtless continue to exist, but its prospects for achieving anything but the most marginal electoral support must be meager.

Other Political Forces

Economic-Interest Groups

Like neighboring Sweden, Norway has a very highly developed system of interest-group representation which plays an important role within the overall political system. Despite the overwhelming ethnic and confessional homogeneity of the population (the Lapps in the far north account for less than 1 percent, and over 90 percent of Norwegians remain members of the Lutheran state church), the earliest voluntary associations to develop were those which articulated emergent cultural differences. In the middle and late nineteenth century, movements associated with religious revivalism, temperance or prohibition, and the promotion of an alternative linguistic standard (New Norwegian) based on rural dialects, gave rise to organizations that have continued to have a significant political impact. In particular these three "counter-cultural" movements with their disproportionate strength in the south and west of the country provided the historic basis for the viability of the centrist parties with their opposition to the industrialism and secularism of the Labor and Conservative parties.

It is the economic-interest organizations—founded around the turn of the century to defend and promote the interest of workers, employers, and farmers—which have had the greatest impact on the style and content of political decision-making. Through a system of regular consultation with government in a wide range of ad hoc and regular committees, commissions, and boards, they have provided a second channel of popular representation alongside that of the *Storting*. The system has been called one of corporate pluralism, and decisions made within it have regularly affected central questions of economic and social policy. The existence of this second tier of decision-making or representation helps to explain the high level of policy consensus and general political stability in a system which for twenty years after the war was dominated by one party, the Labor Party, to the exclusion of all others. The standing of the main interest groups is enhanced by extremely high levels of membership within their respective economic constituencies and a degree of centralization, not least among the trade unions, which has enabled group leaderships to deliver binding agreements.

The major interest-group organizations are the Norwegian Employers' Association (*Norsk Arbeidsgiverforening;* NAF), the Norwegian Trades Union Federation (*Landsorganisasjonen i Norge;* LO), and the Norwegian Farmers' Union (*Norges Bondelag*). No other groups are nearly so important, but two small groups do have some role; they are the Norwegian Smallholders' Union (*Norsk Bonde-og Smabrukarlag*) and the Norwegian Fisherman's Union (*Norges Fiskarlag*).

National Prospects

Despite the benefits of North Sea oil—there have been considerable headaches associated with it, too—the Norwegian economy has been by no means immune from the effects of the world recession. Labor's commitment to maintaining full employment, which exceeded 2 percent only in January 1982, was extremely costly. Traditional industries such as shipping, wood-processing, and textiles have required massive financial support at a time when large loans have had to be raised to finance the development of North Sea oil. The Conservative-led governments of the early 1980s managed to reduce the burden of personal taxation somewhat and to cut back the role of the state in sectors such as broadcasting and the credit system. The 1985 election indicated that a clear majority of Norwegians would not tolerate declining standards of welfare provision, however,

while the collapse of the oil price shortly after faced the government with acute problems of avoiding large budget deficits. Norway's prospects remain closely dependent on the vagaries of movements on the world's oil markets.

Further Reading

Arter, David. *The Nordic Parliaments.* London: C. Hurst & Co., 1984.

Berglund, Sten, and Lindstrom, Ulf. *The Scandinavian Party System(s).* Lund, Sweden: Studentlitteratur, 1978.

Cerny, Karl H., ed. *Scandinavia at the Polls.* Washington, D.C.: American Enterprise Institute for Public Policy Research, 1977.

Eckstein, Harry. *Division and Cohesion in Democracy. A Study of Norway.* New Jersey: Princeton U.P., 1966.

Rokkan, Stein. "Norway, Numerical Democracy and Corporate Pluralism." In *Political Oppositions in Western Democracies,* Robert Dahl, ed. New Haven, Conn.: Yale University Press, 1966.

Storing, James A. *Norwegian Democracy.* Oslo: Universitetsforlaget, 1963.

Valen, Henry, and Katz, D. *Political Parties in Norway.* Oslo: Universitetsforlaget, 1964.

———, and Rokkan, Stein. "Norway: Conflict Structure and Mass Politics in a European Periphery." In *Electoral Behaviour: A Comparative Handbook,* Richard Rose, ed. London: Collier Macmillan, and New York: The Free Press, 1974.

SULTANATE OF OMAN
(Saltanat Oman)

by Sterett Pope, M.A. revised by Jon E. Mandaville, Ph.D.

The System of Government

The Sultanate of Oman, with a population of 1.5 million, is an absolute monarchy ruled by Sultan Qaboos bin Said bin Taimur seventeenth ruler of the house of Al Bu Said. Governed by one of the oldest ruling families on the Arabian Peninsula, Oman is the least developed politically and economically of the Arab monarchies on the Gulf. Oman has no constitution, legislature, or representative institutions in the Western sense of these terms; and only in the last decade have institutions of ministerial and municipal government been developed under the rule of Sultan Qaboos, who is generally credited with bringing Oman "into the twentieth century." Qaboos, who deposed his father in a palace coup in 1970, has since invested the sultanate's oil revenues in economic and social development programs at home and has cultivated strong ties abroad with neighboring Arab monarchies and Western powers.

In the nineteenth century Oman was gradually incorporated into the British Empire as a de facto protectorate. On several occasions, British troops rescued the Al Bu Said dynasty from destruction at the hands of insurgent inland tribes who sought to restore the imamate, Oman's traditional system of theocratic monarchy whose king, the imam, had been elected by tribal leaders and ratified by popular acclamation until Ahmad bin Said's brother usurped the throne. In 1920, the British helped to negotiate the Treaty of Seeb, which gave inland tribes virtual autonomy under a revived imamate.

During the rule of Said bin Taimur (1932–70), the sultanate remained backward and isolated. A man of legendary frugality, Said's principal achievement was the repayment of debts to British merchants which had accumulated during the previous century. During his reign, the sultanate's revenues came almost entirely from customs duties, British subsidies, and near the end of his reign, payments from oil companies.

Convinced that the introduction of modern ways would inevitably disrupt his kingdom and subvert his rule, Said attempted to isolate the sultanate from the outside world; he prohibited his subjects from traveling abroad and refused steadfastly to bring modern education and health services to his people. Under British pressure, an expatriate-staffed development council was established in 1958, but the council could not persuade Said to spend his revenues on any project other than modernization of his military forces, which were composed of tribal levies led by British officers.

Said's policies and his dependence on Great Britain provoked open rebellion in the last two decades of his reign. In 1954 the imam and his followers sought to secede from the sultanate, but in the next three years Said used British troops to crush the revolt and terminate the imamate. In 1965 civil war broke out in the southern province of Dhofar where Marxist insurgents launched an effective campaign of guerrilla warfare. The deterioration of the situation in Dhofar was one of the principal causes of Qaboos's coup, which he undertook with the support of Oman's British-administered army.

In the past ten years, Sultan Qaboos has pursued a policy of balanced development and defense spending. In the years 1978 and 1979, for example, defense, current, and capital expenditures each represented a third of the budget, 95 percent of which comes from the sultanate's oil revenues. Development projects have emphasized infrastructure, education, and health services provided by foreign firms under contract to the various ministries. Defense expenditures have covered the modernization of Oman's 16,000-man army and the purchase of sophisticated weapons systems. The army and security apparatus are still largely staffed and officered by British nationals seconded from the British armed forces. In the wake of the Iranian revolution, Qaboos has successfully promoted

Oman as a "front-line state"; in 1980 he negotiated a defense treaty with the United States in
which Oman received military and economic assistance in return for U.S. military use of
Omani ports and bases. The Omani population
is not amenable to the Iranian regime's Shi'a
propaganda. The great majority of Omanis,
about three-fourths, are Ibadhi Muslims, members of a sect which is neither Sunni or Shi'a.
The remaining fourth is Sunni.

Executive

When Sultan Qaboos came to power in 1970,
he was committed to the design and implementation of a wide-ranging program of social and
economic development to be financed by government revenues from Oman's export of petroleum, which had begun two years previously.
This program required the creation of a planning apparatus and a ministerial form of government, the main structures of which were established between 1971 and 1974.

Policymaking on a national level is conducted through four ministerial bodies: the
Council of Ministers, in which the twenty members of Oman's cabinet convene, and three more
specialized organs—the Councils of Economic
Development, Finance, and Defense. Each body
meets on a weekly basis and is chaired by the
sultan, who directs discussion and has the last
word on all decisions. In practice, however,
councils meet frequently without the sultan,
and ministers are generally free to direct affairs
relating to their respective ministries. The annual budget of the finance and development
councils, approved by the sultan, has imposed financial guidelines on the ministries, but often
ministers do lobby on an ad hoc basis with the
sultan for additional allocations of funds. As of
yet, no legal authority exists for the evaluation
of new laws (which must carry the signature of
the sultan) in light of previous legislation. This
and the lack of formal checks on the prerogatives of the sultan have made the process of
legislation largely one of interpersonal negotiation between Qaboos and those to whom he delegates ministerial power.

Unlike other Arab kingdoms in the Persian
Gulf, the sultan does not hold a traditional *majlis*, or weekly audience, where he may review
the petitions and personal appeals of his subjects. These are handled instead by the *Diwan*,
the ministry which directs court protocols and
the country's embryonic civil service.

Although he initially depended on foreign advisers (both from Britain and other Arab countries) and fellow Al Bu Said clansmen (known as
sayyids), Sultan Qaboos has tended increasingly
to appoint technically trained Omanis and local
prominent businessmen to cabinet-level positions. The sultan himself holds the portfolios of
defense and foreign affairs and still relies
heavily on the advice of foreign nationals in
these areas, while the ministries of interior and
justice and the *Diwan* remain the preserve of
sayyids.

Legislature

No legislature exists.

Judiciary

Legal disputes are handled in the traditional
manner: intratribal suits are resolved by tribal
elders, while disputes between different social
groups are mediated by the regional governor in
consultation with an Islamic judge (these two
officials are appointed by the ministers of interior and justice, respectively). Where disputes
fall outside the scope of Islamic law, the sultan
generally relies on the recommendation of the
local police chief and the regional governor.

Regional & Local Government

Tribal sheiks continue to administer their
groups under traditional rules. Major cities are
administered by appointees of the central government.

Opposition

The only significant opposition to the rule of
Sultan Qaboos is the continuing rebellion in
Dhofar. Several insurgent groups—including
dissident tribesmen, repatriated migrant workers, and some cadres trained in the People's
Republic of China and elsewhere—merged in
1968 to form the Popular Front for the Liberation of the Occupied Arab Gulf (PFLOAG)
which adopted a Marxist-Leninist program and,
with the help of neighboring South Yemen,
gained control of almost all of Dhofar by 1970. A
separate but allied organization, the National
Democratic Front for the Liberation of the Occupied Arab Gulf (NDFLOAG), attempted dur-

ing the same period to mobilize popular opposition in the northern heartland of Oman; its efforts were unsuccessful.

After coming to power, Sultan Qaboos effectively checked the guerrilla movement in Dhofar by reorganizing his army, initiating a comprehensive development program in Dhofar, and calling on other monarchies in the region for assistance against the rebels. Qaboos received military and economic aid from Jordan, Saudi Arabia, and the United Arab Emirates, and in 1973 the Shah of Iran sent troops to Dhofar. By 1975 the sultan had claimed complete victory over the rebels; and in the following year Saudi Arabia mediated a cease-fire agreement between Oman and South Yemen. Although their support within the country has largely been neutralized by the sultan's policies, guerrillas in Dhofar have continued to stage desultory raids and acts of sabotage.

National Prospects

By defeating the Marxist insurgency in Dhofar and sponsoring a popular program of economic and social development, Sultan Qaboos has gained considerable legitimacy for his rule and has reversed the declining fortunes of the Al Bu Said dynasty. Qaboos, however, is as committed to the principle of one-man rule as his father was and has repeatedly stated that his people are not ready for democracy. For this reason, the establishment of representative institutions in Oman seems most improbable in the foreseeable future, while the trend toward oligarchic administration by entrepreneurs, *sayyids*, and the country's few technocrats will probably continue. This form of government will be viable as long as the development programs can be financed by oil revenues, and the sultan himself continues to enjoy the support of Western powers. Given Oman's strategic position at the mouth of the Persian Gulf, this support is likely to be strengthened in the years to come.

Further Reading
Clements, F. A. *Oman: The Reborn Land*. London: Longman, 1980.
Peterson, J. E. *Oman in the Twentieth Century*. London: Croom Helm, 1978.
Townsend, John. *Oman: The Making of a Modern State*. New York: St. Martin's Press, 1977.

PAKISTAN

by William Richter, Ph.D.

The System of Government

Pakistan, a nation of ninety-six million people, operates under a constitution adopted in 1973 but suspended during a period of martial law that lasted from July 5, 1977 to the end of 1985. The constitution established a parliamentary system with key powers residing in a prime minister. The president was given little more than ceremonial responsibilities. Under the military government of Mohammad Zia-ul-Haq, the army chief and chief martial law administrator, the powers of the presidency were greatly strengthened. Zia became president in 1978. A national referendum on the Islamization policies of the martial law government, held December 19, 1984, was interpreted by Zia as a mandate for him to remain president through 1989.

Partyless national and provincial elections in February 1985 paved the way for the reestablishment of civilian governments at the national level and in the four provinces. Parallel electoral processes to restore civilian rule occured later in 1985 in Azad Kashmir, that portion of the former princely state of Jammu and Kashmir administered by Pakistan pending resolution of the decades-old dispute with India.

Executive

The executive role has been crucial in Pakistan since the country's inception. Pakistan's founder, Mohammad Ali Jinnah, chose the post of governor general at the time of Pakistan's independence instead of the more political position of prime minister. In the subsequent two decades, the chief of state (president after 1956) remained the dominant position in government. The prime minister's post, weak and subservient, disappeared entirely during the Ayub Khan and Yahya Khan years (1958-1971). The 1973 constitution, written under Zulfikar Ali Bhutto, changed this distribution of power in favor of a strong prime minister, the position Bhutto assumed after the adoption of the consti-

tution. The president then became a mere figurehead, subject to the directives of the prime minister.

Constitutional changes under martial law have strengthened the position of president vis-à-vis that of prime minister. General Zia continues to hold the presidency, but Mohammad Khan Junejo, the prime minister Zia appointed following the February 1985 general elections, has demonstrated both an independence and a willingness to press his position on major issues, including the legalization of political parties.

Junejo is assisted by a cabinet which in 1986 consisted of twenty-two ministers and thirteen ministers of state. The most important of the cabinet officials are Foreign Minister Sahabzada Yaqub Khan, who held the same post under Zia during the latter years of martial law, Minister for Finance and Planning Mohammad Yasin Khan Wattoo, who previously served as education minister, and Minister for Justice and Parliamentary Affairs Iqbal Ahmad Khan.

Legislature

During the first years of his martial law regime, General Zia governed without the assistance of a legislature. In 1982 he established an appointive Majlis-i-Shura (Federal Council) of approximately 300 members.

Following the 1985 elections, the constitutionally defined National Assembly and Senate were restored in place of the Majlis-i-Shura. The assembly, elected on a non partisan basis from single-member districts, selected as speaker Syed Fakhr Imam, a member of the Shia minority and a highly respected Punjabi lawyer, who had earlier served in the central cabinet during the martial law period. Defeated in the contest for the Assembly speakership was Zia's preferred candidate, Khwaja Mohammad Safdar, former speaker of the Majlis.

The members of the Senate, thirteen elected by each provincial legislature, plus appointed members representing women and special constituencies, chose as their presiding officer Ghulam Ishaq Khan who had served as Zia's financial adviser and finance minister throughout the martial law period.

Judiciary

The Pakistani judiciary has seldom functioned as an independent branch of government. Although the lower courts attempted to save the first constituent assembly (1947–1954), as well as the country's first constitution (1956), from executive onslaughts, the Pakistan Supreme Court discreetly accepted their dissolution and did not challenge the power of the executive. This precedent, with several repetitions, ultimately reduced the prerogatives of the courts to a point where they could be bypassed and ignored.

During his more than eight years of military rule, General Zia weakened judicial institutions further in several ways. Military courts were given jurisdiction over a wide range of civilian offences. In October 1979, a martial law order amended the constitution to establish the supremacy of the military courts. In May 1980, another amendment order barred the high courts from interfering with a judgement of the military courts. In March 1981 Zia issued a Provisional Constitution Order that forbade civilian courts to consider cases that challenged the actions of martial law officials. A new oath of office for judges was issued. Nineteen high court and supreme court justices who refused to sign it either resigned or were dismissed.

Concurrent with the weakening of the secular civilian courts and the strengthening of military judicial institutions, the martial law regime also established an Islamic, or Shari'ah, court system. Panels of judges, knowledgeable in Islamic law, were attached to each of the high courts and the supreme court to render judgements on whether specific laws conformed to the dictates of Islam.

The termination of martial law at the end of 1985 restored to the civilian courts much of the authority usurped by the military, but the Islamic modifications of the judicial system remained intact.

Regional & Local Government

Pakistan is divided into four administrative provinces. With about 60 percent of the country's population, the Punjab is the most influential. Sind (with the exception of Karachi), Baluchistan, and the North West Frontier Province are all economically disadvantaged compared with Punjab. Each province also emphasizes a different language, although minority language groups exist within each province and Urdu and English provide interprovincial communication bridges. Each province is mindful of its separate tradition, and friction among them has historical roots despite the fact that most Baluchis reside outside Baluchistan, more than a million Pathans live in Sind, and Punjabis are scattered throughout the provinces.

Politics is replete with interprovincial squabbling and intraprovincial rivalry: Sindhis, Baluch and Pathans have periodically called for provincial autonomy, and their demands have often led to armed conflict. Sindhis and Punjabis are still dominated by local religious leaders (Pirs and Makhdooms) and by large landlords with countrywide influence; the Baluch still honor their sardars or tribal leaders. Atomization and political fragmentation, not national unity, characterize the Pakistani ethos.

Moreover, there is considerable hostility between the indigenous folk and the Muslim refugees (muhajirs) who emigrated to Pakistan from India. It is important to note that descendents of muhajirs are also perceived as refugees. Sindhi complaints against the muhajirs often have been the loudest. With a majority of refugees settling in Karachi, muhajirs have become the backbone for the commercial development of that port city. Their industry, education, and resources could not be matched by the local Sindhi inhabitants, who have grown to resent the muhajirs as interlopers aggrandizing themselves at the expense of the native population. Under the government of Bhutto, a Sindhi himself, Sindhi nationalism was given new expression, and the refugees were placed under severe strain. The impact of that period continues to reverberate in muhajir circles.

The Muslim League, which received the transfer of power from the British in August 1947, never was interested in the creation of a federal state with substantial responsibilities devolving upon the individual provinces. Parochial attitudes threatened national solidarity. The concentration of power at the center was a direct response to centrifugal forces. On the other hand, the Muslim League's quasi-autocratic performance merely served to justify the perception of the provinces that they were being recolonized and must resist the center's monopoly of power.

Other political parties also attempted to overcome provincialism, but were as unsuccessful as the league. The result was the transfer of authority to the "steel frame" of professional administrators. When the bureaucrats also showed weaknesses, the military establishment moved into the breech.

In July 1979 the martial-law government outlined what was described as a new system of local self-government, with union councils at its base, Tehsil councils above them, and district councils on the summit. The purpose of this arrangement according to government spokesmen, was a desire to return power to the people and to start the process of rebuilding representative institutions from the bottom up.

Elections to local bodies were held in September 1979, and they became operative in November of that year. A second round of local-level elections was conducted in 1983. Although there is a slight variation in numbers among the different provinces, the blueprint for local self-government is essentially the same in all the provinces. In the Punjab, the most populated province, the basic electoral unit ranges between 1,000 and 1,900 people. One representative speaks for each unit. Union councils have fifteen members each, and their chairmen assume positions on the Tehsil councils. District councils are assembled from Tehsil membership, with populations from 5,000 to 10,000, and from fifteen-member councils in towns with 15,000 to 20,000 population. Municipal committees are found in cities with populations ranging from 20,000 to two million. Such committees have from fifteen to seventy-five members. In cities above two million, municipal corporations were created with memberships of one hundred to one hundred fifty persons. The government also has set aside seats on the union councils for special interests, e.g., peasants and non-Muslims. Members of the working class and women also have been reserved seats at the district level.

Countrywide the councils included approximately 50,000 elected local leaders charged with the responsibility of raising food production; promoting education, health, and sanitation; and improving the water supply and road network in their specific region. The people's representatives also were made responsible for developing the livestock and dairy industries on the one side, and welfare and cultural activities on the other. The representatives on the urban committees had some similar tasks, and they were also called upon to help combat floods, develop schemes for economic growth, maintain civic services, and oversee the distribution of electric power. Planning from below was described as the primary goal, and technocrats in the administrative units of provincial governments were instructed to employ the services of the people's representatives.

Given the range of these projects there was the perennial threat that the local bodies would become more dependent on the bureaucrats. Critics of the systems described it as a relic of the past and a holdover from the Basic Democracies (BD) system of Ayub Khan. These detractors noted the failure of the BD system, its manipulation by the bureaucracy, and its ignominious elimination when Ayub fell from power.

In order to avoid the pitfalls of Ayub's BD system, Zia insisted on the transfer of financial resources to the local bodies. The All-Pakistan Local Bodies Convention of March 1980 called for the allocation of approximately $10 million (100 million rupees) to the Union Councils, but it is difficult to determine how much money has actually been transferred to the Union Councils by the central and provincial governments. All indications are that the money is being transmitted from the center, and that other monies are being acquired from provincial governments as well as through local collections.

There is considerable complaint, particularly from among the more sophisticated members of the population in the urban centers, that the local bodies are not receiving the funds pledged to them. On the other hand, there is little complaint from the rural sector. Financial power appears to have added to the prestige of the councils and the provincial governments are now more inclined to draw upon local leadership for their advisory councils. Nevertheless, local bodies that lack real power, that are devoid of political party affiliation, and again come under the supervision of the Pakistani bureaucracy, are not destined to win the confidence of the nation. In an attempt to overcome these objections, the government established, on the recommendation of the Majlis-i-Shura, an ombudsman (mohtasib) to whom individuals may appeal in cases of bureaucratic maladministration.

In one respect at least, the local government institutions functioned as intended when they were established in 1979: they provided hundreds of Pakistanis an outlet for their political activities and aspirations. When the Majlis-i-Shura and provincial cabinets were later established, many of their members were drawn from the ranks of those serving in the local institutions.

The Electoral System

Current election rules provide all adult male and female citizens (age eighteen and over) with the right to vote. In nearly forty years of independence, Pakistan has held general elections only three times. The first, in December 1970, was conducted by the military and led to the civil war of 1971. The March 1977 elections conducted by Prime Minister Z.A. Bhutto were widely regarded as rigged and resulted in a mass protest movement and ultimate military takeover. The February 1985 general elections facilitated the lifting of martial law but final judgement on whether the third attempt at elections will be more successful than the two earlier tries will depend upon the ability of political leaders to deal with the demands of those groups who boycotted the 1985 balloting.

Unlike the earlier elections, the 1985 polls were held on a nonpartisan basis, with separate electorates for Muslims and non-Muslims and reserved seats for women. As in 1970 and 1977, voting for the national assembly was completed in a single day, followed three days later by another single day of provincial assembly elections. Elections are based on single-member districts, although there has frequently been discussion of various forms of proportional representation.

In 1985, over 1,200 candidates registered to contest the approximately 200 national assembly seats and nearly 3,600 competed for the roughly 460 seats in the four provincial assemblies. The elections brought out an estimated 52 percent of eligible voters, despite an active boycott by members of the parties in the Movement for the Restoration of Democracy (MRD). All balloting—conducted by paper ballot—took place under the watchful eyes of government officers and the conduct of the elections was generally regarded as clean and fair.

The Party System

Origins of the Parties

Pakistani political parties have never fully organized. What passed for parties can be better described as movements or personalist factions.

The Muslim League was founded in 1906 to defend Muslim interests on the subcontinent. In 1940, the league, under the leadership of Mohammad Ali Jinnah, called for partition and the establishment of an independent Muslim state. At the time of partition in 1947, the league became the government party of the new Pakistan. It was, however, a movement that never developed a disciplined national organization, and it soon disintegrated into a variety of personalist and regional factions. Its electoral defeat in East Pakistan (now Bangladesh) in 1954 signalled its demise, but it continued to play a role in West Pakistan politics until martial law was imposed in 1958. When party activity resumed in 1962, the league divided into two factions: the Convention Muslim League, the political vehicle of Ayub Khan; and the Council Muslim League, which played a role in the ouster of Ayub in 1969, only to suffer crushing defeat at the polls in 1970.

Other parties of note in the first decade of Pakistani independence—the Awami League, the National Awami Party, the Republican Party, the Krishak Sramik Party and others—were essentially regional in organization and parochial in outlook.

From 1958 to 1971, party activity was more reactive than positive; genuine political power rested with the civilian bureaucracy and the military apparatus. The electoral victory of the Pakistan People's Party in 1970 brought hope of the development of viable political parties, but these expectations were soon dashed by the arbitrary actions of the Bhutto administration.

Parties were allowed to operate during the first two years following Bhutto's ouster, but were banned by General Zia in October 1979. After that time, however, they continued to operate in a somewhat circumscribed fashion—issuing public statements, occasionally holding meetings, and having their activities reported by the press —typically referred to as "defunct political parties." After the 1985 elections and the establishment of a civilian government, Prime Minister Junejo pressed forward with legislation to legalize political parties once again. Early in 1986 his own Pakistan Muslim League became the first of the parties to regain legal recognition.

The Parties in Law

In preparation for promised national elections, political parties were required to register with the government in 1979. All parties on the right and center did so, but the PPP refused, believing that its size and popularity would force the regime to rescind the registration order. Zia's subsequent postponement of the elections and his ban on all political activity (October 1979) was, in part, a consequence of the People's Party's intransigence.

The Political Parties Act, passed in late 1985, legalized parties but retained the requirement that parties register with the federal election commission. The commission would then decide within sixty days whether to let the party proceed with registration of members and election of officers. After a year the party should submit to the election commission a copy of its constitution, names of its national and provincial officers, and details of its accounts, after which the commission may grant full recognition. The election commission was also authorized not to recognize more than one party using the same name. Also, a national or provincial assembly member must resign his seat if he switches parties.

Party Organization

The disorganization of the party system today, though rooted in Pakistani history since 1947, is a direct consequence of the Bhutto years, when moderate political leadership failed to meet the aspirations of Pakistan's diverse populace, often betraying the public trust. With rare exceptions, Pakistani politicians were not dedicated to party ideology or policy or to the interests of the general public. They freely moved from one party to another, usually for opportunistic reasons. Cadres seldom comprised dedicated individuals, and politicians at all levels were quick to grab opportunities for personal gain.

Pakistan Muslim League

History

The Pakistan Muslim League has gone through numerous transformations during the past forty years. Typically, following a factional split in the party, each faction would claim the party name in an attempt to capitalize upon the reputation of the party which brought the Pakistani nation independence. At the time of the March 1977 elections, there were three major Muslim Leagues—one under the leadership of Pir Mardan Shah of Pagara, another led by Malik Qasim, and a third under Abdul Qayyum Khan of the frontier province. The PML (Pagara), largest of the three, was an active component of the Pakistan National Alliance, the nine-party coalition that battled Bhutto's PPP in the 1977 elections.

During the period of Zia's martial law, the PML (Pagara) was generally supportive of the military regime. When civilian politicians were coopted for cabinet posts, they quite often were old Muslim League politicians. The Pagara Muslim League was one of the two major parties (along with the Jamaat-i-Islami) to allow its members to contest the 1985 elections. Although the elections were nominally nonpartisan, the PML (Pagara) was clearly the major winner. The appointment of Mohammad Khan Junejo (a longstanding PML politician from Pagara's own province of Sind) as prime minister reflected the strength of the party in the new assembly.

Following the elections, Prime Minister Junejo established an Official Parliamentary Group (OPG) in the National Assembly. The opposition members, led by partisans of the Jamaat-i-Islami, in turn set up an Independent Parliamentary Group (IPG). After passage of the Political Parties Act, Junejo proceeded to transform the OPG into a revived PML. Nearly two-thirds of the members of the National Assembly attended the inaugural session of the revived party, many of whom had not been associated with the earlier Pagara League.

Organization

Junejo's Muslim League is presently limited to members of the National Assembly and the four provincial assemblies. PML leaders outside Parliament have been specifically excluded from leadership positions within the revived party. In early 1986 the organization therefore remained limited, at least officially, to the legislative party, but ultimately it can be expected to reestablish linkages with one or more of the extraparliamentary Muslim Leagues.

Policy

Reflective of their landed elite social base, the members of the PML are generally conservative. They are supportive of the pro-business economic measures introduced under martial law and of a hardline position against the recognition of the Soviet-supported Marxist government of Afghanistan. On the other hand, they favor the current movement toward total civilian control of Pakistani politics and have, in fact, played a major role in bringing about the degree of civilian rule that has thus far occurred.

The Muslim League assembly members are strongly opposed to recurrence of the Bhutto-type populist authoritarianism that characterized Pakistani politics in the early 1970s. If they are successful in establishing a stable civilian order, which can avoid both populist radicalism and military intervention, they will have accomplished something which has eluded Pakistan for the full four decades of its existence.

Membership and Constituency

Most of the PML members in the assembly are local notables who in the past have shifted their party loyalties to the prevailing party in power. They are able to draw upon the prestige and tradition of the Muslim League name, as well as upon their own long experience in politics. The PML (Pagara), with which the assembly party has its closest affinity, draws its electoral support primarily from the rural clients of the landlords and pirs.

Pir Pagara, in his mid-fifties, has a dedicated following of Hurs (militant devotees) in the Sind districts of Sukkur, Khairpur, Sanghai, and Mirpurkhas, with a sprinkling in other districts. He can personally command the loyalties of voters in at least five national assembly seats in Sind. His brother-in-law, Makhdumzada Syed Hassan Mahmud, holds similar sway over Bahawalpur and Rahim Yar Khan Districts in southern Punjab. Elsewhere, the party relies on the old image of the Muslim League and the memory of its leader, Mohammad Ali Jinnah. The Pagara Muslim League brings together a number of veteran politicians who tend to side with each successive government; many of them are landlords with peasant followings.

Financing

The party is financed primarily from the substantial contributions of its members.

Leadership

The assembly PML selected Prime Minister Mohammad Khan Junejo as its president. For general secretary they selected Iqbal Ahmad Khan, the minister for law and parliamentary affairs. Junejo is a Sindhi and a longtime protegé of Pagara. Iqbal is a Punjabi who was formerly a high court judge and also served as a delegate to the United Nations during the Zia martial law period.

Prospects

In some respects the PML's position is the strongest it has had in many years. Because of the opposition boycott of the 1985 elections, the party enjoys a signficant majority in the National Assembly and in the four provincial assemblies. Its maneuvering with the military to end martial law and restore civil liberties can be expected to garner a considerable amount of public support.

On the other hand, the PML's strength will remain somewhat uncertain, and therefore fragile, until elections are held in which all major parties participate. The PML has demonstrated its vote-getting strength against the Jamaat-i-Islami, but how it would fare against the Pakistan People's Party remains a major question, answerable only when new elections are held.

Pakistan People's Party (PPP)

History

The PPP was founded in 1967 by Zulfikar Ali Bhutto and J.A. Rahim, a former high civil servant and intellectual who formulated the party's original program. Bhutto, the scion of a powerful Sindhi family, had been a rising star in the Ayub government from 1958 to 1966, when he resigned, purportedly angry over the outcome of the 1965 India-Pakistan war. The original leadership of the party was composed of trusted confidants of Bhutto or Rahim. In the 1970 election, the PPP won a majority of the West Pakistan seats in the national legislature. Bhutto's refusal to negotiate with the East Pakistan winner, the Awami League, for a share in the government or autonomy for East Pakistan brought on the civil war, Indian intervention, and the fall of the Yahya Khan government. Bhutto took over the presidency of the truncated Pakistan. The PPP oversaw the writing of the 1973 constitution, and Bhutto became prime minister, the chief executive officer under that constitution. In 1974, Rahim was ousted as secretary general of the party (and given a severe physical beating by police), reportedly after an outburst by Bhutto over the forms of respect due him from the older Rahim. A purge of the Rahim elements in the party followed.

In March 1977, the PPP won an overwhelming majority of seats in the National Assembly amid widespread charges of election rigging, bribery, and violence. The nine-party opposition, the Pakistan National Alliance, refused to cooperate with the PPP, and the country experienced four months of violent political turmoil before Bhutto was ousted by the Zia coup. Bhutto was subsequently arrested and tried for the 1974 murder of a political opponent. After extensive appeals and international agitation for a commutation of sentence, Bhutto was hanged on April 4, 1979. The party today derives considerable strength from this "martyrdom."

Organization

The party has never been well organized, and what little organization there was has been shattered by the Zia regime. As the personal organization of Bhutto, it was not democratically operated: party leaders and local representatives were appointed by Bhutto on the basis of their personal loyalty. Its National Council was convened only once, in 1972. The emergence of Jahangir Badr in Punjab signifies a shift from feudals to lower middle class leadership.

Policy

The party is badly split over its future course. The PPP has a fair number of rightists and wealthy landowning supporters, but the rank-and-file party worker is leftist and the party's public platform will always be leftist. Bhutto's daughter, Benazir, who returned to Pakistan April 10, 1986 after two years in exile, has taken a relatively moderate position with respect to changing the country's political leadership. She has called for a new round of general elections but has forsworn any violent opposition to the government in power.

Membership & Constituency

The party's original strength, as shown in the 1970 elections, was concentrated in the Punjab and Sind. While the party did increase its strength in the more rural provinces during the Bhutto regime, the PPP majority remains primarily with the urban working class. The student population is a particular source of strength, being sharply and almost equally divided between the PPP and left extremist parties on the one hand and the Islamic fundamentalists on the other. No reliable membership estimate exists for the PPP, but until elections are again held it can plausibly claim to be the largest party in Pakistan.

Financing

Money for PPP activities is derived largely from contributions by the organization's supporters.

Leadership

Benazir Bhutto, the Oxford-educated daughter of the late prime minister, has effectively replaced her mother, Begum Nusrat Bhutto, as party leader. Nusrat Bhutto, a Sindhi of Iranian extraction, is in ill health and remains in exile in Europe. Benazir, who spent most of the early years of martial law under house arrest in Karachi or at the family home in Larkana in central Sind, was sent out of the country in early 1984. During the next two years, she was active in London among other PPP exiles and traveled to the United States a number of times to lobby for American support to end martial law in Pakistan. She returned to Pakistan in mid-1985 to make funeral arrangements for her brother Shahnawaz, but was arrested shortly after the funeral when the government overreacted to the large crowds of followers she was drawing. After two months imprisonment she left the country. Since her return her party members have expressed great concern over her personal safety in a country in which many bitter memories—as well as much adulation—remain from her father's period of rule.

Prospects

However divisive the internal party debate may be, the PPP remains a potent force in Pakistani politics. When elections are again held, the PPP will very likely win a solid plurality of the votes, if not a majority. Following her return to Pakistan in April 1986, Benazir Bhutto has drawn mammoth crowds. She has clearly inherited her father's charisma. Her party's propects hinge on whether she can translate such impressive mass support into effective political change without violence and without provoking another military intervention.

Jamaat-i-Islami (Islamic Assembly)

History

The Jamaat was organized in India, prior to the British departure from the subcontinent, by a religious leader, Maulana Abul Ala Maudoodi, who eventually settled in Pakistani Maudoodi orginally opposed the notion of Pakistani independence, but after it became a reality, he strongly advocated its becoming an Islamic state—still the primary aim of the Jamaat. The party's objection to the creation of a secular state made it a target of government suppression. Many Jamaat activists have spent long periods in jail, particularly under the government of Bhutto, who saw the Jamaat as a conspiratorial group. With the collapse of the Bhutto government, however, the Jamaat gained a new importance as a primary supporter of the Zia government.

Organization

The Jamaat has never operated as a conventional mass political party. It is a movement with centralized authority and a well-organized and highly disciplined cadre of some 2,000 members who concentrate on propaganda and elite recruitment.

Policy

The Jamaat is the main proponent of making Pakistan into an Islamic state. It therefore frequently supported and reinforced Zia's Islamization program. Nevertheless, the Jamaat went to some lengths to show that it was not entirely at ease with the Zia government, often by criticizing Zia for not being sincere enough in his Islamization efforts.

Membership & Constituency

The Jamaat has strong support among the industrial elite, merchants, shopkeepers, the laboring masses, and the muhajir community, especially in Karachi. These elements see the Jamaat as their counterweight to the Zia regime, offering a way back to civilian government while continuing the movement toward an Islamic constitution. The movement is particularly strong on university campuses, where its student wing, Jamiat-ul-Tulaba, dominates most student unions, including those of Karachi University (the nation's largest) and Punjab University (the nation's oldest). The student group has also penetrated teachers' associations and has begun to organize labor unions as well. Composed of religious orthodox militants, the Jamiat-ul-Tulaba is not reluctant to use violence.

Financing

The Jamaat is the best-financed party in Pakistan, with some of its revenue rumored to come from Arab oil states and the USA.

Leadership

The Jamaat is ruled by Mian Tufail Mohammad, a man in his late sixties in 1986, who is related by marriage to General Zia. Its chief ideologist is Professor Ghafoor Ahmad; Qazi Husain Ahmad is also an important ideologue.

Prospects

The Jamaat was the only major political party besides the PML (Pagara) to participate actively in the 1985 general elections, albeit without party labels. Although Jamaat partisans did win enough seats to constitute the major opposition group in the National Assembly, their electoral performance was much less than that of the PML candidates and less than might have been predicted on the basis of their cadre and organizational strength. The Jamaat will continue to be an important factor in Pakistani politics, but its influence may diminish rather than grow if civilian rule continues to replace the military.

Tehrik-i-Istiqlal (The Struggle Movement)

History

The Tehrik was founded by retired air marshal Mohammad Asghar Khan in 1966 in opposition to Ayub Khan's government. The party has not done well at the polls. In both the 1970 and the 1977 elections, it was regarded as a minor political organization. Air marshal Asghar Khan played a pivotal role in the Pakistan National Alliance's struggle against Bhutto in 1977 and has been an important actor in the Movement for the Restoration of Democracy (MRD). The Tehrik has acted more as a catalyst for change than as a competitive political organization. In the 1980s, however, the Tehrik has assumed new prominence.

Organization

The Tehrik is the only party with internal democracy, holding national elections every two years. Its elected National Council, with representatives from the provinces, and National Executive meet regularly. Provincial and local leaders are also elected by the membership.

Policy

The party is liberal and democratic, slightly left of center, and projects a major reform program in its party manifesto. Although it opposes the military junta, the party acknowledges the country's need for stability and especially for an effective defense establishment. During the closing years of the martial law period, the Tehrik became increasingly critical of both military rule and the government's refusal to negotiate directly with the Karmal regime in Afghanistan.

Membership & Constituency

The party's firmest adherents are sophisticated professionals and intellectuals, including many high civil servants. Its primary strength is in the Punjab and North West Frontier Province, but it has shown some success in Karachi as well. It has attempted to build a student organization, but Asghar Khan's military background makes him suspect in student eyes, and the party's centrist and moderate policies have little appeal on the polarized campuses.

Financing

The Tehrik's money comes from contributions from members and sympathizers.

Leadership

Former air marshal M. Asghar Khan, president of the party, is not a charismatic figure or a strong leader. Now in his late sixties, he is more a figure-head than an influence in the party. Vice president Mian Mohammad Ali Kasuri, a celebrated lawyer, is in his late sixties; the secretary general, Musheer Ahmad Pesh Imam, is over sixty. A rising young (mid-forties) leader, Asaf Khan Vardag, is from North West Frontier Province. Vardag has strong ties in the Punjab and close family links with elements of the Afghan resistance movement. A former civil servant, he is a major figure in the MRD.

Prospects

The Tehrik probably would do better if the winners were chosen by proportional representation than if they came from "winner-take-all," single-member districts—but even that is not certain. The Tehrik would like to inherit the leftist and centrist support of the PPP, but the party lacks a charismatic leader such as the PPP has in Benazir Bhutto.

Minor Parties

Jamiat-i-Ulema-i-Pakistan (JUP; Conference of Ulema of Pakistan)

The JUP is an orthodox Islamic party, fundamentalist and rightist. It has no program other than the vague aim of Islamization, although it supports the idea of democracy in general terms. The party draws its strength from the Barelvi sect of Sunni Muslims. It also is supported by some of the Urdu-speaking population of Karachi and Hyderabad and by a good number of pirs in the Punjab. The JUP has virtually no support in Baluchistan and only nominal influence in North West Frontier Province. President Maulana Shah Ahmad Noorani is a sharp politician in his fifties. The Punjab president is Maulana Abdul Sattar Khan Niazi, who is in his late sixties.

Jamiatul Ulema-i-Islam (JUI: Conference of Ulema of Islam)

The JUI is the Pakistani successor to the Jamiatul Ulema-i-Hind (Conference of Ulema of India), which played a prominent role in the independence struggle as an ally of the Indian Congress Party. The JUI has a strong base among the Pathans of the North West Frontier Province and Baluchistan, but plays only a marginal role in Punjabi and Sindhi politics. It is primarily a sectarian party of the Deobandi sect of Sunni Muslims, which dominates a majority of the nation's theological institutions.

Maulana Mufti Mahmood, who died in November 1980, was the most important leader of the party in the last decade. He had been chief minister of the North West Frontier Province in 1972 and 1973, and was president of the Pakistan National Alliance during its struggle against the Bhutto government. The president of the party today is Maulana Abdullah Darkhwasti. A learned theologian in his late seventies, Darkhwasti has no real role in national politics. The current secretary general is Maulana Obaidullah Anwar, also in his late seventies, who is a renowned religious leader. Unlike Darkhwasti he is a politician with a strong home base in Lahore. His interest in politics, however, appears to be fleeting; he has already resigned from the party twice, only to be persuaded to rejoin. A looming personality in the party is Maulana Fazlur Rahman, son of the late Maulana Mahmood. He has challenged both the president and the secretary general of the JUI by taking the party into the Movement for the Restoration of Democracy (MRD), and he insists on keeping it there despite government pressure against the move. Fazlur Rahman is in his forties.

National Democratic Party (NDP)

The strength behind this party, which succeeded the National Awami Party (NAP) after its banning in 1975, rests with Wali Khan and his wife, Nasim Wali Khan, who are highly respected among the Pathans. Sardar Sherbaz Kahn Mazari, a Baluch of Dera Ghazi Khan in the Punjab, is the NDP's president. An intellectual in his fifties, Mazari lacks a political base.

Secretary general of the party is Abid Zuberi, an insurance magnate in his mid-fifties. Mazari and Zuberi are pro-West rightists, while Wali Khan, though not a communist, favors the USSR because of its probable future role in the region. The result of this disjunction is considerable vagueness about the NDP's programs and policies; NDP standing today is at its lowest point ever. It lost its Baluchistan wing, which drifted further left in the mid-1970s, and prolonged cooperation with the Zia regime has tarnished its image. It now stands with MRD in opposition to Zia, but it is not very active.

Pakistan Democratic Party (PDP)

The PDP–headed by Nawabzada Nasrullah Khan, one of Pakistan's shrewdest politicians–consists of large landholders and is purely Punjabi in membership. An orator and persuasive speaker, Nasrullah Khan has been a consistent spokesman for democratic causes. He is also quite capable of intrigue and cunning, and many alliances have been forged and later undermined by his actions. He is in his late seventies.

Pakistan Muslim League (Khwaja Khairuddin group, or Malik Qasim group, or Chathha League)

This Muslim League party is led nominally by Khwaja Khairuddin, who was prominent in Calcutta and Dacca Muslim League politics before and after partition. His position in Pakistani politics is very limited. Malik Mohammad Qasim, who is in his fifties, is secretary general and a more influential figure. He is a successful Lahore lawyer and a large landlord of Bahawalnagar. He was an important member of the Convention Muslim League during the Ayub era. During martial law he assumed an important leadership role in the lawyer's movement opposed to President Zia's policies. Another leader of the party is Mohammad Hussain Chathha, also a former Muslim Leaguer, with strong local following in the Punjab. In 1982, the party became a major supporter of MRD. The party is more closely identified with the original Muslim League than its counterpart, the Pagara Muslim League. Nevertheless, it is weaker in electoral strength.

Pakistan National Party (PNP)

The Pakistan National Party was created in 1979 in a split from the NDP. The party is headed by Mir Ghaus Bux Bizenjo, a known communist in his seventies who supports Soviet policy. Reasons for the NDP-PDP split involved both Bizenjo's objections to Mazari's leadership of the NDP and a more leftist policy stance taken by the Baluch leader. Bizenjo is the president of the PNP. Qaswar Gardezi, from Punjab, is general secretary and Shah Mohammad Shah, from Sind, is senior vice president. Although the PNP is the only Baluch party, Baluch leadership generally ignores it. The party advocates a very weak central government and maximum provincial autonomy. It has also consistently supported recognition of the Marxist government of Afghanistan.

Pashtoonkhwa (Pathan Brotherhood)

This was the Baluchistan wing of the NAP-NDP. It was led by Abdul Samad Khan Achakzai until his assassination in 1973; his son Mahmud Khan Achakzai inherited the leadership. The party is found only in the Pathan areas of Baluchistan. It is leftist and Pathan racialist.

Mazdoor Kisan Party (Workers and Peasants Party)

The MKP came into being in 1968 as an offshoot of the peasant committees of the National Awami Party. Afzal Bangash built upon his base in NWFP by forming alliances with other leftist groups in Punjab and Karachi. The party split in 1978, but the Bangash faction formed alliances with other leftist organizations, including the Awami Jamhoori Ittehad (People's Republican Alliance), of which Bangash was elected president. An alliance with the Pakistan Workers' Party (PWP) and a July 1979 unity congress led to further strengthening of the party's worker/peasant base. Bangash was elected president of the reconstituted party, with Fatehyab Ali Khan as senior vice president and Shaukat Ali as secretary general. The KMP was active in the 1981 formation of the MRD and prominent in the MRD's 1983 civil disobedience campaign against martial law.

Other Political Forces

Movement for the Restoration of Democracy (MRD)

Created in 1981 as a loose coalition of diverse parties opposed to martial law, the MRD was modeled upon a similar movement of the same name in 1968–1969 which had succeeded in forcing the resignation of President Ayub Khan. Comprising nine parties in 1981, the MRD had grown to eleven parties by 1986. Included within the movement were both the Pakistan People's Party and most of the parties that had fought against the PPP in the 1977 elections. Ideological and other differences have hampered the organization's effectiveness, with the Pagara PML and the Jamaat-i-Islami dissociating themselves from the movement. The Tehrik-i-Istiqlal, Pakistan National Party, the Jamiatul Ulema-i-Islam, the Pakistan Democratic Party, and the Khairuddin group of the Muslim League have continued to be active participants. The MRD made a major push to topple the Zia regime in August 1983, when it initiated a civil disobedience movement in response to the announcement of Zia's program to restore civilian rule. The program sparked a long-simmering regional discontent in Sind and lasted several weeks before it was subdued. In its next important effort, the MRD led a boycott of the December 19, 1984 referendum which Zia used to secure public endorsement of his Islamization policies and of his retention in office. The referendum boycott was largely successful, despite government claims to the contrary, but a similar attempt to boycott the February 1985 elections backfired. The rapid pace of civilian rule–gains in the latter half of 1985 left the MRD on the sidelines. If Pakistani politics continues to become more free and open, the MRD is likely to continue to lose cohesiveness—its primary raison d'être being its collective opposition to military rule.

The Sind-Baluch-Pakhtoon Front (SBPF)

Minority provinces' long-standing disaffection from Punjabi domination led in December 1985 to the creation in London of the SBPF. Prominent leaders are former PPP figures, such as former law and education minister Abdul Hafeez Pirzada and the late prime minister's cousin Mumtaz Ali Bhutto. Also active are Baluch tribal leader Ataullah Mengal and leftist

Afzal Bangash of the MKP. The SBPF's core policy issue is its advocacy of a confederal system for Pakistan. Arguing that constitutional changes effected under martial law have upset the delicate federal balance of the 1973 constitution, the SBPF calls for decentralization to the provincial level of nearly all governmental functions. In 1986 the major political parties in the MRD, including the PPP, endorsed this position.

The Military

Pakistan's armed forces, particularly the army and air force, are perceived as the bedrock upon which Pakistan's survival rests, and as the primary institution influencing the nation's development as a modern state. Discipline, professionalism, and national consciousness remain key features of the military establishment despite its deep involvement in politics.

Politics, however, has divided the military. During the Bhutto years, some officers were cashiered and replaced with others, Zia among them, thought to be more amenable to Bhutto's control. Professionalism and ability, particularly in the top ranks, are thought by many Pakistanis to have declined. Some lower-ranking officers are embittered by their failure to receive promotions because of the political divisions in the army. Promotion is often based on political considerations, e.g., officers with relatives who were once involved in moderate or left-wing politics may now be passed over. The continuation in the upper ranks of generals associated with the loss of East Pakistan and the humiliation by India is further cause for bitterness.

The officer corps is derived from families with military traditions dating back to the British colonial and Moghul periods. Punjabis and Pathans provide the majority of officers. The ranks also draw heavily from these ethnic groups, especially from the rural areas. The Baluchis have sizeable contingents in the armed forces but the Sindhis and the muhajir (refugee) community have only slight representation. General Zia, however, is a Punjabi muhajir.

Although the army was humiliated in the 1971 war, it retains its reputation as a first-class fighting force. It is highly regarded in the Middle East, and thousands of Pakistani soldiers and airmen have been sent abroad to bolster the forces of other Muslim countries, particularly in the Persian Gulf region. These deployments not only increase Pakistan's influence in the region and contribute to the nation's balance of payments, they also help to defuse tensions within the military by providing opportunities for faster advancement for some and distant postings for other, potentially disruptive, officers.

Religious Groups

The religious establishments in Pakistan are loose congeries of rival groups. Each either supports a particular localized expression of Islam or follows a certain leader. This is true of both Sunni and Shi'a Muslims, the latter comprising about 15 percent of the population. For example, Shi'a Muslims in Lahore do not identify with Shi'a Muslims in Hyderabad or Karachi. By the same token, Sunni Muslims comprising the Jamiatul Ulema-i-Pakistan (JUP) are associated with Sind and the Punjab. The Jamiatul Ulema-i-Islam (JUI) are associated with the Pathans of the North West Frontier Province and Baluchistan. The religious establishments are a cohesive political force, but are more the beneficiaries of popular religious sentiment than an organizational success.

Organized Labor

The trade unions are ineffective, generally poor, and often repressed. Left-wing labor organizers are active, but their organizations are feeble and poor, seldom generating support from the working class. Some of the more extreme left organizations that seek to enlist the industrial and agricultural workers are the Mazdoor Kisan Party (S. Ali Bacha group), the Sind Hari Committee, the Pakistan Socialist Party, and the Mazdoor Kisan Party (Bangash group). None of these parties has much electoral significance.

National Prospects

Under martial law, Pakistan enjoyed a growth rate of approximately six percent per annum, partially because of the pro-business policies of the regime and partially because of the substantial inflow of both foreign aid and worker remittances. Because of this growth, Pakistan is now close to entering the UN-defined category of middle-income nations. Pakistan has always been heavily dependent upon foreign assistance, and, despite an improved economic picture, that dependence continues to grow. Pakistan is one of the largest aid recipients from the International Bank for Reconstruction and Development (World Bank). It is also assisted by loans from the United States Agency for International Development as well as the European Economic Community (Common Market). Saudi Arabia and the Persian Gulf states have also been very generous. Completing in 1986 a five-year American aid program of $3.2 billion, Pakistan anticipated renewal of the package for another five years at a price tag of over $4 billion. The negative side of all of this foreign aid is that Pakistan has an increasingly heavy foreign debt burden, which had grown to about $25 billion by 1985.

This dependency is not one-sided. Pakistan has become the primary exporter of skilled and unskilled labor to Middle Eastern countries. Remittances from these migrants constitute Pakistan's largest single source of foreign exchange, but a leveling-off of the oil boom in the Middle East led in 1985 to a decline in remittances.

The Soviet occupation of Afghanistan remains a major foreign policy concern, as does continued Indian hostility, despite nearly a decade of negotiation to improve and normalize relations. Uncertainty concerning Pakistan's nuclear intentions continues to alarm both India and the United States.

Pakistan's domestic prospects changed dramatically during 1985. Until then it appeared that the military might hold power indefinitely. At the start of 1986, martial law had been lifted, a civilian government established, and preliminary steps taken to reestablish legal political parties. Critics could still point to the fragility of the new system, to Zia's continuance not only as president but as chief of the army staff, and to the ease with which military rule might at any point be reimposed. But the existing freer political system makes prospects brighter than at any point in the previous decade.

Whether Pakistan's latest experiment in democracy will be successful depends upon the skill with which its parties and politicians effect a consensus on acceptable rules of the political game. Pakistan's past record does not offer much basis for optimism, but at least the opportunity is there.

Further Reading

Baxter, Craig, ed. *Zia's Pakistan; Politics and Stability in a Frontline State*. Boulder: Westview Press, Colo.: 1985.

Burki, Shahid Javed. *Pakistan under Bhutto 1971–1977*. New York: St. Martin's Press, 1980.

Callard, Keith. *Pakistan: A Political Study*. London: George Allen and Unwin, 1957.

Choudhury, G. W. *The Last Days of United Pakistan*. Bloomington, Ind.: Indiana University Press, 1974.

Cohen, Steven P. *The Pakistan Army*. Berkeley: University of California Press, 1984.

Feldman, Herbert. *Revolution in Pakistan*. London: Oxford University Press, 1967.

Qureshi, I. H. *Ulema in Politics*. 2nd ed. Karachi: Ma'aref Limited, 1974.

Rizvi, Hasan-Askri. *The Military and Politics in Pakistan 1947–1986*. Lahore: Progressive Publishers, 1986.

Sayeed, Khalid B. *Politics in Pakistan: The Nature and Direction of Change*. New York: Praeger, 1980.

Schofield, Victoria. *Bhutto: Trial and Execution*. London: Cassell, 1979.

Wilcox, Wayne Ayres. *Pakistan: The Consolidation of a Nation*. New York: Columbia University Press, 1963.

Ziring, Lawrence. *Pakistan: The Enigma of Political Development*. Boulder, Colo.: Westview Press, 1980.

REPUBLIC OF PANAMA
(República de Panamá)

by Waltraud Queiser Morales, Ph.D. revised by Sheila Klee

The System of Government

Panama, a Central American nation of two million people, is a unitary republic established November 3, 1903, following a successful revolution of independence against Colombia. The revolution was sponsored by the United States, which gained control of 2 percent of Panama's area for the Panama Canal Zone. The 1972 constitution (the fourth in the country's history) does not mention the Zone, defining the national territory as "the land area, the territorial sea, the submarine continental shelf, the subsoil, and air space between Colombia and Costa Rica." With the ratification of the Panama Canal treaties in 1978, Panamanian sovereignty and ultimate control over the Canal Zone has been established.

The Panamanian political system is presidential. The government is divided into three branches, the executive, legislative and judiciary, with executive power dominating. The 1978 and 1983 amendments to the 1972 constitution expanded legislative powers after the extraordinary rule of General Omar Torrijos Herrera, (officially, 1972–78). The 1983 amendments also reduced the role of the army in governing. However, it remains a central executive force in an ostensibly civilian regime.

Executive

The president of Panama is the official head of state and of government. The constitution vests all executive powers in the president and vice presidents. The post of second vice president was created by a 1983 constitutional amendment. The first vice president assumes executive functions in the absence of the president, but is otherwise powerless. The president initiates most legislation, names one member of the Electoral Tribunal, and, with the approval of the Legislative Assembly, the judges of the Supreme Court. A president and two vice presidents were elected by direct popular vote in 1984. On the resignation of the president in 1985, the first vice president assumed the presidency, the third such succession in three years. The second vice president moved up to fill the first vice presidency, leaving his own post vacant.

Article 277 of the constitution extended special powers for six years (1972 to 1978) to General Torrijos as the chief of government and supreme leader of the Panamanian Revolution. From the expiration of Article 277 in October 1978 to his death on July 31, 1981, General Torrijos remained the de facto executive power. Article 157 of the amended constitution provides for the direct popular election of the president and vice president beginning in 1984. Candidates were required to be at least thirty-five years of age, Panamanian by birth, not have served in the respective offices for the two previous terms, and, by a 1983 amendment, not to be currently serving in the national Defense Forces (*Fuerzas de Defensa Nacional* FDN: formerly named the National Guard).

Legislature

Panama's legislative structure was altered by the constitutional revisions of 1983. The National Assembly of Community Representatives (*Asamblea Nacional de Representantes de Corregimientos*), was abolished, and the National Legislative Council (*Consejo Nacional de Legislacion*) was supplanted by a Legislative Assembly (*Asamblea Legislative*). Representatives of the Legislative Assembly are nominated by parties and elected by direct popular vote. Elections are for a five-year term and are concurrent with presidential elections. Candidates must be at least twenty-one years old, Panamanian citizens by birth or naturalization for a minimum of fifteen years, and must reside in the electoral circuit represented.

The Assembly approves treaties, declares war and initiates some legislation. The Assembly is also empowered to try the president and justices of the supreme court for unconstitutional acts, to supervise the national budget, determine monetary law, and to enact national codes.

The current Assembly comprises sixty-seven members, all of whom were elected in 1984. Parties in the government coalition, the National Democratic Union, won forty-five seats, while the opposition coalition, the Opposition Democratic Alliance, won twenty-two seats. The National Democratic Union seats obtained follow: the Democratic Revolutionary Party, 34; the Labor Party, 7; the Republican Party, 3; and the National Liberal Party, 1. The Opposition Democratic Alliance's seats follow: the Authentic Panameñista Party, 13; the Christian Democratic Party, 6; and the Liberal Republican and Nationalist Movement, 3.

By article 141 of the 1983 constitutional amendments, Panama is divided into Electoral Circuits corresponding to the Administrative Districts of the National Census. Each Electoral Circuit elects one Legislative Assembly representative per 30,000 inhabitants, and one per the remaining number of inhabitants as long as that number is over 10,000. The exceptions are the province of Darien and the territory of San Bals, which have two Electoral Circuits each, and the district of Panama, which has four.

Judiciary

The highest court of the land is the Supreme Court of Justice (*Corte Suprema de Justicia*), whose nine members are appointed for ten-year terms by the president, and, since 1978, with the approval of the legislature. A new Court was appointed in 1983. The court is divided into three chambers which hear civil, penal, and administrative cases, respectively. A permanent justice is assigned to each branch. Justices must have been practicing lawyers for ten years, Panamanian born, and thirty-five years of age. The powers of the court include judicial review and "final, definitive and binding" decisions on the legality and constitutionality of acts. Because of extensive executive appointive power over the Court, the independence of the judiciary will ultimately rest with an expanded and independent role for the Legislative Assembly. However, judges once appointed can only be removed by the Supreme Court, so they are not subject to immediate political influence.

Regional & Local Government

Regional government consists of nine provinces each administered by a governor appointed and removable by the president. A provincial coordinating council includes the local representatives and other members established by law, such as the military-zone commander and local representatives from ministries and national agencies in the province who do not have a vote on the council. The provincial councils are coordinating and advisory bodies. Provincial governments are not autonomous but administrative subdivisions of the national government.

Government on the municipal, or district, level, demonstrates greater self-rule. By law, the nation's sixty-four municipalities are independent of the central government, and Article 210 precludes dismissal of municipal officials by national authorities. Some control of the district-level government exists, however, since the mayor (*alcalde*) of the municipality, elected for a three-year term by direct popular vote, may be dismissed by national authorities. A community governing board of four members assists the municipal council of five or more members (made up of local representatives) and the mayor in district planning, community development, local expenditures, and tax collection. Subdistrict councils (*juntas comunales*) are headed by the local Assembly representative, the subdistrict leader (*corregidor*), and five other members selected by the municipal council. Below the subdistrict councils are *juntas locales*, whose members are elected by the community. The *juntas locales* in turn elect a delegate to present community concerns before the subdistrict council.

In the 1960s, provincial coordinating councils and the *juntas comunales* and *juntas locales* cooperated in grass-roots government and party organization, facilitating community-development projects. The national Agency for Community Development (DIGEDECOM) established permanent local self-help structures and served as a vehicle of popular mobilization for the government and official party. By 1977, DIGEDECOM had established 558 subdistrict councils where members exercised real power. Local councils were less successful since these were essentially powerless. All these council organizations created a new system of provincial and local representation which circumvented the party structures and power networks of the traditional rural elites.

Semiautonomous local rule is exercised by the indigenous territory of San Blas, a reserve for the Cuna Indians, where local *caciques*, tribal chieftains, control politics and deal with the national government directly. General Torrijos established close personal ties with these Indian leaders.

The Electoral System

The Panamanian electoral record has been one of fraud, government manipulation, and military intervention reflected in the maxim: "He who counts, elects." The 1964 and 1968 elections were marked by widespread electoral abuses. Allegations of fraud also attended the vote counting procedure of the 1984 presidential election, in which the government's candidate was accorded victory by a margin of only 1,713 votes after a delay of ten days. A president, two vice presidents, and a Legislative Assembly were elected in May 1984. Municipal elections took place in June of the same year.

The constitution provides for a three-member Electoral Tribunal which oversees the electoral process and is part of the General Council of State, an advisory body in the executive branch. One member of the tribunal is appointed by the president, one by the Legislative Assembly, and one by the Supreme Court. The tribunal oversees voter registration, decides electoral disputes, and may invalidate fraudulent elections.

Elections operate on the principles of majority representation, universal suffrage of all citizens eighteen years or older, secret ballot, and single-member districts. Voting is obligatory and voters must register with the Electoral Tribunal one year prior to an election presenting their identity card showing Panamanian citizenship and one other form of identification. An individual may vote only in his specified district with proof of identity and verification of voter registration from the Electoral Tribunal.

A presidential candidate must win a majority of votes (one vote more than 50 percent) to be elected. If no candidate receives the necessary majority, the outcome of the election is decided in the Legislative Assembly by simple majority. Assembly members are elected by simple pluralities. In the May 1984 elections, in which a Legislative Assembly was elected for the first time, sixty-seven representatives were elected by the new Electoral Circuits, electoral divisions created by the constitutional reforms of 1983. Prior to 1984, National Assembly elec-

tions, one representative and one alternate were elected by each local electoral unit, the administrative subdistricts or *corregimientos*.

While elections on the *corregimiento* level made local representatives more responsive to voters and contributed to higher voter turnout, there were serious districting problems. The electoral units were unequally proportioned to population and discriminated against urban voters in favor of rural ones. In the 1972 elections, a *corregimiento* in Panama City with nearly 20,000 voters elected one representative, while a rural *corregimiento* in Colón province with only 28 voters also elected one representative. Rural overrepresentation restricts the influence of the highly urban provinces of Panamá and Colón, where the political power of the traditional oligarchy and foreign interests are concentrated. The rural vote supports the new populist and agrarian electoral base created by General Torrijos to legitimize his reforms. The substitution of the new legislative electoral system in 1984 was intended to correct the most egregious districting problems without completely undermining either the government's electoral base or the adequate representation of minorities and others previously excluded from political participation.

Since 1968, voter participation increased from 60 percent of the registered voters who voted for provincial representatives to 90 percent in 1972 and fell to 80 percent of the 787,000 registered voters in the 1978 elections. Opposition sources estimated that some 800,000 potential voters failed to go to the polls, an abstention rate of at least 50 percent; the government claimed turnout was as high as 70 percent. Socialist parties and the right-wing Panameñista Party abstained from the election, thus lowering the turnout. In the 1984 elections, with fourteen parties participating, voter turnout was estimated at 70 percent.

The Party System

Origins of the Parties

Historically, Panamanian political parties shared the tradition of the Colombian Liberal and Conservative parties. These parties were more personalistic than ideological, although the Liberals tended to favor anticlericalism, centralism, and Panamanian independence from Colombia. The Conservatives supported clericalism and some degree of regional autonomy within Colombia. These ideological tendencies, weak in Colombia, became confused in Panama, and dissolved during the 1903 revolution when both parties competed for the leadership of the insurrection.

The postindependence party system rested on a Liberal-Conservative coalition. Although Liberals possessed electoral majorities, Conservatives dominated politics until 1912, because they controlled the presidency and because prominent conservative leaders had collaborated with the United States in the revolt against Colombia. Theodore Roosevelt favored the Conservative Party, which represented the propertied white families, over the Liberal Party, which drew support from black and *mestizo* voters. By the 1920s, most of the original Conservative Party leaders had died and with them the first generation of Panamanian parties.

The second generation of parties developed out of numerous personalistic schisms within the Liberal Party. Controlled by a small, landed aristocracy and the National Guard and operating in a system of minimal popular awareness, the parties have been exclusive instruments of elite and personalistic politics. Two party leaders dominated the political scene until 1968: Rodolfo E. Chiari, head of the Liberal Party, and Arnulfo Arias, founder of the populist Panameñista Party.

Until 1978, there was easy entry into and exit from the electoral process. Parties operated in a loose multiparty system in which no one party was dominant or guaranteed an electoral majority. Except for the presidential victory of Ernesto de la Guardia in 1956, elections were won by broad political coalitions. In the 1964 presidential elections, sixteen parties campaigned and seven candidates ran; in the May 1968 elections, ten legal parties participated via two major coalitions. The government candidate, David Samudio, head of the National Liberal Party, ran for the People's Alliance (*Alianza del Pueblo*), a coalition of his Liberal Party, the Agrarian Labor Party, the Progressive National Party, and the Movement of National Liberation. The second coalition, popularly known as *arnulfistas*, after its candidate Arnulfo Arias, was the antigovernment National Union of Opposition (*Unión Nacional de Oposición*), and included Arias' Panameñista Party, the Democratic Action Party, the National Patriotic Coalition, the Third Nationalist Party, and the Republican Party.

Arnulfo Arias narrowly won the presidency in 1968, but long-standing antipathy between his Panameñista Party and the National Guard precipitated a *coup d'etat* on October 11, ten days after Arias had assumed office. The military-civilian junta, headed by General Herrera, banned all party activity in 1968 and abolished political parties in February 1969. Parties were reinstated in October 1978, and a third generation of political parties began to form. General Torrijos influenced their development by creating a new agrarian, populist base for his official government party, the Democratic Revolutionary Party (PRD). His political plan envisioned a Mexican-style, one-party-dominant system, with only "loyal" opposition parties permitted. In the 1984 elections, six parties formed the National Democratic Union (*Union Nacional Democratica*; Unade) in support of the PRD's presidential candidate, Nicolas Ardito Barletta Valarino. Unade comprised the PRD, the National Liberal Party, the Broad Popular Front, the Labor Party the Panameñista Party (a splinter group of the original party of that name) and the Republican Party. A coalition named the Opposition Democratic Alliance (Alianza Democratica de Oposición; ADO) was formed to support the candidacy of, once again, Arnulfo Arias Madrid. ADO included Arias' Authentic Panameñista Party (Partido Panameñista Autentico; PPA,) a regrouping of Arias' former Panameñista Party), the Christian Democratic Party and the Liberal Republican and Nationalist Movement.

Ardito Barletta won the election by a very small margin. When he resigned, under pressure, in September 1985, he was succeeded by his first vice president, Eric Arturo del Valle, of the Republican Party. Second vice president Roderick Lorenzo Esquivel, of the National Liberal Party moved into the first vice presidency.

The Parties in Law

Between 1968 and 1978, all political parties were illegal, although the communist Panamanian People's Party was allowed to operate. After April 1978, exiled political leaders were permitted to return and organize. Under Law Number 81 of October 1978, parties could attain legal status by submitting to the Electoral Tribunal (by June 1979) 30,000 signatures, the party statutes, and a declaration of principles. Parties also had to register ten members in at least 40 percent of the country's districts, a measure which prevented urban-based parties from challenging government control of the interior.

Under the 1979 political-party law, the government Democratic Revolutionary Party was the first to gain legal status with over 50,000 signatures. The National Liberal Party followed soon after. By the 1984 elections, the PRD had registered over 200,000 members, and thirteen other parties had also registered more than the required 30,000. Following the elections, seven of these parties had their official status revoked for their failure to garner the legally required 3 percent of the vote. These were the Broad Popular Front, the Revolutionary Workers Party, the National People's Party, the Panameñista Party, the People's Party of Panama, the Socialist Workers Party, and the Popular Action Party.

The party law represented a balance between the government's need to demonstrate broad popular participation while maintaining political control. While the 1979 law inhibits the formation of small personal political groupings and party schisms, it is not the most prohibitive law in Panamanian history. Under the 1953 party law, all parties required 45,000 signatures for legal status, which only the Liberal Party and official National Patriotic Coalition achieved. The lax 1959 law, on the other hand, recognized political parties with only 5,000 signatures, with the result that legally registered parties increased from two to seventeen.

Party Organization

Panamanian political parties are primarily personalistic, nonideological parties providing electoral vehicles for ambitious politicians. The small communist Panamanian People's Party is a highly disciplined, cadre-type party, while the large official Democratic Revolutionary Party is a mass-based party with extensive grass-roots organization.

Structurally, party organizations are semi-institutionalized, decentralized, and ad hoc, especially on the regional and local levels. Parties are often unstable and transitory, some disappearing in nonelection years. On the national level, parties are elitist with strict recruitment policies and no more than several hundred activists. The party elite decides party policy and chooses candidates privately or at select conventions; there is little or no grass-roots influence on those decisions. Party leaders emerge through family networks, personal ambition, loyalty to older leaders, and charisma. Party unity is uncertain, maintained only as long as the party leader has patronage to distribute and no stronger personality emerges to challenge that leader's authority. The system favors the rise of dominant charismatic figures on the national level, but impedes the development of strong regional and local leadership.

On the local level, party organization has had limited impact. Elites of the traditional parties fear popular mobilization as a threat to their monopoly of politics, status, and wealth. An exception has been the mass mobilization of the Panameñista and Democratic Revolutionary parties. The Panameñista Party drew amorphous mass support because of its populist and ultranationalistic platform and only partially organized this support upward from the grass-roots. General Torrijos initiated extensive local and regional organization for the Democratic Revolutionary Party, based on left-of-center populism.

Campaigning

The 1984 campaign was the first since 1968. Largely a contest between the PRD's candidate, Nicolas Ardito Barletta, and the major opposition candidate, Arias, the campaign itself was quiet and peaceful. Ardito Barletta relied on sending campaign teams throughout Panama to mobilize support for his bid. Arias continued his traditional practice of holding mass rallies. All opposition candidates complained that they were unable to get the amount of media coverage accorded Ardito Barletta. The official party also continued to have the advantage of using government employees as campaign workers.

Independent Voters

In the past, party identification has been weak and ticket splitting common since voters chose individual candidates who often represented multiparty coalitions. In the 1984 elections, many voters chose to back one of the two leading presidential candidates, rather than "waste" their votes on the less viable candidate of their own party.

Broad Popular Front
(*Frente Amplio Popular;* Frampo)

History

More an interest group, perhaps, than a party, Frampo was founded in 1978 as a coalition of independent politicians and bureaucrats who supported the government but did not want to be directly associated with the official Democratic Revolutionary Party (PRD). It grew out of the Broad Front of Lawyers which had been established by the government to counteract the influence of a group of opposition lawyers. When the organization expanded to include other professionals, it was renamed Frampo.

Organization

The Front has only an informal organization. Most of its members are government employees and part of the network of bureaucratic relationships. That network is the core of Frampo's structure.

Policy

Party policy supports the government from a position slightly left of the PRD. It joined the Unade coalition in support of the PRD's presidential candidate in 1984. On the regional level, the party helped mobilize support for the Canal Treaties.

Membership & Constituency

Frampo has been called the "first middle-class party in Panama's history." It has an urban constituency and its members are white-collar professionals and civil servants. It registered over 36,000 members for the 1984 elections.

Financing

No information is available.

Leadership

Renato Pereira was head of the party in 1985.

Prospects

The party's future is contingent on the success and longevity of the PRD and the Torrijos-established coalition. Even with this support, the party has been an empty formality; it elected no delegates to the Legislative Assembly in 1984 and had its official status revoked for failing to get a legal minimum of votes.

Christian Democratic Party
(*Partido Demócrata Cristiano;* PDC)

History

The PDC was officially founded in 1960, emerging from student discussion groups at the National University during the late 1950s. The party ran José Antonio Molino in the 1964 presidential elections, and Antonio González Revilla, a distinguished neurosurgeon, in 1968. In 1984, the party leader ran for vice president in the ADO coalition, and the party won six seats in the Legislative Assembly.

Organization

The PDC is an official party. In 1980, it participated in the elections as a "party in formation." It was fully developed and registered by 1984.

Policy

Center to left-of-center, party policy calls for substantial social reforms and democratic participation based on a philosophy of Christian humanism and Catholic social doctrines. Excluded from the Torrijos coalition in 1968, the PDC offers a programmatic alternative to the government and spearheaded the united opposition to the PRD. With the Authentic Panameñistas, the PDC opposed the official candidacy of Ardito Barlette in 1984.

While the party supports private enterprise, it favors nationalization of basic services and has been active in labor organization. The party supported extension of full Panamanian sovereignty over the canal, but opposed the settlement as too slow and too limited. The Christian Democrats have criticized military involvement in politics and the regime's economic policies.

Membership & Constituency

The constituency base of the party is urban, and members are drawn from the middle and upper middle class of the academic and professional community. The PDC registered over 36,000 members for the 1984 elections, and received almost 47,000 votes for its presidential candidate.

Financing

No information is available.

Leadership

Ricardo Arias Calderón, is party leader. He is in his forties.

Prospects

The PDC has strong chances of growing and electing a presidential candidate within a multiparty coalition. Ricardo Arias Calderon is a strong opposition leader and has been suggested as a successor to Arnulfo Arias as the major opposition leader.

Democratic Revolutionary Party (*Partido Revolucionario Democrático; PRD*)

History

Between 1968 and 1979, before the founding of the Democratic Revolutionary Party, General Torrijos relied upon extraparty support organizations to mobilize the country on the regional level. Torrijos thus circumvented all traditional parties, except for the communist Panamanian People's Party which provided political support through its extensive union and peasant organizations. By the mid-1970s, the importance of the Panamanian People's Party began to decline and regional and local support organizations were linked directly to the government and ultimately to the official Democratic Revolutionary Party.

The PRD was founded by the government in 1978 to provide civilian political support for the policies and support groups of the Torrijos-Royo government.

The PRD presidential candidate in the 1984 elections, Nicolas Ardito Barletta, won by a slim margin. He encountered popular opposition to his economic reforms and FDN opposition to his plans to open an inquiry into the death of Hugo Spadafora, a leading critic of the military. He resigned in September 1985 and was succeeded by first vice president Eric Arturo del Valle of the Republican Party.

The PRD won thirty-four seats in the Legislative Assembly in 1984.

Organization

The PRD is a governing party whose organization overlaps government structures. With government machinery behind it, the PRD is easily the most organized and developed of Panamanian parties, reaching down to the grass-roots. The PRD does not monopolize politics but loosely controls opposition-party activity by its majority in the government and legislature. The party institutionalizes the heterogenous support groups of the coalitions of groups aligned with the government, especially the FDN, which is the real power behind the party. Secondary support organizations were developed by the party or incorporated into it for labor, peasants, white-collar professionals, public employees, the business sector, and youth and women's groups. In the tradition of a long line of official parties, the party and the government are closely interlinked through party organizations in all state ministries and autonomous agencies. A third of the party's 300 directors were selected by party leaders from party representatives to the Assembly to Corregimientos. Under the unifying influence of General Torrijos, intraparty disagreements were minimal.

Policy

The PRD declaration of principles affirms a nationalistic, revolutionary, anti-oligarchical, populist, and democratic program. The party recognizes the National Defense Forces as the "central actor" in national transformation. The party is independent of any foreign influences and favors a multiclass governing coalition. Party-supported policies have included agrarian, educational, and health reforms.

The PRD favored ratification of the Panama Canal treaties and a comfortable working relationship with the United States. Economically, the party protects socially responsible private enterprise while also supporting government intervention and the growth of the public sector. The party and the bureaucracy have spawned a class of *técnicos* (technocrats) who favor the economic policies of the private commercial elite who want to turn Panama and the canal into a free-trade zone and international banking center.

Internationally, Torrijos and the party followed a Third World, developmental foreign policy. This view has generated some intraparty opposition, especially to Torrijos's support of anti-Somoza forces in Nicaragua. Panama and the party have also favored normalization of relations with Cuba and have been diplomatically supportive of reformist and revolutionary groups in Central America. Party policy under Torrijos emphasized closer ties with the newly independent Caribbean ministates and regional Caribbean powers like Mexico and Venezuela. Under the PRD's rule, Panama became one of the four nations in the Contedera Group, which seeks a regional solution to the problems of Central America.

Membership & Constituency

The PRD is the largest Panamanian political party with over 500,000 registered members of all ages, both sexes, and varied class backgrounds. Party support is strong in the *mestizo* and Indian countryside as well as among the large bureaucratic "lower middle class" employed by the government and the semiautonomous public sector. The party has had to appease the banking community and the conservative opposition within its major interest group, the FDN.

Financing

No figures on PRD financing are available.

Leadership

In late 1985, party leadership underwent a major change. The party's five-member executive committee, led since 1981 by Berta Torrijos de Aorsemena (former President Torrijos' sister) resigned. Romulo Escobar Bethancourt, a lawyer and former minister under Torrijos, was elected the new executive secretary and party president. Former vice president Carlos Czores was elected the secretary general of the committee. The other new members were: Alfredo Macharaviaya, Ramiro Vazquez and Hirisnel Sucre. The new committee ranges from right to left ideologically. The new leaders hope to restore party unity which has been fragmented by the crucial need for new social and economic policies.

Prospects

The broad ideological spectrum of the party's right and left wings portends a breakup of its political coalition in the face of growing social and economic crises. The FDN appears to be undermining the authority of the ruling PRD. One political leader observed: "Torrijos was the unifying factor all around. . . . he kept the party alive, and he kept the guard united. Each group owed its loyalty to him, but they were distrustful of each other. He was the godfather figure, and without him things will unavoidably change."

National Liberal Party (*Partido Liberal Nacional;* PLN)

History

The Liberal Party is the oldest traditional Panamanian party with antecedents preceding independence in 1903. Liberals dominated the government off and on between 1912 and 1968, often in coalition with the Panameñistas, also an offshoot of Liberalism. In the 1930s, the party splintered into numerous personalistic factions which all appropriated the title "Liberal." The most enduring wing of the party was the one controlled by the Panamanian *caudillo,* Rodolfo E. Chiari, who was elected president in 1924. The Liberals took the name National Liberal Party in 1940. In the late 1940s, Chiari's son Roberto became the leader of the party. A reformist, technocratic wing of the party, led by David Samudio, developed in 1964 in response to Alliance for Progress pressures for reform and development. Allied with seven smaller parties in the National Opposition Union, the National Liberals ran Marcos Robles as their candidate for president against Arnulfo Arias in 1964. Endorsed by the army, Robles won amid opposition charges of fraud. The party was severely split in 1968 when President Robles and the National Guard endorsed reformist David Samudio for president. The election of Arnulfo Arias in alliance with Chiari's conservative wing of the PLN and Arias's immediate ouster by the National Guard, left both factions of the party on losing sides. In 1984, the PLN was a member of the victorious Unade coalition in support of PRD presidential candidate Nicolas Ardito Barletta, Roderick Lorenzo Esquivel, one of the PLN's own leaders, was elected second vice president of Panama. He became first vice president when Ardito Barletta resigned as president in September 1985. The PLN won one seat in the Legislative Assembly elected in 1984.

Organization

The PLN is one of the two principal pre-1968 parties. Until 1964 the Liberals were a relatively homogenous oligarchical party, repeatedly beset by personalistic schisms. The party had developed no mass organization and most of its decisions were made in the elite Union Club in Panama City, the gathering place for socially prominent politicians. Sharp policy differences superseded personal rivalries in 1964, as the views of the reformist wing were seen as a threat to the traditional party and Panamanian elites. When the party's convention in 1967 chose Samudio for its presidential candidate, Chiari led his faction out of the PLN and formed an alliance with Arnulfo Arias, who won the election with 55 percent of the vote and tepid support from the National Guard.

Party feuding declined when Torrijos banished the PLN to the political wilderness, but with the opening of the system in 1978, the Samudio wing sought to return to the stage through cooperation with the government. In the preceding decade, however, the reformist wing had been weakened by defections to the Torrijos camp and by growing opposition to the government within the PLN. As a result, Samudio was ousted as party leader in 1979 and replaced by the conservative Arnulfo Escalona Rios.

Policy

Although it does not have a clear-cut program, the party has traditionally supported *laissez-faire*, capitalist economics, championing the rights of the private sector. Politically, policy has been individualist and elitist, although in the 1920s Chiari expanded the party electoral base to the urban working class. Sectors of the party favored socioeconomic reforms and revision of the Panama Canal treaties in the 1960s. Under Samudio, the party strongly supported the treaties and the official electoral process. Under the new leadership of Arnulfo Escalona Rios, the party initially boycotted the 1980 elections, but ultimately participated. It became legally registered, with two minor factions remaining unreconciled to the new system.

Membership & Constituency

The PLN is an oligarchical party; core membership is in the urban commercial/business elite. However, like all Panamanian parties, the PLN is supported by a multiclass constituency. Because the Panamanian elite is urban based, the PLN is strongest in the areas of Panama City and Colón. The party registered 49,858 members for the 1984 elections and received 28,568 votes for its presidential ticket.

Traditionally, party support has drawn on urban business and the sugar and cattle barons of the interior. In the 1920s, Rodolfo Chiari, himself an Italian immigrant, expanded the clientele of the party to new immigrants working in railroad and canal construction, and to the predominantly black and mulatto urban working class. The party also cultivated the poor, conservative, and highly nationalistic, white and *mestizo* cattlemen and small rural farmers in the interior (even though these opposed the urban immigrant and "colored" workers). Until 1968, the National Guard was the major interest group allied with the Liberals.

Financing

Financial information on the PLN is unavailable, although given the wealth of its membership, the party undoubtedly has considerable resources.

Leadership

Arnulfo Escalona Rios is head of the majority conservative faction. David Samudio, in his mid-forties is leader of the reformist faction.

Prospects

In 1984, the Liberals reemerged in a ruling coalition with the PRD. Many *tecnico* planners of the Torrijos economic program were Liberals; the economic interests of the government and the business sector have often overlapped since 1978. There is also a long history of Liberal Party-FDN collaboration. At present, however, the party's viability appears to rest with its continued alliance with the PRD.

Panamanian People's Party
(*Partido del Pueblo de Panamá;* PPP or PdP)

History

The party was founded in 1930 as the Communist Party of Panama by a small group of left-wing intellectuals attracted to the ideas of the Spanish anarcho-syndicalist, José María Blasquez de Pedro, who had settled in Panama in the 1920s. In May 1950, the party was declared illegal by Arnulfo Arias's Decree Law 13. To increase its popularity among the workers and to shake an image of foreign influence, the present party name was adopted in 1953. The party achieved semipublic status and was the only traditional party allowed to operate after all political parties were banned in 1968.

Torrijos relied upon the PPP for civilian legitimacy and popular mobilization, but by 1978 had disassociated his governing coalition from the party. Nevertheless, the PPP continued to support *torrijista* policies. The party now operates publicly. The PPP was legally registered with the Electoral Commission in 1981. Carlos del Cid was PPP's presidential candidate in 1984.

Organization

The PPP is a small, well-disciplined, cadre party with extensive organization in labor unions and in peasant and student associations. Under Torrijos, the party controlled the unions (until 1978) and the organization of agricultural cooperatives. It was active in the Federation of Panamanian Students (FEP), the Reformist Front of Panamanian Educators (FREP), the National Federation of Democratic Women (FENAMUDE), and the National Committee for Defense of Sovereignty and Peace (CONADESOPAZ). In 1980 the party held its sixth congress, the first in twelve years.

Policy

The PPP supported government policies even after it was eased out of the Torrijos coalition between 1974 and 1978. The party approved the Panama Canal treaties and official electoral and economic policies. The sixth-congress party platform praised the revolutionary process initiated by the National Guard, and proposed an economic system that would balance government, private, and social sectors of the economy. The PPP upheld the unpopular 1978 Torrijos labor Law Number 95, which weakened the party's labor base. In foreign relations, the party supported improved relations with Cuba and Panama's diplomatic and military assistance to the Sandinistas in Nicaragua. While a Moscow-line party, the core PPP leadership determines internal party policy independently.

Membership & Constituency

The PPP registered 34,990 members before the 1984 elections. Its constituency centers on urban intellectuals, students, and workers.

Financing

No information is available.

Leadership

Secretary general of the PPP is Rubén Dario Sousa.

Prospects

PPP prospects have dimmed since 1978. The PPP belongs to neither progovernment nor opposition party coalitions. Much of the party's earlier success—such as the election of about half of its 120 candidates to the National Assembly in 1972—was the result of Torrijos's patronage and the exclusion of the other traditional parties. In fact, since it received under 5,000 presidential votes in 1984, its official party status was revoked. However, some party members are encouraged, as a result of their success in registration, to believe that they may yet be able to regain some political leverage.

Authentic Panameñista Party
(*Partido Panameñista Autentico;* PPA)

History

The Panameñista Party is the party of the Arias brothers, Harmodio and Arnulfo, who formed the first populist mass party in Panamanian history in the 1930s. Prior to the 1984 elections, the PPA was called the Panameñista Party. That name has been retained by a former faction of the party. The party grew out of a group of urban professionals, engineers, lawyers, physicians, and bureaucrats who founded Community Action in 1923. The group represented a backlash against the expansion of Antillean blacks, the U.S. labor force in the Canal Zone, into the economy, and the threat of these foreign elements to the traditional Hispanic culture. Arnulfo Arias joined Community Action in 1930. His brother, Harmodio Arias, became president in 1932 at the head of his new political party, the Doctrinaire Liberal Party, which represented a mixture of liberalism and the racism and nationalism of Community Action. By 1940 Arnulfo Arias had created, as a new embodiment of Community Action, the National Revolutionary Party, later to become the Panameñista Party, and was elected president for the first time with a vote of 107,750 to 3,022. Through the Panameñista Party, Arnulfo Arias not only became president again in 1949 and 1968, but came to command a group of loyalists, the *arnulfistas*, whose support made Arias more independent of National Guard and U.S. influences than previous Panamanian presidents. In 1984, Arias lost the presidential race by only 1,713 votes. He and other opposition members charged the FDN with intervening in the vote-counting procedure to deprive him of victory.

Organization

The Panameñista Party, as one of the two major pre-1968 parties, is an important mass-based party, perhaps the most powerful within the ADO opposition coalition. Other Panamanian political groups have sought alliances with the PPA to tap its national mass appeal. Since Arnulfo Arias, known on the street as "El Hombre" or "The Man," runs the party, there are no severe intraparty disputes. However, because of its extreme personalism, the party has not developed an institutional structure to parallel its grass-roots appeal.

Policy

The philosophy of the PPA is nationalistic, right of center, and racist. Opponents have labelled the party demogogic and fascist. The party has represented populist policies since the 1940s when it passed agrarian reform and social security legislation. Arias espoused this populist program to associate his party with the

aspirations and animosities of the common people. In that way, it can be compared to Peronism in Argentina. The highly ideological program of Panameñismo has been described as "government by Panamanians for the happiness of the Panamanian people."

Under Arias, the Spanish language was zealously protected from Anglicanization, and the properties of all non-Hispanic racial and cultural groups (blacks and Asians) were confiscated. The Panameñistas often made pacts with other political parties and were allied with the Liberals each time Arias was elected president. When in power, however, Arias and the PP moved to curb the influence of the National Guard. Party economic policy is ill-defined, but not necessarily antagonistic to the private sector. The thrust of the Panameñista position was characterized by the 1941 constitution, promulgated by Arias, which legitimized an interventionist role for the government in the economy. The constitution affirmed the "social function" of private property and government arbitration of labor disputes.

Arias, who had long sought better leasing arrangements for U.S. military bases and whose movement epitomized "anti-Yankeeism," viewed the Torrijos Canal treaties as "giveaways." The Panameñistas also opposed the constitutional arrangements established by Torrijos after 1978 and boycotted the 1980 elections as a "sham."

Membership & Constituency

The Panameñista Party was once the largest single party in the country. It registered over 46,000 signatures before 1984. In the 1984 elections Arias received 299,035 votes.

The PPA claims a multiclass constituency once described as "the alliance of fascist oligarchs" with a growing nationalistic middle class. Arias himself was from a poor cattle-ranching family in the interior, but his Harvard education and charisma drew him into the oligarchy and the select Union Club. His electoral coalition reflected his own diverse background, combining three traditional political groups—the urban working class, rural small holder cattlemen, and the Liberal commercial-business elite. Panameñista strength is the urban, *mestizo,* unskilled and skilled laborers of Colón and Panama City, who feared the economic inroads of the Antillean blacks in the 1940s and 1950s and remained loyal when that threat passed.

Rural strongholds are the provinces of Chiriquí, Coclé, and Veraguas. The major interest groups that have opposed the Panameñistas include the PRD coalition and the National Guard (now the FDN) which has overthrown Arias, governments three times (1941, 1951, and 1968).

Financing

No information on party financing is available.

Leadership

The sole leader of the party since its founding has been Arnulfo Arias Madrid (born 1901 in Penonomé).

Prospects

Arias is an old man and his highly personal party will probably decline with him, particularly since the issues which the Panameñistas addressed in the 1940s and 1950s are no longer relevant. The support he received in the 1984 elections may be divided among several opposition leaders in the future.

Minor Parties

The following parties make up the balance of the fourteen parties that participated in the 1984 elections. Four of them sponsored their own candidates in the presidential election. The others were members of one or the other of the two major coalitions, ADO and Unade.

Labor Party (*Partido Laborista*; Pala)

Pala is a center-right party formed in 1983. It first supported the candidacy of General Reuben Dario Paredes for the 1984 elections, but switched to Nicolas Ardito Barletta when he replaced Paredes as the PRD candidate. A member of Unade, it received 45,384 votes in the May 6 election and won seven seats in the Legislative Assembly. It is led by Carlos Eleta Almaran.

Liberal Republican and Nationalist Movement (*Movimiento Liberal Republicano Nacionalista*; Molirena)

Molirena, a conservative group, is part of the ADO group. It registered over 50,000 signatures and received 30,737 votes in the May elections. Molirena won three seats in the legislature.

National People's Party (*Partido Nacionalista Popular*; PNP)

General Reuben Dario Paredes, former head of the National Guard, formed the PNP in 1983 to support his presidential candidacy after resigning as the PRD's candidate. Paredes came in third in the election, with only 15,976 votes. The PNP won no legislative seats, and its status was revoked.

Panameñista Party (*Partido Panameñista*; PP)

The current PP is a faction of the original party of that name. In 1984, it opposed its founder Arias and joined the government coalition Unade. It registered over 40,000 signatures; but because it garnered only 11,579 votes and no legislative seats, its status was revoked. It is led by Luis Suarez and Alonzo Pinzon.

Popular Action Party (*Partido de Accion Popular*; Papo)

The Papo is a small group of middle-class, urban professionals with a program of social democracy. It ran its own presidential candidate in 1984, Carlos Ivan Zuniga, who proposed the creation of a new constituent assembly. Papo registered over 34,000 signatures and 13,782 votes, but no legislative seats. It was officially revoked as a party.

Republican Party (*Partido Republicano*; PR)

The PR has a middle-class membership of white and Antillean immigrants and *mestizo* workers in the interior. In 1984, the PR's vice presidential candidate Eric Arturo del Valle was elected on Nicolas Ardito Barletta's winning ticket. The PR received 34,215 votes and also won three legislative seats. Del Valle became president of Panama when Ardito Barletta resigned in 1985, increasing the importance of the PR, the smallest member of Unade.

Socialist Workers Party (*Partido Socialista de los Trabajadores*; PST)

Founded in 1933 as the Socialist Party and excluded from political participation in 1953, the party reemerged in 1961 with a small student and university clientele. The PST was highly critical of the government and the Torrijos-People's Party alliance. It ran Ricardo Barria for president in 1984, but won only 2,085 votes. Its official status was revoked.

Workers Revolutionary Party (*Partido Revolucionario de los Trabajadores*; PRT)

This leftist party joined with several trade union organizations in a coalition called the United People's Electoral Front (*Frente Electoral del Pueblo Unidos*; Frepu) for the 1984 campaign. The party's president is Graciela Dixon. It ran Renan Esquival for president in 1984, but he won only 3,969 votes; so the party's official status was revoked.

Socialist Workers Party (*Partido Socialista de los Trabajadores*; PST)

Founded in 1933 as the Socialist Party and excluded from political participation in 1953, the party reemerged in 1961 with a small student and university clientele. The PST was highly critical of the government and the Torrijos-People's Party alliance.

Other Political Forces

The National Defense Forces (FDN)

The National Defense Forces, formerly the National Guard (*Policía Nacional*), a combined military and police force of 10,000 men, has been the most important political factor in Panamanian politics since 1951. Although the Guard formally returned to the barracks in October 1978, when Torrijos, its commander, retired as supreme leader in favor of the civilian president Artistides Royo, the political future of Panama remained within its hands. This was demonstrated in mid-1982, when it appar-

ently forced Royo out and promoted the vice president and again in 1984 and 1985 when it apparently forced out presidents Ricardo de la Espriella and Nicolas Ardito Barletta and promoted their vice presidents.

The history of the Guard is part of the history of U.S. policy and interventions in Panama. As in the rest of Central America, the United States substituted a national police force for a traditional military. It was intended to be an apolitical instrument of law and order under U.S. control. Between 1904 and 1915 Guard forces fluctuated between 700 and 1,150 men and were directly subject to the United States. Repressed nationalism seethed within its ranks and became highly politicized after 1931. When Harmodio Arias became president in 1932, he appointed José Antonio Remón Cantera to command the Guard. Remón forged the independence of the Guard from direct U.S. influence and made it his personal political instrument from 1940 until his assassination on January 2, 1955. Remón literally made and unmade presidents and had himself elected in 1952.

The Guard's most spectacular involvement in politics was the coup of October 11–12, 1968. President Arias, in one of his first acts, forcibly retired the Guard's second-in-command, Colonel José Manuel Pinilla Fábrega, soon after the voluntary retirement of the commander, General Vallarino, who with the Chiari Liberals reluctantly had supported Arias. The Guard leadership felt its independence was threatened and intervened. A provisional junta, led by Colonel José María Pinilla and Colonel Bolívar Urrutia Parilla, was created, but the real power behind the takeover was the Guard commander, Colonel Omar Torrijos Herrera, and Colonel Borís N. Martínez, chief of staff.

To establish control, the Guard battled with urban students and peasants in Chiriquí province, arresting and exiling hundreds of politicians. The National University was closed, political parties banned, and the media censored. Intra-Guard rivalries and opposition to the leftist drift of the junta led to the exile of the more radical Martínez in February 1969, and the replacement of Urrutia and Pinilla after a thwarted centrist countercoup against Torrijos in December 1969.

The character of the Guard is reflected in the middle-class origins of its two dominant leaders—Remón and Torrijos. Both were career officers with a social-reformist tendency. Remón, despite roots in the Panamanian upper class, came from a relatively poor family. When appointed commandant of the Guard, Remón was the only professionally trained officer. His policies in the early 1950s foreshadowed the populist Torrijos alliance of the Guard and the common people against the oligarchy, although many of Remón's policies (again foreshadowing Torrijos) benefitted big commercial-business interests.

Torrijos, whose father was a school teacher, won a scholarship to the Military Academy in El Salvador from 1947 to 1952, when he joined the Guard. He received special counterinsurgency and civic-action training. With Martínez, his major rival, he recognized the command structure of the Guard in 1968.

The officer corps of the Guard is predominantly middle class; recruited from rural areas; and, with the rank and file, represents an ethnically mixed and integrated force. Professional training was initiated under President Harmodio Arias. By the early 1970s the Guard counted some 500 officers, many with academy training and respect for military professionalism. Academy training has affected the ideological orientation of the officer corps. Before 1968 most officers attended conservative Central American academies in Nicaragua and El Salvador; after 1968 many were trained in Mexico, Venezuela, and especially Peru. Those officers trained after 1968 acquired a social-reformist view. The conservative, Central American-trained leadership is often at odds with the reformist-Peruvian group. More recent academy graduates were trained in Brazil, Chile, Argentina, and Uruguay. Broader-based training may increase professionalism, but it could also intensify ideological and generational cleavages within the Guard.

The Guard under Torrijos moved to increase its independence and legitimacy as the nation's ruler. Under the 1972 constitution the Guard's political role is explicitly recognized and legitimized. The president of the republic was denied the role of commander-in-chief with the right to appoint and remove officers. As an outgrowth of the Peruvian experience, the National School for Political Capacitation (ESCANAP) was established in 1974 to bring officers and civilian leaders into dialogue and cooperation.

There have been human-rights abuses in the consolidation of power, and the disappearance of Father Héctor Gallego in 1971 antagonized the Catholic Church and undermined the Guard's legitimacy. The Guard's image also clashes with the traditional involvement of officers in bribery, prostitution, and drug trafficking. The appeal the Guard has had for poorer urban and rural groups might be undermined by this darker side.

After Torrijos's death, the new commander was Colonel Florencio Flórez Aguilar. In March 1982, Colonel Rubén Darío Paredes, chief of staff under Flórez, ousted his boss. Flórez had been seen as loyal to the Torrijos political system and had publicized his political neutrality.

Paredes had more active political aspirations and was seen as a greater threat to civilian rule and the PRD. Paredes was assisted in his coup by Colonel Manuel Antonio Noriega, the second most important man under Torrijos and deputy chief of general staff and head of the intelligence and security services, and by Colonel Armando Contreras, new chief of the general staff. President Royo approved these command changes, officially because Flórez's twenty-five years of active service had expired. However, by this same rule, Paredes was due to retire in September 1982.

After a brief extension of his term Paredes retired to run for president in the elections of 1984. Noriega succeeded him as commander. Paredes was originally the candidate of the PRD but resigned, apparently under pressure, and ran as the candidate of the PNP. He won only 15,976 votes. The FDN backed the PRD candidate.

Students

Students were a vocal and dangerous political force before the 1968 coup and demonstrated their disruptive power in the 1964 Canal Zone riots. Under Torrijos, the student movement was carefully repressed, controlled, or co-opted in the communist-led Panamanian Federation of Students (*Federación de Estudiantes Panameños;* FEP). Student opposition through the newly organized Federation of Revolutionary Students (*Federación de Estudiantes Revolucionarios;* FER) could reassert a political role for students, especially if political interference and repression by their historic enemy, the FDN intensifies. Students have participated in the rallies and strikes called in opposition to the government's economic policies since 1985.

Organized Labor

Prior to 1985 labor activity had been marginal because of the fragmentation of the workers' movement into a moderate, progovernment union, the National Workers' Central (*Central Nacionál de Trabajadores de Panamá;* CNTP); a conservative union with close ties to the United States' American Federation of Labor, the Confederation of Workers (*Confederación de Trabajaderos de la Republica de Panamá;* CTRP); the Marxist-dominated Trade Union Federation of Workers (*Federación Sindical de Trabajadores de la Republica de Panamá;* FSTRP); and several smaller unions. The CTRP was, for years, the officially sponsored union and was dominated by the Canal Zone workers. With some 24,000 members it probably is still the most powerful union. Its U.S. ties, however, caused Torrijos to support the CNTP, which was led by the People's Party. The CNTP counted some 22,000 members in 1978, when Law Number 95 weakened the PPP's hold on the organization. Over 15,000 banana workers from the nationalized United Brands plantations were incorporated into the CNTP. Integration of these labor forces, especially the elite, well-paid Canal Zone workers, has posed political difficulty for the government if the labor movement had continued to develop its independence. Since 1985, it has sponsored broadly supported strikes and other actions in opposition to the PRD's proposed reforms of the labor code and other economic measures.

Peasantry

Until Torrijos came to power, the peasantry had no role in politics and little awareness of that elite process. The Torrijos policy of building local and regional organizations to support his regime, however, was quickly extended into the countryside. In 1970, peasants and subsistence farmers on collective farms and cooperatives (*asentamientos*) were organized in the National Confederation of Peasant Cooperatives (*Confederación Nacional de Asentamientos Campesinos;* CONAC). Through CONAC's pyramidal structure of local, regional, and national bodies, peasants gained a voice in national policymaking for the first time in Panamanian history. Twenty peasant cooperative leaders were elected to the National Assembly in 1972. In spite of the fact that the cooperative movement is relatively small, peasants constitute at least one-third of Panama's population, and the appearance of any peasant group on the national stage is likely to have long-term consequences for political alignments and policy.

National Prospects

The Panamanian political system has experienced extensive changes since 1968, most impelled by the one-man rule of General Omar Torrijos. The regime faces great potential political instability both internally and within the Central American region. The FDN expected to make the transformation from police force to a regular army with responsibility for national defense is still on center stage in the political arena. Labor will probably no longer be divided into an isolated enclave of elite workers and others, and the issue of Canal sovereignty will no longer provide a unifying issue to rouse and appease the masses. Panama faces the immense problem of institutionalizing a civilian and democratic system amid poverty, rising expectations, and high political mobilization with sharp policy divisions. The country is grappling with the dilemmas of growth and economic development in a highly competitive and dependent economy, and with a high external debt which requires tough austerity measures, and their high social and political cost, for its renegotiation.

Further Reading

Austin, Lora, ed. *Panama Election Factbook: May 12, 1968.* Washington, D.C.: Institute for the Comparative Study of Political Systems, 1968.

Brown, Esmeralda, et al. "Panama: For Whom the Canal Tolls." *NACLA Report on the Americas,* Vol. 13, No. 5, September-October 1979.

Goldrich, Daniel. *Sons of the Establishment: Elite Youth in Panama and Costa Rica.* Chicago: Rand McNally, 1966.

Jorden, William J. *Panama Odyssey: From Colony to Partner.* Austin: University of Texas Press, 1983.

LeFeber, Walter. *The Panama Canal: The Crisis in Historical Perspective.* New York: McGraw-Hill, 1979.

Nyrop, Richard F., ed. *Panama: A Country Study.* Washington, D.C.: U.S. Government Printing Office, 1981.

Pippin, Larry LaRue. *The Remón Era: An Analysis of a Decade Of Events in Panama, 1947–57.* Stanford: Stanford University Press, 1964.

Priestley, George. *Military Government and Popular Participation in Panama: The Torrijos Regime, 1968-1975.* Boulder, Colorado: Westview Press, Inc. 1986.

Ropp, Steve C. *Panamanian Politics, From Guarded Nation to National Guard.* Stanford Calif.: Hoover Institution Press and Stanford University Press, 1982; and New York Praeger Publishers, 1982.

Weil, Thomas, et al. *Area Handbook for Panama.* Washington, D.C.: U.S. Government Printing Office, for Foreign Area Studies, American University, 1972.

PAPUA NEW GUINEA

by George E. Delury revised by Bruce Dickson, M.A.

The System of Government

Papua New Guinea, a nation of some three million people on the eastern half of the island of New Guinea and the Bismark Archipelago in the southwest Pacific Ocean, is a parliamentary democracy. Formerly under Australian administration, it became self-governing in December 1973 and achieved full independence on September 16, 1975. Rugged mountains divide the country into small regions in which about 800 different languages and dialects are spoken. As much as 60 percent of the population is illiterate. The area has no previous history of centralized government.

Executive

The British monarch is titular head of state and is represented by a governor general, who must be a Papua New Guinea citizen, appointed on the advice of the prime minister and the approval of the Parliament. The head of government and primary political power in the country is the prime minister, who is the leader of the majority party or coalition in Parliament. He is assisted by a cabinet which he selects from among the members of Parliament.

Legislature

The unicameral House of Assembly has 109 members who are popularly elected for five-year terms. Twenty members are elected at large from each of the nation's nineteen provinces and the National Capital District, while the other eighty-nine represent smaller single-member districts whose boundaries cut across provincial lines. Three additional Assembly members may be elected by a two-thirds vote in the Parliament, but these additional seats have never been filled. The Parliament must approve all legislation and may oust the prime minister on a vote of no-confidence without forcing new elections. The prime minister may request the governor general to dissolve parliament and call new elections.

In the June 1982 elections, the *Pangu Pati* (*Papua New Guinea* Party) won forty-seven seats and, in coalition with the United Party (ten seats) and nine independents, formed a government which returned former prime minister Michael Somare to that office. The new legislature was marked by an increase in the number of members of European ancestry and of well-trained former bureaucrats.

Judiciary

The Supreme Court is the highest court in the land and is the court of first instance in matters requiring interpretation of the constitution. The chief justice is appointed (and may be removed) by the governor general on the advice of the prime minister. Other judges are nominated by a special commission.

Regional & Local Government

The nation is divided into nineteen provinces administered by commissioners appointed by the central government. Amendments to the constitution, however, permit the provinces to establish provincial assemblies and provincial governments responsible to those assemblies with the commissioners' roles reduced to the merely ceremonial. Largely because of the geographical and ethnic diversity of the country and real dangers of secession, the central government has granted provincial politicians considerable power and influence, including control of substantial sums of government money and responsibility for most local and provincial services. In 1983, however, the national Parliament approved a constitutional amendment granting the National Executive Council (Cabinet) authority to suspend provincial governments without parliamentary approval. Port Moresby, the capital, and other cities have elected municipal governments, but the National Capital District, including Port Moresby, remains under direct central government control.

The Electoral System

Candidates for Parliament are elected by simple majority. Since a large number of candidates run for each seat, many are elected with much less than a majority of votes. In the 1982 elections, when over 1,000 candidates ran for the 109 seats, sixty-two won with less than 30 percent of their districts' votes, and one candidate won with less than 8 percent of the vote.

Citizens eighteen years of age and over are eligible to vote. Because of the ruggedness of the country and remoteness of much of the population, the election process takes three weeks. In some cases, voters must walk considerable distances to the nearest voting station; in others, election officials tour the villages to take the votes, which are then sealed in ballot boxes and dispatched to the nearest provincial center. Voting is by secret ballot, but because most of the population is illiterate, election officials are allowed to mark ballots according to the "whispered votes" given them by the voters.

The population takes elections seriously (over 66 percent of eligible voters turned out in the 1977 elections) and there are frequent allegations of electoral fraud, involving improper recording of "whispered votes," destruction of ballots, and tampering with sealed ballot boxes. In the three Highlands provinces, the most remote and politically competitive region, election officials have been assaulted by supporters of unsuccessful candidates.

The Party System

Most of the parties were first formed to contest the 1972 elections, but parties in a Western European sense hardly exist in Papua New Guinea. While there are many parties (seven won seats in the 1982 elections), there are no mass memberships, no national conferences, and no formal procedures for selecting leaders. Many candidates run for office without party affiliation and join a party's parliamentary bloc only after they are elected. Other candidates run under one party's banner and join a different bloc after the election, especially if that bloc can help pay off the candidates' campaign expenses. There are few apparent ideological differences between the parties, and electoral success depends very little on a candidate's policies on the issues. Charisma, status in the community, and a readiness to distribute the wealth that is expected to come from office holding determine victory. Local interests and clan connections are of primary importance. Voters are very demanding; in 1977, less than 40 percent of incumbents who sought reelection were successful. Similar results were reported after the 1982 elections.

Campaigners attempt to influence voters by gifts of cash, pigs, and other valuables, including the provision of local services. Because such services are now largely controlled by provincial governments, members of Parliament have had to develop new government programs to provide them with funds to distribute on the local level.

Pangu Pati
(Papua New Guinea Party)

This urban-based party was founded by Michael Somare (born 1936), who was prime minister from 1975 to 1980, when he was ousted in a vote of no-confidence after a government corruption scandal. He was again prime minister from 1982 until late 1985. The *Pangu Pati* claims the only real party organization, with sixty-five party branches throughout the country. Most of these branches probably operate only during campaigns. Somare stated that the party spent over $700,000 on the party's 1982 campaign, which won forty-seven seats, an increase of sixteen over the 1977 result. In addition, a number of "pro-Pangu" and "pro-Somare" candidates also won. The party draws its major strength from the provinces of Morobe and East and West Sepik.

United Party

This party has its strength in the Highlands provinces, East and West Britain, Madang, and in the Gulf, the home of one of its leaders, Roy Evara. It won only ten seats in the 1982 elections, down from thirty in 1977, but joined with the *Pangu Pati* in Somare's coalition government. Another major leader of the party is Raphael Doa.

National Party

The highlands-based National Party was founded by Iambakey Okuk in 1980 when he broke with the United Party following Somare's ouster as prime minister. Okuk is regarded as one of the most capable political leaders in the country, but he was nevertheless defeated by a *Pangu Pati* candidate in his bid for reelection in 1982. His party won twelve seats and the leadership was taken over by retired Brigadier General Ted Diro. Diro had led a new organization called the Independents' Group during the campaign; the Group won eight seats, primarily in Papua (the southern third of the country). Diro brought the Group into the National Party to give it a total of twenty seats in Parliament. Okuk returned to Parliament after the 1983 by-elections and reclaimed his party's leadership.

People's Progress Party (PPP)

The PPP leader, Julius Chan (born 1939), and Michael Somare had worked together in the government coalition from pre-independence days until Somare's ouster in 1980, whereupon Chan became prime minister. The party is based in the islands north of New Guinea—New Ireland, New Britain, and the North Solomons. It won eighteen seats in 1977, but fell to only ten in 1982.

Papua Besana

Originally founded in the early 1970s as a seccessionist group, this party had two parliamentary seats going into the 1977 election and emerged with six. The increasing autonomy of provincial governments, however, undercut the party's primary program and it was again reduced to two seats in 1982, losing heavily to the Independents' Group. The party's leader and founder, Josephine Abaijah, was not reelected.

Alliance for Progress and Regional Development (APRD)

Commonly known as the Melanesian Alliance, this party was founded in the aftermath of a seccessionist movement in the North Solomon Islands just prior to independence. Based in Bougainville, the center of the country's copper-extraction industry, the movement was led by Father John Momis, who founded and still leads the Alliance. The movement reached an agreement with the government in 1976.

The Alliance fought the 1977 elections and participated in both the Somare government which immediately followed and the Chan government, in which Momis was decentralization minister. It won eight seats in 1982.

The Alliance appears to be the most ideological of the parties, calling for liberation from foreign economic domination. It has not advocated nationalization of foreign interests, but it has emphasized the need for local participation in the development and management of industry. Party adherents appear to be of two types: well-educated professionals and workers in the copper industry and on the docks.

Other Political Forces

The western half of New Guinea island is the Indonesian territory of Irian Jaya. The border artificially divides clan groups and groups which have traditionally made small-scale raids on one another. The Papua New Guinea government has frequently charged Indonesian troops with border violations, but it seeks to improve relations between the two countries and put an end to conflict along the border. It is hindered in this effort by the Free Papua Movement (*Operasi Papua Merdeka*) which has been accused of cross-border raids and the murder and kidnapping of Indonesian citizens near the border. The government has made moves to ban the Movement, but has apparently been stymied by increasing support for it among politicians, academics, and students who dispute Indonesia's claim to Irian Jaya.

National Prospects

Papua New Guinea faces a critical period. The world economic recession has seen a fall in prices for nearly all the country's export commodities—tea, coffee, copra, copper, and timber—and fluctuating prices for its gold. Cutbacks in government employment and in the construction of vitally needed roads and other infrastructure create the potential for unrest among the urban elite and further parochial divisions among the many different groups in the country. Australia provides nearly 30 percent of the nations's annual budget, although the level of aid has been dropping slightly in real terms since 1983. In short, the full range of the problems of independence are just beginning to be felt in the country with the inevitable disappointment of the expectations of a majority of the people. Somare has a strong mandate to govern the country, but whether his charisma and his real abilities as an administrator can ride out the economic crisis remains an open question.

Further Reading

Ballard, J. A., ed. *Policy Making in a New State: Papua New Guinea.* Queensland, University of Queensland Press, 1981.

Fenbury, D. M. *Practice Without Policy: Genesis of Local Government in Papua New Guinea.* Canberra, Australian National University Press, 1979.

Fitzpatrick, Peter. *Law and State in Papua New Guinea* Orlando, Fl.: Academic Press, 1981.

Griffin, James. *Papua New Guinea: A Political History.* Portsmouth, N. H. Heinemann Educational Books, 1980.

Sinclair, James. *Uniting a Nation.* Melbourne, Oxford University Press, 1984.

Woolford, Donald M. *Papua New Guinea: Initiation and Independence.* Englewood Cliffs, N. J.: Prentice-Hall, for University of Queensland, 1976.

PARAGUAY

by Diego Abente, M.A. revised by John Williams, Ph.D.

The System of Government

Paraguay is a presidentialist republic and a unitary state, independent from Spain since May 14, 1811. The history of the Paraguayan political system can be divided into three main periods. The first (1811–70) was characterized by a very rudimentary legal and constitutional system and highly restricted political activity. The second period (1870–1954) was marked by the liberal constitution of 1870, extreme political instability, and the constitution of 1940, a turning point which led back to authoritarianism. The third period, 1954 to date, is characterized by the authoritarian regime of General Alfredo Stroessner, who has presided over the longest-lived dictatorship in the history of Paraguay and one of the longest in world history. In 1967 a new constitution was approved, and in 1977 it was amended to allow the president to run for office beyond the two five-year periods established in the original constitution.

Executive

Executive power rests with the president of the republic, who is head of state and government and commander-in-chief of the armed forces. The president participates in the formation of laws and the preparation of the national budget; is in charge of foreign relations; has the power to appoint and dismiss the members of his cabinet; and designates the members of the Supreme Court (with the agreement of the Senate), the state general prosecutor (with the agreement of the Council of State), and judges (with the agreement of the Supreme Court). The president can veto any law passed by Congress; can dissolve Congress (calling for new elections within three months); and has the authority to dictate decree-laws while the Congress is in recess (December 21 to April 1), although he has to submit them for approval within sixty days of the first meeting day of Congress. The president is not subject to impeachment, and he can decree a state of siege that allows him to detain persons without any legal procedure and forbid meetings and public demonstrations. He has only to notify Congress that such an exceptional measure has been taken.

The president thus holds a vast amount of power. This legal power is increased even more, in practice, by the high degree of formalism of the Paraguayan system. For example, in 1978 Stroessner was supposed to submit the list of members of the Supreme Court to the Senate for confirmation. He delayed doing this, however, for almost a year, leaving the country with a Supreme Court that was illegal, for it sat much beyond its legally established time period. In spite of that, neither Congress nor the Supreme Court did anything to pressure the president to abide by the law. Besides, the country has been living under a state of siege, since the 1954 coup that brought General Stroessner to power.

The Council of State is a consultative body made up of eleven members plus all cabinet ministers. It was established to advise the president, particularly in issuing decree-laws. All members but one, the Catholic archbishop of Asunción (the capital city) are directly or indirectly named by the president. In practice, the Council of State has become a largely decorative body that is maintained by the president as a spare political weapon to be used should difficulties arise in his relations with Congress. Since it is given a semilegislative character, it performs the role of legitimizing the rule of the president. In fact—particularly in the 1960s—the Council has been used extensively to diminish the role of Congress and enhance the power of the president, who rules by systematically enacting laws through the decree-law procedure.

In 1958 General Stroessner faced his first presidential election. He ran and won without any opposing candidate. In February 1963, a new election was held, and he won against a co-op candidate, Enrique Gavilán, from the Liberal Party (PL). A co-op candidate does not represent or offer any real opposition to the government and is, either directly or indirectly, "bought" by the government to be presented as "proof" that opposition to the government is legally recognized. In February 1968, after a new constitution was approved to permit Stroessner to run for office beyond the two periods allowed by the 1940 constitution, he won against three opposing candidates: Gustavo Gonzalez of the Liberal Radical Party (PLR); Carlos Caballero Gatti of the Revolutionary Febrerist Party (PRF); and Carlos Levi Ruffinelli of the PL. In February 1973, he won against two opposing candidates, Gustavo Riart and Carlos Levi Ruffinelli, of the PLR and PL, respectively. In February 1978, after the 1967 constitution was amended again, he won against two co-op candidates, Germán Acosta Caballero and Fulvio H. Celauro, who represented, after a complex splintering process, the minority of the original Liberal and Liberal Radical parties. In 1983, with most parties boycotting the election, only the PLR (Dr. Enzo Doldán) and PL (Hugo Fulvio Celauro), participated with the Colorados. Respectively they won 5.7 percent and 3.2 percent of the vote. This gave them a total of 20 seats in the Chamber and 10 in the Senate.

RESULTS OF THE PRESIDENTIAL ELECTIONS FEBRUARY 12, 1978 and FEBRUARY 10, 1983

	Feb. 12, 1978	Feb. 10, 1983
Eligible voters	1,175,381	N.A.
Turnout	992,817	N.A.
Abstention	169,729	N.A.
Colorado Party	900,774	909,450
Liberal Radical Party	54,984	56,588
Liberal Party	37,059	32,336
Nullified ballots	12,795	N.A.

Legislature

The legislature is composed of two chambers, the Senate and the Chamber of Deputies, with thirty and sixty members, respectively. Both chambers usually meet for an average of two hours per week. Each chamber has a president and two vice presidents, all of them belonging to the majority party. Both chambers have specialized committees, but it is really on the floor where major debates take place.

The Senate is accorded the right to pass laws regarding the approval of international treaties, national defense, and expropriations. The Chamber of Deputies approves banking, taxing, and monetary laws, as well as the annual budget submitted by the president.

The only real power that Congress has vis-à-vis the president is the right to override a presidential veto with the vote of two-thirds of both chambers. However, the president can dissolve Congress and call new elections within three months; or, if the dissolution occurs in the last year of his term, he can govern without Congress until the next general elections are held.

Judiciary

The highest court is the Supreme Court of Justice composed of five members appointed by the president with the agreement of the Senate for a five-year period, coinciding with the presidential and congressional period. Its political role is extremely restricted, and in practice the Court confines itself to strictly nonpolitical matters.

DISTRIBUTION OF SEATS IN THE SENATE AND CHAMBER OF DEPUTIES (1978–85)

	Senate Seats	Chamber Seats
Colorado Party	20	40
Liberal Radical Party	6	12
Liberal Party	4	8
Total	30	60

Regional & Local Government

The country is composed of nineteen political units called departments (departamentos). Each departamento is ruled by an official appointed by the Ministry of Interior, whose title is delegado de gobierno (government's delegate). Their actions are largely oriented toward political and police matters.

Administrative matters rest with a smaller unit, the municipality. Each municipality is ruled by an intendente (mayor) appointed by the Ministry of Interior and by a city council (concejo municipal) elected by popular vote. The president can "intervene" in a municipality, i.e., he may take over its administrative functions, dismiss its mayor and councilmen, and call new elections within sixty days.

The Electoral System

The president, congressmen, and councilmen are elected through direct election every five years. In both Congress and city councils, the winning party gets two-thirds of the contested seats; the remaining are distributed among the other parties through a proportional representation procedure.

In the congressional elections, the country as a whole is considered a single electoral district. In the presidential contest, plurality of votes is enough for a candidate to get elected. The vote is secret, and there is one ballot for each list of candidates. The vote is for a list, or a slate, not for individual candidates, except in the case of the presidential election, in which a single name constitutes a party list.

All eligible voters are required to register for election, usually one year before elections take place. They are given a document (*libreta electoral*), without which they cannot vote, and in which a seal is stamped after voting.

Voting is obligatory for citizens between eighteen and sixty years of age. Legal sanctions against those who do not vote, normally a fine, are largely unenforced, but could be implemented if necessary. The most serious sanction would deprive nonvoters of government jobs. While official figures suggest voter turnout is high (around 80 percent), elections are fraudulent, and a realistic picture would place turnout between 50 percent and 60 percent. Women have been allowed to vote since 1958.

Elections do not carry any suspense at all for the government has already decided what the final figures will be long before they take place. They are largely a political farce instituted by the government to improve its international image and to have a legalistic legitimization of its long stay in power. Fraud is particularly widespread in the countryside. Even government officials, privately, acknowledge that fair play is far from being characteristic of Paraguayan politics.

The Party System

Origins of the Parties

What for over seventy years had been a typical two-party system (liberals and conservatives), has become in the last few years a highly fragmented party system that includes, besides the government party, nine other parties or miniparties. Neither the 1936 emergence of the PRF nor the 1960 founding of the Christian Democratic Party (PDC) did as much damage to the two-party structure as the accelerated process of disintegration of the Liberal Party. Actually, this fragmentation process has been a largely successful political move of the government (begun in 1962 and completed in 1977), as a result of which the old and traditional Liberal Party is now divided into five liberal parties, two of them government-supported and, indirectly, government-financed.

The Parties in Law

The constitution, in Article 117, proclaims the right to organize political parties; but Article 118 establishes that "the formation or functioning of parties whose purposes are to overthrow the republican system, the representative democratic form of government, or the system of competing parties" is not permitted.

Constitutional guarantees notwithstanding, the legal recognition of political parties depends on the Central Electoral Board (*Junta Electoral Central*), which is empowered to grant parties the legal standing known as *personalidad juridica*. In reality, what is supposed to be a merely administrative process has become a highly political one because the government has used this power to decide which sector or faction of a given opposition party will remain legitimate, and which will be considered legally nonexistent. It also allows the government to manipulate party names, a very important factor in a largely traditional country. For example, in 1963 the name Liberal Party was given to a tiny progovernment faction, thus depriving the majority of the party of its own name; they were later (1967) recognized as the Liberal Radical Party. More recently, in 1977, tiny factions of both the Liberal and Liberal Radical parties, following a division, were allowed to use those names, again leaving the majority of both parties with neither name nor legal standing. As of now, the majority Liberal and Liberal Radical parties are known as the Liberal Teeté (PLT) and Authentic Liberal Radical (PLRA), though neither of them has legal recognition.

Party Organization

With the exception of the small and outlawed parties, remaining parties can be considered mass parties with dues-paying memberships contributing 5 percent to 10 percent of their electoral support. With the exception of the Febrerist Party (social-democrat) and the Christian Democratic Party, the ideology of the remaining parties is very vague, varying from very conservative stances to a center ideological position. They are, however, rather than ideological parties, office-seeking parties.

All parties are extremely centralized, but this is particularly true of the governmental Colorado Party. Local and regional leadership is important only to secure support in party elections, and they do not significantly influence important political decisions.

While the local branches of the Colorado Party engage in extensive social and economic activities (in fact, constituting a sort of paragovernmental agency) such as building roads, schools, parks, medical facilities, etc., the opposition parties are restricted to very limited political (small meetings) and social (parties, dancing events) activities. At the national level, opposition parties are confined to the same type of activities, while the Colorado Party has unrestricted access to newspapers, radio and TV programs; it also organizes occasional mass demonstrations.

The selection of candidates for public office varies from party to party. Opposition parties hold relatively open and democratic elections to select delegates to a party convention, which in turn, after all sorts of maneuvering, elects the party slate. The process is exactly the reverse in the case of the governmental party: decisions are made at the very top level without any kind of consultation with grass-roots leaders, and the party convention meets only to ratify such decisions by unanimous vote.

Though the opposition parties are much more open, the elite groups that run the parties are small and quite closed. There is, to be sure, some mobility, but within restricted and very predictable limits.

The membership in the highest executive bodies of the parties overlaps with membership in Congress, so that, generally, the parliamentary party factions quickly implement party decisions. There have been some cases, however, in the opposition parties, in which the internal balance of forces in Congress and in the party were at odds, resulting in strained relations between party members and Congress.

Campaigning

Election campaigns are advertised mainly through newspapers, radio, and TV, as well as through posters which are placed everywhere. Mass demonstrations are not uncommon for the official party, but they are not frequent. In the case of the opposition parties, they have been rare, but are occuring with increasing frequency.

Campaign expenditures are paid for by the party apparatus and membership contributions. There are no spending limits and no state support. Although no official figures are available, the ratio of Colorado Party expenditures to those of all other parties combined would probably be close to ten to one.

Campaigns are highly centralized and hardly a single advertisement or activity is carried out without the agreement of the party campaign committee.

Colorado Party
(Asociación Nacional Republicana— Partido Colorado)

History & Organization

Founded in 1887, the Colorado Party is one of the two traditional parties. It has been in power from its foundation until 1904, and then from 1946 until today. Conservative in ideology, it has become a very homogeneous party. It has a highly centralized organizational structure composed of over two hundred *seccionales* (local branches) spread all over the country. The party is ruled by a small elite group in close contact with the president of the republic, who is also the honorary president of the party. It has no international affiliation. It publishes a daily newspaper, *Patria*. The party has several auxiliary organizations such as the youth movement, the women's movement, and an association for each profession, e.g., the Colorado Association of Lawyers. Through its auxiliary organizations, the party penetrates and attempts to control every area of social, economic, and political activity.

Policy

The domestic policies of the party are very conservative. Its foreign policy is extremely anticommunist, and Paraguay has no diplomatic relations with any communist country except Yugoslavia. As to the relations it maintains with its biggest neighbors, Argentina and Brazil, the party has generally leaned toward Brazil, although in the last five years it has been using a "pendulum" approach, leaning alternately toward one or the other in order to maintain the maximum leverage against both.

Membership & Constituency

The Colorado Party has an alleged membership of nominally around 800,000. However, no reliable figures are available. No one can be an officer in the military or enter public service without being affiliated with the party and receiving a recommendation from a local, regional, or national party leader. The party has no particular area of strength, but the peasants of the central part of the country surrounding the capital city are said to be its most loyal political supporters.

Financing

No reliable figures regarding party finances are available, but its budget is certainly substantial. Contributions come from membership dues and from public employees, who contribute a percentage of their wages. It has unrestricted access to state financing.

Leadership

The Colorado Party leader is Juan Ramón Chaves (born 1902), whose official position is chair of the Colorado Party junta (reelected, 1984). Most of the top leadership is well over sixty-years-old and at the September 1984 party convention, they frustrated attempts by the younger majority to place Stroessner's secretary, the ambitious Mario Abdo Benitez on the junta. Instead, in addition to Chaves as chair, the first, second, and third junta vice presidents were as follows: Sabino Montanaro (minister of the interior), Ruben Stanley, and Adan Godoy Gimenez (minister of public health). Benitez, however, was given a position on the less important Party Political Secretariat. Relatively young Juan Manuel Frutos, director of the Rural Welfare Institute (*Instituto de Bienestar Rural*), is a major force within the party, and, if he can weather the rising unrest, is expected to progress up the ladder.

Prospects

The Colorado Party will remain the single most important political party and political force (leaving aside the military) in the foreseeable future. However, after Stroessner's disappearance, it will probably face a serious process of fragmentation and realignment until a new internal balance of forces is achieved and a new party elite consolidates its position.

MOPOCO
(*Movimiento Popular Colorado*)

Part of the Colorado Party's generational split is reflected in the existence of MOPOCO, formed in 1959 by so-called radical young Colorados whose stated devotion was to the party rather than to Stroessner. Although it was immediately outlawed and its leadership was, until 1984, in exile in Argentina, MOPOCO has slowly gained in strength and membership within Paraguay. In 1984, hesitantly trusting Stroessner's announced policy of *apertura* (opening) MOPOCO leader Miguel Angel Gonzalez Casablanca and some colleagues returned to Paraguay. Although frequently placed under house and other arrest, the MOPOCO leaders have attracted a great deal of support, reflecting the youthful makeup of the Colorado Party membership—60 percent of which is under age 30. MOPOCO might well be permitted to take part in future elections, or if not, influence the party significantly in the future.

Liberal Teeté Party
(*Partido Liberal Teeté;* PLT) and Liberal Radical Authentic Party (*Partido Liberal Radical Autentico;* PLRA)

History & Organization

One of the two traditional parties, the Liberal Party was founded in 1887. It was in power between 1904 and 1936 and again between 1937 and 1939. It is an extremely heterogeneous party and has undergone several divisions. In 1962 the party split into the Liberal Party and the Liberal Radical Party, the latter enjoying the most support and the former constituting a very small fraction which participated in the 1963 elections and won seats in the 1963–68 Congress.

In 1977, after a short-lived reunification, both parties underwent further divisions, as a result of which they became the Liberal Teeté Party and the Liberal Radical Authentic Party. The small factions that succeeded in dividing the party also succeeded—with government support—in keeping the original names for themselves. These factions participated in the 1978 elections, running as *Partido Liberal* and *Partido Liberal Radical.*

Policy

The PLT is a right-wing, *laissez-faire* party, while the PLRA is more center, with its youth leaning towards the left. Both parties abstained from participating in the 1977 convention to amend the constitution and the 1978 presidential and congressional elections. The PLRA is currently the leading force in the *Acuerdo Nacional* (National Pact), an opposition front composed in part of illegal parties; the PRF, the PDC, and the MOPOCO.

Membership & Constituency

No reliable figures regarding membership are available, although it appears that the PLRA has about 80,000 members, or roughly ten times the strength of the PLT. The PLR and PL, which participated in the 1978 elections, are both moribund and have very few members.

Financing

Party finances depend upon members' contributions and dues. Party members occupying elective posts are expected to contribute 40 percent of their pay to the party treasury.

Leadership

The leadership of the PLRA revolves around five major figures. Domingo Laino, an economist expelled from the country in 1984 for writing a novel condemning the Stroessner regime, and Juan M. Benítez Florentín and Hermes Rafael Saguier, both lawyers, represent the left wing of the party, Miguel A. Martínez Yaryes, a physician, and Carlos A. González, a lawyer, represent the center. The first two are in their forties while the last two are in their fifties. The current president of the PLRA is Juan M. Benítez Florentín but this position Laino would probably fill if permitted to return to Paraguay. He was elected in a secret electoral process because the party convention, which was scheduled for May 29, 1982, was forbidden by the government and the place in which it was going to take place was heavily surrounded by uniformed and plainclothes police.

The leadership of the PLT has been reduced to two brothers, Carlos Levi Ruffinelli, a physician in his sixties, and Fernando Levi Ruffinelli, a lawyer in his fifties.

Prospects

The PLRA is likely to remain an important opposition force in the future. There is no evidence, however, that it is going to be able to participate in any capacity in a future government.

The PLT, on the other hand, is not likely to play a significant role by itself, although it will probably merge with other liberal factions to become yet another and new liberal party.

Revolutionary Febrerist Party (*Partido Revolucionario Febrerista;* PRF)

History

In February 1936, a military coup ended thirty years of liberal predominance. The group which plotted the coup, and others who later joined the group, founded what was first known as *Concentración Revolucionaria Febrerista,* and later as *Partido Revolucionario Febrerista.* The founding father, Colonel Rafael Franco, was its main leader until his death in 1975. It participated in government from February 1936 to August 1937 (when a military coup brought the liberals back to power), and in a brief coalition government with the Colorados in 1946.

Organization & Policy

Affiliated loosely with the Socialist International, the PRF is a typically social-democratic party with two major groups, one leaning toward the center (the old guard) and the other toward the left (the youth). In 1973, it ceased participating in national elections, but ten years later again, symbolically entered the lists. In 1979 it joined other opposition parties to form the *Acuerdo Nacional* (National Pact). Its official weekly, *El Pueblo*, has been closed down repeatedly by the government; it is the only regular publication still maintained by an opposition group.

Membership & Constituency

Its membership comes principally from urban intellectuals and students and to a lesser degree from liberal professionals such as lawyers and doctors. The PRF is probably one of the most homogeneous Paraguayan parties. Though it pretends to be national, its main support comes from Asuncion, the capital city, and a few other urban centers.

Financing

Party finances come from membership dues and from the contributions of wealthy members.

Leadership

There are two major factions in the Febrerist Party. The left wing is under the leadership of Euclides Acevedo, a young and ambitious lawyer in his late thirties. The more traditional faction is under the leadership of Alarico Quiñónez Cabral, a physician in his early sixties who is also the current president of the party.

Prospects

The Febrerist Party will remain a force of minor significance as an opposition party likely to draw support from some sectors of the middle class in urban areas. In February 1984, it surprised observers and the government by organizing a mass protest in Asunción to demand a return of democracy which may indicate it has gained strength.

Minor Parties

Apart from the various liberal factions, there are at least five minor parties in Paraguay. In addition to MOPOCO, they are as follows: the Christian Democratic Party (PDC) under Rómulo Perina, the Communist Party (PCP) with less than 500 members, Episanio Méndez Sleitas' *Partido Colorado en Exilio y la Resistencia* (PCELR), seen as coalescing with MOPOCO, and the ultraradical *Organización Político Militar* (OPM). None of these parties has legal electoral recognition and the last three are legally outlawed as revolutionary organizations.

Other Political Forces

Military

Since the late nineteenth century, the military has been a decisive force in Paraguayan politics. Its role has increased over the last three decades. Originally highly politicized, it has gradually moved toward professionalism, especially since the early 1970s. Yet, it is still extremely political and to be an officer is by definition to be a Colorado. As in political parties, factions exist within the army (the navy and air force are miniscule) for the most part along generational lines. The leading traditionalist—apart from Stroessner himself—is aging General Andrés Rodriguez, a cavalryman now heading the strategic Second Corps. A presidential aspirant, he is probably too old and too identified with Stroessner and with the nation's powerful smuggling industry to succeed. Among younger officers—many trained in the United States or in Panama—General Gerardo Johansen, head of the army's training and educational institutions, appears to be the main figure, and it has long been rumored that the army would like him to be Stroessner's successor.

Roman Catholic Church

The Roman Catholic Church has constituted, since the late 1960s, a formidable force of moral opposition to the regime. Its liberal wing—in part ensconced in the Catholic University—controls most of the key positions in the Church. It has organized a people's conscience movement against the government, and Archbishop Ismael Rolón, a member of the Council of State, is a constant embarrassement to the president. Its publication, *Sendero*, (often confiscated as it hits the street) harshly criticizes the government and has accused Stroessner of totalitarianism.

Students

Up until the early 1970s, student organizations were a major opposition force. The *Movimiento Independiente* (Independent Movement) orchestrated mass demonstrations and other forms of protest. Since then, however, government repression and major Colorado Party measures to infiltrate and to take over student groups have seriously weakened the students' power. The last student bastion is the Catholic University (symbolically located on a plaza along with the military school, the police barracks, the Congress building, and the Cathedral).

Peasants

In the late 1960s and 1970s a relatively strong agrarian movement emerged with firm Church support. The increasingly nervous government ruthlessly repressed the movement, arresting thousands, killing some, and outlawing various peasant groups and organizations. In the early 1980s, however, in wake of agricultural recession, growing population, increasing concentration of land in fewer and fewer hands, and severe floods, the peasants reorganized and are again a potent force. They have successfully occupied and defied the government to evict the new squatters. In 1985, a permanent peasant assembly was officially recognized by the regime.

Organized Labor

Long dominated by the *Confederación Paraguaya de Trabajadores* (CPT), a government-controlled labor organization, the few existing Paraguayan workers have had little influence on the regime or its economic policies. However, largely as a result of the massive 1975–1982 building boom, created by the immense Itaipú

hydroelectric project and accelerating inflation, independent labor unions and blocs have organized and become vocal. Still merely an irritant to the regime, these new organizations will no doubt grow in strength and influence.

National Prospects

Alfredo Stroessner, born in 1912, is well into his seventies and his seventh term as president. Until recently, it appeared that he gave no thought whatsoever to his succession, but in 1984 and 1985, party *militantes* (militants), no doubt with his urging, have been backing his son Gustavo for the future presidency. His potential is doubtful. Stroessner will most probably remain in office until he dies or becomes incapacitated, and his successor will have to be a man capable of satisfying (and not threatening) both the Colorado Party and the army.

While General Gerardo Johansen (a rare Paraguayan of Danish ancestry) might fit that bill and be persuaded to do so, it seems more likely that the next president will be civilian Luis Maria Argaña, president of the Supreme Court and a staunch Colorado. He is nationally respected (rare for a major regime figure) and is said to be acceptable to army and party. He might be a suitable—even a good—transition figure, but in the decade after Stroessner's departure, one can expect considerable confusion and probable chaos as a new majority political grouping is created.

Further Reading
Hicks, Frederick. "Interpersonal Relationships and Caudillismo in Paraguay." *Journal of Inter-American Studies and World Affairs*, No. 13, January 1971.
Lewis, Paul H. *Paraguay under Stroessner.* Chapel Hill, N. C.: University of North Carolina Press, 1980.
Pendle, George. *Paraguay: A Riverside Nation.* London: Royal Institute of International Affairs, 1956.
Warren, Harris G. *Paraguay: An Informal History.* Norman, Okla.: University of Oklahoma Press, 1949.

REPUBLIC OF PERU
(República del Perú)
by Henry A. Dietz, Ph.D.

The System of Government

Peru is a multiparty republic of nearly eighteen million people whose successes with electoral politics have been fleeting and irregular. This state of affairs has roots in the nineteenth century when independence in the mid-1820s ushered in a generation of military rule. Not until the 1850s did civilian rule assert itself, and not for a century did Peru's masses have any chance to become involved in the country's political life. Their involvement has not meant stability for the nation. Between 1920 and 1985, only one president had been elected, served his term, and passed power over to an elected successor (Manuel Prado, 1939–45).

The present administration is a second instance of the orderly transfer of power between elected officials. Alan García Pérez was sworn in as Peru's 103rd president in July 1985, following the completion by Fernando Belaúnde of his five-year mandate. Until this time at least, the Peruvian political system thus has displayed a deep-seated incapacity for civilian dominance over a highly institutionalized military establishment. Peru's military, which has held power well over half the time since 1945, is a constant presence that all civilian politicians and parties must take into account in any policy or electoral stategy.

Executive

Basic political power in Peru resides in the constitutional president of the republic. The 1980 constitution provides for direct election to a five-year term and allows reelection only after an expresident has been out of office for at least one term. Unlike the 1933 document, the new constitution calls for a run-off election between the two highest vote getters if no single candidate receives a simple majority. This clause (Article 203) is clearly intended to avoid the sort of constitutional stalemate that occurred in 1962, when none of three major candidates was able to muster the necessary one-third of the popular vote, thereby leading to a desperate round of wheeling and dealing before the military ultimately annulled the election.

As in most Latin American nations, the chief executive is the dominant political figure of Peru. Traditionally and necessarily he maintains a high profile and is the constant target of petitions and demands from throughout society. The fortunes of his administration and of his party primarily ride on his performance.

In the 1985 presidential elections, Alan García took an overwhelming 45.7 percent of the popular vote. Running in a field of nine candidates, García, although only 34 years old at the time, was viewed by many as a refreshing and brisk reformer who offered considerable energy for attacking the country's multiple problems.

Legislature

The Peruvian Congress is comprised of a Senate and a Chamber of Deputies, both of which are elected for five-year terms simultaneously with the president. Its regularly scheduled sessions run from July 27 to December 15 and from April 1 to May 31. When Congress is not in session, it is represented by a Permanent Commission, composed of five senators and ten deputies elected by their peers.

The Senate has sixty members, elected at large throughout the nation by popular vote. The Senate cannot be dissolved by presidential decree, and it cannot censure a minister or the cabinet.

The Chamber of Deputies with 180 members representing *departamentos*, can be dissolved by the president, but it can also formally question cabinet members and enter a vote of no confidence against a minister or an entire cabinet.

The 1985 congressional election results were clearly influenced by García's candidacy and his party's organizational strength. APRA, Peru's oldest political party, rode the wave of García's popularity to take thirty-two Senate (53 percent) and 108 Deputy (60 percent) seats, thereby giving the president strong majorities in both houses.

Judiciary

The Peruvian court system is similar to most others found in Latin America. A clear hierarchy, crowned by the Supreme Court in Lima, descends through superior courts to justices of the peace, who are found throughout Peru. The Supreme Court has the annual duty of preparing a judicial budget for inclusion in the national budget. The court can also initiate legislation in areas of its jurisdiction.

Regional & Local Government

Peru is divided administratively into *departamentos* (twenty-three, plus the constitutional province of Callao, Lima's port), *provincias* (approximately 150), and *distritos* (approximately 1700). While the constitution grants some local administrative and economic autonomy, regional and local power is exceptionally limited, especially regarding powers of taxation. While each administrative level has its own officials, but mayors of major cities have the highest profile in the public eye and the media.

The unpredictability of the electoral process and the fragility of party existence have both contributed to significant histories of self-help among the rural and urban poor (i.e., the peasants, recent migrants to cities, and the urban-squatter population). Rural peasants have for centuries employed various types of local communal activities to provide themselves with labor for basic infrastructure, harvests, construction, and other similar undertakings. In the cities, especially Lima, where the squatter population approaches half the city's total of six million people, neighborhoods have generated spontaneous self-help programs and have elected local leaders for self-governance and as spokesmen for petitioning municipal and national authorities for assistance. Military and civilian politicians have frequently attempted to win over or co-opt those organizations, but without significant success. Political parties tend to pay attention to these urban groups only during campaigns, a fact that may explain why these areas do not vote solidly or predictably as a block.

The Electoral System

The chief executive and mayors are elected by direct majority vote, but members of Congress and of municipal councils come to office through a system of proportional representation. Each political party entered in an election offers a complete list of candidates for each chamber, that is, each party puts up 100 senatorial candidates and a total of 180 deputy candidates. Deputy seats are allotted to each *departamento* according to its population. Each *departamento* has at least one deputy; Lima, the largest, has forty. Each party is awarded deputy seats in proportion to its percentage of the total popular vote cast for that party's list in that *departamento*. Senate seats are also awarded proportionally, except that senators are elected at large by the nation's total popular vote. Typically, the strategy for each party is to place its best-known, strongest candidates toward the top of each list. Voters can vote for one party for president, another for the Senate, and a third for the Chamber, if they wish, but must vote a straight party line within each of these three.

Suffrage restrictions have been loosened recently in two fundamental ways. In 1978, the legal age limit dropped from twenty-one to eighteen, and illiterates were allowed to vote for the first time in 1980. Because of these changes (especially the second), the voting populace has expanded by almost one-third since the 1978 constituent assembly elections. This expansion showed remarkable regional variation. While Lima's vote grew by only 13 percent, voting in rural highland *departamentos* increased by as much as 130 percent.

As has always been the case, the 1985 elections produced a number of blank (494,000, or 6.5 percent of the total) and null (553,000, or 7.3 percent) ballots. However, this 13.8 percent is considerably lower than the 19 percent registered in 1980.

The Party System

Origins of the Parties

Peru's party system does not lend itself to easy characterization. Its intermittent nature reflects the difficulty in agreeing on the rules of the game for itself and for the nation's military. Peru had only six civilian presidents (out of thirty-five) between 1821 and 1872; they served for a total of about five years. In other words, the major split in society was civilian versus military, not liberal versus conservative.

While the twentieth century has seen a much more complex party picture emerge, civilian-military mistrust continues to dominate Peruvian politics. Parties have never had much trouble coming into being; they appear, merge, divide, and disappear constantly. Despite the emergence of populism in the early 1930s, Peru's civilian political leaders have been unable or unwilling to devote their energies to creating institutionalized party structures which can survive the disappearance of a single strong leader.

The Parties in Law

The 1980 constitution allows all political persuasions to form parties and gives no official preference to any party. All recognized parties are permitted free access to state-owned radio and television facilities during campaigns. For the 1980 presidential-congressional elections, new electoral laws required that parties had to collect 40,000 valid signatures to gain recognition by the National Election Board (*Jurado Nacional de Elecciones*). Fifteen parties were finally recognized and placed on the ballot.

Party Organization

Peru's political parties are dependent upon personalist leadership. They vary from loosely organized, middle-of-the-road, and only vaguely ideological to ideological extremism and organizational rigidity. They also vary in their degrees of longevity, regional strength, and organizational capacity. *Alianza Popular Revolucionaria Americana* (APRA) goes back to 1930, and *Partido Acción Popular* (AP) (Belaúnde's party) dates from 1956, but several others (e.g., PRT, PAIS, UNIR, UI, OPRP) came into being solely for the 1980 elections. Most parties tend to pay particular attention in their campaign activities to Lima, which contains about 45 percent of the country's electorate. All parties show regional disparities, and not one can claim consistent national strength.

The strongly personalist favor of most parties tends naturally toward concentrated power within the party. The founder of a party is almost always its head, and decision-making power resides with him and a small coterie of trusted lieutenants. Party discipline varies considerably. Historically, APRA has been determined to maintain purity and has frequently expelled rebellious elements who challenged the direction of Haya de la Torre. The Marxist and Trotskyite leftist parties often disagree among themselves, and issues of ideological probity (as well as of command) have caused innumerable cleavages, splits, coalitions, and factions. The selection of a presidential candidate is usually straightforward: the founder/leader is nominated. Senatorial and deputy candidates are generally the best-known party leaders; while they may be formally named at a party convention, the party elite makes its wishes known beforehand and they are usually heeded. When a severe rupture threatens, leaders of well-established parties may attempt to paper over their differences or to fight matters out rather than bolt the party.

Campaigning

As the Peruvian electorate has expanded since the 1920s, the breadth and style of campaigning has changed. Prior to 1930, politics was a tightly restricted matter that involved perhaps a tenth of the nation's adult population. But the emergence of populism in the 1931 election brought new ways of campaigning to Peru. Burgeoning urbanization, incipient industrialization, and expanding trade unionism facilitated mass meetings and demonstrations, which increased political participation as well.

The 1980 and 1985 presidential elections saw all major candidates travel throughout the country. No longer is it possible to concentrate entirely on Lima; provincial cities and towns now hold an increased percentage of the electorate, thanks to the abolition of literacy restrictions and to the movement of more and more people into urban areas.

Most parties have been influenced heavily by United States campaign techniques that stress full exploitation of mass communications, especially television in urban areas. Afternoon and evening hours programming in 1985 consisted of virtually nonstop political broadcasts for days prior to election day. This saturation was due not only to free air time made available by the government, but also to the determination of all parties to achieve dominance in what could only be described as a "media arms race."

Still, Peruvians—candidates and electorate—place a high value on personal appearances and oratorial abilities. Alan García and his principal opponent, Alfonso Barrantes, were both able to assemble crowds of 100,000 or more in Lima and in the larger provincial capitals as well. In 1985, all candidates and parties ended their campaigns with mass demonstrations.

Independent Voters

Voter identification with a party is a sometime thing in Peru; more often identification is with the individual leader and not the institution. As a result, party identification and the role of the independent (i.e., uncommitted) voter are somewhat slippery topics. For years APRA was the largest single voting bloc in the country; about a third of the electorate appears to have been committed *aprista.* García's youth and vigor allowed APRA to attract large numbers of new and casually interested voters, much to the frustration of both the left and the right.

Popular Action Party
(*Partido Acción Popular;* AP)

History

The Popular Action party came into being in 1956 as a vehicle for Fernando Belaúnde Terry's presidential ambitions, and has been in existence (and served this purpose) ever since.

The party emerged coincident with the end of the eight-year reactionary rule of General Manuel Odría. Until then, political choices had been largely limited to APRA or to a small, dominant, entrenched social and economic elite that had traditionally controlled Peru's politics. While unsuccessful in his bid for power in 1956, Belaúnde clearly appealed to a middle-class, educated electorate in search of new political solutions to the country's problems. Belaúnde finished second in that race to Manuel Prado, who was elected with APRA support.

In 1962, a constitutional stalemate led to a military coup, and new elections were held in 1963. *Acción Popular* took 36 percent of the vote (as opposed to APRA's 34 percent), and Belaúnde assumed the presidency, but with a decided minority in both chambers of Congress. He served amid increasingly difficult political problems (factionalism in the party, majority obstructionism in Congress) until 1968, when another military coup removed him and suspended all civilian electoral politics. By 1980,

the death of APRA's Haya de la Torre, along with the collapse of Peru's economy and with it much of the military's legitimacy as a governing force, carried Belaúnde and his party to resounding presidential and Congressional victories. However, Belaúnde's perceived ineptness in handling extremely severe economic and social problems led AP to a disastrous showing in 1985.

Organization

Acción Popular's national organization has strongly defined horizontal as well as vertical elements. Hierarchically arranged from neighborhood through local, provincial, and national levels, the party has held regular conventions and plenary meetings. Since its inception, Belaúnde has always been in control of the party, but his ability to revive it following the 1985 debacle is open to serious question. Belaúnde's total identification with AP and his unpopularity by the end of his term may make any revival difficult.

Policy

Domestically, AP for twenty years has pushed a program of nationalism, modest reform, self-help, the value of "technical" solutions for social and economic problems, and pragmatic planning. Belaúnde's traditional campaign slogans—"the conquest of Peru by Peruvians"; "the people did it"—illustrate the straightforward thrust of his thinking. Internationally, Belaúnde has always regarded the United States with a friendly eye and has welcomed private investment and sought credit from major lending agencies.

Membership & Constituency

AP's traditional strength has been among Lima's middle-class and white-collar groups; the party has had varying success with the city's low-income sectors. Its national strength in 1980 evaporated steadily during Belaúnde's term in office; the 1983 municipal elections, in which either APRA or a leftist coalition swept Lima and most of the major provincial mayoralties, provided a portent for AP's poor 1985 showing. In that election Javiér Alva Orlandini took 6.3 percent of the popular vote compared to Belaunde's 47 percent in 1980.

Financing

Party sources would reveal no financial information.

Leadership

Fernando Belaúnde (born 1912) is dominant. His immediate coterie of advisors and lieutenants have been with the party since its founding, and several present cabinet ministers were active in the 1963–68 government. Among the more important are Fernando Schwalf Lopez Aldana (born 1916), first vice president; Javier Alva Orlandini (born 1927), Senate president and party secretary general; Manuel Ulloa Elias (born 1923), prime minister, minister of economics and finance, Luis Percovich Roca (born 1931), and Sandro Mariategui (born 1921).

Prospects

Acción Popular's basic concerns are survival and renewal. Belaúnde is still the party's dominant force, but whether he is an asset or a liability is now a real question. If he insists on playing the role of kingmaker, the party could suffer by association with his term in office. Yet if he steps aside, he has no clear successor. Whatever the circumstances, a new generation is clearly needed if the party is to be more than a pale ghost of its past.

Peruvian Aprista Party or American Popular Revolutionary Alliance (*Partido Aprista Peruana;* PAP or *Alianza Popular Revolucionaria Americana;* APRA)

History

The first thirty years of the twentieth century saw rapid changes in Peru in investments, regional imbalances (coast vs. sierra), and the beginnings of rural and urban organized labor. These developments, coupled with the downfall of the conservative dictatorship of Augusto Leguía (1919–30), allowed the nation's first populist movements to establish themselves.

The emergence of APRA at this time as Peru's first truly modern party altered the country's entire subsequent political history.

Always almost winning, almost always persecuted by Peru's traditional civilian elites and the military, frequently underground, politically belligerent and obstructionist, and often cultish regarding Victor Raul Haya de la Torre, its founder and leader (1895–79), APRA's impact on Peru has been profound and controversial. Once *the* radical party of Peru, its search for respectability and victory moved it toward the center and even into coalitions with previously bitter enemies.

In the 1978 constituent-assembly elections, APRA took a 36 percent plurality, and Haya served as the Constituent Assembly president. He guided it through often difficult times and produced a new constitution, only to die before he could run as a candidate under its rules.

APRA is Peru's only indigenous party that has had significant international influence. Originally intended as a pan-Latin American movement, Haya's concepts of a multiclass, highly organized, intensely loyal, antiimperialist party have been adopted by various other nationalist and reformist parties in the region. Haya's death in 1979 has placed the party's future in doubt, but Garcia has given it new life, and its impact on Peru and on Latin America is unquestioned.

Organization

The organizational depth and resilience of the party has for years been the despair and admiration of all of its opponents. Its extremely complex, comprehensive vertical and horizontal structures bind local groups and sectors firmly to the national leadership and (until 1979) to Haya's control, and gave APRA the largest single solid block of votes in Peru for decades. While national in scope and in intent, however, APRA has always been strongly regional in strength, with its base in the rural north.

The party's reach went well beyond voting. It played a fundamental role in the creation of organized labor, where it controlled the nation's largest union for years, and penetrated professional associations and a variety of other middle- and working-class groups. It also attempted to make *aprismo* a way of life by propounding detailed moral codes of thought and behavior for its members; by creating women's, children's, and youth affiliations; and by publishing its own newspaper. Its connections with Latin

American and West European social democratic and other reformist parties are cordial.

Policy

Haya and APRA both mellowed over time. Once Peru's most intransigent radical party, famous for its bloody attempts to unseat numerous administrations, the party since 1950 has been an accepted part of the political spectrum. Many of its early goals—decentralization, a corporatist parliament, new ministries, economic protectionism, and state participation—have been incorporated in one way or another. But the party lost its radical image to new left-wing movements, especially among trade unions and university students, and has found itself competing with Acción Popular for the urban middle-class vote. Nevertheless, its aims and policies (aside from being elected), once considered extremist, have in their eventual adoption given support to the APRA claim that the center of Peru moved toward the party, rather than the reverse. Alan García has shown signs of trying to make APRA appealing to a wide spectrum of the electorate and to claim the democratic left as its natural ideological home.

Membership & Constituency

Since 1930, APRA membership and support have been hard to estimate accurately, since the party frequently chose (or was forced) to support independent candidates (1945, 1956). APRA-supported presidential candidates drew about 567,000 votes (43 percent) in 1956; 558,000 (32.9 percent) in 1962; 623,000 (34.4 percent) in 1963; 1,130,000 (27 percent) in 1980; and then a stunning 3,500,000 (45.7 percent) in 1985, when García reversed a trend that had been in effect since 1956 by carrying the Lima vote for APRA.

APRA's traditional stronghold in northern Peru, where Haya was born and where organized labor really had its start, was thus dramatically augmented in 1985. To what extent this support is evanescent or solid remains an open question, but the party's significant accomplishments in the 1983 municipal elections may offer a hint that APRA's strength and depth go beyond the person of Alan García.

Financing

Party sources would reveal no financial information.

Leadership

Before Haya's death, his control over the party had been complete. His fellow party founders, although now aged, are still important; they include Armando Villanueva del Campo (born 1915), Luís Alberto Sanchez (born 1900), vice president of Peru; and Ramiro Prialé (born 1906). A splinter faction led by Andres Townsend Escurra (1915) was formed following Haya's death but has had no impact on the party or on the national political scene. Alan García is now unquestionably the dominant force in the party and has brought many new faces and much new blood with him.

Prospects

APRA's resurgence since the early 1980s has been truly remarkable. For a party that suffered its worst electoral showing in the 1980 presidential race, it has come back to win its first ever national election by a 2-1 margin and to take strong majorities in both houses of Congress. Its prospects as a political force are now strong indeed. Yet AP had the same sort of apparent strength in 1980, only to collapse. What APRA must do now is to demonstrate that it can confront Peru's massive, profound economic and social problems. If it cannot, it may find that political power can indeed be fickle.

Popular Christian Party
(*Partido Popular Cristiano;* PPC)

The PPC is a conservative following based on the popularity of Luís Bedoya Reyes, the party's founder and leader. Bedoya, a popular two-term ex-mayor of Lima, broke with the Christian Democratic Party in 1966 and has since headed PPC, the most prominent business-backed conservative party in Peru. The party's major electoral triumph occurred in the 1978 constituent assembly elections, where it took twenty-seven of the 100 seats, and where it frequently backed APRA's plurality to create a working majority. In both 1980 and 1985, Bedoya ran a poor third overall (9.6 percent and 10.2 percent, respectively). In 1985, his party (which had been renamed CODE) took seven senate (12 percent) and twelve deputy (6 percent) races.

The Marxist Left

As in most Latin American countries, Peru's leftist parties appear, split, disappear, and coalesce in rapid and often bewildering fashion. (A list of Peruvian Marxist parties—with acronyms—appears below.) It was not always thus; from 1928 to 1956, the Peruvian Communist Party was the only consistent, extreme leftist organization in the country. After that time, the left proliferated into various ideological factions (Stalinist, Castroite, Trotskyite, Maoist), which frequently spent as much time arguing and fighting among themselves as with their more obvious opponents. One group, the MIR, undertook guerrilla warfare in 1965, but was virtually eliminated by the military.

In the 1978 Constituent Assembly vote, six parties (PST, PC–Bandera Roja, FIR–POC, CCP, FEDEP, and POMR) coalesced into FOCEP, a leftist front that took twelve seats. These seats combined with eighteen more won by four other leftist parties, gave a total of thirty seats to the left. However, during the Assembly's deliberations, these thirty virtually never agreed on more than a few issues, and some or all of them frequently walked out.

In 1980, the left split badly and wound up running five candidates, with predictable results: all five combined took 14 percent of the vote. Following this debacle, the left forged a coalition (*Izquierda Unida*; IU) which triumphed in 1983 when Alfonso Barrantes took the mayoral race in Lima. Barrantes then ran as IU's presidential candidate in 1985, finishing a distant second (21.2 percent of the popular vote) to García.

The most spectacular manifestation of radical politics in Peru is Sendero Luminoso , an extreme, avowedly violent splinter group which began its terrorist activities (dynamitings, kidnappings, assassinations, jail-breaks) in 1980 and which caused President Belaúnde no end of difficulties. A prolonged and ruthless military counter-insurgency response to Sendero cost many lives; the final figure for the Belaúnde years exceeded 5,000 dead, and violations of human rights were widespread. Peru's "mainstream" left has for some time renounced Sendero and its tactics, no doubt fearing that its organizational and electoral victories might be jeopardized by any association with Sendero.

Since APRA's victory in 1985, Sendero has shown it plays no favorites; various terrorist activities have continued to plague Lima since García assumed office. The leftist party spectrum, meanwhile, remains highly fluid, as groups shift allegiances, names, and partners frequently.

The left has controlled much of organized labor in Peru for some years, since it founded the General Confederation of Peruvian Workers (CGTP) as a reaction to APRA's dominance of the Workers Confederation of Peru (CTP). Many of the left's movements find core support with Peru's miners in the highland areas, with university students and urban intellectuals, and with various peasant syndicates and organizations.

Predicting the future of any particular party borders on the impossible. As a whole, the left's influence doubtlessly will ride on its ability to maintain a workable coalition and on Peru's economy.

Minor Parties

These parties won at least one senate or deputy seat in the 1985 elections:

Acción Política Socialista (APS); Socialist Political Action.

Convergéncia Democrática — Independientes (CODE-Ind.); Democratic Convergence Movement, dissolved in July 1985. Formerly composed of PPC, MBH, and Independents.

Izquierda Nacionalista (IN); Nationalist Left. Formerly known as FNTC or as FENETRACA.

Movimiento de Bases Hayistas (MBH); Haya Grassroots Movement.

Movimiento Independiente de Madre de Dios (MIMD); Independent Movement of Madre de Dios.

Movimiento de Interes Popular (MIP); Popular Interest Movement.

Partido Democrático Cristiano (PDC); Christian Democratic Party.

Partido de Integración Nacionál (PADIN); National Integration Party.

Other Political Forces

Military

Peruvian politics cannot be understood apart from the military. Since 1919, Peru's presidents have taken office eight times through elections and seven times through coups. Over this period of time, especially during the 1950s and 1960s, Peru's military became increasingly professional, increasingly convinced that national development and national security were inextricably linked, and increasingly doubtful that civilians could do what the country needed. In 1968, with Belaúnde's first term deteriorating economically and the possibility of an APRA victory looming in 1969 (APRA and the military have been bitter enemies since 1932), the military ousted Belaúnde. Its twelve years of strongly activist, reformist rule, however, proved that military regimes need not be right wing.

The military made real efforts, especially between 1968 and 1975, to effect income redistribution, to reorganize citizen-participatory mechanisms, and to escape the United States' dominant role in Peruvian foreign relations. Success was mixed at best, and Peru underwent extremely difficult economic reversals in 1978.

Peru's present army has sharp distinctions between its officer corps and its enlisted men and conscripts. The former has drawn its members since World War II largely from Peru's provincial middle-class families, and prides itself on its training, professionalism, and loyalty to the institution of the military. The lower ranks are in general lower-class and *mestizo* (mixed race) in origin.

The military still maintains a close watch on Peru's civilian leaders, and García more than anyone knows the necessity of watching the military in return. Public blame attached to the military for the economic hardships in the late 1970s reduced their legitimacy a good deal. Nevertheless, the APRA administration has had to tread a narrow path with the military. On the one hand, its overwhelming popular victory has allowed García to fire several high-ranking officers for their involvement in human rights violations during anti-Sendero campaigns. On the other, the military and APRA were bitter enemies for almost half a century dating back to the early 1930s, and García must (as must any Peruvian president) keep in the military's good graces. As of the beginning of his term, for the time being, the civilian government and the military appeared to be on cordial terms.

Social & Economic Elites

Through the 1920s, Peru's economy and society—and politics—were dominated by a small group of related families whose control rested upon their near monopoly of business, commerce, agriculture, and the mass media. Much of this concentrated influence was dispersed under the reforms of the 1968–80 military regime, whose land redistribution and agrarian reform broke the old sierra landowner dominance. The coastal elites, who shifted into urban industrial investments, real estate, and commerce, managed to accommodate themselves to the regime.

Organized Labor

Labor's first major victory in Peru came in 1919, when workers won official recognition of the eight-hour day. Since that time, socialism and *aprista* populism have contended for control of the labor movement. The General Confederation of Peruvian Workers (CGTP), Peru's first national confederation, emerged under the Socialist Party in 1929, but was quickly banned. Not until 1944 did a new group form: the Workers Confederation of Peru (CTP) controlled by APRA. In 1968, as Belaúnde's first administration was toppling, the old CGTP was revived under leftist leadership. When Belaúnde was ousted, the military tried to establish a Confederation of Workers of the Peruvian Revolution (CTRP), but with limited success.

With the economic difficulties of the late 1970s, labor troubles increased. A general strike in 1977 and another in 1978 contributed to the military's decision to step down. Belaúnde's 1980 electoral victory, overwhelming as it was, still lacked any support from organized labor; upon his taking office, Belaúnde faced dozens of strikes and work stoppages by labor and professional groups as inflation and underemployment continued unabated.

Organized labor in Peru still represents a minority of the labor force and often reflects the factions and splits among leftist parties and movements. Some unions, such as the public school teachers' federation (SUTEP), support the far left, while others are more moderate. It remains to be seen if APRA can keep organized labor content enough to prevent the Marxist left from penetrating even further into its ranks.

Students

Prior to 1968, university students frequently occupied an important political place in Peru. The *apristas* controlled university politics until 1956. The party's obvious attempts to ingratiate itself with the Peruvian establishment, along with the emergence of numerous more radical groups, caused APRA's dominance to fade rapidly.

University politics became violent during the 1960s, both in the brief 1965 guerrilla outbreaks and in interparty competition. The 1968–80 military government undermined traditional university autonomy in several ways, but students led and participated in the riots and strikes of the left. Civilian rule may again provide university students with a stage, but it may also give free rein to factionalism among the many splinter groups on the left.

Roman Catholic Church

Peru is nominally and virtually all Roman Catholic. The Church's political influence, dominant during Peru's colonial period, has waned during the twentieth century. Yet while the Church has lost much of its economic and institutional strength, its role in social and political affairs has remained and has resulted in intra-Church and Church-state controversy. A faction, generally among the lower levels of clergy, has pushed for substantial changes, at times along "theology of liberation" lines, but has encountered opposition from within the Church hierarchy and from political and military authorities. This liberal faction at times supported the reforms of the Velasco administration, but the economic hardships of the late 1970s forced caution on such a position. No government can or will knowingly offend the Church today, since it still has much political and social influence.

Peasants (*Campesinos*)

Traditionally the poorest (but also the largest) of Peru's social groups, the peasants had virtually no voice in politics until the 1950s. At that time, peasant federations gained a foothold, and during Belaúnde's first term (1963–68) became a major pressure group for change.

When the Velasco agrarian reform took hold in 1970, many of these federations lost their hegemony momentarily. But as economic conditions worsened in the late 1970s, opposition federations (e.g., the National Agrarian Confederation [CNA] and the Confederation of Peruvian Peasants [CCP]) reemerged and provoked violent clashes with the Belaúnde administration through land seizures.

The peasantry remains at the bottom of the social ladder. Whether the partial agrarian reform and the extension of suffrage to illiterates will induce basic change remains uncertain.

National Prospects

When civilian government returned to Peru in 1980, many observers harbored doubts about its long-term viability. Yet Fernando Belaúnde, under whose term Peru suffered its most severe economic crisis since the 1930s, managed to serve his five years and turn power over to an elected successor. García's popularity at the end of 1985 was widespread and loyal, and his determination to change Peru reflects what must be seen as a mandate in the 1985 vote. If inflation can be slowed, economic recovery initiated, and the various facets of the debt issue brought under control, García and his party may be in the driver's seat for years to come. But the Peruvian electorate has demonstrated its willingness to turn against a popular leader if economic problems cannot be solved, and García himself must realize that charismatic popularity will not be mistaken for economic success.

Further Reading
Becker, David. *The New Bourgeoisie and the Limits of Dependency: Mining, Class, and Power in "Revolutionary" Peru.* Princeton: Princeton University Press, 1983.
Child, Jack, et al. *Peru: A Country Study.* Area Handbook Series. Washington, D.C.: U.S. Government Printing Office, for Foreign Area Studies, American University, 1981.
Dietz, Henry A. *Poverty and Problem-Solving under Military Rule: The Urban Poor in Lima, Peru.* Austin: University of Texas Press, 1980.
Gorman, Stephen M., ed. *Post-revolutionary Peru: The Politics of Transformation.* Boulder, Colo.: Westview Press, 1981.

Klaiber, Jeffrey L. *Religion and Revolution in Peru, 1924–1976.* Notre Dame: University of Notre Dame Press, 1977.

Kuczynski, Pedro Pablo. *Peruvian Democracy under Economic Stress: An Account of the Belaúnde Administration, 1963–1968.* Princeton: Princeton University Press, 1977.

Lowenthal, Abraham F., ed. *The Peruvian Experiment: Continuity and Change under Military Rule.* Princeton: Princeton University Press, 1975.

———— and McClintock, Cynthia, eds. *The Peruvian Experiment Revisited.* Princeton: Princeton University Press, 1982.

Neira, Hugo. "Peru." In *Guide to the Political Parties of South America,* edited by Jean-Pierre Bernard et al. Baltimore: Penguin, 1973.

Palmer, David Scott. *Peru: The Authoritarian Tradition.* New York: Praeger, 1980.

Stein, Steve. *Populism in Peru: The Emergence of the Masses and the Politics of Social Control.* Madison: University of Wisconsin, 1980.

Stepan, Alfred. *The State and Society: Peru in Comparative Perspective.* Princeton: Princeton University Press, 1978.

Thorp, Rosemary, and Bertram, Geoffrey. *Peru 1890–1977: Growth and Policy in an Open Economy.* New York: Columbia University Press, 1978.

Werlich, David. *Peru: A Short History.* Carbondale: Southern Illinois University Press, 1978.

REPUBLIC OF THE PHILIPPINES
(Republika ñg Philipinas)
by H. Monte Hill, Ph.D.

The System of Government

The Philippines, a nation of fifty million people, consists of over 7,100 islands. Ninety percent of the country's 300,000 square kilometers (115,710 square miles) are contained on the eleven largest islands. The national capital, Metro Manila, is the nation's premier city with a population of 7,500,000 and most of the country's transportation, economic, educational, communication, and medical facilities.

Filipinos are predominantly of Indo-Polynesian racial stock. Eighty-five percent are Roman Catholic, 9 percent Protestant, 5 percent Muslim, and 1 percent a variety of other religions.

The 1975 census revealed seventy-two different languages and dialects are spoken in the Philippines. The most important native tongues are Cebuano (24.4 percent) and Tagalog (23.8 percent). The two official languages, Pilipino (a version of Tagalog) and English, are spoken by 55.2 percent and 44.7 percent of the population, respectively. While about 64 percent of the Philippine population is rural and poor, over 85 percent are literate.

The Philippines is richly endowed with natural resources, however, 20 percent of the population controls over 50 percent of the national income. The average annual income is only $457. Most Filipinos engage in subsistence agriculture, the main crops being rice, abaca, coconuts, and corn. The nonsubsistence economy is based upon extractive industries: forestry, mining, fishing, and commercial agricultural plantations which produce pineapples, bananas, sugar, and copra. Local manufacturing enterprises are mainly involved in food and drug processing, textiles, and auto assembly.

After 386 years as a colony—first of Spain (1560–1898) and of the America (1898–1946)—and twenty-six chaotic years as an independent American-style democracy, the Philippines on September 23, 1972, was placed under martial law by President Ferdinand E. Marcos. Personal freedoms were curtailed, the National Congress abolished, political parties banned, and the mass media either shut down or censored. Approximately 12,000 people were detained. The country continued to be governed by Marcos in a nondemocratic fashion until February 1986 when the Philippine electorate (with American assistance) forced him to resign in favor of his chief political rival Corazon Aquino and flee to the United States. While Marcos, his family, and closest advisers are in exile in Hawaii, many of his followers remain in the Philippines where they continue to support martial law policies. The country continues to function under the martial law constitution, which calls for a parliamentary government, a president, a vice president and an independent judiciary. However, the Aquino regime has suspended all arbitrary acts of the government and has established a committee to create a new democratic constitution. In addition, she has released all political prisioners and reopened investigation into the death of her husband, Benigno Aquino.

Executive

Since 1981, ultimate executive power has rested with the president, who is popularly elected for a six-year term with no constitutional limit on the number of terms. Other major executive officers are members of a cabinet appointed by the president and approved by the National Assembly.

While President Aquino relies heavily upon trusted advisers, she appears to make most decisions herself. Her administration is composed of individuals drawn from all parts of the moderate political spectrum, including former Marcos supporters and members of the far left. Aquino maintains her power through widespread popular support, which includes the military, the

Catholic Church, business, and technocrats. The Aquino government tolerates peaceful political opposition, including that of Marcos supporters who, among other activities, have carried out a variety of anti-Aquino public demonstrations in Manila and other urban centers.

Legislature

Since June 1978 legislative power ostensibly has been lodged in unicameral Interim National Assembly (*Interim Batasang Pambansa;* IBP). The IBP has about 200 members, 146 of whom are elected for a six-year term through popular vote. The remaining members are the president; members of the cabinet; and appointed representatives of government-sponsored youth, agricultural, and labor organizations. The IBP no longer is the rubber stamp legislative body that it was under martial law. Instead, the IBP has become under the new administration an independent policy-making body, which includes as opposition remnants of Marcos' KBL political party. Nevertheless, President Aquino retains the power to legislate independently by issuing presidential orders, decrees, and proclamations.

Judiciary

Judicial power ostensibly rests in an "independent judiciary." The court system is headed by a Supreme Court composed of a chief justice and fourteen associate justices. All judges and justices are appointed and can be removed by the president. While possessing the formal right of judicial review of executive and legislative actions, the Supreme Court has lost much of its prestige and impact during recent years by supporting the authoritarian rule of President Marcos. Its image was further tarnished by a recent scandal in which four of the justices rigged the 1981 bar examinations so that Gustavo D. Ericta, son of Justice Vicente G. Ericta, could pass. After resigning en masse, thirteen of the fifteen Supreme Court justices, not including Ericta, were reappointed by Marcos. Since February 1986, all Marcos appointees to the Supreme Court have resigned and been replaced by President Aquino.

Regional & Local Government

Subnational government units consist of twelve regions and seventy-three provinces divided into cities, municipalities, and *barangays* (neighborhoods). Provinces are headed by governors, cities and municipalities by mayors, and *barangays* by chairmen. These officials are assisted by *sangguniang bayan* (advisory councils) which are composed of *barangay* chairmen and vice mayors. All of these institutions function under the control of the ministry of local government and community development. All major regional and local officials are popularly elected, but most elections under martial law were controlled by the government. However, President Aquino has called for new elections in 1987 to select regional and local public officials.

The Electoral System

Present transitional laws provide that popular elections are to be held only when and if the president deems conditions suitable. Voting is compulsory for all Filipino citizens sixteen years of age or older without criminal records (21.5 million voters). Candidates to the Assembly are elected by simple plurality in two-member districts (coterminous with the seventy-three provinces). Political parties are permitted if they register with the Commission on Elections (COMELEC) and are certified not to be subversive by the military.

Six elections have been held under this system: the IBP election of 1978; the Mindanao Regional Assembly election of 1979; the presidential election of 1980; the regional and municipal elections of 1981; the village (*barangay*) elections of 1982; and the national election of 1986..

Only one political party, Marcos's own New Society Movement (*Kilusang Bagong Lipunan;* KBL), fielded candidates in all five elections; it was the only party in the 1979 Mindanao Regional Assembly election. Other urban political groups participated in some but not all of the other elections, as follows: *Laban* (Fight) participated in the 1978 and 1986 elections; *Pusyon Bisaya* (Visayan Faction) contested all but the 1979 election; the Mindanao Alliance party entered the 1978, 1980, and 1982 contests; and the United Democratic Opposition (UNIDO), the Filipino Democratic Party, and the Social Democratic Party (a reincarnation of *Pusyon Bisaya*) participated in the 1982 village elections and the 1986 national elections in alliance with the Laban Party. One small ad hoc group, the National Union for Liberation, entered the 1981 elections, and another, the National Union for Democracy and Freedom, contested those of 1982.

All the elections were marked by fraud and other irregularities. In 1980 Marcos claimed to have won reelection, and the KBL won 152 of the 166 IBP seats, sixty-nine of the seventy-three governorships, and 1,450 of 1,560 mayoral races. Thirteen *Pusyon Bisaya* candidates won IBP seats from the central Philippines; the Mindanao Alliance won one IBP seat, one governorship, and several mayoral races in northeast Mindanao; and the UNIDO leader, Jose Laurel Jr., defeated the KBL candidate for governor of Batangas province.

However, as noted above, Marcos and his party were forced out of office following the February 1986 election because most elements of the Philippine electorate believed Marcos had fraudulently denied Aquino the presidency.

The Party System

Origins of the Parties

From 1898 to 1972, the Philippines had a multiparty system similar to that of the United States. Two vigorous parties, the Liberals and the Nationalists, dominated Philippine political affairs. In addition, two clandestine Marxist groups, the Communist Party of the Philippines (CCP) and the Philippine Communist Party (*Partido Komunista ñg Pilipinas*; PKP) sought to seize power outside the legal political system. One of President Marcos's first acts upon declaring martial law in 1972 was to ban all political parties. This ban remained in effect until February 1978, when the president legalized political organizations.

The old Liberal and Nationalist parties did not regroup in 1978. Some of their former adherents were in exile, most remained inactive, and others became part of the KBL. A few joined the new opposition parties, and others preferred to remain unaffiliated.

The Parties in Law

Political parties are legal if they do not have subversive or other illegal activities and goals,

have a recognized constitution and set of responsible officers, and are formally registered with the Philippine government.

Party Organization

Philippine parties resemble those of the United States in being collections of independent politicians without central organization, formal membership, coherence in policy, or discipline in execution. Leading local notables make alliances with other more or less like-minded politicians to fight elections more effectively by pooling their followers' energies and sometimes their financial resources. Parties have been characterized by considerable factionalism, both personal and moderately ideological, and opportunism. In the pre-Marcos era, shifts of allegiance from one party to the other were not uncommon among elected or hopeful politicians. Voters were and are far more likely to identify with a particular party personality than with the party itself. COMELEC rules have not altered this pattern of non-organization.

Campaigning

The rules for both local and national elections have allowed thirty to forty days for campaigning. During the campaign, the KBL used the enormous resources of the government to stress the accomplishments of the Marcos regime and to attack the opposition groups as being both American backed and communist influenced. The opposition groups were usually denied access to the government-controlled mass media and utilized public rallies and printed material to attack martial law in general and to call for a return to democracy.

Besides the 1986 presidential election, the most notable contest was between Laban led by Aquino's late husband, Benigno (assassinated in August 1983), and the KBL headed by Imelda Marcos for twenty-one Metro Manila IBP seats in 1979. Like other martial law elections, the KBL utilized widespread fraud to defeat the 1979 Laban slate.

New Society Movement
(*Kilusang Bagong Lipunan;* KBL)

History

The KBL was established by Marcos in 1978 to broaden his political base and to reduce his dependence upon the Philippine military.

Organization

The KBL is not formally organized. Marcos planned to establish a permanent national headquarters in Manila.

Policy

KBL policies were the same as those of the Marcos government: a free-enterprise economic system, economic development, strong ties with the United States, and support for the United Nations and the Association of Southeast Asian Nations (ASEAN).

Membership & Constituency

KBL membership still consists of approximately 200 Marcos cronies who were candidates in the 1978 IBP elections.

Financing

The KBL's financial resources until February 1986 essentially were those of the Philippine government. However, since the end of martial law these resources consist only of contributions from Marcos and his wealthy backers.

Leadership

The KBL still is headed by President Marcos and his wife Imelda in exile. Marcos, a much-decorated WWII guerrilla leader and a law graduate of the University of the Philippines, was born September 11, 1917, in Ilokos Norte province. Despite suffering from systemic lupus erythematosis (SLE), a serious vascular and connective tissue disease, Marcos remains a commanding political figure and unlikely to relinquish party power.

Imelda Marcos, the second most powerful party and government leader, is the daughter of the politically prominent Romualdez family of Leyte. A beauty queen in the early 1950s, Mrs. Marcos married the president in 1954. She was a member of the IBP, minister of human settlements, and Metro Manila governor before being exiled.

Marcos exercises KBL party leadership in the Philippines through his 1986 vice presidential running mate, Arturo Tolentino, who also leads the KBL in the National Assembly.

Prospects

The KBL continues to function despite the downfall and exile of Marcos. It retains considerable public support among Conservatives and the Ilokos and Bisayan regions of the Philippines. Nevertheless it is too early to predict what kind of political future the KBL will have in the volatile Philippine political environment.

Social Democratic Party (SDP)

History

Founded in December 1981, the SDP was organized by Marcos's former information minister Francisco Tatad. It is the successor of Tatad's *Pusyon Bisaya* (Visayan Faction) Party, a political group formed in January 1978. Its first and only convention, held in December 1981 in Cebu, attracted only 100 delegates. The SDP has supported candidates in all post-1978 elections, except the 1979 Mindanao contest, and put up Marcos's only 1980 presidential opponent, Alejo Santos. SDP (*Pusyon Bisaya*) candidates won thirteen IBP seats and a number of local offices in the Visayas.

Organization

The SDP, according to COMELEC rules, is headed by a president, vice president, secretary, and a treasurer. It purports to have branches in all major urban centers of the Philippines. As yet, however, the SDP has no national headquarters or staff. It operates out of Tatad's home in Cebu.

Policy

The SDP is oriented along mass-based and socialist lines. It calls for an American-style presidential governmental system. It also calls for a mixed economic system with key economic enterprises owned by the state. Anticommunist, the SDP advocates a pro-American foreign policy.

Financing

SDP activities are funded by donations from its officers and supporters. Its annual budget has ranged from US $1,000 to US $10,000.

Membership & Constituency

The SDP purports to have a membership of 5,000 scattered throughout the archipelago. Most of its strength, however, lies in central Visayas and northern Mindanao.

Leadership

SDP president Francisco Tatad (born 1940) resigned as Marcos's information minister in 1978 in protest against martial-law policies. He is a graduate of the University of Santo Tomas in Manila and was a journalist before he entered government service. The other founder of the SDP is Ruben R. Canoy of Cagayan de Oro City in northern Mindanao. Canoy was a cofounder of the Mindanao Alliance in 1978. He is a writer and a former broadcast executive. He also was former undersecretary of public information and mayor of Cagayan de Oro City.

Prospects

With its regional base in Visaya, the group has more vitality than most of the parties, but it has no prospects of successfully challenging the power of UNIDO or the KBL. Most likely, the SDP will merge with a larger political party such as UNIDO or Laban.

United Democratic Organization (UNIDO)

History

UNIDO is a coalition of five anti-Marcos political groups. Founded in late 1981, the coalition includes the former United Democratic Opposition (also called UNIDO), remnants of the Liberal and the Nationalist parties, and the Pilipino Democratic Party (PDP). The older United Democratic Opposition was founded by IBP assemblyman Salvador Laurel., in 1980 after he split with Marcos over economic policies. *Laban,* also known as *Lakas ñg Bayan* (People's Power), is a band of anti-Marcos opponents originally formed to oppose the KBL in the 1978 IBP election. It has refused to participate in subsequent elections on the grounds that they are not legitimate electoral exercises, but are only designed to defuse foreign criticism and legitimize continuance of martial law. The PDP is composed of the remnants of the pre-martial law Christian Socialist Movement (CSM) created by leading dissident Raul Manglapuz. Founded in 1981, the PDP's first annual convention, held in Cebu, attracted 500 delegates from around the country.

Organization

The United Democratic Organization is an umbrella group led by a committee composed of seven national vice presidents. It has a small secretariat located in Manila. The secretary general is former congressman Abraham Sarmiento. Among its member groups, only *Laban* has a formal headquarters in Manila. The others operate out of the homes of their chairmen and are staffed by volunteers.

Policy

The UNIDO seeks power peacefully within the existing political system by advocating the restoration of freedom and sovereignty, justice for the oppressed and exploited, economic development and social reconstruction, morality and efficiency in government, and friendly relations with all countries.

Membership & Constituency

UNIDO membership includes the 125 to 150 officers and candidates of the five participating groups. In addition, it is supported by a majority of the Philippines's large electorate including important clergymen, pre-martial law politicians, students, industrial workers, and social workers.

Financing

The coalition's budgets have been US$5,000 to US$10,000 annually. These sums have been donated by officers and supporters of the member groups. Annual budgets of the member groups have ranged from US$2,000 to US$50.000 donated by the same officers and supporters.

Leadership

Besides President Aquino and Vice President Salvador Laurel, central figures in the coalition are the chairmen of its five constituent members: Lorenzo Tañada of *Laban,* Jose Laurel, Jr., of the older UNIDO; Diosdado Macapagal of the Nationalist Party; Luis Jose of the PDP. Tañada (born 1903) is a lawyer and former senator from Quezon province. Jose Laurel of Batangas province is a former pro-Marcos IBP member and former senator. Macapagal is a former president of the Philippines (1960–65) and an elder Filipino statesman. Luis Jose is a businessman from Pampanga province and cofounder of the Christian Socialist Movement. Salvador Laurel is a former senator and brother of Jose Laurel. Corazon Aquino comes from a prominent Philippine family, is a natural sciences graduate of American universities, and has had several decades of political experience as the wife of one of the country's most important politicians.

Prospects

UNIDO has the best prospect for dominating future Philippine electoral politics. Nevertheless, its political power will diminish if the coalition's leadership (as it most likely will) follows traditional Philippine political patterns and breaks up into separate competing factions.

Mindanao Alliance

History

The Mindanao Alliance was founded in February 1978 to compete for 3 IBP seats in northeastern Mindanao. It was founded by Ruben R. Canoy, Aquilino Pimentel, and Homobono Adaza. A regional grouping, it has fielded candidates in all elections held in northeastern Mindanao. The Alliance was suc-

cessful in capturing one IBP seat, the governorship of Misamis Oriental province, the mayorship of Cagayan de Oro City, and several other local offices. It is allied with the Social Democratic Party in the region.

Organization

The Alliance is organized to meet minimal COMELEC requirements. It has a chairman, vice chairman, secretary, and treasurer. It has a small secretariat in Cagayan de Oro City, and a secretary general who heads a three-member staff.

Policy

Mindanao Alliance policies focus primarily on local concerns, particularly on greater industrial and infrastructure development on Mindanao. It also advocates the protection of civil and human rights and an end to arbitrary actions by the police and army.

Membership & Constituency

The Alliance consists of about twenty-five officers and candidates, supported by about one million Filipinos in northeastern Mindanao.

Financing

The Alliance's annual budgets have ranged from US$2,000 to US$8,000. Wealthy officers and supporters are the source of funds.

Leadership

The Alliance hierarchy is headed by Homobono Adaza. Adaza, a lawyer and graduate of Silliman University, presently is governor of Misamis Oriental province. Pimentel and Canoy joined the Social Ruben R. Canoy Democratic Party in 1981.

Prospects

The party will continue to be an effective voice in its area, but will have a national impact only in alliance with other groups.

Minor Parties

Moro National Liberation Front

Founded in Malaysia in 1970, the MNLF is a coalition of Muslim separatists operating in the southern Philippines. It has sufficient resources to carry out not only isolated guerrilla acts, but also full-scale conventional military operations against government forces. Since 1972, the MNLF insurrection has caused over 50,000 fatalities, displaced over 200,000 persons, and cost untold amounts of scarce public resources. The MNLF goal is an autonomous Islamic state or an autonomous Muslim region within the existing Philippine Republic.

The heterogeneous groups of the MNLF vary in size from fifty to 1,000 and are loyal primarily to personal leaders rather than any Islamic ideology or cause. The MNLF is led by a revolutionary committee with two headquarters: a field command near Zamboanga City and an administrative center based in Tripoli, Libya. The committee is led by a chairman and several vice chairmen who deal with such specific matters as foreign affairs and finances. The MNLF's military arm, the Bangsa Moro Army (BMA), is organized into six regional commands.

The MNLF has 20,000 troops, mainly of Tausug and Maguindanao Muslims, and some 500,000 supporters spread throughout the five Muslim provinces of Mindanao and the Sulu Archipelago. Since 1978, MNLF manpower has diminished as a result of battlefield casualties, factionalism, and defections. For example, early in 1978, splits occurred between the radical MNLF leadership and the more moderate factions of Hashim Salamat of Maguindanao, Rashid Salipada Pendatun, and Macapantun Abbas, Jr., of Lanao region. Among recent defections to the government are the followers of Abdul Kahyr Alonto and Jamil Lukman of Lanao and Commander "Ronnie" of Cotabato.

Little is known about MNLF funds. Until recently, the most significant amount came from radical Islamic states, especially Libya. The MNLF also is rumored to control large commercial fruit plantations in Cotabato and Lanao.

Very little is known about the MNLF leadership. Its chairman Nur Misuari, a well-known Muslim leftist, was a political science instructor at the University of the Philippines. He is a Tausug from Sulu. Most other MNLF leaders also are Tausugs or Samals from Sulu.

In spite of factionalism and defections, the MNLF will continue to pose serious problems for the Philippine government. The costs of containing the movement constitute a serious drain on the country's resources. It is likely that only some form of autonomy will end the insurrection.

Philippine Communist Party (Partido Komunista ñg Pilipinas)

The PKP is the older and smaller of the two Philippine Communist factions. Founded on November 7, 1930, by Crisanto Evangelista, the PKP is based in the rural areas of Central Luzon. Its military arm, the Hukbalahaps (Huks), was organized in March 1942 as an anti-Japanese guerrilla unit and continued to fight the new Philippine government in 1946. After some growth in the immediate postwar period, the PKP insurgents were crushed by government forces under Ramon Magsaysay. Subsequently, Huk dissidence remained an annoying but minor security problem for the government. In 1974, the main cadre of the PDP gave up armed revolution and surrendered to the government. In return, the Marcos regime gave the PKP legal status and released its imprisoned leaders, who currently serve as advisors to such government programs as land reform and rural cooperatives.

The PKP maintains a central committee and a politburo and recognizes the party's national congress (last held in 1973) as the only legitimizer of party actions and policies.

The party organ is Ang Komunista (The Communist) which is published irregularly in English and the major Philippine dialects.

PKP front groups like the National Workers' Federation (Pambansang Kilusan ñg Paggawa), the Democratic Union of Filipino Youth (Malayang Pagkakaisa ñg Kabataang Pilipinas; MPKP), the Movement for the Advancement of Nationalism (MAN), the Bertrand Russell Peace Foundation, and the Brotherhood for our Development (Ang Kapatiran sa Ikauunlad Natin; AKSIUN) are paper organizations with few or no members.

A pro-Moscow group, PKP demands include a return to democracy; the release of political prisoners; the nationalization of the banking, insurance, and mining sectors; agrarian reform; and the abrogation of all "unequal" treaties with the United States.

PKP membership is estimated at seventy to 250 middle-aged, hardcore members supported by several hundred sympathizers among peasant, labor, and intellectual groups.

No reliable information about PKP finances is available. PKP leadership is dominated by secretary general Feliçismo Macapagal who heads the aging Politburo and Central Committee. Legendary elder statesman Luis Taruc, while a member of the top leadership, has little influence in PKP affairs.

Communist Party of the Philippines (CCP)

The other Philippine communist faction, the illegal CCP, was organized on December 26, 1968, in central Luzon. It was founded by pro-Peking intellectuals dissatisfied with the pro-Moscow PKP leadership. Since 1970, it has been engaged in a "people's liberation war" aimed at encircling cities from the countryside. Enjoying only limited success, many of its followers and leaders have been killed or captured. Nevertheless the CCP remains a security problem for the Aquino regime.

Like the PKP, the CCP is governed by a central committee and a politburo and recognizes the party's national congress as the ultimate policymaker. Currently, the CCP claims to have sixteen regional committees governing over 2,000 local committees. The CCP sponsors one mass-based organization, the National Democratic Front (NDF). Founded in April 1973, the NDF is an umbrella group for three other leftist groups: the Federation of Filipino Workers, the Union of Nationalist Urban Poor, and the United Socialist Party of the Philippines. Largely paper organizations, they serve as recruiting channels among anti-Marcos elements. The party's military arm, the New People's Army (NPA), claims to have 20,000 members operating in sixteen provinces.

CCP clandestine communication resources consist of a domestic news distribution agency, the *Balita ñg Malayang Philippines* (Free Philippines News Service) and two newspapers, *Ang Bayan* (The People) and *Liberation,* which appear irregularly in English and various native dialects.

The CCP's principal policy is to establish a Philippine communist state through subversion.

The CCP has an estimated membership of 60,000 cadre supported by several million sympathizers. The latter are mainly students, intellectuals, and peasants.

Little is known about CCP finances, but it is believed that funds are provided by "people's taxes" levied on residents of areas controlled by the NPA. In addition, materials and supplies are bought or stolen from isolated government military units.

The names and activities of CCP leaders other than secretary general and chief ideologue José Maria Sison (alias Amadeo Guerrero) are virtually never publicized. Sison—son of a wealthy Pangasinan landowner, a university graduate, and a former English instructor of the University of the Philippines—has been in prison since 1978. Other known Politburo members—Antonio Zumel, Satur Ocampo, Victor Corpuz, and José Luneta—also are in prison. Ocampo was once the business editor of the defunct *Manila Times.* Corpuz is a graduate of the Philippine Military Academy and was a lieutenant in the armed forces. Luneta is a graduate of the University of the Philippines in political science.

While the CCP claims its Central Committee and Politburo has been organized, nothing is known about the names or background of the new leadership.

After months of refusal, the CCP leadership has agreed to open negotiations with the Aquino administration toward terminating its armed antigovernment movement. However, most observers speculate that the CCP will not voluntarily relinquish its armed resistance to cooperate with the new regime. As a result, the New People's Army will continue to expand military efforts to overthrow the established government through violent revolution.

Other Political Forces

Military

The imposition of martial law in 1972 elevated the Armed Forces of the Philippines (AFP) to a predominant position in the Marcos regime, which relied upon it to combat armed resistance as well as control many key government and civilian enterprises. Marcos ensured the military's continued loyalty by placing relatives and friends in key military positions. Sizable pay raises, liberal fringe benefits, and frequent promotions, combined with discipline of personnel opposing his policies, help to secure compliance at all levels.

Nevertheless, as a result of problems in morale and discipline, the military has become increasingly ineffective in reducing the communist insurgency. First, in spite of the recent retirement of twenty-five generals, there are few senior slots available for ambitious younger middle-level officers. Second, interservice rivalries have resulted in armed conflict among units of the army, national police, and Police Constabulary. Third, undisciplined military personnel have frequently abused civilians through criminal acts and human rights violations. Finally, there is a growing desertion rate among military personnel engaged in combat against dissident Muslim and communist elements. Since 1972, approximately 6,000 military personnel have been court-martialed.

Concern about the ability of the martial law regime to solve these problems became so great that the military leadership (led by defense minister Juan Ponce Enrile and Police Constabulary Chief Fidel Ramos) played a critical role in the February 1986 ouster of Marcos by throwing its support behind the Aquino movement.

Technocrats

Like Marcos, President Aquino must rely upon technocrats to manage her regime. Trained in the United States, they favor social reforms and enjoy high reputations in international circles.

United States

The United States has unusually powerful influence in its former colony (1898–1946) and enjoys a favorable image among the general Philippine population. The government's bureaucratic, health, legal, welfare, and educational systems are patterned after those in the United States. Most of the country's academic, business, and military elites have been trained in the United States.

The two countries have scores of trade, military, and political agreements, and the United States maintains huge naval and air force bases at Subic Bay and Angeles City. In addition, the United States is the Philippines's largest overall trading partner and the preeminent foreign investor in Philippine business. As a consequence, the United States was able to play a key

role in the February 1986 ouster of Marcos when the Reagan administration withdrew its support in favor of Aquino. For similar reasons, it is unlikely that the Aquino regime can survive for long without the active support of the United States government.

Pre-1972 Politicians

Opposition to the Marcos regime during the martial law years continued among factions controlled by several professional politicians of the pre-1972 democratic era. These included groups headed by former president Diosdado Macapagal, and former senators Benigno Aquino, Gerardo Roxas, Jovito Salonga, Jose Diokno, Salvador Lopez, and Raul Manglapuz.

The most important of these groups is the Movement for a Free Philippines (MFP) and Friends of the Filipino People (FFP), which are based in Washington, D.C. The MFP, a coalition headed by Manglapuz, a former senator and foreign secretary, has 2,000 members belonging to chapters in all major overseas Filipino population centers. The FFP has chapters in seventeen American cities.

Another influential pre-1972 politician is former senator Jose Diokno who along with Benigno Aquino was a serious candidate to succeed Marcos in 1972. Diokno, a lawyer from Batangas province, remains unaffiliated with any political group. He controls a loyal following of thousands of ordinary Filipinos and has close ties with armed dissidents, many of whom he has defended in military courts and tribunals.

The single most prominent and important of the moderate politicians is President Aquino. However, her present political dominance in Philippine politics can be successfully challenged by Vice President Salvador Laurel who, as previously noted, heads a wealthy and prominent family, chairs UNIDO, and enjoys widespread popularity among Philippine voters.

Roman Catholic Church

Although 85 percent of Filipinos are Roman Catholics, severe shortages of priests (one for every 15,000 Filipinos) and funds outside the urban centers mean that most Filipinos never see a priest or attend mass. The Church does have some influence among the urban middle- and upper-class faithful, many of whom are organized in some thirty Catholic Action groups with an aggregate membership of about 250,000. Catholic Action programs vary from group to group, but most of them are engaged in charitable and devotional activities with little or no political content.

The Catholic Bishops Conference of the Philippines was divided in its views on the Marcos regime and proposals for social and ecclesiastical reform. Of the seventy-six bishops, only a small group of thirteen (mostly non-Filipinos), led by Bishop Francisco Clavier of Bukidnon, strongly condemned martial law as well as existing social and ecclesiastical inequities. A moderate group of twenty-three, led by Cardinal Jaime Sin of Manila, adopted a policy of "critical collaboration" with the regime and supported some reform proposals. The remaining forty bishops supported martial law and opposed nearly all reforms. They were led by Cardinal Julio Rufino Rosales of Cebu. Many conservative and moderate bishops are closely affiliated with elite civic and business groups.

The Catholic religious orders, on the other hand, were united in their opposition to the regime and their commitment to reforms. The leaders of the ninety-six orders (thirty-five for men and sixty-one for women) are loosely organized in two Associations of Major Religious Superiors (one for men, one for women) which were founded in 1955. Collectively, the orders are among the wealthiest institutions in the country. With an annual income of $200 million, they control extensive educational and media resources: 430 parishes, 3,017 schools with an enrollment of about two million, 1,500 periodicals, a professional book-publishing industry, and fifteen radio stations. About 2,300 priests and 6,000 nuns manage these operations. Preeminent among the leadership of the orders is Joaquin Bernas, S.J., a U.S.-educated lawyer in his early fifties.

It is difficult to assess the impact the orders will have on the new regime, if any. It is cautious, self-protective, and partly dependent on the goodwill and largesse of the upper and middle classes. Their long-range influence on a future generation of public leaders, however, may benefit the society as a whole.

Organized Labor

While organized labor has roots going back to the American colonial era, it has always been small, fragmented, and concentrated in the Manila region. In 1972, there were one million workers organized into 6,000 unions. These unions in turn belonged to twenty-three federations dealing with single industries or groups of industries.

Marcos's policy during martial law was to discourage the organization of labor and to maintain strict control of its activities through the government-sponsored Trade Union Congress of the Philippines (*Katipunang Manggagawang Pilipino;* KMP) which was launched on December 14, 1975. The KMP includes twenty-nine trade unions with 1.9 million members covering all vital industries. The labor code of May 1, 1974, prohibits strikes in vital industries. Mass action in nonvital industries is allowed, but can only be undertaken after the union gives thirty days' notice. Unresolved labor disputes come under the jurisdiction of the National Labor Relations Commission (NLRC).

The Aquino regime appears determined to dissolve the KMP and permit Filipino laborers to organize independently as before 1972.

Peasants

Peasant movements in the Philippines have an even longer history, dating back to the early Spanish era. While the mass of peasants have remained passive, sporadic uprisings of discontented peasants have been marked by fury and desperation and have been crushed by ruthless government retaliation. These movements all have been localized and personalized cults ranging in size from a few dozen to several hundred. Notable were the Colorosa movement of 1931 in Pangasinan province and the Sakdalista revolt of 1935 in Tarlac.

Government policy under martial law was twofold: a ban on non-government-sponsored peasant organizations and mass actions and a broad program to ameliorate the feudalistic conditions which have led to peasant discontent. A variety of government programs have been launched, including land reform, rural cooperatives, and land banks. Even though these programs have achieved some success, the mass of Filipino tenants and farmers remain unorganized and quiescent. With the exception of the ban on non-government peasant organizations, the Aquino regime seems likely to continue martial law policies toward ameliorating poverty among the rural poor.

National Prospects

It seems likely that the constitutional committee created by President Aquino will reestablish an American-style government. The president and vice president will be limited to one six-year term and local governmental units will be given greater autonomy. While the end of martial law and the reestablishment of democracy undoubtedly has helped relieve many immediate political problems, it has not solved long-term and massive socioeconomic problems which, among other things, have led to widespread poverty and dramatic growth in the Philippine communist armed movement. Therefore, the Philippine political system will continue to experience instability and uncertainty in the foreseeable future.

Further Reading

Asia Yearbook. Honk Kong: Far Eastern Economic Review Publications, Annual.

Machado, Kit. "The Philippines 1978: Authoritarian Consolidation Continues." *Asian Survey,* Vol. 20, No. 1, January 1979.

Neher, Clark D. *Politics in Southeast Asia.* New York: Schenkman, 1981.

Noble, Lela Garner. "Muslim Separatism in the Philippines." *Asian Survey,* Vol. 21, No. 3, March 1981.

Philippine Yearbook. Manila: Republic of the Philippines, 1978.

Youngblood, Robert L. "Church Opposition to Martial Law in the Philippines." *Asian Survey,* Vol. 18, No. 5, May 1978.

POLISH PEOPLE'S REPUBLIC
(Polska Rzeczpospolita Ludowa)
by Suzanne Hruby, M. Phil.

The System of Government

Four years after Solidarity was crushed as a legal movement and martial law was imposed, Poland in 1985 faces the same underlying economic and sociopolitical problems that led to the country's profound upheaval in 1980–1981. The current regime of Gen. Wojciech Jaruzelski has gone to great lengths to demonstrate that Poland's political turbulence has ended and that order has been restored. While remaining party chief, Jaruzelski has turned over the premiership, which he had occupied, to the economist Zbigniew Messner, announced the release of political prisoners (although not an across-the-board amnesty), allowed an open trial of security forces accused of the murder of the Catholic priest Jerzy Popieluszko, and pledged the government's allegiance to economic and technological progress. Many observers inside and outside of Poland agree that although the Polish leader has succeeded in reestablishing control and achieved a semblance of normalcy he has failed largely to reverse the country's protracted economic decline, to resolve the regime's crisis of legitimacy, and to revitalize the Communist Party organization. The sources of Poland's present instability and political impasse lie in its uneasy experience with communism following World War II.

Once a great European power (1386–1696), Poland disappeared from the European map in 1795 after three partitions of her territory by Russia, Prussia, and Austria. The Polish state was reconstituted after World War I, following the collapse of the Russian, Austrian, and German monarchies. Interwar Poland lasted a mere twenty-one years (1918–39) before it was annexed or occupied by Nazi Germany and Stalinist Russia.

During World War II there were three centers of Polish resistance. They were the government-in-exile in London, partisan resistance in Polish areas (both the nationalist Home Army and the smaller communist People's Guard), and the pro-Soviet League of Polish Patriots in the USSR. The restoration of a national government on Polish soil came when the last of these three groups, returning with the Red Army, established, in Lublin in 1944, the Polish Committee of National Liberation, which subsequently transformed itself into a provisional government in 1945.

The Polish state today is approximately 150 miles to the west of the interwar state. It incorporates areas that prior to World War II had substantial German populations (lower East Prussia, Upper Silesia, and the area around Gdansk-Danzig). Areas of interwar Poland with Ukrainian, Ruthenian, Byelorussian populations were incorporated into the USSR. Poland gained approximately 40,000 square miles in eastern Germany and lost 70,000 square miles to the USSR in the east.

People's Poland is the second largest country, both in area and population (36.9 million), in the Soviet bloc. Its politics are unique among the communist countries of East Europe because of geographical position between the USSR and Germany, its peasant smallholder agriculture, its cyclical history of periodic upheaval, and the strength and influence of the Roman Catholic Church.

Historically, political and social resistance to the Polish government has been significant, but it has been a major force in the past eighteen years. Provisionally, modern Polish history can be divided into seven periods. The first period, 1944 to 1948, saw the rise to political power of the Polish communists, who ruled the country along Stalinist lines from 1948 to 1956. From 1956 to 1968, a national communist faction gained control of the party following widespread popular discontent with Stalinism. The period from 1968 to 1976 was characterized by periodic and uncoordinated resistance to the government by various social groups. Since

1976, there has been almost constant opposition to the government by a coalition of dissident forces, articulating broad societal interests. It is this coalition of forces that ushered in the Polish August of 1980 and the Solidarity period of 1980–1981, which was cut short by the imposition of martial law in December 1981. The most recent period is commonly referred to as the postmartial law years or the period of normalization.

The Polish system of government was based on the constitution of 1952. This document resembles the Soviet constitution of 1936, promulgated by Stalin. It classifies Poland as a people's democracy. In Soviet ideological formulations, this corresponds to the period of early development in the USSR and is considered to be a transitional stage between capitalism and socialism. The basis of state power is "the dictatorship of urban and rural workers."

In 1975, the leaders of the communist party, the Polish United Workers' Party (PZPR), and the government proposed a series of amendments to the constitution. Three of these changes brought an outcry from the Polish public. One change that would have constitutionally established "the leading role" of the PZPR in society was toned down. It subsequently defined the PZPR's role as the "leading political force in society in constructing socialism." An amendment that declared that citizen's rights were to be based on the fulfillment of citizen's duties was dropped. Finally, an amendment that mentioned the "unshakeable bonds" between the Polish Peoples' Republic and the Soviet Union was toned down to a commitment to strengthen cooperation between the two nations. This codification of a nation's foreign policy in its constitution is highly unusual and brings the idea of Poland's national sovereignty into question.

Executive

According to the constitution, the Council of State is a collective body that is elected by the *Sejm* (Parliament) from among its own members. It functions as the head of state and handles the business of the *Sejm* when it is not in session. (The *Sejm* is only required to meet twice a year by law.) When the *Sejm* is not in session, the Council of State has the power to issue decrees with the force of law and to interpret all existing laws. The Council also has the power to call the *Sejm* into session, call for elections,

ratify treaties, and to declare war and martial law. It also appoints certain officials such as Supreme Court justices and introduces much of the legislation passed by the *Sejm*. Historically, it has consisted of senior communist politicians.

The second executive body, also elected by the *Sejm* or the Council of State, if the *Sejm* is not in session, is the Council of Ministers. Its members are usually chosen by the party and simply approved by the *Sejm*. The Council of Ministers' chief task is the formulation and execution of state policy. It is similar to most parliamentary cabinets, with portfolios for foreign affairs, trade, defense, interior, etc. Since Polish industry is nationalized, the Council of Ministers contains a large number of ministries which directly oversee industrial production on a sectoral level. Thus it also is responsible for the drafting of the state budget and the national economic plan.

Unlike Western governments, the Council of Ministers has agencies that oversee almost all aspects of the political, economic, social, and cultural life of Poland. Even local government is responsible to the Council of Ministers. The council is headed by a prime minister and several deputy prime ministers. Historically, it has been dominated by the party's Front of National Unity, with a communist majority. Since 1956 there have been some nonparty experts in the cabinet, and in the recent past, one of the deputy prime ministers has been a Catholic independent.

Another important governmental body responsible to the *Sejm* is the Supreme Control Chamber, created by a constitutional amendment in 1957. Its raison d'être was to clean up the widespread corruption and abuse of power among government and party officials discovered during the de-Stalinization period of the mid-1950s. Its function is to investigate irregularities and to report on them to the *Sejm*. It tends to become more active during periods of political volatility. Recently, it has become more active under the stewardship of Mieczyslaw Moczar, an ardent nationalist who challenged both PZPR first secretary Wladyslaw Gomulka for power in 1968 and his successor, Edward Gierek, in the early 1970s. Moczar was relieved of his duties in the ministry of the interior in 1971 and put in charge of the Supreme Control Chamber, supposedly to deny him a power base. With revelations about abuse of power by Gierek and his cronies following the Polish August, Moczar, who had patiently been collecting files on his contemporaries in the party and government, once again rose to national prominence.

Legislature

The *Sejm* is a unicameral body of 460 members (in 1982), each representing about 60,000 voters. Members of the *Sejm* are elected to four-year terms.

More than half the *Sejm* deputies are members of the communist party, the PZPR. The remaining deputies are members of two other small parties and independents. The PZPR's control of the representation accorded these smaller groups is demonstrated by the fact that from 1957 to 1976 the number of deputies in each bloc remained unchanged: PZPR, 225; United Peasant Party (ZSL), 117; Democratic Party (SD), 39; and independents, 49. In the 1976 and 1980 elections, there were slight fluctuations in these numbers. The *Sejm* elected in 1980 consisted of 261 PZPR members, 113 from the ZSL, 37 from the SD, and 49 independents. However, there has been genuine opposition to government and party policies by independent Catholic blocs in the *Sejm*, called the *Znak* (Sign) and neo-*Znak*.

In the aftermath of the Polish August, the *Sejm* engaged in heated debate and criticism of proposed legislation, instead of providing the usual rubber-stamp approval. Technically, Jaruzelski was required to gain the prior approval of the *Sejm* for his martial-law declaration; he received it only after the fact. With the imposition of martial law, debate in the *Sejm* was sharply curtailed.

Judiciary

The Polish constitution calls for an independent court system. However, judges at all levels are chosen by the government and rarely show any independence. The highest court is the Supreme Court. Its justices are chosen by the Council of State for five-year terms and are subject to its recall. Local courts consist of one professional jurist and two citizen judges. The tribunals are selected by the local government. The chief criterion for the selection of judges seems to be their political reliability, although the decision of the Supreme Court to approve Solidarity's application for official recognition, overturning a lower-court decision, may have been an independent act.

The judiciary as a whole is supervised by the prosecutor general, who is appointed by the Council of State. The limits to the power of this office are not constitutionally defined. The prosecutor general can reopen all cases including those of the Supreme Court, control the status of all suits and determine at which level of jurisdiction they will be tried, and can reverse all out-of-court settlements. In criminal suits, the prosecutor general is the prosecutor and chief investigator.

Regional & Local Government

The constitutional amendments of 1975 simplified and centralized the structure of regional and local government. The number of provinces was expanded from seventeen to forty-nine, and the next-lowest tier of government was abolished. The provinces were put under the executive control of prefects (*wojewoda*) appointed by the central government.

At the local level, the people's councils, which had been elected, were abolished in 1975. Many nonparty people had served in these local councils, because the degree of control which the party was able to exercise over the nominating procedure varied from place to place. The people's councils had marginal autonomy from the central government, although they were constitutionally responsible to both the Council of State and the Council of Ministers. The former had the power to annul any decision of a people's council and to dissolve it and hold new elections.

The extreme centralization of the Polish state and the lack of any separation of powers leaves little space in the state organs for opposition to form. Compared to the rest of the communist bloc, however, there has been greater room for political opposition in the state apparatuses.

The Electoral System

The election of candidates to the *Sejm* is not a representative procedure. Nomination is controlled by the electoral committee of the Front of National Unity, an organ of the PZPR. The Front consists of the PZPR and its allied parties, the United Peasant Party and the Democratic Party. The electoral committee is tightly controlled by the PZPR. Prior to 1957, the National Front presented one list of candidates to the voters for approval. It was made up of members of the three parties and a small number of nonparty candidates. The PZPR consistently received better than 50 percent of the seats, thus ensuring its control of the *Sejm*.

Since 1957 the National Front has allowed some contested elections for *Sejm* seats. In 1980, 646 candidates ran for the 460 *Sejm* seats.

Suffrage is universal for all "working people of town and country" eighteen years of age and older. Turnout in 1980 was reportedly 98.87 percent of eligible voters.

Polish United Workers' Party (*Polska Zjednoczona Partia Robotnicza*; PZPR)

History

The roots of the communist party in Poland lie in two parties formed in the 1890s. The Polish Socialist Party (*Polska Partia Socjalistyczna*; PPS) was founded in 1893 in Paris and was a member party of the social-democratic Second International. It had a strong nationalist tendency. The Social Democracy of the Kingdom of Lithuania and Poland (*Socjal-Demokracja Krolestwa Polskiego i Litwy*; SDKPiL), had a strong internationalist and revolutionary bent. It was founded in 1895 by the well-known Marxists Rosa Luxemburg, Leo Jogiches, and Adolf Warski. In 1919 the left wing of the PPS and SKDPiL merged to form the Communist Workers' Party of Poland (*Komunistyczna Partia Robotnicza Polski*; KPRP).

The KPRP was a member of the Marxist-Leninist Third International. It had only a small following because of the anti-Russian sentiments of most Poles. In 1925, the party changed its name to the Communist Party of Poland (*Komunistyczna Partia Polski*; KPP). Following the *coup d'état* of Marshall Pilsudski in the mid-1920s, the party was forced to operate underground. It was further weakened by an unstable leadership and the constant shifting of the strategic line of the Third International. Stalin dissolved the KPP in 1937, charging that it was a center of Trotskyism, Luxemburgism, and police infiltration. Almost all of its leaders, in exile in Moscow, perished during Stalin's purges.

From 1937 until 1942, there was no communist group in Poland recognized by the USSR. In 1942, Stalin permitted pro-Moscow communists to set up the Polish Workers' Party (*Polska Partia Robotnicza*; PPR).

There were two distinct groups in the PPR. One, based in Moscow during most of the war, contained many hardline Stalinists and was led by Boleslaw Beirut. It played a dominant role in Polish groups organized in the Soviet Union, such as the League of Polish Patriots, and in the Polish forces that fought with the Red Army against the Germans. The second group, the "native communists," organized a military arm, the People's Guard, after Germany invaded the Soviet Union. Because of their well-defined goals, disciplined organization, and talented leadership the communists had a disproportionately large influence on the resistance. Its most influential leader, Wladyslaw Gomulka, became first secretary of the party in 1943.

The Moscow communists returned to Poland with the Red Army. In 1944 and 1945, the communists and their allies organized both a new *Sejm* and a provisional government on Polish soil. The government-in-exile in London was denied the right to participate as a group, but some of its leaders were permitted to return to Poland and take part in the new government. In January 1947, elections were held for a Constituent *Sejm*.

The election results were questionable. There were allegations that the communists resorted to stuffing the ballot box. Beyond this, Polish and Soviet security forces did their utmost to disrupt the campaign of the opposition parties and to intimidate their supporters. While the PPR itself captured only one-fourth of the *Sejm* seats, its allied parties won over half of them, so that the coalition altogether controlled more than 80 percent of the seats. The PPR lacked majorities in both the legislature and the government in the period from 1945 to 1948, but was able to maintain firm control of the country by dominating the key ministries, especially interior, and with the support of Soviet occupation forces.

After the utter defeat of the traditionalist Polish Peasant Party in the 1947 elections and the crushing of the remnants of the nonsocialist Home Army, the Stalinist wing of the PPR moved to take control of the party apparatus from the "native communists." Gomulka came under increasing attack for nationalist deviations. In 1948 he was forced to resign as first secretary in favor of Beirut. Gomulka's close associates were removed from top party and government positions in the following months and replaced by supporters of Beirut, such as Edward Ochab and Jakub Berman.

Gomulka, before his resignation, had been exploring the possibility of merging with the PPS. Beirut pursued these plans. After substantial resignations and purges from the PPS, the two parties were merged to form the Polish United Workers' Party in December 1948. Unlike the other communist parties in Eastern Europe, the PZPR did not stage show trials after the Tito-Stalin split in 1948, for reasons which remain unclear. After the death of Stalin in 1953, the party relaxed some of its more excessive practices: political terror was curtailed, censorship relaxed, and the stress on heavy industrial investment was downplayed in favor of more consumer goods.

In the period 1953 to 1956 open dissatisfaction began to develop among the population at large and in some groups in the PZPR, primarily intellectuals. First Secretary Beirut died in March 1956 and was succeeded by his associate Edward Ochab.

Following the beginning of de-Stalinization at the Twentieth Congress of the Soviet Communist Party (1956), opposition to Polish Stalinism among students and intellectuals became visibly widespread. In June 1956, workers in Poznan struck to protest working conditions, living standards, waste, and corruption. A demonstration turned into riots, and battles between police and demonstrators continued for several days. After these events. Gomulka and most of his close associates were rehabilitated, and in October, under the threat of Soviet intervention, Gomulka was again elected first secretary. Gomulka was able to remove or outmaneuver most of his hard-line opponents. He was able to get his own supporters into high party positions and thus resist the demands of the reformist wing of the party. By 1958, the situation had been "normalized."

During the period of unrest in 1956, most of the collectivized farms of Poland began to dissolve on their own initiative. By the time Gomulka came to power, he and the party were faced with a *fait accompli*: the virtual end of collectivized agriculture, a circumstance without parallel in the Soviet bloc. The party lacked the resources and political will to carry out a policy of forced collectivization, a process that had cost millions of lives in the Soviet Union in the late 1920s and early 1930s.

Gomulka's rule remained outwardly stable until 1968 when intellectual ferment over the issues of censorship and academic freedom led to student demonstrations. The police fought pitched battles with students all across Poland. A party faction called the "partisans" used an anti-Semitic campaign to mobilize support for its hard-line and nationalist aspirations. Led by Mieczyslaw Moczar, minister of the interior, the group had a limited but solid base of support in the party, and strong support from elements in the armed forces, the police, and an organization called the Union of Fighters for Freedom and Democracy, formed to involve former anti-Nazi partisans in Polish political life.

Gomulka was able to withstand the Moczar challenge with the help of a new faction in the party. This group, the "economists," was made up of technocrats. While politically conventional, they wanted to reform the Polish economy by the use of monetary incentives and increased managerial autonomy. When workers struck on the Baltic coast in 1970 in response to price rises, Gomulka was removed as first secretary and replaced by a representative of the 'economist' faction, Edward Gierek, the party leader in Silesia.

Gierek and his associates stabilized the situation by repealing the price rises and by talking face-to-face with workers in Szczecin and Gdansk, the two major coastal strike centers. Gierek placed his own associates in the Politburo and replaced Moczar with Stanislaw Kania. Gierek's strongest opposition came from a hard-line group that opposed his policy of increased centralization of the economy and his relatively soft line on opposition outside the party. The most prominent members of this group were Stefan Olszowski and Tadeusz Grabski. Gierek was able to keep this opposition largely in check.

After another attempt to raise prices incited worker unrest in Radom and Ursus in 1976, Gierek's greatest challenge came from outside the party. An opposition comprised of industrial workers and intellectuals, supported by the Catholic Church, began to coalesce. Both the actions of this opposition and the collapse of the economy paralyzed the party. Price rises in July of 1980 brought widespread initially uncoordinated strikes across Poland. Gierek resigned in September and was replaced by Stanislaw Kania.

Kania faced strong opposition on two sides. Grabski and Olszowski made political comebacks, returning to the Politburo, and often abetted by the leaders of the USSR, pressed for a harder line against the independent trade union Solidarity, which emerged during the summer strikes. Kania also had to cope with the fact that nearly one-third of the members of the party joined Solidarity in the next few months. The most serious challenge to his leadership came from the "horizontalists," a group with widespread support among the party rank and file. It called for the rotation of party posts, the separation of the party and the state, greater decision making by elected bodies, no limit to the number of candidates in party elections, secret balloting, and decentralization of party structures to allow local initiative to solve the crisis of both the nation and the party.

There was also rank-and-file pressure for an extraordinary party congress with open nominations and secret ballots. Such a congress was held in July 1981. The delegates were largely first-time participants in a party congress, and Solidarity members made up better than 20 percent of those present. Kania managed to isolate the "horizontalists" and other reformers in precongress caucuses and resisted a power play by Grabski. In the end, even Olszowski and party "liberals" such as Mieczyslaw Rakowski, editor of the influential weekly, *Polityka*, supported Kania.

There was little improvement in the situation of the nation or in the revitalization of the party after Kania's victory, and he was replaced as first secretary by his prime minister, General Wojciech Jaruzelski, in October. Jaruzelski remained both prime minister and defense minister, making him the most powerful party-state official since Beirut. Jaruzelski occupied simultaneously the positions of prime minister, defense minister, and party secretary until 1984 when he stepped down from the post of minister of defense. In 1985, he handed over the premiership to the economist Zbigniew Messner to demonstrate that Poland was returning to normalcy. The transfer did not involve any diminution of his power, however.

Organization

The PZPR's structure is pyramidal. At its base are local party organizations of three to 100 members, concentrated in places of work or residence. Each of these groups vote for representatives for the local administrative area. This procedure continues upward to the provincial level and to the party congress, the national organ of the PZPR. The nomination procedure for representatives to each succeeding level is largely controlled by the local and national secretariats. However, the elections to the last congress, the Extraordinary Ninth, allowed delegates to be nominated by the rank and file.

Although the party congress, which normally meets every five years, is theoretically the ultimate source of authority within the PZPR, its functions are largely limited to approving leadership decisions and nominations to the bodies that exercise real power. The congress elects the Central Committee, which implements party policies between congresses and usually meets several times a year. In practice authority and decision-making are concentrated in the Political Bureau (Politburo) and the Secretariat of the Central Committee.

The Politburo usually includes the most powerful members of the Central Committee Secretariat, the secretaries of the most important provincial party organizations, and the most powerful party members in the government. Often, members will hold a position in each of these bodies. It is the Politburo that normally makes the major political and economic decisions in Poland.

The Secretariat directs the implementation of party resolutions and supervises the selection of cadres. This second function includes recruitment of new members, checking the reliability of old members, and maintaining control of the state apparatus and other key institutions. The Secretariat is a massive bureaucracy that parallels the state bureaucracy and monitors its compliance with the party line. All government bureaucracies are partially staffed by party members whose allegiance to the party exceeds their indentification with their bureaucratic department. In most departments, party members are a majority. The Central Committee also maintains lists of positions which can only be filled with people approved by the local party committee or the Central Committee. This placement system, called *nomenklatura*, ensures that only trusted party members are placed in key posts in the media, industrial and commercial organizations, and other basic social institutions.

All party decisions are made under the Leninist principle of 'democratic centralism.' Originally, the principle meant that decisions were made through a democratic consensus of the party. Once a decision was reached, members were pledged to honor it whatever their personal feelings. Today, democratic centralism in mass parties like the PZPR means little more than local party organizations obeying the decisions of the national leadership and actively working for their realization.

Policy

The main thrust of the Polish party and state policy in the 1980s has been largely a reaction to the social unrest that surfaced in 1980–81. Faced with an unprecedented wave of popular disaffection, the fragmented PZPR appeared paralyzed. It was unable to curb decisively the country's newly developed activism. As rumors of imminent Soviet armed intervention circulated, the Polish military intervened. On December 13, 1981, Gen. Wojciech Jaruzelski declared martial law (technically a state of war) throughout the country. He drastically curtailed personal freedoms, closed universities, suspended Solidarity and unofficial organizations, and interned over 5,000 activists. Press censorship was tightened and the number of periodicals reduced. In an address to the nation, Jaruzelski appealed for cooperation in the name of Polish patriotism and justified the crackdown in veiled language as necessary to prevent Soviet military intervention.

Under martial law the economy showed little sign of improvement. Although the military took over the management of several large-scale enterprises, output continued its downward slide. Indebtedness to the West continued to grow in face of Poland's inability to meet the debt service. Although Poland failed to repay United States Department of Agriculture guaranteed loans in February 1982, the American government waived the right to put Poland in default.

International support for Jaruzelski's maneuver was limited to the Soviet Union, its close allies, the less independent Communist parties and Greece. In the face of West European criticism and economic sanctions imposed by the U.S. administration, the Polish regime painted the United States as the culprit behind its economic difficulties and turned increasingly to its Warsaw Pact allies.

With the announcement of martial law suspension in December 1982, the release of many political internees, and a papal visit in June 1983, the Jaruzelski regime sought to improve its international standing and secure the Western economic assistance needed to rebuild the sagging Polish economy. Unable to pay off the accumulated interest on its loans, the government was forced to plan cuts in imports while adding interest to an already unmanageable debt burden. However, little progress has been made in the drive for normal ties with Western governments because Western banks have consistently refused to extend new funds. Polish economic officials generally concede that the country will be unable to pay its debt or modernize its industry without new credits and greater concessions on outstanding loans. Poland continues to pin its hopes on gaining membership in the International Monetary Fund in 1986.

Closer ties between Jaruzelski and the New Soviet leader, Mikhail Gorbachev, do not appear to have resulted in new economic assistance from Moscow. The Soviets continue to pressure Poland to reduce its trade deficit and debt to the USSR, which has also suffered economic setbacks in recent years. It appears that Polish efforts to win more favorable terms for Soviet energy supplies to Poland have been rebuffed.

The regime's half-hearted attempt to launch economic reforms to introduce some free-market stimulants has been allowed to stagnate. There are also indications that lack of unity within the PZPR and conservatives' concerns that the leadership has been too liberal block the way to significant changes. Despite a short-lived economic rebound, the pace of growth remains sluggish, the enterprises still inefficient, and shortages still rampant.

The regime's domestic policies have been aimed at asserting PZPR control over society while seeking a national dialogue or reconciliation. The government has continued to hold hundreds of political prisoners, has tightened control over intellectual and cultural life, and has intensified its propaganda campaign against the Catholic Church. Although the repression common during martial law has been relaxed to a large extent, a number of restrictions from that period have been quietly incorporated into law. Unable to offer the population much hope of an improved standard of living in the near future, and unwilling to make concessions to its demands for greater autonomy, the regime appears unlikely to make significant headway in establishing a rapprochement with Polish society.

Membership & Constituency

In order to join the party, a citizen must get the recommendation of two party members who have known the applicant longer than one year. There is a one-year period of candidacy, which includes political training. Recruitment has been traditionally high among college students, who begin to receive political training in communist youth groups and in required university courses. (Nevertheless, official student unions have often been disbanded by the party when student unrest and opposition to the regime made even the official unions unreliable.)

The original social constituency of the party was industrial workers. In 1949 they constituted over 60 percent of the party membership. Since that time the proportion of workers (and peasants) in the party has declined. By the late 1950s, the proportion of white-collar workers and others, such as military officers, had risen to about 50 percent. From 1958 to 1976, white-collar workers made up the largest single group of party members.

After the workers' unrest in 1976, the party actively tried to recruit workers. By the late 1970s, industrial workers surpassed the numbers of white-collar-worker members. This influx swelled the party to its largest size ever, over three million members. Yet, the PZPR, relative to other East European communist parties, has a small membership in proportion to the total population.

In the summer of 1980, just before Solidarity emerged, the PZPR claimed 3,149,000 members and candidates. Within the next two years the official figure dropped by a third due to resignations and internal purges. In 1985, 2,115,000 members and candidates have been reported. The decline in membership, despite Jaruzelski's efforts to revitalize the party organization and attract young Poles, remains one of the regime's most critical problems.

Financing

The party has been financed by membership dues and other sources. Details of income are not available, but it is clear that in many cases the party has been better equipped than the state to carry out policy.

Leadership

Until he rose to political power in the 1980s, General Wojciech Jaruzelski (born 1923) pursued a career in the military. Born into a landed family and educated by Jesuits, he rose rapidly through army ranks. After World War II he participated in mop-up campaigns against nationalist anticommunist partisans. By the age of 33 he became the youngest general officer in the Polish army and in 1968 he was made minister of defense and a Politburo member. He played a leading role in the military's political education and in assuring the reliability of the officer corps. As party chief and government leader, he has used the promise of a reformed party and a reform-minded government to spur economic and technological progress, which to some extent parallels developments in Gorbachev's Soviet Union. Moscow's strong endorsement of Jaruzelski's normalization program and his recent aggressive diplomatic initiatives vis-a-vis the West have strengthened Jaruzelski's position before an important Communist Party congress scheduled for June 1986.

Two new top-level government leaders promise to play a key role in future policy and to help Jaruzelski consolidate his power in the face of pressure from both party hawks and liberals.

Marian Orzechowski (born 1931) replaced Stefan Olszowski, widely regarded as Jaruzelski's most harmful hardliner opponent, as minister of foreign affairs in November 1985. A historian with extensive party experience, Orzechowski publicly supports Jaruzelski and enjoys a good relationship with the Soviets. He is considered to be a hawk on the issue of total party dominance, while advocating an even-handed policy to curb the Church and supporters of Solidarity. He helped organize the Patriotic Movement of National Rebirth (PRON) after the declaration of martial law. Since 1984, he served as rector of the PZPR Academy of Social Sciences.

Zbigniew Messner (born 1929), an economist with thirty years' experience in academia and a Politburo member since 1981, became chairman of the Council of Ministers in November 1985. Relinquishing the prime minister's post to Messner has been interpreted as a sign that Jaruzelski intends to concentrate his attention on rebuilding the party, while Messner presides over efforts to resolve the country's economic problems. As deputy premier for the past two years, Messner coordinated economic policies within the government. Regarded as a political moderate, he has not actively supported local self-management organizations or economic decentralization in the past.

Prospects

The party appeared to be moribund in mid-1982. What tendency will prove to be ascendant when the crisis is resolved is impossible to predict. It is probable, however, that the PZPR will reassert itself as the dominant political actor in the country, either through Soviet pressure or the discovery of a *modus vivendi* among the Poles themselves, or both.

Satellite Organizations

The Front of National Unity (*Front Jednosci Narodowej*)

In addition to the Communist Party, the Front includes two other political parties which function as auxiliaries of the PZPR and serve as transmission belts of party policies to the farmers, intellectuals, artisans, and small businessmen whom they nominally represent. They were profoundly affected by the social unrest of 1980–1981. Leadership changes were made and the members debated their role and subordination to the PZPR, frequently openly criticizing government actions. After martial law was declared, their experiment with democratization ended, but they continued to be represented in the *Sejm* and in the new consultative citizen's groups organized by the regime.

The United Peasant Party (*Zjednoczone Stronnictwo Ludowe*; ZSL)

The ZSL first appeared in 1948 with the merger of remnants of the former Polish Peasant Party (*Polskie Stronnictwo Ludowe*; PSL), which had opposed the communists during the early postwar period, and the communist-supported Peasant Party (*Stronnictwo Ludowe*; SL). The new party's program was modeled on that of the PZPR. Its two central tasks were the mobilization of the peasants to fulfil the PZPR's economic plan and the strengthening of peasant solidarity with the working class.

The ZSL has acted to represent rural interests, mainly of private farmers, by assisting in peasant cultural and economic activities. Until 1980 there was no question of its opposing the PZPR by formulating and implementing official agricultural policy. In return, it was fairly well represented in senior government positions and allocated one fourth of the seats in the *Sejm*. The basic organizational unit is the farmers' circle, of which there were about 28,5000 in 1978. Membership in the party was reported to be 478,000 in 1981.

The Democratic Party (*Stronnictwo Demokratyczne*; SD)

Much smaller than the ZSL, the SD was founded in 1938 from a group of democratic clubs with nationalist leanings that appealed largely to intellectuals, white-collar workers and professionals who had opposed Poland's right-wing regimes. After World War II, non-Marxist political groups joined the party and its leaders endorsed communist proposals for land reform and close Soviet ties. The SD's primary purpose was to represent the interests of artisans, small business and service industries, and the intelligentsia and to mobilize these groups to political activism in support of the regime. In 1980, there were 3,400 circles-the party's basic unit-and 110,000 members.

Opposition

The Polish communist government has never succeeded in gaining the allegiance of a substantial number of the Polish people. The serious outbursts of discontent occurring in 1956, 1970, and 1976 were spontaneous rather than organized, and largely confined to specific grievances, without challenging the legitimacy of the party and the government. The regime tolerated a low level of activity by opposition and dissident elements as long as they remained fragmented and did not antagonize the Soviet Union.

The uneasy equilibrium between the communist authorities and the opposition was disturbed in the mid-1970's. Responding to the 1975 Final Act of the Conference on Security and Cooperation in Europe and to dissident activity in the USSR (as well as the climate of detente), many adversaries of the Polish regime surfaced, coordinating their actions with other groups and building bridges between workers, intellectuals, and the Catholic Church. Some of the significant groups that created the social milieu that spawned Solidarity are discussed below.

Committee for Social Self-Defense— "Committee for the Defense of Workers" (*Komitet Samoobrony Spolecznej*—"*Komitet Obrony Robotnikow*"; KSS-KOR)

KOR was organized in 1976, when the state severely repressed strike leaders and other activists after the Radom-Ursus strikes of that year. It organized the workers' legal defense and relief for their families (assisted by the Church), documented state abuses, and struggled for amnesty for the workers. Its efforts were largely successful. After its initial success, it transformed itself into the Committee for Social Self-Defense—"Committee for the Defense of Workers" in 1977.

Following the theories of two of its members, Adam Michnik (born 1946) and Jacek Kuron (born 1934), KSS-KOR's program was to teach the principles and methods of self-governing organization to a variety of social groups while adhering to moderate tactics of dialogue with the PZPR. To aid in this process, KSS-KOR set itself up as an alternative information source, carefully documenting and publishing information on the activities of other opposition groups. It hoped to overcome the isolation that damages the morale of opposition leaders and activists, an isolation which makes it easier for the state to crush opposition groups one by one. The KSS-KOR also documented state violations of the law and organized campaigns to correct these abuses, irrespective of views of those whose rights were violated. The failure of the state to move decisively against KSS-KOR is one of the unexplained puzzles of the period.

During the period of strikes in July and August of 1980, KSS-KOR acted as a contact point for strikers. It kept workers informed about what was going on around the country, thus avoiding isolation of the various strike centers. The KSS-KOR's membership never exceeded fifty, although it had many active sympathizers. Having completed its tasks, KSS-KOR disbanded in 1981; most of its members worked for Solidarity in some capacity.

Students

Following their defeat in 1968, most Polish students returned to the universities and remained politically inactive. With the organization of KSS-KOR, many showed sympathy for the idea of self-defense and others actively helped KSS-KOR collect and disseminate information. In May 1977, the students of Krakow University organized their own Committee for Student Solidarity, as an alternative to the state-sponsored, Polish Socialist Student Union. Within a year, solidarity committees had spread to the campuses of virtually all universities in Poland. They incorporated students sympathetic to KSS-KOR, the human rights movement, and previously unaffiliated students.

After the principle of self-government was established by the formation of the workers' Solidarity, students began to organize an Independent Student Union. When the students' application for recognition by the state was rejected, a major student strike began in Lodz and received support from other campuses. The students had broadbased demands for reforms in the quality of student life, for the restoration of academic freedom, and for sweeping changes in the political life of the country. A compromise worked out with the Ministry of Education in February 1981 brought recognition and some improvement in the quality of life in the universities. The Independent Student Union was disbanded after the declaration of martial law.

Movement for the Defense of Human and Civil Rights (*Ruch Obrony Praw Czlowieka i Obywatela*; ROPCiO)

Detente in the 1970s and the Helsinki Agreement of 1975 played a large role in stimulating awareness of human and civil rights issues in East Europe. Within Poland individuals began to engage in activities similar to those of the Helsinki Watch Committees in the USSR and Charter 77 in Czechoslovakia. In 1975, fifty-nine Polish intellectuals sent a petition to the PZPR criticizing the party's proposed amendments to the Polish constitution. Invoking Poland's participation in the Helsinki conference, the Polish human rights advocates called for the restoration of civil liberties, including the right to work, free speech, the free flow of information, freedom of conscience, and the universal right to education. This "Petition of the 59" elicited considerable support from the public and the Roman Catholic Church.

Inspired by KOR's success at engaging in political activism without attracting official reprisals, the Movement for the Defense of Human and Civil Rights was organized in March 1977. It pursued a policy that was more nationalistic and antagonistic to the regime than KOR's. Some individuals associated with ROP-CiO, including Leszek Moczulski—one of its founders—later formed the Confederation for an Independent Poland (*Konfederacja Polski Niepodleglej*; KPN). It was subjected to police harassment and its leaders were brought to trial in April 1981.

Alternative Information Sources

Since the mid-1970s, a complex network of alternative information sources and cultural institutions has grown despite government raids and arrests. Hundreds of underground publications, ranging from a children's magazine and scholarly journals to worker bulletins, have become an influential source of uncensored information for Polish society. These include the KSS-KOR journals *Robotnik* (Worker) and *Biuletyn Informacyjny* (Information Bulletin); the monthly journal of the human rights movement *Opinia* (Opinion); the literary and political review *Zapis*; the Solidarity weekly *Tygodnik Mazowsze*; and the Catholic intellectuals' *Spotkania*. Several underground publishing houses, including NOWA, continue to operate and expand their operations with the recent introduction of videotapes of censored films. Since the late 1970s, the Society for Academic Courses has organized regular programs of informal courses and lectures (the so-called flying university), despite frequent police disruptions. Churches have provided facilities for performances by banned theater groups and for the screening of banned films.

Peasantry

Since the decollectivization of 1956, about 90 percent of Poland's farm land has remained in private hands, yet the regime has largely neglected the private agricultural sector, concentrating its investments in the state farms.

The communist-controlled United Peasant Party (ZSL), however, was unable or unwilling to represent the interests of the peasants in government or PZPR councils, and the official state organizations for peasants, the Agricultural Circles, were ineffective. In 1978 and 1979, the peasants began to organize on their own. In the summer of 1978, an Interim Committee on Peasant Self-Defense was formed in Lublin. It criticized state agricultural policy, proposed alternatives, and organized to address local prob-

lems on the initiative of its members. Similar organizations of this kind proliferated in 1978 and 1979, particularly in the southeast and central regions of Poland.

Once the precedent for self-governing organizations had been set by Solidarity, peasant activists began to take new initiatives in this direction. A new organization, the Interim Committee for Independent Agricultural Labor Unions, applied for recognition of an independent peasant union, Rural Solidarity. State authorities tenaciously rejected the peasant proposal, and in January 1981, peasants began sit-ins to protest this rejection. State resistance did not let up until a group of peasant activists and local Solidarity leaders were brutally beaten in the town of Bydgoscz. At this point, national Solidarity leaders became involved and a compromise was reached. Rural Solidarity was finally registered in May 1981, eventually attracting a membership of two million. Like Solidarity, Rural Solidarity was suspended and subsequently declared illegal under martial law.

Solidarity (*Solidarnosc*)

During the months of social unrest between August 1980 and December 1981, Solidarity, the independent trade union that took on the larger dimensions of a social, political, and national movement, emerged as an alternative force to the PZPR. At its peak it numbered 10 million Poles. Like earlier popular uprisings, it was sparked by the government's attempt to deal with a troubled economy by raising meat prices. This action provoked a series of factory strikes throughout Poland. Fragmented and demoralized, the political authorities responded by granting wage concessions to individual enterprises.

On August 14, 1980, the Free Trade Union, a group of working-class dissidents in the Baltic coast cities, organized a strike at the enormous Lenin Shipyard in Gdansk. The strike, coordinated by the Inter-Factory Strike Committee, quickly spread to other factories and nearby communities. This committee of workers attracted a group of expert advisers—Roman Catholic intellectuals, academics of the flying university, and members of KSS-KOR and other opposition groups—and signalled a new era of unity and cooperation between Poland's workers and intellectuals. The central figure was, however, Lech Walesa, an electrician who had been dismissed in 1976 for "agitation".

In consultation with their advisers, the workers' demands escalated to a twenty-one point program that included the central demand that the government guarantee free, self-governing trade unions supported by new legislation granting rights to organize and form a single national labor organization. Known as the Gdansk Accord, this program was approved by the PZPR Central Committee and accepted by the government on August 31, 1980. The strikers gained, in addition to economic concessions, important political commitments. These included curtailing of press censorship and allowing broadcasts of Catholic services.

Joined by strikers in other areas, the Inter-Factory Strike Committee became the nucleus of the countrywide Solidarity movement. Founding committees from various regions were represented on a provisional national committee. Walesa and other Gdansk activists remained the dominant members. Relations between the authorities and the new union were marked by tension and confrontation, as the government adoped a hardline approach and procrastinated in implementing the Gdansk Agreement. Threats of strikes were needed to secure legal registration of the union in November 1980 by court acceptance of its internal statutes. Solidarity was denied uncensored access to the mass media. In March, police attacked and seriously injured Solidarity representatives in Bydgoszcz. In response, Solidarity leaders threatened a general strike, which they called off at the last minute when the government agreed to an investigation. But the government's failure to keep that promise or to carry out other commitments contributed to mounting popular frustration and distrust of the authorities.

The First National Congress of Solidarity was held in two sessions between September 5 and October 7, 1981. Walesa was elected chairman with 55 percent of the ballots cast. His election signalled the predominance of more moderate elements within Solidarity over increasingly vocal militants who insisted that the authorities must negotiate with the movement on major social and economic issues. Yet the failure of the popular strike leader to win by a wider margin was attributed to widespread dissatisfaction over his failure to consult others before making policy decisions.

The congress proposed a restructuring of the state to reintroduce democracy and social initiative and proposed a social council for the national economy to ensure that economic reform would fall under public control. Solidarity's effort to reassure the Soviets that its proposals would not violate Poland's international alliances was damaged by its controversial message to the working people of other East European countries, expressing support for their free trade union movements and calling for meetings to exchange experiences.

After the congress, the conflict between Solidarity and the government intensified. The authorities refused to compromise on any major issue and attempts by Solidarity moderates to negotiate seemed increasingly futile. Under pressure from its more radical members, Solidarity escalated its demands, calling for a new trade-union law, free elections, an end to harassment, and free access to the media. At a meeting of the national coordinating commission on December 11–12, a national referendum was proposed to obtain a vote of no-confidence in the government.

The movement was caught by surprise when martial law was declared on December 13, a measure that had obviously been planned ahead for several months. All of Solidarity's leaders who could be located, including Walesa, were interned, most of its records and equipment were impounded, and the union itself was suspended. At first the government indicated that it was prepared to negotiate over the future of Solidarity if it would accept greatly diminished powers, limit its right to strike, and abandon its regional form of organization. The few Solidarity leaders who had avoided arrest rejected any talks as long as their colleagues were imprisoned.

In May 1982, a clandestine wing of the outlawed trade-union movement announced a new leadership structure (a provisional coordinating commission of five former leaders, including Zbigniew Bujak, leader of Solidarity's Mazowsze (Warsaw) branch who had escaped arrest), and prescribed the formation of secret cells of five members and provisional factory committees. Initially, the underground leadership's calls for strikes and demonstrations met with some success, but the government's repressive tactics and displays of force steadily weakened such protests. On October 8, 1982, existing trade unions, including Solidarity, were abolished by law. They were replaced by a new system based primarily on officially sponsored factory-level unions that have not proved successful. In November 1982, Walesa was released from detention but has been subjected to continual police pressure. The authorities have tracked down underground Solidarity leaders as well as clandestine radio transmitters and publications. Jaruzelski's policy of normalization has taken its toll on the now-illegal organization. The national leadership still exists underground and in the open; its statements still have enormous symbolic importance; but it no longer has the capacity to organize effective nationwide actions.

Other Political Forces

Military

The Polish military, the second largest in the Warsaw Pact, has played a major role in modern Polish history, but since the declaration of martial law in 1981, its importance has been increased by the participation of army officers—most prominently Gen. Wojciech Jaruzelski—at all levels of the government. Before 1981, when it assumed a major policy-making and central political role, the Polish People's Army was closely controlled by the state and the party. Since nearly all officers were PZPR members and since party-oriented institutions predominated within the military, Poland's system of virtually universal military training was seen by both party and military leaders as an instrument to provide the country's youth with proper ideological training and discipline.

Between 1948 and 1953, the army was virtually totally controlled by the PZPR and the Soviet military. The most blatant example of Soviet control was the appointment in 1949 of Soviet Marshal Konstantin Rokossovsky, who was ethnically Polish, as minister of defense and commander-in-chief of the Polish armed forces.

The social and political upheavals of 1956 helped the military to recover some of the prestige it had lost earlier. The preparations of several Polish commanders to resist a possible Soviet invasion and the refusal of soldiers to fire on striking Polish workers contributed to the army's reemergence as a political force. Although its direct influence was reduced, Moscow continued to station troops on Polish territory, train Polish officers at schools inside the Soviet Union, supply Soviet-designed weapons, and include Poland in its defense plans.

Gomulka rebuilt and strengthened bureaucratic controls over the army and polonized the officer corps. The professionalization of the officer corps continued after the 1970 workers' riots that led to Gomulka's downfall. Although the military backed the militia's supression of the striking workers, it refused to use its overwhelming force to crush the demonstrations. In the 1970s, it stayed conspicuously away from ideological and political disputes that were not directly related to military issues. By appearing to act as a nationalist apolitical force, the military's prestige rose.

During the Solidarity period, the military continued to keep a low profile, but as the crisis showed no signs of abating, Gen. Jaruzelski emerged as the leading figure acceptable to most factions of the increasingly divided leadership. On February 11, 1981, Jaruzelski became prime minister, thereby increasing military participation in the PZPR Central Committee. By imposing martial law, Jaruzelski and the military claimed to have eliminated the threat of civil war. In July 1983, when martial law was formally lifted, the constitution was amended to permit the proclamation of a state of emergency in the event of an internal crisis. Many military officers retained their top-level government positions.

The armed forces emerged from the martial law period with ostensibly more power than the PZPR and more political influence than armies in other East European countries. But unlike the situation in the 1970s when they had remained aloof from political conflicts, their use of power antagonized hardliners and liberals in the PZPR and key segments of society, costing them politically.

The officially published defense budget, which in the 1970s and early 1980s had varied between five and nine percent of the total state budget, is not seen as an accurate gauge of defense spending. Most Western sources agree that during this period military spending amounted to between five and eight percent of Poland's gross national product. The total is higher than that of all other Warsaw Pact countries (except the Soviet Union) but below average when adjusted to Poland's larger population.

Internal Security Forces

Control of the police is divided between the Ministry of National Defense and the Ministry of Internal Affairs. The former controls the border guards, railroad and industrial guards, and other minor forces. Police forces responsible for the maintenance of public order are under the control of the Ministry of Interior and are known collectively as the Security Services (*Sluzba Bezpieczenstwa*; SB). They are responsible for common police work, internal security, espionage, and counterespionage. The police have a range of arbitrary powers, including the right to search without warrant and to detain anyone for forty-eight hours without charge.

There are three police organizations that play an important role in the political life of the country. The professional police are the Citizens' Militia (*Milicja Obywatelska*; MO). The Motorized Units of the Citizens' Militia (*Zmotoryzowane Oddzialy Milicji Obywatelskiej*; ZOMO) are a highly trained, politically indoctrinated, well-equipped police force, with a high esprit de corps. They specialize in crushing strikes and in crowd and riot control. Their brutal tactics have broken up protest demonstrations several times in recent years, leaving a number of demonstrators dead. They played a major role in the breaking of strikes following the declaration of martial law in December 1981.

The third major police formation is the Voluntary Reserve of the People's Militia (*Ochotnicza Reserwa Milicji Obywatelskiej*; ORMO). This is an unarmed and unprofessional force (380,000 in 1970) that supplements the professional police. The ORMO contains a high percentage of PZPR militants. It is mostly employed in crowd control and surveillance activities. However, in 1968 it played a prominent role in street battles with students all across Poland.

Roman Catholic Church

Despite frequent tensions and confrontations, the Church and the state have established a shaky *modus vivendi* that allows occasional cooperation. Although neither side has accepted the relationship as one of ideological coexistence, each has found cooperation in areas serving the social and economic development and preserving its status as an independent state. This foundation of limited mutual tolerance has provided the Church with the means to develop as a vocal critic of social problems and a champion of human rights. For the communist regime, limited tolerance of organized religion enables it to use the Church as a safety valve for social frustrations and political discontent.

The identification of Poles with the Church is strong and highly emotional. The overwhelming majority of Poles are practicing Roman Catholics for whom the Church has great cultural and historical significance. Following the partitions of the Polish state in the eighteenth century, the Church was the only institution that unified Poles and preserved the national culture. After the formation of the People's Republic, it proved to be the only institution that could resist the state and maintain its independence. Nevertheless, Catholicism in Poland is not monolithic. Members of the clergy take differing positions on how far the Church should go in its support of the recent opposition to the government. The Catholicism of the countryside tends to be more traditional, while that of the cities is more open on such moral questions as contraception and abortion.

The worst period of Church-state relations was that of high Stalinism (1948–56). At this time there were show trials of clerics and the primate of the church, Stefan Cardinal Wyszyński, was under house arrest from 1953 to 1956. In the 1960s and 1970s there were disputes over the construction of new churches, the confiscation of church properties, Catholic education, and censorship of the independent Catholic press.

The selection of the cardinal archbishop of Krakow, Karol Wojtyla, as Pope John Paul II in 1978 was greeted with exultation in Poland. His visit to his homeland in 1979 was a time of national celebration. The visit was organized by the church with minimum help from the state, and was seen by many Poles as a symbol that social initiative was possible on an independent basis. In the period following the Polish August, the Church tried to mediate between the independent social movements and the state; however, these efforts were not as successful as it had been hoped. After the death of Wyszyński in May 1981, the pope appointed Jozef Glemp primate of Poland. As primate, he is also archbishop of Gniezno and Warsaw.

The lifting of martial law and the second papal trip to Poland in the summer of 1983 brought hope for improved church-state relations. However, in 1984 the murder of a pro-Solidarity priest, Jerzy Popieluszko by members of the Polish secret police underscored the difficulty of easing tensions between the Church and the regime. Although four security officers were publicly tried and convicted for the death of the popular young priest—an unparalleled event in the Soviet bloc—Popieluszko's brutal murder and the political authorities' attempts to shift the blame onto the Church brought into sharp focus the regime's deep distrust of the religious community.

Although they have not enjoyed official status as political parties, certain Catholic groups have exerted political influence and adopted positions on social issues. Two of these—the PAX movement, a group of socially progressive Catholics and the Christian Social Association—have generally accomodated themselves with the regime, advocating Christian support of communist policies short of adopting an atheistic philosophy of materialism. The two groups were awarded eleven seats in the 1980 Sejm election. A more representative Catholic group, Znak, which became known as neo-Znak after the government purged its more independent members, was allotted five seats in the Sejm. In February 1981, a new national organization, the Polish Catholic Social Union (*Polski Zwiazek Katolicko Spoleczny*; PZKS) was introduced. It has advocated a "historic compromise" between the PZPR, Solidarity, and the Catholic groups. During the Sejm sessions of 1982 to ratify the imposition of martial law, PZKS representatives advocated the reinstatement of Solidarity.

Many members of the lay Catholic movements joined Solidarity and some rose to positions of prominence. The leading member of this group is Tadeusz Mazowiecki, the former editor of the left Catholic journal, *Wież* (The Link). Mazowiecki served as an advisor to the Interfactory Strike Committee in Gdansk and became the editor of the Solidarity's weekly newspaper. He was associated with the Clubs of Catholic Intellectuals (*Kluby Inteligencji Katolickiej*; KIK). These groups heatedly discussed issues of current interest; undertook some limited social initiatives; and acted as centers for legal advice to independent social movements, including Solidarity.

National Prospects

There is little cause for optimism as People's Poland faces the second half of the 1980s. The historically rooted interrelated problems of economic stagnation and political legitimacy have for a long time defied any quick-fix solutions. The Jaruzelski regime, (or any successor to the present leadership) constrained by a fundamental insecurity, is unlikely to risk far-reaching changes to the society's economic and political structures in light of Poland's strained resources, overburdened population, legacy of social disruptions, the fluctuations of the world economy, and the watchful eye of Moscow.

Poland's strategic importance to the Soviet Union and the strength of its opposition groups have led Moscow to play a particularly strong role in Poland's internal political life. Nearly all Polish groups regard it as axiomatic that, should they adopt a political system or foreign policy inimical to Moscow, Soviet military intervention would follow. Moscow is Poland's largest trading partner, accounting for more than 30 percent of Poland's exports and more than 40 percent of its imports. Payments on the Polish debt to Moscow, estimated at over 4 billion dollars, have been deferred. With little possibility of obtaining needed economic aid from their Soviet ally or from the West, the political authorities recognize that economic reform is essential. But they have proved unwilling to commit themselves to a program, fearing potentially damaging political repercussions. Similarly, discredited by society since the imposition of martial law, the authorities are unlikely to risk the unknown consequences of increased popular participation in economic and political decision-making. Continued social instability, prolonged economic decline, and an incoherent party and state policy of muddling-through are likely to persist in the near future.

Further Reading

Ascherson, Neal. *The Polish August*. New York: Viking, 1982.

Ash, Timothy Garton. *The Polish Revolution: Solidarity 1980–82*. New York: Scribner's, 1984.

Barnett, Clifford R. et al. *Poland*. New York: Grove Press, 1958.

Brumberg, Abraham, ed. *Poland: Genesis of a Revolution*. New York: Vintage, 1983.

Davies, Norman. *God's Playground*. 2 vols. New York: Columbia University Press, 1982.

de Weydenthal, Jan B. *The Communists of Poland*. Stanford, Calif.: Hoover Institution Press, 1978.

Leslie, R.F., ed. *The History of Poland since 1863.* Cambridge: Cambridge University Press, 1980.

Raina, Peter. *Independent Social Movements in Poland.* London: Orbis, 1981.

Roos, Hans. *A History of Modern Poland.* New York: Alfred A. Knopf, 1966.

Singer, Daniel. *The Road to Gdansk.* New York: Monthly Review Press, 1981.

Weschler, Lawrence. *The Passion of Poland: From Solidarity Through the State of War.* New York: Pantheon, 1984.

Woodall, Jean, ed. *Policy and Politics in Contemporary Poland.* New York: St. Martin's Press, 1982.

PORTUGUESE REPUBLIC
(República Portuguesa)
by Jan Knippers Black, Ph.D.

The System of Government

Portugal, a nation of ten million people, is a multiparty parliamentary democracy in a unitary state. Portugal's democracy is new and perhaps fragile. Through a *coup d'état* in 1974 that rapidly took on the characteristics of a revolution, Portugal emerged from a personalist, corporatist dictatorship that had spanned forty-eight years.

The dictatorial style of Antonio de Oliveira Salazar, premier from 1932 to 1968, was low key. A former economics professor and deeply religious, he avoided public appearances and led a frugal life. The governmental system he constructed, however, had many of the trappings of fascism. He banned all political organizations other than his own National Union and attempted to control the populace through youth movements, veterans' associations, and other officially sponsored entities. He also made use of propaganda and censorship and ultimately relied upon a secret-police system to silence dissidents and crush opposition.

Under Salazar's so-called New State and the six-year successor regime of Marcello Caetano, the spiraling costs of maintaining rebellious African colonies were borne by the poor majority of workers and peasants while the profits were closely held by a small commercial, industrial, and landholding oligarchy. By most standards of measurement, Portugal remained Western Europe's poorest nation.

The military coup that forced a sharp break with the past was perpetrated by a group of young military officers known as the Armed Forces Movement (*Movimento das Forças Armadas;* MFA). The initial grievances of the movement had to do with pay and promotions, although disgruntlement over the seemingly endless colonial wars soon became a major issue.

When the young officers made their move, on April 25, 1974, the old regime collapsed like a house of cards, and few could be found to mourn its passing. The Portuguese people surged through the streets in a spirit of euphoria, waving red carnations which soon became the symbol of the revolution. Whether or not there were many in the MFA who had aspired to carry out a revolution, it soon appeared that the people were demanding nothing less.

The new military government, initially headed by General Antonio de Spinola, pledged the release of political prisoners, the dissolution of the secret police, the abolition of censorship, and popular determination of the future of the colonies. It also pledged to bring democracy to Portugal.

Political freedoms soon gave rise to demands for economic justice. The military caretakers initially responded to a spate of strikes by raising wages and instituting price controls. These measures exacerbated the fears of businessmen and contributed to disinvestment, capital flight, and bankruptcy, forcing the government to take over some businesses in order to prevent a sharp increase in unemployment.

Between mid-1974 and the end of 1975, the government nationalized domestic banks and many of the country's vital industries, including the steel, cement, shipbuilding, petrochemical and oil-refining industries, and the country's largest conglomerate, Companhia União Fabril. By the end of this round of government investments and nationalizations, the public sector accounted for about one-fourth of the gross domestic product and 46 percent of gross fixed capital.

Meanwhile, the government announced its intention to expropriate large landholdings, but as it moved slowly in drawing up guidelines, landless peasants took matters into their own hands. In early 1975, peasants in the Alentejo region "liberated" about 2.5 million acres, a fifth of the country's cultivable land.

The revolution's first two years also witnessed political turmoil. During that period the country endured six provisional governments, two abortive coup attempts—one inspired by the right, one by the left—and countless strikes and demonstrations. Nevertheless, on the first anniversary of the "Carnation Revolution," the Portuguese elected a constituent assembly. A new constitution, establishing a parliamentary democracy under the guardianship of the military-dominated Council of the Revolution, was promulgated on April 2, 1976; on April 25, the second anniversary of the revolution, the Parliament, formally known as the Assembly of the Republic, was duly elected.

Executive

Before the constitution was amended in mid-1982, a Council of the Revolution acted as "an advisory body to the president of the Republic, as guarantor of the proper working of democratic institutions, of fulfillment of the constitution and of faithfulness to the spirit of the Portuguese Revolution of 25 April 1974, and as a political and legislative organ in military matters." In essence, the Council supervised the functions of all branches of the government.

The Council, which operated in permanent session, comprised the president of the republic; the chief and deputy chief of the general staff of the armed forces; the chiefs of staff of the three armed services; the prime minister, if he is a member of the armed forces; and fourteen officers, including eight from the army, three from the air force, and three from the navy, appointed by their respective services.

The Council retained sole authority to make laws and regulations concerning the organization, functioning, and discipline of the armed forces. it also was empowered to issue decree-laws with the same validity as laws passed by the Assembly of the Republic.

The Council authorized the president to declare war, make peace, or to declare a state of emergency. It could also pass on the constitutionality of acts passed by the Assembly and, if it chose, make a binding declaration of unconstitutionality.

The Council of the Revolution was an outgrowth of the revolution of 1974. Its functions, as set forth in the constitution of 1976, became subject to great controversy and most civilian political leaders wanted to abolish it. They succeeded in mid-1982.

The Council was replaced by: 1) a Constitutional Commission with a membership of thirteen judges; 2) a Supreme Council of National Defense; and 3) a Council of State. The Council of State was to serve as the supreme advisory body, its meetings to be chaired by the president. The Council is comprised of (i) six ex-officio members, namely, the speaker of the assembly, the prime minister, the president of the Supreme Court, the state ombudsman and the presidents of the regional governments of the Azores and Madeira; (ii) five citizens named by the president of the Republic, who would be members until the end of the president's term of office; (iii) five citizens elected by the Assembly on the basis of proportional representation, who would be members until the end of the Assembly's term; and (iv) all former national presidents elected since the introduction of the revised constitution, provided they had not been impeached.

The full text of a revised constitution was formally approved by the Assembly on August 12 by 195 votes to forty and was signed by President Eanes on September 24. The constitutional reforms entered into force on October 30, shortly after the formal dissolution of the Council of the Revolution and the inauguration of its successor bodies.

The president of the republic, elected by direct and secret universal suffrage by Portuguese citizens, serves as the head of state. He was ex officio president of the Council of the Revolution and is commander-in-chief of the armed forces. The president is elected for a five-year term and is limited to two consecutive terms.

The president is responsible for the promulgation of laws and executive orders. He is empowered to declare a state of siege or emergency in all or part of the national territory. A state of siege or emergency may not last more than thirty days without ratification by the Assembly.

The president is also empowered to grant pardons and commute sentences; to appoint ambassadors and envoys at the proposal of the government; to ratify duly approved treaties; and to declare war, in the case of actual or imminent aggression, and make peace, with the approval of the Assembly.

In accordance with an informal agreement between the armed forces and the political parties in the aftermath of the 1974 Revolution, the president was to be a military officer. General Antonio dos Santos Ramalho Eanes was first elected to the presidency in June 1976 with 62 percent of the popular vote. He was reelected in December 1980 by a 56 percent vote. General

Ramalho Eanes had gained prestige when troops under his command put down an uprising staged by leftists in the armed forces in November 1975. The following month he was appointed army chief of staff.

Presidential elections took place again at the beginning of 1986. No candidate won a majority in the first round, although Diogo Pinto Freitas do Amaral, leader of the Social Democratic Center Party, had a strong lead, with 46 percent in a field of four. In the run-off, however, on February 16, the two leftist candidates who had been eliminated threw their support to former Socialist Prime Minister Mario Soares, giving him a margin of 51 percent to 48 percent for Freitas do Amaral.

The Portuguese government is headed by a prime minister appointed by the president after consultation with the parties represented in the Assembly. Due regard is given to election results and the Assembly majority. Other members of the government are appointed by the president in accordance with the proposals of the prime minister. In mid-1986, Prime Minister Aníbal Cavaço e Silva of the Social Democratic Party headed a minority government.

The prime minister is politically responsible to the president and to the Assembly. Other ministers are responsible to the prime minister and to the Assembly. The prime minister, deputy prime ministers, and other ministers, comprising the Council of Ministers, determine the general lines of government policy and the means of implementation. The government's program is to be presented to the Assembly within ten days of the appointment of the prime minister. Rejection of the program requires an absolute majority of the members of the Assembly entitled to vote. The constitution specifies that in formulating and executing policies the government is to be guided by "the objectives of democracy and the building of socialism."

The government is required to resign if its program is rejected; or it loses a vote of confidence; or two motions of censure are approved at an interval of not less than thirty days by an absolute majority of Assembly members.

Legislature

Legislative power is vested in the unicameral Assembly of the Republic. The Assembly members are to represent the country as a whole, rather than individual electoral districts.

In accordance with the constitution, the Assembly shall have no fewer than 240 and no more than 250 members. The number of members allotted to each electoral district is proportional to the number of eligible voters on that district's electoral register. Nominations are presented by the political parties, either separately or in combination, and may include nonparty members. A duly-elected member may lose his seat if he exceeds a permissible number of absences from Assembly proceedings; joins a party other than the one that presented him for election; or is convicted by a court of participation in any organization with a fascist ideology.

Legislative periods last four years. The president is required to dissolve the Assembly and call new elections when, by withholding its confidence from the government or passing a motion of censure on it, it has brought about a third change of government. New elections must be held within 90 days of dissolution. The Assembly may not be dissolved during a state of siege or emergency. In the event of dissolution and new elections, the newly elected Assembly completes the current legislative period and continues throughout the following one.

Members of the Assembly share legislative initiative with the government and with the assemblies of the autonomous regions. Matters in which the Assembly has sole legislative competence include civil rights and liberties and conditions of citizenship; political parties and elections; the creation of taxes and the revenue system; national and regional planning and agrarian reform; determination of the sectors of ownership of the means of production, including the basic sectors in which private firms are forbidden to operate; and economic intervention, nationalization, and socialization of the means of production and the criteria for determining compensation.

In a general election on October 6, 1985, the Social Democrats (PSD) won eighty-eight seats, the Socialists (PSP) fifty-seven, the newly-formed Democratic Renewal Party (PRD), supportive of then President Eanes, forty-five, the Communist-led United Peoples Alliance thirty-eight, and the Social Democratic Center (CDS) twenty-two. The results represented moderate gains for the Social Democrats and large-scale defections from the Socialists to Eanes's Democratic Renewal Party.

Judiciary

Portugal's court system is independent, subject only to the law. The decisions of the courts are binding on all public and private bodies and prevail over the decisions of all other authorities. Hearings before the court are public, except when the competent court finds cause for deciding otherwise.

The Supreme Court of Justice is the highest court of appeal. Under certain circumstances, the Supreme Court may serve as a court of first or second instance.

The court system is self-regulating. The Higher Council of the Bench, elected by sitting judges from among their own number, appoints judges and dictates assignments and promotions.

The Supreme Court is empowered to rule on the constitutionality of legislation. A finding of unconstitutionality may be appealed to the Constitutional Commission, whose members are chosen by the government, the Assembly, the Supreme Court, and the Higher Council of the Bench. Members of the Constitutional Commission serve four-year terms and are entitled to all the safeguards and immunities proper to judges during those terms.

Regional & Local Government

Pending the establishment of constitutionally mandated regions, eighteen districts continue to be the highest subnational administrative unit. The district is headed by a civil governor appointed by and responsible to the central government. The governor is assisted by a council and by a deliberating assembly comprising representatives of the municipal authorities.

The constitution of 1976 provides that, in addition to the already autonomous regions of the archipelagos (see below), the mainland is to be divided into regions for administrative purposes. They are to be governed by assemblies, committees, and councils. The assemblies will comprise members elected at large and at least an equal number of members elected by municipal assemblies. The regional committee, an executive organ, will be elected by the regional assembly in secret ballot from among its members. The advisory council is to represent the region's economic, social, cultural, and professional organizations. A representative of the national government, appointed by the Council of Ministers, will be assigned to each region.

The archipelagos of the Azores and Madeira already enjoy limited self-rule. These two autonomous regions are governed in much the same manner as the Portuguese Republic.

Their assemblies are elected by direct and secret universal suffrage in accordance with the principle of proportional representation. These regional governments are politically responsible to their respective regional assemblies.

Members of the Council of Ministers of the Portuguese Republic serve as liaisons between central and regional governments. They appoint the chairmen of the regional governments, giving due regard to election results. They also appoint and dismiss other members of the regional governments on proposals of their chairmen.

The autonomous regional governments are empowered to collect and dispose of revenue and to administer and dispose of their own assets. They may enter into contracts and participate in the negotiation of international treaties and agreements of direct concern to them. They may also introduce bills in the Assembly of the Republic. The regional autonomous assemblies have residual legislative powers, but their political and administrative statutes must be approved by the Assembly of the Republic. An Advisory Commission on the Autonomous Regions advises the president on the constitutionality of statutes adopted by the regional assemblies. That commission comprises one citizen appointed by the president, two by the Assembly, and one by each of the regional assemblies.

Parish and municipal governments antedate the constitution of 1976. In practice, however, they had no authority of their own until after 1974. They were generally responsive to the wishes of local landlords and ultimately responsible to the national government.

The parish, as a government unit, almost always corresponds to the pre-existing ecclesiastical parish. Each parish is entitled to a popularly elected assembly and a committee to serve as its executive organ. In the least-populous parishes, the assembly may comprise all eligible voters.

Municipalities are governed by assemblies, chambers, and councils. The municipal assembly comprises the chairmen of the parish councils and at least an equal number of members elected at large from the municipal area. The municipal chamber is the executive organ. Its members are elected at large from the municipality. It is chaired by the candidate heading the party list that received the most votes. In addition, a municipal council, an advisory body, represents local economic, social, cultural, and professional organizations.

Party activity is intense at every level of government. Local and district elections are hard fought by the same alliances that dominate national politics.

The Electoral System

The constitution specifies that "direct, secret and regular elections shall be the general rule in appointing the members of the elected organs of supreme authority, the autonomous regions, and local governments." It also specifies adherence to the principle of proportional representation.

A single registration system is maintained for all elections by direct, universal, adult suffrage.

Multimember electoral districts for the Assembly of the Republic coincide with the country's eighteen administrative districts. The electoral law of 1979 specifies a simple method (d'Hondt) of proportional representation. A party list must contain as many names as the district has seats, plus a number of alternates.

Portuguese voters have gone to the polls ten times since the revolution of April 1974. The first free election in half a century, on April 25, 1975, drew 92 percent of the country's eligible voters to the polls to elect a constituent assembly. Parliamentary elections in April 1976 drew 83 percent. Turnout for the presidential election in June of that year dropped to about 75 percent. About 87 percent turned out for parliamentary elections in 1979, and about 85 percent for separate parliamentary and presidential elections in 1980. The parliamentary elections of 1985 drew a turnout of about 75 percent, and the presidential election of 1986 drew a little more than 80 percent.

Voter turnout for local elections has been somewhat lower. About 64 percent voted for local officials in 1976 and 74 percent in 1979. Although party strength varies by region, national distribution of the vote by party in local elections closely parallels party totals in national assembly elections.

The Party System

Origins of the Parties

Political parties were banned in Portugal from the consolidation of Salazar's dictatorship in the early 1930s until the revolution of April 1974. The Communist Party, however, and to a lesser extent the Socialist Party and a few smaller leftist groups operated clandestinely. These parties were joined by a number of new ones very shortly after the opening of the sytem in 1974. The largest of the new parties, the Popular Democratic Party (later renamed the Social Democratic Party) and the Social Democratic Center Party, were formed by politicians who had been active in the deposed Salazar-Caetano regime. Most of the major parties were organized or reorganized after the revolution with considerable financial assistance from their foreign counterparts.

Within a few months of the revolution, there were about eighty political groups jockeying for position. By the time the first ballot was printed the field had narrowed to twelve.

The Parties in Law

The constitution guarantees freedom of association, including the right to establish or join political associations and parties. No one, however, may be a member of more than one party simultaneously.

Political parties may not use names that contain terms directly related to any religion or church, nor may they use emblems which may be mistaken for national or religious symbols. Parties that are regional in name or program are prohibited, as are fascist and paramilitary organizations.

The Portuguese government subsidizes political parties in accordance with the number of seats each holds in Parliament.

Party Organization and Coalitions

Party organization varies considerably. The parties of the right tend to be loosely structured coalitions of independent politicians and local notables, while those of the left are formally organized and operate with a far greater degree of central control. With the exception of the Communist Party, relatively democratic procedures characterize intraparty organizations.

Between the elections of 1979 and those of 1983 most of the parties were aligned in three coalitions: the Democratic Alliance (AD), led by the Social Democratic Party with eighty-two seats in the Assembly elected in 1980, and including the Social Democratic Center Party with forty-two seats and the Popular Monarchist Party with six seats; the Republican and Socialist Front (FRS), led by the Socialist Party with sixty-six seats and including the Association of Independent Social Democrats (ASDI) and the Union of the Democratic Socialist Left (UEDS) with four seats each; and the United Popular Alliance (APU), led by the Communist Party with thirty-nine seats and including the Portuguese Democratic Movement with two seats. The Popular Democratic Union, to the left of the Communist Party, shunned alliances. It consistently won one assembly seat until the elections of 1983.

The ruling center-right Democratic Alliance disintegrated before the 1983 elections, as did the other two coalitions, and all of the minor parties lost representation in the Assembly. The Portuguese Socialist Party won a strong plurality, with 101 seats. The Social Democratic Party's representation dropped to seventy-five seats, while that of its previous coalition partner, the Social Democratic Center, dropped to thirty. Communist Party representation increased to forty-four. Rejecting overtures from the Communist Party, the Socialists, under the leadership of Mario Soares, formed a ruling coalition with the Social Democrats.

The PSP-PSD coalition also proved unstable. When PSD ministers withdrew from the government in June 1985, it became necessary to call new elections ahead of schedule. In those elections, which took place in October, heavy defections from the PSP to a new party established by supporters of former President Eanes left the PSD in the lead to form a minority government.

Campaigning

Electoral campaigns are characterized by freedom of speech, equality of treatment for the various candidates, and impartiality toward candidates on the part of public bodies. Under the electoral law of 1979, campaigns are limited to a period beginning twenty-one days and ending twenty-four hours before the elections.

Independent Voters

There is very little reliable information on party loyalty or ticket splitting between national and local elections. Indications are that voters identify strongly with one party or alliance and consistently vote for their favorites at all levels.

Social Democratic Party
(*Partido Social Democrático;* PSD)

History

The PSD, originally known as the Popular Democratic Party, was organized a few weeks after the 1974 revolution by former members of the liberal faction of the old regime's National Assembly, including Francisco Sa Carneiro and Francisco Pinto Balsemão. The party was second in strength, following the Socialist Party, in the Constituent Assembly elected in 1975 (eighty seats) and in the first Assembly of the Republic, elected in 1976 (seventy-three seats). It overtook the Socialists in the elections of December 1979, however, gaining eighty seats. The PSD's leader, Sa Carneiro, then became prime minister, but his career was tragically ended by a fatal plane crash on December 5, 1980. Balsemão was sworn in as prime minister on January 9, 1981, but he was not able to hold together the ruling AD coalition. After new elections in 1983, the PSD, with only 75 seats, became the minority partner in a coalition government with the PSP. The 1985 elections placed the PSD in the lead again with 88 seats, heading a minority government.

Organization

The PSD is a loosely structured party based on patron-client relationships that antedate the revolution. The organization shows its greatest strength at the regional level where it is dominated by local notables.

Party headquarters are at Rua Buenos Aires 39, 1200 Lisbon.

Policy

The party's platforms have stressed respect for political democracy and civil liberties and advocates a limited degree of state intervention in the economy. It supports the nationalization of utilities and other "natural" monopolies and limitations on the amount of productive land to be held by a single owner. For the most part, however, the party is responsive to the concerns of private enterprise. It views the distributional schemes of the left as utopian and the nationalizations carried out in the wake of the revolution as excessive. It has supported the return of many businesses to private hands and the return to its original owners of land extralegally seized by peasants. Together with its partners to the right, the PSD has pressed for constitutional reform to delete passages calling for building socialism, protecting nationalized industries, and granting extraordinary powers to the now defunct Council of the Revolution.

Membership & Constituency

The PSD draws its greatest support from the politically conservative and devoutly Catholic middle clsss of northern Portugal, its leadership from among the liberal professionals of the region. The party is also dominant in the archipelagos of the Azores and Madeira. No reliable membership figures are available.

Financing

Party dues are generally spent at the local level. Nationwide operations are dependent on other sources of support, including donations from a foundation associated with the Free Democratic Party of West Germany. The PSD has also become the prime beneficiary of the state subsidy, though this money is used primarily to finance its parliamentary activities.

Leadership

The PSD was weakened by the loss of its original leader, Sa Carneiro, in 1980. Balsemão, who replaced him in 1981, was a man of many talents; but he lacked his predecessor's charismatic appeal. Party leadership has undergone several changes since Balsemão resigned in early 1983. After the 1983 elections, Carlos Mota Pinto became party leader as well as deputy prime minister and defense minister in the coalition government. He had served previously as prime minister from November 1978 to June 1979. In early 1985, Mota Pinto lost a vote of confidence in the party's ruling national council. (Four months later he had a heart attack and died.) He was replaced, both as party leader and as deputy prime minister, by Rui Machete, who had been serving as minister of justice. Machete, however, did not seek reelection as PSD leader at the party's national congress in May 1985. At that time Aníbal Cavaço e Silva (forty-five), an economist serving as minister of finance, was elected by a narrow margin to the party leadership.

Prospects

The party has been weakened by tensions between its social democratic and liberal factions. Nevertheless, with a plurality in the Assembly, it returned to power in 1985. Having alternated in power, or shared power, with the Socialists for a decade, the PSD clearly remained advantageously positioned in the country's political spectrum.

Portuguese Socialist Party
(Partido Socialista Português; PSP)

History

Portugal's first socialist party was founded in 1875, attracting intellectuals but few workers. Between the 1930s and the 1960s several socialist fronts attempted, ineffectively, to oppose the dictatorship of Salazar. The roots of the contemporary party are traced to a front called Portuguese Socialist Action, formed in 1964 by about a hundred militants in exile. It was admitted to the Socialist International in 1972, and in 1973 it became known as the Portuguese Socialist Party.

The PSP proved to be the country's strongest party, by far, in the first two national elections. It won 38 percent of the vote and 116 seats in the Constituent Assembly in 1975 and 35 percent and 107 seats in the Assembly of the Republic in 1976.

The PSP's secretary general, Mario Soares, served as prime minister of the first and second constitutional governments, from mid-1976 to mid-1978. The austerity measures he was obliged to impose, however, in order to obtain a loan from the International Monetary Fund, cost the party dearly. Its representation in the Assembly dropped to seventy-four seats after the elections of 1979 and sixty-six after those of 1980.

Its fortunes rose again in 1983, when with a strong plurality of 101 seats it was able to put together a coalition government with the PSD. Its representation dropped again to fifty-seven seats in the general elections of 1985, but its leader, Mario Soares, was elected president of the republic in 1986.

Organization

The PSP is the best-organized and most highly structured of the larger parties in Portugal. Organized at the neighborhood level in the cities and some smaller towns, party members elect their own leaders and their representatives to district and regional conferences. The regional conferences in turn send representatives to the national congress which elects a national commission (a large oversight body), a political commission (for policy planning), and a small executive commission which comprises the party's top leaders.

Party headquarters are at Rua da Emenda 46, 1200 Lisbon.

Policy

The PSP presents itself as the party of workers and as the defender of all those who have been subject to discrimination or who have special needs, including immigrants and refugees from the former colonies. Its platforms have stressed the need for increasing employment, improving working conditions and extending social benefits, including social security and national health care. It defends the concept of a mixed economy as established by the constitution of 1976, and advocated amending the constitution to suppress the Council of the Revolution and to establish civilian control over the armed forces.

The Socialists consider the agrarian issue to be a crucial one. The land-reform law passed under the Soares government would parcel out the disputed land of the Alentejo region to the tiller, in a pattern more nearly consistent with that of the conservative north.

Membership & Constituency

A mass party with a membership of more than 100,000 the PSP draws wide support from the working class, a sizable portion of the middle class, and many professionals. Its strength is concentrated in urban areas and larger towns, but support from some rural regions, such as the upper Alentejo and the Algarve is firm. The party also has the support of a small workers' federation which it organized in the late 1970s.

Financing

During the first two years following the revolution, the PSP received several million dollars from the Socialist and Social Democratic parties of several Western European countries, particularly those of West Germany, the Netherlands, and Sweden. The United States, seeing the PSP as the strongest opponent of the Portuguese Communist Party, reportedly provided financial backing as well. Today, the party depends primarily on membership dues, special fund-raising events, and a few contributions. Some foreign support continues.

Leadership

Mario Soares (born 1924 in Lisbon) was reelected to the post of secretary general at the party's national congress in May 1981. Soares, a lawyer and writer, had been an active political dissident against the Salazar and Caetano regimes since his student years. After suffering arrest twelve times, he went into exile in 1970, returning to a hero's welcome shortly after the 1974 coup. The leadership is rent by factions, both personal and ideological, but Soares remains the undisputed leader.

The party's political commission, on July 13, 1985, chose as its prime ministerial candidate the man proposed by Soares, António da Almeida Santos, minister of state and parliamentary affairs under the PSP-PSD government.

Prospects

PSP fortunes had followed a zigzag course since the consolidation of the 1974 Revolution. Its terms in government have been politically costly because its austerity measures have been highly damaging to lower–income groups, from which it draws much of its support. However, given the space the party occupies on the ideological spectrum, it is likely to remain a major contender for the foreseeable future.

Other Parties

Democratic Renewal Party
(*Partido Renovador Democrático;* PRD)

On February 24, 1985, supporters of President Eanes launched a new party, the PRD. Under the terms of the constitution of 1978, Eanes was not allowed to seek a third presidential term, but he remained a very popular figure, and he sought to continue his involvement in the political affairs of the country.

The idea of establishing a presidential party had been raised as early as 1978. The new party's structure, however, was based on the organization that had been assembled for Eanes' presidential reelection campaign in 1980. At that time his strongest support had come from the PSP.

The party held its first national congress on June 15–16, 1985 and elected as its president Herminio Martinho, a personal friend of Eanes who had been serving as interim president since February. The PRD program called for electoral reforms; it particularly opposed aspects of the 1982 constitutional changes that diluted the powers of the president.

In general, the party situated itself just to the left of the Socialists, attracting many voters and party activists who had become disillusioned with the failure of the Socialists to remain faithful to the party's platform and to follow through on campaign promises. In the parliamentary elections of October 1985, the PRD won forty-five seats, a stunning performance for a party so new.

Social Democratic Center Party
(*Partido de Centro Democrático Social;* CDS)

The CDS was formed in mid-1974 by officials of the deposed Caetano government, including Diogo Pinto de Freitas do Amaral, Adelino Amaro, and Valentin Pintado. It jumped from sixteen members in the Constituent Assembly of 1975 to forty-two in the Assembly of the Republic elected in 1976. It advanced to forty-three seats in 1979 and forty-six in 1980, but dropped back to thirty in 1983 and to twenty-two in 1985.

The party entered into a brief, informal, and ideologically awkward "partnership" with the Socialists in 1978, giving the Socialists a majority with which to govern in exchange for a pledge to speed up the return of expropriated land to its original owners. The CDS was not pleased with its partner's performance on the agrarian issue, however; and it withdrew its support after a few months, allowing that government to fall. In 1979, the CDS joined forces with the more compatible PSD in the Democratic Alliance.

Like the PSD, the CDS is strongly supportive of private enterprise, but it is rather more conservative, particularly on the agrarian issue. It shares with the PSD the relatively conservative, traditional, and devout constituency of the rural north. Its leadership is drawn from the aristocratic landowning class, and it has strong ties with the prerevolutionary banking community.

It has reportedly received assistance from West Germany's Christian Democratic Union and Great Britain's Conservative Party as well as from wealthy Portuguese contributors.

Its leader, Freitas do Amaral (born 1921 in northern Portugal), has a doctorate in law and was a professor of administrative law of the Lisbon Law Faculty before assuming leadership of the CDS. He served as vice prime minister and foreign minister in the government of Sa Carneiro. He held office briefly as prime minister immediately after Sa Carneiro's death, then became defense minister in the cabinet of Balsemão. In 1985 he was narrowly defeated for the presidency of the republic.

Popular Monarchist Party (*Partido Popular Monarquico;* PPM)

The PPM is as interesting and idiosyncratic as its name. As a miniscule clandestine party, it opposed Salazar, the usurper of royal authority. The postrevolutionary party, however, while advocating a parliamentary monarchy, has become known as the party of ecologists. In addition to the six Assembly seats it held as part of the AD coalition from 1980 to 1983, the party held about 600 seats on municipal councils. In the elections of 1983, it lost all of its Assembly seats and dropped to .5 percent of the vote. One PPM leader, however, was elected to the Assembly as an independent on the PSP list.

The PPM is really a movement and as such has little formal structure. Its leadership, comprising predominantly professionals, is selected by the national directorate on the basis of commitment and ability. Its support is spread fairly evenly throughout the country.

As a participant in the AD government, the PPM held the portfolio for the Quality of Life Ministry. The party joined the coalition in order to acquire a forum, but it sees itself as belonging neither to the right nor to the left. In fact, on a great many issues it stands in opposition to all of the major parties.

It advocates the protection of the environment, the conservation of natural resources, and the preservation of the integrity of small communities. It opposes the development of nuclear energy as well as the construction of huge dams, preferring a number of small dams. It favors the construction of rural roads, but opposes major freeway projects. It opposes the expansion of the paper-pulp export industry as a threat to the fragile forests of eucalyptus.

The PPM favors private enterprise, but within limits drawn in accordance with public interest. It generally opposes concessions to multinational corporations; they are seen as vehicles of a careless and corrupting modernism. The party also takes a strong stand for the protection of civil liberties.

The PPM sees itself as the party of future generations and as the conscience of the party system. Though its immediate following is small, it enjoys considerable respect and influence.

Portuguese Communist Party (Partido Comunista Portugues; PCP)

The PCP, founded in 1921, became a clandestine organization after the republic was dismantled in 1926. The party's courageous opposition to Salazar and Salazar's persistent attempts to crush it contributed to its prestige and popularity following the revolution.

During the first year following the revolution, the PCP enjoyed a close relationship with the Armed Forces Movement (MFA) and participated in the provisional governments of the 1974–1975 period. Its fortunes waned, however, after the electoral process was introduced. The party won only thirty seats in the Constituent Assembly of 1975. It gained at the expense of the Socialist Party in the next two elections, winning forty seats in Parliament in 1976 and forty-four in 1979; but it dropped back to thirty-nine seats in 1980 while its partner in the APU

coalition, the MDP, won two. The PCP, running alone in 1983, won forty-four seats; but in coalition again in 1985, the coalition partners won only thirty-eight seats.

The PCP's basic objective is the socialization of the means of production. It has moderated this line somewhat since the 1974-75 period, but it is still considered by the parties to its right to be Moscow-oriented and dogmatic ideologically.

The PCP was a cadre party of a few thousand members in 1974, but it soon acquired a membership of more than 100,000. The membership is tightly regulated; all applicants are screened by party committees.

The party controls the country's breadbasket, the Alentejo region south and east of Lisbon, which was characterized by large estates and landless peasants under the old regime. Much of the land in the region was seized by the peasants during the first year of the revolution, and some of it is still held by Communist-controlled collectives. Other portions have been returned to the original owners, while some have been distributed to cooperatives.

The PCP also controls most of the labor unions, federated in the Intersyndical. During the period of Communist ascendancy, the Intersyndical was recognized as the only legal labor federation, but that monopoly was ended under the Soares government.

The party is reported to have received substantial sums from the Soviet Union and East Europe and relies heavily on membership dues.

Alvaro Barreirinhas Cunhal (born 1914) has been a member of the party's Central Committee for nearly fifty years and the secretary general for over twenty years. He was reelected by acclamation at the party congress in December 1983. Imprisoned for twelve years under Salazar, he escaped in 1960 and spent the next fourteen years in exile, mostly in Prague. A Marxist ideologue of international repute, he is considered a Stalinist by Eurocommunist leaders. He alone rules the party.

Other Political Forces

Military

Traditionally, Portuguese military officers were drawn from the nobility. Pay was not taken seriously because the gentlemen warriors were not expected to need it. As the country's economy became more complex and large conglomerates developed, military officers augmented their salaries by serving on the boards of directors of private enterprises or in other capacities.

The intensification of conflict in the colonies in the 1960s, however, required the enlargement of the officer corps. Entrance standards were lowered and officers were recruited from the middle class. These *milicianos* had neither family money nor business connections to help them make ends meet. Graft, though rampant, did not suffice to fill the gap between salaries and needs.

By the beginning of 1974, Portugal had committed 80 percent of its armed forces, about 140,000 troops (60 percent of whom were African) to the struggle to maintain its African colonies. The Armed Forces Movement (*Movimento das Forças Armadas;* MFA), which grew out of the African campaigns, did not begin as a revolutionary body. It was a group of young career officers united by professional grievances. Specifically, they resented long tours of duty for meager salaries in remote places in interminable colonial wars. Exposure to the revolutionary ideologies of their opponents led them to an awareness of the need for political and economic change in Portugal itself. The toppling of the old regime coincided with the virtual end of opportunity for employment of young Portuguese in other European countries. The enthusiastic reaction of the Portuguese people to the Armed Forces Movement's seizure of power and the urgency of popular demands completed the radicalization of the movement.

Since the revolution, the large and amorphous MFA has, in general, spoken for the military as a whole. The inevitable political factionalism of the military has been played out within it. During the first two years of the revolution, interaction with civilian political leaders served to intensify that factionalism. General António de Spinola, first president of the new government, resigned on September 30, 1974, having failed in his attempt to build a conservative following sufficient to counter the leftist trend in the MFA. In March 1975, he was implicated in an abortive right-wing coup attempt and fled the country along with fifteen other officers.

For a time resentment of the coup attempt strengthened the positions of military leftists, represented particularly in the Continental Operations Command (*Comando de Operações do Continente;* COPCON). COPCON had been organized in July 1974 as an elite military group charged with protecting the revolution and the MFA program. From March to September 1975,

the leftist faction within the MFA appeared to have the upper hand. It favored what it termed "direct democracy," exercised through people's assemblies of civilian and military representatives. Predictably, most of the civilian parties reacted strongly against such a proposition, and they prevailed upon a more moderate faction within the MFA to steer a different course.

Seeing itself losing ground, the leftist faction attempted a coup in November 1975. Its failure resulted in a far-reaching purge of Communists and other leftist military leaders and left the moderate faction of the MFA with a majority in the military. The moderate faction, in the so-called Document of the Nine, issued in August 1975, called for a gradual transition to socialism, in the context of "political pluralism."

After the purge of the leftists, the moderates split into two factions, one advocating immediate military withdrawal from politics, the other a continuing though limited political role for the military. The constitution of 1976 represented a compromise between the two moderate MFA factions, between the MFA and the political parties, and between the parties themselves.

The general assembly of the MFA, which had been highly influential since the revolution, was given no governmental role. The military-dominated Council of the Revolution, however, retained broad and rather ambiguous powers until it was eliminated by constitutional amendment in mid-1982, with the assent of the military.

In November 1982, a bill transferring responsibility for senior military appointments from the president to the defense minister and restricting the role of the armed forces to the defense of the country against foreign aggression was passed over the president's veto.

National Prospects

The Portuguese Revolution, after a dozen years, must be viewed as incomplete or sharply limited. The reconstitution of the political system has proceeded with remarkable speed and efficiency. The country has disentangled itself from the debilitating vestiges of empire; civil liberties have been restored; free and fair elections have become routinized; and a parliamentary system is functioning. A treaty approving the country's incorporation into the European Community was ratified by parliament on July 11, 1985, and full membership in that community became effective at the beginning of 1986.

The economic promise of the revolution, however, has thus far proved ephemeral. Real wages, after rising by some 15 percent in 1974 and 1975, fell by 25 percent between 1976 and 1982. Much of the land that was "liberated" has been returned to its original owners, and many nationalized companies have been returned to the private sector. By the end of the 1970s, the public sector's share of GDP had dropped to about 15 percent. In 1984, the ban on private-sector banking activity was lifted and in 1985, the ten year old freeze on rents was lifted. Meanwhile, in 1984, GDP had declined by 1.1 percent and inflation had reached almost 30 percent. The foreign debt had doubled in four years. In 1985, the International Labor Organization (ILO) ruled that the Portuguese government was in breach of four ILO conventions, relating mainly to wages owed by public- and private-sector companies to nearly 150,000 workers; in some cases payment was up to two years in arrears.

All of the parliamentary governments, including those of the Socialists, have given higher priority to the resolution of external balance-of-payment problems than to such domestic problems as unemployment, inflation, and slow or negative growth. As a consequence, per capita income has fallen to prerevolutionary levels. Thus far, Portuguese workers and peasants have been surprisingly passive in the face of such deterioration, but sooner or later, their demands that the government make good on its promise of improving the standard of living will surely become more shrill.

Further Reading

Baklanoff, Eric N. *The Economic Transformation of Spain and Portugal.* New York: Praeger Publishers, 1978.

Bruneau, Thomas C. "Discovering Democracy." *The Wilson Quarterly.* No. 1, 1985, pp. 67-83.

———. *Politics and Nationhood: Post-Revolutionary Portugal.* New York: Praeger, 1984.

Fields, Rona M. *The Portuguese Revolution and the Armed Forces Movement.* New York: Praeger Publishers, 1975.

Graham, Lawrence S. *Portugal: The Decline and Collapse of an Authoritarian Order.* Beverly Hills, Calif.: Sage Publications, 1975.

Harsgor, Michael. *Portugal in Revolution.* Beverly Hills, Calif.: Sage Publications, 1976.

Harvey, Robert. *Portugal: Birth of a Democracy.* New York: St. Martin's Press, 1978.

Insight Team of the Sunday *Times. Insight on Portugal: The Year of the Captains.* London: Andre Deutsch Limited, 1975.

Keefe, Eugene K. et al. *Area Handbook for Portugal.* Washington, D.C.: Government Printing Office, for Foreign Area Studies, American University, 1977.

Mailer, Phil. *Portugal: The Impossible Revolution.* London: Solidarity, 1977.

Maxwell, Kenneth. "The Emergence of Democracy in Spain and Portugal." *Orbis.* Spring 1983, pp. 151-184.

Morrison, Rodney J. *Portugal: Revolutionary Change in an Open Economy.* Boston: Auburn House Publishing Company, 1981.

Porch, Douglas. *The Portuguese Armed Forces and the Revolution.* Stanford, Calif.: The Hoover Institution Press, 1977.

Pridham, Geoffrey. "Party Government in the New Iberian Democracies." *The World Today.* January 1984, pp. 12-21.

Szulc, Tad. "Lisbon and Washington: Behind the Portuguese Revolution." *Foreign Policy,* No. 27, Winter 1975–76.

STATE OF QATAR
(Dawlat Qatar)
by Fred H. Lawson, Ph.D.

The System of Government

Qatar, located on the Persian Gulf, is a non-party autocracy whose ruler governs the country's 280,000 people in consultation with a small group of advisers that includes influential members of the royal family as well as a smaller number of Western-educated members of other prominent families. The country's governing elite is descended from one branch of the Bani 'Utub tribal confederacy that was among several that settled on the Arabian Peninsula in the mid-eighteenth century. The political primacy of the Al Thani clan originated less in class or ethnic differentiation than it did by fiat of British administrators during the years after World War I. In fact, Qatari society constituted one of the most ethnically homogeneous communities among all the states of the Arab–Persian Gulf until middle of the present century.

Before the country began producing oil for export in commercial quantities in 1949, most of its inhabitants supported themselves through fishing, sailing, herding, and pearl-diving. Members of the Al Thani family were not markedly richer than their nominal subjects. The small community of wealthy pearl and cloth merchants who resided in ad-Dawhah, the capital, were predominantly native Qataris who occasionally provided the rulers with loans to enable them to meet their expenses. After oil revenues started coming into their hands, however, the country's ruling shaikhs began to move out of ad-Dawhah and set up agricultural estates away from the coast, using farm workers imported from Oman and Baluchistan. This process helped to increase the princes' political strength relative to that of the established commercial elite, and gave them sufficient resources to dominate most aspects of Qatari society. As a way of legitimizing their continued rule in the face of the United Kingdom's withdrawal of its administrative officers from the Gulf region after 1970, Qatar's emir (ruler) issued a provisional constitution for the country that envisaged both a Council of Ministers and an elected Advisory Council which would cooperate with the ruler in enacting national policy.

Executive

Shaikh Khalifah bin Hamad Al Thani became ruler of Qatar in February 1972 following the deposition of his cousin Shaikh Ahmad bin 'Ali by a collective decision of the royal family. Qatar's 1970 provisional constitution requires that the emir be from the Al Thani clan, but sets down no procedures whereby an emir's term of office can be terminated nor any specific guidelines for nominating a ruler's successor. In May 1977, Shaikh Khalifah decreed that his oldest son would be crown prince and serve as minister of defense. This decree has not met with any significant opposition within the royal family, but it is not yet clear that this move will settle the succession question once and for all, since there are precedents for the transfer of the office of emir from brother to brother as well as from father to son.

According to the provisional constitution, Qatar's ruler is to serve as head of state and receive the "absolute obedience" of his subjects. He is given the authority to enact laws for the country and also to amend the constitution "if he deems such revision necessary in the public interest." Moreover, the emir is given the right to appoint the members of Qatar's Advisory Council during the "transitional period" before a final constitution is adopted.

Close relatives of the emir fill the most important posts in the country's national cabinet. The family ties among cabinet members are illustrated in Figure 1. Shaikh Khalifah retains his post as prime minister in this cabinet, as well as serving as emir. Ministers who are not members of the Al Thani family are drawn largely

Figure 1

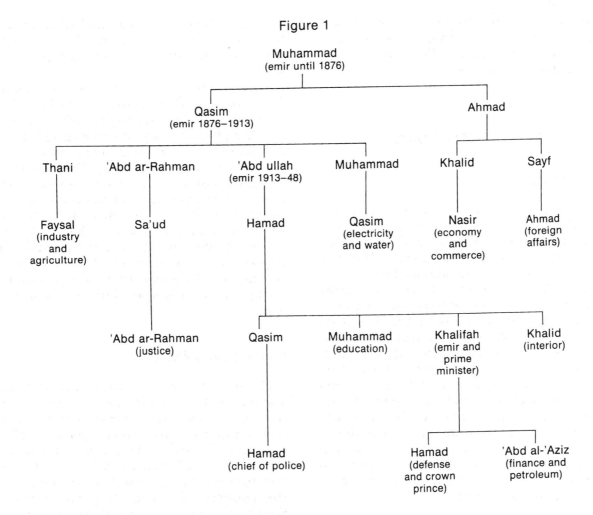

from among those sons of the country's rich merchant families who have received specialized training in Western universities. Khalid Muhammad al-Mani', the minister of health, and Khalid bin 'Abd ullah al-'Atiyyah, the minister of public works, are the most notable of these technocrat administrators. Qatar's largest industrial, commercial, and real-estate concerns are directed and managed by this group of royal family members and influential commoners.

Legislature

Qatar's first consultative assembly and state budget were instituted by order of the emir in May 1972. Twenty members of an Advisory Council were chosen by the ruler from a pool of forty candidates. These candidates had been elected by property-owning Qataris in ten voting districts throughout the country. Those chosen represented the most prominent families within the various communities, all of whom had close ties with the ruling shaikhs. As a result of three extensions of their terms of office decreed by the emir, these same twenty assemblymen remained in the council until at least 1986. In 1975, ten more members, also selected by the ruler, were added to the Advisory Council. When the "transitional period" of Qatar's electoral system is declared to be finished by the emir, all of these offices are to be filled through general elections using secret ballots. But at the present time, no popularly elected governmental body exists in the country.

Judiciary

There are five principal courts in Qatar. These consist of a lower and higher criminal court, a labor court empowered to decide on matters related to the employment and benefits of the country's workers, a court of appeals, and a commercial contract court. Muslim citizens also have access to a system of Shari'ah religious courts for settling personal disputes. The religious courts are run by Sunni clerics whose decisions are made in accordance with the strictures of Islam's fundamentalist Wahhabi sect, to which the Al Thani belong.

Other Political Forces

Rival Families

Prominent local families have continually vied with the Al Thani for predominance both within the Qatari economy and the state's armed forces. Prior to 1963, Hamad al-'Atiyyah controlled not only a large part of the country's treasury but also important sections of its army and police forces. When political unrest among the country's workers precipitated a brief period of demonstrations in April 1963, he joined 'Abd ullah al-Musnad in leading a short-lived National Unity Front. He remains influential within the present regime in his dual roles as the army's chief of staff and maternal uncle to the crown prince. Besides the al-'Atiyyah clan, the al-Muhanidah clan, the al-Mani' clan, and the Darwish clan constitute important clans within the country whose members have had serious conflicts of interest with members of the Al Thani.

Workers

Those native Qataris who had earned their living through sailing and fishing before the expansion of petroleum production have largely become workers in oil-related industries and vehicle drivers. Most of these workers now live in ad-Dawhah, al-Khawr, and Umm Sa'id, where the largest industrial projects are located. Those districts were also the ones in which radical political activity was most evident during the spring of 1963. At that time, demands were made for unionization among industrial workers and drivers, for fair rates on water and electricity, for the opening of a cinema and broadcasting station in the country, and for a representative assembly and a greater degree of fiscal responsibility within the royal family. These demands failed to generate widespread support, as a relatively liberal labor law that gave significant benefits to most workers had been issued the previous year, and oil revenues were readily available for meeting the basic needs of Qatar's small population. Fur-

thermore, during the 1960s and 1970s the country's major firms have been allowed to set up workers' committees to hear complaints and settle minor disputes.

Foreign workers now make up approximately 80 percent of Qatar's total workforce. These workers come from Egypt, Baluchistan, Korea, and Bangladesh, they are concentrated in the agricultural, construction, and commercial sectors of the country's economy. They are permitted into Qatar only if they have a local sponsor. They can own neither land nor buildings in the country. During the summer of 1980, around 250 Indian and Pakistani laborers were arrested on the grounds that their immigration papers were not in order. This move by the regime constitutes one aspect of a general tightening of sponsorship regulations in the shaikhdom.

Foreign Organizations

Qatar's rulers appear willing to allow radical and nationalist organizations to operate within the country as long as their activities are directed toward goals outside Qatar itself. The Palestine Liberation Organization has maintained a regional office in ad-Dawhah for years, and its leading officials make occasional visits to the country. But the People's Democratic Republic of Yemen was refused permission to open a consulate anywhere in Qatar after envoys of that country were arrested in the United Arab Emirates for suspected terrorist activities in the spring of 1978.

National Prospects

Qatar's rulers have so far managed to avoid any serious challenges to their continued dominance. Foreign workers and merchants have been brought into the local economy with virtually no social or political disruption. Native workers who called for unionization or nationalization of the workforce have been isolated and their demands ignored. Middle-income merchants and entrepreneurs have been largely overwhelmed by large businesses having close ties with the regime. The influx of oil money into the local economy has not been accompanied by growing rates of inflation. Consequently, there has been little call for either radical changes or popular participation in the country's government. There is little reason to expect such a movement to arise as long as oil revenues do not dry up completely and indigenous workers remain quiescent.

Further Reading
Halliday, Fred. *Arabia Without Sultans*. Harmondsworth, England: Penguin, 1974.

Nakhleh, Emile A. *Arab-American Relations in the Persian Gulf*. Washington, D.C.: American Enterprise Institute for Public Policy Research, 1975.
Sadik, Muhammad, and Snavely, William P. *Bahrain, Qatar, and the United Arab Emirates*. Lexington, Mass.: D.C. Heath, 1972.
Zahlan, Rosemarie Said. *The Creation of Qatar*. New York: Barnes and Noble; and London: Croom Helm, 1981.

SOCIALIST REPUBLIC OF ROMANIA
(Republica Socialista România)
by Michael Radu, Ph.D. revised by Ivan Volgyes, Ph.D.

The System of Government

Romania, a nation of nearly 22.5 million people, has a communist, one-party, presidential political system. Unlike some other East European countries, Romania does not allow even nominal existence for other parties; the Romanian Communist Party (*Partidul Comunist Român;* PCR) is the only political party and is assigned a "leading role" in society. In addition, the role and powers of the president are far more important than in most communist systems, amounting to autocratic rule by President Nicolae Ceauşescu.

The Romanian political system is an intricate network of institutions, including the PCR, the state administration (government) and state power organs, and the judiciary, with the party and the president in direct and indirect control of all others.

Executive

The presidency has been the center of political power in Romania since the March 18, 1974, amendment of the constitution and the introduction of the presidential system. Nicolae Ceauşescu was sworn in as Romania's first president immediately after the change; he was elected to the office in 1975 and reelected unopposed in 1980 by almost the entire population over eighteen years of age. Since the mid-1970s, Ceauşescu has exercised a personal dictatorship over the country; he and his many relatives maintain a tight grip over Romania's political, economic, social, and intellectual life.

The president is head of the party, state, and government; commander-in-chief of the armed forces; and chairman of the State Council (the former collective presidency). He has the power to appoint and dismiss the members of the government (on the formal proposal of the chairman of the Council of Ministers), the chairman of state central institutions, the members of the Supreme Court, and the prosecutor general.

Ministers are shifted by the president any time he wishes. Even those ministers who are also members of the Politburo or Central Committee are often dismissed or moved from one ministry to another according to the president's whims. At least two very powerful Politburo members, often considered possible successors to Ceauşescu, were first appointed heads of ministries facing structural difficulties and then, in the early 1980s, demoted from both government and the Politburo. Similarly, the relatively popular Minister of Youth, Ion Iliescu, was demoted and appointed a county party leader. In late 1982, Ceauşescu fired his prime minister of three years standing, Ilie Verdet.

In addition to presiding over the meetings of the Council of Ministers at his discretion, the president chairs a number of central state institutions, such as the Supreme Council of Defense, the Socialist Democracy and Unity Front (*Frontul Unităţii şi Democraţiei Socialiste;* FUDS), and the Supreme Council of Economic and Social Development. These last three groups are central bodies which include party and state representatives, as well as representatives of the official trade unions, the judiciary, and mass organizations. They have deliberative powers superior to those of the government. As a result, the president is able to control the government both directly and through these bodies. In short, the president has the decisive role in the most minute details of the national political, economic, and social life.

The president is also the secretary general of the PCR as well as of the Central Committee of the party. This is an important distinction, since the committee secretariat is responsible to the Committee as a whole, while the party secretary is responsible only to the powerless party congress. In addition to these extensive powers, the only Romanian president to date, Nicolae Ceauşescu, is also a deputy of the Grand National Assembly and the president of the Academy of Social Sciences.

The unlimited powers of the president are reflected in the two major characteristics of Nicolae Ceauşescu's rule since his accession to office in 1974: the personality cult and presidential nepotism. The personality cult in Romania has reached proportions unmatched in any other contemporary communist country and it permeates all aspects of national life. The president's picture appears at least once in every issue of every periodical and is present on television daily. His speeches are carried by all newspapers and published in millions of copies as original works; quotations from them appear in publications in all fields—from chemistry to poetry, from literary criticism to history, from philosophy to sociology. He is officially proclaimed Romania's "best son" in the country's history. He is proclaimed a brilliant economist, philosopher, and historian, as well as one of the most important contemporary world statesmen, who gives authoritative advice to specialists in all fields. The loyalty oath required from all state employees—and the state is practically the only employer in Romania—includes a vow of loyalty to him. His name, with that of the party and the country, always appear together in official slogans.

The nepotism characterizing Ceauşescu's rule is demonstrated by the high offices occupied by his relatives. The president's wife, Elena, is the third-ranking member of the PCR Political Executive Committee (Politburo), in charge of party membership. Two successive chairmen of the Council of Ministers, Manea Mánescu and Ilie Verdet, were the second-ranking Politburo members and relatives of the president, as are two other Politburo members. Ceauşescu's youngest son, Nicu, is a Central Committee member and vice-chairman of the Union of Communist Youth. One of the president's brothers is a general; another is a high-ranking member of the editorial board of the party newspaper, Scânteia. Many of the aspects of the presidential personality cult are repeated in the case of Elena Ceauşescu, who is proclaimed a scientist of world renown and is offered as the ideal example of motherhood and creativity combined. Many of her friends are in significant party and government positions, and her control over the scientific life of the country is total.

Legislature

Legislative power in Romania is officially the domain of the Grand National Assembly (Marea Adunare Naţionalâ) and the president is formally responsible to it. In fact, however, the characteristics of the Assembly and the electoral system ensure that the legislature has only formal and nominal powers.

The Assembly's 349 members are elected every five years by universal, compulsory, secret, and direct vote. By law, it must meet at least twice a year in ordinary sessions, usually lasting for a few days. Between Assembly sessions, its activities are carried out by the State Council, a body elected from the Assembly's deputies and chaired by the president. This system enables the president to act in the Assembly's name most of the time, despite his being formally responsible to it. Moreover, the establishment of such bodies as the Supreme Defense Council, the Supreme Council for Social and Economic Development, and the Council of Socialist Culture, all outside the control of the Assembly and endowed with large powers, diminish the Assembly's importance.

In such circumstances, it is quite natural that, since 1948, a law proposed to the Assembly has never been approved by a less than unanimous vote.

Judiciary

The judiciary is as subject to central party control as all other branches of government. The four types of courts—local, district, military, and the Supreme Court—include both elected judges, in the first two instances, and appointed ones. At the local and district levels, judges are elected by the appropriate people's councils on the proposal of the leadership, while the Supreme Court judges are appointed and can be dismissed at will by the president. The public prosecutors are appointed by the government, and the prosecutor general also can be dismissed by the president at his discretion.

Regional & Local Government

Local government is nominally conducted by people's councils in the forty counties, 236 towns and municipalities, and over 2,700 communes. Policymaking power for the local councils is vested in Executive Committees elected by these councils for the duration of their mandates. These councils are directly elected by the populace every five years at the same time as the elections to the Grand National Assembly. At least two candidates acceptable to the party run for most of the seats.

As on the national level, however, the powers of the party and of the local branches of the quasigovernmental councils exceed those of the elected bodies. Local people's council chairmen are often also the local party secretaries but are always responsible to the party, not the electorate. Finally, presidential approval is required for any local legislation to take effect.

The Electoral System

All citizens age eighteen and over have the right to vote. Candidates for deputy are presented exclusively by the FUDS, an umbrella organization which includes representatives of the PCR, government, and all other national organizations. The constitution provides for the possibility of more than one candidate for each elective office, but all candidates are nominated by FUDS. The majorities by which the deputies are elected range between 100 percent in Ceauşescu's own district to over 95 percent in the other cases. National voter turnout regularly exceeds 99 percent. Elections and the counting of votes are supervised by government-appointed officials and no independent observers are allowed. The same pattern is repeated in the local, city, and district elections, with identical results.

Romanian Communist Party (*Partidul Comunist Român;* PCR)

Legally and actually, the supreme institution in Romania is the Communist Party, the political center of power, the undisputed and sole repository of ideological orthodoxy, and the self-proclaimed representative of the entire people. A 1974 constitutional amendment proclaims the PCR "the leading political force of the entire society," thus reiterating and formalizing a situation dating back to 1945. The party Central Committee has the right of legal initiative, and in fact all significant pieces of legislation as well as the major lines of policy in all fields are decided by the PCR. It is the party which nominates the candidate for the presidency, as well as those for the Council of State and the Council

of Ministers. At every level of government administration, from the national level to the local, the relevant party leader is nominated by the party and is also the de facto executive.

History

The Romanian Communist Party was founded on May 8, 1921, when the Socialist Party's minority Bolshevik faction split with the main body. Until at least the mid-1950s, the party was little more than an instrument of Soviet interests in Romania, and until 1951 and 1952 its leadership was ethnically largely non-Romanian: Jews, Hungarians, Ukrainians, Bulgarians. During the 1930s, the PCR openly supported anti-Romanian causes, including the Soviet annexation of the province of Bessarabia. It had virtually no popular base of support. Following the August 23, 1944, *coup d'état* led by King Michael, which brought Romania from the German to the Allied side in World War II, and as a result of the occupation of the country by the Red Army, the party's fortunes suddenly improved. Under Soviet pressure and threats, the first three post–August 1944 national Unity governments had to include Communist ministers in key posts such as transportation and interior. On March 6, 1945, aided by continuing Soviet pressure, the PCR was able to take over the government. The March 6 government included members of small leftist groups under PCR control and members of the minority leftist factions of the democratic parties, as well as Communists and their nonparty supporters.

Once in power, the PCR succeeded in destroying all organized opposition by the end of 1947. Through confiscations and expropriations of property, massive arrests of democratic party leaders, and the use of sympathetic or unscrupulous elements in those parties, the PCR both denied the opposition an economic base and destroyed its coherence. By 1947, the Social Democratic Party was forced to join the PCR, and the largest and most popular party, the National Peasants' Party, was dismantled and its leader, Iuliu Maniu, imprisoned. Maniu died in jail. On December 30, 1947, the PCR forced King Michael into exile and proclaimed Romania a people's republic. At the same time the party changed its name to the Romanian Workers' Party.

Throughout the 1946–56 period, terror was the main instrument used by the PCR to consolidate its position. Victims included members of all classes, ethnic groups, and institutions. Huge concentration camps, the largest and most deadly being along the Danube–Black Sea canal, were set up with the aim of physically exterminating former as well as potential opponents.

The PCR consolidated its control over the workers by taking over the trade unions and using force against strikes. It further strengthened its control by becoming the single significant employer following the nationalization of most of the industry and services sector. Nationalization was complete by 1947. A land-reform program in 1945 was intended to destroy the economic base of the landowner class and to eliminate the most enterprising and wealthy individual farmers. Land was given to the small- and middle-sized farmers, but was taken away again during the forced collectivization campaign that started in 1949 and ended by 1962. All peasants owning more than fifteen hectares (thirty-seven acres) of land were labeled kulaks (*chiaburi*) and declared "class enemies." Many were sent to concentration camps. Onerous delivery quotas were imposed on the remaining individual farmers, ruining them and provoking sharp opposition, which in turn resulted in a concentration camp population of over 200,000 in 1951 and 1952.

Throughout the 1945–52 period the PCR was plagued by factionalism, largely based upon personal ambitions aggravated by ethnic differences which pitted ethnic Romanians against the more cosmopolitan and largely non-Romanian group linked to the Soviet's Comintern. While both factions were staunch Marxist-Leninists, and the ethnic lines were not always clear, the national aspect served as a useful instrument for the Romanian group to both promote its own claims and legitimize the party itself. The two more important ethnic Romanians, Gheorghe Gheorghiu-Dej and Lucreţiu Pătraşcanu, had been jailed during the war, while the non-Romanian Ana Pauker and Vasile Luca were in Moscow. Immediately after August 1944, Pătraşcanu and Gheorghiu-Dej were the most visible and represented the party in the national coalition governments. After the PCR took complete government control, the two Romanians lost their power. Pătraşcanu was tried as a "Titoist" in 1948 and executed in 1954. Gheorghiu-Dej, while retaining the title of secretary general, lost most of his power to Pauker until 1952. In that year, with Russian support, Pauker and Luca were purged by the coalition of Gheorghiu-Dej and Defense Minister Emil Bodnăraş, a Ukrainian-German Soviet citizen. From 1952 until his death in 1965, Gheorghiu-Dej was the undisputed party leader.

By 1956 the party leadership felt secure enough to relax the repression of the previous decade. The remaining concentration-camp prisoners were released and a period of relative liberalization began which lasted until the beginning of the 1970s. Unlike most East European parties, however, the Romanian Communist Party did not fully de-Stalinize after 1956, which could account for the persistence of Stalinist traits, including the personality cult, to this day.

Gheorghiu-Dej's death was followed by a brief struggle between Ceauşescu and Alexandru Drăghici. Ceauşescu, who had been the party official in charge of political control of the military, had the support of the army, while Drăghici, as interior minister, was the head of the security police. Allied with the relatively moderate prime minister, Ion Gheorghe Maurer, Ceauşescu rather quickly emerged the victor and stripped the secret police of much of their autonomy. About this time, the party changed its name back to the Romanian Communist Party. It took several more years to ease Maurer's group out of key positions, but by the early 1970s, Ceauşescu was in firm control of the party and the state. Although Ceauşescu came to power by dismantling the secret police, he soon reestablished secret police powers, but now under his own personal control and in his own personal interests; the secret police continue, to date, to be the mainstay of his personal reign.

Organization

Formally, the supreme PCR body is the congress, which convenes every four years. The congress elects the Central Committee, which in turn elects the twenty-six–member Political Executive Committee. It is, however, a part of the latter group, the eleven-member Permanent Bureau, which is the real center of party and government power.

In principle, congress delegates are selected to reflect the ethnic and social composition of the party. Those selected for the November 1979 XIIth Congress were supposed to be 15 percent peasants, 31 percent workers, 51 percent intellectuals and party activists, over 30 percent women, and 88 percent ethnic Romanians,

8 percent Hungarians, and 1.6 percent Germans. The Permanent Bureau, however, included ten men and only one woman, Elena Ceauşescu, all Romanians. Members of the PCR secretariat cannot, with the exception of Ceauşescu, retain their office once appointed to government, but they do retain their Permanent Bureau membership.

The lowest party unit is the factory, village, or institution cell, including all the party members in the respective group, and led by a cell secretary elected by them after being nominated in close consultation with higher echelons. The local union leader and the enterprise manager are always members of the cell as well. The cell leader is directly responsible to the higher echelon—usually the district party organization—as well as to the central leadership, and is subject to strict discipline according to the principle of democratic centralism. The cells hold regular meetings closed to nonmembers, and are subject to periodical indoctrination courses.

The system of mass organizations in Romania is another form of the PCR drive to control all aspects of the national life. As a general rule, these organizations are intended to provide the party with instruments of mobilization, indoctrination, and regimentation. The party controls them strictly in order to prevent the formation of any autonomous institutional challenge to PCR rule.

The General Confederation of Trade Unions (*Confederaţiă Generala a Sindicatelor;* CGS) is the only legal trade union organization. It includes almost all employees in industry, services, and culture, with a total of over six million members in 1979. Although not legally compulsory, membership in the CGS is actually a necessity, since only its members can obtain access to government-owned health spas, may qualify for scarce government housing, etc. The unions represent the interests of the employer, i.e., the government, more than those of the employees, and are expected to apply the regime's economic and wage policies. The CGS chairman is, *ex officio,* the labor minister. The right to strike is denied, and collective bargaining does not exist, nor are there any means for workers' grievances to be aired legally. The local party leader, the plant manager, and the union leader at factory level form a group whose powers cannot be challenged from below, despite the formal existence of workers' councils—which are usually led by the plant managers.

The Union of Communist Youth (*Uniunea Tineretului Comunist;* UTC) includes the large majority of teenagers and young adults. While the UTC may provide some services, such as dance halls and discos, its main role is one of mobilization and indoctrination. The same applies to the Pioneers' Organization and the Motherland's Falcons, organizations of primary-school children subordinate to the UTC.

A large number of women are members of the Women's National Council (*Consiliul Naţional al Femeilor*), an instrument of party mobilization among women, who form almost half of all employees. Despite official claims, the status of women in Romania is far from equal, although in individual cases women do occupy important positions. Out of twenty-six members of the Politburo, only two are women, while none of the Central Committees secretaries and only two members of the government are women.

The national councils of minorities—Hungarians and Germans—are unrepresentative bodies led by loyal party members who see their task as one of supporting the regime's Romanian nationalist claims, even at the expense of the cultural survival of the minorities. The councils have not even attempted to alleviate the massive discrimination that is practiced against the large minorities of the country, most especially against the some 2 million Hungarians who account for at least 10 percent of the population.

Policy

The policies of the PCR are a combination of strict Marxist-Leninist orthodoxy at home and relative autonomy from Soviet policy abroad.

In economic policy, the Romanian party retains a highly centralized system of planning with a few concessions to local decision making for the sake of efficiency. The major characteristic of the party's policy has been the absolute priority given to industry, especially heavy industry. During the 1970s, almost two-thirds of total investment went to industry, and heavy industry's share grew at the expense of consumer industry. According to official Romanian figures, state expenditure for all consumer industry *and* services fell from 82.4 percent of total expenditures in 1950 to 58 percent by 1984.

From the beginning, Romania lacked sufficient domestic resources to sustain the planned expansion of heavy industry. Though moderately well-endowed with oil, iron, coal and lignite, these resources were limited and, in the case of oil particularly, threatened with depletion. Thus while self-sufficient in oil in 1970, by 1985 the country was importing over 60 percent of its needs at ever higher prices. Even though the 1965–75 GNP growth rate averaged 12 percent annually, one of the highest in the world, this growth was due in large part to the expansion of the steel, machinery, and chemical industries—precisely those areas in which adequate domestic resources are lacking. As a result, the growth rate has been declining sharply since 1975.

Nor did Romania have the skilled labor necessary for the industrialization drive started by Gheorghiu-Dej and continued by Ceaușescu. In the beginning, the policy of industrialization was based on the availability of cheap labor, largely peasants driven off the land by collectivization and attracted to the cities by the prospect of a steady cash income. Although over one-third of Romania's labor force is still engaged in agriculture, rural labor shortages and bad planning still require emergency measures at harvest time, and result in severe and continuous shortages of foodstuffs that should be available in the stores and markets of the country.

Investment in industry, however, depends on acquiring hard currency from the sale of agricultural products, which still constitute the bulk of Romania's exports. With investment capital and labor drawn away from the country's prime export potential, Romania turned to borrowing from Western sources in the early 1970s. By the end of 1981, Romania's debt to Western banks and governments and to international lending institutions was estimated at some $12 billion, about 15 percent of the GNP: the debt service ratio of the country amounted to between 19–22 percent during 1981–1985. At the same time, Romania's industrial products are noncompetitive either at home or abroad because of their poor quality.

Collectivization and decapitalization of agriculture has resulted in a decline in production per land unit. The extremely low productivity and inefficiency of agriculture is demonstrated year after year when soldiers, students, and urban workers are dispatched to harvest the crops. With most agricultural output exported for the hard currency needed for industry, by the mid-1970s widespread shortages of basic foodstuffs appeared throughout the country; these shortages had become permanent by the end of the decade. In November 1981, strict

rationing of food was imposed, and in February 1982, the prices of all food products were sharply raised. However, even these measures failed to alleviate the severe shortages in foodstuffs.

While Romania's economic situation is not unusual in East Europe, the party's foreign policy has no parallel. Under Gheorghiu-Dej, Romania's foreign policy had highly peculiar characteristics: it was used by the PCR to appeal to nationalistic feelings. After 1952, the PCR, while pursuing absolutely orthodox Marxist-Leninist policies at home, succeeded in obtaining a relative degree of national autonomy from the Soviet Union. The purging of some former leading Comintern members during Stalin's lifetime was the first example of such autonomy, and Romania's foreign policy since 1960 has further demonstrated the persistence of this pattern. While supporting the USSR in its conflict with Yugoslavia and in the crushing of the Hungarian Revolution in 1956, by 1960 Gheorghiu-Dej felt secure enough to refuse to take sides in the Sino-Soviet conflict. Romania has continued to retain excellent ties with both Moscow and Beijing.

Under Ceaușescu, Romania refused to participate in the Warsaw Pact invasion of Czechoslovakia in 1968 and loudly but briefly condemned it, refused to go along with the communist bloc when it broke ties with Israel in 1967, and protested Vietnam's occupation of Kampuchea in 1978. On the other hand, while Ceaușescu expressed his opposition to the Soviet invasion of Afghanistan, he supported Soviet initiatives in the Mediterranean and the Indian Ocean, he has also provided help to radical groups in the Third World, and approved the imposition of martial law in Poland in December 1981.

Although a member of the Warsaw Treaty Organization, Romania has not allowed the alliance to undertake military maneuvers on its territory since the late 1960s. In 1977, Romania flatly rejected Soviet and Warsaw Pact calls for an increase in defense spending. Romania is also a member of the Soviet-dominated Council for Mutual Economic Assistance (Comecon), but it has rejected COMECON's requests to concentrate its development on the expansion of the agricultural sector; its foreign trade, instead of being largely conducted within the community, is almost equally divided between the Soviet bloc, the West, and the Third World.

In 1972, Romania proclaimed itself a "socialist developing country," and thus stressed its intermediate position between the Soviet bloc and the Third World. This attitude found widespread acceptance in the world. Romania is now a member of the Group of 77 (a bloc of underdeveloped countries) and has observer status with the nonaligned movement. Romania has greatly expanded relations with such disparate Third World countries as Zaire, Gabon, Zimbabwe, Angola, and Mozambique.

Romania's relations with the West are much closer than those of most communist states and have enabled her to obtain massive credits, favorable tariff treatment for exports, and a significant degree of legitimacy and credibility for Ceaușescu himself. In 1972, Romania became the first COMECON member to gain admission to the International Monetary Fund and the International Bank for Reconstruction and Development (World Bank). Although in 1985–1986 Romania's severe repression of its religious and ethnic minorities has been loudly criticized by the United States, the country — due largely to its foreign policy positions that are often diverse from those maintained by the USSR — still retains its Most Favored Nation status, accorded to it by the U.S. Congress.

Membership & Constituency

In August 1944, the membership of the PCR was less than 1,000, but the general perception that Soviet occupation forces and Western indifference would utimately allow the party to take power helped a massive membership drive; by 1945 membership reached 250,000 and grew to 600,000 by 1948. The membership remained at that level until another massive drive in the 1960s, facilitated by a relative liberalization at the time. At the end of 1981, the PCR claimed 3,150,812 members, or over 30 percent of the total active (employed) population. Of this number, nearly 24 percent were employed by the party. Workers constituted about 42 percent of the membership, peasants 20 percent, intellectuals 22 percent, and women 26 percent.

The PCR membership is divided into two well-defined groups: the general membership, about 75 percent of the total, and the full-time activists, employed by the party. The activists are charged with the permanent surveillance of party, government, and other institutional activities. They are responsible to the higher party leadership only and have the right to impose party views upon industrial managers and institution chiefs. The selection of the activists

is a long process, involving years of careful screening and surveillance, studies at the party institutions such as the Stefan Gheorghiu Academy and the Party Superior School, and periodic reindoctrination. All important party positions are filled by them, and all future PCR leaders are selected from their ranks. In addition to their substantial salaries, the activists have access to special stores, not open to the general public or even to most ordinary members, where prices are lower than usual and rare or otherwise unobtainable goods can be bought.

For the ordinary member, possession of the party card gains few advantages, but it does enable the holder to avoid many of the disadvantages that go with nonmembership. Only a party member can hope to advance in a professional career or to travel abroad, and party members have a better chance at getting scarce housing and sending their children to university.

The popular base of support of the PCR is extremely difficult to assess, since the party has never had to participate in fair and competitive elections. The official structure of membership is less than revealing, both because it does not distinguish between the activists enjoying real authority and the general membership, and because it provides no indication of the degree of party support among nonmembers.

On the other hand, membership figures do indicate that peasants are the least supportive of all social groups, largely because of collectivization, and that half the membership comes from the "new class" of party activists and professionals, with intellectuals overrepresented. Most of the intellectuals and full-time activists are products of the PCR's destruction of the old elites and the promotion of workers and peasants to important positions during the 1950s. In general, it was after acquiring influential positions through party membership that such groups obtained their higher education. In addition to this new elite, during the first two decades of the industrialization drive (1950–70), many peasants were attracted to the cities and formed a block of urban support for the party.

The party's popularity peaked around 1970, when it was largely supported as a nationalist force, and has declined steadily ever since. The children of former peasants, city-bred and with higher expectations, have become dissatisfied with the regime. Most party members are over thirty years of age, an indication that youth are largely apolitical or hostile. Failed economic ex-

pectations, wide-spread shortages of basic consumer goods, and lack of worker rights, along
with the rise of the personality cult and the
power and wealth of the new ruling class have
sapped much of the support the party once had.
Even among party members, what support remains is based more on self-interest than ideological commitment; true Marxist-Leninist believers are an inconsequential and declining
minority.

Financing

All members pay dues in proportion to their
income, but the financing of PCR activities remains a well-preserved secret, since membership dues clearly are insufficient for its extensive activities.

Leadership

Nicolae Ceaușescu was born on January 23,
1918, to a peasant family in the village of Scor-
nicesti in southwestern Romania. He never
completed his secondary education. By 1933, he
was an apprentice shoemaker in Bucharest and,
according to the official biography, already involved in communist activities, for which he
was arrested in 1933 and again in 1941. After
the war, he became the leader of the Union of
Communist Youth and a Central Committee
member. In the early 1950s, he seems to have
undertaken military studies in the Soviet
Union. By the mid-1950s, he was a PCR Politburo member in charge of political and ideological activities in the army. This office allowed
him to build a powerful political base in the
military, which proved decisive in his becoming
Gheorghe Gheorghiu-Dej's successor as secretary general of the party in March 1965.

Ceaușescu has no heir-apparent, although his
wife Elena and his youngest son, Nicu, have
been mentioned as potential candidates. The issue of succession has become important in
1985–1986, with the report that Ceaușescu has
been receiving treatment for cancer, although
the success of such treatment could not be determined. Officially, in the event of the president's death, the prime minister would take
over the country until the party chose a new
leader.

Opposition

Domestic opposition to the PCR and to
Ceaușescu's personal rule remained extremely
insignificant until the late 1970s, and it still
lacks the strength and coordination of opposition in other East European countries. In light
of its most prominent members' isolation from
the general population, its sporadic and localized actions, and its lack of cohesion, the domestic opposition in Romania could more properly
be called dissidence, similar to that in the Soviet
Union and unlike that in Poland.

The initial opposition to communist rule in
the wake of World War II came from the former
elites and political parties, as well as from the
peasants and intellectuals. Disorganized and
lacking external support and a truly national
structure, this opposition fell victim to the secret police. The last of the anticommunist guerrilla groups, operating near the Yugoslav border, were eliminated by the mid-1950s. Until
1977, discontent manifested itself through low
productivity and a high rate of alcoholism and
work absenteeism, rather than through open
dissent. Since then it has become clear that hostility to the PCR is growing among many
groups, the most significant of these being workers, intellectuals, religious groups, and ethnic
minorities.

None of these groups has been involved in
violent activities against the government. Their
opposition is limited to illegal strikes, letters of
protest, manifestos sent to the West, and adherence to nonrecognized religious cults. In all
cases the government's reaction has been
severe—arrests, heavy prison sentences, intern-
ment in psychiatric hospitals, police brutality,
and exile.

Worker opposition has taken a more aggressive form since the August 1977 strike in the
coal mines of the Jiu Valley. After promising
concessions, the government occupied the
mines, arrested the strike leaders, and relocated hundreds of workers to distant mines. At
least one of the main leaders died in unclear circumstances, and a number were confined in labor camps. Since 1977, there have been many
plausible, although unconfirmed reports of industrial sabotage in the cities of Ploiești and
Pitești, further strikes, and some bombings. In
February 1979, a group of intellectuals, immediately joined by some workers and peasants,
proclaimed the formation of a Free Trade
Union of the Working People of Romania (*Sin-
dicatul Liber al Oamenilor Muncii din Româ-*

nia; SLOMR). They were promptly arrested and imprisoned.

The intellectuals' dissatisfaction with the regime has its roots in the disappointment produced by the retreat from the liberalization of the 1960s, particularly after the "mini–cultural revolution" which began in 1971 after Ceauşescu's visits to China and North Korea. The "revolution" saw the imposition of strict ideological requirements on all literary, historical, and philosophical writings; the appointment of party ideologues to the leadership of intellectual associations and institutions; and stricter censorship. The opposition manifested itself by open dissent on the part of such intellectuals as Paul Goma, a writer who became widely known after his publications appeared in the West, and more often, by self-imposed exile to the West by leading writers, literary critics, film directors, and artists.

Ethnic opposition derives largely from the Hungarians, who constitute as much as 10 percent of Romania's population and are largely concentrated in the western part of the country in the Transylvania region. During the first decade after World War II, some of them were quite supportive of the PCR, which they saw as a guarantor of cultural rights, but they have become disaffected by Ceauşescu's vocal Romanian nationalism and policy of hidden forced cultural assimilation. The number of Hungarian-language educational institutions has declined steadily, Hungarian graduates most often are given jobs in purely Romanian areas, and most of the top party and local administrative officials in the Hungarian-inhabited areas are ethnic Romanians. Moreover, Hungarians are underrepresented in the central government and party apparatus. The most important and well-known manifestation of Hungarian dissatisfaction was the public appeal for a change in policy made by a former high PCR official of Hungarian origin, Károly Király, in 1977. Although Király was sent into internal exile, his letter to Politburo member Ilie Verdet became well known and was widely supported by the Hungarians in Romania. At the same time, the policy of assimilation pursued by the party and the repression of those objecting to it had a negative impact on Romania's relations with neighboring Hungary.

The dominant church in Romania, the Greek Orthodox, was historically supportive of the government, and the PCR has largely succeeded in co-opting its leadership, while at the same time pursuing a vigorous, albeit intermittent, antireligious campaign in education, culture, and public life. The officially recognized religious denominations are under the direct control of a ministry of religious cults, and the clergy is dependent upon the government for most of its revenues. Despite cooperation between state and church, some Orthodox priests, such as Gheorghe Calciu, have publicly attacked the party's atheist propaganda; they have been imprisoned. The most important source of religious opposition comes from neo-Protestant churches, some of them dissident factions of legally recognized denominations, such as Baptists and Pentecostalists, and some of them unrecognized and illegal. These groups, with a growing appeal among the youth, are relatively well organized, have links with external churches, and are usually engaged in peaceful civil disobedience and publication of manifestos in the West. In 1977 and 1978 a variety of religious groups founded the Association for the Freedom of Religion and Conscience in Romania, since dismantled by the regime.

The most innocuous but widespread form of opposition to the government takes the form of emigration. Thousands of Romanian citizens, only a minority of whom are Jews or Germans, apply for emigration each year; a similar number attempt to leave the country illegally or refuse to return from travels abroad. Some prospective emigrants are allowed to leave, but most are harassed and see their careers ruined; a number have been interned in psychiatric institutions or jailed after their applications were rejected.

National Prospects

To a very large, perhaps decisive extent, Romania's relatively autonomous foreign policy was a result of and conditioned by the existence of the East-West detente. With the deterioration of detente and Romania's growing economic dependence upon the USSR, particularly for raw materials such as oil and ores, one could expect the country to slowly return to a more orthodox foreign policy of closer cooperation with its Warsaw Pact and COMECON partners.

In March 1982, the price of gasoline rose again to a level over four times higher than it was a decade earlier. In April 1982, strict new limits were placed on electricity use, the cost of housing was increased, and the government asked its Western creditors to reschedule its debts. Romania's economic crisis in part, is, due to unfavorable international economic circumstances, but it is also the result of Ceauşescu's single-minded industrialization drive and skewed investment policy. The population blames Ceauşescu and the party for the situation, and widespread popular discontent is increasingly directed at the leader himself. The long-term future of the Ceauşescu regime, therefore, seems troubled. While an explosion of violence is improbable, the steady erosion of support for the PCR may reach critical proportions and bring concerted open opposition as the economic situation worsens.

The decline of detente, the growing reluctance of Romania's Western creditors to extend new loans, and the rapidly worsening economic situation are all factors which may strengthen the now dormant pro-Soviet group within the PCR and allow Moscow to weaken and ultimately replace Ceauşescu as the price for increased economic assistance. The survival of communism and of the PCR as an institution, however, is the only realistic outcome regardless of Ceauşescu's personal fate as Romania's undisputed ruler.

Further Reading
Bacon, Walter M. "Romania." *In Civil-Military Relations in Communist States*, Dale Her-spring and Ivan Volgyes, eds. Boulder, Colo.: Westview, 1979.

Chirot, Daniel. "Social Change in Communist Romania." *Social Forces*, Vol. 57, No. 2, December 1978.

Cismarescu, Michael. "New Trends in the Development of Constitutional Law in Romania." *Review of Socialist Law*, Vol. 4, No. 2, June 1978.

Georgescu, Vlad. "Romania." In *Dissent in Eastern Europe*, Jane L. Curry, ed. New York: Praeger, 1983.

Gilberg, Trond. *Modernization in Romania since World War II*. New York: Praeger, 1975.

Nelson, Daniel N. and Fischer-Galati, Stephen, eds. *Romania in the 1980s*. Boulder, Colo.: Westview Press, 1981.

Shafir, Michael. *Romania—Politics, Economy and Society: Stagnation and Simulated Change*. Boulder, Colo.: Lynne Rienner, Publisher, 1985.

Tismaneanu, Leonte, and Zaharia, Rolică. *Present and Prospect in Romania's Social and Economic Development*. Bucharest: Meridiane Publishing House, 1977.

Tismaneanu, Valdimir. "Romania." In *Yearbook of Communist Affairs*, 1986, Richard F. Star, ed. Stanford, CA.: Hoover Institution, 1986.

———. "Stalinist Orthodoxy and Byzantine Rituals: The Twilight of Dynastic Socialism in Romania." *Orbis*, Spring, 1986.

SAINT LUCIA

by Indira Jhappan revised by D. Brent Hardt, M.A.

The System of Government

Saint Lucia is a parliamentary democracy which gained its independence from Britain on February 22, 1979, after twelve years of internal self-government. The population of about 124,000 on this Caribbean island is predominantly African or of mixed race. What would technically be called the middle class (businessmen, professionals, technocrats) is the island's elite, with the exception of a few wealthy families. The majority of the population is rural and poor, though industry and tourism are increasingly important elements of the island's economy.

Executive

Executive power is formally vested in the British monarch represented by a governor general whose functions are largely ceremonial. Real executive power belongs to the prime minister, leader of the majority party in the House and head of government. The governor general can dissolve the Parliament and call new elections at the request of the prime minister or in the event of a vote of no confidence.

Legislature

The Saint Lucian Parliament has two chambers, the House and the Senate. The House consists of seventeen members directly elected by simple pluralities from single-member constituencies for five-year terms. At the beginning of each session, a speaker is elected by the House to preside over its sessions. The speaker need not be a member, in which case he cannot vote. If the speaker is a member, he can cast only tie-breaking votes. The attorney general, if not a House member, becomes one by virtue of his appointment, in which case the House has eighteen members.

The Senate has eleven members, all appointed by the governor general. Six are appointed on the advice of the prime minister; three on the advice of the leader of the opposition; and two by the governor general in consultation with economic, social, and religious organizations.

Constitutional changes are made with a two-thirds majority vote of the House, but any bill which would alter the procedure for constitutional amendment must be approved by three-quarters of the House. With the exception of money bills, which can only be introduced in the House, either the House or the Senate may introduce legislation. Certain financial bills can only be introduced with the permission of the governor general. To become law, bills must be approved by both the House and Senate, though if the Senate rejects a bill twice, it may be submitted to a popular referendum and, if approved, sent on to the governor general for his signature. Certain money bills can go to the governor general for signature if the Senate does not act on them within a month after their passage by the House.

Judiciary

Saint Lucia comes under the jurisdiction of the West Indies Associated States and the Eastern Caribbean Supreme Court. The latter consists of a chief justice and a number of judges, one of whom sits in Saint Lucia. Appeals from the Saint Lucia High Court go to the Eastern Caribbean Court of Appeal. Final appeal is to the judicial committee of the British Privy Council.

Regional & Local Government

The island is divided into sixteen parishes with elected bodies responsible for a limited range of local affairs. The political parties are active in local government.

The Electoral System

All adults age eighteen and over are eligible to vote. Registration of voters and the conduct of elections is the responsibility of an electoral commission of three members, one each selected by the governor general, the prime minister, and the leader of the opposition. Elections are generally fair and aboveboard, though the intense rivalry between the two major parties has, on occasion, been accompanied by violence. In the 1979 election, voter participation showed signs of flagging: only 61 percent of eligible voters turned out compared to 83 percent in 1974. The 1979 election was also the first in which there were no independent candidates. Turnout in the 1982 elections showed only slight improvement over 1979. In recent years, the electorate has become better educated, more sophisticated, and more oriented to issues than in the past.

The Party System

The party system is well established and, until 1981, was dominated by two parties. As in many Caribbean nations, the parties rose out of the trade unions in the early 1950s and in their early years were indistinguishable from the union organizations. The unions remain the politicians' political bases, providing them with active supporters and some financial help.

Progressive Labour Party (PLP)

The PLP was founded in 1981, when George Odlum and two other members of the House bolted the Saint Lucia Labour Party (SLP) after a dispute over SLP leadership and policy. The party won 27 percent of the vote and one seat in the May 1982 elections, but Odlum and deputy leader Michael Pilgrim failed to gain reelection. The party stands to the left of center and has been attacked by the current prime minister, John Compton, for its ties to leftist organizations. Compton has accused Libya of recruiting PLP members for terrorist training and has passed laws restricting such PLP activities as the showing of motion pictures and wearing fatigues. The PLP's popularity has declined in the wake of events in Grenada which discredited leftist movements friendly to that country's former government.

Saint Lucia Labour Party (SLP)

The SLP won the first elections in 1951 and stayed in power until 1964. It was first led by George Charles and was based on the Workers Union. It lost to the United Workers Party (UWP) in 1964, but returned to power in 1979, winning twelve seats with 56 percent of the vote.

The party's policy is slightly to the left of center, with some leaning toward socialism, though the party leadership is unwilling to describe the party as socialist. The party has expressed support for Cuba and Grenada under Maurice Bishop and its government attended the conferences of nonaligned nations in Havana, Cuba, in 1979.

The close relationship between the party and some trade unions made it difficult for the SLP governments to deal with both economic problems and union demands between 1979 and 1982. Labor unrest, strong opposition from the Chamber of Commerce to both labor demands and some moderately socialist government measures, and serious intraparty dissension were responsible for the fall of the SLP government in early 1982.

When the party took over the government in 1979, it was led by Allan Louisy, who became prime minister. A struggle for party leadership between Louisy and George Odlum led Louisy to resign as leader and prime minister in April 1981, while Odlum left the SLP to form his own party. Louisy was replaced as leader and prime minister by Winston Cenac.

In late 1982, the party's prospects looked grim. The May elections gave it only 16.5 percent of the vote and two seats in the House. Both Cenac and the party's new leader, Peter Josie, were defeated; Louisy did not run. In August 1984, the SLP elected Julian Hunte, former mayor of Castries, the new party leader. Hunte was not involved in the party's internal disputes and is viewed as a figure who could reclaim some support from the PLP.

United Workers Party (UWP)

The UWP also traces its history to the labor movement and the early 1950s. It first formed a government under John Compton in 1964 and Compton remained in power as premier until the first postindependence election in 1979, when the UWP won only 42 percent of the vote and lost five of its ten seats in the House.

With the elections of May 1982, the party returned to power with an absolute majority of the vote (56.4 percent) and twelve of seventeen seats. The party is led by John Compton (born 1926), the first university graduate to enter St. Lucian politics. It stands right of center and is committed to the development of free enterprise and to free trade. The party leadership has severely criticized the role of Cuba in the region and opposed the former People's Revolutionary Government of Grenada for its failure to pursue a democratic form of government. Compton has devoted considerable attention to attacking the left-wing PLP and he strongly supported the joint U.S.–Caribbean invasion of Grenada in 1983. He is a keen supporter of the U.S. Caribbean Basin Initiative and hopes to derive some economic benefit from the program.

National Prospects

After a period of some political turmoil from 1979 to 1982, Saint Lucia has returned to its traditional pattern of political stability. Recent trends in the Saint Lucian economy have been encouraging: unemployment declined from 27 percent in 1982 to 22 percent in 1984; tourism increased 90 percent in 1983-1984 over the previous season; and inflation remained minuscule at 1.5 percent. Continued stability will depend on the government's ability to expand housing, social services, and employment opportunities, particularly for the young.

As long as the opposition remains divided, the UWP will continue to control parliament.

Further Reading
Emmanuel, Patrick. "Elections in the Eastern Caribbean." *Caribbean Review*, Vol. 10, No. 2, Spring, 1981.
————. *General Elections in the Eastern Caribbean: A Handbook.* Cave Hill, Barbados: Institute of Social and Economic Research, 1979.

Jesse, Rev. C. *Outlines of St. Lucia's History.* Castries: The Voice Press, 1970.
Lowenthal, David. *West Indian Societies.* London: Oxford University Press, 1972.
————. *Saint Lucia at Independence.* Castries: The Voice Press, 1979.

SAINT VINCENT AND THE GRENADINES
by D. Brent Hardt, M.A.

The System of Government

Saint Vincent and the Grenadines is a British-style parliamentary democracy. It gained its independence from Great Britain in 1979 after ten years of internal self-government. The nation of about 110,000 people consists of Saint Vincent and ten smaller islands, the Grenadines, in the eastern Caribbean Sea. The population is predominantly African in origin with a few Europeans, Asians, and Carib Indians.

Executive

Formal executive power is vested in the British monarch represented by a governor-general who appoints as prime minister a member of the legislature's majority party. The prime-minister with his cabinet exercises the effective executive power in the system.

Legislature

The legislature, called the House of Assembly, contains thirteen popularly elected members and six appointed ones. Twelve of the elected members represent Saint Vincent constituencies and one represents the Grenadines. The governor-general appoints the six other members, four on the advice of the prime minister and two on the advice of the leader of the opposition.

Judiciary

The judicial system is based on English common law and is under the jurisdiction of the West Indies Supreme Court, which gives the country's judiciary full independence from political pressure.

Regional & Local Government

The island of Saint Vincent is divided into five parishes; each of the other islands constitute a parish. Each parish has its own elected parish council whose responsibilities are primarily administrative.

The Electoral System

The elected members of the House of Assembly are chosen for five-year terms in single-member districts by simple plurality. Every citizen age eighteen and over is eligible to vote. Elections are regulated by a supervisor who is a nonappointed civil servant and is considered independent of the government.

The Party System

The party system is well developed and highly competitive. There are no barriers to the entry of new parties, but elections typically evolve into a contest between two major parties. Until the early 1980s, the political system was dominated by the Saint Vincent Labour Party (SVLP) and the People's Progressive Party (PPP). In 1966, the PPP ruled with a majority of one seat; in 1972, the two parties each won six seats. The remaining seat was won by an independent, James Mitchell, who became prime minister in coalition with the PPP. The SVLP controlled the House from 1974 to July 1984 when Mitchell led his New Democratic Party to victory over the SVLP in the general elections, winning 51 percent of the vote and nine of the thirteen seats. The 1984 election reflected the competitiveness of the nation's politics as 88.8 percent of the electorate voted—the highest voter turnout in Caribbean history.

The parties are well organized with constituency branches at the local level and annual national conferences. In spite of intraparty democratic procedures, charismatic leadership plays a strong role in determining party policy.

The party system once was characterized by many independent candidacies, but this element has declined sharply since the early 1970s as the political parties have developed into effective organizations. Nevertheless, politicians frequently shift their party affiliation and break with the major parties to form smaller ones. The creation of several small parties, which are often formed at election time and dissolve soon after, is a symptom of frustration with the dominance of the major parties.

Saint Vincent Labour Party (SVLP)

Founded in 1955 by Milton Cato (born 1915), the SVLP first came to power in 1967 when it obtained six of the nine seats in the old legislature. Under SVLP leadership, Saint Vincent became an associated state with Great Britain and was granted full internal self-government over strong objections from the opposition party. In the 1972 elections, the SVLP obtained six out of thirteen seats. The SVLP returned to power in 1974, obtaining 68.5 percent of the vote and ten seats. Four years later, Cato announced that he would seek independence for Saint Vincent, and again over the objections of the opposition, the country became independent in 1979. In the first postindependence election, the SVLP won eleven seats, although its share of votes fell sharply.

While in power, the party pursued a moderate policy, advocating a mixed economy and a conservative foreign policy. Although it supported nonalignment, it retained strong ties with the West.

In the aftermath of its unexpected loss in the 1984 election, Milton Cato resigned as party leader, setting off a struggle for party leadership between the old guard, led by Hudson Tannis, and a disenchanted younger faction, led by former Agriculture Minister Vincent Beache.

New Democratic Party (NDP)

The NDP was founded in 1975 by James Mitchell (born 1931), a former SVLP member and former prime minister as an independent. In its first campaign, in 1979, it won two seats in the House, eliminating the PPP as the formal opposition party. In 1984, the NDP was swept into office by a large and totally unexpected margin, gaining control of nine of the thirteen House seats.

The NDP is fundamentally a centrist party. Mitchell campaigned on a cautious left-of-center program, urging social reform while emphasizing the role of the private sector. His victory established the political center as a major force in Caribbean politics.

United People's Movement (UPM)

The UPM is a coalition of leftist organizations and consists of the United Liberation Movement, the People's Democratic Movement, Arwee (a rural organization), and several smaller groups. In 1979, it gained 14.4 percent of the vote, but failed to win any seats. It did, however, increase the leftist share of the vote over 1974 and contributed to a sharp decline in the SVLP vote and to the elimination of the PPP from the legislature. In 1984, under the leadership of Renwick Rose, the UPM fared poorly in the elections, failing to win a single vote in some districts.

Movement for National Unity (MNU)

A split in the UPM at the end of 1982 led to the formation of the MNU under the leadership of Ralph Gonsalves. The MNU also performed poorly in the latest elections, contributing to the disarray of the left in Saint Vincent. There is speculation of a union between the MNU and the youthful wing of the SVLP.

National Prospects

In spite of a considerable shift in relative party strength in the last decade, the basic political system of Saint Vincent is highly stable and will probably remain so. The NDP inherited state enterprises in poor financial condition and must overcome a number of obstacles to make them viable. Inability to make economic progress could strengthen the opposition to the NDP, either from the SVLP or a new coalition of parties.

Mitchell played a major role in bringing together centrist groups in Grenada to form the New National Party, which triumphed in that country's first post-invasion election. Mitchell opposes the U.S.-backed militarization of the eastern Caribbean.

Further Reading

Brana-Shute, Gary. "An Eastern Caribbean Centrist," *Caribbean Review*, Vol. 14, No. 4. 1983.

Gooding, Earl. *The West Indies at the Crossroads: The Search for a Viable Future.* Cambridge, Mass.: Schenkman, 1981.

Millet, Richard, and Will, W. Marvin. *The Restless Caribbean.* New York: Praeger, 1979.

KINGDOM OF SAUDI ARABIA
(Al-Mamlaka al-'Arabiya as-Sa'udiya)
by Daniel Pipes, Ph.D. revised by Mahmud A. Faksh, Ph.D.

The System of Government

The Kingdom of Saudi Arabia is a monarchy characterized by the exceptionally important role of the royal family, the House of Sa'ud. Members of the dynasty fill most key positions and maintain a near monopoly over political activity in the country.

Saudi Arabia has possibly the least-known political system of any country with international importance. In part, this is due to the region's inaccessibility and, until recently, poverty. No outside power took much interest in central Arabia and the indigenous peoples developed their own political structures, almost without influences from the West. As a result, even though outsiders are now intensely interested in the Saudi system, they know little about it. To make matters worse, the royal family has followed a policy of extreme discretion, making its structures, divisions, and duties more a matter of speculation than of fact. Nonroyal political affairs are equally obscure, because political activity outside the royal family is banned.

The paucity of information means that reports about Saudi political institutions are sketchy, contradictory, and unverifiable. Reputable sources differ on such basic facts as the different types of law courts, the forums of local administration, and the number of King Abd al-Aziz's sons. The following account reflects these uncertainties.

Many of the Saudi state's unusual features can be explained by its relative newness. While some parts of the Arabian peninsula, such as the Yemen or the cities of the Hijaz, on the west coast of the peninsula, have long been governed by constituted governments, the rest of the area has been dominated by tribes which lack even the most elementary forms of state authority (a police force, a fixed capital, written records). Only when their energies were harnessed to a religious cause have the tribes formed anything

more enduring than transient coalitions of warriors. This happened twice, first in the seventh century under Muhammad, the prophet of Islam, and second in the eighteenth century, when the religious leader Muhammed ibn Abd al-Wahhab, founder of the Wahhabi movement, joined forces with the tribal chief Muhammed ibn Sa'ud. From the time of this alliance in 1744, the Sa'udi family has always led a cause with a grander purpose than mere camel raiding or protecting water wells. Religious ideology inspired Sa'udi soldiers to conquer many of the territories of today's Saudi Arabia before the kingdom fell to outside forces in 1818. It was resurrected on a smaller scale between 1820 and 1891, before falling again.

Thus, the Wahhabi-Sa'udi alliance was already 150 years old when King Abd al-Aziz ibn Abd ar-Rahman ibn Faisal as-Sa'ud began to piece the present state together in 1902 in the name of Islamic purification as preached in Wahhabi doctrine. Starting with the recapture of his ancestral home, Riyadh, he expanded his rule to other parts of central Arabia, then to the east and west coasts of the peninsula. These conquests continued over a period of thirty-two years, until his territories reached approximately their present extent in 1934. His achievement, bringing al-Hasa (east coast), Najd (inland), and Hijaz and Asir (southwest) under a single rule, was without precedent.

Abd al-Aziz named his domain the Kingdom of Saudi Arabia in 1932, commemorating his eighteenth-century ancestor and creating a state where none had ever existed before. The notion of a Saudi Arabian nationality no more existed in central Arabia before 1932 than that of a United States existed in sixteenth-century America. As with so many other new states, Saudi Arabia has had to establish itself as a meaningful political entity in a short time. Tribal affiliations are far from eradicated and the Hijaz still retains a sense of separateness (which is moderated, however, by the fact that it benefits from the oil revenues produced on the other side of the peninsula). The fact that the state was created from within, by a local leader, makes tribal and regional ties that much more binding; while most new states were created by European colonial masters—neutral outsiders who disrupted traditional systems and eventually left—Saudi Arabia was the achievement of one local family. As a result, the House of Sa'ud is deeply resented by other tribal leaders for its wealth and power.

Abd al-Aziz relied on an ancient method for consolidating his kingdom: marrying the widows and daughters of his defeated enemies. Exploiting the right of a Muslim man to four wives at once and easy terms of divorce, he wed some three hundred women and had forty-five recognized sons by at least twenty-two mothers. These sons, whose birthdates range from 1900 to 1952, have constituted the dominant political force in the kingdom since Abd al-Aziz's death in 1953 and, assuming the regime stays in power, they will remain in charge for decades to come. Full brothers tend to form groupings against half-brothers; and because of their mother's origins, these disputes have direct tribal and regional implications. Until now, this discord has not created irreconcilable rifts.

Saudi leaders have shown a remarkable devotion to their own way of life, making theirs probably the only country of standing not willing even to make a show of adopting Western ideals and institutions. Islamic law reigns supreme with few concessions to Western sensibilities: women are forbidden to take part in public life, criminal punishments follow traditional forms, and the Koran is claimed to be the constitution of state.

Income from oil has led to a huge increase in the functions which the Saudi government undertakes. Half a century ago it did nothing more than provide a guarantee of social order and a rudimentary form of justice. The central government consisted of the king, his advisors, and some of his relatives; public functions were limited to royal assemblies; and the state treasury was no more than the sacks of gold coins carried wherever the king went. Today, the Saudi state offers among the widest array of services of any in the world, including free education through the doctorate degree, free medical treatment at some of the most-advanced facilities in existence, padded salaries, low-interest loans, subsidies for consumer goods, and guarantees for businesses. It even helps young men pay bride-prices. Some of these social and economic ser-

vices have been reduced in wake of the sharp drop in world oil prices early in 1986.

State functions have required a massive expansion of government bureaucracy, to the point that a large portion of the native Saudi working force is employed by the government. This gives the rulers a vital source of leverage; even more important, state functions have given the government pervasive control over the country, for it disburses nearly all the country's wealth. The Saudi leadership (and the rulers of other thinly populated oil-rich states) enjoy the unique advantage of distributing money to their citizens virtually without taxation. This gives the government an enviable popularity and a most extraordinary source of power over every aspect of life.

The King

The king (*malik*) of Saudi Arabia is an absolute monarch within the constraints of his family's support and the laws of Islam. He is head of state and chief executive of the government.

When Abd al-Aziz took Riyadh in January 1902, he acquired a twin title: imam (religious leader) of the Wahhabis and prince (*emir*) of Najd. He became king of Hijaz after conquering that province in January 1926 and shortly after elevated his title to "King of Najd and Its Dependencies." For five years he retained this cumbersome double kingship; then, on September 22, 1932, he announced that he had taken a new title, king of Saudi Arabia. Since Abd al-Aziz's death in November 1953, four of his sons have succeeded him to this position: Sa'ud (1953–64), Faisal (1964–75), Khalid (1975–82), and Fahd (1982 to present).

The position of king includes several components, dynastic, tribal, and religious. It is as head of the House of Sa'ud that the king derives his power, for the royal family's support determines who rules. Sovereignty resides in the family; whoever leads it is head of state. The selection of an heir-apparent in advance, a tradition established by Abd al-Aziz, is a key decision. Selecting the crown prince is perhaps the single most critical issue in Saudi politics; although it arises only occasionally, it touches on all actions of the royal family. Abdallah is the current crown prince.

The Sa'ud family has no written rule of succession nor even an informal hierarchy. Muslim civilization has never decided whether succession should go by birthright or according to ability; as a result, most dynasties have mixed the two qualifications, often leading to disastrous succession crises. The House of Sa'ud has transferred power nineteen times since the eighteenth century: nine times to a brother, seven to a son, and three to a cousin. A Saudi king typically hopes to pass his rule to a son. However, with thirty-one of Abd al-Aziz's sons alive at this writing, such a succession will be unlikely for some time to come. This issue could easily split the family. Selection of a new crown prince involves such factors as seniority, education, ability, temperament, popularity, the number of his full brothers, and his mother's tribal affiliation. Until now, ideology has played little role in this procedure. So far as can be discerned, the actual decision on matters of succession is taken by the Royal Council.

The king's tribal role (as sheikh) is decreasing, in large part because tribal ties are weakening in the context of a state which provides services once available only from the tribe (such as protection, welfare, and economic opportunities). Abd al-Aziz's style was always that of a tribal leader; even after bcoming ruler of many tribes and immense domains, an international figure and a very wealthy man, he retained the demeanor of a tribal sheikh ruling through his personal authority and accessible to all, almost without intermediaries. As a government bureaucracy developed, the tribal aspect of the king's duties inevitably shrank; also, increases in population and in international concerns now limit the king's accessibility. He still holds audiences, however; he is addressed by his given name; and he is expected to mete out individual justice. The fact that King Khalid had cultivated excellent relations with the tribes was an important factor in his being chosen to rule.

As religious leader (*imam*) of his people, the king is bound to carry out Islamic law, to defend the borders from unbelievers, and personally to set a righteous example for his subjects. Saudi sponsorship of Wahhabi doctrines gives the king an unusually close connection to a religion for a Muslim leader; even more important is his role as "Protector of the Two Holy Cities" (Mecca and Medina).

The Royal Family

Members of the ruling dynasty fill vital positions in the government, both at high and inter-

mediate levels. The following list includes most of the positions held by the sons and grandsons of King Abd al-Aziz in late 1985; it does not include the many other princes holding government posts.

Sons of Abd al-Aziz
* Fahd: prime minister (1982)
  Abdallah: first deputy prime minister (1982) and commander of the National Guard (1963)
* Sultan: second deputy prime minister (1982); minister of defense and aviation (1962)
  Abd al-Muhsin: governor of Medina
  Muta'ib: minister of public works and housing (1975); minister of municipalities and rural affairs (1978)
  Talal: special envoy, UNESCO (1979)
* Turki: formerly deputy minister of defense and aviation until 1979, now in disgrace
  Badr: deputy commander of the National Guard
  Nawwaf: special advisor on Persian Gulf affairs
* Na'if: minister of the interior (1975)
* Salman: governor of Riyadh (1962)
  Majid: governor of Mecca
  Abd al-Ilah: governor of al-Qasim (1980)
  Sattam: deputy governor of Riyadh
* Ahmad: deputy minister of the interior (1978)
  Mugrin: governor of Ha'il (1980)

Grandsons of Abd al-Aziz:
Sons of Faisal
  Muhammad: president, Islamic Bank (formerly head of the Saline Water Conversion Corporation)
  Khalid: governor of Asir
  Sa'ud: foreign minister (1975)
  Turki: director of foreign intelligence
Son of Abd al-Muhsin
  Sa'ud: deputy governor of Mecca
Son of Sultan
  Fahd: deputy minister of labor and social affairs

In all, the direct descendants of Abd al-Aziz numbered nine ministers and three deputy ministers, six governors and two deputy governors, as well as four other major positions.

All princes are entitled to a stipend. Unregulated before 1963, the privy purse once consumed most of government revenues, leading to extravagant consumption and corruption and,

---

* Indicates members of the so-called Sudairi Seven, sons of Hassa bint Ahmad as-Sudairi.

on two occasions, nearly bankrupting the kingdom. Since 1963, stipends depend on a mix of two factors: a prince's age and his proximity by generation and direct descent to Faisal ibn Turki, paternal grandfather of King Abd al-Aziz. Precise figures are of course unknown, but Abd al-Aziz's sons receive something on the order of $100,000 to $250,000 a year and the younger princes about $20,000 to $50,000—handsome sums but nothing like the profits available in business, especially as agents of foreign firms selling to the government. (A deal to install a national telephone system reportedly fell through because the commission was excessive even by Sa'ud family standards; Crown Prince Fahd's son Muhammad reportedly stood to gain $1.3 billion from this one transaction.)

Although King Abd al-Aziz used marriage to bind the country together, bringing daughters of almost every tribe and region to his bed, his descendants increasingly tend toward monogamy (a probable symptom of Western influence) and marriage to cousins (a reflection of their increasing sense of blue-bloodedness). Young princes and princesses are encouraged to marry within the House of Sa'ud or its collateral lines, the Thunayan, Jiluwi, and Sudairi families. The only other family wholeheartedly sanctioned is that of Shaykh, the descendants of Muhammad ibn Abd al-Wahhab, founder of the religious movement. Prince Turki's marriage to the daughter of a rich but undistinguished physician from Jeddah in 1978 contributed to his disgrace.

Royal Council

That the Royal Council (*Ahl al-Aqd wa'l-Hall*, Those who Bind and Loosen) even exists has been barely acknowledged by the government; its composition, functions, and jurisdiction have never been made public. It appears to be the forum in which the leading princes (but not the king) decide matters pertaining to the royal family. Foremost are those questions associated with the monarchy: choosing a crown prince, approving his succession to the throne, or requiring the king to abdicate. In addition, the Royal Council also decides more routine royal matters, such as stipends for princes and princesses, government appointments for princes, and questions of discipline.

Membership in this loosely structured body seems to vary according to the occasion. For example, about seventy princes signed a resolution of the Royal Council in March 1964 which sought to force King Sa'ud to transfer most of his powers to Crown Prince Faisal; almost a hundred princes signed the decree forcing Sa'ud to abdicate in Faisal's favor in October of that year. The March document was signed by the following relatives of the king: two uncles, twenty-three brothers, ten nephews, fifteen cousins, five members of the Jiluwi branch, two members of the Abdallah ibn Turki branch, eight members of the Sa'ud al-Kabir branch, and three other distant cousins.

An "Inner Group" of the Royal Council also exists, about which we know even less; however, it appears to actually implement the full Council's wishes and to make routine decisions. It was this group which actually forced Sa'ud (some say at gunpoint) to transfer his powers to Faisal in March 1964; the Inner Group proclaimed Khalid king within two hours of Faisal's assassination in March 1975. At that time, membership in the Inner Group was said to include Faisal's uncle Abdallah ibn Abd ar-Rahman and four of his oldest brothers: Muhammad, Nasir, Sa'ad and Fahd. This Inner Group, probably the most powerful institution in the country by virtue of its influence within the royal family, including the right to appoint and recall a monarch, is also its least-known organization.

Council of Ministers

Abd al-Aziz had no need for ministers through the first decades of his rule; as a tribal leader with no administrative responsibilities, he waged war, distributed revenues, and adjudicated disputes. In about 1925, when his conquest of the Hijaz virtually ended the wars of expansion and opened a new era of consolidation and bureaucratization, this began to change. Abd al-Aziz kept some of the Hijaz's more developed political institutions (such as its directorates and consultative council), later using some of these as a basis for government institutions for the kingdom. Nonetheless, his rule remained patrimonial; Abd al-Aziz's son Faisal became the first minister in 1930, taking the foreign-affairs portfolio. Abdallah as-Sulayman, the king's accountant, became finance minister two years later. Other ministries followed in due time, particularly in the 1950s and 1970s, marking the increasing size and complexity of the government. From the first, ministers have been both royal and nonroyal.

As the bureaucracy grew, ministers also gained in importance. Although always responsible to the king, they have in fact carved out a good deal of autonomy as the complexity of their offices has increased. With time, functional division has become more pronounced: princes still hold the most sensitive posts (defense, interior, national guard, foreign affairs), with commoners taking the more technical positions (finance, oil, planning). Religious authorities, usually of the Shaykh family, predominate in matters connected to religion, justice, and education.

Skills needed for modern government are still lacking among the Saudis. As a result, foreigners have played key roles in helping the House of Sa'ud adjust to its new bureaucratic and international concerns; these include the "Northern Arabs" (Egyptians, Palestinians, Syrians, etc.), Muslims from other countries (Iran, India), and Westerners (the most famous being a Briton, Harry St. John Philby).

In his last official act, in October 1953, King Abd al-Aziz established a Council of Ministers to meet the "obligations and the diversifications of the responsibilities placed on the state." But the Council had no prescribed functions or effective role until a Royal Decree of May 1958 (inspired by Crown Prince Faisal) specified its policymaking and policyexecuting duties. Like its predecessor, a Council of Deputies, the Council of Ministers has the authority to consider all questions arising in the kingdom, including the budget, treaties, contracts, administrative appointments, and court cases involving the government; however, unlike the Council of Deputies, this new body has to refer its decisions to the king for approval. Its decisions, therefore, are recommendations only, which may be ignored or enacted by the administration, as the king directs. A quorum requires two-thirds of the members, decisions are probably reached by concensus, and the king may veto a Council decision within thirty days. The Council functions, in part, as a legislature by formulating most government decrees.

The increasing volume of state affairs has meant growing authority and freedom of action for the Council. It cannot, of course, override a king's veto, but because no state funds can be paid out except through the Council, it can delay the effect of his positive decrees by failing to authorize the necessary funds.

Consultative Council

The Hijaz had a consultative council (*majlis ash-shura*, a representative body which can have some legislative functions) at the time of its conquest, but it was disbanded in all but name in 1928 when King Abd al-Aziz proclaimed his intent to replace it with a single consultative council for the whole kingdom. Nothing more was heard of this until years after Abd al-Aziz's death, when in 1960 Prince Talal, leader of a group called the "free princes," announced at a press conference that a "national council" was under consideration by the Council of Ministers; the government quickly denied his statement, but Talal had raised an issue which then refused to go away. When Faisal formed a new government in 1962, he promised to institute a consultative council, but again nothing happened. Khalid made a similar statement of intent on becoming king but also did nothing. More talk followed the Iranian upheaval in early 1979, followed by intense discussions after the Mecca siege of November 1979. In January 1980, Crown Prince Fahd promised that a consultative council would be set up within two months. Two months later a committee was formed and charged with establishing a council in accordance with Islamic laws; five years later, its findings have not yet been made public.

Talk of a consultative council surfaces in times of crisis, only to be forgotten with a return to normality. The royal family seems to believe that it can do without such a body and is holding out as long as possible against it. In turn, reformers, both royal and not, have made it the focus of their demands, correctly seeing it as the beginning of popular participation in the government.

Religious Law

Islam has direct bearing on the political life of Saudi Arabia because its sacred law minutely regulates the activities of believers, public (political authority, war, taxation, justice) as well as private (sexual relations, cleanliness, diet). Living by the sacred law of Islam requires an involvement with politics; a Muslim cannot live a wholly righteous life unless his government acts in accordance with Islamic law. Experts in the law, known as *ulema*, are therefore in a position to influence the rulers.

In no Muslim state in modern times have the *ulema* so consistently exercised political influence as in Saudi Arabia (Khomeini's revolutionary experiment in Iran is not really comparable); and nowhere else has Islam been taken quite so seriously as in the deserts of Arabia. According to the fundamentalist Wahhabi ideology, the Koran is the constitution of state (a view almost universally rejected by Muslims elsewhere). This then gives the leading *ulema* an interpretive role somewhat parallel to a supreme court except that these religious scholars are not necessarily government employees. Because the *raison d'être* of the Saudi state is narrowly tied to Wahhabi doctrines, the political leadership has been extremely careful never to stray far from the strictures of the *ulema*, especially those of the Shaykh family, the descendants of the Muhammad ibn Abd al-Wahhab. This family enjoys an authority over matters religious roughly parallel to that of the Sa'udis over matters political. Many religious, judicial, and educational posts in the kingdom are the preserve of the Shaykh family.

Since the eighteenth century, the religious authorities have had a police force, the Committee for Encouraging Virtue and Preventing Vice (*Hay'at al-Amr bi'l-Ma'ruf wa'n-Nahi an al-Munkar*), a vice squad operating in nearly all the cities ruled by the Saudis. It can punish any activity the religious authorities deem harmful, including smoking, drinking, music playing, breaking the fast of Ramadan, or gambling. It can even enforce observance of the daily periods of prayer. Over the years, the Committee's role has decreased, but it still compels storeowners to close shop during prayer periods and runs women off the street when more than their hands and feet are showing.

Relations between the political and religious authorities are cordial, a major strength of the Sa'ud dynasty (in contrast to the Pahlavis in Iran). Nevertheless, tensions have developed as oil revenues transform Arabia's landscape. Tacit trade-offs take place: in return for freedom of action in foreign policy, oil exploration, and economic modernization, the royal family permits the *ulema* greater power over the moral and private lives of citizens. The Iranian revolution spurred a tightening of controls after many years of relaxation: restrictions on women traveling and working, dress codes, and new regulations for foreigners were included. In general, the ruling dynasty, with its finely tuned political sensitivities, has prevailed over the more ideological and inflexible demands of the Wahhabi standard bearers.

During times of crisis, the royal family asks the leading *ulema* to issue religious decisions (*fatwas*) to sanction contemplated government actions. Twelve of them signed the *fatwa* authorizing the transfer of power from King Sa'ud to Crown Prince Faisal in March 1964, including four members of the Shaykh family. In November 1979, leading *ulema* granted the government a *fatwa* permitting it to assault forcibly the Great Mosque in Mecca which had been taken over by religious fanatics.

Regional & Local Government

Provincial government is even more unclear than the central administration. Saudi Arabia is divided into eighteen provinces, two of which, Riyadh and the Eastern Province, make up half the country's expanse. Other leading provinces include Mecca, Medina, Ha'il, and the Northern Frontiers; their governors report directly to the minister of the interior, while governors of smaller provinces (Afif, Asir, al-Bahah, Bisha, al-Jawf, Jizan, al-Khasira, Najran, Northern Region, al-Qasim, al-Qu'ayyat, Ranya) report to the deputy minister. The current governors of Asir, Ha'il, Mecca, Medina, al-Qasim, and Riyadh are princes.

In keeping with the extreme centralization of the government, there are no provincial capitals; administration is direct from Riyadh. Regulations dating from November 1963 call for the creation of provincial councils, but like the consultative council on the national level, they have never come into existence. Each governor holds assemblies in which he grants financial assistance and dispenses justice much as the king does. Larger cities such as Mecca, Medina, and Jidda have general municipal councils whose members are nominated by local citizens and approved by the king. The policies they formulate are then executed by general administrative committees. In tribal areas, district councils are presided over by tribal chiefs. Villages have councils headed by the local sheikh along with three other members; their purpose is to enforce regulations received from higher levels of government.

Other Political Forces

A nearly total ban proscribes political activity outside the government. Demonstrations and strikes are violently repressed; elections are unknown. Political parties, labor unions, or any formal pressure groups are illegal, and no legislature exists (except in the executive, the Council of Ministers). The press is censored to preclude controversy, and many books are blacklisted. Police checkpoints strictly monitor movement between towns and the vice squad has free access to private homes. Surveillance is lowkey but pervasive. No forums exist for dissenting opinions on the royal family, the country's rapid changes, Islam, world politics, or oil policies. The system offers little scope for the expression of competing views, much less for acting on them.

Yet Saudi Arabia is not totalitarian: travel outside the country is common, political crimes are rare, people do not live in fear of the police, and the state does not try to take over all existing organizations. That the leaders have managed to ban political expression without becoming tyrants indicates that features of tribal leadership are still in force. Rulers see themselves in a paternal role, much as a sheikh of old might, in close touch with the concerns of subjects and keeping those concerns in balance. The populace, long used to being looked after in this manner, has not insisted on organized interest groups or popular representation. Reformers calling for a more representative political system have not won much support. With time, as the population becomes better informed, it may claim a greater political role; whether the House of Sa'ud can recognize these aspirations in time will be a central factor in its continued stability.

Significant discontent may come from religious, tribal, regional, military, labor, and radical groups.

Islam

Many of Abd al-Aziz's conquests were accomplished by the Ikhwan (Brotherhood), a force of 60,000 settled Bedouin devoted to the most stringent interpretation of Wahhabi Islam. Growing restive about the king's increasing moderation and statesmanship after his conquest of the Hijaz in 1925, they eventually turned against him in 1929 to 1930. Although crushed, the fanatical spirit of the Ikhwan and the legacy of their armed might are vividly remembered. The attack on Mecca's Great Mosque, which occurred on November 20, 1979, and lasted two weeks, made it clear that this

spirit was still alive and could yet threaten the Sa'ud dynasty. This event shattered royal smugness about knowing the subjects' concerns and inspired more political introspection among the rulers than at any time since the death of Abd al-Aziz in 1953.

Halfway through the Meccan siege, Shi'a riots broke out in Qatif in the far northeast of Saudi Arabia; if the attack on Mecca reminded Saudi rulers of their earliest constituency, the Shi'a disturbances symbolized the anger of their most-dispossessed subjects. Reviled and persecuted for their beliefs, the quarter million Shi'a living in al-Hasa have always suffered under Wahhabi rule. They lack representation in the government (to date, only one minister) and are particularly susceptible to influence from Iran (a group called the Islamic Revolutionary Organization, directed from Teheran, claimed to have instigated the 1979 riots). The Shi'a problem has special importance because it is centered in the oil-producing region; reports reached the West in early 1982 that whole villages of Shi'a had been relocated at the opposite end of the kingdom, in the southwest.

Regional

Oil revenues, which derive from resources in one small portion of the kingdom, have given all the other regions reason to stay within Saudi Arabia; but oil income tends to exacerbate differences between rich and poor regions, creating new dissatisfactions. Also, conflicts over tribal and regional representation at the national level become sharper the more money that the central government has to disburse. An abortive conspiracy to take over the government in May 1969 had a Hijazi character to it, and some have seen a tribal element in the attack on Mecca ten years later. These regional dangers, however, appear to be fading in the face of other tensions.

Military

The Saudi leadership views itself as a major force in the Middle East and Persian Gulf and has undertaken since 1962 to spend enormous sums of money (in 1981–82, $25 billion) on expanding and improving their armed forces. An enlarged military (current levels: 45,000 in the army, 17,000 in the air force, 4,000 in the navy) increases the danger of a challenge to the royal family. Officers were among the key figures of the 1969 coup attempt; and soldiers may have plotted with the fanatics who seized the Great Mosque in 1979, although there has been no clear evidence of military insubordination. Soldiers are privileged and respected; in the short run, this wins their loyalty, but eventually their increased power could lead them to turn against the state.

If so, the Saudi government is prepared. The National Guard, a 20,000-man force recruited and deployed along tribal lines, is considered the most loyal support of the Sa'ud family and of the Wahhabi way of life. It is entrusted with defense of the government itself. In addition, a contingent of Pakistanis and other foreigners (numbering perhaps 20,000 men) guards the oil fields and could have a key role in controlling any internal disturbances.

Labor

A prohibition on labor unions means that all dissent is expressed illegally. Labor in Saudi Arabia divides into three categories: native, non-Muslim, and foreign Muslim. Native Saudis are highly privileged and often overpaid; to the extent that they are discontent, the government usually responds with alacrity to please them. For the foreseeable future, native workers will constitute only about one-third to one-fourth of the Saudi labor force.

Highly skilled workers from the industrial countries pose no problems; they come and go on relatively brief assignments. Other non-Muslim workers can also be contained, for example, the large numbers of South Koreans who come on contract and live in their own compounds, virtually quarantined from Saudi society.

Foreign Muslim workers, Arabs and non-Arabs alike (the latter including Turks, Iranians, Pakistanis, and Indians especially) come to Saudi Arabia for the money, but often reside there for long periods, becoming involved in the life of the country. They feel ties to the Saudis, ties which the government itself encourages with its frequent emphasis on the brotherhood of all Arabs and Muslims. Yet they are consistently paid less than citizens and denied the many privileges citizens receive. Non-native Muslim workers suffer a pervasive, almost systematic discrimination which contrasts glaringly with their expectations, a disparity which has explosive potential. The Saudi government, aware of this, has tried to cut back on employ-

ing non-Saudi Muslims; however, a complete exclusion will never be possible because the annual pilgrimage Muslims must make to the holy places of Islam located in Saudi Arabia brings new waves of illegal migrant workers every year.

Radical Organizations

The Arabian Peninsula People's Union, founded in 1953 in the aftermath of labor troubles in the oil fields, still survives in a minor way, without apparent means to threaten the regime. A Saudi Arabian Communist Party appears to be limited to Saudi citizens in exile. The Vanguard of the Arabian Revolution publishes a magazine, "Voice of the Vanguard," which occasionally gets inside the kingdom, without noticeable effect. Saudi nationals have shown themselves remarkably unreceptive to radical ideologies. Extremist Palestinian organizations have conducted some sabotage in Saudi Arabia—including perhaps the two fires at the Abaqiq oil fields in 1977 which caused over $100 million in damages—but they have almost no appeal to Saudis.

National Prospects

The long-awaited consultative council, if and when it is established, will mark the beginning of a new era in Saudi politics. Even if entirely appointed by the crown and restricted to an advisory role on limited matters, the inclusion of representatives from the population at large will probably lead to increasing popular representation in the government and move it towards constitutional monarchy.

Until this happens, the Sa'ud dynasty will have to try to balance the increasingly conflicting demands of its subjects without any formal guidance. Should the family lose touch—and this seems likely, given its wealth and international orientation—violent change could well sweep them aside. Oil income has created special tensions: rapid changes brought by modernization, a huge foreign presence, and the many problems associated with a boom-and-bust economy. But the Sa'ud family has several factors working in its favor—the country's size, the separation between cities, and the different functions of the cities (press and embassies in Jidda, religious establishment in Mecca and

Medina, administration in Riyadh, oil in Dammam)—all of which make it unlikely that a rebel force could take the country over. In addition, the government has protected itself well against internal enemies. Security is tight and probably effective. The armed forces are institutionally divided and would find it difficult to unite against the government. Princes of the Sa'ud family occupy so many sensitive positions that it would be difficult to organize a conspiracy without their getting wind of it.

But if the government is well prepared for challenges from outside the royal family, it is much less well able to deal with the many hundreds of princes. This is a matter of personalities and currents little known to the outside world, but the fact that King Faisal was assassinated by his nephew (even if he was insane, as the Saudi government claims), strikes an ominous note for the future. Presumably, no one but a prince could have entered the king's assembly hiding a pistol. The "free princes" of the early 1960s point to the sort of ideological splits which can divide the royal family. But the most dangerous problem of all is an irreconcilable division over succession to the throne. The absence of a formula for succession virtually insures that, should the Sa'ud family survive all other threats, it will fall on this inescapable issue.

Further Reading

Dhanani, Gulshan. "Political Institutions in Saudi Arabia." *International Studies* Vol. 19, No. 1, 1980.

Harrington, Charles W. "The Saudi Arabian Council of Ministers." *Middle East Journal,* Vol. 12, No. 1, 1958.

Holden, David and Richard, Johns. *The House of Saud: The Rise and Rule of the Most Powerful Dynasty in the Arab World.* New York: Holt, Rinehart and Winston, 1981.

Kelidar, A. R. "The Problem of Succession in Saudi Arabia." *Asian Affairs,* Vol. 65, No. 1, 1978.

Koury, Enver M. *The Saudi Decision-Making Body: The House of Al-Saud.* Washington, D.C.: Institute of Middle Eastern and North African Affairs, 1978.

Long, David E. *Saudi Arabia.* Beverly Hills and London: Sage Publications, 1976.

Nollet, R. "Regard sur le clan des Al Saud." *L'Afrique et l'Asia Modernes,* 118 (1978).

Önder, Zehra, *Saudi-Arabien: Zwischen islamischer Ideologie und Westlicher Ökonomie.* Stuttgart: Klett-Cotta, 1980.

REPUBLIC OF SENEGAL
(République du Senégal)
by Lucie Gallistel Colvin, Ph.D. revised by Kenneth Menkhaus, M.A.

The System of Government

Senegal, a west African nation of 6.3 million, is a democratic republic, ruled by President Leopold Sedar Senghor after independence from France in 1960 until his voluntary retirement December 31, 1980, and since then by his chosen successor Abdou Diouf. It was the first African country to witness voluntary retirement and peaceful transition to a constitutional successor government. This confirmed its reputation as a leader of the moderate nonaligned nations in international diplomacy and a political and cultural model for Francophone African countries.

Located at the westernmost point of West Africa, the area has been a gateway to the continent by air, sea, and land for centuries. Three medieval empires flourished here, Tekrur, Jolof, and Gaabu (Mandinka), all linked to the trans-Saharan trade with North Africa and the east-west routes across the Sahel/Sudan. Islam has been the dominant religion and cultural influence, and French colonial rule from the 1880s through 1960 laid the groundwork for the modern nation. Senegal's capital, Dakar, was the center of administration for the whole of French West Africa. The formerly British, now independent, Republic of the Gambia forms an enclave within Senegal. A 1981 coup attempt in the Gambia was put down by the Senegalese army at the invitation of the Gambian president, since which time the Senegalese army has remained there. Incomplete arrangements for a Senegambia Confederation have been enacted (see Senegambia Confederation at the end of the Gambia chapter). Some 35 percent of the population of Senegal is urbanized. Nearly one in five Senegalese lives in the capital or its suburbs. Of the six major ethnic groups, Wolof (36 percent), Hal Pular (Tukulor and Pël combined, 21 percent) and Serer (19 percent) are the largest. French is the official language, but Wolof is increasingly the *lingua franca*.

Senegal began independence in 1960 with a constitution providing for a divided executive (president and prime minister) and with multiparty democracy modeled directly on that of the Fifth French Republic. Senghor had tried but failed to keep the French West African Federation unified as self-government approached. Both the French and non-Senegalese political leaders had opposed him. The last of the unity efforts, the Mali Federation (comprising Senegal and Mali) collapsed in August of 1960 during the first election campaign. Each country declared a separate independence, and Senegal decided to celebrate its own on April 4, the day the agreement had been signed with France.

In December 1962, only two and a half years after independence, the two Senegalese chief executives President Senghor and Prime Minister Mamadou Dia (born 1910) came to a showdown in a constitutional crisis, which was resolved with the elimination of the prime ministership. Dia was imprisoned, accused of attempting the overthrow of the government, and kept in prison from 1963 to 1974. The 1963 constitution of the Second Senegalese Republic, issued following the crisis, founded a strong presidential state, which allowed Senghor to make all major decisions and gradually to eliminate opposition political parties. The process by which this was done was peaceful compared to the repressive pattern of single-party emergence in some other countries. Many opposition figures were drawn into the official party and the government.

The current multiparty democratic system dates from the constitutional reforms of 1970 through 1983, which reversed the 1960s tendency toward single-party rule. Parties are now allowed to form and register freely. Press freedom was reintroduced simultaneously, and many small periodicals arose, at least one for each party, along with some independent journals of commentary and satire. Originally, only one party was allowed to represent each major ideological trend, ostensibly to prevent factionalism and personality cults. Under Diouf's presidency that restriction has been dropped. The constitutional reforms of the 1970s reintroduced the office of prime minister, but following his 1983 election, President Diouf proposed a constitutional amendment reform again abolishing the post, a proposal which the National Assembly approved. This move was made to streamline the administration and give more direct power to the president.

Executive

According to the constitution, the president is head of state, chief of the High Council of National Defense, and chief of the armed forces. He is elected by universal adult suffrage (anyone 21 or older may register) for no more than two successive five-year terms. (This rule did not apply to Senghor, who was elected to four successive terms.) Elected in 1983, Diouf is eligible to run for reelection in 1988. The president appoints and dismisses the cabinet at will. The president can dissolve the Assembly and call new legislative and presidential elections after three years of the normal five-year term have been served. He is empowered to declare a state of emergency, a state of siege, or a crisis threatening the institutions of the republic, the independence of the nation, its territorial integrity, or the fulfillment of its international commitments. However, during such an emergency or crisis, he may not amend the constitution, and the National Assembly is automatically called into session for the duration of any of these situations. In practice, the more important presidential perogatives lie in the president's power to initiate legislation and his freedom to regulate by presidential decree in all matters not reserved to the legislature.

Legislature

The National Assembly currently consists of 120 members popularly elected to five-year terms. It normally meets twice a year for two months. Special sessions may be called by the executive or a majority of legislators, and last a maximum of two weeks, unless a budget is being considered, in which case the session lasts until the budget is passed. In 1984 president of the National Assembly, Habib Thiam, resigned following the Assembly's approval of a constitutional amendment reducing the mandate of its

president from five years to one. The current president, Daouda Sow, holds the second most prestigious position in the administration, though it lacks a corresponding political clout. Assembly relations with Diouf have not been smooth.

Deputies have the right to initiate legislation, but they rarely do; most legislative proposals are put forward by the executive. Since Senegalese society regards public acrimony as unseemly, conflicts over legislation are usually settled in committee. Appointed liaisons between each ministry and relevant committees, and between the ruling Socialist Party political bureau and the Assembly, smooth this process. The right to debate the budget, which might theoretically be the key power of the Assembly, has been impaired by Senegal's weak economy, its reliance on French subsidies, and economic strictures laid down by the International Monetary Fund. The government submits all major legislation to the prestigious Economic and Social Council, a representative and scholarly body, for advice and formulation before passage. It is also debated, although not officially, by the Superior Council of Religious Chiefs.

In National Assembly elections, the ruling Socialist Party went from 83 percent of the vote immediately before independence to between 94 and 100 percent from 1963 until 1978. In the last elections, in February 1983, the Socialist Party gained an overwhelming majority, taking 111 of the 120 seats in the Assembly.

Judiciary

The Senegalese judiciary is proud of its independence, although its importance relative to the executive and legislative branches is limited by the prevalence of code-law procedures. Major laws are examined for constitutionality before passage. The judiciary is headed by the ten-member Supreme Court, including a chief justice. The High Court of Justice, consisting of two justices and ten deputies, can be convoked to consider impeachment of the president or ministers; the only impeachable offense is high treason. The High Council of the Judiciary is the nerve center of the system, nominating judges, guaranteeing the integrity of the judiciary, and advising the president on clemency. There are petty courts in departmental capitals, eight tribunals of first instance in regional capitals, four courts of assize, and the Supreme Court of Appeal. Civil and criminal cases are heard by the same judges and assessors in all except the courts of assize, where felonies are heard by juries.

Regional & Local Government

The territorial administration comprises ten regions headed by governors, thirty departments headed by prefects, and eighty-five *arrondissements* (districts) headed by subprefects. All officials are civil servants appointed by the Minister of the Interior. A successful career in the administration, a common path for the young elite, typically begins with a degree in law or economics from the university and continues with the National School for Administration. The civil servant then moves into the territorial administration and tries for advancement to and through the central administration. Territorially elected representative bodies include regional assemblies, municipal councils, and rural councils (villages or village groupings), all with budget authority over the personal taxes collected in their area by the central government. However, the centrally appointed territorial administration disburses the funds.

The Electoral System

Legislation passed in August 1982 increased the number of deputies in the National Assembly from 100 to 120. Prior to 1973 there were eighty. The new code, developed with the assistance of West German political consultants and against the vehement protests of opposition parties, introduced the principle of election by simple majority in legislative districts (*départements*) for the first time. The new system obtains for only sixty of the seats, in thirty *départements;* the remaining sixty continue to be elected by proportional representation from national lists presented by each party, as in the past. The new legislation apparently has abrogated a provision that reserved twenty seats for specific social and economic groups. The president continues to be elected simultaneously with deputies by direct universal suffrage.

Until 1978 secrecy was universal. That year the secret ballot was made optional, to the dismay of the newly formed opposition parties conscious of peasant conservatism and local leaders' surveillance. In the 1983 elections, eight parties participated, while six recently legalized smaller parties boycotted the election to protest a ruling prohibiting parties from forming coalitions. Initially, the two opposition parties which gained representation in the Assembly, the *Parti Democratique* (PDS) and the *Rassemblement National Democratique Senegalais* (RND), refused to sit in the new Assembly, alleging that electoral fraud had occurred. The Supreme Court, which oversees election campaigns, rejected this accusation. Voters must register well ahead of time, with village chiefs or urban district leaders. In August 1982, there were 1,923,483 registered voters, up from 1,556,250 in 1978. Voter turnout is typically over 85 percent even in uncontested elections, as voting seems to function more as a traditional pledge of clientship than for making decisions. All citizens age twenty-one and over are eligible to vote.

The Party System

Origins of the Parties

Although Senegal has the longest tradition of electoral politics in black Africa (the French first organized elections in the trading centers of Saint-Louis in 1848 before they conquered the rest of the country), political parties are a relatively recent phenomenon. Elected leaders in the early twentieth century depended on their political clubs, such as the "Aurora of Saint Louis," which helped launch the career of the first black Senegalese deputy to the French National Assembly, Blaise Diagne (1872–1934) and his patron and later rival Galandou Diouf (1875–1941). In 1929 Lamine Guèye founded the first Senegalese political party, the Senegalese Socialist Party (*Parti Socialiste Sénégalais;* PSS). Its members were urban intellectuals, including local French socialists. In 1937, Guèye led his followers into the Socialist International; his party became a Senegalese branch of the French Section of the Labor International (*Section Française de l'Internationale Ouvrière-Sénégal;* SFIO-Sen). Electoral politics were suspended during World War II by local representatives of the Vichy regime, so it was not until 1945 and 1946 that the SFIO-Sen won its first electoral victories. Guèye sponsored poet Léopold Senghor as a candidate for deputy from the rural areas, while he himself stood in the urban elections. The protégé quickly surpassed his patron, however, and in 1947 formed his own mass-based political party, the Senegalese Democratic Bloc (*Bloc Démocratique Sénégalais;* BDS). His rural stumping, alliances with Muslim and Catholic religious leaders (the most powerful rural authorities), and attention to particular needs at all levels paid off in the 1951 and 1952 elections, in which the BDS handily defeated the SFIO. As the demand for self-government became more intense, the BDS absorbed the SFIO and most of the other small parties, always finding honorable posts within the party and administration for the leaders thus eclipsed. In a major merger in 1958, the party name was changed to Senegalese Progressive Union (*Union Progressiste Sénégalaise;* UPS). In the tense early years of independence from 1960 through 1963, those parties whose leaders refused merger offers were gradually banned. National coalitions of ethnic mutual aid associations were also disbanded; Senghor feared they could become bases for separatist aspirations.

The UPS reigned over a single-party state until 1973, when, in connection with a move to join the Socialist International, which requires member parties to participate in multiparty democracy, Senghor decided to legalize a limited number of opposition parties and change the name of his own to the Socialist Party (*Parti Socialiste;* PS). First, the centrist Senegalese Democratic Party (*Parti Démocratique Sénégalais;* PDS), then one branch of the long underground Marxist-Leninist African Independence Party (*Parti Africain de l'Indépendance;* PAI), and finally the conservative religious Senegalese Republican Movement (*Mouvement Républicain Sénégalais;* MRS) were legalized. In 1981, President Diouf allowed complete freedom to organize and formally register parties, producing sixteen parties by 1985. Intraparty politics in the PS continues to attract more attention than interparty rivalries, and no opposition party has yet found a candidate to oppose Diouf for the presidency.

Party Organization

The PS is the only party that has a mass membership nationwide. Most of the smaller parties are based and have most of their members in Dakar, although several have local power bases in the far southern province of Casamance or in the Sine-Saloum.

Parties typically have political bureaus elected at their annual national conventions, but the basic mechanisms of politics are intraparty cliques, locally dubbed "clans," and patron-client networks. The latter comprise a political leader's relatives, their traditional dependents, adherents, religious disciples if the leader is a marabout (Islamic leader), and organizations the leader has founded or won over. The style and internal functioning of the networks and clans grew out of precolonial extended-family and lord/vassal ties, with modern twists. Patrons buy large blocks of party membership cards and distribute them to their followers. Trade unions, cultural associations, and vocational organizations sometimes adhere to a single patron or form a clan. Within the network, adherents turn to one another for help in getting jobs, promotions, and political favors, and in coping with the cumbersome Senegalese bureaucracy. Only at election time do most networks have enough coherence to be identified individually; then they are expected to vote as a bloc with the patron.

Campaigning

Campaigning is officially limited to the two weeks preceding an election, but candidate decisions and publicity begin much earlier. The choice of candidates takes place through intraparty elections well ahead of time. Election campaigns, until recently, were not contests and tended to take on the aura of precolonial royal tours: candidates gleaned news of local problems and collected expressions of client loyalty. Television and radio news and the government daily *Le Soleil* (The Sun) focus on presidential and cabinet activities year round, and incumbents tour the country at government expense. The new electoral code obliges the media to provide equal time or space to the opposition parties as one group and the ruling parties (at present, only the PS) as another group.

Socialist Party
(*Parti Socialiste;* PS)

The ruling party, PS practices a brand of African socialism combining private sector with nationalized economic development. President Abdou Diouf (born in Louga in 1935) serves as secretary general. The first, second, and third assistant secretaries, and political secretary are, respectively, Amadou Cisse Dia, president of the National Assembly; Magatte Lo, president of the Economic and Social Council; and Minister of State for Foreign Affairs Moustapha Niasse. Léopold Senghor is honorary president for life. In keeping with his own recent and untested succession, Diouf has staffed the party with a combination of elder statesmen (Dia and Lo) and trusted companions with limited power bases of their own. Potential rivals, such as former Minister of Finance Babacar Ba of Kaolack, have been excluded from the formal leadership.

The PS remains structurally, as it was in its BDS and UPS days, a curious amalgam of patron networks cutting across a formal territorial hierarchy of committees. All urban wards and most rural *arrondissements* have local committees, which send delegates to district, regional, and national meetings. Individual membership cards are sold for 300 CFA francs ($1), but patrons and marabouts buy large blocks for distribution to followers, which renders membership figures meaningless. Ruling-party membership claims have generally been about one-third of the registered voters. The party also has labor unions, peasant, women's, youth and student units at various levels, rivalling, often successfully, independent voluntary associations. It publishes the weekly *l'Unité africaine* and the satirical *Caaxan faaxee* (Wolof: The Game's Up!).

In foreign policy, Diouf continues Senghor's roles as leader of the moderates in the nonaligned Group of 77; advocate of Francophone unity; close ally of the Socialist regime in France; and prominent member of the Socialist International, the Saudi-sponsored Islamic Conference, and the Organization of African Unity. Domestically, Diouf's African socialism continues to be pragmatic. He is moving away from the uneconomic parastatals (corporations partially owned by the state) as quickly as he moved to establish the sector in the midseventies; the new emphasis is on decentralization of economic planning and initiatives.

Democratic Popular Movement (*Mouvement Démocratique Populaire;* MDP)

The MDP is former prime minister Mamadou Dia's party, registered in 1981. Its journal, *Ande Sopi* (Unity for Change!), began appearing earlier, but since the end of his imprisonment (1963–74), Dia had not settled on a party allegiance. With a flexible African socialist platform and strength in Dakar and his northern homeland in the Senegal River Basin, Dia is now working to unite the opposition through the Coordination of the United Senegalese Opposition (*Coordination de l'Opposition Sénégalaise Unie;* COSU).

National Democratic Assembly (*Rassemblement National Démocratique;* RND)

Cheikh Anta Diop (born 1923), a noted historian, founded this pan-African socialist party in 1977, after a decade and a half in internal exile as head of a radiocarbon-dating laboratory. Together with assistant party secretary Babacar Niang and linguist/economist Pathé Diagne, he publishes *Taxaw!* (Stand up!), one of the first all-Wolof journals in Senegal.

Senegalese Democratic Party (*Parti Démocratique Sénégalais;* PDS)

Lawyer Abdoulaye Wade (born about 1930) left the ruling party to found this centrist labor party in 1974, the first in Senegal's recent experiment in multiparty democracy. His was the only party to mount a presidential campaign in 1978 (he won 17.7 percent of the vote), and the only one to win Assembly seats (eighteen). Ideologically it is similar to the African socialism of the ruling party, yet opposed to nationalization. Its journal, *le Démocrate,* harshly criticizes government corporations. Wade has refused to recognize Diouf's succession, pointing out that it was engineered through a constitutional amendment and that Diouf has never stood for election. When he launched the PDS, Wade apparently expected to receive Senghor's blessing to inherit the presidency. He originally styled the PDS a party of "contribution." It did not become a party of opposition until the constitution was amended to allow for Diouf's succession. The government, in turn, brought criminal charges against the leadership when it learned the PDS had sent the party's bodyguards to Libya for training. Wade stayed in exile in the latter half of 1981. This, and the defection or expulsion of eight of its eighteen deputies, diminished its chances in the 1983 elections. Its greatest strength in 1978 was in urban areas and the Casamance, both of which now have other opposition parties wooing them.

Minor Parties

African Independence Party (*Parti Africain de l'Indépendance;* PAI)

Founded in 1957 by pharmacist Mahjmout Diop (born about 1920), this Marxist-Leninist party advocated independence at a time when other leaders were still seeking a formula for association with France. Banned for sedition in 1960, it remained intellectually active underground until it was again legalized in 1976. It publishes *La Lutte* (The Struggle) sporadically. A faction split off in 1965 to found the Independence and Labor Party. Both factions were recognized by the Communist International. Numerous Marxist-Leninist and Maoist-inspired factions formed in the last five years have dissociated themselves from the older Senegalese Marxist leadership and from international affiliations.

African Party for the Independence of the Masses (*Parti Africain de l'Indépendance des Masses;* PAIM)

Founded in 1982 by Aly Niane, PAIM is Marxist-Leninist.

And Jef: Revolutionary Movement for the New Democracy (*And Jef* [Unity for Action!]: *Mouvement Revolutionaire pour la Démocratie Nouvelle;* AJ/MRDN)

And Jef is an Asian-style communist movement registered in 1981 by demographer and former director of statistics, Landing Savane (born 1948 in Casamance), and colleague Amadou Top. It publishes the important journal *Jaay Doole Bi* in Wolof and French.

Communist Workers' League (*Ligue Communiste des Travailleurs;* LCT)

The LCT is an independent Marxist faction founded in 1982 by Mahmoud Saleh.

Democratic League—Popular Labor Movement (*Ligue Démocratique— Mouvement Populaire et du Travail;* LD/ MPT)

This Marxist movement, registered in 1981, is led by Abdoulaye Bathily and Mbaba Guisse. This younger generation of Marxist intellectuals, born in the 1940s, avoids the international orientation of the PAI and its factions, concentrating on local issues. Its journal, *Vérité* (Truth), focuses on ridding Senegal of French and International Monetary Fund influence. Its leadership is active in the teachers' union, SUDES, but lost the 1982 union elections.

Independence and Labor Party (*Parti de l'Indépendance et du Travail;* PIT)

A 1965 offshoot of the then underground PAI, the PIT is led by Seydou Cissoke and Amath Dansokho, with Maguette Thiam. It was legalized and registered in 1981.

People's Liberation Party (*Parti pour la Libération du peuple;* PLP)

Formed in 1983 by RND dissidents, the PLP is led by Babacar Niang, and advocates antiimperialist, neutralist policies.

Senegalise Democratic Union (*Union Démocratique Sénégalaise*)

Led by Mamadou Fall, this party was founded in 1985 by PDS dissidents; its platform is nationalist and progressive.

Senegalese Popular Party (*Parti Populaire Sénégalais;* PPS)

Founded in 1981 in Diourbel by Marxist Amadou Dia, this is the only party which does not have its headquarters in Dakar.

Senegalese Republican Movement (*Mouvement Républicain Sénégalais;* MRS)

The MRS is a conservative religious (Islamic) traditionalist party founded in 1978 by lawyer Boubacar Guèye, nephew of post-World War II nationalist leader Lamine Guèye.

Socialist Workers' Organization (*Organisation Socialiste des Travailleurs;* OST)

A Marxist-Leninist faction without international affiliation, the OST was founded in 1982 by Mbaye Bathily.

Union for Popular Democracy (*Union pour la Démocratie Populaire,* UDP)

This small democratic Marxist party was founded in 1981 by Hamedine Racine Guissé and is comprised of former supporters of the And Jef party.

Other Political Forces

Military

Senegal's armed forces are relatively small for a country of its size, comprising approximately 8,000 troops. They have been increased significantly from about 6,000 members in 1976. The military is noted for its professionalism and, thus far has been consciously and consistently apolitical under the firm control of the civilian government. In service of Senegal's foreign policy, it has been part of the United Nations peacekeeping forces in Zaire's Shaba province in 1978, in Lebanon, and with Organization of African Unity forces in Chad. It also moved into the Gambia at the request of Gambian President Jawara when rebels attempted to overthrow that government in August 1981. Senegalese troops are still stationed there, and the two countries have signed a pact of confederation. There is no known disaffection in the Senegalese armed forces at present, nor has there been a known threat of military takeover in the history of Senegal since independence. During the constitutional crisis of 1962, when Prime Minister Mamadou Dia called in the national guard to close down the National Assembly, the army under the order of President Senghor forced the guard to back down without serious open conflict. The continued presence of French troops, small as it is, and the traditions of multi-ethnic recruitment and French officer training all contribute to a tradition of abstention from politics in the Senegalese armed forces.

Organized Labor

Trade unions have been regulated and politically controlled by the government as much as possible. The original General Confederation of French Workers-Senegal (*Confederation Générale des Travailleurs Français-Sénégal;* CGTF-Senegal) merged with the ruling party's National Union of Senegalese Workers (*Union Nationale des Travailleurs Sénégalais;* UNTS) in the 1960s. It worked closely with the ruling party until 1968, when it broke those ties and led demonstrations against the government. At that time, Senghor was able to split its leadership. The new Union of Free Senegalese Workers (*Union des Travailleurs Libres Sénégalais;* UTLS) is independent, while another union, General Confederation of Senegalese Workers (*Confédération Générale des Travailleurs Sénégalais;* CGTS) is closely tied to the ruling UPS. These unions focused their efforts on getting contractual and minimum-wage legislation to improve conditions for their membership, which is limited to the small number of Senegalese who earn salaries in the modern sector of the economy.

It is in education that the next significant independent union activity emerged. This came with the formation of the independent Unique and Democratic Syndicate of Senegalese Teachers (*Syndicat Unique et Démocratique des Enseignants Sénégalais;* SUDES), which is both a labor and political alternative to the existing teachers' union affiliated with the Socialist Party. Since 1979, SUDES has built a substantial following among public school and university faculty throughout the country. While its focus is mainly on working conditions in the educational system, education in itself is one of the major political concerns of any regime in Senegal. In the present budgetary crisis, the government can do little to improve the low salaries and large classes found throughout the educational system. Diouf dealt deftly and openly with this immediately after his assumption of the presidency, by calling an Estates General for education. This national convention effectively shifted the focus from the particular tensions in the educational system to global questions of educational philosophy.

Religious Brotherhoods

Marabouts—whose roles include teacher, scholar, landowner, and leader in worship—are the most widespread and effective local political powers in the countryside. Discipleship, or the patron-client relationship, is the key to their political power. People become their adherents either through having studied with them or having joined their movement as adults. In either case, the political ties and religious allegiances are generally strong and lifelong. As a literate and landed group, with an elaborate political philosophy expressed in the history and law of Islam, they offer a complete political alternative. According to their own ethic, however, they should normally abstain from politics and there should be separation of church and state. Barring a full-scale crisis of the secular leadership or the emergence of a charismatic religious leader, the religious leadership normally is a stable complement rather than a threat to the existing political leadership. While there is a serious economic crisis in Senegal today, there does not appear to be any viable charismatic movement. Ahmad Tijani Niasse, who briefly threatened to form one, with Libyan backing, has been under surveillance and periodically jailed. The main brotherhoods—Mouride, Tijani, and Qadiri—all support the government.

National Prospects

The economy is weak, with annual per capita income averaging under $300 and the modern sector dependent on groundnut and phosphate exports. The great drought from 1968 to 1973, followed by escalating fuel costs and stagflation, plunged the government into recurring budgetary crises. Economic development strategies in the 1960s relied on national corporations and in the latter 1970s on parastatal development agencies. Neither has proved effective, so now the government is attempting to decentralize economic initiatives while operating under a budgetary reform plan negotiated with the IMF.

A pragmatic outlook by its leadership has allowed Senegal to evolve a stable democracy despite chronic economic crisis. Ethnic and religious factors have blended into political life without overt conflict. The recent multiparty system and Diouf succession passed their first test in the elections of 1983. Yet long term success would require an economic turn-around, alleviating domestic inflation, stimulating production, and ending government recourse to IMF and French bail-outs.

Further Reading
Colvin, Lucie Gallistel. *Historical Dictionary of Senegal.* Metuchen, N. J.: Scarecrow Press, 1981.
Foltz, William J. "Senegal." In *Political Parties and National Integration in Tropical Africa,* James S. Coleman and Carl G. Rosberg, Jr., eds. Berkeley: University of California Press, 1964, 1970.
Gellar, Sheldon. *Senegal,* Boulder, Colo.: Westview Press, 1982.
Nelson, Harold D., et al. *Area Handbook for Senegal.* 2nd ed. Washington, D.C.: U.S. Government Printing Office, for Foreign Area Studies, American University, 1974.
O'Brien, Donal B. Cruise. *Saints and Politicians: Essays in the Organization of a Senegalese Peasant Society.* New York and London: Cambridge University Press, 1975.
Traoré, Bakary; Lo Mamadou; and Alibert, Jean-Louis. *Forces politiques en Afrique noire: Sénégal,* (no. 2). Paris: Presses universitaires de France, 1966.
World Bank. *The Economic Trends and Prospects of Senegal.* 4 vols. Washington, D.C.: World Bank, 1979.
Zuccarelli, François. *Un parti politique africain: l'Union progressiste sénégalaise.* Paris: Pichon et Durand-Auzias, 1971.

REPUBLIC OF SIERRA LEONE

by Steven Metz, M.A. revised by Shiela Elliot, M.A.

The System of Government

Sierra Leone is a one-party republic with an executive form of government. The West African nation of about 3.5 million people became a republic in 1971 when the parliamentary system, which had been created before independence from Great Britain in 1961, was replaced. The current political system is codified in a constitution ratified in 1978.

Executive

Most political power in Sierra Leone is vested in the executive branch of the government. The executive is composed of the president; the first and second vice-presidents; and a cabinet of more than twenty ministers.

The president is the leader of the single constitutionally legal party and is the sole candidate in a presidential election. His term of office is seven years. The president appoints the vice-presidents and cabinet from among the members of the House of Representatives.

The president is both head of state and head of government and has wide-ranging legislative powers. He has the constitutional right to dissolve the House and call new elections. The president is also commander-in-chief of the armed forces.

Legislature

The House of Representatives is a unicameral body of 104 members. Eighty-five seats are filled by popular election in single-member districts; twelve seats are held by paramount chiefs selected by the chiefdom council (a body of elders) in their district; and seven members are appointed by the president. The members appointed by the president are usually leaders of the police and military. All representatives except the paramount chiefs are required to be active members of the official party. Representatives are elected for five-year terms. Bills pass in the House with a simple majority, but a two-thirds majority is required for measures which would change the constitution.

Judiciary

The judicial system includes a Supreme Court, Court of Appeals, High Court of Justice, and Magistrate's Court. Judges to all but the Magistrate's Court are appointed by the president. There is a system of local courts which rules on questions of tribal and traditional law.

Regional & Local Government

Sierra Leone is divided into three provinces (Northern, Southern, and Eastern), and the Western area which includes Freetown, the capital and largest city.

Local government in the Western area is directed by a council, part of which is elected and part appointed. The mayor of Freetown is also appointed by this council. Each of the three provinces has a governing minister appointed by the president with the rank of a cabinet officer.

The most important position on a local level is that of paramount chief of one of the 148 chieftaincies. These chieftaincies are administrative units of a similar size, and are not the same as traditional tribal divisions. The 148 chieftaincies are grouped into twelve chieftaincy districts, each of which is represented in the House by one of its paramount chiefs. The chiefs are selected by the chiefdom council of their districts, which are elected by the taxpayers of the district. The office of paramount chief is restricted to members of "chiefly families." Since most districts have more than one of these noble families, competition for the chieftaincy is vigorous. Most of the political power of the paramount chiefs comes from their role of government administrators, which allows them to allocate government funds and jobs.

The Electoral System

Sierra Leone has universal adult (age twenty-one) suffrage, and voting is by secret ballot. Since there is only one legal party, the candidates in any election have been chosen by that party. The electoral system, therefore, is less important in the selection of national leaders than the system of party primaries. Under this primary system, two candidates—chosen from each district by the executive council of the party in that district—stand for office in a general election. Voter turnout is usually low.

All People's Congress (APC)

History

The APC was formed by Siaka Stevens in the pre-independence period. As a businessman and a union organizer, Stevens developed close ties to the more modern elements of Sierra Leonean society, so the APC came to represent modernization and a sense of opposition to the traditional power of the chiefs.

From independence in 1961 until 1968, the country was governed by the Sierra Leone People's Party (SLPP), originally an alliance of Northern and Southern provincial elites opposed to political control by the Creoles of Freetown, a mixed-race group which had dominated the political system under the British. When the first SLPP leader, Sir Milton Margai, died in 1964, his brother Albert took over the party. The Margais were from the Mende tribe of the Southern province and their continuing hold on the party leadership alienated the ethnic groups of the Northern province, chief of which was the Temne. Albert Margai's attempts to alter the political system to solidify his power raised fears in the north that the Mende would come to dominate the country. These fears gave Stevens and the APC the victory in the 1967 elections. Stevens was arrested by the army on Margai's orders and subsequently went into exile. The following year a military coup deposed Margai and invited Stevens to return to Sierra Leone and form a government, which he did.

During the mid-1970s, the electioneering of the SLPP and other opposition parties was gradually curtailed, and, after 1973, Sierra Leone was a de facto one-party state.

The 1978 constitution banned all parties in Sierra Leone except for the ruling APC. Most of the leaders of the SLPP were absorbed into the APC and competition between parties was ended. Several leaders of the SLPP resigned from politics rather than join the APC.

The government has stifled all criticism; opposition to the APC is now carried on only by ineffective and splintered expatriate groups.

Organization

The national party is highly centralized and is not effectively organized at the local level. Local political organization is carried out by the district-chieftaincy faction supported by the party leadership.

Party politics in Sierra Leone is an outgrowth of competition for the 148 chieftaincies. While the chiefs have little impact on national policies, their ability to allocate government funds, projects, and jobs on the local level makes control of the chieftaincy extremely valuable. Before 1978, rival factions for a chieftaincy formed an alliance with one of the national parties, with the victorious national party installing their candidates in the chieftaincies. Since the 1978 constitution abolished party competition, factions in a struggle for control of a chieftaincy often align with factions within the central organs of the APC.

Since public criticism of the government is not allowed, differences in ideology or policy are not important in competition among factions on either the local or national level. The major issue is control of political office. For this reason, political groups in Sierra Leone tend to be loose alliances of factions and not groups organized around a common theme or set of beliefs. Although the tribal aspects of party competition were used to mobilize support during the period of party competition, the tribes are of less political importance than in many other areas of Africa. The major political division is between those who hold office and those who wish to hold office.

Policy

The policy of the APC is centered on the twin problems of tribal fragmentation and poverty. The creation of the one-party state and the allocation of development funds on a political basis have both helped to stabilize the political system in general and the party in particular.

Membership & Constituency

Theoretically, membership in the APC is universal—equivalent to citizenship. Party activists probably number no more than one thousand.

Financing

Nothing is known of party financing. Gifts from wealthy supporters in Freetown, the private funds of chiefly families (used to advance their own interests as much as the party's), payments from APC-indebted office holders, and some government support probably cover all expenses. After the creation of the one-party state, the distinction between government and party revenues was no longer clear-cut.

Leadership

Siaka Stevens (born 1905) was the president of Sierra Leone until August 1975. That year, citing his age and health, Stevens designated Major General Joseph Saidu Momoh as his successor. On Oct. 6, 1985, Momoh won 2,784,591 out of 2,788,687 votes cast to become president. President Momoh (born 1937) has spent much of his career as leader of the army.

The current first vice-president of Sierra Leone is S. I. Koroma (born 1930); the second vice-president is Francis Minah. Dr. S. S. Banya is the minister of finance.

Other Political Forces

Military

Despite a past history of support for civilian rule, the military is seen as a potential political force in face of its opposition to President Momoh and the country's economic problems.

National Prospects

The future political climate of Sierra Leone hinges greatly on three factors. First is the role played by the military. The election of an army officer to the presidency could affect the outlook of the army toward the office. This is particularly significant since it has been asserted that Momoh does not enjoy the full backing of the military elite. Second, although former president Stevens has claimed to be retired from politics, he has retained his post as chairperson on the governing council of the APC. Stevens, therefore, can still maintain his influence over the decision and policy-making process of the Momoh government. Third is the many campaign promises Momoh made to end Sierra Leone's economic problems, especially the pervasiveness of smuggling. A declining economy might encourage the military or Stevens to intervene or even to assume power.

Further Reading

Barrows, Walter. *Grassroots Politics in an African State: Integration and Development in Sierra Leone.* New York: Africana, 1976.

Cartwright, John R. *Political Leadership in Sierra Leone.* Toronto, Canada: University of Toronto Press, 1978.

Clapham, Christopher S. *Liberia and Sierra Leone: An Essay in Comparative Politics.* Cambridge, England: Cambridge University Press, 1976.

Tangri, Roger. "Central-Local Politics in Sierra Leone." *African Affairs,* Vol. 77, No. 307, April 1978.

THE REPUBLIC OF SINGAPORE

by Donald M. Seekins, Ph.D.

The System of Government

Singapore is a parliamentary republic in which one party, the People's Action Party (PAP), has been dominant since it first came to power in 1959. The territory of the republic consists of Singapore Island and about fifty offshore islets located at the southern tip of the Malay Peninsula, with a total area of about 230 square miles. The Johore Strait, less than a mile wide at its narrowest, separates Singapore from the Malaysian state of Johore; the Singapore Strait, less than five miles wide at its narrowest, separates it from islands belonging to the Republic of Indonesia. The City of Singapore, located on the southern coast of Singapore Island, is the economic, political, and administrative center of the country, although all parts of the island are densely populated. In 1979, the population was estimated at 2,362,700. Chinese make up 76.2 percent of the population, 15 percent is Malay, 6.8 percent is Indian or Sri Lankan, and 2 percent consists of Westerners and other ethnic groups.

The present republic had its origins in the British colony established by Sir Thomas Stamford Raffles in 1819. In 1957, Britain granted independence to the Federation of Malaya and Singapore attained home rule two years later. Malayan leaders were reluctant to attempt a union with Singapore because of its large Chinese population and active left-wing movements, but in August 1963, Malaya, Sarawak and Sabah, and Singapore united to form the Federation of Malaysia. This arrangement lasted only two years. Differences between the state government of Singapore and the central government in Kuala Lumpur and their governing parties, the People's Action Party and the United Malay National Organization, led to the departure of Singapore from Malaysia in 1965. Separation was announced on August 9, 1965, and Singapore became an independent nation. Prime Minister Lee Kuan Yew had hoped to keep the federation viable, but with its collapse, he set about with great determination to assure the survival of the new Republic of Singapore. His policy was to create a "multiethnic, multilingual, secular state." In the words of Sinnathamby Rajaratnam, People's Action Party leader, speaking in 1965, if "we of the present generation can steadfastly stick to this policy for the next thirty years, then we will have succeeded in creating a Singaporean of a unique kind. He will be a man rooted in the cultures of four great civilizations [China, Malaya, India and Europe], but not belonging exclusively to any of them."

Singapore's constitution is embodied in four documents: the Constitution of the State of Singapore when it was a part of Malaysia, certain articles of the Constitution of Malaysia considered applicable to the republic, and the 1965 Singapore Independence Act and Constitution (Amendment) Act. With separation, the governor of the State of Singapore was renamed the president of the republic, and the State Legislature became the national Parliament. Singapore is unusual in that it shares with another state certain provisions of its constitution, but this is not meant to compromise its independence. According to Article 52J of the Constitution (Amendment) Act, the surrender or transfer of sovereignty is prohibited "whether by way of merger or incorporation with any other sovereign state or with any Federation, Confederation, country or territory or in any other manner."

Executive

The head of state of the Republic of Singapore is the president, elected by Parliament for a term of four years. The first president was Inche Yusof bin Ishak; he was succeeded in 1970 by Dr. Benjamin Henry Sheares, who died in office in May 1981 and was succeeded by Devan Nair. Nair resigned in March 1985. After an interim period, Parliament selected Wee Kim Wee as the republic's fourth president. Parliament may reelect the president for an indefinite number of terms and can remove him from office with a two-thirds vote. He is in theory the chief executive, and has the authority to appoint the prime minister and deny his request to dissolve Parliament. All parliamentary bills are submitted to him for approval. Yet his position is only formal, and he does not participate actively in the political process. An office of vice president was created in 1968.

Below the president is the Presidential Council for Minority Rights, established in 1967, which reviews all legislation to determine whether it discriminates against the rights of any ethnic or religious group in the republic. The constitution requires that all parliamentary bills, with the exception of those involving the budget, national defense, or public security, be examined by the Council, which also serves as an advisory body to the government on ethnic affairs. The Public Service Commission, appointed by the president, deals with civil service personnel matters. The attorney general has three responsibilities: he acts as public prosecutor, advises the government on legal matters, and drafts all legislation.

The cabinet, headed by the prime minister, is the focus of real political power. He is designated by Parliament and answers to it for government policy. There is a Prime Minister's Office, which contains the Anti-Pollution Unit, the Corrupt Practices Investigation Bureau, the District Offices, the City District Secretariat, and the Election Department. It is responsible for the Citizens' Consultative Committees (see below, *Local Institutions*). First and second deputy prime ministers assist the prime minister in his responsibilities. In 1985, Lee Kuan Yew remained the prime minister, while the first deputy prime minister was Goh Chok Tong and the second deputy prime minister was Ong Teng Cheong.

The government has established a number of statutory boards and public corporations, of which the most important include the Housing and Development Board, the Singapore Institute of Standards and Industrial Research, the Economic Development Board, the Jurong Town Corporation, the Port of Singapore Authority, and the Singapore Tourist Promotion Board. Important policy decisions are made not by elected representatives in Parliament, but by bureaucrats in the upper echelons of the civil service, statutory boards, and public corporations in consultation with the party leadership. The creation of what Chan Heng Chee of the University of Singapore calls an "administrative state," whose personnel have a high

reputation for honesty and efficiency, has produced impressive results in the economic and social spheres. There have been generous investments in education, health services, housing and social welfare; the country's standard of living is the envy of the rest of Asia.

Legislature

Singapore has a single-chamber Parliament of seventy-nine popularly elected members, up from sixty-nine in 1980. The legislature is presided over by a speaker, who is elected by the members but is not necessarily a member himself. Bills are passed by a simple majority before being given to the president for approval. Parliamentary business can be conducted in one of four official languages: Chinese, Malay, Tamil, or English. Members serving as cabinet ministers retain their parliamentary seats. Parliament has a term of five years, although the government can be dissolved and general elections held before that time; by-elections are frequent.

Since independence there have been general elections in 1968, 1972, 1976, 1980, and 1984. With the exception of a bi-election in 1981 and 1984, the People's Action Party has won all the seats in Parliament. Voter support for the PAP, some of whose candidates ran in uncontested districts, reached a high of 86.7 percent in 1968; in the 1972 general election, it fell to 70.4 percent, increasing to 72.4 percent in 1976 and 75.5 percent in 1980, and a low of 62.9 percent in 1984. In the December 22, 1984 general election, the PAP won seventy-seven out of seventy-nine seats.

Judiciary

Singapore's judicial system is based on the British model, and the Judicial Committee of the Privy Council, in London, is the ultimate court of appeal, which can reverse decisions of the Singapore Supreme Court. Within the republic, the highest court is the Supreme Court. Lower courts include the High Court and the district and magistrate's courts. A special Shari'ah Court is attached to the Ministry of Social Affairs and hears cases involving certain aspects of Muslim law. The Industrial Arbitration Court, under the Ministry of Labor, settles disputes between management and unionized workers. The Labor Court, also under the Ministry of Labor, handles disputes between employers and nonunion employees. Both are considered of great importance, since the maintenance of labor peace is seen as vital to the republic's economic health.

The constitution provides for the independence of the judicial branch, and the Supreme Court has the power of judicial review.

Local Institutions

Singapore, given its compactness, does not have formal structures of local government. The national government, however, has established a number of institutions which serve to keep it in touch with the grass roots. The most important are the Citizens' Consultative Committees, found in each electoral district. These are theoretically nonpartisan groups which are the responsibility of the Prime Minister's Office. Committee members, about twenty to fifty in each district, are nominated by the local member of Parliament and approved by the Prime Minister's Office. In essence, they serve as a medium through which the government can educate local people on programs and policies and through which the people can make their needs known to the government. They are also responsible for certain public works projects, and often serve as arbitrators in local disputes, an especially delicate task in racially mixed constituencies where tensions between Chinese and Malays can lead to confrontations. In some cases, the committees have taken over several of the functions traditionally performed by Chinese clan associations or Malay *kampong* (village) headmen. The government has found them extremely useful for the promotion of a wide variety of campaigns designed to make the people better citizens, e.g., movements to eradicate bad habits like spitting or littering and to encourage courtesy, neatness, and "gracious living." Many of these functions are also performed by PAP branch offices, however, and committees and party branch offices often find themselves in competition.

The People's Association was established as a statutory body in 1960 and is responsible for running some 160 community centers which conduct educational, social, cultural, and recreational programs throughout the country. They sponsor kindergarten classes, folk-dancing troupes, social education programs, and drug addict rehabilitation services. A People's Association Youth Movement, with 30,000 members in 1978, and a National Youth Leadership Training Institute, established in 1964, train People's Association staff in youth and community work.

Since 1977, residents' committees have been established in the numerous high-rise apartment blocks which have been built throughout the republic. Their purpose is to encourage neighborliness and security consciousness in these otherwise impersonal surroundings.

The Electoral System

Candidates for Parliament are elected by simple plurality in single-member districts. According to the Parliamentary Elections Act, voters must be twenty-one years of age, citizens and residents of Singapore, and not owing allegiance to or enrolled on the electoral lists of another country. Voting is secret and compulsory.

In July 1984, Parliament passed a constitutional amendment creating three "non-constituency" seats to be occupied by opposition parties if their candidates fail to win any of the single-member districts in a general election. The three candidates who won the largest percentage of votes in any constituency would be selected (if two opposition candidates won in constituencies, then one non-constituency seat would be granted; and if one won, two would be granted.) The non-constituency members of Parliament, however, would not be allowed to vote on such important matters as the national budget, constitutional amendments, and motions of no confidence.

The Party System

Origins of the Parties

Political parties in Singapore had their origins in the post-World War II years, when Singapore and Malaysia were struggling to make the transition from a colonial to an independent status. After the separation of Singapore from Malaysia in 1965, the system evolved rather rapidly into one in which one party, the People's Action Party led by Lee Kuan Yew, became dominant. Through its control of Parliament, the PAP was able to mold the state in its own image, keeping the opposition parties completely outside the policymaking process.

The Parties in Law

Singapore is not a one-party state. Opposition parties have legal status, and as many as sixteen have been registered at one time—although many of these are little more than paper entities. Yet PAP leaders have not hesitated to use repressive measures in order to sharply inhibit opposition-party activities. In the words of Second Deputy Prime Minister Rajaratnam, "the people are more interested in what is good government than in having an opposition."

Party Organization

With the exception of the highly organized PAP, there is little formal party structure in Singapore. Party activity traditionally has concentrated on grass-roots development around community and cultural issues. The smaller parties have followed this tradition, but under PAP and state pressure, have remained fragmented and disorganized at the national level.

People's Action Party (PAP)

History

The PAP was founded in 1954 by a small group of lawyers, journalists, educators, and trade unionists. The party was socialist in orientation, relying largely on the support of union workers and promoting an anticolonialist ideology. From the very beginning, it was composed of both communist and noncommunist factions. At first they cooperated with each other and with other leftist groups. Thus, in the 1955 Legislative Assembly elections, held while Singapore was still a British crown colony, the PAP, with the support of the Malayan Communist Party, ran four candidates and won three seats. In the 1957 City Council elections, PAP won thirteen of the fourteen seats it contested. Two years later, it was able to gain a strong majority in the Legislative Assembly, winning forty-three out of a possible fifty-one seats. The PAP has remained in power ever since.

Tensions between the noncommunist and communist factions increased over a number of issues, of which the most prominent was that of union with Malaya, until July 1961, when thirteen leftists bolted the party and formed the *Barisan Sosialis* (Socialist Front). Despite the fact that the leftists took with them as many as 80 percent of the party's members, the noncommunist PAP under Lee Kuan Yew was able to win the 1963 legislative elections with the support of moderates. The party since has become strongly anticommunist and antileftist.

Organization

The highest organ of the party is the Central Executive Committee (CEC), which consists of the top party leaders. The CEC has six policy bureaus—Malay affairs, welfare, women's issues, culture, publicity, and foreign affairs—and a Central Political Bureau which trains party cadres. It publishes *Petir*, the party newspaper. Domination by the PAP of the political system has made the CEC virtually synonymous with the government. Its members are elected by cadres at the biannual party conference.

The basic unit of the party is the local party branch. It is established in each electoral district and works closely with the local member of Parliament. Each branch has a committee responsible for its activities, and although its members must be approved by the Central Executive Committee, it has great latitude in carrying out the CEC's general directives. In some districts, there are sub-branches; and, below the sub-branches, "liaison stations," which are often located in the houses of cadres and party members. Sub-branches are often established in localities where opposition parties have set up branches.

The most important function of the branch is similar to that performed by the Citizens' Consultative Committee: providing a medium through which the government and people can communicate. Members of Parliament hold weekly "meet the people sessions" at branch offices where citizens can present petitions and receive free legal aid and information about government policies. A member of Parliament is sometimes asked to mediate local disputes.

Policy

A country small in territory, surrounded by hostile or suspicious neighbors, divided internally along ethnic lines, and lacking natural resources, Singapore's future at first seemed to be very much in doubt. Prime Minister Lee and the other party leaders saw their most urgent tasks in terms of the nation's very survival. Two basic themes have been central to PAP and, therefore, government policy: the development of a modern economy which would enable the republic to survive and prosper, and the creation of a genuine sense of national identity and commitment among Singapore's citizens.

The PAP has seen development in terms of planning and administration rather than politics. According to the political scientist Chan Heng Chee, a "depoliticization of a politically active and aggressive citizenry" and a "shift in emphasis from politics to economics" have occurred. The party has gained the confidence and support of the civil service, and encourages the outlook of the technocrat and manager, rather than that of the politician or journalist.

Labor peace is seen as especially important, as a compliant and undisputatious work force is attractive to foreign investors. To assure this, the Employment Act and the Industrial Relations (Amendment) Act were passed in 1968 to restrict trade union activity, prevent strikes, and increase productivity. Labor-management disputes have to be handled through the arbitration courts of the Ministry of Labor. Unions are organized into a federation, the National Trade Unions Congress, which is under the firm control of the PAP. Independent or leftist trade unions have been suppressed, especially those associated with the *Barisan Sosialis.*

The government has initiated tight curbs on dissent in the face of what PAP leaders see as the threat of foreign or communist subversion. A special police, the Internal Security Department, has broad powers of arrest and detention, and publications can be banned if they are judged not to be in the "public interest." The government has been intolerant of even mild criticism from journalists. Prime Minister Lee's attitude toward the press is neatly summed up in a statement he made to the *Straits Times* in 1972: "Every morning, my task begins with reading five, four, now, newspapers. I note the scurrilous and the scandalous. I can live with that. But when any newspaper pours out a daily dose of language, cultural or religious poison, I put my knuckledusters on."

Students at Singapore's colleges and universities, once rather active politically, have been tamed after *Barisan Sosialis*–inspired student movements were broken up in the late 1960s. At present, students are required to hold "suitability certificates" before being allowed to enter college, and, as a result, most steer clear of political issues. However, in 1976 there was an activist student union at the University of Singapore which was subsequently banned. Overall, a fear of subversion, not entirely unjustified, has led to a kind of "fortress Singapore" mentality. Criticism of the PAP's attitude toward individual rights by European socialists led to its withdrawal from the Socialist International in 1976.

Complementing tight government controls is a puritanical emphasis on individual self-sacrifice and the building of a "rugged society," a constant theme in PAP pronouncements. Party leaders are especially explicit in their rejection of individual-centered Western social mores. Singapore's leaders have hit upon a theme that is familiar in the histories of China, Japan, Korea, and other Asian nations: the combination of "Western technology" with "Eastern ethics." Whether a Confucian-inspired moralism can survive the distractions of Singapore's new affluence, however, is difficult to say.

Ethnicity is one of the most delicate issues faced by the PAP-led government. The region is one of great cultural, linguistic, and religious heterogeneity. Not only are there Chinese, Malay, and Indian groups, but these are further subdivided so that among Chinese there are Hokkien, Teochew, Cantonese, Hakka, and other dialect and regional groups; among Malays, those from Sumatra, the Celebes, Java, and the Malay Peninsula, although their common Islamic faith gives them a great degree of unity; and among Indians, those from Pakistan, South India, and Sri Lanka, who may be Muslim, Hindu, or Christian. Hostility between these groups has been intense in the past, and Malays have especially resented the Chinese for their dominance of the economy. The PAP has committed itself to being a multiracial party and to building a "Singapore consciousness" that would transcend old ethnic divisions. It has been careful to respect ethnic sensitivities, as is seen in the establishment of the Presidential Council on Minority Rights and the Muslim Shari'ah Court. The issue of Malay rights is especially salient since the government does not wish to see Singapore depicted as a Chinese-dominated island in the middle of a "sea" of over 150 million Malays. On the other hand, the government has attempted to integrate the different groups into a common national life. Thus, a universal national-service obligation was established in 1967, not only to provide manpower for the republic's armed forces, but to give young men from different ethnic groups the experience of working together. Old, racially segregated communities, such as the Malay *kampongs* and "Chinatowns" have been torn down and replaced with ethnically integrated high-rise apartment complexes. The government has been zealous in suppressing overt expressions of ethnic chauvinism. In 1970, a Malay-language newspaper was closed, and the following year four staff members of one of the largest Chinese-language newspapers were arrested for publishing articles which allegedly stirred up racial passions. In 1980, Nanyang University, which had been founded as an institution for overseas Chinese from all parts of southeast Asia in 1956, was absorbed into the University of Singapore in order to form a new National University of Singapore. This action was taken in part because Nanyang was seen as a stronghold of Chinese chauvinism and opposition to the PAP's multiracial policies.

Singapore has four official languages: Chinese, Malay, Tamil, and English. The government hopes to make all citizens bilingual, and Chinese have been strongly encouraged to use Mandarin Chinese rather than their native South Chinese regional dialects not only at school and work, but also in the home. In schools, English, seen as an international language and the key to employment in the high-paying modern sector, has rapidly become the chief medium of instruction. Persons educated in Malay- or Chinese-language schools are left at a comparative disadvantage. The relatively disadvantaged status of the Malay population as a group remains one of the government's most difficult problems.

In recent years, Prime Minister Lee has expressed concern that the quality of Singapore's gene pool (and thus, supposedly, the quality of its future citizens) was declining because educated women were having fewer children and poor, uneducated women, more. He has made highly controversial statements that eugenic policies are necessary to preserve the country's vitality. In 1984, measures were introduced that give places in the most desirable primary schools to the children of educated mothers who have more than two children, and cash stipends to low-income, non-graduate mothers who agree to undergo sterilization.

Singapore is a member of the United Nations, the British Commonwealth of Nations, and the Association of South East Asian Nations (ASEAN), of which it is a strong supporter. Foreign policy is dominated by the need to maintain friendly relations with trading partners and the desire to encourage more foreign investment. The republic's ethnic composition makes relations with Indonesia, Malaysia, and the People's Republic of China particularly delicate. The government has stated that relations with the last would not be established until it was sure that Chinese Singaporeans were fully loyal to Singapore rather than China. Relations with the United States and the Soviet Union are based on the principle of nonalignment .

Membership & Constituency

The People's Action Party is not a mass party. Its membership was estimated at around 43,000 in 1971, and there does not seem to have been a great concern to increase that number. Most members are of Chinese origin, reflecting the composition of the population, and they come from the lower as well as middle classes. One observer states that a number of poor and unemployed persons have joined the party in order to obtain influence and financial security. Union workers are still an important component of the party's membership. There are actually two kinds of PAP members: regular members and an elite core of several hundred cadre members; the latter category is considered especially reliable and plays an important role in maintaining intraparty discipline and organization. One commentator has called the PAP "almost a secret society," because no list of elite cadres has been made public, although it is known that they are active in branch activities and that some are invited to attend meetings of the Central Executive Committee (CEC).

Financing

Party branches are expected to be financially self-sufficient; they raise much of their revenue through the operation of kindergartens. Other sources of funds include the holding of commemorative dinners and the sale of publications. The PAP as a whole is supposed to be supported by the annual dues paid by members, but these are small. Larger monthly contributions are made by members of Parliament and cabinet ministers, which are collected by the CEC. Contributions are given by private individuals and groups, especially during election years, but details on these are scant. The need for political contributions is perhaps less than in other political systems since the PAP has at its disposal the resources of the government, including state-owned television and radio stations, with which to press its point of view.

Leadership

The most important party leader and political figure in Singapore is the tough and outspoken Lee Kuan Yew, born in 1923. He, along with Toh Chin Chye, born in 1921, and Goh Keng Swee, born in 1918, is of Chinese descent. The most important non-Chinese leaders have included Sinnathamby Rajaratnam, born in Sri Lanka in 1915, and Edmund W. Barker, born in 1920. All were educated at the elite Raffles College in Singapore, and studied at various universities in Britain. The leadership is close and coherent, and observers have not detected serious rifts in it.

Since 1980, Prime Minister Lee has been concerned with promoting the emergence of a new generation of political leaders. In 1984, he announced his decision to retire in 1988. Observers believed he would be succeeded as prime minister by a member of the new generation, Goh Chok Tong (in 1985, first deputy prime minister and minister of defense).

Prospects

Overall, the people have supported PAP rule. The sharp, 12.6 percent, decline in its share of the vote in December 1984 and in the election of two opposition legislators, however, may signal the beginning of a new stage in Singapore politics, one in which the PAP government and its policies will be more seriously challenged. The near future may see the appearance of genuine parliamentary politics, if the ruling party is willing to give up its monopoly and tolerate a new pluralism.

Opposition Parties

The Workers' Party

The Workers' Party , established in 1957 as a noncommunist, leftist group, has advocated greater freedom for labor unions, stronger safeguards against government infringement of personal liberties, the abolition of "suitability certificates" for university students, and the loosening of restraints on the press, including abolition of the annual press-license system. The party, led by J. B. Jeyaretnam since 1971, appealed at first only to a small following of intellectuals; but it made history in an October 31, 1981 by-election, when Jeyaretnam defeated a PAP candidate in the low-income electoral district of Anson to become the first opposition member of Parliament in Singapore's history. The party put up a total of fifteen candidates in the 1984 general election, but only Jeyaretnam was elected, returned by his Anson constituency.

Singapore Democratic Party

The Singapore Democratic Party put up four candidates in the 1984 election; Chiam See Tong, the party leader, won a parliamentary seat.

Malay National Organization of Singapore (*Persatuan Kebangsaan Melayu Singapura;* PEKEMAS)

Originally the Singapore branch of the United Malay National Organization of Malaysia, PEKEMAS sees itself as the spokesman for the republic's Malays. Its strength was allegedly weakened in 1967 by the redrawing of electoral boundaries in which Malay districts were combined with areas containing non-Malay majorities. Many critics accused the government of gerrymandering. Its support has also been undermined by many younger Malays, who for reasons of career advancement have preferred to join the PAP. In recent years, PEKEMAS has functioned more as a social, cultural, or charitable organization than a political party, sponsoring kindergartens for Malay children, mosque building, Koran competitions, lectures on Islam, and the maintenance of Malay gravesites. It ran one candidate in the December 1984 election.

Socialist Front (*Barisan Sosialis*)

After the party schism in 1961, *Barisan Sosialis* was the bitterest rival of the People's Action Party. Until "Operation Cold Storage," conducted in 1963 by the Internal Security Department, put many of its most important leaders in jail, it was a serious threat to PAP rule. In 1966, *Barisan* members resigned from Parliament and embarked on a strategy of "street democracy," which included occasional bombings and acts of arson. The strategy proved to be a fatal mistake, losing the party most of its popular support. Arrests continued and pro-*Barisan* unions, with minor exceptions, were decertified. By the mid-1970s, the party had only a few thousand members. It ran four unsuccessful candidates in the 1984 election.

Other Parties

Other parties which participated in the 1984 general election but failed to win parliamentary seats were: the Singapore United Front, which ran thirteen candidates; the United People's Front, which ran eight; the Singapore Justice Party, which ran two; and the Angkatan Islam (Islamic Movement) which ran one. There were also three independent candidates.

National Prospects

Despite early predictions that Singapore could not survive economically outside of union with Malaysia, the republic, in the years since 1965, has done remarkably well in terms of both social and economic development. Its people enjoy a per capita income second only to that of Japan in Asia. Standards of health, education, and other social services are high. Singapore has become a major center for trade, manufacturing, and finance, not only on a regional, but also on a world scale. The PAP can take much credit for this progress, having provided a stable environment for foreign investment and taking an active role in promoting economic expansion.

Problems remain in the area of national integration, but, in the words of Prime Minister Lee, speaking in 1980, "we are becoming one people much sooner than I had dared to hope." In the view of the leadership, the most pressing problem in the future is nurturing a new generation of able and dedicated citizens and statesmen. Recent electoral results raise two questions, however: is the PAP losing touch with the voters, and is a new era of genuine opposition politics beginning?

Further Reading
Asia Yearbook. Hong Kong: Far Eastern Economic Review, Ltd. Published annually.

Bedlington, Stanley S. *Malaysia and Singapore: The Building of New States*. Ithaca, N. Y.: Cornell University Press, 1978.

Chan Heng Chee. *The Dynamics of One Party Dominance: The PAP at the Grassroots*. Singapore: Singapore University Press, 1976.

Quah, Jon S. T. "Singapore in 1984: Leadership Transition in an Election Year." *Asian Survey*, Vol. XXV, No. 2, February 1985.

———. "Singapore in 1983: the Continuing Search for Talent." *Asian Survey*, Vol. XXIV, No. 2, February 1984.

Republic of Singapore. *Singapore '80*. Singapore: Ministry of Culture, Information Division, 1980.

Seah Chee-Meow, ed. *Trends in Singapore*. Singapore: Singapore University Press, 1975.

Turnbull, C. M. *A History of Singapore 1819–1975*. Kuala Lumpur and London: Oxford University Press, 1977.

Vreeland, Nina, ed. *Area Handbook for Singapore*. Washington, D.C.: U.S. Government Printing Office, 1977.

SOMALI DEMOCRATIC REPUBLIC
(Al-Sumhouriya Soomaaliya Al-Democradia)
by Sally Healy, M.Sc. revised by Mark DeLancey, Ph.D.

The System of Government

The Somali Democratic Republic, a nation of 3.7 million people on Africa's east coast, is a one-party socialist state formed by the unification of the British Somaliland Protectorate and the United Nations Trust Territory of Somalia at independence in 1960. It was known as the Somali Republic until 1969. The political system does not conform to one particular model but is officially said to be evolving towards "democratic centralism" similar to that of the Soviet Union. At present the system is an amalgam retaining features of its authoritarian origins combined with a party organization formed in 1976, the addition of a constitution adopted in 1979, and an elected assembly dating from 1980.

The present regime came to power in a bloodless coup on October 21, 1969, under the leadership of the head of the armed forces, General Mohammed Siad Barre. The previous multiparty parliamentary system was abolished. For the next seven years Siad Barre ruled at the head of a twenty-five–man Supreme Revolutionary Council (SRC), consisting largely of military men, with the assistance of a civilian council of advisers. The SRC was dissolved in July 1976, but all its members retained positions of influence on the Central Committee of the newly formed Somali Socialist Revolutionary Party (SSRP) of which Siad Barre became the secretary-general. The party devised a new constitution which was approved by referendum in July 1979. This made provision for a representative assembly which was duly elected in December. The People's Assembly held its first session at the beginning of 1980. Later that year, Siad Barre declared a state of emergency and reinstated the SRC (reduced to seventeen men) to function directly under his instructions and with a full mandate to govern. In April 1981, ten members of the SRC were dismissed, but most of them were reinstated in the new government formed in March 1982 when the state of emergency was lifted and the country formally returned to constitutional rule.

Executive

President Siad Barre is the head of state and personally holds all the key positions in the formal political system in his capacity as secretary-general of the SSRP, chairman of its Central Committee and Political Bureau, president of the Council of Ministers in the People's Assembly, head of the SRC, and head of the armed forces. (He is publicized as the father of the nation of which the revolution, which he instituted, is the mother.) He appoints his own close associates, who have remained remarkably consistent during the twelve years of his rule, although some were dismissed from the SRC in 1981. At the opening session of the new People's Assembly in January 1980, he was acclaimed president for a further six-year term. Constitutionally, the president is elected by direct universal suffrage for a seven-year term. Any successor to President Barre would be chosen by national referendum. The Central Committee of the SSRP has the power to remove him from office. The president may appoint a prime minister, although Siad Barre has not chosen to do so. He selected the first Council of Ministers from the People's Assembly in February 1980.

Article 83 of the constitution gives the president extraordinary powers "to declare a state of emergency . . . and to take appropriate measures whenever he is confronted with grave matters endangering the soverreignty and the internal and external security of the country." It is on this basis that President Siad Barre ruled by decree from October 1980 until March 1982.

Legislature

The People's Assembly consists of 171 elected and six appointed members. Seventy-four are members of the Central Committee of the SSRP and the remainder were nominated by the party to stand for election in the districts of the country. The first election took place on December 31, 1979. Voters were not presented with a choice of candidates but were asked to endorse or reject the official party candidate. The result of this election was 3,982,532 approving votes, 1,826 negative ones, and 1,480 spoiled ballots. This result must be viewed with some caution since the total exceeds the most recent estimates of the total Somali population (3.7 million in 1978). While these figures are open to question—such a turnout is astonishing in an electorate which is still about 70 percent nomadic—it is probably fair to say that in the absence of any organized opposition and with the encouragement of party officials most voters did endorse the party candidate.

According to the constitution, all legislative power is vested in the People's Assembly. The deputies have a five-year term of office and hold two sessions a year. The Assembly may be dissolved either with the approval of a two-thirds majority or by the president, but in either case new elections must be held within three months. The restoration of the SRC ten months after the installation of the People's Assembly and the return to rule by decree suggests that the Assembly proved to be not entirely compliant with Siad Barre's wishes.

Judiciary

A Higher Judicial Council is responsible for the direction of the policies and the general administration of the judiciary, including the appointment of the attorney general and the judges. The president is, ex officio, president of this council. The courts are constituted as follows: the Supreme Court, courts of appeal, regional courts, district courts, judicial committees at places of work, and tribunals of the armed forces. The judiciary constitutes a single unit and has a insignificant role in the political process.

Regional & Local Government

Until 1972 the Somali Democratic Republic was divided into eight provinces which bore some relation to the clan divisions of the Somali people. One of the earliest reforms of the revolutionary government was to reorganize the country into fifteen regions, comprising seventy-eight districts, in an effort to discourage the persistence of clan identification. Until the formation of the SSRP, regional and district administration was controlled by local councils, frequently headed by military officers, in imitation of the SRC which governed nationally. After 1976, the regional governors became, ex officio, regional party secretaries (likewise the district governors) and continued the work of local government with the assistance of a first secretary for party affairs and a second assistant for administrative affairs. Locally elected councils are intended to advise the regional rulers, but have not yet been established everywhere. Local elders, renamed "Peace Seekers" (Nabaddoon) since the revolution, act as intermediaries between the officials and the people. Local government is supervised by a Regional Inspectorate which reports directly to the president. Additional supervision is carried out by local branches of the National Security Service.

The Electoral System

Article 61 of the constitution provides that "the People's Assembly shall consist of Deputies elected by the people by free, direct and secret ballot." Voting is open to men and women over eighteen years of age, but registration procedures used in the last election have not been made clear. Although the nomadic lifestyle of the great majority of Somalis poses difficulties in organizing elections, a high level of interest was shown in the elections which took place in 1964 and 1969—1,002 candidates competed for 123 seats in 1969. The mobility of the society is combined with a high degree of communication, which is helped by a common language. In the December 1984 elections a turnout of 99.8 percent of eligible voters was reported. Of these, 99.91 percent voted in favor of the SSRP candidates.

Somali Socialist Revolutionary Party (SSRP)

The constitutional position of the SSRP is unassailable. Article 7 prohibits the formation of any other party and gives the SSRP "supreme authority over the leadership of the political, economic and social affairs of the Somali Democratic Republic." Article 8 states: "The country's leadership shall be based on the unified political leadership of the Party and the State."

History

The SSRP was formed in July 1976, possibly as a result of pressure from and certainly with the active assistance of the Soviet Union, which exercised considerable influence in Somalia at that time. The party served to legitimize the military regime of Siad Barre and to ensure the continuation of his revolutionary policies. The initial party congress was attended by 3,000 people selected by the National Political Bureau of the outgoing SRC for the active role they played in the implementation of the Somali Revolution.

It must be stressed that the regime had not confined its activities to the capital city. Great efforts had been made to spread the message of the revolution, notably through the creation of orientation centers in all the towns, set up by the Ministry of Information and National Guidance. An ambitious literacy campaign to teach the writing of the newly adopted Somali script and a Rural Development Campaign which turned into a massive drought-relief operation were important events of 1972 to 1975. A people's militia known as the Victory Pioneers (*Gullwadayall*) was formed to organize and participate in local self-help projects such as building and road construction. The leaders of these activities were appointed by Siad Barre and included many military officers. It was they, together with the Victory Pioneers, who formed the nucleus of the new party.

Organization

The party largely took over the countrywide organization created by the president. The leadership of the party also remained in the hands of the previous rulers. All the members of the SRC and its civilian advisers found places on the Central Committee (with one exception), and the Political Bureau of the party consisted of Siad Barre, his three vice presidents from the SRC, and the head of the National Security Service. The party did provide a somewhat enlarged setting for the continuation of the Siad regime, but in 1981 it was decided on the advice of the SRC to postpone the annual party congress, scheduled for July, for one year.

Policy

Party policy is to implement the Somali revolution, the principles of which are enunciated by Siad Barre. The main thread of this philosophy is the achievement of socialism (literally "wealth sharing through knowledge" in Somali) through mass education and collectivization of production. The goal of "scientific socialism" dropped the scientific quality after the demise of Soviet influence in 1977. A certain amount of nationalization took place after the coup, and private enterprise and private property were discouraged rather than abolished. Under pressure from the United States government and because of poor economic performance, the Somali government has begun again to encourage private entrepreneurship and the profit motive.

The foreign policy of party and state, outlined in the constitution, includes adherence to the general principles of cooperation between nations, nonalignment, and respect for international law. Special reference is made to the principle of self-determination, which holds particular relevance to the Somalis. It has been a long-standing wish of Somalia to unite all Somali people within one state.

This claim has inevitably created tension with neighboring Kenya and Ethiopia, which both contain Somali-inhabited regions. The problem has been most acute with Ethiopia, which the Somali government considers to be in colonial occupation of the Ogaden. Somalia committed its armed forces to the Ogaden War (1977–78) to wrest this territory from Ethiopian control. The attempt was unsuccessful, but Article 16 of the new constitution reaffirms the government's commitment to "the liberation of Somali territories still under colonial occupation" by "legal and peaceful means." The country now relies on close economic and military relations with the United States while retaining its previous close ties to Italy and Saudi Arabia.

Membership

Party membership has been open to any Somali recommended by two party members. By 1977, membership had risen to 12,000. The great majority of these are classed as "workers and employees" and about 5 percent as "peasants." Women's and youth organizations created in the early years of the revolution have been grafted onto the party organization. The party produces a monthly journal called *Halgan*.

Financing

There is no information on party funding, but the party's "complementary role" clearly suggests that it is funded by state revenues.

Leadership

Siad Barre (born 1919) appears to be in firm control of all elements of the party and government. It would be fair to say that the second most powerful man in Somali politics is Brigadier General Ahmed Sulieman Abdullah, who is Siad's son-in-law, was head of the National Security Service for many years, and is now Minister of Planning. If Siad were to disappear from the scene without any other changes, Abdullah would probably replace him. If Siad were to be removed through political action, the support of the army would be essential. The minister of defense is General Mohammed Ali Samater, who has no clan backing and is generally viewed as being completely loyal to Siad Barre. Some rumors suggest Samater as the most likely successor to President Barre. Umar Haji Masseleh, once seen as a possible successor, was removed from his post as head of the armed forces and has been under house arrest since mid-1982, in spite of the fact that he is a close clansman of the president.

Opposition

Both opposition parties are Islamic in character, favor a return to neutralism in international affairs, and criticize Siad Barre for his participation in the Ogaden war and his management of the economy. Above all they object to his personalistic rule and his exclusive dependence on his own kinsmen in the government of the country. Both parties are in exile. The SNM is in a better position to influence events inside the country, but either party could become significant in the event of Siad Barre losing control of the state. A third group,

the Somali Patriotic Front, is reported to exist in Aden.

Democratic Front For the Salvation of Somalia (DFSS)

The DFSS was formed in October 1981 and is an amalgamation of three leftist opposition movements of which the Somali Salvation Front (SOSAF) was much the most important. The party is based in Addis Ababa, from where it beams hostile radio broadcasts into the Republic. SOSAF was formed in 1978 following an unsuccessful coup attempted which was attributed by the president to the Mijjertayn clan. The core of its supporters are members of that clan, but it has attracted various other Somalis in voluntary exile in Ethiopia. It has the backing of the Ethiopian government and financial support from the Soviet Union. Libya has discontinued its support of Somali dissident groups since the opening of friendly relations between the two states. It was responsible for a series of bomb explosions in the capital, Mogadishu, in the early part of 1981. The DFSS has stepped up its military activities and in 1981 and 1982 has claimed responsibility for several attacks on military installations on the Ethiopian borders, although the Somali government has attributed these to Ethiopian armed forces. The Party's first congress, held in March 1983, established a constitution, a 21-member central committee, and a nine-member executive council. Reports in May 1984 indicated that the DFSS was involved in a power struggle, but that it continued to exist. Its current chairman is Colonel Abdullahi Yusuf Ahmed.

Somali National Movement (SNM)

This is a newly formed (1981) party based in London. Its core members are members of the Ishaaq clan, but it attracts supporters from dissidents from the northern (ex-British) part of the country. The SNM receives support from Ethiopia. The Party publishes a newspaper, *Al-Moujahid*, in English, Arabic, and Somali. Party chairmanship is variously reported to be held by Ahmed Silanyo and Yusuf Ali Madar. The SNM appears to have been increasing its strength in the northern portions of the country where discontent with the Mogadishu government is very strong. Reports of territorial gains by the SNM, though difficult to confirm, appear frequently.

Other Political Forces

Ethnic Groups

The Somali people constitute one ethnic group and share a common language, culture, and history. There is, however, a problem of "tribalism" which has been opposed in principle by civilian governments and repeatedly denounced (as well as officially abolished) by the present regime. Particularism in Somalia takes the form of affiliation to the clan groupings of the traditional Somali social structure, based on kinship. There are six clan families: Darod (of which the Mijjertayn are a part), Dir, Ishaaq, Hawiye, Digil, and Rahanweyn; each clan is divided into several subsidiary clans quite capable of opposing one another and forming alliances with other clans. This capacity for flexible, cross-cutting alliances underlies the overall unity of the Somali people, but when effective political power is limited to members of only a few clans, the consequences of alienating the others can be severe. While all Somali governments have contained representatives of each of the clan families, President Siad Barre has been accused of allocating key positions to members of three Darod clans—his own (Marehan), and those of his mother (Ogaden) and his son-in-law (Dolbahante). Somalis from the Marehan clan make up the greater part of the president's personal bodyguard; Dolbahante are associated with the National Security Service, which was headed by his son-in-law, Brigadier General Ahmed Sulieman Abdullah, until April 1981. Siad Barre's connections with the Ogaden have been blamed in part for the involvement in the Ogaden war, with disastrous consequences for most Somalis. Both the parties in exile have a recognizable clan base, but this would not preclude their acceptance by other Somalis opposed to Siad Barre.

Religious Groups

Virtually all Somalis are Moslems, and Islam is enshrined in the constitution as the religion of the state. While religious leaders have not yet taken a prominent part in politics, they do continue to enjoy the respect of a deeply religious people. It is inconceivable that any ruler could reject Islam. President Barre stresses the importance of Islam and has often emphasized the compatibility of Islam with his own brand of socialism, at times invoking Koranic authority for his utterances. However, Siad Barre did deal firmly with opposition from religious leaders in 1975 when he ordered the execution of ten shaikhs who preached against the acceptance of a new law which gave women the same inheritance rights as men.

National Prospects

Respect for Islam and attempts to overcome remnants of the divisive clan system will be enduring features of any Somali political system in the future. Whether the present political system could survive the disappearance of its founder would depend on the circumstances of his removal from office. All existing institutions are of his creation, and the fact that he has found it necessary to override these structures within a year of their inception has prevented them from taking any firm root and suggests a high level of discontent with them. It is difficult to conceive of his removal from power by constitutional means, but since he has already survived defeat in war, his capacity to remain in control should not be underestimated.

Further Reading
Davidson, B. "Somalia: Towards Socialism." *Race and Class* Vol. 17, No. 1, 1975.
Decraene, Philipe. *L'expérience socialiste somalienne.* Paris: Berger-Levrault, 1977.
Hoben, Allen. *Somalia: A Social and Institutional Profile.* Boston: African Studies Center, Boston University, 1983.
International Labor Organization. *Economic Transformation in a Socialist Framework: Somalia.* Addis Ababa: ILO, 1977.
Laitin, David D. *Politics, Language, and Thought: The Somali Experience.* Chicago: University of Chicago Press, 1977.
——————, and Said S. Samitar. *Somalia: A Nation in Search of a State.* Boulder, Colorado: Westview Press, 1985.
Lewis, I. M. *A Modern History of Somalia.* (Rev. ed.). London: Longman, 1980.
——————, and Kim Il Sung. "The End of Tribalism in Somalia?" In *Politics in Leadership*, Percy S. Cohen and William A. Shack, eds. Oxford: Clarendon Press, 1979; and New York; Oxford University Press, 1979.
——————, ed. *Nationalism and Self-determination in the Horn of Africa.* London: Ithaca Press, 1983.

REPUBLIC OF SOUTH AFRICA
(Republiek van Suid-Afrika)
by B. David Meyers, Ph.D.

The System of Government

On September 14, 1984, Pieter Botha became the last prime minister of South Africa's First Republic and the first executive state president of its Second Republic. South Africa's version of Westminster-style parliamentary government, which had existed since the formation of the then Union of South Africa in 1910, was replaced by an executive president over a unique, racially determined tricameral legislature. Persons of Indian and couloured (mixed racial) descent could now participate in national politics, previously the exclusive domain of the white population. The state president called *apartheid* (a policy of white supremacy legitimized as separate development and the centerpiece of internal politics since 1948) an "outdated" concept and promised reforms guaranteeing citizenship and, as yet undefined, political rights to the black majority. From some perspectives, South Africa experienced institutional change unequaled since 1910 and an unparalleled rethinking of the basic tenets of its racial policy.

To others, including South Africa's black majority and many foreign observers, the change was less dramatic. The constitutional revision had been determined by a bill drafted and passed in a whites-only House of Assembly and approved solely by white voters in a November 1983 national referendum. The political system remains dominated by the white minority, particularly the Afrikaans-speakers organized in the National Party, which has held power continually since 1948. Blacks remain barred from the national political arena, and government statements of planned reforms have explicitly excluded majority (i.e., black) rule.

The contitutional transition has been accompanied by increased and often violent expression of dissatisfaction throughout many parts of the country since summer 1984. Estimates of violent deaths during the eighteen months end-ing in December 1985 range from 670 to upwards of 1,000. Under a State of Emergency proclaimed in 1985, over 8,000 people have been arrested and held without trial. Despite the lifting of the emergency, similar violence and harsh official responses continued during 1986.

Underlying most South African political issues is the racial diversity of its population and the continued disenfranchisement of the majority of its population. In 1985, South Africa had a population of 32.5 million people. The politically dominant whites number 4.8 million or 15 percent of the total population. This white minority consists of 2.9 million Afrikaans-speakers (a unique cultural group descended from sixteenth-century Dutch settlers) and 1.9 million people of English descent. There is also a total of 2.8 million coloureds (8.6 percent of the national population) and 890,000 Asians (2.7 percent), most of whom are Hindu Indians. The vast majority of the population consists of 24 million blacks (73.8 percent), all of whom have been denied participation in the nation's political process. The blacks are primarily Zulu and Xhosa tribesmen (about 6 million members each). Of equal political importance are the residence divisions within the black population: approximately 5.8 million live in four nominally "independent" tribal-based homelands, 7.2 million in "self-governing" homelands and 11 million in the areas of the country legally reserved for white ownership.

Executive

From 1910 until 1984, South Africa had been a parliamentary political system with a ceremonial head of state. Until 1961, it was a constitutional monarchy with the Queen of England as its nominal head. When it changed to a republic, the former monarch was replaced by a president who possessed equally few discretionary powers. Real power was located in the executive council of the all-white House of Assembly. The prime minister and cabinet members were all members of the Assembly's majority party (since 1949, the National Party). Because he was leader of the majority party, head of government, and, in effect, the leader of the Afrikaner nation, the prime minister was able to exercise great power. Under the new constitution essentially these same powers are now given to the state president who is the ceremonial head of state, the chief executive officer, and the dominant legislator.

The state president is elected for a five-year term by majority vote of an electoral college comprising eighty-eight members of the legislature. Of this number, fifty individuals are chosen from the majority (i.e., National) party in the all-white Assembly; twenty-five from the majority in the coloured's House of Representatives; and thirteen from the majority in the Indian's House of Delegates. This method of selection assures that the president will be white and, for the foreseeable future, the National Party's leader.

Basic throughout the constitution is the distinction drawn between each racial group's own affairs and general (common) affairs. A group's own affairs are those matters which specifically or differentially affect the maintenance of its identity and furtherance of its way of life (e.g., education, community development, and local government). Matters which are not a group's own affairs are general affairs. Any question arising as to whether matters are own or general affairs is decided by the state president.

Executive authority is designated to the state president, a cabinet, and three (white, coloured, and Indian) minister's councils. The cabinet is appointed by the state president from all three population groups that are represented in Parliament. For the first time in South Africa's history, the cabinet that was appointed in September 1984 included two non-white members. In keeping with recent practice, it also included one English National Party Member. The cabinet exercises executive authority in consultation with the president on matters of general interest such as constitutional development, defense, finance, and foreign affairs. The president also appoints the chairman and members of the three ministers' councils from members of the majority party in each house. The ministers' councils have executive power over their own affairs, such as education and housing. The designation of executive departments into government ministries is also the president's prerogative.

There is also a president's council that advises the executive on matters of public interest. The council also arbitrates legislative deadlocks that occur when the different houses pass differing versions of the same bill, or when one or two houses pass a bill rejected by the other house or houses. Of the sixty members who make this final judgement, fifteen are appointed by the president and another twenty are selected by the majority (i.e., National) party in the white House of Assembly. Of the remaining members, ten are chosen by the majority in the House of Representatives, five by the majority of the House of Delegates, and ten proposed by the opposition in the three houses. There have been discussions of adding black members to the council in the future.

Legislature

Until 1984, legislative power rested with a unicameral Parliament (a Senate having been abolished in 1980), which was made up exclusively of white members chosen by a white electorate. Under the new constitution, legislative authority is vested in the state president and a tricameral Parliament with separate houses for whites, coloureds, and Asians.

The House of Assembly (whites) comprises 178 members: 166 are directly elected, four (one representing each province) are nominated by the president, and eight are chosen by the directly elected members. The House of Representatives (coloureds) comprises eighty-five members: eighty are directly elected, two nominated by the president, and three chosen by the elected members. The House of Delegates (Indians) is composed of forty-five members, of whom forty are directly elected, two nominated by the president, and three chosen by the elected members.

Each house is solely responsible for legislation affecting only the affairs of that specific population group. Legislation on general or national affairs must be passed by majority vote in all three houses. In dealing with either type of legislation, the president can withhold his assent only if the act was not passed in accordance with constitutional procedures. This veto authority could be important if there are conflicting claims of chamber jurisdiction.

Parliamentary joint standing committees, comprising members of all three houses, including members of opposition parties, try to achieve consensus on legislation. The president

South African Parliament: Party Strength, 1985	
House of Assembly (white) 178 members (12 indirectly elected)	
Parties	Seats
National Party	126 (10 indirectly elected)
Progressive Federal Party	27 (1 indirectly elected)
Conservative Party	18 (1 indirectly elected)
New Republic Party	5
Reconstituted National Party	1
vacant	1
House of Representatives (coloured) 85 members (5 indirectly elected)	
Parties	Seats
Labour Party	81 (5 indirectly elected)
People's Congress Party	3
vacant	1
House of Delegates (Indian) 45 members (5 indirectly elected)	
Parties	Seats
National People's Party	23 (4 indirectly elected)
Solidarity	21 (1 indirectly elected)
Progressive Independent Party	1

may also seek solution to disputes in deliberations with the cabinet or the ministers' councils. The president has the power to refer any point of difference or dispute to the president's council for a final ruling.

The political parties are disciplined and individual members of Parliament's legislative role is largely predetermined by party directive.

Judiciary

Judicial authority is vested in a national system made up of an Appellate Division (the supreme court) and several provisions and local divisional courts. Appellate Division judges are appointed by the state president and can only be removed for misbehavior or incapacity. They do not have the power of judicial review of acts of Parliament. There are also over 300 local magistrate's courts and specialized tribunals to hear cases involving riparian rights, tax appeals, and child neglect.

In both civil and criminal matters, blacks are generally subject to the ordinary laws and courts. Some civil matters which arise from traditional indigenous law are heard in courts of chiefs and headmen.

The administration of justice is under the control of the minister of justice. Parliament is not legally restrained from infringing on individual rights and liberties. Civil liberties, such as protection from detention without trial or search without warrant, are severely circumscribed or nonexistent. South African police are tacitly immune from prosecution for any actions taken "in good faith" to terminate internal disorder. The exercise of such police powers often contributes to further disorders and further alienation from the government.

Within the limits of the legal system, the higher court judges have often served as a bulwark against arbitrary or unwise use of executive power. In 1982, the supreme court disallowed a government agreement to transfer the NaNgwame homeland and part of the KwaZulu homeland to Swaziland, and thus remove a large black population from South Africa. During 1985, the higher courts substantially reduced bail restrictions on Rev. Allan Boesak, thus allowing him to resume leadership in the campaign against government policies. The court also granted Wendy Orr, a district prisons doctor, an injunction preventing police from assaulting detainees.

Regional and Local Government

South Africa comprises four provinces: Cape Province, Natal, Orange Free State, and Transvaal. These were separate British colonies before 1910 and the latter two were independent Afrikaner republics until 1902. The South African Act joined the four in what was essentially a unitary political system with a few concessions to provincial interests. Although power increasingly moved toward the national level, the provincial governments retained authority to levy taxes and to legislate on provincial and local issues as long as such legislation was not contraindicatory to that passed by Parliament.

The new constitution includes little mention of the provinces whose future courses of development will be clarified later. Provincial executive authority will consist of an administrator and an executive committee appointed by the state president and responsible to Parliament.

It is expected that there will be some devolution of power from the provincial to local level authorities.

At the local level, elected authorities legislate and administer their own racial group's affairs, while those issues that affect more than one ethnic community are handled by regional services councils, which include representatives of all races. Since November 1983, there have been elected mayors and councils in the black townships outside of the tribal homelands. For the first time in South Africa's history, within the regional services councils, elected blacks met with representatives of the other racial communities to make decisions about matters of local mutual concern.

The Homelands

Since coming into power in 1948, the National Party government has promulgated the doctrine that the black population is composed of ten distinct tribal nations. It has created ten "homelands" where each tribal nation is to exercise its own political rights. The Bantu Homelands Citizen Act of 1970 provided that every black would not be a citizen of South Africa but rather—regardless of actual place of residence—of his tribe's national state. The Bantu Homelands Constitution Act of 1971 empowers the government to grant independence to any national state.

Transkei (a Xhosa tribal homeland) was declared independent in 1976. This was followed by Bophuthatswana in 1977, Venda in 1979, and Ciskei in 1981. South Africa has been unable to convince any other country of the validity of this "independence." No nation—other than South Africa and each independent homeland in relation to the others— has recognized these states. Opponents, both within and outside of South Africa, consider this "independence" a scheme to deprive blacks—approximately half of whom do not reside in the homelands—of South African citizenship and further to relieve the South African government of welfare obligations while continuing to reap the benefits of abundant black labor. Among the most outspoken opponents have been South African white businessmen who believe that the policy has clearly proven itself an economic failure.

Although a sixth homeland (KwaNdebele) is scheduled for independence in December 1986, the future of the homelands policy is uncertain.

Chief Gatsha Buthelezi, Chief Minister of KwaZulu, and at least two other homeland leaders have stated that they will not accept independence for their territories, and the government has agreed that independence would be a matter of their own free choice. Chief Buthelezi has recommended that the KwaZulu government and the Natal provincial government establish cooperative institutions to govern the combined area; the South African government has had no objection in principle to this suggestion. The political future of persons currently residing in independent homeland states is also uncertain. President Botha has suggested that South African citizenship is no longer necessarily lost to those who accepted independence.

The Electoral System

The 1984 constitution greatly expanded an electorate which had, since 1960, excluded all nonwhites. This exclusion had been a gradual process. At South Africa's establishment in 1910, nonwhites were completely barred from the Orange Free State and Transvaal. There were approximately 23,000 enfranchised blacks and coloureds in Cape Province and some Indian and other nonwhite voters in Natal. After 1936, a series of laws progressively eliminated black suffrage and representation until, in 1959, blacks were completely disenfranchised. A similar process, which included a constitutional amendment, disenfranchised coloured and Indian voters by 1960.

Under the new constitution, whites choose 166 members of the House of Assembly, coloureds choose eighty members of the House of Representatives, and Indians choose forty members of the House of Delegates. For this purpose, South Africa is divided into three overlying but separate sets of electoral districts for white, coloured, and Indian voters. Members of each house are selected from these single-member districts by a simple plurality vote. Every white, coloured, and Indian who is a citizen over 18 years of age is entitled to vote.

The seats in each house are constitutionally assigned by province in proportion to each race's numbers therein. Each province is then divided into three sets of electoral districts. The number of voters in most districts may vary by 15 percent above or below the provincial average and, in a few large but sparsely inhabited areas, it may fall 30 percent below the average.

Historically, these variances have favored the rural Afrikaners (and the National Party) at the expense of the more urbanized English-speaking populace. Blacks cxontinue to be excluded from voting except at township level and in the tribal homelands.

On November 2, 1983, the constitution was approved by voters in an all-white referendum. Over 76 percent of the eligible voters turned out and almost 66 percent cast affirmative votes. Originally, it had been the government's plan to test coloured and Indian opinion in similar referendums but these referendums were shelved in early 1984. Thus, elections to the House of Representatives and the House of Delegates became the first test of nonwhites' reactions to the recent political changes.

The first elections to the two new chambers were widely boycotted. Only 18 percent of the voting-age coloured population and only 16.6 percent of the eligible Indian population cast ballots. The elections were marked by calls for boycott and outbreaks of violence, which made it impossible to differentiate nonvoting as an expression of political dissatisfaction from that due to intimidation.

Political groups that opposed the new constitution also urged blacks to boycott the first elections in the townships. The turnout for these elections averaged only about 20 percent and in Soweto, the largest township, it was only 10.7 percent.

The Party System

Origins of the Parties

Historically, South Africa's electorate has been overwhelmingly white and the political parties have reflected the cultural-linguistic cleavage within the white community. The original stimulus for the emergence of parties before the Act of Union was the growth of Afrikaner identity to oppose British imperialism. Since 1910, there have been three types of white parties: those dedicated to the exclusive interests of Afrikaners; those representing English-speakers' interests; and those including members from both communities trying to reconcile their divergent interests. Because Anglo-South Africans have been a minority, exclusively English parties have usually been excluded from control of government. From

1910 until 1948, the main partisan struggle had always been between an Afrikaner party and a reconciliation party. Elections tended to be close, usually decided by the swing of Afrikaner voters between these two choices; party splits and mergers were frequent. Control of government alternated between the two types of parties and among a number of coalitions. From 1948 to the present, the National Party—originally representing Afrikaner interests but more recently moving somewhat toward reconciliation—has controlled the government. It currently holds more than two-thirds of the seats in the Assembly and controls the state presidency, the majority of the cabinet, and the president's council.

Nonwhite political groupings can be traced back to the founding of the National Indian Congress by Mahatma Ghandi in 1894 and the African National Congress in 1912. Such groups were regularly limited or excluded from political participation. Currently, nonwhite political groups are divided between those that participate in the new institutions and those, including some banned and in exile, that oppose the system.

The Parties in Law

In 1985, Parliament repealed the 1968 Prohibition of Political Interference Act, which confined membership in each political party to a specific ethnic group, and thus allowed multiracial party membership. The only provision of the Act that has been retained—and the only law concerning party finance—prohibits political parties from receiving money from abroad. This provision is a major concern as some South African organizations are well-funded by overseas sources.

The Communist Party has been outlawed since 1950, and the African National Congress, Pan-African Congress and the Indian National Congress since 1960.

Party Organization

The dominant National Party (NP) is a mass party of over one-million members, organized nationwide, with active local branches in every polling district. The party has four separate organizations (one in each province), each led by a provincial head committee and an annual provincial congress. Although the provincial congresses are supposed to approve all party decisions to make them binding, in actuality, there is less decentralization than may first appear. Key decisions have often been made and implemented by the national caucus of party MPs and their leader, the state president or, formerly, the prime minister.

The four white opposition parties are resource-poor in comparison with NP. The Progressive Federal Party has branches in all four provinces and holds seats from three of them. The other white opposition parties have predominantly regional power bases and relatively few branch organizations.

Of the nonwhite parties that participate in the political system, the best organized is the Labour Party, which has strong central leadership, branches in all four provinces, and has nominated candidates for all eighty elected seats in the House of Representatives. The Indian parties have tended to be looser coalitions of individuals, many of whom began their careers as independents. Most of the parties that oppose the current political system have gone underground or into exile. Little is known of their organization.

Campaigning

Until the recent political changes, parliamentary campaigns involved only white parties and politicians. The intensity of these campaigns depended primarily on whether the constituency was a traditionally safe one or highly competitive. Campaigns lasted a few months and consisted largely of political rallies, pamphleteering, and public appearances by candidates. Radio and television are state-owned and cannot be used for campaigning.

The 1983 local elections in the black townships and those in 1984 for the coloured House of Representatives and Indian House of Delegates were marked by calls for boycott and by threats of violence. The real choice was seen by many to be between voting (expressing support for the enacted reforms) and not voting (expressing disapproval). Thus, the campaigns were as much directed toward influencing this choice as toward promoting the various candidates.

Independent Voters

From 1948 until 1984, party loyalty among white voters was generally strong and stable, except for a segment of Afrikaners who some-times shifted their support from the National Party to one of the more conservative parties. There has been no general election for whites since the implementation of the new constitution, but closely watched by-elections suggest that such a shift to the right is now occurring. There may also be a rightward shift of Progressive Federal Party supporters, 20 percent of whom ignored their party leader's advice and voted "yes" on the constitutional referendum. It is not yet known if coloureds and Indians will prove stable in either voting patterns or in maintaining a non-participatory stance.

National Party (*Nasionale Partie;* NP)

History

In 1975, then Prime Minister Pieter Botha stated that "the National Party is an instrument in the service of Afrikanerdum." The party came into existence in 1914, under the leadership of General James Hertzog, to oppose an Anglo-Afrikaner coalition pledged to reconciliation between the white ethnic groups. After being the parliamentary opposition to three successive reconciliation governments, NP was part of government coalitions in 1924, 1929, and 1933. These coalition governments sought to counter' white poverty by passing legislation that protected white workers by excluding blacks from certain skilled and semiskilled jobs.

During the Great Depression (1930s), the majority of the Nationalists merged with the South African Party to become the United Party (UP), representing Anglo-Afrikaner reconciliation. While the UP overwhelmingly won the 1938 and 1943 general elections, Afrikaner nationalists rebuilt a Purified National Party under the leadership of Dr. D.F. Malan.

The 1948 general election was decisive; the NP won seventy seats against sixty-five won by the UP. It formed a government in coalition with the small Afrikaner Party, which it soon absorbed. NP's success partly stemmed from appeals to Afrikaner nationalism and partly from exploitation of appeals to white supremacists. The National Party strengthened its position by changing parliamentary representation and voting eligibility laws and by skillful electoral redistricting. The NP has won the overwhelming majority of parliamentary seats in the eight general elections held since 1948.

Organization

The National Party is made up of four provincial party organizations and a Federal Council composed of the national leader, a youth representative, and seven delegates from each province. All decisions of the council must be approved by the provincial party congresses to be binding. The provincial organizations are divided into constituencies and further divided into branches in every electoral district. These local branches nominate candidates, recruit members, and raise money.

The national caucus of National Party MPs chooses the party's leader and thus, in effect, simultaneously chooses the state president. Although the caucus is a party organization, it functions as a quasi-governmental body and it is closely consulted by the president and cabinet.

In recent years, powerful party leaders have, on occasion, bypassed both the provincial congresses and the party caucus in implementing major policy changes. President Botha has sometimes tried to circumvent the normal party procedures in developing race-reform policies; on some occasions, he apparently has been forced to retreat by provincial leaders and/or caucus members.

Policy

The National Party's control of the government since 1948 has meant that party policy and official government policy are virtually one and the same. When the NP came into power, its policies were intended to achieve Afrikaner supremacy within the white community and to maintain white supremacy throughout South Africa.

Once in power, NP appointed Afrikaners to almost all important positions in the bureaucracy, military, and the police. With the exception of the business community, where positions were independent of government control, Afrikaners became the dominant elite within the white community.

Most Afrikaners had traditionally sought to sever South Africa's special ties to the United Kingdom, and during the 1930s, NP had committed itself to replacing the British sovereign with a republican government. Not until 1960, however, did Prime Minister Hendrik Verwoerd submit the republican question to a popular referendum where 52 percent of the voters supported the proposed change. Parliamentary legislation followed, and South Africa became a republic on May 31, 1961.

All of South Africa's major parties espoused the continuation of white supremacy, and all of them, when in power, enacted legislation toward this end. Even so, one of the factors in NP's rise was its success in presenting itself as the party best able to maintain white supremacy through a new policy of *apartheid* (separateness).

The central core of the *apartheid* policy was the separate development of the black national homelands, comprising approximately 13 percent of the country. The homelands would, in theory, provide residence for blacks not otherwise employed in the white areas and would allow the development of separate black political institutions. This policy would remove the black majority from South African political citizenship without the loss of their labor. Despite overwhelming international condemnation, the *apartheid* policy moved toward fulfillment with the independence of four homelands during the years 1976–1981.

The National Party contains two intraparty factions. These are popularly differentiated as the *verligtes* (enlightened ones), who support Anglo-Afrikaner reconciliation and some interracial cooperation, and the *verkramptes* (closed ones), who favor Afrikaner domination and complete racial exclusiveness. During the years of NP government, the *verligtes* had gradually grown in strength within the party. In 1961, an English South African was appointed to the cabinet, beginning a tradition that has been continued to date. During the mid 1970s, a special government-appointed commission of experts and a special cabinet committee (headed by then Minister of Defense Pieter Botha) proposed the extension of political rights to coloureds and Indians. These proposals were pushed by Botha, who became prime minister in September 1978. He immediately reshuffled the cabinet to promote *verligtes*, a move that utlimately led to the new constitution with its tricameral Parliament. In 1969, and again in 1982, *verkrampte* National Party MPs were purged after refusing to support the leadership's reform legislation.

There are clear limits to the *verligtes* reforms; white supremacy still remains a cornerstone of policy. Despite parliamentary legislation that allows multiracial membership, the NP is seen remaining an exclusively white party. Under the new constitution, whites, who outnumber coloureds and Indians combined, have preserved control over their own affairs and—by control of the state presidency and the majority of the cabinet and president's council—of general affairs as well.

From the perspective of the country's black majority, the National Party's political reforms promise little. President Botha has stated that *apartheid* is a dead issue and that blacks will be included in the continuing constitutional development with a role in decision making at the local, provincial, and national levels. He has, however, also made clear that there will be no one-man, one-vote in a unitary system, no fourth house of Parliament, and no constitutional development that would allow "the domination of one population group over another," In most public discussion of plans for future political changes, blacks' participation in national-level politics would be limited to a consultative or advisory role granted to a limited number of individuals. Clearly, the enacted and proposed reforms, although promising major changes from past practices, do not threaten continued white political supremacy.

Outside of the political arena—despite recent efforts to liberalize some of the most objectionable aspects of *apartheid*—many of the cornerstones of South Africa's racial policy have been retained. These include the Population Registration Act, which racially tags every South African; the Group Areas Act, which determines by race where anyone may live; and the Reservation of Separate Amenities Act, which determines what public facilities (e.g., schools and hospitals) anyone may utilize.

The NP's reforms in civil rights areas have included the acceptance of the black urban population as permanent, the discontinuation of forced resettlement, and the legalization of urban black home ownership. Black and multiracial trade unions have been made legal and given the right to bargain collectively and to strike. The ban on racially mixed marriages and intimate relations has been abolished. The president's council has recommended that current influx control laws, which halt further black movement to the urban areas, be replaced by liberalized controls that will allow "orderly urbanization."

Membership & Constituency

Throughout its history, the National Party has been seen as the political embodiment of the Afrikaner community and most of its electoral support has come from that group. More recently, however, there has been an effort to attract conservative English-speaking members, and a 1977 opinion poll found that over 23 percent of English-speakers preferred the NP. One or two cabinet appointments have been reserved for Anglo-South African members and a few English candidacies have been supported in various elections. The Afrikaner-Anglo membership distribution within the NP may be further changed by Afrikaner defections to the new parties of the ultra-right and by new recruits into NP from English-speakers who support the constitutional reforms.

Once almost solely a party of rural people, the NP now receives the majority of its support from urban industrial workers, businessmen, civil servants, and bureaucrats. Total party membership is estimated at one million.

Financing

The party's financial support comes from individual membership dues, fund raising drives, and corporate donations. No figures are made public on the amount of money raised.

Leadership

The leadership of the National Party has been exclusively Afrikaner throughout its history. The early leaders were predominantly war heroes, farmers, and church leaders; more recently they have been educators, lawyers, and lifelong professional party politicians. Increasingly, leaders have come from the *verligte* faction.

Pieter Botha has served as party leader since September 1978. Other party leaders include minister of constitutional development and planning, J. Chris Heunis; minister of home affairs and national education, F.W. deKlerk; and minister of cooperation and development, Dr G.N. Viljoen.

Prospects

The National Party won the overwhelming majority of parliamentary seats in the most recent (1981) white general election and received the implicit support of almost two-thirds of the white voters in the 1983 constitutional referendum. More recently, however, economic recession, internal violence, and white backlash have weakened some of the party's electoral support.

As the results of five October 1985 parliamentary by-elections came in, it was clear that NP, while losing only one seat, had suffered a 17 to 20 percent loss of support to two ultra-right wing parties. At the same time it picked up some strength at the expense of the Progressive Federal Party and the dying New Republic Party. Following the elections, Botha announced that despite the losses he would continue his policy of gradual reforms.

The next general elections are scheduled for 1989. It is expected that the NP will continue to lose some support to the right-wing Conservative and Herstigte (Reconstituted) National Parties, but that its strength will predominate for the foreseeable future.

Other Parliamentary Parties

Progressive Federal Party (PFP)

The PFP was established in 1977 through the merger of the disbanded United Party's liberal wing with the tiny Progressive Reform Party. In the 1977 general election, it won seventeen seats—all in urban English-speaking districts—and became the largest opposition party to the NP. The election of Dr. Frederick van Zyl Slabbert, an Afrikaner, as party leader attracted some liberal Afrikaner support and its strength increased to twenty-seven seats in 1981.

The most liberal of the white opposition parties, the PFP advocates universal suffrage and abolishment of all racial discrimination. It opposed the 1983 constitution, claiming that it excluded "70 percent of the population, namely the Blacks." The PFP has advocated constitutional referendums for the coloured and Indian communities and for new general elections for whites. The party has recently opened its membership to all races and will field candidates for all three houses of Parliament in the next election.

The PFP has suffered a number of recent setbacks: many of its members voted in favor of the constitution, party support slipped in the 1985 by-elections, and its liberal Afrikaner leader resigned. It will, however, continue to be supported by the more liberal whites and may gain some new members from coloureds and Indians.

Colin Eglin has resumed the role of party leader, which he held previously until 1976.

New Republic Party (NRP)

When the United Party disbanded in 1977, many of its members joined PFP or NP, while others formed the NRP. The party's support comes primarily from Anglo-South Africans concentrated in Natal Province who advocate white supremacy but oppose the harsher and uneconomical aspects of *apartheid*. In 1983, it urged support of the new constitution. NRP's seats in Parliament declined in the 1981 general election and its candidate fared poorly in a Natal by-election in 1985. The party is dying and may soon be disbanded.

Herstigte (Reconstituted) National Party (HNP)

The HNP is the most conservative party represented in Parliament. It was formed in 1969 by Dr. Albert Hertzog, a former NP cabinet member, when he and a few followers were purged from the NP caucus over issues of Anglo-Afrikaner reconciliation, opposed by HNP. HNP wants Afrikaans to be the sole national language and believes that South Africa must be built around a purely Afrikaner cultural core. It supports white supremacy and the continuation of *apartheid* and has opposed the new constitution.

HNP received only 3.5 percent of the total popular vote in 1969 but over 14 percent in 1981. It has shown great strength in the more recent by-elections and won its first parliamentary seat in 1985. Together with the growth of the Conservative Party, the HNP has turned a number of previously safe NP seats into marginal constituencies. Continued growth on the right might force NP leaders to slow down or discontinue its reform program.

HNP is led by Jaap Marais.

Conservative Party of South Africa (CPSA)

The CPSA supports a policy of Anglo-Afrikaner cooperation, white supremacy, and strict racial separation. It was formed by former NP members who had been expelled in 1982 after refusing to support proposals for power-sharing with coloureds and Indians. Since its founding, the party has been led by Dr. Andries Treurnicht, who had previously been a National Party M.P. The party holds eighteen seats in Parliament and has demonstrated widespread popular support in recent by-elections. Along with the HNP, it may force the NP to slow the pace of reform.

Labour Party of South Africa (LP)

The Labour Party, founded in 1966, has been the predominant party among the coloureds. Throughout most of its history, LP has opposed separate development and has worked with black groups backing their demands for universal equal political rights. In 1983, it rejected the new constitution because it excluded blacks, but then, in 1984, agreed to participate in elections to the House of Representatives to ensure having some influence on further reforms. LP holds eighty-one of the eighty-five seats and its leader, Rev. H.J. Allan Hendriekse, serves as chairman of the Ministers' Council of the House of Representatives and as a member of the cabinet. The party plans to enroll Indian members and support candidates for seats in the House of Delegates.

Despite its current strength, the party's future may be determined by the majority of coloured voters who boycotted the 1984 elections and have been skeptical of Labour's ability to influence the government from within.

National People's Party (NPP)

The National People's Party was formed in the early 1980s to support candidates for the advisory South African Indian Council. The NPP initially decided to support the new constitution only if it were first approved by the Indian community in a referendum. It later changed its position, participated in the 1984 elections, and currently holds the majority of seats in the House of Delegates. The party's leader, Amichand Rajbansi, is the chairman of the Ministers' Council in the House of Delegates and is a member of the cabinet.

Solidarity

Solidarity was founded in 1984 to contest elections to the House of Delegates where it now serves as the official opposition. Most of its leaders want to extend power to South Africa's black majority. The future of both Solidarity and NPP is difficult to assess because the majority of Indians boycotted the 1984 elections and because the PFP and the Labour Party plan to contest the 1989 elections to the Indian chamber.

Other Political Forces

African National Congress (ANC)

The African National Congress was organized in 1912, making it the oldest political organization in South Africa today. For many years it worked within the system to support multiracialism and to oppose peacefully white domination. During the 1950s, under the leadership of Albert Luthuli—a devout Christian, nonviolent activist, and recipient of a Nobel Peace Prize—the ANC greatly increased its national and international visibility. Together with the South African Indian Congress, the South African Coloured People's Organization, the predominantly white Congress of Democrats, and the multiracial South African Congress of Trade Unions, the ANC campaigned for mass opposition to government policies. Throughout the country, local groups collected lists of grievances and elected 3,500 representatives to a Congress of the People, which was held on June 26, 1955. Here they adopted the Freedom Charter, which remains the political platform of the ANC. It announced the goal of a democratic state based on the will of the people, with no distinctions of color, race, sex or belief. It explicitly demanded that members of all races be given the right to vote and to stand as political candidates.

The ANC's campaign made little headway against stiff government resistance and, in 1959, a number of its younger, more activist members broke with the organization to form the Pan-African Congress (PAC). The leaders of the new organization believed that blacks' cooperation with other ethnic groups, particularly the whites, had weakened the ANC. This split over the effectiveness of multiracial cooperation against *apartheid* policies has continued to divide the government's opponents.

Events in 1960 encouraged ANC leaders to reverse their previous nonviolence policy. On March 21, passive resistance to the pass laws triggered the "Sharpeville massacre," in which the police opened fire, killing sixty-nine unarmed blacks. During the following weeks, the ANC, PAC, and the Indian National Congress were banned; most ANC leaders and many members went underground or into exile. Luthuli, whose freedom of movement was restricted by government order, was replaced as ANC president by Nelson Mandela. In exile under Mandela and his lieutenant (ANC's current acting president) Oliver Tambo, the party developed a military wing which has trained insurgents to sabotage strategic and, more recently, civilian targets. The South African army has frequently entered neighboring independent states to pursue ANC forces, and South Africa's military strength makes it unlikely that ANC can topple the government by force.

In 1962 when Mandela secretly returned to South Africa, he was arrested and sentenced to life imprisonment. His wife, Winnie Mandela, has defied government bans and become a leading spokesperson for ANC policies. The Free Nelson Mandela campaign has developed extensive support across the otherwise significant divisions within the government's collective opposition.

In exile, ANC has continued its multiracial tradition and includes coloureds, Indians, and whites as well as blacks in its national executive committee. It has also maintained—and perhaps even increased—its popularity among blacks, particularly those in the urban areas. Surveys show that ANC has more support than its rival black organizations and that Nelson Mandela remains the most popular black leader. The ANC party colors (black, green, and gold) are frequently displayed in public, particularly at the funerals of prominent opponents of *apartheid*.

Bishop Desmond Tutu and the South African Council of Chruches (SACC)

In 1984, the Right Reverend Desmond Tutu, now the Anglican bishop of Johannesburg, was the recipient of the Nobel Peace Prize. Throughout his career, and especially during his term as the first black general secretary of the South African Council of Churches (1978–1984), he prominently advocated nonviolent measures to end *apartheid*, called for racial reconciliation, and prophesied a potential blood bath ahead.

The South African Council of Churches represents 13 million Christians, approximately 80 percent of whom are black. Conspicuously absent from its membership are the Dutch Reformed churches of the white Afrikaners . With the main African nationalist parties banned, the SACC, under Tutu and his successor, Beyers Naude (a liberal Afrikaner), became an important vehicle of black protest. Much of the SACC's budget is used to provide legal and other services for imprisoned blacks and those detained without trial.

United Democratic Front (UDF)

The United Democratic Front was organized in 1983 to promote and coordinate the widest possible opposition to the new South African constitution. It is a loosely organized multiracial alliance of over 600 affiliated organizations, including community associations, trade unions, and women's and student groups. The Front's national presidents are Albertina Sisulu and Archie Gumede. Dr. Allen Boesak, a coloured minister in the Dutch Reformed Mission Church, is its best-known spokesperson. The UDF is avowedly nonracial and welcomes support from members of all races. It includes somes predominantly white organizations among its affiliates, a fact that has caused clashes with supporters of black consciousness.

There is a strong convergence at both the personal and ideological level between the UDF and the ANC. Most UDF leaders were supporters of the ANC before it was banned in 1960 and many of the UDF-affiliated organizations have endorsed the ANC's Freedom Charter.

The UDF's Declaration of Purpose states that its objective is a democracy in which all South Africans will participate in the governing of a single unfragmented country, free of tribal homelands and racial group areas. The Front claims an unswerving commitment to combating *apartheid* peacefully, but members have sometimes been involved in violence with government authorities and with supporters of AZAPO and Inkatha (two rival opposition groups).

The South African government has repeatedly used the Internal Security Act to ban meetings of the UDF and its affiliates on the grounds that such gatherings were likely to endanger public peace. The South African courts usually have overturned such bannings. Most of UDF's leaders were jailed at least once during 1985, often being detained for many months without access to lawyers or the courts. Although the government has accused the UDF of fomenting popular unrest, it has, to date, hesitated to ban the organization.

The UDF claims a membership of 1.5 million and is the only nationwide opposition group. It has thus become the most effective legal opposition to the NP government.

Inkatha

Inkatha was founded in 1975 by Chief Gatsha Buthelezi, the chief minister of the KwaZulu homeland. Although the movement is open to all South African blacks and has tried to foster cooperation with the Labour Party and some Indian leaders, it has remained overwhelmingly a Zulu political organization.

Buthelezi has refused independence for the Zulu homeland, condemning the government's separate-development policy. He has called for the release of Mandela, opposed the new constitution because it excluded black participation, and refused appointment to the president's council.

The movement and its leader are considered to be moderates because they have worked within the system and are willing to accept a racial power-sharing formula short of majority rule. Inkatha's inability to expand beyond its tribal base and the failure of its alliance with the Labour Party and Indian leaders, may limit its future role to that of protecting Zulu tribal interests. Nevertheless, with 1.1 million members, Inkatha remains a potent political force.

National Forum

The National Forum, established in 1983, is an umbrella movement of over 200 black organizations that oppose *apartheid* but reject cooperation with liberal and radical whites. Forum policies are built upon the black consciousness philosophy of the late activist Steve Biko, who died in prison allegedly at the hands of the police. The National Forum opposes both racism and capitalism and seeks a democratic, antiracist and socialist Anzania (i.e., South Africa). The movement cooperates with coloureds and Indians, but it condemns the ANC and UDF for their cooperation with liberal whites.

The largest and best-known affiliate within the National Forum is the Anzanian People's Organization (AZAPO), which was formed in 1979 after the government had banned a number of predecessor black consciousness groups because of their alleged instigation of violent uprising in Soweto.

National Prospects

During the first half of the 1980s, the South African government has shifted away from the policy of *apartheid*—its goal being the political removal of blacks to the homelands—to a new policy that retains white control but extends political participation to coloureds, Indians, and —at the local level—blacks. Newer policies are also removing many of the harsher aspects of social and economic *apartheid*, while retaining the legal cornerstone for continued racial separation.

It is difficult to know if promises of continued reform will be kept in wake of significant opposition from segments in all of South Africa's racial communities. The growing political strength of the ultraconservative white parties may slow the pace of current reforms, which many Indians, coloureds, and liberal whites wish to extend to the blacks. It also seems evident that black leaders would not be satisfied with the current modest political reforms even if they were extended to blacks. The government of the National Party (and its coloured and Indian allies) can be seen as balancing on a tightrope as it tries to maintain order with the hope that over time its reforms will be more widely accepted in all of the racial communities.

To date, despite the reforms, both internal and international opposition to the South African political system is growing. During 1985, in both Western Europe and the United States public awareness of the South African situation greatly increased as did calls for action against that government. Although the United States has remained South Africa's major trading partner, limited and largely symbolic economic sanctions were imposed in late 1985. Many U.S. municipalities, churches, and universities have divested themselves of stocks in companies doing business in South Africa. Public protests outside of the South African Embassy in Washington, D.C. occur daily.

Even more significant is the increased popular opposition within South Africa; organizations that oppose the current political system have become major and seemingly permanent political fixtures. Both despite and because of stiff government resistance, there has been a growing animation of the black disenfranchised.

Meanwhile, largely as a result of unmet demands and frustrations, political violence has escalated. Black unrest in the urban areas and increased attacks on civilian as well as strategic targets by the ANC have been countered by white vigilante groups as well as by the police and army. The South African police and military can contain but not end the violence—only maintaining the current uneasy situation for the foreseeable future.

Further Reading

Boulle, L.J. *Constitutional Reform and Apartheid: Legitimacy, Consociationalism and Control in South Africa.* New York: St. Martin's Press, 1984.

Department of Foreign Affairs and Information, *South Africa 1985: Official Yearbook of the Republic of South Africa.* Johannesburg: Chris van Rensburg Publications, 1985.

Lodge, Tom. *Black Politics in South Africa Since 1945.* London and New York: Longman, 1983.

Parker, Frank J. *South Africa: Lost Opportunities.* Lexington, Mass: Lexington Books, 1984.

South African Digest (weekly). Pretoria: Bureau for Information, Government Printer.

South African Institute of Race Relations. *A Survey of Race Relations In South Africa* (annual). Johannesburg: South African Institute of Race Relations.

Stulz, Newell. "Interpreting Constitutional Change in South Africa," *Journal of Modern African Studies* Vol. 22, No. 3 (September, 1984) 353-379.

The Report of the Study Commission on U.S. Policy Toward South Africa, *South Africa: Time Running Out.* Berkeley: University of California Press and the Foreign Policy Study Foundation, 1981.

Thompson, Leonard M. *The Political Mythology of Apartheid.* New Haven: Yale University Press, 1985.

————, and Prior, Andrew. *South African Politics.* New Haven: Yale University Press, 1982.

NAMIBIA/SOUTH WEST AFRICA

by Richard Dale, Ph.D. revised by Jack Parson, Ph.D.

The System of Government

Namibia is a territory of over one million people that has yet to become an independent sovereign state. It was once a German colony and subsequently a League of Nations–mandated territory called South West Africa and administered by South Africa. When the United Nations converted the League-mandated territories into United Nations trust territories in 1946, South Africa refused to recognize the U.N.'s authority in South West Africa. From 1946 to 1977, South Africa governed the territory almost as if it were a fifth province, extending South Africa's *apartheid* and security laws to the territory. In 1966, the U.N. General Assembly terminated the area's mandate status and shortly thereafter established a Council for Namibia which was supposed to take over the administration of the territory and lead it rapidly to independence. In 1970, the U.N. Security Council condemned South Africa's "illegal" control of the area, and in 1971 the International Court of Justice, in an advisory opinion, also declared the South African occupation illegal.

South Africa still governs the region and has been waging a war against the guerrilla forces of the People's Liberation Army of Namibia (PLAN), the military arm of the South West Africa People's Organization (SWAPO) since 1966. PLAN operates out of sanctuaries in Angola, where Cuban troops have helped to combat incursions against the sanctuaries by the South African Defence Force (SADF). Five Western states (Canada, France, Britain, the United States, and West Germany), known as the Contact Group, have been trying since 1977 to negotiate a settlement between South Africa and SWAPO under the aegis of the United Nations and with the concurrence of six neighboring African nations called the Front Line States (Angola, Botswana, Mozambique, Tanzania, Zambia, and Zimbabwe). The achievement of a negotiated settlement based on the UN Security Council resolution 435 has been stalled by the insistence of South Africa and the United States that a withdrawal of South African armed forces from Namibia be linked to a simultaneous withdrawal of Cuban forces from Angola . The Angolan government and other Front Line states reject the absolute and direct linkage of Namibian independence to the presence of Cuban troops in Angola.

Although South Africa maintians administrative control over the territory, it has attempted to create internal governments that would represent all races and major ethnic groups, excluding SWAPO. The 1975–1977 "Turnhalle Conference" of the country's major ethnic groups produced an internal government of twelve "second-tier" ethnic authorities in which ethnic groups, including whites, were separately represented. The national "Turnhalle" government was composed of a twelve member Council of Ministers chaired by Dirk Mudge of the DTA, the dominant party in a National Assembly. This National Assembly was composed of seventy-two members, representing the "second-tier" legislatures. However, the South African administrator general had the power to veto Assembly acts.

The "Turnhalle" government lost support as South Africa refused to allow it to drastically reduce racially discriminatory legislation and ignored it in international negotiations on Namibian independence. Dirk Mudge and other members of the Ministers' Council resigned in January 1983. The administrator general resumed all the powers of the central government and exercised those powers until June 1985 when South Africa created a new internal government based on the views of a Namibian Multi-Party Conference created in late 1983 and composed of SWAPO-Democrats, SWANU, the DTA, the Damara Council, and the Rehoboth Liberation Front. The MPC was committed to internal self-determination and recognized Resolution 435 as the only concrete plan for independence recognized by South Africa, the UN, and the western contact group; but it also argued that implementation of the resolution should depend on a Cuban withdrawal from Angola. The new unelected and non-representative government in Namibia, consisting of six anti-SWAPO parties, technically could pass laws; but the administrator general retained the power of the veto and South Africa continued to directly control foreign affairs, defense, and internal security. The new government was denounced by SWAPO, and the United Nations and United States regarded it as an additional obstacle to achieving a settlement in terms of Resolution 435.

South West Africa's ethnic groups are many and varied, with most groups living in geographically distinct areas. The largest group by far is the Ovambo, about 47 percent of the population, who live in the north central area along the border with Angola. The next-largest group, whites, makes up about 11 percent of the population and includes Afrikaners (70 percent), Germans (18 percent), and English (10 percent). The Kavango in the northeast, the Damara in the northwest, and the Herero, most of whom live in the east central region, each comprises less than 10 percent of the population. Smaller groups include the Nama and the Tswana in the south, Bushmen in the east, several groups called Kaokolanders in the extreme northwest, and East Caprivians in the extreme northeast near the Zambian border. There are two groups of mixed racial origin: the so-called coloureds who immigrated to South West Africa from South Africa's Cape Province and the Rehoboth Basters, Afrikaans speakers who are concentrated just south of Windhoek.

Executive

The Cabinet is composed of six persons, three from Mudge's DTA and one each from each of the other parties including SWANU and SWAPO-Democrats. The cabinet may make policy and supervise the bureaucracy subject to the fact that South Africa is responsible for foreign affairs, defense, and internal security and the fact that the administrator general may veto the actions of the government.

Legislature

The National Assembly is made up of sixty-two members, all of whom are nominated. Thus, neither the legislature nor the executive are elected and therefore directly representative of the population as a whole.

Judiciary

South Africa established a territorial Supreme Court in 1960. It consists of four judges appointed by the South African administrator. The court is the final court of appeal, but it does not have the right of constitutional review of legislation, a juridical concept foreign to the South African (and British) tradition.

Regional & Local Government

Elections of some of the second-tier authorities were held in November 1980. These authorities enjoy limited executive and legislative powers for specific ethnic groups, most of which live in clearly demarcated geographical areas. In the few urban areas, elected councils and mayors, mostly white, exercise limited administrative authority over municipal affairs.

The Party System

Contemporary formal parties in Namibia are primarily outgrowths of the Turnhalle conference. The parties are largely personal followings of ethnic leaders who, although all anti-SWAPO, constantly maneuver for possible United Nations support or South African patronage and for favorable coalitions with other parties. Essentially, each group and leader is struggling for a place in whatever political system finally emerges, and each fears that failure will mean total political eclipse.

Most of the parties seem convinced that the United Nations will ultimately prevail and that UN-supervised elections will be held. The DTA, for example, seems to be trying to put some distance between itself and the South African administration on the assumption that only an independent profile will enable it to outpoll SWAPO in future elections. The DTA and other independence-oriented parties try to influence negotiations on the structure of the system to be used in those elections (e.g., whether they are to be based on regions alone, ethnic group alone, or some combination of the two).

According to one count made in early 1982, there were forty-five political parties representing a variety of inter- and intra-ethnic divisions. Out of this welter of parties, a number of umbrella organizations have emerged, of which only the DTA and Aktur are politically significant within the Turnhalle system. Outside of that system and aiming at its overthrow, SWAPO is the primary contender for political power with the other non-Turnhalle force, the South African government and security forces.

Action Front for the Preservation of Turnhalle Principles (Aktur)

Aktur appeals to conservative elements of several groups, most notably whites, Rehoboth Basters, Damaras, and Kavangos. The party favors a close relationship with South Africa and is opposed to black majority rule, which some minority black groups regard as essentially Ovambo rule. Aktur is the majority party in the white second-tier Legislative Assembly.

Democratic Turnhalle Alliance (DTA)

The DTA appeals to moderate elements among whites, to anti-SWAPO Ovambos, and to segments of most other ethnic groups. The DTA includes twelve component parties and supports independence with a multi-ethnic government. In May 1982, the DTA president, Peter Kalangula, an Ovambo notable, bolted the party and formed his own, Christian Democratic Action for Social Justice, thus tending to undercut Ovambo support for the DTA, support the Alliance needs to offset the popularity of SWAPO among many Ovambos. The driving force behind the DTA is Dirk Mudge.

Minor Parties

Three smaller parties that are important are: the *Herstige Nasionale Partie* (Reconstituted National Party), a branch of the conservative Afrikaaner party of the same name in South Africa and firmly opposed to independence; the South West Africa National Union (SWANU) which is active among the Herero; and SWAPO-Democratic, led by a former SWAPO leader. The latter two parties were included in the new government installed in June 1985.

Other Political Forces

South West Africa People's Organization (SWAPO)

SWAPO was founded in 1960 to work for independence for the territory. It is led by an Ovambo, Sam Nujoma, a former migrant laborer, now in his mid-fifties. Its armed force has been estimated at some 6,000 men, and most of its support comes from less traditional elements of the Ovambo people. SWAPO has attempted to secure the allegiance of other black groups, but with negligible success, although the chairman of the party, David Meroro, is a Herero. The organization of SWAPO is similar to that of a communist party, with a central committee and smaller policy bureau which determines policy. Its public rhetoric is markedly Marxist-Leninist, and its avowed aim is to establish a one-party socialist state in Namibia. SWAPO is recognized by both the United Nations and the Organization of African Unity as the sole legitimate liberation movement in Namibia. This external legitimation provides SWAPO with forums in the United Nations and at international conferences, with access to funds and arms from the Soviet bloc, and with the attention of the Contact Group and the Front Line States. In spite of its diplomatic successes, it is not yet a match for South Africa's security forces and has been unable to mount any major sustained campaigns against the SADF within Namibia itself.

South African Defence Force (SADF)

South Africa's forces in the territory are estimated at up to 75,000 men. Black ethnic units have been used in the counterinsurgency efforts. Officially, the SADF stays out of domestic politics, but it could become a major political actor in any area deemed to be a matter of South African national security.

National Prospects

A probable scenario for Namibia's future is the continuation of low-level guerrilla and counterinsurgency war as international talks drag on. The preferred outcome in the West is to have the SADF leave Namibia at the same time that the Cubans withdraw from Angola. A demilitarized zone along the northern border would then be set up under a United Nations peacekeeping force, and the United Nations would supervise elections for an assembly which would draft a constitution for the new state. Such an assembly would reflect the relative balance of power between SWAPO and South African–oriented groups, tempered by any political concessions the Contact Group and the Front Line States could extract from the two dominant forces. The critical issue is the degree to which SWAPO could establish complete hegemony over the country in the absence of the South African military. An unqualified SWAPO victory, even if achieved primarily through outside negotiation, would be a critical psychological blow to the white oligarchy of South Africa. The future of Namibia has concerned the United Nations, in one form or another, since 1946, an indication of both the significance of the issue and the difficulty of reaching a lasting conclusion.

Further Reading
Green, Reginald H.; Kiljunen, Marja-Liisa; and Kiljunen, Kimmo, eds. *Namibia: The Last Colony.* Burnt Mill, Harlow, Essex, England: Longman Group Limited, 1981.
International Defence & Aid Fund. *Namibia: The Facts.* London: International Defence & Aid Fund, 1980.
Leistner, Erich; Esterhuysen; Pieter, and Malan, Theo. *Namibia/SWA Prospectus.* Pretoria: Africa Institute of South Africa, 1980.
South African Institute of Race Relations. *A Survey of Race Relations in South Africa.* Johannesburg: South African Institute of Race Relations, annual.
Tötemeyer, Gerhard. *South West Africa/ Namibia: Facts, Attitudes, Assessment and Prospects.* Randburg, South Africa: Fokus Suid Publishers, 1977.

KINGDOM OF SPAIN
(Reino de España)
by Jan Knippers Black, Ph.D.

The System of Government

Spain, a nation of 38.6 million people, is a parliamentary monarchy. The government is headed by a prime minister. The king serves as head of state and as commander-in-chief of the armed forces. The central government recently completed the process of granting limited autonomy to the country's historic regions.

The Spanish political system is a system in transition. One aspect of the system—especially the bureaucracy, the courts, the armed forces and the Civil Guard, a rural constabulary—represents the vestigial remains of the quasitraditional, quasicorporatist dictatorship maintained by Generalissimo Francisco Franco y Bahamonde from his victory over the republicans in 1939 until his death in 1975.

The other aspect includes organizational and ideological survivals of the short-lived Second Republic and reflects demographic changes, economic modernization, the democratic political models of Europe, and the lure of Europe's Common Market. It consists of the parliamentary and electoral systems, the political parties, the labor unions, and other modern associations and interest groups. The most important agent of transition and the seemingly indispensable link between the so-called two Spains has been the monarchy.

The monarchy itself has been discontinuous in recent Spanish history. Besieged by enthusiasts of the republican cause, King Alfonso XIII renounced the throne in 1931. The pretender thereafter, Don Juan de Borbón y Battenberg, became a severe critic of Franco's policies and lived in exile. Seeking a successor, Franco bypassed Don Juan and, in 1969, named the pretender's son, Don Juan Carlos de Borbón y Borbón (born 1938), prince of Spain and king-designate.

Franco was confident that the young prince, schooled at all three of Spain's military academies as well as the University of Madrid, would carry on his policies and maintain the authoritarian system he had established. But either as a matter of principle or of pragmatism, King Juan Carlos has chosen to identify himself with the unmistakable aspirations of the overwhelming majority of the Spanish people and to move the government, albeit gradually and cautiously, in the direction of democracy.

The Spanish political system is characterized by a number of major cleavages. The most important one during the early years of transition has been that between the advocates of civilian democratic rule and the advocates of military-imposed authoritarianism. The former category includes the king, both of the major parties and most of the minor ones, the unions, and most business interests, in effect, most of Spanish society. The authoritarian groups include a few violence-prone organizations of the extreme left, several more on the extreme right; and more importantly, influential factions of the armed forces and the Civil Guard, the national police. Though the advocates of democracy are overwhelming in numbers, their opponents' command of arms and their willingness to use them means that they cannot be written off as inconsequential.

A second major cleavage is that between the proponents of political modernization and the defenders of traditionalism. Although the groups and categories on opposing sides of this cleavage and of the democratic/authoritarian one often overlap, the issues and motivations involved are different and the overlap is only partial. This cleavage coincides more nearly with one of urban versus rural or of political participants versus nonparticipants. It groups on one side members or supporters of political parties, unions, or other modern organizations and institutions and on the other those who are disinclined to participate in elections and whose primary allegiance is to the Roman Catholic Church or to the king.

A third cleavage is that between centralists and regionalists. It pits the king, the armed forces, all of the national parties and other national organizations and institutions against the regional parties and other advocates of extreme decentralization and regional self-determination. The most readily justifiable claims for regional autonomy are those of Catalonia, while the most extreme are those of the Basque country. The national parties of the left have supported limited regional self-rule, but not absolute self-determination.

The final major cleavage is that between right and left within the community of political participants and modernizers committed to the process of transition to constitutional rule. The line in this case fell initially between the center-left Spanish Socialist Workers Party (PSOE) and the now defunct, center-right Union of the Democratic Center (UCD). Since 1982, that line has fallen between the PSOE and the right-wing Popular Alliance (AP). This cleavage defines the issues governing the particulars of the electoral process, of constitutional provisions, and of laws.

These cross-cutting cleavages have militated against the very dangerous prospect of polarization; but they have also rendered extremely difficult the process of identifying areas of consensus. The new constitution, therefore, has tended, on many issues, to record conflicting aims rather than to resolve them.

A new bicameral legislature, the *Cortes,* was brought into being by a 94.2 percent majority in a popular referendum on the Law for Political Reform in December 1976 and the Electoral Law (1977). The new *Cortes* served as the constituent assembly for the drafting of a new constitution. That *Cortes* was dominated by the UCD, with the PSOE in a strong minority position.

All of the national parties were in agreement that the constitution should be one that would allow for alternation of governments and permit any of the parties to govern in good conscience. Rather than limiting the document to an expression of broad and basic principles, however, they chose to address themselves in detail (169 articles, 15,000 words) to highly controversial issues. However, these issues are often dealt with in ambiguous and, in some cases, seemingly contradictory language that may in time result in serious problems of interpretation.

Article 1 of the constitution declares that the highest juridicial values of the state shall be liberty, justice, equality, and political pluralism. It further states that national sovereignty is vested in the Spanish people, from whom emanate the powers of the state. The political form of the state is declared to be that of a parliamentary monarchy.

Article 1 seems clear enough, but Article 8, suggesting a special mission for the armed forces, has been a source of concern to some. It states that, "The Armed Forces, comprising the Army, Navy, and the Air Force, have as their mission the guaranteeing of the sovereignty and independence of Spain and of defending her territorial integrity *and the constitutional order.*" [Emphasis added] Whether explicit or implicit, the demands of the military could not be ignored in the drafting of the constitution.

The issue of church-state relations proved highly controversial. The final wording, discomforting to the advocates of a secular state as well as to those of an established church, is found in Article 16. It guarantees freedom of religion and worship and declares that there shall be no state religion. But it further states, "The public authorities shall take the religious beliefs of Spanish society into account and shall maintain the consequent relations of cooperation with the Catholic Church and the other confessions." The displeasure of the Socialists with this clause was reinforced by a clause in Article 27 that appears to pledge continuing government subsidy to private schools. Historically, the private Catholic schools, subsidized by the government, have attracted the children of the affluent, creating a class-based, separate and unequal educational system.

The nature of the economic order was also a source of controversy, pitting the advocates of unfettered free enterprise against the advocates of socialism. The controversy was resolved for constitutional purposes through ambiguity. Article 38 guarantees respect and protection for "free enterprise within the framework of a market economy." Article 128, on the other hand, calls for "public initiative in economic activity." It allows for legislation whereby "the public sector may be granted funds or basic services, especially where there is a monopoly." It further authorizes the state to "intervene in enterprises when this is demanded by the public interest." Article 131 says that "the state may through legislation plan general economic activity in order to meet collective needs, to balance and harmonize regional and sectoral development, and to stimulate the growth of income and wealth and their more equitable distribution."

Civil rights and liberties are spelled out in some detail in the constitution, including freedom of the press, recognition of conscientious objection to military service, and the right to organize political parties and trade unions. Equality before the law is guaranteed regardless of "birth, race, sex, religion, opinion, or any other personal or social circumstance." The death penalty is prohibited except in military trials in time of war.

The new constitution was approved in 1978, first by the *Cortes* on October 31, then by national referendum on December 6. With 345 of the 350 members of the Congress of Deputies present, 325 voted to approve it. In the Senate, with 239 of the 248 members present, 226 voted approval. Opposition came primarily from the extreme right, the extreme left, and the extreme regionalists, particularly the Basques.

For the referendum, turnout was 67.7 percent of eligible voters, of whom 87.8 percent voted approval. Turnout was lowest in historically apathetic Galicia; opposition was highest in the historically separatist Basque country.

Executive

The king is "the head of state and symbol of its unity and permanence" according to the constitution. He sanctions and promulgates laws and is commander-in-chief of the armed forces. After consulting with representatives of the political parties, the king nominates a candidate for president of the government (prime minister). The candidate must then win a vote of confidence in the Congress of Deputies. If after two months no candidate has been able to win a vote of confidence, the king must dissolve the *Cortes* and call for new elections.

Executive authority is vested in the prime minister (formally, president of the government) and the vice presidents, ministers, and other officials whom he chooses. The prime minister and his cabinet are collectively responsible to the Congress of Deputies. The government is subject to a vote of censure, but the motion of censure must include the name of the candidate who is to succeed to the prime ministry. This "constructive" censure, borrowed from the West German constitution, was favored by both of the major parties as a stabilizing feature.

Legislature

Legislative power is vested in the bicameral *Cortes*. The lower house, the Congress of Depu-

ties (*Congreso de Diputados*), presently has 350 members who are directly elected to four-year terms by proportional representation from the fifty provinces. Barcelona and Madrid have thirty-three and thirty-two deputies, respectively; the forty-eight other provinces have from three to fifteen. The North African enclaves, Ceuta and Melilla, have one deputy each. The upper house, the Senate (*Senado*), presently has 208 members directly elected to four-year terms by simple plurality. The forty-seven mainland provinces elect four each and the enclaves two each. The two Canary island provinces elect eleven senators, and the Balearic islands province elects five.

The Congress of Deputies has by far the stronger role. Bills passed by the Congress must be approved by the Senate, but the Congress can override a Senate vote by a simple majority. Nor can the Senate long delay legislation. It is required to act on Congressional bills within two months and, in some cases, within twenty days.

The role and composition of the Senate was a subject of great controversy during the constitutional debates. The initial proposal of the UCD, that all senators be elected indirectly by the legislative assemblies of the autonomous regions, was unacceptable to the PSOE and other parties of the left. Even the formula ultimately accepted left the more conservative rural areas greatly overrepresented. Thus, the left, fearing that the Senate would block any progressive measures initiated in the Congress of Deputies, refused to agree to grant significant powers to the Senate.

Popular initiative is permitted with a minimum of 500,000 signatures. The constitution also provides that "political decisions of special importance may be submitted to all citizens in a consultative referendum." A referendum may be called by the king at the proposal of the prime minister following authorization by the Congress of Deputies.

The constitution may be amended by a three-fifths majority of each of the two chambers of the *Cortes*. On the petition of one-tenth of the deputies or senators, an amendment may be submitted to referendum. Amendments to Articles 1 to 9, 15 to 29, and 56 to 65, defining civil liberties and the basic characteristics of the state, call for a more nearly consensual procedure. They would require a two-thirds majority of both chambers, the immediate dissolution of the *Cortes*, new elections, a two-thirds majority of both chambers of the new *Cortes,* and a national referendum.

While the *Cortes* is elected to a four-year term, the prime minister can advise the king to call new elections earlier. This happened in 1982, when Prime Minister Calvo Sotelo's ruling party, the UCD, disintegrated, and he could no longer rely on a majority in the Congress.

	CORTES ELECTIONS RESULTS, 1979 AND 1982 (Partial and Unofficial Figures)					
	Congress of Deputies				Senate	
	1979		1982		1979	1982
Party	% of Votes	Seats	% of Votes	Seats	Seats	Seats
Socialist Workers Party (PSOE)	30.50	121	46.07	202	70	134
Popular Aliance (AP)	5.76	9	25.35	106	3	54
Democratic Center (UCD)	34.96	168	7.26	12	119	4
Communist Party (PCE)	10.81	23	3.87	4	1	—
Social Democratic Center (CDS)	2.89	2	—			
Convergence and Union (CiU)	2.70	8	3.73	12	1	7*
Basque Nationalist (PNV)	1.54	7	1.91	8	8	7
Herri Batasuna	0.96	3	0.97	2	1	—
Basque Left (EE)	0.48	1	0.47	1	—	—
Republican Left (ERC)	0.69	1	0.66	1	—	(1)
Independents and others	—	—	—	—	5	3

* The seven Senate seats won by the CiU were won in alliance with the Republican Left.
Source: El Pais, October 31, 1982, Barcelona.

Judiciary

Judicial authority is vested in an independent court system. Ultimate recourse on most matters of ajudication is to the Supreme Court, but constitutional questions are to be referred to the Constitutional Court consisting of twelve judges serving nine-year terms. Two of its members are to be named by the government, two by the General Council of the Judiciary, four by the Congress of Deputies, and four by the Senate. The Constitutional Court, a relatively conservative body, has been kept busy as a consequence of the many ambiguities of the constitution.

The judiciary has been one of the last institutional vestiges of the Franco regime. Even by the mid-1980s, about half of the judges were holdovers. But changes can be seen. In the fall of 1985, the Judicial Council was reconstituted. It was elected, for the first time, by Parliament, and, also for the first time, it included a woman.

Extraordinary political tribunals are prohibited, and the jurisdiction of military courts is limited to members of the armed forces, except in the event of a state of siege. The jurisdiction of military courts over members of the armed forces has already proved troublesome, as military conspirators against the democratic system have been dealt with in very lenient fashion.

Regional & Local Government

Prior to the Franco regime, Spain had a long history of regional autonomy and, under the Second Republic, local self-government. Under Franco, all regional autonomy was abolished and the central authority was paramount at all levels. With the restoration of democracy, the new government found itself under intense pressure to restore regional autonomy.

Article 2 of the constitution addresses itself to the state's territorial jurisdiction: "The constitution is based on the indissolubility of the Spanish nation, the common and indivisible country of all Spaniards, and recognizes and guarantees the right to self-government of the nationalities and regions of which it is composed and to solidarity amongst them all." The article recognizes Catalonia, the Basque country, and Galicia as "nationalities." Article 2 might be seen as a self-contradiction rather than a compromise. It represents an attempt to bridge an essentially unbridgable gap between the centralists and the most extreme proponents of regional self-determination, particularly the Basque nationalists. Nevertheless, in mid-1981 agreement was reached among the major parties on the broad outlines of a plan for the reinstatement of regional autonomy, and in 1982 the Organic Law on the Harmonization of the Autonomy Process was enacted. In accordance with the legislation, seventeen more or less "historic" regions were to gain varying degrees of autonomy.

On May 8, 1983, elections were held for the first time to regional parliaments in thirteen of the new autonomous regions. The PSOE won absolute majorities in the parliaments of Aragón, Asturias, Canaries, Castille-La Mancha, Extremadura, Madrid, Musica, La Rioja, and Valencia. The party took half of the seats in the Balearics and Castille-Leon, and won a plurality in Navarre. The Popular Alliance–Popular Democratic Party–Liberal Union (AP–PDP–UL) coalition won control of the Cantabrian parliament.

February 26, 1984 elections to the 75-member Basque regional parliament resulted in a 32-seat plurality for the Basque Nationalist Party (PNV). PSOE strength increased to nineteen seats. In elections to Catalonia's regional parliament on April 29, 1984, the center-right Convergence and Union Party (CiU) won a majority. New measures of autonomy for the Basque and Catalan regional governments included the opening of television stations with programming entirely in the regional languages. The more extreme regionalists were not satisfied, however, with all aspects of the new organic law and successfully challenged some of its provisions in the Constitutional Court.

All top municipal offices and council seats are filled by direct election. Municipal elections were held in conjunction with the 1979 and 1982 general elections and with the regional parliamentary elections of 1983. Among the national parties, the more conservative ones are strongest in the smaller towns, while the Socialists and, to a lesser extent, the Communists tend to sweep the major cities. After the 1979 elections, the PSOE governed the more populous cities in coalition with the Spanish Communist Party (PCE) and other smaller or regional parties. Since increasing its lead in the 1983 elections, however, the PSOE has generally been able to govern alone.

In the 1983 elections, the PSOE and its Catalan branch (PSC) won 43 percent of the vote, with majorities in twenty-six of the fifty-two provincial capitals (including those of the North African enclaves of Ceuta and Melilla) and pluralities in seven other capitals, almost doubling its number of councilors. The AP–PDP–UL Coalition won 26 percent of the vote, with majorities in seven capitals and pluralities in three others. The PNV won 2.6 percent of the vote, with pluralities in Bilbao, San Sebastián, and Victoria. The PCE vote was 7 percent nationwide, but the party won a majority only in one capital, Córdoba. Mayoralties of the fifty-two provincial capitals were distributed as follows: PSOE/PSC 35; AP-PDP-ULI O; PNV 3; independents 2; PCE 1; Canary Islands Party (ATI) 1.

The Electoral System

The constitution specifies that each province is to have a minimum number of deputies (presently two), the remainder to be allocated in accordance with population. It also requires that seats be allocated in accordance with a relatively simple form of proportional representation (modified d'Houdt). These provisions represent a compromise between the UCD and the PSOE. The minimum representation for each province establishes overrepresentation of the rural areas where the more conservative parties are stronger. In return for accepting that disadvantageous provision, the PSOE insisted upon proportional representation in order to avoid being forced into a formal electoral alliance with the Spanish Communist Party (PCE).

In lower-house elections, the voter can indicate his preference only for a list, not for a particular candidate. Parties are required to obtain at least 3 percent of the vote in any given province to win a seat in that province. For the Senate, voters mark their ballots for individual candidates, who may be party nominees or independents. The four candidates in each province receiving the largest number of votes are the winners.

For the general elections of 1982, 80.2 percent of the 26.5 million registered voters turned out. Regional and municipal elections in 1983 drew a 65-percent turnout.

The Party System

Origins of the Parties

The only national parties to have survived the three and one-half decades of the Franco dictatorship are the Socialists (PSOE) and the Communists (PCE). Their organizations were maintained underground and in exile, and many of their members suffered severe persecution. Franco tolerated no parties other than his own, originally the Falange and later an amorphous group known as the National Movement, which subsumed the Falange. Although several individuals who were associated with it have emerged as leaders of new parties. The National Movement, as such, died with Franco.

Carlos Arias Navarro, appointed prime minister by Franco at the beginning of 1974, shared Franco's aversion to party politics, but felt that a measure of liberalization before Franco's death would ease the mounting tension in the system. Thus, as one aspect of the *apertura*, or political opening, he promised to permit the creation of political "associations." However, as the associations were required to pledge allegiance to the principles of the National Movement, only supporters of the regime bothered to form such associations. One of these was Adolfo Suárez, who established the Union of the Spanish People (UDPE).

After Franco's death, the Arias government proposed and the *Cortes* (then comprised, for the most part, of Franco appointees) approved, in June 1976, a very selective legalization of political parties. A centrist group known as the Popular Party (PP) requested and received recognition under that legislation.

The government of Adolfo Suárez, appointed by King Juan Carlos in mid-1976 to succeed that of Arias, was reluctant to recognize the Communist Party fearing that such a move would provoke a strong reaction from the military. The PSOE, however, and other left-of-center parties refused to apply for legal status, denying credibility to the process of liberalization, until the government agreed to legalize *all* parties. Under this pressure, the government, in February 1977, finally announced new legislation whereby it renounced its discretionary power in the granting of legalization.

Since the promulgation of the electoral law of 1977, more than 200 parties have been registered. Of those, however, only eighteen parties or coalitions have had parliamentary representation, and only ten maintained seats after the general elections of October 1982.

The Parties in Law

Article 6 of the Constitution of 1978 addresses itself to political parties: "Political parties express political pluralism, concur in the formation and manifestation of the popular will and are a fundamental instrument for political participation. Their creation and the exercise of their activities are free in so far as they are compatible with respect for the constitution and the law. Their internal structure and operation must be democratic."

Parties are partially subsidized by the state in proportion to the vote they receive in the parliamentary elections.

Party Organization

Party organization varies widely. Policymaking is highly centralized in the parties on the left and right extremes. Local initiative and participation in party policymaking is more common in the PSOE. Only in the leftist parties, including the PSOE, is party organization highly structured and formalized. Although all the parties are formally membership parties, the Civil War and forty years of authoritarian rule have made many Spaniards reluctant to become openly involved in politics. As a result, formal party memberships are quite small in proportion to voting strength. This failure of open political association hurts the parties on the left more than those on the right.

Campaigning

Formal campaigning in parliamentary elections is limited to a three-week period. Television is the most important campaign medium. The state provides free television time to the parties on the basis of the number of seats they hold in the Congress of Deputies, with special provisions made for smaller parties which are unrepresented. Radio speeches and personal appearances are also common. Campaigns are oriented more to personalities than to issues.

Independent Voters

The level of party identification is quite low compared to that of other European countries. According to a 1982 survey, 54 percent of the electorate does not identify with any party. Only about 6 percent of the population actually belongs to a specific party. Because Spain has had only three national elections, data on voter identification is sparse. Comparison of the results of these elections suggests that voter loyalty to one party or another is fairly strong, but that a large bloc of voters in the center cannot be counted on by either party. Some 9 million voters transferred their votes from one party to another between the second and third national elections. A rough comparison of votes for deputies and senators indicates a considerable amount of ticket splitting in 1979, i.e., some voters cast their ballots for PSOE deputies and UCD senators and vice versa, and much less splitting in 1982.

Popular Alliance
(*Alianza Popular;* AP)

History

The AP was organized shortly after Franco's death and won sixteen seats in the 1977 elections. Before the 1979 elections, it drew a few smaller right-wing groups into an electoral alliance called the Democratic Coalition, but the coalition only managed to win nine seats in the Congress. With defections to it from the center and from parties to its right, the AP returned in 1982 to take over 25 percent of the vote and become the major opposition party to the Socialists.

Organization

The AP is weaker at the mass level than the leftist parties. Its organizational structure is relatively loose and local strength depends on the prestige and activity of local notables. The more powerful of these notables have considerable influence on party policy, particularly in their regions.

AP headquarters are at Silva 23, Madrid.

Policy

Many party leaders see themselves as guardians of the traditional order that the Franco regime championed. The AP has distinguished itself from ultraright groups by conceding the need for political reform and renouncing violence. Its shrill anti-Marxist rhetoric, however, has been viewed as provocative by some who might otherwise sympathize with its stress on "law and order."

Membership & Constituency

Originally based on firm supporters of the Franco regime, the AP has come to include many other conservatives since the break-up of the UCD, winning votes in all provinces and a plurality in six. It is stronger in the rural and semirural areas than in the major cities, showing particular strength in the northwestern region of Galicia. In a nation in which political activity was systematically discouraged for over a generation, the AP's deference to traditional and economic elites gives it an advantage among voters who are politically passive.

Financing

The party is very well financed by members' contributions and by gifts from banking and industrial interests.

Leadership

The party is led by sexagenarians who occupied important positions in the Franco regime. The party leader, Manuel Fraga Iribarne (born 1922) served as Franco's minister of information and tourism from 1962 to 1969. Iribarne reportedly stands slightly nearer the center of the political spectrum than most of the party.

Prospects

Since the party congress of January 1983, the AP has defined itself as "liberal-conservative," based on the model of the British Conservative Party. It has sought to modify its ideological profile and public image so as to appeal to the entire right-of-center electorate. The outcome of that strategy remains to be seen.

Spanish Socialist Workers Party (*Partido Socialista Obrero Español;* PSOE)

History

The PSOE was founded in 1874 and grew rapidly in the north, especially in Asturias where the General Union of Workers (*Unión General de Trabajadores;* UGT) had been most successful in organizing the working class. It participated, with other groups of the democratic left, in the coalition government of the Second Republic (1931–36). Socialists and other republicans put up a valiant defense in the Civil War of 1936 to 1939, but suffered devastating defeat.

By the time of Franco's death the party had splintered, and while socialistic leanings were widespread, organization, as such, was weak. With technical assistance and financial support from other European socialist parties, however, it grew very rapidly, attracting reform-oriented Spaniards who distrusted the UCD because of its ties to the Franco regime. It won 29 percent of the vote and 118 seats in the Congress of Deputies in the elections of 1977, slightly more in 1979, and major victories in regional elections in Andalusia in May 1982. Finally, on October 28, 1982, the PSOE won absolute majorities in both houses of the *Cortes.*

Organization

The organizational structure of the PSOE is highly elaborated with strong democratic procedures. Delegates are elected from local chapters to provincial and regional conferences which, in turn, elect delegates to the national conference, the party's highest formal authority. The national conference elects the party leadership, though there has been little real competition for these posts since the party leader is in undisputed control of the organization.

The Unified Socialist Party of Catalonia (*Partido Socialista Unificado de Cataluña;* PSUC) is an autonomous affiliate of the PSOE. The Andalucian Socialist Party is *not* affiliated with the PSOE.

National PSOE headquarters are at Joaquin García Morato 165-2, Madrid.

Policy

At its Twenty-seventh Congress, the first in Spain since the Civil War, held in Madrid in December 1976, the PSOE defined itself as a class party and its ideology as Marxist socialism. The leadership selected at the congress, however, was considerably less radical than the party's popular base.

The PSOE would have preferred a clean break with the past and reform from the bottom up—responding more directly to the demands of grass-roots organizations—rather than reform from the top down. It advocated a secular republican state, rather than a monarchy in which the Catholic Church retains official status. Nevertheless, there is unspoken support among party leaders for a continuation of the monarchy as an essential element in support of Spain's fragile democracy.

The party advocates autonomy for historical regions within a federal system, while opposing the unfettered self-determination demanded by the Basques. The PSOE has sought to protect the interests of workers and of the disadvantaged against excesses of the capitalist system and favors economic planning and government intervention to improve the economy and facilitate income redistribution.

Taking office in late 1982, the PSOE government, headed by Felipe Gonzalez, proposed a program including: implementation of the establishment of the *comunidades autónomas,* or autonomous regions; the introduction of new codes governing the penal system, judicial power, legal aid, military justice and conscientious objection, and antiterrorism measures; reform of legislation concerning employment, social security, and taxation; a ban on further construction of nuclear power plants and nationalization of the country's power-supply grid; and the establishment of a system of university autonomy.

Membership & Constituency

Membership in the PSOE is "regulated," as opposed to "open." Candidate members must accept the party platform and be willing to pay dues. They must also be nominated by members and must be accepted by local party assembly. Party membership doubled between the elections of 1977 and 1979. It stabilized in the early 1980s at about 100,000 (only about 1.8 percent of its voters) in 2,900 local chapters. The membership, almost equally divided between manual laborers on one hand and white-collar workers, professionals, and the self-employed on the other, is older on average than either the party's leadership or its electoral base. The party's historical ties with the UGT have been maintained.

The PSOE is strongest in the major cities and in the north, east, and south. Its constituency, compared to that of the AP, is young, urban, more active politically, and less devout, but not necessarily anticlerical. It is predictably less affluent than the AP, although the distinction is not a sharp one. The PSOE draws support from a broad range of occupational and income categories. The leftward shift of the electorate since Franco's death suggests the increasing complexity of the social structure rather than polarization.

Financing

Membership dues account for a major proportion of the party's income. Contributions from some businesses and assistance from other European socialist parties add to revenues.

Leadership

The virtually unchallenged leader of the party since 1974 has been Felipe González (born 1942 in Seville), who became prime minister in late 1982. A labor lawyer from Andalucia, González is a political moderate and a highly charismatic figure. Public opinion polls have shown him to be second only to the king in personal popularity.

Party leadership in general is highly educated, upwardly mobile, and professionally or technocratically oriented. Working-class backgrounds are virtually absent among the party elite, and even at party congresses manual workers are in a tiny minority.

Prospects

The PSOE's shift toward the center, en route to electoral victory, had the desired effect of attracting new voters, among them about 30 percent of the disintegrating UCD. The price, however, has been further disgruntlement on the part of the party's formally recognized and highly critical left wing, *Izquierda Socialista* or Socialist Left, and within the PSOE's trade union affiliate, the UGT.

The referendum on participation in NATO, which took place in March 1986, can be expected to deepen that rift. The 53.4 percent vote to maintain NATO membership which was arranged by the UCD government in May 1982, was seen as a victory for Prime Minister Felipe Gonzalez, who had reversed his position, once in office, to favor such membership. It was believed to augur well for his prospects of winning another four-year term in general elections expected in October. Among the 38.6 percent who voted against NATO membership, however, are bound to be a great many Socialists who will find means of expressing their disaffection on election day.

Minor Parties

Union of the Democratic Center (*Unión del Centro Democrático*; UCD) and its Successors

The UCD emerged on the eve of the 1977 elections as a convergence of the Democratic Center (CD), a coalition of liberal, Christian democratic, and social democratic groupings marginally associated with the Franco regime, and the personal following of Prime Minister Adolfo Suárez. Its space on the political spectrum was residual, marked by the parties to its right and to its left. Its support was weakest around the northern, eastern, and southern perimeters of the country, strongest in the geographical center and in the west. It drew support, in particular, from the more rural, the more devout, and the older generations.

The UCD won 34.72 percent of the vote and a plurality of 165 seats in the Congress of Deputies in 1977. Suárez was elected prime minister in 1977 and reelected in 1979. Despite his association with the Franco regime, Suárez was identified with the social-democratic faction within the UCD. Under pressure from several quarters, including bankers and other financial backers of the UCD, Suárez resigned in early 1981 and temporarily "retired" from politics. He was succeeded by Calvo Sotelo, a party bureaucrat lacking charismatic appeal.

Lacking then both ideological coherence and strong leadership, the party disintegrated. Its few successes in the 1982 elections were limited to the Canaries and conservative Galicia. Sotelo was not reelected in 1982, and the party leadership fell to a little-known deputy from Madrid, Landelino Lavilla. In February 1983, he dissolved the party. The twelve UCD deputies and four senators elected in 1982 were authorized to join other parties. Several were allocated senior posts with the Popular Democratic Party, which had contested the 1982 elections in coalition with the AP.

Social Democratic Center (*Centro Democrático y Social*; CDS)

The CDS was founded by Adolfo Suárez (born 1932), the former UCD leader, in mid-1982, too late to make an effective showing in the elections, if, indeed, Suárez had the popularity and support that many observers believed he did.

Born in 1932, Suárez studied law in Salamanca and Madrid and held several bureaucratic posts before obtaining a seat in the *Cortes*. In the late 1960s and early 1970s, he served as civil governor of Segovia province and as director general of radio and television. In 1975 he became secretary general of the National Movement. Juan Carlos selected him in 1976 to serve as president of the government, reportedly because the king wanted someone who would be personally loyal to him and who would be able to maneuver among the existing institutions manned by Franco appointees.

Suárez was reelected from Madrid in 1982. If his earlier success rested on anything more than the king's favor, he could again become a rallying point for social democratic forces if the Socialists move toward more aggressive leftist policies.

Democratic Reformist Party (*Partido Reformista Democrático*; PRD

At the end of 1983 a new centrist formation, the Democratic Reformist Party (PRD), began to take shape under the leadership of Antonio Garrigues Walker, until then president of the Liberal Democratic Party (PDL). The PRD, which held its constituent congress on November 25, 1984, sought to recapture the center abandoned by the UCD. The party line is "progressive liberal" and its structure is federalist, reflecting the country's traditions of regionalism.

Spanish Communist Party (*Partido Comunista de España*; PCE)

The PCE was fast becoming the strongest political force in the coalition government of the Second Republic before the victory of Franco's forces. It remained the strongest—in fact, virtually the only—core of opposition to the dictatorship until Franco's death. Its courageous stand had attracted many Spaniards who were not necessarily enthused by its creed and who, after the political opening, transferred their allegiance to the Socialists or other more "acceptable" parties.

While holding the socialization of the means of production as an ideal, the party's short-term goals have been the successful transition to a democratic system and the legitimization of its own participation in that system. Its platform is virtually indistinguishable from that of the PSOE, but to combat greater skepticism from the public and the threat from the armed forces and other reactionary groups, it compromised even more readily than did the PSOE with the center-right UCD government. While the PSOE, in the voting on constitutional provisions, abstained, the PCE voted in favor of retaining the monarchy and recognizing the special status of the Catholic Church. Since the 1979 elections, however, the PCE has gradually adopted a more radical posture.

Since 1960, the party has been dominated by its Eurocommunist faction and by Santiago Carillo. Born in 1916 in Asturias, the son of a socialist union organizer, he joined the PCE in 1936 and became a member of its central committee the following year. He has repeatedly declared his commitment to majority rule, has sought coalition among opposition groups, has disassociated the party from all extremist elements, and has urged it to avoid provoking its enemies. Carillo briefly resigned from the leadership in June 1982 after the party lost badly in autonomous-region elections in Andalusia and resigned again after the party's miserable showing in the Cortes elections. These resignations reveal serious intraparty disputes over Carillo's authoritarian style and firm Eurocommunist commitment. Replacing Carillo after his 1982 resignation was Gerardo Iglesias. Iglesias was reelected in 1983 for a three-year term.

With coherent, experienced, and disciplined leadership, and with a solid base in the Workers' Commissions (*Comisiones Obreras*; CCOO)—the labor confederation that operated extralegally but effectively during the last years of the Franco regime—the PCE is likely to retain a major role on the left.

Regional Parties

The forcefulness of the claims to regional autonomy have derived more from the economic strength of Catalonia and the Basque country, the regions with the strongest claims, and from the intransigence of the Basques, than from the electoral strength of regional parties. Furthermore, representatives of the PSOE and the PCE elected from those regions have also supported the principle of regional autonomy.

Catalan interests have been represented by a coalition known as Convergence and Union (*Convergencia i Unió;* CiU). Its position on regionalism has been moderate compared to that of the Basque parties. In 1982, the CiU and the Catalonian Republican Left (*Ezquerra Republicana de Catalunya;* ERC) ran a combined slate for the Senate and won nearly half the Catalonian seats.

The Basque Nationalist Party (*Partido Nacionalista Vasco;* PNV) was established in 1893 as the first modern political expression of Basque regionalism. It is a conservative, Catholic party with middle-class leadership and a constituency of peasants. Its goal is the preservation of the Basque language and social customs through self-determination. During the Franco years, the party survived in exile in France.

The PNV faces more radical competition from two parties to its left: the Basque Left (*Euzkadiko Ezquerra;* EE) and a coalition of Basque leftist groups under the name United People (*Herri Batasuna;* HB).

The Socialist Party of Andalucia (*Partido Socialista Andaluz;* PSA) emerged from the 1979 elections with five deputies, but won none in 1982, possibly because the PSOE's Gonzalez is an Andalucian. Regional parties in Navarre and Aragon, which won Senate seats in 1979, were closed out in 1982. A regional party in the Canaries and one in Majorca did win one senate seat each in 1982.

Other Political Forces

Military

The Spanish armed forces constitute a virtual caste. Most officers are the sons of officers, and many trace their professional lineages back several generations. The castelike structure and mentality of the armed forces has been reinforced by the maintenance of a military court system, which permits the military to operate virtually independently of civil authority. Military officers tend to keep to themselves socially as well as professionally, to read the same newspapers, such as *Alcázar,* and to otherwise avoid "contamination" by civilian society. There is some evidence, however, that this system is gradually being broken down by the lure of higher salaries in business. The developing trend appears to be for the sons of high-ranking officers to opt for careers in business and for new officers to be the sons of noncommissioned officers.

There is also a regional bias in the armed forces. Since the times of the *conquistadores,* officers and military families have come disproportionately from the more nearly feudal areas of Estremadura, Castile, and Andalusia. There are relatively few officers from the more prosperous and more nearly autonomous Basque country and Catalonia.

The Spanish army, in general, is highly traditional in the sense of commitment to a centralized state; to conservative Catholic values; to the ideas of monarchy, authority, and order; and, of course, to an important and privileged position for the army in society. It is hardly surprising that the officer corps feels threatened not only by socialism but by liberalism and democracy as well. The navy and air force are less traditional, more technocratic, and more closely associated with the U.S. military, but they are not necessarily less political nor more liberal.

The Civil Guard is a more clear-cut vestige of Francoist Spain and, even more than the regular armed forces, feels threatened by the transition to democracy. The Guard is unlikely, however, to undertake such an ambitious project as a *coup d'état* on its own initiative. Its command structure is integrated with that of the regular armed forces and, in a conspiracy, the Guard could be expected to be acting under the orders of well-placed military officers.

There are several identifiable factions within the armed forces. The largest group, while conservative, is relatively apolitical and disinclined to take initiatives, but also relatively uninfluential. Of the politically committed factions, the largest is Francoist, that is, reactionary and authoritarian, inclined to flaunt fascist values and resist the dismantling of Francoist institutions.

The next-largest faction is committed to the institution of monarchy, but more commonly to absolute monarchy than to the constitutional variety. In that sense, it is more monarchist than the king. The smallest faction is liberal, committed to the process of transition and to the establishment of links with democratic Western Europe. The king has placed officers of this inclination in military intelligence where they can keep track of developing conspiracies.

Budget competition is not a major source of friction between military and civilian leaders. The armed forces have not suffered financial loss under the parliamentary monarchy. In fact, officers' salaries have been raised substantially and perquisites have remained intact.

For the military establishment as a whole, the most readily articulated grievances with the transition process have been the centrifugal force of demands for regional autonomy and legal constraints on the ability of the armed forces to combat Basque terrorism. At least two soldiers have been arrested after suspected members of the Basque revolutionary separatist organization, ETA, died under "interrogation." Thus, while civilian institutions attempt to protect the Basques from the violation of their civil and human rights by the military, ETA terrorism provides military conspirators with continuing pretexts for attacking those civilian institutions.

Four military conspiracies were foiled between mid-1977 and late 1982. The severest challenge to date came on Feb. 23, 1981, when Lieutenant Colonel Antonio Tejero Molina of the Civil Guard, accompanied by a band of 288 guardsmen assembled ad hoc from the Guard's motor pool and traffic control division, forced his way into the Congress of Deputies and held parliamentarians and cabinet members at gunpoint for eighteen hours.

At the same time, in Valencia, Captain General Jaime Milans del Bosch, commander of the Third Military Region, broadcast a communique that he was assuming civil control of the region under quasi-martial law. In Madrid, General Alfonso Armada, deputy army chief of staff and a former tutor of the king, reported to Army Chief of Staff General Gabeiras that

other military regions supported Milans. With virtually all civilian leaders literally under the gun, Armada had believed that his own selection as head of government might be made to appear as a reasonable negotiated solution. In their haste, however, the conspirators had failed to reach accord on details. Tejero insisted on holding out for Milans rather than Armada as the new head of government.

Most other military officers were waiting for word from the king. Juan Carlos, however, refused to see Armada. He telephoned the regional commanders, made clear his opposition to the coup, and demanded and received their pledges of loyalty. He subsequently appeared on television to inform the country of what had taken place and to repudiate the attempted coup.

Once it was clear that support was not forthcoming, Milans withdrew his declaration of civil control in the Third Military Region. Tejero and his guardsmen withdrew from the *Cortes,* and Armada fell back on his claim of being a disinterested mediator.

Four days after the assault on the *Cortes,* leaders of all the significant national parties, from Manual Fraga of the Popular Alliance on the right to Santiago Carillo of the Communist Party on the left, together with other influential figures, such as Rafael Termes, president of the bankers' association, paraded arm in arm through the streets of Madrid to the cheers of some two million demonstrators. A public opinion poll conducted shortly after the putsch of February 23 showed 81 percent favoring democracy and only 4 percent in sympathy with the conspirators. Nevertheless, there have been a number of provocative acts by groups of military officers and Civil Guardsmen since the incident of February 23.

Thirty-three officers and one civilian involved in the coup attempt were arrested and tried before a military court. On June 3, 1982, Milans and Tejero were given maximum sentences of thirty years in prison, while all the other officers received sentences of six years or less. Armada was sentenced to six years in jail. Ten junior officers were absolved. The armed forces were sharply divided over these results, with the hardliners calling for the reduction or suspension of all the sentences. Civilian authorities on the other hand demanded harsher penalties for those who had received the lightest sentences and appealed their case to the Supreme Court. On April 28, 1983, the Court handed down a verdict that increased Armada's sentence to 30 years, increased thirteen other sentences, and imposed sentences of one to two years on eight Civil Guardsmen who had previously been acquitted.

Meanwhile, shortly before the 1982 elections, another military conspiracy had been uncovered. It involved some of the same men as the abortive coup of 1981. Some observers believe the disclosure of the conspiracy not only added to the PSOE's will to win a majority, but also contributed to the party's landslide victory. In April 1984 three colonels found guilty of engaging in that conspiracy were given the minimum sentence of twelve years and one day by a military tribunal. Under legislation passed in December 1984, as part of a new code of military justice, members of the armed forces accused of rebellion would henceforth face a civilian court, and no future defense could be based on merely obeying orders.

Other aspects of the so-called Serra reforms, named after Defense Minister Narcis Serra and enacted in 1984, were addressed to the establishment of overall political control. The armed forces were placed under the control of the prime minister. A new post was created, Chief of the Defense Staff, to report directly to the defense minister, and the Joint Chiefs of Staff were demoted to an advisory role. The king, however, remains supreme commander of the armed forces.

Plans for the modernization and depoliticization of the armed forces in the 1980s were to bring them into line with the forces of other European countries and to align their salaries with those of civilian government employees. The army was to be reduced in strength by one-fourth of its officers and one-third of its men, and promotion was to be on merit rather than seniority. Whereas during the Franco era the armed forces had been concentrated around Madrid and other major cities to deal with threats from the "internal enemy," those forces were to be redeployed and to be oriented toward external defense planning. Conscripts were to be allowed to serve in their native regions.

Basques

While the cultures of other "nationalities" in Spain are variants within the Spanish nation—and their languages related to the Latin—Basque culture is different. The Basques are thought to have been in Spain since paleolithic times, and their language is apparently unrelated to any other known language.

Basque nationalism surfaced with the founding of the PNV in 1893, but it did not become a major factor in Spanish politics, until a part of the PNV's youth wing left the party in 1959 and founded the Basque Nation and Liberty (*Euzkadi ta Azkatasuna;* ETA). The ETA seeks to achieve independence through revolutionary violence. There is no reason to believe the Basque majority is in sympathy with either the means or the goals of the ETA. Nevertheless, there is widespread sympathy for the ETA as a result of the violence employed by the Franco government to repress it, violence so indiscriminate that it was seen as an attack on the Basque people as a whole.

The ETA's terrorism is most often directed against the army and the Civil Guard. Terrorists are tried in civil courts and, from the military's point of view, are treated too leniently. Military casualties from terrorist action combined with a perceived disparity between the treatment of terrorists and conspiratorial officers is a primary element in the friction between the civil government and the military. Continued terrorist activity, therefore, only increases the military's frustration and the danger of a coup.

The PSOE government, with AP concurrence, in late 1983 adopted a set of new measures to deal with ETA terrorism. Judges were empowered to ban political associations that supported terrorism and to order detention of suspects without trial for up to two-and-a-half years. Penalties for terrorist crimes were increased, police were given extended powers of search and surveillance, and incentives were offered for prisoners to turn informer. Taking a different tack, the government announced in late 1984 that it was willing to enter direct negotiations with the ETA, hinting that there might be a prospect of amnesty for those not guilty of crimes.

Neither approach proved effective, nor did the establishment of a regional government with considerable autonomy and with its own Basque police force. Separatist violence continued, with the killing of at least six Civil Guards and more than a dozen policemen in 1983 and 1984 and several kidnappings for ransom. Meanwhile, the ETA had split into two branches, ETA-m and ETA-pm, and it was being "balanced" on the far right by a death squad, the Anti-Terrorist Liberation Group (GAL), which ETA spokesmen claimed was a parapolice force.

National Prospects

By the mid-1980s, most observers of Spanish politics believed that the greatest danger to the process of transition to democracy—that of reversal by military coup—had been overcome and that there remained among the politically articulate little fundamental disagreement as to what the basic outlines of the political system should be. The party system, however, was still in the process of formation.

Political fragmentation had diminished, but voters retained a wide range of options. These ranged from the PCE on the left to the PSOE at the center-left, the remnants of and splinters from the UCD covering center to center-right, and the AP and its coalition partners, the PDP and UL, on the right. There were also regional parties ranging across the left-right spectrum and from moderate to radical on issues of regional jurisdiction. Some Spaniards were discomfited, however, by the system's increased polarization and volatility.

Sociological and public opinion studies over the past decade have found that most of the population on most issues locates itself at the center-left; thus, the position of the PSOE remains strong. Nevertheless, the recession of the early 1980s has left in its wake an unemployment rate of 21 percent by the end of 1985. Adjustments in industrial and labor policies necessitated by entry, on January 1, 1986, into the European Community have been costly to the party's credibility. The very fact that fear of a successful coup and return to authoritarianism fades with the passage of time also means that the austerity measures Gonzalez has deemed necessary may meet steadily increasing resistance as the next election approaches.

Further Reading

Anderson, Charles W. *The Political Economy of Modern Spain.* Madison: University of Wisconsin Press, 1970.

Bar, Antonio. "The Emerging Spanish Party System: Is There a Model?" *West European Politics,* October 1984.

Cortada, James W., ed. *Spain in the Twentieth Century World.* Westport, Conn.: Greenwood Press, 1980.

Coverdale, John F. *The Political Transformation of Spain after Franco.* New York: Praeger Publishers, 1979.

Keefe, Eugene K., et al. *Area Handbook for Spain.* Washington, D.C.: Government Printing Office, for Foreign Area Studies, American University, 1976.

Medhurst, Kenneth N. "Spain's Socialist Government." *Contemporary Review,* June 1983.

Penniman, Howard, ed. *Spain at the Polls.* Washington, D.C.: American Enterprise Institute, 1980.

Pollack, Benny. "The 1982 Spanish General Election and Beyond." *Parliamentary Affairs,* Spring 1983.

Share, Donald. "Two Transitions: Democratization and the Evolution of the Spanish Socialist Left." *West European Politics,* January 1985.

Wigg, Richard. "Socialism in Spain: a Pragmatic Start." *The World Today,* February 1983.

DEMOCRATIC SOCIALIST REPUBLIC OF SRI LANKA
(Prajathanthrika Samajawadi Janarajaya Sri Lanka)

by Thomas J. Nossiter, Ph.D.

The System of Government

The unitary state of Sri Lanka, an island nation of 14.8 million people on the former Ceylon south of India, is a parliamentary democracy with a directly elected executive president. Sri Lanka has been unusual in the Third World in enjoying a viable competitive democracy. It owes this to the institutions and traditions developed while under British colonial rule, its high levels of literacy (80 percent), the role of Western-educated political families such as the Bandaranaikes and Senanayakes, and to the small size of the armed forces. However, since 1979 conflict between the majority (74 percent) Sinhala community and the minority (18 percent) Tamil community has placed the system under great stress. In 1983 the Constitution was amended to make the advocacy of separatism illegal. There has also, since 1982, been increasing concern about the institutionalization of political violence under ruling party auspices.

The current French-style Gaullist system was established by constitutional amendment in 1977 after the United National Party (UNP) electoral victory. Its chief architect is Julius R. Jayewardene who became Sri Lanka's president on February 4, 1978 through parliamentary election. The first popular presidential election took place on October 20, 1982 after Parliament approved a constitutional amendment permitting Jayewardene to call the election after four years not six. Jayewardene won with 53 percent of the votes. His nearest rival, Hector Kobbekaduwa of the Sri Lanka Freedom Party (SLFP), led by Anura Bandaranaike, is the UNP's only serious rival.

A new constitution was promulgated in September 1978. Jayewardene's aims in reforming the constitution were to preclude future prime ministerial abuse of power such as occurred under the previous Bandaranaike government; to promote political stability and economic growth; and to encourage national unity. The septuagenarian president has had only limited success.

Executive

Besides being head of state, the president exercises executive authority directly and through the prime minister. Ministers hold their office at the president's pleasure, and the president himself may hold any ministerial portfolio. He can dismiss Parliament, call new elections, and submit bills of national importance to a referendum. He may also declare a national emergency. The presidency is open to any Sri Lankan citizen thirty years of age or older who is not (as Mrs. Bandaranaike has been) deprived of their civil rights.

While it is possible for a president to transform himself into a dictator, there are real restraints on presidential power: the president may not be strictly accountable to Parliament, but he is responsible to it; his term of office is limited to six years and can only be renewed once; and the Supreme Court has genuinely independent powers. In the last resort, Sri Lanka is a pluralist society and the citizens are politically sophisticated and articulate—two of the best defenses against arbitrary government.

Legislature

The Parliament is a unicameral body composed of 169 elected members. The presidentially appointed Delimitation Commission demarcates multimember electoral districts (at present twenty-four) on the basis of population. There are no appointed members. Parliament must meet once a year, but normally meets for one session of up to four months. Its powers are of the usual kind: to enact legislation—including (with some provisos) constitutional law—and to control public finance. Elections must be held once every six years, but they may be called by the president any time after one year of Parliament's term. In 1977 the UNP won a sweeping victory with 50 percent of the vote and 140 of the seats, the most lopsided result in Sri Lanka's history. The SLFP suffered from the effects of the simple-plurality electoral system, winning only eight seats from 30 percent of the vote. The Tamil United Liberation Front (TULF), representing the geographically concentrated minority community, became the official opposition with eighteen (now 16) seats from 6 percent of the vote. Since August 1983, it, together with the Communist Party, the JVP (People's Liberation Front) and the LSSP (Equal Society Party) has been banned. The remaining seat was won by the Ceylon Workers' Congress, a party representing tea workers of Tamil origin. The CWC's leader, Savumyamoorthy Thonadaman, joined the government in 1978. Outright single-party majorities are rare and governments have normally been coalitions, though the present UNP ministry has a four-fifths majority in parliament.

In late 1982, the life of the present Parliament was extended until 1989, after a government-sponsored referendum to that effect was approved by 55 percent of the voters after a controversial campaign. Normal elections had been scheduled for August 1983 and were to have been held under proportional representation for the first time.

Judiciary

The Supreme Court of Sri Lanka is composed of a chief justice and six to ten associates, who serve until retirement. Under the 1978 constitution, the judiciary is fully independent though doubts have been expressed as to whether or not this is true. The Supreme Court may determine whether legislation violates the constitution (a court decision has been overruled by amending the constitution) and whether a proposed constitutional amendment should be put to referendum, and adjudicates charges against the president.

Regional & Local Government

Devolution of regional powers has been a contentious issue largely because of Tamil fears of Sinhala domination. In early 1981, the District Development Councils Act appeared to give considerable autonomy over economic development to the twenty-four districts. The consequences of the act are as yet unclear. The council members themselves are elected, but their officers are appointed by the central government through the Public Service Commission. In addition, each district has a minister of state appointed by the central government; currently, all ministers are UNP members of Parliament. Their precise powers are uncertain, but it is likely that they will function principally as representatives of the central government and ruling party. The balance between centralization and decentralization has yet to be struck, and it is likely to be different in the north, with its Tamil population, than in the rest of the country. Such cases, which include the receipt of block grants for the district councils from the central government, may help to overcome ethnic discrimination, backwardness in some localities, and the general lethargy of the civil service. The impact of the 1981 reorganization remains largely hypothetical in view of the security situation. Negotiations between the TULF and the government with Indian mediation are stalemated.

The Electoral System

All citizens eighteen years of age and over are entitled to vote and are registered efficiently by the local authorities. Turnout has been high, especially for a Third World country; it was 87 percent in 1977. In the presidential election of 1982; however, it fell to 71 percent.

Through 1977, Sri Lanka's elections were conducted on the British system—victory through a simple plurality in single-member districts, with the underpopulated rural areas overrepresented. In 1978, a proportional-representation system was adopted, with multimember districts represented on the basis of population and proportionality determined at the district, not the national, level. The first election under this system is scheduled for 1989. Voting is to be by secret ballot for lists of candidates prepared by recognized political parties or independent groups. Coalitions or "united fronts" would appear to be precluded from offering joint lists. In counting the votes, those parties or groups which do not achieve 12.5 percent of the vote in the electoral district will gain no seats, although this figure may be reviewed.

By-elections will have no place under the new system. In the event of a vacancy, the party concerned nominates a successor from its election list. Parties may also expel an M.P. and replace him as if the seat has become vacant, a provision aimed to prevent M.P.s from changing sides.

The Party System

Origins of the Parties

The party system is of recent origin, but in the thirty years since independence, it has become truly competitive and part of the fabric of society.

The first modern party was the Lanka Samasamaja Party (LSSP), a Marxist independence party founded in 1935, which has fathered a number of other left-wing groupings and is now the only Trotskyite mass party in the world. At independence, the moderate and pragmatic UNP was the dominant party, and it was out of the UNP in 1951 that the left-of-center SLFP was formed, soon to establish itself as the opposition within the parliamentary system.

Virtually all the top leaders of the major parties—and most of the minor ones—have come from a network of political families who have kinship connections and are drawn from the upper castes (*goigayama*) with access to Western education. This is just as true of the Marxists as of the UNP, which has been known as the "Uncles and Nephews" party. In the 1980s, leaders have emerged from less favored backgrounds, but the system is still dominated by the old elite.

The Parties in Law

There is a specific constitutional guarantee of freedom of association, and any party which calls itself such has legal status unless banned under a state of emergency, or for advocating separatism or indirectly through a variety of laws designed to combat terrorism and criminal activity.

Official recognition—by the Commissioner of Elections—of a party or an "independent group" is based on having engaged for five years in political-party activity or having two members elected to Parliament. Since every conceivable political tendency has received a label at one time or another and there are a number of empty shells of old organizations that can be taken over, it is unlikely that the provisions of the new constitution will appreciably change the ease with which political parties can form and contest elections.

There are no limits on campaign expenditure, though those costs typically are low.

Party Organization

Party organization exhibits patrimonial elements in part because of the hierarchical character of traditional social relations in the island. The major parties have the form of mass democratic parties—primary members are enrolled for a nominal fee, branches cover the country, conferences are held regularly—but not the substance. At the local level it is the MPs and district leadership and not party membership who make the decisions. In turn, the national leaders treat district leaders as patrons might treat clients. For instance, it is the national leadership which selects candidates for constituencies. Ideology—despite appeals to Marxism and socialism—plays a subordinate role in the operation of the party system. Centrally determined programs are treated pragmatically, and in office the differences in practice between governments have been modest. There is a measure of policy continuity: as a UNP leader observed on nationalization, "one cannot unscramble eggs." Personal rivalries and quarrels are as important as political belief; and only the UNP has been relatively immune from factionalization. In the case of the SLFP, the feuding extends into the family life of the controlling Bandaranaikes: in December 1981 Mrs. Bandaranaike expelled her son, Anura. After forming a breakaway party, Anura and other leaders rejoined the SLFP in 1982.

Campaigning

Campaigning is controlled almost entirely by the top party leadership and most of the work—canvassing, fund raising, mobilizing crowds for rallies—is done by the parties' auxiliary organizations, that is, trade unions and youth wings.

These auxiliary groups are generally more important and effective than the organizations to direct party members. The auxiliaries are not affiliated formally with their respective parties and are not incorporated into the decision-making structures of the parties.

The costs of campaigning are slight because the public is politically conscious, the constituencies are small, and there is no tradition of bribery or the buying of votes. Officially, costs are estimated at about $1,000 per candidate and are probably not more than three or four times that in actuality.

Independent Voters

The independents' share of the vote has declined from 29 percent in 1947 to less than 5 percent in 1977. Independent MPs are now a rarity. The splitting of tickets is not an available option.

Ceylon Equal Society Party
(*Lanka Samasamaja Pakshaya;* LSSP)

History

Formed in December 1935 by Western-educated young intellectuals from elite families, this Marxist party had turned to Trotskyism by the late 1930s in reaction to Stalinism and Comintern domination of colonial Communist parties. Its peak impact was in the late 1940s. The emergence of the SLFP has since robbed it of its postindependence role of principal opposition to the UNP. It adopted united-front tactics and shared in the government formed in 1970. It now seeks to forge an alliance of Marxist parties to form a third alternative.

Organization

The LSSP is organized on socialist lines with a hierarchy extending from the locals (branches), through party conferences and congresses to the Central Committee and Politburo. Intraparty democracy is vigorous and genuine. The Ceylon Federation of Labor and the Youth League are important auxiliaries; LSSP headquarters are in Colombo.

Policy

The party is a mission-oriented Trotskyite party with long-range socialist aims including popular ownership of the means of production and collectivized agriculture. Although slowly becoming more pragmatic, it has maintained electorally unpopular stances.

Membership & Constituency

Membership numbers some 4,000. The party is highly selective and the members are committed ideologically. From 1952 to 1963, the party's electoral support was stagnant or declining, and although it increased its seats in Parliament in 1970, the party continued to lack popular appeal. In 1977, it took only 4 percent of the total vote and won no seats. Its principal constituency is the small Sinhala urban working class, especially in the coastal belt from Colombo south to Kalutara. It has had no impact on the rural Sinhala.

Financing

The party is financed by dues, contributions, and the sale of publications.

Leadership

The dominant figures have been N. M. Perera (died 1979) and Bernard Soysa (born 1914), but the Politburo is a collective leadership.

Prospects

The LSSP's prospects of returning to government are minimal.

Sri Lanka Freedom Party (SLFP; *Sri Lanka Nidahas Pakshaya*)

History

The SLFP grew out of Solomon W. R. Bandaranaike's *Sinhala Maha Sabha* (founded 1937). It was founded by him in September 1951, after his resignation from the UNP government, to be a left-of-center alternative to the parent party and a democratic alternative to the Marxist forms of socialism. In 1956 Bandaranaike led a Sinhala Buddhist–oriented united front to a major electoral victory and became prime minister. He was assassinated by a Buddhist monk in 1959. After a period of upheaval in which conservative elements were replaced by Marxist ones, Solomon's widow, Sirimavo Bandaranaike, took over the leadership and won the 1960 election. From 1960 to 1964 and again from 1970 to 1977, Mrs. Bandaranaike headed increasingly left-wing governments which undertook land reform and nationalization, pursued welfare policies and state intervention, and sought to accommodate Sinhala Buddhist revivalism. Her last administration faced grave difficulties including a 1971 insurrection of unemployed youth in the interior and economic decline. Corruption and illegality flourished, and in 1977 the SLFP suffered an overwhelming defeat.

Organization

The SLFP is nominally a mass party, but direction is highly centralized and there is little actual rank-and-file participation in decision making. Control rests with the parliamentary leadership and the Bandaranaike family. Party headquarters are in Colombo.

Policy

The SLFP is a left-wing democratic socialist party committed to nationalization, state intervention, and redistributionist policies. It adopts a neutralist foreign policy but inclines to an anti-West posture. It supports Sinhala as the official language but accepts minority safeguards.

Membership & Constituency

Party membership is about 65,000, but the trade union and youth league auxiliary organizations are more significant. Its main appeal is to the poorest Sinhala of the Dry Zone, an area of irrigated agriculture in the north. A bloc of safe seats surrounds the Bandaranaike and Ratwatte estates.

Financing

The party's income comes from dues, contributions, and the sale of publications.

Leadership

The leadership is dominated by the Bandaranaike clan. Sirimavo Bandaranaike (born 1916) dominated even though she was expelled from Parliament in the early 1980s for her abuse of power as prime minister between 1972 and 1977. After family feuding in 1981-2, her son, Anura, who espoused a relatively right-wing position, became leader. Mrs. Bandaranaike's daughter, Mrs. Chandrika Kumatunga, who supported her mother has subsequently (1984) founded a left-wing splinter from the SLFP, the Sri Lanka People's Party.

Prospects

The SLFP is the obvious alternative to the UNP, combining, as it does, Sinhalese-Buddist nationalism and, historically, a left-of-center stance. Under proportional representation an SLFP-led leftist coalition could defeat the UNP in the 1989 elections if Jayewardene's policies have proved unsuccessful, particularly on the economic front.

Tamil United Liberation Front (TULF; *Tamil Vimukthi Peramuna*)

History

The TULF is an ethnic party formed by the alliance of several political groups representing Tamil interests. A Tamil Liberation Front was formed in 1970. It consisted of the Federal Party (*Illankai Tamil Arasu Kadchi*) and the (All-Ceylon) Tamil Congress. In May 1972, this group was replaced by the Tamil United Front which also included the National Liberation Front (*Jatika Vimukthi Peramuna*), the Muslims United Front (primarily appealing to Tamil Muslims), and the Tamil Congress. The Tamil United Front was organized to support S. J. V. Chelvanayakam, the most important of the Jaffna Tamil leaders, in a by-election which he precipitated by resigning the contested seat in 1972 in order to force an election on the issue of regional autonomy, which Mrs. Bandaranaike refused to discuss. Chelvanayakam won the election (delayed until 1975) overwhelmingly, but Bandaranaike still refused to discuss the issue. This in turn prompted the Tamil parties to form the TULF, a sign of their full commitment to united Tamil action, in 1976. (Chelvanayakam died in 1977.)

Of the constituent elements, the Federal Party had traditionally favored autonomy within Sri Lanka. The Tamil Congress advocated collaboration with the UNP to secure concessions. The Ceylon Workers' Congress, as a trade union cum political party, represented the interests of the Tamil workers on inland tea estates.

Approximately one-fifth of the Sri Lankan population is of Tamil (Indian) origin: slightly more than half of the Tamils are Jaffna Tamils who migrated to Sri Lanka many centuries ago and are concentrated in the extreme north, the Jaffna peninsula; the rest are the Indian Tamils, imported by the British in the nineteenth century as indentured labor for the tea plantations. Many of the latter are not Sri Lankan citizens and some are stateless.

Historically, there has been tension and sometimes overt conflict between the well-educated, largely Hindu, Jaffna Tamils and the dominant Sinhala Buddhist community. After independence the Sinhala majority sought to establish cultural supremacy, and there have been intermittent bloody clashes culminating in July–August 1983 in the worst comunal outbreak in Sri Lanka's history. Following the murder of 13 soldiers (all Sinhalese) on the night of August 23 by Tamil Terrorists, civil disorder broke out in Colombo, the capital, leading on August 29 to the massacre of several hundred Tamils. This, and other attacks on the minority community, particularly in the northern area of Jaffna, led to strong diplomatic intervention by India. However, the TULF, under pressure from the clandestine terrorist movement, the Tamil Tigers, and the Sri Lankan government, caught between principle and its Sinhalese support base, have been unable so far to reach any agreement.

Organization

The TULF is a loose coordinating body in which the constituent elements retain their separate identities. Each party provides a vice-president. Although the (moderate) Federal Party is the dominant force, the Front is increasingly unpredictable as militant elements, inside and outside Sri Lanka, gain support. The TULF has been banned since August 1983; previously its headquarters were in Jaffna. The terrorist Tamil Tigers are alleged to maintain training camps in the south Indian state of Tamil Nadu and to receive funding from Tamil migrants in the West. At least five factions are known within the Tiger movement. Party headquarters are in Jaffna.

Policy

The TULF aims to establish a separate autonomous region known as Eelam with the right of self-determination. Its extremist wing seeks outright independence which, however, without improbable Indian support, is scarcely a practical proposition. The Front may well be satisfied with a real measure of district autonomy and security for Tamils resident elsewhere in the island.

Membership & Constituency

The party's membership is unknown, but its constituency embraces virtually all the Jaffna Tamils who live in the geographically isolated north. Support among the Indian Tamils of the central region is limited.

Financing

The TULF is financed by dues and contributions and possibly by funding from sympathizers in India and the United States.

Leadership

The TULF's president is M. Sivasithamparam (born 1923) and its secretary general Appapillai Amirthalingam (born 1927), both skillful and experienced politicians.

Prospects

Communal antagonism between Sinhalese and Tamils is now profound and although there are wise, secular politicians in both the UNP and the TULF, they are prisoners of the situation. The TULF's best hope is Indian intercession, coupled with an improvement in the performance of the Sri Lankan economy which would reduce the tendency of the ordinary Sinhalese to scapegoat the minority community. India would undoubtedly not tolerate the forcible expulsion of the Tamils from Sri Lanka but a lasting accommodation may be difficult to achieve.

United National Party
(Eksath Jathika Pakshaya; UNP)

History

The UNP was founded in September 1946 by Don Stephen Senanayake and other conservative notables with the support of some ethnic groups. It won clear victories in the 1947 and 1952 elections. In 1952 Dudley Senanayake succeeded his father as leader. However, his cosmopolitan liberal democratic policy and concern with long-range agricultural development failed to capture the Sinhala imagination. That and the UNP's failure to understand the intensity of the Sinhala Buddhist revival led to its defeat in 1956. The electoral setback led to the adoption of a new democratic socialist program in 1958.

During a further term of office between 1965 and 1970, the UNP neglected its organization and a heavy defeat in the 1970 election precipitated a major party crisis. Jayewardene argued that the UNP had no future as a party of the propertied classes and should support the government in its unpopular measures for economic renewal. Failing to affect the party's policy, he turned his attention to reviving its organization and democratizing the UNP. On the death of the indecisive Senanayake in 1973, Jayewardene took full control and forced the UNP into adopting a broad-ranging reform program including *dharmishta* (a just and righteous society), popular participation, and a presidential-style constitution. His victory in 1977 was its vindication. At the first popular presidential election in 1982 Jayewardene was returned with an absolute majority (53 percent) of the votes cast but the Tamil boycott and the less-than-free campaign suggest that the UNP does not command the widespread support it did in the late 1970s.

Organization

The UNP is a mass party. Jayewardene remains the elder statesman but is by no means total master. Prime Minister Premadasa and Cyril Matthew, Industries Minister, are powerful and arouse anxiety by mobilizing populist gangs to intimidate rivals and political opponents. Party headquarters are in Colombo.

Policy

Democratic socialism, according a significant role to private enterprise and foreign investment, is the party's policy. While national reconciliation and accomodation with the Tamils is a UNP aim, not all the cabinet is necessarily committed to these objectives.

Membership & Constituency

The UNP's support base was originally high-caste privileged groups with some backing from minority interests. During the 1970s it successfully sought to extend its appeal and organization to the majority rural poor. It now has well over 100,000 members. Electorally it is dominant in the urban areas, especially around Colombo, the capital, and Kandy. It also has some safe seats in Catholic-dominated rural areas. Like the other major parties it has trade-union and youth-front organizations.

Financing

The UNP's income is derived from contributions, dues, and party publications.

Leadership

Julius Richard Jayewardene (born 1906) is leader of the party and exercises charismatic authority; the chairman of the party is N. G. P. Panditharatne. The deputy party leader, prime minister, and possible successor to Jayewardene, is Ranasinghe Premadasa (born 1924), who is unusual in being of low caste. Among the younger leaders, Gamini Dissanayake (born 1942), minister in charge of the great Mahaveli river valley scheme; Lalith Athulathmudali (born 1936), minister of national security; and Cyril Matthew, industries minister, are important.

Prospects

The UNP will remain an important element within the Sri Lankan party system, but its prospects depend on its economic achievements in the years to come.

Minor Parties

Not counting the constituent elements of the TULF, there are at least nine minor parties in Sri Lanka. Ideological factors play a minor role in their formation, with the exception of the Communist Party. For the most part they are personalist political vehicles, or represent ethnic or caste interests.

Ceylon Workers' Congress

A member of the TULF, the Ceylon Workers' Congress operates independently of the trade-union front in the inland regions where, as a trade union and political party, it represents the interests of the Indian Tamils who work on the tea plantations. Its leader and sole member of Parliament, S. Thondaman (born 1913), is not fully committed to the Front; he joined Jayewardene's government in 1978 as minister of rural industrial development.

Communist Party of Sri Lanka (CPSL)

The CPSL was founded in 1943 by a breakaway pro-Soviet group of LSSP members. In 1963 it split into pro-Moscow and pro-Maoist factions. The Moscow group remains the dominant force, but except on the trade-union front, it is politically insignificant. A cadre party organized along Leninist lines, it has a membership of some 1,500. In 1977 its total vote was 2 percent, concentrated in the Matara area around the estates of its late leader, S. A. Wickremasinghe, and among Colombo dock workers. The party is led by K. P. Silva and Peter Keuneman and since August 1983 has been banned. Its prospects are nil.

Jathika Vimukthi Peramuna (JVP)

The JVP, or People's Liberation Front, has its origins in a group of Marxist youth disillusioned by the policies of the SLFP-LSSP government in 1964. They organized a secret network of cells. It appealed mainly to the jobless Sinhala Buddhist youth of the lower and lower middle class, and its eclectic views embraced Marxist ideas from China, Cuba, and Albania. In April 1971, it staged an insurrection which was savagely repressed. Many of JVP's followers were killed, and its leaders jailed for long terms. The UNP commuted the sentences after 1977, and its leader Rohana Wijeweera has re-turned to politics. The JVP has been banned since August 1983; and, despite government allegations, is not a significant force.

Other Political Forces

Organized Labor

Labor is well organized in three sectors—docks and transport, the plantations, and government service. The majority rural areas, which contain some 70 percent of the population, are totally unorganized. Parties seek to embarrass their political opponents by strike action, but both the Bandaranaike and Jayewardene ministries have adopted tough stances and exploit the high level of unemployment. Marxist influences are significant in the union movement. Since 1977 the UNP-controlled Jatika Sevaka Sangamaya (National Workers' Organization) has become the biggest single union and dominates the government offices. Its methods have evoked criticism.

The Press

Press support for the UNP attracted the ire of Mrs. Bandaranaike between 1970 and 1974. Two of the four main press groups were closed in 1973 and 1974; one was restored to private ownership in 1977, and the other, the Times of Ceylon, was reopened as a government concern in the same year. Under the UNP there is tight press censorship.

Ethnic Groups

Ethnic and religious groups other than the Tamils have been important, notably the Sinhala Buddhists through the medium of Buddhist seminaries and the All-Ceylon Buddhist Congress. The Christians through their bishops and Muslims through their League also seek to pressure politicians.

National Prospects

The year 1977 marked a major watershed in Sri Lankan history with the inception of an economic liberalization program, the shift to a Gaullist-style executive system, and a serious effort to accomodate the minority Tamils. These measures were interconnected; ultimate success in each could make the accomplishment of the others more likely. Conversely, problems in the economy would make the resolution of the communal conflict more difficult. Failure to reincorporate the Tamils in the political system would strengthen the hand of its most militant elements, the Tamil Tigers.

Since 1979, Sri Lankan politics have been dominated by the Tamil issue. After the destruction of Tamil life and property in Colombo in mid-1983, with attendant Tamil terrorist reprisals, the gulf between the communities appears to be unbridgeable. Compromise negotiations still continue under Indian auspices but, as of early 1986, they appear to be stalemated, and it seems doubtful that either the TULF or the government could guarantee to implement any agreement.

The security situation has damaged a burgeoning tourist industry, which was a major stimulation of Sri Lanka's balance of trade. In general, the economic record has been mixed. After twenty years of increasing state intervention and socialism, Jayewardene has turned to private enterprise—domestic and foreign—for the island's salvation, most notably through the formation of an industrial promotion zone near Colombo. At first the impact of the new orientation was marked—GNP rose by 8, 6.5 and .5 percent in the years 1978 to 1980. Since then, progress has slowed and, in 1981, the International Monetary Fund imposed stern terms in financing Sri Lanka's requirements. The industrial promotion zone has been a disappointment. The improvement in food production has been more successful. Agriculture has been revived, thereby reducing food import costs. Lacking natural resources and heavily dependent on the vagaries of world markets for its staple export crops of tea, rubber, and coconut, Sri Lanka's economic performance is modest. In addition, the country has an acute population problem. Inflation has outstripped wage and salary increases, and both the urban poor and the middle classes have turned to populist chauvinism, encouraged by the political elite. Factions in the ruling party have misused their governmental power for partisan and opportunistic ends. In Sri Lanka theoretical democracy does exist, but its substance may have been attenuated.

Further Reading

Jupp, James. *Sri Lanka—Third World Democracy.* London and Totowa, N. J.: Frank Case, 1978.

Kearney, Robert N. *The Politics of Ceylon* [Sri Lanka]. Ithaca and London: Cornell University Press, 1973.

Phadnis, Urmilla. *Religion and Politics in Sri Lanka.* London: C. Hurst & Co., Ltd., 1976.

Robinson, M. S. *Political Structure in a Changing Sinhalese Village.* Cambridge, Eng.: Cambridge University Press, 1975.

Silva, K. M. de, ed., *Sri Lanka: A Survey.* London: C. Hurst & Co., Ltd., 1977.

Wilson, A. Jeyeratnam. *The Gaullist System in Asia: The Constitution of Sri Lanka (1978).* London: Macmillan, 1978.

———. *Politics in Sri Lanka, 1947–1979.* 2nd ed. London: Macmillan, 1979.

DEMOCRATIC REPUBLIC OF SUDAN
(Jumhuriyat al-Sudan al-Dimuqratiyah)
by Kenneth J. Perkins, Ph.D.

The System of Government

Sudan, the largest country in Africa, covers nearly one million square miles in northeast Africa, and shares borders with eight other countries. About one-fifth of Sudan's 22 million people are urban or semi-urban, most of whom live in the Nile Valley centered on the capital city of Khartoum. Culturally and linguistically, Sudan is divided into two distinct regions: the northern two-thirds of the country is largely Muslim Arab, while the southern part is composed of heterogeneous ethnic groups culturally and religiously akin to Black Africa. The Dinka are the most populous and politically prominent of the southern peoples.

Until its conquest by Egypt in the 1820's, Sudan was little more than a variegated collection of independent states and tribal polities. A revolt in 1881 by the Mahdi, a messianic Muslim leader, resulted in the establishment of an independent theocratic state in the north. An Anglo-Egyptian force eventually defeated the Mahdist state in 1898, and in 1899 Sudan was declared a joint Anglo-Egyptian Condominium. This arrangement was merely a facade for British rule. In 1953 Britain and Egypt agreed to allow self-government and self-determination in Sudan, which became independent on January 1, 1956.

Independence was marred by a low-intensity war of secession which erupted in the south in 1955 and continued for the next seventeen years. The multiparty parliamentary government was overthrown in a 1958 army coup led by Lt. General Ibrahim Abboud. Six years later the military regime collapsed in a wave of strikes and riots, clearing the way for a second period of parliamentary politics (1965-69) which lasted until Ja'far Muhammad Numeiry's 1969 coup.

After an initial two-year "radical" period, Sudan under Numeiry pursued a policy of reconciliation at home and abroad. A new constitu-tion was promulgated in May 1973, recognizing the Sudan Socialist Union (SSU) as the only legal political organization. The establishment and popularization of the SSU, the progressive devolution of government functions and powers to an ever-increasing number of regional and provincial structures, and close ties with Egypt and the United States were the hallmarks of Numeiry's regime. The Sudan is now ruled by a Transitional Military Council (TMC) which toppled Numeiry's government in a bloodless coup led by General Abd al-Rahman Siwar al-Dahab on April 6, 1985. Numeiry was on his way back from a visit in the U.S. when he was deposed. He has since lived in Cairo as an exile. Dr. Dafalla al-Ghazouli, a civilian, was appointed to the position of Prime Minister on May 22, 1985.

Implementation of the Charter of Integration with Egypt, which was signed in October 1982 and included plans for a binational Nile Valley Parliament and an Integration Fund for joint development projects, was set aside pending the emergence of a new socio-political order in the Sudan. The Transitional Military Council, which suspended the 1973 constitution upon taking power, scheduled elections for a constituent assembly for April 2, 1986 as the first step in the return to parliamentary democracy.

Executive

General Siwar al-Dahab is the head of state and chairman of the TMC. A professional soldier who rose through the ranks, General Siwar al-Dahab is a devout Muslim with no overt political ambitions. While favoring the inclusion of the *Shari'ah* (Islamic law) as a firm part of Sudanese life, General Siwar al-Dahab deplored the brutality with which it was imposed and enforced by the Numeiry regime.

The Council decreed a statutory transition period of 12 months. The cabinet included a civilian prime minister, three ministers from the south, ten from the ranks of the independents, a minister of defense chosen by the military, and a minister of the interior nominated by the police and vetted by the military.

The 1973 constitution provided for a strong presidential and federal form of government. The president, who had to be at least thirty-five years of age, was nominated by the SSU for a six-year term as head of state and could be reelected. He was empowered to appoint vice presidents, a prime minister, and a cabinet, all of whom were responsible to him. He had the power to dismiss the legislature at will and was supreme commander of the People's Armed Forces and Security Forces.

The president could also declare a state of emergency and suspend all constitutional rights. After a 1975 coup attempt, the constitution was amended to give the president broad powers to take whatever measures he deemed "suitable". Numeiry was reelected to a second term as president by national referendum in 1977 and to a third in 1983.

Numeiry manipulated rather than managed, balancing various factions and institutions. He frequently promoted and demoted, reshuffled and reorganized, reconciled and purged, all of which prevented the formation of power blocs and the accumulation of followers or any institutional backing for potential rivals. Numeiry was the single constant and the prime mover in a political system in perpetual motion.

Legislature

The Transitional Military Council dissolved the unicameral National People's Assembly and ruled by decree until the April 1986 elections. The Assembly, which had undergone a series of alterations under Numeiry, had consistently supported, if not subordinated itself to, the president. Its members routinely upheld the increasingly frequent presidential decrees that undermined the powers of the Assembly. The last Assembly of the Numeiry era convened in 1982. Its 151 members included fifty-two from the north, sixteen from the south, seventy representatives of mass organizations, and thirteen presidential appointees. About a third of its members were sympathizers of the Islamic Charter Front, a collection of Islamic groups including the Muslim Brotherhood.

Judiciary

Prior to 1983, the Sudanese legal and judicial system was based primarily on English common law and Islamic law (*Shari'ah*), with the jurisdiction of the *Shari'ah* courts limited to the personal affairs of the Muslim population. Although theoretically independent, the judiciary, like the rest of the government, was subordinate in practice to the SSU.

In September 1983, Numeiry decreed the *Shari'ah* and punishments sanctioned by the Qur'an to be state law throughout the Sudan, despite the fact that some 30 percent of the country's population, concentrated especially in the south, was non-Muslim. The president used his broad powers to make appointments to the bench to name new judges, many of whom were affiliated with the Muslim Brotherhood. These men imposed harsh penalties, including amputations and floggings, in the name of Islam.

Shortly after seizing control of the government, the Transitional Military Council abolished the special courts applying Islamic punishments. The TMC did not, however, rescind the *Shari'ah* as Sudan's state law, at least in part to avoid alienating Muslim religious elements who wish to retain some form of Islamic law. Instead, the TMC left the decision of this issue up to the constituent assembly to be elected in April 1986.

Regional & Local Government

In March 1972, a seventeen-year low intensity north-south civil war ended, paving the way for the creation of an autonomous Southern Region consisting of the provinces of Equitoria, Bahr al-Ghazal, and Upper Nile. The Southern Region had its own constitution (entitled the Law for Regional Self-Government in the Southern Provinces), its own High Executive Council and Regional Assembly, and a regional president responsible to the Assembly.

Until 1981, Sudan's northern provinces were largely controlled from Khartoum. In that year, in an effort to devolve greater powers on local and regional structures, the government established five regions in addition to Khartoum Province, the seat of government. The new arrangement provided for regional governors and councils of ministers appointed by the president on the recommendation of the regional assemblies and governors, respectively. The regional assemblies had from fifty to seventy seats. Regions were, in turn, divided into provinces with provincial commissioners appointed by the president on the recommendation of the regional governors. These governors represented their regional governments, chaired the people's province executive councils, and headed the local government services. District councils were elected by rural and urban councils and, in turn, elected the provincial executive council.

In June 1983, Numeiry announced the redivision of the Southern Region into three separate regions. This was ostensibly done to lessen the concentration of power in Juba, the regional capital, and also to dilute the influence of the Dinka tribe. As the largest single group in the unified Southern Region, the Dinka had enjoyed considerable political power. Many southerners viewed Numeiry's proposal as an unconstitutional tactic to divide and rule the south, deprive it of its hard-won security and autonomy, and subject it to the same laws as the Arab Muslim north—a problem which became particularly acute with the imposition of the *Shari'ah* in the same year.

This situation, combined with the conviction of many southerners that they were not benefiting from economic development as much as northerners (despite the fact that large oil reserves, the country's most important natural resource, were located in the south), sparked an open insurrection. Anya Nya II, a guerrilla group taking its name from the organization which had led the armed battle for southern autonomy between 1956 and 1972, formed in 1983 and began attacking government installations.

More significant was the emergence of the Sudan People's Liberation Movement (SPLM) and its military component, the Sudan People's Liberation Army (SPLA). Under the leadership of John Garang, the SPLA engaged government forces in the south in a series of battles. Its attacks succeeded in crippling oil exploration in the area and halting work on the Jonglei Canal irrigation project, both serious setbacks for the Khartoum goverment. The SPLM also went further than other southern groups in attempting to rally nationwide support for its resistance to the Numeiry regime.

After Numeiry's ouster, General Siwar al-Dahab invited Colonel Garang to participate in the transitional government, but the SPLM leader declined. To administer the south, the TMC established a National Transitional High Executive Council composed of military and civilian southerners. The Council supervised the work of a seven-member transitional cabinet, also composed of southerners. Although this policy resulted in a de facto return to the status quo prior to the 1983 redivision, the SPLM rejected it, claiming that the High Executive Council's members represented the TMC in Khartoum, not the wishes of the southerners themselves.

The TMC struggled to curb the war in the south through both military means and diplomatic maneuvers. The latter included a rapprochement with Libya which, along with Ethiopia, had strongly supported Garang during the Numeiry era. Nevertheless, the SPLM remained powerful in much of the south, as evidenced by the fact that civil unrest and insecurity prevented the April 1986 elections from being contested in thirty-seven southern constituencies.

The Electoral System

The 1973 constitution provided for citizen suffrage for all those eighteen years of age and over. All candidates for elected office in the assemblies ran on a nonpartisan platform and were approved by the SSU, although they did not need to be SSU members. Some candidates represented geographical constituencies, while others represented professional groups and mass organizations. The Transitional Military Council's abolition of the SSU enabled other political parties to field candidates for the April 1986 elections. The system of geographical and organizational constituencies was, however, retained.

The Party System

Origins of the Parties

Historically, the first political parties in Sudan emerged from the Graduates' General Congress, founded in 1936. The first true party was *Ashiqqa* (Bloodbrothers), established in 1942. It advocated independence from British rule under some kind of union with Egypt. Members of *Ashiqqa*, backed by the Khatmiyyah (a religious brotherhood associated with the important al-Mirghani family), were instrumental in founding the National Union Party (NUP) in

1952. Khatmiyyah partisans withdrew from the NUP in 1956 to form the People's Democratic Party (PDP), but the two groups merged into the Democratic Unionist Party (DUP) in 1968. The conservative rural and tribally based counterpart of *Ashiqqa*-NUP was the *Ummah* Party, established in 1944 by the *Ansar*, followers of a brotherhood centered on the al-Mahdi family. The party sought independence, but without ties to Egypt. These parties dominated Sudanese politics during periods of parliamentary rule (1953–1958 and 1964–1969). In the April 1986 elections, the *Ummah* Party and the DUP together won a total of at least 162 seats out of the 264 contested, suggesting their continuing strength and influence.

The Parties in Law

Under Numeiry, the SSU was the only legal political organization. All parties except the Communist Party of Sudan (CPS) were abolished following the 1969 coup; the CPS was suppressed after the Communist-supported coup attempt in July 1971 and the formation of the SSU. Remnants of the old parties and many other ephemeral parties either went underground or into exile. A few participated in the fluid political process without party labels.

The Transitional Military Council permitted the parties to reorganize and contest the April 1986 elections. Some forty formal parties or groupings of independent candidates participated in the polling.

Sudan Socialist Union (SSU; *Al-Ittihad al-Ishtiraki al-Sudani*)

The SSU was founded in late 1971 after an abortive coup attempt by leftists. The constitution of May 1973 declared it the sole legal party in the country. After taking control of the government in April 1985, the Transitional Military Council abolished the SSU.

The SSU was conceived as a mass party espousing a vague political philosophy combining elements of nationalism, democratic centralism, and Afro-Arab socialism. It emphasized national unity rather than class struggle, elimination of exploitation and corruption, and advancement of socio-economic development. Membership was open to all citizens with few restrictions or requirements. The party claimed

as many as five million adherents. Many of those, however, did not actively participate in SSU activities.

The SSU was hierarchically organized from the bottom to the top of the Sudan's political structure, starting at the village or neighborhood level and proceeding upwards through district, area, provincial, and national levels. At each level there was an SSU congress of lower-level delegates and government-nominated people and a committee of officers to conduct day-to-day party business.

The supreme SSU body was the General Congress of approximately 1,500 members which convened every three years. It elected a Central Committee of several hundred members which met annually to determine major policies. Real power, however, was concentrated in the presidentially appointed Political Bureau whose membership varied in size, but usually consisted of some twenty persons.

Nation (*Ummah*)

The *Ummah* party is a political organ of the *Ansar*, a religiously and politically conservative group which originally drew its strength from the rural and nomadic elements in the central belt of the country. After independence, it formed a coalition with the PDP, and *Ummah* leader Abdallah Khalil served as prime minister from 1956 to 1958. In the 1958 election *Ummah* won a plurality of seats and formed a ruling coalition which was overthrown in General Abboud's 1958 coup.

The *Ummah* reemerged under Sadiq al-Mahdi (born 1936) after the 1964 parliamentary restoration. It won seventy-six of the 173 seats in the 1965 elections and allied with the NUP to form a coalition government. The *Ummah* was split from 1966 until 1969 by a clash between the westernized, Oxford-educated Sadiq and his more traditionalist uncle al-Hadi al-Mahdi, who had assumed the spiritual leadership of the Ansar. Nevertheless, the party provided Sudan's prime ministers until the 1969 coup ended party politics again.

After 1969 the *Ummah* was transformed from the party of government to a base of strong opposition to Numeiry. When al-Hadi died in a violent antigovernment Ansar uprising in March 1970, Sadiq became undisputed Mahdist leader and threw his support behind the National Front, a coalition of conservative dissidents. After supporting the Front's 1976 coup attempt, Sadiq went into exile and was sentenced to death in absentia. He returned in 1977 after a reconciliation with Numeiry.

A formal agreement in April 1978 led to the release of many political detainees, a general amnesty, repeal of security laws, and return of exiles. Many former opposition leaders were reappointed to government and SSU posts. But Numeiry's embrace of Sadat's Egypt, support for the Camp David Accords, pro-Western leanings, estrangement from the Arab world, and failure to keep all his reconciliation promises led Sadiq to resign from the SSU and Political Bureau. He left the country in late 1978, but returned in 1982. Sadiq criticized Numeiry's introduction of *Shari'ah* law, denouncing it as a political tactic to intimidate the president's opponents rather than a truly Islamic policy. He spent the last two years of the Numeiry era in prison or under house arrest.

The *Ummah* Party is very well organized. Its national committee of 400, elected by party members, elects a Political Bureau of fifty, at the heart of which is the party secretariat, composed of Sadiq and a small cadre of loyal *Ummah* supporters.

Democratic Unionist Party (DUP; *al-Hizb al-Dimuqratiyah al-Ittihadi*)

In 1952 various groups under the leadership of Ismail al-Azhari merged to form the National Union Party (NUP). The party's primary platform was a call for Nile Valley unity. The NUP won a parliamentary majority in 1953 and led Sudan to independence. In 1956 the *Khatmiyyah* wing defected to form the People's Democratic Party (PDP). In the late sixties, the PDP and the rump NUP rejoined to form the Democratic Unionist Party (DUP) led by al-Azhari until the 1969 revolution terminated parliamentary government. Although Numeiry dissolved the DUP along with other political parties, individual party members remained active in the political process.

With the ouster of Numeiry in 1986, the DUP was immediately reorganized under the leadership of Muhammad Osman al-Mirghani. The al-Mirghani family has traditionally provided leadership for the *Khatmiyyah* Brotherhood, and that group provided the party with strong support and an effective organizational network.

Muslim Brotherhood (*Ikhwan al-Muslimin*)

The Brotherhood, originally founded in Egypt in 1928, established a branch in Sudan in the early 1950's. This militant fundamentalist religious and political movement advocated the creation of an Islamic state, close relations with the conservative Arab states, and proselytizing the non-Muslim southern minority. Drawing its support largely from students and intellectuals, the Muslim Brotherhood entered electoral politics in 1964 through the Islamic Charter Front. Although kept outside the political process for years by Numeiry, the Brotherhood remained highly influential. Its leader, Dr. Hasan al-Turabi, was held without trial for eight years until his release after reconciliation in 1977. In February 1978, he was appointed to the SSU Central Committee and later to the Political Bureau. In 1979, he assumed the post of Attorney General.

The Brotherhood supported the decision to impose *Shari'ah* law and many of its members actively participated in both the government and the SSU in the closing years of the Numeiry regime. Shortly before the April 1985 coup, however, Numeiry purged Brotherhood members from the government and the party, maintaining that they were plotting against the regime. Many observers, however, viewed the president's assault on the Brotherhood as an effort to saddle it with responsibility for the increasingly unpopular implementation of the *Shari-ah.*

Under al-Turabi's leadership, the Brotherhood resumed its political activities after Numeiry's ouster. Supporters of the Brotherhood participated in the April 1986 elections under the banner of the newly formed National Islamic Front.

Communist Party of Sudan (CPS; *Al-Hizb al-Shu'yu'i al-Sudani*)

The Communist Party of Sudan traces its origin to the 1946 founding of the Sudan Movement for National Liberation, an offshoot of the

Egyptian communist movement. At first it operated and contested elections through various front organizations, but in the 1960's it openly sought electoral support. The party drew its strength primarily from intellectuals, students, and members of trade unions, especially the powerful railway workers. Two factions emerged within the CPS, one orthodox and pro-Moscow, and the other nationalist and Arab socialist. Both advocated state control of the economy. The CPS played an important role in the 1964 revolution, and reached the peak of its influence during the two years after the 1969 coup. Effectively suppressed after a coup attempt in July 1971, the CPS was the only party actively persecuted by the Numeiry government. Like the other parties, it benefited from the easing of political restrictions following Numeiry's removal. Running as Communists, party members participated and won seats in the April 1986 elections.

Minor Parties

A number of smaller parties, some of which had come into existence during the Numeiry era but had been denied a role in the political process, became active in the period between Numeiry's fall and the April 1986 elections.

Several regional parties succeeded in winning seats in the elections for the constituent assembly. The Sudan National Party, led by Philip Abbas Qabbush, represents the interests of the Nuban people of Kordofan. The Beja Congress, originally established in 1965, claims to speak for the tribes of the Red Sea highlands area. The People's Progressive Party, which supports the division of the Southern Region, met with considerable success in Equatoria Province. Regional parties based in Darfur and Blue Nile Provinces, however, failed to gain enough votes to enable them to participate in the constituent assembly.

Though not strictly speaking a political party, the Republican Brotherhood does have political influence. An Islamic reformist group founded in the 1940s by Mahmud Muhammad Taha, it attracted support from intellectuals and students who saw its policies as viable alternatives to the more radical programs advocated by the Muslim Brotherhood. Numeiry's decision to permit the execution of the highly respected Taha in early 1985 on charges of "heresy" symbolized his unwillingness to tolerate even moderate opposition or criticism and helped contribute to his downfall.

Other Political Forces

Military

The People's Armed Forces (PAF) were both the backbone and the nemesis of Numeiry's government. Formed during the Anglo-Egyptian condominium period as the Sudan Defense Force, the PAF now numbers about 70,000. The army is the largest element and is composed of infantry, armor, and parachute brigades, and artillery, air defense, and engineering regiments. The PAF is outfitted with a combination of Soviet, Chinese, European, and, more recently, U.S. equipment. In addition to a small navy and air force, there is a paramilitary National Guard, a Republican Guard, and Border Guards. During the 1970's military expenditures accounted for 10 to 20 percent of the government budget and 3 to 4 percent of the GNP, a relatively heavy burden on a weak economy.

The army has been a major actor in recent Sundanese history, and remains the ultimate arbiter of political power. It fought in the civil war in the South from 1955 until 1972 and again after 1983 when new fighting erupted. The army has also ruled the country for most of its independent existence (1958–1964, 1969–1986). Although the military provided the main institutional base for Numeiry's rule, there were numerous coup attempts after 1969, some of which briefly succeeded before loyalist forces restored Numeiry. Numeiry tried to keep the army in check by frequent reassignments, retirements, and purges of its leadership.

The Numeiry government entered into a mutual defense treaty with Egypt leading to efforts to integrate the two nations' armed forces. After Numeiry's deposition and the improvement of relations between Sudan and Libya, however, the military integration program with Egypt came to a halt. In the last several years of the Numeiry era, the PAF was also organized into production and service units to make some of its own equipment and clothes, grow food for itself and for domestic consumption, and provide public transportation in Khartoum.

Since the army was the only institution that had an independent base of power and the means to exercise it, and since many soldiers had become disillusioned with government policies, especially concerning the war in the South, few observers were surprised when the military intervened to bring the deteriorating political and economic situation under control in the spring of 1985.

Organized Labor

Sudan has a strong labor-movement tradition dating back to at least the 1940's. The Sudanese labor force now numbers about ten million, of which some 70 percent is in agriculture and 30 percent in industry, commerce, services, etc. Unemployment and underemployment are serious problems, although labor shortages are common in most high-skill areas.

The 1973 constitution gave the right to form trade unions, and most workers are organized and affiliated with the Sudanese Workers' Trade Union Federation (founded 1950) or the Federation of Employees and Professionals Trade Unions. Numeiry sought to control organized labor through SSU penetration and ideological blandishments, but labor remained a major source of opposition to his regime to the end.

Sudanese unions have been prone to strikes and political activism, the most dramatic being the 1964 general strike which brought down the military government of General Abboud. Numeiry responded to a series of walkouts by railway workers in 1979 and 1981 by imposing stiff penalties on organizers and strikers alike.

As the debt-ridden and fragile Sudanese economy continued to flounder and austerity measures imposed additional short-term hardships in the mid-1980's, labor unrest mounted. Many unions and professional organizations were in the forefront of the demonstrations which ultimately brought down the government in 1985.

Students

Students have been a key component of Sudanese political movements for decades, at times acting as catalysts for political action, as in the downfall of the Abboud regime. Student organizations have always been active in the universities and the secondary schools. Even when they were officially banned in the Numeiry era, the religious brotherhoods and political parties maintained strong links with the student population.

Students frequently resorted to demonstrations and strikes to protest government policies, especially the series of economic austerity measures in the closing years of the Numeiry era. Serious riots over price increases for food and fuel accompanied the labor strikes of 1979. In early 1982, schools in Khartoum Province were closed for forty-five days following student riots over sugar price hikes. Similar disturbances erupted just before Numeiry's overthrow when the price of bread rose by 33 percent without warning.

In February 1980, police dispersed 6,000 students in Khartoum for protesting Egypt's exchange of ambassadors with Israel, and in January 1981, all universities and public schools were closed in the wake of student demonstrations in Khartoum over the dissolution of the university students' union.

As their discontent over Numeiry's political and economic policies mounted with no evidence that their grievances were being addressed, students gravitated increasingly toward the extreme right or left. Alone they did not pose a terribly severe challenge to the government, but when they made common cause with labor and professional organizations, they were often able to force government reorganizations, cabinet reshuffles, and policy alterations. In 1985, as in 1964, they played an important part in bringing about the downfall of an unpopular regime.

National Prospects

Political tensions in Sudan were greatly eased by the Transitional Military Council's assumption of power and by its adherence to its promise to hold elections for a constituent assembly in April 1986. Nonetheless, extremely grave social, economic, and political problems confront Prime Minister Sadiq al-Mahdi and the coalition government, based primarily on the *Ummah* and the DUP, which he heads.

The Sudanese economy has been plagued for years by poor agricultural performance, inflation, balance of payments deficits, and very onerous international debts. In order to reschedule debts to Sudan's commercial creditors and to qualify for continued International Monetary Fund support, Numeiry imposed painful belt-tightening measures which aggravated short-term hardships, especially for urban consumers. The Transitional Military

Council was able to do little more than maintain the economic status quo and the new government faces the same bleak picture which prevailed at the end of the Numeiry era.

Related to the general economic troubles are critical food shortages resulting from a drought that has lasted nearly three years. Between 8 and 10 million Sudanese are affected by the drought; 4 million are starving. Repeated crop failures in the western provinces of Kordofan and Darfur have spawned massive internal migrations from those areas to the Nile Valley. Khartoum and other urban centers near the Nile have been overwhelmed by the influx of people from outlying regions. The cities' capacities to provide shelter and other basic services have been strained to the breaking point and temporary communities with sub-standard housing surround the capital.

Furthermore, Sudan hosts well over a million refugees from neighboring countries, especially Ethiopia, Chad, and Uganda. Public and private international relief agencies and foreign government aid programs are attempting to provide for the refugees, but their presence in the country places additional strains on the already reeling economy. Clearly, the revival of the Sudanese economy will be a lengthy and arduous process, but one which must have a high priority for the new government.

The questions of Islamization and the role of the *Shari'ah* in Sudanese society must also be addressed. The Transitional Military Council did not enforce Qur'anic punishments, but neither did it abrogate the *Shari'ah*. Large numbers of Sudanese Muslims appear to want some form of Islamic state, but there are considerable discrepancies among the leaders of the political parties and religious organizations over what characteristics are essential for an Islamic state.

Until the central government stabilizes the situation in the South, however, it will have great difficulty in marshaling the resources and backing needed to cope with its other problems. Southern grievances go well beyond religious differences to fundamental disputes over the proper allocation of political and economic power and the role of the non-Arab, non-Muslim population in the Sudanese state. A military solution to this dispute has never appeared feasible, nor does it seem so in the foreseeable future. Some form of political accommodation with the SPLM, which is the major, but not the sole, vehicle for the expression of southern discontent, must rank high on the new government's agenda.

Finally, the Transitional Military Council improved relations with Libya and Ethiopia, much to the distress of Egypt and the United States, both strong partners of Numeiry. This required considerable political maneuvering on the part of the TMC. The civilian government must decide on the relationships it wishes to develop with its immediate neighbors, as well as the impact those relationships will have on international links developed in the Numeiry years.

Sudan has long been regarded as a country with enormous potential, both in terms of material and human resources. The exploitation of that potential, however, is likely to occur only when a popularly elected government begins to come to grips with the crucial international and domestic problems which have faced the country, in one form or another, since independence.

Further Reading

Abdel-Rahim, Muddathir. *Changing Patterns of Civilian-Military Relations in the Sudan*. Research Report No. 46. Uppsala: Scandinavian Institute of African Studies, 1978.

Allum, Percy. "The Sudan: Numeiry's Ten Years of Power." *Contemporary Review*, Vol. 235, No. 1366, 1979.

Bechtold, Peter K. *Politics in the Sudan: Parliamentary and Military Rule in an Emerging African Nation*. New York: Praeger, 1976.

Beshir, Mohamed Omer. *The Southern Sudan: From Conflict to Peace*. London: C. Hurst, and New York: Barnes & Noble, 1975.

———. *Revolution and Nationalism in the Sudan*. New York: Barnes & Noble, 1974.

Lees, Francis A., and Brooks, Hugh C. *The Economic and Political Development of the Sudan*. London: Macmillan, 1977.

Nelson, Harold D., et al. *Sudan: A Country Study*. 2nd ed. Washington: U.S. Government Printing Office, for Foreign Area Studies, American University, 1979.

Sylvester, Anthony. *Sudan under Nimeiri*. London: Bodley Head, 1977.

Voll, John O. *Historical Dictionary of the Sudan*. Metuchen, N. J.: Scarecrow Press, 1978.

Wai, Dunstan M. *The African-Arab Conflict in the Sudan*. London and New York: Africana Publishing Co., 1981.

————. "Revolution, Rhetoric, and Reality in the Sudan." *Journal of Modern African Studies*, Vol. 17, No. 1, 1979.

————. "The Sudan: Domestic Politics and Foreign Relations under Numeiry." *African Affairs*, Vol. 78, No. 312, 1979.

Warburg, Gabriel. *Islam, Nationalism and Communism in a Traditional Society: The Case of Sudan.* London: Frank Cass, 1978.

Woodward, Peter. "Nationalism and Opposition in Sudan." *African Affairs*, Vol. 80, No. 320, 1981.

SWAZILAND

by Jack Parson, Ph.D.

The System of Government

The Kingdom of Swaziland, a nation of nearly 600,000 people (over 90% of them Swazi), between South Africa and Mozambique, was governed by the longest-reigning monarch in the world, the *Ngwenyama*, Sobhuza II (born July 22, 1899) until his death in 1982. His reign, beginning in 1921, spanned the colonial, nationalist, and independence eras, generating an unusual and potentially unstable political system. Landlocked (surrounded by South Africa and Mozambique), relatively poor, and buffeted by unstable international factors, Swaziland's political system and development are uncertain.

Executive

The political system is a monarchy and unitary state, although of a hybrid variety. The kingdom became independent in 1968 as a constitutional monarchy with a liberal democratic Parliament. By 1973 the strains of operating parallel monarchical and liberal democratic institutions in Swaziland's circumstances threatened the stability of the state and provoked a constitutional crisis. The king suspended the constitution, including Parliament, and ruled by decree, consulting primarily with his own traditional advisors. In 1978, a new Parliament was elected, but the king retained the right to nominate and appoint ministers and deputy ministers, and to dismiss them. He could also veto any action of Parliament. Recruitment to positions of leadership and the determination of policy therefore closely depend on a traditional hierarchy, the apex of which is the king. Following the king's death, the government was taken over by a royal family regency. The family chose a new king, Mswati III, whose coronation took place on April 25, 1986.

Legislature

In late 1978, a unicameral National Assembly of forty members was elected by indirect methods. Political-party representation was forbidden during the process. Besides the elected representatives, the king appointed an additional ten members (senators). The Assembly appears to have little or no substantive power.

Judiciary

A multilevel court system is headed by a chief justice. All judges are appointed by the king, but they are relatively independent of political pressure.

Regional & Local Government

Swaziland is divided into four districts administered by appointed officials.

The Electoral System

In the 1978 elections, nominations of 160 candidates for an electoral college of eighty members were made in public meetings of tribal councils. The king had the right of final approval of the nominations. The eighty members of the college were chosen by public ballot. The final list of candidates was not made public until the day of the vote. About 55 percent of the adult population actually voted. The college then chose the forty members of Parliament.

Political Forces

Although political parties as such no longer function, informal groupings follow the previous major party orientations. One was the king's party or Imbokodvo National Movement.

The other is the banned Ngwane National Liberatory Congress, the leader of which was Dr. Ambrose Zwane. Dr. Zwane was detained, then fled to Tanzania in 1978. He was granted amnesty and returned to Swaziland in 1979 on condition that he not engage in politics.

The primary political split which underlies the policymaking process, and formerly political parties, is that between the traditionalists and a more loosely knit group outside of traditional social and political hierarchies. The traditionalists include the far-flung Swazi royal family led by the king (including the hierarchy of princes) and the chiefs. Their power lies in control of land and an ideology of traditional legitimacy which binds the peasantry to them. The modernizing elite includes those who by education and occupation control the skills for developing the economy, but who do not have traditional status. This elite includes many in public service and white-collar employees in the private sector.

The traditional hierarchy has maintained firm control through the new constitution. But its power also rests on the channeling of resources, on locating policymaking power in the "Swazi Nation," and on its institutionalization in the Swazi National Council and the Tibiyo Fund. The Swazi Nation, personified by the king, controls revenue from mining and land, and has its own investments and businesses, rivaling the state as a national decision maker. Operating outside formal governmental institutions, the Swazi Nation through the Tibiyo Fund constitutes an alternative policymaking structure. Even if the modernizing elite controlled the institutions of government, therefore, a very important area of economic decision making would be outside its authority.

National policymaking must also take into account an array of external factors. Large parcels of land were transferred during the colonial period, such land and its European owners are still important political factors. In addition, Swaziland's geopolitical position requires that an accommodation be reached with South Africa and Mozambique. South Africa is Swaziland's main trading partner and a major foreign investor in Swaziland, particularly in tourism. Further, Swaziland is perceived in South Africa as a security risk because of its potential as a base for African liberation groups, banned in South Africa. Considerable pressure has been successfully put on Swaziland by South Africa to reduce to insignificance the presence of the African National Congress in Swaziland.

Mozambique provides an outlet to the Indian Ocean.

Finally, foreign investors play a significant role in the Swaziland economy, particularly in mining and agriculture. Pineapple and sugar plantations, with significant foreign participation, are important foreign-exchange earners and employers of Swazi labor. Each of these noninstitutional factors influence the policymaking process.

National Prospects

The Swaziland political system is unstable. Perhaps the primary source of instability involves the tensions between and among Swazi political groups and the question of what is likely to occur subsequent to the coronation of a new king. The succession is now clear, creating the potential for social and political upheaval. Internal political conflict is therefore endemic in the system, and its management will determine the system's ability to survive in its present form.

In addition, the situation in southern Africa, particularly regarding the pace and direction of change in South Africa, will closely affect national policy in Swaziland. The processes of economic and political change in Swaziland will depend in a significant way on what happens in South Africa.

Further Reading

Booth, Alan R. *Swaziland: Tradition and Change in a Southern African Kingdom.* Boulder, Colo.: Westview Press, 1983.

"Kingdom of Swaziland." In *Africa Contemporary Record*, Colin Legum, ed. New York: Africana Publishing Company. Published yearly.

Kowet, Donald. *Land, Labour Migration and Politics in Southern Africa: Botswana, Lesotho, and Swaziland.* Uppsala, Sweden: Scandinavian Institute of African Studies, 1978.

Potholm, Christian P. "Swaziland." In *Southern Africa in Perspective*, Christian P. Potholm and Richard Dale, eds. New York: The Free Press, 1972.

———. *Swaziland: The Dynamics of Political Modernization.* Berkeley: University of California Press, 1972.

KINGDOM OF SWEDEN
(Konungariket Sverige)
by Neil C. M. Elder

The System of Government

Sweden is a parliamentary democracy, a constitutional monarchy, and a unitary state with a population approaching 8.5 million.

The principle of cabinet responsibility to Parliament won final acceptance in 1917; universal suffrage was achieved by 1921. Earlier, executive power had been vested in the king under the constitutional arrangements of 1809, and that power was exercised by him in large, though diminishing, measure.

The Swedish constitution comprises three separate documents: the Instrument of Government (*Regeringsform*) of 1974, which is the most important of the three; the Act of Succession (for the present royal family), dating from 1810; and the Freedom of the Press Act of 1949. An amendment of 1979 to the Act of Succession represented a victory for sex equality by allowing female succession, so that the first-born now has the right to the throne irrespective of gender. In addition to these documents, there is also the 1974 Parliament Act which contains some of the most important rules regulating the legislature and which has a status half-way between constitutional and ordinary statute law.

The new constitutional document of 1974 and effective January 1, 1975, ended all opportunity for the monarch to influence the political process while at the same time confirming the king as head of state (*Statschef*). Otherwise, this reform in large measure simply gave formal recognition to prevailing constitutional practice.

The power to govern the country is vested in the cabinet (*Regering*) headed by the prime minister (*Statsminister*) under accountability to Parliament. All political power is declared to emanate from the people. Primary legislative power is vested in Parliament (*Riksdag*), which is elected at least once every three years.

Executive

The cabinet is the key policymaking center in the political system as long as it can maintain its parliamentary support. In periods of minority government, crucial decisions are taken in talks among party leaders and also in Parliament and its standing committees. The first phase of Swedish parliamentarism, through the 1920s to 1932, was marked by a rapid succession of minority governments. The second, from 1932 to 1976, was one of Social Democratic dominance and, for the most part, majority government, although some of the governments were coalitions. The period from 1976 to 1982 saw a series of nonsocialist governments. Two majority combinations (1976–78 and 1979–81) broke up through internal dissension, and were replaced by minority governments. In 1982 and again in 1985, the Social Democrats returned to power in effect as a majority government.

Nearly all cabinet ministers are representatives of the party or parties in power and also members of Parliament, but occasionally an independent expert may be called upon to serve. All ministers may address Parliament; none may vote in it. A substitute from the same party takes over the parliamentary duties of any member of Parliament (MP) who has been appointed to the cabinet for as long as that MP remains in office. The substitute has full voting rights in Parliament and, although under party discipline, is independent of the minister he replaced.

When a cabinet resigns, Parliament votes on a proposal for a new prime minister submitted to it by the speaker of the Parliament, after consultations with the leaders of the parliamentary parties and with the deputy speakers. This function passed from the king to the speaker under the 1974 Instrument of Government. The proposal of a new prime minister fails only if an absolute majority votes against it. The speaker then appoints the prime minister, who in turn appoints all the other members of the cabinet. If the prime minister so requests, the speaker can discharge him. The same applies if Parliament declares that the prime minister does not enjoy its confidence. Other cabinet ministers may be dismissed either by Parliament or the prime minister.

Ministries are small units, with an average staff of 100, including clericals. The preparation of major legislative measures is thus usually entrusted to commissions of inquiry within guidelines approved by the cabinet. The membership of these commissions is variable at government discretion and may include representatives of interest groups, MPs from both the government and the opposition sides, civil servants, and independent experts. The inquiry stage commonly lasts two to three years. The final report is circulated to relevant administrative agencies and nongovernmental organizations for official comment (*Remiss* procedure). A summary of the material thus assembled is included as background in the formal papers introducing a government bill to Parliament. The process, though cumbersome, is valued as a contribution to informed public debate and to responsible government.

Similarly, the small ministries provide a framework for steering through laws and regulations for the seventy to eighty administrative agencies which are charged with the day-to-day enforcement of government decisions. These agencies often suggest proposals for change in their respective fields arising out of practical experience. Their recommendations are also customarily circulated for comment in the same way as commission of inquiry reports and are included in any bill that may be later submitted to Parliament.

Legislature

The Parliament (*Riksdag*) consists of 349 members. Unlike most parliaments, in which deputies are seated in party blocs along a left-right spectrum, Swedish MPs are seated by constituency, regardless of party.

The ordinary session of Parliament runs normally from early October until May 31 the following year. It may be prolonged until June 15 by parliamentary decision if necessary. Extraordinary sessions may be held at other periods of the year, but eight months is the usual annual span for parliamentary work.

Parliament elects a speaker and three deputy speakers. These posts are shared by agreement among parties and collectively form the Presidium of the *Riksdag*. The management of the parliamentary agenda is in the hands of the Speaker's Conference, consisting of the Presidium together with one representative from each party caucus, the chairmen of the parliamentary standing committees, and the deputy chairman of the *Riksdag* Board of Administration. Committee chairmanships are shared by agreement among the political parties in the same way as presidium posts.

Private members' proposals (*Motioner*) are some ten times as numerous as government bills (*Propositioner*). Most, however, are in effect amendments to government bills; some are party alternatives to government proposals; some seek to have the issue they raise investigated by the government. Most fail. The bulk of the legislative program is determined in accordance with the wishes of the prime minister and his cabinet.

The process of constitutional amendment reflects the legislative primacy of Parliament, although a modest measure of direct democracy has recently been introduced. Until 1980, all constitutional amendments had to be passed by two successive Parliaments, with a general election thus taking place between the first and second votes. Now, in addition to this procedure, a third of the members of Parliament can force an amendment to be put to a referendum after one favorable parliamentary vote. This referendum is held at the same time as the general election, and the amendment fails if the votes against equal more than one half of valid votes cast in the general election. If the amendment passes, Parliament again takes up the issue for final decision.

The 1974 Parliament Act consists of a number of important regulations each supplemented by detailed prescriptions. The key passages are amended in the same way as other constitutional documents, except that an amendment takes immediate effect if it is passed by a three-fourths majority of those MPs voting, and provided that the pro-amendment vote comprises a majority of the whole Parliament. The subsidiary clauses are amended in the same way as ordinary statute law. It is for these reasons that the Parliament Act has an intermediate status in the hierarchy of laws.

A measure of direct democracy had been countenanced in the Swedish political system long before the 1974–75 constitutional reform continued it. Parliament may enact a law requiring a consultative referendum to be held, which has happened on four occasions to date. The first referendum, in 1922, narrowly rejected Prohibition. The second, in 1955, rejected a switch from left- to right-hand driving by a four-to-one majority. The third, in 1957, approved a compulsory supplementary pensions scheme. The most recent, in 1980, approved the building of nuclear reactors. Only in the second case was the referendum verdict overturned, by a conference of party leaders.

The 1973–76 Parliament, like its predecessor, had 350 members but was remarkable in being split exactly evenly between the socialist and nonsocialist blocs. On major questions, the minority Social Democratic government shopped around successfully for support. On minor matters, over 100 decisions were resolved by recourse to the lottery prescribed in the case of tied votes. The speaker, like ministers, has a parliamentary substitute and no personal vote. After experience of this legislature, the *Riksdag* was reduced in size to 349 members.

General elections must be held every third year. If the government dissolves Parliament between the ordinary elections, the mandate of the ensuing election is valid only for the remaining portion of the regular three-year parliamentary term of office. No such extraordinary election has been called since a three-year term was substituted for the previous four-year term in 1970.

ELECTION RESULTS (1982 and 1985)				
	1982		1985	
Party	% Vote	Seats	% Vote	Seats
Social Democrats	45.6	166	44.7	159
Communists	5.6	20	5.4	19
Center	15.5	56	12.4	44
Liberals	5.9	21	14.2	51
Moderates	23.6	86	21.3	76

Judiciary

The highest courts in Sweden are the Supreme Court (*högsta domstolen*) and the Supreme Administrative Court (*regeringsrätten*). The five-member Supreme Court is the final court of appeal for cases raising important issues of legal principle in civil and criminal law. The Supreme Administrative Court performs a similar function for cases arising from the decisions of administrative authorities. These latter cases can only be pursued through a special system of administrative courts. The members of both supreme courts are appointed by the government from the ranks of qualified judges only.

A constitutional amendment passed in 1979 states that governmental and parliamentary enactments shall not be enforced if they are in "obvious" breach of the constitution. This may be viewed as reinforcing the special section on basic rights and freedoms that was written into the new Instrument of Government of 1974.

Regional & Local Government

Regional government comprises twenty-three counties (*län*), in each of which the national government is represented by a governor (*landshövding*) and a county administration (*länsstyrelse*). The governors are appointed by the national government for six-year terms. Politicians commonly are chosen, and quite often they come from parties in opposition. As a rule, they give up active political involvement when appointed. County councils (*landsting*) are the elected regional units of self-government. The most important business of the national government's county administration is conducted in a board of which the governor is chairman. Since 1977, the fourteen board members of each county have been appointed by the county council. Previously, some members of each board were appointed by the councils and some were appointed by the national government. Municipalities (*kommun*), of which there were 279 in 1980, constitute the basic units of local self-government.

Local government functions fall into two main categories: those within the general powers granted by statute, and those based on special legislation. The general powers enable local authorities to "conduct their own affairs" and include, for example, cultural matters, leisure activities, parks, and electricity generation. The widest range of these is exercised by the municipalities. The specially regulated tasks are usually mandatory and include the school system, child care, public assistance, treatment of alcoholics and drug addicts, and public health and medical care, and so on. This last function is by far the most important task of the county councils which are responsible for running most of the country's hospitals.

The importance of the local government sector has gradually increased and the degree of national supervision of local authorities has been relaxed. Municipalities and county councils together account for some two-thirds of total consumption and investments within the Swedish public sector. The municipalities accounted for 69 percent of total local-government external expenses in 1978, compared to the county councils' 31 percent. For both types of local authority, the largest item of revenue is a local income tax. Some decisions of local government still require confirmation by the regional branch of national government, for example, urban planning.

The Electoral System

The Swedish Parliament is directly elected on a proportional basis (St. Laguë). Of the 349 seats, 310 are divided among the country's twenty-eight multimember constituencies in proportion to the number of registered voters in each constituency. The remaining thirty-nine seats are divided between the parties *and* allocated to constituencies through a complex formula (St. Laguë), which tries to ensure that party representation in Parliament corresponds as closely as possible to the national distribution of votes. A party must obtain 4 percent of the national vote to win a seat, unless it wins a seat in a specific constituency with at least 12 percent of that local vote. The Christian Democratic Party has to date been the most prominent sufferer under the 4 percent barrier; no party has as yet benefited under the 12 percent local rule.

Any Swedish citizen age eighteen or over on polling day and not legally disbarred has the right to vote. Aliens resident in the country for over three years have been entitled to vote in all local government elections since 1976. Electoral registers are kept for inspection at the local tax office, and voters' cards are sent out in advance to all electors with details of their local polling stations. The ballot form is a party candidate list. Each party contesting the election distributes these at the polling station. The voter selects the party list of his choice and seals it into a special envelope in a screened-off area (the envelope is provided on production of the voter's card), then hands it to the election officer for immediate deposition in the ballot-box.

Electors may add or remove names on a party candidate list, but this right has little or no practical political significance. More importantly, a party can run more than one list under its party label and votes for these lists are aggregated when calculating the total party vote. Multiple lists are more commonly run by the nonsocialist rather than by the socialist parties. Thus a party may put forward different lists in different regions of a constituency, or a list may be drawn up with one eye on a particular category of voters (e.g., free church voters). After the vote, the multiple lists are merged to form one rank-ordered list. No by-elections occur under this electoral system. In case of a vacancy, the seat passes to the candidate next in line on the list.

Elections are held on the third Sunday in September and take place at national, regional, and local levels simultaneously. Consequently, ballot papers (candidate lists) of different colors and markings are employed: plain white papers for municipal elections, blue with a black corner line for county council elections, and yellow with two black corner lines for parliamentary elections. Voting is optional, but voter participation levels are high.

VOTER PARTICIPATION LEVELS, BY PERCENT			
	1973	1976	1979
Parliamentary	90.8	91.8	90.7
County Council	90.6	90.3	89.0
Municipal	90.5	90.4	89.0

NOTE: Voter participation in the 1985 parliamentary elections was 89.9%

The Party System

Origin of the Parties

Sweden adopted a proportional system of representation in 1909. At this time Conservatives and Liberals dominated the political scene, with Social Democrats a rising third force. Proportional representation enabled the farming population to set up their own Agrarian Party to protect their interest, and the Russian Bolshevik revolution led to the emergence of a Communist Party. In the 1930s, these political groupings became the components of a remarkably stable five-party system.

The basic line of cleavage within this system lies along the left-to-right axis: Communists-Social Democrats/Agrarians/Liberals-Conservatives. An urban/rural cleavage has on occasions cut across and softened this pattern, especially during the period from 1933 to 1956. The balance between the socialist and nonsocialist sides has often been a narrow one in terms of electoral strengths. The generally pragmatic temper of the four largest parties (i.e., excluding the Communists until the post-1945 era) meant that accommodations have periodically been made across the basic divide. The four parties entered into a national coalition government in 1939–45 with the aim of preserving the country's neutrality. They had earlier proved capable of heading off extremist political movements generated by the economic depression of the 1930s. Among them, they have managed to articulate and contain dissatisfactions arising out of the most recent manifestations of economic recession.

The Parties in Law

The constitution restricts the distribution of parliamentary seats to registered parties. The major parties protect their names by registering these with the National Tax Office, which serves also as the central authority for the administration of elections. For registration purposes in a parliamentary election, a party must show that it has the support of 1,500 electors (for county council elections the figure is 100; and for municipal elections, fifty). The party must also show that it can field a certain number of candidates and produce their written consent to nomination. The nomination process is not subject to legal regulation, but is left to the parties themselves to manage.

Since 1966, state subsidies have as a general rule gone to parties overcoming the 4 percent barrier to parliamentary representation. These subsidies are paid partly in the form of a "party support grant" or Skr 173,000 (about $36,300) per seat per year and partly in the form of a "secretariat grant" which is paid at a higher rate per seat to opposition parties as compared with parties in office. No condition is attached to these subsidies, nor is there any public audit of their expenditure. Voluntary compacts among parties are the sole limit on campaign expenditure. By 1976, state contributions to parties far

outweighed their income from membership dues and other sources. There is no legal requirement that party finances be disclosed. The general tenor of these rules is to recognize parties as essential to the democratic process while at the same time providing some reinforcement to barriers against the emergence of new groupings at the parliamentary level. Similarly, the youth organizations of the established parties have received state support grants without strings attached since 1964. Also, since 1969 the parties contesting municipal and county elections have been able to claim subsidies from public funds on the basis of a tariff per seat that varies from one locality to another. Finally, the costs of the ballot papers in all elections are charged to the state.

Party Organization

Swedish parties are generally associations of dues-paying individual members. The Social Democrats have collective affiliations of trade unions at the local level. Individuals who might be collectively affiliated have the right to opt out.

The basic organizational structures and the functions of the three main levels of party organization are similar for all five parties. The sets of specialized working groups at national level and minutiae of procedure for the nomination of candidates do differ, however. In this last case, indeed, procedures often vary *within* the same party, yet certain crucial characteristics are common throughout the system. By longstanding convention, for example, national party authorities do not seek to interfere in the nominating process for parliamentary candidates, which takes place at the constituency (county) level. So strong is this practice that even the Left Party Communists have conformed, abandoning their earlier practice of "democratic centralism," i.e., central dictation.

Party cohesion is strong, though MPs do occasionally break ranks when constituency interest requires it. Genuinely maverick behavior is likely to result in failure to win renomination. Stricter measures may on rare occasions be applied, especially on the left. Thus in 1981, the Social Democratic Party National Executive supported the expulsion of twenty-four party members by the party's youth organization on the grounds that they were Trotskyites.

On the local level, party organizations choose local candidates and campaign for them. While this is the main local activity, the amalgamation of local government authorities into larger units has tended to increase the liveliness of party debate about local issues. In varying degrees, depending on the party, local party associations are also linked into the process of nominating and ranking constituency candidates for parliamentary elections. They may also originate motions for submission to party regional or national congresses. Since the late 1960s, complaints about the ineffectiveness of some aging local party caucuses have led to the formation of nonpolitical community action groups, especially by younger voters.

At the regional level, party lists are established for parliamentary elections by the regional (county) party oligarchy in consultation with representatives from the local organizations and/or other party figures, or through a regional conference (Social Democrats). Party regional executives and full-time party officials play a crucial role in shaping the outcome. Through compromises and accommodations, they balance out interest groups, occupational categories, etc., on the final ticket. Otherwise, they replicate the functions of local party organizations one rung higher up the hierarchy.

At the national level, the Swedish system is characterized by a generally high level of cooperation between the parliamentary blocs and their respective national party organizations. As a rule, the leader of the party is also elected leader of the parliamentary group. In 1981, however, the Moderate Party reverted to a practice that had always been more common with them than with the other parties, that is, the retiring party leader carries on as leader of the parliamentary caucus. The actual process of choosing a new leader when a vacancy occurs has varied greatly, but commonly a special committee representing the top echelons of both the parliamentary and membership sides of the party plays an important role.

Nominally, the most important national party organs are the periodic congresses of 200 to 350 delegates which elect key party functionaries, draw up election manifestoes, discuss constituency motions, review the stewardship of party executives, etc. By no means rubber-stamp bodies, they can and quite often do take a stand independent of the party leadership, usually by asking it to examine the issue further or to take certain facets of the question into special consideration.

In practice the real steering of the party's work—except in the case of nominations—comes from the party leader, the party's national executive, and the parliamentary caucus. The growth of the mass media has encouraged the process of centralization of authority in the hands of party leaders who, because of television appearances, are both better known and more important to the parties' electoral success than was the case twenty years ago.

Campaigning

Issues are generally more important than personalities in Swedish elections, but the importance of issues varies from election to election. In 1976 and again in 1982, the Socialist proposal of "worker funds," urged by the labor federation, was a major issue. The funds would be accumulated by appropriating a percentage of the profits of private companies. Controlled by unions, the funds would be used to purchase shares of corporate stock which would be owned by the workers collectively, not individually. Over a period of time, the unions would become majority shareholders in many private businesses. The nonsocialist parties, of course, were vehemently opposed to the proposal, and polls showed that it was not popular with many Social Democratic voters. In the 1982 campaign, the nonsocialist parties emphasized their campaign against the idea, while the socialists concentrated on the problem of rising unemployment. A much-diluted funds reform was enacted in 1983, and in the 1985 electoral campaign taxation was a major issue.

Television time for campaigning is allocated equally to all parties represented in Parliament. The highlight of the television campaign is a long session on election eve in which the leaders of all the parties participate. The moderator of the session tries to achieve a proportional allocation of time with the use of a stopwatch!

In general, issues are sharpened on television and radio and obscured in elaborate poster campaigns. The posters show the influence of mass marketing campaigns and stress generalized images: "Peace," "Work," "Safeguard the Family," etc. The posters come in series, and one party's poster will occasionally be a "response" to that of another party.

Independent Voters

Roughly 10 percent of the voters split their votes between parties in national and local elections, which occur on the same day. About half of this splitting occurs between one or another of the nonsocialist parties; the rest occurs between leftist parties, or across the left-right cleavage, or between a national and a local party.

Center Party
(*Centerpartiet*)

History

The Center Party is the modern successor of the Agrarian Party (*Bondeförbundet*), which began life in 1913, chiefly to represent small farmers. Larger farmers formed their own party in 1915. Both organizations returned their first parliamentary representatives in 1917. In 1921 they merged, under the name Agrarian Party. For the next three decades, the Agrarians polled some 11 to 14 percent of the total vote. They remained first and last a party to protect agricultural interests. In pursuit of those interests, they came to an understanding with the Social Democrats during the Depression (1933). Later they took part in two "Red-Green coalitions" with the same party (1936–39 and 1951–57), both times as the junior partner, but both times in control of the Ministry of Agriculture.

During the second of these coalitions, the party's vote fell to just over 9 percent, a record low. At the same time, a rapid drift out of agriculture threatened the party's support base. Gunnar Hedlund, the farmer-politician who led the party from 1949 to 1971, supported the change of name to Center Party in 1958 as one move in a major shift of strategy designed to widen the party's appeal. The strategy resulted in a series of successful elections, culminating in a 25.1 percent vote in 1973. Since then support has ebbed. Nevertheless, the party has provided the prime minister in three nonsocialist coalitions in the person of Thorbjörn Fälldin, its leader from 1971 to 1985. Fälldin I (1976–78) was a tripartite nonsocialist majority government resulting from a victory for the nonsocialist bloc in the 1976 elections. This government fell because of internal dissension, more specifically because of Center Party opposition to the nuclear power program. Fälldin II (1979–81) was a similar combination, made possible by interparty agreement to hold a referendum on the

nuclear issue in the wake of the incident at the Three Mile Island reactor in the United States. The coalition came to power in an election in which the Center Party fell to 18.1 percent and second place in the narrowly successful nonsocialist camp. The coalition disintegrated in May 1981 over a tax-reform scheme, and Fälldin III, a minority coalition with the Liberals, took its place.

Organization

The Center Party holds a national conference annually. It is one of two parties which issue central directives about the procedure to be followed for making nominations on the party ticket.

The party press is not prominent in the country's mass media. The biggest paper is *Skgnska Dagbladet*, published in Malmö. The chief party journals are *Svensk politik* and *Politisk Tidskrift*. The youth organization publishes a paper called *Ung Center* and the womens' organization has a paper called *Budkavle* (The Fiery Cross).

The National Farmers' Association (*Lantbrukarnas riksförbund*; LRF) is formally a nonpolitical organization. In practice it has many close links with the party, both at the voting and membership levels and in the composition of the parliamentary caucus.

National headquarters are at Scheelegatan 8, 10422 Stockholm.

Policy

The Center Party program adopted in 1970 reflects the wider appeal of the party since its change of name. Stress is laid on decentralization, egalitarianism, and environmental protection; political decisions should be made as near to grass-roots level as possible. The party favors small businesses and an increased measure of codetermination in industry. It opposes regional imbalances in the quality of life, urban overdevelopment, and rural underdevelopment. Its concern for the environment resulted in an opposition in principle to the nuclear power program, which consequently became a dominant issue in Swedish politics from 1976 to 1980.

Membership & Constituency

The Center Party's membership is approximately 140,000, some 14 percent of its total vote in the 1979 election.

The success of the Center Party's drive to widen its appeal is reflected in the fact that from 1956 to 1973 it made gains among all social classes. Recently, over a third of its support has come from industrial and other workers, and just under a third from white-collar workers. It also has won the vote of almost one in five of the country's small businessmen. It is still a class party in the sense that it retains the loyalty of a large majority of the country's farmers; estimates vary from two-thirds to over four-fifths. Nevertheless the farmers, who accounted for over three quarters of the Center vote in 1956, are now down to less than a quarter of its total support.

The Center polled some 15 percent of the vote in the major cities at its peak in 1973; by 1979 this had fallen to 10 percent. Much of the party's urban support comes from those whose home background was originally in a farming community. The concern with environmental issues attracted many younger voters, while the opposition to nuclear power attracted women voters. The party's strongest areas cover two broad swathes of counties just to the north and to the south of central Sweden. In general it is a significant political factor in rural areas throughout Sweden.

Financing

No details of party financing are available, but state support far outweighs income from membership dues and other sources.

Leadership

Thorbjörn Fälldin, a farmer from northern Sweden, was ousted as leader by his party in December 1985 after the Center in September had had its worst election results in 29 years (12.4 percent): Karin Söder, party vice-chairman, replaced him on a stand-in basis until the party conference can make a final decision on the leadership in summer 1986. She is the first woman to lead a Swedish political party.

Prospects

The signs are that the Center Party has entered a period of decline following its earlier phenomenal successes. In early 1980, the nuclear question disappeared from the political agenda with a vote in favor of continuing the nuclear energy program. The Center has thus lost the issue which gave it a sharp profile in the mid-1970s. Its appeal has also weakened as some of the incoherence of its program has become more evident. For example, the equalization of regional living standards requires increased central direction, yet the party stands for increased decentralization. Only the farmers remain a dependable source of support: its other voters are more volatile. The decline has been severe and continuous since 1976, with polls in early 1982 showing it at 10.5 percent. The party's support among low-income groups helped push it towards a deal with the Social Democrats in May 1981 on the question of tax reform. The Liberals went along with the Center on this, and the Moderates left the government. The crisis can be seen as an attempt by the Center and Liberals to make clear to the voters their differences with the Moderates' conservatism. In 1985, the Center formed an electoral alliance with the Christian Democrats, without which it might well have lost even more seats than the twelve it did.

Left Party Communists
(*Vänsterpartiet Kommunisterna;* VPK)

History

The VPK is a descendant of the Left Socialist Party of 1917. From 1921 to 1967, it had the name Swedish Communist Party, having joined the Third International in 1919. The Communists have experienced repeated schisms—in 1921, 1924, 1929, 1967, and 1977—and have averaged only some 3 percent of the vote in the 1930s and 4.5 percent in the post-World War II period. In 1944 Soviet prestige helped them to an isolated peak of 10.3 percent (11.2 percent in the local government elections). In 1970 and 1976, they barely scraped over the 4 percent barrier to representation, but in 1979 recorded their best result in recent times, 5.6 percent.

Organization

The VPK party congress must meet at least once every third year. Additional congresses may be convened by the party executive or by local organizations representing at least a third of the total membership.

The party's main newspaper is *Ny Dag*. Its theoretical debate is conducted in the journal *Socialistisk Debatt*. The youth organization, *Kommunistisk Ungdom* (KU) publishes a paper called *Stormklockan* (The Tocsin).

National headquarters are at Kungsgatan 84, 11227 Stockholm.

Policy

The Communists have a Marxist program, but subscribe to parliamentary principles for the achievement of party goals. They seek public ownership of big business, banks, insurance companies, and credit institutions, and constantly attack the Social Democrats for being too friendly to capitalism. In practice they have repeatedly had to support the Social Democrats in order to keep the nonsocialists at bay. They therefore have been subject to internal rifts and, ultimately, to splits for being too parliamentary or not friendly enough to the Soviet line. They have to put much effort into elections in order to get over the 4 percent barrier: calls for rent and price freezes and lower taxes on foodstuffs are staple electoral appeals. The party joined the Center Party in opposition to nuclear power.

Membership & Constituency

The membership of VPK is approximately 18,000, some 6 percent of the votes cast for it in the 1979 elections.

Since 1968, VPK has changed character from a party of blue-collar workers to a party of white-collar workers and students, with about 40 percent of support coming from the working class. In the 1979 elections, one out of every two VPK voters was under age thirty. The party's attraction for the highly educated is reflected in the fact that in those elections it polled a bigger share of university graduates than of blue-collar voters. It still has above average strength in "red" Norrbotten, Sweden's most northerly county, and in the country's docklands and heavy industrial communities.

Financing

No details on party financing are available.

Leadership

The VPK's transformation began in 1964 under the leadership of C. H. Hermansson (1964–75), himself a university graduate and a talented television debater. Since 1975 the party has been led by Lars Werner (born 1935), originally a stonemason by trade; he entered Parliament in 1965 and became vice chairman of VPK in 1967.

Prospects

The VPK's strength among younger voters does not necessarily imply that it is the party of the future. It has a volatile electorate, and the polls show it hovering around the 5 percent mark. It cannot hope to enter government in the foreseeable future. It is essentially a party of protest, with a marked New Left–environmentalist strand in its make-up.

Liberal Party
(*Folkpartiet*)

History

The Liberal Party began life as a parliamentary caucus in 1895. It created a national party organization in 1902. It was then one of the two major actors on the Swedish political scene, rivaling the Conservatives in voting power and alternating with them in government. Under the leadership of Karl Staaff at first and later of Nils Edén, the party concentrated its energies on expanding suffrage and on parliamentary reform. With final victory on these issues between 1917 and 1921, the Liberals lost impetus, falling away from a majority of votes at the turn of the century to slightly over a fifth in 1920 and a mere 11 to 12 percent throughout the 1930s. Their decline was accelerated by a 1923 schism on the prohibition issue between a rural, Free Church temperance wing and an urban radical "Wet" wing. The two factions were not reunited until 1934. From 1948 to 1956, the party revived to become the strongest on the nonsocialist side with almost a quarter of the total vote. Since

1956, it has lost ground to its numerous competitors, recording an all-time low of 5.9 percent in 1982, before rallying strongly to 14.2% in 1985.

From 1945 to 1976 the Liberals, in common with the other nonsocialist parties, were in opposition. From 1976 to 1982, however, they have been the only such party continuously in office. Not only have they served in all three of Fälldin's ministries, but they also formed a minority government of their own in 1978 with their then leader Ole Ullsten as prime minister.

Organization

The Liberal Party's national congress normally takes place annually except for election years. The party is by far the strongest in terms of the circulation figures for newspapers sympathetic to it. These papers include a number of the leading dailies, notably *Dagens Nyheter*, and are read by a much wider circle than the party's voters. The youth organization also publishes a newspaper.

National headquarters are at Luntmakargatan 66, 11383 Stockholm.

Policy

Under the leadership of Bertil Ohlin, party leader from 1944 to 1967, the Liberals finally moved away from their old attachment to *laissez-faire* economic policies and towards "social liberalism." This implies a partnership between the state and private enterprise to remedy the ills of the market economy, but no more than is required for that purpose. The party opposes both socialists and conservatives in principle, although in practice it has reached accommodations with both at times. It is strongly in favor of vigilant constitutional defense of civil rights and liberties, of equal rights for men and women, and of generous aid to underdeveloped countries.

Membership & Constituency

The Liberal Party has approximately 54,000 members, slightly more than 9 percent of its total vote in the 1979 elections.

The Liberals have lost strength in their old rural Free Church bastions, notably Västerbotten county in northern Sweden and Jönköping county in south-central Sweden. Secularizing trends in society at large do much to account for

this decline, together with rural depopulation and, to a lesser extent, competition since 1964 from the new Christian Democratic Party. Liberal support now comes fairly evenly from both town and country. Their urban support comes from all classes, especially from white-collar workers, professional people, and small businessmen. In no class, however, are they predominant. The more radical young intellectuals who joined them during their postwar peak (1948–56) tended to drift away to the Social Democrats and Left Party Communists under the influence of the New Left wave in the second half of the 1960s. Since 1970 they have lost support to the Center Party and the Moderates. Their geographical spread is remarkably evenly distributed among the country's regions, with a mild concentration (5 percent or so above the average) in Gothenburg and along the western coast. They still preserve something of their old character of an amalgam of Free Church members and what might be called "cultural radicals."

Financing

No details are available on party financing, but like the other parties, the Liberals rely on state support as the largest part of their income.

Leadership

The Liberals have had five different leaders since 1967, after the long tenure of Bertil Ohlin. In October 1983, Ole Ullsten (prime minister 1978–1979) was succeeded as party leader by forty-year-old Bengt Westerberg, a talented debater and TV personality from the right wing of the party. Westerberg has had political administrative experience under the nonsocialist governments of 1976–1982. With him as leader, the party's fortunes have shown a dramatic improvement.

Prospects

The September 1982 elections were a disaster for the Liberals. Their tactic of siding with the Social Democratic position on taxes in an effort to distinguish themselves from the conservative Moderates appears to have worked in favor of the Moderates. The Liberals have greater difficulty than any other party in the system in maintaining voter loyalty and a sharp political profile. Cooperation with the Social Democrats across the bloc boundary is a constant temptation to the more radical party members, but it is a high-risk option in terms of voter support.

Moderate Party (*Moderata Samlingspartiet*)

History

The Moderate Party has since 1969 been the name for what used to be the Right (*Högern*), the Swedish Conservatives. At the beginning of this century, the Conservatives represented the power-holders in Swedish society: higher civil servants, entrepreneurs, large landowners. They polled almost half the total vote on a restricted franchise and alternated in office with the Liberals. They were in large measure a party of resistance to change, opposing suffrage reform, parliamentary democracy, and high expenditure on social welfare. The adoption of the present name was designed to break with the old image of a party of reaction.

The Conservatives began as a parliamentary caucus and created a nationwide party organization in 1904. They began to lose ground after the final modernization of the political system between 1917 and 1921. They polled a quarter of the national vote, however, throughout the 1920s and remained the strongest party on the nonsocialist side until 1948, when they received only 12.3 percent of the vote. Since then they have had a checkered career. In 1958 they again became the largest nonsocialist party with a 20.4 percent vote. By 1970 they were down to 11.5 percent, but they made a steady recovery throughout the 1970s and reached 23.6 percent in 1982, when they won more seats than the other nonsocialist parties combined.

After forming two minority governments in the 1920s, the Conservatives were out of power for thirty-one years before they participated in Fälldin's tripartite coalitions of 1976 to 1978 and 1979 to 1981.

Organization

The Moderate Party normally holds a national congress every third year in the year preceding a general election.

The party newspaper is *Medborgaren* (The Citizen). The Moderates have their own educational and training establishment for party members, the *Medborgarskolan*. The youth organization runs the paper *Moderat debatt*. There is a student organization, technically autonomous, which has a journal called *Svensk Linje*.

National headquarters are at L. Nygatan 13, 11182 Stockholm.

Policy

The Moderate Party is the strongest advocate among the Swedish parties of restraint in public-sector expenditure, of tax reforms to encourage individual enterprise, of a property-owning democracy, and of a powerful national defense. In principle it supports a free-market economy and is hostile to collectivization. In particular it attacks compulsory profit-sharing schemes. In 1969, concurrently with changing its name, it came out for the first time in support of an expansion of social welfare provisions. It now stresses the avoidance of wasteful expenditure in this sector and greater matching of resources to needs. It supports the nuclear power program. In foreign policy, it does not view potential Swedish membership of the European Community as necessarily incompatible with the country's traditional neutrality. It regards itself, justifiably, as the polar opposite of the Social Democrats on domestic policy. This stance has to date made it impossible for the Moderates to assume a leading position in a nonsocialist coalition, because both of the other nonsocialist parties fear loss of public support if they are identified with too firm a right-wing stance.

Membership & Constituency

The Moderate Party has some 160,000 members, slightly less than 15 percent of its support in the 1979 elections. They are, in the main, an urban-based party, although they are quite strongly supported in the more prosperous agricultural areas of southern Sweden. In the cities, they command approximately a quarter of the vote of white-collar workers and almost a half of the vote of higher civil servants and professional people. In addition they have strong backing among entrepreneurs, both large and small. They may be characterized as the party of the upper-income brackets in Swedish society. Their insistence on reduced levels of direct taxation and on the careful management of the public sector helped bring them over a third of the poll in 1979 in the metropolitan areas. They are weak in working-class support, and weak also in the northern half of the country, which is traditionally more radical.

There is a considerable membership overlap between the Moderate Party and associations of Swedish industry. Nevertheless, the Federation of Swedish Employers (SAF) and the Federation of Swedish Industry (SI) are not affiliated with the party, and since 1976, the party has not accepted financial contributions from firms or industrial enterprises.

Financing

Like the other parties, the Moderates depend heavily on state support, but no details are available. In 1976, the party announced that it would no longer accept contributions from private industry.

Leadership

Gösta Bohman (born 1911), the fifth party leader since 1945, was elected in 1970 and resigned in 1981. He continued as leader of the parliamentary caucus. He presided over the party's upswing, is a clear and forceful debater, and has a military and business background. His successor as party leader is Ulf Adelsohn (born 1942), earlier prominent as a party leader in Stockholm city.

Prospects

The Moderates have gained much support in the past decade at the expense of their nonsocialist competitors, not least among younger voters. A future victory by the nonsocialist parties would raise the issue of a Moderate-led coalition, a very awkward prospect for the Center and the Liberals, who might well prefer to support a Moderate minority government on an ad hoc basis without actually joining a coalition. But the recent success of the Liberals under Westerberg has produced the alternative of a Liberal-led coalition.

Social Democratic Party
(*Socialdemokratiska Arbetarepartiet;*
S or SAP)

History

The Social Democratic Party came into being in 1889 with Hjalmar Branting as party leader. In 1896 Branting became the party's first MP, although he was elected on a Liberal list. In 1897 the party adopted a modified version of the orthodox Marxist Erfurt Program developed by the German Socialists in 1891. Practice, however, was already at variance with theory. The party collaborated with the Liberals in pursuit of the modernization of the political system and gave full support to the parliamentary principle. By 1914, the SAP was polling over a third of the vote. After 1932, it never fell below 40 percent and became the dominant party in the system. In 1940 and 1968 it gained an absolute majority of the votes cast, although the earlier of these two results was achieved in the shadow of Nazi domination elsewhere in Scandinavia. After 1968, it experienced a number of electoral setbacks, the worst of them in 1976 with a 42.7 percent poll, but it returned to full strength in 1982 when it won more seats than the three nonsocialist parties combined. In 1985 its strength was reduced slightly, but not enough for it to lose power.

The SAP has generally proved extremely resistant to splits on its left. Their pragmatic policies led in 1917 to a breakaway of radicals to form the Left Socialist Party (*Vänstersocialistiska Partiet*), but their voting support fell off only briefly as a result. In 1917 they entered government for the first time, in coalition under a Liberal prime minister. In the 1920s, they took turns with the nonsocialist parties in forming unstable minority administrations. In 1932 they came to office on an expansionist economic program to meet the Depression. In 1933, agreement with the Agrarians began what proved to be an almost uninterrupted tenure in power until 1976. The party's position was not quite so impregnable as this record might suggest. Sometimes coalition was necessary (1936–39, 1939–45, 1951–57), and often the balance of advantage over its adversaries was finely poised. Nevertheless, the party appeared to be the natural party of government during this period. Even in opposition between 1976 and 1982, they were the single strongest party by a wide margin.

Organization

The SAP holds a national congress every third year, in the year preceding a general election. The procedure to be followed in making nominations to the party ticket is centrally controlled.

The party controls a number of newspapers; however, the one with the biggest circulation, *Aftonbladet*, is owned by the umbrella union federation. The party journal, *Tiden*, is the main vehicle for intellectual debate. The youth organization runs a newspaper called *Frihet* (Freedom); the women's organization operates one called *Morgonbris* (Morning Breeze). Christian Social Democrats have their own organization within the party, *Broderskapsrörelsen* (The Brotherhood Movement).

National headquarters are at Sveavagen 68, 10560 Stockholm.

Policy

Social Democratic Party programs steadily diluted their Marxist content between 1920 and 1960. The party has come to stress the welfare state; increased egalitarianism; and especially in the last fifteen years, "economic democracy" to complete the political democracy already achieved. In pursuit of this aim, the party has considerably strengthened union powers vis-a-vis management, notably by the passage of a Co-Determination Act in 1976. The SAP also supports the introduction of the worker funds scheme which would be likely to have further radical effects on the industrial power balance. This project was an important factor in the party's loss of office in 1976, largely because the party and the union movement for once spoke with discordant voices. (In 1981, however, they came to an agreement in principle on the proposal.) A second important factor in that defeat was the nuclear power issue. The party supported the nuclear program in the interests of full employment and economic growth, for once in agreement with the Moderates. The U. S. economist John Galbraith rather than Marx has been the inspiration to the SAP since the 1950s. Nevertheless, some radicalizing tendencies have been apparent since the mid-1960s.

Membership & Constituency

The SAP has approximately 1.1 million members, or about 46 percent of its 1979 poll. Over 70 percent of the membership, however, is collectively affiliated, and many of these members are politically apathetic. Nevertheless, the party has more loyal supporters, relatively and absolutely, than any other in the system.

The Social Democrats generally win more votes than any other party throughout most areas of the country, although competition from the Moderates has been stiff recently in the larger cities. The SAP is still predominantly a workers' party, but its support among trade-union members has fallen from four-fifths to just over two-thirds since 1968. The increased social mobility of labor has reinforced a tendency for issue-oriented voting to bulk larger than loyalty voting. At the same time, the party has made compensating gains in the white-collar sector, especially among younger voters in the lower echelons. Northern Sweden is a fortress of the party, with an absolute majority of votes coming to the party despite a weakening of strength since 1968 in other parts of the country.

The Swedish Confederation of Trade Unions (*Landsorganisationen;* LO) is formally independent of any party, but in fact it has a natural relationship with the SAP. The two partners regularly hold top-level meetings, and the LO Secretariat has inspired numerous important policy initiatives, e.g., the principles for labor market policy, a compulsory supplementary pensions scheme, and in 1976, the worker funds scheme. The General Secretary is commonly a Social Democratic MP. His weight in the party leadership derives from a union movement with 1.8 million members and near-complete coverage of the blue-collar work force. At the same time, it should be stressed that the individual unions which may affiliate with the party have no formal representation at the party's national congresses or in its other governing bodies.

The Cooperative Movement (*Kooperativa förbundet;* KF) has significant overlapping membership with the SAP but not as close a relationship as the LO, despite the degree of affinity between the two.

Financing

No details on financing are available. The party is probably less dependent on state support than any other party.

Leadership

The Social Democrats have only had five party leaders since their foundation: Hjalmar Branting (1889–1925), Per Albin Hansson (1925–46), Tage Erlander (1946–69), Olof Palme. (1969-86), and now Ingvar Carlsson. Palme (born 1927) was a close political confidant of Erlander, serving under him in the Cabinet Office and later in ministerial capacities. At age forty-two, he was the youngest prime minister in Europe when he took over upon Erlander's retirement.

Prospects

The SAP is far too strongly entrenched in Swedish life to ever be in danger of serious loss of electoral support. Its return to power in the elections of 1982 was primarily due to the non-socialist government's inability to deal with the unemployment problem, which, according to official figures, had reached 3 percent, with perhaps another 1.5 percent concealed unemployment. Whether the Socialists will be able to do any better is uncertain. It is certain, however, that the difficulties of governing are greater today than ever before.

Minor Parties

The Christian Democratic Party (*Kristen Demokratisk Samling;* KDS)

Founded 1964, the KDS has contested most constituencies in parliamentary elections since then, winning 1 to 2 percent of the national vote and some municipal and county council seats. The KDS opposes the permissive society and has the support of fundamentalist churches. Electoral alliance with the Center Party in 1985 enabled it to return its first-ever M.P., the party leader Alf Svensson.

Ecology Party (Miljöpartiet de gröna)

Founded 1982, this party seeks a six-hour day, low interest rates, and less economic growth. It received 1.5% of the total vote in 1985.

Pensioners' Party (*Pensionärspartiet*)

The Pensioners' are another new party and fought the 1982 elections in alliance with the Ecology Party as "The Cooperating Parties." They won a miniscule portion of the vote.

Swedish Communist Party (*Sveriges Kommunistiska Parti;* SKP)

A Maoist splinter from the Left Communist Party in 1967, the SKP originally called itself the Communist League of Marxist-Leninists (not to be confused with the Revolutionary Communist League [now Party], a tiny Gothenburg faction). The party won 0.4 percent of the national vote in 1970 and 1973. It adopted its present name in 1973, much to the resentment of the Left Party Communists.

Worker Party Communists (*Arbetarpartiet Kommunisterna;* APK)

This Moscow-aligned faction, based in the far north, broke with the Left Party Communists in 1977, taking two of the latter's MPs with it. It lost those seats in 1979.

National Prospects

The return of the Social Democrats to a second term in office after the September 1985 general election was eventually followed by the most traumatic event in Sweden's post-1945 history, namely the assassination of prime minister Olof Palme on February 28, 1986, as he was walking home from a Stockholm cinema. Political violence had hitherto been unheard of in modern Sweden, except on rare occasions by foreign terrorists against foreign embassy staffs in the pursuit of imported quarrels. Ingvar Carlsson, the party's deputy leader, was subsequently confirmed as successor both by his party and then by Parliament, the nonsocialist parties abstaining in the parliamentary vote to demonstrate a measure of national unity. Carlsson then reappointed the outgoing cabinet as a sign of continuity.

The Social Democrats have had mixed success in grappling with Sweden's considerable economic problems. Industrial production has been slightly above the western European average and unemployment has been reduced to below the 3 percent level (the 5 percent level of youth unemployment also represents an improvement). The large budgetary deficit inherited from the nonsocialist governments in 1982 has been cut by stringent public expenditure measures. On the debit side, real-interest rates of 8 percent are above the western European average; inflation is proving difficult to decrease below the 8 percent level, and the balance of payments deficit has increased to an awkwardly high figure.

The Liberals under Westerberg's new-style leadership appear to be displacing the Conservatives as the main opponents of the Social Democrats. In summation, the country's underlying political stability remains unshaken by the violent removal of its best-known political leader.

Further Reading

Bäck, Pär-Erik, and Berglund, Sten. *Det svenska partiväsendet*. Stockholm: Awe/Gebers, 1978.

Berglund, Sten, and Lindström, Ulf. *The Scandinavian Party System(s)*. Lund: Studentlitteratur, 1978.

Elder, N. C. M. "Bipolarity or Indeterminacy in a Multi-Party System?" Hull Papers in Politics No. 14. Hull, England: University of Hull, Department of Politics, 1979.

Elvander, Nils. *Scandinavian Social Democracy: Its Strength and Weakness*. Acta Universitatis Upsaliensis No. 39. Uppsala: Almqvist and Wiksell, 1979.

Hancock, M. Donald. *Sweden: The Politics of Postindustrial Change*. Hinsdale, Ill.: Holt, Rinehart and Winston, Dryden Press, 1972.

Petersson, Olof. *Partier Och Väljare, Känn Ditt Land*, serie No. 11. Stockholm: Svenska turistforeningen, 1981.

Ryden, Bengt and Bergstrom, Villy, eds. *Sweden: Choices for Economic and Social Policy in the 1980s*. London: George Allen & Unwin, 1982.

Särlvik, Bo. "Recent Electoral Trends in Sweden." In *Scandinavia at the Polls*, Karl H. Cerny, ed. Washington, D.C.: American Enterprise Institute for Policy Research, 1977.

Worre, Torben. "Class Parties and Class Voting in the Scandinavian Countries." *Scandinavian Political Studies*, Vol. 3 (new series), No. 4, 1980.

SWISS CONFEDERATION
(Schweizerische Eidgenossenschaft)
by C. F. Schuetz, Ph.D.

The System of Government

The Swiss Confederation had its beginning in 1291 when Schwyz, Uri, and Unterwalden entered a perpetual alliance. While other areas in the region gradually became associated with them, a federal consciousness did not evolve until the fifteenth century. With the federal constitution of 1848, which has since been extensively revised, especially in 1874, the Swiss Confederation assumed its present structure as a republican, democratic federation composed of twenty-six states (twenty full and six half-cantons). In September 1978, this number rose to twenty-six with the creation of a new canton, Jura, comprising the French-speaking areas of the predominantly German-speaking canton Berne. Of the nation's 6.3 million people, about 65 percent speak German as their mother tongue, 18 percent speak French, and 12 percent speak Italian, and 0.8 percent speak Romanche.

Executive

Executive authority rests with a seven-member body, the Federal Council (*Bundesrat*). The members are chosen individually by a joint meeting of the two houses of Parliament at the commencement of a new legislative term or whenever a vacancy must be filled. Constitutionally, any Swiss citizen who satisfies the requirements to become a candidate for election to the Parliament may be chosen. In practice, only people with considerable experience in public affairs are selected. The appointee must resign all other offices, private or public, which might create a conflict of interest. With few exceptions, federal councillors who have been willing to remain in office have been reconfirmed after four years. The size of the reconfirmation vote is an indicator of a candidate's performance and political support.

In a similar manner, a different member of the Federal Council is selected annually to serve as president of the Swiss Confederation (*Bundespräsident*). This person fulfills the dual role of head of state and chairperson of the executive. The role is mostly ceremonial and quite different from the presidency in a presidential system or the presidency and prime ministership in a parliamentary democracy. According to the federal constitution, the Federal Council is the supreme directing and executive power in the Confederation, but no personal leadership role is evident. Not even the president of the Confederation enjoys a special status. Like every federal councillor, the president is required to administer one of the seven federal departments. Another executive role is fulfilled by the federal chancellor (*Bundeskanzler*) who is the principal liaison officer between the Parliament and the administrative machinery.

Generally, the Swiss style of executive decision-making is collegial. The entire membership of the executive meets about ninety times a year. Although there is a certain deference to the opinion of the federal councillor in charge of the matter under consideration, decisions are made by all members of the executive as a team. The general effect of collegial decision-making is a limitation on power, a concentration of information, coordination of policy, and continuity despite changes in personnel.

In addition to collegiality, the Swiss executive is characterized by ethnic minority representation and diversity of partisan membership. From its very beginning in 1848, the Swiss executive has provided representation to minority populations. Over the entire period, the average ratio of minority representation has been somewhat higher than the actual percentage of these populations taken together. Following the election of 1891, the Federal Council has also included members from more than one political party. As a rule, the partisan composition of the executive has reflected party strength in the legislature. Since 1959, the "magic" formula for coalitions has been 2 : 2 : 2 : 1 with the three largest parties getting two seats while the remaining seat goes to one of the smaller parties.

The current executive was selected in 1983. As of 1986, the distribution of departments and functions was:

President of the Confederation and Department of the Interior: Alphons Egli (Christian Democratic Party—elected as president in December 1985 by 198 of 211 valid votes cast);

Vice President and Department of Foreign Affairs, Pierre Aubert (Social Democratic Party);

Department of Public Economy: Kurt Furgler (Christian Democratic Party);

Department of Finance, Otto Stich (Social Democratic Party);

Department of Transport, Communications and Energy, Leon Schlumpf (People's Party);

Department of Justice and Police, Elizabeth Kopp-Iklé (Radical Democratic Party);

Military Department, Jean-Pascal Delamuraz (Radical Democratic Party).

Legislature

With the exception of those powers reserved to the people and the cantons, the federal constitution declares that the "supreme authority of the Confederation" is exercised by the bicameral Federal Assembly (*Bundesversammlung*), which is composed of the Council of States (*Ständerat*) and the National Council (*Nationalrat*). The two chambers enjoy equality of status and can veto any piece of legislation passed by the other chamber. In addition, the legislative authority is subject to a wide range of obligatory and optional referenda provisions, the former applying specifically to constitutional amendments.

Generally, the legislature tries to avoid optional referenda, but opposition groups can relatively easily gather the 30,000 signatures (on provided postcards) required to put an issue to a national vote. Eight cantonal governments can also initiate a national referendum, but that process has never been used. Fifteen to eighteen referenda take place each year at all three levels of government combined. They are decided by a majority of those voting. Turnout for referenda depends on the issue, but it is usually well below that for Federal Assembly elections.

The National Council is composed of 200 members elected to four-year terms. The 200 seats are allotted according to a canton's population. To prevent any of the smaller cantons from losing their legislative representation, they are assured of at least one seat. As a rule, party discipline in the National Council is not very strong. While like-minded members form party groups (*Fraktionen*), that does not mean that the parliamentary representatives elected under the same party label will also adhere to the same party group in the legislature. In the selection process for the membership of the executive, this loose organization has at times produced a situation where a political party has been unable to get its official candidate elected to the party's seat in the Federal Council. In turn, a federal councillor cannot always count on the political support of his parliamentary *Fraktion*.

Initially, the forty-six member Council of States (two members for each full canton) was to represent the cantons in the central decision-making process. Over the years, however, this function has not been fulfilled. In consequence, the Council of States has become a second popular chamber. It differs from the National Council primarily in that it tends to have a higher percentage of conservative or bourgeois members.

Contrary to the usual parliamentary system, the Swiss legislature is not characterized by a competitive relationship between government and opposition. The executive, for example, does not face votes of confidence. Everything is geared towards cooperation on behalf of the people. The executive functions in close accord with the National Assembly in the preparation of reports and legislative proposals and in the implementation of decisions of the Assembly.

The two chambers also aim at complementing each other's efforts. After each election, the presidents of the two councils meet to draw up a plan of legislative action identifying the priorities of each chamber. Each council in turn reviews the plan and approves it or makes adjustments which, at times, are decided by lot. The successful operation of the bicameral system is also facilitated by the close association of the respective party groups in the two chambers. Due to the numerical advantage of the *Fraktionen* in the National Council, their influence tends to be more prominent than that of Council of States members in the formulation of party policy.

For certain specific purposes such as the election of the Federal Council, the judges of the

ELECTION RESULTS BY CANTON (1983)

Canton	CVP %	CVP Seats	FDP %	FDP Seats	SPS %	SPS Seats	SVP %	SVP Seats	Others %	Others Seats	Total Seats
Zürich	9.1	3	21.8	9	23.0	8	13.8	5	32.2	10	35
Berne	2.1	—	15.1	5	28.3	9	29.0	9	25.5	6	29
Lucerne	49.6	5	28.6	3	11.7	1	—	—	10.0	—	9
Uri	—	—	84.7	1	—	—	—	—	15.3	—	1
Schwyz	46.6	2	26.0	1	21.0	—	6.5	—	—	—	3
Obwalden	91.0	1	—	—	—	—	—	—	9.0	—	1
Nidwalden	97.2	1	—	—	—	—	—	—	2.8	—	1
Glarus	—	—	—	—	—	—	92.3	1	7.7	—	1
Zug	39.9	1	33.6	1	22.8	—	—	—	3.8	—	2
Fribourg	45.5	3	20.0	1	24.0	1	8.9	1	1.7	—	6
Solothurn	26.7	2	37.2	3	27.8	2	—	—	8.4	—	7
Basle City	9.9	1	13.5	1	30.0	2	—	—	45.6	2	6
Basle Land	10.8	1	25.1	2	32.5	3	11.2	1	20.4	—	7
Schaffhausen	6.3	—	26.2	1	35.3	1	22.7	—	9.5	—	2
Appenzell (OR)	14.5	—	36.0	1	23.6	—	—	—	25.9	1	2
Appenzell (IR)	95.6	1	—	—	—	—	—	—	4.4	—	1
St. Gallen	40.8	5	27.5	4	16.3	2	1.9	—	13.5	1	12
Grisons	33.3	2	20.1	1	24.7	1	22.0	1	—	—	5
Aargau	21.5	4	20.2	3	27.5	4	14.1	2	16.7	1	14
Thurgau	21.6	2	18.3	1	19.5	1	22.8	2	17.8	—	6
Ticino	33.9	3	37.9	3	13.8	1	2.1	—	12.3	1	8
Vaud	4.5	—	30.4	7	21.9	5	6.2	1	37.0	4	17
Valais	57.7	4	25.1	2	14.1	1	—	—	3.2	—	7
Neuchâtel	—	—	19.4	1	33.1	2	—	—	47.4	2	5
Geneva	12.3	1	16.2	2	19.2	2	—	—	52.2	6	11
Jura	36.8	—	28.8	1	17.8	1	2.0	—	14.5	—	2
Total	20.6	42	23.3	54	22.8	47	11.1	23	22.1	34	200

NATIONAL COUNCIL ACCORDING TO PARTY GROUPS (1959–1983)

	1959	1963	1967	1971	1975	1979	1983
Christian Democratic	47	48	45	44	46	44	42
Radical Democratic	51	51	49	49	47	51	54
Social Democratic	52	53	51	46	55	51	47
People's Party	23	22	21	23	21	23	23
Independent Alliance (includes EVP after 1975)	10	10	16	13	11	11	12
Democratic Party et al.	6	6	6	—	—	—	—
Labor Party	—	—	5	5	5	7	5
Unaffiliated and transitory	7	10	7	20	15	13	17
Total number of seats	196	200	200	200	200	200	200

Federal Tribunal and, in time of impending war, the general of the army, as well as the deci-sions regarding pardons and conflicts of competency, the Federal Assembly meets in joint ses-

COUNCIL OF STATES ACCORDING TO PARTIES (1959–1983)							
	1959	1963	1967	1971	1975	1979	1983
Christian Democratic	17	18	18	17	17	18	18
Radical Democratic	13	13	14	15	15	11	14
Social Democratic	4	3	2	4	5	9	6
People's Party	3	4	3	5	5	5	5
Independent Alliance	—	—	1	1	1	—	—
Liberal Party	3	3	3	2	1	3	3
National Action and Unaffiliated	4	3	3	—	—	—	—
Total number of seats	44	44	44	44	46	46	46

sion (*Vereinigte Bundesversamnlung*) under the president of the National Assembly as presiding officer.

Judiciary

On the whole, the Swiss judiciary is thoroughly separated from the political sphere. The administration of justice is regulated by the cantons while the content of law is primarily determined by the central authority. Since the 1920s, a progressive system of administrative courts has been developed both on the federal and on the cantonal level.

The highest court in Switzerland is the Federal Tribunal (*Bundesgericht*) with its seat in Lausanne and Lucerne. Its thirty members are elected by the National Assembly for six-year terms with reelection readily available for any judge whose performance is satisfactory who wishes to remain in office. Parliament selects the court's president and vice president for two-year terms from among the members of the court.

Although Switzerland is a federation, the function of judicial review on the national level is quite restricted as a consequence of the use of referenda in determining norms. According to the federal constitution, laws passed by Parliament and its general decisions are binding on the Federal Tribunal. The judiciary's constitutional jurisdiction deals principally with cantonal constitutions and laws.

Regional & Local Government

Understanding self-government on the local level is the most important key to a full compre-hension of the peculiar character of the Swiss political system. In Switzerland, individual citizenship is determined by membership in the local community, which is also the source of other legal, political, and even economic rights of the individual. In turn, most individuals feel a special attachment to their home communities.

Though the federal and cantonal governments delegate such functions as relate to elections, policing, education, taxation, health, and military training to the local communities, they are not merely administrative districts of the higher governments, but autonomous units of democratic self-government. In larger municipalities, the direct participation of the people is replaced by representative communal or city parliaments with all kinds of administrative officers being subject to election by the people.

In Obwalden, Nidwalden, Glarus, Appenzell Outer Rhodes, and Appenzell Inner Rhodes, the cantonal government is exercised on the basis of direct democracy (*Landsgemeinde*). With a relatively small number of eligible voters, ranging from 8,174 in Appenzell Inner Rhodes to 29,485 in Appenzell Outer Rhodes, and with a participation that has not exceeded 10,000 in the largest assemblies, it is possible for these cantons and half-cantons to have their electorate meet in a public place on one day each year to decided on issues and to select officials. As time constraints make it impossible to debate plans and policies on these occasions, the *Landsgemeinden* have been supplemented with small representative bodies.

Federation has provided uniform political structures in all the cantons, despite their extensive diversity in terms of culture, language, and religion. Although they are "sovereign" according to the constitution, they must all have constitutions in accord with the federal constitution and provide democratic government on the basis of general equality. In most cases, cantonal institutions reflect those of the federal level, except that all representative assemblies are unicameral. Cantonal executives are not responsible to these assemblies and conduct business in a collegial manner like the Federal Council.

With the exception of the executive of Appenzell Inner Rhodes, which has a one-party government formed by the Christian Democrats, all cantonal executives are coalitions reflecting the strength of the parties in the representative assemblies. The number of parties in coalition ranges from two (Obwalden, Nidwalden, Appenzell Outer Rhodes and Valais) to five in the canton of Zürich where the Christian Democrats, the Independent Alliance, the Radical Democrats, the Social Democrats and the People's Party manage to work together to form the government. The majority of the coalitions, however, are composed of three or four parties with the Radical Democrats in twenty-five cantonal executives, the Christian Democrats in twenty, and the Social Democrats in nineteen.

The Electoral System

Unlike nations where parliamentary representatives enjoy a virtual monopoly over political legitimization, in Switzerland, the more critical legitimizing function is fulfilled through initiatives and referenda. Both are used extensively and more frequently than elections on the cantonal and federal levels. In a few cantons, a form of direct democracy is still in use, while in others, parts of the entire legislative program and major financial matters are subject to approval in referenda.

As a consequence of this separate legitimizing process, the election of parliamentary representatives tends to be less competitive and more concerned with the degree to which the personality and opinions of candidates are in harmony with public perceptions. A satisfying performance in office or as a representative is also essential to election. Popular candidates are not the exclusive property of any one party. Such people can appear on any number of party lists of candidates who may benefit from a coat-tail effect.

The Swiss electoral system is characterized by inclusiveness. This feature is enhanced by the ease with which small groups are admitted to the electoral process. All that is required is the submission of the signatures of fifteen qualified voters to the appropriate cantonal authorities.

On the federal level, two types of electoral procedures—proportional and majority—exist side by side. Although the cantons determine when and how their two seats in the Council of States are filled, direct election by simple plurality is most common. Prior to 1919, this method was also used for elections to the National Council.

Following the lead of a number of progressive cantons which abandoned majority rule in their cantonal elections, the method of electing the members of the National Council was changed in 1919. With the exception of those cantons which have only one seat in the National Council, the electoral system is one of proportional representation (primarily d'Hondt).

Under this system, the voter has to make two decisions: which group or party to vote for and whether to leave the list of candidates as proposed or to change it. In the latter case, several options exist. A voter may strike out a name; rearrange the order of listing the names; emphasize a name by writing it in a second time; or add new names, including those taken from other party lists. Indeed, a voter can obtain a blank list and fill in his own candidates.

This arrangement benefits particularly popular candidates running for smaller parties. But popularity is a factor that tends to overrule the purposes of proportional representation, especially in a setting where only a few seats are open. The major parties, of course, try to prevent voter manipulation of their lists of candidates. The extent to which they are successful indicates the relative control these parties are able to exercise over their supporters. In this respect, the Social Democrats are most successful; only slightly more than a quarter of their lists are changed. In the case of the Radical Democrats and the People's Party, the rate exceeds 50 percent.

Under the Swiss electoral system, political parties are also allowed to form electoral coalitions or to combine their lists of candidates. Inasmuch as the federal government is already composed of representatives of the major parties in the National Assembly, these electoral combinations are not formed to control the executive as is usually the case in other countries. They are rather a consequence of the proportional system which creates a situation in which most parties have more votes than needed to elect their share of candidates. If parties pool these leftover votes, they can gain an extra seat. Accordingly, electoral combinations can only be formed in a single electoral district which, for elections to the National Council, are the cantons. Moreover, it is only in the larger cantons that a combined list has a chance to win a seat by producing the largest leftover parcel of votes. It has been estimated that, on the average, between 2 and 3.6 percent of the seats are affected by such combinations. But as far as the parties are concerned, the picture is more definite. Inasmuch as the Radical Democrats find it easier to combine with a kindred political group, they usually profit from the arrangement at the expense of the more ideologically inclined Social Democrats.

Since the establishment of the "magic formula" for the executive in 1959, special electoral coalition lists have increased in number. In the election of 1983, the Radical Democrats profited most from the arrangement by winning three additional seats despite a 0.8 per cent reduction in electoral support. In contrast, the Social Democrats lost four seats despite a 1.6 per cent increase in voter strength. Other parties gaining one additional seat on this basis were the Independent Alliance, the Liberal Party and the Progressive Swiss Organizations.

Switzerland has universal suffrage for its citizens who have reached the age of twenty. (Federal suffrage for women was approved in 1971.) Eligibility is determined almost automatically on the basis of membership in a local community. There are, however, cantonal regulations which disenfranchise certain categories of people. Although these regulations follow generally the commonly accepted grounds for exclusion (criminal record, insanity), there are also places where drunkenness can lead to the loss of the franchise.

Although the introduction of proportional representation brought a sudden jump in electoral participation with a high of 80.4 percent in 1919, it has also been blamed for the gradual decline since then. In 1979, the voter turnout fell to a low of 48.1 percent—uncomfortably close to the lowest point ever recorded—44.6 percent in 1848. In 1983, the percentage improved slightly to 48.9 percent.

The Party System

Origins of the Parties

The evolution of the Swiss party system falls into four major segments: a period of ideologies generally polarized in two main camps; the organizational struggle to establish national parties; the confrontational period involving working-class interests; and finally, the current condition of consensus democracy.

Prior to the establishment of the federation in 1848, the ideological pattern was characterized by the conservative camp supporting religious views and cantonal sovereignty, and the liberal camp favoring a centralist organization and secular views. Although neither side had an organization, they still managed to fight the Sonderbund War of 1847. The victorious side, the liberals, became the dominant political influence for the next few decades. Political organization was quite loosely structured and localized. Concrete issues would occasionally divide ideological groups into warring sections. In the efforts at constitutional reform during the early 1870s, the centralist-federalist polarization once more assumed national proportions.

After the constitutional issue had been settled in 1874, the political groups attempted to organize themselves nationally. For most of them, it was a very difficult struggle as many of the local differences were deeply rooted in past conflicts. The organizational process started on the parliamentary level. The need to control the appointment of the executive particularly induced the formation of more disciplined groups. Only gradually and after several false starts did national mass parties emerge. With their international experience to guide them, the Social Democrats, in 1888, became the first party to organize itself nationally, at least in form if not in spirit, for it, too, had to contend with the problems of local diversity and independence.

An unintended side effect of these organizational efforts was the creation of new divisions. In particular, the liberal camp suffered from the consequences of tighter organization. Traditionally, the Radical Democrats followed a very inclusive ideological line. Following their establishment of a national organization, they tried to retain wide support by following a centrist line. But their flexibility was sufficiently impaired to induce the less moderate wings to separate and to form their own groupings. With the introduction of proportional representation, which terminated the dominant position of the Radical Democrats, the multiparty pattern of the present Swiss party system emerged. During the first few decades of its existence, this pattern was also characterized by a confrontational relationship between the bourgeois parties and the Social Democratic opposition.

This political cleavage was finally resolved when, following the election of 1959, the Social Democratic party began to participate in the government coalition in accord with its electoral strength. This development meant the establishment of the *Konkordanzdemokratie*, a political system where all the major parties have been involved in running the government. As a consequence of this system, opposition is rather limited and restricted to small parties and protest groups which become more active and numerous in periods of national stress.

In addition to the major parties, this type of democracy provides also for the involvement of interest groups, especially the "big four": the Swiss Association of Commerce and Industry (*Schweizerischer Handels- und Industrieverein;* founded 1870), the Swiss Association of Arts and Crafts (*Schweizerische Gewerbeverein;* founded 1879), the Swiss Federation of Trade Unions (*Schweizerische Gewerkschaftsbund;* founded 1880), and the Swiss Agricultural Union (*Schweizerische Bauernverband;* founded 1897).

The Parties in Law

Constitutionally, the political parties have so far been ignored. During World War II, there was a prohibition of extremist parties. Financial compensation is provided only by a very small number of local communities and the canton Geneva. In practice, however, the political parties are recognized in their role of interest aggregation (they have the right to be involved in the process of public consultation), in their activities during election campaigns, and in parliamentary procedure. In line with the ideals of direct democracy, it is extremely easy for small groups to be recognized as parties for electoral purposes.

Party Organization

Most Swiss mass parties are heavily dependent on interest-group organizations. Indeed, the accusation has been made that these organizations overshadow the party system. The situation differs, of course, from party to party: some are sustained primarily by dues-paying members while others receive contributions from the associated interest groups to supplement the income from dues.

Structurally, most mass parties are federations of local or regional parties. Some commentators feel that Switzerland does not have one party system but as many systems as there are cantons. Though central organs resemble those of parties in other countries with congresses of party delegates, central committees, and secretariats, these organs are relatively weak. Recently, efforts have been made to improve the involvement of the rank-and-file members at national party conventions.

Locally, most parties are organized in residential cells, the smallest unit. In these cells, efforts are made to keep the party spirit alive, to relate current issues to the party platform or guidelines, and to get involved in initiatives and referenda especially on the local level. Party officials, however, are faced with a growing fatigue among ordinary people who feel that political involvement is too demanding.

In most large parties, the residential cells are linked to the cantonal organization through membership congresses. Aside from dealing with policy issues, these congresses elect the central party committee and its secretariat for the canton. The main influence of these organizations on the national party lies in granting or withholding support and in selecting candidates, who are usually chosen from party activists who have proven themselves in lesser positions. If, however, a representative fails to meet the expectations of the party, he is usually induced to resign by a sudden withdrawal of support. There are really no outstanding leadership personalities in Switzerland who can count on the blind adherance of their supporters.

Campaigning

As most Swiss voters are highly independent in their attitudes, and as there is no confrontation between government and opposition leaders in the elections, campaigns are generally characterized by less emotion and greater clarification of issues than is usually the case in Western Europe. Due to the lack of public funding, there is relatively less use of radio and television while a greater portion of the campaign funds is used for direct appeals, newspapers, and posters. The media, however, do provide time for public discussion, statement of views, and analysis to help in the process of public information.

Independent Voters

While Swiss voters are very independent with regard to individual candidates, they are relatively consistent in their choices of party. Party electoral support remains relatively consistent from election to election and between cantonal and national elections. This is probably less an indication of deliberate choice than of habit and a lack of volatility.

Christian Democratic People's Party of Switzerland (*Christlichdemokratische Volkspartei der Schweiz* [CVP]; *Parti démocrate-chrétien suisse*)

History

Although the Catholic and conservative elements were a major political factor prior to the establishment of the Swiss Confederation, their defeat in the Sonderbund War of 1847 destroyed whatever organizational structure they had and forced the leadership to leave the country. Still, about eight or ten members of the first Federal Assembly represented this segment of the population. These men were clearly a minority and were not involved in the government of the day.

Diversity of opinion kept the conservatives from constituting themselves as a national party until long after the other major parties had been established. Although several attempts at national organization were made between 1874 and 1894, only in 1912 did a founding convention of representatives from various rightist groups succeed in setting up a national structure. Even then dissent was strong, especially with regard to the name of the new party. The convention decided to avoid using the term Catholic in the hope of becoming more acceptable to a wider range of potential supporters. After the name of Conservative People's Party (*Konservative Volkspartei*) was approved by the delegates, all the opponents of that name left the convention.

Since the election of 1919, this party has been a major force in Swiss politics. Its first president, who guided the party for twenty years, National Councillor Heinrich Walther of Lucerne, frequently played a critical role in the election of the executive. The party changed its name to the Christian Democratic People's Party in 1957.

Organization

The CVP has retained its peculiar structure since its foundation in 1912. Unlike other parties, it is not composed of a network of local associations even though the party is organized in cantonal and local sections. These sections, however, consist of only a few members and frequently of single individuals. The majority of partisan supporters are members first of various Roman Catholic organizations collectively associated with the party. Although the emergence of the national organization was more difficult—and probably delayed by at least twenty years by this kind of structure—the arrangement offers considerable advantages in its range of public appeal, the flexibility of organization, and the satisfaction of diverse interests. In addition to the interests of small businessmen, artisans, and farmers, the CVP has also brought labor groups and youth movements under its umbrella. One technique which has proved to be quite effective in revitalizing this associational party structure is the use of study groups for various concerns and problems. The principal exponents of these groups have usually been given special representation in the party leadership.

In most geographical areas, the local CVP organizations are subject to the party convention, whose delegates are drawn from the individual as well as the collective membership. Official representatives of various intercantonal organizations and other affiliates and study groups, as well as party functionaries, outnumber direct party members by two to one at the convention. The convention elects the party Presidium which, according to the statutes, constitutes the central organ of the party. Its size, however, about 120 members, makes it difficult to satisfy that function. Actual power seems to lie with an informal leadership cluster including the most prominent members of the parliamentary group. According to the party statutes, this group may act independently on its own responsibility. In practice, however, it tends to coordinate policy with party officials.

The mailing address of the party is Postfach 1759, 3001 Berne.

Policy

The basic program of the CVP has remained surprisingly stable. It is based on the ideas of natural law and the main concepts of Roman Catholic teaching on society and the state. The main elements are protection of the individual person against state intervention, particularly with respect to belief, education, and family; preservation and development in a pluralist context of free associations such as religious institutions, interest organizations, political parties, communes, and cantons; subsidies on the basis of need to permit subordinate groups to fulfill their functions (e.g., education); and a basic solidarity among the independent social organizations to facilitate the amicable settlement of differences, especially in labor disputes.

In particular, the CVP has been advocating a more consistent national leadership on the part of the Federal Council on the basis of clearly articulated principles of action; a reorganization of the military establishment; improvement of pensions for the aged and invalids; reform of provisions relating to the ownership of land; maintenance of jobs and of the buying power of the Swiss currency; strengthening of the family unit; and development of professional education facilities and scientific research, especially through cantonal universities.

In the international context, the party strongly insists on the continuation of armed neutrality, while also advocating a close association with international organizations, possibly even Swiss membership in the United Nations, and a form of European confederation allowing small countries a voice in determining their destiny. Other ideas include a wider acceptance of the right to asylum and a world fund for economic aid.

At the national convention of March 26, 1983, meeting in Berne, the party's platform for the 1983—1987 session of the National Assembly tried to overcome a conceptual erosion due to the all-encompassing image associated with the CVP's center party position by reaffirming the party's lasting Christian values and through a special policy focus on federal balance, protection of the family unit, and economic risk-taking.

Membership & Constituency

Due to its peculiar organization, it is difficult to determine party membership. It is estimated that members and sympathizers number about 90,000. The CVP is politically strong because of loyal and consistent support by Roman Catholics. This segment of society has grown from 41 percent in 1919 to close to 50 percent in 1980. This growth generally parallels the increase of electoral support for the Christian Democrats. The party's greatest political strength is located in rural areas, especially in northeastern and northwestern Switzerland, and in a few larger urban areas such as Lucerne, Zürich, and Fribourg. There are also "diaspora areas," such as the city of Basle, where migrant Catholic workers have helped the party to win up to 20 percent of the cantonal seats.

The CVP has been described as the party of the little man. It is supported by farmers, small businessmen, artisans, employees, and workers, as well as by a sizable segment of young people.

Financing

It is relatively easy to obtain information on particular aspects of party financing in Switzerland, but with the complexity of the party system, the diversity of structures and the peculiarities of local fund raising, it becomes virtually impossible to obtain a national or general picture. Within most parties, the arrangement of dues and the amounts paid vary considerably from region to region.

As far as the CVP is concerned, the estimated operating budget of the national organization was 760,000 Swiss francs (about $325,000) in 1975 and that of all cantonal sections about twice as much. In the election of 1983, the party spent about 600,000 francs (about $300,000) nationally and a slightly higher amount through cantonal sections. Primary support comes from dues and from contributions from affiliated groups.

Leadership

In 1985, the leader of the party's parliamentary group was National Councillor Paul Zbinden (born 1936) from Appenzell Inner Rhodes. During the legislative sessions of 1985, he presided over the Lower Chamber, while his party colleague Markus Kuendig (born 1931) chaired the Upper Chamber. Of the two CVP Federal

Councillors, Kurt Furgler (born 1924) has been the most senior member of government, having been first elected in 1972. In 1985 he served as President of the Swiss Confederation. The second CVP member of the Federal Council, Alphons Egli (born 1924) was elected in 1983.

In the past, the parliamentary group of the Christian Democrats has generally been in the forty-to-sixty age bracket with only a few members older than sixty. The president of the party, Flavio Cotti (born 1939) is a member of the National Assembly and the first Italian-speaking leader of the party. Cotti is also a possible candidate for the Federal Council. Other leading party members are: Julius Binder (born 1925) from Aargau, Franz Muheim (born 1923) from Uri, and the director of justice and police of the canton of Geneva, Guy Fontanet (born 1923). The president of the youth wing of the party is Bruno Vanoni.

Prospects

Over the years, the electoral strength of the CVP has varied less than that of other large parties. Increases in its share of the national vote have generally been in line with demographic growth in the party's main areas of support. Although the party had three positions in the executive between 1954 and 1959, there is no indication of a return to this arrangement; nor are there indications that might point to an impending loss of electoral support. In all likelihood, the Christian Democrats will continue to participate in the government coalition with two representatives.

Independent Alliance
(*Landesring der Unabhängigen* [LdU]; *Alliance des Indépendants*)

History

The Independent Alliance is the youngest of the major parties. It was the only new political organization to emerge from the Great Depression as a continuing influence. In contrast to the other parties, the LdU was unique in existing as a protest movement and as a parliamentary group for over a year before the foundation of the formal organization. The founder and most prominent leader, Gottlieb Duttweiler, was a commercial genius who had organized a grocery retail chain, MIGROS AG, in the 1920s. During the Depression, various government regulations attempted to blunt his competitive edge. In reaction to that treatment, Duttweiler entered politics. The Radical Democratic Party in canton Zürich offered him a safe position on their electoral list, but barely four weeks before the election of 1935, Duttweiler set up his own independent list. Although running candidates in only three cities, Berne, St. Gallen, and Zürich, the movement managed to elect seven national councillors and to become the second-strongest political group in canton Zürich. Duttweiler hoped to pursue his political aims through one of the established parties, but none of them, particularly not the logical ally, the Radical Democratic Party, responded in a positive way. Consequently, the LdU was founded on December 30, 1936. Although the party already had a membership of 10,000 by the end of 1937, it has, to date, been active only in the parliamentary opposition.

Organization

The organizational structure of the LdU is characterized by its close association with that of the MIGROS enterprise. Party statutes resemble those of other parties and do not spell out this association, but the corporation plays an unusual role with regard to finances, personnel, and leadership. MIGROS pays 1 percent of its annual profits to support various LdU activities. During the first four decades of its existence, nearly half of the fifty-three parliamentary representatives of the party have been employees or functionaries of MIGROS, although this proportion has been declining recently. Duttweiler presided over the MIGROS enterprise, the LdU, and its parliamentary group until his death in 1962, whereupon his nephew, National Councillor Rudolf Suter, assumed all of these functions. At present, the party is led by National Councillor Walter Biel who is only a MIGROS director.

This tightly knit structure produces a high level of party cohesion and homogeneity. Only once, in 1943, did a serious organizational crisis arise when a segment of the party questioned Duttweiler's public acceptability and tried to get him to retire. The dissident group was forced out of the party and disintegrated.

The LdU has its headquarters at Herten-steinstrasse 40, 6004 Lucerne, and uses the paper, *Die Tat* (Action), to publicize its ideas.

Policy

The LdU calls itself *Landesring* (meaning literally "ring of the land") in reference to the traditional form of direct democracy, the *Landsgemeinde*, which used to arrange participants in a huge circle. This symbolism is meant to indicate that the LdU wants to play a unifying and not a divisive role.

Although party policy has not been consistent, it has been a center party, able to attract support from parties to its right and left. The essential principle of the LdU, which Duttweiler distilled from what he perceived to have been the American experience of the 1930s, represents a paradoxical combination of capitalism with welfare concepts. It rejects the negative manifestations of capitalism and wants to achieve the well being of the masses by lowering consumer costs through fair competition and increasingly efficient production.

In particular, the LdU advocates balanced budgets in order to avoid hurting future generations through compounded debts; commercial and entrepreneurial freedom to stimulate the economy; restriction of state intervention in the economy; reduction of working hours to combat unemployment; promotion of the feeling of usefulness and importance on the part of workers and employees; preferential hiring of heads of families in time of crisis; promotion of personal education and development; encouragement of a healthy family life in a dwelling owned by the family and preferably located in a rural setting; expansion of democracy and human rights; and absolute neutrality both in political and economic terms guaranteed by military preparedness.

In its election program of 1983, the party also stressed environmental issues, improvements in health services, and greater concern for young people.

Membership & Constituency

There have been efforts to find correlations between the growth of the MIGROS empire and the electoral strength of the LdU. Although the former includes some two million shareholders, electoral support of the party lies somewhere between 50,000 and 120,000 voters. Indications are that the vast majority of persons associated with the firm and its customers vote for other parties. The LdU is primarily an urban party which has had some success in rural areas. Its membership of about 8,200 comprises, in fairly equal numbers, workers, employees, and business people. Principal areas of support have been the cantons Zürich, Basle, Aargau, Lucerne, and St. Gallen.

Financing

Aside from voluntary contributions, the main source of party income has been the MIGROS enterprise. In 1982, for example, the LdU received a contribution of 2,700,000 francs (about $1.3 million). In the election year of 1983, this amount was increased to nearly four million francs. About half a million was used for administrative purposes and about an equal share for publicity, including the party paper, *Die Tat*. The remaining money was channelled into direct political action, particularly in referenda and popular initiatives, which the LdU has been using as an instrument to influence government action.

Leadership

Since it is not as democratically selected as other mass parties, the leadership of the LdU shows less susceptibility to change. One of the consequences of this situation is a higher retirement age than is common in most parties. In the parliamentary group, about half the members are over age sixty. The party revitalizes itself by recruiting new candidates in the thirty-to-forty age bracket. In May 1985, a new party president, National Councillor Franz Jaeger (born 1941) was elected. His opponent was Hans Ramseier (born 1939), the president of the cantonal party of Zurich.

Prospects

With its support ranging from 9.1 percent of the popular vote in 1967 to 4.0 percent in 1983, the LdU has little chance of participating in the government coalition. On the basis of cantonal results in 1985, the party may experience a slight 5 per cent increase in electoral support. Programmatically inconsistent at times and moralistic about the corrupting influence of power, the LdU seems destined to continue its role as the largest opposition party.

Radical Democratic Party of Switzerland
(*Freisinnig-Demokratische Partei der Schweiz* [FDP]; *Parti radical-démocratique suisse*)

History

The Radicals differentiated themselves from the Liberals over the problem of changing the confederal structure established in 1815. The Liberals were quite willing to seek constitutional change only in accord with the requirement of unanimity among all the member states. The Radicals appealed to the higher law of national unity. They became proponents of greater centralization even to the point of military action as in the Sonderbund War of 1847. Despite their military success and their majority in the Constituent Assembly, the Radicals did not impose their centralist conceptions fully in the constitution of 1848. As a consequence, groups opposed to the federation were nevertheless won over, enabling the new structure to continue with a broad base of support.

Given the independent disposition of the membership, it was not until 1894 that the mass organization was founded. Initially, the party structure was not as consolidated as a political organization would be today. The "early Liberals," for example, formed the *Zentrum* faction with a strong inclination towards a separate course. Nevertheless, the Radicals were the predominant party at that time, with a majority in the Parliament and all seven seats in the Federal Council. Even though individual federal councillors represented different sections of the party, when it came to overall policy, they agreed among themselves and with the parliamentary majority. In retrospect, perhaps the most significant feature of the Radicals' progressive disposition was their advocacy of measures which in other countries were exclusively proposals of the Socialists. In particular, the Swiss Radicals supported the idea of state intervention for social purposes. In the beginning of the twentieth century, this openness to social needs and diverse interests waned. With the introduction of proportional representation in 1919, the FDP lost its predominant position.

The party has remained a major force in Swiss politics. It is still one of the largest parties in the Parliament and usually wins about a quarter of the seats in the National Assembly.

At present, the Radicals have fifty-four seats following the election of 1983. In the Council of States, the party has fourteen of the forty-six seats. In the government, the Radicals are represented by two federal councillors.

Organization

The organization is a federation of cantonal sections. On the national level, the party has a party convention, a central party organization, and a general secretariat. In the absence of strong membership cohesion, the party officials tend to be more powerful than party rules suggest. In turn, however, the parliamentary group of the Radicals also enjoys considerable independence. Compared to the other three parties participating in the executive, FDP voting in the Federal Assembly shows the highest rate of partisan deviation, with an average of 40 percent.

The mailing address of the party is Postfach 2642, 3001 Berne.

Policy

The FDP wants to promote the general welfare on the basis of freedom, equality, and popular sovereignty. In principle, the party is also committed to free enterprise and private property. In particular, the party aims at improving the federal features of the constitution while protecting the cultural diversity and political autonomy of the cantons; at strengthening democratic legitimacy through increasing the channels of citizen recourse against harmful or arbitrary administration; at increasing the role of women in society and state; and at improving research, educational, and artistic endeavors.

Internationally, the FDP favours an efficient, well-trained defense force; an extension of civil defense measures; and strong links with all Swiss citizens living abroad. It is a strong supporter of Swiss neutrality and cool to the idea of Swiss United Nations membership.

In the FDP objectives for 1983-1987, reduction in government control and excessive taxation; environmental protection, and ecological energy supplies; economic stimulation against recession; as well as peace with freedom in a world of coercion were the main points emphasized.

Membership & Constituency

The number of party members and sympathizers, people who support the party but refuse to pay dues, for instance, has been estimated at 121,000, or about 28 percent of the electoral support. More than half the membership is composed of high- and middle-level employees and public servants, and about a quarter is businessmen and artisans. Workers account for about 12 percent, while membership of rural interests is quite negligible.

Among the major parties, the FDP constituency has the highest level of linguistic minority support; 26 and 6 percent of electoral support coming from French- and Italian-speaking voters, respectively. The main areas of party strength are in the cantons Zürich, Berne, Lucerne, St. Gallen, Aargau, Vaud, Geneva, and Ticino.

Financing

The basic principle of FDP financing is that of voluntarism. Although there are no set dues, the party occasionally engages in fund-raising drives among its middle-class supporters. On one occasion, it was found that such an effort in the area of Zürich netted an average individual contribution of 70 francs (about $34).

In 1975, the budget of the national party amounted to 760,000 francs (about $375,000) and that of the cantonal sections to 1.7 million francs (about $850,000). For the election of 1983, the national FDP organization budgeted 550,000 francs (about $275,000). The cantonal organizations were estimated to have spent approximately three times that amount for the same purpose.

Leadership

Early in 1984, national councillor Dr. Bruno Hunziker (born 1930) was elected as president of the party. Later in 1984, after federal councillor Rudolf Friedrich (born 1923) had to resign his government position (elected 1982) for health reasons, the FDP nominated both Bruno Hunziker and Elizabeth Kopp-Iklé as official candidates to replace Friedrich. In a dramatic election, the Federal Assembly selected Kopp-Iklé as the first female member of the Federal Council in Swiss history. The second FDP seat in the executive was filled in 1983 by Jean-

Parcal Delamuraz (born 1936) of Longirod in Vaud.

Other leading personalities of the party are the national councillors Franz Eng (born 1928), the leader of the parliamentary faction, and Ulrich Bremi (born 1929), and the councillors of states Hans Letsch (born 1924) and Jean-Jacques Cevey (born 1928) who was elected president of the upper chamber in 1985, as well as the leader of the cantonal FDP organization in Ticino, Pier Felice Barchi (born 1929).

Prospects

Although the party considered an opposition role following the defeat of its financial proposals in 1967, there is every likelihood that it will continue its leading position as a government party. On the basis of cantonal elections in 1984, however, a slight decline in electoral support of about 3.7 per cent has been projected for the FDP in the next national election in 1987.

Social Democratic Party of Switzerland
(*Sozialdemokratische Partei der Schweiz* [SPS]; *Parti socialiste suisse*)

History

After attempts to organize a national party in 1870 and 1880, the third and finally successful effort took place in 1888 through Albert Steck, a member of a patrician family living in Berne. He was not a Marxist ideologue, but wanted to establish a national community based on economic justice along the lines of traditional Swiss ideas.

This moderate view still seemed too radical to the Swiss majority to generate significant popular appeal. Nevertheless, with the particular prompting of the Swiss Federation of Trade Unions, the party moved to adopt a still more radical program in 1904. This trend accelerated in response to the economic difficulties that came with World War I. Increased tension between the moderate and the revolutionary wings culminated in the *Zimmerwalder Manifest,* under the inspiration of Lenin, passed by the left wing in 1915. It proposed to change the world war into a revolutionary civil war of the

European proletariat against the establishment. Although no action was taken on this manifesto, the move to a more radical response led to an unsuccessful general strike in 1918. A schism was inevitable: the Swiss Communist Party was founded after the moderate wing of the Social Democrats declined to join the Moscow-oriented Third International.

Upon realizing how easily a rightist extremist was able to destroy the Weimar Republic, the Swiss Social Democrats abandoned doctrinaire Marxism and returned to the moderate disposition of the late nineteenth century. The program of 1935 still favored economic planning to overcome the massive unemployment of the day, but it rejected the Soviet model of state control. Further moderating trends were shown in the programs of 1943 and 1959; the latter had considerable similarities with the contemporary Godesberg Program of the West German Socialists.

In institutional terms, the more moderate program also helped in electing in 1943 the first Social Democrat to a seat in the Federal Council. However, the permanent involvement of the SPS in the government coalition was only achieved in 1959 with the introduction of the "magic formula." Late in 1983, this arrangement was severely tested when the Federal Assembly failed to fill a SPS vacancy in the Federal Council with the official party candidate, national councillor Lilian Uchtenhagen, who would have been the first woman member of the federal executive. At a national party convention in early 1984, the more moderate wing with the overwhelming support of trade unionists decided to continue SPS participation in the government coalition.

Organization

In contrast to the majority of Swiss parties, the SPS enjoys a more centralized structure. It is based on sections and cantons, with the number of party members in each section determining the size of its delegation to the party convention. According to the party statutes, the conventions elect the party Presidium, the supreme organ of the organization. In practical terms, however, the Presidium is not able to fulfill that role due to its extensive membership. Accordingly, party officials, particularly the president, exercise strong leadership. The dominant position of the party leadership results in strict control over the parliamentary party caucus, whose voting record shows the least deviance from the party line among all the groups in the National Council. Sanctions available to the leadership include recall and even expulsion from the party.

Party headquarters are at Eigerplatz 5, 3000 Berne. The party paper is called *Tagwacht* (Sentinel).

Policy

Party policy has remained fairly constant since World War II. Perhaps the most significant policy over the recent past has been the promotion of female suffrage and women's role in society. In economic terms, the party no longer advocates nationalization of large enterprises as in 1943, but rather represents itself as the trustee of various groups on whose behalf a fair share in the national wealth should be obtained. While accepting private property, the party advocates a rationally "guided" economic policy ensuring full employment and constant growth at a stable level of prices. There is also a clear recognition of the need for efficiency and productivity enhanced through technical and scientific research, improved methods of education and training, updating of production methods, fair competition, and freedom of economic initiative. The party also aims at prevention of price increases; reduction of interest rates; protection of tenants and consumers; assimilation of immigrant laborers; land-planning for recreation and industrial parks; reduction of pollution; improvement of agricultural yield; fiscal rearrangements between federal and cantonal jurisdictions; modification of indirect taxes affecting vital consumer goods; secure energy supplies; vigorous pursuit of highway construction; financial support for education (especially adult education); and a rationalization of university services, which are now a responsibility of the cantons.

In international issues, the SPS favors the limitation of nuclear weapons, the creation of a civil guard which would help in various disasters and emergencies and permit conscientious objectors an alternate form of service, the extension of foreign aid to underdeveloped countries, membership in the United Nations, and increased cultural and economic cooperation between Eastern and Western Europe.

In preparation for the electoral campaign of 1983, the SPS presented a program containing thirty-nine specific items, ranging from a concern over the condition of the individual person in economic, national and international contexts, to the relationship of socialism to democracy, the ecology, labor, and the state.

Membership & Constituency

Although the SPS is the kind of membership party all the other Swiss parties would like to be, there is still no absolute certainty as to the size of the membership; the estimate of 55,000 members has the best claim to accuracy among all the Swiss parties. With nearly a half million SPS voters, the party's voter-to-member ratio is the highest among the major parties.

Well over half of the party's constituency is composed of workers. About a quarter of it is employees and clerks, with the remainder being made up of teachers, pensioners, and small businessmen. Territorially, the party is strongest in the urban areas, especially around Berne, Zürich, Basle, Aargau, Solothurn, Vaud, and Geneva.

Financing

With its strong membership orientation, the SPS is also the party with the relatively clearest picture on financing. National party dues amount to 24 francs (about $12) annually. These contributions are responsible for a major portion (almost 90 percent) of the party's national budget. In the different localities, annual membership dues range from 0.4 to 70 francs (about 20 cents to $34). In 1975, the national party had a budget of 723,000 francs ($360,000), while all the cantonal sections operated on about 1,400,000 francs ($700,000). For the parliamentary election of 1983, the national organization had a budget of 340,000 francs ($170,000).

Leadership

The two members of the Social Democrats in the government are Pierre Aubert (born 1927), who has been a member of the government since 1977 and the president of the Confederation in 1983, and Otto Stich (born 1927) who entered the government in 1983. Walter Buser (born 1926), federal chancellor since 1981, was considered a prime candidate for a government position in 1983. The other leading personalities of the party are national councillors Felicien Morel, president of the parliamentary group and representing Fribourg; Helmut Hu-

bacher (born 1926) chairman of the party, Lilian Uchtenhagen, and Martin Bundi (born 1932), a representative of the Romanche minority who has been elected in 1985 to preside over the National Council.

Prospects

After the party gradually reconciled itself to the realization that it would probably never achieve an absolute majority, it settled down to play the role of coalition partner in government. With its fairly extensive electoral support of about a quarter of the vote, the SPS is likely to continue that role. On the basis of cantonal elections in 1984/85, however, an erosion of up to ten percent of the electoral base has been projected for the election of 1987.

Swiss People's Party (*Schweizerische Volkspartei* [SVP]; *Parti suisse de l'union démocratique du centre*)

History

With the major parties gradually fixing their positions along fairly definite lines, various interests and ideologies found it difficult to fully identify with the established parties. These amorphous concerns would float through the organizational spectrum at times affiliating with congenial parties, at times existing independently and at times fading into oblivion. One category of such interests related to the economic views of people involved in such activities as farming, providing rental accommodations, or running small business or artisan-based enterprises. Socially, these people were not a homogeneous group. Territorially, they did not enjoy adequate density to be politically effective, except in the canton Berne where these interests formed an organization as early as 1919. It was not until late in 1936 that a national organization was able to unify the different local and cantonal groups. At that time, the party took the name Farmers, Artisans, and Bourgeois Party (*Bauern-, Gewerbe-, und Bürgerpartei;* BGB) indicative of the complex interests it tried to unite. In 1971, the name was simplified to Swiss People's Party.

At present, the party is the fourth-largest group in Parliament with about half as many seats as each of the three major parties. The People's Party has also been given one seat in the executive.

Organization

With the establishment of a national organization, the difficulty of holding the diverse groups together did not disappear. The party is still quite heterogeneous and loosely structured. The national party depends heavily on the organizational services of member groups. There is a considerable range of independence within the party with the highest level of flexibility in the canton Berne and the lowest in the canton Schaffhausen.

The party has only been able to organize itself effectively in those areas where its interests have been clearly neglected by the major parties. Thus, despite the fact that the party represents farming interests, it has been unable to replace the Christian Democrats in those rural areas where the CVP has been the traditional representative of agricultural concerns. Nor has the SVP been able to prevail in areas with strong ideological contrasts such as Solothurn or Lucerne. It has been able to succeed wherever the Radical Democrats have laid too much stress on industrial or consumer concerns such as in the cantons Ticino, Fribourg, Vaud, Basle-Land, and Aargau. But the importance of the party's base in the canton Berne has remained and is reflected in the fact that about half of the party officials are provided by that area. Another important feature is the prominent role played by the younger generation of farmers who, aware of the importance of their contribution to Swiss well-being, are frustrated by the way they are treated by government and the major parties.

Party headquarters are located at Ahornweg 2, 3000 Berne.

Policy

The SVP has a deliberately defensive orientation. From its beginning, there have been few variations in its policy. Typically, the motto of the 1967 parliamentary action program was: "courage for conformism." Contrary to the Social Democrats, the members of the SVP do not want to change their economic condition; they want to defend it in the face of the neglect by other parties. The key principle of SVP policy is the "social buffer" theory, that is, the rural and middle classes provide the best protection against excessive and destructive industrialization, against depopulation of rural and mountain areas, and against the destruction of private ownership through nationalization. Positively, the party aims at preventing increases in government obligations, at balanced budgets, and at promoting fiscal honesty.

At a party convention in 1983, an action-program was approved to guide party policy in the upcoming election and in the legislature. It placed special emphasis on helping people who have economic or social problems, such as small businessmen, or family farmers, or those who are dependent upon drugs. It also stressed the need to enhance the federal structure so that communal and cantonal authorities can better help individuals in need.

Membership & Constituency

Party membership is estimated at about 54,000, with about three times as many people supporting the party in general elections. Nearly half of the SVP's constituency lies in the canton Berne and a quarter in the canton Zürich, with some support in the cantons Aargau, Schaffhausen, Thurgau and Vaud.

Financing

As a rule, the SVP collects membership dues amounting to 2 percent of an individual's taxable income. In 1975, the budget of the federal party amounted to 235,000 francs ($115,000) and those of the cantonal sections to 350,000 francs ($170,000). For the 1983 election, the party spent close to 180,000 francs (90,000). Twenty percent of this amount was provided by the federal payments to the parliamentary group of the party.

Leadership

Since 1980 the party has been represented in the executive by Leon Schlumpf (born 1925), formerly a National Councillor from Grison.

National Councillor Adolf Ogi (born 1930) was elected president of the party in 1984. Walter Augsburger (born 1922) has been the leader of the parliamentary group. National Councillors Hanspeter Fischer (born 1930) from Thurgau, and Werner Martignoni (born 1927) from

Berne are considered as having the most promising leadership potential. In 1985 Peter Gerber, president of the Swiss Agricultural Union, was chosen to chair the Council of States.

Prospects

Compared to its electoral support, the SVP has played a very large role in Swiss politics. One reason for this effectiveness has been the party's ability to attract outstanding personalities. There is no sign that the party's place in the system will change appreciably.

Minor Parties

With the Swiss political system deliberately facilitating the participation of small groups, it becomes difficult to deal with the many small parties. In the general election of 1983, as many as 187 candidates' lists were entered in the campaign by 39 parties covering 1880 candidates. Yet the minor parties are quite significant in providing a breeding ground for issues too uncomfortable to be dealt with by the established parties.

Due to the inclusiveness of the government coalitions, 77.8 percent of the votes in the election of 1983 fell to the government parties. Of the remaining 22.1 percent, 4.0 percent was obtained by the Independent Alliance. Six minor parties won 13.2 percent, with each getting between 0.9 and 3.5 percent. All the other groups won 4.9 percent. With low voter turnout, however, these figures could be deceptive. Potentially, even a very small group could grow sufficiently to challenge the established pattern.

Generally, the minor parties and groups fall into three main categories: petrified leftovers of Swiss party struggles, ideological quibblers, and protest groups.

In the first category, one of the grand old traditions of Switzerland is represented by the Liberal Party of Switzerland (*Liberale Partei der Schweiz;* PLS). Founded by a group of men of quite diverse backgrounds, it fought against the restoration of feudal privileges in 1815, achieving its greatest success in the 1830s with the wide acceptance of individual and political liberties. During the rest of the nineteenth century, the Liberals formed a parliamentary group which included a number of leading personalities. By tradition opposed to regimentation, the Liberal Party constituted itself only in 1913 as a national organization. Still, over its entire history, the party has faithfully adhered to its basic six principles: supremacy of the voice of the people, the need for national commitment, centralism, anticlericalism, equality, and social welfare. More recently, the party has espoused the concerns of ethnic and cultural minorities. Accordingly, with a party membership of about 9,000, the Liberals obtained 2.8 percent of the national vote in 1983. As the vote was mostly concentrated in the cantons of Vaud, Neuchâtel, and Geneva, it also resulted in eight seats in the National Council.

The Protestant People's Party of Switzerland (*Evangelische Volkspartei der Schweiz;* EVP) received 2.2 percent of the vote in 1979 and 2.1 percent in 1983. It was initially founded in 1917 in the canton Zürich in response to the introduction of proportional representation there. In 1945, a national organization was established. With its program of deepening Christian values, the party differs little from the Christian Democratic Party. Yet due to latent confessionalism and continued distrust of Roman Catholics, the EVP has been able to exist as a separate party. Whenever it sought political affiliation, it tended to associate with the Independent Alliance.

Remnant parties also fade away if they find no new causes for which to fight. A case in point is the Democratic Party (*Demokratische Partei der Schweiz*). It evolved from the left wing of the Radical Democrats and established itself as a separate party in 1896 for the purpose of solving social problems in pragmatic terms. Attacked from both sides by the Radical Democrats and the Socialists, the Democrats never blossomed as a major political force. With declining support, they entered an alliance with the Protestant People's Party in 1951 to form a parliamentary group. After receiving only 0.8 percent of the vote in the election of 1971, the Democrats stopped contesting national elections and joined various cantonal parties such as the FDP in Zürich and Glarus or the SVP in Grison.

The category of ideological quibblers is populated particularly by various strains of Marxist groups. They could, of course, also be characterized by criteria other than ideology. The oldest of these groups is also a remnant of Swiss party struggle in the context of efforts to radicalize the Social Democratic Party. Prior to the general strike of 1918, the more radical wing of the SPS formed a separate organization in Zürich with about 2,000 members. Later known as Old Communists (*Altkommunisten*), this group was closely associated with the Communist Party of the Soviet Union and attempted to induce the SPS to join the Third International. Failing in this attempt, the *Altkommunisten* and the left wing of the SPS joined in founding the Swiss Communist Party (*Kommunistische Partei der Schweiz*) in 1921. Forming alliances and fronts with various groups, the party was able to get as many as 15,000 votes in 1925 and 1928, mostly in Zürich, Basle, and Schaffhausen.

But success and cohesion were short-lived. Following Stalin's demand for partisan purity in 1928, a new group was formed, the Communist Party Opposition (*Kommunistische Partei Opposition;* KPO), which was more loyal to Moscow and rejected electoral alliances. When Stalin changed his mind about forbidding such alliances, most Socialists were no longer enthusiastic about sharing their electoral support. Indeed, during the 1930s, a strong anticommunist sentiment began to develop in Switzerland. It led to popular initiatives on the local level which resulted in the prohibition of a number of cantonal sections of the Communist Party including the one in Geneva. In November 1940, the Federal Council applied the prohibition to the national organization together with a number of organizations on the extreme right. A similar fate overtook the *Fédération socialiste suisse* which the Communists and radical Socialists set up later on in the French-speaking areas of Switzerland in order to reconstitute their party organization.

Toward the end of the Second World War in 1944, the various fragments united in organizing the Swiss Labor Party (*Partei der Arbeit der Schweiz;* PdA). Once more pursuing an open-arms policy, the party scored a number of electoral successes and managed to reach a membership of 20,000 by 1947. The negative effect of Soviet foreign policy, however, soon caused disintegration and splintering. A Titoist section was the first to separate. The suppression of the Hungarian uprising in 1956 decimated membership and public support. Following the Sino-Soviet split a Maoist group organized itself in 1963. It chose the name Swiss Communist Party (*Kommunistische Partei der Schweiz;* KPS), the name of the original organization of the 1920s, in order to demonstrate its claims to orthodoxy. Still another group, the Organization of Swiss Communists (*Organisation der Kommunisten der Schweiz;* OKS) constituted itself in 1964 with a seemingly more independent line. Today,

there are two more Labor Party associates appealing for electoral support: the Progressive Swiss Organization (*Progressive Organisationen der Schweiz*) POCH and the Autonomous Socialist Party (*Partito Socialista autonomo*) aimed at voters in Ticino. In addition, to complete the main outlines of a complex situation, there is also the Revolutionary Marxist League (*Revolutionäre marxistische Liga*) with a Trotskyite program. Electorally the POCH was able to win 2.2 percent of voter support in 1983, while the PdA got only 0.9 percent.

The third category, the protest parties, emerges especially during periods of crisis relating to minorities, political conditions, or the economy. Encouraged by low requirements for electoral recognition, these groups are occasionally able to achieve political prominence far in excess to the significance of the dissatisfaction they claim to represent. In a way, the Independent Alliance has been a typical example. There had been several such groups during the Great Depression; it was the only one to survive.

More recently, the question of the number of foreigners residing in Switzerland became an issue. In 1961, a nationalistic protest movement was founded, the National Action against Alienation of the People and Homeland (*Nationale Aktion gegen Überfremdung von Volk und Heimat*). The movement, led by Valentin Ochen, was able to win one parliamentary seat in each of the elections of 1967, 1971, and 1975. But in 1979, its electoral support fell from 2.5 percent in 1975 to 1.3 percent. Internal dissent was also damaging. In 1970, a splinter group established the Republican Movement (*Republikanische Bewegung*), appealing to the ancient Swiss tradition of "republicanism," which opposed foreign influence and interference in Swiss affairs. The movement managed to win four seats in the National Council in 1971 and two in 1975, with an electoral support of 10.4 and 6.2 percent of the vote. In 1979, however, the surprising strength of the Republicans fell to a mere 0.6 percent of the vote. For the election of 1983, the NA and the Republicans combined forces to take advantage of resentment caused by an increasing stream of people seeking asylum in Switzerland. Moreover, the NA used ecological concerns in a rightist context to appeal to voters including some of the younger generation. Together, the two groups managed to obtain the support of 3.5 per cent of the electorate, and win five seats in the National Council. As a consequence, they also became a parliamentary group which received 33,000 francs from the public treasury in 1984. Projections on the basis of 1984/85 cantonal and municipal elections indicate further growth for the next national election of 1987 which may even see a doubling of NA/Republican representation in the National Council.

Environmental problems are also expected to play a major role in the next election. But the issue is not the exclusive preserve of any one party. In some areas, e.g. canton Schaffhausen, the parties of the right have been promoting ecological policies for a long time. Nationally, the CVP demanded already in 1979 more environmental protection and better utilization of agricultural land. As a consequence, ecological groups find it hard to establish a separate political organization, particularly as they are also split ideologically into left and right.

The earliest foundation took place in 1973 with the formation of the Green Party of Vaud (*Grüne Partei der Waadt*) with a membership of about 600 people. Other cantonal foundations followed in Zuerich, Geneva, Neuchâtel and Thurgau. Prior to the election of 1983, these groups formed a non-leftist national organization, the Federation of Green Parties of Switzerland (*Föderation der grünen Parteien der Schweiz*; GPS). It obtained 1.7 per cent of the vote and one parliamentary mandate each in Zürich, Geneva and Vaud. Further gains are expected in 1987.

Subsequently, there was also the formation of a national ecological organization on the left, the Green Alternative of Switzerland (*Grüne Alternative Schweiz*; GAS). Being numerically very weak, this group has allied itself with the Communist POCH and PdA. On the cantonal level, this association was able to increase the normal POCH/PdA voting strength by about 20 per cent in elections held during 1985. If that growth could be maintained, it would project to an increase in the national vote in 1987 by 0.7 per cent with possibly one or two additional parliamentary seats.

National Prospects

Switzerland has generally been considered to have one of the best forms of democracy. The political system has evolved an inclusive and accommodating decision-making pattern. Past stability and a reasonably fair distribution of benefits seem to be promising indicators for the future. Yet, there is also an agitation for a com-

plete revision of the constitution, a general fatigue with the demands of democracy, and even the spectacle of youths rioting in the streets of major cities and of distributing leaflets suggesting the destruction of symbols of wealth. The constitutional innovators argue that all these negative manifestations are the consequence of ordinary persons being confused by the meaning of the often amended constitution. A new draft constitution published in 1977, with a revised model published in 1985 by the Federal Council, may remove most of these problems. But one could also argue that the constant decline in voter turnout and the growth, not necessarily in numbers but in intensity, of a polarized radical fringe have causes that lie beyond the constitutional remedy. Conceivably, the very absence of tension and conflict may provide the conditions for the growth of a revolutionary dissatisfaction that may yet challenge the great accomplishments of the political system in Switzerland.

Early in 1986, Switzerland made a major international decision. Although the country has been a long-standing member of the International Court of Justice and most U.N. agencies, full membership in the United Nations Organization required the approval of the people and the cantons. After lengthy debate in Parliament, the question was finally submitted to a referendum in March 1986. With a relatively high voter participation rate of 50 percent, the proposal was defeated in every canton with a national rejection by 75 percent of the voters. The result was a clear statement about the popularity of the world body. Still, the government which had supported membership, pledged to continue the policy of armed neutrality as well as efforts toward international solidarity, and availability for international service, especially in the context of good offices.

Further Reading

Codding, George A. *The Federal Government of Switzerland.* Boston: Houghton Mifflin, 1961.

Gruner, Erich. *Die Parteien der Schweiz.* Berne: Franke Verlag, 1977.

Hughes, Christopher. *The Constitution of Switzerland,* Oxford: Clarendon Press, 1954, and Westport, Conn.: Greenwood Press, 1970.

———. *Switzerland.* London: Ernest Benn, 1975.

———. *The Parliament of Switzerland.* London: Cassell, 1962.

McRae, Kenneth D. *Conflict and Compromise in Multilingual Societies*. Vol. 1, (Switzerland). Waterloo, Ont., Canada: Wilfrid Laurier University Press, 1983.

———. Switzerland: *Example of Cultural Coexistence*. Toronto: Canadian Institute of International Affairs, 1964.

Schmid, Carol A. *Conflict and Consensus in Switzerland*. Berkeley, Calif.: University of California Press, 1981.

Steiner, Juerg. *Amicable Agreement Versus Majority Rule*. Chapel Hill: University of North Carolina Press, 1974.

SYRIAN ARAB REPUBLIC
(Al-Jumhuriya al-'Arabiya al-Suriya)
by Judy Barsalou, M. Phil. revised by Mahmud A. Faksh, Ph.D.

The System of Government

The Syrian Arab Republic, a nation of nine million people, is a pseudo parliamentary system dominated by its president, Lt. General Hafez al-Asad, and by the two institutional pillars of Syrian society—the armed forces and the Arab Socialist Renaissance (Ba'th) Party. Ostensibly a multiparty democracy, Syrian political history since the end of the French mandate over Syria in 1943 has been characterized more by authoritarian rule and internecine struggle for power than by orderly succession and parliamentary debate. President Asad's years of rule (beginning in November 1970) have brought relative stability to this country, which, since its independence, has averaged a coup every three years. Yet chronic factionalism in the Ba'th party and periodic widespread opposition to the regime, which has taken the form of assassinations and demonstrations, have presented the regime with severe challenges.

The formal distribution of political power among legislative, executive, and judicial institutions is enumerated by the Permanent Constitution promulgated on March 13, 1973. Declaring the people to be the ultimate repository of national sovereignty, the constitution outlines a democratic, socialist system whose main feature is a very dominant executive. Prefatory to the description of the three branches of government is the articulation of basic principles of the Syrian state. Included among them is the provision that all legislation be based on Islamic doctrine, despite the fact that no Syrian constitution since independence has declared Islam the state religion. An earlier draft of the constitution, circulated in January 1973, sparked protracted rioting by its failure to state that the president must be a Muslim—an ommission rectified in the final version. The constitution also commits Syria to socialist development, to the pursuit of economic justice, and affirms Syria's identity as a part of the larger Arab "nation" comprised of the whole of the Arab world.

These formal constitutional arrangements of Syria are misleading, however. The actual distribution and exercise of political power is determined far more by personal and sectarian relationships than by formal legal provisions.

Executive

The constitution confers broad executive and legislative powers on the president, who is elected to a seven-year term in a mass plebiscite after receiving the recommendation of the Ba'th party and the nomination of the People's Council (Parliament). In the event of the president's death or permanent incapacity, elections are to be held to determine his successor. It should be noted, however, that preeminent political position in the Syrian ruling hierarchy since independence has been achieved through behind-the-scenes power struggles and/or outright military coups. Hafez al-Asad himself, as minister of defense in 1969, gradually consolidated his position as chief executive through these means. At the head of the powerful armed forces, by March 1969 he had already established the military superiority of his "nationalist" faction over the radical Ba'th regime led by Salad Jadid. But rather than seize power immediately at the risk of losing legitimacy and threatening the facade of Ba'th party rule over Syria, Asad bided his time until September 1970 when, as head of the air force, he refused orders to give air support to Syrian units entering the civil war in neighboring Jordan. Soon after the completion of his takeover of power in November 1970, he created the People's Council and was nominated president by this body. A mass plebiscite held March 12, 1971, elected him president of the republic. Asad was reelected to a second seven-year term in February 1978 by 99.6 percent of those who cast votes, and to a third seven-year term early in 1985.

As chief executive, head of state, and commander-in-chief of the armed forces, Asad exercises awesome power. His position as secretary-general of the Ba'th party and president of the Progressive National Front, the latter a coalition of nationalist and socialist political parties represented in the People's Council, is further indication of the remarkable extent of his control over the Syrian political order. Furthermore, the constitution grants him the power to choose and dismiss his prime minister and the members of his cabinet, known as the Council of Ministers. Asad may also dissolve at will the main parliamentary body (the People's Council) and take over its legislative functions during its adjournment—with the proviso that his legislative acts be approved in its next session. In times of national emergency the president may assume legislative functions even when the People's Council is in session. The Council's power to veto or amend presidential decrees by a two-thirds vote has not been exercised effectively during Asad's rule. When moved by the need to submit political questions to a "higher" authority, the president may circumvent the People's Council altogether by holding mass referenda whose results cannot be challenged by the Council. Yet for all his titles and powers, President Asad cannot make important policy decisions, such as that to enter the Lebanese civil war in August 1975, without reference to crucial interest groups and political forces. His power is limited by the very real need to consult regularly, if indirectly, with members of the Ba'th party's National and Regional commands, and with high officers of the armed forces.

Aiding the president in the administration of state policy is the Council of Ministers, led by Prime Minister Dr. Abdul-Rauf Kassem. These ministers are entirely dependent on the president for their positions, and few actually have access to real power. They are overshadowed by the inner circle surrounding President Asad which includes, among others, Vice President Rifa'at al-Asad, brother of the president and commander of the 20,000-strong Defense Brigades, an internal security organization; Vice President Abdul Halim Khaddam; and Minister of Defense Mustafa Tlas. None of the ministers is constitutionally required to answer questions raised by legislators in the People's Council.

Over the years, President Asad has tried to achieve the appearance of representative government by appointing ministers from several parties and from a wide range of regional locations and ethnic and religious backgrounds. Since 1972 Asad has made a practice of appointing non-Ba'thists to roughly half the cabinet posts, but the most important posts are still occupied by Ba'th party members and a significant number is held by military officers and technocrats. Since Asad's accession to power, Sunni and urban representation in the cabinet has been stressed at the expense of the religious minorities and rural dwellers. With regard to religious representation, between November 1970 and August 1976, for example, 82 percent of the cabinet ministers were Sunni, while 'Alawi representation trailed far behind at 9 percent. Christian representation during this period was almost 4 percent, while Druze and Ismaili representation was slightly over 2 percent.

Legislature

Created February 16, 1971, only three months after Asad's assumption of power, the People's Council began as an appointed assembly. Its 173 members, four of them women, were appointed by President Asad for two-year terms. Seats were distributed among five political parties: the Ba'th party (eighty-seven seats); the Arab Socialist Union (eleven seats); the Syrian Communist Party (eight seats); the Socialist Unionist Movement (four seats); and the Arab Socialist Movement (four seats). Remaining seats were reserved for independents and members of the opposition. Early in 1972 the People's Council set to work drafting a constitution, a revised form of which became the Permanent Constitution approved by plebiscite on March 12, 1973. It provides for a People's Council whose elected members serve four-year terms. During their terms members have the responsibility to debate government policy, consider development and budgeting plans, pass legislation, and ratify international treaties. While the Council possesses the power to vote no confidence in the government or in any individual minister, presidential prerogatives over the legislative process—including the right to dissolve the assembly and to enact legislation in its stead during its periods of recess—have rendered the People's Council the weakest of government institutions. Low voter turnout and the running of candidates on slates organized by the Progressive National Front have further minimized the role of the People's Council.

The most recent elections for the People's Council were held on August 1 and 2, 1977. Voter apathy was widespread and turnout in the cities may have been as low as 16 percent. The slate of Progressive National Front candidates who were fielded in almost every electoral district won all of the 159 seats they sought in a house of 195 seats. Representation in the People's Council after the August 1977 election was divided among five parties in the following manner: Ba'th, 125; Socialist Unionist Movement, twelve; Arab Socialist Union, eight; Arab Socialist Movement, eight; Syrian Communist Party, six. The remaining 36 seats were won by independent candidates. Ninety-nine members were "peasants" and "workers" in accordance with a constitutional provision which requires that at least half of the seats be set aside for persons of that description. Ordinarily the People's Council meets in three sessions per year, but may sit in special sessions at the request of the president, one-third of the Council's members, or the speaker of the Council.

Judiciary

Nominally independent of the government, the judicial branch also feels the power of the chief executive. Justices of the Higher Constitutional Court, which rules on the constitutionality of laws and resolves electoral disputes, are appointed by the president. So too are the members of the Higher Judicial Council whose purpose it is to ensure the independence of the judiciary. While religious courts are still to be found, they have been largely supplanted by secular courts. The highest secular court, called the Supreme Court, serves as a court of ultimate appeal. Below it are the courts of appeal and the local level "magistrate" or "peace" courts.

Regional & Local Governments

Government at the subnational level is organized along provincial lines. Each of the thirteen provinces has a governor (appointed by the central government) and a provincial council consisting of both elected and appointed members who serve four-year terms. Provinces are further subdivided into districts, each with its own elected district council and appointed district officials. Local governments collect taxes, resolve disputes, direct public services, and license businesses; they also convey information

and ideology to local populations. On occasion they may also carry back up to the central government the opinions of individual citizens. Government administration is performed by a somewhat politicized civil service, many of whose members belong to the Ba'th party.

The Electoral System

Representatives to the People's Council are chosen by direct elections from single-member districts. Suffrage is universal and citizens must be at least eighteen years of age to vote. Ballots are secret and equal. Voter turnout, despite these democratic privileges and safeguards, is very low. It was reported by the foreign press that only 40 percent of those eligible to vote did so in the May 1973 elections for the People's Council, despite an extension of the voting period. Even official Syrian estimates put voter turnout for the August 1977 People's Council elections at no more than 50 percent.

The Party System

It is misleading to speak of a Syrian party system for, while several parties do operate, all but one exercise only nominal influence over policymaking. The preeminent party—in fact the only party requiring sustained attention—is the Arab Socialist Renaissance (Ba'th) Party. Since 1972 it has been the dominant member of a five-party coalition, the Progressive National Front. The Front's charter, issued March 7, 1972, proscribes political activity by parties other than the five belonging to the Front, yet such activity does exist. The five members of the Front include the Ba'th party, the Syrian Communist Party, the Arab Socialist Union, the Socialist Unionist Movement, and the Arab Socialist Movement. Illegal political forces existing outside the Front include the Muslim Brotherhood, the Communist Action League, and the National Democratic Grouping.

While it would appear that the coalition of parties in the Front is extensively involved in legislating and policymaking, it was fashioned by President Asad primarily to end the Ba'th's isolation as the ruling party without actually diminishing the Ba'th's primacy. Indicative of its status is the clause of the Front's charter recognizing the Ba'th's exclusive right to mobilize students and members of the armed forces. The Central Command of the Front, on the other hand, is given the responsibility of helping formulate foreign and domestic policy and promoting national unity, but here too Ba'th representation far outweighs that of the other four parties. Of the eighteen members of the Front's Central Command, ten are Ba'th members, including the Central Command's president who is also secretary-general of the Ba'th party and chief executive of the Syrian state. The remaining four parties are each allotted two positions on the Central Command of the Front.

Arab Socialist Renaissance (Ba'th) Party

History

Established in the early 1940s by two Damascus schoolteachers, Michel 'Aflaq and Salah al-Din al-Bitar, the Ba'th party came to power in March 1963 in the wake of military coup. The Ba'th party did not directly engineer the coup itself but dominated the regime shortly after its takeover by virtue of its status as the best-organized political force.

The origins of the party lay in the desire of its founders to break with the methods and failures of the traditional order. The party's ideology is an eclectic mixture of nationalist, socialist, and pan-Arab ideals vague enough to have wide appeal but with the disadvantage of giving rise to conflicting interpretations. Radical change, according to party ideology, is achieved through rebellion against the structural foundation of traditional society; freedom, socialism, and Arab unity (the so-called Ba'th trinity) is the ultimate goal.

Initially the party attracted leftist university students who, clustering around its two founders, discovered them reluctant to enter the rough and tumble of political life. 'Aflaq hoped to shape the thinking of the younger generation but was afraid to sully the ideology of the party of actively entering politics. At first he believed that spiritual transformation of Arab society could not be imposed by force or achieved through unprincipled political coalition. The turning point came in 1953 when the Ba'th merged with the Arab Socialist Party of Akram Hawrani, whose insistence on socialism and mobilization of landless peasants helped reori-

ent the party's focus toward active politics. In the meantime, the debacle of the 1948 Arab-Israel War and the series of military coups in Syria which followed in rapid succession after the first coup in March 1949 provided further impetus for action and demonstrated a method conducive to rapid change—military takeover. Hawrani's excellent connections with influential military officers proved useful, and a quadrupling of the party's membership between 1952 and 1954 (from 500 members to 2,000) revealed its new energy. But the Ba'th and Arab Socialists never formed a cohesive union, each choosing instead to cultivate its own following. And while Bitar and 'Aflaq continued to think in terms of a transformation of the Arab societies throughout the Levant, Hawrani and his followers focused on political and social change in Syria. As a result, a factionalization of the Ba'th party along civilian and military lines and between moderate and radical forces became an entrenched feature of the party. Exacerbating this factionalism in the 1950s was the loose cellular organization of the party and the minimal coordination among cells.

Scarcely a month before the March 1963 Ba'thi coup in Syria, a coalition of Nasserists and Ba'thists took power in Iraq. In response to this almost simultaneous Ba'thi acquisition of power in an adjoining country, the National Command of the Ba'th party was created to direct Ba'th policy across national borders. Regional commands, one each for Syria and Iraq, were also set up as the supreme party organ in each state. The Syrian Regional Command over the next several years increasingly was dominated by radical Ba'th military officers whose disagreements with Bitar and 'Aflaq, leaders in the National Command, soon became apparent. A "neo-Ba'th" coup led by radical Syrian officers, with the ideologue Salah Jadid at their head, ousted the Ba'thi government of Salah al-Din al-Bitar on February 23, 1966, and imposed a program of rapid land reform and nationalization of industry. Shortly thereafter, Syria established its own National Command, as a rival to the one already operating in Baghdad. The new government's radical policies and blatant 'Alawi favoritism fed widespread discontent which erupted in antigovernment riots. Taking advantage of this unrest was one of Jadid's more moderate colleagues—a man crucial to the success of the February 1966 coup, Lieutenant General Hafez al-Asad—who became recognized as a rival of Jadid. As minister of defense, Asad gained control of the internal security forces and gathered considerable support among military officers. By November 1970, Asad's consolidation of power was complete. In deposing Jadid he established a more moderate regime which has been the most long-lived of all those formed since Syria's independence. Both Jadid and Asad are members of the 'Alawi religious sect, but Asad recognized the necessity of stabilizing the country by appealing power to Syria's most numerous Muslim sect, the Sunnis; by tempering Jadid's more extreme economic policies; and by establishing better links with other Arab regimes.

Organization

Under Asad, the Ba'th party has been consolidated and expanded. Originally the Ba'th was to imitate the Leninist model of organization, but it has never fully achieved its founders' aim of creating a party of rigidly disciplined cadres organized into hierarchical cells which would form the exclusive pool for recruitment into the highest party and government positions. During different periods over its roughly thirty-five–year history it has achieved some approximation of the ideal but it has always been plagued by factional rivalry, ideological disputes, and irregular recruitment and advancement patterns and nepotism.

Party cells have been established in a variety of settings—villages, schools, and factories. Cells are the lowest unit in the party and consist of less than ten members. A hierarchy of cells, divisions (three to seven cells), and branches (two or more divisions), comprise the basic structure of the Syrian Ba'th party. At the apex are the Regional and National commands. Party ideology and interpretation of political affairs are disseminated by the party's newspaper, *al-Ba'th* (circ. 20,000), and by the government paper, *al-Thawra* (circ. 20,000). (Syria has no privately owned newspapers of major importance.) Young people are reached through the Revolutionary Youth Federation, which recruits them into the party.

Under Asad, central party organs have exercised more control over lower levels of the organization. Local party leaders, for example, are appointed to their offices by the central government. Top members of the party may reach down into the lower levels and promote or purge members and suspend or impose party rules. Delegates to central congresses, however, are elected at the local level, and representatives to top party organs, such as the Regional Command, are elected from among the ranks of central congress delegates. Asad's rise to power has also been associated with a more prominent distinction between military and civilian wings of the party, and his imposition of separate control over the military wing has meant some loss of influence for the civilian sector of the party.

The quadrennial national congress of the Ba'th party, the Seventh Regional Congress, met in Damascus from December 22, 1979 to January 5, 1980. Widespread concern among its 771 delegates about political instability and pervasive government corruption contributed to an atmosphere in which these problems were discussed in an unusually frank manner. Elections of members to the twenty-one-seat Regional Command resulted in the elevation of fourteen persons who had never previously served in the Regional Command. A central committee consisting of seventy-five Ba'th members was also created to supervise the Regional Command between party congresses. What intraparty disagreements there are, which mostly take the form of personal rivalries, appear to have been well contained by Asad's control over the party's hierarchical structure.

The address of party headquarters is National Command, P.O. Box 849, Damascus.

Policy

The Ba'th party has always strongly advocated pan-Arabism, although its actual commitment to it considerably declined following the failed Syrian–Egyptian union (1958–61). The old guard of the Ba'th party, led by 'Aflaq and Bitar, continued to pursue reunion with Egypt even after the 1961 military coup which broke Egyptian dominance over Syria. But with the rise of the neo-Ba'this to power in 1966, Asad among them, the desire to unify the Arab world gave way to an almost exclusive preoccupation with Syrian and regional problems and interests. The predominant commitment to socialist development was rapidly translated into radical land reform and nationalization policies. President Asad's economic policies, while more moderate than those pursued by Jadid, have been conceived and executed within the framework of socialist development for Syria. Furthermore, lip service has continued to be paid to Arab unity even during the most prolonged periods of isolation from the Arab and world communities.

Syrian foreign-policy considerations have been dominated by the Arab–Israeli conflict and related problems, such as the civil war in Lebanon. Close American ties to Israel, coupled with American provision of the most advanced military equipment to the Israeli armed forces, has been paralleled by Syrian dependence on Soviet technical and military assistance. Since the Ba'th took power in 1963 a constant tension has existed in the party between those advocating greater alliance with Moscow and those championing stronger ties with the Arab states, including the more conservative Arab monarchies.

While President Asad has been associated with the effort to improve relations with the Arab states, he has also maintained close links to the Soviets. Perhaps as many as 2,600 Soviet advisors are stationed in Syria. American–Syrian relations, while not warm, nonetheless have improved since the mid-1960s, subject to the ebb and flow of events in Lebanon. Syria belongs to the Steadfastness and Confrontation Front of Arab states opposed to the late Egyptian president Anwar Sadat's peacemaking efforts with Israel, and has heartily condemned the Camp David peace process.

Indicative of Syria's better relations with conservative Arab regimes is the probability that the Saudis initially paid the bill for Syria's involvement in the Lebanese civil strife. Since mid-1975 Syrian soldiers have been stationed in Lebanon, and as many as 30,000 served there in 1985. Syria's entry into the 1975–76 Lebanese civil war initially had the effect of bolstering the leftist and Palestinian forces. But Syria switched its support to the right-wing Christian militias when a leftist-Palestinian victory appeared imminent. Such shifts in alignment have continued on a regular basis.

On the whole, Syria's presence in Lebanon has served to maintain the status quo. Syria's relations with Iraq have been very bad. Enmity between the Ba'thi regimes in Baghdad and Damascus has existed since the 1966 neo-Ba'th coup in Syria, and Syria has lent some surreptitious support to Iran in its war against Iraq. Relations with Jordan soured in early 1981 because of Syrian suspicion that Jordan was providing assistance to members of the Muslim Brotherhood who were launching terrorist attacks against Syrian officials, prominent 'Alawis, Soviet advisors stationed in Syria, and President Asad himself. Early in 1986 relations with Jordan were improved following exchange of visits by government officials of both countries.

Membership & Constituency

By 1970 party members numbered more than 100,000, or approximately one of every thirteen adult males. As these figures would indicate, the party has become a significant tool for indoctrination and mobilization, especially of those groups most influenced by the party—the lower middle class, the lower class, and the rural population. All are welcome except the offspring of the old aristocratic ruling class and members of illegal political organizations.

Membership is not automatic. Candidates must undergo a period of study and participation in various activities before being elevated to full membership status. Requirements for membership, however, have eased the Asad's ascent to power. Recruits no longer must be from working-class families, nor must they be recommended by two full members of the party. But the party remains limited and has no mass appeal.

Financing

Information about party financing is unavailable.

Leadership

While Sunnis form a majority in all Syrian provinces except Suwayda and Latakia, Syria is dotted with concentrations of minority groups living in mostly rural areas. Almost three-quarters of the Syrian 'Alawis, for example, live in Latakia where they constitute over half the population. Similarly, over 90 percent of the Druze are clustered in Suwayda province, which they dominate numerically. Eighty percent of Syria's Ismailis live in rural settings in Hama province, while most of Syria's Kurds are scattered along the northern border with Turkey. Greek Orthodox and other Christian minorities also tend to reside in concentrated rural towns and villages. On the whole, demographic statistics for Syria are inadequate, but population estimates indicate that roughly 90 percent of Syria's eight million people are Arabs. Kurds (8 percent) and Armenians (3 percent) constitute the principle ethnic minorities. The 'Alawis, Christians, and Druze who form the bulk of the religious minorities constitute perhaps 25 percent of the population.

The core of the Ba'th party elite has been drawn mostly from the rural, lower socioeconomic, and minority (non-Sunni) groups. By contrast, elites of the preindependence period tended to be wealthy, well-educated Sunnis based in the cities. It is highly significant that one of the few avenues of social mobility open to members of the minority religious and ethnic sects during the French-mandate period was the military profession. The 'Alawis especially looked upon enrollment in the military academy as a means of advancing their social position. Further contributing to the concentration of minorities in the military was the fact that, unlike most Sunnis, the members of minority groups often were too poor to come up with the fee that would exempt them from military service. Many of them rose through the ranks and some estimates indicate that by late 1965 more than 70 percent of all army units were under the command by 'Alawi and Druze officers. This is an important statistic when one considers the primacy of the military wing of the Ba'th party over its civilian counterpart. Furthermore, there are strong indications that most military officers belong to the Ba'th party. In a 1975 speech, President Asad indicated that of the officers killed in action during the October 1973 Arab–Israel War, 80 percent were Ba'th party members.

The Ba'th elite is not comprised exclusively of individuals from minority sects. There are many highly placed Sunnis, including Vice President Khaddam and Minister of Defense Tlas, who have enjoyed the confidence of President Asad for many years. But the 'Alawis, who constitute only 11 percent of the total population, nonetheless hold such a disproportionate number of the most crucial posts that there is a widespread perception that the government is predominantly an 'Alawi preserve. Some of its most important members are:

Lt. Gen. Hafez al-Asad: 'Alawi, born October 6, 1930, in Qardaha, Latakia province. Head of state and chief executive of the Syrian Arab Republic; secretary-general of the Ba'th party, president of the Progressive National Front. His power base lies in the party, the military, and among the 'Alawis.

Lt. Col. Rifa'at al-Asad: 'Alawi, born 1937 in Qardaha, Latakia province. Brother of Hafez al-Asad; commander of the Defense Brigades whose presence helps protect the regime from military overthrow. Member of the Ba'th Regional Command.

Abdul Halim Khaddam: Sunni, born in Banias, 1933. Vice President, member of the Ba'th Regional Command.

Lt. Gen. Mustafa Tlas: Sunni, born in Rustan City, Homs, May 1932. Minister of Defense and member of the Ba'th Regional Command. Active member of the military wing of the party.

Prospects

The Ba'th is firmly entrenched in the Syrian system as the ruling party. No other political party poses an immediate threat to its monopoly of power, or seems able to lead a successful coup. Even the military, because of its predominance in the party, need not openly intervene in day-to-day politics because it is assured a voice in making the most important policy decisions. Nonetheless, especially in the early 1980s, the Ba'th regime has encountered widespread and intense opposition to its rule. Common complaints about the regime have to do with its largely 'Alawi character and with rampant corruption at all government levels. Especially vulnerable to attack is the Ba'th's essentially secular ideology; the regime's critics have taken heart from the Iranian revolution, which gave evidence that even an apparently indomitable regime can be toppled by its own people.

Much of the antiregime opposition has taken the form of terrorist attacks carried out by the Muslim Brotherhood and other fundamentalist groups. Perhaps the Muslim Brotherhood's most dramatic attack was the June 1979 killing of sixty Aleppo military academy cadets, most of them 'Alawi. Demonstrations and riots in that city, beginning in December 1979, widened by March 1980 into a general strike of merchants throughout Syria protesting price controls and calling for democracy, an end to secularism, and the release of political prisoners.

The regime's response was repression. In April 1980, the Defense Brigades commanded by Rifa'at al-Asad swept through Aleppo, Hama, and other centers of opposition. Summary executions became commonplace, especially after an attempt on President Asad's life June 27, 1980. Nevertheless, during the first three weeks of February 1982, severe fighting raged in Hama where at the very least 5,000 civilians and members of the *Ikhwan*—The

Muslim Brotherhood —died in battles with government troops, which suffered perhaps as many as 1,000 killed. The battle began when troops attacked in force after thirty or forty of their members were ambushed and killed in what was to have been a surprise raid on a cell of the *Ikhwan* in Hama. Rebellion against the government then quickly spread throughout Hama as officials and members of the ruling Ba'th party were sought and killed. Two brigades were dispatched to stem the tide of rebellion. After surrounding the city with tanks and artillery and isolating it from the rest of the country, the troops proceeded to damage or destroy at least half of the city. One Western diplomat was quoted as saying that the Asad regime had "decided to finish with its Hama problem once and for all," by leveling entire sections of the city and making an example of the city that other centers of rebellion in Syria would long remember. This strategy appears to have succeeded in the short term; few acts of rebellion have been reported since. However, the government's brutal action against its own population may become a rallying point for operation leaders in the future.

Minor Parties

Arab Socialist Union

Headed by Jamal Atassi, this Nasserist party claims to have, and may indeed control, a larger membership than the Syrian Ba'th party. Yet it has only eight seats in the People's Council and three portfolios in the Council of Ministers. Benefiting still from the considerable enthusiasm and reverence generated by former Egyptian president Gamal Abdul Nasser in Syria, the ASU aspires to be a mass party like its namesake in Egypt in order to promote socialist development.

Arab Socialist Movement

Abdul Ghani Kannout is the leader of this party, which is what remains of the Arab Socialist Party originally led by Akram Hawrani, and which merged with the Ba'th party in 1953. Hawrani himself has rejected the party out of a determination to have nothing to do either with the Progressive National Front or the Ba'th. The ASM has eight seats in the People's Council and holds three portfolios in the Council of Ministers.

Socialist Unionist Movement

This Nasserist party is led by Sami Soufan. It was established in 1961 by ex-Ba'this who hoped to restore the union between Egypt and Syria. A member of the Progressive National Front, its possession of twelve seats in the People's Council and two portfolios in the Cabinet probably does not reflect the full extent of its popularity.

The Syrian Communist Party

Led for many years by Khalid Bakdash, this is one of Syria's older parties. It participates uneasily in the Ba'th regime because of their ideological differences and its relations with the Soviet Union. Recently, the party split into two factions when one of its members, Riad Turk, challenged the pro-Moscow leadership of Bakdash. Both factions have been recognized by the regime and take part in the government, sharing six seats in the People's Council and two portfolios in the cabinet. The party commands less popular support than the two Nasserist parties.

Other Political Forces

Military

The Syrian armed forces are not only becoming a formidable fighting force but also constitute one of the most powerful interest groups in Syria. Indicative of the importance given to internal and external defense is the fact that the 1980 military budget was raised to 55 percent of the national budget. In the wake of domestic insurrection, Asad in January 1980 also doubled military pay (compared to a 50 to 75 percent hike in civil servant salaries), probably to maintain the loyalty of the troops. Officers also enjoy substantial fringe benefits, such as travel allowances, duty-free imports, interest-free loans, and free medical care. Two well-armed military intelligence and security units carry out frequent purges of officers suspected of disloyalty. Well over half of the officers are Ba'th party members, and it is estimated that, in the mid-1970s, eighteen of the top twenty-five officers were 'Alawis. President Asad finds it necessary to include as members of his inner circle the army chief of staff and the minister of defense, and consults regularly with them, especially on foreign affairs.

Muslim Brotherhood (*Ikhwan al-Muslimin*)

This shadowy fundamentalist organization was established in Egypt by Hassan al-Banna in 1929. It is comprised of a network of small Sunni Muslim organizations whose aim it is to reorganize the state and society according to Islamic doctrine. Its terrorist tactics have had the effect of articulating a broad mass resentment against the government. No single individual can be identified as the leader of the Muslim Brotherhood, although Marwan Hadid and Essam Attar—the former dead and the latter in exile—may have been important figures in it. Captain Ibrahim al-Khatib apparently was responsible for the June 1979 massacre of 'Alawi cadets in the Aleppo military academy. Repression seems to have dampened Brotherhood activity for the moment, but it is doubtful that the regime's assertions to have entirely dismantled the organization are correct. Government countermeasures have included the killing of an unknown number of political prisoners in Palmyra prison—perhaps as many as four hundred—two days after the assassination attempt on President Asad in June 1980. Membership in the Brotherhood is now punishable by death.

National Prospects

Hafez al-Asad's regime is now approaching its sixteenth year in power—a long period relative to the instability of Syrian governments between 1944 and 1970. Yet these have been difficult years for the regime, punctuated by internicine strife between the Ba'thi groups of Syria and Iraq, widespread insurrection against the Syrian government, and prolonged involvement in the Lebanese conflict. With Iraqi President Saddam Husain's attention now riveted on his own survival in the struggle with Iran, President Asad has felt less pressure from his neighbor to the east. Asad also appears to be seeking a way gracefully to withdraw from Lebanon the approximately 30,000 Syrian troops which have suffered severe losses at the hands of Israeli forces, which invaded Lebanon

on June 6, 1982. Asad can claim to have led the only Arab defense against the Israeli onslaught, even though his troops engaged the Israelis only when they entered Syrian-held territory in Lebanon. Finally, Asad's brutal response to rebellion among the citizens of his own country appears to have derailed at least for the moment the growing grass-roots movement against his regime. In the general turmoil of the Middle East, an uneasy quiet reigned Syria in late 1985, but the root causes of potential rebellion have yet to be addressed by the regime. The severe economic crisis facing the country in the mid-1980s will make the situation increasingly difficult for the regime.

Further Reading

Dawisha, A. I. "Syria under Asad, 1970–78: The Centres of Power." *Government and Opposition,* Vol. 13, No. 3, 1978.

Devlin, John F. *The Ba'ath Party: A History of its Origins to 1966.* Stanford, Calif.: Hoover Institution Press, 1976.

Drysdale, Alasdair. "Syria's Troubled Ba'thi Regime." *Current History,* Vol. 80, No. 462, 1981.

Faksh, Mahmud. "The Military and Politics in Syria." *Journal of South Asian and Middle Eastern Studies.* Vol. 8 (Spring, 1985).

———, "The Alawi Community of Syria: A New Dominant Political Force." *Middle Eastern Studies.* Vol. 20 (April, 1984).

Hinnelbusch, Raymond A. "Political Recruitment and Socialism in Syria: The Case of the Revolutionary Youth Federation." *International Journal of Middle East Studies,* Vol. 11, No. 2, 1980.

Hudson, Michael C. *Arab Politics: The Search for Legitimacy.* New Haven and London: Yale University Press, 1977.

Kaylani, Nabil M. "The Rise of the Syrian Ba'th, 1940–1958: Political Success, Party Failure." *International Journal of Middle East Studies,* Vol. 3, No. 1, 1972.

McLaurin, R. D.; Mughisuddin, Mohammad; and Wagner, Abraham. *Foreign Policy Making in the Middle East: Domestic Influences on Policy in Egypt, Iraq, Israel, and Syria.* New York and London: Praeger, 1977.

Reed, Stanley. "Dateline Syria: Fin de Regime?" *Foreign Policy,* No. 39, 1980.

Torrey, Gordon H. "The Ba'th—Ideology and Practice." *The Middle East Journal,* Vol. 23, No. 4, 1969.

Van Dam, Nikolaos. *The Struggle for Power in Syria: Sectarianism, Regionalism, and Tribalism, 1961–1978.* London: Croom Helm, 1979.

Van Dusen, Michael. "Political Integration and Regionalism in Syria." *The Middle East Journal,* Vol. 26, No. 21, 1972.

———. "Syria: Downfall of a Traditional Elite." *Political Elites and Political Development in the Middle East,* Frank Tachau, ed. New York: Wiley and Sons, 1975.

TAIWAN (REPUBLIC OF CHINA)
(Chung Hua Min Kuo)
by Helen Andrews, revised by Joseph Miller, Ph.D.

The System of Government

The government of the Republic of China is a government in exile on the island of Taiwan. It asserts that it is the legitimate ruler of all China. Since 1949, the government has maintained a "state of emergency" and martial law which, the government says, will continue until the "temporary" exile is ended and the mainland again comes under its control.

The effect of this "national emergency" is to impose on the province of Taiwan and its native citizens—some fifteen million people of Chinese descent—a government which primarily represents the interests of some two million exiles and their descendants. Any native Taiwanese claim to greater participation in the national government is tantamount to a claim that the government really only rules Taiwan. Such Taiwanese demands, therefore, present a genuine and serious challenge to the legitimacy of the Republic of China government.

Although it allows some degree of Taiwanese self-rule at the local level, the ruling party, the Kuomintang (KMT), controls all the organs of national government in Taiwan. It controls the vast majority of seats in the nationally elected bodies, most of those seats being held by "life-term" members from the mainland. The KMT controls the military and security apparatus; national president Chiang Ching-kuo is both leader of the KMT and commander-in-chief of the armed forces. Most of the press and media is under government control; those that are not tend to be short-lived. All meetings, demonstrations, and assemblies of a political nature occur only with government permission. Protests such as strikes or boycotts are forbidden. Any opposition to KMT rule runs the risk of being construed as a "communist subversion and incitement to rebellion," a crime punishable in military courts by sentences of seven years to life and, in some cases, death. There are presently several thousand political prisoners on Taiwan.

The present government structure is based on a 1946 constitution designed for the whole of China. At the federal level, the government consists of five *Yuan* (branches)—Executive, Legislative, Judicial, Examination, and Control—and a National Assembly.

Executive

The Executive Yuan, the cabinet, is the highest administrative organ. Its president is the head of government or premier. He is appointed, with the consent of the Legislative Yuan, by the president of the republic. The vice president of the Executive Yuan, the ministers and chairmen of commissions are appointed by the president of the republic on the recommendation of the Executive Yuan. There are three special commissioners on the Executive Yuan in charge of Mongolian, Tibetan, and Overseas Chinese Affairs.

The main function of the Examination Yuan is the recruitment, testing, and management of the civil service. In general, its processes are considered fair, with placement and advancement based on merit.

The Control Yuan is a powerful oversight body charged with hunting out corruption in government. It may impeach or censure officials at any level of government. It also supervises national budget preparation. Its members are indirectly elected by the Taiwan Provincial Assembly and the smaller assemblies of Taipei and Kaohsiung cities. Representatives of Mongolians, Tibetans, and Overseas Chinese also participate in electing Control Yuan members.

Legislature

The Legislative Yuan is the principal law-making body. Its members are elected to three-year terms and meet regularly for about eight months each year.

The National Assembly's powers are limited to electing the president and vice president, amending the constitution, and altering the official boundaries of the country (China). It is popularly elected and meets only once every six years, although it may be called into extraordinary session.

Judiciary

The Judicial Yuan administers the court system and is responsible for the conduct of all trials except those involving national security offenses which, under martial law, are tried by the Taiwan Garrison Command.

Regional & Local Government

The Taiwan Provincial Government consists of twenty-one commissioners appointed by the central government. By the early 1980s, eleven of these commissioners were Taiwanese and their designated chairman, who functions as provincial governor, by tradition has also been Taiwanese, although that is not constitutionally required. The provincial governor is subject to the national government and to the Provincial Assembly; his decision- and policy-making powers are substantially restricted.

Members of the Taiwan Provincial Assembly have been popularly elected since 1959. Currently, there are seventy-seven seats and seventy-four are filled by persons born on Taiwan. Most of them are members of the ruling party, the Kuomintang (KMT). The Provincial Assembly determines the provincial budget and administrative policies within the framework of national law. The Provincial Government can appeal Assembly decisions to the central government which may rescind them.

Since 1950, sixteen counties and five cities have elected their own governments. The mayors of the two major cities, Taipei and Kaohsiung, however, are appointed by the central government. Both these mayors are KMT members of Taiwanese descent.

In the most recent local elections, held in November 1985, there was a voter turnout of more than 71 percent. This election was for members of the Provincial Assembly, the Taipei City Council, the Kaohsiung City Council, and mayors and chiefs in city and county governments. While the ruling Kuomintang retained firm control of local politics (winning 146 of the 191 contested seats), the *tangwai* opposition (candidates endorsed by coalitions of non-KMT forces) continued its impressive election performance begun in 1980.

Tangwai candidates won seventeen seats in the Provincial Assembly, a loss of three. Of twenty-one mayors and chiefs, the KMT retained seventeen while independents (including *tangwai* candidates) won four. In the capital city of Taipei, all eleven opposition candidates won seats on the Taipei City Council, resulting in a loss of three seats by the Kuomintang. Even though the number of victorious *tangwai* candidates is small, these continued minor successes have even KMT spokespersons talking about the new growth of "political democracy" in the Republic of China.

There are nine identifiable tribes of an aboriginal people of Malay origin on Taiwan. About half of them (150,000) still live in traditional villages in the mountains in eastern Taiwan. These villages are under central government administration, but exercise a large measure of local autonomy. In the Provincial Assembly, two members represent the mountain groups, and two other members are tribesmen from the western plains.

The Electoral System

The first and only general elections for *all* seats in the Legislative Yuan, National Assembly, and Control Yuan were held in 1947–48 in those parts of China then controlled by the Kuomingtang. About 525 of the 933 members of the Legislative Yuan fled the mainland. Less than half of the 3,330 members of the National Assembly did so. Nevertheless, the official government position is that the originally elected members of the National Assembly and the Legislative and Control Yuan are to remain in office "for the duration" of the "national emergency." Since 1949, even the membership that moved to Taiwan has been halved by death, emigration, and in some cases, return to the mainland.

To cope with these losses, the central government in 1969 held "partial elections" in the "free district," meaning Taiwan. Two new seats were added to the Control Yuan, fifteen to the National Assembly, and eleven to the Legislative Yuan. Subsequently, another set of regulations provided for "supplementary elections" for the National Assembly and Control Yuan every six years and for the Legislative Yuan every three years. These elections apply only to "limited-term seats," that is, those representing districts currently under central government control. The majority of seats in all three bodies remain "life-term seats" representing areas under communist control.

In December, 1983, Taiwan held the fifth national supplementary election (the fourth since 1969), in which seventy-one candidates were chosen to serve in the Legislative Yuan, along with twenty-seven members chosen from among Overseas Chinese communities. The tangwai candidates campaigned hard, but won only six seats (three of these were won by women). This election did, however, continue the process some have called the "Taiwanization" of ROC politics, since sixty-six of the victorious candidates were native Taiwanese.

Limited-term members comprise 17 percent of the Legislative Yuan; 34 percent of the National Assembly, and 6 percent of the Control Yuan, or about 10 percent of the total. Nevertheless, limited-term members have more power than their numbers would suggest, because so many life-term members fail to attend sessions or are incapacitated by age from taking an active role.

There was a new election law passed in July 1983, which was expected to deal with some of the problems of vote buying, bribery, and illegal campaign activities seen in the 1980 election. As elections seemed to become more competitive, the earlier hopes placed in the election law of 1980 were dashed by fears of rising emotionalism and violence. The two-week limit on campaigning was continued, but more severe restrictions were placed on the use of media, making it illegal for political candidates to use television, other mass media, parades or demonstrations. Many of the independent candidates favored such restrictions since this would seem to negate the advantage held by those with more money to spend on media. Further, penalties for vote buying and bribery were made more severe and were clarified over those in the 1980 law. Ceilings were also placed on campaign spending, and candidates were not permitted to accept any contributions from foreign sources.

With the establishment of the 1980 and 1983 election laws, the actual mechanics of balloting and vote counting are generally conceded to be relatively fair and honest, though some irregularities do persist. For example, it was alleged that some 20 percent of the vote in 1985 could have been influenced by money or gifts.

National People's Party (*Kuomintang;* KMT)

History

The KMT had its origins in China under the leadership of Sun Yat-sen in the early 1910s. In 1923–24, the KMT, then a revolutionary force advocating democratic and socialist reforms, allied itself with the Soviet Union and reorganized itself along the model of the Soviet Communist Party. Its internal structure and functioning still resembles that model.

After Sun's death in 1925, the anticommunist general Chiang Kai-shek ended the KMT-Soviet alliance and began his long, losing attempt at a military unification of China, turning to the United States for aid and, after fleeing the mainland, for diplomatic support of the KMT claim to legitimacy as the government of China.

Organization

The KMT congress meets every five years to elect the Central Committee and ratify leadership decisions. Membership in the Central Committee is actually determined by the party leader, who also controls nominations to the Central Standing Committee, the real policy-making body.

In spite of this highly centralized structure, the KMT is not rigidly controlled from the top, particularly at the local level. For example, candidacy for election to the party congress and the nationally elected bodies is not always determined by the central leadership and is left to individual and local initiative within the party. In elections to county and local government bodies, the KMT does not always present a candidate.

Policy

The KMT defines its return to the mainland as the sole government of China as the only acceptable solution to the "China problem." To protect its claim to legitimacy, it has denounced all demands by the Taiwanese for greater representation in the government and imposes various forms of mainland culture on the local population, most noticeably the restriction of the use of the Taiwanese dialect. The KMT professes support for the values of freedom and democracy, and places strong emphasis on capitalism, free trade, and industrial development.

In recent years, a split in the party between "hard-line" military leaders and more moderate "technocrats" has become evident. The technocrats, who include some native Taiwanese, favor cautious political reforms. The hard-liners continue to control the levers of power, but the moderates have time and reality on their side.

Given the serious international setbacks suffered by the KMT in the 1970s, the party has shown some willingness to consider a compromise regarding its status as the ruler of China. Though it continues to govern strictly and to use repressive controls, there is evidence of greater tolerance for dissent within the party, of increased interest in Taiwanese participation in the party, and even of a decrease in automatic suppression of Taiwanese opposition to KMT policies.

Membership & Constituency

The party claims that 70 percent of the adult population of Taiwan belongs to the KMT, and the party has made real efforts to attract Taiwanese to its ranks. Political and professional advancement appears in part to be dependent on KMT membership, which makes it difficult to assess genuine Taiwanese support for the party under the present circumstances.

Financing

Much of the Kuomintang's finances are provided by party dues, as well as from sizable contributions from wealthy industrialists on the island. A significant supplement to these sources, however, is the income generated by large investments of party capital, managed by the Central Party Holding Company. This firm makes substantial income-generating investments in large, successful Taiwanese business ventures.

Leadership

Chiang Ching-kuo (born 1910), the son of Chiang Kai-shek, assumed leadership of the KMT on his father's death in 1975 (he has been President of the Republic of China since 1978, reelected to a second six-year term in 1984). He previously held posts in the party apparatus in internal security. In recent years, his health seems to be failing; consequently, there is growing concern about future leadership.

At this time, Chiang has no chosen successor, and the three most prominent individuals thought only a few years ago to be potential successors are no longer in contention. General Wang Sheng (mainlander, born in 1917), former Director of the General Political Warfare Department, was retired from the military in mid-1983 and appointed ambassador to Paraguay later that same year in what many consider to be a "double demotion" stemming from fears about the extent of his political ambitions. Dr. Tsiang Yen-shih (mainlander, born in 1915) was forced to resign as secretary general of the KMT in February 1985, in the wake of a major financial scandal known as the "Tenth Credit crisis." He has been replaced by Ma Shu-li (mainlander, born in 1909), who may be seen as merely an interim party leader until a younger person can be groomed to take over as secretary general. Former Premier Sun Yun-suan (mainlander, born in 1913) was forced to retire from public life in 1984 after he suffered a stroke. He has been replaced by Yu Kuo-hwa (mainlander, born in 1914), whose lack of political base and experience would probably make him an unlikely candidate for successor to Chiang.

It is suspected that immediately upon the death of Chiang his vice president would temporarily act as president while a successor is chosen. The person currently holding that position, Lee Teng-hui (native Taiwanese, born in 1923), has been seen for some time by many observers as one of the most likely successors to Chiang. He is native Taiwanese, former Mayor of Taipei, and a member of the KMT's Central Standing Committee (the party's "inner circle"). Of course, it is also possible that no one individual will replace the president, that a committee of sorts might rule instead. Such a ruling committee would most likely be a coalition of representatives from the military, the party, and the government.

Minor Parties

Two parties besides the KMT fled from China in 1949. These were the Young China Party and the China Democratic Socialist Party (CDSP). In 1981, Young China had eighty members in the three nationally elected bodies, while the CDSP had forty-four. Both parties are led by mainlanders, both are subsidized by the KMT, and neither one opposes KMT policy. They are part of a "front" controlled by the ruling party, although this is not their official status. Neither party actively recruits new members and, unless they are revived as opposition parties, it is likely they will die out with the passing of the generations which fled the mainland.

Opposition

On February 28, 1947, there was a mass uprising on Taiwan against the newly installed KMT government's corruption and incompetence. It was brutally repressed at the cost of an estimated 20,000 Taiwanese lives. Again, in the early 1950s, Chiang Ching-kuo, now president, carried out a massive purge against anti-KMT personalities and groups. Since then the local population has been reluctant to question KMT authority and notably cautious in their attempts at political opposition. The KMT has continued to imprison, deport, and sometimes execute opposition figures, whether they advocated reunion with the mainland under the communist regime there, or far more frequently, called for Taiwanese self-determination.

Despite such repression, there was an increasing amount of independent political activity in the 1970s. The new election system permitted non-KMT candidates, thirteen of whom won seats in the Legislative Yuan. These candidates ran as individuals without any visible organizational support beyond their district. While some of them were supporters of KMT policy, many were *tangwai,* that is, advocates of democratic freedoms and a multiparty system. *Tangwai* views were not limited to the nonparty candidates; some KMT candidates were also *tangwai.*

Tangwai activity in the 1970s was particularly visible in a number of journals and magazines critical of the government. This tendency culminated in the *Meili Tao* (or Formosa) magazine, which was the product of a broad coalition which called itself the Democratic Movement and included in its ranks legislators, lawyers, writers, and former political prisoners. By the time its fourth issue appeared, in November 1979, *Meili Tao's* circulation had reached 110,000.

On December 10, 1979, *Meili Tao,* together with the newly formed Taiwan Human Rights Committee, held a rally in Kaohsiung in recognition of International Human Rights Day. The demonstration ended in a bloody clash with the military and police and the subsequent arrest and imprisonment of the magazine's staff. The key organizers were convicted of sedition in military courts and received sentences of several years to life. Many of these persons were released on parole in February 1986. This is generally seen as a major concession to the reality of a vital political opposition in Taiwan.

Meili Tao and the other most popular unofficial publications called for basic freedoms and civil rights, such as free speech and assembly. Other issues raised by the opposition candidates include objections to the rapid buildup of nuclear power plants, government corruption, and excessive military spending.

It is difficult to measure the extent of support for non-KMT political forces on Taiwan, although it is certain that a strong sympathy exists for them. There is a definite fear of the "mainland threat" among the population, which may keep the Taiwanese from pushing harder for political reforms. Generally, there is greater support for opposition politicians in the south of the island and in the cities, especially Taipei and Kaohsiung. The KMT denies the existence of any noncommunist opposition.

The Presbyterian Church in Taiwan is another focus of potential opposition. Founded in 1865 by British missionaries, it today includes nearly 200,000 members. Unlike other Protestant denominations, which came to Taiwan in 1947 to 1949 with the Chinese nationalists, the Presbyterian Church had always been closely allied to the interests and views of the native Taiwanese. In the 1970s it became more vocal on issues such as human rights, self-determination, and use of the Taiwanese dialect. Despite government attempts to undermine its authority, the Church continued to serve as a voice on political issues under the leadership of Rev. Kao Chun-ming, its general secretary, until 1980, when Rev. Kao was arrested and sentenced to seven years' imprisonment for harboring the fugitive Shih Ming-teh, one of the *Meili Tao* organizers.

National Prospects

In the coming decades several factors will probably contribute to loosening the KMT's iron grip on political power in Taiwan. One of these is the age of its leaders, most of whom are in their sixties and seventies. Another is the increasingly evident split within the party between the hard-line, military leaders and the generally younger and more moderate "technocrats," many of whom are native Taiwanese. The latter group favors some cautious reforms and will undoubtedly grow in power. A third factor is the international setbacks suffered by the KMT in the 1970s and early 1980s, the latest being the 1984 murder of Chinese-American writer Henry Liu in California by people working for Taiwan intelligence services. Although Taiwan's immediate response to such setbacks and embarrassments has been a reiteration of its claims to sovereignty, the situation is changing gradually, and the party is showing more signs of willingness to compromise, as well as increasing tolerance of dissent within its own ranks. So, while the KMT will probably remain the dominant power in Taiwan for some time, it appears that a Taiwanese voice within the party will grow and that, in time, legitimate political opposition will be increasingly tolerated.

After several decades of steady economic growth, Taiwan has felt the worldwide business slump of the 1980s. Increasing energy costs, a rising budget deficit, decreasing export orders, rising labor costs (factory wages rose 20 percent from 1976 to 1980), high interest rates, and inflation have contributed to the slowdown. Despite these problems, Taiwan is one of the Asian countries for whom economic expansion and prosperity have been forecast in the coming generation. Taiwan's private industrial sector is traditionally powerful and secure, but the decisions of its political leadership will probably determine its economic progress.

Further Reading

Clough, Ralph N. *Island China*. Cambridge, Mass.: Harvard University Press, 1978.

Copper, John F., with George P. Chen. *Taiwan's Elections: Political Development and Democratization in the Republic of China*. Baltimore, Maryland: Occasional Papers/Reprint Series in Contemporary Asian Studies, 1984.

The Democratic Movement in Taiwan. Hong Kong: Asian Forum on Human Rights, 1980.

Gregor, A. James, and Maria Hsia Chang. *The Republic of China and U.S. Policy: A Study in Human Rights*. Washington, D.C.: Ethics and Public Policy Center, 1983.

Han Lih-wu. *Taiwan Today*. Taipei: Cheng Chung Book Co., 1977.

Hinton, Harold C. *An Introduction to Chinese Politics*. New York: Holt, Rinehart and Winston, 1978.

Hungdah Chiu, ed. *China and the Taiwan Issue*. New York: Praeger, 1980.

Lasater, Martin L. *The Taiwan Issue in Sino-American Strategic Relations*. Boulder, Colorado: Westview Press, Inc., 1984.

The Letter on Taiwan, Nos. 1–3. Manhattan, Kan.: Taiwanese-American Society, May 1979–May 1980.

Mendel, Douglas. *The Politics of Formosan Nationalism*. Berkeley and Los Angeles: University of California Press, 1970.

SPEAHRhead, quarterly. New York: Society for the Protection of East Asian Human Rights.

Taiwan Communique, monthly. Seattle, Wash.: International Committee for the Defense of Human Rights in Taiwan.

U.S. Congress. Senate. Committee on Foreign Relations. *Oversight of the Taiwan Relations Act. Hearing before the Subcommittee on East Asian and Pacific Affairs, May 14, 1980*. Washington, D.C.: U.S. Government Printing Office, 1980.

UNITED REPUBLIC OF TANZANIA

by Nadine Epstein, M.A. revised by Bernard Nzo-Nguty, Ph.D.

The System of Government

The United Republic of Tanzania, a one-party socialist state governing some seventeen million people, was formed in 1964 by the union of Tanganyika and the islands of Zanzibar. The two countries, which experienced very dissimilar political development before the union, achieved independence from Great Britain in 1961 and 1963, respectively.

From 1884 until 1919, Tanganyika was under German rule. After the German defeat in World War I, Tanganyika was administered by Britain under a League of Nations mandate. The country became a UN Trusteeship Territory in 1946. Tanganyika was granted full independence on December 9, 1961, under Julius K. Nyerere, president of the country's only party, the Tanganyikan African National Union (TANU).

At first, Nyerere worked within the bounds of the parliamentary system the country had inherited from the colonial period and cooperated closely with the largely British bureaucracy. However, relations with Britain soon became strained, and radicals within TANU became stronger and more vocal, particularly over the issue of Africanization of the bureaucracy. At the same time, Nyerere objected to elitist attitudes among black leaders and to increasing social stratification. To cope with these problems, he gradually instituted reforms in party policy and government structure which radically changed the relationship between party and government.

From independence, Tanganyika was de facto a one-party state. In his 1965 treatise, *Democracy and the Party System,* Nyerere stated that in a country such as Tanzania, where the vast majority of the population was unfamiliar with politics, voters were not prepared to choose from among many candidates. He argued that a democratic one-party system would more appropriately meet the needs of the nation. TANU's status as that one party was written into the 1965 Interim Constitution.

Party supremacy was written into the constitution in 1975.

Government and party leadership structures are generally parallel on the national, regional, and district levels. A great deal of overlap of party and government leadership exists on all levels, particularly in the higher echelons. Since 1977, efforts have been made to bring the Zanzibari party and government structures into conformity with those on the mainland, but this process is still in its early stages.

Political developments on Zanzibar were significantly less peaceful than on the mainland. The islands had been ruled by an Omani sultanate since the early nineteenth century and had been a British protectorate since 1890. When independence came on December 10, 1963, the island's politics were characterized by sharp antipathy between a minority Arab elite and the majority Africans, with a large mixed-race group, the Shiraz, split between the two camps.

Shortly after independence, the Arab-dominated government cancelled elections which the Afro-Shirazi Party (ASP) was expected to win easily; a bloody revolution followed in January 1964. The ASP, led by Abeid Karume, took over the government. Three months later, Karume arranged the union with Tanganyika. Karume ruled Zanzibar with a handful of men through the Zanzibar Revolutionary Council (ZRC). Their rule was marked by paranoia, corruption and by violence against the Arab and Asian minorities. There were no elections.

The 1964 union was superficial. Karume made little attempt to work with Nyerere and was indifferent to TANU policies. He showed little interest in his constitutional role as union vice-president. Zanzibar remained politically and economically autonomous, while receiving more tangible political benefits from the union than did the mainland. The 1965 Interim Constitution dealt with issues primarily of concern to TANU and the mainland; it had little application to Zanzibar.

Karume was assassinated in 1972. He was succeeded by Aboud Jumbe, who took steps to broaden the government's basis of power within Zanzibar. He strengthened the ASP and relegated many of the powers of the Revolutionary Council to the ASP and to ministerial positions. In addition, he attempted to moderate abuses of power and curtail corruption.

Jumbe also proved more willing to cooperate with Nyerere, and the relationship between the two parts of the country significantly improved. Jumbe took his role as Tanzanian vice-president seriously and became active in national politics.

The rapprochement between Zanzibar and the mainland culminated in the merger of the ASP and TANU in 1977 in the Revolutionary Party (*Chama Cha Mapinduzi;* CCM), the first step towards a full national integration.

Early in 1984, Jumbe's resignation was forced by a political crisis instigated by Zanzibari pressure for a better deal under the Tanzania constitution. Some Zanzibaris intended to use this conflict to lead to the creation of an independent state. Ali Hassan Mwinyi was chosen by the ruling Revolutionary Party to fill the vacancy and was later elected president of Zanzibar which automatically qualified him to be nominated as vice president of Tanzania and vice chairman of the party. On August 15, 1985, President Nyerere announced to delegates of a special congress of the ruling Chama Cha Mapinduzi (Revolutionary Party) that Mwinyi was his successor and the sole candidate for the presidential election which was scheduled for October 27, 1985. He was duly elected by a 92.2 percent of the total votes cast.

Mwinyi was sworn in as Tanzania's new president on November 5, 1985. During the swearing-in ceremony, Nyerere handed over to Mwinyi the instruments of power, including the country's 1984 constitution and the election manifesto of the Chama Cha Mapinduzi. President Mwinyi's new cabinet consisted of a vice president and prime minister, Joseph Warioba; second vice president, Idris Abdul Wakil; deputy prime minister and minister of defense, Salim Ahmed Salim; fourteen ministers and six ministers of state. Wakil had previously been elected Zanzibar president on October 15, 1985 to replace Mwinyi in that post. He heads Zanzibar's twelve-member cabinet, in addition to his responsibilities as second vice president of Tanzania.

Zanzibar still has its own administration for internal affairs, and a separate constitution for the islands was adopted in October 1979, providing for an elected president and a Council of Representatives elected by party members. The amended Zanzibar constitution of 1984 came into force in January 1985. It provides for the post of a president, elected by universal adult suffrage for a maximum of two five-year terms, and for a House of Representatives of forty-five to fifty-five members, also directly elected by universal adult suffrage. The president of Zanzibar appoints the chief minister, and the two cooperate in choosing the twenty other members of the Revolutionary Council, which will have up to twenty members. The members representing Zanzibar in the Union Parliament will also be elected from among the members of the House of Representatives by universal adult suffrage.

Executive

Constitutionally, the president is head of state, commander of the armed forces, and chairman of CCM. He has broad powers to arrest and pardon, to deport, and to dismiss students from the university. Nyerere has himself admitted that he had sufficient power under the constitution to be a dictator. He was, however, an extremely popular president who invoked his harsher powers only occasionally. The president is elected every five years by popular vote. A single presidential candidate is nominated by CCM.

The president appoints a vice-president from the members of the National Assembly. The vice-president must also be chairman of the Zanzibar Revolutionary Council, unless the president is from Zanzibar, in which case the vice-president must be from the mainland. The president also chooses the prime minister and all other ministers from among the members of the National Assembly. The vice-president and the ministers comprise the cabinet, which is presided over by the president. The prime minister represents the president in the National Assembly and the regional commissioners in the cabinet.

Newly independent Tanzania inherited a largely British civil service, but by the early 1970s, over half of civil service posts were held by Africans. The civil service has grown immensely since independence, however, and still includes many Asian and white Tanzanians. Many of the most educated and qualified people in Tanzania are in the civil service, attracted by relatively high salaries. Civil servants may run for political office only if they resign their positions after being nominated. Few choose to do so. As in most developing countries, the overall quality of the civil service is erratic.

Legislature

The National Assembly or *Bunge* is a unicameral body which has legislative jurisdiction only for the mainland and for foreign affairs. The president cannot legislate without the Assembly, but the Assembly is not a truly deliberative body which formulates legislation. It is, instead, an important forum of debate and a platform for broader explanation and defense of party policy. It acts as a sounding board and a support gatherer for party policies, and its primary function, ultimately, is to ratify those policies.

Nearly all major political figures in Tanzania are members of the National Assembly. All members of the Assembly are required to be party members in good standing; if an Assembly member goes too far in opposing party policy, he can be expelled from the party and automatically loses his Assembly seat. The party first asserted this authority in 1973 when a group of assemblymen rallied to defeat an income tax bill which would have sharply increased their own taxes. Nyerere used his powers as party chairman to expel some members of the group.

According to the constitution, the Assembly consists of 204 members, though the actual number varies because of appointed members. In a 1981 count, there were 214 members. The distribution of seats was as follows: 101 members elected directly from the mainland; fifteen national members elected from the Designated Mass Organizations; up to ten members from the mainland appointed by the president; twenty-five ex officio members (regional commissioners); up to thirty-two members appointed by the Zanzibar Revolutionary Council; ten members elected directly from Pemba and Zanzibar; up to twenty members appointed by the president to represent Zanzibar; and the national vice-president.

Judiciary

The High Court, consisting of a chief justice appointed by the president and fifteen additional judges appointed by the president after consultation with the chief justice, is the final court of appeal and the interpreter of the constitution. There is also a national appeals court. District and primary courts of first instance are presided over by appointed magistrates on the mainland. In Zanzibar, the people's courts were introduced in 1970. In these courts, the magistrates were popularly elected, defense lawyers prohibited, and accused persons compelled to defend themselves. A newer judicial system in Zanzibar, which became effective on January 14, 1985, permits defense lawyers in the people's court. Under this system, a defendant is innocent until proven guilty by the prosecution. The system is similar to that in other Commonwealth countries. The Permanent Commission of Inquiry, provided for in the constitution, is empowered to investigate abuses of authority.

Regional & Local Government

Tanzania is divided into twenty-five regions; twenty on the mainland, five on Zanzibar. Each region contains from two to six districts with 120 districts nationwide. Top leadership on each level includes a representative of the government, a civil-service head, and representatives of the party. Individual ministries also have offices on each level.

There are approximately 8,325 registered villages, each with an assembly made up of everyone eighteen years of age and older. The assembly elects twenty-five residents over age twenty-one to a village development council. The council can legally do anything necessary for the economic and social development of the village. When a village reaches the later stages of social development, the council, according to party policy, will own all village capital goods and a large portion of the village's economic activities will be carried out communally.

Unlike many countries in modern Africa, where traditional tribal structures often compete with the national government, no one tribe in Tanzania has sufficient political or economic power to stand against the government; of the over 120 tribes, the largest, the Sukuma, comprises only 13 percent of the population. The disintegration of the tribes' traditional organization under German and British rule has deprived them of even local power, and, in most areas, traditional functions have been taken over by the party and government.

An important element of national government disintegration has been the attempts by some Zanzabari political leaders to secede from the union with mainland Tanganyika. Under the union, Zanzibar is autonomous except in areas of defense, foreign relations, domestic affairs, and finance.

The Electoral System

Each of the 120 districts elects one member to the National Assembly for a five-year term. There is universal adult (age eighteen) suffrage. Nominees for directly elected seats in the Assembly are chosen at the district level by the party conference. A candidate has to be nominated by at least twenty-five registered voters in the district to be eligible for consideration by the district conference. The district conference then culls the list and passes it on to the National Executive Committee, which designates the two nominees who will finally compete for the seat. The Committee tries to take local preferences into account.

Revolutionary Party (*Chama Cha Mapinduzi;* CCM)

History

African political groups began to develop in Tanganyika as early as 1934. The first group, the African Association , was primarily a social-welfare organization formed by educated Africans. In 1948 this group evolved into the explicitly political Tanganyikan African Association (TAA). Conflict between Africans and Great Britain centered around the issues of "majority representation" and a timetable for independence. In July 1954, the TAA became the Tanganyikan African National Union (TANU), led by Julius K. Nyerere, an eloquent, British-educated teacher and political activist. The party adopted its current name when TANU and Zanzibar's ASP were united in 1977.

Organization

Party organization has five levels: national, regional, district, branch, and cell. Local organization is not uniformly present or effective throughout the country. Parts of the country are not easily accessible and illiteracy and non-participation in politics are higher in some areas than others. The party's presence and activities often depend on the attitudes and skills of local leaders.

The chairman of CCM is the former president of the republic, Julius Nyerere. The vice-chairman is Ali Hassan Mwinyi, president of the nation and formerly head of the state of Zanzibar. The chairman and vice-chairman are elected to five-year terms by the delegates to the party's National Conference. They can be removed by two-thirds vote of both mainland and Zanzibari National Conference members. A chief executive secretary and two deputy chief executive secretaries are in charge of party administration.

Although the National Conference is officially the supreme organ of CCM, policymaking and power is in the hands of the Central Committee, which meets at least twice a month, more frequently than any other national party organ. Its membership consists of the CCM chairman and vice-chairman, thirty high-ranking party leaders nominated by the National Executive Committee (NEC), and up to ten members nominated by the chairman. Four major standing subcommittees of the Central Committee oversee government activity, while a fifth supervises party activities. The Central Committee is also responsible for preparing the National Executive Committee agenda, reviewing candidates for leadership posts at all levels, appointing party secretaries and commissioners, routine party administration, and political education programs.

The NEC is the chief executive organ of the CCM. Officially, it decides on and initiates policy. However, its agenda is set by the Central Committee, and, in reality, it does little in the area of policy initiation. The NEC is a large body consisting of all Central Committee members, all regional chairmen and secretaries, all chairmen and secretaries of the Designated Mass Organizations, twenty members from the mainland elected by the National Conference, and twenty from Zanzibar elected by the Zanzibar Revolutionary Council. The NEC, then, is made up of the inner ruling group and a sizeable body of middle-level party officials. It meets every six months.

The NEC's prime function is to review Central Committee decisions on development, defense, and security activities. It monitors the conduct and performance of party members and has the power to dismiss members from leadership positions. It also gives final approval of the nominations of candidates for the National Assembly. Decisions in the NEC are made by consensus or, failing that, by majority vote of those present and voting. Decisions on the relationship between Zanzibar and the mainland require the approval of two-thirds of both the mainland and Zanzibari delegations.

The National Conference meets once every five years and is, formally, the supreme organ of CCM. The infrequency of its meetings and its size make it difficult for the conference to be a genuine policymaking body. It has become less important over the years. The conference functions mainly to confirm or repudiate any decision of any organ or officer of the party. It is also the body which is responsible for amending the constitution and electing the chairman and vice chairman of the party.

The conference is chaired by the party chairman and consists of all the members of the Executive Committee, all members of the Assembly, all members of the Zanzibar Revolutionary Council, all district chairmen and secretaries, ten members elected from each party district conference, and one member from each Designated Mass Organization.

The conference has two standing committees in which the power of party over government is outstandingly clear. The first committee consists of all members of the Assembly. Its responsibility is to ensure implementation of party policies in Parliament. The second committee consists of all members of the Zanzibar Revolutionary Council and is responsible for ensuring that party policies are carried out in Zanzibar.

Region and district boundaries are the same for both the party organization and the government. Party responsibility for each region or district is in the hands of a secretary who is appointed by the national party chairman. The secretary convenes all meetings of party organs in his area.

Regional and district chairmen are elected to five-year terms by regional and district conferences. They preside over working committees responsible for the routine administration of party affairs and over executive committees, which supervise defense, security, and developmental affairs in the area and monitor the conduct of party members and government institutions. Responsibility for approving nominees for party leadership at the next lowest level falls to the working committees. Both bodies contain representatives of the next lower level of party organization; the executive committees also include the National Assembly members of the region of district and representatives of the Designated Mass Organizations. The working committees meet at least every two weeks; the executive committees every six months.

Regional and district conferences meet every thirty months to elect the regional and district chairmen and representatives to the working and executive committees. The district conference also elects representatives to the regional and national conferences. While these bodies are formally the supreme organs of the party in the regions and districts, they function more to promote party cohesiveness and facilitate the transmission of party objectives to the local, or branch, level.

Party branches are of three types—those formed of whole villages, those formed in the workplace (industrial), and those formed in the larger towns and cities (ward). A branch is supposed to have at least fifty members. The branch secretary is appointed by the party's Central Committee, while the branch chairman is elected by all branch members (in large branches by all cell leaders) for a five-year term. The branch executive committee membership includes the chairman, the secretary, six persons elected by the branch, all district conference members in the branch, and representatives of designated mass organizations in the branch. The committee's primary function is to transmit and explain party directives to the rank and file and to convey local public opinion up the ladder to the higher organs of the party. Larger branches are divided into cells which have primary responsibility for neighborhood and workplace security and political education.

In 1977 there were five Designated Mass Organizations (DMOs): the Youth Organization, the Union of Tanzanian Women, the Union of Tanzanian Workers, the Union of Cooperative Societies, and the Tanzanian Parents Association. The DMOs replaced the independent unions and organizations of the sixties. Their primary function, in government eyes, is the political mobilization of the people. Each mass organization can make rules governing its own operation, but the rules must be approved by the party's National Executive Committee. Their activities are conducted under the supervision of the party Central Committee. The organizations are represented on all levels of party organization and in the National Assembly. Their chief officers on all levels are appointed by the party chairman or the Central Committee.

Policy

To avoid what Nyerere saw as the negative aspects of industrialization—inequality between rural and urban areas, the development of an economic elite, and consumerism—the party has emphasized rural development. In 1967, in a landmark speech known as the Arusha Declaration, Nyerere formally put forth his alternative to industrialization. He provided an "ideology" called "African Socialism" based on *ujaama,* which is translated literally from Swahili as "familyhood." *Ujaama,* in the sense that Nyerere uses it, refers to a pattern of equality, cooperation, interdependence, and sharing which he believes to be characteristic of traditional African families and rural communities.

Ujaama villages, as opposed to the traditional isolated *shambas* (small farms), were to be the foundation on which the Tanzanian society and economy would be built. They would be cooperative communities in which the majority of Tanzanian citizens would live and share scarce agricultural equipment and health and education facilities. Economically, cooperative farming was supposed to be more efficient. In addition, citizens living in villages would be easier to mobilize politically.

Among the other policies introduced at this time, "self-reliance" and a leadership code were the most important. "Self-reliance" was a slogan created to discourage Tanzanians from being excessively reliant on foreign and government assistance. A strict leadership code was adopted to stem corruption and elitism among government leaders.

Policy implementation in both sections of the country has not proceeded smoothly. People have not flocked to the *ujaama* villages, and in some cases, officials have resorted to force to meet their quotas for advancing *ujaama.* The government has also sometimes used force to remove rural migrants from urban areas where a new, moderate industrialization policy has created a demand for labor. The overall economic situation is dismal. Crop production has been stymied by droughts and ineffective cooperative organization. International market prices for Tanzanian export crops have remained low, while prices for imported necessities, especially oil and fertilizers, have remained high. A difficult foreign-exchange problem, therefore, has become worse not better, and Tanzania has become more dependent on foreign aid.

Mwinyi can afford slow progress in domestic and economic affairs, because the country's interest seems focused on foreign issues. Nyerere was one of the most important leaders of the "front-line" nations, the African states which support black liberation movements in southern Africa. Nyerere's direct intervention in Uganda to aid the overthrow of Idi Amin, however, caused concern both at home and abroad. The action depleted the country's cash reserves and probably did not improve the nation's security. Indeed, it may create a new activism in the army which could lead that body to intervene in Tanzanian politics.

Membership & Constituency

No reliable figures are available for CCM's membership. It is a mass, not an elite or a "vanguard" party, and is not interested in excluding people. Any citizen eighteen or older can apply for membership after taking a course of instruction in the party creed, policy, and objectives. The citizen's application is considered by the branch executive committee, which forwards its recommendation to the district executive committee. This body has the power to accept or reject applicants, but rejected applicants can reapply. If members are dismissed for poor conduct, they can reapply later.

Nyerere and other top leaders of the party seem to truly desire broad support for party policies. Efforts have been made to decentralize the party (as well as the government), to delegate responsibility, and to encourage debate within the membership as long as the basic policies of socialism and egalitarianism are not questioned. Communication between and among party levels appears to be encouraged and is facilitated by the extensive overlap of leaders from the local to the national level. In fact, the party is highly centralized and its policies require national direction. Finally, at present there are simply not enough qualified people at the party's lower levels to sustain a truly decentralized system.

Financing

Party members must pay an inexpensive entrance fee and monthly dues; how effective the party is in collecting the dues is uncertain. Given the intermingling of party and government affairs and personnel, it is probably safe to assume that most party activities are heavily subsidized by the government.

Leadership

The current party chairman is Nyerere. He inspires and initiates most party policy and has significant powers of appointment. But because Nyerere has had this role since before independence, it is difficult to distinguish the powers of the office from those of the man. A lesser figure might not be such a dominant force in the party.

Julius K. Nyerere was born in 1921 and is from one of the smaller tribes, the Zanaki. He attended Makerere College in Uganda, where he received an M.A. degree, and studied social science at the graduate level at the University of Edinburgh, Scotland. He taught in Tanzania until his political activities in the Tanganyikan African Association cost him his job. His personal integrity and discipline have made him a model for his countrymen, who call him *Mwalimu,* an honorific for a teacher.

Nyerere so dominates the government and party that no other outstanding figures have emerged. Personnel have moved up and down the power ladder at Nyerere's behest, and no single person has developed a permanent base of power. Many older traditional leaders are being replaced by younger, better-educated ones who are only now beginning to return in significant numbers after years of study abroad.

Nyerere, as the chairman of the ruling party — a post he plans to retain until 1987 — will continue to wield considerable power in the government. His successor, Mwinyi, is conscious of the fact that "Mwalimu Nyerere is around," but hopes that he will not interfere with the functions of the new government. It is envisaged that Mwinyi will follow some of the reform plans of his predecessor.

Mwinyi was born on the mainland at Kivure, in Kisarawa district, on May 8, 1925. His family moved to Zanzibar when he was a child. He began his primary education there in 1933 and later trained as a teacher. He became principal of Zanzibar's teacher-training college and, from 1963 to 1964, was acting permanent secretary of the Zanzibar Ministry of Education. He was assistant general manager of the Zanzibar State Trading Corporation, and received his first political appointment in 1970 as minister of state in the Tanzanian president's office in Dar es Salaam. Later, he served as minister of health for three years, then minister of home af-

fairs, ambassador to Egypt, and minister of state in the vice president's office.

The choice of Mwinyi for the presidency appears to be a compromise after the party failed to agree on other main candidates such as Prime Minister Salim Ahmed Salim, once a candidate for the post of United Nations Secretary General, and Rashidi Kawawa, the secretary general of Tanzania's ruling party. Mwinyi is perceived as a potentially effective factor in consolidating the union between the mainland and the isles of Zanzibar. His choice as the sole candidate for the presidency was seen as a source of great relief and pride to Zanzibaris and as a potential antidote to antiunion sentiments in the country.

Opposition

The only known opposition to Nyerere's rule has been a clandestine campaign to detach Zanzibar from the union. It culminated in the resignation of Jumbe from the posts of vice president of Tanzania, president of Zanzibar, chairman of the Zanzibar Revolutionary Council and vice chairman of the Chama Cha Mapinduzi. Nyerere's nominated successor, Mwinyi, is a Zanzibari but a staunch supporter of the union. He has been credited with adroit handling of a delicate situation that could have damaged relations between Zanzibar and the mainland. Most Tanzanians, therefore, regard Nyerere as an outstanding statesman (despite the nation's economic problems) because of his exemplary leadership, commitment to national unity and stability, honesty, and humility.

Other Political Forces

Military

The military in Tanzania does not play an important role in politics. However, in 1964 the military staged a revolt, taking over communications in the then capital city of Dar es Salaam, forcing the president to flee and sparking violence in the streets. The military took this action to protest the slow Africanization of the officer corps and to demand higher wages. The revolt was quickly put down with the help of the British, and the military was subsequently reorganized. Nothing similar has occurred since, but the army probably retains a potential for disruptive action if it becomes sufficiently dissatisfied.

The military is commanded by the president and is subordinate to the government. Total armed forces in July 1979 was 51,700, of whom an estimated 50,000 were in the army. There is also a paramilitary police force of 1,400 and a 35,000-man Citizen's Militia.

National Prospects

It is difficult to predict what will happen when Nyerere's chosen successor begins changing some of his predecessor's policies and structures. So far, President Mwinyi seems to be taking a cautious, gradual approach to Tanzania's domestic politics. As a devout Muslim and, like his predecessor, a reformist socialist, Mwinyi is anticipated to introduce innovative economic policies beneficial to the country's overall growth and prosperity. Diffusion of both the secession threat and the succession struggle for the presidency sets the stage for national reconciliation and consensus-building in Tanzania's external relations. Whether the political elite of mainland Tanganyika will cooperate with the leadership of the new Zanzabari–dominated government, remains a matter of speculation.

Further Reading

Barkan, Joel D., and Okumu, John J., eds. *Politics and Public Policy in Kenya and Tanzania.* New York and London: Praeger Publishers, Praeger Special Studies, 1979.

Bienen, Henry. *Tanzania: Party Transformation and Economic Development.* Princeton: Princeton University Press, 1970.

Kaplan, Irving, ed. *Tanzania: A Country Study.* Foreign Area Studies. Washington, D.C.: American University, 1978.

Nyerere, Julius. *Ujaama: Essays on Socialism.* Oxford and New York: Oxford University Press, 1968.

THAILAND
(Prathet Thai)
by David Morell, Ph.D. revised by H. Monte Hill, Ph.D.

The System of Government

Thailand, a nation of about forty-seven million people, is a constitutional monarchy with the king as head of state. Legislative power is vested in the National Assembly composed of the elected House of Representatives and the Senate appointed by the king. According to the constitution, the legislature selects the prime minister, who controls the armed forces, the national police, and the civilian ministries.

The armed forces—especially the Royal Thai Army—have dominated the exercise of political power almost continuously for over fifty years, since June 1932, when a group of young military and civilian leaders overthrew the nation's centuries-old absolute monarchy in a bloodless coup. Since the 1950s, the military has been increasingly dependent on the monarchy for its legitimacy as a political force, and relations between palace and garrison have grown increasingly tense. By the early 1980s, the monarchy had once again become a powerful force in its own right. The military's legitimacy is also limited by its pervasive corruption, which renders the armed forces increasingly vulnerable to pressures not only from the monarchy but from an occasionally aroused population as well. The large and politically powerful civilian ministries, however, have generally been coopted into accepting military leadership. Their fragmented structure renders the ministries incapable of acting effectively as a cohesive political force.

Legislatures, political parties, and elections are of dubious importance in Thai politics. Although the military elite and its allies have never been willing to share significant power with legislative institutions, neither have they been willing to abolish them. In essence, the parliamentary process provides a way to limit the monarchy's political power, and popular sovereignty thus provides a convenient facade for continued military rule. Parties and elected assemblies are abolished after each army coup, but each time the process is soon reinstituted. Between 1932 and 1985 Thailand has witnessed sixteen coups (nine successful), and a bewildering succession of cabinet changes, constitutional reforms and new elections. While participant political institutions are certainly not irrelevant, they are at most supplementary to the primary locus of power and authority, which is the military.

A brief outline of recent political history follows:

1957— Elections marked by fraud were followed by a coup. Field Marshal Sarit Thanarat* became prime minister; parties were outlawed until 1968.

1963— Sarit died; Field Marshal Thanom Kittakachorn succeeded him and served as prime minister until 1973. Field Marshal Praphat Charusathien was the real power behind Thanom.

1969— Elections were won by the government's United Thai People's Party; many independents were also elected.

1971— Thanom reimposed martial law, parliament was abolished and parties outlawed.

1973— Popular demonstrations against the Thanom government led the king to exile Thanom and Praphat; Sanya Thammasak, former chief justice, was appointed prime minister, and parties were legalized.

1975— Elections. Seni Pramoj (Democrat) became prime minister, but was replaced after two weeks by Kukrit Pramoj (Social Action).

1976— Preceding elections in April, many left-wing leaders were assassinated. Seni Pramoj became prime minister. Thanom and Praphat returned from exile,

---

* Thai names have the surname last, but by Thai custom people are referred to by their given name.

sparking major demonstrations by both left and right. Thanin Kraivichien became prime minister after a coup in October. Parties were outlawed.

1977— General Kriangsak Chomanan became prime minister after a coup.

1978— Parties legalized again.

1979— Elections were won by a coalition supporting Kriangsak.

1980— Kriangsak was replaced as prime minister by General Prem Tinsulanonda in a peaceful exchange of power.

1983— General Prem retains control of the government by forging a coalition between the Democrat, Social Action, and National Democrat parties.

1985— Coup of regular and retired army officers failed to overthrow Prem government. Democrat Party and Prem strengthened in by-elections.

Executive

The monarch, a descendent of the 200-year-old Chakkri dynasty, is formal head of state. Although the monarchy's absolute power was broken by the 1932 coup, the throne remains a major force in Thai politics, a force of increasing importance as other political institutions appear unable to lead successfully. The monarchy's residual power is based on its overwhelming prestige and unquestioned popular acceptance. Fundamentally all legitimacy throughout the Thai political system emanates from the traditional royal institution, even in 1986. King Phumipon Adulyadej (born 1927) ascended to the throne in 1946.

The head of government, the prime minister (*hayoke rathamontri*), wields the executive power. For thirty-nine of the fifty-four years of constitutional monarchy, a military officer—typically an army general—has held this post. At times, the leader of the military coup group (*khana thahan* or *khana batiwat*) has simply assumed this position, receiving the king's formal blessing. During those periods when the constitution has allowed an elected legislature, this body has chosen the prime minister. The prime minister and members of the cabinet need not be popularly elected, and only rarely has the prime minister stood for election to the legislature.

As head of the dominant military group, the prime minister can dominate Thai politics. Field Marshal Sarit Thanarat, for example,

prime minister from 1957 to 1963, ruled in a highly autocratic manner. More often, though, competition within the military, the need to share power with the monarchy, complicated relations with the business community, and competition within the elected Assembly have combined to constrain the prime minister's actual power. The prime minister in 1986, General Prem Tinsulanonda, exemplifies this situation. Prem came to power in 1980 and retained his post in the face of a military coup in April 1981 only by relying on direct intervention by the king, thus involving the monarchy even more deeply in politics.

Legislature

In October 1976, a military coup with extensive bloodshed ended a three-year period of open politics. The elected legislature was abolished, political parties were prohibited, and martial law was proclaimed. Military leaders named conservative civilian Thanin Kraivichien as prime minister. A new National Assembly was appointed. In 1977, General Kriangsak Chomanan seized power in his own right. Among other actions, Kriangsak sponsored the development of a new constitution which set forth an appointed Senate of 225 members and an elected House of Representatives of 301 members.

The Senate and the House meet in joint session on matters of national security, the throne, the budget, the national economy, and, most importantly, votes of no-confidence. All but thirty-one of the 225 senators appointed in early 1979 came from the armed services, primarily the army, thus ensuring Kriangsak's subsequent selection as prime minister, a post he held until Prem took over in March 1980.

Judiciary

The nation's court system is characterized by high institutional integrity, unusual for a political system with extensive corruption. While administrative decisions are rife with favoritism and bribery, the judiciary has typically been insulated from such pressures. The members of the Supreme Court (*san dika*) are appointed by the king (normally but not always on the recommendation of the prime minister). In October 1973, in the wake of extensive violence in Bangkok that forced the king to order top military leaders into exile, King Phumiphon selected

ELECTION RESULTS (1975–1983)
(Number of Seats Won in Legislature)

Party	Jan. 1975	April 1976	April 1979	April 1983
United Thai People's	*	*	2	19
Democrat	72	114	34	100
Social Justice	45	28	*	*
Thai Nation	28	56	44	63
Social Agrarian	19	9	8	0
Social Action	18	45	85	51
Social Nationalist	16	8	*	0
Socialist	15	2	*	*
New Force	12	3	8	1
Socialist Front	10	1	*	*
Thai People's	*	*	32	24
Seritham	*	*	23	*
Other parties	34	13	25	49
Independents (no party affiliation at time of election)	0	0	40	40
Total	269	279	301	347

* Party not in existence.

retired chief justice Sanya Thammasak as the new prime minister.

Regional & Local Government

The powerful Ministry of Interior is the heart of a system of centralized public administration. The country's seventy provinces are headed by governors (*phuwaratchakan changwat*) who report to the ministry's undersecretary. Each province has between five and ten districts, each under the supervision of a district officer (*nai amphoe*). This is the lowest level at which central-government officials are present permanently. Each village has an elected chief (*phuyaiban*) who can be removed by the district officer. Appointed provincial assemblies (*sapha changwat*) advise the governor and top province officials, who are directly responsible to their superiors in the Bangkok ministries.

Municipal government (*thesaban*) is significant only in the enormous Bangkok/Thonburi capital area, where some 10 percent of the nation's population lives. At times, depending on national politics, Bangkok's mayor and the municipal council have been directly elected. At other times, these posts are filled by appointees of the Ministry of Interior. Control of Bangkok is crucial to stability and order in Thai political life.

The Electoral System

All Thai elections have used direct suffrage, usually from single-member districts. All adults age twenty-one and over may vote. The January 1979 election law removed the franchise from voters with alien fathers, however; effectively disenfranchising nearly one-quarter of the previously eligible electorate (mostly Chinese) in Bangkok. Secret ballots are used, although rural voters typically respond to guidance from their village chief, who himself is often beholden to the district officer.

Voter turnout has declined consistently since 1969, as follows: February 1969, 50 percent; January 1975, 47 percent; April 1976, 46 percent; April 1979, 40 percent; July 1983, 39 percent. This decline has occurred despite increased literacy; more candidates; more parties; and more vigorous campaigning in newspapers, radio, and television. The decline reflects continuing voter perceptions of the legislature as ineffectual and faction-ridden, likely to be overthrown in another army coup, and lacking the power to improve the lot of the ordinary voter. Turnout increases with the distance from the capital; rates in Bangkok declined from 35 percent in 1969 to 21 percent in 1983, reflecting voter cynicism and apathy in the central city.

The 1975 constitution mandated that all candidates be affiliated with a legally registered political party. This was prompted by the aftermath of the 1969 election, when many "independent" members of the National Assembly blatantly sold their affiliation to the ruling coalition. The government's political party then, the United Thai People's Party, had to purchase the allegiance of some seventy independents to secure its House majority and form a cabinet. In the 1978 constitution, however, the rules were changed once again to permit Kriangsak to work with independents rather than rely solely on a few strong parties with which he had minimal ties. After his resignation from the prime ministership in 1980, General Kriangsak reentered politics by winning a hotly contested by-election the following year. By-elections often indicate party strength, and thus induce large contributions from wealthy party supporters.

The Party System

Origins of the Parties

Only two existing political parties predate the 1974 constitution, which once again legalized noncommunist political assemblies of over five people. The oldest is the illegal Communist Party of Thailand (CPT) which dates to 1925. The oldest legal party, the Democrat Party, took its present form in 1946. Of the sixty new parties created to contest the 1975 and 1976 elections, three remained important in 1983: the military-dominated Thai Nation Party, the moderate Social Action Party, and the progressive-left New Force Party. The right-wing Thai People's Party won a stunning upset in Bangkok in 1979, the first election in which it participated. Kriangsak formed the centrist National Democracy Party after the 1979 election. By incorporating several smaller groupings, it has become the largest political party outside the present coalition government.

The Parties in Law

All political parties must register with the Ministry of Interior. In order to register, 5,000 members nationwide are required by law. Each party has to identify a party leader, a secretary general, and other members of its central committee.

Party Organization

In spite of the formalities of the law on membership and organization, Thai parties are generally loosely structured coalitions of relatively independent politicians whose positions in the parties depend on the strengths of their personal local campaign organizations. Only the Democrats and, perhaps, the Social Action Party have local party organizations. The parties do not maintain full-time offices, even in Bangkok.

The 1983 party situation resembled that of 1970–71: party ties were weak; members of the National Assembly changed their party affiliation at will; the press was full of allegations that candidates and legislators were being bought outright to join one party or another. Because patronage and influence are more important than substantive policy differences in parliamentary maneuvering, neither large party groupings nor flexible independent legislators, who demand individual arrangements, seem to provide the basis for acceptable and stable coalition government.

Campaigning

Thai electioneering occurs in three different arenas. First, a small number of nationally known political and military personalities attract large crowds at rallies and garner significant press and media attention. The election rhetoric from national party leaders is amazingly consistent, if vague and contradictory. Typical national party platforms call for higher produce prices for farmers and lower food prices for consumers, a free economy and greater social services, support for democracy and a strong military, an independent foreign policy, an end to corruption, and loyalty to the king.

National election campaigns managed by the party leadership do not exist. Candidates from each district are provided with financial support, but have to devise their own local structure for campaigning. Much of the money for the campaigns is collected by the national party leadership from Bangkok business and military sources. While restrictions limit the amount each candidate may spend, these are frequently ignored. In 1975, the Thai Nation Party, probably the biggest spender in the election, was reported to have spent $2,500 per candidate. Overall it was estimated that the 2,199 candidates for the House spent $40 million. By 1979, average expenditures were estimated at nearly $10,000 for each independent candidate. The Democrat Party, traditionally a low-spender, raised $9,000 for each of its 200 candidates in the April 1983 election.

The second kind of electioneering consists of "money-dumping"—the use of campaign funds in rural constituencies. These expenditures take many forms: direct purchase of votes; the provision of free social services in the period immediately preceding the election; and the use of party funds for roads, wells, free meals, and medical care.

Finally, campaigns involve village-to-village appearances. Village campaigning involves numerous speeches to anywhere from twenty-five to a few hundred potential voters. (Each district contains about 150,000 people.) Additional communication is achieved by the use of mobile loudspeakers placed on car tops and advertising at movie theaters. A great deal of printed literature is distributed; posters are put up everywhere. Because of the weakness of the parties, the strength of the individual candidate is a vital determinant of electoral success.

Campaigning is relatively nonviolent, particularly as compared with other Third World countries. The notable exception was the 1976 election in which over thirty leftist politicians—including the secretary general of the Socialist Party of Thailand, Dr. Boonsanong Punyodyana—were assassinated. The polarization between student and labor groups on the one hand and the military, reactionary businessmen and clerics on the other was unprecedented in Thai politics and culminated in a military coup six months after the election.

Despite Thailand's image as a homogeneous country, campaigns are affected by regional variations: Bangkok was carried by the Democrats until 1979; the poor northeast region has typically elected Socialists; the south has consistently returned liberal Democrats to the National Assembly. Additionally, all parties are now running Muslim candidates in the districts bordering on Malaysia. The influx of refugees along the Lao border has discredited leftist parties there. Large concentrations of politically disciplined military personnel in certain Bangkok districts and on the Kampuchean border outvote indigenous populations. Modern campaign techniques—polls, for example—are beginning to be introduced in Thailand, especially in Bangkok.

Democrat Party
(*Prachatipat*)

History

Originally called the Progressive Party (the name was changed in 1948), this party was founded in 1946 by former prime minister Khuang Aphaiwong soon after he lost a vote of confidence in Parliament. He was joined by the brothers Seni and Kukrit Pramoj, distant relatives of the king. Khuang led the party until 1968, when Seni took over the leadership. (Kukrit played little role in party politics until he founded his own party, Social Action, in 1974.) The Democrats positioned themselves between army leaders and progressive civilians, their primary aim being to keep power in the hands of the civilian aristocracy and away from the military and less conservative civilians.

In the 1975 elections, the Democrats became the largest party in the House, with a program Seni called "mild socialism": legalization of trade unions, enhanced powers for local government, and public assistance for farmers. Seni formed a government but was ousted two weeks later by a coalition of the right.

In 1976, the Democrats won their biggest victory, and Seni formed a coalition government with three military-supported parties. Intense right-left factionalism within the party, however, weakened Seni's ability to cope with events, and he was ousted in the coup of October 1976. When the party reformed in 1978, its right wing was forced out, and Thanat Khoman, a former foreign minister, became party leader. The Democrats suffered a great defeat in the 1979 elections when the former right wing, now the basis of the Thai People's Party, carried most of Bangkok. However, the Democrats regained some Bangkok legislative seats in 1983 when the Thai Peoples Party lost eight positions. The party maintained its strength in the 1985 by-elections. Democrats in the House have supported the Prem governments, and Thanat has served as deputy prime minister.

Organization

The Democrats are the only national political party with a broad-based local organization. The party claims to have over 100 branches in all regions of the country. Their organization is strongest in the south, the home of most of their current members of Parliament.

The party is still split between left and right factions, though the disagreements between the two sides are not as profound as in 1976. The left, by far the dominant faction, is centered in the south and includes most of the party's parliamentary bloc. Chuan Leekpai, agriculture and cooperatives minister and a confidant of Prime Minister Prem, is its head. The right includes most of the party's financiers, primarily from Bangkok. Its leader is businessman Chalermphand Srivikorn. Former secretary general Damrong Lathipipat, part of the left grouping in 1976, is now allied with Chalermphand.

Policy

The Democrat Party entered the 1983 election in the weakest position since its founding. However, the party's emphasis on avoiding alienating major segments of the electorate apparently paid off as it managed to retain control of the government in 1983 with the assistance of the Social Action and National Democracy parties.

Membership & Constituency

The Democrat Party remains the best known of the parties, primarily because of its long history. Information on the party's membership is not available. It has been widely assumed that the Democrats' most consistent support has come from professionals and workers in Bangkok and the large towns, and from a broader range of people in the south.

Financing

The Democrats have never had much money. Annual party expenses are about $120,000. As party leaders approach Bangkok business interests for money, they can highlight the party's support for a cut in the current 40 percent corporate tax. An indication of the party's financial situation is its rule requiring monthly donations of $50 from Central Committee members and $125 from cabinet members.

Leadership

Thanat resigned as party leader in March 1982, although he remains a deputy prime minister in the Prem government. He was replaced by Bhichai Rattakul, foreign minister under Prime Minister Thanin and a compromise choice for leader between the left and right factions. Other party members of importance are discussed below.

Lek Nana is the secretary general and former deputy foreign minister.

Chuan Leekpai is a deputy leader and agriculture and cooperatives minister. Leader of the party's liberal southern faction, he stepped aside for Bhichai for the sake of party unity.

Marut Bunnag, a deputy leader and justice minister, was defeated by Lek for the secretary general's post.

Chalermphand Srivikorn is leader of the party's right faction and a former member of the Prem cabinet; he blocked Chuan's bid to be party leader.

Kraisorn Tantipong is a House member and former industry minister, as well as chief campaign manager for the 1983 elections.

M. R. Seni Pramoj is the former prime minister and party leader.

Prospects

The Democrats' performance in the July 1986 elections exceeded all expectations and may suggest renewed strength in the party. In particular, in Bangkok the traditionally strong Thai People's Party weakened considerably and the Democrats gained ground. It remains to be seen how permanent a shift this represents in the notoriously fickle Bangkok electorate. In the northeast, the Social Action Party (SAP) defeated the Democrats in a 1982 by-election and the 1983 election in a constituency won by the Democrats in 1969, 1975, 1976, and 1979. Hopes that the Democrat Party can regain from SAP seats they lost in 1979 seem unrealistic.

National Democracy Party (NDP; *Chat Prachathippatai*)

History

The NDP is General Kriangsak Chomanan's personal political vehicle. He formed the party in the spring of 1981 and was elected to Parliament in a hotly contested by-election in the poor northeastern constituency of Roi-et in August 1981. Upon Kriangsak's election, several disparate groups within the National Assembly threw their support behind the NDP, which has fluctuated between thirty to fifty adherents in the House ever since. While the NDP is now the largest party outside the current coalition government it has only three seats of its own in the national legislature. Kriangsak, prime minister from October 1977 to February 1980, serves as the unofficial leader of the opposition.

Organization

The party is a conglomeration of several competing factions linked to Kriangsak, apparently with the hope of advancing their interests or ideology under his banner. Specifically, each group hopes to use Kriangsak's national stature to elect their own allies to the next Assembly.

Only the general himself holds these groups together. The factions battle vigorously for control of the NDP, making the party by far the most diverse in the Parliament. Kriangsak tries to stay above the factions, hoping to hold onto each while not alienating the others. This is the same style he used to lead his cabinet after the 1979 elections.

The most conservative NDP group is centered around Thawit Klinprathum, House member from Mahasarakham. Thawit was a leading member of the United Thai People's Party (UTPP), the government party under Field Marshals Thanom and Praphat. Later, he was leader of the Social Justice Party, one of four military-supported parties which grew out of the UTPP to contest the 1975 and 1976 elections.

Wattana Asavahem, a legislator from Samut Prakan, is perhaps second in power to Kriangsak. Wattana was a deputy industry minister in the Thanin regime. A wealthy businessman, he gave substantial funds to the Red Gaurs, a violent right-wing vocational students' organization. (A gaur is a huge wild ox native to Thailand.) Wattana led the Mass Line Party (*Naew Mahachon*) in the 1979 election; he then brought thirty-four winners (including Thawit's group) to the new NDP. Thawit has supported Wattana, but on the whole his faction acts independently of Wattana. Also in Wattana's grouping, but with independent ties to Kriangsak, is Police Major General Sa-nga Kittikachorn, a House member from Chiang Mai.

A third group directly opposes Wattana. It is headed by Ob Vasuratna, a wealthy businessman who was commerce minister under Kriangsak. Several members of this faction were prominent in the Seritham Party which was formed by the "technocrats" in the first Kriangsak cabinet to contest the 1979 elections and to provide Kriangsak with a base in the House. The Seritham Party (translated either as Freedom and Justice Party or Just Liberal Party, but almost never referred to by its English name) won twenty-one seats in 1979. It has since ceased to function.

Another faction in the party is headed by Dr. Arthit Urairat, a cofounder of the liberal New Force Party and now general secretary of the NDP. Arthit and a group of other former New Force members recruited to serve in Kriangsak's government have stayed with him as the most realistic way to achieve an active role in the political system. Allied with them are a group of lower-ranking military officers who have supported Kriangsak since 1977. Many of these "Young Turks" allied themselves with General Prem in the second Kriangsak cabinet, but have since returned to his side, especially after their participation in the coup of April 1981. They are an important source of military support for the NDP.

Policy

Given the diversity of its constituent parts, it is difficult to know how the National Democracy Party would govern if it came to power. The nature of the ruling coalition would probably determine which NDP faction emerged dominant.

Kriangsak's policies can be surmised from his twenty-eight-month tenure as prime minister. At first, Kriangsak received accolades for his appointment of one of the most skilled, nonpolitical cabinets in memory. People also applauded his carefully paced return to a modified constitutional democracy. Kriangsak's postelection cabinet in May 1979, on the other hand, came under heavy criticism. Kriangsak was attacked both for his lack of strong support in the elected House and for making the political accommodations necessary to gain the support he did have. After Vietnam's invasion of Kampuchea in December 1978, Kriangsak's accommodationist policies toward Asian communist governments were perceived to have left Thailand weak and vulnerable.

Thailand faced economic difficulties based on its reliance on imported Iranian oil. Kriangsak raised petroleum prices several times to account for increased costs, but encountered consumer resentment. He also tightened credit to bring down the inflation rate, then hovering between 18 and 20 percent, causing business to join the chorus of opposition. A final round of oil-price increases brought the government down in February 1980. One economic policy deemed a success was Kriangsak's distribution of nearly $1 billion to local agricultural development projects. If the past is any indication, Kriangsak's hard-nosed economic policy would be good for the country in the long term, but painful and unpopular in the interim. However, if the Vietnamese presence in Kampuchea proves intractable to military pressure, or the anti-Vietnam sentiment in the Association of South East Asian Nations (ASEAN) weakens, Kriangsak's diplomatic skills may once again be in demand.

Membership & Constituency

The National Democracy Party has a small membership base, owing to its relatively recent formation. Its popular support appeared to be relatively weak since it won only three seats in the 1983 elections.

Financing

The party's funding comes primarily from the businessmen surrounding Ob, whose faction's power is based on their financial contributions. Wattana's group provides the primary political and parliamentary support. The party gives a stipend of $300 per month to each of its legislators. Total party expenses amount to about $240,000 a year.

Leadership

All positions are temporary until an upcoming party congress. Kriangsak (born 1917) is unchallenged for party leader. Ob is chairman of the Central Executive Committee, and Wattana is its secretary.

Prospects

General Kriangsak has the closest ties to the United States government of any Thai military or political leader, and he has support from many of the diverse constituencies that affect Thai politics. As such, he will remain a potent threat to any government for the foreseeable future. He is also one of the few men of sufficient stature and reknown to lead the country.

Kriangsak also has a number of liabilities. His policies, particularly improved relations with the Soviet Union and Vietnam, are out of step with the current foreign-policy consensus. The issue on which the country is in greatest need of competent leadership, economic policy, was the area of Kriangsak's greatest vulnerability as prime minister. He has little support in the army and engenders active enmity from the monarchy. If Kriangsak and the NDP are able to achieve a strong popular endorsement in the next election, however, he will be the obvious choice to replace Prem.

New Force Party
(*Palang Mai*)

History

The New Force Party is considered here not because of its electoral or political strength, nor because of its likely future impact. It has only one seat in the National Assembly. The party's significance lies in its unique ideological and symbolic position in the parliament. Moreover, its development reveals much of the promise and the failure of recent Thai political history.

The New Force Party was founded in 1974 by a group of intellectuals, teachers, and students, many of whom had been involved in the unrest which brought down the military regime in October 1973. The party was seen by many of its founders as the natural outgrowth of the Developing Democracy Program, an activity sponsored by the government of Prime Minister Sanya which sent thousands of university and secondary school students into rural areas to promote election participation and citizenship. Moderate student activists joined the New Force Party; others joined one of six other new leftist parties or the Communist Party of Thailand. The party's first head was Dr. Krasae Chanawongse, noted for his rural health work.

The first party platform called for the immediate withdrawal of all United States troops from Thailand, normalization of relations with Vietnam and the People's Republic of China, land reform, nationalization of key industries, and repeal of the Anti-Communist Law. With the exception of the nationalization issue, this program was shared by several parties, including the Democrats. Although it ran a strong second to the Democrats in Bangkok, overall the party did poorly in the 1975 elections, winning only twelve seats, seven of them in the northeast.

In the four months preceding the April 1976 elections, Thailand's progressive political parties were virtually destroyed, and with them, perhaps, the notion of incremental change through the electoral system. Over thirty left-wing politicians were killed in the period immediately prior to the election. The headquarters of the New Force Party were bombed by two members of the Red Gaurs. A large propaganda campaign was conducted to discredit the left parties. All distinctions between socialists and communists were blurred in the public's mind. Socialists were portrayed as being opposed to sacred institutions, particularly the monarchy. A group of right-wing Buddhist clerics emerged; one of them, Kittiwuttho, declared that "killing communists is not sinful." The campaign also played upon external events. The forced abdication of the king of Laos by the Pathet Lao and the destruction of the *ancien regime* in Kampuchea were used to scare conservative rural voters.

The New Force Party parliamentary bloc was reduced from twelve to three. Total left representation went from thirty-seven to six, as a percentage, the lowest in any House since the end of World War II. Nevertheless, the election returns were ambiguous. The New Force Party increased the number and percentage of the votes it received from 1 million, constituting 5.9 percent in 1975, to 1.3 million, constituting 7 percent in 1976.

The New Force Party reemerged to contest the 1979 elections, while the Socialist and Socialist Front Parties combined to form the Social Democratic Party (*Prachathipat Sangkhom*). Kriangsak's new coalition was supported by three parties, with a combined voting strength of seventy seats, and the New Force Party was one of these three.

Since the accession of Prime Minister Prem, the New Force Party has voted with the opposition. Several members switched their allegiance to Kriangsak's National Democracy Party, leaving New Force with only one adherent in the Assembly following the 1983 election.

Organization

The New Force Party claims to have a number of active branches, particularly in the northeast and south. A Youth Union of New Force was established in 1981 to strengthen the party's base in the universities and to recruit volunteers for the April 1983 election. While this effort has had some success it has not attracted as much support as party leaders originally had anticipated.

Policy

The party claims "not to have forsaken its original ideology." No other information is available.

Financing

The party has traditionally suffered from inadequate financing in election campaigns. Several industrialists who made major contributions in 1975 were intimidated from further support by the anti-left campaign in 1976. The party is taking the unusual approach of making regional branches responsible for their own election expenses, though this may be more a matter of facing reality than of choice.

Leadership

Krasae resigned as party leader in 1980, although he remains an influential advisor. Somwang Srichai took over as party leader in 1981 in a contentious intraparty election. The new Central Committee was elected in the beginning of 1982, with House member Suthep Wongkamhaeng as secretary general. Anuparb Choon-on, a former leader of the Thammasat University Student Union, is secretary general of the Youth Union.

Prospects

The party fielded a large number of candidates in the 1983 election but, as noted above won only one seat. There are no reasons to expect any dramatic improvements in the party's future electoral record.

Social Action Party (SAP; *Kit Sangkhom*)

History

The SAP was founded in 1974 by Kukrit Pramoj in preparation for the 1975 elections. Kukrit had been speaker of the indirectly elected National Assembly just prior to forming the SAP. Kukrit brought into the party many associates from his business activities, and the SAP was known in its early days for its technocrats. Prime among these was Kukrit's colleague in the Bangkok Bank, its vice chairman, Boonchu Rojanasathien, who became SAP's secretary general. Other people joined the party from the Democrats and the military-supported United Thai People's Party.

SAP's program for the election, as described by Kukrit, contained some jingoistic elements as well as some proposals for economic reform. For example, Kukrit blamed "clever Chinese businessmen" for poverty in the countryside. He supported labor unions while decrying "communist-inspired" union leaders. He also attacked student activism. On the other hand, SAP proposed a number of specific programs to alleviate poverty, including a floor on the wholesale price of rice, free education and medical care for the poor, slum clearance, housing construction for Bangkok workers, and a minimum wage. The party won eighteen seats in the election. All except one (Kukrit's) came from outside Bangkok. Boonchu reportedly spent $1,000,000 to win his seat.

After the defeat of Seni's brief government, Kukrit became prime minister in a coalition with Thai Nation, Social Justice, and seven smaller rightist parties. Boonchu and Kukrit initiated many of the social programs outlined in the SAP's election platform. The Parliament passed an enormous budget for fiscal year 1976; it included a 29 percent spending increase and a commensurate increase in government borrowing. Much of the country's foreign currency reserves were depleted. SAP began perhaps the most innovative and politically popular program ever—the Tambon Development Funds effort, which distributed $25,000 to each of 5,000 *tambons*, an administrative unit of ten to fifteen villages. These monies were used to build roads, bridges, irrigation systems, schools, health centers, or electrification projects as the local tambon council decided. The Tambon Development Funds program is the political flag of the Social Action Party; it accounted in large part for SAP's ensuing success in 1976 and 1979 and remains its prime selling point to Thailand's 80 percent rural population.

The SAP-led government was also distinguished by its diplomacy with the communist nations. Relations were established with the Soviet Union, China, North Korea, Vietnam, Laos, and Kampuchea, and Kukrit began to play off Soviet and Chinese interests. Relations with the United States were less successfully handled. Military aid to Thailand was cut drastically. Deteriorating relations with the United States caused a sense of alarm in Thai military ranks about the will of the Kukrit government to protect Thailand from communist threats. This alarm was instrumental in forcing the government's collapse.

The fall of the coalition came when opposition to Kukrit's policies, particularly urban opposition to a floor on wholesale rice prices, the one campaign promise Social Action ultimately failed to fulfill, caused defections within the right-wing parties. Kukrit was forced by the military to call new elections when it became clear that a center-left coalition might gain a majority position in the National Assembly.

The April 1976 election made the SAP the third-largest party in the House. Ironically, it was also rendered politically impotent: Kukrit ran fourth in his constituency in Bangkok, defeated by a right-wing Democrat who was supported by the military-backed parties.

In 1979, the party ran a vigorous campaign, well-financed and supported by strong local candidates. Kukrit travelled nationally to ridicule Kriangsak's economic program which had resulted in high inflation, and to remind voters of his successful term in office and of the heralded Tambon Fund. Social Action won nearly twice as many seats as the next-largest party in the House. However, Kukrit could not topple Kriangsak, as the constitution allowed the Senate to vote with the House in forming the government. Kriangsak, as prime minister, had controlled the appointment of the Senate.

Kukrit organized continual trouble for Kriangsak in the House, where the prime minister had little support. At one point, Kukrit engineered a 155 to zero vote censuring Kriangsak in his role as agriculture minister. However, Kukrit's situation was delicate, since strong pressure on Kriangsak might lead to another army coup. Kriangsak ultimately resigned for lack of parliamentary support, but his post went to his defense minister, General Prem, rather than to Kukrit.

Social Action joined the Prem cabinet. Boonchu became deputy prime minister in charge of economic policy; Amnuay Virawan became finance minister; and Tamchai Khampato was appointed commerce minister. Boonchu designed a policy intended to restore the rapid rates of economic growth that Thailand had enjoyed before the rise of foreign oil prices. The policy, which he labelled "Thailand Incorporated" and which won widespread praise from Western economists, removed government economic controls and provided for greater reliance on market forces. The Social Action Party's control over economic policy, though, was limited by Thai Nation's control of the agriculture and industry portfolios. A sharp dispute occurred in March 1981, when Thai Nation defied Boonchu's right to oversee economic policy in those fields. Prem sided with Thai Nation, and Social Action withdrew from the cabinet. Social Action rejoined the Prem government in December 1981, over Boonchu's objections and without a position for him in the cabinet. Boonchu thereupon resigned his position in the party. Although it lost thirty Assembly seats in the 1983 elections, it remains a potent force in Thai politics.

Organization

The party is second only to the Democrats in its local organization. It has maintained and nurtured its relations with members of the local *tambon* councils which administered the Tambon Development Funds. Its eighty-six House members have the reputation of being particularly attentive to the needs of local constituents, thereby extending the party's base in rural areas.

Policy

Social Action is committed to achieving a more equitable distribution of wealth without resorting to nationalization or socialism. The party continues to endorse national government support for decentralized rural development. Boonchu is presently stressing the need for regional economic cooperation within ASEAN.

Membership & Constituency

No information is available.

Financing

Financial support in the past has come from the banking and business communities surrounding Kukrit and Boonchu. The party has been the best funded of any of the non-military-backed parties.

Leadership

Kukrit Pramoj (born 1910), long the dominant figure in the Social Action Party, resigned in the wake of the party's poor showing in the 1985 by-elections. He was replaced by Deputy party leader Siddhi Savetsila as part of a reor-

ganization of the party in preparation for the 1987 general elections.

Prospects

The aging Kukrit did not seek a House seat in the 1983 elections. Moreover, his inability to campaign actively for Social Action candidates was an important factor in the party's losses in the 1983 election. In general, the party will need a leader to give it identity and appeal at the polls. The party's appeal in rural areas remains strong. While it should maintain its current influence in future elections it does not appear sufficiently powerful to replace Prem and the Democrats.

Thai Nation Party
(*Chat Thai*)

History

Four of the parties which contested the 1975 elections had significant support from the military. Three of the four, Social Justice, Social Nationalist, and Social Agrarian, were alike in that their backing came from the military leadership that had ruled Thailand from 1957 to 1973. The fourth party, Thai Nation, founded in 1974, was centered around a group of military men who had been on the losing side of the 1957 coup.

In the 1975 elections, Thai Nation ran particularly well in the central and northeast regions, the source of twenty-two of their twenty-eight seats. The surprise and disappointment of the 1975 election for Thai Nation was the defeat by Boonchu of party deputy leader Siri Siriyothin in Siri's home constituency. On the whole, Thai Nation ran young civilians rather than military officers in most districts, a successful tactic that it continues to the present. The Thai Nation Party played the major role in defeating the Seni coalition and the Democrats in the House immediately after the election; it was given the greatest number of portfolios in the new Kukrit cabinet—seven. The 1976 election campaign was filled with strident verbal attacks on the left parties, much of it carried on state-controlled media under Siri's direction. It is also thought that the physical violence against the left was financed and directed by the Internal Security Operations Command, the military's anti-insurgency unit controlled by Thai Nation leader Praman Adireksan. Praman made two now-famous statements during the campaign. The first was his exhortation on state radio, "Right kill Left." The second was his suggestion that a bombing of the headquarters of the New Force Party had been done by their own supporters to attract sympathy. Thai Nation won 18 percent of the national vote and doubled the number of seats they held from twenty-eight to fifty-six, advances made largely at the expense of the other right-wing parties. Thai Nation had become the largest of the military-backed parties and the second-largest party overall.

Thai Nation engineered one more event of consequence in the 1976 election. By running a combined slate with the Democrats in the Dusit constituency in Bangkok, and through active solicitation of local military commanders, the party was able to ensure the defeat of Kukrit by right-wing Democrat Samak Sundaravej and thus destroy any chance of a coalition led by the Social Action Party.

Thai Nation was in many ways the critical factor that immobilized the government in the six months from April to October 1976. The presence of Thai Nation prevented Seni from purging the right from his party, and it gave the right the strength to resist Seni and to act independently. With his own party and the coalition split, Seni was incapable of acting decisively.

The Thai Nation leadership did not fare well over the following year and a half of military rule. The military factions that functioned as the National Administrative Reform Council and the Revolutionary Party were opposed to Praman's clique. None of the top three Thai Nation leaders served in the Thanin and Kriangsak cabinets, but it has participated in all four Prem coalition governments since. Thai Nation demanded the right to run its ministries free of outside interference. At times this has meant being independent of Prime Minister Prem as well.

Organization

The party is commonly reported to continue to have extensive influence over the nation's media. In the 1974–76 period, Praman was supposed to control all television and most radio broadcasts through his contracts with a small group of station managers. The party is controlled by its three leaders and consists of their personal followers and clients.

Policy

The party is in accord ideologically with Prem's austerity budgets and strong anti-Vietnam foreign-policy stance. Having moved somewhat closer to the center of the political spectrum, it still emphasizes strict law and order, while supporting modest social welfare programs.

Membership & Constituency

Active and retired military officers form the most important part of the party's membership, although it has recently made an active attempt to recruit support from other sectors of the society in an attempt to broaden its base for future elections. The party's power derives from its influence in the military and the business community as much as from its representatives in the National Assembly.

Financing

Thai Nation is by reputation the wealthiest party and the largest spender in election campaigns. Much of the money is reported to come from Japanese business interests which want to see General Praman remain in the government. Much of the party's success is attributed to its ample funding.

Leadership

The three men dominant when the party began in 1974 still control the party today. Major General Praman Adireksan is deputy prime minister in the Prem cabinet and leader of the party. He served as deputy communications minister from 1951 to 1955 and minister of industry from 1956 to 1958. He then became the leading figure in Thailand's huge textile industry as president of the Association of Thai Industries and of the Thai Textile Manufacturers' Association. The leading spokesman for Japanese economic interests in Thailand, Praman's business practices earned him a fiercely antilabor reputation.

Major General Chatichai Choonhawan is minister of industry in the Prem government.

He was deputy foreign minister in Sanya's government.

Major General Siri Siriyothin, deputy leader of the party, was elected to the House from Chonburi in 1969 with the United Thai People's Party. He was speaker of the House from 1969 to 1971 and president of the appointed National Assembly established after the 1971 coup.

Prospects

Thai Nation is the second-largest party in Thailand, and by many criteria, it has been the most powerful political party in recent years. The Thai Nation's Party increased its seats in the National Assembly to sixty-three in the 1983 election and participated in all three Prem coalition governments before 1983. However, it was not a part of the Prem coalition in 1983 and is unlikely to lead a government in the near future. The party has neither an individual capable of assuming the prime minister's post, nor the potential of gaining enough seats to become the largest party in the parliament. Nonetheless, the party will in all likelihood remain an important force, continuing to win in a significant number of districts.

Thai People's Party
(*Prachakon Thai*)

History

The Thai People's Party was founded just prior to the 1979 election by its present leader, Samak Sundaravej, a former right-wing Democrat. The party fielded forty-three candidates and won thirty-two seats, immediately establishing itself as the third-largest party in the House. Especially notable was its sweep of twenty-nine of thirty-two constituencies in Bangkok, the traditional stronghold of the Democrats. Samak, a highly charismatic figure, ran an aggressive campaign, making numerous speeches on behalf of each of his party's candidates, few of whom were known in their own right. Samak ridiculed Prime Minister Kriangsak's economic policies, particularly those reflected by rising food and petroleum prices. Samak was thought to have been aided by the extremely low turnout in Bangkok. Samak has been one of the leaders of the opposition to the Prem cabinets, although he is even more scorn-

ful of fellow opposition leader General Kriangsak than of Prem.

Organization

Samak is closely tied to three right-wing vigilante groups—*Nawapon*, the Red Gaurs, and the Village Scouts—which are supported by the military and which have played a critical role as opponents of the leftist-oriented university student movement. These three groups form the organizational base of the Thai People's Party. The Village Scouts took many of Samak's supporters to the polls in Bangkok in 1979.

Policy

The party is closely associated with the military and is the farthest right of any of the major parties in the present Parliament. Samak has been quoted as saying that coups are inevitable, traditional, and to some degree desirable. He has been compared to European fascists of the 1930s in that he caters to the economic concerns of the lower middle class and is strongly identified with law and order and extreme forms of nationalism and militarism. Samak's strong personality and authoritarian values have an appeal in times of economic or social unrest.

Membership & Constituency

No information is available on membership. The party's primary strength is in Bangkok.

Financing

No information is available.

Leadership

Samak's biography is illustrative of the ideological position of his party and is important because he is likely to remain a significant figure in Thai politics. Samak was elected in 1976 as a Democrat from the Dusit constituency in Bangkok with strong support from the military. He was deeply involved in the struggle for control of the Democrats and served on the Democrat Party Central Committee and as deputy interior minister in the 1976 Seni cabinet until Seni, under pressure from the party's moderates, dropped Samak in a cabinet reshuffle.

Samak helped to engineer the disruptive return from exile of Field Marshal Thanom in 1976, which spurred large student and labor demonstrations demanding Thanom's ouster from the country. Allegedly, he also orchestrated much of the violence against those same demonstrators and the popular agitation for a crackdown on leftists which immediately preceded the military coup in October. Samak was appointed minister of the interior by Prime Minister Thanin Kraivichien in late 1976 and implemented Thailand's most brutal repression in this century. His political strength apparently derives in part from his friendship with Queen Sirikit, who at times supports the extreme right in the military. Samak's disdain for General Kriangsak stems from the general's leadership role in overthrowing Thanin.

Prospects

Samak fielded candidates in most of the country's constituencies in the April 1983 elections. Because of his previous electoral success, his close ties with the military, and his valuable base in the nation's capital, Samak has been able to attract strong candidates and ample financial backing. Given the state of Thailand's economy, Samak's prospects seem excellent, both to keep his base in Bangkok and to extend his support into the countryside.

Minor Parties

In the last four elections perhaps as many as ninety different political parties were registered with the Ministry of Interior. Few survived to contest more than one election. None of the minor parties listed below is expected to have a significant impact on the parliament, the political system, or the polity, but they are worthy of mention because they once had some importance or because they are indicative of some aspect of Thai political culture.

Social Democratic Party (*Sangkhom Prachathipatai*)

A coalition of the Socialist Party of Thailand and the Socialist Front Party, the Social Democrats draw their strength from the northeast. The SDP contested the 1979 and 1983 elections, winning three seats. It is moderate socialist.

Social Agrarian Party (*Kaset Sangkhom*) and Social Justice Party (*Dharama Sangkhom*)

Two of the four military-supported rightwing parties to emerge in 1974, both parties have since been eclipsed by Thai Nation.

Freedom and Justice Party (*Seritham*)

This centrist group sponsored apolitical "technocrat" candidates from the first Kriangsak cabinet to give Kriangsak a base in the House after the 1979 election. It was eclipsed by Kriangsak's National Democracy Party, and became defunct in 1983.

Pro General Kriangsak (*Sanap-Sanoon Kriangsak*)

This group is an example of numerous onetime tiny parties formed to advocate a particular position, in this case the policies of Prime Minister Kriangsak.

Other Political Forces

Military

Even since the overthrow of the absolute monarchy in 1932, the military—especially the army—has dominated Thai political life. No other force is capable of challenging army dominance successfully. The armed forces have offered an attractive opportunity for upward mobility to young men of lower-middle-class backgrounds. By passing competitive examinations to attend the cadet academy and then the Chulachomklao Royal Military Academy, they have been able to gain great career potential.

While military professionalism is certainly evident in Thailand's modern officer corps, factional conflict and pervasive corruption are even more striking institutional characteristics. Indeed, Thai politics revolve around the competition among various factional groups led by senior army generals. These groups compete not only for government power but also for access to enormous private wealth.

Students

Student activism and participation in the political process are recent phenomena in Thailand. From 1932 to about 1968, students played a minimal role, either remaining silent politically or responding to manipulation by military leaders. By the early 1970s, however, students had become a major force on the Thai political scene. They were able to articulate growing public disaffection with corruption under military rule and with the growing gap between the wealthy beneficiaries of economic development and the masses of the poor who were being left behind.

In 1973, students led the nation in ending military rule; at least temporarily. From then to 1976, the National Student Center of Thailand (NSCT) influenced most important government decisions. Yet the student movement lacked cohesion and lost power through factional competition. When the military seized power again in October 1976, their violent attack on the NSCT caused hundreds of student activists to flee from Bangkok to join forces with the Communist Party of Thailand. By 1978–79, however, most had decided to accept the government's offer of amnesty rather than to continue to face tensions within the revolutionary party. In 1983, the students' political presence was again minimal, though their awesome power during the 1970s suggested that this group may well be heard from again in Thailand.

Organized Labor

The extent to which labor groups have been organized, and thus able to wield effective political power, fluctuates with the vagaries of overall Thai politics. Under military rule, labor's influence has been relatively modest. Only those unions acceptable to the military leadership are allowed to organize. The unions' strongest influence is in the public utility sector: electricity, water, transportation, and so on.

During the period of open politics in the 1970s, however, labor organizations burgeoned in size, level of activity, and political influence. Strikes became a daily event in the Bangkok area. Extensive labor demands for increased wages and improved working conditions, along with the growing power of organized labor in the Socialist Party and in the parliament as a whole, contributed directly to the growing fears of the middle class and to the violence of 1976. Yet labor unions by then had attained such po-tential power that no government—elected or military—could outlaw them entirely, as army leaders had done in the 1950s and 1960s. While the 1976 coup group dissolved the more radical labor organizations, it left the Federation of Labor Unions of Thailand intact as a moderate, nonideological spokesman for the country's workers.

Communist Party of Thailand (CPT)

The revolutionary movement in Thailand, led by the Communist Party, faced major challenges in 1983. Yet its political base in many rural villages remained quite strong, and the Communists continued to pose a potent long-term threat to the continued hegemony of the conservative power structure entrenched in Bangkok.

The party's weakness in 1983 was due to the unprecedented intense conflict among its fraternal Communist allies. Vietnam's invasion of Democratic Kampuchea at the end of 1978, the overthrow of Pol Pot and his replacement by Heng Samrin, and China's invasion of Vietnam shook CPT leadership badly. The Vietnamese expelled Thai party cadres from Laos and ordered their training base closed. The party's leadership felt closer to China than to Vietnam, but bitter disputes arose within the party's Central Committee not only over external relations, but over the very basis of revolutionary strategy in Thailand, the nature of ideology, cadre leadership and the role of "intellectuals" in a mass movement, the importance of armed struggle versus political action, and over the relative priority of social unrest and revolutionary power in rural and urban areas, respectively. As a result of these tensions, nearly all of the student converts of the late 1970s left the revolutionary movement to return to Bangkok, confused and disillusioned.

Before this chaos, the CPT had risen to national prominence. Its military bases were centered in remote parts of the northeast, north, and south; and party cadres controlled daily life in several hundred organized "combat villages." While no threat to Bangkok in the immediate future, the party's combination of unified central leadership committed to long-term struggle, its potent guerrilla capabilities, and its sensitivity to village political grievances all suggested a growing capacity to vie with the Bangkok regime for control of important parts of the realm.

The party's disarray since 1982 provided time for the central government to devise effective mechanisms to cope with the nation's many political and social problems. Yet, ironically, this adversity may turn out to have been a gift to the Thai Communist Party, forcing it for the first time to develop a truly Thai rather than a Chinese or Soviet approach to revolution. In the end, only such a Siamese conception of revolution can hope to succeed in Thailand.

Buddhism

Political activism entered the ranks of Thai Buddhism in the 1970s, as it entered all other major institutions in the country. Some monks with nationwide reputations adopted an aggessive anticommunist stance, even to the extent of justifying violence and murder. Other monks openly affiliated themselves with the new groups on the left, a few joining in street demonstrations, and an activist Young Monks Movement became significant in the 1970s. While miniscule in size compared to the overall monkhood, this unprecedented development of political consciousness is reflected in other areas of Thai society.

National Prospects

In past decades, Thailand's politics were characterized by a remarkable degree of political passivity and conservatism. Mass acceptance of hierarchical paternalism, especially in the villages, was matched by co-optation of the elite under military leadership. In general, Thais felt satisfied with their status in the land of royal plentitude. In recent years there have been increasing questions raised about the roles of both the monarchy and the military in Thai politics.

The next few years seem most likely to witness a gradually declining spiral of government performance in economic and political spheres. One or more army coups are nearly certain, as military factionalism remains unchecked. Infla-

tion will continue to trouble economic policymakers, and the troublesome gap between rich and poor will widen rather than shrink. Production of natural gas from the Gulf of Siam will be helpful, but overall demands for economic equity and political participation will threaten the military elite and its commercial allies, as they did in the early 1980s. Most profoundly, Thais have to resolve the dilemma of their traditional royal institution's role in the modern era. Can the increasing politicization of the monarchy in recent years be blunted, or will the basic structure of the Thai polity have to change to accommodate an activist royal institution? Can this traditional source of political legitimacy be fused with new approaches to popular participation, or will it remain attached to military power and bureaucratic authoritarianism? These are the most significant questions facing Thai politics for the remainder of the 1980s.

Further Reading

Banks, Arthur S., and Overstreet, William, eds. *Political Handbook of the World: 1981.* New York: McGraw-Hill Book Co., 1981.

Chai-anan Samudavanija. *The Thai Young Turks.* Singapore: Institute of Southeast Asian Studies, 1982.

Girling, John. *Thailand: Society and Politics.* Ithaca, N. Y.: Cornell University Press, 1981.

Keyes, Charles F. *Thailand.* Boulder, Colo.; Westview Press, 1986.

Marks, Thomas A. "October 1976 and the Role of the Military in Thai Politics." *Modern Asian Studies,* Vol. 14, No. 4, 1980.

Morell, David, and Chai-anan Samundavanija. *Political Conflict in Thailand: Reform, Reaction, Revolution.* Cambridge, Mass.: Oelgeschlager, Gunn & Hain Publishers, Inc., 1981.

Neher, Clark D., ed. *Modern Thai Politics: From Village to Nation.* Cambridge, Mass.: Schenkman Publishing Co., 1979.

Thak Chaloemtiarana. *Thailand: The Politics of Despotic Paternalism.* Bangkok: Social Science Association of Thailand, 1979.

Turton, Andrew; Fast, Jonathan; and Caldwell, Malcolm, eds. *Thailand: Roots of Conflict.* Nottingham, England: Spokesman, 1978.

REPUBLIC OF TOGO
(République de Togo)
by Peter Schraeder, M.A.

The System of Government

Togo, a nation of nearly three million people, has a highly centralized, one-party political system with nearly all power held by the president. The current president and leader of the Assembly of Togolese People (RPT), the official party of the Nation, is Gnassingbe Eyadema. Eyadema seized power in 1967 in a military coup that ended seven years of parliamentary government in Togo.

The current constitution of Togo was enacted in December 1979. This constitution began what is called the Third Republic of Togo, ending twelve years of emergency military rule under which Togo had no constitution or legislature.

Executive

Under the current system, the president is head of state, government, administration, and the military. The power of the president is nearly unlimited, with much of the governing process taking place through executive decree rather than through legislation. The president has the power to appoint a cabinet, which serves primarily as a body of specialized experts, and to appoint all other civil and military officials. The president may dissolve the legislature after consultation with the Political Bureau of the official party. After the legislature is dissolved, the president must hold new elections within three months.

The president is chosen by direct national election for a seven-year term. He may stand for an unlimited number of reelections. In the elections held in December of 1979, which were the first in Togo since 1960, Eyadema was the only candidate for the presidency. He received 99.7 percent of the votes cast.

Legislature

The legislature of Togo, which is called the National Assembly, was dissolved following the 1967 military coup and re-created by the constitution of 1979. The elections of 1979 were the first held since 1960. The process has now become institutionalized, as a second set of legislative elections was held in March of 1986. New election laws allowed 216 candidates to present themselves for seventy-seven seats (only 131 names remained on the list at election time). Participation of the electoral roll was 78.8 percent, with only twenty out of sixty-six deputies reelected.

The National Assembly is a unicameral body with seventy-seven seats; members serve for five-year terms. The National Assembly meets in two ordinary sessions per year, one convening in April and one in October. Extraordinary sessions may be called by the president. These extraordinary sessions meet with a fixed agenda, ending when the agenda is completed.

The realm of the National Assembly's lawmaking power is strictly limited by the constitution. All powers not explicitly given to the National Assembly are considered administrative issues, and thus are decided by the executive. While members of the National Assembly have the power to initiate legislation, the issues placed before the National Assembly are tightly controlled by the president. Thus, the National Assembly usually serves as a rubber stamp for policies instigated by the president and the leaders of the official party.

Judiciary

The judiciary of Togo played a partially independent political role before 1976, but after that date Eyadema tightened his control over the judiciary. The current judiciary usually follows the president's policies closely.

The highest court in Togo is the Supreme Court. This body is made up of a Constitutional

Chamber, a Judicial Chamber, an Administrative Chamber, and an Audits Chamber. Each of these rules on issues within its field of expertise.

All judicial officials are appointed by the president.

Regional and Local Government

For administrative purposes, Togo is divided into four provinces governed by inspectors appointed by the president. The provinces are divided further into districts, each with a district chief and a ruling committee called a special delegation. These officials, too, are appointed by the president. The six major urban areas of Togo are governed by elected councils who appoint mayors.

Local government in Togo serves primarily as a means of administration. All local political policy is made at the national level by the president and the Political Bureau of the official party.

The Electoral System

Elections in Togo are direct, with the president and the deputies to the National Assembly representing the nation as a whole. Suffrage is universal and automatic for all. For the presidential elections, a single candidate is nominated by the party. Nominations for legislative elections have changed. Whereas under the 1979 constitution legislative candidates were nominated by the party, in 1986 individuals were able to present themselves and canvass for votes throughout the country. Eyadema has called this change the second stage of the process of democratization of Togolese institutions (the first being the adoption of a constitution in 1979). The goal is to involve the people more in choosing their political leaders. Eligibility for office is straight forward: one must be at least twenty-five years of age, have asked for and received the approval of the RPT'S political bureau, and have deposited 50,000 CFA (reimbursements are given to those obtaining at least 10 percent of the popular vote).

Assembly of Togolese People (*Rassemblement du Peuple Togolais; RPT*)

The constitution states that the RPT forms the framework for all political activity in Togo. All citizens are encouraged to participate in party activities.

Before the 1967 coup there were four major parties in Togo. These parties were organized on regional and tribal lines, as the tribes of northern Togo attempted to prevent the numerically dominant Ewe tribe from controlling the government.

History

The RPT was formed after the 1967 coup to integrate the various tribal factions and to replace the military officials in the government with civilian ones. The RPT has largely succeeded in these goals because the urban Ewe elite has become involved in the party-sponsored development projects, and because of great popular support for Eyadema.

Organization

The organization of the RPT is pyramidal, and policymaking power is concentrated at the higher levels of the party. At the base of the party's organizational pyramid are numerous local and village groups along with auxiliary party organizations for labor, youth, and women. At the apex is the Central Committee of the party and the nine-member Political Bureau. The Political Bureau, which is chaired by Eyadema, is the chief policymaking body of Togo.

The primary purpose of the RPT has not been to provide a forum for political discussion and debate, but rather to mobilize popular support for policies created by the party elite. Most of these policies have dealt with the economic development of Togo. Recent changes in the electoral laws may provide for greater mass participation in the political process.

Policy

The policy of RPT is centered mainly on the tasks of economic development, political education, and the creation of a sense of national unity through the deemphasis of local and ethnic issues.

Membership & Constituency

Membership is universal for eligible voters. No data is available on the number of party activists.

Financing

The RPT is financed by compulsory "contributions" from the members, in effect, a tax on eligible voters.

Leadership

As the leader of both the government and the RPT, Eyadema is by far the most powerful figure in Togolese politics. Enjoying wide popularity, he has encouraged a personality cult in which he is pictured as the "Guide" and political savior of Togo. Eyadema was born in 1937 of peasant stock in northern Togo. He joined the French army in 1953, serving in Indochina and Algeria. While a noncommissioned officer, he was instrumental in the 1963 coup which ousted President Sylvanus Olympio. When a civilian government was reinstated after this coup, Eyadema quickly rose in rank. He was chief of the general staff at the time of the 1967 coup which brought him to power.

Eyadema is a member of the Kabre tribe, and thus his support is strongest in the northern, Kabre regions of the country. Northerners from Eyadema's ethnic group and family occupy influential positions in the government. Eyadema's half-brother, Lt. Toi Donou, heads the presidential guard, and the president's cousin, Yaya Malou, heads the police academy. Southerners also have influential posts in the government. Kpotivi Tevi Lacle, for example, is minister of the interior. It is rumored Eyadema is grooming his son as his potential successor.

Eyadema began delegating power in 1985, leaving daily operation of the government to Gbegnon Amegboh, a southerner heading the Ministry of Information. It is reported that Eyadema's public appearances are decreasing, with the president spending more time in his home village of Pya.

National Prospects

Economic difficulties, coupled with bombing attacks and human rights abuses, have marred the political stability Togo enjoyed during the 1970s. Togo has suffered economically due to a world slump in phosphate prices since 1975; that commodity provides one-half of the nation's hard currency earnings and one-third of its budgetary revenues. Also, the Eyadema regime has been accused of trying to cover up gross economic mismanagement of the economy. Even more unsettling to the regime was a wave of bomb attacks in late 1985, one of which exploded at RPT headquarters. Serious political challenges to the still popular Eyadema, however, seem distant. For example, over 150,000 Eyadema supporters were brought together in September of 1985 to demonstrate mass support for him. Critical to the regime will be economic challenges which may have an impact on the political realm; such challenges include reorganization of the para-statal sector, continued negotiations with the IMF, and the continued slump in world phosphate prices.

Further Reading
Hodges, Tony. "Eyadema's Unchallenged Rule," *Africa Report*, Vol. 22, No. 4, July–August 1977.
    Steinholtz, Manfield. "West Africa's Middleman in a Pinch," *Africa Report*, Vol. 30, No. 4, July-August 1985.
U.S. Dept. of State, Bureau of Public Affairs. *Togo*. Background Notes Series, no. 8325.

TRINIDAD AND TOBAGO

by Indira Jhappan revised by D. Brent Hardt, M.A.

The System of Government

Trinidad and Tobago is a parliamentary democracy which achieved independence from Great Britain in 1962. While several parties compete in elections, one party, the People's National Movement (PNM), has won all elections since 1956.

The population of these two southernmost Caribbean islands is nearly 1.2 million, of which about 43 percent are of African descent, 40 percent of East Indian descent, 14 percent of mixed race, and the remainder of Chinese and Middle Eastern origins. As in the rest of the Caribbean, color and class have been closely related in the past, but the dominance of light-colored groups is diminishing as the middle and upper classes become racially more mixed. The economy is dependent on petroleum and natural gas deposits which provide a base for current industrial development.

Executive

The head of state is a president elected to a five-year term by a joint session of the bicameral legislature soon after legislative elections. The president appoints as prime minister the leader of the party which obtains the majority of seats in those elections. The prime minister is head of government and exercises effective executive power through his cabinet, which is made up of members of the legislature.

Legislature

The bicameral House of Assembly includes a thirty-one-member Senate and a thirty-six-member House of Representatives. The Senate members are appointed by the president: sixteen on the advice of the prime minister; six on the advice of the leader of the opposition; and nine on the advice of community, social, and economic bodies consulted by the president. Representatives are elected by direct popular suffrage to five-year terms. The speaker of the House of Representatives is elected by the House from outside its membership. After the 1981 elections, the lower house seated twenty-six PNM members, eight United Labour Front (ULF) members, and two Democratic Action Congress (DAC) members. The DAC members held the two seats assigned to Tobago.

Bills can be introduced in either house with the exception of money bills which must be introduced in the House of Representatives. Constitutional amendments and money bills must be passed by both houses to become effective, but other legislation may be passed without Senate approval if the House of Representatives passes them twice.

Judiciary

The system of justice is based on English common law and practice. The Supreme Court of Judicature consists of the High Court and the Court of Appeal. The chief justice of the High Court is appointed by the president on the advice of the prime minister in consultation with the leader of the opposition. He is assisted by ten other judges appointed by the president on the advice of the Judicial Service Commission, which is chaired by the chief justice. The Court of Appeal, which consists of the chief justice and three other judges, is the highest court in the land; further appeals go to the Privy Council in London.

Regional & Local Government

The country is divided into three self-governing cities, eight counties, and the Ward of Tobago. The cities are administered by elected mayors and city councils who are elected for one-year and three-year terms, respectively. The counties are administered by county councils of aldermen chaired by councillors. County councillors and aldermen are elected in the same one-year and three-year pattern as city mayors and councils. Tobago, whose population is less than 5 percent of the total, has its own fifteen-member National Assembly which chooses the island's administrator.

The Electoral System

Members of the House of Representatives are chosen by direct popular vote of citizens eighteen years of age and over. They are elected by simple plurality in single-member constituencies. Elections and constituency boundaries are overseen by the Elections and Boundaries Commission. In 1981, turnout amounted to 56.3 percent of eligible voters, slightly lower than the turnout in 1976.

The Party System

While one party has dominated the system, it is relatively easy for new parties and independents to get on the ballot. Party organization is well developed and democratic procedures are used extensively, though in practice charismatic personalities play the major role in determining party policy. A continuing feature of the system is attempts by the minor parties to find a formula for electoral alliances and joint campaigning that will challenge the overwhelming appeal of the PNM. With the formation of the National Alliance for Reconstruction (NAR) in September 1984, the opposition finally appears capable of mounting a serious challenge to the PNM's dominance in the 1986 general elections. In the past, the parties were partially based on the major ethnic division in the country—African and East Indian—but this division is of decreasing importance as both the PNM and the ULF have broadened their appeal.

People's National Movement (PNM)

The PNM was founded in 1956 by the late Dr. Eric Williams, a well-known Caribbean historian. The party had its roots in the Teachers' Economic and Cultural Association, an organization of African professionals with political interests. They made Williams their spokesman. From the beginning, the party organized by constituencies with lines of communication running up to a general party council selected by an annual national convention. The party has

dominated the legislature since the first national elections in 1956 and in the 1981 elections it won twenty-six of the thirty-six House seats. The party is supported by membership dues and has its base of support in the African middle class, although Williams and the party made a considerable and ultimately successful effort to broaden its appeal. In the beginning the party had a nationalistic, pro-independence platform, and has always been moderate to conservative in foreign and economic policy. It has encouraged foreign investments. When Eric Williams died in 1981, party leadership passed to George Chambers (born 1929) with minimal intraparty conflict.

The decline in international oil prices has sharply reduced government revenues, forcing the PNM to curtail governmental expenditures, devalue the currency, and ration foreign exchange. These actions, though necessary, have been extremely unpopular and have given rise to complaints that party leaders have mismanaged Trinidad's oil wealth. The PNM is therefore more vulnerable to opposition challenges than at any time in its history.

National Alliance for Reconstruction (NAR)

In September 1984, four main opposition parties—the United Labour Front, the Democratic Action Congress, the Organization for National Reconstruction, and the Tapia House Movement—united to form the NAR and to contest the 1986 elections. The NAR is a successor to the National Alliance for Trinidad and Tobago (NATT), which contested the 1981 elections and won ten House seats (eight for the ULF mainly in rural East Indian areas and two for the DAC in its stronghold of Tobago). The original Alliance was strengthened in 1983 when Karl Hudson-Phillips brought his Organization for National Reconstruction into the coalition. The ONR had won 22 percent of the vote in 1981, but no seats. In the first test of the new Alliance's strength in the 1983 municipal and county elections, the Alliance won sixty-six seats and 54 percent of the vote compared with the PNM's fifty-four seats and only 40 percent of the vote. The NAR was further strengthened by the DAC's trouncing of the PNM in the 1984 Tobago House of Assembly elections in which it won eleven of twelve seats. In September 1985, the four member parties reached agreement on where each should field candidates in the next general election. If the parties remain united and avoid a divisive leadership struggle, the NAR stands a good chance of ousting the PNM in 1986.

United Labour Front (ULF)

The ULF was founded in 1976 as an outgrowth of an alliance between the oil and sugar workers' unions. The party claims about 100,000 members and is highly organized. A central executive is elected by an annual national congress of constituency organizations; the congress elects a central committee which meets four times a year to decide policy and plan strategy. The party has been torn by disputes over leadership and ideology. In 1977, Basdeo Panday and Raffique Shaw, a more radical member, fought for the leadership. Panday (born 1933) won, but continuing disputes caused him to resign in 1980. The rank and file soon forced his return to the leadership. The party has traditionally campaigned on a platform calling for the nationalization of foreign interests and for workers' participation in the management of enterprises. The PNM and the Organization for National Reconstruction (ONR) have made serious inroads into its traditional area of support, the sugar-growing areas where the majority of the East Indian population lives. In the 1981 elections, the ULF first joined with other opposition parties in the National Alliance. Though the ULF won eight seats, the coalition as a whole received fewer votes than the parties had received independently in 1976. The ULF is now a major component of the strengthened NAR coalition.

Democratic Action Congress (DAC)

The Democratic Action Congress (DAC) was founded in 1971 by A. N. R. Robinson (born 1926), a former PNM member who resigned from that party over the government's suppression of a surge of black nationalism in the 1970s. The DAC was the product of a merger of the Action Committee of Dedicated Citizens and part of the defunct Democratic Labour Party. The party has had most of its success in Tobago where it has held the island's two seats in the House of Representatives since 1976, and where

it won eleven of twelve seats in the 1984 House of Assembly elections. As a result of the DAC victory in Tobago, Robinson is a strong favorite to emerge as leader of the NAR. The DAC is administered by a national committee responsible to a national congress. Officials of the party are elected. The party is well organized at the constituency level and claims about 18,000 members.

Organization for National Reconstruction (ONR)

The ONR was founded in 1980 by Karl Hudson-Phillips, a former PNM member and once attorney general of Trinidad. Hudson-Phillips was seen as a possible successor to Williams as leader of the PNM, but when this did not materialize, he left the party. The ONR fought the 1981 election alone and took 22 percent of the national vote, cutting sharply into UFL strength. It did not win any seats, however, and Hudson-Phillips decided to enter into an accommodation with the original National Alliance. This accommodation led to the formal formation of the NAR.

Minor Parties

A small leftist party, the National Joint Action Committee (NJAC) took part in the 1981 elections, winning 3.3 percent of the vote. The Tapia House Movement, a black nationalist group, has also run candidates without success.

National Prospects

After thirty years of uninterrupted rule, the PNM is showing signs of political vulnerability. Its poor performance in municipal elections, growing doubts about its ability to manage the economy, and the impact of its budgetary austerity measures have eroded public confidence in the PNM's leadership and point the way to a potential opposition victory in 1986.

Trinidad is highly vulnerable to shifts in the price of oil and natural gas. A long-term decline in prices could threaten Trinidad's political stability. Likewise, a resurgence in prices could solidify the political system.

Another issue of importance in the next few years will be Tobago's effort to redefine its relationship with Trinidad in the direction of greater autonomy, if not complete separation. Many in Tobago accuse the PNM of undermining its cooperative rural traditions. A PNM victory in 1986 would increase Tobago nationalism, whereas a NAR victory would likely defuse secessionist sentiments.

Further Reading

American University. *Area Handbook for Trinidad and Tobago*, 1976.

Brereton, Bridget. *A History of Modern Trinidad, 1783–1962*. London: Heinemann, 1981.

Deosaran, Ramesh. *Eric Williams: The Man, His Ideas and His Politics*. Port of Spain, Trinidad: Signum, 1981.

Gooding, Earl. *The West Indies at the Crossroads: The Search for a Viable Future*. Cambridge, Mass.: Schenkman, 1981.

Johnson, Caswell. "Political Unionism and Autonomy in Jamaica and Trinidad." *American Journal of Economics and Sociology*, Vol. 39, No. 3, July 1980.

Malik, Yohendra K. *East Indians in Trinidad: A Study in Minority Politics*. London: Oxford University Press, 1971.

Panday, Basdeo. "The Role of the Opposition in Trinidad and Tobago." *Caribbean Review*, Vol. 7, No. 4, Fall 1977.

Ryan, Selwyn, et al. *The Confused Electorate: A Study of Political Attitudes and Opinions in Trinidad-Tobago*. Port of Spain, Trinidad: Institute of Social and Economic Research, 1979.

———. "Tobago's Quest for Autonomy: From Colony Ward to..." *Caribbean Review*, Vol. 14, No. 2.

Williams, Eric. *History of the People of Trinidad and Tobago*. New York: Transatlantic, 1970.

REPUBLIC OF TUNISIA
(Al-Djoumhouria Attunusia)
by Sterett Pope, M.A. revised by Ronald Bruce St John, Ph.D.

The System of Government

The Republic of Tunisia, a nation of 7.0 million people, is a presidential republic in which a single party, the *Parti Socialiste Destourien* (PSD) has monopolized bureaucratic and electoral politics at all levels. Although the constitution of 1959 was modeled on the principle of separation of powers and provided for an independent judiciary and an elected unicameral legislature, the presidency has effectively dominated the formulation and execution of national policy. A distinctive feature of the Tunisian political system is the overlapping of the formal government and party structures by which elected officials are selected both on the basis of centralized party control and popular support.

Executive

Executive power is vested in the office of the president and his appointed cabinet. Previously elected by universal suffrage to the presidency for three five-year terms, Habib Bourguiba was affirmed as president for life by the National Assembly in 1974. He is empowered by the constitution to direct general policy, instruct the National Assembly, and submit an annual budget. As chief of the Tunisian armed forces, he conducts foreign policy in consultation with the National Assembly. He may veto any legislation proposed by the Assembly; his own legislative proposals may be overridden by a two-thirds majority of the Assembly, though this has never happened. When the National Assembly is not in session, he may issue decree-laws subject to ratification by a standing committee of the Assembly.

Legislature

The National Assembly consists of 365 deputies, each elected from a regional district, but responsible to the nation at large and also to the PSD. Once in session, the Assembly elects four standing committees which review and draft legislation. The real work of the Assembly is done on these committees, which have on occasion stopped or modified bills proposed by the president. By and large, legislative debate has not played an important role in drafting legislation. General policy lines have usually been determined at PSD national congresses, and President Bourguiba has generally been free to use his executive prestige to make specific policy through the promulgation of decree-laws after informal negotiation among top party cadres.

Judiciary

Like the legislative branch, the judiciary is subject to the initiative of the president. All judges and judicial committees are appointed directly by the president, who is authorized by the constitution to consult judicial bodies, but is not limited by powers of independent judicial review.

Regional & Local Government

Coordinating councils administer the country's thirteen governorates. A governor heads each council. The governor has his own budget and commands the governorate's National Guard units and police. In the latter function, he reports directly to the Ministry of Interior. The governors are appointed by the president on the recommendation of appropriate party and government bodies. At the local level, rural districts are administered by roughly 1,000 shaikhs, usually local notables, in consultation with the local party branch. These local organs have little power to do more than enforce the policies handed down from the governors and higher party councils. Large cities, which may include many party branches organized both by geographical location and economic activity, have separate municipal administrations, which are built into the three-tier system of national party organization.

The Electoral System

Since the drafting of the constitution in 1959, members of the National Assembly have been elected every five years (the last election of 1981 being irregular), while local and municipal officials have been elected for three-year terms. According to electoral law, voters are allowed to choose among various lists representing the candidates fielded by competing parties, and may substitute competing candidates for those offered by the list of their choice. Voting is not completely secret, since the individual voter is required to select a list, differentiated from the others by color, in a public voting station. While such a system implies a substantial margin of free choice, the system has in practice permitted the PSD to capture all the seats in each election since competing parties have either been banned, chosen to boycott elections, or had very poor showings. Within the PSD, nomination of candidates at all levels is carefully controlled by party cadres from above; only in 1979 was the selection process liberalized to offer the voters a choice by requiring the nomination of twice as many candidates as elected offices.

Voter registration and participation in national elections has been strong. All Tunisian citizens age twenty and over are entitled to vote, and between 60 percent and 70 percent of all eligible voters have registered for each election. Of these, approximately 80 percent voted in the elections for the National Assembly in 1979 and 1981, a sharp decline from the average of 95 percent who voted in previous national elections.

Constitutional Socialist Party (*Parti Socialiste Destourien*; PSD)

History

Influenced by liberal democratic ideas from France as well as by the success of nationalist movements in other parts of the Middle East, a group of Tunisian notables formed the Destour

Party in 1920 and called for a self-governing constitutional government with an elected legislative assembly. The movement was criticized by a younger generation of Tunisian nationalists as collaborationist vis-à-vis the French colonial authorities and as representative only of the conservative landed and commercial elites. In 1934 these nationalists, under the leadership of Habib Bourguiba, a lawyer, formed the Neo-Destour Party. In the next twenty-two years, Bourguiba and his colleagues organized a mass-based nationalist movement, founding party cells in every region of the country. Bourguiba balanced step-by-step negotiation with the French authorities with politics of mass agitation and confrontation through demonstrations, general strikes, and guerrilla warfare at various times. The Neo-Destour found a powerful ally in the General Union of Tunisian Workers (*Union Générale des Travailleurs Tunisiens;* UGTT), founded in 1946, which agitated for national independence as well as the promotion of the rights of native workers under the French protectorate.

In 1955 Bourguiba successfully negotiated for an autonomous Tunisian government; the following year Tunisia was accorded full independence. Success precipitated the first serious rift among the membership of the Neo-Destour, when the party's secretary general, Salah Ben Youssef, rejected Bourguiba's 1955 autonomy negotiations as collaborationist. Relying on strong support from organized labor, Bourguiba quickly isolated Ben Youssef. Following independence, the Neo-Destour captured all ninety-eight seats of the Constituent Assembly and 98 percent of the vote, in general elections which the Ben Youssefists and the Old Destour boycotted. Bourguiba was immediately elected president by the Assembly.

During the period of nationalist struggle the Neo-Destour had created a loosely organized structure of local party cells in order to form a broad coalition of nationalist groups in each region and maximize the local effectiveness of its clandestine command structure. After independence, President Bourguiba tightened party structure by limiting the number of proliferating party cells and replacing elected regional officials with appointed ones. The party structure was made parallel to government organization at all levels. In 1961 President Bourguiba announced a program of economic centralization as well. At the Seventh Party Congress in 1964, the party's hierarchical command structure was further strengthened by a series of reforms which made candidates for office down to the local level subject to selection and censure by higher committees. The Seventh Congress also approved Planning Minister Ahmed Ben Salah's program for land reform, and the name of the party was changed to the *Parti Socialiste Destourien*.

The centralization process was weakened in the 1960s and 1970s as competing factions within the party split over national policy and dissident groups came increasingly to advocate liberalizing Tunisia's political structures so as to allow greater popular participation and freer public debate of national issues. Ahmed Ben Salah's drive to introduce land reform and agricultural cooperatives antagonized rich landlords as well as small landowners, leading in 1969 to the reversal of his policies and his trial and imprisonment the following year.

Opposition within the administration surfaced from another quarter when Ahmed Mestiri was appointed minister of the interior in 1970 and began to advocate liberalization of the regime, and in particular constitutional reforms to check abuses of presidential power. Mestiri was removed from his cabinet post and stripped of his party membership the following year. In 1974, when the Ninth Party Congress met to discuss constitutional reform, it gave even greater powers to Bourguiba and his protege, Prime Minister Hedi Nouira, by amending the constitution to make Bourguiba president for life to be succeeded by the prime minister, who could be appointed or dismissed by the president. (These actions were later affirmed, pro forma, by the National Assembly.)

Perhaps the most serious threat to the PSD emerged in January 1978 when the party's labor union, the General Union of Tunisian Workers, led by Habib Achour, called a general strike to protest workers' low salaries and the absence of popular participation in government. Achour and his collaborators, who included ex-members and critics of the PSD, were soon tried and imprisoned.

In early 1981, the new prime minister, Mohammed Mzali, announced his support for a policy of *ouverture* (opening), or liberalization of the regime. Three ministers who had left the government during the 1978 crisis rejoined the cabinet, and a general pardon of political prisoners and exiles was announced. In an extraordinary labor union congress, eleven dissident union leaders were reelected to the thirteen-member executive committee, including Habib Achour, who was still under house arrest. Ac-

hour was replaced as secretary general of the union in late 1985 but later reinstated.

Organization

The smallest unit of the PSD pyramidal structure is the cell or local branch, which may represent a village, municipal precinct, or professional association. Cells are primarily engaged in community service and political education of their constituencies, supervising such programs as voter registration, birth-control distribution, and the maintenance of mosques and irrigation works. Every two years, dues-paying party members elect an executive committee of between ten and twenty members, who in turn participate in the election of thirteen regional coordinating committees (which correspond to Tunisia's thirteen governorates), each headed by the regional governor and two higher party officials appointed by the party's Political Bureau.

While local party members are free to nominate their comrades for seats on local committees, their lists of nominees are submitted to the regional coordinating committees which may eliminate undesirable candidates or propose others, and so limit the scope of local elections. A similar process takes place at the regional level where nominees for membership of the coordinating committees are vetted by the Political Bureau, itself elected through a similar process of negotiation between members of the National Party Congress and the president of the republic. In this way, party representatives at the local, regional, and national levels are chosen by a process in which the free choice of electors is tempered by central control.

The broadest representative body at the national level is a party congress to which each local executive committee elects a delegate. The party congress elects from among its number the eighty-member Central Committee which in turn elects the twenty-member Political Bureau from a list of nominees submitted by the president. The Central Committee is considered the highest council for the formulation of party doctrine and general direction, while the Political Bureau frames party statutes in consultation with the president and submits them for ratification to the party congress.

Although party statutes stipulate that a party congress should meet every three years, national congresses have in practice convened on an irregular basis, the last three being held in 1974, 1979, and 1981. Debates on national issues have on occasion been candid and intense, but the outcomes have generally secured the status quo against political currents seeking to restrain presidential power, separate formal administration from party structure, and liberalize the regime in general. The 1974 Party Congress won greater initiative for itself by trimming some presidential prerogatives of appointment, and the 1981 Party Congress was notable for the substantial turnover of high-level party personnel which it produced.

Policy

During the French Protectorate, Neo-Destour ideology was shaped by two countervailing tendencies: French liberalism with its traditions of parliamentary pluralism and trade unionism, and Tunisian nationalism based on party discipline and the building of a broad front to combat French colonialism. Since independence, the latter tendency has been reinforced by the charismatic leadership of Habib Bourguiba and the challenge of building a strong national economy. Like its Nasserist Destour Party counterpart in Egypt, Destourian socialism is predicated on the cooperation of different classes and social groups within Tunisian society and places emphasis on state initiative in economic planning and development.

The 1970s saw the development of a more laissez-faire economy with emphasis on exploitation of mineral resources and the courting of foreign investment. State investment has generally favored industrial expansion over agricultural development: the former, it is hoped, will boost exports and create jobs for Tunisia's rapidly growing population. The current government of Prime Minister Mohammed Mzali has shown increased concern for social welfare and has established agricultural self-sufficiency as a national priority. The 1982–86 Economic Plan targeted 12 percent of state funds in agriculture versus 25 percent for industry.

In foreign policy, Tunisia has always maintained a posture of nonalignment, although in the past twenty years President Bourguiba has charted a course of "moderation" which has consistently favored the Western alliance over the Soviet bloc. Bourguiba has continually advocated a negotiated settlement of the Palestinian question. An exponent of Maghreb (Arab

North African) unity, Tunisia has often had strained relations with its larger, more radical neighbor Algeria. The Tunisian leadership has rebuffed several offers from Libyan president Qaddafi for a national merger or federation between the two states. Libyan relations continue to have a high place on Tunisia's foreign-policy agenda.

Membership & Constituency

In the early 1970s, PSD membership was estimated at roughly 600,000, about one-third of the country's adult population. The organizational style of the party is to involve the mass of the population at as many points as possible; to that end, it has affiliated mass organizations for workers, women, students, and farmers. Given the absence of effective opposition parties, it is difficult to gauge popular support for the ruling PSD and its policies, but most observers agree that the PSD commands the loyalty of the populace.

Financing

No information is available on party financing.

Leadership

President Bourguiba (born 1903) is aged and ailing. The constitution provides for his replacement as head of state by the prime minister who, in 1985, was Mohammed Mzali (born 1925). Whether Mzali, who is also secretary general of the PSD, commands sufficient support within the party to become its leader in fact is uncertain, but observers anticipate a relatively smooth transfer of power.

Opposition

Opposition groups are subject to periodic repression by the government, are inchoate in organization, and ideologically vague. The government allowed three of these opposition groups to participate in the 1981 general elections. The results were disappointing for the opposition and gave credence to its charges of electoral manipulation by the PSD. According to the rules set up for that election only, a party had to win at least 5 percent of the vote to win a seat and gain recognition as a legitimate party. None of the opposition groups reached this threshold; the MDS with 3.28 percent came closest.

Movement of Social Democrats (*Mouvement des Démocrates Socialistes;* MDS)

The MDS was founded in 1972 by Ahmed Mestiri, a former minister of interior who had been stripped of his party membership in 1971. Mestiri's platform includes greater press freedoms and freer public political debate, a multiparty parliamentary system, separation of the PSD organization from the state administration, and more social legislation.

Movement for Popular Unity (*Mouvement pour l'Unité Popular;* MUP)

MUP was founded in 1974 by Ahmed Ben Salah, a former leader of the party's labor organization (UGTT) and architect of a discredited land-reform program. The MUP advocates a planned economy under greater state control, greater commitment to social reform, and a nonaligned foreign policy. The MUP later split into two factions with MUP-II, which enjoys official support, being the only one legally allowed to function.

Tunisian Communist Party (*Parti Communiste Tunisien;* PCT)

For many years after independence, the PCT was the nominal opposition to the Neo-Destour. It was founded in 1933 by members of the Tunisian branch of the French Communist Party, and its public platform remains close to that of its French progenitor.

Islamic Tendency Movement (*Mouvement de Tendance Islamique;* MTI)

The MTI was established in the early 1970s and has shown increasing strength. Its ideology is vague—a return to Islamic law, particularly in the domain of social legislation, and staunch anti-imperialism (i.e., anti-Western). The strongest of the opposition groups, MTI is popu-

lar among students and the lower middle class. As an illegal political party, it is not allowed to hold public meetings, and its activities are closely watched by the police.

Other Political Forces

Organized Labor

The only significant opposition to PSD rule has come from its own labor movement, the General Union of Tunisian Workers (*Union Générale des Travailleurs Tunisiens;* UGTT). Independently founded in 1946, the UGTT soon became the principal ally of the Neo-Destour Party in the struggle for independence. Bourguiba used the UGTT, then headed by Ahmed Ben Salah, to isolate his political opponents within the party, notably, the secretary general, Salah Ben Yousseff. After independence, Bourguiba incorporated the union into the party as its largest mass organization. With a strong tradition of radical syndicalism, the UGTT became increasingly critical of the conservative policies of the PSD associated with Hedi Nouira in the late 1970s. In 1978, the UGTT revolted by calling a general strike. The strike was crushed by the army and many of the UGTT leaders were jailed. Most of these leaders, however, have returned to the top ranks of the union, a result of a liberalization within the regime. The UGTT maintains links with the MUP and MDS and continues to press for greater social legislation. It remains the primary focus of intraparty opposition and, as such, has won concessions from the government.

Military

The army has never played a role independent of Bourguiba and the party. Although the army was instrumental in checking the 1978 general strike as well as the 1984 riots, army leaders have maintained a low political profile. There have been few reports of unrest among junior officers, but this may change as younger officers tend to be more politically conscious and ideological.

National Prospects

The poor health of President Bourguiba and the growth of opposition outside the PSD pose grave questions for the political future of Tunisia and its one-party system. Should Bourguiba die, the constitution provides for his succession by Prime Minister Mzali with a presidential election to follow in 1986. A relatively smooth transition of power seems in prospect, since the PSD still commands the loyalty of the populace, and the opposition groups, none of which present radical alternatives (with the exception of the MTI), will probably be inclined to work through party or UGTT channels. The regime seems to fear the MTI most, and it is likely that the government will try to check this threat by working more closely with the UGTT, which enjoys strong support among the working class. Greater attention to issues of social welfare and further, more credible initiatives in the direction of *ouverture* are likely to result from such a partnership.

Further Reading

Debbasch, Carles. *La Tunisie.* Paris: Editions Berger-Levrault, 1973.

Lawless, Richard and Allan Findlay, eds. *North Africa: Contemporary Politics and Economic Development.* London: Croom Helm, 1984.

Salem, Norma. *Habib Bourguiba, Islam and the Creation of Tunisia.* London: Croom Helm, 1984.

REPUBLIC OF TURKEY
(Türkiye Cumhuriyeti)
by Paul J. Magnarella, Ph.D.

The System of Government

After three years and two months of military rule, Turkish voters went to the polls on November 6, 1983 to elect a civilian government. The event marked a major step toward a return to political democracy.

The 1980 military coup had transformed Turkey from a democratic republic with a bicameral legislature and a multiparty political system to a country under the temporary rule of a five-man military junta. After almost a decade of escalating political terrorism, economic recession, violent labor strikes, and impotent coalition governments, the Turkish military seized power in a bloodless coup on September 12, 1980, for the declared purpose of saving the country from internal war and reestablishing the foundations of democracy. Subsequently, the military ruled the country through the National Security Council (NSC; *Milli Güvenlik Konseyi*), headed by General Kenan Evren, chief of the General Staff. General Evren acted as both head of the NSC and head of state (*Devlet Başkanı*). The NSC took over the legislative functions of Parliament, which it dissolved, and appointed a mixed civilian-military cabinet headed by retired admiral Bülent Ulusu to handle the day-to-day business of government.

In its effort to restore order and discipline throughout the country, the NSC declared martial law, prohibited all political-party activity and labor strikes, disbanded the left- and right-wing trade unions, placed restrictions on the news media, and replaced hundreds of civilians in government posts with military officers. On October 27, 1980, the NSC approved the "Law Regarding Constitutional Order," which defined the NSC's duties and authorities and superceded various parts of the 1961 constitution.

The NSC also dissolved all political parties on October 16, 1981, and had their monies and property confiscated.

The NSC convened a Consultative Assembly in Ankara, the capital, on October 23, 1981, and charged it with the responsibility of drafting a new constitution, a new election law, and a new law on political parties. The new constitution was approved by over 90 percent of 20 million voters in November 1982. In the same referendum, General Evren was elected president of Turkey for a seven-year term. The constitution gives the president extensive powers of appointment and decree and sharply curtails the power of Parliament. It bars all members of the last Parliament from political activity for five years and major political leaders for ten years.

Traditionally, the Turkish military has regarded itself as the guardian of the secular and democratic reforms of Kemal Atatürk, the republic's founder. The 1980 coup was the third time the military deemed it necessary to intervene to save democracy. In 1960 the military seized power from the ruling Democrat Party after its leaders had suppressed political expression by the opposition. Among other things, the military supervised the writing of a new, more liberal constitution during its seventeen-month rule and then turned the government over to the democratically elected political parties. In March 1971, the armed forces again stepped into the political arena because it believed the civilian government could not effectively deal with the country's spreading anarchy. The military issued a memorandum (March 12, 1971) which intimidated the ruling Justice Party government into resigning. Then, rather than govern themselves, the military leaders supervised the formation of a civilian government dominated by independents and technocrats. Following this, the military and civilian police made what proved to be an ineffectual attempt to bring an end to political violence and anarchy.

The 1980-83 military rulers believed Turkey's stability depended on their ability to root out extremists and improve the country's economy. They succeeded in sharply reducing terrorism: just prior to the takeover, for example, anarchists were murdering an average of twenty persons a day; a year later the figure had dropped to a few persons a month. By June 1982, martial law authorities reported they had arrested over 40,000 suspected terrorists and other alleged law breakers, including over 1,000 suspected Kurdish separatists. Of these, 23,145 were tried and convicted by martial law courts, of whom 6,091 were convicted of "ideological offenses," such as promoting the creation of a Marxist-Leninist state. Over 6,500 cases were continued.

On the economic front, the military fully backed the recovery program designed by Turgut Özal (a member of the previous civilian government) and endorsed by the International Monetary Fund. By 1982, all indicators pointed to the program's success. The annual inflation rate had been reduced from 100 to 40 percent; industry was operating at a much higher capacity; emigrant workers' remittances and exports were sharply up; and international confidence in Turkey's economy had grown.

By 1983, the NSC felt confident enough in Turkey's social and economic stability to allow the creation of new political parties and the holding of new elections. But the NSC exercised strict control over the entire party formation and election process. It permitted only three of fifteen newly created parties to participate in the election. It also dissolved the Great Turkey Party, charging it was simply a continuation of former Premier Demirel's banned Justice Party.

The 1983 parliamentary election resulted in a victory for the conservative Motherland Party of Turgut Özal. With a 92.9 percent voter turnout, the Motherland Party took 45 percent of the vote, winning 212 seats in the new 400-member Parliament. The social democratic Populist Party of Necdet Calp, a former provincial governor, received 30 percent of the vote for 117 seats. The law-and-order Nationalist Democracy Party of Turgut Sunalp, a retired general, won only 23 percent of the vote for seventy-one seats.

Executive

Executive power is vested in the president of the republic (*Cumhurbaşkanǐ*) and the Council of Ministers (*Bakanlar Kurulu*). According to Turkey's original 1924 constitution, the presidency was a party office; the chief of state was elected by each Assembly for a concurrent term. Until the 1960 coup, all presidents were members of the majority party. The 1961 constitution, however, separated the presidency from party politics. Henceforth, each president was to be elected for a single seven-year term by the Grand National Assembly from among its own members. Once elected, he had to resign from the Assembly and disassociate himself from his party. In fact, since 1961 all elected chiefs of state had been presidential appointees to the Senate without party affiliation.

The president is the head of state. He presides over the Council of Ministers; sends representatives to foreign states and receives the representatives of foreign governments; ratifies and promulgates international treaties; and exercises power of pardon and commutation. He appoints the prime minister (*Başbakan*) as well as members of the Council of Ministers and can dissolve Parliament.

With the single exception of Celal Bayar (1950–60), all presidents came from the highest ranks of the military. After 1961, especially, they played a critical extraconstitutional role as mediators between the leaders of the military and the political parties. The first president under the 1961 constitution, General Cemal Gürsel, had headed the National Unity Committee, the junta that governed Turkey after the 1960 coup. He was succeeded by General Cevdet Sunay, the former chief of the General Staff. Each had been recommended to the Assembly by the armed forces chiefs.

The prime minister is head of government. He and his cabinet compose the Council of Ministers. The president designates the prime minister from among the members of the Grand National Assembly. Although the president usually designates the leader of the majority or plurality party, he has occasionally designated an independent to form an "above party" government.

With the exceptions noted above, prior to 1983 real executive power belonged to the prime minister and the council. The prime minister designate chose the candidates for the various ministries in his cabinet from within or without parliament. The president formally appointed them. In recent decades, the Council of Ministers usually consisted of the prime minister, one to three deputy prime ministers, twenty to twenty-four ministers, and up to seven ministers of state without portfolios. Except for the "above-party" governments of 1960 to 1961, 1971 to 1973, and 1980 to 1983, all ministers were drawn from the Grand National Assembly. In addition to considerations of skill and experience, they were selected for reasons of political expediency. In 1978, for instance, Prime Minister designate Bülent Ecevit was able to form a government only after detaching ten deputies from the rival Justice Party and awarding them with cabinet posts.

Since 1983 the prime minister designate presents his government's program to the new unicameral Assembly for a vote of confidence. Only with an affirmative vote can the government be formed. Thereafter, the Council of Ministers maintains close contact with the legislature, with individual ministers appearing before the house to debate legislation and to respond to questions.

The 1982 constitution greatly increased the president's powers on the model of de Gaulle's Fifth Republic. When he deems necessary, the president may call Parliament into special session or dissolve it and call for new elections. He may initiate challenges to legislation in the Constitutional Court. In addition to appointing and dismissing ministers, he appoints the justices of the Constitutional Court, the Military Court of Appeals, and the Supreme Military Court, as well as members of the Supreme Council of Judges and Prosecutors. He also controls higher education by appointing members of the Higher Education Council and university presidents.

In times of crisis, the president together with the cabinet is empowered to declare a state of emergency, martial law, or military preparedness and issue decrees carrying the force of law. Significantly, presidential decrees may not be challenged by the Constitutional Court.

Legislature

The Grand National Assembly (GNA; *Büyük Millet Meclisi*) is the legislative organ of the Turkish republic. The 1924 constitution established a unicameral legislature, but the 1961 constitution created a senate in order to introduce some additional checks and balances into the law-making process. The lower house or National Assembly (*Millet Meclisi*) had 450 members elected for four-year terms. Male and female citizens literate in Turkish who were at least thirty years old were eligible for office.

The Senate (*Senato*) consisted of 150 members elected for six-year terms, fifteen "contingent senators" appointed by the president (for distinguished service in their fields), and a varying number of ex officio life members, who were former members of the 1960–61 National Unity Committee and former presidents of the republic. Because ex officio members were meant to be nonpartisan, they lost their life-membership status upon joining a political party. Every two years, one-third of the Senate (excepting its ex officio members) stood for reelection. All Senate members were required to have had a "higher education" and were to be at least forty years of age.

Members of both houses were elected from individual provinces, with each province's number of deputies and senators being determined by its population size. Once elected, however, legislators were supposed to represent the entire country. During the early years of the republic, members with civil service and military backgrounds were most numerous. In recent decades, however, members with legal, professional (especially medical), and business backgrounds predominated. Because the GNA had a turnover rate exceeding 50 percent in practically every election since 1961, the opportunity for the development of expertise based on experience was limited for most of its members.

The GNA was empowered to enact, amend, and repeal laws, to mint currency, proclaim pardons and amnesties, ratify treaties, declare war, confirm or revoke death sentences passed by independent courts, and elect the president from among its members. While any member could initiate legislation, most bills actually originated with the Council of Ministers. All members had parliamentary immunity. Although the GNA was obliged to be in session for a minimum of seven months a year, its extended debates and inability to reach major decisions required it to operate almost year-round in recent times.

The National Assembly enjoyed more power than the Senate in that it received and debated bills first and could override Senate or presidential disapproval of a bill. The lower house also had the exclusive right to pass motions of censure and call for new elections before the termination of the four-year term.

Each house elected a chairman at the beginning of the legislative year for a two-year term. During their time in office, the chairmen were to remain above politics by excluding themselves from general debates and political-party activities. In accordance with the constitution, membership in the Chairman's Council

ELECTION RESULTS: 1961–1977
National Assembly
(Lower House)

	1961	1965	1969	1973	1977
PERCENT OF ELIGIBLE VOTERS VOTING	81.0	71.3	64.3	66.8	72.5
REPUBLICAN PEOPLES PARTY founded 1922: Kemal Atatürk successor: Ismet Inonu 1980 leader: Bulent Ecevit	173 seats 36.7%	134 seats 28.7%	143 seats 27.4%	185 seats 33.2%	213 seats 41.4%
JUSTICE PARTY founded Jan. 1961: Gen. Ragip Gümüspala 1980 leader: Süleyman Demirel	158 seats 34.8%	240 seats 52.9%	256 seats 46.5%	149 seats 29.8%	189 seats 36.9%
DEMOCRATIC PARTY founded: Dec. 1970: Saadettin Bilgic 1980 leader: Ferruh Bozbeyli				45 seats 11.8%	1 seat 1.8%
NATION PARTY founded June 1962: Osman Bölükbaşi		31 seats 6.3%	6 seats 3.2%	0 seats .6%	not eligible to run
NATIONAL ACTION PARTY (previously Republican Peasants Nation Party) founded Feb. 1954: Osman Bölükbaşi 1980 leader: Alparslan Türkeş	54 seats 14.0%	11 seats 2.2%	1 seat 3.0%	3 seats 3.4%	16 seats 6.4%
NATIONAL SALVATION PARTY founded: Oct. 1972: Süleyman Emre 1980 leader: Necmettin Erbakan				48 seats 11.9%	24 seats 8.6%
NEW TURKEY PARTY founded Feb. 1961: Ekrem Alican	65 seats 13.7%	19 seats 3.7%	6 seats 2.2%	dissolved of its own initiative	
REPUBLICAN RELIANCE PARTY founded May 1967: Turhan Feyzioğlu 1980 leader: Turhan Feyzioğlu			15 seats 6.6%	13 seats 5.3%	3 seats 1.9%
TURKISH LABOR PARTY founded March 1961: Avni Erkalin 1980 leader: Behice Boran		15 seats 3.0%	2 seats 2.7%	closed by courts	0 seats .1%
TURKISH UNITY PARTY founded Oct. 1966: Gen. Hasan Berkman 1980 leader: Mustafa Timisi			8 seats 2.8%	1 seat 1.1%	0 seats .4%
INDEPENDENTS	0 seats .8%	0 seats 3.2%	13 seats 5.6%	6 seats 2.8%	4 seats 2.5%

(*Başkanlik Divani*) and other parliamentary committees were distributed among the parties in proportion to their size.

Each house chairman met regularly with an advisory council, which was composed of the heads of the political-party groups in his house. Any political party with at least ten members in a given chamber could form a group. In the Senate, independents could also form a group with a minimum of ten members. Committee assignments were made and parliamentary debate was normally conducted on the basis of party groups, with each group having a designated spokesman. Party discipline was generally strong and most issues were debated along party lines. The Turkish legislature was no place for the timid, as insults and physical assaults during times of heated argument were common.

Joint meetings of the two houses were chaired by the chairman of the National Assembly and were held to decide declarations of war,

ELECTION RESULTS: 1961–1977
The Senate
(Upper House)

	1961	1964	1966	1968	1973	1975	1977
PERCENT OF ELIGIBLE VOTERS VOTING	81.4	60.2	56.2	66.3	65.3	58.4	73.8
REPUBLICAN PEOPLES PARTY							
Seats won	36	19	13	13	25	25	28
% of vote cast	37.2%	40.8%	30.0%	27.1%	33.6%	43.8%	42.4%
cumulative seat total	36	45	50	34	41	60	75
JUSTICE PARTY							
Seats won	71	31	35	38	22	27	21
% of vote cast	35.5%	50.3%	56.3%	49.9%	31.0%	40.8%	38.3%
cumulative seat total	71	77	92	101	80	78	64
DEMOCRATIC PARTY							
Seats won					0	0	0
% of vote cast					10.4%	3.1%	2.2%
cumulative seat total					6	0	0
NATION PARTY							
Seats won		0	1	1			
% of vote cast			5.9%	6.0%			
cumulative seat total		3	1	1			
NATIONAL ACTION PARTY							
Seats won	16	0	1	0	0	0	0
% of vote cast	13.5%	3.0%	1.9%	2.0%	2.7%	3.2%	6.6%
cumulative seat total	16	3	1	1	0	1	1
NATIONAL SALVATION PARTY							
Seats won					3	2	1
% of vote cast					12.3%	8.8%	8.5%
cumulative seat total					3	5	6
NEW TURKEY PARTY							
Seats won	27	0	1	0			
% of vote cast	14.0%	3.5%	2.3%				
cumulative seat total	27	9	1	1			
REPUBLICAN RELIANCE PARTY							
Seats won				1	1	0	0
% of vote cast				8.6%	5.9%		1.9%
cumulative seat total				11	10	4	3
TURKISH LABOR PARTY							
Seats won			1	0	0	0	0
% of vote cast			3.9%	4.7%			
cumulative seat total		1	1	0	0	0	0
TURKISH UNITY PARTY							
Seats won					0	0	0
% of vote cast					2.1%	.5%	
cumulative seat total					0	0	0
INDEPENDENT							
Seats won		1	0	0	1	0	0
% of vote cast		2.3%	.5%	1.7%	2.0%	.1%	.1%
cumulative seat total		11	4	0	10	2	1

* Coincided with general elections to the lower house.

the sending of troops abroad, the acceptance of troops on Turkish soil, a declaration of martial law, and the election of a new president. On this last issue, the GNA came into direct conflict with the military.

The GNA elected the military-backed presidential candidates on the first ballot (requiring a two-thirds majority) in 1961 and 1966. In 1973, however, the parliamentarians balked. They asserted their independence from the military by rejecting its candidate, General Faruk Güler (an author of the March 12, 1971, memorandum). It took fourteen inconclusive rounds of balloting before the GNA and the military heads finally compromised on retired admiral Fahri Korutürk (a contingent senator since 1968).

Upon the expiration of President Korutürk's term in 1980, however, the GNA was so splintered by inter- and intraparty feuding that even with a hundred rounds of balloting it was unable to elect a successor (even though only an absolute majority is needed after the second round). For this reason among others, the military dissolved parliament and took over the government in 1980.

The 1982 constitution eliminated the senate by creating a unicameral assembly consisting of 400 deputies, elected to five year terms. Deputies lose their right to run for reelection if they switch parties. When a president's term of office ends, Parliament must elect successor within 30 days. If it fails to do so by the fourth ballot, Parliament must dissolve itself.

GRAND NATIONAL ASSEMBLY ELECTION RESULTS: 1983

Party	VOTES BY %	SEATS
Motherland Party	45.1	212
Populist Party	30.4	117
National Democracy Party	23.2	71
Independents	1.1	

Judiciary

The Turkish Republic, which was founded in 1923 upon the crumbled remains of the Ottoman Empire in Asia Minor and Thrace, shed itself of Islamic law (*shari'ah*) and adopted a secular constitution as well as several legal codes from Europe: the Swiss Civil Code (1926), the Italian Penal Code (1926), and the German Commercial Code (1926). This was one of many ways in which Turkey distinguished itself from other Muslim Middle Eastern countries.

Although Turkey's 1924 constitution proclaimed the independence of the courts, alleged interference with the judicial system by the Democrat government (1950–60) led the framers of the 1961 constitution to institute strict guarantees against outside pressures on the judiciary. According to law, no institution, agency, or individual could give orders or instructions to courts and judges in connection with the discharge of their duties.

The Constitutional Court (*Anayasa Mahkemesi*) was established in 1962 and charged with the responsibility of reviewing legislation to ensure its constitutionality. A 1980 decree by the National Security Council, however, stated that the court could not question the constitutionality of laws, decrees, or communiques approved or issued by the NSC after its takeover on September 12, 1980. The court could continue to review previous legislation, and it remained the supreme court for trying high state officials.

Previous to the 1980 coup, opposition political parties, especially the Republican People's Party, used this court to challenge the government's legislation and regulations. "Autonomous establishments," such as the state universities, also resorted to the court to protect themselves from new, infringing regulations.

The Council of State (*Danistay*), reorganized in 1964 and modeled after the French *Conseil d'Etat*, serves as the highest administrative court and the "organ of advice" to the executive. The High Court of Cassation (*Yargitay*) is the highest court of appeal. It confirms or reverses verdicts rendered by lower civil and criminal courts.

In addition to the civilian courts, there are military courts charged with handling all cases related to terrorism and anarchy in areas under martial law.

The 1982 constitution emphasizes national security and presidential power. It established State Security Courts with jurisdiction over crimes against Turkey's internal and external security. It also places outside the scope of judicial review the decisions by the Supreme Military Council and the acts by the president in his own areas of competence.

Regional & Local Government

The responsibility and authority for local government is centralized mainly in Ankara, especially in the Council of Ministers and the various state ministries. Administratively, Turkey is divided into sixty-seven provinces (sing., *il*), which are further divided into subprovinces (sing., *ilçe*), districts (sing., *bucak*), and villages (sing., *köy*). Each of these administrative units, with the exception of the village, is headed by an official who is appointed by the president and responsible to the Ministry of Interior. Although the village chief (*muhtar*) is popularly elected, he too is answerable to the Ministry of Interior.

The office of the provincial governor (*vali*) is located in the province's largest city, while subprovincial seats with subprovincial governors (sing., *kaymakam*), are located in smaller cities, towns, and in some cases villages. District seats are mostly in villages. Locally elected councils are attached to the offices of *vali* and *kaymakam*, but they advise only; authority descends from Ankara.

Except for the Ministry of Foreign Affairs, all ministries have departments on the provincial level. Because their provincial officers are responsible in the first instance to the local *vali* and in the second instance to their own ministries, a certain confusion and ambiguity often results. This situation developed historically out of the Ottoman tradition when governor-generals were in charge of the provinces. Today, many *valis* are retired generals. No data are available as to who usually has the last word, although in matters of internal security, it is probably the *vali*.

In addition to these national units of administration, Turkey had 1,719 municipalities in 1980, each with an elected mayor (*belediye başkanï]* the council (*belediye meclisi*). The relationship between the municipality and the national government is one of tutelage; practically every decision made by municipal officials can be altered or negated by the *vali* or Ministry of Interior.

The Electoral System

During the early years of the republic, the voting franchise was limited to males over eighteen years of age, and the national electoral system was indirect. Men voted for secondary electors who selected the actual deputies to the unicameral assembly. In 1934 women received the right to vote and to run for national office. Consequently, the Fifth Assembly, elected in 1935, had eighteen female deputies. In 1946, the electoral system became a partially direct one.

Since 1950, elections have been based on fully direct suffrage. All votes are equal, ballots are cast secretly, and results are openly counted. Citizens twenty-one years of age or older are eligible to vote: in 1977, there were 21.2 million registered voters. Enlisted men, corporals, sergeants, and military-academy students cannot vote, nor can those who have been convicted of or who stand accused of a serious crime. Each province constitutes an electoral area.

Since 1950, when the electorate turned the authoritarian Republican People's Party out of office, voters have taken elections seriously and voter participation has been high. Curiously, voter turnout has been somewhat greater in rural areas than in urban ones. Among the many theories attempting to account for high voter participation are these: competitive support for political patrons by rival client groups; the need to express local rivalries through political-party support; and the utilization of parties to promote religious, nationalistic, or other ideologies.

Elections are supervised by the High Election Board, which both certifies election results and serves as the original and final court for all complaints of irregularities regarding election matters. The board has eleven members; six elected by the general assembly of the Court of Cassation and five by the general assembly of the Council of State from among its own members.

From 1946 to 1960, national elections were based on a "majority system"; the party receiving a majority of votes in a given province won all of that province's seats. This system favored the Democrat Party, which ruled from 1950 to 1960. Consequently, the 1960–61 military government changed the election law and instituted a proportional system, known as the "d'Hondt System with Quota"; hereafter, seats were to be distributed to a party in proportion to its votes in each province. However, a party not receiving a stipulated minimum number of votes in a province received none of that province's seats. The "quota" or minimum number was determined by dividing the number of votes cast in a province by its number of seats.

Because this system still appeared to favor the Justice Party (heir to the outlawed Democratic Party), the opposition parties, led by the

Republican People's Party, enacted a change called the "National Remainder System." This new system permitted the votes for parties which had failed to meet provincial quotas to be pooled on the national level for the purpose of acquiring seats not already won on the provincial level. This system aided small parties. For example, in 1965, the Republican Peasant's Nation Party met the quota in only one of the provincial constituencies, but received eleven National Assembly seats, ten of them derived from the party's national remainder total.

In 1969, the ruling Justice Party pushed through a new law which restored the previous quota system. However, the small Turkish Workers Party, which relied heavily on the national remainder system, challenged the new law in the Constitutional Court. The court ruled that by hindering the expression of small-party movements, the quota requirement contradicted the constitution. Hence, the quota again was abolished and a revised proportional system (the "Simple d'Hondt System") remained in effect from 1969 to 1980.

This proportional system also applied to local elections in which officials filled four-year terms, the exceptions being mayors and village headmen who were elected by a simple majority.

The Turkish system was very democratic and liberal. Its current critics say it was too democratic to work. It permitted divisive right- and left-wing radical groups to operate in the open as legitimate political parties. Rapid urbanization, high inflation, high under- and unemployment, coupled with a poorly developed sense of civic responsibility among politicians and the inability of any party to win a majority in the 1970s, led to the creation of fragile coalition governments unable and unwilling to implement the strict economic and social measures required to stabilize the country.

The 1983 electoral law is based on the d'Hondt system, preserving proportional representation, but disadvantaging small parties. The law assigns one GNA seat to each of Turkey's sixty-seven provinces and allocates the remaining 333 by the populations of electoral districts. Political parties failing to win at least 10 percent of the national vote get no seats, while the party receiving a plurality of the vote wins an additional bonus of seats. In 1983, this feature enabled the Motherland Party to win 53 percent of GNA seats with only 45 percent of the vote.

The Party System

Origins of the Parties

The Republican People's Party (RPP) of Atatürk was Turkey's first and oldest political party. It was formed in 1923 out of the Associations for the Defense of Rights, which had been organized in 1918 by Turkish nationalists opposed to foreign demands on Turkey. The RPP dominated the one-house National Assembly created by the 1924 constitution, and for twenty-one years it governed Turkey as a one-party regime.

There were two brief experiments with opposition parties during this period. In 1924 a small group of Assembly deputies formed the Progressive Republican Party (*Terakkiperver Cumhuriyet Firkasi*), which criticized the RPP's authoritarianism and opposed its interference with religion. This party was abolished in 1925 after being accused of involvement with a Kurdish rebellion in eastern Turkey.

In 1930, President Atatürk encouraged the formation of the Free Republican Party (*Serbest Cumhuriyet Firkasi*) in the hope of creating a loyal opposition in the Assembly. But it too was dissolved within a year, because it seemed to have stirred up religious reactionaries. The Assembly maintained a ban on new parties until 1946.

At the end of World War II, the government's desire to conform to the practices of the victorious Western democracies and the demand by Turkey's emerging business class for greater political expression combined to convince the Assembly to lift the ban on new parties. After 1946, multiparty politics became the norm.

The Parties in Law

The 1965 Political Parties Law regulated parties from the time of its enactment until the 1980 coup. According to this law, a political party could be formed without government authorization by fifteen qualified persons, provided its statutes and programs did not violate the constitution. Parties had to support the 1960 revolution, Atatürk's reforms, and the principles of democracy and republicanism. They had to be secular, and could not exploit religion for political purposes. Their titles could not contain words such as communist, anarchist, fascist, or national socialist. They could not conduct training or educational activities for military purposes, nor could they recruit school children. They could involve university professors only in their central organizations. All parties had to report their sources of income and expenditures to the Constitutional Court, which was empowered to examine the parties and ban those which violated the law. In order to enter candidates for national office, a party had to organize a local headquarters in a minimum of fifteen provinces at least six months prior to the election date; parties were required to hold primary elections to select candidates.

The 1983 Political Parties' Law increased the minimum number of provinces in which a party must organize to thirty-four. It also prohibited the involvement of university professors in party affairs.

Party Organization

Prior to 1983, practically all political parties originated in the National Assembly and grew from factions in earlier parties. Parties were of the cadre type, led by a small group of men with established political status, financial strength, and often charismatic personalities.

Because various provisions in the 1965 Political Parties Law dealt with organizational requirements, political parties shared many structural similarities. A party's central organs included a general congress, central executive committees, disciplinary committee, and women's and youth wings. In accordance with the 1965 law, the by-laws of all parties stated that the general congress was the party's highest authority and was required to meet at least bi-annually. In practice, extraordinary congresses were also convened.

Delegates to the general congress included representatives elected by the party's provincial congresses and ex officio members. The latter generally included members of the central executive and disciplinary committees, Assembly deputies and senators, cabinet ministers, and the officers of the women's and youth wings. The general congress's main activities included the election, by secret ballot, of the party chairman and members of the central executive committees as well as the approval of the party's program. Party executives explained the party's national policies and strategies to the delegates; in turn, the delegates described local political and economic conditions. The congress served both to communicate and legiti-

mize decisions already reached by a small group of the party's elite.

The party's organization was hierarchical: because top party leaders controlled the decision-making process, an individual's advancement within a party depended on his ability to associate himself with the "inner circle" of party leaders.

Parties maintained disciplinary committees on both the national and provincial levels which took action against members who deviated from either the party's programs, by-laws, or executive-committee directives. Challenges to the leadership's decisions were rare; successful challenges even rarer. All major parties expelled unsuccessful challengers to the inner circle if such challengers continued to criticize the leaders' policies.

The parties' organizational structures paralleled Turkey's administrative divisions. Parties had congresses, executive committees, as well as women's and youth wings on the provincial and subprovincial levels. The 1965 law prohibited party organization on the district and village levels, because its framers feared formal political divisions in the villages would disrupt community life. Parties were allowed one representative in each village who checked the voter registration list and worked to get out the vote during election times. In practice, local party organizations dealt mostly with electoral mobilization, candidate selection, and, when possible, patronage distribution. Locally, however, party membership lists were not accurately kept, and membership dues were neither regularly paid nor insisted upon. Only about 6 percent of the registered voters were party members in 1977.

Provincial and subprovincial congresses were held every two years to elect members of their corresponding executive committees. These committees were extremely influential in determining who went to the general congresses, who ran for local political office, and who was supported in the provincial primaries for national office. Local party leaders were commonly members of major landowning families, doctors, lawyers, and businessmen. Prominent local status, wide-ranging kinship ties, and personal patronage were key qualifications for the attainment of office. Control of the mayor's office was especially important to parties and their local elites because it facilitated the distribution of municipal jobs to party supporters.

For most parties, membership in the provincial women's wings tended to be confined to the wives of party officials. The youth wings consisted mostly of males, ages twenty-one to twenty-nine, and served to recruit party helpers and future leaders. Local youth-wing officers campaigned for party candidates, did clerical work, watched voting boxes on election day, and attended the general congress.

The selection of party candidates for national office involved both the local and national levels through provincial primaries and central executive committee nominations. All aspiring candidates had to file an application with the party central executive committee and pay a fee, which in 1977 ranged from TL 5,000 to TL 15,000 (about $278 to $833) for most parties. The central executive committee had veto power over all applications. No details of filing fees in 1985 were available.

Voting in the primaries, which were held two months before the general election, was restricted to a portion of a party's membership. Though individual party by-laws varied, most granted voting rights to members of local executive committees, locally elected municipal and provincial officials, as well as district and village representatives. The more votes a candidate received, the higher on the final election list his name would appear and the better his chances of being elected.

In addition to the primaries, a party central executive committee exercised the legal right to nominate twenty-three candidates (i.e., 5 percent of 450) for National Assembly seats in the general election and to place those nominees at the top of the party's provincial election lists, even above the names of those who had won the primaries.

This practice sometimes led to friction between local and national party leaders. In 1969, for example, local heads of the RPP in Diyarbakir Province refused to support the RPP list when its central executive committee imposed an unwanted candidate on them. As a consequence, the RPP's share of the vote in that election dropped to 7.3 percent as compared to 23.2 percent in the previous 1965 election.

The legal requirement for party primaries did not democratize the political parties as had been hoped. Of Turkey's almost 17 million registered voters in 1973, only an estimated one million were party members, but because of party restrictions, only about half of these actually voted in the primaries.

Because most parties were founded by men already in the National Assembly, party and parliamentary leadership usually overlapped. In addition to the party organization, major

parties with parliamentary groups (formed with ten or more members) had an additional organization to deal with. Each such parliamentary group had a chairman, usually the party leader. The group held a party caucus at the opening of each legislative term and elected an executive committee. The executive committee designated a party spokesman for legislative debates, decided party strategy, and enforced party cohesion. Historically, conflict between a party's parliamentary group and its party leadership only occurred when members of the party's central executive committee who were not elected to parliament still insisted on directing the parliamentary group's activities.

The 1982 constitution imposed additional restrictions on political parties. It prohibits them from establishing ties with, aiding, or receiving aid from associations, unions, foundations, cooperatives, or public professional organizations. It also prohibits parties from forming auxiliary bodies, such as women's and youth branches, and from having university professors among their members.

Campaigning

Although Turkish law prohibited campaigning in primary contests, candidates still competed intensely to influence party voters and win the backing of local party leaders. Legal, open campaigning for the election began after the primary and progressively intensified up to election day. Parties arranged for their nationally known candidates to address mass rallies in the major cities; lesser figures, and sometimes energetic national leaders, toured small towns and villages.

In the cities, party helpers distributed propaganda leaflets and pasted up wall posters. Newspapers supported their chosen party with news articles and editorials. Some parties and individual candidates took out paid print advertisements. Each party utilized the free radio and television time provided by Turkish law by putting forth their most prominent figures—cabinet ministers, party chairmen, allied intellectuals and professors. Each party's central executive committees instructed its candidates in the party line and strategy. Economic issues were most commonly addressed, with small parties attacking the policies of the large ones, and the two major parties attacking each other.

The amount of financial and personnel support a party gave its candidates depended on its organization and budget. Well-organized parties enjoying a state subvention could offer help; others could not. Practically all candidates had to pay for either some or all of their campaigning expenses out of pocket, often preventing persons of modest means from entering politics. A post 1980 coup campaign pattern has yet to develop but will probably resemble that of the past.

Independent Voters

Although the vast majority of voters are not formal party members, most identify with a party or with political figures who are party members. Hence, with the exceptions noted below, the independent vote has been insignificant.

Turkish law permits independent candidates for national and local offices. For the five National Assembly elections occurring between 1961 and 1977, the percentage of the total vote for all independent candidates ranged between 0.8 percent (1961) to 5.6 percent (1969), and the number of independents elected ranged from none (1961, 1965) to thirteen (1969). On average, only 1 percent of the 450 National Assembly seats went to independents. In 1985 Independents received 1.1% of the vote and no seats in the assembly.

Generally, independents performed much better in the less developed provinces of eastern Turkey where Kurdish and Arab voters often supported independent local notables. In 1969, for example, of the nineteen provinces which gave independents more than 10 percent of their vote, thirteen were in the east. The remaining six were also less developed economically. It has been hypothesized that party institutionalization and identification are more important in Turkey's developed provinces than in the less developed provinces where voters are more responsive to appeals based on local status and popularity.

In terms of forming governments, elected independents played a minor role. One exception was the 1978–79 coalition government headed by Bülent Ecevit of the Republican People's Party. His thirty-four–person cabinet included nine independents from the National Assembly. Most of these, however, had been elected on party tickets and subsequently resigned their parties to join the coalition.

Interestingly, until 1984 voters had been more supportive of independent mayoral candidates than of parliamentary ones. For example, in the mayoral elections of 1963 and 1968, they respectively gave independents 9.7 percent and 13.2 percent of their vote. In 1968, seven of sixty-seven provincial capitals returned independent mayors, and one of these was Bursa, a highly developed city in the west. In 1973, eight independent mayors were elected, but in 1977 the number dropped to two, and in the 1984 mayoral elections no independents were elected to office.

Parties before the 1980 Coup
Justice Party (*Adalet Partisi*)

History

The Justice Party was formed in February 1961 by former members of the Democrat Party, which had been dissolved by the military junta after the 1960 coup. The JP's founder, former general Ragïp Gümüşpala, had been one of the 5,000 officers involuntarily retired by the junta in order to "rejuvenate" the armed forces.

Having inherited much of the Democrat Party's extensive local organization, the JP emerged from the 1961 general elections with 34.8 percent of the vote and 158 National Assembly seats. With no party winning a majority, a series of four coalition governments followed, and the JP participated in two of them.

Internally, the party had two major interest groups or factions: the "extremists" and the "moderates." The extremists opposed the 1960 military coup and demanded immediate amnesty for former Democrat Party members convicted of crimes against the state. Some also opposed Atatürk's secular reforms. The moderates regarded the 1960 coup as a fact of life, believed compromise with the military was politically necessary, and accepted secularism.

The party's Second General Congress, held in 1964, elected moderate Süleyman Demirel party chairman to succeed the recently deceased Gümüşpala. Demirel continued in that post until the 1980 military takeover. Demirel led the JP into the 1965 national elections. By then, the JP was generally regarded as the true successor to the once-popular DP. It emerged from the election with 52.9 percent of the vote and 240 National Assembly seats. The JP formed its first majority government with the forty-one-year-old Demirel as prime minister. From 1965 to 1971 Demirel headed three JP governments, and from 1977 to 1980 he led three JP-dominated coalition governments.

The party's heterogeneous makeup eventually led to two major splits. In 1970, twenty-six JP deputies, including JP Parliamentary Speaker Ferruh Bözbeyli, were expelled from the party for their failure to support the JP government's budget proposal. They formed the rival Democratic Party, which favored the emerging provincial bourgeoisie over the large urban capitalists allegedly supported by Demirel. The dissenters also defended rural landowners against Demirel and his proposed tax on rural land profits. In the same year, a small group of religious conservatives left the party to organize the pro-Islamic National Order Party under the leadership of Necmettin Erbakan, an independent deputy, but former JP member. In 1969, Demirel had vetoed Erbakan's application to enter the National Assembly primaries as a candidate on the JP list.

Organization

The JP was one of the two major parties to organize in all provinces, subprovinces, and districts. Like other parties, its chairman and central executive committees determine party policy, direction, and strategy. The JP's central executive committees were somewhat more balanced and less elitist than those of the rival Republican People's Party (RPP). From 1961 to 1970, 89 percent of JP central executives had university educations; 36 percent were professionals (18 percent lawyers, 12 percent doctors, and 6 percent engineers); 15 percent were government employees; 12 percent had had military careers; 10 percent were businessmen; 9 percent were educators; and 8 percent were agriculturalists.

In many ways, the party's strength lay in its diversity. After becoming chairman in 1964, Demirel so successfully balanced party factions that his leadership was seldom seriously challenged. He tended to consult with the executive committees on major decisions, but was firm in expelling rivals who failed to support the party in parliamentary votes.

Among the major independent dailies supporting the JP were *Tercuman*, *Son Havadis*, *Adalet*, and *Yeni Asir*. The party was also supported by the Freedom Youth Association (*Hürriyetçi Gençler Derneği*).

Policy

Domestically, the JP's approach to politics was adaptive and anti-elitist. It was more likely to utilize political patronage to win votes than was the RPP. The JP occupied a right-of-center (liberal-conservative) position on the political spectrum. It strongly favored private enterprise (large and small) within a mixed economy and advocated tolerance for traditional religious expression. It also advocated rural development and educational expansion, especially in the villages. It appealed to many sectors of society by promising a better standard of living through economic development rather than through wealth redistribution. It was ardently anticommunist.

In terms of foreign policy, the JP promoted Turkey's memberships in the European Economic Community, NATO, and CENTO. It encouraged exports and welcomed foreign capital on condition that such capital be controlled by the state. It was cautiously pro-American.

Membership & Constituency

The party no longer exists. It is estimated to have had a membership of 450,000 in 1977.

The JP's liberal economic policies, its stress on rural development, and its religious tolerance appealed to a wide variety of voters in terms of class, age, and sex. Hence, it succeeded in becoming a mass party, supported by peasants, artisans, businessmen, conservative urban dwellers, and families of the aspiring middle class. The party's share of the vote in the five general elections between 1961 and 1977 ranged from 30 percent (1973) to 52.9 percent (1965). Geographically, its major support in relative order of strength came from the Aegean, Mediterranean, Black Sea, Marmara and Central Anatolian regions. The first two of these areas are typified by middle and large landowners, extensive cash cropping, a growing commercial class, and high levels of religiosity.

Financing

The JP's share of the vote in national elections qualified it for large state subventions, the amounts varying with the size of the vote and the amount of the national revenue. Party dues were not regularly collected, and candidates financed parts of their own campaigns. Exact figures are not available.

Leadership

Süleyman Demirel (born 1924) is a professional engineer without military affiliations. After graduating from Istanbul Technical University in 1949, with a degree in hydraulic engineering, he went to the United States for further study on an Eisenhower Exchange Fellowship. Back in Turkey, he was appointed general director of the State Water Works in 1955, at the age of thirty-one, by then prime minister Adnan Menderes of the Democrat Party. Demirel proved to be a capable manager. After the 1960 coup, he went into private business, becoming a successful engineering consultant. He joined the newly formed JP in 1961 and was party chairman from 1964 until it was dissolved in 1980. In post 1980 coup politics, he became the power behind the Correct Way Party.

Republican People's Party (RPP; *Cumhuriyet Halk Partisi*)

History

Formed originally in early 1923 as the People's Party under the chairmanship of Mustafa Kemal (later surnamed Atatürk), its name was changed to the Republican People's Party in November 1924. Atatürk continued as chairman until his death in 1938. Retired general Ismet İnönü—Atatürk's close comrade—held the post until his resignation in 1972. He was followed by Bülent Ecevit, who chaired the party until the 1980 coup.

From 1923 to 1946, the RPP ruled Turkey as a single-party regime and perceived itself as the architect of the modern nation-state. The party was authoritarian and tutelary, devoted to strict secularism, Western-style reform, and state intervention in the economy. Its power was reenforced by its alliance with the military and civil bureaucracy.

Between 1923 and 1950, the RPP's domestic policy was devoted to the legitimation, control, and direction of the modernization program initiated by Atatürk and continued by İnönü. The policy's main principles of republicanism, nationalism, populism, secularism, reformism, and statism became the party's "six arrows." However, the party lacked a formal ideology or comprehensive doctrine. Its stress on urban economic development and its radical secularism accentuated the elite-mass cleavage during the one-party period, alienating many of the country's peasants. This legacy adversely affected the RPP electoral performance in the era of competitive party policies. The RPP eventually was defeated by a group of its own dissenters in 1950—the year of Turkey's first fairly contested election. Thereafter, the RPP failed to return to power as the majority party.

In the mid-1960s Ecevit and his faction moved the party to a left-of-center position and designed a new party image. Politically, the party attempted to broaden its support base by appealing to the lower economic classes; economically, it favored development in the rural areas where most of the people lived. Ecevit criticized the condescending attitude that the RPP elitists had exhibited toward the peasants. He argued that the party should play down its secular stand and identify more with the common Turk. He set an example by touring the villages and recruiting craftsmen and workers into the party. Ecevit also terminated the party's long-standing alignment with the military by criticizing the generals' interventions in 1971 and 1980.

During the Atatürk years, the RPP followed a neutral foreign policy. Atatürk often spoke against entangling alliances and opposed extensive foreign borrowing or foreign investment in Turkey. He promoted an era of revolutionary cooperation with the Soviet Union, but forbade the formation of a Communist Party in Turkey. Although Turkey had close economic ties with Nazi Germany, the RPP kept the country out of World War II. The Soviet demand for joint control of the Turkish Straits at the end of the war caused the RPP government to turn to the United States for help. Subsequently, the party promoted Turkish–American alliances and followed a pro-American, pro-NATO , and pro-CENTO foreign policy.

Organization

The RPP had the basic organizational form prescribed by the 1965 Political Parties Law. After 1950, the RPP was one of the two major parties to be organized in all of Turkey's provinces, subprovinces, and districts. From 1960 to 1970 its central executive committees were dominated by men with university educations (96 percent). Approximately one-third were lawyers; about 15 percent were university professors; 10 percent were retired military officers; and only 3 percent had agricultural occupations. It was an elitist party.

In the late 1960s, however, more workers, peasants, and young urban intellectuals were attracted to the party. This trend accelerated after Ecevit took over the party in 1972 and turned it in a social-democratic direction. Grass-roots participation in the party councils, though not extensive, probably exceeded that of other Turkish parties at the time of the military takeover.

The party published the key speeches of its chairmen and other top leaders in book form and also published a daily called *Ulus* (Nation). The RPP was favored by *Cumhuriyet* (Republic), Turkey's fifth-largest daily newspaper.

Policy

A major struggle within the party occurred in 1971 and 1972. Then secretary general Ecevit and his left-of-center faction strongly opposed the 1971 military intervention in government, refusing to participate in the "above party" coalition government that the military demanded. Party Chairman Ismet Inönü and his centrist supporters, on the other hand, supported the military, and one member of this faction even resigned from the party in order to become the independent prime minister of the coalition. This caused a break between the party's two top men.

In the RPP's 1972 Extraordinary Congress, Ecevit opposed Kemal Satir, Inönü's candidate for secretary general. Inönü, then almost eighty-eight years old, announced he would resign the chairmanship if Satir were not elected. Ecevit won; Inönü resigned. (Inönü died December 25, 1973.) Ecevit subsequently was elected party chairman, and the defeated Satir and his faction left the RPP to form the Republican Party. Thereafter, Ecevit promoted his left-of-center or social-democratic philosophy and took the party into the Socialist International.

The RPP and the country reexamined the policy of almost exclusive reliance on the West when Turkey came into conflict with Greece (a NATO partner) over Cyprus in the 1960s and 1970s. After Turkey intervened militarily in Cyprus in 1974, world reaction caused the nation to feel isolated. The United States embargoed arms shipments to Turkey because of the intervention, and European allies refused to rally to Turkey's side against Greece. Conse-

quently, the RPP, led by Ecevit, proposed that all alliances and bilateral agreements (especially those with the United States) be reexamined. Ecevit also advocated strengthening diplomatic and economic ties with Arabs, the Eastern Bloc, and Third World countries. He favored détente between the superpowers, while continuing to support Turkish memberships in the European Economic Community and NATO.

Membership & Constituency

The party is no longer in existence. At its height in 1977, it had an estimated membership of 500,000.

Historically, the RPP drew its support from civil servants, military officers, urban professionals and intellectuals, large landowners, and religious minorities, who believed the party's secular policies protected them from the Turkish Sunni Muslim majority. From the mid-1960s on, the party directed its appeal more to young urban intellectuals and to workers and peasants.

In the five general elections for the National Assembly (1961–77) before its reformation in 1983, the RPP's portion of the total vote ranged from 27.4 percent (1969) to 41.4 percent (1977). Geographically, its main support came from the major urban areas of Istanbul, Ankara, Izmir, and Adana, and from provinces in the Black Sea, East Central, Mediterranean, and Aegean regions.

Financing

Because of its percentage of the national vote, the RPP always qualified for comparatively large state subventions. The amounts varied with vote totals and the state's fluctuating annual revenue. Party dues were not systematically paid or collected, and candidates financed parts of their own campaigns. Exact figures are not available.

Leadership

Bülent Ecevit (born 1925) differed from the party's previous leaders. During the late 1940s, he had served in London as a Turkish press attaché. While there he developed an admiration for the British trade-union movement and democratic socialism. In the 1960s, he served as minister of labor in three coalition governments headed by Inönü. In the seventies, Bülent Ecevit led three short-lived coalition governments. His denouncement of the military's curtailment of press and speech rights in 1981 earned him a court conviction and a four-month prison sentence. After his release from prison, he continued to criticize the government, spent another two months in prison, and faced further charges for his outspokenness. In addition, Ecevit and the RPP were charged with collusion with left-wing terrorist groups, with complicity with DISK (Confederation of Revolutionary Labor Unions), and with insulting a judge. While officially banned from participating in politics until 1990, Ecevit retains influence through his wife's role in the Democratic Left Party.

Minor Parties

Most minor parties appeared after 1950, growing out of the two major parties. During the 1970s, when neither the JP nor the RPP could win an electoral majority, some of the small right-wing parties gained inordinate political power because of their participation in coalition governments and control of various ministries. Below are brief descriptions of the five minor parties which competed in both the 1973 and 1977 general elections. The Turkish Labor Party, also described, was banned during the 1973 election.

Democratic Party (*Demokratik Parti; DP*)

The DP was formed in 1970 by forty right-wing members of the Justice Party who opposed Demirel's leadership. They were headed by Ferruh Bözbeyli (born 1927), a lawyer and former president of the National Assembly. The DP defended the emerging provincial bourgeoisie against large urban capitalists and promoted greater respect for Islam. The party placed itself midway between the Justice Party and the National Salvation Party on the political spectrum.

With the backing of Celal Bayar—former president of Turkey (from 1950 until the 1960 coup) and former leader of the outlawed Democrat Party—the Democratic Party managed to win 11.8 percent of the vote and forty-five National Assembly seats in the 1973 election. In 1975, however, about a dozen deputies left the DP (among them Bayar's daughter, Nilüfer

Güsoy) to join the Justice Party and support Demirel's National Front Coalition Government. Additional defections followed. In the 1977 general election, the DP returned only one deputy, Faruk Sükan. Bözbeyli resigned the party's chairmanship, and Sükan became acting chairman. Sükan served in the RPP Ecevit-led coalition cabinet from May 1978 until September 1979, when he resigned. The DP Congress of May 1980 decided to dissolve the party.

National Action Party (NAP; *Milliyetçi Hareket Partisi*)

The NAP had its roots in the Republican Peasants Nation Party (RPNP) founded in 1954 under the leadership of Osman Bölükbaşi. In 1962, when the RPNP executive committee voted to join a coalition government with Inönü, Bölükbaşi and twenty-eight other RPNP deputies bolted and established the Nation Party. Subsequently, in 1965, former colonel Alparslan Türkeş and his supporters gained control of the RPNP and gave it a new mission. In 1969, the RPNP renamed itself the National Action Party.

Türkeş has been one of the fourteen radical members of the 1960–61 ruling junta who were expelled because of their insistence on prolonged military rule. Seeking a vehicle for political leadership, he and some of the other "fourteen" joined the RPNP in 1965. Subsequent to being elected party chairman, Türkeş firmly established his one-man rule over the party and imposed strict military discipline on its members. The party's ideology took on a fascist character, favoring the state over the individual, exalting Turkish nationalism, and promoting the union of Turkic peoples all over the world. The party's program was antisocialist, but favored the nationalization of heavy industry and the promotion of small private enterprise. In its foreign policy, the party opposed all "imperial alignments," but sided with the West against the communist East.

The NAP gained distinction for its violent opposition to the left in Turkey. Türkeş promoted the Idealist Youth Associations (*Ülkücü Gençlik Dernekleri*)—right-wing militants who clashed with their left-wing counterparts throughout the 1970s. Under Türkeş' leadership, the party's best electoral performance was in 1977 when it received 6.4 percent of the vote and sixteen National Assembly seats. Geographically, the party's main support came from Adana—the province in which Türkeş ran—several Central Anatolian provinces, and two eastern provinces (Kars and Van). The NAP participated in three right-wing coalition governments headed by JP leader Demirel in 1971 to 1973, 1974 and 1975, and 1975 to 1977.

After the 1980 coup, Türkeş and over one hundred NAP members were arrested and charged with crimes against the state and its citizens. Türkeş was charged with personally ordering the murders of the former president of the Confederation of Revolutionary Labor Unions (DISK) and of a police chief. He also was accused of conducting activities under the cover of a political party to overthrow the constitutional order and establish a dictatorship. The indictment went on to say that the NAP divided the country into mutually hostile camps of right and left, and Türkeş supplied arms to and directed the right-wing extremists, called "idealists," who engaged in terrorist acts for the purpose of establishing the dictatorship. The prosecution asked for the death penalty. The trial was still in process in 1986.

National Salvation Party (NSP; *Milli Selamet Partisi*)

Formed in October 1972, the NSP was actually a rejuvenation of the National Order Party (*Milli Nizam Partisi*), which had been banned by the Constitutional Court in 1971 on grounds of "antisecular activities." Its leader, Necmettin Erbakan, was not arrested, however, and was permitted to join the NSP in 1973. His supporters, the actual founders of the NSP, quickly made Erbakan its chairman.

The party was pro-Islamic, favoring government support for religious education and proreligious legislation. It opposed both communism and large-scale capitalism. Its foreign policy advocated disengagement from alliances with the West and closer attachment with other Muslim countries. Erbakan made no secret of his opposition to Atatürk's reforms. He was always conspicuously absent from official ceremonies honoring Atatürk's achievements.

The party received enough support from poorly educated, provincial Muslim conservatives living in underdeveloped regions of Turkey to become the largest of the minor parties. It was the only minor party to form parliamentary groups after both the 1973 and 1977 elections, when it received 11.9 percent of the vote

for forty-eight National Assembly seats and 8.6 percent of the vote for twenty-four seats, respectively. The NSP entered into a strained coalition with the RPP in 1977 and then with the JP and other right-wing parties in 1975 to 1977, 1977 and 1978, and 1979 to 1980.

After the 1980 coup, Erbakan and thirty-three other NSP members were arrested and charged in military court with using the NSP to establish a theocratic state based on Islamic law. They were convicted in 1983, but acquitted on retrial in 1985.

Republican Reliance Party (RRP; *Cumhuriyetci Güven Partisi*)

The RRP originally was formed as the Reliance Party in 1967, a year after its leader, Turhan Feyzioğlu, had been defeated by Bülent Ecevit in the RPP election for the post of secretary general. Feyzioğlu and forty other parliamentarians quit the RPP in protest over Ecevit's and the RPP's new left-of-center position and established the Reliance Party. In 1972, Kemal Satir, who had also been defeated by Ecevit in an RPP election for secretary general, left the RPP with his right-of-center followers and formed the Republican Party. In 1973, the Reliance and the Republican parties merged, creating the Republican Reliance Party with Feyzioğlu as its chairman.

The RRP's right-of-center domestic and foreign policies were similar to those of the JP. It was strongly anticommunist and opposed left-wing movements in Turkey. However, it failed to compete successfully against either major party. The RRP's vote in general elections progressively dwindled from 6.6 percent (for fifteen National Assembly seats) in 1969 to only 1.9 percent (for three seats) in 1977. During the last legislative term, it was unable to form a parliamentary group. In earlier terms, the RRP participated in two "above party" interim governments (1971–73 and 1974–75) and in one Demirel-led coalition government (1975–77).

Although the RRP was heading for extinction in the late 1970s, Feyzioğlu continued to be regarded highly as a politician. Born in 1922 in Kayseri, he later studied law and joined the political science faculty of Ankara University. There he established a reputation as a brilliant professor of constitutional law. He joined the RPP in the 1950s and became İnönü's right-hand man. His political experience included serving as minister of education and as deputy prime minister in several cabinets. After the 1980 coup, Feyzioğlu was appointed rector of Ankara's Middle East Technical University.

Turkish Labor Party (TLP; *Türkiye Işçi Partisi*)

Founded in 1961 as an expressedly Marxist party (an act permissible under Turkey's liberal 1961 constitution), the TLP became the country's only significant radical left-wing party. Former law professor Ali Mehmet Aybar became party leader in 1962 and sought to disseminate Marxist principles through an effective organizational network supported by a dues-paying membership. The party failed to win the support of *Türk-Iş*—Turkey's largest confederation of labor unions—but still did well in the 1965 elections, winning 3 percent of the vote and fifteen National Assembly seats (thanks to the national remainder system). In 1967, it allied with DISK, the newly formed confederation of radical trade unions.

The party soon became divided into three factions: Aybar's European Marxist faction; Behice Boran's pro-Moscow faction; and a Maoist group. After the 1969 election in which the TLP got 2.7 percent of the vote, but only two seats (the national remainder system had been dropped), Boran and her faction gained control of the party.

The Constitutional Court banned the party following the 1971 military intervention on the grounds that the TLP had made communist propaganda and encouraged separatist movements among the Kurds in the East. Boran received a fifteen-year prison sentence, but was released in 1974, thanks to an amnesty bill. She and her supporters reestablished the TLP in 1975, but it mustered only 0.14 percent of the vote and won no seats in the 1977 election. Party supporters traditionally had been leftist intellectuals, radical union members, and some Kurds and Alevis (Shi'a Muslims). By the late 1970's most of them had switched their support to the leftward-moving Republican People's Party.

After the 1980 coup, Boran and some other Marxists fled to Eastern Europe. Since then, the government has deprived Boran of her Turkish citizenship and a military court has convicted her in absentia of crimes of subversion. The TLP was charged with instigating left-wing terrorism for the purpose of establishing a communist state.

Turkish Unity Party (TUP; *Türkiye Birlik Partisi*)

The TUP was founded in 1966 by former Nation Party members and Alevi (Shi'a) businessmen for the purpose of protecting Turkey's Alevi minority population. The party enthusiastically supported Atatürk's secular reforms and the principle of separation of state and religion.

Alevi grievances against the Sunni majority were especially pronounced in the mid-1960s, when the Sunni-dominated State Religious Bureau promoted policies favoring the religious rights of the majority over those of the Alevi minority.

Because the 1965 Political Parties Law prohibited parties from making claims about the existence of religious or linguistic minority groups in Turkey, the TUP was cautious in its approach. Instead of mentioning the Alevis directly, it stressed the principle of equal rights for all Turkish citizens in matters of education and religion. However, the party's emblem, with its twelve stars standing for the twelve Shi'a imams, was a clear sign of its purpose.

Politically and economically, the party was left of center, advocating state planning and the nationalization of large-scale industry, banking, and insurance, as well as land and tax reform. In 1973, its chairman, Mustafa Timisi, accused the Republican People's Party of being a bourgeois organization and made overtures to the Turkish Labor Party to form an electoral alliance. Originally, the TUP was strong among Alevi voters in several Central Anatolian provinces (winning a high of eight National Assembly seats in 1969). Thereafter, however, support for the party declined. It suffered a severe defeat in the 1977 election, taking less than one percent of the vote and losing its only parliamentary seat. It never participated in a government cabinet.

Parties after the 1980 Coup

Following its 1980 takeover, the NSC announced new laws on political parties and elections. These laws stipulated that leaders and administrators of the parties active on September 11, 1980 (the eve of the coup), are prohibited until 1992 from engaging in political activity. In addition, persons who were members of Parliament on January 1, 1980, may not form parties or serve as administrative officers in them until 1987. Consequently, when the NSC permitted the formation of new parties in 1983, many new faces appeared on the scene.

Motherland Party
(*Anavatan Partisi*; MP)

The MP is politically conservative, favoring liberal economic policies, private enterprise, and alliances with both Western and Muslim countries. It won a plurality of the vote in both the 1983 parliamentary and the 1984 local elections. Party chairman Turgut Ozal is a traditional Muslim. Born in the eastern province of Malatya in 1927, he graduated as an electrical engineer from Istanbul Technical University. He later headed Turkey's State Planning Organization and worked with the World Bank in Washington, D.C. He designed and directed the economic recovery program in ex-Premier Demirel's last government. When the military took control in 1980, the NSC promoted him to Deputy Prime Minister in charge of the economy.

Social Democrat Populist Party
(*Sosyal Demokrat Halkci Partisi*; SDPP)

The SDPP resulted from the November 1985 merger of the Populist Party (PP) and the extraparliamentary Social Democracy Party (Sodep). Both had been formed in 1983, but the NSC had prevented Sodep from entering that year's election. In the 1984 local elections, however, Sodep entered and won 23.4 percent of the vote versus only 8.8 percent for the PP.

Both were social democratic parties comprised primarily of former Republican People's Party supporters. Necdet Calp, the PP's first chairman, had served as the late Ismet Inönü's private secretary. Sodep's chairman was Erdal Inönü, Ismet Inönü's son. Erdal entered politics in 1983 after teaching physics in Turkish universities for many years.

The SDPP is chaired by Aydin Gurkan, a deputy from Aydin, who had been elected PP chairman at that party's June 1985 Congress. The two left-of-center parties merged to become

a strong opposition and viable alternative to the ruling Motherland Party.

Minor Parties

Of the several minor parties, only one—the National Democracy Party (NDP)—holds seats in Parliament. This conservative, law-and-order party was originally headed by retired general Turgut Sunalp. However, after the party's poor showing in the 1984 local elections, the party congress elected Ülkü Söylemezoğlu, a deputy from Kahramanmaras, as its new chairman. In August 1985, Söylemezoğlu announced that he and Husamettin Cindoruk, head of the small Correct Way Party (CWP), had entered into party merger talks. The CWP, which had outperformed the NDP in the 1984 local elections, is the unabashed front for ex-Premier Süleyman Demirel—a resilient and still popular politician.

Two other new parties on the right, but of little consequence, are the Islamic Welfare Party and the Nationalist Activity Party. The first represents the policies and symbols of the defunct National Salvation Party, while the second is a successor to the pre-coup National Action Party. In addition, in late 1985, Rahsan Ecevit, wife of ex-Premier Bulent Ecevit, announced the formation of the Democratic Left Party, hoping to attract her husband's old supporters.

Other Political Forces

Military

Traditionally, military officers have acted as Turkey's windows to the West. The Turkish military under Atatürk was largely responsible for the creation of the Turkish Republic in 1923 and for those trends in Turkish society which aim at a secular, democratic state.

There are three major reasons for the military's persistent involvement in politics: (1) the tradition of Atatürk; (2) the bitterly hostile relationships between the political parties, which rarely cooperated for the good of the country; and (3) the military's determination to protect its own social status and economic interests.

The 1950–60 period of Democrat Party rule was the one in which the military enjoyed the least political power. Under the Democrats, the military's budget received less priority than formerly, inflation eroded officers' fixed salaries, and officers' status declined markedly relative to those of the rising urban and provincial commercial entrepreneurs. When the Democrat Party became repressive and ordered the military to put down antigovernment demonstrations, the officers staged a coup on May 27, 1960, declaring they had acted in the name of Atatürk and democracy.

During its period of rule (lasting until October 25, 1961), the junta (National Unity Committee, or NUC) banned the Democrat Party and had its leader jailed. The NUC set about establishing a new legal framework for democratic government; it also increased salaries and benefits for the military.

The 1961 constitution more securely institutionalized the military's role in government by making NUC members lifetime senators and by creating a National Security Council comprised of government ministers, the chief of the General Staff, and representatives of the armed forces. This council provided the formal context in which military leaders could communicate their views directly to the prime minister and his cabinet. Informally, military leaders also believed they had the right to pick the country's presidents.

In addition, former military officers were conspicuously present in all the major and most of the minor parties. Of the RPP and JP central committee members from 1961 to 1970, 11 percent and 12 percent respectively were former officers. Two generals and a colonel were instrumental in the formation of minor parties. Factions within the armed forces reflect the divisions in the society as a whole as expressed in its political parties, but the dominant military faction has always been the moderate, Atatürkist one.

Since the 1960s, the military has developed several of Turkey's major investment institutions. The largest is OYAK, the Army Mutual Assistance Foundation. Headed by retired general Nazmi Yavusalp, OYAK has invested large amounts of capital (obtained through voluntary deductions from the salaries of military personnel) in numerous Turkish industries, from automobile and tire manufacturing to retail outlets. With so many officers and enlisted men relying on Turkey's economic development for investment and retirement incomes, the military can have little patience with radical labor unions or ineffective governments which appear to mismanage the economy.

Organized Labor

Throughout his life, Atatürk opposed all class-based organizations, including labor unions, believing they would divide the country. Labor unions were first permitted in 1947, but they were denied the right to strike. After legislation in 1963 legalized strikes, lockouts, and collective bargaining, labor unions began to grow in size and political importance. The number of unions climbed from 432 in 1960 to 863 in 1977, while their estimated total membership jumped from 283,000 to about 3.8 million. Unions continued to be prohibited from having organizational affiliations with political parties.

In the late 1970s, about 70 percent of union members belonged to *Türk-Iş* (Confederation of Turkish Labor Unions), the oldest and most moderate major confederation. It pursued a pragmatic "above party" strategy. About 20 percent of union members belonged to the militant, leftist DISK (Confederation of Revolutionary Labor Unions), established in 1967 by *Türk-Iş* dissidents desiring a more active political policy. It alternately favored the Marxist Turkish Labor Party and the Republican People's Party. About 100,000 workers belonged to MISK (Confederation of National Labor Unions), founded in 1969 as a right-wing, pro–National Action Party confederation. Only about 20,000 workers belonged to *Hak-Iş* (Confederation of Right Labor Unions), founded in 1977 as a right-wing, pro–National Salvation Party organization.

During the 1970s, many unions, especially those associated with DISK, engaged in frequent and violent strikes, forcing the government to declare martial law in the major industrial areas. In June of 1980, about three months before the coup, there were almost 48,000 workers on strike affecting 203 work places. Almost 90 percent of the strikers were DISK members.

After the coup, the National Security Council suspended many labor-union rights and banned all confederations and most of their member unions with the exception of the moderate *Türk-Iş*. The leaders of the other confederations were placed under arrest pending the outcome of investigations into their alleged illegal activities. In June of 1981, the last DISK chairman, Abdullah Baştürk (a former RPP deputy), and fifty-one other DISK officials were formally charged with instigating violent demonstrations and conducting other illegal activities with the aim of establishing a Marxist–Leninist state.

Students

During the early decades of the republic, university students were a small, politically moderate elite. By the 1950s, their numbers had increased markedly and they gained prominence by playing a leading role in the opposition movement against Prime Minister Adnan Menderes and the Democrat government. The government had alienated the students and the historically pro–Republican People's Party faculty by refusing to promote teachers critical of the government, by curbing unfavorable political expression by the press and individuals, and by ordering the army to suppress antigovernment campus demonstrations. Many students believed their activities were critical to the military's decision to stage the 1960 coup.

During the following decades, political activism among university students accelerated. From the later 1960s to the late 1970s, the number of university students doubled to 315,000. The period was also one of rising inflation, high unemployment, and a decline in the quality of the expanding educational system. The massive influx of students in certain fields of education such as law, political science, sociology, and history, was grossly disproportionate to the employment opportunities available in those fields. Student discontent was critically heightened and expressed itself in the formation of numerous radical right- and left-wing organizations. These included *Dev Genç* (Revolutionary Youth), *Dev Yol* (Revolutionary Path), *Türk Halk Kurtuluş Ordusu* (Turkish People's Liberation Army), and the rightist *Komandolar* (Commandos).

The militant leftists proclaimed that Atatürkism had no relevance to contemporary conditions. Armed revolution was the only solution. Rightists and leftists clashed violently for control of university and even high school campuses. Political parties on the right and left encouraged and protected their favored student organizations. By the late 1970s, the students' main contributions to the political scene were violence and chaos.

After the 1980 coup, the military government quickly disbanded the radical student organizations and rounded up their members. Many were tried and convicted of crimes ranging from murder and kidnapping to armed robbery. The mass of moderate students, who had been caught up in the crossfire, welcomed the peace that finally returned to their campuses. Since 1983 all political student organizations have continued to be outlawed. Only educational and cultural associations are allowed.

Interest Group Organizations

Turkey's major private business interests are promoted by several associations. Two of the most important are the Turkish Union of Chambers of Commerce (*Türkiye Odalar Birliği*) and TÜSIAD (Turkish Industrialists and Businessmen's Association). The first handles private-business contracts with foreign firms and has established the Supreme Negotiation Council to study the role of the private sector in Turkish–EEC relations. Established in 1971 by prominent industrialists, TÜSIAD operates a respected research center that produces economic studies and forecasts which influence government policy.

Both organizations favored the Justice Party because of its pro-private-sector attitude. However, they became impatient with the JP-led coalitions in the late 1970s and welcomed the 1980 military action. They supported the postcoup economic-recovery program. Now they tend to support the Motherland Party.

Ethnic Groups

Approximately 80 to 85 percent of Turkey's 50 million population in 1985 is ethnically Turkish. The rest are Kurds, Arabs, Slavs, Bulgars, Greeks, Armenians, Jews, Gypsies, Circassians, Georgians, and others. According to law, all share the same rights of Turkish citizenship. But because Turkish is the only official language, some of the minorities are disadvantaged educationally, socially, and economically.

With an estimated population of six to eight million, the Kurds constitute the largest and politically most important ethnic minority. Most Kurds of Turkey live in the underdeveloped eastern provinces, and organized for the most part into tribes of pastoral nomads and peasant farmers. Their Indo–Iranian language is unrelated to Turkish. Because of their geopolitical separation as well as internal social and dialect variations, the Kurdish people have never unified into a single national movement, although separate national movements have existed among them in Turkey, Iraq and Iran.

In Turkey, about two-thirds of the Kurds are Sunni Muslims of the Shafii rite (as opposed to the dominant Turkish Sunni Hanafi rite) and one-third are Alevis (Shi'a). Hence, Kurds differ from the Turkish majority linguistically, religiously, geographically, and socially.

In its desire to develop a unified Turkish nation-state, the government under Atatürk prohibited the use of Kurdish and certain other minority languages in schools, government affairs, and the public media. Kurds were referred to as Mountain Turks, and Kurdish was regarded as a crude Turkish dialect. However, educational and economic opportunities were insufficient to foster full Kurdish integration into Turkish society.

During the multiparty period, local Kurdish notables entered into alliances with various political parties, especially the New Turkish Party in the sixties, the JP, the RPP, and the Marxist TLP. Such alliances did little to develop the Kurdish area economically or free it culturally. In the 1970s, many left-wing radical groups appealed to the Kurds for support, describing them as economically exploited and culturally suppressed people in a capitalist system. About fifteen small and uncoordinated Kurdish separatist organizations allegedly existed at that time. After the 1980 coup, the military quickly disbanded them and rounded up their leaders. Over 2,000 Kurds were prosecuted in 1982 for a variety of separatist activities. In early 1985, 25 of these defendents received death sentences and hundreds were sent to prison.

Religious Groups

During the republic's early decades, Atatürk was determined to disestablish Islam as the state religion. He abolished the caliphate, closed religious schools and religious lodges (*Tarikat*s), and prohibited religious dress in public. A number of Muslim orders—such as the Ticanis, Nurcus, and Kurdish Nakshibendis—revolted and were crushed. In recent times, the only serious move against secularism came from the National Salvation Party.

Turkey is 98 percent Muslim: 80 percent Sunni and 18 percent Shi'a (mostly Alevi). Conservative Sunni Muslims tended to support the religiously tolerant Democrat Party from 1950 to 1960, and its successor, the JP, thereafter. Very conservative Sunnis backed the NSP. They regarded the Alevis not only as heretics, but as fifth-column communists. Many of the Alevis (who are Turks, Arabs and Kurds) favored the RPP, believing its strong stand on secularism protected them from the Sunni majority. Some supported the short-lived Turkish Unity Party, which was founded by Alevis for Alevis.

During the chaotic 1970s, provocateurs, probably of both right and left, inflamed tensions between the two sects in low-income urban areas and in a number of eastern provinces. Clashes became so violent, that martial law had to be declared and extended to maintain peace. Martial law in many of the eastern provinces continued into 1986.

National Prospects

During the 1980-1983 period of military rule, Turkey's political anarchy and violence ended. The country achieved political and social stability. Despite notable economic improvements, the annual inflation and unemployment rates during the eighties have been running at about 50 percent and 20 percent respectively. Various public opinion polls show that enthusiasm for the Motherland Party and its economic policies has declined, while support for the new Social Democrat Populist Party and its left-of-center predecessors has increased. In a late 1985 poll, conducted by the *Milliyet* newspaper, the percentages of voters favoring the four leading parties were as follows: SDPP, 39 percent; MP, 30 percent; Correct Way, 18.5 percent; and National Democracy Party, 6.5 percent.

The right-of-center NDP, which holds seventy-one parliamentary seats, will probably merge with the CWP before the 1988 elections. If so, that contest will involve two strong parties on the right and one on the left. Should the economy fail to improve, the social democratic SDPP will probably win a plurality of the vote.

Of the deposed political leaders, Suleyman Demirel of the old Justice Party appears to be the most influential. His popularity explains the sudden rise of the Correct Way Party. Whether this popularity can be sustained until 1992, when Demirel can once again run for office, is an open question.

Further Readings

Ahmad, Feroz. *The Turkish Experiment in Democracy 1950–1975.* Boulder, Colo.: Westview Press, 1977.

Bianchi, Robert. *Interest Groups and Political Development in Turkey.* Princeton: Princeton University Press, 1984.

Dodd, C. H. *Democracy and Development in Turkey.* New York: Humanities Press, 1980.

Hale, William. *Political and Economic Development in Modern Turkey.* New York: St. Martin's Press, 1981.

Karpat, Kemal H. *Turkey's Politics: The Transition to a Multi-Party System.* Princeton, N. J.: Princeton University Press, 1959.

———, ed. *Social Change and Politics in Turkey.* Leiden: E. J. Brill, 1973.

Landau, Jacob M. *Radical Politics in Turkey.* Leiden: E. J. Brill, 1974.

———; Ozbudun, Ergun; and Tachau, Frank eds. *Electoral Politics in the Middle East.* London; Croom Helm, 1980; and Stanford, Calif.: Hoover Institution, 1980.

Magnarella, Paul J. *Tradition and Change in a Turkish Town.* 2d rev. ed. Cambridge, Mass.: Schenkman, 1982.

Ozbudun, Ergun. *Social Change and Political Participation in Turkey.* Princeton, N. J.: Princeton University Press, 1976.

Tachau, Frank. *Turkey: The Politics of Authority, Democracy and Development.* New York: Praeger, 1984.

Turan, Ilter. "Political Perspectives." *Current Turkish Thought,* Nos. 44–45, Fall-Winter, 1980.

Weiker, Walter F. *The Modernization of Turkey from Ataturk to the Present Day.* New York and London: Holmes and Meier, 1981.

REPUBLIC OF UGANDA

by Jeanne Marie Col, Ph.D.

The System of Government

Uganda, a nation of about 13.5 million people, is a unitary state with a mixed presidential-parliamentary democracy. A former British colony, Uganda gained self-governing status in 1961 and full independence the following year. In 1967, a new constitution altered the Westminister system inherited from the British, giving the president full executive authority. In 1971, President A. Milton Obote was ousted by General Idi Amin in a military coup. After nearly eight years of tyrannical misrule, Amin was overthrown by a combined force of Ugandan exiles and Tanzanian troops. In 1980, Obote was reelected to the presidency, the first African executive to be restored to office by election after having been ousted in a coup. In 1985, Obote again was overthrown in an intramilitary ethnic struggle by an Acholi group which remained in power for only six months. In 1986, the Uganda Patriotic Movement, which had been engaged in guerrilla struggle for four years, overthrew the government in a protracted military action led by Yoweri Museveni.

The Ugandan population has been divided by sharp ethnic, linguistic, and religious differences. About two-thirds of the population is Bantu speaking. (Bantu uses prefixes to designate people [Ba-], an individual [Mu-], land [Bu-], and language [Lu-], thus: Baganda, Muganda, Buganda, Luganda.) The largest Bantu group, about 15 percent of the total population, is the Baganda, whose separate monarchical government was retained during the colonial and early independence period, and whose king, the Kabaka Mutesa II, served as president of Uganda from 1963 to 1966. The other major Bantu groups, all of whom live in the southern part of the country, are the Basoga, Banyankole, Banyoro, and Batoro. Northern Uganda is about equally divided between Nilotic (Acholi, Lango, Alur) and Nilo-Hamitic (Karamojong, Teso) peoples with a few groups, such as the Madi and the Kakwa, being of Sudanic origin. Sixty-three percent of the population is Christian, of whom approximately 55 percent are Catholic, and 45 percent are Protestant. Muslims, primarily Nilotic, comprise about 6 percent of the population. Before the Amin regime, there was also a large South Asian (Indian and Pakistani) community which was the core of the nation's commercial life. Amin forced the vast majority, some 75,000, to leave the country.

A north-south, Nilotic-Bantu split became increasingly apparent during the 1960s. The Baganda resented the loss of their autonomous kingdom in 1967, while the northern peoples and smaller Bantu groups resented the dominance of the Baganda in the civil service. Nationally elected leaders have come principally from the smaller northern groups: Amin was a Kakwa Muslim; Obote is a Langi Protestant. In 1986, Yoweri Museveni became the first Bantu president in twenty years. Although these divisive factors of ethnicity and religion are still important elements in Ugandan politics, increased regional mobility and intermarriage and the demoralizing effect of Amin's regime have contributed to efforts to promote unity and cooperation.

Executive

Executive power is vested in the president, who is elected by the National Assembly for a five-year term. The president selects the prime minister and cabinet from among the members of the Assembly. The cabinet meets to discuss policy options and coordination between ministries. Legislative proposals originate with the cabinet.

Legislature

Before Museveni took power, the National Assembly had 146 members, 126 of whom were elected from single-member electoral districts for five-year terms. Ten military representatives were nominated by the president, and another ten members were appointed by majority vote in the Assembly. The Assembly-appointed members enhanced the majority party's strength and permitted the president to recruit ministers from among nonparty experts and party figures who failed to get elected in their districts.

The most recent Assembly was elected in December 1980. Obote's Uganda Peoples' Congress (UPC) won seventy-four seats, the Democratic Party (DP) won fifty-one, the Uganda Patriotic Movement (UPM) won one, and the Conservative Party was closed out. The UPM victor, in protest against the electoral outcome, refused to take his seat, so the Assembly had only 125 sitting members. It is not clear when the next election will be held, or what the make-up of the next assembly will be.

An unusual feature of the Uganda political system has been the common practice of MPs "crossing the floor," i.e., changing parties. Many opposition MPs changed to the UPC in the late 1960s, and the practice emerged again in the most recent Assembly. Six DP members, all from Busoga, crossed to the UPC after their election. The most genuine reason for crossing is the MPs' perception that the majority party is performing better than the opposition. The crossing MP may also expect to gain influence, prestige, or political rewards for his switch. Whether from constituency pressure or personal ambition, Ugandan MPs can and do change parties after their election. Military destabilizations often result in dissolution of Parliament.

Judiciary

Uganda's High Court, composed of three judges including a chief justice, is the final court of appeals in Uganda. It hears in the first instance cases concerning electoral, national, and international disputes. Local magistrate courts in large district headquarters handle most civil and criminal cases concerning private citizens. Justices at all levels are appointed for life by the president. Although constitutionally separate from the political branches of government, the High Court occasionally seems to bow to political pressures and justices occasionally are removed for what appear to be partisan political reasons. At the county and subcounty levels, chiefs hear private disputes and lessen the burden of the official courts of record.

Regional & Local Government

The 1967 constitution established a strong central government at the expense of regional and local governments. This tendency was strengthened when Amin abolished local councils and administrative bodies. These local councils have yet to be reinstated in most areas, and the local administrations continue to be under the strict control of district commissioners. Although recruited and promoted through the civil service, the district commissioners are the direct representatives of the president and responsible for carrying out presidential policy.

Uganda has been plagued by disruptive competition between politicians, civil servants, and military men at the local and regional level. During the period between Amin's overthrow and the elections of 1980, local people were confused as to who was in charge, as party leaders, army officers, and bureaucrats gave contradictory orders and often worked at cross-purposes. This roughly paralleled the situation in late 1960s, when the district commissioners and the secretaries general of the UPC competed for community respect and influence. During Amin's regime, civil servants generally deferred to military personnel. Since the 1980 elections, civil servants have gained new authority, though the government party has firm control of policy decisions at all levels.

The Electoral System

Suffrage in the 1980 election was universal for all citizens eighteen years of age and older. Elections were direct and voting was by secret ballot. Voters chose between individual candidates in each electoral district. Turnout was approximately 60 percent of the voting-age population, and 78 percent of the registered voters.

Leaders of the DP and UPM have charged that the elections were rigged. They cite the facts that seventeen UPC candidates ran unopposed when opposition candidates were "disqualified"; that fourteen district commissioners were replaced shortly before the elections; and that the announcement of results was interrupted and delayed forty-eight hours by Paulo Muwanga, the head of the Military Commission. In two constituencies, Kabale Central and Iganga Northeast, results were announced nearly a month late. Although the Returning Officers in each case had declared the results null and void due to election irregularities, the

Electoral Commission, after visiting the constituencies and reviewing the election documents, decided to announce the available results and allow the losers to petition, rather than to leave the seats vacant and the constituencies unrepresented. It is impossible to assess the impact of these facts on the actual results; both parties appear to have maximized their vote in their areas of strength, and the results may not have been significantly different if none of these incidents had occurred. A non-Ugandan Commonwealth Observer Group present at the time of the elections vouched for their fairness. Petitions alleging irregularities and intimidation have been filed in High Court by losers from both major parties. Preparations for the 1985 election, including voter registration, were interrupted by two military coups (1985 and 1986). The UPM government has announced that new elections will be held in a few years.

The Party System

Uganda's political life has run the gamut of no-party, one-party, two-party, and multiparty systems. After the liberation from Amin's regime, two main parties emerged to capture the loyalties of most Ugandans; both were centrist and emphasized development issues. Ideologically, DP was to the right of center, emphasizing private enterprise and individual and ethnic freedoms; the UPC was to the left, advocating government control of an open economy and national unity and discipline. Both parties have been opposed by extremists groups on both right and left; both were national parties with supporters throughout the country. Although electorally weak in 1980, the UPM converted its four-year guerrilla war to a regime takeover in 1986. The UPM president has a history of interpreting events in terms of class conflict, and before he took power, organized the people in the countryside into revolutionary cells. However since heading the government he has sought ties with the West.

Campaigns have been as much an exercise in local pork-barrel politics as forums for developing national issues and leadership. All candidates emphasized what they have done or would do for their constituencies. Parties have promised to give small ethnic groups separate administrations in order to win support. National politicians have courted the favor of local elites—tribal, religious, and economic—who exert a strong influence over their neighbors. Better communications, more formal education, and more regional mobility will have to develop before national issues override local ones. All political parties, their meetings, and the "wearing of party colors," have been banned by the current UPM government.

Democratic Party (DP)

History

Founded in 1954 in reaction against the Protestant political leadership in Buganda, the Democratic Party appealed first to Catholics suffering from discrimination in Buganda and later to Catholics throughout the country. The DP strength outside Buganda was concentrated in those areas where the French Roman Catholic missionaries had set up schools and hospitals. The first party manifesto, "Forward to Freedom," was published in 1960 during pre-independence political maneuverings. The DP won the first nationwide general election in 1961, which the Buganda Protestants boycotted. Led by Benedicto Kiwanuka and Basil Bataringaya, DP ran the government until the first independence elections in 1962 were won by the Uganda People's Congress.

The DP assumed the role of Opposition, and lost four of its MPs including Basil Bataringaya to the Uganda Peoples' Congress through crossovers. Because of DP criticism of UPC leadership and alleged plots against the UPC, all opposition parties were banned in 1970. Some DP leaders were imprisoned. While vocal opposition to the government was stilled, DP party loyalty was not eliminated. When elections returned to Uganda in 1980, DP received forty-one of the seats with 42 percent of the votes. Again led by Baganda, the DPs' focus of support shifted from Catholics outside Buganda in 1962 to Baganda within the boundaries of Buganda in 1980. Becoming more regionally focused, the DP appealed to those elements opposed to centralization and nationalization. A few prominent DP leaders have joined the 1986 UPM government.

Organization

The DP was structured hierarchically with national leaders drawn from all parts of the country. Because the DP did not have primary elections to choose party nominees for the general elections, its grass-roots organization was relatively weak. The DP national leadership chose local candidates, thereby denying local participation. As an organization, DP was strong and well-organized in Kampala, but weaker in the hinterlands.

Policy

The 1980 DP manifesto emphasized security, respect, and dignity for the individual. Opposing tight control by the state, the DP advocated a mixed economy in which the private sector is as free as possible. In proposing a commission to study the 1967 constitution, the DP indicated some dissatisfaction with the excessive powers of the presidency, the indeterminate tenure of the presidency, and the current predominance of a powerful central government. The DP also campaigned on the issue of keeping the military out of politics.

Membership & Constituency

The DP won seats in fourteen of the thirty-three administrative districts of Uganda. In nine of these districts it was the only winner and derived 65 percent of its total national vote from those nine districts. Of the total vote of these nine districts, 79 percent went to the DP. The DP did best in Bantu areas in and around Kampala, in the Masaka region in the far south, and in some Busoga districts. It did worst in Acholi and Teso areas, where it got less than 10 percent of the vote.

No membership figures are available.

Financing

Due to its firm stand in favor of private enterprise, most of the DP campaign money was contributed by wealthy businessmen who sought to operate in a climate free of government control.

Leadership

In precampaign conferences, three candidates competed for their party's nomination for the presidency: Professor Yusufa Lule, Mr. Godfrey Binaisa, and Dr. Paul Ssemogerere. Lule and Binaisa held responsible positions in Ugandan government in the 1960s, and Ssemogerere worked as a journalist for a Catholic newspaper

and as DP publicity secretary. Dr. Ssemogerere got the nod, perhaps because he was the only one inside Uganda's borders at the time. After the election, Dr. Ssemogerere's faction in Parliament took on the role of loyal opposition. Other factions reportedly were involved in violent antigovernment guerrilla activity (the so-called militant wing).

Prospects

The DP had a strong base of support and its parliamentary wing served as an effective opposition party. The DP leader Ssemogerere served the two post-Obote regimes as Minister for internal affairs. While DP supporters seem to be cooperating with the 1986 UPM leadership, only a token number of DP's have actually been invited to join the cabinet.

Uganda Peoples' Congress (UPC)

History

The UPC evolved from a collection of sectionalist nationalist groups. The earliest, the Uganda National Congress (UNC) formed in 1952 by Enoch Malira, was Baganda-led throughout its eight-year existence. In 1958, the Uganda People's Union (UPU) was formed outside Buganda as the first party not led by Baganda. By 1959, the UNC had split into two factions led by Ignatius Musazi and Obote, respectively. The Obote faction of the UNC allied with the UPU to form the Uganda People's Congress in 1960. Skillfully led by Obote, this UPC coalition of local interests and local notables led the non-Baganda, non-Catholic population into a prominent role in postindependence politics.

In a risky but successful alliance with the Kabaka Yekka (KY), a monarchist movement, Obote promised Kabaka Mutesa II the ceremonial presidency and near-autonomy for Buganda in return for the KY votes which helped to form the constitutional majority, making Obote prime minister. In order to consolidate government and party control, Obote then worked at eroding the power of the Kabaka and Buganda. In 1966, Obote's parliamentary and military maneuvers caused the Kabaka to flee the country. Obote assumed the presidency and revised the constitution to strengthen the presidency and the central government. In an attempt to build a unitary government and a one-party state, all parties other than the UPC were banned.

Organization

In the 1960s, the UPC was split into several factions—the southern, non-Baganda Bantu and the northern Nilotics, the youth and those personally close to Obote. Only a few prominent Baganda such as Binaisa and Muwanga, aligned themselves with the UPC. Regional and personal antagonisms were displayed openly within the party debates. As the nation developed economically, the major issue remained pork-barrel allocation of development projects and the distribution of jobs among people of various affiliations—religious, ethnic, regional. The need to appeal to voters on local development issues furthered the identification with factions and subverted development of national spirit.

The structure of the UPC was dependent upon constituency parties organized around the UPC candidates. These local groups developed from coalitions of supporters for the candidates in the UPC primaries. In many areas, such as Teso, the primaries were more hotly contested than the general election. Delegates' conferences, inaugurated a month before the 1980 elections, were now held on an annual basis until the UPM coup. Constituency parties meet before and after the delegates' conferences to discuss issues of party philosophy and policy. In addition, there are meetings for women, youth, and other interest groups within the party. These grass-roots activities contributed to the higher turnout in districts with UPC majorities.

Obote's strong leadership held together a party organization which was nearly as factional as it was in the 1960s. The divisions in 1980 were many: those that were in exile and those who stayed inside Uganda during Amin's regime; those that fought in the Liberation War and those that did not actually fight; those who are formally educated and those who are not; those who were in Obote's previous government (1962–71) and those who are new to government; soldiers and civilians; southerners and northerners. Fortunately for the UPC, there are many young persons whose alliegences cut across these lines and whose presence and activities served to unify the party. With the help of these cross-cutting individuals, Obote attempted to forge a new alliance designed to pull the country together for the redevelopment effort. The cabinet represented a cross-section of Uganda. Even among Obote's closest circle of advisors, there were representatives from north and south, army and civilians: old guard and new faces.

Policy

The UPC party platform in the 1960s slowly evolved from a purely nationalist independence document into a socialist manifesto stressing equality, central government planning, and nationalization of the economy. "The Common Man's Charter" and the Nakivubo Pronouncements in 1970 clearly stated these socialist goals.

Ten years later, and with most of the sociopolitical and economic development of the 1960s destroyed by Amin, the UPC manifesto is more pragmatic and less ideological. The 1980 manifesto tempers the ideal of the socialist equality with a call for vigorous private efforts to rebuild the economy. Focusing on raising the standard of living, Obote calls for national reconciliation, no revenge, cooperation with all religious leaders, and moderate economic policies to support a mixed ecomomy.

Membership & Constituency

In the 1980 elections, the UPC won seats in twenty-four of the thirty-three administrative districts of Uganda. In eighteen of these districts it was the only winner and derived 70 percent of its total national vote from those eighteen districts. Of the total vote of these eighteen districts, 86 percent went to UPC. The UPC did best among the Nilotic, Sudanic, and non-Baganda southern groups. Of the seventeen UPC candidates who ran unopposed, all but two were in the northern districts; those two ran in Kasese, where the UPM won the third seat by a margin of 52 percent to 48 percent for the UPC. Some observers assert that the UPM victory was due solely to DP voters having been denied a chance to vote for their party's candidates. Other observers note that the presence of a DP candidate on the ballot would have split the anti-UPC vote and allowed the UPC to win. The UPC's victories in Bantu areas were in the far southwest in Kigezi, in the extreme southeast in Bukedi and Bugisu, and in one Ankole district, Bushenyi. Several districts were split, including Iganga, Mbarara, and Rukungiri. The UPC did worst in and around Kampala; in Mpigi, a populous district near Kampala in which the DP leader Ssemogerere ran, it received less than 5 percent of the vote.

No membership figures are available.

Financing

The UPC was financed by fund-raising efforts in the constituencies. Farmers, business persons, and salaried workers contributed to the party's coffers. A large percentage of the funds were returned to the constituency in the form of development projects. Businesses were urged to contribute to the financing of party conventions.

Leadership

Dr. A. Milton Obote, the former president of Uganda and founder of the UPC, was born in 1925 in Akokoro village in Lango. After attending Makerere University in Kampala, he participated in the trade-union movement in Kenya before returning to Uganda in 1957. He was first elected to the pre-independence Legislative Council by the Lango District Council.

Since Obote's overthrow in 1985, several UPC members claim to be leading the UPC. In Kampala, Paulo Muwanga argues that as ex-vice president of Uganda, he is the current UPC president, while the UPC Secretariat, run by Kagenda-Atwokii, still recognizes Obote as party president because there has been no party Congress to vote on a change. In addition, Anthony Tiberondwa, in exile in Nairobi, claims to be the rightful heir to UPC leadership.

Prospects

The 1985/86 military destabilizations have removed the UPC from power. Susceptible to overthrow due to internal factionalism, the UPC is badly divided, with internal and external wings (Nairobi and Lusaka).

Uganda Patriotic Movement (UPM)

History

The Uganda Patriotic Movement is based in the western Bantu part of Uganda and led by Yoweri Museveni, now President of Uganda. Museveni was instrumental in the Liberation War and served in several capacities in the transition government, including the posts of minister for defense and member of the Military Commission. The appeal of the UPM is strongest among younger Ugandans who sought positions of power and viewed the DP and UPC as controlled by older politicans who had already had a chance to run the government. After losing his bid for the presidency in the 1980 elections, in which the UPM contested seventy-five seats and won only one, Museveni and his most militant followers went into the bush to work for a violent overthrow of the UPC government. They achieved this overthrow in 1986. UPM has since aligned with various military and civilian opposition groups to form the National Resistance Movement (NRM).

Organization

The NRM and its parent group, the UPM, have formed a National Resistance Council to make decisions for Uganda. The council is composed of thirty-five soldiers and politicians. There seems to be no distinction between the party and the government policy-making machinery.

Policy

The NRM seeks to restore the industrial sector, as well as the roads and agricultural exports. They seek external aid that will lead to self-reliance. They deplore corruption.

Membership & Constituency

Although there is currently no party registration information, the elites of the government have come from several sources besides UPM: two small guerrilla groups—the Uganda Freedom Movement and Federnu—the Democratic Party, the Uganda Peoples Corps, and the minor Conservative Party. Cooperation with UPM by members of other parties can be interpreted as a form of "crossing-over." Museveni has stated that he prefers a one-party system.

Finance

Although it is alleged that the UPM and its fighting wing were financed by non-Ugandan sources, they now control Uganda's treasury and make no distinction between party and government funds.

Leadership

Yoweri Museveni, a Bantu from Ntungamo in the South West of Uganda, is in firm control of the party and the government. A radical Marxist who followed a traditional Marxist approach to struggle and local organization, apparently he seeks a nationalist coalition. He has trained in Mozambique and North Korea. He has served in several past governments, but was especially effective as a guerrilla leader.

Prospects

The UPM must face the usual challenge of organizing under conditions of extreme ethnic factionalism.

Conservative Party (CP)

The Conservative Party is a small Buganda-based group of staunch traditionalists who prefer a return to monarchy in Uganda. Their loyalties are purely regional, in 1980 they contested only forty-seven seats and won none. The CP leader, Mayanja-Nkangi, spoke throughout Buganda during the campaigns, but attracted only small crowds. The CP is a throwback to the now-defunct Kabaka Yekka party formed with the sole purpose of keeping Buganda's king the preeminent personage in all of Uganda. The CP's potential supporters voted for the DP which advocated increased regional control, if not actual kingdoms. The CP is perceived as neotraditional and out of touch with modern Uganda.

Other Political Forces

The bureaucracy and the army rival the political parties in power and influence. Even though the government is legally headed by a president and sometimes by the National Assembly, the members of the civil service have a near-monopoly on formal education, technical expertise, and knowledge of government rules and regulations. On the other hand, the army has a near-monopoly on the use of force and has been instrumental in maintaining and disrupting the political status quo. The bureaucracy has been dominated by members of the Baganda ethnic group, who were the first to receive formal education in colonial times. The army has been composed mainly of northerners, who had a reputation for being fierce warriors. Politicians, bureaucrats, and soldiers establish themselves either through wealthy connections or salaried occupations thereby setting themselves apart from the masses, both rural and urban. Competition among politicians, bureaucrats, and soldiers is a constant source of tension in Uganda's politics.

National Prospects

Stability and progress in Uganda depend upon strict economic measures and a reduction in political violence. Post-Amin economic improvement was halted by the military destabilizations. Coffee exports had quadrupled; cotton was replanted in large quantities; and tea and sugar production was revived. Agricultural and other production was stimulated by floating the shilling, increasing producer prices, and following other IMF–World Bank recommendations. Several governments have canceled or rescheduled debts. Although development assistance flows mostly from multilateral donors such as the EEC, UNDP, and the World Bank, individual governments have increased assistance when the security situation is stable.

Both guerrilla attacks and pacification campaigns continue to delay reconstruction in several districts. Constant violence breeds personal insecurity, contributes to political polarization, and encourages nearby farmers and businesses to refrain from cooperating with the government. While UPM's military controls the southern (Bantu) part of Uganda, a ragtag military group, which ruled for six months in 1985 and is largely composed of Acholi and ex-Amin soldiers, still controls sections of the north. Other paramilitary guerrilla groups have allied with either the UPM government or this ragtag northern group.

The 1986 ban on all political activities and the resurgence of military destabilizations have discouraged organized political activity. Although Uganda has great potential for both economic self-reliance and export, and considerable experience with partisan politics, twenty-five years of experiments have been repeatedly marred by ethnic factionalism, which is likely to continue in the future.

Further Reading

Apter, David. *The Political Kingdom in Uganda*. Princeton, N. J.: Princeton University Press, 1961.

Gingyera Pinycwa, A. G. G. *Apolo Milton Obote and His Times*. New York: NOK Publishers, 1978.

Ibingera, Grace. *The Forging of an African Nation*. New York: Viking Press, 1973.

Law, D. A. *Political Parties in Uganda, 1949–1962*. London: Athlone Press, 1962.

Kasfir, Nelson. *The Shrinking Political Arena. Berkeley: University of California, 1976*.

Mamdani, Mahmood. *Politics and Class Formation in Uganda*. New York: Monthly Review Press, 1976.

Mittelman, John. *Ideology and Politics in Uganda*. Ithaca, N. Y.: Cornell University Press, 1975.

Welbourn, F. B. *Religion and Politics in Uganda: 1952–1962*. Nairobi: East African Publishing House, 1965.

UNION OF SOVIET SOCIALIST REPUBLICS
(Soiuz Sovetskikh Sotsial'isticheskikh Respublik)
by Donald D. Barry, Ph.D.

The System of Government

The Union of Soviet Socialist Republics (Soviet Union) is a one-party state which is described in its constitution as having achieved "developed socialism." This is a transitional stage between socialism (which was declared achieved in 1936) and communism. The "constitution of developed socialism," which was adopted in 1977 to replace the 1936 constitution, sets out the basic principles of the present state structure. The Soviet state came into being in November 1917, when the provisional government which had replaced the Tsarist system in March 1917 was overthrown.

The USSR is a federal system made of fifteen republics, known as Soviet Socialist Republics (SSRs) or Union Republics. Each is typically named after the dominant nationality in the republic. In addition, a variety of smaller territorial subdivisions, some of which are also associated with particular nationalities, exist within the union republics.

The Communist Party of the Soviet Union is the foremost political organ in the USSR. It exercises decisive control over the legislative and executive opertions of the Soviet state apparatus.

Executive

Executive power is vested in the USSR Council of Ministers, which is chosen by the USSR Supreme Soviet. The chairman of the Council of Ministers is considered head of government. The functions of head of state are performed by the Presidium of the USSR Supreme Soviet. The chairman of the Presidium is accorded the highest protocol status in the country and may be considered the head of state.

The Council of Ministers is a large body, typically containing over 100 persons of ministerial status. This is largely explained by the great number of economic ministries of rather narrow specialization found in the Council (ministries of gas industry, cellulose-paper industry, food industry, etc.). Ministry-level departments in the Council of Ministers are basically of three types: all-union ministries, union-republic ministries, and state committees and other departments.

All-union ministries exercise direct control of the branch of administration under their jurisdiction throughout the country. Union-republic ministries administer their affairs through ministries of the same name located in the capitals of the fifteen union republics. Although the all-union ministry suggests greater central control, no logical rationale appears to exist for placing a ministry in one or the other categories. While ministries are responsible for "branch administration" (i.e., a branch of economic administration, such as the oil industry, or of public administration, such as health), state committees carry out "interbranch administration," meaning that they supervise activities common to several branches of administration. A typical example is the State Planning Committee (Gosplan). In addition to over sixty ministries and more than twenty state committees (in the 1980s), the USSR Council of Ministers has a chairman and a number of first vice chairmen and vice chairmen. The chairmen of the fifteen union-republic councils of ministers serve as ex officio members of the USSR Council of Ministers.

Because of the large size of the Council, it cannot serve as a true executive body, and its meetings are infrequent (the 1978 law prescribes Council meetings "not less than once per quarter"). The Presidium of the Council of Ministers includes the chairman, first vice chairmen and vice chairmen of the Council of Ministers and numbers about fifteen. It performs the executive functions of the Soviet state apparatus. Although the Presidium existed prior to 1977, it was not given official constitutional recognition until that year.

The Council of Ministers has the authority to issue legal acts pursuant to legislation adopted by the Supreme Soviet. On some matters, it appears that the Council of Ministers takes initiative in areas where regular legislation has not yet been adopted. A frequent practice is the issuance of joint Council of Ministers–Party Central Committee decrees on important public-policy matters. The chairman of the Council of Ministers has the authority in urgent cases to make decisions in the Council's name.

Members of the Council of Ministers are appointed and removable by the USSR Supreme Soviet. The constitution gives the chairman the authority to recommend the slate of candidates for ministers as well as to recommend the discharge of ministers. Since the chairman of the Council of Ministers has always in recent years been a full member of the party Politburo, the highest policy-making body of the Communist Party of the Soviet Union, it is likely that party control over the appointment and dismissal of ministers is maintained through the chairman of the Council of Ministers.

Legislature

Legislative power is vested in the bicameral USSR Supreme Soviet, which is elected every five years. A smaller body, the Presidium of the USSR Supreme Soviet, performs legislative functions during the periods between the infrequent meetings of the Supreme Soviet. Analogous legislative bodies exist at the lower levels of the Soviet state structure.

The Supreme Soviet consists of two houses (the Council of the Union and the Council of Nationalities) of 750 members each. All members are elected at one time for nonoverlapping five-year terms. Apportionment of seats in the Council of the Union is based on population. The Council of Nationalities provides representation to the various national territorial units in the following way: thirty-two deputies for each union republic, eleven deputies for each autonomous republic, five for each autonomous province, and one for each autonomous district.

The Supreme Soviet usually meets twice a year, often in June and December. The sessions typically last two to three days. Often the two houses meet in joint session. It is clear that little genuine legislative activity can take place in such a short period of time. And although the Supreme Soviet is provided an impressive list of powers and duties by the constitution, most of its activity involves providing the official stamp of approval for policies already adopted and laws that have been prepared in advance.

Such advance work may emanate from several sources, including the organs of the party bureaucracy as well as the Council of Ministers. Two types of bodies that may also play some role are the standing committees (or commissions) of the Supreme Soviet and the Presidium.

Each house of the Supreme Soviet has sixteen standing committees made up of thirty-five deputies each (the Planning Budget Committee of each house has forty-five members each). It is not likely that these bodies contribute much to the process of policy formation, since most committee members, like other ordinary Supreme Soviet deputies, are not full-time legislators or public servants and devote all but a few days each year to other occupations. However, the committee chairmen are typically officials from fairly high levels of the bureaucratic apparatus, and they may play important roles in policy discussion in lieu of the committees which they head. And it is likely that the committees' advisors from various state organs (for example, the law institutes and the Ministry of Justice in the case of legislative drafting) play a considerable role in drawing up alternative policy proposals.

Because of the infrequency and shortness of Supreme Soviet sessions, the Presidium of the Supreme Soviet is assigned a number of important functions. An impressive list of powers and duties are granted to it by Articles 121, 122, and 123 of the constitution. These include the typical functions performed by heads of state in other countries, such as the granting of pardons, the awarding of titles of honor, and the certification of diplomatic representatives, as well as the little-used power of issuing interpretations of laws. The most significant power is that of issuing edicts (*ukazy*) which have the force of law. They are often given permanent status by being transformed into statutes (*zakony*) at the next session of the Supreme Soviet.

The Presidium of the Supreme Soviet, elected by the Supreme Soviet, is composed of a chairman, a first vice chairman, a secretary, and a number of regular members, usually around twenty. In addition, the chairmen of the fifteen union-republic supreme soviet presidiums are ex officio members, and are designated as vice chairmen of the USSR Supreme Soviet. Although several important politicians sit on the Presidium, it is not considered an important political organ. Its actual meetings occur no more frequently than once a month, which suggests that the edicts and other acts issued in its name are in fact the work of a small number of members aided by the Presidium staff.

Judiciary

The highest court in the Soviet Union is the USSR Supreme Court, a body of some thirty-five members chosen by the USSR Supreme Soviet for five-year terms. The Court can act as a whole (the plenum) or in separate panels of judges: the Civil Law Chamber, Criminal Law Chamber, and the Military Law Chamber. The Supreme Court meets in plenary session at least once every four months. It is headed by a chairman. The chairmen of the fifteen union republic supreme courts are ex officio members of the USSR Supreme Court.

The Supreme Court has no authority to declare acts of the legislature or the executive contrary to the constitution, and decisions of Soviet courts are not considered legal precedents. The USSR Supreme Court does have some broad influence on Soviet law, however, through its authority to issue "guiding explanations," decrees on general questions of law which are designed to aid lower courts in deciding cases.

Each of the fifteen union republics has a supreme court, which is constituted similarly to the USSR Supreme Court. Below the union republic are two further court levels. The people's court is the main court of original jurisdiction in the USSR. The first appeal level above the people's court is at the level of the province, autonomous republic, or large city.

Another organ with broad legal authority is the Procuracy. The Procuracy is an organization with a unitary structure within the federal system. It is headed by the USSR Procurator General, who is appointed by the USSR Supreme Soviet for a five-year term. The Procurator General and his deputies have direct control over lower-level procurators, instead of these officials being responsible to the legislatures of the federal subunits. This is intended to insulate lower-level procurators from regional and local influence. The Procuracy is charged with guaranteeing "socialist legality" in the USSR, and is given broad authority over a wide range of legal functions in order to carry out this mandate.

Regional & Local Government

Regional and local subdivisions are basically of two kinds: those identified with nationality groups which dominate the population of a given territory and those which are strictly territorial units. Below the national level there are four levels of territorial units associated with nationalities: fifteen union republics (Soviet Socialist Republics or SSRs), twenty autonomous republics (Autonomous Soviet Socialist Republics or ASSRs), eight autonomous provinces, and ten autonomous districts.

As mentioned, representatives of these units comprise the membership of the Soviet of Nationalities. The union republics are the most important and include territories in which the country's major nationalities are concentrated. They vary significantly in both population and land area. The Russian Republic (RSFSR) contains almost 52 percent of the Soviet population and covers almost three-fourths of the total territory of the USSR. It is almost twice the size of the continental United States and has a greater population than France, West Germany, and the Benelux countries combined. The remaining union republics are much smaller, both in size and in population. Tiny Estonia occupies a territory about the size of the state of Maryland and has about 1.5 million people.

POPULATION OF THE USSR BY UNION REPUBLIC (1985)		
Union Republic	Population (in thousands)	% USSR Population
RSFSR	149,090	51.8
Ukraine	50,840	18.4
Uzbekistan	17,974	6.4
Kazakhstan	15,842	5.7
Byelorussia	9,942	3.6
Azerbaidzhan	6,614	2.4
Georgia	5,201	1.9
Tadzhikistan	4,499	1.6
Moldavia	4,111	1.5
Kirghizia	3,967	1.4
Lithuania	3,570	1.3
Armenia	3,317	1.2
Turkmenistan	3,189	1.1
Latvia	2,604	0.9
Estonia	1,530	0.6
Total USSR	276,290	99.8

The union republics, unlike the three lower-level nationality units, have the theoretical right to secede from the USSR (USSR constitution, Article 72). This right has never been exercised and seems to be obviated in any case by provisions elsewhere (Article 75) that the territory of the USSR "is a single entity and comprises the territories of the union republics," and that "the sovereignty of the USSR extends throughout its territory." The governmental structure of the union republics very much parallels that of the USSR. Each republic has its own constitution and elects a supreme soviet (of one chamber rather than two) which chooses a presidium and a council of ministers.

Autonomous republics (ASSRs) have been created to represent nationality concentrations within union republics. The intention is to give limited autonomy to medium-sized nationality groups. The ASSRs have their own constitutions, supreme soviets, and other organs of state, but they are not accorded the theoretical right of secession which the union republics possess. Even less autonomy is provided to the autonomous province and autonomous district. Except for the nationality concentrations in these areas, they differ little in state or party structure from the regular territorial-administrative subdivisions which exist throughout the USSR.

Local government in the USSR includes a confusing variety of names and types, ranging from the sprawling, largely rural territory (*krai*) to the province (*oblast'*) to the village, city, or big-city district. In terms of structure, what they have in common is the elected local *soviet* or council, from which the local executive committee is chosen. It is at this level that the local people's courts and the first-level appellate courts (e.g., Moscow City Court) are found. Very few powers are granted to the exclusive competence of the local organs. It appears that the higher authorities can interfere frequently in local affairs if they choose to.

The Electoral System

The USSR constitution (Article 95) guarantees "universal, equal and direct suffrage by secret ballot" to all Soviet citizens eighteen and over. The electoral system now in use was created in 1938 on the basis of provisions of the constitution of 1936. It has been changed only in minor ways since that time. All members of legislative bodies, from local soviets to the USSR Supreme Soviet, are elected under this system. This amounts to about 50,000 popularly elected bodies containing some 2.3 million persons. In addition, all judges at the people's court level are popularly elected. To be elected, a candidate must secure a majority of the total votes

cast. In some countries where a majority system is used (e.g., France), a second round of voting is available in those constituencies where a majority is not achieved on the first ballot. Because of the particular characteristics of Soviet elections, no such arrangements are necessary in the USSR.

The most salient features of the Soviet electoral system are elections without competition and almost unanimous voting for the single candidate for each seat. The only choice available to the voter is to cross out the name of the single candidate, since writing in another person's name voids the ballot. Under these arrangements, only a miniscule number of candidates do not receive the required majority of the votes cast. On the rare occasions when this happens, it is at the local levels rather than the national or union-republic level. Election, therefore, depends largely on nomination.

At first glance the nomination arrangement might suggest the possibility of more than one candidate for a given seat. Six kinds of bodies are permitted to make nominations: Communist Party organizations, trade unions, *Komsomol* (Young Communist League) organizations, cooperatives and other public organizations, work collectives, and meetings of servicemen in their military units. These organizations may provide an initial screening process by which several potential candidates are put forward, but always in the end only one candidate is announced for each seat. A process that takes place beyond public view, no doubt coordinated by Communist Party authorities, results in the single candidate being nominated.

The actual voting process is also highly organized and controlled. Upon identifying oneself at the voting place and receiving a ballot paper, the voter need only place the paper in the ballot box. No marking of the ballot is needed to make it valid. As pro forma as this procedure undoubtedly is, the Soviet government expends considerable effort, time, and money on the electoral process. Election commissions are established all over the country, and significant media attention is devoted to coming elections, including coverage of a campaign speech that each candidate delivers to his or her constituency. All of this activity acts as a prelude to election day itself, when the efforts of millions of volunteers and public officials are devoted to mobilizing the populace to vote. As suggested, official reports routinely state that the voting record of Soviet citizens is nearly unanimous. Apparently this high level of voting is looked upon by Soviet authorities as evidence of the legitimacy of their rule. Certainly it can provide little support for those who would challenge the regime, not necessarily because the election legitimates anything, but rather because it appears to indicate how successful the authorities are in mobilizing the population.

Until recent years, the tendency among Western analysts of Soviet elections was to accept the reported electoral results, but to dismiss them as largely meaningless. Lately greater skepticism has been expressed about the figures for voter turnout. As one analyst has pointed out, for instance, official figures claim that in Uzbekistan, in the 1979 USSR Supreme Soviet elections, only fourteen voters out of a total electorate of over seven million failed to vote. Evidence from recent emigrés suggests that the pressure on local Soviet officials to produce near-unanimous results can frequently lead to practices that considerably overstate voter participation. Among these are the occasional stuffing of the ballot box, allowing one member of a family to vote for all members, and the covert avoidance of voting. This last practice is accomplished by obtaining a certificate to vote elsewhere on the grounds that the voter expects to be away on election day, and then not voting. On the basis of information of this kind, a former member of a local Soviet election commission estimated that about three-quarters of Soviet electors actually vote, rather than the 99-percent-plus figure routinely reported.

During some periods of recent Soviet history, recommendations have appeared infrequently in Soviet publications that voters be allowed some choice among candidates. Several of the Soviet Union's East European neighbors combine limited electoral choice with the absence of alternative governments or policies. It is fair to say that Soviet leaders have not seriously entertained this idea as a possibility in the Soviet Union, and by the 1980s it had been many years since the proposal had been mentioned in the open Soviet press.

Although the Communist Party of the Soviet Union (CPSU) exerts great control over Soviet elections, not all members of those elected bodies are party members. News releases at election time refer to the "bloc of Communists and nonparty candidates" running for various legislative bodies, and the slates of candidates always contain a certain number who are not party members. Apparently the proportions of party and nonparty members of the various bodies are arranged in advance in what amounts to a quota system. In recent elections, party members (or candidate members) have constituted between 71 and 75 percent of the USSR Supreme Soviet membership. At the union-republic level about two-thirds of those elected are party members, approximately the same figure as in the autonomous republics. But at the local-soviet level, the corresponding figure has consistently been below 50 percent (usually between 43 and 45 percent) for the past several decades. This suggests that the local soviet is probably considered a training ground for nonparty members as well as an avenue for broadening political participation without creating much risk for the authorities in terms of political control.

The apparent quota arrangement with regard to nonparty members also applies to other nonfavored categories of persons (i.e., women, younger persons, persons without higher education). At the USSR level, women now constitute about one-third of all Supreme Soviet members. At each succeeding lower level this figure rises until it is about 50 percent in the local soviets. Deputies below age thirty constitute about one-fifth of the USSR Supreme Soviet but one-third of the membership of local soviets. Over half of the deputies at the higher levels have partial or complete higher education, while this is true of less than one-quarter of the deputies in the local soviets.

Soviet data indicate that about half of the members of the USSR Supreme Soviet are workers or collective farmers (a figure that surpasses two-thirds in the local soviets), which may appear inconsistent with the information just cited concerning a high level of education among Supreme Soviet deputies. Soviet spokesmen also claim a relatively high turnover among Supreme Soviet members from election to election (typically over 50 percent). But this still leaves hundreds of slots for returnees from previous legislatures, including a great number of high political leaders who have been members for many years. Leonid Brezhnev, for instance, served continuously in the USSR Supreme Soviet from 1960 until his death in 1982. All of the most important party and government officials and a number of top scientists and intellectuals are regularly elected to the Supreme Soviet. Outstanding workers in less exalted positions may also be chosen to serve a term or two. Since the Supreme Soviet meets only a few days a year, it does not interfere seriously with one's full-time job. It constitutes a measure of prestige and material reward for those found worthy of such honors. In addition to expenses-paid visits to Moscow twice a year, Supreme Soviet deputies also receive 200 rubles per month salary (about $270 at the official rate of exchange in 1985). Deputies to union-republic supreme soviets receive 120 rubles per month. It should be added that the top party leaders typically serve in both the USSR Supreme Soviet and a union-republic supreme soviet, in addition to receiving the salary for their regular position.

Communist Party of the Soviet Union (CPSU; *Kommunisticheskaia Partiia Sovetskogo Soiuza*)

A one-party state has been in existence in the USSR virtually since the beginning of Soviet power in 1917. Unlike some of its neighbors in socialist East Europe, which have permitted the nominal operation of other parties, the Soviet Union has not condoned even an appearance of the sharing of power.

The CPSU is not merely the only party in the USSR; it is the most important organization in the country. This is proclaimed by no less a source than the constitution, which describes the party as "the leading and guiding force of Soviet society and the nucleus of its political system, of all state and public organizations." The party is charged with determining "the general perspective of society's development and the line of domestic and foreign policy of the USSR." Given the nature of the Soviet system, the party clearly does not derive its authority from these provisions. They constitute rather an official affirmation of the party's leading role.

History

The Communist Party of the Soviet Union had its origins in the Marxist movements in Russia in the late Nineteenth Century. The Russian Social Democratic Labor Party (RSDLP) was founded before the turn of the century. Many of its members lived abroad to avoid harrassment by the Tsarist police. At the Second Congress of the RSDLP held in Brussels and London in the summer of 1903, the party split into two competing Marxist groups: the Bolsheviks ("majoritarians") led by Lenin and the Mensheviks ("minoritarians") led by Martov. The differences between them largely involved disagreement about the internal organization of the party. Lenin argued for a centralized, disciplined party led by an elite group of professional revolutionaries. The Mensheviks favored a mass organization in the tradition of European social-democratic parties. Later a split surfaced over the nature of the future Marxian revolution in Russia. The Mensheviks saw socialism coming to Russia as the result of a long process of development, including a bourgeois revolution which would precede the proletarian revolution. Lenin and the Bolsheviks eventually embraced a position which saw the possibility of telescoping the two revolutions. They also considered the peasantry in Russia a potentially revolutionary force, a position rejected by more traditional Marxists.

For years the Bolsheviks and the Mensheviks regarded themselves as factions of the same party, and periodically they made attempts to restore party unity. The Bolsheviks, Mensheviks, and other groups succeeded in overthrowing the provisional government in November 1917, and for a time thereafter several political groupings participated legally in the exercise of political power. Soon after the Revolution, a dispute developed within Bolshevik ranks on the question of cooperation with other parties. Lenin's skepticism toward coalition government eventually prevailed, and the elimination of other parties proceeded. By the end of the Civil War in 1921, only the Bolsheviks remained. The party created by Lenin changed names several times after the revolution, retaining "Bolshevik" in the name until 1952, when it adopted its present name.

During Lenin's lifetime the party remained an elite group of relatively small size. By the time of his death in 1924, there were still fewer than one-half million members, considerably less than 1 percent of the population. Under Stalin, the party took on different characteristics. It became a ruling bureaucracy and grew considerably in size. In these respects the present-day CPSU owes much more to Stalin than to Lenin. By Stalin's death in 1953, party membership totalled nearly seven million and was well over 3 percent of the Soviet population. It reached 4 percent by 1960, 5 percent by 1965, and 6.5 percent in 1985.

Organization

The Party Rules amount to a kind of constitution for the party. This 10,000-word document sets out the structure and organization of the party, describes its rules of operation, and prescribes conditions and requirements for admission and continued membership.

Democratic centralism is referred to in the Party Rules as "the guiding principle of the organizational structure of the Party." The concept is made up of four parts, the first two democratic, the last two centralist: (a) election of all leading party bodies, from the lowest to the highest; (b) periodic reports of party bodies to their party organizations and to higher bodies; (c) strict party discipline and subordination of the minority to the majority; and (d) the obligatory nature of the decisions of higher bodies for lower bodies.

In practice, the application of democratic centralism is much more centralist than democratic. To take only the first element as an example, although election of all party bodies is called for, it has already been shown with regard to the Politburo and the Secretariat that this amounts in practice to a prearranged ritual controlled by the entrenched leadership. In addition, there are other parts of the Party Rules which effectively negate the democratic elements of the principle. An example is this passage from the introduction to the Rules: "Ideological and organizational unity, monolithic cohesion of its ranks, and a high degree of conscious discipline on the part of all communists are an inviolable law of the CPSU. All manifestations of factionalism and group activity are incompatible with Marxist-Leninist principles, and with party membership."

What remains of the democratic substance of the principle is essentially this: On some issues party members may be accorded the right to free discussion "until a decision has been made" (as an earlier description of the concept of democratic centralism put it). After a decision has been reached, continued opposition is improper under prevailing party practices.

The CPSU is a highly structured, strictly organized party. At the lowest level is the primary party organization (PPO). The PPOs are found typically in factories, stores, and other places of work, but may also be established on a residential basis in housing complexes or villages. The PPO is the basic organization, to which all party members belong. It serves as the main point of contact between the individual member and the party. To establish a PPO at least three members are required. Over 400,000 PPOs are said to exist in the country. Every PPO has a cadre of leaders, but only the larger PPOs (150 or more members) qualify to have full-time paid workers. In the smaller PPOs, leaders are excused from part of their regular employment to perform party duties. They vary considerably in size, but the overwhelming majority are rather small. According to official data, over 80 percent have fewer than fifty members and only 7 percent have over 100 members. The highest organ of the PPO is the general meeting, which is required by the Party Rules to convene once a month. Reportedly, this rule is frequently ignored.

Above the PPO, the party is organized on a territorial basis which essentially follows the levels of state administration. The levels include the rural or urban district (*raion*), the city (*gorod*) or autonomous area (*okrug*); the province (*oblast'*), territory (*krai*) or ASSR; the union republic; and the national party organization. As with the state apparatus, structural similarities are to be found at the various levels of the party organization. The main organs of the national party, which will be discussed below, are the Party Congress, the Central Committee, the Politburo, and the Secretariat (the last organ headed by the general secretary, the highest party official). All lower levels have their own congresses (called conferences below the union-republic level), committees, bureaus, secretariats, and first secretaries. The hierarchy of organs at each level is prescribed by the Party Rules: the congress (or conference) is considered the highest organ; it selects a central committee (or committee), which in turn chooses the bureau, the secretariat, and the first secretary. In terms of actual authority, however, the order is reversed, with the greatest power in the hands of the elite bureau and secretariat. This can be best shown by examining the national party organization in more detail.

The Party Rules identify the all-union congress as the supreme organ of the party. Delegates to the congresses represent subordinate party organizations throughout the USSR. In reality there is no possibility that the congress can play this role. It meets too infrequently (once every five years for about ten days), and is too large (its membership has been above 5,000 at recent Congresses) to exercise real power. Rather, the congress serves as an occasion when important issues can be discussed by the top leaders, and it provides a time for rallying the faithful to the important tasks the leaders have set forth. At each congress, the party general secretary gives an "account" speech to the congress in the name of the Central Committee, which is charged under the Party Rules with running the party between congresses. In recent years, a discussion of the new five-year economic plan has also been a feature of the congresses.

A major function of the congress is naming the Central Committee. Like everything else which takes place at the congress, this function is planned well in advance. In effect, the congress is presented with a slate of Central Committee members and candidate members, which it approves. The Central Committee then retires to choose the Politburo and the Secretariat, a task which is accomplished in a similarly orchestrated manner.

The Central Committee (CC), according to the Party Rules, "directs the activity of the party" between congresses, "selects and appoints leading functionaries, directs the work of central government bodies and social organizations of working people through the party groups in them, sets up various activities, appoints the editors of the central newspapers and journals operating under its control, and distributes the funds of the party budget and controls its execution." It is clear, however, that the Central Committee *as a body* can perform no such function. Typically it meets only two days a year, in two one-day sessions just before the convening of the Supreme Soviet. Given the Central Committee's size (over 300 full members and another 150 or so candidates or non-voting members in recent years), it cannot possibly perform the above-mentioned duties. In effect, the authority provided the Central Committee by the Party Rules is exercised by the more elite organs of the Central Committee, the Politburo and the Secretariat.

This is not to say that the members of the Central Committee are not important and influential people. In addition to the Politburo and Secretariat members, the Central Committee includes the most important leaders from party organizations around the country as well as prominent representatives from the military, the diplomatic corps, science, journalism, and other important spheres of Soviet life. (The membership of the CC is leavened by a token number of actual industrial workers and collective farmers.) But as important as these individuals are in their own areas of activity, their functions as Central Committee members are necessarily limited because of the large size of that body and the infrequency of its meetings.

A considerable amount of activity takes place in the name of the CC. This can include a speech by a party leader at a regular meeting of the Central Committee, a decree by the CC adopted at such a meeting, or a simple CC decree. The CC decrees are issued at times when the Central Committee is not in session, and clearly emanate from some more exclusive part of the party, probably the Politburo. Sometimes these decrees are issued jointly by the CC and the USSR Council of Ministers. In subject matter and form they often closely resemble regular legal acts and might be considered a kind of party legislation.

Another central party organ, of considerably less importance than the CC, is the Central Auditing Commission. It is charged with several administrative matters, including auditing the party's financial accounts. It seems to be largely an honorary body of moderate size (about seventy-five members in recent years), whose members are somewhat less highly placed in the hierarchy than those on the Central Committee.

The Politburo and the Secretariat are organs of the Central Committee. Their functions are described briefly in the same provision (Article 38) of the Party Rules: "The Central Committee of the Communist Party of the Soviet Union elects a Politburo to direct the work of the party between plenary meetings and a Secretariat to direct current work, chiefly the selection of cadres and the verification of the fulfillment of party decisions. The Central Committee elects a General Secretary of the CC CPSU." It is generally said that the Politburo is the policymaking organ while the Secretariat is the administrative arm. There is no established number of members of either body. In recent years the Politburo has had about fifteen full members and five to eight candidate (nonvoting) members. The number of Central Committee secretaries has usually been about ten, including the general secretary. Typically, several persons (including the general secretary) serve on both the Politburo and the Secretariat.

As the administrative arm of the party, the Secretariat, is in charge of the party bureaucracy. The Secretariat is divided into over twenty departments which specialize in important areas of economic activity and foreign policy, as well as culture, propaganda and agitation, science and education, government administration, and personnel. It is through these departments, several of which are headed by CC secretaries, that the party oversees the political, economic, and social life of the country. The staff workers of these departments, who may number several hundred thousand, constitute the bulk of the party bureaucracy.

Both the Politburo and the Secretariat meet about once a week. The general secretary, with overall responsibility for day-to-day concerns of the party, appears to be in a crucial position in terms of agenda-setting for Politburo meetings. This, as well as his responsibilities in the personnel field, are considered major factors in making the general secretary's post the key one in the Soviet political system. Other CC secretaries may not rank near the top of the Soviet political hierarchy, however, unless they also have positions on the Politburo. Most Politburo members achieved that status by gaining high positions in other areas of Soviet politics, positions which they often retain. Several Politburo members are also members of the Secretariat. The late Mikhail Suslov, one of the most important Soviet politicians in recent decades, held a position on the Secretariat from 1947 and a seat on the Politburo from 1955 until his death in 1982.

In addition, the Politburo in recent years has had within its ranks the ministers of defense and foreign affairs, the head of the KGB (security police), and the heads of important republic or urban party organizations such as those in the Ukraine, Moscow, and Leningrad. By having represented in the Politburo the chief politicians from these crucial sectors, the authorities seek to assure both that powerful interests will have a voice at the highest levels, and that the central political authorities can maintain control over influential and potentially dangerous subgroups in Soviet society.

Criticism and self-criticism is mentioned several times in the Party Rules, in connection with both the free discussion of party policy and the uncovering of shortcomings in Soviet society. It is obviously designed to control abuse of authority in various areas of Soviet life. This function, one that might be performed by opposition parties in other political systems, must be handled within the single party in the Soviet system. But restrictions on freedom of expression clearly limit the usefulness of this device. It is sometimes used to criticize party leaders at lower levels, but public criticism of higher party leaders, unless they have fallen from favor, is strictly forbidden.

An important device used by the party in running the Soviet system, though not, strictly speaking, a principle, is *nomenklatura*. The term refers to a list of positions for which party approval is required before a person holding such a position can be dismissed or a replacement named. All party levels above the PPO have *nomenklatura* lists, but the national level covers the most important posts. Not all positions are in the party apparatus. They also include high positions in the military, the government, communications media, trade unions, Komsomol, and other important organizations in Soviet life. Party membership is not required for appointment to *nomenklatura* posts, but communists undoubtedly predominate among those selected. It is in part through the *nomenklatura* system that the party is able to maintain its dominant position. And the general secretary's considerable responsibility for cadres' policy is thus related to the centrality of *nomenklatura* in party operations.

One of the muted criticisms of the *nomenklatura* system is that it provides a haven for incompetents. It is difficult to determine to what extent this is the case. There does seem to be a reluctance, however, to demote people from *nomenklatura* to non-*nomenklatura* positions. And there have been occasional reports of persons being shunted from one *nomenklatura* position to another, and doing an incompetent job each time.

As a ruling party with effective control over all sanctioned media of communications, it might be said that all publications in the USSR are party publications. In a narrower sense, however, there are numerous publications—of national, regional, and local importance—that are specifically identified as organs of the party. Some of these are devoted largely to party matters. The most important newspaper in the country is *Pravda* (The Truth), an organ of the Central Committee of the CPSU. Its average circulation, the largest in the country, was about twelve million in the mid-1980s. Two of the major magazines associated with the party are the theoretical journal *Kommunist* (Communist) and *Partiinaia Zhizn'* (Party Life).

The major auxiliary organization of the CPSU is the Komsomol. The term is an acronym based on the Russian words meaning "Young Communist League." The age range for Komsomol members is fourteen to twenty-eight. At the upper age levels, persons may join the party but remain in the Komsomol if they hold a leadership position in the youth group. A Komsomol member can join the party at age eighteen; the earliest age for party membership for non-Komsomol members is twenty-three.

By the mid-1980s, the Komsomol had some forty-two million members organized in nearly one-half million primary Komsomol organizations in schools, factories, military units, and other places of work or study. The Komsomol organization parallels the party structure in numerous ways. Each primary organization is headed by a secretary, nominally elected by the membership at large. A hierarchy of Komsomol levels culminates in a Central Committee located in Moscow. The leaders of the Komsomol are party members trained to work with young people. The highest-ranking Komsomol members are sometimes accorded membership in the party Central Committee.

The Komsomol is a less elite body than the party. Over half of all Komsomol members are women, for instance, as against about one-fourth in the Party. Clearly, not all Komsomol members eventually become party members. But it is said that over 70 percent of all persons admitted to the party enter through the Komsomol. The Komsomol publishes a number of newspapers and other publications designed to appeal to young people. The most important of these is *Komsomolskaia Pravda*, a daily newspaper with a circulation of about ten million.

Below the age level of the Komsomol are two organizations for younger children: the Pioneers for ages ten to fifteen and the Little Octoberists for ages five to nine. The organizations include virtually all school-age children.

Policy

While truly impressive accomplishments have been achieved in the Soviet economy during the sixty-five years of the country's existence, the economy's rate of growth has dropped significantly in recent years. With the traditional stress on capital-goods production still emphasized, the development of the consumer sector has been retarded. By the mid-1980s the average monthly wage or salary in the Soviet Union was over 180 rubles (about $250 at the official rate of exchange). This compares unfavorably not only with West European countries, but also with some of the USSR's East European neighbors (e.g., German Democratic Republic, Czechoslovakia). In spite of this rather low average wage, sums in savings accounts in the Soviet Union have grown to record levels, in part because of the shortage of consumer durables for Soviet citizens to buy.

Planning is at the basis of Soviet economic activity. The five-year plan, the fundamental planning document (the Twelfth Five-Year Plan covers the years 1986 to 1990) is broken down into annual and quarterly plans and, at the actual production level, into monthly plans. Each production unit is assigned quotas to meet, and success is determined largely on the basis of fulfillment or overfulfillment of plan targets. Relative to planning systems in some other socialist countries (e.g., Hungary), Soviet planning is quite rigid and centralized, leaving little discretion or initiative at the lower levels of the system. Several attempts have been made over the years to decentralize and provide incentives at the production level in order to increase economic efficiency. The most notable of these efforts was the 1965 economic reform. But such reforms have typically been met with resistance from the central economic bureaucracy and have largely failed.

If Soviet industrial development has experienced a slowdown in recent years, this problem is minor in comparison with that of agriculture. Agriculture has long been the weak link in the Soviet economy, and by the 1980s the situation had reached crisis proportions. Only about 10 percent of the vast Soviet land mass is designated as arable, and much of this is ill-suited for farming. Undependable weather conditions make crop yields uncertain even on the better lands. As a result, even good years do not produce large surpluses, and in poor years when conditions are unfavorable large amounts of food must be imported. Several particularly bad harvests occurred in the late 1970s and 1980s. Since 1981 the Soviet authorities have declined to announce the size of the grain harvest, apparently because it has often been so low.

Agricultural difficulties have a spillover effect on the rest of the Soviet economy. Large annual imports of grain constitute a substantial drain on Soviet hard-currency reserves, preventing the import of other needed goods from the West. And the need to improve agricultural production has taken investment funds away from other areas. The small private sector in Soviet agriculture (private plots held by collective farmers and others) produces a disproportionately great amount of certain products, such as eggs, vegetables, meat, milk, and wool. The authorities have shown some inclination recently to provide more encouragement for this type of production. But ideological considerations make it clear that the great bulk of agricultural activity will remain under state control.

In May 1982, a special plenary meeting of the Party Central Committee was called to address the agricultural problem. The Central Committee adopted a "Food Program of the USSR for the Period to 1990," aimed at eliminating the worst of the problems of food production and distribution which have plagued the country for decades. The Food Program and a series of accompanying joint Central Committee–Council of Ministers decrees designed to implement the Program received the most intensive media coverage given to any Soviet domestic program in years. To administer the program, "agroindustrial associations", will be established on a regional basis all over the country. These agroindustrial associations, which have operated on an experimental basis in some parts of the country for several years, will coordinate the work of collective and state farms and all other organizations and persons involved in agricultural pursuits. Oversight of the work of the agroindustrial associations will be provided by regional agroindustrial councils, which will report to similar councils at the union-republic level. A national agroindustrial council is attached to the USSR Council of Ministers. It remains to be seen whether this latest reorganization will deal better with the problems that earlier reforms in the agricultural sphere have failed to solve.

Another major problem area in Soviet domestic policy is the nationalities problem. Over 100 different nationalities are represented in the Soviet population, twenty-three of which numbered over one million in the 1979 census. Generally speaking, the most populous nationalities are the ones for whom the fifteen union republics are named. In addition to these fifteen, the other eight nationalities of more than one million persons are: Tatars (6.3 million), Germans (1.8 million), Jews (1.7 million), Chuvash (1.7 million), peoples of Dagestan (1.6 million), Bashkirs (1.4 million), Mordvins (1.1 million), and Poles (1.1 million).

Over half of the Soviet population is Russian (52.3 percent in 1979). But Russian dominance is decreasing as several other ethnic groups, particularly those concentrated in Soviet Central Asia, have grown much more rapidly in recent years. It seems likely that the census at the end of the 1980s will show the Russians to be a minority of the Soviet population. One of the traditional ways of maintaining Russian dominance in the USSR has already been mentioned: the occupation of a disproportionately large percentage of positions in the leading central party and government organs by Russians. Another method is the settling of significant numbers of Russians in non-Russian areas of the USSR. Although over 82 percent of Russians lived in the Russian Republic (RSFSR) in 1979, this was a drop of 3.2 percent from twenty years earlier, indicating a continuing effort to settle Russians in other areas of the country. This effort has been only partly successful: in recent years the percentage of Russians has grown in most of the European republics of the USSR (excluding the Russian Republic itself), but it has dropped in each of the Asian and Transcaucasian republics. Still, the *total* Russian population in other republics remains impressive. The Russians constitute the largest nationality group in two of the fifteen republics (their own and the Kazakh SSR), are second in nine republics and third in the other four. Only in four republics was the percentage of Russians under 10 percent in 1979. In addition to sheer numbers, the Russian presence is felt in other ways. While the party first secretaryship in each republic is usually held by a member of the native ethnic group, the second secretary is often a Russian. The same pattern is typically followed in key state positions such as the republican security police (KGB).

Evidence of a recent intensification of national (and, by implication, anti-Russian) feeling in the USSR has been manifested in a number of ways. Complaints about linguistic and cultural russification appear from time to time in the dissident literature. Numerous examples of overt dissent by members of nationality groups, including some violence, have been documented. And a theme that has been present in center-periphery relations for decades, i.e., "localism," continues to be mentioned from time to time in the Soviet press. In its simplest form, localism merely means local officials favoring local interests over national interests. But the term can also carry overtones of nationality tension.

Unlike current ecomonic difficulties, however, the nationality issue remains largely a potential rather than an actual problem. The central authorities have been quite successful in co-opting local leaders and preventing threats to central control. Moreover, most of the nationality groups are too small to constitute a serious problem on their own. Among Soviet nationalities, only the Ukrainians pose any major numerical challenge to the Russians. With over forty-two million people they are second behind the 137 million Russians and constitute about 15 percent of the total Soviet population. The Ukrainians are close to the Russians in language and cultural traditions, but there has long been enmity between the two nationalities, based in large part on Russian efforts at domination. The Ukrainian Republic, with over fifty million people, is about half again as large as Poland, the largest East European socialist state. Moreover, it contains much of the best farm land and many of the important industrial centers in the country. It is natural, therefore, that Moscow would be particularly concerned about preventing the development of excessive national feeling in the Ukraine. Recent Soviet history manifests several examples of such concern. For instance, among the reasons advanced by Western analysts for the 1972 removal of Pyotr Shelest, Ukrainian party leader and member of the CPSU Politburo, was that he allowed too much expression of Ukrainian nationalism. One of the many important considerations that entered into the Soviet decision to invade Czechoslovakia in 1968, according to some scholars, was the disturbing effect the "Prague Spring" was having across the Slovak border in the Soviet Ukraine.

In the post-Stalin period the USSR has manifested interest and gained influence in many parts of the world, well beyond its own borders and those of neighboring communist states. In the process, its relations with the West, and particularly with the United States, have gone through several stages. Khrushchev's policy of "peaceful coexistence" led only to minimal relaxation of tensions with the West, and the Cuban Missile Crisis of 1962 brought the USSR and the United States close to military confrontation. After Khrushchev, his successors reached a series of important agreements with the West in the period from the late 1960s to the mid-1970s. Among these the most notable were the Nuclear Non-Proliferation Treaty (1968); a new agreement on Berlin in 1971, accompanied by more relaxed Soviet–West German relations; and the agreement reached at the thirty-five nation European Security Conference in Helsinki in 1975.

The latter part of the 1970s saw the beginning of a deterioration in the period of détente (relaxation of tensions) which had lasted for several years, particularly with regard to Soviet-American relations. In 1975 Moscow cancelled the long-negotiated 1972 bilateral trade agreement with the United States. The United States had linked most-favored-nation status for the USSR with the adoption by the Soviet Union of relaxed emigration policies, an arrangement that the Soviet Union would not accept. Soviet activities in Angola and Ethiopia in the late 1970s worsened relations further, and its invasion of Afghanistan in 1979 brought the period of détente definitively to a close. The mid-1980s saw the possibility of improved Soviet-American relations, a development highlighted by the summit meeting between President Ronald Reagan and Party General Secretary Mikhail Gorbachev in Geneva in November 1985.

Soviet relations with Western Europe became less cordial in the late 1970s and early 1980s, but did not deteriorate as much as those with the United States.

While most West European governments condemned the invasion of Afghanistan and Soviet interference in Polish affairs, several of them have taken the position that these events should not impede normal trade relations with the USSR, particularly the purchase of Soviet petroleum products. This has caused some friction between West European governments and that of the United States, which has expressed fear concerning possible West European dependence on Soviet oil.

Ultimately, Soviet-Western relations depend upon the mutual perceptions of each side about the other. An aggressive move by one party tends to produce a like reaction by the other. Neither side has given consistently clear signals of its intentions. Generally speaking, Moscow's objective seems to be to build its military strength at least to a point where it can be perceived as an equal and then to negotiate agreements with the West that will not undermine the status it has achieved. At the same time, it seems intent on exploiting differences in the Western alliance to its advantage. Thus, with the United States taking a confrontational posture toward the USSR, Moscow has placed great emphasis on economic cooperation with Western Europe, accompanied by gestures designed to reduce West Europe's fear of the Soviet military threat.

The Soviet Union's closest allies are several East European states, namely Bulgaria, Czechoslovakia, East Germany, Hungary, and Poland. The Soviet Union's primary military pact, the Warsaw Treaty Organization, is with the above-mentioned states, plus Romania, which has developed a degree of independence from the Soviet foreign policy.

The 1968 Soviet invasion of Czechoslovakia (with token participation by forces from Bulgaria, East Germany, Hungary, and Poland) led to what is sometimes referred to in the West as the "Brezhnev Doctrine" or "doctrine of limited sovereignty." This concept holds that (as Brezhnev put it) "the borders of the socialist commonwealth are inviolable." It is the Soviet Union that decides when intervention is required to preserve socialism. Events in Poland have numerous times caused concern in Moscow, most notably in 1956, 1970, and 1980. In the last instance the Soviet Union brought great pressure on the Polish authorities to neutralize Solidarity, the free-trade-union movement.

The USSR's most important challenge in the communist world comes from China. The dispute between the two countries came into the open in 1961, and has continued, at varying levels of intensity, since then. Armed confrontations along the Sino-Soviet border have taken place a number of times, the most serious coming in 1969. As the first and senior member of the world communist movement, the USSR has sought to be the sole authority on the interpretation of Marxism-Leninism, and has resented China's unwillingness to follow its lead.

The conflict has not been only over doctrine. Moscow and Beijing have developed differing priorities in the foreign-policy arena, as well as rivalries in their attempts to extend their influence around the world. A particular source of discord has been the USSR's assistance to India, especially after the Sino-Indian war of 1962. Moreover, there is a genuine great-power rivalry between the two countries. The USSR stopped helping China develop its nuclear capability in 1959, intent, apparently, on keeping China a second-rate military power. China was able to detonate its first nuclear explosion on its own five years later, however. Long-standing border disputes between the two nations, going back to a series of treaties imposed by Russia on China beginning in 1858, constitute a continuing grievance. As a result, there seems to be considerable concern among the Soviet leadership about the Chinese threat, and the Soviet communications media has quite successfully exploited latent anti-Chinese feeling among the Soviet population. The Soviet Union is well fortified along the 4,000-mile border with China, and regularly maintains some forty-six divisions of troops there. At times the two countries have indicated willingness to try to reconcile their differences, but little progress has been made so far.

One of the several points of contention between China and the USSR involves competing claims for leadership of the world communist movement. Of some ninety-five communist parties in existence in the world in 1985, the overwhelming majority could be classified as pro-Soviet, while only a few could be identified as pro-Chinese. Moscow expends considerable effort on maintaining this preeminent position, but some erosion of its overall influence is evident. A number of communist parties, both ruling (e.g., Yugoslavia, Rumania) and nonruling (e.g., Italy, Spain) maintain or advocate policies that are independent of Soviet domination. "Eurocommunism" is the term coined to describe the pluralistic, autonomous socialism advocated by several West European communist parties, most notably those in Italy and Spain. Soviet spokesmen have denounced Eurocommunism, and outside observers see it as a cause for concern for the USSR because of its potentially disruptive effect on Moscow's position as leader of the world communist movement.

In terms of the Third World, the USSR has not pursued a single policy but a set of policies, all designed to extend its presence and influence. It has trained a large number of specialists for work in the developing areas, and produces a large volume of literature on them. Clearly its influence in parts of Asia, Africa, and Latin America has grown considerably in recent years. While its efforts have not been without failure (e.g., Indonesia in 1965, Egypt in 1972), the Soviet Union clearly intends to continue to extend its influence at every point of the globe that offers an opportunity.

Membership & Constituency

By 1985 there were some 19 million party members. This amounts to about 6.5 percent of the Soviet population and about 9 to 10 percent of the adult population.

The size of the party presents certain dilemmas for the Soviet leadership. The leaders feel the need to increase membership so that the party can maintain its leading role and perform its oversight functions of all major aspects of Soviet life. But the recent growth of the party has considerably exceeded general population growth. Given the potential advantages, psychological and material, that may accompany party membership, there is a problem of persons seeking admission purely for selfish motives.

The party has tried to cope with this problem in several ways. Admission to the party is by no means automatic. Applicants must have recommendations from three party members of five or more years standing who have known the applicant for at least a year. The Party Rules provide that the recommenders will be considered responsible by the party for their endorsements. Admission is for a year-long probationary period as a candidate member before full membership is achieved. Once admitted, the member is expected to (quoting the Party Rules) "master Marxist-Leninist theory," "serve as an example of the communist attitude toward labor," "put party decisions firmly into effect," "take part in the political affairs of the country," etc. In short, there is an expectation of political activism. The member is required to support the party's positions without question and to give up a fair amount of otherwise free time for party work. It is not surprising, therefore, that a large number of Soviet citizens choose not to apply for membership. Still, the party apparently admits some persons unworthy of membership, and official reports issued from time to time indicate that large numbers of members have been dropped for "acts incompatible with the designation communist." In addition to expulsion, another process for thinning party ranks is known as "exchange of party cards." This amounts to a thorough membership review, and was last carried out in the 1970s. It was reported that some 350,000 people were dropped from the party in the exchange.

Another dilemma involves the social composition of the party. Ideological precepts hold that a communist party ought to be basically a workers' party. At the same time, in order to meet the challenges of the day and maintain its preeminent position, the party needs large numbers of highly educated members. During the 1970s, it was made more difficult for white-collar workers, especially intellectuals, to join the party, but several Western analysts believe that this practice will not continue.

Information on social groups in the USSR includes only three broad categories: workers, collective farmers, and employees. The last category embraces white-collar workers, including party, government, and economic functionaries, as well as intellectuals. Workers and collective farmers comprise about 80 percent of the Soviet population and are reported to make up 56 percent of the party membership. A problem with this latter figure is that it is based on the status of individuals when they joined the party and may not reflect changes in status based on job advancement or education. On this basis, many of the top party leadership are still listed as workers or collective farmers, their status when they joined the party. This practice appar-

ently serves to mask the fact that the CPSU is a party overwhelmingly composed of persons who are not workers or collective farmers. Persons with partial or complete higher education comprise less than 7 percent of the Soviet population but about 25 percent of the party; those with little or no formal education number over 35 percent of the Soviet population but only 14 percent of the party.

Other aspects of social composition involve sex and nationality. Women make up over 53 percent of the Soviet population but only about one quarter of the party. Russians constitute just over half of the Soviet population but comprise over 60 percent of party members. At the other end of the scale are nationalities such as the Tadzhiks, with over one percent of the Soviet population but less than one-half of one percent of the party membership.

Financing

Party dues are not likely to keep many people from seeking admission. An entrance fee of 2 percent of one month's earnings is paid by each new candidate member. Monthly dues thereafter are based on salary level. The lowest-paid workers (under fifty rubles per month—the ruble was set at about $1.35 at the official rate of exchange at the end of 1985) pay only ten kopecks (100 kopecks = 1 ruble). Above fifty rubles, dues range from one-half of one percent of one's salary to a maximum of 3 percent for salaries over 300 rubles per month. At these dues levels, it seems unlikely that the party could run its wide-ranging activities on the basis of dues alone. The Party Rules (article 70) provide: "The funds of the Party and its organizations are derived from membership dues, income from Party enterprises, and other revenues." The last-mentioned category probably includes a rather sizable subvention from the state budget, although no such item may be found in the sketchy official budget figures which are published.

Leadership

The imbalances in CPSU membership mentioned above become greater at the top of the party: only one woman has served on the Politburo/Secretariat, and none has held such a position since the early 1960s. The proportion of Russians on the Politburo is typically about 75%; when Russians are combined with the other two major Slavic nationalities, the Ukrainians and the Byelorussians, only a few token places remain for other ethnic groups. The average age of the thirteen full members of the Politburo at the end of 1985 was just over 66. This suggests a picture of a rather old elite. Actually, however, several years earlier the average age of this body had reached slightly over seventy. The advent of Mikhail Gorbachev to the top party post in 1985 marked the beginning of a rejuvenation of higher party ranks, a development that promises to continue for the foreseeable future.

Another dominant characteristic of the top leadership has to do with educational level. Unlike earlier generations of leaders, virtually all of the present top leaders are said to have complete higher educations. For some this training was achieved on a part-time basis while engaged in full-time party or other work. The norm is training in the technical or engineering fields rather than in the humanities or social sciences. The study of law, the path to politics for so many leaders in Western countries, has not been a fruitful avenue for advancement in the Soviet Union. Lenin, the founder of the Soviet state, has been almost the only leader of importance who studied law. Gorbachev graduated from the Law Faculty of Moscow University in the 1950s but did not work professionally at this specialty. Most leaders spend some time working at their specialty, but the typical path to the top appears to involve rather early transfer to full-time party work. The following tables provide information on members of the Politburo and the Secretariat as of the end of 1985.

The major characteristics of top leaders, then, usually include Slavic ethnic background, higher education in a technical specialty, transfer to party work early in one's career, and elevation through party ranks. To sum up the traits of the higher authorities so briefly suggests a rather narrow profile for the typical member of the elite. This no doubt involves, at least in part, a conscious effort on the part of political leaders to recruit like-minded individuals who can be expected to maintain the essential features of the system. Some Western analysts have wondered whether reliance on this rather restricted pool will deprive the top leadership of the diverse talents needed to meet the political, economic, and technological problems increasingly facing the Soviet state. The answer to that question is not clear at present. Studies indicate, however, that the middle level of party leadership, which once contained large

numbers of "party generalists" with no particular specialized training, has been largely replaced by more highly trained functional specialists. Moreover, many Western analysts have commented upon the increasing tendency in recent years to call upon scholars and other specialists in such fields as economics, management, law, and other areas to provide informed policy alternatives which the political elite can use in making decisions. What this suggests is that the top leaders recognize the problem and are seeking to cope with it in ways which will not threaten the preeminent position of the entrenched elite.

Collective leadership suggests that important policy decisions should be made collectively, and that a single person should not hold the top two positions of general secretary of the party and prime minister (chairman of the Council of Ministers). This principle is obviously designed to discourage the concentration of excessive power in one person's hands. It was disregarded by both Stalin and Khrushchev, but after each of them ceased to be the top leader (Stalin died in 1953 while still holding the general secretary's post; Khrushchev was ousted from both positions in 1964), calls for a return to collective leadership were made. The Central Committee even adopted a resolution after Khrushchev's dismissal that the two positions should not be held simultaneously by the same person. In 1977 Brezhnev took the position of chairman of the Presidium of the Supreme Soviet while retaining the post of party general secretary. The Presidium chairmanship is considered the equivalent of being head of state. In assuming this post Brezhnev did not violate the letter of the CC resolution. After Andropov had succeeded Brezhnev as Party General Secretary in late 1982, he assumed the Presidium Chairmanship a short time later. The same thing happened in 1984 when Konstantin Chernenko followed Yuri Andropov. And when Mikhail Gorbachev was chosen to the top party post early in 1985, it was widely assumed that he too would take over the Presidium Chairmanship. It came as some surprise when Andrei Gromyko, the longtime minister of foreign affairs, was named Presidium chairman in mid-1985. As for the aspect of collective leadership which relates to collective decision making, it has already been shown that the general secretary enjoys advantages over his Politburo colleagues which make him at least first among equals. The example of Khrushchev's 1964 ouster, however, by the Politburo suggests that

POLITBURO AND SECRETARIAT OF THE CPSU CENTRAL COMMITTEE (December 31, 1985)

Politburo Members	Elected	Elected to Secretariat	Responsibilities, Other Positions
Full			
Aliev, Geidar Ali Rza Ogly (May 10, 1923)	Nov., 1982	—	First Deputy Chairman, USSR Council of Ministers
Chebrikov, Viktor Mikhailovich (Apr. 27, 1923)	Apr., 1985	—	Chairman, Committee for State Security (KGB)
Gorbachev, Mikhail Sergeevich (Mar. 2, 1931)	Oct. 1980	Nov. 1978	General Secretary, CPSU Central Committee
Grishin, Viktor Vasil'evich (Sept. 18, 1914)	Apr. 1971	—	Member, Presidium, USSR Supreme Soviet
Gromyko, Andrei Andreevich (July 18, 1909)	Apr. 1973	—	Chairman, Presidium, USSR Supreme Soviet
Kunaev, Dinmukhamed Akhmedovich (Jan. 12, 1912)	Apr. 1971	—	First Secretary, Central Committee, CP of Kazakhstan
Ligachev, Egor Kuz'mich (Nov. 29, 1920)	Apr. 1985	Dec. 1983	Chief, Organizational Party Work Dept., CPSU Central Committee
Ryzhkov, Nikolai Ivanovich (Sept. 28, 1929)	Apr. 1985	—	Chairman, USSR Council of Ministers
Shcherbitsky, Vladimir Vasil'evich (Feb. 17, 1918)	Apr. 1971	—	First Secretary, Central Committee, CP of Ukraine
Shevardnadze, Eduard Amvrosievich (Jan. 25, 1928)	July 1985	—	USSR Minister of Foreign Affairs
Solomentsev, Mikhail Sergeevich	Dec. 1983	—	Chairman Party Control Committee, CPSU Central Committee
Tikhonov, Nikolai Aleksandrovich (May 14, 1905)	Nov. 1979	—	
Vorotnikov, Vitalii Ivanovich (Jan. 20, 1926)	Dec. 1983	—	Chairman, RSFSR Council of Ministers
Candidate			
Demichev, Petr Nilovich (Jan. 3, 1918)	Nov. 1964	—	USSR Minister of Culture
Dolgikh, Vladimir Ivanovich (Dec. 5, 1924)	May 1982	Dec. 1972	Chief, Heavy Industry Department, CPSU Central Committee
Kuznetsov, Vasilii Vasil'evich (Feb. 13, 1901)	Oct. 1977	—	First Deputy Chairman, Presidium, USSR Supreme Soviet
Ponomarev, Boris Nikolaevich (Jan. 17, 1905)	May 1972	Oct. 1961	Chief, International Department, CPSU Central Committee (responsible for foreign affairs and relations with nonruling Communist parties)
Sokolov, Sergei Leonidovich (July 1, 1911)	April 1985	—	USSR Minister of Defense
Talyzin, Nikolai Vladimirovich (Jan. 28, 1929)	Oct. 1985	—	Deputy Chairman, USSR Council of Ministers
Other Secretaries			
El'tsin, Boris Nikolaevich (Feb. 1, 1931)		July, 1985	First Secretary, Moscow City Party Committee
Kapitonov, Ivan Vasil'evich (Feb. 23, 1915)		Dec. 1965	Responsible for consumer goods production, food industry, and light industry
Nikonov, Viktor Petrovich (Feb. 28, 1929)		Apr. 1985	Responsible in Secretariat for agriculture
Rusakov, Konstantin Viktorovich (Dec. 31, 1909)		May 1977	Chief, Department for Liaison with Communist and Workers' Parties of Socialist Countries, CPSU Central Committee
Zaikov, Lev Nikolaevich (Apr. 3, 1923)		July, 1985	Responsible in Secretariat for defense industry
Zimyanin, Mikhail Vasil'evich (Nov. 21, 1914)		Mar. 1976	Responsible in Secretariat for questions of propaganda, ideology, and culture

other leaders, acting in concert, may be able to overcome these advantages if circumstances require it.

The principle of renewal has had an interesting history. It was first written into the Party Rules under Khrushchev in 1961. It required that a certain proportion of turnover in the party leadership organs takes place at each new election of party leaders (e.g., at least one quarter at the all-union level, at least one-third at the union-republic level, etc.). Exceptions could be made for individual leaders in recognition of their "high political, organizational, or other qualities." At the first post-Khrushchev party congress in 1966, however, this provision was abolished. A passage was retained stating merely that the principle of systematic renewal shall be observed. But the extraordinarily high degree of stability in higher party ranks during the 1970s and 1980s indicates that the principle of renewal has little significance at present.

No established rules exist for political succession in the USSR. Leaders emerge as a result of political activities that take place well beyond public view. Outsiders draw conclusions about possible succession to top leadership positions on the basis of such factors as present position, career pattern, nationality, age, and, to the degree that such information is available, policy positions and political alliances. Despite the lack of ground rules, it is usually clear who the small number of potential successors for the top leadership post will be. The rapid turnover of top leaders in the mid-1980s (four men held the post of party general secretary in the 28 months between November 1982 and March 1985—Brezhnev, Andropov, Chernenko, and Gorbachev) produced no real surprises to sovietologists. Gorbachev's accession did reverse a trend toward older leaders, however. When he assumed the general secretary's position in March 1985, he was barely fifty-four, the youngest top leader since Stalin consolidated his power in the late 1920s. Gorbachev moved quickly to bring younger men into positions of responsibility, and within a year he had effected extensive personnel turnover at the top.

Other Political Forces

One of the traditional preoccupations of the CPSU is with keeping its dominant position in the one-party system. The objective, therefore, is to prevent other organizations from rivaling the party's status. This goal is achieved in various ways, depending upon the organizations involved.

Military

With over 3.6 million persons in uniform, the USSR has one of the largest military forces in the world. Organized into five services (army, strategic rocket forces, air defense forces, air force, and navy), the Soviet military functions administratively under the Ministry of Defense. The minister of defense has traditionally been a career military officer. The recent exception, Dmitry Ustinov, was a civilian member of the Politburo with long experience in military equipment production. The minister of defense is not automatically accorded a seat on the Politburo, but since 1973, perhaps in acknowledgment of the important place of the military in Soviet foreign policy, military representation on the Politburo has been almost continuous. When Ustinov died in late 1984, he was replaced as minister of defense by Marshal Sergei Sokolov, a career military officer with minimal political experience. Sokolov was given candidate Politburo membership a few months later. Since 1973, Politburo membership has also usually been accorded to the minister of foreign affairs and the chairman of the Committee for State Security (KGB, the security police).

The party has long been concerned about the maintenance of political control over the military. Shortly after the Bolshevik takeover, the new regime instituted a system of political commissars brought from the ranks of the party to serve as equals with regular commanding officers. If this division of authority did not enhance military efficiency, it was thought to serve well the purpose of preventing military independence from the party. Political leaders have also, on occasion, sought to discredit famous military leaders. Stalin purged a number of top military men on the eve of World War II, and after the war he banished Marshall Georgy Zhukov, a military hero, to obscurity in the provinces. Khrushchev brought Zhukov back into prominence, naming him minister of defense and allying with Zhukov to support his political authority. In 1958, however, Zhukov was accused of "Bonapartist tendencies" and "curtailment of the work of party organizations" in the armed forces. He was dismissed from his posts and retired in disgrace.

In recent years, the party has used several means to maintain its ascendent position. As mentioned, the minister of defense since 1976 has been a civilian. Military councils, consisting of leading party functionaires, oversee the work of all large military units. As noted above, all important military leadership posts are on the party's *nomenklatura* list. Each commanding officer of a military unit has a deputy, a "political officer," who is in charge of political and ideological education in the armed services. All military units contain primary party organizations and Komsomol organizations. And finally, virtually all career officers are now party members.

Obviously the party leaders have made these efforts to maintain control because they see the military as a force of potential political importance. The military must not only be controlled but also courted and consulted. High military officers are among the most privileged members of the Soviet elite, entitled to the best of the material perquisites the society has to offer. And their views on military and political-military matters cannot be ignored. Khrushchev's ouster in 1964 is generally attributed to policies which alienated a number of powerful interests, including the military. A large contingent of military leaders is regularly represented on the party Central Committee. Perhaps more important is military input on the Defense Council (*Sovet Oborony*), a body composed of high military and civilian leaders who develop basic material policy.

In general, party and military interests seem to have largely coincided in recent years. It is probably fair to say that on most issues the party is closer to the military than it is to virtually any other actual or potential group in Soviet society.

Organized Labor

Trade unions are the major group in a category known as "mass organizations of workers" (which also includes smaller organizations such as a scientific-technical society, an inventors' organization, and others). Unions cover virtually all employed persons and students in higher education in the USSR. By the mid-1980s, over 130 million persons belonged to trade unions, more than 98 percent of all workers. About 85 percent of union members are classified as manual or white-collar workers. In recent years, however, there has been great em-

phasis placed on collective farmers joining trade unions. By the mid-1980s, twelve million (over 96 percent of all collective farmers) were enrolled, compared with 3.2 million (21 percent) in 1976. Like the Komsomol, trade unions are an organization which nearly all students in higher education are required to join. In 1980, over 99 percent of such students were in unions.

During the 1920s, unions became the focus of a struggle that could have challenged party control. But the so-called "workers' opposition" was outlawed under Lenin, and before the end of the decade unions had been effectively neutralized as an independent political force. They have become, in effect, an appendage of the party bureaucracy and perform few of the functions typically associated with labor unions in the West. Strikes are forbidden and collective bargaining is not considered a legitimate union activity. The rare attempts to create independent labor organizations which have advocated such rights have been suppressed by the authorities.

In their present form, unions perform some of the functions formerly associated with the ministry of labor (abolished in 1933) such as control over observance of safety rules and administration of some aspects of the social insurance system. In addition, the commissions on labor disputes, to which workers may appeal grievances against management, include representatives of both local unions and management. Unions serve a social function for workers, managing the factory "club" and other social and cultural events and helping to administer health and vacation resorts maintained by many enterprises for their workers.

The lowest trade-union level is the primary organization established in the factory or shop. Like its party counterpart, it elects a committee of leaders. Above the primary level are several higher levels, similarly organized, culminating in the All-Union Central Council of Trade Unions or ACCTU (*Vsesoiuznyi Tsentralnyi Sovet Professionalnykh Soiuzov;* VTsSPS). An indicator of party influence in the trade-union organization is the level of party membership. In the committees of the primary organizations less than 30 percent are party members, but at the ACCTU level the corresponding figure is about 80 percent. The chairman of the Presidium of the ACCTU, the national union leader, is always a high-ranking party member.

Interest Groups

Western scholars have expended considerable effort in attempting to apply interest-group analysis to Soviet politics. Agreement is lacking as to whether it is even appropriate to speak of interest groups in the USSR, given the party's considerable success in monopolizing political power. A number of studies have demonstrated how aggregations of like-minded people have been able to influence policies adopted by the political authorities. Often these have been specialists such as economists, jurists, industrial managers, educators, and other professionals who can bring expert views to bear on policy discussions. In all of these examples, the party leadership sets the ground rules for specialist participation, and the specialists acknowledge, implicitly and explicitly, the party's leading role.

Dissent

Most analysts agree that the dissident movement in the Soviet Union dates from the 1960s. Occasional instances of dissent before that time have been documented, but widespread recognition of the movement is traced to the post-Khrushchev period. It is thought to have originated largely in the frustration growing out of limitations on expression after the partial liberalization achieved during the Khrushchev period.

The dissident movement has demonstrated considerable diversity and has found a number of forms of expression. In a sense, all Soviet dissent is political. But it can also be said that most dissident activities have at their base either political, religious, or ethnic concerns. Political dissent ranges across the spectrum. Examples would be "Leninist" Roy Medvedev, who believes in a Marxist socialist system with the Stalinist excesses removed; people of centrist persuasion such as Andrei Sakharov, who basically favor the social-democratic political arrangements of Western Europe; Aleksandr Solzhenitsyn, whose prescriptions emphasize Russian nationalism and Orthodox Christianity and the elimination of the alien communist ideology; and rightist dissidents whose Russian nationalism is more extreme than Solzhenitsyn's and contains anti-Semitic overtones. Some political dissent has also concentrated on narrower concerns such as women's rights, free trade unions, and the rights of the handicapped.

A number of religious groups have been active in dissent for several years. Foremost among these are the Catholics in Lithuania, but also included are smaller groups such as Pentecostalists and Baptists. Groups within the Russian Orthodox Church have also pushed for greater freedom of religious expression. Ethnic dissent is often intermixed with religious dissent. Both religious and nonreligious Jews have been involved in protesting against what they consider official anti-Semitism in the USSR. A number of these people, along with many thousands of Soviet Jews who have not engaged in overt protests, have been allowed to emigrate from the USSR in recent years. But a great number of Jews have been refused exit visas. Soviet policy on this matter appears to be tied to the status of Soviet-Western relations, and fewer exit visas are granted when such relations are bad. Among other ethnic groups, the Crimean Tatars are notable. Forcibly removed from the Crimea during World War II, groups of Crimean Tatars have protested the refusal of the authorities to allow them to return to their homeland.

Over the years a wide range of forms of dissent has been manifested. The more violent forms such as arson, bombings, self-immolation, and airplane hijacking are infrequent, but there are a few documented examples of these activities. More frequent, but still rare, are public protests in the form of demonstrations, mass signing of protest letters, and the like. By far the most common form of dissent is *samizdat*, an acronym that literally means "self-publishing." *Samizdat* includes all manner of unofficial, clandestinely circulated writings, often typewritten in multiple copies. A number of *samizdat* journals have appeared over the years, many of which existed only briefly and then disappeared. The best known is undoubtedly *The Chronicle of Current Events*. This publication began in 1968, and although several generations of its editorial staff have been arrested and imprisoned, other dissidents have taken over editorial duties. By the mid-1980s, however, even this hardy publication had been silenced.

Official response to the various dissident activities has depended to some extent on the times and the perceived threat. When the number of protest letters began to grow in the mid-to-late 1960s, threats from the authorities were enough to convince most signers to cease their activity. For more persistent dissenters, various forms of harassment, including imprisonment and incarceration in mental institutions, have been used. A number of well-known dissenters were forced to leave the USSR (Solzhenitsyn, for example, was arrested and flown to Switzerland in 1974), while Sakharov was exiled from Moscow and confined in the city of Gorky in 1980. Several Soviet Armenians accused of planting a bomb in a Moscow subway train in 1977 were executed. By the mid-1980s, while sporadic manifestations of dissident activity could still be observed, it seemed clear that the tactics of the authorities had reduced such movements to quite modest proportions.

National Prospects

The fact that the Soviet system has celebrated sixty-five years of existence testifies to the stability that the communist regime has created. During that time the USSR has been transformed into an impressive economic and military power. It has gained numerous allies through the spread of Marxist socialism to many parts of the world, and it has secured a buffer zone of compliant (if not completely reliable) allies in Eastern Europe against the threat to its historically vulnerable western border. In spite of the evidence of political dissent, the overwhelming majority of the Soviet population has remained relatively passive. As a result, the Soviet regime has not had to face the rather widespread upheavals that have taken place in several neighboring states in East Europe over the past decades. Preoccupied as they are with internal and external security, it is reasonable to expect that the Soviet authorities will continue to place great emphasis on maintaining the stability of the system.

This is not to suggest that the road for the next few years will be completely smooth. Significant internal and external problems, which past regimes have shown little ability to solve, will continue and even intensify. First among these is the Soviet economy, particularly the agricultural sector. As long as investments go disproportionately to industrial and military production, it is not likely that any reform measure, including the 1982 "Food Program," will do much to improve agricultural efficiency.

As ethnic Russians move toward minority status in the Soviet population at large, greater restiveness among the other nationalities can be expected. At the very least this is likely to necessitate greater efforts toward equalizing the regional economic imbalances that have long characterized the USSR.

Great-power status in the international sphere is also likely to require escalating commitments and costs. The amount of aid required to maintain friendly regimes in such countries as Cuba and Afghanistan is a considerable drain on the capacities of the domestic economy. If the Soviet leaders are determined to maintain such efforts in the international sphere, they must be counting, in part, on the continued passivity of the Soviet population in the face of a stagnating or perhaps even declining standard of living. Perhaps the greatest problem the Soviet leadership will have to face in the next few years will be a growing unwillingness of Soviet citizens to remain passive.

Further Reading

Barry, Donald D., and Barner-Barry, Carol. *Contemporary Soviet Politics: An Introduction.* 2nd ed. Englewood Cliffs, N.J.: Prentice-Hall, Inc., 1982.

Byrnes, Robert F., ed. *After Brezhnev: Sources of Soviet Conduct in the 1980s.* Bloomington, Indiana: Indiana University Press, 1983.

Harasymiw, Bohdan. *Political Elite Recruitment in the Soviet Union.* New York: St. Martin's Press, 1984.

Hill, Ronald J. and Frank, Peter. *The Soviet Communist Party.* 2nd ed. London: George Allen & Unwin, 1983.

Lane, David. *State and Politics in the USSR.* New York: New York University Press, 1985.

Lowenhardt, John. *The Soviet Politburo.* New York: St. Martin's Press, 1982.

Medish, Vadim. *The Soviet Union.* 2nd ed. Englewood Cliffs, N.J.: Prentice-Hall, Inc., 1985.

Vozlensky, Michael. *Nomenklatura: The Soviet Ruling Class.* New York: Doubleday & Company, Inc., 1984.

UNITED ARAB EMIRATES
(Dawlat al-Imarat al-'Arabiyyah al-Muttahidah)
by Fred H. Lawson, Ph.D.

The System of Government

The United Arab Emirates (UAE) is a federation of nonparty autocracies in which a variety of federal institutions have been set up that are intended to supplement and eventually to supplant the personal regimes of its member states. This federation was created in December 1971 by the rulers (emirs) of six of the autonomous principalities lying along the southwestern coast of the Arab/Persian Gulf: Abu Dhabi, Dubai, Sharjah, 'Ajman, Umm al-Qaiwain, and Fujairah. The ruler of Ra's al-Khaimah initially refused to join the federation on the grounds that Abu Dhabi and Dubai were being given a disproportionate amount of influence in the federal government's institutions. In February 1972 this principality became the seventh member of the union, which has a total population of about one million people.

Unity among the individual shaikhdoms that make up the UAE has been buttressed by a measure of complementarity among their respective economies. Abu Dhabi and Dubai produce significant quantities of petroleum for export, bringing in considerable amounts of foreign exchange that can be used by the federation to fund industrial and infrastructural construction programs. Ra's al-Khaimah and Fujairah produce fruits and vegetables for sale to the more arid parts of the union, while Sharjah and Dubai are important centers of commerce and finance. Fishing remains the most important sector of the economies of 'Ajman and Umm al-Qaiwain. These economic complementarities are reinforced by the emirs' shared political interests in maintaining both their autonomy from more powerful Gulf countries and their dominance over the professional administrators and large communities of expatriate workers within the union. Consequently, the UAE has been able to survive as an integrated political unit in spite of persistent tribal and other conflicts among the federation's member states.

Executive

Executive authority for the federation is vested in three closely related federal institutions: the Supreme Council of the Union (SCU), the president and vice president of the union, and the Council of Ministers. Of these, the SCU is the most important, as its approval is required for virtually all significant governmental activities. This Council consists of the rulers of each of the federation's seven member states and meets on a regular basis beginning in October of each year. Decisions by the SCU on substantive policies must be reached with the consent of five of the seven rulers including those of both Abu Dhabi and Dubai. Among the most vital of this body's powers are those of ratifying all federal legislation, supervising the disposition of federal monies, electing the union's president and vice president, approving the appointment of all other federal officials, and ratifying all international agreements and declarations of war or national emergency.

Since its founding in 1971, the UAE's president has been Shaikh Zayyid bin Sultan an-Nuhayyan, the ruler of Abu Dhabi. As president, Shaikh Zayyid is empowered by the draft constitution both to call and to chair the meetings of the SCU, to select and dismiss the country's premier and other cabinet ministers as well as its federal judges, and to supervise the implementation of all federal laws and decrees. In November 1979, the SCU adopted a measure which placed the president in charge of the federation's unified public security and intelligence services and gave him control over the issuing of immigration and residence permits. These powers, in conjunction with his close supervision of the country's armed forces, have put Shaikh Zayyid in a dominant position within the UAE's central government. The term of office for both president and vice president is five years. In 1982, both Shaikh Zayyid and Vice President Shaikh Rashid bin Sa'id al-Maktum, the ruler of Dubai, were reelected to their third consecutive terms.

The Council of Ministers draws up initial drafts of all laws and decrees and submits them to the Federal National Council for discussion. It also prepares the union's annual budget and supervises the day-to-day operation of all administrative agencies. Initially, Abu Dhabi was given six of the cabinet positions, Dubai the prime ministership and three other portfolios, Ra's al-Khaimah four posts, Sharjah three, Umm al-Qaiwain and 'Ajman two apiece, and Fujairah one. Virtually all of these offices were held by members of these principalities' ruling families. By January 1977, when the UAE's third cabinet was announced, both the size and the composition of the council had changed significantly. Although several new ministries—such as those of petroleum and mineral resources, fisheries, and Islamic affairs—had been created in 1974, others were disbanded or consolidated; the total number of cabinet positions dropped from twenty-seven to twenty-two. Furthermore, the proportion of ministers not related to the region's ruling families rose from eleven of twenty-seven in December 1973 to twelve of twenty-two, with the an-Nahayyan family of Abu Dhabi suffering the greatest loss of representation. This decline in Abu Dhabi's presence within the cabinet was compensated for in the winter of 1977–78 when Minister of the Interior Shaikh Mubarak bin Muhammad an-Nuhayyan was delegated wide-ranging powers to ensure internal security, and the president appointed his son Shaikh Sultan as commander in chief of the UAE's armed forces. As partial compensation for these changes, Shaikh Rashid was made prime minister in June 1979 in addition to his being the vice president of the federation. Feuding among the union's other rulers prevented Shaikh Rashid from forming a cabinet until late in the summer. This new cabinet included nine ministers from Abu Dhabi, five from Dubai, three each from Ra's al-Khaimah and Umm al-Qaiwain, two from Sharjah, and one each from 'Ajman and Fujairah.

Legislature

Members of the Federal National Council are appointed by the ruler of each emirate for two-year, renewable terms. Abu Dhabi and Dubai each send eight delegates to this assembly; Sharjah and Ra's al-Khaimah each send six; and 'Ajman, Umm al-Qaiwain, and Fujairah each send four. The Council is empowered to make recommendations on laws and decrees submitted to it by the Council of Ministers and to debate issues of national concern. But it may not enact legislation on its own, and any actions it takes with regard to proposals that are submitted to it can be overruled either in the Council of Ministers or in the SCU. During periods in which the Federal National Council is not in session, the cabinet is permitted to send draft laws directly to the SCU for approval without convening the assembly for discussion. The National Council can be dissolved by the federation's president at will, but such an order must include a call for the convening of a new National Council within sixty days.

In recent years, this body has discussed the disposition of the federal budget, the effects of the federation's immigration policies on its economic development, and the social implications of rising fuel costs within the union. More significantly, during the term of Tiryam 'Umran Tiryam as its speaker, it called for closer integration of the UAE's member states and the adoption of a permanent federal constitution, despite clear signals from the SCU that most of the union's rulers favored an extension of the draft constitution of 1971. The SCU in late 1976 firmly rejected a proposal that at least some members of the Federal National Council be appointed in ways other than by the federation's individual rulers. Calls such as those made in mid-1979 for the direct election of the assembly's membership have not received a positive response from the SCU.

Judiciary

Three sorts of courts operate within the UAE. First, on the federal level, a Supreme Court, consisting of five judges appointed by the union's president, adjudicates disputes among the member states and those between individual principalities and the central administration. It also decides whether or not proposed laws and decrees are constitutional. Lower federal courts handle civil and commercial disputes when these involve aspects or agents of the federal government. Judges for these courts have come primarily from larger Arab countries, notably Jordan, the Sudan, and Iraq. Second, in Abu Dhabi, Sharjah, and Fujairah, local courts are administered by the federal Ministry of Justice. Third, in the remaining four shaikhdoms, judicial matters are handled largely by their respective rulers, who benefit both financially and socially from adjudicating local disputes that do not involve federal issues.

Emirate & Local Administrations

According to the UAE's draft constitution, any powers and responsibilities not explicitly relegated to federal authorities are to be considered perogatives of the administrations of the member states. Thus each emirate is free to determine its own internal political affairs, retains control over its own natural resources, and is permitted to maintain its own armed forces. But in each of these areas, federal institutions have begun to extend the scope of their own authority at the expense of local officials.

When the ruler of Sharjah was killed during the course of a coup attempt led by his brother in January 1972, the SCU responded by sending federal troops into the emirate to suppress the revolt. The federal government then recognized another of the slain ruler's brothers, Shaikh Sultan, as his successor; all without the participation or the prior consent of Sharjah's ruling family.

Similarly, in an effort to achieve some measure of coordination with regard to production and pricing policies among the UAE's oil-producing members, the Council of Ministers created an Energy Commission in September 1980 to augment the largely impotent federal Ministry of Petroleum and Mineral Resources. The Energy Commission, in cooperation with the much more successful Central Bank established in December of the same year, has been able to increase the level of integration in the UAE's economic relations significantly. However, Ra's al-Khaimah and Umm al-Qaiwain have continued to oppose the extension of centralized control over members' natural resources in the expectation that they can have a greater degree of influence in setting national policy if and when sizable oil or gas reserves are discovered within their own territories.

Finally, it was announced by the Supreme Defense Committee in 1976 that the armed forces belonging to each of the UAE's member states would be merged into three federal commands led by sons of the rulers of Abu Dhabi, Dubai, and Ra's al-Khaimah. Although the implementation of this project has been subject to various delays, work was begun in the spring of 1981 on three consolidated army bases and two unified airbases within the union. The resignation of Shaikh Sultan bin Zayyid an-Nuhayyan as the commander of the Union Defense Force at the end of February 1982, and his replacement by another of Shaikh Zayyid's sons, does not appear to have derailed the central government's efforts to create a unified armed forces under federal control.

Despite these trends toward greater unification among the UAE's members, major differences in local administration across these principalities remain. In Abu Dhabi, the ruling family as a whole retains considerable influence over public policymaking and occupies predominant positions in the Abu Dhabi Investment Authority, the ruler's consultative council, the emirate's larger economic concerns, and its burgeoning civil service. In Dubai, on the other hand, Shaikh Rashid deals with the ruling family in a more authoritarian fashion, allying himself instead with members of the city's merchant elite, Western-educated technocrats, and representatives of foreign firms, while keeping the number of administrative agencies in the shaikhdom to a minimum. In Ra's al-Khaimah, there is a third type of local rule in which the ruler functions primarily as a mediator among rival bedouin and village factions within his domain. Finally, in 'Ajman there is a long political tradition of limiting the power of the ruling shaikh by means of a local council meeting on a daily basis.

Other Political Forces

Radical Organizations

In the larger emirates within the UAE, support for radical organizations such as the Popular Front for the Liberation of Oman and the Arab Gulf (PFLOAG) and the pan-Arab Ba'th party has come primarily from well-to-do families such as the Shurair family in Dubai and the al-Oweiss family in Sharjah. Pro-Nasserist sympathies are also found among certain influential members of the royal families in these two principalities, including Shaikh Maktum bin Rashid, Dubai's heir apparent. But in Ra's al-Khaimah and the smaller emirates, where the gap between rich and poor is not as great as it is in Abu Dhabi or Dubai, settled bedouin are the people most likely to provide support for radical movements. In January 1976, for instance, a violent demonstration broke out in one of Ra's al-Khaimah's northern villages. The demonstrators protested not only the lack of water and electricity, but also a new federal law that reduced the requirements for foreign Arabs to obtain local citizenship. Leaders of this demonstration charged that rich foreigners were buying up land in the emirate and charging higher rents to the local inhabitants. Similar sorts of nationalist and socialist activity have been evident in other rural areas of the UAE's poorer member states, while PFLOAG sympathizers have been active in Dubai's public high schools and Abu Dhabi's state militia as well.

Minority Communities

Ethnic Persians, Indians, and Baluchis constitute influential communities within virtually all of the UAE's urban districts. These communities have dominated commerce and finance in towns like Sharjah and Dubai for many years, and their influence in these areas has led to repeated social disorders both by the members of these communities themselves in support of their own interests and by poorer Arabs against what they perceive as foreign dominance over the local economies. When Iran occupied the islands of Abu Musa and the Tumbs off the UAE's coast at the end of 1971, demonstrators in Sharjah and Ra's al-Khaimah set fire to banks and shops owned by both resident and nonresident Persians. On the other hand, a violent demonstration by indigenous Persians in support of the Islamic Republic of Iran occurred in Dubai during February of 1979.

Workers

Industrial disturbances on the part of workers in these shaikhdoms during the early 1960s were firmly and quickly suppressed by the local rulers and their British advisers. But with the influx of expatriate laborers into the UAE after the mid-1970s, protests by workers in the union's larger principalities became more frequent and widespread than ever before. In February 1976, Indian and Pakistani workers at the dry dock in Dubai struck for higher wages and better working conditions; ten months later riot police in that emirate broke up a larger

strike by South Asian workers involved in constructing a new sewer system for the city. By 1981, indigenous government workers and professionals had adopted similar tactics. These demonstrators have merged demands for economic betterment with calls for greater popular representation in the Federal National Council and for an end to foreign control over the federation's economic affairs.

National Prospects

The rulers of the UAE have so far managed to suppress both tribal and radical violence within the federation's boundaries with little effort. Shaikh Saqr bin Muhammad al-Qasimi of Ra's al-Khaimah remains a sort of political maverick on a wide range of political and economic issues. However, Shaikh Zayyid and those of his allies who favor a more comprehensive unification among the member states of the federation appear to have beaten down the primary opponents of greater integration either by co-opting them through judicious use of Abu Dhabi's immense oil revenues or by skillfully manipulating the delegation of offices within the federal apparatus. It is probably reasonable to expect that as long as oil prices do not collapse completely and economic difficulties can be avoided by increasing levels of production of oil and natural gas, political grievances will find expression primarily in the form of sectarian conflict. This circumstance will have the contradictory effect of enhancing the unity of the UAE as a whole, even as it threatens to disrupt social relations within the more urban of its constituent members.

Further Reading
Anthony, John D. *Arab States of the Lower Gulf: People, Politics, Petroleum.* Washington, D.C.: Middle East Institute, 1975.
Khalifa, Ali Mohammed. *The United Arab Emirates: Unity in Fragmentation.* Boulder, Colo.: Westview Press, 1979.
Sadik, Muhammad, and Snavely, William P. *Bahrain, Qatar, and the United Arab Emirates.* Lexington, Mass.: D. C. Heath, 1972.
Sahr, Naomi. "Federalism in the United Arab Emirates." In *Social and Economic Development in the Arab Gulf,* Tim Niblock, ed. New York: St. Martin's, 1980.

UNITED KINGDOM OF GREAT BRITAIN AND NORTHERN IRELAND

by William G. Andrews, Ph.D.

The System of Government

Great Britain and Northern Ireland (Ulster) are governed by the United Kingdom, a democratic, parliamentary monarchy in a unitary state. On the island of Great Britain (population: about 54.9 million) are the countries of England, Scotland, and Wales. Northern Ireland (population: about 1.5 million) is composed of the six northeastern counties on the neighboring island of Ireland. The British political system dates at least to William the Conqueror in 1066, and has evolved in character with several abrupt constitutional breaks since then. The most recent was the Glorious Revolution of 1688 and the settlement it produced. The regime of coordinate executive and legislative branches that was founded then was transformed gradually into a parliamentary system by the mid-nineteenth century. By the mid-twentieth century, further evolution had given the queen's prime minister such ascendancy over the government and Parliament that the regime was being labeled "prime-ministerial" by some observers. However, in the past generation, Parliament has recovered some power.

Because of the evolutionary nature of the regime, it lacks a written constitution. The closest the British have come to framing such a document was the Instrument of Government of Oliver Cromwell and the Puritan Commonwealth of the seventeenth century. Its failure provided little incentive to make another such attempt.

The absence of a single integrated constitution has not, however, left the British without a clearly defined set of principles to regulate the conduct of their politics and government, much of which may be found in formal legislative and executive acts. The earliest and best known of these principles is the Magna Carta of 1215 by which the nobility imposed limits on King John's authority. Others emerged from the great constitutional struggles of the seventeenth century: the Petition of Right (1628), Habeas Corpus Act (1679), Bill of Rights (1689), Act of Settlement (1701), Act of Union with Scotland (1707), and the Place Acts (1740s). Other such statutes of constitutional standing are the series of nineteenth-century reform acts that expanded suffrage. British constitutional principles have undergone much additional codification in this century through such laws as the Parliament Acts (1911 and 1949), the Statute of Westminister (1931), the Ministers of the Crown Act (1937), the Life Peerages Act (1958), and the renunciation of Peerages Act (1963).

The British constitution has been framed even more by convention than by statute. Some of its most fundamental features have become established through the elevation of practice into principle. Such cornerstones of the system as the unitary state, ministerial responsibility, the role of Her Majesty's Loyal Opposition, and the suprapolitical monarchy have all emerged in that way.

A constitution of such origin would seem likely to be highly unstable, as an ordinary act of Parliament or executive action might alter it. Nevertheless, the British political class has worked with this system for so long that it rarely makes changes abruptly or without deliberation, and it seldom disagrees in significant ways on the content of the constitution.

Executive

The executive branch of the system has five main components: the monarch, the prime minister, the cabinet, the government, and the civil service. The monarchy provides the head of state, the ceremonial chief executive. The prime minister is the head of the government, the effective chief executive. The cabinet is the collective chief executive; the government is the leadership of the administration; and the civil service is the administrative staff that implements the decisions of the cabinet and government.

The British monarchy is among the most venerable institutions of its type in the world. It has survived since Roman times, the only interruption in its reign having been the brief period of the Puritan Commonwealth (1649–60). The House of Windsor has been on the throne since 1714, but its hereditary connections to the crown can be traced through collateral lines much further back. The present monarch, Queen Elizabeth II, has reigned since 1952.

The monarchy has a broad range of important formal powers. They include the power to appoint and remove all civil and military officers, an absolute veto over all laws, authority to make foreign and defense policies and to implement them through the diplomatic corps and armed forces. However, the gradual retreat of the institution to the status of a nonpolitical office has cost it the effective use of those powers, except in the most extraordinary circumstances.

In practice, the monarch plays a public and a private role. In public, she is the symbolic embodiment of the state and nation. She and other leading members of the royal family represent those elevated abstractions on all sorts of ceremonial occasions, from launching ships and dedicating buildings to receiving ambassadors and opening sessions of Parliament. In private, she acts as a confidential advisor to the prime minister. She receives a constant flow of official dispatches on all important public business and has "the right to be consulted, the right to encourage, the right to warn" (Walter Bagehot [1826–77]). As Queen Elizabeth has tended seriously to business throughout her long reign, she draws on a background of information and experience unmatched by most of the eight prime ministers she has counseled.

Almost never in recent decades, so far as is known, has the monarch used her own discretion in performing a political act. In 1957, Sir Anthony Eden resigned as prime minister without recommending a successor, leaving the Conservative Party with a parliamentary majority but no titular leader. While either R. A. Butler or Harold Macmillan would have been accepted by the party, the Queen consulted two elder Conservative statesmen and appointed Macmillan. Had she chosen to consult others who would have given different advice, she might well have named Butler. That exception underlines the normally nonpolitical character of the institution.

In contrast to the queen, prime ministers are in the vortex of politics. Although they have been called "first among equals," their actual power is much greater than that, though not as great as that of American presidents. The prime minister's power is based on the role of chairing the cabinet. He or she controls its membership and the attendance of nonmembers at its meetings, schedules its meetings, drafts its agendas, directs and summarizes its deliberations, draws the conclusions from them, and supervises the implementation of its decisions. That power is further enhanced by the process of democratic election. British national elections turn largely on the issue of the incumbency of the prime ministership. Voters select members of Parliament (MPs) largely on the basis of their preferences for the prime ministerial candidates of the major parties. Thus, the winner has a popular mandate that cannot be matched by other members of the government.

However, the prime minister's power is restricted by the principle of collective responsibility. The prime minister's actions require the acquiescence of the other members which is usually obtained. Revolt is very rare, for the cabinet members know that the electorate tends to impose severe penalties on disunited governments. On the other hand, disgruntled influential party members can inflict heavy political costs on prime ministers without open rebellion. A prime minister's awareness of this vulnerability acts as an important restraint.

According to the concept of collective responsibility, all political decisions of the government are taken by deliberation and agreement in the cabinet. All members of the government must support all cabinet decisions loyally, regardless of their own opinions or views expressed in cabinet. Usually, the decisions are reached by consensus.

The principle of collective responsibility has been attenuated somewhat in recent decades. Some new practices have reinforced the traditional reality of prime ministerial preeminence in the meetings. In some cases, cabinet committees have been permitted to make decisions binding on the whole cabinet without review by it. In others, the prime minister has taken important action without prior reference to the Cabinet. In still others—notably the decision to join the European Economic Community—the cabinet has been unable to agree and its members have been permitted to take opposing positions publicly. The rise of a cabinet secretariat responsible to the prime minister and a decline in cabinet secrecy has undermined the concept of collective responsibility still further.

A typical British cabinet includes about twenty senior ministers. Its exact size and composition depend on the circumstances of the moment and the preferences of the prime minister. The heads of the principal ministries are always members, as is the leader of the House of Commons. Often, one or two cabinet members will be ministers without portfolio or ministers on short-term assignment, such as negotiating entrance to the European Economic Community.

The cabinet is part of the much larger government. In recent years, the government has numbered about one hundred members. Most of them are members of the majority party in the House of Commons, but a few are always drawn from the House of Lords. In addition to the cabinet members, the government includes noncabinet ministers, ministers of state (deputy heads of major ministries), junior ministers (administrative assistants to ministers, usually called parliamentary secretaries or undersecretaries), and parliamentary private secretaries (constituency and parliamentary assistants to ministers). Finally, the chief whip and assistant whips of the majority party (officers responsible for liaison between the government and Parliament) are de facto members of the government.

The prime minister is appointed formally by the monarch. However, normally, this is not a discretionary decision. Usually, the House of Commons has a single-party majority, and that party has a designated leader. In such cases, the monarch must appoint that leader. If no party has a majority in the Commons or the majority party has no designated leader, the monarch may use some small measure of discretion in selecting a prime minister. Even that must be done so carefully and be so generally acceptable that no suspicion of political manipulation by the monarch arises.

The other members of the government are appointed by the monarch on the nomination of the prime minister. Most members of a new cabinet that has been formed by a transfer of power come from the opposition's shadow cabinet. The non-cabinet members of the government are selected by the prime minister from among the old warhorses and the able, ambitious younger MPs, taking into account factional and electoral considerations, the preferences of the cabinet, and personal compatibilities, and political and personal competence.

Legislature

The dominant chamber of the British Parliament is the House of Commons. It has 650 members, 523 representing England, seventy-two Scotland, thirty-eight Wales, and seventeen Northern Ireland. Like most legislatures, the House is not an accurate cross-section of the British population occupationally. Business management and consulting was the most common occupation of MPs in the 1983 Parliament, being listed by more than one-quarter of them, including more than one-third of the Conservatives. Law is a distant second, followed by teaching and manual labor. The most common occupation for Labour MPs is manual worker. Educationally, MPs are also atypical. About 75 percent of those in the 1979 Parliament listed some form of higher education, including Oxford or Cambridge universities for 229, and more than half received their secondary education in private schools, including fifty-one at Eton. Similarly, only nineteen women (3 percent) were elected in 1979 and twenty-three (3.5) in 1983.

OCCUPATIONAL BACKGROUND OF BRITISH MPs (1983 PARLIAMENT)				
Occupation	Con.	Lab.	Other	Total
Law	82	17	7	106
Journalism, Writing	31	9	5	45
Business, Management	142	19	6	167
Teaching	24	52	7	83
Medicine, Dentistry	2	2	1	5
Agriculture	19	1	4	24
Architecture, Surveying	6	–	1	7
Engineering	7	1	2	10
Scientific Research	3	2	–	5
Civil service/Local Govt.	16	12	2	30
Misc. White Collar	6	14	2	22
Manual labor	4	70	–	74
Housewife	6	–	–	6
Politics/Political Staff	12	7	1	20
Armed Services	18	–	1	19
Clergy	–	–	3	3
	397	209	44	650

The Commons is headed by the speaker, its presiding officer. The speaker is a nonpolitical nonpartisan officer, responsible mainly for ensuring order and decorum in the proceedings. By tradition, to ensure the nonpolitical character of the office, the speaker is not opposed for reelection by major party candidates. The present speaker, Bernard Weatherill, has served in that office since 1983 and held the second-ranking office in the Commons, chairman of Ways and Means and Deputy Speaker, from 1979 to 1983. He had been a Conservative MP for nineteen years before becoming Speaker.

The chairman of Ways and Means presides over the House when it meets in committee of the whole. The chairman is assisted by a deputy chairman and by the panel of committee chairmen appointed by the speaker at the beginning of each Parliament. All of these officers are expected to conduct the sessions of the House in the same spirit as the speaker.

Besides presiding over the committee of the whole on occasion, the members of the panel of chairmen preside over the standing committees of the House on specific assignment by the speaker. The other members of the standing committees are nominated by the eleven-member Committee of Selection which, in turn, has been selected by the party whips and is controlled by the government. Usually, seven or eight standing committees denominated A, B, C, D, etc., are required at a time. They contain from sixteen to fifty members, composed on a basis that takes into account their qualifications, their special interests, and the partisan composition of the House. Also, the members include the minister in charge of the bill to be considered by the committee and one or more of his junior ministers, plus their counterparts on the Opposition front bench (leaders). Each standing committee is reconstituted and a new chair is appointed each time a new bill is assigned.

The role of the standing committees is mainly to provide a forum for the expression of the various viewpoints and to advise the government on technical aspects of the bill. Rarely does a committee recommend substantive changes in a bill that are not acceptable to the government. In a sense, the committee stage is a dress rehearsal for the more public performance in plenary session. In addition to the general-purpose standing committees, two Scottish Standing Committees, a Scottish Grand Committee, and a Welsh Grand Committee handle bills and other matters that pertain exclusively to those countries.

Another part of the Commons' committee system is the select committees. Although they may be appointed only for one session, they tend to be renewed frequently and to acquire the character of standing committees. The present system began in 1979 with twelve committees and has grown to over thirty. They deal especially with oversight of the executive branch. Some are oriented functionally. They include committees on public accounts (to audit

the expenditure of parliamentary appropriations), expenditures (to seek economies in the state budget), nationalized industries (to audit the accounts of those enterprises), statutory instruments (to ensure that some 2,000 to 2,500 executive regulations per year conform to legislation), and the parliamentary commissioner for administrations (to review action taken on citizens' complaints). Others "shadow" various ministries, such as Treasury and Civil Service, Home Affairs, Agriculture, Defense, Employment, Foreign Affairs, etc. Select committees are appointed by the whips in proportion to the partisan division of the House. The use of subcommittees and expert advisers has increased in recent years, though it still falls far short of American practice. Select committees have become more common, active, and important recently, and have produced an increasing volume of reports. In a recent survey, 90 percent of the MPs considered the select committees "very or fairly successful" in obtaining information from the departments, but they were not regarded as very helpful in controlling the Government.

The Commons has an officer, the parliamentary commissioner for administration, to assist it in dealing with complaints by citizens against the bureaucracy. The commissioner receives complaints on referral from MPs, investigates them, and recommends corrective action where appropriate. About 1,000 cases are handled in a typical year, about one-third of which are found to have merit.

The most important organizations in the Commons are the political party caucuses, the main instruments for the organization of the business of the House. The government works through its party caucus to ensure that its agenda receives the necessary attention. Opposition to and criticism of the agenda is organized by the other major party's caucus. The distribution of floor time, the referral of bills, the scheduling of parliamentary activities, the designation of debaters and committee members, etc. are arranged by the party whips within the caucuses and by negotiations between them. The whips use the caucuses to ensure party voting discipline.

In a sense, the work of the House in plenary session resembles that of its committees, writ large and more public. It debates bills and resolutions mainly to ventilate the leading political issues publicly with a view to influencing the voters at the next general election. Only rarely does a Commons debate affect the content or fate of a bill. Most of the time, dissenting MPs suppress their personal preferences and those of their constituencies in the interests of party unity, and votes are cast along straight party lines.

That behavior underlines the subordinate role of the backbench MPs. They are, in effect, party soldiers who must obey orders or face expulsion. However, they serve as virtually the only reservoir of political leadership in the country. The Commons has been the sole route to the prime ministership throughout this century and, with two or three exceptions, the only way to reach the cabinet.

One small legislative sop left to the backbenchers is private members' time, the eight to ten Fridays per session that are reserved for consideration of private members' bills, which usually deal with narrow personal items and matters of conscience. However, that hardly affects the government's dominance. In fact, the government initiates about 80 percent of the bills enacted. Also, over 90 percent of the government's bills become law in the same session compared to about 15 percent of private members' bills. Even those figures understate the government's control. As a practical matter, nothing is passed that the government is determined to prevent and nothing fails that the government is determined to pass.

In addition to its legislative work, the House in plenary session holds a question period at the beginning of each day's session. For about an hour, ministers respond to inquiries and follow-up questions posed by MPs. From 100 to 150 questions are submitted for oral answer each day and about a third of them get responses. In addition, several hundred questions are submitted for written answers each day. As with debates, questions that deal with policy matters are aimed more at public opinion than at substantive change in policy.

The Commons rarely—only once since 1924—exercises its constitutional prerogative to remove a government from office by defeating it on a vote of confidence or motion of censure. The exception was the overthrow of the government of James Callaghan by a margin of one vote on March 28, 1979. That Labour government had been formed by Harold Wilson in October 1974 with a majority of three seats, but lost seven seats in by-elections, three by defections, and one to the speakership. Also two were vacant by the end of March 1979. Thus, even that exception resulted from the erosion of party strength, not a breakdown of party discipline. It still conformed to the underlying principle of British government that MPs are elected to support their party leaders and may break ranks only on insignificant matters and only in the most extreme circumstances.

In most decades, the Commons has sat about 160 days each year. The legal term of each Parliament is five years. It may be dissolved early by the monarch on request of the prime minister. Usually, the prime minister decides to dissolve after very limited consultations with the most senior leaders of the government; it is not usually a matter for cabinet discussion. Most dissolutions are called because Parliament is near its end and the prime minister believes the moment is propitious electorally for the Government party (June 1983, February 1974, June 1970, October 1959, May 1955, February 1950, July 1945). Others prorogue Parliaments without working majorities (May 1979, October 1974, March 1966, and October 1951). Since 1945, only the 1959 Parliament has run full term.

The upper chamber of the British parliament is the House of Lords. Traditionally, it included all of the hereditary peers of the realm. Since 1958, there have been peerages limited to the life of the bearer. All peeresses also now have the right to sit in the Lords. Hereditary peerages still can be created, but none has been since 1964. At the present time, the Lords is composed of about 800 hereditary peers and peeresses, and nearly 400 life peers and peeresses. Only about 300 of them attend a typical sitting. In addition, the Lords includes twenty-six bishops of the Church of England and nine active Lords of Appeal, who form the highest appellate court in the realm. Since 1963, peers have been able to renounce their titles, and fifteen have done so, mainly to continue political careers in the House of Commons.

The House of Lords was once the dominant Parliament chamber, but its power declined with the rise of democracy. The Parliament Acts of 1911 and 1949 left it with only a suspensive veto. It can delay money bills only thirty days and other bills one year. Recent efforts to reform the Lords have failed, but the Labour Party is committed formally to its abolition, the Liberal Party to its replacement, and the Social Democrats to its reform. Nevertheless, the absence of constituency pressures and party discipline sometimes enables the Lords to play an independent legislative role, which it has done increasingly in recent years.

GENERAL ELECTION RESULTS (1959–1983)

| | Conservatives | | Labour | | Liberals | | Others | | |
	Percent of Votes	Seats	Percent of Votes	Seats	Percent of Votes	Seats	Percent of Votes	Seats	Total Vote
1959	49.4	365	43.8	258	5.9	6	0.9	1	35,397,080
1964	43.4	304	44.1	317	11.2	9	1.3	0	35,892,572
1966	41.9	253	47.9	363	8.5	12	1.7	2	35,964,684
1970	46.4	330	42.9	287	7.5	6	3.2	7	28,344,807
1974 (Feb.)	38.2	297	37.2	301	19.3	14	5.3	23	31,340,162
1974 (Oct.)	35.9	277	39.3	319	18.3	13	6.6	26	29,189,104
1979	43.9	339	36.9	268	13.8	11	5.5	17	31,222,279
1983	42.4	397	27.6	209	25.4*	23*	4.6	21	30,670,905

* Alliance of Liberals and Social Democrats.

The organization of the House of Lords is much less formal than that of the Commons. The Lord Chancellor, a member of the cabinet, is its speaker, and its Lord Chairman of the committees; another government supporter serves as deputy speaker. The committee system is much less elaborate than in the Commons. Only one standing committee is used for the review of government bills and occasional sessional and select committees report on special matters. Parties are less important, also, although each has a leader and whips. Not all lords join a caucus: during one recent session, the Conservative caucus had 518 members, the Labour caucus 127, the Liberal 42 and the Social Democratic 41. "Independents" numbered 172 and 281 peers were listed without status.

Judiciary

The British courts are nonpolitical institutions with no authority to review acts of Parliament or the executive for constitutionality. Although the head of the system in England and Wales is the Lord Chancellor, a member of the government and speaker of the House of Lords, he exercises the judicial functions of that office without political considerations. All judicial appointments are made for life by the monarch on recommendation of the Lord Chancellor and the government. Scotland's judicial system varies considerably from the English, but is equally nonpolitical. The Law Lords in the House of Lords are the highest court of appeal in the United Kingdom.

Regional & Local Government

The present system of local government for England and Wales went into effect in 1986. The seven metropolitan councils that had existed since 1974 were replaced by coordinating committees and a set of functional authorities. Besides the metropolitan counties (London, Manchester, Merseyside, South Yorkshire, West Yorkshire, Tyne and Wear, and West Midlands), England and Wales have thirty-nine nonmetropolitan or "shire" counties. London is divided into thirty-two borough councils and the Corporation of the City of London (the historical and financial core of the city) and the other metropolitan counties contain thirty-six districts. The shires are formed of 296 districts in England and 37 in Wales. Below them are more than 8,000 parishes.

In the metropolitan counties, the functional authorities are responsible for fire protection and civil defense, passenger transport, police, and (in London only) education. The coordinating committees handle roads, waste disposal, and voluntary bodies and arts. In addition, transitional residuary bodies in the metropolitan counties are supposed to deal with a miscellaneous assortment of matters pending definitive arrangements by 1991. The metropolitan boroughs and districts cover housing, education (except London), environmental health, and personal social services. The distribution of tasks in the shires and their districts is the same except that the shires are also responsible for education and personal social services. The principal sources of revenue for local government are property taxes and grants from the central government.

Scotland is divided into nine regions and three island areas (Orkney, Shetland, Western Isles). The regions are further subdivided into districts. The distribution of government functions is similar to that of England, except that the councils at the lowest level, the community, are not independent authorities.

The government of Northern Ireland is discussed in detail in a separate chapter.

At all levels, local government units are directed by councils that are elected every four years. The regional and local units are, within their spheres, relatively independent. Government at the lower level is not supervised by that at the next-higher level.

The Electoral System

The only national popular elections in Britain are for members of the House of Commons. MPs are elected by simple plurality in single-member districts. By-elections are used to fill interim vacancies and are watched closely for clues to trends in public opinion.

Since 1948, legislation has required that constituency boundaries be adjusted for population changes every ten to fifteen years on the basis of recommendations by a nonpolitical commission. Such adjustments were made in 1948, 1954, 1971, and 1983. The most recent redistribution took sizable steps toward equalizing the constituencies, but large disparities remain. In 1983, they ranged from 22,822 registered voters to 94,226 and 21.8 percent of them deviated from the national average (64,919) more than 15 percent. Also, substantial differences remain among the countries. English districts averaged 67,201 registered voters in 1983, Scottish 53,985, Welsh 55,628, and Northern Irish 61,778. For perfect equity, twelve Scottish, five Welsh, and one Northern Irish seat should go to England.

Suffrage extends to all British subjects who are at least eighteen years of age, with certain minor exceptions. Peers and peeresses, convicted felons, and the insane are not eligible to vote. Voter registration is usually through postcard forms sent out by the government. The register is open at certain specified times and qualified voters who have been omitted may be enrolled. Nevertheless, an estimated 5 to 10 percent of the eligible voters do not register. Turnout of registered voters since World War II has ranged from 72 to 84 percent, averaging 76.7.

Polling day is always a Thursday. Official paper ballots are provided under rigorous controls at the polling stations. On each ballot are printed the name, address, and party affiliation of each qualified candidate for the seat from that district.

The only two national referenda in British history were held June 5, 1975, and March 2, 1979. The former decided that Britain should join the European Community; the latter, held only in Scotland and Wales, gave insufficient support to a proposal that those two countries should be given more autonomous status with the United Kingdom. Legally, both referenda were only consultative, but the parliamentary majorities were committed to giving effect to the decisions expressed. The law that called the 1979 vote included the unusual requirement that an affirmative decision would not be given effect unless supported by at least 40 percent of the registered electorate, a condition not met in either country. The results of the referenda were:

NATIONAL REFERENDA	
June 5, 1975	March 2, 1979
Yes 17,378,581 (67.2%) No 8,470,073 (32.8%) Abstentions 14,183,483 (35.5%) Registered Voters 40,086,677	Scotland Yes 1,230,937 (32.85%) No 1,153,502 (30.78%) Abstentions 1,362,673 (36.7%) Registered Voters 3,747,112 Wales Yes 243,048 (11.9%) No 956,330 (46.9%) Abstentions 838,671 (41.2%) Registered Voters 2,038,049

The Party System

Origins of the Parties

The British have had basically a two-party system since the Whigs and Tories (Royalists) emerged in the late seventeenth century. They were replaced by the Liberals and Conservatives after the Reform Act of 1832, and Labour supplanted the Liberals in the late 1920s. However, the Liberals survived as a minor party, and since 1970, have been joined in the House of Commons by several other minor parties. In the Parliaments of 1910, 1923, 1929, and 1974, the major parties were so evenly matched that minor parties held the balance of power.

Britain has a two-party system in the sense that the two major parties have won 97 percent of the seats in general elections since World War II. However, that figure declined slightly to 94.4 percent in the elections after 1970. The system is also bipartite in that the two major parties are substantially equal in strength and frequently alternate in power. The Conservatives held a 55-45 edge over Labour in terms of time in office between 1945 and 1983.

The Parties in Law

British law is virtually silent on political parties. No laws deal exclusively with political parties as organizations and general legislation on associations make no explicit distinctions with respect to them. Laws on charitable societies expressly exclude organizations that are primarily political. Election laws deal almost entirely with candidates, rather than parties; party affiliations could not even be mentioned on the ballots until 1969. The governmental subsidies for the opposition are paid to the parliamentary groups, rather than the parties themselves. In practice, those funds are used mainly to support extraparliamentary activities. Beyond these oblique references, parties as such are untouched by British law.

Party Organization

British parties all have dues-paying memberships and elaborate organizational structures which generally provide for a considerable degree of intraparty democracy and local influence on party policy. The basic working organization of parties (with a minor variation in the Social Democratic Party) is the constituency organization based on the parliamentary district. The constituency organizations are responsible for nominating and electing the candidates for Parliament. The candidate does not need to be a resident of the constituency, and the national party makes sure its major figures are nominated in "safe" districts, a practice which seldom causes friction with the constituency organization.

Campaigning

Parliamentary election campaigning in Great Britain falls into two clearcut phases and is conducted mainly at two levels. The precampaign begins when a general impression forms in the political elite that an election is likely within a few months. The official campaign begins when Parliament is dissolved and continues through the seventeen days until election eve. The precampaign phase can last for two years or more; at other times it may be very short, or, in the case of a "snap" election, nonexistent. The campaigns are conducted mainly at the national and constituency level, though regional party offices perform certain coordinating functions.

The national party organizations are responsible for reviewing and endorsing the constituency nominees. In the case of the Social Democrats and the Liberals, who conducted their 1983 campaigns as a formal alliance with joint candidates, the national bodies must also agree on which constituencies each will contest. The national organizations prepare campaign broadcasts; publish party election manifestoes; arrange national tours for party leaders to appear at rallies, press conferences, and other public occasions; prepare posters, stickers, and other campaign material that is not specifically local in content; and continuously review campaign strategy and tactics and coordinate changes with the local organizations. Finally, the national organization places advertisements, especially in newspapers; these advertisements do not endorse any specific candidate and thus are not chargeable against candidate expenditure.

The constituency organization handles local campaigning, which includes the candidate's tours of the district with speeches, question periods in local meeting halls, and handshaking in public places. Local party workers canvass door-to-door, distributing national party materials as well as brochures on local issues and the candidate's election speeches.

The principal means by which those activities are regulated by the state are financial. A legal limit—varying somewhat by constituency—is placed on the amount of money that can be spent on behalf of each parliamentary candidate. In 1983, it averaged £4,700 ($7,050) for the rural districts and £4,200 ($6,400) for the urban ones. However, the law has three major loopholes. First, the restrictions apply only during the seventeen-day official campaign. Thus, as long as the party nominees are called "prospective candidates," expenditures on their behalf during the precampaign are not charged against the legal limit. Second, the law applies only to money spent on behalf of a specific candidate. In effect, this exempts almost all expenditures by the national headquarters of the parties. Third, some campaign resources are provided by the government without cost to the candidates. These include one free mailing to each registered voter in each district by each candidate in that district, the use of public meeting halls, and television and radio broadcast time for the national parties.

In practice, campaign costs are several times as great as those specified by law. Precampaign expenses vary greatly by election, tending to be quite substantial if an election comes later than anticipated. For instance, the October 1964 election had been expected as early as spring 1962. As a result, the precampaign extended intermittently for more than two and one-half years and its expenses at the constituency level may have totaled as much as $8 to 10 million. On the other hand, the "snap" elections of 1970 and February 1974 had virtually no precampaign expenses. Firm estimates are not available, but precampaigns probably cost the constituency organizations as much, on the average, as the official campaigns. In 1983, about $9.2 million was spent in the constituencies during the official campaign and a somewhat smaller amount during the precampaign. Expenditures by the national parties were nearly $6 million for the Conservatives, $3.75 million Labour, and about $2 million for the Alliance. Probably, campaign expenditures by the State exceeded $20 million. Thus, total costs of the campaign, not counting the government's expenses in maintaining the electoral rolls and organizing the polling topped the $40 million mark. In addition, an indeterminate amount was spent by nonparty groups and individuals apart from direct support of individual candidates.

Party funds for campaigning come from three main sources: membership dues, donations, and candidates' payments of personal expenses. The parties vary greatly in their reliance on the different categories.

Independent Voters

In the past, about two-thirds of the constituencies have been considered "safe," that is, virtually certain to give a majority to the same party in every election. There are signs, however, that the number of voters who feel free to switch parties from election to election, previously about 10 percent of the electorate, is increasing. Independent candidacies are not rare but are generally unsuccessful except in cases where long-time MPs have been dropped by their parties and run as independents in their usual constituencies.

Conservative and Unionist Party

History

The Conservative Party was formed under the leadership of Sir Robert Peel after enactment of the Reform Act of 1832 by conversion of the Tory Party, which had emerged in the late seventeenth century as the political ally of the king. In 1834, Peel established local "registration societies" which evolved gradually into constituency Conservative Associations. In 1867, about fifty of those organizations formed the National Union of Conservative and Constitutional Associations and called for annual conferences. Three years later, Benjamin Disraeli created the Conservative Central Office. In 1912, a faction of the Liberal Party opposed to Irish Home Rule allied itself to the Conservatives and "Unionist" replaced "Constitutional" in the name. In 1948–49, the party underwent sweeping reorganization into its present structure. It controlled the government during most of the period between the end of World War I and the end of World War II. Since then, it has alternated in office with Labour. Its most important leaders in this century have been Stanley Baldwin (1923–37), Winston Churchill (1940–55), Harold Macmillan (1957–63), Edward Heath (1965–75), and Margaret Thatcher (since 1975).

Organization

The Conservatives have the best partisan organization in Britain. They have constituency committees in all districts in Great Britain and Northern Ireland. Nearly half of them have full-time paid agents (320 in 1983), seven times as many as the Labour Party.

At the national level, the constituency committees are joined together in the National

Union of Conservative and Unionist Associations. The Union holds an annual conference that is, in theory, the sovereign decision-making organ of the party. In fact, the Conservatives usually keep their factional and personal rivalries behind the scenes. Also, they tend to accept the decisions of the official leadership with little open questioning. As a result, the conferences are more like pep rallies than deliberative assemblies. The Conservatives maintain a well-staffed, well-financed Central Office and a network of eleven area offices in England and Wales. The Scottish Conservatives have a separate organization, and the Northern Irish Official Ulster Unionists are an entirely independent party closely allied to the Conservatives. The principal official Conservative periodical is the monthly *Conservative Newsline* (circ. 150,000). Internationally, the party belongs to the European Democratic Union. The party's auxiliary organizations include the Bow Group (about 1,000 left-wing, younger Conservatives); the Monday Club (2,000) and Selsdon Group (200) on the right wing; and Young Conservatives (25,000), Federal Conservative Students (12,000) the women's auxiliaries, and Conservative clubs. Also, the party is associated closely with a number of business organizations such as British United Industrialists; the Economic League; and Aims, a confederation of business groups opposed to nationalized industry.

Power is highly concentrated in the national party. The leader appoints the chairman and other officials of the Central Office and indirectly controls the executive organs of the National Union. The Conservative Leader appoints the party's shadow cabinet.

Until 1963, the leaders of the Conservative Party were said to "emerge" through informal processes. That year, Lord Home was picked through an elaborate series of "soundings" of the party elite. The present selection system was adopted in 1965. It calls for balloting by the Conservative members of the House of Commons. A candidate may win on the first ballot only with an absolute majority of the votes and 15 percent more than the runner-up. Failing that, a second ballot is held four days later which may be won simply by an absolute majority. If a third ballot is required, only the three top candidates on the second round may run and a preferential voting system is applied to ensure a decision. The winner of that balloting must be confirmed in office by a meeting of Conservative members of the Commons and Lords, prospective parliamentary candidates, and the members of the Executive Committee of the National Union.

National headquarters are at 32 Smith Square, Conservative Central Office, London SW1P 3HH, England.

Policy

Current Conservative policies are most distinguished by their emphatic commitment to monetarist economics. Otherwise, its domestic policies follow the general line of reducing the involvement of government in the affairs of individuals. It advocates closer control of industrial disputes, lower taxes, stronger measures against crime, and tighter limits on immigration and the public owned sector of the economy. It favors reduction of the public-owned sector of the economy, import controls, and abolition of the House of Lords. It supports maintaining British rule in Northern Ireland. Internationally, it wants to strengthen Britain's military defenses and remains firmly committed to NATO and the European Economic Community.

Membership & Constituency

The Conservative Party has much the largest dues-paying membership in Britain and the largest in the democratic world, with about 1.2 million members, about 9.2 percent of its voting strength in the 1983 elections. Using the higher figure, its members were about 11 percent of its voting strength in the 1979 election. The party acquired its mass-membership character in the years after its 1945 defeat and has been quite stable in size for a number of years.

The party draws its support disproportionately from people of professional and business backgrounds, but it also has a substantial following among skilled and semiskilled workers. A survey of voters in the 1983 elections showed that its electorate included 61 percent of the professional and managerial occupations, 55 percent of the office and clerical workers, 40 percent of skilled manual workers, and 32 percent of semi and unskilled workers. Because the latter two categories are the largest occupational groups in Britain, they provided 59 percent of the Conservative voters in 1983. The party is weakest among trade union members. Nevertheless, its support there has risen from 22 percent in October 1974 to 31 percent in 1983.

In terms of class, the Conservative vote in 1979 was close to 100 percent in the upper class, 84 percent in the upper middle class, 79 percent in the middle class, 76 percent in the lower middle class, 48 percent in the upper working class, 28 percent in the working class, and 23 percent in the lower working class.

Religiously, the Conservative party is strongest among members of the Church of England, 41 percent of whom support it. This is followed by 39 percent of Church of Scotland (Presbyterian) members, 23 percent of Methodists, 37 percent of other nonconformists, 24 percent of Catholics, and 31 percent of those with no religious preference.

Geographically, the Conservatives are very English. Indeed, its strength is concentrated very much in southern England outside inner London. In that most populous region of the United Kingdom, with about one half of the seats in Parliament, the Conservatives consistently outdraw their rivals by wide margins. In every other region, they almost always trail Labour.

Interest-group support for the Conservatives comes mainly from the business and agricultural communities. The Confederation of British Industry and the National Farmers Union, the dominant organizations in those sectors, have close ties to the party. In addition, many corporations, smaller groups, and political-action organizations are allied with it.

Financing

Traditionally, the Conservative party has been very secretive about its finances. Although it has begun releasing some information in recent years, much remains private. The budget of Central Office seems to run about $6-7 million in non-election years and its expenditures in the 1983 election campaign have been estimated at perhaps $6 million. About 90 percent of its income is derived from donations, mainly from business corporations and the remainder comes from affiliation fees paid by the constituency associations. Those associations raise and spend an average of about $20,000 in non-election years, most of which goes for their agents' salaries. One-third to one-half of that comes from members' dues, which are set by the associations individually, and the rest is donations, again mainly from businesses. A small amount is earned from gambling games and bazaars. When in opposition, the parliamentary

delegation receives a government subsidy of about $500,000 per year.

Leadership

Traditionally, Conservative leaders came from upper and upper-middle-class backgrounds and were educated in private schools and at Oxford and Cambridge universities. However, the two most recent leaders, Edward Heath and Margaret Thatcher, have come from more modest circumstances.

Current leadership includes: Margaret H. Thatcher (born in Grantham, Lincolnshire, in 1926), leader since 1975 and prime minister since 1979, is head of the ideological-monetarist faction of the party.

Edward Heath (born in Broadstairs, Kent, in 1916), party leader from 1965 to 1975 and prime minister from 1970 to 1974, is head of the moderate European integrationist movement in the party.

Sir Geoffrey Howe (born in Port Talbot, Glamorgan, in 1926), chancellor of the exchequer 1979-1983 and foreign secretary since then, was a candidate for party leadership in 1975 and has been a protégé of Thatcher since then.

Francis Pym (born in 1922), defense secretary 1979 to 1982 and foreign secretary 1982-1983, is a leader of the party moderates in the House of Commons, through the factional organization, Centre Forward, formed in 1985.

Norman Tebbitt (born in Enfield, Middlesex, in 1931), junior minister 1979-1981, employment and industry secretary 1981-1983, trade and industry secretary 1983-1985, party chairman since 1985, responsible for preparing for 1987-1988 elections.

Cranley Onslow (born in Bexhill in 1926), junior minister in Foreign and Commonwealth Office 1982-1983, chairman of 1922 Committee since 1984 and, thus, leader of backbench MPs.

Prospects

The Conservatives won a larger majority in the 1983 parliament than any party has held since World War II. If Thatcher remains in office until the legal end of the present Parliament in 1988, she will have served longer than any prime minister in more than 150 years. Her standing in public opinion polls has been low and the severe unemployment problem seems intractable. Grumbling against her autocratic style and dogmatic policies persists among her governmental and parliamentary colleagues. Yet, she and her party have weathered similar situations in the past and emerged triumphant. Moreover, the party's prospects are complicated by the existence of the Alliance parties as the first "third force" in at least fifty years of British history to have realistic prospects of playing an important role in government and of disrupting the normal alternation in office between the two main parties.

Labour Party

History

The British Labour Party was formed in 1906 as the successor to the Labour Representation Committee that had been founded in 1900 by trade unions, the Independent Labour Party, the Fabian Society, and other socialist societies. Two Labour MPs were elected in 1900 and thirty in 1906. By 1922, Labour had become the second-largest party. In 1924 and from 1929 to 1931, minority Labour governments held office with the support, but not the participation, of the Liberal party. After World War II, Labour governments held office in 1945 to 1951, 1964 to 1970, and 1974 to 1979. Besides MacDonald, the principal Labour leaders have been Clement Attlee (1935–55), Hugh Gaitskell (1955–63), Harold Wilson (1963–76), and James Callaghan (1976–80). The party's left wing won control in 1980 and installed Michael Foot as leader. After the disastrous Labour showing in 1983, Foot was succeeded by Neil Kinnock.

Organization

The Labour Party's structure is unusually complex. It includes two types of membership: individual and collective. Many of the collective members are trade unions, but others are cooperative or socialist societies, Young Socialist groups, and women's societies. Collective members may join at the constituency, regional, or national levels. For instance, local trade unions may affiliate with local Labour branches while the national federations, of which they are part, join the national party.

The structure rises from local branches through about 630 constituency associations to eleven regional councils and the national party. The main elements in the national party are the annual conference, National Executive Committee, head office, and the Parliamentary Labour Party, which is always called the PLP. This last group elects an executive committee whose members are assigned by the leader to represent the party in various policy areas, becoming its shadow cabinet.

The annual conference is the highest policymaking body in the party; it is composed of delegates from the constituency associations, the cooperative and socialist societies, and the national trade unions. In conference balloting, delegates cast numbers of votes equal to the number of their members for which dues or affiliation fees have been paid. Thus, millions of votes are cast. In practice, a few large unions, each with hundreds of thousands of members, dominate the conferences. However, until 1980, they rarely acted in concert against the parliamentary leadership. In that year, sufficient numbers united behind Tony Benn and the party's left wing to force Callaghan to resign as leader and to make sweeping changes in the party's procedures and policies.

Until recently, the Labour Party used a method similar to the Conservatives to elect their leader. However, in late 1980, Labour shifted control from its parliamentary caucus to the annual conference of the party. The leader is now chosen by weighted voting arrangements that give the trade-union members of the party 40 percent of the votes, the MPs 30 percent, and the constituency associations 30 percent. Balloting continues until a candidate wins an absolute majority.

Among the conference's functions is the election of the National Executive Committee (NEC) which exercises policymaking and managerial authority between conferences. The composition of the NEC reflects the federated character of the party. Twelve members are elected by the unions, seven by the constituency associations, and one by the cooperative and socialist societies. Five women and the party treasurer are elected by the conference as a whole, and the leader and deputy leader are ex officio members. The NEC appoints and supervises the general secretary, who manages the day-to-day affairs of the party.

Labour has a long history of factionalism, partly a result of the federated structure of the party. The trade unions, socialist societies, cooperative societies, and constituency associations tend to foster divergent viewpoints within the party. The main dividing line has lain between the leftist ideological socialists and the moderate pragmatic social democrats.

In recent years, the leftists have become increasingly strong, taking control in 1980. Their principal factional organizations are the Tribune group of MPs associated with the left wing magazine of that name, the Campaign of Labour Party Democracy of Tony Benn which is supported by 40–50 MPs, the Labour Coordinating Committee of London leader Guy Livingstone, and the Young Socialists which are dominated by Trotskyites. The leaders of the moderate wing of the party defected in 1981 to form the Social Democratic Party, but their tradition is being carried on by a small faction called the Labour Solidarity Group. A Trotskyite faction, Militant Tendency, was declared illegal in 1985 as being a party-within-the-party and was dissolved and five of its leaders expelled, but leaders and members remain active in the party. The present leader, Neil Kinnock, was a member of the "soft-left" Tribune Group and the deputy leader, Roy Hattersley, of the moderate Solidarity faction.

The party is a member of the Socialist International and the Confederation of Socialist Parties of the European Community. Its principal periodical publication is *Labour Weekly* (circ. 18,000). Its main auxiliaries are the Young Socialists (5,000 members), the National Organization of Labour Students (7,000 members), the Fabian Society (4,000 members), and the Young Fabians (2,000 members).

National headquarters are at 150 Walworth Road, London, S.E., 17.

Policy

For most of the period since World War II, the Labour Party has pursued moderate reformist policies. In the immediate aftermath of its 1945 victory, it pushed through a series of measures nationalizing key industries and expanding the social welfare system. It implemented a more limited additional nationalization program from 1964 to 1970. Throughout that period, it gave unstinting support to NATO and to the dismantling of the British colonial empire. More equivocally, it favored European integration and reform of the House of Lords. It gave consistently greater emphasis than its rivals to public housing, unemployment relief, social welfare programs, reflationary economic policies, protection for immigrants and other minorities, the interests of organized labor, and equality of educational opportunity.

In the late 1970s, however, the party moved decisively to the left while continuing to adhere to most of its traditional positions, it now advocates, also, British withdrawal from the European Economic Community, unilateral nuclear disarmament, and abolition of the House of Lords and of private schools. It favors a sweeping new nationalization program and workers' control of industrial enterprises.

Membership & Constituency

The Labour Party claims about 6.2 million members. However, some 5.8 million of them are indirectly affiliated through their trade unions and another 60,000 through cooperative and socialist societies. Only 300–325,000 persons belong directly. That is less than one-third of the party's peak membership in 1952. The decline since 1952 has been quite steady and largely reflects waning enthusiasm after the first burst of party success and growing disillusionment over its internecine squabbling. Directly-affiliated members constituted about 3.5 percent of the party's electorate in 1983.

In member and supporter demographics, the Labour Party is a close mirror image of the Conservatives. Its strength lies disproportionately in the lower economic categories, among men, and in the younger age groups. It draws slighty more support from trade unionists than do the Conservatives. Labour voters are more likely to dwell in public housing than are Conservatives and are less likely to own their own homes. The party is weak in most rural areas and strong in major cities and where Catholics are concentrated. Geographically, the party is strongest in Northern England (40.2 percent of the vote in 1983), Yorkshire (40.8), inner London (38.6), Wales (37.5), and Scotland (35.1). Its weakest area is England south of the Midlands. The main interest group supporting the party is, of course, the trade unions. Another major interest group associated closely with Labour is the nationalized sector of the economy.

Financing

The annual dues for individual membership in the Labour Party are about $10. That should produce about $3 million per year. About $700,000 of that goes to the national party. The balance is about 12 percent of the income of the constituency parties. The rest of their income comes from trade union contributions and gambling games. About 75–80 percent of the national party's revenues come from trade union affiliation fees of about $1 per member. In 1984, the national party also received about $40,000 from cooperative and socialist societies, $225,000 in donations, $150,000 from the parliamentary subsidy, and over $40,000 from other sources. The trade unions made a special contribution of over $3 million for the 1983 election campaign, which was slightly more than the national party spent in that effort. In addition, local trade union branches contributed heavily to the constituency campaigns. The aggregate annual budgets of the constituency associations total about $6 million and they spend another $1.25–1.5 million during a parliamentary election campaign.

Leadership

The principal Labour Party leaders are:

Neil Kinnock (born in Tredegar, Wales in 1942), chairman of the party executive and leader of the party since 1983 and member of the NEC since 1978; junior minister 1974 to 1975; chief Opposition spokesman for education and shadow cabinet member 1979 to 1983; a member of the "soft-left" Tribune Group and a trade union-sponsored MP.

Roy Hattersley (born in Sheffield in 1932), deputy party leader and shadow chancellor of the exchequer since 1983; junior minister 1964 to 1970 and 1974 to 1976; cabinet member 1976 to 1979; chief Opposition spokesman on the environment 1979 to 1980 and on home affairs 1980 to 1983; election campaign director 1983, co-chair of moderate Labour Solidarity faction.

Denis Healey (born in London in 1917) Foot's chief rival for leader in 1980 and deputy leader 1980 to 1983, elder statesman of Labour moderates in 1983, but did not challenge Kinnock; defense minister 1964 to 1970, chancellor of the exchequer 1974 to 1979, shadow foreign secretary since 1981; a leader of the "center-right" faction and former Fabian Society leader.

Tony Benn (born 1925), has been a member of the National Executive Committee since 1962. He is a former chairman of the Fabian Society and leader of the party's left wing. Benn was formerly the Viscount Stansgate, but renounced his title in order to return to the House of Commons.

Peter Shore (born 1924), has been economics minister (1967–69), minister without portfolio (1969–70), deputy leader of the House of Commons (1969–70), trade minister (1974–76), environment minister (1976–79), shadow foreign secretary (1979–1981), and Opposition treasury spokesman since 1981; contested the party leadership as a moderate in 1983, but polled only 3 percent of the vote.

Larry Whitty (born in West London in 1943), party general secretary since 1985, was trade union research official previously and secretary of Trade Unions for Labour Victory, an organization formed by trade unions to raise funds for the 1983 Labour Party general election campaign, "soft-left", supported by Kinnock and Benn, opposed by Hattersley, committed to streamlining the party to make it a more effective campaign organization.

Prospects

The Labour Party is in the throes of a slow recovery from its diastrous electoral defeat in 1983 and adverse spinoff from the bitter miners' strike of 1984 to 1985. Public opinion surveys indicate that it is making some progress and that Kinnock is beginning to establish an image as a mature, competent political leader. However, the continuing factional squabbling, especially involving left-wing extremists damages its prospects considerably. Also, the sharp tilt to the left since 1980 has shifted the party away from the central marketplace of British elections and exacerbates its difficulties in attracting voters. The presence of an increasingly viable Alliance coalition between Labour and Conservatives on the political spectrum is another major obstacle in the path of Labour resurgence.

Liberal Party

History

The Liberal Party today is a pale shadow of the organization that evolved out of the seventeenth-century Whigs and that dominated British politics during much of the nineteenth century. It declined early in the twentieth century as a result of its inability to agree on a solution to the Irish problem, the squabbling among its leaders, and the emergence of the Labour Party. Since 1945, its share of the vote in general elections has varied widely, between 2.5 and 19.3 percent, and its parliamentary delegation ranged from six to fourteen. In 1979, it won 13.8 percent of the vote and eleven seats. It has not held government office since the National Coalition of World War II, but it supported the minority Labour government in 1977–78. In 1981, it formed an alliance with the newly formed Social Democratic Party (SDP). They ran joint candidates in the 1983 elections, winning 25.4 percent of the vote but only 23 seats (3.5 percent) of which 17 are held by Liberals.

Organization

The Liberal Party is a complex and loosely joined federation. The Scottish, Welsh, and Northern Irish branches are autonomous national parties. The basic units of the party are the constituency associations, which are grouped into twelve regional organizations. The constituency, regional, and national parties send delegates to the annual assembly, the formally sovereign organ of the party. Between assemblies, the party is run by a council that meets quarterly and the National Executive Committee that meets as needed in the interim. The Finance and Administration Board for party management and a standing committee for policy have special responsibilities in those areas. The leader is elected by the constituency associations, with their vote weighted in proportion to their membership and electoral strength. The only contested election under this system in 1976 produced 12,541 votes for David Steel and 7,032 for John Pardoe.

The main split in the party lies between its urban associations, which have most of the members, and its outlying rural associations, which nominate most of the party's MPs. The party also has been deeply divided on the question of its successive alliances with Labour and the Social Democrats. Especially, Liberals are divided on whether to merge with the SDP in a single party or remain separate but allied.

The Liberals are affiliated internationally with the Liberal International and the Federation of Liberal and Democratic Parties of the European Community. Its principal publication is *Liberal News*, a weekly with a circulation of 8,000. Its main auxiliary organizations are the National League of Young Liberals (8,000 members) and the Union of Liberal Students (3,000 members, federated as the Young Liberals), the Women's Liberal Federation (1,000 members),

the Association of Liberal Trade Unionists, and the Association of Liberal Councilors.

National headquarters are at 1 Whitehall Place, London SW1A 2HE.

Policy

Traditionally Liberal policies have occupied a middle ground between Labour and the Conservatives. The party has firmly resisted social and political polarization between big trade unions and big business. It advocates the introduction of a proportional representation electoral system, governmental decentralization, worker participation in industrial management, replacement of the House of Lords, fixed dates for parliamentary elections, an end to official secrecy, a written constitution and bill of rights, a supreme court, additional protection for minorities, reform of the taxation and social welfare systems, and sweeping new measures for environmental protection. Liberals pioneered proposals for urging British membership in the European Community and are firm supporters of NATO.

Membership & Constituency

Total membership of the separate English, Welsh, and Scottish parties is about 180,000, up from about 100,000 in 1979. Undoubtedly, the rise resulted largely from enthusiasm over the prospects of the party's new alliance with the Social Democrats. Because the party ran candidates only jointly with the SDP in 1983, its ratio of members to voters cannot be calculated.

The most distinctive demographic characteristics of the Liberals are that they are disproportionately lower middle class, religiously nonconformist or atheist, and geographically in the Celtic fringe (Wales, Scotland, Cornwall, and the islands) and the London suburbs. Liberal voters are notably volatile in their electoral behavior, often forming a protest current. Indeed, the most typical characteristic of the Liberal may be an unwillingness to conform to British social and political stereotypes. They tend to be workers at odds with salient positions of the Labour Party or middle-class members with similar attitudes toward the Conservative Party.

Financing

The budget for the national organization was about $500,000 in 1983, including about $100,000 from constituency association affiliation fees and $80,000 from fund-raising appeals to its members. The rest comes from donations, mainly from businesses. The annual membership dues are $9. In a typical year, the local units will spend perhaps $2.5-3.0 million on routine activities and $0.7–1.0 million on campaigning. About $650–700,000 is received in dues and $1.0–1.5 million is raised through lotteries, bazaars, etc. Most of the remainder comes from donations. Also, while in the Opposition, the parliamentary party receives government grants of about $65,000 per year.

Leadership

Current Liberal Party leadership includes: David Steel (born in Scotland, in 1938), has been leader of the party since 1976 after serving as whip. He is the principal instigator of the alliances with Labour and the SDP.

David Alton (born in London in 1951) chief party whip, "Young Turk" of the party, antinuclear urban radical, youngest city councilor in British history 1971, youngest MP 1979, Steel's political assistant 1982.

Prospects

The prospects for the Liberals are brighter than at any time since the 1920s. Their alliance with the SDP seems solid and viable. By the end of 1985, the two parties had already agreed on their parliamentary candidates for the 1987–1988 elections. The Alliance came tantalizingly close to overtaking Labour in popular vote in the 1983 elections, with 25.4 percent to 27.6, even though it won only 23 seats. Although public opinion polls are not consistent, they do indicate that the Alliance is persistently in the running for major-party status. As the Liberals are the larger and more senior partner in the Alliance, they can expect to derive the greater benefit from its successes. Britons seem to be finding the Alliance an increasingly credible and comfortable haven between Labour's left-wing platitudes and Thatcher's dogmatism.

Social Democratic Party (SDP)

History

The SDP was founded in January 1981 by four defecting leaders of the Labour Party who were dissatisfied with the leftward shift of that party in recent years. It got off to a fast start, chalking up a number of successes in its first eighteen months. By December 1981, public opinion polls gave it 46 percent support, well ahead of the two major parties, and its alliance with the Liberals was winning two of every three local council by-elections. Between July 1981 and March 1982, the alliance won three of four parliamentary by-elections and lost the fourth narrowly. Two of the new MPs were Social Democrats. By March 1981, it had 78,000 dues-paying members and twenty-eight MPs, more than any party except Conservative and Labour since 1935. By mid-1982, its momentum had flagged somewhat, and by September its share of public support in opinion polls had fallen to 8.5 percent. Its showing in the 1983 elections was disappointing, as it won only six seats in Parliament.

Organization

The basic unit of the SDP is the area, which may include from one to seven parliamentary constituencies. England has 181 areas, Scotland 19, Wales 9, Northern Ireland 1, and the British staff and officials of the European Community 1. Although local branches may be formed, the area party selects parliamentary candidates and is the basis of representation in the party's main decision-making body, the 435 member Council for Social Democracy. Each area that includes up to three constituencies has two delegates in the Council; the larger areas have three. The Council may add up to 5 percent more members by co-optation. The party President and the Leader are chosen by postal ballot of the entire membership. The Council meets three times a year. In the interim, the highest organ of the extraparliamentary party is the National Committee, one-third of whose members are MPs selected by their fellows. The remaining two-thirds are mostly chosen by the area parties, though local government councilors, members of the House of Lords and European Parliament, and the youth organization are also represented. The parliamentary leader is a member ex officio. A subcommittee of the

National Committee composed of the party president, elected by postal vote of all members, and equal numbers of MP and non-MP members of the National Committee is responsible for preparing policy statements, including election manifestoes, for approval by the Council. Consultative assemblies, open to all party members, are called at least once a year by the Council. The sovereign policy-making body, the 1,200-delegate Annual Conference, meets each Autumn.

National headquarters are at 4 Cowley Street, London SW1.

Policy

The SDP is a moderate, reformist social-democratic party. It advocates a proportional representation electoral system; stronger measures against inflation, including wage controls; continued membership in the European Community and NATO; an end to the independent British nuclear force, but not to NATO nuclear weapons on British soil; government decentralization; and a moderate approach to social welfare and economic management.

Membership & Constituency

Because the party is new and ran joint candidates in its first parliamentary election, information on the characteristics of its members and electorate is scant. It seems to draw its members heavily from the middle class and its voters broadly across the social-economic spectrum. Its main appeal seems to be to Britons who are dismayed by the increased polarization of the Conservatives and Labour and who are favorably impressed by the SDP leaders.

Financing

The budget of the SDP national organization in 1984–1985 was about $900,000. About $300,000 came from donations and about $150,000 from appeals. Four companies contributed a total of about $13,000. The rest came from its 80 percent cut of members' dues. The membership-recommended subscription is set at about $20 and about half the members pay that amount. The minimum subscription is about $6. The parliamentary party receives a small State subsidy.

Leadership

Current leadership includes: David Owen (born in South Devon in 1938), party leader and parliamentary leader since 1983; deputy parliamentary leader, 1982 to 1983; one of the four founders of the party in 1981, after having been a junior minister in the Labour government 1974–79.

Shirley Williams (born 1930), is party president. She was Labour home secretary from 1969 to 1970 and minister of education and science from 1967 to 1969 and from 1976 to 1979, and was also a member of the Labour NEC from 1970 to 1981. She leads the reformist socialist wing of the party.

Roy Jenkins (born in Wales in 1920), another of the four founders and the elder statesman of the party; the first party leader and parliamentary leader 1982 to 1983; deputy leader of the Labour Party and second-ranking member of the cabinet in the 1970s; president of the European Community 1977 to 1981. He leads the centrist wing of the party.

William Rodgers (born 1928), one of the founders and a follower of Jenkins; transport minister and junior minister in defense in 1974–1979; Labour government and shadow defense minister 1979 to 1980; defeated in 1983 parliamentary elections.

Prospects

The poor showing of the SDP in the 1983 elections interrupted its early momentum and it has not recovered. Although its support undoubtedly contributed importantly to the success of the Alliance in popular votes, the Liberals derived the greatest benefit. This has clouded the party's future. Although it has a public image of greater freshness and dynamism than the Liberals, it lacks the grassroots organization and experience and has seemed to be the tail on the Liberals' dog. Its prospects seem to depend largely on its ability to establish a clearcut public image distinct from that of the Liberals in the Alliance.

Minor & Regional Parties

Scottish National Party (SNP)

The SNP was founded in 1934 and won parliamentary seats in by-elections in 1945, 1967, and 1973. Except for one seat in 1970, it won no representation in general elections before February 1974. In that election, it captured seven of Scotland's seventy-one seats with 21.9 percent of the Scottish vote. It rose to eleven seats and 30.4 percent in October 1974, but fell to two MPs in 1979 and 1983, with 17.3 and 11.8 percent of the vote respectively. It supported the minority Labour government until the failure of the devolution referendum of March 1979. Those two disappointments of 1979 seem to have signaled the end to the SNP's threat to major-party dominance in Scotland. The SNP is a social-democratic party whose distinctive appeal is its advocacy of "self-government" for Scotland. Membership: 50,000. President: Donald Stewart. National Headquarters: 6 North Charlotte St., Edinburgh EH2 4JH Scotland.

Plaid Cyrmu (Welsh Nationalist Party)

The Plaid Cyrmu is a Welsh counterpart of the SNP. Although it was founded in 1925, it neither contested parliamentary elections until 1945 nor won a seat (in a by-election) until July 1966. Its first general election wins were in February 1974, when it took two of Wales's thirty-six seats and 10.8 percent of the Welsh vote. It won three seats with the same percentage in October 1974, but fell to two seats in 1979 and 1983, with 8.1 and 7.8 percent of the vote respectively. Its program advocates self-government for Wales and promotion of Welsh language and culture. Membership: 30,000. President: D.E. Thomas. National Headquarters: 51 Cathedral Rd., Cardiff CF1 9HD Wales.

See NORTHERN IRELAND, below, for descriptions of its parties.

National Front (NF)

The NF was founded in 1967 through the merger of several extremist parties of the right. Although it has contested all parliamentary elections since then, it has not come close to winning a seat. In 1983, it nominated 60 candidates and polled only 27,065 votes (0.09 percent). The party is mainly an anti-immigrant movement, but also takes other policy positions typical of right-wing extremism. Membership: 20,000. Chairman: Andrew Brons. National headquarters: 50 Pawsons Rd., Croydon, Surrey.

Communist Party of Great Britain

This party was founded in July 1920. In 1922, one of its parliamentary candidates was elected and a successful British Labour Party candidate was also a CP member. One Communist candidate was elected in 1924, another in 1935, and two in 1945. Since 1964, it has entered between 29 and 58 candidates in each election. In 1983, thirty-five candidates received an aggregate total of 11,606 votes, 0.04 percent of the national poll and a substantial further decline from its meager result of 1979. The party follows Marxist-Leninist doctrine as defined by the Soviet Union despite the lip service it pays to a peculiarly British "road to socialism." Membership: 20,600. Executive Committee Chairman: Ron Halverson. National headquarters: 16 St. John St., London EC1M 4AL.

National Prospects

Great Britain's decline in relative economic strength, international importance, social cohesion, and political and governmental efficiency seems to be continuing, although perhaps at a slower rate since 1983. No recent government has made significant progress in solving its fundamental problems. The excessively high inflation rate that dogged the economy for years has slackened appreciably, but unemployment remains abnormally high. Britain has no realistic aspiration of recovering great-power status. The violence in Northern Ireland and occasionally in England's principal cities and the persistent grumblings of the Scottish and Welsh over English rule, combined with class tensions provoked by the economic squeeze, augur ill for social harmony. Political manifestations of those phenomena appear in the recent partisan fragmentation, increasing resort to coalition politics, and the rising ideological tone of political discourse. Unless Thatcher Toryism, Bennite radicalism, or Alliance moderation produces some sudden and dramatic turnaround, the next few years are likely to continue to confirm the decline of "right little, tight little" Britain.

Further Reading

Ashford, Douglas E. *Policy and Politics in Britain.* Philadelphia: Temple University Press, 1981.

Beer, Samuel H. *British Politics in the Collectivist Age.* New York: Knopf, 1965.

Brennan, T. *Politics and Government in Britain.* Cambridge, England: Cambridge University Press, 1972.

Butler, David, and Kavanaugh, Dennis. *The British General Election of 1983.* London: Macmillan, 1984.

————, and Stokes, Donald. *Political Change in Britain.* 2nd rev. ed. New York: St. Martin's Press, 1976.

Drucker, H. M. *Multi-Party Britain.* New York: Praeger, 1979.

Headey, Bruce. *British Cabinet Ministers.* London: Allen and Unwin, 1974.

Pinto-Duchinsky, Michael. *British Political Finance, 1830–1980.* Washington, D.C.: American Enterprise Institute, 1981.

Ranney, Austin, ed. *Britain at the Polls, 1983.* Durham, N. C.: Duke U. P., 1985.

Young, Roland. *The British Parliament.* London: Faber and Faber, 1962.

NORTHERN IRELAND
(Ulster)

by William G. Andrews, Ph.D.

The System of Government

Northern Ireland is a political division of the United Kingdom and consists of the six northeastern counties (population over 1.6 million) of the island of Ireland, most of the traditional Irish province of Ulster. Founded in 1921 by the Government of Ireland Act, Northern Ireland was governed until 1972 by a locally elected Parliament and government located at Stormont responsible to the central government in London. In March of 1972, because of the increase in sectarian rioting, the British government assumed direct authority over internal security. This precipitated the resignation of the Stormont government, dissolution of its Parliament, and assumption by London of direct control over all governmental functions through a cabinet-level Northern Ireland Office headed by a secretary of State and three or four junior ministers. Since then the British have ruled directly, pending agreement of both major Ulster political communities (British unionist and Irish nationalist) on a governmental arrangement to which they would then devolve their powers. Successive British governments have initiated a series of projects designed to effect that transfer, but none has achieved the requisite support so far. The most recent effort was the 1985 Hillsborough agreement between the British and Irish prime ministers for a joint consultative "Conference" for continuing coordination of their policies toward Northern Ireland.

The origins of the link between Great Britain and Northern Ireland can be traced back to the twelfth century when large parts of Ireland came under the control of Henry II of England. After 1537, the indigenous Irish remained Catholic, while most of the settlers from England and Scotland turned Protestant. Under James I, Cromwell, and William III, Catholic Irish were driven off the land, especially in Ulster, and the land was turned over to Protestant settlers. In 1800, the British Act of Union provided for Irish representation in both Houses of the British Parliament and abolished the Irish Parliament. In the nineteenth and early twentieth centuries, agitation against British rule grew throughout the island. As the "home-rule" movement increased in strength, supported mainly by Catholics, Protestants formed the Orange Order, which provided the leadership for an effective opposition to home rule. By 1905, that opposition had united the various unionist (supporters of union with Great Britain) groups in the Ulster Unionist Council. In 1921, they were able to block the inclusion of Ulster in the new independent Ireland. Although Catholics are a majority in the island as a whole, Protestants have nearly a two-to-one majority in the six northeastern counties. However, the Catholic minority in the north, as well as many citizens of the Irish Republic, have never been reconciled to the division of Ireland.

The tension between the two communities generated a militant Catholic civil rights movement in the late 1960s and sporadic violence. The Stormont and, later, London governments responded by increasing the size of the security forces and by suspending certain civil liberties and procedural rights. Violence escalated to a peak of 10,628 shootings, 468 deaths, and 4,876 injuries in 1972. Since then, the disorder has diminished gradually, dropping to fifty-four deaths and 845 injuries in 1985, the lowest since the current troubles began. Nevertheless, the two communities are far away from real accomodation and their antipathy dominates Ulster politics. Nothing political in Northern Ireland can be understood, except against that background.

Executive

The Northern Ireland Office is under the direction of the secretary of state for Northern Ireland who is assisted by a minister of state and two parliamentary under-secretaries of state. In addition to constitutional developments, law and order, and security, the secretary of state is also directly responsible for the Northern Ireland departments of Civil Service and Finance. The other ministers have special responsibility for the remaining six departments—agriculture, education, commerce, environment, health and social services, and manpower services.

Legislature

Of the 650 members of the British House of Commons, ten are from Ulster. Ulster is divided into twelve single-member constituencies (for a detailed description of this system see UNITED KINGDOM, Electoral System). Members are elected by a simple plurality. The 1983 parliamentary election results gave the Official Unionists 34 percent of the vote and eleven seats, the Democratic Unionists 20 percent and three seats, other unionists 3.1 percent and one seat, the Social Democratic and Labour Party 17.9 percent and one seat, the Provisional Sinn Fein 13.4 percent and one seat, and other parties 1.7 percent and no seats. In November 1985, the unionist members resigned their seats to protest the Hillsborough agreement. All were reelected in subsequent by-elections, except that the SDLP took one seat from the DUP.

Judiciary

The three-tiered court system of Northern Ireland consists of the Supreme Court (comprising the Court of Appeal, the High Court, and the Crown Court), the county courts, and the magistrates' courts. Twenty-five petty sessions districts form eight county court divisions and four county court circuits. The Lord Chancellor, appointed by London, is responsible for administration of all courts in Northern Ireland through the Northern Ireland Court Service, and is specifically responsible for the appointment of judges and resident magistrates.

Appeals from the Court of Appeal may go directly to the British House of Lords only in those matters which the House or the Court think to be of overriding importance. In criminal cases, the Court must certify that a point of law of general public importance is involved. These restrictions effectively minimize the number of cases going to the House of Lords.

Provincial & Local Government

The provincial governmental system of Northern Ireland consists of ten government offices and the Northern Ireland Assembly. Six of the offices (finance and personnel, education, environment, health and social services, economic development, and agriculture) are departments headed by permanent secretaries. The others are the Industrial Development Board, the Civil Service Secretariat, the Exchequer and Audit Department, and the Northern Ireland Trade Centre. All offices are supervised by the Northern Ireland Office in London and the departments are "scrutinized" by parallel committees of the Assembly. The 78-member Assembly was set up by the Northern Ireland Act of 1982 as a scrutinizing, consultative, and deliberative body to which executive and legislative authority would be transfered when the rival communities could agree on its form. This was assumed to mean support by seventy percent of the reconstituted Assembly membership. In the first elections to the reconstituted Assembly in October 1982, the OUP won 29.8 percent of the vote and 26 seats, the DUP 23.0 percent and 21 seats, the SDLP 18.8 percent and 13 seats, the Alliance Party 9.3 percent and 10 seats, PSF 10.1 Percent and five seats, and other unionists 5.8 percent and two seats.

The local governmental system consists of six counties and twenty-six municipalities. Each of the former is governed by a lord lieutenant and a high sheriff. Each of the latter has a district or borough council, ranging in size from sixteen to fifty-one members. The 566 councilors are elected for four-year terms by proportional representation. In the 1985 elections, the unionist parties won a majority of the seats on seventeen councils, the nationalist parties won control of eight, and one was "hung". Since most government power is concentrated in London without an effective intermediate regional government, any residual powers go directly to the district councils. The councils are responsible for provision of recreational, social, community and cultural facilities, and refuse collection. They nominate representatives to various bodies which administer regional functions such as library services, fire protection, and electricity supply. They also present the views of the population on regional affairs to the appropriate section of the Secretary of State's Office. The latter is meant to assure that no district suffers discrimination.

RESULTS OF THE 1985 COUNCIL ELECTIONS		
	Votes	Seats
Official Unionist Party	30%	190
Democratic Unionist Party	24	142
Social Democratic & Labour Party	18	101
Provisional Sinn Fein	12	59
Alliance Party	7	35
Others	9	39

The Electoral System

Local district elections absorb much of the energies of the political parties. Even though the powers of the district councils are not significant, these elections indicate the sentiments of the people at the grass-roots level. Also, they are the pivot of the Irish tradition of political localism in which municipal politicians intercede with government for their constituents in return for their votes. This localism, in turn, is the basis of provincial political organization.

In order to vote in local elections one must be a British subject, be eighteen years old before the election, be born in Northern Ireland (or have resided continuously in the United Kingdom for a period of seven years ending on the qualifying date), and have resided in the constituency or elsewhere in Northern Ireland for a period of three months ending on the qualifying date. There are differences between the voting requirements for the local and parliamentary elections (see UNITED KINGDOM, The Electoral System, for voting requirements at the parliamentary level). Each registered voter who presents himself at the polling station with one of the prescribed identification documents is given an officially stamped paper ballot which lists candidates in alphabetical order. The presiding officer of the polling station marks the register opposite the voter's name to indicate that a ballot was issued. Voting is secret.

The election system used is that of the single transferable vote; the voter has the option of ranking all the candidates on the ballot. If his vote is not needed to elect his first choice, or if his first choice has been eliminated, his vote will go to his second choice. This form of proportional representation was instituted in 1977.

In order to be placed on the ballot, a candidate must put up a deposit of £150. If a candidate does not poll votes equal to one-fourth of the number needed to be elected, his deposit is forfeited. This law is meant to eliminate candidates who lack substantial backing and to prevent the ballot from becoming unmanagably long.

The population of the districts varies greatly. The largest, Belfast, has about 318,000 voters and fifty-one councilors; the smallest, Moyle, has only some 15,000 voters and sixteen councilors. Thus, overall, small towns and rural areas are overrepresented in the councils. Protestant and Catholic populations, though generally concentrated in specific areas, are nearly evenly distributed along the urban-rural spectrum.

The Party System

Origins of the Parties

The political parties of Northern Ireland were all born out of and relate to the sectarian strife of the province. There are legal parties which take part in elections as well as the illegal parties which represent various proscribed organizations. A party may be legal one year and illegal the following year, depending on the political situation. Such organizations as the Provincial Irish Republican Army (PIRA) and the Irish National Liberation Army (INLA) are significant factors on the political scene but are illegal.

The legal parties fall into three categories. The unionist parties (OUP, DUP, and their spinoffs) are based in the Protestant community and favor close governmental ties with Great Britain. The nationalist parties (SDLP, PSF, and Workers' Party) are Roman Catholic and advocate the incorporation of Ulster into the Republic of Ireland. Also, the unionist parties are staunchly conservative socially and economically, while the nationalists have a pronounced leftist bent. The Alliance Party (not to be confused with the Alliance of the Liberals and Social Democrats in Great Britain) stands alone in appealing to members of both sectarian communities and urging a constitutional solution acceptable to both. Its social and economic policies are centrist. On each side of the sectarian divide, the parties differ mainly in their degree of militancy, the OUP and SDLP being the more moderate.

The Parties in Law

See under UNITED KINGDOM.

Party Organization

Parties are extremely active at the local level, and are strongly influential in such areas as job allocation, housing, street cleaning, and general public services. Local and national party structures are closely integrated. The national leadership has a strong hand in deciding who is to run in the local election; however, they must keep in tune with the members at the local level or they are likely to lose votes to another party. Ian Paisley's Democratic Unionist Party has gained support since 1973, at the expense of the Official Unionist Party, because many of the traditional supporters of the Official Unionists do not perceive the party as being aggressive enough in denouncing terrorism and cooperation with the Republic. Also, the PSF emerged as a major party in the early 1980s largely because it built an elaborate grassroots organization and appealed to the sense of injustice of the more radical members of the Catholic community.

In the major parties, the party leader is selected from among the elected representatives to the local councils. In minor parties the procedure varies (i.e., those parties controlled by paramilitary groups choose their leadership through "unofficial" channels; parties failing to elect members or electing very few members,

choose their leader through a vote of all dues-paying members). Those members sent to the British House of Commons usually have been active at the local level before being elected.

Campaigning

Campaigning varies depending upon whether the party is one of the major parties or one of the minor parties. There are certain similarities, i.e., mass mailings, posters, rallies, attendance of candidates at local functions, television and radio talk shows, and house-to-house canvassing. The larger parties have nominal control over expenditures. However, since campaign funds are raised from local contributors, the party at the local level has a good deal to say about how the money is spent. Splinter groups tend to exert tighter control.

Alliance Party (AP)

History

The AP was formed in 1970 in reaction to the civil rights militancy and sectarian strife of the late 1960s. It has never elected an MP to Westminster, but has had greater success in provincial and local politics. Its main purpose has been to bridge the sectarian communities and foster a climate in which they can agree on a constitutional solution. It rose quickly to a peak of 14.9 percent of the vote in the 1977 council elections, but has declined slowly, with the increased communal polarization since then. It drew 9.3 percent of the vote in the 1982 Assembly elections, 8.0 in the 1983 parliamentary poll, and 7.0 in the 1985 council vote. It has been more successful than most Ulster parties in maintaining the cohesion of its organization.

Organization

From its beginning the AP was the least homogeneous of the four major parties. Since it tried to be "non-doctrinaire," it attracted members from all parts of the sectarian divide. The party is organized around thirty-three geographically based associations that send six delegates each to the party council, the governing body which meets quarterly. The council appoints the party executive committee which meets frequently; there is an annual conference.

Because of the sectarian nature of Ulster politics, the AP is always in danger of having the middle ground cut out from under it. "Its organization tends to be strongest in areas where the two religious communities are fairly evenly balanced in population, especially the more affluent and intellectual neighborhoods. A prime example is the integrated quarters around Queen's University, Belfast. The AP has little organization in such areas as Fermanagh and Armagh where Republican sentiment is strong, and is not strongly supported in heavily Loyalist areas. Its official publication is the *Alliance Newspaper* (circulation 7,000).

Party headquarters are at 88 University Street, Belfast ET7 1HE.

Policy

The party policy is to be nondoctrinaire. The AP can best be characterized as a nonsectarian moderate Unionist group, committed to maintaining ties with Britain, but also believing that Ulster's political system must be reformed. Specifically it believes Catholics must be involved in all phases of government operations if they are to support the state. This has led it to endorse the Hillsborough agreement but to be skeptical of the NIA as now defined. It advocates NIA reforms, including question time, broadcast of debates, and more time spent on review of legislation. It believes in retaining the present social-welfare programs. It favors government discouragement of sectarianism so as to improve the business climate, get people off the welfare rolls, and decrease government expenditure. The party has avoided internally divisive issues such as divorce laws.

Membership & Constituency

In 1981, the AP had approximately 10,000 members (about one of every six votes cast for the party in the 1983 Parliamentary elections and about one of every ten votes cast in the 1981 local council elections). Membership was down from 1977; AP officials attributed that to the exacerbation of sectarian tensions. Many of the Protestants moved over to the various other Unionist parties, while some Catholics were lost to the SDLP.

The most loyal supporters of the AP tend to be of moderate religious persuasion and from the commercial and industrial interests of the north, either from Belfast or from the larger towns in the more prosperous areas. A large proportion of the membership consists of academics (students and faculty) from Queen's University; the party headquarters are only three blocks from the university. The Alliance is the only party with a fairly even religious balance among its supporters. A 1983 survey found them to be 54 percent Protestant and 45 percent Catholic. Also, it was the only party to draw a majority of its support from the middle class, having 54 percent in that category and 46 percent working class.

Financing

Members are encouraged to contribute as much as they can afford. No fixed scale has been set. Contributions are solicited from businesses, individuals, and associations. Exact figures are not available.

Leadership

Party leadership is concentrated in the forty-to-sixty-year-old age group. The average age for AP candidates in the local council elections falls within the forty-to-forty-nine age bracket. Party leaders are:

Oliver John Napier, founder, born 1935; elected to the Belfast City Council in 1977, stood unsuccessfully for the East Belfast seat in the 1979 and 1983 British parliamentary elections; retired as party leader, 1984.

John Cushnahan (born 1948), party leader since 1984; general secretary 1974–82, contested North Belfast in 1979 and North Down in 1983 parliamentary elections.

Present leadership includes Alec Boyd, chairman; Susan Edgar, general secretary (1982 to date), born 1960; no prior political experience (she is the youngest leader of a major political party).

Prospects

The secretarian conflict in Northern Ireland appears to be too deeply rooted to permit a nonsectarian party like the Alliance ever to develop as one of the principal parties. However, if the Hillsborough agreement becomes a plausible vehicle for movement toward a solution of the constitutional issue and if sectarian strife continues to diminish in violence, the Alliance Party may be able to broaden its appeal. One of its worst handicaps in recent years has been the decreasing credibility of its conciliatory approach. If that trend is reversed, it may have an important role to play in the future. Otherwise, it may continue to dwindle until it loses all viability as a political force and its supporters seek refuge in the more moderate of their respective sectarian parties.

Democratic Unionist Party (DUP)

History

The DUP was founded in 1971 by Reverend Ian Paisley and the then MP for Shankill, Desmond Boal, who had been expelled from the Unionist parliamentary bloc. Its original name was the Popular Unionist Party. It was formed specifically to oppose the politics of the government of Terence O'Neill of the Ulster Unionists, whose attitude toward the Republic was viewed by Paisley and Boal as being too conciliatory. The party changed its name to the Democratic Unionist Party in 1971. In an April 1970 by-election, Paisley defeated O'Neill for the Bannside seat in the Northern Ireland House of Commons. Although Boal was the first party chairman (1971–74), Paisley was the real leader from the beginning. The DUP increased in strength rapidly from its founding through the 1981 local elections, winning 2.5 percent of the seats in 1973, 14.1 percent in 1977, and 27.0 percent in 1981. It peaked in the 1984 European Parliament elections as the largest party with 33.6 percent of the vote, but dropped back in the local elections the following year with only 25.1 percent of the seats.

Organization

The party structure is based on the twelve Westminster constituencies. Each of these local branches elects delegates to a central delegates' assembly, which is dominated by Paisley. It has been said that "Paisley is the driving force of the DUP," and it is unthinkable that anyone would challenge him.

Party headquarters are at 296 Albertbridge Road, Belfast BT5 4GX.

Policy

The main plank in the DUP program is militant and adamant opposition to any moves toward the integration of Ulster into the Republic of Ireland or to the involvement of the Republic, overtly or covertly, in the affairs of Northern Ireland. The DUP credo was summed up in Paisley's statement, "If the Crown in Parliament decreed to put Ulster into a United Ireland, we would be disloyal to Her Majesty if we did not resist such a surrender to our enemies." The party strategy to avoid that capitulation is support for expeditious devolution with majority rule. For that reason, it has been the strongest supporters of the Assembly.

The DUP supports welfare spending, especially when Protestants are the beneficiaries. It recognizes that the depressed Ulster economy needs government support, but blames the weak economy on the Catholics. (Proportionately more Catholics are on welfare, but this is because tradition has barred them from many areas of employment.) Many of the DUP's platform points are similarly anti-Catholic. Paisley's extreme pro-Unionist, anti-Catholic position and rhetoric has alienated moderate Protestants.

Membership & Constituency

In 1979 the DUP had approximately 40,000 members, about one out of every two of its supporters in the 1979 parliamentary elections. By 1981, membership had increased to 44,000 or one in fifteen of its 1981 local government electoral supporters. The DUP leadership claims that its support is due to the fact that people are losing faith in the Ulster Unionist Party (UUP) and Alliance, and that government has not been tough enough in its stance against terrorism.

The DUP was originally the most homogeneous of the four major parties and appealed to the extreme right wing of the Unionist movement. While it has since broadened its base, its most loyal supporters continue to be lower-class factory workers and members of the lower middle class. A 1983 survey gave it a composition of 70 percent working class and 30 percent middle class. Also, its supporters were 95 percent Protestant, two percent Catholic, and three percent "other."

Financing

No exact information is available. However, the general mechanism for soliciting funds is similar to that of the UUP, and member contributions are close to 100 percent of operating revenue.

Leadership

The DUP has had only one leader: Ian Paisley, moderator of the Martyr's Memorial Free Presbyterian Church, born 1926; MP for North Antrim (1970 to date), representative to the European Parliament (1979 to date); member Northern Ireland Assembly 1973-75 and since 1982. His power base is in the Raven Hill area of Belfast.

Lesser leaders are:

Peter David Robinson, general secretary (1975 to date), born 1948; MP for East Belfast (1979 to date); member Northern Ireland Assembly since 1982.

William James McClure, chairman (1978 to date), born 1927; Coleraine District Council member; past grand master of the independent Orange Institution; member Northern Ireland Assembly since 1982.

Prospects

After a decade-long rise at the expense of the OUP, the DUP seems to have stabilized below the strength of its senior rival. Moreover, the twin threats of the Hillsborough accords and the rise of the PSF put it under great pressure not to split the unionist community. This may restrain it somewhat from its accustomed role of playing the Orange card to the hilt, i.e., encouraging sectarianism and discouraging any form of cooperation with the Irish Republic. This demagoguery may backfire if the British tire of hearing themselves vilified for trying to find an acceptable solution. There is also the possibility that the people of Northern Ireland may tire of living in a "state of siege." If either of these came to pass, the DUP would lose much of its support. The strength of the party would also be greatly diminished if Paisley were to disappear from the scene.

Provisional Sinn Fein

History

The Provisional Sinn Fein (or simply Sinn Fein) is the legal, political arm of the Provisional Irish Republican Army (see below). (Sinn Fein is Gaelic for "we ourselves.") Until 1981, the PIRA abstained from political, especially electoral, action on the grounds that only military force could "drive the British from Ireland" and that participation in the politics or governments of Ireland (north or south) was inconsistent with its position that those governments were illegitimate. In April 1981, PIRA militant Bobby Sands contested and won a parliamentary by-election while on a hunger strike in a British prison. He died of starvation less than a month later and his election agent won the consequent by-election. Nine other prisoners died before the strike was called off in October. Buoyed by their success in the by-elections and by the wave of sympathy that the deaths evoked in some parts of the Catholic community of Northern Ireland and, perhaps, by the realization that the hunger strike had failed to achieve political objectives that required other tactics, young and aggressive leaders of the Ulster wing of the PIRA gained control of the organization at its annual conference in November and pushed through a basic policy change. The PSF would now participate in elections in both parts of Ireland, but its successful candidates would abstain from assuming office. Later, that ban was relaxed to permit full involvement in the work of local councils in Catholic municipalities of Northern Ireland and in the European Parliament, but the boycott of the NIA and Westminster continues.

Organization

The PIRA (and, thus, the PSF) is organized on an all-Ireland basis with headquarters in Dublin. Its executive body is the Army Council and includes, as executive officers, a president, a chief of staff, two joint vice presidents, and two joint secretaries. The duality is designed to provide parity between the northern and southern branches of the organization. The council and officers are elected at a conference in Dublin each autumn. The PIRA has support affiliates in a number of foreign countries, most notably the Irish Northern Aid Committee (NORAID) in the United States. They channel assistance through An Cumann Cabrach, with headquarters in Dublin.

The PSF has made strenuous efforts since 1981 to organize an elaborate grassroots structure in Northern Ireland. For instance, it is said to have the best political machine in Belfast. In particular, it has established "advice centers" in Catholic areas to provide assistance to residents in their dealings with the government. It endeavors with considerable success to show concern and ability to solve such everyday problems as housing, pensions, welfare aid, etc. On the other hand, it does nothing political in Protestant neighborhoods and very little in integrated communities.

Policy

The overriding goal of the PSF is the establishment by revolutionary means of a unified, democratic, neutralist, socialist Irish republic. To achieve that end, it seeks to drive out the British by force and overthrow the constitutional government of the Republic of Ireland. Its entry into the political arena was not intended to detract in any way from the continuing military struggle. Indeed, the political effort was designed to "broaden and popularize" support for its armed struggle. According to one of its leaders, "With a ballot in one hand and an Armalite [rifle] in the other, we can take power in Ireland." Consequently, since 1981, the PSF has made great effort to reassure its prospective electoral clientele that its violence is concentrated on British and Ulster security forces rather than on civilians.

The addition of the political dimension also led the PIRA to modify its economic and social policies, or at least its presentation of them. It starts from a Marxist or crypto-Marxist basis. Before 1981, it pursued openly a practice of "immiserization," deliberately sabotaging the economic and social programs of the government to sap the British treasury and discourage capitalists. Since then, its stance has been more constructive, advocating positive measures and criticizing specific shortcomings of the government. Nevertheless, its basic economic goal remains the overthrow of capitalism and the installation of a Marxist-type socialist economy. Also, in keeping with that Marxist orientation, it abjures the religious commitment that is otherwise so pervasive in Irish politics, north and south.

Membership and Constituency

Membership is a cloudy concept for a semiclandestine organization such as the PIRA/PSF, especially as it has close affinity to Lenin's "professional revolutionary" cadre structure. Its supporters are the most radical and disaffected elements in the Catholic community, especially in those areas where Catholics are concentrated most heavily and are poorest, such as West Belfast. One survey showed them to be 98 percent Catholic and two percent "other," with none at all professing protestantism. Also, it is the most solidly working class of the Ulster parties, 80 percent in that category and 20 percent middle class.

Another striking characteristic of the PSF voters is their background of political abstention. The PSF rise did not erode SDLP support appreciably, contrary to early expectations, and coincided with an increase in turnout. This suggests that it appeals mainly to Catholic electors who had found none of the older parties sufficiently attractive to warrant a vote.

Finances

PSF finances are shrouded by even more mystery than its membership rolls. It appears to be the most affluent of the Ulster parties, despite its working class character. For instance, it outspent all the other parties in the 1982 NIA elections, despite fielding fewer than half as many candidates as some of them.

Also, its local organizations seem well-funded, to the point of staffing about a dozen "advice centers" within two years of their founding.

Probably, the PSF relies much less than its rivals on such traditional sources of party funds as dues and donations, nor does it have formal trade union subsidies. On the other hand, its unconventional sources seem abundant. Its foreign affiliates send money, $3 million from NORAID alone in thirteen years. Its critics allege that it also raises funds by tax swindles, protection rackets, kidnap ransoms, bank robberies, blackmail, and extortion.

Leadership

In the 1981 coup, aging stalwarts of the IRA cause, mainly southerners, were pushed aside—but not out—by admiring, but impatient "young Turks" from the north:

Gerry Adams, born 1948 in Belfast, president since 1983, joint vice president 1978–83; member NIA since 1982, MP since 1983 without taking his seat; allegedly PIRA chief of staff 1976–78.

Ruairi O'Bradaigh, president 1969–83, "old guard" leader.

Martin MacGuinness, chief of staff since 1978, member NIA since 1982, "young Turk."

Danny Morrison, publicity director, member NIA since 1982, "young Turk."

David O'Connell, joint vice president, former chief of staff, "old guard."

Prospects

The PSF seems to be well established as a major force on the Northern Irish political scene. Its radicalism is a key factor in any future Ulster political equation. This has tended to polarize the electorate to the extent that the centrist Alliance Party has lost support. On the other hand, it has politicized important segments of the Catholic population and, thereby, given the situation better balance. Moreover, the necessity to compete in a peaceful contest for the votes of reasonable human beings may have had a moderating effect on the PSF. If this process continues, the PSF may eventually provide an essential building block for the foundation of a permanent solution to the "Irish problem"—at long last.

Social Democratic and Labour Party (SDLP)

History

The SDLP was founded on August 21, 1970, absorbing most of the members and other supporters of the old Nationalist Party, the Republican Labor Party, and the National Democratic Party. The party was started by seven members of the Northern Ireland government: Gerald Fitt of the Republican Labour Party, three independent MPs—John Hume, Ivan Cooper, and Paddy O'Hanlon; Austin Currie, a Nationalist MP; Paddy Devlin, a Northern Ireland Labour Party MP; and Paddy Wilson.

It shares with the Provisional Sinn Fein and the Workers' Party the ultimate goal of the unification of Ireland, but favors a more conciliatory and gradual approach than does the PSF. It is the principal representative of the Catholic population. It has avoided major schisms, but there have been numerous minor arguments and splits over tactics. For example, the controversy over whether to attend the constitutional conference on North Ireland, called by Humphrey Atkins, the secretary of state for

Northern Ireland, in December 1979, led to the resignation of Gerald Fitt as party secretary when the party's Executive Committee voted not to support his stand in favor of attending the conference. Fitt was replaced by John Hume. The change had no noticeable effect on the party's general direction, although Fitt quit the party and held on to his Westminster seat for West Belfast.

The party's popularity declined after 1977, especially after the PSF began to take electoral politics seriously in 1981. This was due largely to the increasing polarization of the political scene. The SDLP appeared to be more middle class and "incremental" than either the PSF or the Workers Party trying to work within the system to change it rather than to overthrow it by violent means. The party has elected two MPs to the Westminster Parliament.

Organization

The SDLP is a homogeneous party with a very strong local base. The twelve Westminster constituencies are subdivided into branches with a membership range of thirty to fifty. There is no fixed boundary to the geographic area of a branch so it can be stretched as far as necessary to comprise thirty to fifty members. The goal in this type of arrangement is to encompass as much of the province as possible. The branches are geographically smaller in such areas as Londonderry with a high concentration of Catholics. The branches report through various intermediary organizations to the Executive Committee.

In practice the elected representatives rule the party. Because membership is small, these elected representatives must pay more attention to the wishes of the Catholic electorate.

The SDLP is a member of the Socialist International and the Confederation of Socialist Parties of the European Community. It cooperates with the Irish Congress of Trade Unions and is also a member of the Council of Labour, an all-Ireland association of labor parties and trade unions formed in 1968.

Party headquarters are at 41/43 Waring Street, Belfast BT1 2EY.

Policy

Officially, the SDLP stands for partnership between Protestants and Catholics and between Ulster and the Irish Republic. Its stated goal is "reunification by consent" and it calls its program "constitutional nationalism." This presupposes that the party will someday be able to build a strong base among the Protestant electorate, but the party is divided on the issue of appealing to Protestants. It is committed to socioeconomic reform, i.e., improving the lot of both Catholic and Protestant workers.

It has very strongly supported constitutional reform. Its primary political tactic aims at powersharing: allowing Catholics into the Northern Ireland government until they reach the same proportion as their distribution in the general population. The SDLP also calls for the formation of a Council of Ireland to oversee gradual integration of the two parts of the island and gives qualified support to the Hillsborough agreement. However, because of sectarianism, the SDLP is a Catholic party with little hope of Protestant support. The task of attracting Protestant support has been rendered virtually impossible by the involvement of the PSF in electoral politics. The SDLP has been forced into more sectarian positions to defend its support within the Catholic community against PSF depredations. Thus, it has abandoned hope for an eventual solution within a British framework and insists that full participation of the Republic is essential. Also, it has abstained from the work of the Assembly, though not from its elections. In the 1983 parliamentary election campaign, it promised to call attention to Ulster's plight by disrupting proceedings in the British House of Commons. On the other hand, it speaks out loudly against the PSF's advocacy of the use of violence.

Membership & Constituency

In 1976 the SDLP had 6,000 members, the smallest membership of the major parties. More recent figures are not available, but reliable estimates put the figure at about the same. There was approximately one member for every sixteen supporters in the 1979 and 1983 parliamentary elections and one member for each nineteen supporters in the 1981 local council elections. SDLP leaders blame this low figure on the increased polarization of the political situation.

The SDLP supporters are predominantly working class, with 63 percent in that category, compared to 37 percent middle class. However, its middle class strength is greater than that of the PSF and Catholic intellectuals are its most

loyal supporters. The blue-collar membership has tended to remain steady, but it is the most likely group to bolt the party as polarization intensifies. The party has appealed for labor-union support, but as the unions are overwhelmingly Protestant and Loyalist, these appeals have fallen on deaf ears. Its strongest areas of support are West Belfast, South Down, and Armagh, all areas with large Catholic populations. Ninety-six percent of its supporters are Catholic and only 4 percent Protestant.

Financing

The financial structure of the SDLP is very different from that of the other main parties. Annual membership fees for individuals are £1.50. Because of the small membership this provides only a miniscule portion of operating expenses. The "troubles" have dampened personal canvassing and necessitated appeals for donations through expensive advertisements in daily newspapers. The largest source of funds since 1972 has been from a small group of executive and professional expatriate Ulstermen living in Dublin ("Dublin Fund"). Contributions are also received from other private individuals in the Irish Republic. The fact that so much of their money comes from the Republic restricts the party's freedom to comment about matters in the Republic, as well as raising suspicion among Protestants that the SDLP may only be a "front organization" for southern interests.

Leadership

The SDLP age profile is somewhat lower than that of the other major parties with the largest number of elected representatives (40–43 percent) in the thirty-to-thirty-nine age bracket.

Gerald Fitt (born 1926), founding leader 1970–79; deputy chief minister Northern Ireland Executive 1974; MP as Republican Labour 1966–70, as SDLP 1970–1979, as Socialist 1979–1983; Independent MP candidate 1983.

John Hume, (born 1937), deputy leader 1970–79; leader since 1979; member NIA 1969–1972 and since 1982; MP since 1983; power base in Londonderry; member European Parliament since 1979.

Other leaders are:

Seamus Mallon (born 1939), deputy party leaders since 1979; contested parliamentary seat October 1974, 1979, and 1983, elected by-election 1986; elected to NIA 1973 and 1982.

Prospects

The SDLP seeks radical change through moderate means and can find support only within the Catholic community. This was difficult enough before the PSF began to compete electorally. Now, it must show, also, that its approach promises greater success than the extremism of the PSF. So far, it has fared surprisingly well and the PSF support seems to have come mainly from former abstainers. However, its commitment to a peaceful nationalist solution makes it heavily dependent on forces beyond its control, especially the ability of the British and Irish governments to work expeditiously toward an accomodative resolution acceptable to the bulk of the Ulster Catholics.

Ulster Unionist Party (UUP)

History

More commonly known as the Official Unionist Party or OUP, the party has been the largest and most powerful since the formation of Ulster in 1921. The party originated in prepartition times and was the strongest element in the Unionist movement. From 1921 until the introduction of direct rule from London, it provided all the governments of Northern Ireland and always held a majority of the fifty-two seats in the old Northern Ireland Parliament.

It normally held ten of the twelve Ulster seats in the British House of Commons. Since pre-"state" times, it has been affiliated with the British Conservative Party, entitled to send full voting representatives to party conferences. It has relied on the Conservative Party to strongly support the link with Great Britain.

The OUP remained closely united until the rise of alternative forms of Unionism in 1970 to 1973 (i.e., Democratic Unionist Party, Alliance Party, Vanguard Movement). In 1974 the United Ulster Unionist Council (UUUC) was set up, consisting of the traditional Unionist groupings with the OUP as the dominant party. The event that brought the Unionist parties together was the signing of the Sunningdale Agreement (December 1973) between the British and Irish governments and representatives from Northern Ireland. This was a power-sharing agreement designed to bring Catholics into the government. However, the Sunning-

dale Agreement collapsed, the Unionist parties started bickering again, and in 1977 the UUUC broke up. The DUP split off and ate rather deeply into OUP support for several years. However, the OUP decline seems to have been stemmed at a level somewhat higher than its community rival. Recent leaders of the party have been: Captain Terence O'Neill (1963–69); James Chichester-Clark (1969–71); Arthur Brian Faulkner (1971–74); Henry William West (1974–79); James Henry Molyneaux (1979 to present).

Organization

Traditionally the OUP has been highly homogeneous (Protestant and propartition) with strict control exerted by the party leadership. The leadership has always placed very high importance on unity: anyone suspected of opposition was expelled from the party. During its fifty years in office, it acquired influence over the more important industries (shipbuilding and engineering), and members suspected of disloyalty could lose their jobs as well as their party affiliation.

The OUP is governed by the Ulster Unionist Council which is subdivided into twelve constituency associations. Such affiliated bodies as the Ulster Women's Unionist Council, the Young Unionists, the County Grand Lodges, and the Associations of Official Unionist District Councillors provide additional support.

The suspension of the Northern Ireland government in the early 1970s thrust the OUP into the unaccustomed position of being out of power at the provincial level. However, it retreated into the local fiefs that had always been the bulwark of its strength and has continued to hold office in the House of Commons and, more reluctantly, in the European Parliament and the NIA. Despite the erosion, office-holding remains an important factor in its organization.

Party headquarters are at 38 University Street, Belfast BT7 1FZ.

Policy

On the one hand, the cornerstone of the OUP's long-term program is full integration of Northern Ireland in the United Kingdom. On the other, its immediate objectives are the end of direct rule from Westminster, devolution of authority to a majority-rule government at Stormont, and reform of the NIA to eliminate the 70 percent requirement. It rejects "power sharing" with the nationalists or any involvement by the Republic of Ireland. It insists on rigorous enforcement of law and order and included withdrawal from the European Community in its 1983 election manifesto. It trumpets its commitments to Protestant principles and takes a conservative stand on economic and social policies.

Membership & Constituency

In 1979, the OUP had approximately 75,000 members, about one out of every three of its supporters in the 1979 parliamentary elections. Because of the constant splitting it is difficult to get an exact, current membership figure. OUP officials claim to stand for the solid Protestant (middle-class artisans and shopkeepers, factory workers) and the party's 1983 composition was 57 percent working class to 43 percent middle class. Yet, the DUP is tipped more heavily toward the working class and the OUP has been seen from the beginning as a vehicle for the interests of the Protestant upper class. Its critics say that it has rallied the Protestant workers in support of upper class interests by using the party's power to improve their lot compared to that of the Catholics. Its supporters are 98 percent Protestant and 2 percent Catholic.

COMPOSITION OF THE ULSTER UNIONIST PARTY	
White-collar workers	35%
Women	25%
Self-employed	15%
Blue-collar workers	35%
Persons of private means (pensions, investments)	6%
Protestants	95–100%
Catholics	0–5%

The most loyal supporters are likely to be those Protestants who own sizable businesses and who have direct family ties to the other sections of Great Britain. The party has its heaviest support in Protestant counties such as Antrim and its lowest level of support from such Catholic counties as Fermanagh. Many of the blue-collar and some of the self-employed members might be considered "floaters"; i.e., if they perceive the OUP to be doing anything that might damage their immediate economic interests, they are likely to switch to another Unionist group.

Among organized interest groups, the Orange Order has had very close ties with the OUP. All but three ministers in the OUP governments of the last fifty years were members of the Orange Order. This staunchly Unionist organization has had a very strong hold over the OUP. If a member of the OUP started to moderate his position, he was expelled from the Orange Order and thus rendered ineffective in the party.

Financing

No exact information is available, but the general mechanism for soliciting funds can be described. All members are expected to donate a fixed proportion of their income to the party. Before the suspension of local government, almost all employed people were expected to donate to the party coffers. Contributions to the party have always amounted to close to 60 percent of operating revenue, with membership dues covering the remainder. Before 1972, it was hard to discern where voluntary contributions ended and unofficial government support began.

Leadership

The Unionist party leadership is roughly in the forty-to-sixty age bracket (forty to forty-nine, about 31 percent; and fifty to fifty-nine, about 29 percent). The party leadership comes from the "squireocracy," i.e., traditional land-owners or wealthy industrialists. The party leader controls the formulation of policy until he is deposed.

Present leaders are:

James Henry Molyneaux (born 1940), parliamentary leader since 1977; party leader since 1979; MP since 1970; power base in Armagh.

James Howard McCusker, born 1940; chief whip since 1977; MP since 1974; power base in Armagh.

Prospects

The OUP will probably have to become more extreme if it is to maintain its current levels of support and lure supporters away from the DUP. The chance of the UUP obtaining power again will depend on events outside its control, i.e., devolution of power from London.

Minor Parties

Irish Independence Party (IIP)

The IIP was founded in 1977. Its primary tactic is to place anti-Unionist candidates in Westminster and local council elections. It won 3.3 percent of the votes in the 1979 Westminster election and twenty-one seats in the 1981 local council elections. It contested several seats unsuccessfully in the 1982 NIA elections but none in the 1983 parliamentary elections. For all practical purposes it is no longer an electoral force.

The IIP organization is very centralized, revolving around the leaders: Frank McManus (born 1942), anti-Unionist MP for Fermanagh-South Tyrone (1970–74), and cofounder of the IIP; and Fergus McAtear (born 1939).

The IIP's stated policy is British withdrawal from Northern Ireland by nonviolent means at the earliest possible date. It lobbies with the government of the Irish Republic and believes that Ireland must play a significant role if reunification is to be achieved. They do not appear to be controlled from Dublin.

Exact membership figures are not available, but it is probably no more than 3,000 with the average age under forty. Its main support is in West Ulster, North Antrim, and South Down.

Financing comes through contributions (65 percent) and membership dues.

The IIP is a marginal force without any prospects for achieving national power in a devolved government. However, it may occasionally play a minor role in local politics.

Ulster Progressive Unionist Party (UPUP)

The UPUP is the personal political organization of the highly individualist James Kilfedder (born 1928), formed after his 1979 break with the OUP and given its name in 1980. In the 1981 local council elections, it received 2.1 percent of the vote and five seats (two of them in Antrim). Kilfedder was its only candidate in the 1979 and 1983 parliamentary elections, retaining his North Down seat with 59.6 percent and 56.1 percent of the vote, respectively. He was elected speaker of the NIA in 1982, defeating the OUP candidate and precipitating a boycott by his former colleagues.

The UPUP strongly supports the union with Great Britain, devolved government, proportional representation in all elections, desegregated housing and schools. It believes Catholics should be integrated into all areas of government, but ultimately supports Protestant ascendancy.

The UPUP has a very small membership, approximately 1,500, most of them under forty years of age. The party's strength is concentrated in North Down, Kilfedder's base, and in neighboring Antrim.

Workers' Party Republican Clubs (WPRC)

This organization is the Northern Ireland wing of Sinn Fein, the Workers' Party in the Irish Republic, which was formed in 1926 by Roderic Connolly, Captain James Robert White, and members of the Irish Communist Party. The clubs were declared illegal in 1967. After the split in the Republican movement in 1970 between the IRA and the Provisionals, the Republican Clubs became the official political front of the Official Irish Republican Army (OIRA). In 1973 the ban was removed and the clubs were allowed to organize legally. They received 2.6 percent of the total vote in the May 1977 local elections, allowing them six seats. They fielded seven candidates in the 1979 parliamentary elections, but polled only 1.7 percent of the vote. They won only three seats in the 1981 local elections and none in the 1982 NIA elections. They entered fourteen candidates in the 1983 parliamentary elections, but finished dead last in all but two contests. They beat out only an Ecologist and a Noise Abatementer, polling only 1.9 percent of the vote.

The party is tightly organized in the Catholic areas of Belfast, Londonderry, and along the border. During elections party leaders from the Republic come over for electioneering.

The party tends to concentrate on strictly local issues such as employment, alleged police brutality, education, housing, and development. They work through community groups, primarily in the urban areas. They are officially Marxist, their ultimate goal being the establishment of a "socialist republic" in a reunited Ireland. In practice, they are more reformist, concentrating on bread-and-butter issues and leaving violence to the PIRA. They advocate a bill of rights as a step toward devolution, but reject both power-sharing and abstentionism.

Membership figures are not available, nor is any financial information. Since the party is a wing of the southern Sinn Fein, much of the money to cover day-to-day operating expenses comes from the Republic.

Thomas MacGiolla has been president of the Official Sinn Fein from 1970 to the present and formerly president of Sinn Fein (1962–70). Headquarters are in Dublin; the Northern Ireland headquarters are in Belfast.

The idea of a "socialist republic," which is part of the WPRC doctrine, is anathema to all religious leaders, most politicians, and most Irishmen in general. The achievement of a united Ireland might damage the WPRC because part of their *raison d'étre* is the fight against partition. The party's prospects are nil, though it will probably continue to survive as a minor force in local politics.

Other Political Forces

Orange Order

The Orange Order was founded in 1875 and is the largest Protestant organization in Northern Ireland with 100,000 members there and over 5,000 in the Irish Republic. When the Unionist Party was formed in 1886, the seven founders were all Orangemen. Many members of the British Conservative Party are also Orangemen and this made for strong ties between the Conservative Party and the Unionist Party; there is a lodge in the British House of Commons.

The Order strongly opposes power sharing and anything else they think may lessen Protestant control of the state machinery. Although the Order remains close to the OUP, the rise of the DUP in the 1970s forced it to adopt a neutral stance between the parties. Some of the Order's members are supporters of the DUP. The Order is primarily committed to Unionism, not to any particular party. The position of the Orange Order was summed up by James Craig, a former North Ireland prime minister, in 1932: "I am an Orangeman first and prime minister and a member of the Northern Ireland Parliament second."

Irish Republican Army (IRA)

The IRA has played an active role in opposing partition since the 1920s. In 1970 it split into two sections over the issue of how to achieve reunification. The Official Irish Republican Army (OIRA) stresses reformist policies with the ultimate goal of a Marxist state. It works through neighborhood committees to improve housing, schooling, etc. The OIRA believes in uniting Ireland, but rejects violence as a means to that end, working legally through the WPRC. After the split in 1970, most of the IRA membership went with the Provisional Irish Republican Army (PIRA).

The members of PIRA are purists whose only goal is the establishment of a united Ireland through violence. They have been responsible for most of the violence committed against the security forces.

Discipline in the PIRA is strict. Kneecap smashing and assassination are the ultimate sanctions. Even while the PIRA abstained from participation in the political process before 1981, it has a great deal of influence over that process. Catholic politicians that appear overly moderate must fear for their lives. In addition, the PIRA murders Protestants in retaliation for murders of Catholics. It is difficult to gauge PIRA support. It is estimated that it has approximately 3,000 members in the north with many more sympathizers. Since 1981, the PIRA has sponsored the PSF as its legal, political arm (see above).

Any proposed political solution to the conflict will have to be acceptable to both branches of the IRA if it is to succeed.

Ulster Defense Association

The UDA is the largest Protestant paramilitary organization. Founded in 1971 it had approximately 40,000 members at its peak in 1972. By 1980 membership had dropped to about 10,000. The UDA is an umbrella organization for the many local defense associations that had been formed in Belfast and Londonderry to fight the IRA. These defense associations are tightly controlled and local intragroup power struggles wasted much of the groups' energy. Illegal paramilitary organizations, such as the Ulster Freedom Fighters and Red Hand, are alleged to be part of the UDA, but this has not been conclusively proven.

Membership in the UDA is drawn largely from blue-collar workers in the thirty-to-thirty-nine-year-old age bracket. It created a political arm in the New Ulster Political Research Group (NUPRG), which advocated independence from Great Britain and the establishment of a separate state in Northern Ireland.

The political group had a very small following and disbanded in 1981.

Irish National Liberation Army

An extreme Republican paramilitary group which arose after the split in the IRA, it combines the Marxist rhetoric of the OIRA with the terrorist tactics of the PIRA. Its most noted action was the assassination of Airey Neave, the Conservative spokesman for Northern Ireland in March 1979. It will probably merge with the PIRA at some time in the near future. Its political wing is the Irish Republican Socialist Party (IRSP), which probably has no more than 500 members while the INLA has no more than 200.

Police Forces

British Army

The British army, with about 11,000 men stationed there, is presently the most important element of the Northern Ireland security system. With the suspension of the Northern Ireland Parliament in 1972, London assumed direct responsibility for security.

Army headquarters is in Belfast and the commanding general reports directly to London. It has been the policy of the army to keep as low a profile as possible. It is the ultimate goal of the British government to remove the army, or reduce the contingent to as low a number as possible, and turn over primary peacekeeping responsibilities to the RUC. The army coordinates its activities with the RUC and UDR.

The Royal Ulster Constabulary (RUC)

The RUC, established in 1922, is the official Northern Ireland police force. It is charged with dealing with regular crime as well as with the IRA and terrorist activities. Since its formation, members have been recruited primarily from the Protestant segment of the population. One of the strongest complaints of the Catholic minority is that the police force is less than objective in enforcing the law. In some cases, there were alleged connections between Protestant paramilitary groups and the RUC. The RUC had approximately 8,200 members on full-time, active duty, 2,600 full-time reservists, and 1,800 part-time reservists.

Auxiliary Police

In 1921, at the height of the "troubles" between Irish nationalists and the British, the Ulster Special Constabulary (USC) was established to supplement the regular police forces. The USC was entirely Protestant and many of its members belonged to the Orange Order. Of its three branches—A, B, and C—the "B Specials" were regarded as particularly obnoxious by Catholics; their mere appearance in Catholic neighborhoods sparked many riots.

The USC was disbanded in 1970 and replaced with the Ulster Defense Regiment (UDR) whose function was to assist the RUC and the British army in controlling IRA terrorism. It had hoped to recruit Catholics, but as of 1980 fewer than 3 percent of its 8,000 members were Catholic. In spite of this fact, the UDR's relative discipline made it a great improvement over the old USC. By 1986, its size had fallen to 6,400 members.

National Prospects

Northern Ireland faces a dilemma in that a majority of its voters wish to remain part of Great Britain and have no desire to be incorporated into the Irish Republic. At the same time a hard core of this majority adamantly refuses to concede equal political and economic rights to the Catholic minority. A portion of that Catholic minority is determined to fight as long as necessary to undermine the state and achieve a "united" Ireland. The conflict appears unresolvable. The best that can be hoped for is that the level of violence can be kept down, and that in turn could make it possible for a more normal political situation to develop.

There is some slight cause for optimism. The Northern Ireland Assembly has been functioning since 1982, however weakly and fitfully. It may be the vessel for sectarian accommodation. Also, the Hillsborough agreement may signal greater resolve on the part of the British and Republican Irish governments to twist the arms of their recalcitrant protégés. Those developments may have taken some of the wind out of the sails of the more extreme branches of the political movements. In any case, both the DUP and the PSF seem to have leveled off after several years of rising support. Some sort of federal relationship with the Republic of Ireland seems the most likely eventual solution, but the unionist majority would certainly require very convincing guarantees that it would not be oppressed by the Catholics with whom it has shared such long and heated antipathy. Perhaps détente might be hastened by differential birth rates. One recent study claims that the Catholic share of the population has reached 42 percent already. If it were to reach near-parity, the Protestants might be induced to settle matters more readily.

Further Reading

Arthur, Paul. *Government and Politics of Northern Ireland.* New York: Longman, 1980.

Bell, J. Bowyer. *The Secret Army: The IRA 1916–1979.* Cambridge, Mass.: MIT Press, 1979.

Elliot, Sydney. *Northern Ireland Parliamentary Results: 1921–1972.* Chichester, England: Political Reference Publications, 1973.

———, and Smith, F. J. *Northern Ireland Local Government Elections of 1977.* Belfast: Queen's University, 1977.

Evelegh, Robin. *Peace Keeping in a Democratic Society: The Lessons of Northern Ireland.* Montreal: Queen's University Press, 1978.

Farrell, Michael. *Northern Ireland: The Orange State.* London: Pluto Press, 1980.

Flackes, W. D. *Northern Ireland: A Political Directory 1968–1979.* New York: St. Martin's Press, 1980.

McAllister, Ian. *The Northern Ireland Social Democratic and Labour Party: Political Opposition in a Divided Society.* New York: Holmes and Meir, 1977.

Probert, Belinda. *Beyond Orange and Green: The Political Economy of the Northern Ireland Crisis.* London: Zed Press, 1978.

BAILIWICKS OF GUERNSEY AND JERSEY
(Channel Islands)
by George E. Delury revised by William G. Andrews. Ph.D.

The Channel Islands, which lie off the coast of Normandy about 100 miles from England, are not part of the United Kingdom, but direct possessions of the British monarch. The islands consist of two bailiwicks: Jersey (population about 76,050) and Guernsey (total population about 53,313). Guernsey consists of the main island and two associated territories, Alderney (population about 1,800) and Sark (population about 600). The islands belong to the crown by virtue of inheritance from the Duke of Normandy, William, who conquered England in 1066. The islands have never been considered colonies; their business with the United Kingdom has always been conducted through the Home Office in London.

The titular executive of each bailiwick is a lieutenant governor, the personal representative of the monarch. The head of government in each bailiwick is a bailiff, a senior member of the local legal profession, who is appointed by the monarch in accordance with special procedures in each bailiwick. The bailiffs function as both the chief judicial officers and the presidents of the parliaments, or States, of the two

dependencies. The bailiff of Guernsey is also president of the States of Alderney and of the equivalent body on Sark, the Chief Pleas.

The States of Deliberation of Jersey consists of fifty-two popularly elected members, the dean of Jersey, the attorney general, the solicitor general, and the lieutenant general. Only the elected members may vote, although the bailiff may cast a tie-breaking vote in most circumstances. The elected members consist of twelve senators, half of whom are elected to six-year terms every third year; twelve constables, or heads of local parishes, elected by their parishes to three-year terms and twenty-eight deputies elected at large for three-year terms.

The States of Deliberation of Guernsey consists of the bailiff, two crown appointees, thirty-three people's deputies popularly elected at large for three-year terms; ten *douzaine* representatives elected by their local parishes (*douzaines*); two representatives elected by and from the States of Alderney, and twelve *conseillers* elected to three-year terms by the States of Election, which consists of all of the above plus additional *douzaine* and Alderney States representatives and twelve *jurats* (court officers comprising a standing jury). The States of Alderney consists of twelve popularly elected members and the Guernsey bailiff, while the Chief Pleas of Sark has twelve popularly elected deputies and forty tenants designated by the feudal suzerain of the island, the *seigneur,* plus the bailiff.

All candidates for these bodies run as independents; there are no parties, although several members of the States are members of the Jersey Democratic Movement.

Almost all island domestic legislation is made by these legislatures but requires the approval of the monarch on the advice of the Privy Council, which in island matters is generally guided by the Home Secretary. Legislation enacted by the British Parliament (in which the islands are not represented) does not apply to the islands without express provision or "necessary implication." Items of the latter type usually deal with very practical matters such as merchant shipping, aerial navigation, and telegraphy.

The bailiwicks' judicial systems operate under old Norman common law, which in some cases differs markedly from English common law. The bailiff is the chief magistrate. The Royal Courts have full civil and criminal jurisdiction, but the final court of appeal is the judicial committee of the British Privy Council.

Major issues in the bailiwicks have recently turned on questions of the legal rights of the citizens to redress against alleged wrongs by the bailiwick governments. Some citizens have charged that local attorneys will not pursue such cases, and the local attorneys do not permit outsiders to practice in the Royal Courts. Another major issue is the rate of immigration to be allowed. The bailiwicks have low taxes and no death duties (inheritance taxes) and are thus very attractive to wealthy persons looking for a tax haven. At the same time, however, the island's resources are limited and cannot support populations much larger than they have. Jersey permits only fifteen wealthy persons per year to buy houses on the island, while both bailiwicks use housing and job controls to limit all immigration.

ISLE OF MAN

by George E. Delury revised by William G. Andrews, Ph.D.

The Isle of Man (population 64,679), located in the Irish Sea, is not part of the United Kingdom, but a dependent territory of the British monarchy. Once a possession of the kings of Norway, it was ceded to the king of Scotland in 1266 and passed to the British monarchy when James I (VI of Scotland) ascended to the throne. It was granted to a noble family in 1405, but returned to the direct administration of the monarchy in 1765.

The executive of the island is the governor, appointed by and representing the monarch. The governor has delegated power to approve domestic legislation by the Court of Tynwald, the island's legislature.

The Tynwald consists of two chambers that usually meet together. The Legislative Council is formed of the lieutenant governor, the bishop of Man and Sodor, the attorney general (without vote), and eight members chosen by the House of Keys, one of whom presides. The House of Keys, one of the oldest legislative bodies in the world, has twenty-four members elected from ten districts for five-year terms. An Executive Council, composed of two members of the Legislative Council and five members of the House of Keys, advises the lieutenant governor. The Manx electoral system provides voters in some districts with multiple votes, but recent Tynwald legislation calls for a system of "one man, one vote" in single-member districts. The practical application of this system has been left to the governor. Candidates for the Tynwald are generally independents, but parties do play a minor role in the political process. Three parties are organized. The Manx Labour Party (chair, Alan Clague) resembles its British counterpart. The Manx National Party (chair, Audrey Ainsworth) advocates greater internal autonomy. The Mec Vannin (Sons of Man) advocates complete independence. Its officers are president Lewis Crellin, chair Jack Irving, and secretary Hazel Hannan. In the 1981 elections, with fifty-four candidates competing for the House of Keys seats, the Labour Party won four seats, a Manx nationalist party (*Mec Vannin;*

Sons of Man) won two, and independents took the rest.

Subject to the governor's approval, the Tynwald has full authority to legislate for the island in domestic matters. British parliamentary acts apply to the Isle of Man only if they contain express provision or "necessary implication" to that effect or have been imposed by an Order in Council.

The top level of the island's judiciary is appointed by the crown, and the final court of appeal is the Privy Council's judicial committee in London.

A major issue on the island is the question of taxation. While Manx taxes are already much lower than those in the United Kingdom, the inhabitants want to become as free of taxation as residents of Guernsey and Jersey. Instead, they face the possibility of a more thorough imposition of British taxes.

Other recent issues have been banking regulations, the customs link with Britain, the death penalty, and corporal punishment. A popular referendum on the last-named matter gave the practice firm approval.

HONG KONG
(Xianggang)
by Donald M. Seekins, Ph.D.

The System of Government

Hong Kong is a colony of Great Britain whose principal administrator, the governor, is appointed by the queen and is responsible to the government in London, although in practice he and his subordinate officials enjoy a good measure of autonomy. Hong Kong is located on the coast of the southern province of Guangdong (Kwangtung) of the Peoples's Republic of China, some ninety-five miles southeast of the provincial capital of Guangzhou (Kwangchou or Canton), and forty miles east of the Portuguese colony of Macao across the estuary of the Pearl River (in Chinese, Zhu Jiang or Chu Chiang). The colony is 404 square miles in area with a population of some five million. It was originally part of the province of Guangdong and its inhabitants had been subjects of the Chinese emperor since the Qin (Ch'in) Dynasty (221–206 b.c.). However, the territory which now comprises Hong Kong was taken from China by Britain during the nineteenth century.

The legal basis for the existence of the colony is found in three treaties which Britain imposed on China following the latter's defeat in war. The first, the Treaty of Nanjing (Nanking), which followed the First Anglo-Chinese War or "Opium War"—so called because hostilities broke out when Chinese officials destroyed supplies of the drug which British traders were attempting to import into China illegally but at big profits—was signed in 1842 and ceded the island of Hong Kong to Britain; the colony of Hong Kong was formally established in June 1843. In 1860, the Kowloon Peninsula and Stonecutter's Island were annexed by the British under the First Convention of Beijing (Peking), which followed China's defeat in the Second Anglo-Chinese War in that same year. In 1898, after China's defeat in the Sino-Japanese War, the British pressed the Chinese to agree to the Second Convention of Beijing which allowed them to occupy 365.5 square miles of territory north of the Kowloon Peninsula and on islands adjacent to the colony which were designated the "New Territories." Hong Kong Island and the Kowloon Peninsula south of Boundary Street (totaling some 32.75 square miles) were considered by the British to have been ceded "in perpetuity." The New Territories, some 90 percent of the total land area of the colony, are held under a ninety-nine–year lease which expires in 1997. The future of Hong Kong remains rather uncertain, not only because reversion of the New Territories would render the rest of the colony economically unviable, but also because the People's Republic of China , which has been in control of the mainland since 1949, has not recognized the legitimacy of the "unequal treaties" which created it. The colony remains a symbol of the great humiliation China has suffered in modern times at the hands of foreign imperialists. The Chinese could recapture it with little difficulty, but tolerate its existence for economic and political reasons.

Despite its uncertain international position, its small size, lack of natural resources, and the fact that it is one of the most crowded places on earth, Hong Kong has thrived economically, particularly in the years after World War II. Its people, nearly all Chinese, have one of the highest average per-capita incomes in Asia. However, crowding, high prices, poor housing, and the lack of social services have depressed the standard of living, and income is in fact distributed very unequally. Hong Kong was established as a base for the British Royal Navy and a free port in the nineteenth century, rapidly developing into a prosperous center for trade between China and the West. Between the establishment of the Republic of China in 1911 and the Japanese occupation in 1941, it was an island of stability on the periphery of a China embroiled in civil war. The years after the establishment of the People's Republic of China in 1949 have seen Hong Kong emerge as a formidable producer of light-industry goods, particularly textiles, and, most recently, as a center for Asian and world banking and finance.

On July 1, 1997, Hong Kong is scheduled to be restored to Chinese sovereignty after a history of more than a century-and-a-half as a British colony. Internal political changes are expected to take place as a result of the Sino-British Joint Declaration, which was signed by Prime Minister Margaret Thatcher and Premier Zhao Ziyang in Beijing on December 19, 1984; the nature and extent of these, however, cannot be fully determined in the mid-1980s. On the date that British sovereignty ends, Hong Kong will become a "Special Administrative Region" of the People's Republic of China. China has promised, under the "one country, two systems" principle, to preserve the territory's social, legal, and financial institutions for fifty years after 1997.

As of this writing, the principal administrator of the colony is the governor, who is appointed by the British monarch and is responsible to the government in London. According to the 1984 joint declaration, the future chief executive will be appointed by the central government in Beijing following "elections or consultations to be held locally."

Executive

Hong Kong's government structure, with a colonial governor at its apex working in consultation with the nonelective official and unofficial members of the Executive and Legislative councils, is typical for a British colony. The chief executive and head of government is the governor, whose full title is governor and commander-in-chief of Hong Kong. Formally, he is appointed by the queen, but in actuality is chosen by the secretary of state for foreign and commonwealth affairs, the foreign-affairs minister in the British cabinet, to whom he is responsible. The governor's official term is five years, although many have served longer, especially when unstable conditions have required a certain continuity of administration. Thus, Sir David Trench served from 1964 to 1971, and Sir Murray MacLehose from 1971 to 1982. Governors have usually been high officials in the colonial administrations of other parts of the British Empire, but these are an increasingly rare breed. Sir Murray and his successor, Sir Edward Youde (born 1882), are former diplomats.

The powers of the governor and the colony's constitutional framework are defined by the Letters Patent and Royal Instructions to the Governor of Hong Kong, documents drawn up in 1917 and since amended several times. The governor is responsible for the administration of the colony and the conduct of its officials. He has the power to make laws "for the peace, order and good government of the Colony," although he must do so in consultation with the Legislative Council. He is responsible for the establishment of the Executive and Legislative councils and the appointment of their members, although these are formally approved by the secretary of state in London. The governor has the power to dispose of crown lands (that is, government lands) under certain circumstances; holds the power of pardon; and appoints officials, including judges.

The British government has the power to make laws for the colony and to veto those passed in the colony, although the latter has not happened since 1913. Formally a subordinate of the secretary of state for commonwealth and foreign affairs, the governor is regarded in practice as Hong Kong's "head of state" rather than simply as a functionary of the British government. The governor represents Hong Kong's interests in London.

The Executive Council, meeting weekly, advises the governor on administrative matters; he is expected to consult with it on all but emergency or trivial issues. The Council consisted in 1985 of seventeen members: four official members (the chief secretary, the financial secretary, the commander of British forces, and the attorney general), two other officials nominated by the governor and eleven unofficial members. Official or "ex officio" members, as their name indicates, are appointed to the Council by virtue of being high officials—in fact, the most important outside of the governor himself. Unofficial members are prominent persons in private society who are expected to represent the interests of significant sections of the population. At present, more than half of the unofficial members are Chinese. They are appointed formally by the secretary of state after nomination by the governor.

The governor has the final decision in all matters discussed by the Council, but if he disagrees with a majority of its members, he must report this to the secretary of state. The Executive Council has been compared to the British cabinet in function. It considers new legislation proposed by government departments or the Government Secretariat and can veto those which it considers inappropriate before they reach the Legislative Council.

Financial matters usually are not considered by the Executive Council but by the governor in consultation with the financial secretary. Below the governor is the chief secretary, whose Government Secretariat oversees and coordinates the work of the different departments of the civil service.

Legislature

The legislature of Hong Kong, the Legislative Council, is a consultative rather than a lawmaking body. According to Article VII of the Letters Patent, it is the governor who makes laws, and submits bills to the Council only in order to obtain its "advice and consent." New legislation ordinarily originates in the departments of the civil service and is drafted by the Government Secretariat; then, it is approved by the Executive Council before being presented to the Legislative Council. The latter very rarely rejects bills which are presented to it.

Another significant feature of the Legislative Council is that until 1985 none of its members have been popularly elected. Like the Executive Council, it has both official and unofficial members, the former being high-ranking civil servants, several of whom serve simultaneously on the Executive Council, and the latter being appointed, formally by the queen, but in fact by the governor with the approval of the secretary of state. They come from among the most prominent and influential members of Hong Kong's financial, industrial, and professional elites. The unofficial members perform a sort of representative function. They are responsible for sounding out public opinion on certain issues, and presenting it to the government. If a certain piece of pending legislation is offensive to the interests of a significant section of the population, the unofficial members are charged with thrashing out a compromise between those protesting and the government department from which the bill originated.

In September 1984, the Hong Kong government published a White Paper on reforms designed to extend the scope of representative government. Its major proposal was to include an elected component in the Legislative Council. The body would have ten official members, twenty-two unofficial members appointed by the governor, and 24 members chosen in indirect elections. Some of the elected members would be chosen by electoral colleges in ten geographical constituencies, and the remainder by occupational constituencies composed of professional or business groups. Elections were held on September 26, 1985.

Judiciary

The chief justice, judges of the High Court and justices of appeal are appointed by the governor on approval from the secretary of state, while district judges are appointed by the governor on his own. English common law is practiced, insofar as this applies to the conditions of Hong Kong.

Regional & Local Government

The Urban Council is a local government body with fifty percent popularly elected members. In 1981, it had twenty-four members, twelve of whom were appointed by the governor and twelve of whom were elected. Both appointed and elected members serve for a four-year term.

The authority of the Urban Council is limited both in geographical area and in responsibility.

It has jurisdiction over Hong Kong Island, Kowloon and New Kowloon, but not over the New Territories, where only 20 percent of the population lives. Its responsibility is the formulation of policies dealing with the maintenance of public sanitation and cleanliness; the inspection and licensing of all restaurants and food stalls, as well as markets, slaughterhouses and cemeteries; the management of City Hall, museums, stadiums. beaches, and public parks; and the granting of liquor licenses. Its electorate was limited to about 300,000. Qualifications for voting are stringent. Persons wishing to vote for members not only must meet age and residence requirements, but must meet further criteria defined by education, profession, or eligibility to pay taxes. Given the limited powers of the Urban Council, very few of those eligible to register and vote actually do so. The decisions of the Urban Council are carried out by the Urban Services Department of the government.

In the New Territories, an advisory body known as the Heung Yi Kuk is designed to express the interests of the local residents and works closely with the New Territories Administration. Its members are the chairman and vice-chairmen of the twenty-seven Rural Committees found in communities throughout the New Territories, as well as unofficial justices of the peace and special councillors who are chosen every two years by the Rural Committee leaders and the justices, or by a broader electorate.

In 1982, the government held elections for a new local government institution, sixteen District Boards—eight in the urban areas and eight in the New Territories. The electorate was broad: all adults over twenty-one years of age who have lived at least seven years in the colony. In this first District Board election, only 12 percent of the eligible electorate participated; but in the second election, held in March 1985, this figure rose to 37.5 percent. The boards will have only an advisory function in local government, and of the thirty members on each board, only ten will be elected, the rest being government appointees.

Other Political Forces

Except for a brief period after the World War II, the Hong Kong government made little attempt to establish even the facade of elective institutions outside of the very limited scope of the Urban Council, the Heung Yi Kuk, the District Boards and the modest reform of the Legislative Council outlined in the 1984 White Paper. Moreover, there has been very little popular support or pressure for the creation of democratic reforms. No significant political parties have been organized in the colony. Two associations, the Civic Association and the Reform Club, put up candidates for Urban Council elections and there are a few small groups toying with the idea of Hong Kong self-government, but political parties have not developed as a means of obtaining political power or expressing public aspirations. One reason for this is the nature of colonial government with its stress on executive authority and hierarchical administration. However, other colonies have developed strong party movements as one of the decisive steps toward independence, and the lack of this sort of political action in Hong Kong is a reflection of its unique internal and international conditions.

Observers stress that the Chinese, who comprise 98 percent of the population of Hong Kong, have no tradition of parliamentary institutions, preferring to work within and through their own voluntary associations rather than make demands directly on government. The Tung Wah Hospital is a good example of this sort of institution, providing not only medical care but also serving as what one writer calls a kind of "unofficial 'government' of the Chinese community," recognized as such by British and Chinese Communist authorities alike. Other groups such as neighborhood associations, chambers of commerce, charitable foundations, and clan or regional associations also serve as intermediaries between the people and their colonial rulers. The government has found this voluntaristic tradition extremely useful. The associations generate resources to satisfy needs that otherwise would fall within the responsibility of government, and, being rather conservative, they do not attempt to mobilize the people politically.

The Chinese community has striven to be self-sufficient, avoiding contact with government officials when possible. Hong Kong has a well-established tradition of what in Western countries might be considered corruption—gifts of money or favors being used to keep low-level (and sometimes high-level) officials content, cooperative, and at a distance. In 1973, the Independent Commission Against Corruption (ICAC) was established, and since then has carried out a number of highly controversial investigations, especially within the Hong Kong police force.

An important factor in the people's apparent political apathy has been their lack of a citizen consciousness. Strongly aware of their identity as Chinese despite often superficial Westernization, the people, many of whom are refugees from the People's Republic who came to the colony for its greater freedom and range of opportunities, have little attachment to Hong Kong itself as an entity. It is often remarked that Hong Kong has "belongers" but not citizens. The lack of a sense of allegiance to the political unit in which they live no doubt contributes to a lack of interest in political participation.

Another factor is the tremendous leverage which the People's Republic of China exercises over Hong Kong. With the adoption of the 1984 Joint Declaration, Beijing has an interest in preventing the emergence of a strong democratic movement that could challenge its authority after 1997. The Communists insist that the loyalties of the people as Chinese are exclusively with them, although there are a number of people who continue to support the Nationalist regime on Taiwan.

Nevertheless, the government has been aware of the dangers of leaving the ordinary people completely out of the political process. This awareness has become particularly acute since recently the traditional Chinese voluntary associations have suffered a decline in vitality, reflected in lower membership and revenues. A number of official bodies have been established which serve to listen to and, if possible, act on individual grievances. These include the Office of the Unofficial Members of the Executive and Legislative Councils (UMELCO), the City District Offices of the Home Affairs Department, and the ward offices of the Urban Council. These bodies, provide information and assistance to those who find themselves dependent upon government for housing, medical care, or welfare services; or who wish to lodge a complaint about the behavior of government officials.

National Prospects

Ironically, the very success of Beijing's modernization plans and the viability of the Special Economic Zones may make Hong Kong less vital for China's future. Other cities and regions, especially along the China coast, will begin to assume its functions. But this will be a gradual process. Other Chinese cities may be able to compete with Hong Kong in light industry (particularly since their labor is much cheaper), but the territory has sophisticated financial institutions that cannot easily be duplicated elsewhere. Its capitalist managers and entrepreneurs, moreover, are a source of much-needed expertise.

Some observers fear that the relatively liberal "one country, two systems" concept will fall victim to the political rivalries between leftists and rightists that have marked the history of the People's Republic since its inception. Death of the pragmatic leader Deng Xiaoping, an octogenerian, could give radicals the opportunity to seize power, initiate a second Cultural Revolution, and strangle Hong Kong's capitalist system.

Radicalism in China, however, is largely a spent force. A more likely turn of events after Deng's death would be the imposition of tighter central controls over China's economy and society in a manner similar to that of the Soviet Union. For the reasons suggested above, this could actually help the territory. It might survive as it always has—a useful enclave of free enterprise serving a socialist hinterland. Even the Soviet Union has, in a sense, its own Hong Kongs: Hungary with its "market socialism," and the relatively freewheeling Soviet Baltic republics. A new generation of Chinese leaders, standing on the pulpit of Marxist-Leninist orthodoxy, could choose to ignore the Declaration's promise of administrative, economic, and social autonomy, but shutting down Hong Kong would damage China's economy and its international standing. Socialism could be imposed by force, but the costs both in terms of prestige and resources would be high.

The basic principle that underlies the 1984 Sino-British Joint Declaration on the Question of Hong Kong and associated agreements is the "one country, two systems" concept: that China will exercise full sovereignty over Hong Kong after 1997, but that the territory's unique social and economic institutions will be preserved and its active role in the international economy will continue. As a Special Administrative Region, Hong Kong will—according to the Declaration—enjoy "a high degree of autonomy," although the central government will be responsible for defense and foreign affairs. Its chief executive will be a Beijing appointee, but he will be chosen "on the basis of the results of elections or consultations to be held locally." The territory will be able to issue its own visas for entry and exit. The local authorities will be responsible for public order. Hong Kong's legal system will remain basically the same as before 1997, and the territory will exercise final adjudication. Freedom of speech, press, assembly, movement, religion, and the right to strike are guaranteed.

The Declaration also assures that the integrity of Hong Kong's capitalist system will not be disturbed. There will be legal safeguards for private property, inheritance rights, and foreign investment. The Special Administrative Region will have budgetary autonomy, will be exempt from taxes imposed by the central government, and will continue to issue its own freely convertible currency — the Hong Kong dollar. Hong Kong "will retain the status of an international financial center, and its markets for foreign exchange, gold, securities, and futures will continue." It will also continue to operate as a free port, with its own customs system.

With Britain running a lame duck colony and unable to influence the course of events even before 1997, Hong Kong's future is China's future. The Joint Declaration states that socialism will not be established in Hong Kong for fifty years after China takes over. By the end of the transition period, China will have developed its own economy sufficiently that complete integration of the territory will occur without disruption. This assumes, however, that China's economic growth will continue and that the present leadership's policy of economic liberalization will be successful. Models for the future Hong Kong already exist: the Special Economic Zones that have been established on Chinese territory in Guangdong and Fujian Provinces.

Further Reading

Asia Yearbook. Hong Kong: Far Eastern Economic Review, published annually.

Bernstein, Thomas B. "China in 1984: the Year of Hong Kong." *Asian Survey*, Vol. 25, No. 1, January 1985.

Endacott, G. B. *Government and People in Hong Kong, 1841–1962: A Constitutional History.* Hong Kong: Hong Kong University Press, 1964.

Harris, Peter. *Hong Kong: A Study in Bureaucratic Politics.* Hong Kong, Singapore, and Kuala Lumpur: Heinemann Asia, 1978.

King, Ambrose Yeo-chi. "Administrative Absorption of Politics in Hong Kong: Emphasis on the Grass-Roots Level." *Asian Survey*, Vol. 15, No. 5, May 1975.

Lau, Siu-kai. "The Government, Intermediate Organizations, and Grass-Roots Politics in Hong Kong." *Asian Survey*, Vol. 21, No. 8, August 1981.

Miners, Norman J. *The Government and Politics of Hong Kong.* Hong Kong and London: Oxford University Press, 1977.

"Can Hong Kong Survive 1997?" *Asia Pacific Community*, No. 6, Fall 1979.

Rabushka, Alvin. *Hong Kong: A Study in Economic History.* Chicago: University of Chicago Press, 1979.

UNITED STATES OF AMERICA

by Robert Schneider, Ph.D.

The System of Government

The United States of America, a nation comprised of fifty states and over 240 million people, is a federal republic with a democratic system. It was created when thirteen British colonies declared their independence in 1776 and secured that independence after winning a war against the British government.

The United States national government deals with its populace directly. But each of its fifty states has substantial and autonomous domestic powers. A written constitution, adopted in 1789 after an earlier one proved to have given inadequate authority to the federal government, delineates the powers and responsibilities of the different levels and branches of government. Certain powers, conducting foreign policy for example, are granted exclusively to the national government. Other powers are reserved for the states. Still others, taxation for example, overlap and can be exercised by both national and state governments.

The written constitution, along with the constitutional convention as a means for devising constitutions, is an American invention. The 1787 convention in Philadelphia, acting as the sovereign people, drafted a document that is best characterized by the principle of checks and balances. The framers, fearful of excessive governmental power, sought to prevent tyranny by vesting overlapping responsibilities in three separate branches of government. The president is both head of state and chief executive, but the agencies of the executive branch depend on the two houses of the Congress to appropriate funds and pass enabling legislation. The president conducts foreign policy, but the upper house, the Senate, must ratify treaties, confirm ambassadorial appointments, and the lower body, the House of Representatives, must provide the funds necessary to conduct foreign policy. The president has the power to veto legislation, but his veto may be overridden by a two-thirds vote in both the House and Senate. The third branch, the judiciary, exercising its power of judicial review, may invalidate laws or presidential actions that conflict with the constitution. Thus the constitution establishes shared powers between three equal branches of government: no area of public policy is the exclusive responsibility of just one branch.

As originally written, the constitution limited political participation. The president and members of the Senate were indirectly elected: an electoral college voted for the president and state legislatures for their national senators. Only the House of Representatives was chosen directly by the people. But this electorate was also restricted to people who were white, male, and could meet property qualifications set by each state. Formal amendments have subsequently made the constitution more democratic by expanding political participation. In 1913 direct election of senators was enacted, In 1920 women were empowered to vote. Legislation such as the 1965 Voting Rights Act enfranchising southern blacks, and conventions such as electoral college candidates' commitment to a specified presidential candidate have also contributed to the immediacy of the political process.

Constitutional amendments are proposed by a two-thirds vote in both chambers of the Congress, and then ratified by the legislatures of three-fourths of the states. But in theory, amendments could be proposed by a national constitutional convention called on the request of two-thirds of the state legislatures and ratified by constitutional conventions in three-fourths of the states.

Executive Branch

The president of the United States is its chief executive. The powers of the president under the constitution are extensive but in many instances imprecisely defined. It is possible, however, to provide a generalized account of the contemporary chief executive's powers.

The president nominates the heads of the major executive branch agencies and departments.

These include some 4,000 political appointees, all of whom may be removed when the presidency changes hands. In addition, the president appoints all federal judges (including Supreme Court justices). The Senate must confirm or reject the president's nominees. The latter rarely happens inasmuch as the Senate traditionally defers to the necessity of presidential appointees who are nominally sympathetic with administration goals and policy preferences. The president has the power to dismiss political appointees without deference to Congress, although this may diminish his popularity. President Jimmy Carter's dismissal of well-known department heads in 1979 was widely interpreted as an admission of his administration's flaws.

The chiefs of the major departments are called secretaries and together are known as the cabinet. The size of the official cabinet is fixed by law. It presently contains thirteen secretaries. This number may be changed through legislative action as new departments are created or as existing departments are consolidated or eliminated.

In addition to the cabinet, the president presides over the Executive Office of the President. The EOP includes the Office of Management and Budget, the National Security Office, the Council of Economic Advisers, and several other advisory groups. While not formally a part of the cabinet, many heads or directors of EOP offices are given cabinet rank and, as such, attend cabinet meetings. There are also a number of independent agencies in the executive branch such as the General Services Administration and the Veterans Administration. They report directly to the president, but they do not have cabinet rank.

Perhaps the most important presidential attribute is the political skill to direct the vast machinery of the bureaucratized executive branch. Agencies and departments often experience political pressures that may detach them from presidential policy. Funds and legislation must be obtained from Congress, but both Congress and the executive departments are subject to pressure from the interest groups representing the constituents of various governmental programs. To gain passage of legislation, departments may try to appease these interest groups. In this process, both the permanent civil service and the political appointees in a department may develop ideas and policies at variance with the president's. Thus a president must use the

powers of his office skillfully if he is to maintain control.

The president's power to appoint and dismiss the senior officials of the executive branch is an important basis for presidential control of the executive branch. This power is limited by the major extension of the merit civil service. Federal employees under this system—the overwhelming majority of all public servants—can be removed only for narrowly proscribed offenses, not including presidential displeasure. Still, by appointing or removing department heads, the president exerts considerable influence. This does not guarantee that each civil servant in the more then 1,800 divisions, branches, offices, and other sub-units in the executive branch will loyally and effectively implement presidential policy. But it does place persons in posts of control who will tend to see things the president's way. To the degree that these appointees remain responsible to the president and avoid political pressures from within and without, they can at least keep the president's priorities foremost and thus influence a department's range of activity. On the other hand, political pressures may restrict both the president and his appointees. President Ronald Reagan, for example, entered office with the intent of abolishing the Department of Education. Pressure from educators and from Congress coupled with a perceived crisis in American education have rendered this objective politically unattainable.

There are several groups or agencies within the White House that are of particular importance as instruments of presidential control over the executive branch. Two of the most important are the Office of Management and Budget (OMB) and the National Security Office (NSC). The OMB has two major powers over executive branch agencies and departments: first, the OMB examines their budgets and recommends cuts or increases in spending to the president; second, the OMB examines all legislation that an agency or department intends to submit to Congress to determine whether it conforms to the president's program. The OMB, which employs about 500 people, is staffed primarily by civil servants. The fact that OMB is part of the permanent Washington scene makes some presidents distrust it. Moreover, the OMB is most useful to presidents who wish to contain or reduce the scale of government; it is of little use to presidents who wish to promulgate new programs. The National Security Council is the chief source of foreign policy advice within the

White House. The head of the NSC, the national security adviser, is often the most important individual adviser to the president on foreign policy. President Richard Nixon's NSC adviser, Henry Kissinger, was considered the primary formulator of foreign policy during the Nixon presidency. The NSC adviser briefs the president daily, often shapes a president's conceptual thinking on foreign policy, and has the further advantage of being independent of the State Department bureaucracy. For these reasons, the NSC adviser is often perceived as a rival to the secretary of state who reigns over the deparment that is supposed to conduct foreign affairs. Other agencies of continuing importance within the Executive Office of the President include the Council of Economic Advisers, while other groups such as the Domestic Council and the Council on Wage–Price Stability have occasional importance.

The White House staff is another important group whose numbers and powers have increased in recent years. The White House staff refers to the 400 or so people who work directly for the president in the White House and in the adjoining Executive Office Building. This group includes close confidants of the president, often people who have worked with him throughout his political career, who are assumed to be personally loyal, and have no power base beyond him. They are appointed by the president without congressional confirmation and can be removed by the president at his pleasure. The White House staff controls the flow of people and paper to the president's Oval Office, considers problems from the president's (not an agency's) perspective, ensures that the widest range of options is developed, and keeps the president in touch with all major developments, including political factors. In practice, White House staffs have also been criticized for acting as a buffer between the president and reality. President Lyndon Johnson's staff was said to have shielded him from news or opinions damaging to his Vietnam policy. They have also been criticized for overzealousness in serving the president's interests. President Nixon's staff, which was involved in the planning and, after the fact, conspiring to cover up the illegal activities symbolized by Watergate, is the example of overzealousness most often cited. Finally, White House staffs have sometimes been accused of controlling presidents. This is to suggest that staff members, who technically are not supposed to make policy, use their positions and influence to shape a president's thinking and

thereby shape policy. Because he has tended to delegate many functions to staff members, some of his critics have suggested that President Reagan has been controlled by his staff.

Legislative Branch

The U.S. Congress consists of 535 members–100 in the Senate and 435 in the House of Representatives. House members are elected every two years and represent districts that are more or less equal in population. Senators are elected every six years, with one-third of the Senate seats being subject to election every two years. Senators are elected on a statewide basis, and each of the fifty states elects two senators.

Members of Congress typically come from high-status occupations. In 1985, nearly half of the total members of Congress, 190 in the House and sixty-one in the Senate, were lawyers. Many others, thirty in the Senate and 144 in the House, have backgrounds in business and banking. Most senators and representatives have been elected more than once to the office they currently hold. In fact, members who seek reelection are successful approximately 90 percent of the time.

There are two major structures which engage the time and attention of representatives and senators. First, nearly all members of the Congress are aligned with the two major parties. Though party blocs in Congress do not exercise tight discipline over their members, they do influence a congressman's votes to a significant degree. The party may help or hinder legislators in many ways, including providing the legislator a better set of offices or a seat on an important congressional committee.

The bulk of the work of Congress is done in committee. The most important congressional committees, called standing committees, are permanent. Each committee specializes in one or a few closely related policy areas. Committees handle most of the legislative, appropriations, and investigative work of Congress. The hearings, deliberations, and votes of committees are likely to settle the majority of issues. There are currently fifteen standing committees in the Senate and twenty-two in the House. Almost all standing committees have subcommittees, which have jurisdiction over specific aspects of a full committee's work. Very few issues, usually the most controversial, are decided in debate on the floor of the House and Senate.

Every senator and representative has one major—or powerful—committee assignment. Senators, because they are fewer, sit on several major committees. The work of the committees is much influenced by the chairman, who is usually selected on the principle of seniority, i.e., the person from the majority party with the longest continuous service on the committee is chairman. In recent years, the seniority system has been weakened. Democrats and Republicans, in each house, have adopted reforms which allow members to vote on committee chair and ranking minority member selections. Except among the Democrats in the House, these reforms have not resulted in selections which depart from the norm of seniority. These reforms, the result of a 1975 revolt by junior members less willing to serve an apprenticeship and defer to party and committee leaders, have served to keep chairmen more responsive to rank-and-file legislators than they once were.

Theoretically, Congress is the equal of the president and the executive branch. In practice, the Congress is at its strongest when reacting to proposals, including the president's. In fact, most legislative proposals come from the president. Since Congress is insufficiently coordinated to launch its own program, the president is usually the agenda-setter. There is an old saying "the president proposes and the Congress disposes." Only three-fourths of the legislation a president supports is likely to be enacted. Yet, it is the president's program which is usually the basis for legislative action.

Legislating is only one of the functions Congress performs. Overseeing the executive branch is a function of equal importance. Oversight is exercised in a variety of ways. The power of the Senate to deny confirmation of key presidential appointees is used sparingly, but committee meetings with the nominees give Congress a chance to review and criticize executive policy. However, the "power of the purse" through authorizations to spend and appropriation of actual monies is more important. Different congressional committees first authorize agencies to spend money and then approve legislation providing the money. This process provides Congress with important opportunities to influence agencies. Agencies may be called to account by Congress in committee and, through legislation, directed to change policy.

Another particularly powerful oversight tool which Congress exercises is the special investigative committee. These special or select committees, which may be established by either house, examine a particular problem to determine if new legislation is needed. Often such committees are set up to investigate and expose corruption or scandal. The 1973 Senate Committee on Watergate, which exposed to public view the corrupt and illegal activities that eventually brought about President Nixon's resignation from office, is a prime example of a special committee.

Congress has been dominated by the Democratic Party since the 1932 elections. The Republicans have enjoyed a majority in Congress only briefly (both houses, 1947–49, 1953–55; and the Senate, 1981 to the present).

The Democrats have gained important privileges from this dominance, as all the leadership positions in the Congress (speaker, committee chairmen, subcommittee chairmen) are held by members of the majority party. However, the apparent dominance of the Democrats can be misleading. Only 40 percent of the recorded votes in the Congress are votes in which a majority of Democrats opposed a majority of Republicans. On almost every vote some Democrats and Republicans voted with the opposing side. Often many, though not all, southern Democrats have joined with Republicans to form a conservative coalition on issues of economic policy, civil rights, and welfare legislation. The conservative coalition is a factor in about a quarter of all recorded votes and usually wins. President Reagan benefited from a conservative majority in the House as he secured deep cuts in federal government funding of welfare, education, and health care early in his first term. Southern Democrats have historically been more conservative than northern Democrats. (This is especially true today in the areas of economic policy, welfare programs, and national defense.) So long as these differences persist, the Democratic majority in the House (and past majorities in the Senate) gives a misleading impression of the power of the party.

Judicial Branch

The judiciary of the United States is involved in political questions to a degree uncommon in most Western democracies. The reason for this is that American judges not only interpret the laws (as judges everywhere do), but they also may declare laws invalid if they conflict with

PARTY STRENGTH IN CONGRESS 1968–1984 ELECTIONS

	House				Senate		
	Dem.	Rep.	Other	Vacant	Dem.	Rep.	Other
1968	243	192			58	42	
1970	255	180			54	44	2
1972	242	192	1		56	42	2
1974	291	144			61	37	2
1976	292	143			61	38	1
1978	277	158			58	41	1
1980	242	190		3	46	53	1
1982	269	166		3	46	54	
1984	253	182			47	53	

the constitution. The power to invalidate laws, known as the power of judicial review, is not spelled out explicitly in the constitution. It has been asserted frequently in case law, beginning with Chief Justice John Marshall's first use of the doctrine in *Marbury* v. *Madison* in 1803. Thus, with the power of judicial review, American courts not only enforce the norms of American society (they mete out punishments, award damages, issue orders, etc.) but are also involved in policymaking or lawmaking. Courts and judges not only enforce, they actually create or establish norms. For example, it was not a legislative act or executive order which decided that U.S. House districts should be approximately equal in population; a Supreme Court decision established this rule. Some critics contend that federal judges, because they are not elected, should not make policy, a power reserved for the president and Congress, elected by the people. The fact remains, however, that judges and courts do make policy and policymaking is one of their legitimate functions.

There are two major types of courts in the United States: state and federal. The state courts, acting under state constitutions and the laws enacted by state legislatures, hear most of the criminal and civil cases. (Every state has its own constitution.) State judges are usually elected by the public. Federal courts have jurisdiction over matters pertaining to the U.S. constitution and federal law. Some criminal offenses may be tried both in state courts, under state law, and in federal court, under federal law. For example, a person charged with possession of heroin could be tried both in a state court and a federal court. Given the two separate jurisdictions involved, such an instance does not constitute double jeopardy. The trial courts in the federal system are called district courts. There are eleven mid-level courts of appeal, which review cases brought on appeal from the district courts. The Supreme Court of the United States is the court of last appeal in the federal system. The Supreme Court may also review the rulings of the highest state courts in cases where federal constitutional issues are in dispute. All federal judges are nominated by the president and must be confirmed by a two-third vote of the U.S. Senate. Political factors are often important in these appointments. Senators from the president's party are often allowed to pick the federal district judges for their states. The president, in return, may expect a favor, perhaps in the form of a senator's vote on a crucial piece of legislation. The nine justices of the Supreme Court are selected more on the basis of policy criteria. The president will generally choose someone who will be in agreement with his views on judicial and social policy.

As the court of last appeal, the U.S. Supreme Court is the chief judicial policymaker. The problems that have concerned the Supreme Court have varied greatly over the years. From the 1860s to 1937, the Supreme Court emphasized defending property rights, including the freedom of business from government regulation. Since 1937, the Court has been more innovative on the issues of democratic fairness and individual freedom. It has also been less concerned about defending laissez faire economics. Indeed, it has gone on to support government regulation of business in which the use of private property may have a public consequence. The Court's policymaking was most assertive under Chief Justice Earl Warren (1953–1967). During this period of Supreme Court activism, racial segregation was declared unconstitutional, the rights of the criminally accused were substantially expanded, the "one man one vote" principle (equal population for congressional and legislative electoral districts) was articulated, and the protections of the First Amendment regarding free speech were greatly enhanced. In addition, the Warren Court completed a process, begun in the 1920s, of incorporating the Bill of Rights into the Fourteenth Amendment. This means that federal constitutional rights must be observed and protected by state courts. Thus, for example, the exclusionary rule of *Weeks* v. *United States*, which held that any evidence gathered in a federal criminal case through illegal means is inadmissible in court, was incorporated in *Mapp* v. *Ohio*, thereby establishing that state and federal officials must abide by the same rule. Any departure from federal standards in a state court would generally justify an appeal to federal courts to quash the state court's decision.

During his period in office, President Richard Nixon tried to restrain Supreme Court policy-making and to reverse many Warren Court decisions by appointing conservative justices. Presidents Gerald Ford and Ronald Reagan, the only other presidents subsequently to make Supreme Court appointments, have also sought more conservative justices. It is probably fair to say that their acts have had a significant impact. The Warren Court's decisions on race and apportionment have survived, but they have been slightly weakened. The decisions on the rights of the accused have been partially reversed and, where not reversed, considerably weakened. Moves which the Warren Court made to promote equality through judicial action have been halted altogether.

Independent Regulatory Agencies

Independent regulatory agencies, most established by acts of Congress in this century, have such unusual power that they might be termed a fourth branch of government. The agencies are supposed to operate without political interference and their executive boards contain nearly equal numbers of Republicans and Democrats. In the case of most of the major agencies, this political parity is set by law. These agencies are designed to protect the general public interest, but because their executives and staffs are often drawn from among the experts of the industries they are supposed to

regulate, they are often seen as more receptive to the narrow interests of the regulated.

Chief among the independent agencies in terms of power is undoubtedly the Federal Reserve System (essentially, the U.S. central bank), which through its control of the credit market, exercises direct and enormous influence on the American economy. Other major agencies include the Federal Trade Commission (FTC), which oversees the competitiveness and fairness of business practices; the Security and Exchange Commission (SEC), charged with the supervision of investment markets; the Federal Communications Commission (FCC), which assigns broadcasting channels and grants licenses to private broadcasters; the Nuclear Regulatory Commission (NRC; formerly the Atomic Energy Commission), responsible for the licensing and safety of all civilian nuclear operations, including power plants; several agencies charged with a variety of labor matters from union certification to fair employment practices to occupational health and safety; and a host of others regulating everything from such vital matters as truck and airline traffic to the care of battle monuments.

Most of the agencies are run by commissions of from five to seven people appointed by the president with the consent of the Senate. The commissioners' terms of office are fixed, generally ranging from five years in the case of the SEC to fourteen years for governors on the Federal Reserve Board. Once confirmed, they cannot be removed from office except for personal delinquency. The chairmen of the commissions are named by the president from among the commissioners; the president can demote a chairman, but the political price in congressional and public outcry is usually so great that few presidents attempt it. While the general responsibilities of an agency are set by law, an activist chairman can usually stretch his legal mandate to include additional related areas or contract the mandate to avoid interfering with some area of industry concern. In general, the agencies have tended to expand their mandates. Congress can set new guidelines, as it recently did to rein in FTC consumer-protection activities, but again, only at a high political price.

Among the more powerful, but less noticed independent agencies is the General Accounting Office (GAO), which functions as an arm of Congress. The GAO is directed by the Comptroller General of the United States, who is appointed to a fifteen-year term by the president with the consent of the Senate. Among many other duties and powers, the GAO is entitled to examine the accounts and operations of any government body (except most intelligence agencies) including those state and local governments that receive money from the federal government, i.e., all but a handful of small municipalities. It monitors many federal government operations on a regular basis, but may look into any area at the request of a congressional committee or individual congressman. Because of these formidable powers, the GAO has been well insulated from partisan manipulation and is generally regarded as dispassionate, fair, and rigorous.

Regional and Local Government

State governors and legislatures are elected by direct popular vote in each state after nominating processes and campaigns that resemble their federal counterparts. State legislatures, with the exception of Nebraska's unicameral one, each have an upper and lower house patterned closely after the federal House and Senate.

The United States remains in theory a federal system. The fifty states retain the power to make and enforce any law without permission of the federal authorities provided only that the law does not breach the federal constitution or attempt to legislate on a topic already covered ("pre-empted") by federal laws. Until recently, however, state governments seemed unimpressive to many commentators. State governors have to share control of the state executive branch with other directly elected officials, who not infrequently are from the opposite party. State legislatures were amateurish and poorly staffed, met briefly, and were overinfluenced by pressure groups and, too often, by bribes. States lacked the will to raise income both for fear of driving corporate and individual taxpayers out of the state and for fear of the political consequences of imposing efficient taxes (such as the income tax). The systematic overrepresentation of rural, conservative areas in state legislatures, the fact that some states virtually disenfranchised poor whites and blacks, and some notable scandals involving governors of states in corruption convinced many Americans that only the federal authorities could provide effective government. One-third of state funds came from federal grants by 1980.

More recently, there has been something of a resurgence in state government. Nearly all states now have a more modern and adequate tax structure. The malapportionment of seats in state legislatures has ended, admittedly at the behest of federal courts. The executive branches of state governments have been reformed and their structure simplified. The reemergence of governors as presidential candidates (a role they had lost in the 1960s, among other things), marked the resurgence of state governments.

Of course, this resurgence has its limits. It is probably still the case that without federal supervision many states—particularly in the South—would provide inadequate services on a discriminatory basis. States still fear that if they tax too heavily in order to provide services or are otherwise seen as having an "anti-business" attitude, they will lose taxpaying corporations to other states. A number of state "taxpayers' revolts" have resulted in cuts in state taxes, once again weakening the fiscal base of state governments, and at a time when recession was already reducing tax revenues. However, whatever their limitations, the state governments are in better shape now than in the past.

Beneath the states are city and country governments operating under charters or laws passed by the state legislatures. Some of the biggest cities, such as New York, are larger in population than many states, but cities are legally inferior to states and enjoy only those powers entrusted to them by states.

Typically, control of a city is divided among numerous elected officials, the best known of which is the mayor. Most cities have an elected city council and appointed board of auditors. The ordinary citizen is often unaware of who is in control within the city, and may also be confused as to whether a specific sphere is a federal, state, county, or city responsibility. Two very different alternatives to this fragmented pattern have been known. The first is when a city is controlled by a "machine," a tightly disciplined political group commanding citizens' votes in return for patronage, such as jobs or contracts. The machine has become rare in American politics: the death of Mayor Richard Daley of Chicago in 1977 was seen as marking the end of the last machine. The second and very different attempt to integrate city governments has been through the appointment by the city council of a city manager. City managers were supposed to provide efficient, honest, and depoliticized administration. Much favored by middle-class reform movements, the city manager form of government is rarely found in major cities.

Cities suffer even more than states from inappropriate boundaries and insufficient tax bases. It is easy for an individual to move to a suburb outside the city boundary to escape city taxes, while still working in the city and depending on it for certain services. In the 1970s, the affluent tended to move to the suburbs, leaving the center of cities with an unusually high proportion of the poor who needed services and an unusually low proportion of middle-class people, who paid the bulk of the taxes. Recently, however, the ability of major cities, especially in the northeastern sector of the country, to restructure their economies away from manufacturing and toward communications, finances, and other technological white-collar occupations, has led to a revival of the urban middle and upper class. This, in turn, has improved the tax base and allowed for some civic improvements.

The Electoral System

Voting is a basic right in the United States. But that right has been selective over the years. Today, however, legal barriers to voting based upon race, sex, age, property, literacy, and ability to pay poll taxes, have been removed by law. The federal constitution, as amended, proclaims that the right to vote is available to all citizens over the age of eighteen. (Prior to an amendment in 1971, the voting age was twenty-one.) The 1965 Voting Rights Act allows the Justice Department to appoint inspectors to conduct all voter registration where there is clear evidence of attempts to prevent voters from registering. Otherwise, the mechanics of registering are controlled by the states. Some states require voters to register at frequent intervals, just before elections. Some states have a permanent registration system under which citizens continue to be registered. Some states, such as Wisconsin and Minnesota, register voters on election day on the production of evidence of identity and residence. Voting is secret and is usually done by machine. Voters select the individual candidates of their choice.

All general elections in the United States are decided by simple plurality. The great exception is the presidential election. Voters do not choose a president directly. They do vote for the candidate of their choice on the ballot, but that vote actually selects delegates to an electoral college. Each state has a number of electors equal to its number of U.S. senators and members in the House of Representatives. All the electors on a slate are pledged to vote for the candidate of their party. Thus, while there have been elections in which one or two electors voted for someone else, the candidate who wins a state's popular vote will be awarded *all* of its electoral votes. To win the election, a candidate must receive a majority of the electoral votes.

Because the electoral college seats are (like congressional districts) allocated to states on the basis of population, it is possible to win a presidential election by winning the popular vote in only seven (the most populous) of the fifty states. It is even possible, under this system, that the college could elect a candidate who did not win a plurality of the nation's popular vote. This has happened only once—in 1888. Usually, the electoral college vote simply magnifies the victor's margin. In 1984, for example, Ronald Reagan won 59 percent of the popular vote and 98 percent (525) of the electoral vote. Walter Mondale's 41 percent popular vote total was not at all reflected in his 2 percent (13) electoral vote. The electoral college originated at the Constitutional Convention as a compromise between those favoring direct election by the people and those favoring selection by Congress. Opponents of this institution, and there are many in the United States, have periodically sought to win support for abolishment or reform of the electoral college.

Federal elections are held every two years (e.g., 1984, 1986) in early November. Presidential elections are held every four years (e.g., 1980, 1984, 1988). The elections in the middle of a presidential term are called midterm elections and are often interpreted as a barometer of public opinion about the president's effectiveness. Presidential elections begin with a long nominating process. The two major parties, the Democrats and the Republicans, hold a series of primary elections and/or caucuses in each of the fifty states. The first caucuses are held in January and the first primaries in March. The nominating process usually concludes in June and, later in the summer, both parties hold national conventions to confirm the results of the spring primaries/caucuses by officially nominating their candidate for president.

The Voters

People who register to vote are, in most states, required to declare themselves Democrats, Republicans, or independents. In some states independents may vote in either the Democratic or Republican primary; in others they are excluded from primaries. Declared Democrats and Republicans usually must vote in the primaries of their respective parties. There are a few states where cross-over voting has been permitted (i.e., Democrats may choose to vote in the Republican primary and vice versa).

Americans believe in the idea of political participation, especially voting. Yet, belief in the importance of voting aside, the United States ranks last among the world's major democracies in actual voter turnout. Only about 53 percent of America's voters went to the polls in the 1984 presidential election. Voter turnout for midterm elections generally falls to under 40 percent. These figures compare to 70 percent and 80 percent turnout rates for European national elections.

Many reasons have been advanced to explain the low turnout in American elections. First, it should be noted that the turnout figure is expressed as a percentage of the adult population and not, as in Europe, as a percentage of eligible voters. Therefore, the American figure looks even worse than it is in a comparative setting. However, the greater difficulty of registering to vote in the United States than in, say, Great Britain does reduce the number of potential voters on election day; many who would vote find that they are ineligible, and the high mobility of Americans exacerbates this problem. Many older citizens may have been accustomed not to vote, for example, while growing up as blacks in the South. Two other factors are much discussed.

The fact that nonvoters are disproportionately from low socioeconomic groups has been linked to the absence in the United States of a significant social-democratic party which might appeal to such people. And the fall in turnout in the United States in recent years seems to be associated with a considerable decrease in the confidence of Americans in their government.

The Party System

Political parties emerged in the early republic. The Federalists and anti-Federalists, factions which supported and opposed the adoption of the constitution, were not organized as actual political parties. They did not run candidates for office under party labels, but they were divided on many issues. Most of the framers of the U.S. constitution opposed the formation of political parties, but they found them to be necessary almost as soon as the new government became operational.

In the first Congress, the Federalist faction grew stronger and more like a political party. Led by Alexander Hamilton, secretary of the treasury under President George Washington, the Federalists favored a strong national government to promote the financial interests of merchants and manufacturers. Thomas Jefferson formed an opposition party, called the Democratic-Republicans, and with his election to the presidency in 1800, it controlled the presidency for twenty-eight years. During this period, the Federalists disappeared from the scene. By 1828, however, the Democratic-Republican party was splintered into factions. Two of these factions, Democrats and Whigs, grew into parties. The Democratic Party, founded in 1828, is thus the oldest political party in the world. Led by Andrew Jackson, the Democrats reached out and attempted to involve ordinary citizens in their affairs through national campaigns and conventions. (The first presidential nominating conventions were held in 1832.) In 1854, a coalition of Whigs and antislavery Democrats joined to form the Republican Party. The Republican nominee for president in 1860, a darkhorse named Abraham Lincoln, was the party's first successful candidate. The Whigs soon disappeared. The Democratic and Republican parties have dominated American politics for the past 125 years.

The Republican Party during the nineteenth century acquired many characteristics still associated with it. It was the party of the North, with the exception of recent immigrants (such as the Irish) in central cities. The Republicans, who had favored confining slavery to the South and keeping other agricultural areas for the family farmer, acquired a strong grip on the Midwest. Since it dominated national politics during the Civil War and Reconstruction periods (1860–77), which coincided with the initial emergence of the United States as the world's foremost industrial power, the Republican Party also became the party of business. The modern image of the Republican Party as the party favoring business was fixed in the 1920s and early 1930s by a series of presidents—Harding, Coolidge and Hoover—who favored laissez faire economic policies.

The Democrats gradually emerged as one of the most amazing coalitions ever to form a political party. After the Civil War, the southern states were solidly Democratic because the Union government during and after the war was Republican. Southern politics tended to be dominated by rich elites and their clients. In the North, the Democratic Party appealed to recent immigrants—such as the Irish—who associated the Republicans with the native-born Protestant elites. The loyalty of the immigrants was often reinforced by political machines—organizations which gave voters help in finding jobs, housing, and even food—in return for their votes. In the twentieth century, the Democrats attracted groups which were ever harder to reconcile. The New Deal social reforms of Franklin Roosevelt helped the poor, the unemployed, and the labor unions, which grew dramatically in this period. For the first time in American politics, social class, rather than ethnicity or region, played an important part in shaping political allegiance. Finally, the social and civil rights policies of Democratic presidents from Roosevelt onwards won the Democrats the overwhelming support of black voters. On paper, the Democrats had an enormous advantage. But their coalition of city, ethnic, union, poor, black, and Southern white voters—sometimes referred to as the New Deal coalition—was hard to keep together.

The Parties in Law

Political parties exist, and are legally protected, under the "freedom of association" clause of the U.S. constitution's First Amendment. Beyond this general guarantee, the legal position of U.S. parties is set forth in state law, court decisions, and laws relating to campaign financing.

State laws regarding political parties concentrate on several issues. State laws govern access to the ballot. Each state has a set of requirements which candidates must meet to be included on the ballot. Each state also has laws pertaining to primary elections, and many have laws on campaign financing.

Variations among the states are immense and many of the laws are complex. The laws on primaries and candidate inclusion are also frequently changed as parties and factions jockey for advantage in each state. Generally, the laws on candidate inclusion do not set up serious barriers—several thousand signatures on formal petitions for candidacy and the payment of a small fee are usually all that is required. Yet, a candidate of a third or minor party can often be kept off the ballot by representatives of one or both of the two major parties who raise legal objections to the validity of signatures on petitions or take other legal actions in courts presided over by politically partisan judges.

Court decisions have concentrated on the question of which takes precedence—state law or party rules—in the selection of delegates to the parties' national conventions. The courts have determined that the parties have virtually unlimited freedom to make their own rules and that those rules take precedence over state law in cases of conflict.

Campaign finance has been a major issue in the United States. Until the 1970s, candidates for office raised money primarily from a small number of wealthy contributors. These contributors were often acting on behalf of corporations or special interests who employed them. Although campaign contributions were generous under this system, it seemed to many that special interests were buying influence. This system also was an open door for bribery and corruption. It enabled politicians to extort campaign contributions by threatening to initiate policies or legal suits unfavorable to a corporation if it did not make a satisfactory contribution. The Nixon campaign organization engaged in such practices on a massive scale in raising funds for the 1972 election.

In 1974, Congress passed the Campaign Finance Reform Act in an effort to reform the system. Candidates for a party's presidential nomination now receive federal grants to match their privately obtained contributions, so long as these contributions are obtained in at least twenty states in the form of small contributions from individuals. After winning the party's nomination, a candidate qualifies for a federal grant—around $27 million—to cover campaign expenses. In accepting this grant, the candidate must agree not to accept any private funds. Much smaller payments are made available to minor party candidates who receive at least 5 percent of the popular vote—a rare occurrence.

Congressional campaigns are not publicly financed. Congressional candidates are thus free to accept private contributions. The size of these private contributions are, however, limited by law. Individuals may give candidates only $1,000 in each campaign. Group contributions (e.g., organized labor, business groups, etc.) may contribute only $5,000 to a candidate.

Recent decisions by the Supreme Court have weakened the campaign finance reforms to some degree. The original legislation placed a limit on the expenditure of personal or family funds ($50,000) in campaigns. The Court has ruled that this limitation is unconstitutional inasmuch as it constitutes a limitation of political free speech. Individual candidates thus may spend unlimited amounts of their own money on campaigning. This would seem to give rich candidates the kind of advantage the Campaign Finance Act had attempted to remove. The Court has also allowed independent groups to act on behalf of candidates in ways which would be illegal if undertaken by a candidate's own organization. In effect, an independent group may spend whatever it wishes as long as its activity is not directly linked to a specific candidate's campaign organization. This has led to the creation of political action committees (PACs) by corporations, special interests, and ideological groups. Since they are not limited by the laws that restrain candidates and their campaign organizations, PACs have been able to spend millions of dollars to influence election results. Ronald Reagan, for example, was greatly assisted by a supposedly independent group in his 1980 campaign. This independent organization, in fact run by friends, campaigned against Reagan's opponent (President Carter) rather than for him. In this guise, the group was able to spend $11 million. Reagan himself could not have spent this money without losing his federal grant.

Business and trade PACs are now the largest source of election funds, followed by unions. The number of PACs has increased from around 600 in 1974 to over 3,000 by 1984. Over this same period of time, PAC contributions to congressional candidates has increased from $12.5 million to $102 million. It can be argued, therefore, that special interests have not been weakened by the Campaign Finance Reform Act. They have not only maintained a crucial role in election finance, but have done so in a more open, organized, and regulated manner.

Party Organization

Decentralization and fragmentation are the words which best describe the organization of political parties in the United States. There is no Democratic Party or Republican Party per se. Just as federalism means shared sovereignty between the states and the federal government, it extends in practice to each party having a national organization and separate state and local organizations. (No formalized relationship exists between a Democratic governor, for example, and a Democratic president.) A political party does not have a single position on all issues that all of its officials, national or state, must embrace. There is no official membership or leadership and no clear policy. Parties do play a crucial role as organizations in the electoral process. No president and only a handful of congressmen have been elected without party backing. Political parties in the U.S. are perhaps best understood as vehicles for the recruitment and selection of candidates. The fragmentation of power within the American political system makes it very difficult for political parties to be united on all policy questions.

It is said that national parties exist only every four years when they meet to nominate their presidential candidates. Candidates for nomination compete in primaries and caucuses for delegates to these conventions. About 80 percent of the delegates to national conventions are selected in primaries and 20 percent in caucuses.

Until 1972, the caucus system of selecting delegates was common; the importance of presidential primaries is relatively recent. The expansion in the number of primaries was prompted by the feeling of many—particularly rank-in-file Democratic voters in the late 1960s—that party leaders were not responsive to the public in the nominating process. Primaries have weakened party control of the nominating process and given the ordinary party voter more opportunity to participate in the selection process. Under the old system, party leaders (primarily state and local) determined who could serve as delegates, and the party conventions were deliberative bodies, which chose party nominees in an atmosphere of power brokering and deal making. With the expansion of primaries and the democratic selection of convention delegates, conventions today do little more than ratify the outcome of the primaries and caucuses. Critics of the new system argue that it gives too much power to the voters who are unable to assess the abilities of candidates, who are too easily manipulated by clever media campaigns, and who are, in some cases, too ideological.

Conventions have functions other than to nominate presidential candidates. They also adopt party platforms. The platform, a manifesto of party beliefs and issue positions, is not binding on the candidates, but the platform commitments of the party do enable all factions to exert some influence on the nominee. In addition, research has shown that a significant portion of the party platform does find its way into a president's program once he is elected.

Campaigning

Candidates for office at all levels, from the presidency down, have to raise the majority of their campaign funds themselves, hire their own experts, and attract their own supporters to run campaigns. The parties as organizations have few activists and little money to share among the candidates. Wages for the campaign staff of non-incumbents rarely cover more than expenses and subsistence. The fulltime members of a candidate's staff hope to gain influential positions on congressional staffs or in the White House if their candidate is elected.

Campaigns are long, especially those for president. A presidential aspirant will begin informal campaigning soon after the midterm elections. The race for the presidency in 1988, for example, will be well under way by late 1986. Formal announcements of candidacy may be made at any time, but usually are made well before January of the election year. This is to enable a candidate to organize, raise funds, and prepare to compete in the early caucuses and primaries.

Campaigning takes the form of parades, motorcades, and media events intended to reach a wide audience with symbolic messages. A visit to a plant of a bankrupt corporation, dutifully recorded by television news crews, is an excellent opportunity to express concern for the unemployed or the plight of industry. Speeches are carefully scripted and usually have segments designed more for use as excerpts on television news programs than with the immediate audience in mind. Campaigns usually disappoint those who wish to see issues debated. Even though presidential campaigns— most extensively visible in newspapers and on television—are covered in great detail, the views of the candidates do not emerge clearly. Most reports of an election campaign treat it as a sporting event, concentrating on who appears to be winning and what tactics are being used. Issues are rarely highlighted. Candidates also obscure the issues in the interest of winning. While running for office in 1976, Jimmy Carter was criticized for not being specific on the issues. Responding to this criticism, in a private conversation with a reporter friend, Carter is supposed to have said, "Oh, you want me to be specific. . . like Presidents Goldwater and McGovern!" Senators Barry Goldwater and George McGovern, both of whom were quite specific on issues, were among the biggest landslide losers in presidential election history. Ambiguity, safe promises, and pointless remarks are a valuable part of any campaign strategy. The goal is to win by capturing as many voters as possible. The best way to do this, most candidates feel, is to avoid clearcut and divisive policy statements.

The Democratic Party

History

The modern Democratic Party emerged with the presidential victory of Franklin Delano Roosevelt in 1932. Roosevelt's New Deal, an economic and social policy of federal support for the poor, aged, and unemployed combined with increased regulation of business and agriculture, became the policy benchmark for all subsequent Democratic administrations. The Roosevelt coalition of northern and southern poor, labor, ethnic groups, the white southern elite, and many small farmers gave the Democrats control of the presidency for thirty-two of the next fifty years and control of both House and Senate for forty-four of those years. Since about 1965, however, the coalition has begun to break up as its various elements have objected to civil rights legislation, rising welfare and social security costs, and extensive government involvement in health care, job safety, and environmental protection.

Organization

In theory, the party has a pyramidal structure, starting at the ward or precinct level and progressing upward through county and state committees to the national committee. But this structure exists only on paper. Since the demise of the machine in nearly every city, precinct organizations have virtually disappeared, and county and state committees are little more than loose coalitions of office holders and their supporters whose primary task is the negotiation of patronage assignments if the party is in power at the state level.

The Democratic National Committee with representatives from each state is essentially powerless. Its primary function is to make the rules for the national conventions and serve as a coordinator for fund-raising activities. The committee does not make policy, let alone issue instructions to Democratic office holders. The chairmanship of the committee is a personal appointee of the president if the Democrats are in the White House; otherwise, he represents a compromise of the party leaders, who expect him to show no favoritism to any faction of the party or potential presidential candidate. The chairman's role is purely administrative, though a strong chairman may occasionally serve as a negotiator between party factions.

In 1970 the Democratic Party reformed (i.e. made more democratic) its rules for delegate selection to the national convention in an attempt to ensure representation for ordinary party adherents and to decrease the control of party "bosses." Quotas were established for minimum acceptable representation of minority and other socially handicapped groups, including women. All delegate seats were to be proportionately allocated to the candidates according to the outcomes of the state primaries, and all delegates were to be committed to a candidate. The consequences of these rules increased the amount of citizen participation in the nominating process. From the point of view of party regulars, they also rendered the party vulnerable to well-organized and -financed primary campaigns by relative unknowns such as Jimmy Carter.

In early 1982, the Democratic National Committee altered the rules to ensure that party office holders and officials would be represented at the conventions and free to vote as they choose. The changes will also permit a candidate to win all the delegates within an election district by a simple plurality. At the same time, the Committee decided to shorten the primary season from twenty weeks to fifteen. All these measures were taken to enable party regulars and officeholders to regain some nominal influence in the presidential nominating process. Theoretically, in the case of a closely contested nomination, these party regulars could hold in reserve enough votes to sway the nomination. In reality, given the dynamics of the primary/caucus system of delegate selection, it is quite likely that nominations will continue to be locked up before the National Convention formally convenes. The address of the Democratic National Committee is 1625 Massachusetts Avenue NW, Washington, D.C. 20036.

Policy

Democratic Party policy is best understood as a tendency for most Democrats to differ from most Republicans on certain issues. By and large, Democrats are more likely than Republicans to favor welfare programs, government management of and intervention in the economy, and greater use of federal (as opposed to state) power to address economic and social problems. Democrats have been more receptive to movements concerned with women's rights, the environment, and civil liberties and rights. Most modern liberal-reform movements have found their natural home in the Democratic Party. The civil rights movement, the campaign against U.S. involvement in the Vietnam War, and the feminist movement found it natural to direct their energies through the Democratic, not the Republican, Party. The Democratic Party, with some hesitation, found a home for such movements. There is no clear difference between the parties on foreign policy, though supporters of a lower U.S. military profile abroad are more likely to be Democrats than Republicans.

Southern Democrats —one-third of the party's strength in Congress—are much more conservative on these issues than northern Democrats. Indeed southern Democrats on many issues constitute the swing group whose support can be gained by either northern Democrats or Republicans to provide the margin of victory in Congress. Southern Democrats have been the most hostile group to civil rights legislation, although this opposition has been moderated since the 1965 Voting Rights Act produced, for the first time since Reconstruction (1865–1877), a substantial number of black votes in the South. In short, Democrats often disagree on policy: Representative Morris Udall, a contender for the Democratic presidential nomination in 1976, once remarked that when Democrats form a firing squad, they form it in a circle. This major ideological division between southern, usually conservative, and northern, usually liberal, Democrats makes any attempt to build a disciplined national organization virtually impossible.

Membership and Constituency

Membership in an American party is a very informal thing. An American may say, "I am a Democrat," even though he or she has never attended a meeting, paid any party dues, or participated in a political campaign. Membership is purely a matter of self-identification. Anybody may register as a Democrat and vote in the party primaries. American parties, as such, have no control over membership. This is not to suggest that membership is unimportant. Analysts of voting behavior consider voter identification with one or the other party to be the single most reliable way to predict how an American will vote.

Altogether, some 44 percent of American voters identified themselves as Democrats in early 1986. Traditional Democratic identifiers include blacks (some 85–90 percent of black voters have supported Democratic presidential candidates in recent elections), Catholics and Jews, people on the lower end of the economic scale, southerners, union members, and northeastern urban dwellers. While these groups tend to vote Democratic, few (with the exception of blacks) can be counted on to vote predictably. As the following table shows, the Republican presidential candidate (Reagan) attracted some traditional Democratic voters in the past two elections.

Financing

Financial support for Democratic candidates comes from many economic groups, particularly labor unions, some special interest groups, and many small contributors, the last being the most important source of funds. Labor union PACs contribute about half of all Democratic income from PACs. Labor unions supplied more than a third of Jimmy Carter's campaign funds in 1980 and were of even greater importance to Walter Mondale in 1984.

Once the best financed of the two political parties, the Democrats have fallen on hard times. In 1982, for example, the Democratic National Committee had a budget less than one-fourth of its Republican counterpart. The reasons for this change in fortune are fairly clear. In general, Democrats have been slower and less successful than Republicans in organizing direct-mail fund-raising campaigns and in forming political action committees to put these funds to effective, focused use. The ideological incoherence of the Democrats also impedes party fund-raising. In addition, the party that does not control the presidency generally receives less financial support than the party in the White House. Finally, a majority of the PACs are conservative oriented—sponsored by business and industrial corporations, trade associations, and ideological groups. In general, Republican candidates tend to be favored where PAC contributions are concerned.

Leadership

There is no single position, official or unofficial, which could properly be labeled leader of the Democratic Party. There are, rather, a number of influential Democrats in the Senate, the House, some state governorships, and the private sector. When a Democratic president is in the White House, he is quite naturally the most influential Democrat. When the Democrats do not control the White House, other politicians who are national figures emerge as more influential and, in many cases, as the focus of discussions about the party's future.

The most influential Democrats at the beginning of 1986 were as follows:

Thomas P. (Tip) O'Neill of Massachussetts (born 1912) has served in the House since 1952 and has served as speaker of the House since 1977. A highly partisan man, O'Neill represents the Democratic liberal approach to government. While he has decided to retire after the 1986 election, O'Neill will remain through the remainder of his current term the most influential Democrat in the House.

Edward M. (Ted) Kennedy of Massachussetts (born 1932) is the youngest brother of former President John F. Kennedy. He has been a senator since 1962 and throughout his career has represented the more liberal wing of the party. While he is often mentioned as a presidential candidate and did seek the party nomination in 1980, personal and family problems have diminished his ambitions and chances. He nevertheless remains, as the last of his generation of a very important political family, a powerful national figure and a potent representative of the liberal position in American politics.

Gary W. Hart of Colorado (born 1937) defines himself as a "pragmatic idealist." First elected to the Senate in 1974, he is one of the new breed of Democratic politicians who has been somewhat critical of the orthodox liberalism of older Democrats. Without abandoning the party's commitment to its traditional values, he has emphasized that the national agenda is not a

1980 AND 1984 PRESIDENTIAL VOTES BY DEMOGRAPHIC CATEGORIES

Group	1980 %			1984 %	
	Carter	Reagan	Anderson(Ind.)	Mondale	Reagan
All	41	51	7	41	59
Men	38	53	7	37	63
Women	44	49	6	44	56
Whites	36	56	7	33	67
Blacks	86	10	4	91	9
Hispanics	54	36	10	53	47
Professional/ Manager	32	57	9	37	62
White-collar	40	51	9	40	59
Blue-collar	46	47	5	46	53
Union Households	50	43	5	52	48
East	43	47	8	41	59
South	44	51	3	42	58
Midwest	41	51	6	41	59
West	35	52	10	41	59

federal government agenda. He stresses the need for policies that rely on the initiatives of the private sector as much as governmental initiatives. As a presidential candidate in 1984, Hart did surprisingly well in the Democratic primaries. Though he eventually lost the nomination to Walter Mondale, he is considered to be among the front-runners for the 1988 nomination. He will not seek reelection to the Senate in 1986, presumably to devote more time to his presidential bid.

Jim Wright of Texas (born 1922) was first elected to the House of Representatives in 1954. He is currently the majority leader in the House. Throughout the 1950s Wright was the most liberal member of the Texas delegation. He is today considered a moderate Democrat and has proven himself as a skilled legislative tactician. When O'Neill retires, Wright will most likely be the new speaker of the House.

Mario Cuomo of New York (born 1932) is the current governor of New York. He is considered to be an oldline liberal. In 1984, he stirred the Democratic National Convention with a keynote address, which stressed traditional ethnic values and Democratic philosophy. Many consider him to be a possible presidential candidate in 1988.

Joseph R. Biden (born 1942) was first elected to the Senate in 1972. Biden is seen by many as one of the Democratic Party's younger leaders with a bright future. He may in time become the first Delaware Democrat since Thomas Bayard (secretary of state under President Cleve-

land) to be a serious candidate for president. His work on both the Foreign Relations and Judiciary committees has been highly praised. Biden is a man who tends to run against the establishment and, like other young Democrats, sees limits to traditional Democratic liberal approaches.

Prospects

Some observers thought that the election of Ronald Reagan, together with the fact that the Republicans gained a majority in the Senate, signaled a partisan realignment (i.e., a permanent shift in the ratio of Democratic and Republican identifiers). This has not altogether come to pass. Yet, the Democratic Party has cause for concern. In the recent past, almost twice as many Americans identified with the Democrats as the Republicans. This margin has shrunk. By the beginning of 1986, 44 percent of Americans identified themselves as Democrats and 36 percent as Republicans. President Reagan's immense popularity has been cited as one explanation for increasing the number of Republican identifiers. It is doubtful, however, that this is the only explanation. The Democrats face some major problems. First, they are very vulnerable in the South as the Republicans increasingly become the more appealing party in this conservative region. The same can be said of the West. Second, while Democrats can still rely on substantial union support, a declining proportion of Americans belong to unions. Finally, although Americans are strongly attached to government services, they have reacted in the past several elections against what they perceive as high taxation, government budget deficits, and waste in government spending. Cutting the federal budget has become such a priority and the deficits such a problem that many Democrats are worried about the party's reputation for big spending and big government. In recent years, even liberal Democrats have attempted to propose deficit-reduction programs. To the degree that the Democrats can be perceived as having viable alternatives in this area, they may maintain their advantage among party identifiers. Barring a serious loss in popularity by President Reagan or a public perception that budget cuts have been excessive and unfair, this is the nature of the challenge facing the Democratic Party in the near future.

Republican Party

History

The Republican Party was founded in 1854 as a party opposed to the spread of slavery into the frontier areas of the West. It immediately became the party of northern industrial interests and of those who stood to profit by uninhibited westward settlement. With only three brief intervals (Grover Cleveland, 1885–1889 and 1893–1897; Woodrow Wilson, 1913-1921), the Republicans controlled the presidency from 1861 to 1933. During the same period of sixty-four years, the Republicans controlled the House for fifty years and the Senate for fifty-four. After 1933, the party fell into sharp decline, and after 1960, appeared to be in such hapless disarray that some commentators doubted it would survive. Since 1969, however, the party has gained increasing organizational strength, voter support, and financial well-being.

Organization

The Republican Party is no more organized than the Democrats and most of what has been said about the latter applies equally to the Republicans. In the 1970s, however, the party made an effort to develop better machinery to recruit and help candidates and to raise money for them. In general, the Republican National Committee provides candidates with better ser-

vices, such as campaign planning, opinion polling, and development of campaign materials, than do the Democrats.

The Republican National Committee serves much the same functions as its Democratic counterpart, but it has been far less busy with rulemaking for the national convention. The Republicans have maintained the winner-take-all system for the selection of delegates to the convention, e.g., the winner of the state primary wins all the state's delegates. This ensures that the most influential state and congressional leaders will be voting delegates.

Republican National Committee headquarters are at 310 First Street SE, Washington, D.C. 20003.

Policy

In general, it is possible to say that Republicans are more conservative than Democrats on economic and social issues. While a belief in the superiority of a free-market economy dominates both parties, Republicans are generally much less willing to accept government intervention in the economy and very likely to oppose aid to specific industries, including agriculture.

Republicans have been generally unsupportive of legislation favoring organized labor. The National Labor Relations Act, which made mass unionism possible in the United States, was passed by the Democrats during the New Deal. Republicans generally opposed the act, supported union reform amendments to it in 1947 and 1959, and resisted attempts to remove some restrictions on unions in the 1970s.

Historically, Republicans have been divided between moderates who have accepted the necessity of some social programs created by the Democrats and true conservatives who favor cutting or abolishing these programs. The moderate wing, loosely associated with the party's old base in the Northeast, was the party establishment (i.e., dominant group) until the middle 1960s. From that point on, beginning with Barry Goldwater's nomination in 1964, the conservative wing has become more dominant. As early as 1968, in wake of the growing importance of the South and West to the Republican Party, moderates were vetoed off national tickets by southern delegates. With the 1980 election of President Reagan, the conservative wing had ascended. While a few moderates do remain, the party is generally considered to be conservative.

Republicans, especially in recent years, have been generally opposed to movements seeking change in American society. For example, reversing its moderate stand on the issue of earlier years, the Republican conventions of 1980 and 1984 opposed the Equal Rights Amendment to the constitution (which was supported by women's rights groups seeking full legal equality). On the other hand, conservative reform movements have been quite welcome in the recent Republican Party. A substantial element within the Republican Party, including President Reagan, has been associated with such Moral Majority proposals as outlawing abortion, restoring prayer in public schools, and banning sex education. (The Moral Majority is an association of conservative Christians, nearly all Protestant, in southern, rural, and suburban areas. They combine religion and very conservative political objectives.)

Although the two parties each contain advocates of both hawkish and dovish positions on relations with the USSR, military expenditures, and the use of U.S. power abroad, Republican leaders are more generally inclined to the hawkish position. They are more likely to advocate getting tough with the Russians, expanding the military budget, and planning a more assertive role overseas, including the use of military force.

Membership and Constituency

Currently about 36 percent of Americans identify themselves as Republicans. Traditionally the person most likely to vote Republican is a well-educated, white, business or professional person. Republican strength has been growing in the southern and western portions of the United States. In the past two presidential elections, white males have been the most likely to vote Republican. In fact, President Reagan's popularity remains highest among this group. Women are more likely to vote and identify as Democrats. This is a recent development.

Financing

Republican funds, like Democratic, come from contributions by major economic interests, some special interest groups, and smaller individual contributions. With the exception of the Teamsters Union (a conglomerate in a variety of industries, but based on truck drivers and warehouse employees), the Republicans get little support from organized labor.

Republicans are better financed than the Democrats, and by a very wide margin. The Republican advantage stems in part from better-planned and more aggressive direct-mail campaigns. It also can be attributed to PAC contributions that exceed those made to the Democrats because a majority of PACs are conservative and represent business and corporate interests.

There have been attempts, such as in 1977, to propose a system of public financing for congressional candidates. Republicans have presented a cohesive front in opposing such legislation because they know that public financing would help Democrats far more than Republicans.

Leadership

As with the Democrats, there is no real leader of the Republican Party, only influential Republicans, of whom President Reagan is the first among equals.

Ronald W. Reagan (born 1911) is now into his second presidential term. He is clearly the most popular American president since World War II. Some say his popularity is based more on his personality than his policies, but the fact remains that he has dramatically reversed the course of policy debate. Through budget cuts and his new federalism, President Reagan has sought to reduce the role of the federal government and to shift many basic responsibilities back to the states. Even Democrats have accepted the need for some reorientation of the federal government. He also ended the period of detente with the Soviets, which had reached its height under President Nixon, and has escalated both military expenditures and anti-Soviet rhetoric. He became a Republican in 1964 when he supported Barry Goldwater's unsuccessful drive for the presidency. Since then he has represented the right wing of the party. A former film and television actor, he entered politics as a candidate when he was elected governor of California in 1966.

George H.W. Bush (born 1924) is vice president of the United States. A New Englander turned Texan, Bush represents the moderate Republican position. Before being elected vice president in 1980, Bush had twice been elected to the House (1966, 1968). His influential position in the party developed out of a career of loyal service to the party and to presidents Nixon and Ford. A frontrunner for the 1988 presidential nomination, Bush will be hard pressed by conservative Republicans to prove he is a worthy successor to the popular Ronald Reagan.

Robert Dole of Kansas (born 1923) is the Senate majority leader and a member of that body since 1968. With a reputation for craftiness, he first came to national prominence as a staunch Nixon supporter. He was the party's nominee for vice president in 1976. Dole is very conservative, but has also been quite independent. Aside from his general conservatism, Dole does demonstrate, in the opinion of some observers, a compassion for the poor and those with problems. He is said to be considering a bid for the presidency in 1988.

Jack F. Kemp of New York (born 1935) was a physical education major in college and was once a professional football player. He was first elected to the House in 1970 and has served there since. Kemp's primary concern has been about the creation of wealth. He believes that the nation has been overtaxing the productive (i.e., rich) people in the economy. In conjunction with economist Arthur Laffer and others who became identified as supply-side economists, he developed the Kemp-Roth tax cut proposal (to cut taxes by 10 percent for each of three years). This tax cut, he believed, would bring government more, not less, revenue as it would encourage production. Accordingly, there would be no need for major cuts in federal spending. Kemp's ideas were a potent influence on the Reagan administration in 1981. Since then, Reagan has placed greater emphasis on budget cuts than on Kemp-Roth. Kemp is young, articulate, and is perceived as a presidential prospect.

Jesse Helms of North Carolina (born 1921) represents the extreme right in American politics. He entered national politics in 1972 when he was first elected to the Senate. Helms has been called an ineffective extremist but, in fact, is a powerful exponent of conservative ideas. He is the purest of political conservatives. He feels government should promote his conception of the proper religious values and personal morality. Helms is unlikely ever to contend seriously for higher office, but his leadership of the conservative self-acclaimed Christian and vehemently anti-Soviet elements of the party make him a force with which to contend.

Prospects

In the early 1980s, Republican fortunes were higher than they had been in years. The popular Reagan presidency, majority status in the Senate, and the growing acceptance of conservative economic policies combined with Moral Majority demands for conservative social policy have given Republicans some feeling of control over public debate. Finally, Republican identification is up to 36 percent (from a low of 21 percent in 1977) thus narrowing to 8 percent the once commanding Democratic lead. These developments cause some to believe that the Republican Party may soon emerge as the dominant party for the first time since 1932. There are problems, however. It remains to be seen if Republican gains will be held in the aftermath of the Reagan years. Once this popular president has left office, it is possible that some of the Republican policies will be less popular. This is especially true if any period of high unemployment should occur. Even without a crisis, some of the president's policies are already less popular than he is personally. It must also be remembered that Moral Majority ideas appeal to a vocal minority, but not to the general public. Nevertheless, Republican strength has grown and this has brought about a remarkable transformation in American politics. The 1986 and 1988 elections will be very important to both parties.

Independent Voters

About 20 percent of American voters identify themselves as independents and tend to believe that parties have little relevance or meaning. They are not actually hostile or negative toward parties so much as neutral. The number of independents has increased in recent years as, according to some experts, party ties have been loosening. Interestingly enough, the percentage of independents is higher among people under thirty years of age. Generally speaking, it has always been true that partisan identification is weakest among younger voters. Independents tend to vote more for attractive personalities or specific policies than for the candidates or policy trend of one party. Some Democrats and Republicans, a small proportion, will do the same.

Minor Parties and Third Parties

Roughly speaking, minor parties in the United States are usually parties of ideology and issue. Some have a highly specific commitment (e.g., the Vegetarian Party) which is apparent in their name. Others are single issue parties such as the Liberty Party of the 1840s, which sought the abolition of slavery. Most, but by no means all, have a very short life span. The Socialist Party, U.S.A. was founded in 1898 and continues to run candidates for office. Electoral victory is not the first or most important objective of minor parties. Many are symbolic and wish to make a protest statement. Others wish to crusade on a single issue and, over time, influence the two major parties to pick it up. Still others, Marxist and some conservative parties for example, wish to serve as a rallying point for the promotion of a particular ideology.

The term third party is usually applied to groups or candidates who temporarily split off from one of the two major parties, frequently supporting a presidential candidate who failed to win the nomination of one of those parties. Thus, the candidacy of John Anderson in 1980 represented a split in the Republican moderate wing, while the candidacy of George Wallace in 1968 was based on the southern wing of the Democratic Party.

Third parties tend to appear only in presidential elections and tend to run only presidential candidates. Minor parties are usually active at the state and local level as well as the national level and run candidates for a variety of offices. Finally, third parties tend to be ideologically incoherent, as are the two major parties, whereas minor parties are notable for their ideological consistency.

All third and minor parties combined seldom win more than 5 percent of the national vote. The largest third party vote in modern times was 16.6 percent for the Progressive Party candidate in 1924; George Wallace won 13.5 percent in 1968 and John Anderson about 7 percent in 1980. In local elections, minor parties occasionally get a candidate elected.

Interest Groups

Alexis de Tocqueville, as an observer of the American system, noted in 1835 that Americans have a tendency to form associations for the purpose of pursuing and protecting their individual interests. The interest or pressure group is a type of association. Its members pursue a common interest by exerting pressure on the political process. Because interest groups are tightly organized to pursue specific objectives, they fill a void not filled by American political parties. American parties, being less well organized and less ideologically consistent, are not as able to express specific interests and positions.

Unlike political parties, interest groups do not compete for public office. They may, through the formation and funding of political action committees, try to influence the outcome of elections. They may also, through lobbying efforts (applying pressure on government decision makers to decide in their favor), influence policy.

Economic interest groups, which include business, professional, labor, and agricultural groups, are the largest and possibly most important type of interest group.

Business interest groups, which include such well-known organizations as the Chamber of Commerce, the National Association of Manufacturers, and the National Small Business Association, have an interest in supporting policies that will enhance their profits. Larger and powerful corporations such as General Motors or Mobil often act as interest groups by themselves. Nearly 3,000 business groups and trade associations, about a third of all national interest groups, have headquarters in Washington, D.C. The various business groups are not united on all issues, but they are fairly united on major issues such as lowering business taxes, reducing government regulation, weakening labor unions, and reducing federal spending.

Professional groups such as the American Medical Association and the American Bar Association are also powerful groups in Washington. The American Bar Association, for example, regularly makes recommendations concerning presidential nominees for federal judicial positions. The American Medical Association has considerable influence on health-care issues. It opposes, for example, adoption of a national health-care program. Its PAC, like all other PACs, makes contributions to candidates who support it on this and other issues. The National Education Association, which represents schoolteachers, works for legislation designed to improve (i.e., generally spend more federal money on) the educational system.

Organized labor is perhaps the most influential liberal interest group in the United States.

The American Federation of Labor–Congress of Industrial Organizations (AFL–CIO) contains unions that represent three-quarters of the total union membership in the United States. The AFL–CIO runs one of the most respected lobbying organizations in Washington as well as the Committee on Political Education (COPE), which provides favored candidates with funds, volunteer help, and lists of potential supporters. Individual unions such as the National Education Association and the United Auto Workers also maintain extensive lobbying and campaigning units. The AFL–CIO and most individual unions have worked for a variety of liberal domestic causes. In addition to working for legislation directly benefiting their members or the unions as organizations, most unions have worked for more general liberal measures such as civil rights and antipoverty legislation.

A substantial minority of unions cling to a policy of taking political action only to defend the union itself. The craft unions within the AFL-CIO, representing groups such as plumbers and carpenters, are noted in union circles for taking the narrowest view of their political interests. The Teamsters, the largest single union in the United States, have supported many Republican candidates for office in recent times, whereas most unions and the AFL-CIO have nearly always supported Democrats. However, the AFL-CIO has been sharply divided on foreign and defense policies. The United Auto Workers and certain particularly liberal unions within the AFL-CIO have opposed policies such as American involvement in the Vietnam War. The leader of the AFL–CIO at the time was an enthusiastic supporter of an aggressive foreign policy. Indeed, the UAW withdrew from the AFL-CIO for over ten years because of such differences.

Unions in the United States have been weakened by political differences, but they have been hurt even more by their industrial weakness. Only one in five workers in the United States belongs to unions, and union membership is concentrated in certain regions, being particularly low in the South and Southwest.

Agricultural interest groups are not, relative to other economic interest groups, very powerful. There are not as many farmers as there once were. This is often cited as a reason for the declining importance of farm groups. The largest farm group is the American Farm Bureau. It is a conservative organization, and its members own large farms and are aligned with agribusiness. It favors the free market and opposes government regulation. The National Grange, the oldest farm group, lobbies for government price support. The National Farmers Organization, formed in 1956, seeks to provide collective bargaining for the sale of produce. The National Farmers Union favors price supports and generally takes liberal positions on social and economic issues. There are some militant farm groups, which favor government intervention to protect family farmers, and many other specialized organizations and/or cooperatives. The fact that there are many groups, sharply divided on policy or objectives, and fewer farmers has meant less influence for agricultural interests.

In addition to economic interest groups, there are many special-interest groups. Interest groups are formed on almost every issue. Some struggle for political, social, and economic equality. Some are concerned primarily with social and moral issues and seek, as such, governmental policies in accord with their morality. The groups advocating and protesting women's right to an abortion are one example. Women, blacks, consumers, environmentalists, churches, right-wing religious fundamentalists, and others have well-organized groups working on their behalf.

Lobbying

Lobbying refers to the methods and tactics employed to pressure governmental decision-makers. The 1946 Federal Lobbying Act requires groups to register with the clerk of the House and the secretary of the Senate if they wish to influence legislation. Interest groups maintain professional staffs, often including former members of Congress, in Washington.

There are two types of lobbying activity that should be noted. Direct lobbying refers to lobbying that takes place in congressional committees and executive agencies. Most groups provide experts to testify before the committee. They also work one to one to provide information to win support from individual members of Congress or heads of executive departments. Very often, groups PACs will reward sympathetic representatives and senators with campaign contributions. Indirect lobbying usually involves massive letter-writing campaigns directed by lobbyists in Washington. Every time gun control legislation comes before Congress, for example, the National Rifle Association organizes a letter-writing campaign. NRA members from throughout the nation write their congressmen and/or senators to oppose the legislation. Many lobbying efforts are more subtle and non-political. Public relations campaigns, complete with television advertisement, are often used to raise public support or dampen public criticism of a group's interests and goals.

PACs and Campaign Contributions

Interest groups are very much involved in electoral politics. Through campaign contributions, they reward candidates for past support and encourage them to give support in the future. Another tactic is to work for the defeat of candidates they oppose. Through the formation of independent committees (not linked directly to a specific candidate's organization), some groups spend huge amounts of money to this end. A prime example is the Moral Majority's 1980 election campaign against what they called moral decay, and promotion of their view of Christian values. Of the six liberal senators targeted for defeat, all but one lost. Neither the Moral Majority, nor any other group for that matter, has enjoyed this level of success since 1980, but the threat of an organized group running negative ads and campaigning against a candidate has more than a few members of Congress concerned. Interest groups also organize their members in get-out-the-vote drives. A part of this effort includes convincing members to vote for a specific candidate in a given election.

As noted earlier, in the discussion of campaign finance, PAC campaign contributions are very significant. In the 1950s, organized labor established a political action committee, the Committee on Political Education, which has served as a model for others. Now almost all interest groups have such an organization. In 1984, PACs contributed over $100 million to congressional candidates. The largest contributors were corporate PACs followed closely by trade, member, health, and labor PACs. Lesser contributors were ideological PACs, followed at some distance by agricultural PACs.

Because of their increasing importance in the U.S. political process, some economic groups, particularly business, have improved their organizations in recent years, responding in part to the success of environmental and consumer-protection groups. The changes in the electoral-finance laws have enhanced the importance of interest groups' political action committees. It would appear that many Americans find political participation through involvement in an interest group more congenial than through involvement in a political party.

National Prospects

The American political system is one of the world's most stable. The U.S. constitution, written in 1787, provides an elastic framework that sustains the system even through periods of systemic changes.

The 1980s has been such a period of change in the United States. On a superficial level, the Republicans have enjoyed their greatest success in nearly thirty years. They maintain control of the executive branch and continue to hold a slight majority in the Senate. Assisted to no small degree by President Reagan's personal popularity, the Republicans have significantly altered the direction of public policy. The Reagan years can be compared to Roosevelt's New Deal years in this respect. The Reagan administration, more than most others, has had a clear vision of what it wishes to accomplish. Much of this vision is a function of the president's conservative agenda for redirecting the nation's domestic policies. In pursuing an American governmental system based on less governmental control and more individual enterprise, the Reagan administration has been both distinctive and controversial. The moderate and liberal consensus of the past several decades has been rejected. The administration has won significant budget cuts (primarily in social programs) and has sought, with some success, to diminish the regulatory functions of the federal government. In foreign policy, there has also been redirection. In the face of what it has perceived as a growing Soviet threat, and in an attempt to restore U.S. pride and power in the aftermath of the Vietnam era, the Reagan administration has shown a more aggressive American posture to the world. This has meant ending the period of detente (which some argue had ended already), increasing tensions with the Soviet Union, greatly expanding the military budget, and increasingly using military options to deal with international problems. A new wave of patriotism across the nation, symbolized to some extent by American reaction to the 1984 Olympics, suggests that this new aggressive policy is popular. But questions about the future remain. How extensive has the redirection of American policy really been? Will it leave a lasting imprint? What consequences has it produced?

Traditionally, America has been more pragmatic than ideological. It is thus possible that the conservative trend will have its limits. It is also possible that the current trend will continue as, according to many analysts, the nation has grown basically more conservative. The immediate future may provide some clues. The 1986 and 1988 elections will be critical for both parties. Republicans hope not only to solidify their gains but, sensing this may be a period of partisan realignment, attain majority status. Democrats, seeking to regroup and revise, hope to recapture the Senate in 1986 and the presidency in 1988. It is quite possible, as the popular Reagan leaves office, that the battle for control over the policy agenda will become very intense. The debate regarding the direction of American policy may become sharper and more divisive. The results of the next two elections may decide the direction of American policy for the next thirty years.

Further Reading

Abraham, Henry J. *The Judicial Process*. 4th ed. New York: Oxford University Press, 1980.

Dodd, Lawrence, and Oppenheimer, Bruce. *Congress Reconsidered*. 2nd ed. Washington, D.C.: Congressional Quarterly Press.

Edwards, George, and Wayne, Stephen. *Presidential Leadership*. New York: St. Martin's Press, 1985.

Goldman, Sheldon, and Jahnige, Thomas. *The Federal Courts as a Political System*. 3rd ed. New York: Harper & Row.

Hinckley, Barbara. *Congressional Elections*. Washington, D.C.: Congressional Quarterly Press, 1981.

———. *Outline of American Government, The Continuing Experiment*. Englewood Cliffs, N.J.: Prentice-Hall, Inc., 1981.

Jacob, Herbert. *Justice in America: Courts, Lawyers, and The Judicial Process*. 4th ed. Boston: Little, Brown, 1984.

King, Anthony, ed. *The New American Political System*. Washington, D.C.: American Enterprise Institute, 1978.

Nelson, Michael. *The Presidency and the Political System*. Washington, D.C.: Congressional Quarterly Assoc., 1984.

Polsby, Nelson, and Wildavsky, Aaron. *Presidential Elections*. 6th ed. New York: Charles Scribner's Sons, 1984.

Sorauf, Frank J. *Party Politics in America*. 4th ed. Boston: Little, Brown, 1980.

Wilson, Graham K. *Interest Groups in the United States*. London: Oxford University Press, 1981.

COMMONWEALTH OF PUERTO RICO
(Estado Libre Asociado de Puerto Rico)
by Kal Wagenheim

The System of Government

Since July 25, 1952, the Caribbean island of Puerto Rico has been a commonwealth, "freely associated" with the United States of America, with local autonomy, but at the same time subject to the laws of the United States. Puerto Ricans are U.S. citizens by birthright (since 1917) and move freely between the island and the continental United States. There are now 3.3 million people in Puerto Rico and 2.4 million persons of Puerto Rican birth or origin in the United States. The Commonwealth government is similar to that of the states of the United States, with a governor and a bicameral legislature, elected every fourth November concurrent with the U.S. national elections.

The current political status of Puerto Rico is a complex one that has evolved over a number of years. Puerto Rico was opened to European settlement shortly after the voyage to the island by Christopher Columbus in 1493. The island remained a Spanish possession for four centuries.

During the latter part of the Spanish colonial period, in the nineteenth century, as the island's population grew, there emerged a distinct sense of Puerto Rican cultural and political identity. During that period, three solutions to the question of Spanish colonialism emerged. One favored total assimilation with the mother country, and the conversion of Puerto Rico into an overseas province of Spain. Another movement, smaller but nevertheless fervent, sought independence from Spain, following the route of the other Spanish colonies in the hemisphere. The third favored a midway path—autonomy—allowing Puerto Rico a certain international "identity" (the right to draft trade treaties, for example), while retaining ties with Spain. In 1897 an "autonomic charter" was granted by Spain, permitting the formation of an insular government that would further define and begin to exercise autonomy. But in early 1898 the Spanish-American War erupted. Puerto Rico was invaded by the United States and came under the sovereignty of the United States by the Treaty of Paris, signed on December 10, 1898.

On April 12, 1900, after two years of U.S. military occupation, President McKinley signed the Foraker Act, providing Puerto Rico with a civilian government (the governor, an American, to be appointed by the U.S. president), and a popularly elected House of Delegates (lower house). Puerto Rico was declared an "unincorporated territory" of the United States. On March 2, 1917, the Jones-Shafroth Act (also known as the Puerto Rico Organic Law) provided for a popularly elected Senate and U.S. citizenship for all Puerto Ricans. The people of Puerto Rico were not consulted at the time, and there was considerable sentiment for independence or autonomy among the island's political leadership.

As a colonial possession of the United States, there remained the same three options for the island's political future: becoming a state of the union; independence; or some form of autonomy, while staying under the political "umbrella" of the United States. The last option gained favor during the years following World War II, when there arose a worldwide movement to end colonialism.

On July 21, 1946, President Truman named Jesús T. Piñero as the first native governor of Puerto Rico. On August 4, 1947, Truman signed the Crawford-Butler Act, permitting Puerto Rico to elect its own governor, and Luis Muñoz Marín, the Senate leader of the Popular Demo-

crats won the 1948 elections, becoming the island's first popularly elected governor.

On July 4, 1950, President Truman signed Public Law 600, permitting Puerto Rico to draft its own constitution. On October 30, armed nationalists sparked uprisings in several island towns, killing twenty-seven and wounding ninety. On November 1, two Puerto Rican nationalists tried to kill President Truman in Washington; a White House policeman and one of the assailants were killed, and nationalist leaders in Puerto Rico were given long prison terms for complicity.

On June 4, 1951, Puerto Ricans voted on Public Law 600, with 387,000 for and 119,000 against. Some 200,000 voters abstained. On March 3, 1952, the new constitution of Puerto Rico was approved in a referendum, 374,000 to 82,000, and was subsequently approved by the U.S. Congress. The Commonwealth Constitution went into effect on July 25, 1952. That November, in the gubernatorial elections, the Popular Democrats (who advocated commonwealth status) won the election with 429,000 votes against 232,000 votes for other parties. The Independence Party, with 125,000 votes, came in second.

In 1953, the United Nations authorized the United States to cease transmitting to it information on Puerto Rico as a non-self-governing territory, finding that achievement of commonwealth status meant that the island was engaged in the process of self-determination.

On March 1, 1954, four nationalists opened fire in the U.S. House of Representatives, wounding five congressmen. This occurred almost thirty-seven years to the day after Congress granted U.S. citizenship to Puerto Ricans.

In 1959, the Popular Democratic Party sought to amplify Puerto Rico's autonomy with the Fernos-Murray bill, but it was rejected by the U.S. Congress. On July 23, 1967, in a status referendum, commonwealth status received 60.5 percent of the votes, compared with 38.9 percent for statehood, and 0.6 percent for independence. Many supporters of the independence option boycotted the plebiscite.

Since then, the commonwealth status has remained unchanged. Governors favoring U.S. statehood won three of the last five elections—1968, 1976, and 1980—thus blunting the thrust of the commonwealth movement, which seeks to expand the island's autonomous powers.

Under commonwealth status, Puerto Rico and the United States share a common defense, common market, and common currency. The official languages of Puerto Rico are Spanish and English. The commonwealth exercises virtually the same control over its internal affairs as do the fifty U.S. states, differing from the states in its relationship with the federal government.

For example, although the people of Puerto Rico are U.S. citizens, they do not vote in national elections, and they are represented in Congress only by a resident commissioner who has a voice in the House of Representatives, but no vote.

On the other hand, most federal taxes (except those such as Social Security taxes, which are imposed by mutual consent) are not levied in Puerto Rico. No federal income tax is collected from commonwealth residents on income earned from local sources in Puerto Rico, except for federal employees, who are subject to taxes on their salaries. Federal excise taxes on shipments of alcoholic beverages (chiefly rum) and tobacco products from Puerto Rico to the continental United States are returned to the Puerto Rican treasury.

Executive

The governor of Puerto Rico is elected every four years with no limit on reelection. (Muñoz Marín served four consecutive terms—1949 to 1964—and at age sixty-six voluntarily retired.) Candidates for governor must be thirty-five years old and during five preceding years be a U.S. citizen as well as a "citizen and bona fide resident of Puerto Rico." In emergencies, the governor is succeeded by the secretary of state, whose appointment requires the approval of both houses of the legislature. The commonwealth government is much more centralized than that of any state of the United States, and perhaps more centralized than that of many nations.

The executive branch encompasses the governor's office and several large agencies, departments, and corporations. Such key services as education, health, police, fire protection, electricity, and water are under the executive branch. (If workers in these services are added to federal, legislative, and municipal employees, about one of every four workers in Puerto Rico holds a government job.) The governor is also the nominal commander-in-chief of the state militia (which is actually the federally funded National Guard).

The current governor of Puerto Rico, Rafael Hernández Colón, head of the pro-autonomy Popular Democratic Party (*Partido Popular Democrático*; PPD), took office January 2, 1985. This is his second four-year term as governor; he occupied the office previously from 1973 through 1976. In two tightly contested reelection bids, in 1976 and 1980, Hernández Colón was defeated by Carlos Romero Barceló, head of the New Progressive Party (*Partido Nuevo Progresista*; PNP), which favors U.S. statehood. But in a third try against Governor Romero Barceló, in November 1984, Hernádez Colón returned to power. He won 47.8 percent of the vote, compared to 44.6 percent for the PNP. Third place in the election, with 4.1 percent of the vote, was taken by the Puerto Rico Renovation Party (*Partido de Renovacíon Puertorriqueña*; PRP), a new group headed by San Juan Mayor Hernán Padilla, which had split off from the PNP. In fourth place, with 3.6 percent, was the Puerto Rico Independence Party (*Partido Independentista Puertorriqueño*; PIP). Hernández Colón's victory ended eight consecutive years of rule by the PNP and slowed down what appeared to be an inexorable trend toward U.S. statehood. During his campaign, Hernández Colón stressed that, if elected, he would not focus upon the perennial issue of political status, but would seek to resolve the island's critical social and economic problems.

PUERTO RICO GUBERNATORIAL ELECTION (1984)		
	% of Votes	Number of Votes
Rafael Hernández-Colón (PPD)	47.75	822,783
Carlos Romero Barceló (PNP)	44.62	768,742
Hernán Padilla (PRP)	4.05	69,865
Fernando Martín (PIP)	3.55	61,316

The U.S. government plays a decisive role in the government of Puerto Rico. Several thousand federal government employees are based on the island. The post office and the customs and quarantine services are operated by the federal government. Flight procedures are controlled by the Federal Aviation Agency. Radio and television stations are licensed by the Federal Communications Commission. Almost every federal agency or department, from the Weather Bureau to the Peace Corps, is represented. A substantial amount of federal money is also spent on the island, ranging from Social Security payments to grants and loans. United

GUBERNATORIAL ELECTIONS (1952–84)*

Year	Registered Voters	Voters	%	PPD	PNP**	PIP
1952	883,219	664,947	75.3	429,064	85,172	125,734
1956	873,842	701,738	80.3	433,010	172,838	86,386
1960	941,034	796,429	84.6	457,880	252,364	24,103
1964	1,002,000	839,678	83.8	487,280	284,627	22,201
1968	1,176,895	922,822	74.4	367,903	390,623	24,713
1972	1,555,504	1,250,978	80.4	609,670	524,039	52,070
1976	1,701,217	1,464,600	86.1	634,941	682,607	58,556
1980	N.A.	1,609,311	N.A.	756,889	759,926	87,272
1984	1,953,496	1,741,905	89.1	822,783	768,742	61,316

* Several other parties have taken part in Puerto Rican elections over the years, but few have drawn significant numbers of voters. The People's Party, for example, drew 87,844 votes in 1968, but has since disappeared. The Puerto Rican Socialist Party (PSP) took part in the 1976 and 1980 elections, drawing 9,761 and 5,224 votes, respectively.
**The PNP first took part in elections in 1968. Prior to that the principal statehood party was the Republican Statehood Party (RSP), whose figures are shown for 1952 through 1964.

States minimum wages apply in Puerto Rico, which is also subject to federal labor legislation.

The U.S. military operates from bases on the island, and the U.S. Federal Bureau of Investigation and the Secret Service maintain offices there. Also, from Washington, the United States manages all of the island's external affairs. Consulates of foreign nations are located in San Juan, but the island has no official diplomatic relations with any country.

Legislature

Puerto Rico's bicameral legislature has twenty-seven senators and fifty-one representatives. Two senators are elected from each of eight senatorial districts and eleven others are elected for "at large" seats, which have no specific local constituency. There are forty representative districts, with one House member from each, and eleven "at large" house seats. The legislature meets each year from January through April, but one-month extensions to complete last-minute business are usually required.

Legislators must "read and write Spanish or English," be citizens of the United States, and have resided in Puerto Rico for two years prior to election. The minimum age is thirty for senators and twenty-five for representatives. Although an Anglophone with no Spanish does, in theory, qualify for a legislative seat, the working language of both houses is Spanish. Since 1900, three North Americans have been elected to the legislature, but all were long-time residents of the island.

Bills approved by both houses become law when the governor signs them or if he fails to act on them within ten working days. The legislature may overrule the governor's veto if it passes the bill for a second time by a two-thirds majority.

In the 1984 elections, the Popular Democratic Party not only regained the governor's mansion, but also won majorities in both the Senate and the House of Representatives. In the Senate, the PDP won sixteen seats, with ten held by the PNP and one by the PIP. In the House, the PDP swept thirty-four of the seats, leaving sixteen to the PNP and one to the PIP.

Judiciary

Puerto Rico has its own Supreme Court, composed of a chief justice and eight associate justices. It also has nine superior courts, thirty-seven district courts, and forty-two justices of the peace in rural areas. The island's official courtroom language is Spanish, except in San Juan Federal District Court, where English is required. The courts are under the jurisdiction of the U.S. Circuit Court in Boston, but appeals may go as high as the U.S. Supreme Court.

The island's judicial system was unified in 1952 by reforms written into the new constitution. United States legal authorities have described the change as "an almost revolutionary reorganization, which embodies reforms well in advance of those adopted by even the most progressive states." The 1952 reform required the appointment, rather than the election, of judges. It forbade judges to engage in political activity, and guaranteed them substantial independence from the executive and legislative branches.

Regional & Local Government

Each of Puerto Rico's seventy-eight *municipios* has a mayor and a municipal assembly elected during the general voting every fourth November. Until 1968, the capital city of San Juan was an exception; its assembly appointed the mayor, who was really a city manager. San Juan now conforms to the other cities, except that the governor appoints five members of its assembly, in addition to the twelve who are elected. Many of Puerto Rico's "cities" are quite small. Outside of the three largest cities—San Juan, Ponce, and Mayagüez—the average population of the other municipalities is about 25,000. The minority-representation law described under *The Electoral System*, below, also holds true for municipal assemblies.

The Electoral System

Puerto Rico has about two million registered voters and at least 80 percent of them participate in elections, among the highest such percentages in the world. A referendum in 1970 lowered the voting age from twenty-one to eighteen.

Puerto Rico's constitution safeguards a minority voice in the legislature. If two-thirds or more of the seats in either house are won by a single party, the number of seats is increased (by a maximum of nine in the Senate and seventeen in the House). These "at large" seats are reserved for minority-party legislators. If there is more than one minority party, the extra seats are apportioned according to the electoral strength of each group.

Although Puerto Ricans on the island cannot vote in the U.S. congressional and presidential elections, the U.S. Democratic and Republican parties allow voting Puerto Rican delegations at their nominating conventions, and prior to the 1984 elections local primaries of the two U.S. parties were held on the island.

The Party System

Origins of the Parties

The three party tendencies—autonomy, integration, and independence—can trace their origins to the period of Spanish colonialism, and the first political groupings appeared just prior to the Spanish-American War. The autonomy charter of 1897 was achieved largely through the efforts of the group around Luis Muñoz Rivera, the father of Muñoz Marín. The integration or statehood tendency arose immediately after the war and quickly identified itself with the dominant party in the United States, the Republicans. The Republican Statehood Party, the ancestor of the modern PNP, was formed in 1899. Pro-independence sentiment was expressed as early as 1868, in a brief, unsuccessful revolt against Spain (*El Grito de Lares*), but did not manifest itself in a political group until 1912, and then only briefly. Today's independence movement was not clearly identifiable until 1930.

The Parties in Law

In order to register for elections, a new party, or one that failed to earn 5 percent of the votes in the previous election, must gather notarized signatures in at least three-fourths of the voting precincts; total signatures must exceed 5 percent of the total votes cast for governor in the previous election. The usual technique for a party to register is to staff tables at town plazas or shopping centers with a party official and a notary public and ask passersby to sign the necessary forms.

An electoral subsidy law, passed in 1957, provides public funds for party campaigns. The established parties receive $75,000 per year and $150,000 in an election year. Newly registered parties also receive public funds according to the number of votes they poll. The law prohibits personal gifts to parties in excess of $600 a year; to get around this, donors sometimes cosign bank loans to the parties.

Party Organization

Political parties in Puerto Rico have a highly centralized leadership, based in San Juan, the capital. However, some mayors in island towns have established local power bases, and the same is true of leaders at the *barrio* (village or neighborhood) level. Parties do not have formal membership or dues. In the two major parties, party organization is comparable to that in the United States, i.e., relatively loose coalitions of independent local politicians. Power is to a large extent exercised through patronage, which often means doling out federally funded jobs. While there is a professional civil service in Puerto Rico, thousands of jobs at all levels are subject to the influence of the party in power. Other forms of patronage include providing government goods and services, such as materials to help repair homes in poor *barrios*, improving roads in remote rural areas or urban slums, providing electricity and water in such areas where they do not exist or are deficient, and giving preferred access to Puerto Rico's free health services.

Campaigning

Political campaigns are major events. Widespread illiteracy until about two decades ago prompted parties to develop symbols that attract the voter's eye. These symbols are used on posters, flags, car decals, lapel pins, and TV commercials. The PPD since 1940 has used the *pava*, the broad-rimmed straw hat of the rural peasant as its symbol; PPD colors are red and white. The PNP uses *la palma* (coconut palm) and employs blue and white colors on all of its materials. People commonly remark that "I voted with the *pava*," or "with *la palma*."

Television, radio, and newspapers are heavily employed in campaigns. The major parties have hired skilled (and expensive) political consultants from the United States to advise and shape their strategies, but there are also highly sophisticated local consultants who influence the media blitz.

Much use is made of catchy musical jingles. As election day nears, long caravans of cars—horns blaring and banners waving—snake along the highways, creating enthusiasm and a festive atmosphere. There is occasional violence, neither major nor widespread, as a result of these public displays of support for each party.

Independent Voters

The overwhelming majority of the voters have strong party affiliations, although in recent years there appears to have been considerable crossover voting. This is one way to explain why the two major parties get voted in and out of office. Also, the actual number of voters has more than doubled in the past twenty-five years (from 700,000 to 1.6 million) which could partially explain the apparent shift in loyalties. Ticket splitting is possible, but not widespread.

Popular Democratic Party (*Partido Popular Democrático;* PPD)

The PPD was founded in 1938 by Luis Muñoz Marín and a group of left-of-center populists, most of whom favored autonomy or independence for Puerto Rico. The party won a narrow victory in 1940 and continued to dominate the island's political scene until 1969. From its beginnings, the PPD has maintained formal ties with the U.S. Democratic Party.

When Muñoz retired as governor in 1964, he designated his longtime aide Roberto Sánchez Vilella as the party candidate for the 1964 elections. Sánchez won handily, but towards the end of his four-year term became embroiled in party factionalism and personal problems (divorcing his wife of many years and marrying a young aide). Sánchez was not named the PPD candidate at the party convention prior to the 1968 election. With the short-lived People's Party, he drew about 10 percent of the 1968 popular vote, enough to spell defeat for the PPD, whose candidate for governor was Luis Negrón Lopez, a veteran legislator. In 1972, with the young lawyer and former justice secretary Rafael Hernández Colón as its leader and candidate, the PPD returned to power. But Hernández was defeated in 1976 and again in 1980 by Carlos Romero Barceló and the New Progressive Party, but he regained his post in 1984. Born in the southern city of Ponce in 1936, Rafael Hernández Colón is a graudate of Johns Hopkins University, and earned his law degree from the University of Puerto Rico.

The PPD is a major political force in Puerto Rico, in part due to the strong memory of the recently deceased (1980) patriarchal figure, Luis Muñoz Marín, and also because of its long list of accomplishments—a successful economic development program in the late 1940s and the achievement of commonwealth status in 1952, which, despite its shortcomings, gained additional self-government for Puerto Rico.

The PPD favors "permanent association" with the United States while seeking maximum autonomy within that linkage. "Autonomy," however, is subject to many interpretations. Within the ranks of the PPD are those who would support statehood or independence, if an increased-autonomy option were to become totally impossible. Thus, in a sense, PPD support largely rests on a fragile base.

In ideological terms, the PPD would be viewed as centrist or slightly left of center, advocating an important role for the private sector. It was under PPD control that Puerto Rico's "Operation Bootstrap" industrial development program was founded, offering liberal tax incentives to attract outside investment. The PPD also advocates government control of key services.

PPD support is found throughout the island, but in general appears stronger in rural areas, as well as certain sectors of the western end of the island.

Puerto Rico Independence Party (Partido Independentista Puertorriqueño; PIP)

The PIP, an offshoot of the PPD, was founded in 1946. Until that time, the PPD had focused upon economic development and avoided pronouncements on political status. But when Muñoz Marín managed a PPD consensus favoring autonomy, a group of independence supporters bolted to form the PIP. The peak of the PIP's strength, under its founding president, Dr. Gilberto Concepción de Gracia, was in the 1952 gubernatorial elections, when it won almost 20 percent of the vote. Since then it has not drawn more than 6 percent.

Dr. Concepción died in the late 1960s. The party is now led by Ruben Berríos, in his fifties, a lawyer and skilled debater. Berríos won a seat in the Puerto Rican Senate in 1976, but resigned in 1980 to run for governor under the PIP banner. In 1984, he ran again for a seat in the Senate and won. The PIP also won a seat in the House.

The PIP has close ties with the Social Democratic parties of Europe and Latin America, and seeks international support for Puerto Rican independence. The party calls for democratic socialism and is careful to draw a distinction between itself and the rival Marxist PSP. It proposes a peaceful ten-year transition to independence, gradually weaning the island away from its heavy dependence on the U.S. economy.

New Progressive Party (Partido Nuevo Progresista; PNP)

The PNP was formed in 1967 following the plebiscite on the island's political status. Industrialist Luis A. Ferré, a three-time loser as gubernatorial candidate of the Republican Statehood Party, formed the PNP. He called for voters of all political persuasions to support him and on November 4, 1968, he was elected when his PNP edged in with 44 percent of the 875,000 votes cast, compared with 42 percent for the PPD and 81,000 votes for Sánchez's People's Party.

The PNP is the successor of the old Republican Statehood Party, which has long maintained formal ties with the U.S. Republican Party. The PNP no longer maintains such exclusive affiliations. While Ferré is still closely linked to the Republicans, his successor, Governor Romero, in 1976 changed his national party affiliation and became a Democrat, acting on the notion of many younger members of the party that both U.S. parties should be cultivated in support of the statehood idea.

The PNP has strong support throughout the island, at all socioeconomic levels, but seems to enjoy particular strength in the modern, upwardly mobile suburbs. Nevertheless, the PNP does not fit entirely within the common image of the U.S. Republican Party. While it is the preferred party of many conservative businessmen, it has a strong populist element and appeals effectively to certain lower income urban barrios. The latter support has come about because the PNP has consistently said that "statehood" is for the poor, meaning that such a permanent tie with the United States would guarantee generous benefits for the island's needy.

Ferré, now in his eighties, although a popular "father figure," is no longer considered a potential candidate for political office. Former Governor Romero had been the unquestioned leader of the PNP for several years, but a series of government scandals during his incumbency encouraged others in the party to challenge his position. The first was Hernán Padilla, the mayor of San Juan from 1976 through 1984, who is affiliated with the U.S. Republican Party and also served briefly as alternate U.S. delegate to the United Nations. When he sought the PNP nomination for governor prior to the 1984 elections, he was harshly rebuffed by Romero's forces, and abandoned the party to form his own group, the PRP, which siphoned votes from the PNP. The most likely PNP gubernatorial candidate in 1984 (although Romero has not totally renounced his own ambitions) is Baltasar Corrada del Río, who served as Puerto Rico's resident commissioner in Washington, D.C. during the eight years of the Romero administration, and in 1984 won election as mayor of San Juan.

Puerto Rico Renovation Party (*Partido Renovación Puertorriqueño*: PRP)

The PRP was formed shortly before the 1984 elections, splitting from the pro-statehood PNP. Its candidate, Hernán Padilla, won 4.1 percent of the vote. It is unclear whether the PRP will take part in the 1988 elections or whether its members will rejoin the PNP.

Puerto Rican Socialist Party (*Partido Socialista Puertorriqueño*; PSP)

The PSP, founded in 1972, has a Marxist-Leninist philosophy and maintains close ties with Cuba. The PSP was formed from the Pro-Independence Movement (PMI), which had years before (Sept. 22, 1959) broken off as a militant leftist wing of the PIP.

As the PMI, and later as the PSP, the party maintained a policy of boycotting Puerto Rico's elections on the grounds that these were futile "colonial" exercises. However, it took part in the 1976 and 1980 elections, receiving about 3 percent of the vote in 1976 and less than 1 percent in 1980.

The PSP has an estimated core of 5,000 activists, but wields far more influence than that, partly through its widely distributed weekly newspaper *Claridad*.

The PSP actively seeks international support for Puerto Rican independence and, with the assistance of Cuba, is perhaps the main force in keeping the issue alive at the United Nations.

Juan Mari Bras, a lawyer, was for years the key leader of the PSP. But in recent years he has been succeeded by a younger man, Carlos Gallisá, also a lawyer. Gallisá came to the PSP from the PIP, where for a time he shared the leadership with Rubén Berríos and also won a seat in the Commonwealth House of Representatives in the 1976 elections, serving four years.

Minor Parties

The Nationalist Party, a major force between the 1930s and the 1950s, has been disbanded, but some of its older members, considered heroes by many pro-independence youth, continue to make public appearances and pronouncements.

The Puerto Rican Communist Party and the Puerto Rican Socialist League are tiny organizations which make appearances during pro-independence rallies, such as the annual pilgrimage to Lares, site of Puerto Rico's *grito* (literally, "cry"; figuratively, "revolt") for independence against Spain in 1868.

Other Political Forces

Organized Labor

A number of labor unions are active in Puerto Rico, including local organizations as well as affiliates of major U.S. unions. However, union membership in Puerto Rico is not particularly high, due in part to high unemployment (nearly 25 percent in 1982). An estimated 11 percent of the labor force is unionized, compared with 19.7 percent in the United States. The more aggressive unions are in the public sector, perhaps because job security there is greater. The private sector is dominated by subsidiaries of large U.S. corporations which can move elsewhere with relative ease if faced by a hostile labor environment.

The unions with the greatest political influence are those of government employees, particularly those of the Puerto Rican government as opposed to the federal government. If both groups are added together, approximately one in four workers in Puerto Rico is employed by government. Political candidates are quick to point out their support for government wage and benefit increases, and the teachers' union among others is avidly courted by party leaders.

Students

Student organizations, particularly at the university level, while not playing a decisive role in Puerto Rico's politics, have an impact. Most student activists are supporters of independence for the island. The best-known group, formed some years ago at the University of

Puerto Rico, is the Pro-Independence University Federation (*Federación Universitaria Pro Independencia;* FUPI). These student groups have led strikes and protests at universities, sometimes resulting in a partial or complete shutdown. There was considerable foment on campus in the late 1960s and early 1970s as pro-independence students also focused upon the question of U.S. involvement in Vietnam and protested the drafting of Puerto Rican youth into the U.S. military. More recently, in 1981–82, there was a major protest, resulting in a weeks-long shutdown, sparked by tuition increases at the University of Puerto Rico, which operates with heavy government subsidies.

Interest-Group Organizations

The Puerto Rico Manufacturers Association and the Puerto Rico Chamber of Commerce are among the most important interest groups on the island. Also exercising some influence are the Puerto Rico–U.S.A. Foundation and the Puerto Rico Chamber of Commerce in the United States, two organizations of major corporations that have subsidiaries on the island. Other groups having an impact on public opinion and to some degree on government are the Bar Association (*Colegio de Abogados*), which frequently issues studies or pronouncements on major political issues; and the Industrial Mission, a twenty-year-old group largely subsidized by labor and religious leaders, which focuses mainly on issues of environmental conservation and has sometimes lodged class action suits.

Terrorist Organizations

Over the years, clandestine groups causing violence in Puerto Rico have gone by different names. The *Macheteros* (Machete Wielders) first appeared in 1978; since then they have claimed responsibility for killing an island policeman and two U.S. sailors, as well as for raids on U.S. military installations. In 1981, the group blew up nine fighter planes at a Puerto Rico Air National Guard base in San Juan. The Armed Forces for National Liberation (*Fuerza Armada Liberación National;* FALN) is another clandestine group, operating in the continental U.S. and responsible for numerous bombings that have resulted in deaths and injuries. Federal officials have arrested and jailed several persons believed to be key members of the FALN. These violent clandestine groups are

dedicated to gaining independence for the island.

National Prospects

Following the 1984 elections, the victorious PPD sought to reinvigorate the proautonomy movement after eight years of rule by the PNP, which supports U.S. statehood.

Led by Governor Hernández Colón, Puerto Rico immediately became more active in efforts to increase trade and cultural relations with its Caribbean neighbors, and with Central America. This coincided with the Reagan Administration's Caribbean Basin Initiative, a program to boost the economy of the region by promoting trade and investment; and Puerto Rico's efforts were praised by the White House.

Prospects for the 1988 gubernatorial elections remain unclear. A substantial swing vote among the electorate rejected the Romero Barceló government after eight years, because of a combination of factors: a depressed economy; numerous incidents of government corruption; and the scandal resulting from the Cerro Maravilla incident of 1978, when insular police entrapped and killed two young pro-independence activists. Thus far, the economy has recovered slightly, but unemployment remains in the 20 percent range, and crime (caused largely by the widespread use of drugs) continues to seriously diminish the quality of life on the island.

Puerto Rico's unresolved political status is—and will be for years to come—a cause of continuous and fierce debate. Every U.S. administration since the conclusion of World War II has publicly supported the principle of self-determination for Puerto Rico. In August of 1979, the U.S. Congress reaffirmed its commitment to "respect and support the people of Puerto Rico to determine their own political future and to change their relationship with the U.S. through a peaceful, open and democratic process."

However, U.S. presidents have not remained strictly nonpartisan. Because of traditional links between the Popular Democrats and the U.S. Democrats, the Democratic presidents have been the strongest supporters of the autonomy solution. The island's statehood movement has much stronger ties with the U.S. Republican Party, and presidents Eisenhower, Ford and Reagan have come out openly supporting statehood, despite the official U.S. position of allowing Puerto Rico to exercise self-determination.

United States rhetoric on self-determination will only be put to the test when, in the future, a strong mandate is developed for a particular political status solution, and then submitted to Washington for its reaction and ratification.

It appears, however, that such a strong popular mandate will be difficult to achieve. Puerto Rican voters seem to have demonstrated in recent elections that they are less interested in the political status (which appears to many a problem that is virtually beyond resolution), and more concerned about social and economic issues and the effectiveness of candidates as leaders.

This appears to be borne out by the election results since Muñoz Marín stepped down. Voters elected a Muñoz protegé for four years (1965–68); then a Statehood Republican (1969–72); then a young Popular Democrat (1973–76); then a young backer of statehood (1977–80); and in 1980, although the statehood advocate was finally declared the winner, the election was virtually a draw.

Further Reading

Anderson, Robert W. *Party Politics in Puerto Rico.* Stanford, Calif.: Stanford University Press, 1965.

Cruz Monclova, Lidio. *Historia de Puerto Rico (Siglo XIX).* 3 vols. Rio Piedras: University of Puerto Rico Press, 1958.

Figueroa Diaz, Wilfredo. *El Movimiento Estadista en Puerto Rico.* San Juan: Editorial Cultural, 1979.

Lewis, Gordon K. *Puerto Rico: Freedom and Power in the Caribbean.* New York: Monthly Review Press, 1963.

Lidin, Harold J. *History of the Puerto Rican Independence Movement.* Vol. I. San Juan: Author, 1982.

Maldonado Denis, Manuel. *Puerto Rico: A Socio-Historic Interpretation.* New York: Random House, 1972.

Mathews, Thomas. *Puerto Rican Politics and the New Deal.* Gainesville, Fla.: University of Florida Press, 1960.

Pagán, Bolivar. *Historia de los Partidos Politicos Puertorriqueños.* 2 vols. San Juan: Librería Campos, 1959.

Tugwell, Rexford Guy. *The Stricken Land.* Garden City, N. Y.: Doubleday & Co., 1947.

United States–Puerto Rico Commission on the Status of Puerto Rico. *Status of Puerto Rico.* Washington and San Juan: U.S. Government Printing Office, 1966.

Wagenheim, Kal. *Puerto Rico: a Profile.* New York: Praeger, 1975.

———, ed., with Olga Jiménez de Wagenheim. *The Puerto Ricans: A Documentary History.* New York: Praeger, 1973.

Wells, Henry. *The Modernization of Puerto Rico: A Political Study of Changing Values and Institutions.* Cambridge, Mass.: Harvard University Press, 1969.

ORIENTAL REPUBLIC OF URUGUAY
(República Oriental Del Uruguay)
by Richard J. Collings, Ph.D.

The System of Government

Uruguay, a nation of nearly three million people, has recently emerged from eleven years of military dictatorship. After being governed by decree by the senior officers of the armed forces from 1973 through 1984, the country has reinstituted its 1966 constitution and its tradition of democratic rule. Since 1985, the country has returned to a presidential, unitary state with a powerful bicameral legislature.

Uruguay has a long democratic tradition and one of the oldest political party systems in the world; the Colorado and National (Blanco) parties trace their origins to the early nineteenth century. Its democratic institutions, extensive social welfare programs, use of a plural executive, and relative wealth once earned Uruguay the title "Switzerland of South America."

Beginning in the 1950s, however, the economy entered a period of decline from which it has never recovered. Prolonged inflation, economic stagnation, and political corruption contributed to the rise in the 1960s of a leftist urban terrorist group known as the Tupamaros. The army was used to combat the Tupamaros, and by 1972 they had been neutralized. Disgusted with the inability of civilian governments to deal with Uruguay's problems, the military began to actively intervene in politics for the first time in this century. In 1973, the legislature was dissolved and all leftist political parties outlawed. In 1975, all remaining parties were proscribed, and in 1976 the president was deposed and virtually all prominent political figures were stripped of their political rights for fifteen years. Repression was severe and torture of political prisoners was common.

In an attempt to institutionalize and legitimize its rule, the military proposed a new constitution in 1980 that would give it a legal veto over all major public policies. Somewhat surprisingly, the ban on political activity was partially lifted and the document was presented for ratification in a national plebiscite in November 1980. Despite government harassment, elements of the long-suppressed political parties delivered a resounding 58 percent no vote. Apparently stunned by their defeat, the military retained control of the government, but began negotiations with elements of the major nonleftist parties to allow a gradual liberalization of the political process. In 1982, the military lifted the ban on the Colorado, National, and Civic Union parties and allowed them to reorganize. In July 1984, several leftist parties from the Broad Front coalition were also allowed to reconstitute themselves. The Communist Party and several smaller leftist groups remained banned. However, the Communists simply renamed themselves Advanced Democracy and rejoined the Broad Front.

Executive

On November 25, 1984, the first presidential, legislative, and local government elections were held since 1971. Julio Sanguinetti of the Colorado Party was elected president. The Colorados won pluralities in the Senate, Chamber of Deputies, and provincial governments.

Uruguay has experimented with a variety of executive arrangements. While the single presidency has been the most common arrangement, twice the country has experimented with plural executives (1918–33 and 1951–66). The 1950 constitution created a nine-man executive council (*colegiado*); six of its members were from the majority party and three were from the largest minority party. In 1966, the nation returned to a single president elected directly by the people for a single five-year term. During the recent period of military rule, the president was appointed by a Council of the Nation, a body made up of civilians from the legislative Council of State and military officers from the Junta of Generals. Julio Sanguinetti was elected president in November, 1984, with 39 percent of the vote and is scheduled to serve until 1990.

Legislature

The General Assembly consists of a ninety-nine–member Chamber of Deputies and a thirty-one–member Senate (including the vice president, who serves as a voting presiding officer). All legislators are elected directly by proportional representation for five-year terms. Senators are elected from the nation at large and deputies from the regional subdivisions of the country (nineteen departments). Sessions are eight to nine months long. The powers of the General Assembly are extensive and it is one of the few Latin American legislatures whose strength rivals that of the executive branch. Although the Colorado Party has won majorities in the General Assembly for most of the twentieth century, the major political parties are so factionalized that party control of the legislature has been sporadic.

Judiciary

The Supreme Court is the apex of a well-developed, independent judiciary. The five members of the Court are elected for ten-year terms by the General Assembly. The Supreme Court supervises the judicial system, has appellate jurisdiction over cases from lower courts, has original jurisdiction in constitutional cases, and under certain circumstances can declare laws unconstitutional.

Regional & Local Government

Uruguay is a unitary state divided into nineteen administrative departments. The executive power in the departments is exercised by an elected *intendente* and the legislative functions by elected departmental boards. Local powers and functions are quite limited, however.

The Electoral System

Uruguay has one of the most dynamic and complex electoral systems in the world. Most offices are filled by direct election, using proportional representation from multimember districts. With minor exceptions, all citizens at least eighteen years old were required to regis-

ter and to vote. Voting is carried out on secret paper ballots provided by each political party. Voter turnout typically ranges from 75 to 85 percent of the eligible electorate.

The most significant part of the electoral system is the "Law of the Lemas," adopted in 1925. Also known as the "double simultaneous vote," it combines primary and general elections into one contest. Each political party (*lema*) can be divided into officially recognized factions (*sub-lemas*). In national elections, each party faction presents its own candidates for president and the legislature. Voters choose from slates of candidates offered by *lemas* or *sub-lemas* and ticket splitting is impossible.

In presidential elections, the votes of each party's factions are totalled to determine the winning party, and the nominee of the faction that receives the most votes within the winning party is declared president; this often resulted in the nominee receiving the most votes losing the election. For example, in 1971, Wilson Ferreira of the National Party received 383,113 votes, while his nearest competitor, Juan Bordaberry of the Colorado Party, received 325,246. However, the votes of all the Colorado factions totalled 595,408, while the total National Party vote was 584,865. Therefore, as the nominee of the largest Colorado faction, Bordaberry was the winner. During the 1951–66 plural-executive era, the largest party got six seats on the executive council, while the runner-up party received the other three. Each of the parties would then divide its seats among its factions. In legislative races, seats are divided proportionally among the parties, and then proportionally among the factions within each party. Local elections are conducted in a similar faction.

The Party System

Origins of the Parties

The two major parties originated in the armed struggles of the nineteenth century. While the Colorados have their firmest base in the capital city of Montevideo, and the National Party is strongest in the countryside, each party's membership cuts across geographic, class, and occupational lines. The Colorado victory in the last civil war and its pursuit of public policies that brought peace, democracy, and prosperity to Uruguay kept it in power from 1865 to 1959. While the Nationals (Blancos) became a perpetual opposition party, they were a large minority and received significant votes and elective offices. In addition, the factionalization of the two major parties made possible alliances among *sub-lemas* across party lines in the legislature.

The Parties in Law

Political parties are regulated by both constitutional and statutory law. Party activities and elections are supervised by a National Electoral Court. A party that wishes to participate in national elections is required to register with the Court, a relatively easy process. The General Assembly allocates campaign funds for the Electoral Court to distribute among the parties in proportion to the number of votes they received during the election.

Party Organization

Uruguay's two major parties are mass parties. Traditionally, about 90 percent of the population have considered themselves Colorados or Blancos. While some pay dues, this is not strictly enforced. Historically, both parties had significant elements of personalism. For example, José Batlle y Ordóñez (whose father was a party leader and president of Uruguay) led the majority faction of his party until his death in 1929, and his followers were commonly called *batllistas*. After his death, the party leadership was split between his sons, Lorenzo and César, and his nephew, Luis. Jorge Batlle, the son of Luis, is now a prominent Colorado politician. The National Party was dominated for most of the twentieth century by Luis Alberto de Herrera; after his death in 1959, a portion of the party followed the leadership of his grandson. A major faction of the party is still known as the *herrerista* wing.

Because of the proliferation of *sub-lemas* in the two major parties, party organization is somewhat chaotic. Although ostensibly governed from the bottom up through the mechanism of conventions, in fact, each *lema* is divided into *sub-lemas* dominated by a strong political figure elected to the executive or legislative branch and/or associated with one of the highly partisan newspapers. A striking feature of the system is the existence of a large number of neighborhood political clubs maintained by the various Colorado and National *sub-lemas*. The clubhouses serve as social centers, focal points for campaign activity, and as headquarters for the local party boss to distribute patronage (usually providing government jobs or expediting bureaucratic problems).

Campaigning is vigorous: the political clubs pass out handbills, put up wall posters, and operate sound trucks; while the central party organizations make use of television, radio, and their partisan newspapers.

Colorado Party (*Partido Colorado*)

History

One of the oldest political parties in the world, the Colorado Party traces its origins to a successful revolt in 1836 against the government led by Fructuoso Rivera. Named for the color of their headband, the Colorados (reds) gradually evolved from Rivera's armed band into a legitimate political party. During the leadership of José Batlle y Ordóñez (1903–29), the party's military domination of Uruguay was transformed into electoral domination. Since 1865, the party has controlled the executive and legislative branches except for the period from 1959 to 1966 and during the years of military rule (1976–84).

Organization

While the party's greatest strength is in metropolitan Montevideo, it has followers in all parts of the country. The party has a well-developed structure and makes some attempts to encourage internal democracy, but the national leaders of its various factions tend to dominate. Intraparty disagreements are long standing and institutionalized by the Law of the Lemas. While some differences are ideological (e.g., support for or opposition to the plural-executive concept), most are essentially personalistic. The number of major *sub-lemas* within the party has varied from four to six in recent years. No one person has been able to dominate the party for many years. Several highly partisan daily newspapers are publications of the various *sub-lemas* (e.g., *El Día, El Diario, La Mañana,* and *Acción*).

Policy

Colorado domestic policies have been oriented toward industry and the urban middle and working classes, and have tended to neglect the countryside. The party has consistently supported pro-labor union legislation, the expansion of government services and welfare measures, the protection of domestic industries, and a significant role for the government in the economy. In foreign affairs, the party has consistently supported the West and democratic liberalism, but is tolerant of leftists domestically and maintains relations with communist-bloc countries when in power.

Membership & Constituency

The size and composition of party membership is difficult to ascertain. It is safe to say, however, that during the twentieth century, a plurality of Uruguayans have identified with the party. The party's strength has been among the urban middle and working classes, with labor unions, government employee organizations, and many businessmen (especially in government-protected industries) serving as major sources of support. In the late 1960s and early 1970s, however, many young, well-educated members of the urban middle class began to be disillusioned with the traditional parties and gravitated toward the leftist parties and even the Tupamaro terrorist organization. Also, it has been estimated that some 300,000 people, about one-tenth of the population, have left the country for political and/or economic reasons in recent years. As these tend to be members of the urban middle classes, this emigration may hinder the future growth of the party.

Financing

Exact figures on finance are not available, but the largest single source of party revenues is the funds provided by the government to help finance campaigns. Membership dues and contributions from business and labor groups are also important.

Leadership

Since the military takeover, the party's leadership is in flux. Former presidents Juan Bordaberry and Jorge Pacheco appear to have been discredited by their collaboration with the military regime, and many potential leaders were in exile for many years. Jorge Batlle is one of the few party veterans who still commands respect. New leaders include President Sanguinetti, Carlos Manini Ríos, and Vice-President Enrique Tarigo.

Prospects

The Colorado Party emerged from the 1984 elections once again as the largest single party in Uruguay. While it will remain a major political force, internal dissension and its inability to stop the deterioration of the economy will probably prevent it from dominating the country's politics in the second half of the twentieth century as it did in the first half.

National Party
(*Partido Nacional* [Blancos])

History

The National Party also has its origins in the 1836–1838 civil war. The followers of General Manuel Oribe were known as the Blancos (whites, for the color of their headband). While the group formally changed its name to the National Party in 1872, it is still commonly referred to as the Blanco Party. The military and then electoral defeat of the Blancos turned them into a perpetual opposition party. However, as Blanco military and electoral strength remained substantial, the victorious Colorados were forced into a system of "coparticipation." Through a series of "party pacts," the Blancos were given minority representation in the plural executive, on the boards of directors of government-monopoly enterprises, and in appointments to bureaucratic jobs in executive agencies. Thus, although the Blancos were a minority party from 1865 until 1959, they always had substantial numbers of elective and bureaucratic positions at all levels of government. Their leader for much of the twentieth century was Luis Alberto de Herrera. He dominated the party for almost forty years, and was its presidential candidate six times. He died less than six weeks after the Blancos finally took office as the majority party in 1959, and no one of his stature has been able to so dominate the party since.

Organization

While the party's greatest strength is in the rural areas, Blancos are in all parts of the country. Intraparty differences are basically those of personality, and have been less numerous than in the Colorado Party. The number of major *sub-lemas* has ranged from two to four. Organizational discipline has been tighter and internal democracy more limited than in the Colorado Party, with major national leaders exercising more control over their *sub-lemas*. *El País* is the major daily newspaper of the party.

Policy

The National Party has had few opportunities to influence public policy decisively. Usually it has opposed the idea of the plural executive and supported somewhat more conservative economic and social policies than the Colorados. During its eight years in power it made no radical breaks with the past, but attempted to implement policies more favorable to its rural supporters, slow the growth of government spending, and pursue deflationary economic policies. It was unable to reverse Uruguay's economic stagnation, however. In foreign affairs, it has tended to be somewhat more nationalistic than the Colorados, was pro-Axis in World War II, and has been consistently anti-communist. However, no substantial changes were made in Uruguay's foreign policy from 1959 to 1966.

Membership & Constituency

The present size and composition of the party is difficult to determine. Traditionally, most Uruguayans who do not consider themselves Colorados identify with the National Party. Wealthy ranchers, owners of large farms, businessmen involved in the export trade, rural workers, and inhabitants of small towns are the party's staunchest backers. The Blancos appeared to be growing in strength before the military coup. After winning presidential and legislative majorities from 1959 through 1966, the Blancos lost the 1966 election badly, but rebounded in 1971, losing the presidential election by less than one percent of the vote. In 1984, it received 33 percent of the vote, versus 39 percent for the Colorados.

Financing

Like the Colorado's, National's major source of party revenues has been government subsidies. It also has collected dues and contributions from ranchers, businessmen, and farmers.

Leadership

The military coup has destabilized the party's leadership. Wilson Ferreira Aldunate is the leader of the major *sub-lema* and was the party's leading vote getter in the 1971 elections. Ferreira represents a new progressive influence in the party and was one of the most popular political figures in the country in the 1970s. However, he was vehemently opposed to any cooperation with the military regime and was not permitted to participate in the 1984 elections. Ricardo Rocha and party veteran Alejandro Zorilla de San Martín remain influential. Alberto Sáenz de Zumaran, and Gonzalo Aguirre Ramírez were the party's presidential and vice-presidential nominees, respectively, in 1984.

Prospects

The future of the party is uncertain. Party loyalties are so entrenched in the population that large numbers of citizens will continue to consider themselves Blancos, but whether or not the party can sustain the increase in popularity it enjoyed in the 1960s and 1970s is impossible to predict.

Minor Parties

A number of minor parties have had a long life in Uruguay, but have had little electoral impact. In the 1971 elections, the leftist parties tried to break the monopoly of the two major parties by uniting as the Broad Front (*Frente Amplio*). Composed chiefly of the Christian Democratic Party (founded 1962), the Communist Party (founded 1921), and the remnants of the defunct Socialist Party (founded 1910), the Broad Front gained 18 percent of the vote. It received twenty percent of the vote in 1984, receiving twenty-one seats in the Chamber of Deputies and six in the Senate. Its leader, Líber Seregni, was banned from the election. Other influential members of the coalition include

Hugo Batalla, Francisco Otonelli, and José Diaz. The Civic Union (*Unión Cívica*) was founded in 1872 as a Catholic party. Originally conservative, it gradually moved to the left and was transformed into the Christian Democratic Party in 1962. It was revived as a conservative party in 1981 and ran Juan Chiarino as its candidate for president in 1984. He received less than three percent of the vote, but the party obtained two seats in the House of Deputies.

Other Political Forces

Military

Uruguay's armed forces personnel are all career soldiers, who are well trained and highly disciplined. They are primarily equipped to maintain internal order, as their chances of defending themselves against neighboring Argentina or Brazil are slim. The enlisted men come from the lower classes, and the officers from the middle classes (more than half from the rural areas). Before the 1970s, the military establishment was small, poorly paid, and had low prestige and little political influence. During the struggle against the Tupamaros, the armed forces' size and salaries went up dramatically. Today, with approximately 28,000 men under arms, Uruguay's military establishment is twice the size it was in the middle 1960s.

Before the 1970s, Uruguay's military was reputed to be one of the most apolitical in Latin America. Uruguay's *coup d'états* of 1933 and 1942 were staged by incumbent civilian presidents and involved no violence. The officer corps was gradually politicized in the 1960s and 1970s. Dissatisfied with civilian rule and impressed with its success in restoring internal stability, the military overthrew the government and declared its intention to reform the political and economic systems of the country.

No single figure arose after the coup to dominate the armed forces or the government. A number of officers, especially in the Navy, were opposed to the intervention and the torture and repression that followed. Many of these officers were forcibly retired or arrested. Continuity of leadership was made difficult by continuation of the long-established procedure of the top generals and admirals serving only two years before retiring.

The military will probably retain some sort of veto power over government policies, and a return to an apolitical stance is highly unlikely.

Organized Labor

It is estimated that as many as one-third of Uruguay's one million workers were unionized by 1970. Union members were found in virtually all sectors of public and private employment in the urban areas, and included both blue- and white-collar workers. The only true rural union was that of the sugar workers.

For most of this century the labor movement was fragmented among unaffiliated unions and competing labor federations. Despite the Colorado Party's pro-union stance, as the state became one of the country's largest employers, clashes between government and labor increased. By the 1940s, the major labor federation was dominated by communists. Strikes over economic issues and for political purposes were frequent. In 1966, the communist-dominated National Workers Convention (*Convención Nacional de Trabajadores*; CNT) was created. This federation quickly became the dominant element in organized labor. It was outlawed in 1973 when it called a general strike to protest the dissolution of the legislature. The CNT was revived in 1985 and reelected José D'Elía as its leader (as it has since 1966).

Interest Groups

The Rural Federation (*Federación Rural*) is the major political pressure group of the large ranchers. It is well financed and conservative in orientation. Less influential are the business groups, the Chamber of Commerce and the National Chamber of Industries being the most important.

Despite the fact that most Uruguayans are nominally Roman Catholics (approximately 78 percent), the Church has never been a powerful pressure group. Jose Batlle was strongly anti-clerical and succeeded in establishing public policies that restricted the Church's already-limited role in Uruguayan society.

National Prospects

The military gave the government back to the civilians in 1985 because of domestic and foreign opposition to its heavy-handed rule and because it was unable to deal with Uruguay's serious economic problems. However, the generals are seen likely to retain some form of control over leftist governmental activity. Colorados and Blancos are returning to politics as usual, with the charismatic Wilson Ferreira trying to lead the Blancos to victory in the next election. From the left, the Broad Front attacks both parties. Regardless of who ultimately controls the government, it is unlikely that Uruguay will ever return to the relative peacefulness and prosperity that it knew in the first half of the twentieth century. The prospects for its economy look bleak and the forces of extremism appear to be a permanent part of the political landscape.

Further Reading

Biles, Robert E. "Political Participation in Urban Uruguay." *Political Participation in Latin America: Volume I, Citizen and State.* John A. Booth and Mitchell A. Seligson, eds. New York: Holmes and Meier, 1978.

Kaufman, Edy. *Uruguay in Transition: From Civilian to Military Rule.* New Brunswick, N. J.: Transaction Books, 1979.

McDonald, Ronald H. "Confrontation and Transition in Uruguay." *Current History,* Vol. 84, February 1985. "The Rise of Military Politics in Uruguay." *Inter-American Economic Affairs,* Vol. 28, Spring, 1975.

———. "Legislative Politics in Uruguay." *Latin American Legislatures.* Weston H. Agor, ed. New York: Praeger Publishers, 1971.

Taylor, Philip B., Jr. *Government and Politics of Uruguay.* Tulane Studies in Political Science, Vol. 7. New Orleans: Tulane University Press, 1960.

Washington Office on Latin America. *From Shadow into Sunlight: A Report on the 1984 Uruguayan Electoral Process.* Washington, D.C.: 1985.

Weil, Thomas E., et al. *Area Handbook for Uruguay.* Washington, D.C.: U.S. Government Printing Office, 1971.

Weinstein, Martin. *Uruguay: The Politics of Failure.* Westport, Conn.: Greenwood Press, 1975.

REPUBLIC OF VENEZUELA
(Republica De Venezuela)
by David W. Dent, Ph.D.

The System of Government

The Republic of Venezuela is a presidential democracy of twenty federated states plus the Federal District, and two territories and seventy-two islands in the Caribbean Sea. Venezuela achieved independence from Spain in 1821 and in 1830 became a separate republic. Until the late 1950s, Venezuela experienced considerable political instability and long periods of authoritarian rule by members of the armed forces. Democratic governments were incapable of legitimizing their authority and inevitably broke down. The overthrow of General Marcos Pérez Jímenez in 1958 paved the way toward the creation of a viable democratic system that has witnessed five peaceful transfers of power and effective competition between government and opposition parties.

The basic design of the current system stems from interparty agreements and the understandings on moderate reform, conciliation, and reconciliation reached by key elites (including military leaders) during the 1957 to 1961 period. The January 23, 1961, constitution was constructed to reflect these understandings and provide the rules of the political game. The current government of Jaime Lusinchi was elected on Dec. 4, 1983, and took power on Feb. 2, 1984.

Executive

The president of the republic is both the national executive and the head of state. He has the right to declare a state of emergency and to order the restriction or suspension of constitutional guarantees; however this right requires the approval of congress. The president is the commander-in-chief of the national armed forces and is expected to control them. The president also has the power to appoint and remove the governors of the states and federal territories. Finally, the president plays a key role in the politics of the budgetary process.

Despite the relative lack of effective constitutional limitations on the exercise of presidential power, the last six presidents have found that heavy political costs can be incurred by exercising power indiscriminately without a congressional majority. The president must pursue political goals through carefully crafted interparty coalitions that involve negotiation, persuasion, and consultation among a wide variety of legitimate party interests. The president also is circumscribed by a single five-year term; no incumbent is eligible for reelection until ten years after the end of the first term. Presidential hegemony also is weakened by several veto groups such as the armed forces and the corporate and governmental bureaucracies. The media and the president's party also put limits on presidential power. Finally, according to Article 150 of the constitution, the Senate has the power to authorize a court trial of the president, a form of impeachment.

The president is elected by a plurality of votes cast through direct, popular suffrage; he must be Venezuelan by birth, over thirty years of age, and a layman. If the president-elect is unable to take office before the designated inauguration date, the president of Congress takes charge of the chief executive's position until the Congress in joint session sets a date for a new general election. If the presidential office becomes vacant after the inauguration, the Congress in joint session elects a new president by secret ballot to fill the remainder of the constitutional term. There is no permanent vice-president; however, when the president is abroad, the minister of the interior is sworn in as acting president.

Legislature

Venezuela's National Congress consists of a Senate and Chamber of Deputies, both elected by popular vote on the basis of proportional representation. As currently constituted, the Senate (*Senado*) has a total of fifty members and the Chamber of Deputies (*Cámara de Diputados*) a total of 201. Senate candidates must be of Venezuelan birth and over thirty years of age. Two senators are elected from each of twenty states and from the Federal District for a total of forty-two. This is known as the "fixed number of senators." The remaining seats are reserved for minor parties and ex-presidents, who automatically become senators for life.

DISTRIBUTION OF SEATS IN THE SENATE, 1979 AND 1983

Party	1979	Senate Seats (Former Presidents)	1983	(Former Presidents)
AD	22	(2)	26	(1)*
COPEI	20	(1)	14	(2)**
URD	2	—	2	—
MAS	2	—	2	—
TOTAL	46	(3)	44	(3)

* The former president with an AD seat is Carlos Andrés Pérez
** The former presidents with COPEI seats are Rafael Caldera and Luís Herrera Campíns.

PRESIDENTIAL ELECTION, 1983: POPULAR VOTE TOTALS AND PERCENTAGES

Candidate & Party	Total Valid Vote	Percent
Lusinchi (AD)	3,770,647	55.2%
Caldera (COPEI)	2,292,637	33.5
Petkoff (MAS)	276,263	4.1
Rangel (Alliance for Popular Unity)*	220,207	3.2
Others**	272,620	4.0
TOTAL	6,632,374	100.0

* The Alliance for Popular Unity is made up of five parties: MEP, Nueva Alternativa, PCV, Liga Socialista, and GAR.
** The "other" votes include: 32,048 (Jorge Olavarría); 19,282 (Pérez Hernández); 5,999 (Velásquez); 8,719 (Burgoín); 1,111 (Alcala); 1,382 (Ibarra Riverol); 1,640 (Solano); and 2,439 (Romero).

The size of the Chamber of Deputies, whose members must be Venezuelan by birth and at least twenty-one years of age, is determined by a mathematical formula which uses the national population figure to establish the number of deputies in each of the twenty-three electoral districts. The total of these is the "fixed number of deputies": 187 in 1983. At least two deputies must be elected in each state, and one is elected in each territory. The Chamber is also allotted additional deputies for minority parties.

PARTY REPRESENTATION IN THE CHAMBER OF DEPUTIES, 1983

Political Party	Total Valid Vote	Percentage	Direct Seats	National Quotient Seats	Total
AD	3,284,166	50.26	109	—	109
COPEI	1,887,126	28.88	60	—	60
MAS	337,795	5.16	7	3	10
OPINA	130,022	1.98	2	1	3
MEP	129,263	1.97	1	2	3
URD	125,458	1.92	6**	2	8
PCV	115,162	1.76	2	1	3
MIR	103,923	1.59	—	2	2
Other*	421,310	6.48	—	3	3
Total	6,534,225	100.00%	187	14	201

* The "other" minor parties that received seats were Nueva Alternativa (1), Liga Socialista (1), and MIN (1). Thirty-eight other political parties and groups contested the Congressional elections.
** Five URD seats were won through joint URD-AD tickets in five states.

The Venezuelan Congress sits for approximately six months in two sessions: from March 2 to July 6 and from October 1 to November 30. This timetable is modified slightly during the first year of each presidential term when legislative sessions begin on January 23.

The congressional design in the 1961 constitution resembles that of the United States Congress, but in practice Venezuelan congressmen are controlled more by their party caucuses than by interest groups and individual personalities. Furthermore, the power of party delegations (*fracciones*) is not offset by a committee system. Thus, the more rigid separation of powers found in the U.S. Constitution is blurred in Venezuelan political reality.

While the constitution spells out numerous powers of both the Senate and Chamber of Deputies, the Congress is essentially a vetoing agency. It may be a policy initiator only when the president's party is in the minority. Thus, Congress plays its most prominent role in shaping the budget during periods in which the president's party holds a congressional minority or there is a coalition government. The most significant powers of Congress include legitimation of government decisions and allowing for a political catharsis through the rhetoric of debates and delay. The Congress also demonstrates to the general public the democratic values of tolerance and pluralism.

Judiciary

The judicial system's highest court is the Supreme Court of Justice (CJS), organized into three panels—criminal, politico-administrative, civil— of no fewer than five members each. The Congress elects each of the judges for a nine-year term; one-third of the judges retire every three years. In addition, each justice is elected with an alternate (*conjuez*), who sits in for the regular justice in cases where a conflict of interest is perceived.

The powers of the Supreme Court are limited by Venezuela's code-law system of justice. This means that judges have little leeway to make law from precedents. The Supreme Court's authority to rule on the constitutionality of executive decrees and congressional acts is severely limited by its susceptibility to political influence.

Regional & Local Government

The 1961 constitution divides Venezuela into states (*estados*), the Federal District, two federal territories, and seventy-two island dependencies. The governor of each state is appointed by the president and serves at his discretion. Thus, the federal arrangement described in the constitution tends to operate more like a unitary system where legitimate authority is derived from above rather than below. The gov-

ernor's powers center on law enforcement, budget formulation, and national executive policy administration.

The governor of each state is assisted by a unicameral legislature that is popularly elected on the basis of proportional representation. Assembly size varies from state to state within a range from eleven to twenty-three deputies. Neither the Federal District nor the federal territories have legislative assemblies. The most important activity of an assembly is voting on the governor's budget and approving the report of activities and expenditures, but because of constitutional limits on taxation, the states remain dependent on the national government for most of their income.

Local government is carried out below the state level through 156 districts, which are in turn divided into 613 municipalities. The number of districts is determined by the size of the state. They are governed by popularly elected councils that have little in the way of decision-making power. The 1978 Organic Law of the Municipalities instituted greater citizen participation in local government, but national policies continue to dominate local administration.

The Electoral System

Elections are directed and supervised by the Supreme Electoral Council (CSE) composed of thirteen members chosen every two years by Congress. In addition to registering voters, the CSE is responsible for operating the polling booths, tabulating the votes, settling controversies between parties, and ruling on appeals from electoral boards.

Senators, deputies, state legislators, and members of municipal councils are elected on the basis of proportional representation plus a quotient system that provides some representation for minor parties. The electorate votes for party lists rather than individuals. The more prominent members of the party, or independents, are placed at the top of the list; a legislator does not have to be a resident of the legislative district from which he or she is selected.

The CSE determines additional Senate representation for minority parties in the following way. The "national electoral quotient" for the Senate is determined by dividing the total number of valid votes cast in the entire country for legislative candidates by forty-two, the fixed number of senators. Next, the number of valid votes obtained by each national political party is divided by that quotient. That quotient then determines whether a party is awarded one or two senators. For example, if the result is one, then the party is awarded one senator. If the result is two or more, the party receives two senators. However, no party can receive more than two senators. Choosing each pair of state senators by proportional representation makes it likely that the two winners will be of different parties. Thus, population, voting turnout, and party strength determine the level of party representation in the Senate.

Deputies are elected according to a formula similar to that used for the Senate. By dividing the fixed number of deputies (187) into the total number of valid votes cast for legislative candidates in the election, a national quotient is produced. The quotient is then divided into the total number of valid votes obtained by each national party. This calculation can produce as many as four additional deputies per party, depending on the difference between the quotient and the number of seats already won. The two major parties won all their seats directly, while the minor parties can receive direct seats and seats from the national quotient. In practice, the quotient serves to reduce the representation of the second and third largest parties, and slightly increases the number of seats held by the smaller parties.

Citizens are eligible to vote once they have reached the age of eighteen—there are no restrictions in terms of sex, property ownership, or literacy. However, while on active duty, members of the armed forces may not vote. Between the ages of eighteen and seventy, Venezuelan citizens are required to vote; those who fail to comply are subject to a variety of penalties and possible fines. The large voting turnouts have made it unnecessary to enforce this law. With the exception of the 1978 turnout, Venezuelans have always turned out in excess of 90 percent. The reasons for this are only partly attributable to the mandatory voting law. The best scholarly estimates would place voluntary suffrage turnout in the 60–80 percent range.

The voter receives a *boleta única,* or "single ballot," the size of a full newspaper page; it contains a rainbow of colors, pictures, party initials, and symbols. There are large squares for the presidential candidates and small ones for legislative candidates. The voter marks one small and one large square, called a "card" because they resemble the separate cards once used in elections.

The system also allows for "blank" and "null" voting. Blank voting occurs when the voter places an empty ballot in the ballot box. Null voting is the result of placing an improper ballot in the ballot box. Although there is no way of determining whether a nullified or blank ballot is the result of error or intent, the most probable cause is voter dislike of the candidates or parties. Venezuelans have adopted a very favorable attitude toward elections, but approximately 10 percent of the votes are null or blank.

A general profile of Venezuelan attitudes toward the political system would reveal an electorate highly supportive of elections, strongly opposed to one-party rule and military coups, and committed to the need for some form of opposition criticism. The perception of the electoral system as an equitable and fair way to provide representation for large and small parties is certainly a major factor in political legitimacy. Yet at the same time, many are critical of the democratic reformist regime and certain aspects of the government's social-welfare performance. These attitudes reflect on Venezuela's political culture where policy and ideological give and take resemble the dynamics of a "national sport."

The Party System

Origins of the Parties

The roots of Venezuelan political parties can be found in the student and Labor-led opposition to the dictatorship of General Juan Vicente Gómez who ruled with an iron fist from 1908 to 1935. The two oldest parties, Democratic Action and the Communist Party, grew out of the 1928 student uprising against the government's efforts to stifle antigovernment rallies in the universities.

Following the death of Gómez in 1935, political parties began to take a permanent place in Venezuelan politics. Today, the system is marked by two dominant parties, one third party on the left, and several minor parties.

The Parties in Law

The Venezuelan constitution states that "competing political parties have the right to guide national policy through democratic methods." A new party gets on the ballot by submitting either a presidential candidate or list of legislative candidates to the CSE for approval. However, the Law of the Parties states that a political party must obtain one percent of the national vote to maintain its legal status. This process makes for a constant ebb and flow of minor parties in the political system.

Venezuelan parties are financed mostly by private sources; however, the Supreme Electoral Council contributes directly and indirectly to the financing of campaign advertising. Direct assistance is given in postelection grants to parties that have obtained at least 10 percent of the valid votes for congressional candidates. The CSE distributes funds among such parties according to their percentage of total valid votes, which means that Democratic Action (AD) and the Christian Social Party (COPEI) received all government contributions since 1978. Indirect financing stems from the CSE's role in contracting and distributing radio and television time and newspaper advertising space to those parties that received more than 5 percent of the valid votes cast in the prior congressional election. The CSE expenditures represent only a fraction of the total costs of the campaign. Unofficial and extralegal support is also provided indirectly by government employees who work on the campaigns of both major parties while being paid from public funds. The party in power, of course, will have more workers on the public payroll. The partisan advantage the governing party brings to bear on the election campaign is referred to as *ventajismo* (advantage of incumbency).

Party Organization

Party organization varies considerably. The two larger parties aim at being mass-membership bodies with internal democratic procedures. In fact, the traditional style of personalistic coteries around a dominant leader or leaders persists. National conventions and other mechanisms for popular participation serve more to build enthusiasm for the leadership and its policies than to promote grass-roots influence on party policy. COPEI and AD are well-organized nationwide, with branches extending down to the municipal level and even into neighborhood groups in much of the country. Party administration is controlled from the top by a handful of leaders who often compete

for control of regional and local organizations. The smaller parties have very complex organizations, but find it difficult to staff party offices throughout the country. Party penetration reaches into all sectors of society except the military and the church. This makes professional organizations, student groups, labor unions, and many other voluntary organizations susceptible to manipulation by the national party leadership.

There is no uniform method by which parties, coalitions, or other groups select their presidential and legislative candidates. The national convention, where party members and their leaders decide who will represent the party, is most common. In 1967 and 1977, Democratic Action experimented with primary elections to choose their presidential candidate. In both years, these efforts weakened the party and contributed significantly to COPEI victories. Most minor-party candidates are either self-selected or endorsed by "mock conventions."

Campaigning

Venezuelan election campaigns are quite similar to those in Western Europe and North America, but they are longer and more expensive. Recent elections have relied upon extensive use of public-opinion surveys and modern polling techniques with heavy amounts of money allotted for radio and television campaign commercials. The two major parties hired David Garth and Joseph Napolitan, two internationally known campaign media managers. And the Italian Communist Party assisted the Movement Toward Socialism (MAS) by providing expertise in the areas of party organization and publicity.

Although exact figures are difficult to obtain, Venezuela's campaign expenditures are the most expensive per capita in the democratic world. The best estimates place campaign expenditures in 1983 at close to $250 million. At that figure the per-vote rate would be considerably higher than in the United States in 1984.

Venezuelan campaigns are also extremely long, which may explain the heavy costs of campaigning. In 1983 the CSE announced that the official campaign began on April 1 and ended with the election on December 4. However, for most parties the 1983 campaign was well underway by the end of 1981. By that time, the parties had chosen their respective leaders, some of whom became frontrunners for the party nominations. Formal nominations were made during the summer and early autumn of 1982.

Independent Voters

The fact that Venezuelans do not have to declare a partisan preference at the time of registration makes party identification and independent status rather cloudy. Recent studies show that 50–55 percent of the population identified themselves as party sympathizers, 15 percent said that they were not interested, and the rest considered themselves to be independents. The two major parties draw support from all classes, though AD does appear to draw more heavily from those at the top and bottom of the social scale than does COPEI, whose support is more evenly distributed. The left does not gain as much support from the lower classes as the major parties do. Thus voting behavior cannot be reliably predicted from demographic variables. In this regard Venezuela is more like the United States than most other countries in the world. Ticket-splitting—voting for one party's presidential candidate and another's congressional candidate—is possible but not common.

Christian Social Party
(*Partido Social-Cristiano/Comité Organizado Pro Elecciones Independientes;* COPEI)

History

Venezuela's Christian Social Party (COPEI) was officially founded in 1946 by Rafael Caldera, leader of a Catholic student movement opposed to the reform-minded AD party. Since the end of the Pérez Jiménez dictatorship in 1958, COPEI has participated in the coalition government of Rómulo Betancourt and captured the presidency under Rafael Caldera (1968) and Luis Herrera Campíns (1978). The number of people who voted for COPEI's presidential candidate in 1978 represented an increase of 10 percent since the 1973 election. The 1978 victory did not include control of Congress, but the party managed to win a decisive majority of local elections in 1979.

Organization

The party is a relatively homogeneous organization, even though several *ad hoc* groups and organizations have allied themselves with the party. The party apparatus is highly centralized with the highest authority formally vested in the National Convention. The decisions of the National Convention are carried out by the nineteen-member National Committee. Below the National Committee are regional, district, municipal, base, and hamlet committees. Local influence on the national party is minimal. Functional organizations for workers, women, peasants, youth, teachers, professionals, and technicians are maintained.

Intraparty disputes center on generational and ideological differences—the distribution of political power and the economic role of the state. The differences are muted by the need to achieve as much unity as possible in order to defeat the AD party.

A member of the Organization of Christian Democrats of America, COPEI maintains close ties with other Latin American Christian democratic parties.

Party headquarters are at Edificio Santa Ana, Calle Santa Ana, Boleita, Caracas.

Policy

COPEI is identified with policies of educational reform; participatory democracy; the "promoter state;" and specific issues such as housing, agriculture, and administrative corruption. In the past election, Herrera paid relatively little attention to foreign policy. COPEI's victory over Democratic Action in 1978 was based on its ability to gain poor and working-class votes without alienating its middle-class supporters. The emphasis on educational reform appealed to the masses and was presented as a way to enable them to participate more meaningfully in the democratic process. The idea of a "promoter state" was designed to shift power slightly in favor of the private sector while maintaining a creative and socially stimulating public sector.

Foreign policy is based on the principles of international social justice and ideological pluralism. The Herrera administration supported the government of José Napoleon Duarte during the civil strife in El Salvador and moved closer to the United States because of its emphasis on political and economic solutions to the conflict. In the "Falklands Fracas" Venezuela sided strongly with Argentina. Petrodollar aid to select Central American and Caribbean nations, developed under the AD government of Carlos Andrés Pérez, has continued under Herrera and Lusinchi with less gusto. After the precipitous decline in oil prices in early 1986, its importance greatly diminished.

Membership & Constituency

Formal membership in COPEI is approximately 800,000, but only 600,000 are considered to be active in party affairs. While COPEI attracts a broad base of support, the most loyal supporters are urban middle class. In the 1978 election, COPEI drew its support from all regions, but it was proportionately stronger in the heavily populated northwest and weaker in the east. A broader spectrum of lower-class voters gave their vote to COPEI in 1978 than in previous elections, but the winner, Luis Herrera Campíns, drew as much support from the upper class as he did from the poor.

Financing

COPEI party activities are financed by payments from members who hold elective and appointive positions at all levels and by contributions made by foreign and domestic industrialists; COPEI politicians are expected to pay a percentage of their salaries determined by the party convention. Regional committees and individual party members also contribute financially to the party. A small amount of funding comes from the West German Christian Democratic Union.

Leadership

Dr. Luis Herrera Campíns (born May 4, 1925), president from 1978 to 1983, leads the reformist wing of the party.

Dr. Rafael Caldera Rodríquez (born January 24, 1916), former president of the republic, leads the centrist position within the party.

Dr. Godolfredo González is acting president of the party, while Eduardo Fernández is secretary general. Oswaldo Alvarez Paz heads the COPEI bloc in Congress.

Much of what COPEI is today stems from the work of past-president Caldera. Caldera is the only figure from the 1936 generation to retain importance in COPEI. The 1945–1958 generation is more closely aligned with Herrera's group than the generation of 1958 which is now firmly in control under Caldera. It is the post-1958 generation of leaders, such as Eduardo Fernádez and Oswaldo Alvarez Paz who will be expected to carry forward the tradition of democratic give-and-take established by Betancourt and Caldera.

Prospects

COPEI is now facing two serious problems as the 1988 elections approach. The first problem centers on yielding the mantle of power to the younger generation of leaders within COPEI. Internally, the question of succession is causing hardening of the organizational arteries. If Caldera wants the nomination, it will no doubt be his, but this would more firmly entrench the old guard and exacerbate the ultimate problem of transfering power. The second problem is how to present itself as a real alternative to the larger AD party. This means that it must generate a consensus as to how it is going to present itself as a major opposition party. Some leaders insist on a more strident populist approach while others advocate constructive criticism in the mode of a loyal opposition. If COPEI is going to win in 1988, it will also have to modify its elitist image to widen its appeal.

Democratic Action
(*Accion Democrática*; AD)

History

Venezuela's Democratic Action Party was officially founded in 1941 by Rómulo Betancourt, leader of the opposition to military rule and a major advocate of political reform. From 1959 to 1964, AD ruled Venezuela in coalition with three other parties; this was followed by its second victory in 1963 under Raul Leoni, a third victory in 1973 under Carlos Andrés Pérez, and a fourth victory in 1983 under Jaime Lusinchi. The non-titular head of AD was Rómulo Betancourt until his death in 1981.

Organization

Democratic Action is a relatively homogeneous organization with *ad hoc* links to groups of independents associated with the party. The party apparatus is highly centralized, with administrative organs at the state, district, and municipal levels. Vertical control is exercised from the party's National Executive Committee located in Caracas. Democratic Action's regional (state) organization consists of base committees at the grass-roots level. Ideally, these base committees function as channels for demands upon politicians at higher levels and a source of electoral support during election time. The party maintains functional organizations for professional workers, peasants, youth, and women. With the election of Manuel Peñalver as secretary general in 1981, the labor wing of the party has become especially prominent in party affairs.

Intraparty differences have put strains on the efforts of the party stalwarts to maintain unity during periods of national elections. Major schisms in the AD party led to the COPEI victory in 1968. The differences, centered on policy, generational conflicts, personalities, and ideological purity, were eventually resolved by prudent leadership and the necessity of appealing to the broad political center. Economic policies of income redistribution and industrialization have split the party at times, but these disputes are usually linked to personal antipathies and ambitions.

Officially, AD is run by the secretary general and those who head the regional, district, and municipal executive committees. In fact, all political parties are run by a small group of party notables known as the *cogollito*. This informal group usually consists of former presidents and party candidates, the secretary general, secretary of organization, the Strategy Commission chairman, and several talented leaders from interior cities.

As AD has become more explicitly social democratic in ideology, it has established schools for the doctrinal and organizational training of leaders at different levels of the party hierarchy. It has also established loose ties to Social Democratic leaders in Europe, among them Spain's Felipe González and West Germany's Willy Brandt.

Party headquarters are at Edificio Blanco y Azul, Casa Nacional de AD, Avenida Los Cedros, La Florida, Caracas.

Policy

With a majority of the electorate occupying the center-right position within the political-party spectrum, both AD and COPEI compete with each other to see who will dominate this "space." The differences that AD has with COPEI center more on policy implementation than on policy substance or national goals. Two areas of sharp difference, however, are in creation of employment and in the utilization of resources for regional development.

As a social democratic party, AD has been a strong advocate of rapid economic development, gradual nationalization of petroleum production, broad-based welfare policies, and adherence to the Western alliance. The party heavily stresses the need to balance industrial-manufacturing development with growth in the agricultural sector. It is moderately anticommunist, in favor of a mixed economy, and committed to education and agrarian reform.

Past-president Pérez leads the party's "statist" development wing, whose policies stress production over distribution and a more aggressive role in foreign policy. The AD *cogollito*, in contrast, has tended to emphasize a restrained state role, some liberalization of the economy, and a more cautious role in foreign affairs.

The last AD government of Carlos Andrés Pérez pursued policies designed to increase Venezuela's image as a middle-level power in Latin America with its own "sphere of influence." Pérez tried to project himself as a spokesman for the Third World, advocated a new international economic order, and spoke out sharply against military dictatorships. To counter the United States–dominated Organization of American States, Pérez and Mexican President Luis Echeverría created the Latin American Economic System (SELA) to coordinate regional economic-development policies. To further the policy of "ideological pluralism," Pérez reestablished diplomatic ties with Cuba and led the effort to reincorporate Cuba into the inter-American system. However, Venezuela's increased international role led to opposition criticism of AD for not devoting enough attention to domestic problems.

Perhaps the most interesting innovation in Venezuelan foreign policy was the use of petrodollars to further national interests in Central America and the Caribbean Basin. Through a series of bilateral agreements, Venezuela and neighboring countries agreed to allow roughly half of a payment for oil imports to remain in the purchasing country as a long-term loan to promote national development. All six Central American countries (except Nicaragua) plus Guyana, Jamaica, the Dominican Republic,

Peru, and Bolivia receive such developmental assistance. Venezuela also contributes large sums to international and hemispheric banks and lending institutions.

Membership & Constituency

Almost one million members are claimed by AD, representing approximately 40 percent of its total vote in 1978. It draws support from all groups and regions, but its major regional strength can be found in the plains, the Andes, and the east. The defeat of AD in 1978 is at least partially attributable to a decline in urban middle-class support. The party continues to draw considerable strength from workers, peasants, and the poorer sectors of the middle class—in 1973 they provided 80 to 90 percent of its vote. Democratic Action tends to get proportionally more of the rural vote because of its role in pursuing agricultural-development policies such as land reform and rural credit.

Financing

Democratic Action is financed by membership dues, substantial contributions from elected officials, economic interest groups, and wealthy private sector individuals and organizations. Campaign needs also are met through fund-raising dinners, raffles, and social gatherings with the candidates.

Leadership

Carlos Andrés Pérez (born October 22, 1922), former president of the republic, leads the "statist" development wing of the party.

Jaime Lusinchi (born May 25, 1926) president of the republic since 1984, leads the Betancourt faction within the party. He was formerly secretary general of AD.

Dr. Gónzalo Barrios is president of the party; Manuel Peñalver is secretary general. Luis Piñerúa Ordaz, presidential candidate in 1978, is associated with the Betancourt faction of the party and a strong supporter of Lusinchi. Reinaldo Leandro Mora is president of the Congress.

Prospects

The death of Rómulo Betancourt in September of 1981 united AD internally and coalesced forces behind Lusinchi to help him win the largest democratic majority in Venezualan history. In that 1983 election, Lusinchi promised a new social pact that would eventually produce a wider distribution of oil wealth. By the end of 1985, Lusinchi's promise was largely unfulfilled, but the blame goes far beyond either the president or AD party leadership.

AD must continue to maintain its appeal to independents and the politically disinterested if it is to succeed itself in office—something that has not happened since 1964. The Lusinchi administration also must keep its partisans from monopolizing access to government and maintain its appeal to new voters. These are but a few of the factors that make party incumbency in Venezuela a disadvantage rather than advantage for reelection. Thus, if Carlos Andrés Pérez manages to capture the party's nomination for president in 1988, he may be in a rather weak position to carry the party to victory.

Movement Toward Socialism (*Movimiento al Socialismo;* MAS)

History

The MAS was formed in 1970 by former communists who split with the Communist Party of Venezuela over the 1968 Soviet invasion of Czechoslovakia. Led by Teodoro Petkoff, the MAS managed to capture two Senate and ten Chamber seats in 1983. However, as a presidential candidate, Petkoff captured only 4.1 percent of the total vote, a decrease from 5.2 percent for the MAS in 1978. This decline occurred despite the fact that Petkoff was supported by the Movement of the Revolutionary Left (MIR).

Organization

The MAS is a loosely organized party under central control, which means that each presidential candidate assumes personal direction of the party during the election process. The MAS maintains close ties with the Italian and Spanish Communist parties but rejects the label of Eurocommunist; it stresses a nonviolent, evolutionary Marxism associated with the Italian philosopher Antonio Gramsci. Its goal is to establish a distinctly Venezuelan socialist party.

Party headquarters are at Centro Empresarial Miranda, Avenida Francisco de Miranda, Las Ruices, Caracas.

Policy

The MAS has had its problems with intraparty disagreements over strategy, tactics, and leaders. Domestic policy stresses the need to "socialize" most of the means of production and to pursue a more radical program of wealth redistribution. If the MAS were to succeed in capturing power in a future presidential election, efforts would be made to meet the needs of the very poor and to increase worker participation, as well as to nationalize domestic capitalism.

In foreign policy, the MAS espouses the principle of "active nonalignment." This means that the party opposes superpower intervention of any kind (for example, in Grenada in 1983 and in Afghanistan in 1979) because one intervention invariably leads to another as the United States and the Soviet Union seek to maintain their spheres of influence. The MAS expresses solidarity with the Sandinista revolution in Nicaragua, support for the Contadora peace process, and an end to the U.S. economic blockade of Cuba. The MAS supports the Revolutionary Democratic Front of Guillermo Ungo over the U.S.-supported government of José Napoleon Duarte in El Salvador. The MAS would attempt to extend relations to all socialist regimes, while at the same time isolating the United States in hemispheric organizations such as the Organization of American States.

Membership & Constituency

Membership is estimated at 40,000, with perhaps 4,000 activists. The MAS draws heavily from intellectuals, students, and unionized voters in the large urban centers in both the center— Caracas—and other major urban areas.

Financing

There is no reliable information on party financing; most of its resources come from the members.

Leadership

Teodoro Petkoff (born August 15, 1938), is the leader of one faction of the party. Pompeyo Márquez, a senator, is secretary general and moderates between party factions. José Vincente Rangel, the MAS presidential candidate in 1973 and 1978, was the candidate for the Alliance for Popular Unity coalition in the 1983 presidential election.

Prospects

The success of the MAS in attracting voters in future elections depends on its ability to shed its communist image while forming coalitions with other parties on the left. The MAS has done much better in municipal elections but its chances of winning the presidency are remote within the foreseeable future.

Minor Parties

Movement of the Revolutionary Left (*Movimiento de Izquierda Revolucionaria;* MIR)

MIR was founded in 1960 by members of a student movement that split with the Democratic Action. Legalized as a political party in 1973, MIR became sharply divided into two factions, one led by Américo Martín and the other by Moisés Moleiro. The 1981 split eventually led to adjudication of the party name (since both claimed to represent the real MIR) with the court deciding in favor of the Moliero faction because of its more orthodox Marxist-Leninist orientation. As a minor left-wing party, the MIR draws most of its votes from university students and urban workers. It has some regional strength in the states of Lara and Yaracuy. Membership is estimated at 6,000 after the loss of the more charismatic Américo Martín faction of the party.

People's Electoral Movement (*Movimiento Electoral del Pueblo;* MEP)

The MEP was founded in 1968 by disgruntled left-wing members of AD who disagreed with the Betancourt-Barrios choice for president in 1967. The MEP is currently led by Luis Beltrán

Prieto Figueroa(president) and Jesús Angel Paz Galarraga (secretary general). MEP has support among urban union workers and intellectuals, but only obtained one Chamber seat in 1983. MEP considers itself a democratic socialist party with a Marxist orientation, although less radical than that of the MAS. Membership is estimated at 30,000 and activists at 3,500.

Democratic Republican Union (*Unión Republicana Democrática*; URD)

The URD was founded in 1947 by Jóvito Villalba; he still leads the party despite leadership struggles with such figures as Leonardo Montiel Ortega. A personalistic party with democratic nationalist credentials, the URD's policies often mirror those of AD and COPEI. In the 1978 elections URD supported Luís Herrera Campíns (COPEI) and in 1983 supported Jaime Lusinchi (AD). By teaming up with AD in 1983, URD won five seats in five states. Those who vote for the URD do so because of a strong attachment to Villalba; it also has strong regional support in Nueva Esparta.

National Integrationalist Movement (*Movimiento Integracionista Nacional*; MIN)

The MIN was founded in 1977 by the late entertainer and showman Renny Ottolina. His daughter, Rhona, is trying to keep the party and its policies alive by continuing her father's attacks on AD and COPEI as inefficient, corrupt, and overly bureaucratic.

Communist Party of Venezuela (*Partido Comunista de Venezuela*; PCV)

The PCV was founded in 1931 as a Marxist-Leninist party. It has never had any success at the polls. Many of its former members have broken off to form new parties such as MAS and the Communist Vanguard. The PCV is led by Gustavo Machado (president) and Jesús Faria (secretary general), and generally adheres to the Soviet line while rejecting revolutionary violence. The party's history is one of internal dissension over political and ideological matters. Membership is estimated at 10,000.

National Opinion Movement (*Opina*)

Opina was formed in 1967 by the political gadfly Amado Cornielles, who had supported Uslar Pietri in the 1963 elections. As a center-right party with three Chamber seats, it stresses conservative economic policies and the protection of Venezuela's borders. Jorge Olavarría was Opina's candidate for the presidency in 1983.

Other Political Forces

Military

The military became a major force in national politics during the Gómez dictatorship and remained so until the end of the Pérez Jiménez dictatorship in 1958. Since 1959, the armed forces have come to accept civilian rule while continuing to act as a player in the political game. The legacy of past military rule led the architects of the 1961 constitution to define the armed forces as a "non-political, obedient, and non-deliberative institution" designed to protect the newly created democratic institutions. Both the military and democratic institutions have been strengthened by the growth of strong political parties and the acceptance by major groups of the new rules of the political game.

Military leaders come from mostly middle-class families and are trained at the military academy in Caracas, one of the most elaborate career school systems in Latin America. Professionalism is maintained through specialization, a fair system of promotion, relatively high pay, and substantial fringe benefits. High-ranking officers usually attend the Institute for Higher Studies for National Defense in Caracas. The major source of manpower for the armed forces is a system of conscription which tends to draw mostly from the lower classes. Large amounts of money are allocated for literacy training for the more than 20 percent of recruits who can neither read nor write and others with incomplete secondary educations. The military thus serves an important educational function.

The Venezuelan armed forces enjoy considerable autonomy within the political system, at times acting as a corporate pressure group on military matters and occasionally on foreign policy or frontier development. The exercise of military power can be observed in policy struggles over the retention of its share of the national budget (about 6 percent of total government spending). This is one of the lowest relative shares in Latin America and has been cut steadily under democratic rule. Despite boundary disputes with Guyana (Venezuela claims two-thirds of its territory) and Colombia (exacerbated by the discovery of light oil in the subaqueous trench in the Gulf of Venezuela), Venezuela is the only South American nation never to have gone to war with one of its neighbors.

Organized Labor

The role of labor unions in the Venezuelan political system derives from the active role of AD and COPEI in building a network of representational mechanisms for urban and rural workers. At the present time there are three major labor confederations in Venezuela.

The Confederation of Venezuelan Workers (Confederación de Trabajadores de Venezuela; CTV) is the product of AD's early efforts to expand its influence by embracing the labor movement in the 1940s. Today, the CTV represents over 650,000 skilled and unskilled workers in twelve urban federations, and its aims have been integrated into the programs of both major parties.

The Peasant Federation of Venezuela (Federación Campesina de Venezuela; FCV) is also an offshoot of AD's early organizing efforts associated with its land-reform program. Today, it represents over 800,000 peasants in all regions of the nation. The FCV is less active and militant than the CTV.

The United Workers' Confederation of Venezuela (Confederación Unitaria de Trabajadores Venezolanos; CUTV) arose in the 1960s when antigovernment labor leaders split from the CTV to form a union of workers with a more leftist orientation. However, leftists and smaller parties in particular unions or regions may be dominant. It has a small membership of 40,000.

Students

University students in Venezuela have been a catalyst for political change for over a century. Most of the political activity of students now stems from the youth wings of the major parties. But COPEI usually competes with the left within university politics and AD remains a minor force. The parties have their own youth directors at the national and regional levels and the parent parties exercise little control over them. With the rapid expansion of university education over the past twenty years, student politicization has declined to the point that the non-activist half of the student body is more important.

Interest Groups

Among special-interest groups only commercial and industrial interests have a decisive impact on national policy, particularly in economic development issues. The viewpoints of businessmen and manufacturers are made known to the government through the Federation of Chambers of Commerce (Federación de Cámaras de Comercio e Industria; FEDECAMARAS).

The influence of the Catholic Church has never been very strong in Venezuela despite the growth of Christian social movements, the dominant role of the Church in education, and the overwhelmingly Catholic population. Finally, the landed oligarchy has suffered a sharp decrease in power through structural economic reform.

The United States

United States investors and major companies are heavily involved in mining, industry, banking, commerce, and construction. North American influence can also be observed in Venezuela's mass media, various foundations, and a few private voluntary organizations such as the Pan American Development Foundation. Venezuela's role in OPEC and its Caribbean policy have contributed to political conflicts with the United States; currently, relations between the two countries could be best described as cordial.

National Prospects

The future of Venezuela's democratic reformist system will depend on its ability to settle a variety of policy issues—petroleum dependency; foreign debt repayment; industrial growth; economic distribution; agrarian reform; and social-welfare measures such as health, housing, and education—without stagnation or reversion to military rule. The relative legitimacy of AD-COPEI party competition and alternation in power, combined with the limited access provided nongovernmental elites, is likely to continue into the foreseeable future. Yet political legitimacy is still fragile, the rules of the political game are not universally accepted, and uncertainties in the price of petroleum will continue to plague the policy-making process. The way to judge Venezuelan democracy is not to use the United States or Western European governments as a standard, but to assess how far Venezuela has come since 1958 in solving problems of power distribution and organization, governmental legitimacy, and national identity—all without threatening a breakdown of democracy. There is no doubt that the strength of the party system will enable the Venezuelan political system to muddle through future difficulties.

Further Reading

Alexander, Robert J. *The Communist Party of Venezuela.* Stanford, Calif.: Hoover Institution Press, Stanford University, 1969.

Baloyra, Enrique A., and Martz, John D. *Political Attitudes in Venezuela.* Austin: University of Texas Press, 1979.

Bigler, Gene, and Tugwell, Franklin. "Banking on Oil in Venezuela." Andrew Maguire and Janet Welsh Brown, eds. *Bordering on Trouble: Resources and Politics in the Americas.* Washington, D.C.: The World Resources Institute, 1986.

Blank, David Eugene. *Venezuela: Politics in a Petroleum Republic.* New York: Praeger, 1984.

———."Oil and Democracy in Venezuela." *Current History,* Vol. 78, No. 454, February, 1980.

Blutstein, Howard I. *Area Handbook for Venezuela.* Washington, D.C.: U.S. Government Printing Office for Foreign Area Studies, American University, 1977.

Constitution of the Republic of Venezuela, 1961. Washington, D.C.: Pan American Union, 1968.

Ewell, Judith. "Venezuela: Interim Report on a Social Pact." *Current History,* Vol. 85, No. 507, January, 1986.

———. *Venezuela: A Century of Change.* Stanford, Calif.: Stanford University Press, 1984.

Gil Yepes, José Antonio. *The Challenge of Venezuelan Democracy.* New Brunswick, N. J.: Transaction Books, 1981.

Herman, Donald L. *Christian Democracy in Venezuela.* Chapel Hill: University of North Carolina Press, 1980.

Levine, Daniel H. *Conflict and Political Change in Venezuela.* Princeton, N. J.: Princeton University Press, 1973,

Martz, John D., and Myers, David J., eds. *Venezuela: The Democratic Experience.* Revised Edition. Praeger Special Studies. New York: Praeger, 1986.

Martz, John D., and Myers, David J., eds. *Venezuela: The Democratic Experience.* Praeger Special Studies. New York: Praeger, 1977.

Merten, Carole, "Venezuela." *Yearbook of International Communist Affairs.* Richard F. Staar, ed. Stanford, Calif.: Hoover Institution Press, Stanford University, 1984.

Oropesa, Luís Jose. *Tutelary Pluralism: A Critical Approach to Venezuelan Democracy.* Cambridge, Mass.: Harvard University Press, 1983.

Penniman, Howard R., ed. *Venezuela at the Polls.* Washington, D.C.: American Enterprise Institute for Public Policy Research, 1980.

SOCIALIST REPUBLIC OF VIETNAM
(Cong Hoa Xa Hoi Chu Nghia Viet-Nam)
by William S. Turley, Ph.D.

The System of Government

The Socialist Republic of Vietnam (SRV), a nation of some sixty million people, is a communist state reuniting the northern and southern halves of the country. From the Geneva Conference in 1954 to the victory of communist forces in the south in 1975, Vietnam had been divided into the Democratic Republic of Vietnam (DRV) north of the seventeenth parallel and the Republic of Vietnam south of it. The communist victory paved the way to nationwide elections of the National Assembly and the formal pronouncement of reunification under the country's current name in June 1976.

A new constitution was adopted in December 1980, replacing the one that had been in force in the north since 1959. This constitution defines the SRV as a proletarian dictatorship and vests the highest executive and administrative authority in the Council of Ministers. The Council of State serves as the "collective presidency" with a combination of ceremonial and oversight functions. Sole constitutional and legislative authority formally belongs to the National Assembly, the highest popularly elected body. The primary responsibility of the state structure, however, is to give concrete form to policies laid down by the Vietnam Communist Party (VCP) which, in the words of the constitution, "is the only force leading the state and society."

Executive

The chairman of the Council of Ministers is elected by the National Assembly. On his recommendation, the Assembly also elects the vice-chairmen, ministers, and chairmen of state commissions, a total of nearly fifty members. The Council drafts legislation for submission to the National Assembly, oversees all routine administration, manages foreign relations, and performs other functions previously performed by ministries subordinate to a premier. The continuity of the Council chairmanship with the premiership is underscored by the fact that Pham Van Dong, who had been premier since 1955, was chosen in 1981 to be the Council's first chairman. The Council's direct command over the state's bureaucratic resources makes it the most powerful organ in the state structure and a significant resource of power for whomever chairs it.

The Council of State combines the ceremonial functions of a presidency with a role in legislative leadership that formerly was assigned to the National Assembly Standing Committee. Its most important substantive function is to serve as the Assembly's highest continuously functioning organ. It has the power to call the Assembly into extraordinary session, elects the National Defense Council, can issue decrees when the Assembly is not in session, and reviews the work of both the Council of Ministers and the Assembly for compliance with the constitution. The chairman and members of the Council of State are elected by the Assembly from its own delegates, with Council members elected on the recommendation of the chairman.

The first chairman of the Council of State, elected in July 1981, was Truong Chinh, a senior party leader ranked just ahead of Pham Van Dong. Chinh had served as the party's secretary general from 1941 to 1956, and his principal base in the state structure since 1960 had been the National Assembly Standing Committee. His election to the chairmanship in effect enhanced his leadership within the Assembly and added to this a share in the "collective presidency." It is speculated that the distribution of state offices under the new constitution is intended to keep power dispersed among the top party leaders.

Legislature

The Seventh National Assembly elected in April 1981 had 496 deputies, an increase of seventy-six over the number that sat in the National Assembly of the Democratic Republic up to 1975. The constitution endows the Assembly with the "highest state authority" in the SRV. Theoretically, it not only has the highest formal authority to make law and amend the constitution, but also to choose the chairman and members of the two councils. In practice, however, the Assembly's authority is quite limited. Assembly sessions mainly serve to ratify legislation prepared by the Council of State and other organizations over which the party has effective control. Seven "standing committees" and the Nationalities Council take the lead in drafting legislation, and the chairmen of these committees are invariably party stalwarts. The Assembly chairman presides over the Assembly when in session (twice a year, usually for less than two weeks) and serves as its speaker. In 1981, the chairman was Nguyen Huu Tho, who previously had been chairman of the National Front for the Liberation of South Vietnam and then vice-president of the SRV.

Since the Assembly exists in large measure to give legitimacy to party policy, the selection of delegates is carefully controlled. Local committees of the Vietnam Fatherland Front, a constitutionally established instrument of mobilization, nominate candidates "in consultation" with the "working people" and mass organizations and under the supervision of local party committees. Limiting the number of nominations (in 1981, there were 614 candidates for 496 seats) further assures the election of specific individuals whose presence in the Assembly is regarded as necessary. Substantial numbers of party leaders, uniformed soldiers, and state officials typically are among the delegates elected, although care is taken to secure a putatively representative cross section of the population. The Seventh Assembly elected in 1981 was reported to contain the following groups (A delegate will often fall within several categories.):

Workers	100	Prominent	
Peasants	92	personalities	
Soldiers	49	and religious	
Political		people	15
cadres	121	Members of	
Intellectuals	110	handicrafts	
Ethnic		cooperatives	9
minorities	74	Women	108
		Youth aged 23–35	90

Judiciary

The highest juridical body of the SRV is the Supreme People's Court, whose chief justice,

judges, and popular representatives ("people's assessors") are chosen by the National Assembly. Local people's courts consisting of indirectly elected judges and assessors adjudicate criminal and civil cases. An entirely separate procuraturate called the Supreme People's Organs of Control has powers of public prosecution against the state administration. The procurator general is chosen by the National Assembly and administers a system of People's Organs of Control that roughly parallels the state structure.

Regional & Local Government

The SRV is a unitary state consisting of thirty-six provinces, three municipalities, and one special zone. These are further subdivided into 443 districts. Below district level, organs of government are present at village and township levels in rural areas and at precinct and ward levels in urban areas. The formal organs of state authority in each of these subnational levels are people's councils, popularly elected bodies which vest executive authority in people's committees chosen from their own membership. In principle, the people's councils and committees exercise the "working people's right to collective mastery" over the state administration in their respective jurisdictions, and indeed they sometimes enjoy considerable latitude to determine how centrally determined policies will be implemented. However, the rule that their work is subject to review by the next higher level in accordance with the principle of democratic centralism assures that they will act principally as instruments of central policy. Local party organs, moreover, supervise the work of the people's councils, and it is common for the secretary of the local party organ to serve concurrently as chairman of the people's committee.

The Electoral System

The 496 delegates to the National Assembly are directly elected at-large in ninety-three multimember electoral units, with seats distributed among the units in proportion to population. Election for the five-year terms is by secret ballot on the basis of universal suffrage for all citizens age eighteen and over. Citizens can stand for election to the Assembly at age twenty-one. The nomination process is tightly controlled and about four-fifths of all candidates are guaranteed election. The elections are supervised at the national level by an Electoral Council appointed by the Council of State. The Electoral Council oversees the work of electoral committees appointed at subordinate levels by local people's committees. This structure organizes all the mechanical aspects of the election from posting voter name lists and setting up polling booths to counting the ballots. The electoral committees also take responsibility for motivating people to vote and are instructed to assist voters to get to the polls and to take ballot boxes to the homes of invalids, which helps to account for the claim that, in the 1981 elections, 97.96 percent of all registered voters cast ballots.

Elections for people's councils at the various subnational levels proceed in much the same way as for the National Assembly. Delegates are chosen in direct elections every four years for provincial and municipal councils and every two years for councils at other levels. These elections frequently have been postponed on the grounds of extenuating national emergency, however. As with the National Assembly, effort is made to secure the election of council members representing a cross section of the population in order that the Councils can lay claim to exercising "collective mastership" over the instruments of state. Thus women, youth, ethnic minorities, and other groups previously excluded from political participation have attained an enlarged role in public affairs.

Vietnam Communist Party (VCP; *Dang Cong San Viet-Nam*)

History

The Vietnam Communist Party was founded on February 3, 1930, following Comintern instructions that three nominally communist groups then laying competitive claim to Comintern recognition should form a single party. In October 1930, again in response to Comintern instructions, the party changed its name to Indochinese Communist Party (ICP) to reflect the Comintern assignment of responsibility for all of colonial French Indochina. The ICP received the Comintern's grant of national-section status the following year.

The party at its founding had 211 members and perhaps up to 2,000 active collaborators in front groups and the trade-union movement. The principal leader was Ho Chi Minh, who had

been present at the founding of the French Communist Party in 1920, studied in Moscow in 1923, and was a major figure in the Comintern's East Asia bureau at the time of the ICP's founding. Other founders tended to be relatively youthful middle-class individuals with above-average education and nationalist inclinations. Prominent among the founders were descendants of mandarins who had led a violent resistance to French rule in the nineteenth century. To this group, the initial appeal of Marxism-Leninism was its critique of colonialism and the embodiment of that critique in an international organization committed to the end of colonial exploitation.

The party led a furtive existence in its early years. A peasant uprising which led to the isolated creation of village soviets in Nghe An and Ha Tinh provinces during 1930 and 1931 provoked harsh repression: many leaders were arrested or forced to seek refuge abroad. But the party was able to reconstruct itself, finding trained cadres among the thirty to fifty individuals who annually attended the so-called Stalin School in Moscow from 1928 to 1934. With 800 members, the party held its first national congress in 1935. A shift in Comintern strategy and the installation of a socialist-led Popular Front government in France allowed the party to build openly a broad coalition of nationalist movements from 1936 to 1939. At the decade's close, with an estimated 2,000 members and 40,000 followers, the party was the most effective and perhaps the largest organization in Vietnam opposing French rule.

In 1941, the party shifted to a strategy of armed struggle similar to that of Mao Zedong in China. During the four years that the Japanese army occupied Indochina, the party built a front organization called the *Viet nam doc lap dong minh* (League for the Independence of Vietnam, or Viet Minh for short) and gradually assembled a small guerrilla force. In August 1945, a popular uprising spearheaded by party and front activists swept the Japanese-inspired puppet government from power and paved the way for the declaration of independence and establishment of the Democratic Republic on September 2, 1945. France refused to recognize the republic and moved to reestablish its colonial rule, precipitating in December 1946 an eight-year war of resistance. The party's Second National Congress in 1951 adopted the name of Lao Dong (Workers') Party and separated the Laotian and Cambodian sections into nominally independent national parties. On May 8, 1954, as the Geneva Conference opened to negotiate an end to the war, a major French force fell to the People's Army of Vietnam at Dien Bien Phu. The settlement reached in July provided for the regrouping of forces north and south of the seventeenth parallel and elections on the question of unification two years later.

The party left a small core of activists behind in the south, but chose to concentrate on building socialism in the north. One component of this effort, land reform, was successful in its goal of redistributing land and laying a basis for cooperativization. However, the reform provoked such opposition over the way it was conducted that in 1956 the party secretary general, Truong Chinh had to resign. Le Duan, a leader closely identified with southern interests, took over administration of the party. In the same period, the Saigon government refused to hold discussion on reunification and mounted a campaign to stamp out all opposition. By the late 1950s, the party organization in the south had dwindled to about 5,000 members, or one percent of the national total. After a sharp debate, the Central Committee decided in early 1959 to commence preparations for a reunification struggle, by armed means if necessary. This decision received ratification at the party's Third National Congress in September 1960, at which Le Duan was formally elected first secretary. A subsequent Central Committee decision in December 1963 authorized the introduction of People's Army regulars into the south a year later. Due to the intensity of the war that followed, highlighted by massive American intervention in the south and bombardment of the north, the party was able to make only very slow progress developing socialism. When the war ended, pressures within the party were strong for resuming socialist construction in the north and integrating the south into a single socialist framework. The Fourth National Congress in December 1976 ratified this program, adopted the current name of Vietnam Communist Party, and reelected Le Duan as head of the party with the title of secretary general.

Organization

Growing out of a struggle for national independence and unity, much of it in conditions of enforced clandestinity, the VCP is a highly unified, ideologically uniform, cadre party organized on the Leninist model. Its leaders, who participated in the party's founding or joined during the 1930s and have ruled the party up to the present, exhibit a high degree of solidarity. Shared experience has been an important bond among these leaders. Stability and consensual decision making have been hallmarks of VCP leadership at the highest levels, but are not likely to remain so when new leaders come to power.

The party rules place ultimate authority in the National Congress. In theory delegates are to be chosen by indirect election through a pyramid of congresses every five years, conditions permitting, which has never been the case. Indeed, the failure to ever hold a congress on schedule and the gaps of sixteen, nine, and sixteen years between the congresses up to 1976 have few parallels in the communist world. Since then a congress was held in 1982 and another is scheduled for late 1986.

The National Congress ratifies broad policy guidelines and elects the Central Committee, the executive authority of the party between congresses. The Central Committee is the center of formal authority in the party: the party regulations give it the power to determine when national congresses will be held, to specify what issues will be discussed at congresses, to conduct relations with other communist parties, and to make policy decisions that are absolutely binding on all party members. The Committee also elects the secretary general, a Secretariat to oversee routine administration of the party, and the Political Bureau which is charged with executing Committee resolutions. However, while the Central Committee seldom meets more than the stipulated minimum of two times a year, the Political Bureau is frequently in session and normally turns to the Committee only for broad policy guidelines and approval of decisions it already has made. The Political Bureau, whose membership is coterminous with the highest-ranking and most prestigious core of leadership, has considerable latitude to rule as it sees fit.

Disagreements within the Political Bureau, as throughout the party, have on occasion been sharp. The most durable disagreement concerns the relative weight to be assigned to the socialist reform of society as opposed to meeting immediate production needs, a disagreement which may be characterized crudely as dividing "ideologues" and "pragmatists." Another disagreement which lasted from 1954 to 1975 was over reunification, with the high point occurring in the late 1950s when some members, particularly those associated with southern affairs, perceived the line emphasizing political rather than armed struggle as verging on a sellout of the cause. And since 1975, foreign policy issues have been quite divisive. At one time some analysts claimed to discern stable factions in the Political Bureau based on individuals' supposed "pro-Moscow" or "pro-Beijing" orientations. It is now generally agreed that differences over Sino-Soviet issues always have been more reflective of differing assessments of the Vietnamese national interest than of ideological quarrels. Moreover, other issues have been equally or more compelling, and these issues have created alliances which are cross-cutting and shifting rather than stable. While disagreements among Political Bureau members occasionally have been sharp, they have not been polarizing. Were the Politburo to become deadlocked, the Central Committee conceivably could be called upon to arbitrate, but such a situation seems not to have arisen. The consensual orientation of Political Bureau members, their exceptional personal status, and the Central Committee's cumbersome size help to keep the locus of decision within the Bureau.

The Fourth National Congress in December 1976 undertook to rejuvenate a Central Committee whose composition had changed little over the preceding sixteen years. Of the 101 full members and thirty-two alternates elected, raising the total membership from seventy-seven to 133, 65 percent were new to the Committee. Many of the new people had worked their way up through the southern party organization during the war or had education that qualified them for leadership in peacetime development. The percentage of military officers declined from 30 to 23.

That Central Committee in turn elected a Political Bureau of fourteen full and three alternate members. The one member who did not win reelection, Hoang Van Hoan, evidently had refused to support the consensus on foreign policy and eventually defected to China. Five of the six new members represented a slightly younger transitional generation and included three who, years earlier, had been elected in secret while serving in the war in the south.

At the Fifth Congress in March 1982, the changes in leadership were equally far-reaching. Forty-nine members of the Central Committee failed to win reappointment and sixty-eight new members were elected, giving the Committee 116 full members and thirty-six alternates for a total of 152. Six men, including four senior leaders (of whom the best known was General Vo Nguyen Giap, followed by Nguyen Duy Trinh, Le Thanh Nghi, and Tran Quoc Hoan), were dropped from the Political Bureau and four new ones were appointed. The number of full bureau members dropped to thirteen and alternates to two for a total of fifteen. No general pattern was discernible in these changes other than a continuing effort to ease some older leaders into retirement and bring in younger people. From statements made by leaders at the congress, it may be surmised that a few individuals lost their positions due to association with failed programs, opposition to current policies, or corruption, but the identity or number of such cases cannot be determined with much precision. One member who was dropped, Nguyen Van Linh, an advocate of controversial reforms, was reinstated in June 1985 (raising the membership to sixteen). Two new members of the Political Bureau were military officers in charge of operations in Kampuchea and of communication and transportation, apparent concessions to the army's paramount role in these areas. Perhaps most noteworthy, however, was the absence of any change at all in the inner circle of five septuagenarians who hold the highest posts. These men obviously chose to exclude themselves from the process of generational succession, and due to their extraordinary prestige in the party, it is unlikely that anything but their own mortality can remove them from office against their will.

The authority of the party's central organs passes down through party committees for each province, municipality, township, district, and urban precinct or ward. These committees are chosen every two years in local congresses and in turn elect their own secretaries, subject to approval by the next-higher echelon. At still-lower levels—industrial enterprises, villages, state agencies, cooperatives, and military units—the party is further articulated into "basic level committees" or "chapters" depending on whether there are more or less than thirty members present. Through overlapping membership between party committees and the leadership of other organizations throughout society, the party assures that its policies are carried out.

All mass organizations are at least indirectly subject to the party's guidance, but one qualifies unambiguously as an auxiliary: the Ho Chi Minh Communist Youth Union, provision for which is made in the party regulations. Described as a "school of communism for youth," the union has its own vertical structure of committees extending down into schools, military units, or wherever people under thirty are concentrated. Participation in union activities is designed to instruct youth in Marxism-Leninism, to elicit support for party policies, and to determine eligibility for admission to the party.

The most important publications dealing with party affairs are the daily newspaper published under the auspices of the Central Committee, *Nhan dan* (The People), and the monthly political and theoretical journal, *Tap chi Con san* (The Communist). The Youth Union has its own organ, *Thanh nien* (Youth).

Policy

The VCP seeks to transform Vietnam into a modern, industrialized, socialist society more or less along Soviet–East European lines through three simultaneous "revolutions" in (1) the relations of production, (2) ideology and culture, and (3) science and technology. Of the three, the "scientific and technological revolution" is the "key."

In June 1977, the central Committee authorized an accelerated program of agricultural cooperativization in the south and the consolidation of cooperative management at the district level in the north. A campaign in March 1978 sought to abolish private trade in the south. But these policies provoked popular resentment and contributed to a per capita decline in agricultural production. Failure to attract foreign aid in the amount originally anticipated coupled with the economic costs of military conflict with Cambodia and China added to the factors that forced the leadership to reconsider its policies. At its sixth plenum in September 1979, the Central Committee approved a major policy shift permitting the enlargement of the free market under state supervision and emphasis on material incentives. These reforms and an agricultural production contract system that was launched in 1980 improved the economic situation but sparked ongoing controversy.

In foreign affairs, the VCP's central preoccupations have been Vietnamese national independence and unity within the context of an international communist movement. Up to 1975, party leaders maintained that Vietnam held center stage in the global conflict between communist and capitalist "camps" and therefore was entitled to the support of other communist parties. Their decision in 1959 to prepare for

armed struggle opposed them to the Soviet line on peaceful coexistence and aligned them with China's position on wars of national liberation. A brief tilt toward China on Sino-Soviet issues resulted. More typically the Vietnamese attempted to mediate the Sino-Soviet dispute in the belief that they stood to gain more from bloc unity (and cooperation in aiding Vietnam) than from division. But China's rapprochement with the United States and stake in the maintenance of American power in Asia convinced the Vietnamese that China's strategic interests were incompatible with those of Vietnam. Lingering suspicions of Han chauvinism and the Soviet Union's superior ability to contribute to Vietnam's development provided additional incentives for VCP leaders to accept Soviet offers of a closer relationship. The Soviet Union provided the relatively sizable sum of $2.5 billion for the SRV's 1976–80 state plan; in June 1977 the SRV acquired full membership in the Council for Mutual Economic Assistance (CMEA, or Comecon); and in November it joined the Soviet Union in signing a Treaty of Friendship and Cooperation.

Toward the noncommunist states of Southeast Asia, VCP leaders harbor distrust. They regard the other states as ideological foes, but have adopted an ostensibly conciliatory attitude. They hold Thailand responsible for destruction caused by American planes based on Thai soil during the last war and recognize the Thai as traditional rivals for power on the Southeast Asian mainland. But since 1978, in an effort to dissuade noncommunist Southeast Asian governments from deepening their dependence on the United States and China and to win their acceptance of the Vietnamese-installed regime in Cambodia, they have found it expedient to express interest in the concept of a Southeast Asian zone of "peace, freedom, and neutrality" advocated by the noncommunist states.

The VCP's exact intentions and motives regarding Laos and Cambodia are the subject of speculation. The party was charged by the Comintern at its founding with responsibility for all of Indochina, party resolutions up to 1951 indicated an aim to establish an Indochina Federation, and the Vietnamese assumed a tutelary role in the development of communist movements in Laos and Cambodia. Since 1975 VCP leaders have insisted upon establishing a "special relationship" among the three states of Indochina. While they now vehemently disavow the federation concept and there is no evidence of movement toward institutional integration, the "special relationship" does call for coordination of policies through consultations in which the Vietnamese are dominant. Vietnamese behavior over the years suggests that VCP policy has been motivated primarily by strategic requirements rather than by an ideological imperative or urge to territorial expansion. Chinese hostility and Thai collusion with outside powers to influence events in Laos and Cambodia are seen by VCP leaders as requiring Vietnam, in the interest of its own security, to maintain client regimes in these states.

On issues of importance to the Soviet Union, the VCP follows the Soviet line. It supports Soviet initiatives on arms control, identifies the United States as the principal enemy, and echoes the Soviet interpretation of events in Afghanistan and Poland. The SRV joined the Conference of Nonaligned Nations, but has followed Cuban initiatives in that movement. However, Vietnam also is one of the few CMEA countries to hold membership in the International Monetary Fund and the World Bank, which it attained by succeeding to seats previously held by the Saigon government. These involvements suggest a desire, thus far unrealized, to diversify economic contacts and avoid excessive dependency on any one country.

Little is known about intraparty opposition aside from the fact that some divergent tendencies exist. An influential group centered upon Truong Chinh was reluctant to accept the relaxation of socialist controls in 1979 and opposes any suggestion that supposedly emergency measures be made permanent parts of the development model. And in foreign affairs, there are misgivings about Soviet reliability, the costs of dependence, and the wisdom of prolonged confrontation with China. Such opposition, however, is insufficient to compel major policy changes in the circumstances which have prevailed since the late 1970s.

Membership & Constituency

The VCP in 1976 had 1,553,500 members, or 3.13 percent of the population, almost double the membership a decade earlier. The party's rapid growth in that period was attributed to wartime requirements and lax admission standards. Of the total, 273,000 were enrolled in the party's southern organs, a figure which represented enormous growth despite the loss of

many thousands to death, defection, and fatigue.

In 1976 the party initiated a review of the membership which continued up to the Fifth National Congress in 1982. The purpose was to weed out "substandard" members based on infirmity, incompetence, corruption, or lack of zeal in supporting current policies. At the same time, a campaign was launched to recruit new members, particularly educated ones, between the ages of eighteen and thirty. Just over 90 percent of all new members were from this age group (the majority from the armed forces), which brought the average age down to thirty-nine. Total membership in 1982 remained at the same level as in 1976, reflecting the shift from quantity to quality in recruitment priorities.

Due to the agrarian character of Vietnamese society, the party historically has had to rely heavily on the rural population for members and on persons of middle-class background for educated leadership. The majority of members has been depicted as "middle peasant" and "petit bourgeois intellectual" in origin. This state of affairs has been seen as inappropriate since the shift in priorities from national reunification to socialist reform, and so in 1976 the party intensified efforts to enlarge the proposition of workers in its ranks. The small size of the industrial proletariat, however, severely limits this effort, and in 1982 individuals classified as workers accounted for only 9 percent of the membership.

Financing

All members pay a percentage of their basic incomes (i.e., excluding rations and special allowances) in party dues. The Central Committee fixes this percentage, imposes special levies, and administers party finances. The percentage of income to be paid in dues and the amount collected from all sources are unknown.

Leadership

The membership of the Political Bureau elected at the Fifth National Congress in March 1982 averaged sixty-nine years of age, if four members whose ages are not known are excluded. Le Duan and Truong Chinh were 74 and Pham Van Dong 76. With all five members of the inner circle aged seventy and older, a decisive shift of power toward younger leaders is inevitable in the next few years. Six members were born in the northern third of the country (Tonking), five in the center (Annam), one in the south (Cochinchina), and the origins of two are unknown. As of July 1985, Political Bureau members' rank order and positions were as shown in the accompanying table.

MEMBERS OF THE VIETNAM COMMUNIST PARTY POLITICAL BUREAU AND THEIR RESPONSIBILITIES
(July 1985)

	Position in Central Party Organs			Position in Central Government			Other Positions
	Secretariat	Central Committee Department headed by	Central Military Party Committee	State Council	Council of Ministers	National Defense Council	
FULL MEMBERS (year of birth) Le Duan (1908)	Secretary General		Secretary				
Truong Chinh (1908)		Research on Party History		Chairman		Chairman	
Pham Van Dong (1906)					Chairman	Vice-Chairman	
Pham Hung (1912)					Vice-Chair.; Minister of Interior	Member	
Le Duc Tho (1910)	Member		Deputy Secretary				
Van Tien Dung (1917)			1st Deputy Secretary		Minister of National Defense	Member	
Vo Chi Cong (1912)	Member						
Nguyen Van Linh (1915)							Sec'y Ho Chi Minh City Party Committee
Chu Huy Man (1920)			Deputy Secretary	Vice-Chair.			Head, Army General Political Directorate
To Huu (1920)					Vice-Chair.	Member	Vice-Pres. VN Arts and Letters Federation
Vo Van Kiet (n.a.)					Vice-Chair.; Chairman of State Planning Commission		Chair, Joint Party/ Gov't Committee on Zoning Economic Areas
Do Muoi (1910)					Vice-Chair.		Commander, People's Army in Kampuchea
Le Duc Anh* (n.a.)			Member				
Nguyen Duc Tam* (n.a.)	Member	Organization					
ALTERNATE MEMBERS Nguyen Co Thach* (1920)					Minister of Foreign Affairs		
Dong Si Nguyen* (n.a.)				Vice-Chair.; Minister of			

* New members elected at the Fifth National Party Congress in March 1982.

The Political Bureau contains two distinct leadership generations: one composed of men over seventy who joined the party at its founding or shortly thereafter, the other of men in their sixties who joined in the late 1930s and 1940s. Successors to the senior leadership no doubt will come from the latter group, though by the time they accede to the top posts many of them will themselves be quite old, so their leadership may be only transitional. The younger figure who has risen most rapidly is To Huu (born 1920), who appears to be a protege of Le Duan.

Satellite Organizations

The VCP guides the work of several organizations whose purpose is to mobilize broad national support for party policies. These are the Vietnam Fatherland Front, the Vietnam Confederation of Trade Unions, the Vietnam Association of Collective Peasants, the Vietnam Women's Union, and two supposedly independent political parties. The Fatherland Front succeeded the Viet Minh in 1955 as the principal institutional expression of the united-front concept. It is responsible for securing broad-based popular participation in public affairs and building the alliance of workers, peasants, and intelligentsia which is the supposed bulwark of the regime. In 1976, the Front absorbed two organizations which performed similar functions during the war in the south—the National Front for the Liberation of South Vietnam (1960–76) and the Alliance of National Democratic and Peace Forces (1968–76)—to form a National Unity Front. The name reverted to Vietnam Fatherland Front following a congress in February 1977 at which the Front dedicated itself to uniting "all the people in the name of building a peaceful, independent, united, and socialist Vietnam."

The Confederation of Trade Unions, the Association of Collective Peasants, and the Women's Union fulfill much the same purpose as the Fatherland Front but within their appropriate groups. These organizations also sponsor campaigns in support of specific programs, such as agricultural cooperativization or improvements in the status of women. The two political parties, the Vietnam Democratic Party and the Vietnam Socialist Party, purport to represent the interests of bourgeois elements in society, but have little substance and function as constituent parts of the Fatherland Front.

Other Political Forces

Military

The VCP organized the first unit of the People's Army of Vietnam (PAVN) in December 1944 out of guerrillas and political cadres it had been preparing to lead an armed struggle since 1941. The first commanders, who went on to hold the highest positions in the Vietnamese Communist military establishment, had joined the party prior to that time and already had established themselves as party leaders. Very few had had any professional military training. The fusion of party and military leaderships and the homogeneity of their experience have helped to temper civilian-military conflicts even while they have guaranteed that the military will have a large role in the political process.

Disputes involving the military have not divided civilian and military leaderships so much as they have divided generations or functional groups. Thus a sharp disagreement during the mid-1960s over strategy and tactics pitted advocates of guerrilla-style "people's war" against proponents of "big unit" semiconventional war. The dispute cut across civilian-military lines. The characteristics of PAVN leadership began to change, however, with the emergence in 1975 of a professionally oriented generation of top commanders, many of them trained in the Soviet Union . Such officers resisted the decision made by state planners at war's end to assign military units and resources on a vast scale to economic work. The tendency of professional officers to focus on their strictly military mission and to resist political supervision has grown more pronounced, but firm traditions of military subservience to the party and civilian-military integration at leadership levels help to guarantee that the PAVN's political role, although influential, will remain legitimate.

Ethnic Groups

The regime recognizes 54 ethnic minorities comprising 16 percent of the population. Most of the minority population is scattered throughout the mountain chain that stretches from the Chinese border to the edge of the Mekong delta. The nine largest groups number from 200,000 to 900,000 people each, and two of these, the Tay and Nung, were important bases of support for the communists in the war against France.

The ethnic groups traditionally have resisted intrusion by the lowland Vietnamese and traded their political allegiance for guarantees of autonomy. Several northern groups that sided with the French in the First Indochina War continued to fight the Hanoi government until 1956. In the south, an alliance of minorities called the *Front Unifié pour la Lutte des*

Races Opprimées (FULRO) revolted against the Saigon government in 1964. The tendency of some minority groups to resist central control and to accept external support for this purpose has not completely disappeared. Following its "punitive attack" across Vietnam's northern border in 1979, China had some success in turning border-straddling minorities against the Hanoi government. Further south, armed bands claiming to be FULRO units, with the moral and possible material support of Cambodia's Khmer Rouge, for a time harassed roads, lines of communication, and security forces.

Minority grievances usually focus upon government efforts to populate highland areas with lowland Vietnamese and to exploit the highlands' economic potential under central administrative direction. However, the minorities are too diverse and dispersed ever to form a unified bloc against these policies. The government seeks to minimize minority dissidence further by assimilation through education, employment, resettlement, and economic development.

Religious Groups

The single largest religion in Vietnam is Buddhism, claiming a majority of the population as adherents. Buddhism traditionally has lacked unifying structures, and only rarely provided a basis for organized political action, as when monks immolated themselves and led demonstrations to help bring down the Saigon Ngo Dinh Diem regime in the south in 1963. Partially successful attempts to build such structures were made during the 1950s and 1960s, but sectarianism, personal rivalries, and divergent political allegiances remained obstacles to clerical unity.

The Communist Party claims to have no quarrel with the Buddhist faith, its practice, or its educational and welfare activities. However, refusal by some orders to cooperate with the regime has resulted in the conversion of their pagodas to public use and the "reeducation" of their clergy. In November 1981, the country's nine Buddhist organizations and sects, with the party's blessing, formed a single Vietnam Buddhist Church. Its charter makes clear that it is a constituent element of the Vietnam Fatherland Front charged with mobilizing its followers to support the regime as well as with propagating the faith. In return for political acquiescence, the regime guarantees freedom of religious observance and provides modest support for the education of clergy.

Better organized and more cohesive than the Buddhists are the Catholics, who comprise 8 to 10 percent of the population. Once a strong factor in the north, many Catholics sided with the French during the First Indochina War and roughly 600,000 of them found it expedient to join the exodus to the south at war's end. The Church organization that remained behind was much weakened, and its activities were severely restricted. Northern refugees swelled the Catholic community in the south to form the bulwark of Saigon's anticommunist regimes.

Since reunification, some Church leaders have indicated willingness to cooperate with the regime so long as basic religious freedoms are preserved, but the regime has closed many Church-related institutions and placed a number of clergy in "reeducation" camps. The Communist Party maintains that the Catholic Church represents an exploitative elite allied with imperialism which must be "reformed" so as to make it harmless to national security and an instrument of state on the lines of the Vietnam Buddhist Church. The clergy itself is divided over how to adapt, if at all, to the new circumstances, and the party seeks to exploit these "contradictions" between "inveterate reactionaries" and "progressives and partisans of adaptation" in order to increase its influence in the Church's internal affairs. By securing the appointment of cooperative clergy to Church bodies, reducing Church income, and restricting Church social activities, the party hopes to turn it into a compliant, preferably supportive component of the new socialist society.

Two other religious groups that have played important political roles in the past are the Hoa Hao and the Cao Dai sects. Both sects originated in the south, had millinerian and traditionalist tendencies, once maintained their own armed forces, and flirted with the Communists, but ended on the side of the Saigon government. Moreover, both sects' members were geographically concentrated, giving each a degree of territorial autonomy which made them difficult for any government or political movement to control. Since 1975, the regime has extended its administrative apparatus into Cao Dai areas and promoting its development programs there, but the Hoa Hao, or elements of it, have offered resistance and members of the hierarchy have been imprisoned. Figures which show cooperativization to be proceeding more slowly in the two provinces where the Hoa Hao and Cao Dai are concentrated (An Giang for the Hoa Hao, Tay Ninh for the Cao Dai) confirm the refractory character of these sects.

National Prospects

The Vietnamese revolution brought about an improvement in economic equity for the Vietnamese people, but the SRV is likely to remain for a long time one of the poorest countries in Asia. Vietnam's significant lag in growth behind its neighbors, due in part to internal factors over which the regime has had limited control, is exacerbated by foreign policies which placed up to 200,000 Vietnamese troops (reduced to 100,000 in 1985, according to a Hanoi source) in Cambodia, provoked a Chinese policy of "bleeding" Vietnam into submission, incurred the enmity of other Southeast Asian states, and alienated noncommunist aid donors. The VCP leadership adopted more flexible development policies in 1979 partly to gird the country for a prolonged period of hardship in a context of international hostility. The SRV must in consequence maintain a close relationship with the Soviet Union, which has a strategic interest in transforming Vietnam into a strong ally against China and as a base from which it can enhance its naval presence in the western Pacific and Indian oceans. These policies, and the indefinite deferral of popular material aspirations that they imply, have a corrosive effect on the morale of party members and on the party's hard-won legitimacy, but not so much as to endanger the party's control. Though a new generation of leaders could succeed to top posts at the Sixth Party Congress tentatively scheduled for November 1986, major policy changes on either the domestic or international fronts are unlikely.

Further Reading
Communist Party of Vietnam. *Fifth National Congress: Political Report.* Hanoi: Foreign Languages Publishing House, 1982.

Duiker, William J. *Vietnam Since the Fall of Saigon.* Athens, Ohio: Ohio University Center for International Studies, Southeast Asia Series Number 56, rev. ed., 1985.

————. *The Communist Road to Power in Vietnam.* Boulder, Colo.: Westview Press, 1982.

Elliott, David P. "North Vietnam Since Ho." *Problems of Communism,* Vol. 24, No. 3, July–August 1975.

————. *The Third Indochinese Conflict.* Boulder, Colo.: Westview Press, 1981.

Porter, Gareth, "Hanoi's Strategic Perspective and the Sino-Vietnamese Conflict," *Pacific Affairs,* vol. 57, no. 1 (Spring 1984), pp. 7-25.

————*Indochina Issues.* Washington, D.C.: Center for International Policy, 1979 to present.

Moise, Edwin E., *Land Reform in China and North Vietnam.* Chapel Hill: University of North Carolina Press, 1983.

Pike, Douglas. *History of Vietnamese Communism, 1925–1976.* Stanford, Calif.: Hoover Institution Press, Stanford University, 1978.

Porter, Gareth, ed. *Vietnam: A History in Documents.* New York and London: New American Library, 1979.

Turley, William S. "The People's Army of Vietnam." In *Communist Armies in Politics.* Jonathan Adelman, ed. Boulder, Colo.: Westview Press, 1982.

————*The Second Indochina War: A Short Political and Military History, 1954-1975.* Boulder, Co.: Westview Press, 1985.

————"Hanoi's Domestic Dilemmas," *Problems of Communism,* Vol. 29, no. 4 (July-August 1980), pp. 42-61.

————, ed. *Vietnamese Communism in Comparative Perspective.* Boulder, Colo.: Westview Press, 1980.

United States Information Service. "Bases of Power in the DRV," and "VWP-DRV Leadership 1960–1973." Viet-Nam Documents and Research Notes, Nos. 107 and 114, Saigon, 1973.

Zasloff, Joseph J. and Brown MacAlister, eds. *Communism in Indochina: New Perspectives.* Lexington, Mass.: D.C. Heath, 1975.

YEMEN ARAB REPUBLIC
(al-Jumhuriyat al-Yamaniyat al-Arabiyah)
by Jon E. Mandaville, Ph.D.

The System of Government

The Yemen Arab Republic (YAR), known as North Yemen, is a mountainous country of some 8 million people, including several hundred thousand refugees from its communist neighbor, South Yemen. The head of state is a president, who appoints the prime minister and ministerial cabinet. He also appoints the 159-member People's Consultative Council from among the traditional regional leaders of the country.

The YAR might best be described as a government-in the making. In 1962, the traditional absolutist Imamate which had ruled since World War I without any modern governmental structure was overthrown by a revolutionary front spearheaded by army officers and leading civilian politicians. A republic was proclaimed. In the ensuing eight years of civil war between republicanists and monarchists, more than 100,000 died; little could be done in that period to build a full unitary government.

Although the republican front had won the war by 1969, moderates forced a compromise upon both the radical left and the monarchists; and in 1970, a coalition government resulted. A constitution was drawn up and indirect nonpartisan elections held for a 149-member Consultative Assembly in that year. A council emerged dominated by conservative tribal and regional leaders who worked to limit the emergence of a strong central government. The council also regionalized the army and divided it against itself; tribal units were incorporated whole into divisions, and officers with primary regional loyalties recruited.

The inability of this civilian government to build a strong center from which to develop the country economically triggered the Correctionist Movement of 1974, led by Colonel Ibrahim al-Hamdi. A Military Command Council was put in place of the suspended constitution and Consultative Assembly. Using it and a few loyal army divisions, continuing the civilian prime ministership and ministerial cabinet with an enlarged and strengthened Central Planning organization, al-Hamdi, now President, moved over the next three years to curtail tribal and regional power while strengthening the central government. Significant progress toward that goal was dealt a setback in October 1977 with the assassination of al-Hamdi, apparently at the hands of conservative leadership. After a brief term by his successor Ahmad al-Ghashmi, Lt. Colonel Ali Abdullah Salih was elected president in July of 1978 by the newly reconstituted People's Consultative Assembly (PCA). He was reelected in a national referendum in 1983 for a six-year term.

Executive

The president of the YAR is formally elected by the People's Consultative Assembly. The current office holder was ensured a six year term by national referendum in 1983, pending completion of a new constitution.

Though the president theoretically has a monopoly of the state's authority, in practice his power is sharply limited by the need to negotiate compromises among the many factions within the government and society. Few actions are taken by him without formally or informally consulting the leaders of these factions, most of whom sit or are represented in the PCA.

Legislature

In May of 1979, President Salih strengthened his political base by appointing a fifteen-member Advisory Council and expanding the membership of the PCA from ninety-nine to 159 members. In May of 1980, he appointed the fifty-two-member Committee for National Consultation to draft a new constitution. In July of 1985, nationwide non-partisan elections were held for Local Development and Municipal

Councils. Both men and women over the age of 18 voted, and 17,507 councilpersons were elected. Each council then chose delegates to a new People's General Congress, which is expected to replace the People's Consultative Assembly with stronger legislative powers.

Judiciary

Since 1974, a series of presidential decrees have rationalized both civil and criminal proceedings and introduced a limited appeals system. The codes adhere closely to Islamic legal principles while, as in the case of the Family Law of 1979, reflecting a modernist interpretation. In outlying rural areas most matters of litigation are settled by traditional communal mediation in preference to state courts.

Regional & Local Government

The YAR is divided into ten provinces whose governors are appointed by the president. In recent years the governors have been chosen on the basis of ability rather than local connections, a fact which indicated the increased strength of the central government.

Political Forces

Zaydi/Shafi'i Division

Approximately 40 percent of the population of the YAR are Zaydi Shi'i Muslims (no theological or political connection with the Shi'i of Iran). They live primarily as farmers in the northern mountains and interior. Their counterparts, the Shafi'i Sunni Muslims, live on the coastal plains and southern hills. Historically, the Zaydis dominated the country under the leadership of a Zaydi Imam who relied on their support to govern the Shafi'i population. With the deposition of the Imam in 1962, many Zaydi tribes rallied to the monarchist cause in the civil war that followed; others sold their military services to the highest bidder, switching sides frequently, accumulating gold, arms, and political power in the course of the conflict.

The Shafi'is, their society and economy strongly influenced by proximity to Aden and other port towns, supported the republican cause in the civil war.

Most Zaydis are members of two large tribal confederations, the Hashid and Bakil, which are in turn split into many smaller tribal units.

While they have not always acted in concert, Zaydis share common conservative political interests where national policy is concerned. Making common cause with conservative Shafi'i leaders, the Zaydis dominated the national legislature elected in 1970, and the head of the Hashid Federation, Abdullah al-Ahmar, became the assembly's first speaker. This conservative bloc, supported clandestinely with arms and money by Saudi Arabia, is adamantly opposed to unity with the PDRY, publicly a main goal of government policy.

National Democratic Front (NDF)

Groups committed to the twin goals of social reform and Yemeni unity have played an important role in North Yemen's politics since the country's republican revolution in 1962. They have recruited partisans from the Shafi'i and Zaydi population, officers, and civil servants, and have consistently enjoyed the military and political support of South Yemen. During the civil war, leftists organised farmers coops and trade unions and made an abortive bid for power in 1968. Leftists were critical but on the whole sympathetic to al-Hamdi's attempt to reduce the influence of conservative Zaydi leaders and move away from Saudi Arabia.

This entente was upset in 1977 with al-Hamdi's assassination and the reversal of his policies by his successor al-Ghashmi. This led to a short-lived revolt in 1978 by leftist officers and the launching of a guerilla campaign in the south under the leadership of the NDF, which was officially founded in that year by Marxist leaders, southern Zaydi elements, and numerous dissident army officers.

Taking advantage of the turmoil in the south, the PDRY invaded in February 1979 in support of the NDF. Within a month, however, a peace agreement was signed on a status quo ante basis. While guerrilla activities by the NDF continued, the army moved steadily over the next several years to crush the NDF; by 1985, the movement controlled no significant territory.

National Prospects

President Salih has over the past seven years achieved relative political stability by relying on a centrist coalition of Zaydi leaders, Shafi'i civil servants, and military officers. This policy is unlikely to change. Relations with the PDRY is likely to prove the most troublesome issue facing the YAR in the near future. Though North-South national unity is a major national goal, both the conservative bloc and Saudi Arabia vehemently oppose it as long as the PDRY remains communist. Salih has attempted to find a middle ground by pursuing a nonaligned policy in economic and military assistance programs, and talking (inconclusively) with the PDRY on specific unity issues.

The discovery of oil in the YAR in commercial quantities in mid–1985 introduces a major new factor in domestic and foreign policy. It seems likely to lend new confidence to the central government, decreasing its dependence on Saudi Arabia and the domestic conservative bloc while simplifying the cooption of remaining NDF supporters.

Further reading

Bidwell, Robin. *The Two Yemens*. Boulder, Colorado: Westview Press, 1983.

Nyrop, Richard F. et al. *Area Handbook for the Yemens*. Washington, D.C.: U.S. Government Printing Office, for Foreign Area Studies, American University, 1977.

Pridham, B.R.. *Contemporary Yemen: Politics and Historical Background*. London: Croom Helm, 1984.

Stookey, Robert. Yemen: *The Politics of the Yemen Arab Republic*. Boulder, Colorado: Westview Press, 1978.

PEOPLE'S DEMOCRATIC REPUBLIC OF YEMEN
(Jumhuriyat al-Yaman al-Dimuqratiyat al-Sha'abiyah)

by Sterett Pope, M.A. revised by Jon E. Mandaville, Ph.D.

The System of Government

The People's Democratic Republic of Yemen (PDRY), or South Yemen as it is more commonly called, is a one-party state which relies on a highly centralized party apparatus to implement its policies of "scientific socialism." The population of the PDRY is 2.2 million. The ruling Yemen Socialist Party (YSP) in recent years has sought to widen its political base by creating popularly elected councils which are supervised by and cooperate with the party's hierarchical structures.

Executive

The formal executive is an eleven member presidential council chaired by the nation's president and including the vice president, the secretary general of the YSP and representatives of trade, women's and farmers' unions. Council members are chosen by the party's leading body, the Political Bureau. The larger Council of Ministers and a fifty-one member presidium are elected by the Supreme People's Council.

Legislature

Formally, the highest legislative authority is the Supreme People's Council, a 111-member body directly elected by the people. Forty Council members were elected as independents, with no affiliation with the YSP.

Judiciary

In 1968, the Supreme State Security Court was set up to establish a unified legal system and integrate within it the state's political and social programs. A secular code influenced by Islamic law governs civil proceedings; criminal law is adjudicated by secular lower magistrate courts in conjunction with the local people's committees.

Regional & Local Government

Subnational government is conducted according to the Marxist-Leninist principle of democratic centralism whereby the national party leadership maintains close control over lower-level officials, who have little scope for individual initiative and are subject to review and censure by their superiors. The country's six governorates and their administrative subunits are each staffed by a chief executive (governor, director, and district commissioner), an executive committee, and a people's council. At each level, the people's councils are directly elected from lists of nominees screened by higher party authorities. The people's councils are then charged with choosing the executive committees, whose membership is generally reserved for party loyalists often named by the national leadership. The chief executive at each level is usually directly appointed by the executive committee at the next level.

The Electoral System

The electorate comprises all citizens, men and women, above the age of 18. While elections at all levels are carefully controlled by the party, there is considerable scope for free choice by voters. In the 1978 elections for Supreme People's Council, for example, several candidates ran for each seat including many independents without YSP affiliation.

Yemen Socialist Party (YSP)

History

In 1963 the NLP, the forerunner of the YSP, launched a campaign of guerrilla warfare against British rule in the crown colony of Aden and the adjacent British protectorate, the South Arabian Federation. Originally a loose grouping of Yemeni nationalists of diverse political persuasions and social backgrounds, the NLF gradually developed a revolutionary ideology strongly influenced by Marxism-Leninism. From the start, the NLF cooperated, uncomfortably, with other less radical nationalist organizations. In 1965 the non-NLF factions merged in the Front for the Liberation of the Occupied South Yemen (FLOSY). This moderate group enjoyed the support of Egypt which had sent troops to North Yemen in 1962 to defend the embattled republican government there against the monarchists.

Two months after the British withdrawal in 1967, the NLF and FLOSY were drawn into an armed confrontation from which the NLF emerged victorious with the help of the South Arabian Army, a less radical nationalist organization made up remnants of Britain's Yemeni militia. The result was a ruling coalition dominated by moderate elements which elected Qahtan al-Shaabi as the first president of the new republic. Al-Shaabi's autocratic rule and his refusal to address the socialist platform of the NLF's left wing led to his dismissal by the Corrective Movement of 1969 under the leadership of Salem Ali Robea.

Confirmed as president of the republic by a party congress in 1970, Ali moved quickly to implement the congress's platform, which included the nationalization of nearly all foreign assets, a sweeping program of land reform, and cooperativization of agriculture. Impressed by the Cultural Revolution in Communist China, which he visited in 1970, President Ali undertook a thorough purge of the army and the civil service and orchestrated a series of popular uprisings to mobilize South Yemen's rural population and strike at what he viewed as the overly hierarchical and urban-biased structure of the party itself. Ali advocated "permanent revolution" at the expense of party organization and preferred Chinese developmental models and assistance programs to those of the Soviet Union. His views split the party and in 1978 Ali was removed and then executed following an attempted countercoup by his followers in the army.

The new leadership under former party secretary general Abd al Fattah Ismail moved to broaden its political base in the country. In 1976 Ismail had organized the Unified Political Organization-National Front (UPO-NF) which brought together the FLN and two independent communist and Arab nationalist parties; following Salem Ali Robea's removal, the UPO-NF was transformed into the new YSP, which held national elections the same year. Ismail was replaced as Yemen's president by Ali Nasser Mohammed in 1980. He pursued over the next five years a more flexible program of accomodation with moderate domestic constituencies and with the PDRY's non-socialist neighbors. Ismail's return from Moscow in 1985 signaled a renewal of tension between the pragmatist/doctrinaire wings of the leadership.

Organization

Party organization parallels the four-tier system of the government: national council, regional governorates, subregional directorates, and local districts. At the national level, a party congress, whose delegates are drawn from the three lower administrative levels, convenes every two years to elect a fifty-one-member Central Committee and a eleven-member Political Bureau.

Real power in the country rests with the Political Bureau which controls the presidency and cabinet-level posts, orchestrates political debate, and submits legislation for ratification by the SPC. Decisions by the Political Bureau are reached through an informal process of negotiation and consensus among members and their intraparty constituencies.

These constituencies are extremely diverse, reflecting a nation in the first generation of radical change. Old party loyalties left over from NLF guerilla war days may also be discerned as divisive factors. Arab nationalist sentiment crosses and sometimes undermines the Soviet socialist international line. More potentially disruptive of party discipline than any of the above are local and tribal loyalties. These loyalties are the best reflection of South Yemen's local, grass-roots constituencies, and may be seen in various cliques and personal factions permeating all traditional aspects of government.

Policy

In the field of foreign affairs, the present regime has maintained close ties with the Soviet Union, with which it signed a twenty-year Treaty of Friendship and Cooperation in 1979. The PDRY is a member of the Steadfastness Front, a group of Arab states which are opposed to a negotiated settlement with Israel on the Palestine question; and in 1981 South Yemen signed a regional mutual defense pact with Ethiopia and Libya under Soviet sponsorship. The most pressing diplomatic issue for the PDRY is that of national union with its neighbor, North Yemen. The governments of North and South Yemen are committed in principle to the merger, and signed national unity pacts in 1972 and 1979, in each case after the outbreak of war between the two countries. The PDRY supports with financial and military assistance the National Democratic Front, an armed opposition organization which advocates Yemeni unity and social reform within North Yemen. Given the ideological and structural differences of the governments of the two Yemens, and countervailing regional pressures, the prospects for Yemeni unity in the near future are not promising.

Although committed to the full realization of "scientific socialism," the government of the PDRY has managed a mixed economy with an emphasis on central planning for rapid social and economic development. More than half of the country's factories are state owned and managed; and in the countryside the PDRY has distributed over half the country's cultivated land to farmers whose produce is marketed by state-run cooperatives.

Membership & Constituency

Party membership in 1977 stood at 26,000, over 3,000 of which had been trained by the YSP's political academy in Aden. The party also fields a number of mass organizations, the most important of which are the General Union of Yemeni Workers (84,000 members in 1978), the Democratic Yemeni Youth (31,000), and the General Union of Yemeni Women (10,000). Party membership itself stands at less than three percent of the population.

Financing

No details on financing are available. The party's resources are probably indistinguishable from those of the state.

Leadership

Ali Nasser Mohammed remains the head of the party and government, as first among equals. Haydar al-Attas is Prime Minister, and Ali Antar, considered by many to be second in power, is Minister of Local Governments. Abdul-Fattah Ismail has recently returned from Moscow and certainly will press for an important government role.

Other Political Forces

Military

The strength of the South Yemeni army has been estimated at 27,000 by Western authorities, supplemented by 15,000 effective militia. Although Soviet and Cuban military advisors have worked continuously since the early 1970s to create a disciplined professional army, most of the officers corps is still staffed by guerrilla veterans with the same legacy of political division as civilian leadership. Party cadres, also divided on policy issues, influence promotion and demotion. As a consequence, military factions fought each other openly in the crises of 1969, 1978, and 1980.

National Prospects

It appears unlikely that the PDRY policy will undergo a radical shift in the near future; its direction will continue to be guided by the Soviet Union. At the same time, struggle between the pragmatic/doctrinaire wings of leadership will also continue. Given the close identification of military leadership with these issues, it seems certain that the disputes will also continue periodically to be the occasion for internal coups and concommitant, more or less contained, war between army and militia factions.

Further Reading

Bidwell, Robin. *The Two Yemens.* Boulder, Colorado: Westview Press, 1983.

Halliday, Fred. "Yemen's Unfinished Revolutions: Socialism in the South." *MERIP Reports,* Vol. 9, No. 8, October 1979.

Nyrop, Richard F., et al. *Area Handbook for the Yemens.* Washington: U.S. Government Printing Office, for Foreign Area Studies, American University, 1977.

Pridham, B.R. (ed.). *Contemporary Yemen.* London: Croom Helm, 1984.

Stookey, Robert W.. *South Yemen: A Marxist Republic in Arabia.* Boulder, Colorado: Westview Press, 1982.

SOCIALIST FEDERAL REPUBLIC OF YUGOSLAVIA
(Socijalisticka Federativna Republika Jugoslavija)
by Stephen C. Markovich, Ph.D.

The System of Government

Yugoslavia is a one-party, socialist federal republic comprised of six republics and two autonomous provinces. The six republics are Serbia (pop. 5,687,000), Croatia (4,601,000), Bosnia and Herzegovina (4,125,000), Macedonia (1,912,000), Slovenia (1,891,000), and Montenegro (583,000); the two provinces, both within the republic of Serbia, are Vojvodina (2,028,000) and Kosovo (1,584,000). Yugoslavia's nearly 23 million people represent six nationalities, cultures, and languages; and three religions. Besides Slovenians, Croatians, and Serbs—the last being the primary population of Montenegro, Bosnia and Herzegovina, as well as Serbia—Yugoslavia contains Hungarians (less than half the population of the autonomous province of Vojvodina), Albanians (a large portion of the autonomous province of Kosovo), and Macedonians (related by culture and language to people in both western Bulgaria and northern Greece). Croatians and Slovenians (the latter ethnically identical to the Slovenians of far southeastern Austria) are Roman Catholic, as are the Hungarians; the Serbs, Montenegrins, and Macedonians are Eastern Orthodox Christians; and sizable portions of the population of Kosovo, Bosnia and Herzegovina, both Serbs and Albanians, are Muslim. The Croatians and Slovenians were long under the rule of Austria, while the rest of the country experienced centuries of Turkish suzerainty. These differences among the nationalities have contributed to a chronic turbulence that no leader or system has permanently calmed. The country has no official language, though Serbian and Croatian, which are closely related, predominate.

Since the postwar inception of the socialist state, the communist party—the League of Communists—has been the dominant political institution, and, until his death in 1980, Josif Broz Tito was the dominant political force. With Tito's passing, no one individual has been able to assume the same degree of personal control; instead, collective leaderships, set up by Tito to provide stability after his death, head both party and state organs. Fully aware of the national differences that have threatened to shatter the country throughout its history, the late Yugoslav leader hoped that the collective bodies would reduce ethnic rivalries and ensure the country's continuance as a national entity. Consequently, in all party and governmental organs, a "nationalistic key" is employed in appointing and electing officials in order to approximate a balance among the various nationalities.

Executive

When Tito was alive, he was president of the republic and president of the League of Communists; with his death, both of these offices were abolished. Now the governmental executive branch consists of the presidency, the collective head of state, and the Federal Executive Council, the collective head of government.

The presidency (also referred to as the Presidium) has nine members, one from each republic and province, and one representing the League of Communists. The League representative is an ex officio position assumed by the nominal head of the party, the president of the party Presidium, who is elected for a one-year term by the party. The eight regular members are elected by the legislative branches of their respective republics and provinces.

From its own membership, the presidency annually elects a president and vice president. While these posts are formally filled by election, in practice they are decided by a prescribed rotation of nationalities; thus, on May 15, 1982 Petar Stambolic from Serbia became president, was succeeded in 1983 by Mika Spiljak from Croatia, who was followed in 1984 by Veselin Djuranovic from Montenegro, who was replaced in 1985 by Radovan Vlajkovic from Vojvodina. Although the president of the presidency is the nominal head of state for a year and officially exercises the prerogatives of a head of state, the constitutional powers in fact rest with the collective rather than the individual. Accordingly, the constitution states that the presidency shall represent Yugoslavia at home and abroad; command the armed forces; propose policies; promulgate statutes; and make ambassadorial, judicial, and military appointments. In addition, the presidency has the difficult task of effecting adjustments in nationalist differences to forge a consensus among the several governments.

The Federal Executive Council (FEC) has twenty-nine members including the prime minister (officially titled president of the FEC), fourteen representatives elected by the republics and provinces (two by each republic and one by each province), and fourteen federal secretaries appointed by the prime minister in consultation with party, governmental, and other sociopolitical organizations.

The present prime minister, Milka Planinc from Croatia, was proposed for the office by the presidency and confirmed by the Federal Assembly for a four-year term beginning May 15, 1982. Under Article 349 of the constitution, Planinc would be permitted to serve two consecutive terms, but an amendment adopted in 1981 now limits an individual to a single term; the amendment also provides that candidates for prime minister and other government posts will be nominated by the Socialist Alliance of the Working People of Yugoslavia (SAWPY), a mass organization led by the League of Communists. Planinc is the first female prime minister in the history of Yugoslavia and presently holds the highest position of any woman in a communist country.

Of the fourteen members from the republics and provinces, three of them are elected vice prime ministers (officially vice presidents) of the FEC, and eleven are designated FEC members without portfolio. The fourteen federal secretaries, appointed and confirmed in adherence to the "nationalistic key," are placed in charge of specific administrative agencies.

As the executive organ of government, responsible to the Assembly, the FEC is constitutionally charged with proposing policies, drafting a budget, enforcing federal statutes, executing policies, implementing defense policy, and directing the administrative agencies. Since some of the powers given to the FEC are similar to those granted to the presidency, this apparent duplication can and does cause confusion in the system. Such confusion was limited when Tito was alive since his positions, power, and prestige enabled him to act as arbiter in the transition to collective leadership. Since his death there has been no arbiter and in consequence there has been more confusion within and among the national branches of government. The political momentum generated by Tito's strong leadership plus the more concentrated power in the collective presidency has enabled the presidency to overshadow the FEC. Vladimir Bakaric made this point publicly in a 1981 interview in which he suggested that the FEC and the Assembly were unable to handle the problems, particularly the economic ones, facing the country, and therefore the presidency had to step in "even though it has no right to do so according to the constitution."

Confusion and tension in the federal branches are partially alleviated by the influence of the League of Communists (LCY). All key positions in the federal government, that is, all members of the presidency and the FEC, and senior officers in the Assembly have high standing in the LCY. While few individuals are permitted to hold important administrative positions in both party and government, all high governmental officials have a commitment to the party line. However, interpretations of the party line itself may vary, thereby spawning divergent views and policy differences.

Legislature

The national legislative branch is the bicameral Assembly of the Socialist Federal Republic of Yugoslavia composed of the Federal Chamber and the Chamber of Republics and Provinces. The Federal Chamber has thirty delegates from each republic and twenty from each province for a total of 220; the Chamber of Republics and Provinces has twelve delegates from each republic and eight from each province for a total of eighty-eight. All of the delegates are elected for four-year terms through a complicated, indirect system introduced in the 1974 constitution. Delegates to the Federal Chamber are elected by secret ballot by the members of the commune assemblies within the respective republics and provinces. Delegates to

While all citizens eighteen years of age and over are enfranchised, most of them vote only in the initial phase. But it is possible to vote in more than one capacity; some citizens, for example, will participate in three capacities: as workers, as members of local communities, and as members of sociopolitical organizations.

This indirect electoral system, which supplanted the direct system established under the 1963 constitution, obviously permits the LCY to influence heavily the electoral process and the political system. Members of the party and its ancillary organizations directly control the sociopolitical chambers, and through their participation in industry, agriculture, bureaucracy, and other areas strongly influence the delegate elections in the remaining chambers. Party dominance increases at each successive level. While more than one candidate might occasionally be nominated for a seat in the communal assemblies, the LCY front organization, the Socialist Alliance (SAWPY), presents single slates for election to the higher assemblies, although often only after considerable debate over potential candidates.

The League of Communists of Yugoslavia; LCY
(*Savez komunista Jugoslavije;* SKJ)

The LCY does not have the same monopoly of power that its counterparts have in other communist countries. The LCY is the most important political institution in the country, but the extent of its control and the degree of its influence are less than that of other ruling communist parties. This situation is due in part to the decentralization and liberalization that were inaugurated by the LCY itself in the fifties and sixties, and in part to the nationalistic and related cleavages that have historically divided the country. The LCY has to exert considerable effort to sustain its own unity and political primacy.

History

The First Congress of Yugoslav Communists took place in April 1919 under the name of the Socialist Workers Party of Yugoslavia (Communist). The participants at this congress passed several policy measures including a resolution to join the Third Communist International.

Just over a year later, in June 1920, the Second Congress was held, a program adopted, and the name of the party changed to the Communist Party of Yugoslavia. The future of the young party looked bright; it had some 60,000 members, and in elections that year did well at all levels, gaining control of several local governments and winning enough seats in the federal legislature to become the third-largest party. Soon after, the ruling government outlawed the CPY.

During the 1920s and 1930s the party was wracked by disunity, disorganization, and uncertain leadership, due in part to harassment by the government, but more to dissidence among the members themselves. With the party in disarray, membership dropped, eventually falling to a low of 200 in the early thirties. In 1937 Stalin appointed Josif Broz Tito general secretary of the party. Under Tito's leadership, the party resumed its growth, reaching 12,000 in 1941, on the eve of Yugoslavia's involvement in the war. These 12,000 Communists, 9,000 of whom perished during the war, provided the nucleus around which Tito successfully massed his partisan army, an army whose numbers swelled to 900,000 by the end of the war. In addition to serving effectively as a military force, the army also became a rich source for party recruitment; when the fighting ceased, 141,000 of the partisans were members of the party.

From the beginning of the conflict, Tito emphasized an all-Yugoslav theme, stressing equality among the nationalities, and opted to fight the German troops occupying the country despite heavy reprisals. The strategy worked, for Tito soon increased his power and influence within the country and eventually gained recognition and assistance from Britain and the United States. Although there was an official Yugoslav government-in-exile, Tito boldly established a provisional government to replace the prewar monarchy. With the war's end, his provisional government became permanent. All opposition was eliminated or neutralized.

Tito then set out to duplicate the Soviet system in Yugoslavia. The 1946 Yugoslav constitution was based on the 1936 Soviet constitution; and the Soviet party organization, governmental structure, and economic system, apart from agricultural collectivization, were emulated. Yugoslavia appeared to be Stalin's model satellite, especially as viewed from the West. Under the facade of imitation, however, Tito and his colleagues had real differences with Stalin's economic, foreign, and party policies; differences which became so fundamental that Stalin had the Yugoslav Communists expelled from the COMINFORM in 1948 and subsequently did all that he could, short of military intervention, to topple Tito. By uniting his support within the country and getting some help from external sources, mostly from the United States, Tito and his party survived Stalin's pressures.

The break with Stalin resulted in the Titoists concluding that they had to find their own road to the communist utopia, a road which would take into consideration their country's particular national conditions. The basic principles were worked out in theory and practice over the next few years and formalized at the Sixth Congress in 1952. The key points were a diminished role for the party, economic decentralization, and worker's self-management. To symbolize the new road, the name of the party was changed to the League of Communists of Yugoslavia. The Titoists further formalized these changes in a new constitution introduced in 1953 and in the LCY program presented in 1958. Also in the 1950s, they underscored their independence in world affairs and their neutrality between East and West by cofounding the nonaligned movement.

Another constitution, promulgated in 1963, laid the groundwork for rapid changes. As the role of the LCY diminished, other centers of power surfaced. Specifically, in the republics and provinces, governments, economic enterprises, and Leagues of Communists all improved their political positions at the expense of federal institutions and national party organs. Decentralization, liberalization, and pluralism appeared to be irrevocable.

Toward the end of the sixties, the positive developments of the decade were threatened by rumblings of political unrest. When the unrest exploded into nationalist riots in Croatia in 1971, Tito stepped in forcefully. Although Croatia's atavistic nationalism was singled out as the main culprit, none of the regional governments escaped Tito's wrath. Wholesale changes were made in League and government organs at all levels throughout the country. Popular leaders who had presided over the pluralistic governments of the preceding decade were replaced by individuals who would be more hardheaded.

Tito's main aim was to resurrect the LCY as the dominant political institution in the country and make the party, with the support of the army, a force for integration and stability. Most of the 1970s were devoted to this task. The party organization was tightened, Communists were

urged to exert more influence in all areas, the Tenth and Eleventh Congresses emphasized the leading role of the LCY, and the 1974 constitution reiterated that the LCY "shall be the prime mover and exponent of political activity." Progress was made in achieving Tito's task, but it was not completed by the time of his death. The national cleavages with all their related complications remained. These cleavages, now frequently reinforced by overlapping economic cleavages, continued to plague the Yugoslav nation and Tito's collective successors, as riots in Kosovo in 1981 demonstrated.

Organization

The statutes of the League state that the supreme organ of the party is the congress convened every four years. The congress, with about 2,000 participants, elects the Central Committee of 165 members to act on its behalf when it is not in session. Although the congress votes for the members of the Central Committee, the candidates are actually proposed by the republic, provincial, and military party congresses; each of the Leagues at the republican level propose twenty candidates, and the provincial and army conferences each submit fifteen candidates for election to the Central Committee. From the members of the Central Committee, the Presidium is elected composed of twenty-three individuals representing the various nationalities and groups. The president of the Presidium, elected by secret ballot for the first time at the Twelfth Congress in 1982, is now considered the head of the LCY for his one-year term. For its administrative duties, the Presidium has a secretary and nine executive secretaries. All of the major offices in the LCY are formally filled by election, but in practice are determined by a scheduled rotation among the nationalities.

A few months prior to the national congress, the republics, provinces, and army hold their congresses and conferences at which they select *their* central committees, presidiums, and other organs. Likewise the communal Leagues of Communists hold conferences every four years to set up committees and executive organs. At the lowest level are the 71,000 basic organizations which are formed in associated labor groups, self-management units, local communities, and military institutions; each of the basic organizations is headed by a secretary and/or secretariat to implement decisions and organize meetings.

Although the hierarchical structure of the LCY resembles that of other communist countries, this hierarchy has not consistently reflected the power distribution within the party. As noted earlier, when the national party organization relinquished some of its power in the sixties, the republican and provincial organizations assumed some of this authority and stubbornly resisted giving back any of it. As a result, the LCY has at times looked like a federal organization of eight regional parties rather than a solid unitary League. Even after Tito swung the pendulum back to the national level, the intraparty competition for power continued.

The LCY promotes its policies through its own publications and seeks mass support through several auxillary organizations. The major publications are *Komunist*, a weekly newspaper, and *Socijalizam*, a monthly journal. The most important sociopolitical organizations tied to the party are the Socialist Alliance of the Working People of Yugoslavia (SAWPY), the Confederation of Trade Unions of Yugoslavia (CTUY), the Federation of Associations of National Liberation War Veterans of Yugoslavia (FANLWVY), and the League of Socialist Youth of Yugoslavia (LSYY).

The Socialist Alliance (*Socijalistički savez radnog naroda Jugoslavije;* SSRNJ) is the most extensive mass organization with an individual membership of over thirteen million and an institutional membership encompassing all other sociopolitical organizations. Through meetings at several levels and through the Alliance's newspaper *Borba* (Struggle), the Communists use this organization to publicize their policies, implement their programs, and promote national unity. More specifically, the SSRNJ plays a dominant role in nominating delegates for the several assemblies in the political system and in sending delegates directly to the Sociopolitical Chamber.

The Confederation of Trade Unions (*Savez sindikata Jugoslavije;* SSJ) is supposed to act on behalf of its 5.7 million members by protecting workers' interests, participating in self-management agreements, and resolving labor disputes. But judging from the number of strikes in Yugoslavia, the workers have often chosen more direct means to voice their complaints and gain economic benefits. Theoretically, the development of self-management and the existence of the CTUY should make strikes superfluous in a proletarian society. Yet according to a Yugoslav study, in the previous decade there has been an average of 200 strikes a year in the country, and the author of the study puts most of the blame on ineffective trade unions. In the 1980s the number of strikes has increased with nearly 400 in 1984 and over 500 in 1985; according to Yugoslav officials 90 percent of these strikes were organized to protest low wages.

The Federation of Veterans Associations (*Savez udruženja boraca narodnooslobodilačkog rata;* SUBNOR) has generally backed the LCY, particularly when the party has taken authoritarian stances. Comprised mostly of old-guard partisans and army personnel who were instrumental in the war effort and influential in the early postwar years, this organization has consistently held conservative positions and has been uninhibited in expressing them. Its members were intensely loyal to Tito, and he often sought their help at critical times. When, for example, Tito moved to restore the stature of the LCY in the early seventies, he sought and received SUBNOR's full and enthusiastical support.

In terms of numbers, the League of Socialist Youth (*Savez socijalistički omladine Jugoslavije;* SSOJ) has been a successful auxilliary organization of the LCY. Presently the youth organization has over 3.5 million members, two-thirds of the country's young people between the ages of fifteen and twenty-seven. Of the 3.5 million, 572,000 are already members of the LCY; in fact, they make up approximately 25 percent of the party's total membership. On the other hand, the LSYY does not always attract the ablest youth in the country; only a small number of university students have been attracted to the party and been supporters of its policies. One party official complained that the students seem to shy away from anything structured.

Policy

Within the ideological context of Marxism-Leninism-Titoism, the domestic aims of the LCY have been to strengthen the economic base in Yugoslavia as a foundation for the further development of socialism and to increase citizen participation in the politico-economic system through progressive development of social self-management. Yugoslavia's foreign policy has long been based on the concept of nonalignment.

Party policies initially had considerable economic success. Under a system combining elements of socialism and capitalism, described as "market socialism," economic growth doubled in the 1950s and again in the 1960s, raised living standards for a majority of Yugoslavs, and lifted the country out of its less-developed status. Subsequently, however, the growth rate slowed in the 1970s and stagnated in the eighties dropping to one percent in 1985.

Offsetting initial successes are several problems that chronically weaken the economy. Among the most critical are unbalanced investments, a huge foreign debt, uneven development, and inflation and unemployment. The agricultural sector, for example, has suffered investment shortages as a result of a capital-investment policy that concentrated on industry. Even though 85 percent of the farms are privately owned, the nation cannot consistently produce enough to feed itself, and in years of poor harvests must purchase foreign grains with precious hard currencies.

An annual balance-of-payments deficit has constantly hindered the Yugoslav economy. Although the country has successfully diversified its trade pattern—40 percent with the developed nations, 43 percent with COMECON members, and 17 percent with the less developed—it still imports more than its exports. In recent years, the trade deficit plus other external transactions have caused a rapid rise in Yugoslavia's foreign debt, from $4 billion in the early seventies to $23 billion in the mid-eighties.

Gross disparities between developed and undeveloped regions in the country not only cause economic dissatisfaction but create morale problems among the ethnic groups. Albanian students who precipitated the riots in Kosovo in 1981 were aware that the per capita income in their province was under $1,000, whereas in Slovenia it was over $6,000. Efforts to correct the disparities have not been successful and sometimes cause problems of their own. Citizens in the developed areas are not favorably disposed to having the profits from their enterprises invested in the poor regions, while attempting to achieve regional equality increases economic costs through inefficient duplication. As one Yugoslav official put it to an American reporter, "We have six steel mills, one for each republic. We have five auto plants, each in a different republic. Yet our total production of steel and autos is less than the minimum output required to run just one steel or auto plant efficiently."

Finally, the party leaders have not been able to manage inflation and unemployment. For the average Yugoslav, this has meant a drop in his standard of living over the past few years as the inflation rate has soared as high as 80 percent and the unemployment figure has hovered around 15 percent. These economic woes, should they persist, can turn into political unrest, especially if they reinforce ethnic rivalries.

The problems described above are not supposed to exist in any communist country, let alone one which is based on social self-management. The LCY made self-management the foundation of the economic system in the 1950s in order to avoid state exploitation as practiced in the Soviet Union and to involve the Yugoslav workers in economic decision making. When the concept was introduced, it applied only to workers in economic enterprises, but it was later broadened to include other organizations as well. Self-management permits individuals employed in small enterprises and institutions to participate directly in policy-making; those in larger firms elect a council to act on their behalf. Over the years, the system has generally been praised at home and abroad, but the results have been mixed. Successful operation varies with the quality of workers, ability of directors, type of facilities, and other factors. Judging by the many comments made at preparatory meetings preceding the Twelfth Congress, party members themselves had doubts about the system as their speeches were filled with phrases calling for "the proper development of self-management" and expressing a need for "genuine self-management." For the party there has also been a contradiction between its wish to maintain political control and its desire to extend self-management freedoms. Usually the party has resolved this contradiction by the party's placing limits on self-management freedoms.

Tito made nonalignment the basis of Yugoslav foreign policy in the 1950s. Ever since he founded the movement with Nehru of India and Nasser of Egypt, Yugoslavia has used nonalignment to exert its influence and reinforce its independence in world affairs.

Tito's stature within the nonaligned movement and among Third World countries gave Yugoslavia greater influence internationally than the size and power of the country warranted. Much of this influence rested on Tito's own prestige and much has evaporated with his passing, but there is a residue that continues to benefit Yugoslavia in its relations with the

Third World. It is with the radical left-wing members of the movement, Cuba, for example, that Yugoslavia has had the most difficulty. The Yugoslavs have insisted that the movement should be genuinely neutral between East and West.

In its relations with the Soviet Union, Yugoslavia has steadfastly defended its position as an independent communist country. All overtures by the Kremlin aimed at persuading the League of Communists to recognize Moscow as the center of international communism have been rejected by the Yugoslav leaders on the grounds that there are as many centers as there are communist parties. Relations with the Soviet Union, as with other countries—communist or otherwise—are to be based on respect of equality and noninterference in internal affairs. Consistent with these principles, the Yugoslavs have repeatedly condemned the Soviet Union for its military interventions and diplomatic pressures. Despite these ideological and political differences, party and government relations between Moscow and Belgrade have been normal. In its relations with other communist nations, Yugoslavia has for the most part maintained normal ties. With some countries, Romania and China in particular, relations have been excellent; with others, such as Albania and Bulgaria, recurring differences have strained vacillating relations.

After the war, Yugoslav leaders were very belligerent toward Western governments, but their attitude changed when the United States and its allies helped Yugoslavia survive the COMINFORM expulsion. With emergency aid at first and long-term assistance later, the American government became Yugoslavia's biggest supporter in its fight for independence from the Soviet Union. These aid agreements opened the way for expanding trade agreements and improved diplomatic relations. Today, the developed countries of the West still make up the largest segment in Yugoslavia's trade pattern and are its major source of financial assistance; over 90 percent of Yugoslavia's $23 billion foreign debt is owed to Western sources. It should be pointed out that some of these sources now have a stake in Yugoslavia; after the Yugoslavs enacted a law in 1967 that permitted foreign ownership of Yugoslav enterprises, several hundred Western corporations invested in Yugoslavia.

Membership & Constituency

When the war ended in 1945, the Communist Party of Yugoslavia had a membership of 141,000. Seven years later, by the Sixth Congress, membership had increased to 773,000. For a few years, the numbers decreased and then resumed their climb, surpassing one million in 1960. The upward trend continued through the sixties, reversed in the early seventies—paralleling the difficulties of that period—and dropped to 947,000 by 1972. Following this brief slowdown, steady rises and a spurt in new enrollments after Tito's death lifted the membership to an all-time high of 2.2 million in 1982.

The statistical breakdown of membership according to nationality shows that the Serbs are the largest group with 49 percent of the total membership. The Croats have 15 percent, and the Slovenes, Montenegrins, Macedonians, and Moslems each have approximately 6 percent. Individuals who identify themselves as "Yugoslavs" make up 5 percent, the Albanians hold under 4 percent, and the Hungarians and other minorities contribute 3 percent. When the nationality percentages on party membership are compared with the nationality percentages on population, the data shows that the Serbs and Montenegrins are the most overrepresented group, while the Croats and Albanians are the most underrepresented.

The LCY has a changing age distribution and an uneven sex distribution. Generally the number of young people interested in the party is diminishing. Whereas five years ago members twenty-seven years old or under made up 34 percent of the party, presently they make up 25 percent. Women, whose numbers increased in recent years, account for over half a million members, about 25 percent of the total membership. However, in the upper echelons of the party hierarchy, the women and young people are underrepresented.

According to occupation, 29 percent are blue-collar workers, 42 percent white-collar personnel, 4 percent peasants, 4 percent in the army, 10 percent students and pupils, with 11 percent for "others." Party heads ritually deplore the relatively low number of workers in their proletarian party, but invariably fail to effect any substantial change in their representation. Moreover, as with women and youth, few workers hold high offices in the party; in the nine party presidiums on the national, republican, and provincial levels, which together have more than 100 positions, only one member is a worker; in the 165-member Central Committee of the LCY, less than 5 percent are workers. Most underrepresented are the peasants who make up over 30 percent of the population yet account for only 4 percent of party membership.

Over the years popular support for the party has varied. It has tended to increase at critical turning points, such as Yugoslavia's expulsion from the COMINFORM and President Tito's death, and diminish in more normal times. Lack of consistent data makes it difficult to measure accurately the extent of popular support, but the demographic statistics do reflect some strongholds and soft spots. Obviously the peasants have not been enamoured with the party, nor have the workers been strongly attracted, and the underrepresented Croats have not been as enthusiastic as the overrepresented Serbs and Montenegrins.

Financing

Party members pay monthly dues on a graduated scale based on income. For students, senior citizens, and others without income derived from employment, the fee is a small, flat sum. Payment of dues is a condition of membership, and failure to pay them for three consecutive months results in the delinquent member being dropped from the party. The dues' scale undergoes frequent upward adjustment partly because of high inflation and partly because the League wants to become self-supporting.

According to party reports, membership dues are the principal source of revenue, accounting for over 90 percent of the party's income. The remaining revenues come from grants made by sociopolitical communities and work organizations. When the party undertakes special activities, these communities and organizations are usually called upon to finance them. Normally about 25 percent of the revenues go to the LCY Central Committee to cover national expenses, but the percentage has varied from a low of 15 percent to a high of 63 percent. Almost half of the revenues collected are used to pay the salaries of full-time employees of the party.

Leadership

The objective of collective leaderships in the leading organs of party and state was to assure a balance of nationalities and a consensus of views. With all republics, provinces, and na-

tionalities participating in decision making, the possibility of one region exercising hegemony over other areas was considerably reduced. And the likelihood of one individual replacing Tito was seen as highly improbable, if not impossible. Consequently, in the two years since Tito's passing, no one individual has come close to taking over, no one individual has even approached the status of first among equals.

There are certain leaders who are political heavyweights, such as Branko Mikulic (born 1928), of Bosnia; General Nikola Ljubičic (born 1916), of Serbia; and others. But neither the system nor the circumstances have permitted any one official's star to rise significantly above his colleagues'.

The members of the executive organs in party and state are primarily older party veterans, but there have been moves to make room for younger aspirants. On the Central Committee Presidium, the highest executive organ of the LCY, the average age is sixty-one. In the government, where the high offices are also held by party members, the average age of the nine-member presidency is sixty-four, but on the Federal Executive Council appointed in 1984 the average is only fifty with the oldest sixty-three and the youngest thirty-five.

Other Political Forces

Although there have been periodic recurrences of repression in Yugoslavia, the overall trend in the country has been one of pluralism and liberalization. As a result, there are other groups besides the party that influence or attempt to influence the system in practice. Among the most important are the intellectuals, clerics, and ethnic nationalists, all of whom try to exert influence through criticism and/or opposition to the regime. But the most influential group by far, one whose position does not stem from pluralism and one which is highly supportive of the regime, is the army.

Military

The Yugoslav People's Army has always had a close relationship with the League of Communists. The party and army grew together in the wartime partisan units; most party leaders today—at least those over 60—joined the partisans before they became party members. Today, over one-third of the 250,000-man army belongs to the party. The army is presently seen as a protector of revolutionary achievements, a force of unity, and the defender of independence. Beyond its military and supportive functions, the army is directly involved in the political process. On the LCY Central Committee, it has the same number of representatives, fifteen, as an autonomous province. In the state system, a military man holds the position of defense minister, a powerful, influential office. The military-political career of former defense minister Nikola Ljubičić typifies the army's influence: while rising through army ranks, he served for two decades in the federal legislature, was a member of the LCY Central Committee and Presidium, and on leaving the ministry of defense in 1982, was elected president of Serbia. The symbiotic relationship between League and army will endure. The only risk in such a close relationship is that army officers may some day decide to take control of the government rather than be controlled by civilian authorities, as the League statutes and Yugoslav constitution require.

Intellectuals

Unlike the army, the intellectuals have neither a disciplined organization nor direct political influence. They may be dissidents whose stature enables them to criticize effectively, or they may be academics who have outlets for expressing their ideas. On the changes that should be made in the system and on the methods for effecting these changes, they vary widely. What they have in common is a degree of dissatisfaction with the present system and a desire to express this dissatisfaction publicly. Illustrative of this group is Milovan Djilas, the country's most prominent dissident. Once considered Tito's most likely heir, Djilas has not hesitated to issue critical appraisals of the regime. Since he has been denied access to Yugoslav media, he fires his salvos through foreign publications and reads the authorities' counterattacks in the domestic press. Other dissidents have joined the fray, sometimes criticizing the existing system, other times censuring each other. Professors have used their lectures and seminars, conferences and journals to convey their thoughts and criticisms. Most notable among them has been a group of Zagreb and Belgrade intellectuals who founded their own Marxist journal, *Praxis*. Though the journal was banned in 1975 and several of them lost their academic positions, they have continued their philosophical criticisms of the system and have made attempts to renew their journal. Students have emulated their professors by using university publications for their opinions. But they have also initiated critical movements of their own, including strikes and sit-ins which have mushroomed beyond the campuses into broader expressions of dissatisfaction. Actions by Zagreb students began the Croat revolts in 1971, and Priština students triggered the rebellions in Kosovo in 1981. All the critics have been harrassed, and some incarcerated, but this repression has not been sufficiently intensive or extensive to quiet the critics. Only by returning to Stalinist measures could the authorities neutralize the verbal opposition, but there is not enough support for such drastic action among the collective leaders themselves.

Religious Groups

Religious groups, particularly the Roman Catholic hierarchy, have been at odds with the party and state ever since the communist takeover. Although the Christian Orthodox and Moslem clerics have more often accommodated themselves with the authorities, the Catholics have consistently collided with them. The state argues that religious orders must stay within the sphere of Church affairs and that only when Catholics overstep this sphere are they persecuted. The Catholics reply that they are only exercising their religious rights as guaranteed by the constitution.

Catholic clerics have made a few concessions to the government and have repeatedly stated that they are willing to work out an accommodation provided the regime treats them with respect and recognizes their constitutional rights. Communist leaders are uneasy about the Church, in part, because it has traditionally had close ties with Croatian nationalism. They are also sensitive to similar ties that mesh Serbian nationalism with the Orthodox Church. As for the Moslems, the Communists have satisfied them by officially recognizing them as a nationality.

Ethnic Groups

Remnants of ethnic organizations with turbulent backgrounds have been incessant irritants for Communist Yugoslavia. Loyal supporters of the Yugoslav nationalist Serbian Chetniks and separatist Croatian Ustashi, intensely nationalistic organizations that have never accepted the Communist victory, have dreams of rescinding that victory and gaining control of the existing Yugoslav state or seceding. While these organizations no longer exist as such within the country, supporters in Yugoslavia have ties with friends abroad who maintain loose organizations and who, in the case of the Croatians, have resorted to terrorist tactics to shake the present regime and to gain international publicity for their causes. These organizations have not been serious threats to the state, but they are stubborn dogmatics who, considering the traditional centrifugal forces in the country, do pose a latent danger.

National Prospects

One of the most enduring facts about Yugoslavia is that it has always been a country of several nationalities and minorities. When the nationalities were part of the Austro-Hungarian Empire, their ethnic squabbles beset the monarch in Vienna, and each succeeding Yugoslav state has had to deal with the threat these centrifugal forces present. Neither Tito nor his successors could make the "nationalities question" a thing of the past. For Yugoslavia to survive as a nation, the nationalities problems must be made manageable, but this task is becoming harder rather than easier. When Tito was present, he could periodically put forceful

clamps on ethnic-inspired rumblings, but no one has emerged with the authority to assume his unifying role. Indeed, as noted earlier, the system of collective leadership was set up to preclude anyone from assuming such overreaching authority. The collective leaders, backed by the army, have kept the nation intact for five years, but only with difficulty. Severer tests are yet to come.

Further Reading

Banac, Ivo. *The National Question in Yugoslavia: Origins, History, Politics.* Ithica, New York: Cornell University Press, 1984.

Clissold, Stephen, ed. *A Short History of Yugoslavia.* Cambridge, England: Cambridge University Press, 1968.

Djilas, Milovan. *The New Class: An Analysis of the Communist System.* New York: Praeger, 1957.

Ramet, Pedro. *Nationalism and Federalism in Yugoslavia, 1963-1983.* Bloomington, Indiana: Indiana University Press, 1984.

———ed. *Yugoslavia in the 1980s.* Boulder, Colorado: Westview Press, 1985.

Rusinow, Dennison. *The Yugoslav Experiment: 1948–1974.* Berkeley: University of California Press, 1977.

Singleton, Fred. *Twentieth Century Yugoslavia.* New York: Columbia University Press, 1976.

Stankovic, Slobodan. *The End of the Tito Era: Yugoslavia's Dilemmas.* Stanford, Calif.: Hoover Institution Press, 1981.

Wilson, Duncan. *Tito's Yugoslavia.* Cambridge, England: Cambridge University Press, 1979.

REPUBLIC OF ZAIRE
(République du Zaire)
by Thomas M. Callaghy, Ph.D.

The System of Government

Zaire, a nation of nearly thirty-one million people, is a highly personalistic, single-party, unitary state which has developed out of a military coup d'état of November 24, 1965, led by General Mobutu Sese Seko (changed in 1971 from Joseph-Désiré Mobutu). Formerly known as the Democratic Republic of the Congo, the country emerged from Belgian colonial rule on June 30, 1960, and immediately disintegrated into chaos marked by secession, civil war, rebellions, rampant political instability, and intervention by United Nations troops. Peace and order were slowly achieved after the coup d'état.

Executive

Zaire is ruled by Mobutu Sese Seko. After his coup d'état in 1965, he commenced a search for order and sovereignty, and in the process created the current authoritarian, centralized, single-party state. In short, he is the state and controls nearly everything in it. The structure of political power exists because he exists; he created it. He controls a highly personalized administrative machine, especially the councils of the party-state and his *"créatures,"* the political elite who staff them. As supreme head of all party-state organs—Political Bureau, Executive Council, Legislative Council, Central Committee, Party Congress, the military, and the territorial administration—all political power is centralized and concentrated in his person. He has used police and military forces and territorial administrative cadre to control all key societal groups and emasculate the power of traditional authorities.

Although his formal title is president of the republic, he has in fact become a presidential monarch with the power and style of an early modern European absolutist king. He has shrewdly played upon the widespread belief that only a strong ruler can guarantee order and maintain the unity of the Zairian state.

Mobutu has said, "Cite me a single Zairian village where there are two chiefs, with one in opposition. It does not exist. For Zairians, two heads on one body make a monster. The notion of chief is beyond discussion." Mobutu portrays himself as a powerful neotraditional king or chief and as savior of his people. Traditional notions of kingship remain potent, and Mobutu has clearly drawn on them. As part of that style, Mobutu attempts to maintain paternalistic personal contacts with his "citizens," although the contact is usually one way. During frequent trips in the interior of the country, he holds mass meetings to explain his ideas, policies, and successes; he often grants the local people personal gifts or donations, such as vehicles, hospital equipment, etc.

As head of state and president-founder of the only political party—the *Mouvement Populaire de la Révolution* (MPR), he has almost unlimited personal discretion in policymaking and personnel selection and control. In fact, there is no distinction between the man and his political role, just as there seems to be no distinction between his personal finances and those of the state. According to one estimate, Mobutu controls between 17 and 22 percent of the annual national budget for his exclusive personal use. Between 15 and 20 percent of operating expenditures and 30 percent of capital outlay annually go through the presidency without any budgetary control. Reputedly, Mobutu is now the richest head of state in Black Africa, although the actual size of the fortune is subject to some controversy.

Mobutu is not invulnerable, however; opposition to him and his policies does indeed exist within the party-state apparatus and the military. The remarkable fact of his personal power, and indeed the basis of it, is his sophisticated ability to manage successfully the shifting international and domestic coalitions which give him support. Any evidence of ethnic and regional unrest, so apparent during the early

1960s, is quickly suppressed, and all legal means for the expression of ethnic or regional sentiment or opposition have been systematically abolished. Beyond the focus on order and personal profit, there have been a series of loudly proclaimed socioeconomic and welfare policies, but they have never been implemented in any sustained or serious manner. The welfare of the people has progressively declined since the collapse of copper prices in 1974. Recently, Mobutu has attempted to mask this decline by resurrecting his concept of "authenticity" (expelling foreign influences from Zairian life).

After seizing full power in 1965, Mobutu was first "elected" president in 1970. He was the only candidate, and the "ballots" were green for hope and red for chaos. He won with a vote of 10,131,699 to 157. In 1977 he was "reelected" for a second seven-year term. Again he was the only candidate, and again the vote total was overwhelming. In July 1984, he was "reelected" for a third time, capturing 99.16 percent of the vote. The unopposed candidate ran a five-week "campaign" in an election he had moved up from November, fearing more intense unrest later in the year. Under a new decree, Mobutu had made voting compulsory, and it was announced that the military would check identification papers to ensure that everyone had voted. This time a voter wishing a red ballot had to specifically request one and then hand it to a soldier at the polling place. In many polling places, red ballots were simply not available. One official said, "There is no need for them. Everyone is voting green." Mobutu declared that "the voting was a real election and could not be considered a referendum or plebiscite." Essentially, he has become president for life.

Mobutu maintains direct personal links between himself and the staff of the fused party-state apparatus. Party-state personnel are completely dependent on him for selection, appointment, and maintenance in power. An oath of loyalty to the president himself is taken by all officials. His wide powers create constant uncertainty for state personnel, which helps to maintain their loyalty to and fear of Mobutu. In order to increase this personal dependence, Mobutu constantly rotates the membership of the highest organs of power. This is essentially true within the Political Bureau and the Executive Council, the powers, composition, and size of which change frequently. A close body of relatively stable collaborators does exist, but its members are often rotated from position to position.

Another important method used by Mobutu to maintain loyalty is to allow participation in the "politics of appropriation," a tolerated corruption, formal and informal, which allows the political elite to enrich itself and indulge the lavish lifestyle that has become its trademark. This system has an added advantage in that, when necessary, any official can be removed for indulging in "pervasive corruption which harms the nation." Mobutu also makes use of awards and honors, such as the Order of the Leopard, and periodic amnesties for those who have fallen from grace. The hope that a return to the good life is possible is a powerful factor in controlling opposition.

Constant and intense glorification of Mobutu is another key manifestation of this highly personalistic rule. Mobutu is very concerned with his dignity, glory, greatness, and reputation. He believes that his will embodies that of his "citizens." The president-founder has many titles ("Guide," "Helmsman," "Father of the Nation," "Savior of the People," etc.) and is glorified in the press, on radio and television, and in specially staged activities called animation sessions, mass meetings, and marches of support throughout the country. Even his name is used for political glorification. In 1971 when he declared that all Zarians must adopt "authentic" Zairian names, he changed his name from Joseph-Désiré Mobutu to Mobutu Sese Seko Kuku Ngbendu Wa Za Banga. The Ngbendu translation is "The warrior who knows no defeat because of his endurance and inflexible will and is all powerful, leaving fire in his wake as he goes from conquest to conquest." The Baluba translation is more succinct but just as potent: "Invincible warrior, cock who leaves no chick intact."

Indeed, the cult of Mobutu has taken on distinctly religious and neotraditional overtones. In 1974 his thoughts and actions became the official doctrine or gospel of the country—Mobutuism, the teaching, thoughts, and actions of the president-founder. The propagation of this doctrine is seen as an important link between Mobutu and the masses. It even was decided that places that have marked the life of Mobutu would become "high places of meditation." In 1975 one regime official announced; "Henceforth, the MPR must be considered as a church and its Founder as a Messiah."

Mobutu also uses the politics of grandeur in his style of rule and style of life. Mobutu measures all in terms of himself, his interests, prestige, and glory, which are equated with those of the country. Examples of the politics of grandeur include the massive Inga dam project, an uneconomic steel manufacturing complex, the creation of Zaire's own airline and shipping fleet, and "events" such as the Ali–Forman "Fight of the Century" in October 1974. There is, of course, the personal grandeur–two palaces in Kinshasa; an estate outside the city (N'Sele); chateaux in Belgium, Switzerland, and France; presidential mansions in each region; cars; the presidential riverboat; the personal use of Air Zaire's 747 and DC-10; and so on. There is even a royal politics of the arts: Mobutu gives a prize in literature, *Le Grand Prix Littéraire Mobutu*.

The power of the presidential monarch is organized primarily through the Office of the President, which is staffed by loyal and often well-educated officials. It coordinates the activities of the major decision-making councils of the fused party and state apparatuses–the Political Bureau and the Executive Council. It also controls several specialized services, including the secret police (*Centre National de Recherches et d'Investigations*), the diplomatic corps, and research and development and data-processing services. The size and powers of the Political Bureau and the Executive Council have varied widely over the years. More recently, the Executive Council has predominated in major decision-making. It has more administrative functions since it directly controls the departments of the state administration. As head of both organs, President Mobutu makes the final decisions on all important issues.

Legislature

Formal procedures for selecting Legislative Council members as well as formal designations of their powers and responsibilities can be changed by Mobutu to fit his momentary needs. Any detailed outline of such formalities, which might suggest that they are operative and stable, would be misleading.

After coming to power in 1965, Mobutu quickly emasculated the power of the Parliament; he later abolished it and created a unicameral Legislative Council. As with everything else in Zaire, the Legislative Council is controlled by President Mobutu. Its purpose is to control popular participation, not to represent the views of the populace. Selected by the Political Bureau and nominated by Mobutu, the members range from close colleagues and relatives of Mobutu to former state officials, businessmen, politicians from the pre-Mobutu era, and traditional authorities. In October 1975, the Political Bureau selected 244 candidates for the Legislative Council, and the "election" was held on November 2. In the true style of pseudodemocracy, the voting was by acclamation at popular meetings throughout the country.

The Legislative Council was a docile, rubber-stamp body until 1977. After the first invasion of Shaba Region in 1977, President Mobutu, under substantial pressure from his Western supporters, undertook a "political liberalization." As part of this process, members of the Legislative Council were no longer to be selected by the Political Bureau, but competitively elected directly by the people. Elections were duly held in October 1977. Although in theory almost anyone could run for office, regime officials and prefects closely scrutinized candidates, in some instances eliminating them because they were not sufficiently committed to the MPR or for some "technical" reason. More than 2,000 people ran for the 268 seats in the Legislative Council, but those with regime connections or wealth (usually one and the same) fared best.

Mobutu took the "liberalization" process an important additional step in early 1978 when he granted the Legislative Council the power to question regime officials about governmental matters (*interpellation*). This process was strongly urged on the regime by Western, particularly American, officials, and encouraged by them once allowed. In early 1979 the Council started to seriously question members of the Executive Council about their departments and had the audacity to reject the national budget (something it had never done before). Still playing the "reform" card, Mobutu undertook a minor reshuffling of the government in at least partial response to the *interpellation*. In late December 1979, a major three-day *interpellation* took place, giving an indication that at least some Council members wanted to alter the Council's role as a control mechanism aimed at pseudodemocracy rather than participation. A number of state commissioners, the secretary general of the Political Bureau, and six top parastatal officials were grilled about their activities. Although he was not directly implicated, Mobutu clearly realized that much of the criticism was actually aimed at him.

In a major speech to the Legislative Council on February 5, 1980, Mobutu scolded its members for the "excesses" of the *interpellations*, and announced that henceforth they could be held only with his express permission. Then in August 1980 Mobutu took another step to emasculate the few remaining powers of the Legislative Council by creating a new institution—a 121-member party Central Committee whose functions are only advisory. It can, however, overrule the Legislative Council. In short, it is meant to effectively overshadow, if not replace, the Legislative Council.

By December 1980, Mobutu, despite the continuation of a severe economic and fiscal crisis, began to feel more secure in power again, and on December 30 moved against his critics in the Legislative Council. Five legislators were arrested, among them Tshisekedi wa Muluma. Tshisekedi, a Luba from the Kasai area, had once been minister of the interior. He had been very active in efforts during 1979 calling for real democracy. University students had been strongly supportive of these efforts and had staged strikes and demonstrations in favor of them. Tshisedeki had close ties with the students. In November 1979, he had joined a group of other legislators calling for an inquiry into the alleged massacre of young people near the city of Mbuji-Mayi by government troops in July 1978. He also had the audacity in October 1980 to criticize Mobutu's rule and call for reforms in an interview with a Belgian newspaper. Then, in November, he joined twenty-two other Council members who either voted against or abstained on a measure dealing with the creation of the new party Central Committee. Apparently it was at this point that Mobutu decided to move against his Legislative Council critics. The actual triggering event reportedly was criticism of the finances of Mobutu and one of his sons, Colonel Mobutu Niwa, in the Legislative Council by Mpanda Ndjila, one of the five arrested on December 30.

In early January 1981, thirteen more members of the Legislative Council were arrested and charged with subversive activities, inciting revolt, and insulting Mobutu by having issued a lengthy and highly critical document calling for Mobutu to resign and the holding of free and open elections. Six people reportedly were arrested in March just for reading the document. Most of the Legislative Council members arrested in January were from regions long opposed to Mobutu's rule—the two Kasais, Shaba, Kivu, and southern Bandundu. The arrests reportedly touched off violent demonstrations in Kasai Oriental Region, which included the sacking of the regional commissioner's house.

The dissidents were eventually released, but in 1982 the core of them, now known as "The Thirteen," were rearrested for forming an illegal opposition party, the *Union pour la Démocratie et le Progrès Social* (UDPS), "tried," and sentenced to long prison terms. Although several of them have since "recanted" their actions, most of them have continued to oppose the regime internally and, as a result, have been in and out of detention several times.

New Legislative Council elections were held in September 1982 and again in September 1985.

Judiciary

The judiciary has always been controlled by Mobutu. He created the Judiciary Council, composed of all courts and tribunals, and served as its president. The independence of the judiciary was abolished, and it became merely another arm of the state apparatus. This was justified as being in line with the traditional African concept in which the chief is also a judge. Judicial appointments are directly or indirectly controlled by President Mobutu, especially to the Supreme Court, Court of Appeals, and the special Security Court which deals with all cases affecting state security and certain criminal matters. As part of the "liberalization" generated by the first invasion of Shaba Region in 1977, the Judiciary Council was abolished and replaced by a Department of Justice in the Executive Council. The longtime head of the Judiciary Council, Kengo wa Dondo, had come under severe internal and international criticism for harrassing judges and lawyers and for political manipulation of public prosecutors. With the creation of the Department of Justice, Kengo was appointed to the important post of ambassador to Belgium where he could closely observe the increasingly active exile opposition groups.

Regional & Local Government

After coming to power in 1965, Mobutu quickly recentralized the structure of the state along the lines of the Belgian colonial state. This included reducing the number of provinces from twenty-one to eight, abolishing their autonomy, including their assemblies, and renaming them regions. All territorial administrators henceforth were appointed and tightly controlled by the central state apparatus.

Formally, Zaire is a highly centralized administrative state in which regime prefects or territorial commissioners control the population at four administrative levels: regions, subregions, zones, and the local collectivities. The first three levels are structures of the centralizing state; the last—the collectivities—constitute local authorities (traditional, semitraditional, and newer, partially urbanized ones) which frequently remain beyond the complete control of the Zairian state. The prefects operate at each of the first three levels. The core of this prefectoral cadre are the subregional and zone commissioners. They are the ones who attempt to increase central control on a daily basis over the authorities in the local collectivities. Roughly 740 prefects operate at these two levels. They usually have administrative and clerical personnel under them, and they also supervise the numerous but often moribund state services operating in their jurisdictions.

All of the territorial commissioners are appointed by and are directly dependent on Mobutu. They swear an oath of loyalty to him and to the state. They key criterion of selection, maintenance, and promotion is loyalty to Mobutu, commonly referred to as *militantisme*.

The personal bond between Mobutu and his prefects is constantly emphasized. Although they report to the state commissioner for territorial affairs, they are directly responsible to Mobutu. Education is clearly a criterion of selection, but education without loyalty is not sufficient. Loyalty with little education or training, however, has frequently been sufficient. The prefects usually are not assigned to their region of origin and are rotated frequently so they will not develop ties with the local population.

Their primary tasks are those of maintaining order, extracting resources, controlling and slowly emasculating the power of traditional and semitraditional authorities, and performing a number of "party" mobilization functions.

The local population has no real opportunity for political participation. Mobutu has stated, "Our masses must understand that if every person does what pleases him and seeks to satisfy his ambition, anarchy will be the inevitable result."

Popular Movement of the Revolution (*Mouvement Populaire de la Révolution;* MPR)

The MPR is not a political party but rather an arm of the state designed to control and mobilize the populace. The state and party are fused, the former absorbing the latter despite the official rhetoric which proclaims the primacy of the party. State officials are party officials and vice versa. Although for a number of years the constitution formally permitted the existence of a second party, Mobutu never allowed one to form. In a major speech in February 1980, he emphatically declared, "As long as I live, I will never tolerate the creation of another party."

History & Organization

In 1966 Mobutu created the Corps of Volunteers (CVR), a quasipolitical party, to begin institutionalizing his new regime. The creation of a "real" party, the MPR, came in April 1967, and the CVR was abolished. The new party issued the Manifesto of N'Sele—the major programmatic and ideological statement of the infant party. The party was to be controlled by the Political Bureau and was to exist alongside the structure of the government. In a major control move, a youth wing of the party was also created, the *Jeunesse du MPR* (JMPR), which was designed to integrate and control all youth political groups and act as the vigilance committee of the party.

During 1968 attempts were made to improve party organization in the provinces, and measures were taken to assure the close integration of the JMPR into the party. In 1969 the presidency and the Political Bureau of the party increased in importance and scope of powers. The latter began to assume ascendancy over the governmental Council of Ministers (later to become the Executive Council).

During the first party congress in May 1970, the MPR was designated the sole party and supreme institution of the country, thereby theoretically absorbing the state. A constitutional reform in early December ratified the dominant role of the MPR and of its president-founder, Mobutu Sese Seko. By November 1972 the fusion was formally recognized. In fact, the reality was not so clear-cut. At the center, in the high levels of power, the MPR may well have absorbed the state in terms of decision-making power. But in terms of the implementation of policy, even in the center, the state structure remained intact. In the periphery, where the party had not become well institutionalized, the state administration clearly absorbed the party. The state apparatus remained, and state administrators took over all party functions.

The next major changes came in 1974. After a three-day meeting of the Political Bureau on the presidential boat in July, several important measures were announced: a new official doctrine (Mobutuism) a new constitution, a major reshuffle and enlargement of the Political Bureau, and the creation of a party school—the Makanda Kabobi Institute. The new constitution simply ratified in law the results of past centralization efforts and gave Mobutu the preeminent position in the fused party-state as chief of state and president-founder of the party with full and direct control of the major institutions. The MPR was declared the sole institution of the republic. Special clauses in the constitution concerning the removal of the president and the number of presidential terms were not to apply to Mobutu as president-founder. The Legislative Council was called into immediate special session to ratify the new constitution.

During the 1977 "liberalization" process, even the party's Political Bureau was opened to direct elections. Eighteen of the thirty members of the bureau were now to be elected, two from each region and two from Kinshasa, the capital. For the eighteen positions, there were 167 declared candidates, but most of those elected were well-known regime figures, including several members of the "presidential family" and other close collaborators. In the 1980 retrenchment from "liberalization," Mobutu announced that the election of some members of the Political Bureau would not be repeated and that after the bureau's current term expired in 1982, he would again appoint all its members. He earlier had expanded its size to thirty-seven so that the eighteen elected members became a minority rather than a majority.

The new Central Committee was designed by Mobutu "to conceive, to inspire, to orient, to decide and to see to respect for discipline within the Party and to supervise the activities of the MPR." It is headed by a permanent secretary and divided into a number of commissions: economy and finance (with several subcommissions), agriculture and rural development, industry and commerce, and transport and communications. The Central Committee met three times in 1981 to discuss a wide range of policy issues, including "economic reactivation through reactivation of agriculture, well-being and health," educational reform, party discipline, the rights and duties of "citizens," and administrative reform. This docile new institution clearly was meant to eclipse the more conten-tious Legislative Council. Nonetheless, in the summer of 1982, the Central Committee carefully screened and "approved" candidates for new Legislative Council elections which were held in September. In 1985 the Central Committee was reduced to 80 members.

Policy

The party has no real program for the country. Its sole policy is to serve Mobutu. What development or reform policies are announced by the party from time to time are more in the nature of internal and external propaganda than realistic plans.

Membership & Constituency

By definition every Zairian "citizen" is a member of the MPR, but genuine support for the party is minimal. Where it does exist, it has a highly opportunistic character: people actively support the party in order to improve their economic and social condition. On the whole, "participation" is administratively induced and coerced.

Zairian prefects have "party" mobilization and propaganda tasks in their local areas. The four main types of activities are (1) mass meetings (reassemblements populaires) held at all levels of the administrative hierarchy; (2) animation; (3) marches of support (marches de soutien); and (4) constructing and dedicating monuments, signs or other symbols glorifying the state, the party, and, above all, Mobutu.

Administrators at all levels of the state hierarchy conduct mass meetings, usually on subjects dictated from above. These range from the latest grandiose policies decreed by Mobutu (agriculture "number one priority," state takeover of the schools), to local administrative changes (a new collectivity chief, new tax collection procedures), the content of the latest Mobutu speech, and general ideological themes of the regime (authenticity, economic independence, "radicalization of the revolution"), and to the propagation of Mobutuism—the political religion. The meetings involve only one-way communication—from state to subject. Policies and dramatic decisions come and go; each is grandly announced in turn. But the basic themes remain remarkably constant with the emphasis on order, control, and the duties of the subjects.

Meetings often are preceded by *sessions d'animation* to warm up the crowd that has been assembled by local officials and notables, usually on the orders of prefects. In *animation*, groups of men and women sing and dance political slogans and messages and songs of praise. Traditional songs and dances have been systematically collected and adapted to a new political medium. More than any other form of "party" activity, *animation* is principally focused on the glorification of Mobutu. One chant says, "We sing and dance to honor our Guide and express our love for him."

Marches of support are held for Mobutu or his policies at all levels, from the smallest collectivity up to the major cities such as Lubumbashi, Kisangani, and Kinshasa. All the various groups of the country are carefully organized to participate in the marches—school children, state and private workers, soldiers and police, the churches, the JMPR, veterans, and businessmen, as well as ordinary "citizens." For example, in April 1974, marches of support were held throughout the country to thank Mobutu for the victory of the Léopards, the state soccer team, in the Africa division of the World Cup competition.

The prefects also are responsible for distributing and explaining the significance of various symbols of the regime, notably the picture of Mobutu that must hang in all buildings open to the public, the national flag, and the party emblem. Little cement pillars with a picture of Mobutu, the party torch, and the inscription "Long Live President Mobutu" can be found in small urban parks, crossroads, and the smallest rural villages. Other signs say things like "MPR = Service," "The MPR First, the Rest After," and "Mobutu Sese Seko Our Only Guide."

Financing

Financial support comes from the state budget, tax revenues, and "party dues" collected by the territorial administration.

Leadership

President Mobutu was born October 14, 1930, in the Equateur Region river town of Lisala. His father was a cook for Catholic missionaries and eventually for a Belgian magistrate in Lisala. Mobutu is Ngbandi, both of his parents coming from the area of Mobayi-Mbong (Banzyville).

The Ngbandi are a small and isolated group from the northern savanna of Zaire along the border with the Central African Republic; Mobutu is related to Jean-Bedel Bokassa, the former president and later emperor of that state. For most Zairians, the Ngbandi are not a widely recognized group, and Mobutu is thus generally perceived as being Ngala because his primary African language is Lingala.

Mobutu attended Catholic primary and secondary schools in Mbandaka (Coquilhatville) and briefly in Kinshasa. Although a good student, he was expelled from the school in Mbandaka for disciplinary reasons, and, as a result, was automatically conscripted into the *Force Publique*, the Belgian colonial army, in February 1950. Trained in administration and accounting in a special military school in Kananga (Luluabourg), he rose to the highest African rank of sergeant major before being released at the end of 1956. Pursuing earlier interests, Mobutu went to work as a journalist in Kinshasa for *L'Avenir* and later as a writer and editor for *Actualités Africaines*, the first newspaper by and for Africans. He helped Patrice Lumumba to organize the *Mouvement National Congolais* (MNC). In 1958 and again in 1959 Mobutu visited Brussels as a journalist, and in 1959 enrolled as a trainee in *Infocongo*, a Belgian propaganda agency for the Congo, while pursuing other studies. He also reportedly had contacts with the Belgian *Sûreté* during this period. After Lumumba's arrest in the Congo in November 1959, Mobutu worked for his release in Brussels, and he was later an MNC delegate to the Round Table Conferences which negotiated Zaire's abrupt independence in June 1960. Just before independence, Mobutu returned to Kinshasa and acted as Lumumba's senior private secretary. Right after independence, Mobutu helped to contain the mutiny of the *Force Publique*, and Lumumba made him a colonel and appointed him chief-of-staff of the army under Commander-in-Chief General Victor Lundala.

In September 1960, Mobutu staged his first coup, neutralizing both President Joseph Kasavubu and Prime Minister Lumumba. In February 1961 he returned power to Kasavubu who promoted him to major general and appointed him commander-in-chief of the army. Although he attempted to assume the mantle of Lumumbaism after 1965, Mobutu has been implicated in Lumumba's arrest and murder.

While in the *Force Publique*, Mobutu met and later married a woman from Banzyville; by

1974 they had seven children. Marie Antionette Mobutu died in 1980, and Mobutu has remarried. Although a self-proclaimed Catholic, Mobutu has had serious conflicts with the Catholic Church in Zaire. Tall, good looking, and immensely proud, Mobutu can be both disarmingly charming and very cruel and imperious. This shrewd and pragmatic ruler has always had a burning ambition for both himself and his country, the fates of which he sees as inextricably mixed. After the 1965 coup, he told a foreign journalist, "I want to make the Congo a country that the world will no longer laugh at." He is vain and very sensitive to criticism, yet courageous, and a prodigious worker who also greatly enjoys high living.

Mobutu has not allowed any regime official to develop long-term autonomy or a viable power base. When an individual appears to be moving in that direction, he is replaced. Most regime officials come from Equateur Region; one of the few exceptions was the former ambassador, foreign and prime minister, Nguza Karl-i-Bond, a Lunda from Shaba Region, who went into exile in 1981. Despite Mobutu's techniques of elite control, the officials of the regime are beginning to constitute a veritable ruling class, but one heavily dependent on Mobutu himself.

Satellite Organizations

President Mobutu has sought to control all key societal groups and organizations. Almost immediately after the coup in 1964, he suspended the right of unions to strike. In June 1967 all unions were forced to merge into a party-state union federation, the *Union Nationale des Travailleurs Zairois* (UNTZa). All ethnic associations were banned in 1968. Student riots in 1969 led to the abolition of all student associations; the JMPR became the sole representative of the students. But the regime had major trouble with the students again in 1971, 1979, and 1980 when demonstrations had to be put down with force. In 1971, this unrest led directly to the nationalization of the universities and much closer surveillance of the students by the JMPR and the secret police.

The party-state also attacked another major source of autonomous power—the press. It was reorganized in 1972 to become a vehicle for the thoughts and ideas of the party and its president-founder. The number of periodicals was greatly reduced, and strict control applied to those that survived. In Kinshasa the number of newspapers went from thirteen to two eventually, and in the interior from about twenty down to two dailies and three weeklies. In January 1974, the regime announced that the "hypocritical distinction between information and propaganda" was to disappear in Zaire. Control measures were also applied to sports, the arts, music, and literature, all to be directly controlled and channeled by the party-state structure and its president-founder. Finally, in September 1975, the Political Bureau decided that MPR committees would be installed in all large economic enterprises.

Opposition

As a result of the economic, military, and political crises since 1975, opposition to the Mobutu regime has increased substantially. In January 1978, a small uprising took place near the town of Idiofa in the Kwilu area of Bandundu Region, near the native village of Pierre Mulele, an early 1960s revolutionary leader. Followers of a local millenarian religious sect attacked two villages, and the army was brought in to stop them. Fourteen leaders of the uprising were publicly executed without trial, and Amnesty International estimates that about 500 other people were killed. An attempted military coup allegedly took place in March 1978. In July 1979 about 200 young people were killed by soldiers near the city of Mbuji-Mayi in Kasai Oriental Region, apparently for failing to pay the army for permission to engage in illegal digging for diamonds and for refusing to cease digging when so ordered by troops.

Students staged violent strikes and riots on all of the national university (UNAZA) campuses in February 1979. The specific causes were related to the conditions of student life, but heavy political overtones hung over the actions of the students. Regime troops ended the disturbances. Throughout 1979 students and teachers took part in efforts to push liberalization efforts in a substantive direction, particularly with a call for two additional political parties. These actions led in large part to the downfall in January 1980 of Mungul-Diaka, the state commissioner for higher education, apparently because of his sympathies for the students. He subsequently escaped into exile and headed a new umbrella organization of opposition groups, the Committee for the Liberation of the Congo (CLC), founded in July 1980. In April

1980 university students again mounted a major strike at all three UNAZA campuses. In addition to university-related demands, the students called for the removal of the entire Political Bureau and the establishment of a multiparty system. Army troops violently stopped the demonstrations and closed the campuses, the students were evacuated to the interior, and the university shut down until October. Primary-school teachers also staged a large-scale strike between March and June 1980. In 1981 UNAZA reorganized as three separate universities, and important protests by university students took place again in 1984 and 1985.

External opposition to the Mobutu regime has always been poorly organized, factionalized, and generally ineffective. Groups come and go, hardly more than loosely organized cliques. Few have real roots inside the country, much less coherent policy programs or opposition activities. Political terrorism is as yet nonexistent. No recognized leader dominates the opposition, and no opposition ideology unites it. This is in part due to the fact that, at least so far, Zaire has not produced an effective anti-Western Marxist intelligentsia. About the only thing the opposition can agree upon is referring to the country by its former name of the Congo. The major opposition parties and organizations are:

Front de Libération Nationale du Congo (FLNC)

Founded in 1968 by Nathaniel Mbumba and based in Paris and Angola, the FLNC has its roots in the refugees (largely Lunda and Chokwe) who fled into Angola after the failed Katanga secession attempt in the early 1960s. With the alleged help of Angola and other countries, the FLNC organized and carried out the two invasions of Shaba Region in 1977 and 1978. Neither invasion triggered the expected mass uprisings against the regime, but Mobutu survived only because of direct combat assistance by Moroccan troops in 1977 and French and Belgian troops in 1978. After the failure of the second invasion and its subsequent reconciliation with Zaire, Angola moved key FLNC personnel to Guinea-Bissau and its armed units away from the border. The ideological orientation of the FLNC is unclear, and it has several internal factions.

Parti Révolutionnaire Populaire (PRP)

Laurent Kabila, a leader of the rebellions of the early 1960s, founded the PRP in 1967. For years it has carried on intermittent guerilla activity in the South Kivu–North Shaba area near Lake Tanganyika. Although it has Lumumbist roots, it professes a Marxist-Leninist ideology. In 1977, the PRP formed a loose coalition with the FLNC, called the *Conseil Supérieur de Libération* (CSL), of which little came. The PRP was apparently responsible for armed attacks on the town of Moba on the shores of Lake Tanganyika in November 1984 and again in June 1985.

Mouvement d'Action pour la Résurrection au Congo (MARC)

Based in Brussels, MARC was particularly active among Zairian students and some intellectuals in Belgium in the 1970s. An outgrowth of the *Mouvement du 4 Juin,* an underground student movement commemorating the student revolt of 1969, MARC published an important opposition magazine called *Miso Gaa* which drew widespread attention and was outlawed in Zaire. Its president and secretary general were condemned to death in absentia in March 1978 for allegedly fomenting internal dissent. Later in the year the secretary general died under mysterious circumstances.

Mouvement National Congolais-Lumumba (MNC-L)

This group is Marxist in orientation and uses the name of Patrice Lumumba's old political party; it is in fact sometimes referred to as the MNC-L *Rénouvé.* Based in Paris, it has worked with French Amnesty International in issuing reports on human rights violations in Zaire. Hostile to the PRP, it reportedly also has had a small military presence in northeastern Zaire. Lumumbaism remains a latent and potentially important force of opposition, despite Mobutu's attempts to co-opt it.

Comité pour la Libération du Congo (CLC)

The Brussels-based CLC emerged from a three-week congress in Belgium in June 1980. It represented the first attempt of several of the most serious opposition groups to create an umbrella organization. It was headed by Bernardin

Mungul-Diaka, the former state commissioner for higher education. Despite being sentenced in absentia to eleven years forced labor and having his properties confiscated in August 1980, he remained a controversial figure because of a history of compromise with the regime. This controversy was refueled when he returned to Zaire from exile. At various points the CLC included the FLNC, the PRP, and the *Mouvement National de l'Union pour la Reconciliation* (MNUR), a small group founded by Mbeka Makosso, a former ambassador to Iran who went into exile in June 1978. He, too, subsequently returned from exile. Other groups in the CLC have included a small group headed by Valère Nzamba, and the *Etudiants Congolais Progressistes*, a student group focused primarily on the University of Louvain-la-Neuve in Belgium. Both MARC and MNC-L stayed out of CLC.

Apparently, the CLC replaced an earlier umbrella effort called the *Organisation pour la Libération du Congo* (OLC), founded in 1978. The FLNC and the PRP were not members of the OLC, which faded away like so many other anti-Mobutu groups. Problems of organization and policy cohesion constantly plagued the CLC.

Most of the main opposition groups have received assistance from the *Comité Zaire* made up of exiled Zairian academics and intellectuals and Belgian sympathizers, Flemish socialists in particular. The exile opposition has fluctuated in size over the years. For example, ten Zairians requested asylum in France in 1978, five hundred in 1979, and about one thousand in 1980. In April 1981 the Mobutu regime was dealt its most spectacular blow when Nguza Karl-i-Bond, the prime minister and former foreign minister, resigned while overseas and went into exile. Giving only personal reasons for the move, Nguza at first took no antagonistic actions towards the regime. In public statements in June, however, he sharply attacked Mobutu's rule while declaring his opposition. He called for the overthrow of the regime by the West in its own interests, and charged Mobutu himself with massive corruption and systematic efforts to emasculate the control measures of the IMF. In testimony before a committee of the U.S. House of Representatives in September 1981, he repeated his charges, and among other things, declared that the Amnesty International reports about Zaire were accurate despite attempts he had made while in office to denigrate them. In 1982, Nguza published a book entitled *Mobutu ou l'incarnation du Mal Zaïrois*

(*Mobutu or the Incarnation of the Zairian Disease*), which was highly critical of the regime. In October 1982 Nguza helped to form a new coalition organization of opposition groups, called the Congolese Front for the Restoration of Democracy (FCD), which replaced the CLC. He became the head of the FCD, which included the UDPS and the PRP. In 1985, however, Nguza also decided exile opposition politics was not for him. His quiet return to Kinshasa was timed to coincide with the celebrations of the 25th anniversary of Zairian independence in June. Full restoration of "the prodigal son" came in 1986 when Mobutu selected Nguza to be his new ambassador to the United States.

Other Political Forces

Military

Mobutu has maintained his direct and personal control of military affairs as commander-in-chief and often as head of the Department of National Defense. The military, now called the *Forces Armées Zairoises* (FAZ), has always been a major pillar of his support, more prominently in the beginning, but still very important in succeeding years. However, it has occasionally troubled the regime and has never functioned as a truly effective combat force when confronted with a major threat. Immediately after the coup, states of emergency and exception were instituted which allowed extensive intervention of the military into politico-administrative affairs. Initially, the provinces remained effectively under military administration and control. Provincial police units were brought under the supervision of the army until 1966, when they were reorganized as a national police force under the Ministry of the Interior (now the Department of Territorial Administration).

Right after the coup, the *Sûreté* was reorganized and brought under the control of Colonel Singa, a close collaborator of General Mobutu. In 1969 it was again reorganized, becoming the *Centre National de Documentation*. It has been reorganized several times since then, eventually becoming the *Centre National de Recherches et d'Investigations*. This secret police has complete financial and administrative autonomy from the rest of the government and is directly controlled by Mobutu through the presidency. In August 1969 Mobutu created the

National Security Council to assure coordination between all the forces of order.

After the formation of the MPR in 1967, some tension existed between it and the military. President Mobutu made increasingly persistent efforts in succeeding years to integrate the military into the MPR, to little avail. In 1972 the national police was transformed into a gendarmery which was integrated into the military structure of FAZ. At the same time, Mobutu modified the FAZ command structure and made important personnel changes, and the party congress has tried to give new social and educational functions to the military. In July and August 1974, Mobutu again instituted a new command structure and created a general military intelligence service within the president's office. At the same time, five military officers were appointed to the Political Bureau, thus giving the military strong representation in the highest circles of the party-state. Military representation in the Political Bureau has fluctuated over time, however. At the end of 1974, Mobutu severely attacked the military as a scourge of society because it consumed resources without being productive. Vague measures were announced that would give it a more active social role. As a result, some unrest was generated in the military which may have been manifested in an alleged attempted coup in June 1975. Another shakeup was instituted by Mobutu which seems to have restored his full control. Several alleged coups, plots, and subsequent purges and reorganizations have taken place since, however, especially after the disastrous performance of the army during the invasions of Shaba Region in 1977 and 1978.

In 1984 FAZ consisted of an army of 22,000, a navy of 1,500, an air force of 2,500, and the gendarmery of about 22,000. But after the two military embarrassments at Moba in November 1984 and June 1985, Mobutu announced a shakeup of his senior military staff, the enlargement of his armed forces by about 30 percent, the creation of a new military intelligence unit, and the formation of a new civil guard to be trained by West Germany. Most military equipment and training are supplied by Belgium, the United States, France, China, and Israel. The military remains one of the most important, if precarious, pillars of support for Mobutu, but it is clearly not an effective fighting force despite considerable external efforts to improve combat capability. The military is, however, an effective, if brutal and undisciplined, internal-control instrument. In these efforts, it is assisted by the JMPR. Opposition within the military most likely exists, but it is difficult to verify.

Religious & Fraternal Groups

In July 1971, organizations such as the Templars and the Free Masons, which were seen as threats to public order, were banned. (The Free Masons were reinstated in April 1972, but most of the other organizations remained dissolved.) In a major party-state control effort in December 1971, the government announced a law regulating all churches in Zaire. The state recognized only three main churches: (1) the Catholic Church, (2) the Church of Christ in Zaire (a grouping of various Protestant denominations and sects), and (3) the Kimbanguist Church. Islamic, Greek Orthodox, and Jewish groups were later also recognized. But all other religious groups were abolished in a major effort to control the rapid proliferation of new syncretic religious sects which the regime viewed as covers for political opposition.

The Catholic Church is the strongest non-state organization in Zaire. It is so because it possesses a clear doctrine, a body of faithful who believe that doctrine (about 40 percent of the population); good organization throughout the country; a clearly established and recognized hierarchy; immense resources; control of much of the country's health, welfare, and educational activities; and strong external ties. It was not long before Mobutu and those around him began to view the Church as an opposing protostate structure. Given this situation, state-Church tension was almost unavoidable.

The only important leader in Zaire with a clearly autonomous power base who has been able to stand up to Mobutu consistently over time is Joseph Albert Cardinal Malula. Born in Kinshasa on December 17, 1917, of a Baluba father and a mother from Equateur Region, he was educated at the Petit Seminaire in Bolongo and the Grand Seminaire in Kabwe, where he studied classics and humanities. He started his ecclesiastical career as a vicar in a Kinshasa parish. He became auxiliary bishop of Kinshasa in 1959, archbishop in 1964, and cardinal in 1969. In 1968 he began to speak out vigorously within the Church for increased "authenticity," calling for more rapid Africanization of the clergy and African expression in the forms of worship. Ironically, one of his first conflicts with the state was over Mobutu's own political and social version of authenticity.

Church and state have come into conflict on numerous occasions: in 1971 over student protests and the subsequent nationalization of the Church-run Lovanium University and the government's decision to establish JMPR branches in Church seminaries; in 1972 over Mobutu's decision to ban the use of Christian first names in favor of "authentic" Zairian ones and also to ban all religious and television broadcasts and all religious youth groups; in 1973 when the government banned thirty-one religious publications so that "the national masses (would) be oriented by one and only one source"; in 1974 over government controls on the travel and meeting rights of Church officials because of their criticism of the regime and over the proclamation of Mobutuism as the official national ideology; and in 1975 and 1976 over the nationalization of Church schools and the teaching of Mobutuism in them (the schools were returned to the Church in 1976). In addition, Church officials have periodically and eloquently attacked the regime for its brutality, rampant corruption, authoritarian manner, and lack of real social-welfare content to its policies. At the time of the 1984 presidential election, Cardinal Malula suggested that people "should vote according to their souls and consciences, keeping in mind the past, the present, and the future of the country." Mobutu responded by curtailing religious services.

In the mid-1980s the regime became increasingly concerned about the rapid proliferation of independent religious movements, whose actions it viewed with suspicion and hostility. It called them a "plague" and an "hysterical craze" exploited by enemies of the state and announced that all "sects" would be investigated "in order to protect the people from all practices that are contrary to the interests of the community and to the party's ideals."

External Groups

Zaire was born in the international arena, and it has remained there. International assistance has been a continuous and pervasive factor supporting the emergence, consolidation, and survival of President Mobutu's regime since 1965. Military, economic, and political support by Belgium, the United States, France, Great Britain, China, Israel, and other states has been crucial, especially in attempting to cope with the severe economic and fiscal crisis commencing in 1975, the two invasions of Shaba Region in 1977 and 1978, and subsequent political unrest and opposition. The International Monetary Fund, World Bank, and numerous private international banks have also played very important roles in attempting to cope with the regime's enormous economic and fiscal problems.

The causes of the economic crisis were multiple: a dramatic fall in the price of copper, the closure of the Benguela Railroad in Angola, the disastrous economic effects of the "Zairianization" of many foreign-owned businesses (1973–75), and rising oil prices. All of these conditions were made far worse by other factors. Political factors are very important: massive and rash spending and borrowing when revenues were high, rampant corruption, fiscal and economic mismanagement, and a lack of understanding or concern about the rapidly deteriorating situation by Mobutu and his political elite. High regime officials have traditionally known and cared little about economics. They are political, not economic, men.

The regime has borrowed extensively and often unwisely able to do so because of its vast potential wealth. By the end of 1973, 67 percent of the total external debt was of the hard-term variety which created severe debt-service problems. The government tried to hide the actual amount of debt-service payments, but in the first half of 1973, actual payments exceeded 80 percent of the budget estimates for such payments for the entire year. In 1975 the regime did not even have a roughly accurate list of how much it owed or to whom. The World Bank and the United Nations finally provided personnel to sort things out. The figures were staggering. In 1976, the total debt was more than a third of Zaire's total expenditure and 12 percent of its GDP. By 1977 the total debt was estimated at over $4 billion; debt-service payments were the equivalent of 43.4 percent of export earnings and 49.5 percent of total state revenue.

Under external pressure, particularly from the International Monetary Fund (IMF), Mobutu put together three stabilization plans (*Les Plans Mobutu*), the first in March 1976, the second in November 1977, and the third in August 1979. In each case the IMF extended substantial standby credit (SDR 118 million, about $153 million, for the third stabilization plan in 1979). The plans aimed to cut corruption, rationalize expenditures, increase tax revenues, limit imports, boost production in all sectors, improve transportation infrastructure, eliminate arrears on interest payments, make principal payments on time, and generally improve financial management and economic planning.

The results of early efforts by Zairian officials proved meager; so in 1978 the IMF decided to send its own team of experts to Zaire to take over key financial positions in the Bank of Zaire, the Department of Finance, and the Customs Office. In December of 1978, the head of the Bank of Zaire team took dramatic measures which struck at the heart of the power of the political elite. He cut off credit and exchange facilities to companies owned by key members of the political elite, including some of Mobutu's closest collaborators, and imposed strict foreign-exchange quotas. Efforts to impose budgetary control over the presidency were circumvented, however. Former foreign and prime minister, Nguza Karl-i-Bond, charged from exile in June 1981 that Mobutu himself had siphoned off up to $100 million in World Bank and IMF assistance.

In June 1981, the IMF approved an extended fund facility (EFF) for Zaire of about $1.2 billion to be allocated over three years in return for new reform efforts. The next month Zaire's creditor countries (the Paris Club) met for the fourth time in five years and rescheduled $3.34 billion. In April of the previous year its commercial bank creditors had rescheduled $434 million in syndicated debt. The IMF canceled the EFF in June 1982 for noncompliance and forced Zaire to follow a "shadow program" for over a year before it agreed to a new standby agreement in December 1983. The "shadow program" included significant new policy measures, including a 77.5 percent devaluation. The Paris Club also rescheduled Zairian debt again in December 1983. The new IMF agreement worked better than in the past and was followed by another standby agreement and a sixth Paris Club rescheduling in 1985. Despite the much touted "success" of these efforts, an IMF official noted that "these measures have considerably improved the image of Zaire abroad, but the economic recovery at home has remained modest so far."

National Prospects

Compared with most other African countries, Zaire has vast resources and enormous economic potential—substantial and important mineral deposits (copper, cobalt, industrial diamonds), huge hydroelectric potential, and more than adequate arable land to feed its roughly 31 million people. Zaire also has relatively high foreign-exchange earnings, but the country is nevertheless nearly bankrupt. Its total foreign debt is now about $4.5 billion, economic growth has all but stopped, and the mass standard of living has fallen precipitously in recent years. Agricultural output is down dramatically; nutrition levels and literacy rates are falling dangerously; and social welfare services and the transportation network have seriously deteriorated. Unemployment and underemployment levels are dangerously high, inflation is rampant, and corruption permeates the political structure, particularly at the top. Mobutu and his political elite live grandly, while the vast majority struggle from day to day. Periodically, the regime grandiosely announces sweeping "policies" to deal with these problems, but they are never implemented in any serious way. For example, agriculture has been "priority of priorities" for years now, while rural decline continues. The regime's real substantive thrust is that of control and personal aggrandizement, despite its revolutionary rhetoric and Mobutu's attempt to wear Lumumba's mantle.

Without international support the regime would collapse, but the countries and the banks cannot afford to let it do so for both economic and politico-strategic reasons. Mobutu has gone to great lengths to avoid paying the country's debts and to avoid the penalties for not paying. He knows that lending is a two-way street, and he has played the debt-repayment game shrewdly. However, for the majority of Zairians, the cost of internationally imposed reforms and austerity measures is very high indeed. Recovery depends on reestablishing the productive capacity of the economy, but the prospects are not bright despite the recently alleged "success."

In November 1985, the Mobutu regime loudly celebrated its twentieth anniversary. In 1965, most observers would not have been willing to forecast that this regime would last five years, much less twenty.

Mobutu most likely can rule as long as his will to dominate lasts, he is blessed with *fortuna*, external assistance remains available, his opposition continues to be divided and ineffectual, and his control of the military continues. But change in one or two of these conditions might well lead to a change in regime. Mobutu has made no real preparation for a succession, and, if something were to happen to him, Zaire might well disintegrate again as it did during the early 1960s. Although highly authoritarian in nature, the unity of the Zairian state is fragile. A power vacuum in Kinshasa, however temporary, might well release ethnic, regional, and class unrest which the military might not be able to control. International intervention, possibly by opposing forces, might well follow.

Further Reading

Callaghy, Thomas M. *The State-Society Struggle: Zaire in Comparative Perspective.* New York: Columbia University Press, 1984.

————. "The Political Economy of African Debt: The Case of Zaire." In *Africa in Economic Crisis,* John Ravenhill, ed. New York: Columbia University Press, 1986.

Gould, David J. *Bureaucratic Corruption and Underdevelopment in the Third World: The Case of Zaire.* New York: Pergamon Press, 1980.

Gran, Guy, ed. *Zaire: The Political Economy of Underdevelopment.* New York: Praeger, 1979.

Kaplan, Irving, ed. *Zaire: A Country Study.* 3rd ed. Department of the Army. Washington, D.C.: U.S. Government Printing Office, 1979.

Naipaul, V. S. *A Bend in the River.* New York: Random House, 1980.

Nzongola-Ntalaja, ed. *The Crisis in Zaire: Myths and Realities.* Trenton, N.J.: Africa World Press, 1986.

Schatzberg, Michael G. *Politics and Class in Zaire: Bureaucracy, Business, and Beer in Lisala.* New York and London: Africana Publishing, 1980.

Willame, Jean-Claude. *Patrimonialism and Political Change in the Congo.* Stanford, Calif.: Stanford University Press, 1972.

Young, Crawford. *Politics in the Congo.* Princeton, N.J.: Princeton University Press, 1965.

————, and Thomas Turner. *The Rise and Decline of the Zairian State.* Madison: University of Wisconsin Press, 1985.

REPUBLIC OF ZAMBIA

by Marcia M. Burdette, Ph.D. revised by Elizabeth Normandy, M.A.

The System of Government

Zambia, a nation of over 5.6 million people in southern Africa, is a one-party presidential democracy whose present leader, Dr. Kenneth D. Kaunda, brought the country to independence in 1964. Kaunda advocates a doctrine called "Humanism" which functions as the official ideology of the governing party, the United National Independence Party (UNIP). The doctrine purports to describe a path to noncapitalist development. The regime, bolstered by the one-party political system, has slowly come to control most of the productive sector of the urban economy. The form of government is a combination of the British parliamentary system and the presidential model; over the years, the presidential elements have come to outweigh the parliamentary ones. The one-party system was instituted with the constitution of December 1972, which inaugurated the Second Republic. The First Republic began with Zambia's independence from Great Britain in 1964.

Executive

Executive power resides with the president, the cabinet, the prime minister, and also with the party hierarchy in the Central Committee of UNIP. President Kaunda (often called KK) is also president of UNIP.

The president's powers are extensive under both the Zambian and UNIP constitutions; in practice, his powers and prerogatives are larger still. As head of state, he appoints and dismisses the prime minister and, in consultation with the prime minister, appoints and dismisses ministers and junior ministers. He appoints (but cannot dismiss) the chief justice, the auditor general, permanent secretaries, and the secretary to the cabinet, as well as the boards and managing directors of various state-owned companies. He commands the armed forces and has extensive emergency powers. His office also encompasses several key portfolios. In the 1969 takeover of the mines, for example, President Kaunda was the minister for state participation.

In his daily routine, the president presides over cabinet and Central Committee meetings; greets foreign dignitaries; and acts as chairman of ZIMCO, the government holding company with shares in various enterprises. With his political advisors, the president is instrumental in various domestic and foreign policy decisions. Kaunda is an active and resourceful politician and head of state. As head of the party, the president has the aid of a corps of personal assistants, advisors, and politicians located in Freedom House, UNIP's headquarters.

The Zambian cabinet consists of the secretary general of UNIP ex officio, the prime minister, and a varying number of ministers as heads of departments. As a whole, the cabinet is responsible for advising the president in respect to government policy and implementation. The degree of responsibility that the cabinet has to Parliament is unclear. Under the 1972 constitution, the cabinet is to be in charge of "policy implementation rather than policy formation." Ministers of state and permanent secretaries are senior administrators of the ministries; the latter as the apex of the civil service and the former often as political appointees. President Kaunda and his advisors have attempted to balance the politicians and civil servants serving in the cabinet in terms of their regional origins. A pattern of frequent shuffles and reshuffles of portfolios among politicians means that few ministers or junior ministers serve in any one ministry for over eighteen months.

The president selects a prime minister from within the National Assembly to serve as titular head of government. Although not a particularly powerful figure, the prime minister oversees a series of important portfolios or functions located within his office, e.g., the Provincial and Local Government Administration Division and the Personnel Division. He also defends government policy in the Assembly, often against loud criticism from backbenchers. The post of prime minister is of less importance in the Second Republic than the secretary general of UNIP, who takes precedence over the prime minister in policy and acts for the president when he is out of the country.

The Central Committee of UNIP plays a vital role in the executive functions of the state. Under the 1971 party constitution and the Zambian constitution, the Central Committee of the party is superior to the cabinet and acts as the primary policymaking body for government. As the Central Committee is potentially so powerful, the president and his advisors are careful to see that its membership (twenty-five, officially) displays a regional balance. Most of the Central Committee's work is done in subcommittees. The chairpersons of these subcommittees outrank the ministers whose portfolios fall within their competence. In addition nine members of the Central Committee, since 1976, have served as representatives of the provinces and thus take an advocacy role for their home districts and indirectly for their own linguistic or ethnic group.

Conflicts between cabinet and Central Committee are rare. Because the cabinet is in direct control of the bureaucracy, which is quite strong, it usually prevails in policymaking as well as policy implementation. However, there have been cases where the Cabinet has been overruled, for example, the 1974 cabinet decision to raise the prices of bread and cooking oil, which brought a great outcry from the population and was overturned by the Central Committee. To diminish the chances for conflict, the Central Committee and the cabinet hold joint meetings approximately every two weeks.

Legislature

Legislative power is vested in the Parliament which consists of the president and the National Assembly. The National Assembly has 125 elected members, up to ten additional members appointed by the president, and a speaker. The president tends to appoint technically skilled men or people from specific regions who can then be drawn into his cabinet.

The National Assembly has a term of five years and must meet at least once a year. The Assembly must approve any alterations of the constitution and can confer on any person or authority the power to make statutory instruments, which have the force of law. Officially, bills originate in the Assembly and are passed onto the president for his opinion. In practice,

bills and amendments usually begin in the various ministries, go to the cabinet office and UNIP headquarters for clearance, and only then to the National Assembly. The president can halt the passage of any measure by withholding his assent; there is no way for the Assembly to override the president's final opinion on a parliamentary matter.

Members of Parliament can question ministers on their performance in office and have exercised considerable freedom in so doing. In the recent past, the National Assembly has shown some pugnacity on issues arising in Parliament and has subjected government representatives to close questioning on such matters as budget, government expenditures, and a new local administration bill. Despite its weakness relative to the executive, the National Assembly must approve taxes and levies, although it cannot, by itself, increase taxes or impose charges upon the general revenues of the republic.

In the National Assembly the proportion of educated and professional women and men has been increasing in recent years. Businessmen, commercial farmers, and civil servants have joined the diminishing percentage of teachers, professional politicians, and trade unionists in the latest Assembly. This new character of the Assembly contributes to the more combative tone of parliamentary debates, because many members, if they lose office, can now return to other professions. Nonetheless, the National Assembly serves primarily to legitimize government policy through debate and passage of bills rather than as a law-making body.

Another group sometimes involved in the legislative process is the House of Chiefs. Established in the Second Republic, it is composed of traditional leaders elected by the chiefs' provincial councils. The House of Chiefs has the rather imprecise mandate to consider and discuss any bills in the National Assembly or other matters referred to them by the president. It seems to have been created in order to pacify traditional authorities who are otherwise bypassed in the modern system. So far, the House has acted as a rubber stamp for all government proposals. The administration of House affairs is managed by the prime minister's office.

Judiciary

The legal system in Zambia derives primarily from the British colonial tradition. The highest court is the Supreme Court of Zambia which is the final court of appeal and the superior court of record. The High Court is one step below the Supreme Court but is more active, having unlimited original jurisdiction and in most legal matters has the final word. Judges to both sets of courts are appointed by the president; under the constitution the president can revoke the appointment of a justice only after investigation by a tribunal.

In 1981, the High Court heard a charge of false arrest brought by four trade-union officials who had been jailed in June. Despite the sensitive nature of the case, the court ruled in favor of the trade unionists, who were subsequently released. Equally controversial is the so-called treason trial of various highly placed officials, including a former governor of the Bank of Zambia, a prominent Lusaka lawyer, a former general manager of the National Building Society, and four high-ranking military officers. The state alleged that these individuals had participated in a plan to abduct the president and force him to resign. The plan was said to have been the idea of a white Zambian lawyer, a man who was a friend of Simon Kapwepwe, the late opponent of the president. Others involved in the plot apparently disagreed with the socialist-type policies of Kaunda and the UNIP.

In January 1983, seven persons, including three prominent Zambians were found guilty of treason and sentenced to death. A Zambian air force officer was given a ten-year prison sentence for misprison of treason. On the appeal, the Supreme Court ruled in 1985 to uphold the convictions except in two cases where evidence had been obtained under duress, and the interrogators had overstepped their authority. Despite charges from some of the defendants about lack of court neutrality and government interference in the trial, the defendants seem to have received a relatively free and fair trial, with the court following established legal procedures in the longest criminal case in Zambia's history to date. President Kaunda may still pardon the convicted men.

The Judicial Service Commission oversees the behavior of the judiciary and consists of the chief justice, the attorney general, the chairman of the Public Service Commission, the secretary to the cabinet, and one other member appointed by the president. An Anti-Corruption Commission was appointed in 1981; headed by Supreme Court Justice William Bruce-Lyle, it has been given wide-ranging powers but, so far, has been inactive. It will operate parallel to the formal judiciary and follows a set of procedures that places the burden of proof on the accused rather than on the prosecution.

Regional & Local Government

The nation is divided into nine provinces, each with its own hierarchy of officials. Below the provinces are the districts; the smallest unit of government is the local government authority. Each layer of government is, in turn, connected to a set of lateral bodies such as provincial and district development committees which are meant to be mobilizing forces in the countryside and the urban and periurban areas. Traditional authorities—chiefs, headmen, and various familial and lineage authorities—arbitrate most disputes over domestic and inheritance questions.

In December 1980, a new Local Administration Bill (LAA) was passed by Parliament. It included provisions for a greater devolution of power and authority to the subnational levels of government, as well as an alteration in the relationship between the party and the civil service at the local level. The slogan used was "decentralization in centralism." The important portfolio for local government, however, is still in the prime minister's office, and most vital services—education, welfare, police, and health—are still controlled by central ministries in the capital. Thus, the move towards more autonomous local government is still to be realized, but after a five-year transitional period, there may be more local control.

Under the new plan, which was implemented in 1981, mayors and district chairmen were to be replaced by district governors, and town clerks were to become executive secretaries. The trade unions objected to these changes because they increased party control over local government and thus diminished the areas in which the trade unions might exercise influence. Despite a boycott threat by the trade unions, the new system was implemented with few power struggles among local officials, and with some confusion about the new roles.

Local governments in the urban, periurban, and rural areas consist of district councils and a local civil service headed by a district secretary. Councillors are elected by local UNIP membership and vetted by the Central Committee. A district governor is appointed from the capital; this individual also chairs the district development committee which consists of civil servants, UNIP regional officials, and representatives of local authorities, para-statal organizations, and other interest groups. Thus, the district governor heads both the political bodies and the administrative ones and is a powerful subnational political actor.

In face of insufficient finance and staff as well as the more mundane items such as transport, the governors have been only partially successful in their roles as facilitators of district development. A major constraint on the district level of government is that all their projects must be cleared at the next level of government which is the province—the provincial development committee must release any funds for district-level development. Provincial government is also in a state of flux in Zambia. Until 1978, three authorities—a cabinet minister for the province, a member of Central Committee for the province, and a provincial political secretary—contended for power over a rather frail and understaffed provincial civil service headed by the provincial permanent secretary. After December 1978, the cabinet minister's post was eliminated.

The provincial permanent secretary is the key actor in that he or she presides over the provincial development committee and is essential to the approval of development projects, the allocation of funds to various districts, and the preparation of reports to central government. The central government retains final authority; provincial bodies receive only a very small proportion of the central government's annual revenue.

The Electoral System

The president is elected in a two-step process. A primary election by the party at a party general conference elects the sole candidate, who is approved by the Central Committee as well as the party's National Council. This individual is now the president of the party and stands for election to the nation's presidency by universal adult suffrage. The candidate must obtain at least a 50 percent "yes" vote to be elected.

In the 1978 election, former opposition leaders joined UNIP and then contested the leadership with Kaunda. Simon Kapwepwe, former leader of the banned UPP and once vice president of Zambia under the First Republic, along with Harry Nkumbula, former head of the defunct ANC, and Robert Chiluwe, a Lusaka businessman, announced their intentions to run

against Dr. Kaunda in the party primary. In a precedent-setting move, Kaunda was nominated by the National Council of June 1978 instead of by the general conference scheduled for September. After various parliamentary and party maneuvers, the challengers were stopped, although Nkumbula and Kapwepwe took the matter to court.

In the 1983 elections, Dr. Kaunda won a "yes" from 94 percent of the voters. Turnout was 67 percent of the registered voters. Although voters could have expressed their disapproval of Kaunda, no constituency recorded a majority "no" vote. However, the disapproval rate reached 18 to 19 percent in the Copperbelt districts because of the mine workers' discontent with wages and living conditions. It was the first election since independence in which there was no alternative to Kaunda. Even so, Kaunda's overwhelming victory was attributed more to his personal appeal than to the effectiveness of his policies.

The nation's 125 electoral constituencies each selects one member of Parliament. The number of seats per province varies depending on population quotas and allocations by the Electoral Commission. Provinces show wide variations in the proportion of seats to registered voters because of the UNIP leadership's attempt to maintain regional and ethnic balance in party and government institutions.

In the parliamentary elections of 1983, 750 candidates, all UNIP members, contested the 125 seats. Seven ministers of state, one political secretary, and two district governors lost their seats. Also in 1983, an electoral bill was introduced which proposed dropping primary elections. Government opponents charged that the measure's purpose was to ensure that only persons approved by the Central Committee of the UNIP could be candidates for office. Prior to 1983, parliamentary elections had been held in two stages, a primary by party officials followed by a national election. After the primary, local-level candidates were reviewed by the Central Committee which could then remove candidates from the rolls. In the 1978 elections, twenty-eight candidates were removed from the rolls, but a few of them contested the action and were restored to the list.

In presidential and parliamentary elections, all citizens of Zambia eighteen years of age and older are eligible to register and vote in their constituency. Immediately following the introduction of a one-party system, the number of voters declined precipitously. In the 1973 general election, out of 1.7 million registered voters, only 39.8 percent voted. However, voter apathy was seemingly turned around in the 1978 election where out of nearly 1.9 million registered voters, 67 percent voted. Registration and voting procedures are straightforward, and are not linked to the possession of a UNIP party card. Elections in Zambia are among the most free in Africa.

United National Independence Party

History

The UNIP began as a breakaway party from the parent African National Congress (ANC) led by Harry Nkumbula. Younger and more radical members were led by Kenneth Kaunda to form the Zambian African National Congress (ZANC) which in 1960 evolved into the United National Independence Party (UNIP). In the election of 1964, UNIP won a majority of the National Assembly seats, forming the first government with Kaunda as head of state.

Many sectional, ethnic, and personal battles characterized the first decade of multiparty politics in Zambia, and the UNIP leadership wanted a change. The ANC had a strong following in the southern and eastern provinces, while UNIP popularity was greater in the Copperbelt and northern provinces. In 1971, Simon Kapwepwe, then vice president, stepped down to lead a new opposition party, the United Progressive Party (UPP) which gained adherents in former UNIP strongholds. In 1972, the UPP and the ANC were banned and a one-party state was introduced by UNIP. Dissent now takes institutional form in nonparty organizations such as labor unions and student groups. The UNIP is the sole legal party, and the phrase "the Party and its Government" is used in common parlance.

Organization

While certain party leaders have become increasingly powerful since independence, UNIP's organization base has atrophied. The decline varies with the districts and is halted as national elections approach. Before elections, new life and funds are poured into the lower levels of the party. Linguistic and ethnic divisions that characterized politics in Zambia's first decade have given way to growing class differentiations in the country, differentiations which are also visible within UNIP. For example, provincial, regional, and district party officials are compensated for their efforts with salaries and various privileges, while branch, ward, section, and constituency cadres receive no salaries. Yet these subdistrict members are expected to be active proponents of the party, translators of national policies to the local level, and mobilizers of voters at elections.

At the base of the party pyramid are the branch, section, and village political committees. Directly above them are the constituency and ward committees, and above these are the regional committees which eventually supply individuals to the National Council of UNIP. Auxiliary bodies are the Women's Brigades and the Youth Brigades which exist to inspire party loyalty within their constituencies. Individuals from these brigades sit on constituency and regional political committees and make up a sizable number of all party representative bodies.

The UNIP is a relatively democratic organization at the branch and constituency levels, which feed candidates to the higher party jobs. Members of provincial and regional committees are supposed to be appointed by the Central Committee; however, in practice, they are often chosen by the president himself. Freedom House is the secretariat for the party, and the National Council and General Conference are the most populous institutions.

The Central Committee consists of twenty-five members who are elected by secret ballot by the general conference. In practice, Kaunda has presented a slate of candidates to the conference which approves his choice en masse.

The National Council of UNIP encompasses the members of the Central Committee and Parliament, district governors, three officials from each region, representatives of the security forces, the Zambian Congress of Trade Unions and the brigades, as well as a variety of party administrators and ministers of state. The final party authority is supposed to be the general conference which meets once every five years and has well over 6,000 members. Because of its size and the infrequency of meetings, the general conference serves mostly to legitimize the actions or decisions already taken by the president, Central Committee, and National Council. Presidential speeches to the National Council and the general conference form the substance of party policy. The most important compendium of party ideology and current policies can be found in President Kaunda's book *Humanism in Zambia, Part II* (1974).

Policy

As government is considered the implementing wing of the party, their policies are the same. In the domestic sphere, party policies are incorporated in the national development plans (NDPs), the party constitution, and presidential addresses. The UNIP claims to be struggling to bring the standard of living of the rural peoples up to urban standards, to lessen the gap between rich and poor in the society as a whole, and to "Zambianize" the economy. Prominent in all party proclamations are intentions to build a more productive African agricultural sector to enhance the economic independence of the nation. Despite this supposed emphasis on agriculture, the First and Second National Development Plans directed most capital investment into the mines and the urban sector in general; conditions in the rural areas have continued to deteriorate. The Third National Development Plan (TNDP) was postponed until 1980 in recognition of the severe economic straits of the country. The TNDP postulates a shift of investment in favor of the agrarian sector as well as diversification of the mining and manufacturing enterprises. An expected gap between government finance and expenditures is said to be bridgeable by mobilization of foreign assistance and the encouragement of direct foreign investment.

At present, the party and its government are banking on a series of agricultural schemes to boost food and export crop production. Because officials expect Zambia's copper reserves to be exhausted in the next fifteen to twenty years, they see agriculture as the new base of the country's economy. Substantial resources have been diverted to the agricultural sector, and the past emphasis on mining has been downplayed as poor development strategy. Concurrently, the government has lifted subsidies from most food products, except maize. This major agricultural policy change was motivated by the country's poor economy and the necessity for IMF assistance. The resultant food-price rise has stimulated production, but hurt urban consumers.

The UNIP's foreign policy has consistently had two connected themes: anti-racialism and nonalignment. Zambia became involved heavily in the struggle over Zimbabwe at con-

siderable cost to the Zambian people and economy. UNIP backed Joshua Nkomo's ZAPU, but there was government support for Mugabe's ZANU as well. Zambia pressured both liberation movements to present a united front against the Rhodesian regime. Zambian policies included informal talks with the Rhodesian and South African authorities, which came to nothing, but damaged Zambia's antiracist image among the Front Line States (black states in southern Africa opposed to the South African regime). With Zimbabwe now independent and under majority rule, Zambia has been able to normalize trade links, and UNIP is backing the new regional integration thrust embodied in the Southern African Development Coordinating Conference (SADCC).

Zambia has worked with the major Western powers to end white rule in Namibia. However, Zambia's relationship with South Africa has been ambivalent. On the one hand, Zambia opposed South Africa's internal policies and has supported the liberation movements operating in Southern Africa. On the other hand, Zambia has adopted a pragmatic, less ideological approach to actual relations with South Africa. A 1982 meeting between President Kaunda and Prime Minister P.W. Botha marked another occasion in which Zambia broke ranks with the Frontline States. Zambia's attitude toward South Africa is conditioned by its reliance on South Africa for transport routes, harbors, consumer goods, and food imports.

Zambian politicians and diplomats have also tried to increase their ability to maneuver in international politics by participating in the nonaligned movement. They try to balance relations between East and West in order to obtain some economic and military benefits from them while maintaining neutrality. The overall slant to Zambian foreign policy, however, is pro-West. A few top-level UNIP leaders with long-term ties to Eastern bloc countries can be vocal in their socialist sentiments, and these sometimes find their way into party manifestoes. But in terms of economic and aid ties, Zambia is strongly linked to the industrial states of the West and Japan.

Factions within UNIP reflecting cleavages of ethnicity, language, and region have given way to a struggle between factions identified with business and in favor of more private enterprise and direct foreign investment and those of a more social democratic or egalitarian character in favor of state ownership of the means of production and the availability of social services to the citizenry. Individuals such as former Parliament member Arthur Wina and former minister of finance John Mwanakatwe belong to the former category, while the latter viewpoint is represented by the minister for the national commission for development planning, Dr. Henry Meebelo, and Dr. Alexander Kwibisa, director of the Industrial Participatory Democracy Agency located in the prime minister's office.

Membership & Constituency

Figures on total UNIP membership are unavailable, but there are some informed estimates. One scholar says that 25 percent of the population were UNIP members in 1968 when the population was four million. Only 8 percent of the population were still members in 1974, which meant about 376,000 UNIP card holders; there were even fewer members in 1976. On the district level, in 1982 the Ndola Urban District had 30,921 UNIP members out of a district population of 300,000, and these party membership figures had been constant for three years despite population growth.

The UNIP's popularity varies widely over the country and reflects regional loyalties during the period of multiparty contestation. No demographic breakdown of UNIP membership is available, but Northern and Luapula provinces as well as North-Western province, and parts of Copperbelt, Lusaka, and Central provinces are the strongholds. Western, Southern, and Eastern provinces have remained distant from UNIP and often receive less government largesse.

In addition to individual members, various organizations, such as the Women's and Youth Brigades, the security forces, and the Zambia Congress of Trade Unions are affiliated with UNIP.

Financing

According to the UNIP constitution and a manual produced in 1975 for party officials, the party can derive funds from entrance and annual subscription fees; membership card fees; grants, loans and donations or levies permitted under the constitution; a monthly contribution of 5 percent of salaries from top-level government and party officials; and other methods, which seem to include UNIP's total or partial ownership of various enterprises. State monies are allocated to UNIP by vote of the National Assembly. These amounts are listed in the national accounts under constitutional and statutory expenditures, which came to 312,800,000 kwacha (about $306 million) in the 1981 budget. However, UNIP expenses are not the only ones included in this category, so it is impossible to know how much money the party gets from the state.

Leadership

Indisputably, the most important party official is Kaunda himself (born 1924). His father was a pastor from Malawi, though he was raised in the northern part of Zambia and speaks Bemba. In the most recent cabinet reshuffle in mid-1985, President Kaunda made changes in senior positions in the government and the party. Former finance minister Kebby Musokotwane was made the new prime minister replacing Nalumino Mundia, a longtime confidant of the president and a prominent figure in the party. Grey Zulu, secretary of state for defense and security, was named secretary-general of the UNIP replacing Humphrey Mulema, a key party man who had been viewed as Kaunda's possible successor. With these changes, Musokotwane and Zulu became the leading candidates to succeed Kaunda, who, in announcing the changes, made his first public reference to his retirement and spoke of the changes as necessary to maintain political stability in facilating the succession process.

Other Political Forces

Military & Police

A great unknown in Zambian politics is the possibility of direct involvement of the military, paramilitary, or police in politics. Generally, these bodies have stayed out of government and politics, except for a few individuals such as General K. Chinkuli, who serves as a minister. Sometimes a military group may be given temporary control over a business or public service that has collapsed. A certain amount of behind-the-scenes politiking goes on as shown by the detention of several military men including a general in the army and general in the air force in the recently concluded "treason trial." In

1974, a few high-ranking police officers were implicated in another possible coup attempt.

By and large, the president and political leaders have been careful to give officers good salaries as well as various privileges of rank. The lower levels of the services and the police are less well off. Generally, the military in Zambia has a reputation for professionalism, a claim difficult to assess as the forces have so rarely been used except in some defensive battles against Rhodesian and Portuguese forces. An adjunct body is the Special Branch, which is the intelligence wing of the government and operates from the Office of the President. Although widely feared in Zambia, Special Branch agents have limited their political activities to an occasional arrest of someone charged with sedition.

Organized Labor

Labor unions date back to the 1940s when workers organized a series of strikes for improvement of conditions of life and work. In 1943, shop assistants formed a union, and in 1949, the African mineworkers were permitted to form their union, a lineal ancestor to today's very powerful Mineworkers Union of Zambia (MUZ). In pre-independence years, the unions tended to play a supportive role in relation to the nationalist parties. In general, the mineworkers backed UNIP, although this allegiance weakened in the 1970s when the government became the major shareholder in the mines and thus the employer of the workers.

Government restrictions on wage increases added fuel to this growing disenchantment. Opposition leaders such as Simon Kapwepwe and John Chisata began to draw support from the mineworkers and other workers. Finally, the party began a concerted effort to place leaders loyal to UNIP at the top level of the umbrella labor organization, the Zambia Congress of Trade Unions (ZCTU).

However, in 1981, seventeen ZCTU leaders were expelled from the party over the issue of decentralizing local administration which union leaders felt would put more power in the hands of local UNIP cadres. Although the issue was resolved with the ZCTU leaders pledging their allegiance to UNIP, withdrawing their objections to decentralization, and being readmitted to the party, a series of strikes in the Copperbelt affected the output and prices of copper and threatened to halt the economy. In response to the strikes, President Kaunda jailed four trade unionists and charged them with inciting labor unrest to overthrow the government. These officials included the chairman and vice chairman of the ZCTU and the head of MUZ. They were later released, and President Kaunda arranged a truce with the unions to prevent further strikes.

Nonetheless, party-labor friction remained. The ZCTU, which claims a membership of 300,000 or 80 percent of Zambian workers, is the most powerful organization not controlled by the party. Its leadership has often been critical of the party and outspoken in its desire to curb its growing power. The trade unions have become the focal point of demands for political change as well as the instrument through which many Zambians can express their frustration over the poor state of the economy. In recognition of the key role played by the unions, Kaunda has often taken a conciliatory stance toward union leadership. In 1983 he even promoted union leaders to management positions in the parastatal holding corporation, ZIMCO. By this move, he hoped not only to enhance the unionists' participation in top-level policy-making but also to make it more difficult for the union leadership to be militant.

Students

Students in Zambia have played a prominent political role in the past decade. The University of Zambia (UNZA) was closed four times by the government between 1971 and 1984. Other campuses such as the Zambia Institute of Technology and Evelyn Hone College have also been the sites of sporadic student protests. The issues which have brought about conflict between the students and the party and its government have been a mixture of campus politics and student criticism of state policies. UNZA students in particular have a history of radical criticism of the party. In spite of their often radical-sounding rhetoric, university students are a very privileged lot. They have to pass a series of rigorous examinations to obtain entrance to university and receive an annual stipend which is greater than most peasants' yearly income. Although students come from all parts of the country, a sizable proportion come from Lusaka and the Copperbelt towns where their parents have jobs in the public or private urban sector. Often, upon leaving university, they find employment in the civil service or parastatal organizations, and their criticism seems to die away under a blanket of security and bureaucracy. Nonetheless, the UNZA students have a bold tradition of criticism and analysis which seems to be passed on to each new generation. In a political system which has muffled or enclosed most criticism of the party, this external voice can be threatening to those in power.

Ethnic Groups

Zambia contains over seventy separate ethnic or linguistic groups, but there are fourteen major groups (Bemba, Bisa, Ila, Chewa, Kaonde, Lala, Lamba, Lenje, Lozi, Lunda, Luvale, Ngoni, Nsenga, and Tonga) and eight major languages (Bemba, Tonga, Nyanja, Lozi, Kaonde, Lunda, Luvali, and English). Zambia is also home to 50,000 to 60,000 people of European or Asian origin. Although ethnic or home village identifications of the various players in Zambian politics can be strong, the major area in which they affect the political scene is in patronage and nepotism. At various times, one group or the other has been accused of being too dominant, for example, there were claims that UNIP was the party of the Bemba in the 1960s. More often the lines of power and resistance seem to follow class distinctions.

Religious Groups

Most Zambians are members of some form of Protestant church, although a sizable portion of Roman Catholics and Muslims live there as well. The largest churches are the Baptist, Anglican, Methodist, and various evangelical sects such as the Watch Tower and Bible Tract Society ("Jehovah's Witnesses") and the Seventh Day Adventists.

Two religious groups which have come into conflict with the party and its government are the Lumpa Church of Alice Lenshina and the Jehovah's Witnesses. Both sects believe in the sole authority of God and reject the temporal authority of the state, thus leading to an obvious battle against politicians bound on centralizing control over the country and unifying its peoples. Many of the churches in Zambia have objected to the introduction of scientific socialism into the school curriculum. They fear the decline of spiritual values in the country if Marxism is taught in the schools and the demise of religious tolerance if Marxism becomes part of official policy. President Kaunda has tried to reassure church leaders that, under scientific socialism, no one will be persecuted for their religious beliefs.

National Prospects

The UNIP's chances of staying in power are greatly enhanced by the lack of an organized and committed opposition as well as by the party's ability to coopt dissident groups under the UNIP umbrella. The trade unions and the military present two poles of possible opposition, but so far these bodies have either been penetrated by UNIP or their leaders have simply been unwilling to engage in a major struggle for control of the state.

Nonetheless, UNIP seems to be in a slow decline, not unlike many other African one-party systems. The centripetal forces drawing more and more decisions to the center rob local party officials of much autonomy and even their *raison d'être*. Worsening economic circumstances will limit the patronage that the party can hand out and diminish the ability of the government to deliver on various political promises to the regions. A steady increase of corruption will tend to make the lower-level officials eager to get what they can, given the example of their superiors. Finally, as the possibility of salaries for local UNIP officials fades, so too does their eagerness to regenerate the party.

In many ways, modern Zambian politics has been characterized by a smooth transition towards centralized power and an uneven but distinct growth of apathy or lethargy of the masses towards politics in general. The stability of the regime is remarkable, and President Kaunda is held in great regard and affection by many of the people. Party leaders have been quite skillful and, despite occasional lapses, have respected the citizen's human and legal rights. The future is more problematic as the economy seems bound on a downward track and contradictory pressures grow within the society for social welfare and personal aggrandizement. Because open dissent is not possible outside the party, the next decade may reveal serious rifts within UNIP or a violent and abrupt change of regime.

Further Reading
Burdette, Marcia. *Zambia*. Colorado: Westview Press, 1985.

Dresang, D. L. *The Civil Service in Zambia: Entrepreneuralism and Development Administration.* Nairobi: East African Publishing House, 1975.

Gertzel, Cherry J. (ed.) *The Dynamics of the One-party State in Zambia.* Dover, New Hampshire: Manchester University. 1984.

International Labor Organization. *Basic Needs in an Economy under Pressure.* Geneva: United Nations, 1981.

International Labor Organization and Jobs and Skills Programme for Africa. *Narrowing the Gaps.* Geneva: United Nations, 1977.

Mulford, D. C. *Zambia: The Politics of Independence, 1957–64.* London: Oxford University Press, 1967.

Ollawa, Patrick. *Participatory Democracy in Zambia: The Political Economy of National Development.* Devon, England: Arthur H. Stockwell Ltd., 1979.

Roberts, Andrew. *A History of Zambia.* London: Heinemann, 1976.

Tordoff, William. *Administration in Zambia.* Manchester: Manchester University Press, 1980.

———, ed. *Politics in Zambia.* Berkeley and Los Angeles: University of California Press, 1974, and Manchester: Manchester University Press, 1974.

Turok Ben, ed. *Development in Zambia.* London: ZED Press, 1979.

REPUBLIC OF ZIMBABWE

by Timothy Dunmore, Ph.D. revised by Sheila Elliot, M.A.

The System of Government

Since 1980 Zimbabwe, a nation of over eight million people, has been a multiracial parliamentary republic. Its government of national unity is dominated by the majority party, Robert Mugabe's Zimbabwe African National Union-Popular Front (ZANU-PF), but it also contains representatives of other parties with both black and white support. However, some politicians among the minority parties feel that the situation is unstable and foresee the development of a one-party state in Zimbabwe.

Zimbabwe is the former British colony of Southern Rhodesia which since 1923 had been ruled by a virtually independent government of European settlers. While the British government granted independence to its other southern African colonies in the 1960s, it refused to do the same for southern Rhodesia unless the government of Ian Smith's Rhodesian Front Party would agree to make provisions for an end to white-minority rule in the country.

Smith's reaction was a unilateral declaration of independence (UDI) in November 1965. The Labour government in Britain retaliated by declaring the Smith government illegal and arranging economic sanctions against Rhodesia through the United Nations. However, the Rhodesian Front government managed to survive for fifteen years, principally because of help from its white-dominated neighbors in South Africa, Angola, and Mozambique. The fall of the Portuguese colonial governments in Angola and Mozambique in 1974–75 and the establishment of independent black governments there, signalled the beginning of the end of white rule.

A guerrilla war begun several years after UDI, with black armies aided by many of Rhodesia's neighbors sought the overthrow of the white government. The main guerrilla groups were linked to Joshua Nkomo's Zimbabwe African People's Union (ZAPU) and Robert Magabe's Zimbabwe African Nationalist Union (ZANU). In spite of their differences, the two movements joined forces in the Patriotic Front (PF) in 1977. More peaceful opposition to the Smith regime came from Methodist Bishop Abel Muzorewa's United African National Council (UANC).

It was only in 1977 that Smith declared his acceptance of the principles of universal suffrage and a rapid transition to black-majority rule and thus legal independence from Britain. However, the guerrilla forces still did not trust the Rhodesian Front government and refused to cooperate. In May 1978, Muzorewa's UANC and Smith joined forces with the two other black movements, Rev. Ndabaningi Sithole's faction of ZANU and Chief Chirau's Zimbabwe United Peoples Organization (ZUPO) to form an interim government to guide the country towards majority rule.

In 1979 a new constitution was approved (by white voters) and multiracial elections held, with Muzorewa's UANC achieving a clear victory in renamed "Zimbabwe-Rhodesia." However, without the agreement and participation of the PF and its guerrilla forces, the new constitution stood little chance of domestic or international acceptance. Real hope of a lasting solution came with negotiations arranged in London in September 1979. The PF agreed to accept special representation for the white minority; Smith and Muzorewa in turn consented to free multiracial elections under British-government supervision.

In November 1979, the Parliament of Zimbabwe-Rhodesia voted to return the nation to its pre-1963 status as a British colony. This paved the way for a British-controlled voluntary disarming of the guerrillas and for elections in February 1980. Mugabe's ZANU-PF won an absolute majority of the seats in Parliament.

The new prime minister, Robert Mugabe, then led Zimbabwe to full independence in April 1980 with a coalition government consisting not only of ZANU-PF ministers, but also of four PF (formerly ZAPU) men (including Nkomo himself), and two white representatives.

In its first two years the coalition was dominated by quarrels between Nkomo and Mugabe. These culminated in Mugabe's dismissal of Nkomo and other members of his cabinet after the discovery of caches of arms on property belonging to prominent PF supporters. However, at least two deputy ministers from the PF chose to stay in Mugabe's government, splitting Nkomo's party. The white Rhodesian Front Party has also split over the issue of support for the government.

Executive

The head of state is a president chosen by an electoral college consisting of the members of both houses of Parliament (the House of Assembly and the Senate). The president appoints a prime minister who can command a majority in the House of Assembly. He also appoints the members of the cabinet on the advice of the prime minister. The prime minister is head of government and the real chief executive. The president's responsibilities are mainly ceremonial. While the president is titular commander-in-chief of the armed forces, real responsibility for the military belongs to Mugabe who is also minister of defence. The president's term of office is six years and he may stand for reelection. President Canaan Sodindo Banana, a member of one of the minority Ndebele tribes, was elected unopposed.

The tenure of the prime minister is limited by the term of his Parliament, normally five years. His cabinet consists of departmental ministers, a deputy prime minister, and two ministers without portfolio. Most are members of the House of Assembly and the rest are Senators. They all have extensive experience and support in their respective parties (ZANU-PF, PF, and RF) and several also have a proven record in trade-union or guerrilla organizations. If the government ceases to command a majority in the House, the constitution calls for the resignation of the prime minister and his cabinet. Given Mugabe's control over ZANU-PF and the party's strength in the House, such an event is unlikely in the near future.

Legislature

The legislature consists of two houses, the House of Assembly and the Senate. The House is directly elected and is much the more important organ; the powers of the Senate enable it to advise on and delay, but not reject, legislative proposals.

The House consists of 100 members. Eighty are directly elected by black votes only from common-roll constituencies, with the other twenty chosen by white, colored (mixed race), and Asian voters (white roll). Its members are elected for a term of five years. It has the power to reject or amend legislation, but it generally supports the government. In the June 1985 election, the Conservative Alliance of Zimbabwe (CAZ) won fifteen of the guaranteed twenty Eurpoean seats. The Independent Zimbabwe Group (IZG) won four, and an independent won the final seat.

ELECTION RESULTS BY PARTY (1985)			
Party	Votes	Percent	Seats
ZANU-PF	2,199,057	77	63
ZAPU-PF	517,654	19	15
ZANU-S	35,737	2	1
UANC	65,603	2	1
Others	376		

The Senate has forty members. Fourteen of these are chosen by the MPs elected in the common-role constituencies and ten by those elected in the white-roll constituencies. Five senators are chosen from among the Mashonaland chiefs by the chiefs themselves and five more in a similar fashion by the Matabeleland chiefs. The other six senators are appointed by the president on the advice of the prime minister. Mugabe has appointed senators who are either elder statesmen (such as former white premier Garfield Todd), representatives of small minorities (such as colored leader Joseph Culverwell), or cabinet ministers without a seat in the Assembly. The Senate thus overrepresents the more traditional power elites in Zimbabwe (the white minority and the chiefs).

Judiciary

The highest judicial authority is the High Court, which is divided into appellate and general divisions. There is also an ombudsman advised by a Judicial Service Commission and appointed by the president to investigate complaints against employees of the government and local authorities. Neither form of judicial authority represents any real challenge to the government. In 1980, a cabinet minister, Edgar Tekere, was tried for the murder of a white farmer and acquitted by the courts on the grounds that as a minister he was entitled to take action against those committing unconstitutional acts. The decision was widely regarded as politically rather than judicially based. Tekere was, however, forced to resign his cabinet post, a sign that Mugabe himself did not approve Tekere's actions.

Regional & Local Government

Zimbabwe is a unitary state. Its local government is still organized along preindependence lines which are based on British structures. ZANU-PF's political dominance was reflected in the 1985 elections to municipal councils as it maintained its control of all the black seats.

The Electoral System

The House of Assembly is directly elected; the president and Senate are chosen by elected legislators and traditional chiefs. The twenty white roll seats are based on the districts set up by the "Delimitation Commission" in 1978. The constituencies are divided according to regional and ethnic criteria, as was agreed before the 1979 elections. Each province has approximately one representative for each 35,000 voters.

In the white-roll constituencies all whites, Asians, and coloreds registered before December 31, 1979, were allowed to vote. In the common-roll constituencies, all black Zimbabweans over the age of eighteen and black noncitizens resident in the country for two years were allowed to vote. To prevent multiple voting each person had to dip his hand in an indelible fluid once he had voted. Voter turnout in the common-roll constituencies was 93.7 percent; in the white roll it was only 57.6 percent.

Voting in the white roll constituencies is preferential, i.e. the voter ranks the candidates according to his preference. If no candidate gains an overall majority of first preferences, the candidate with the lowest vote is excluded and the second-preference votes on those ballots are redistributed among the others. Further candidates are excluded until someone has an overall majority.

In black constituencies each party presents a ranked list of candidates for each electoral province and voters choose a party list, not an individual. In each province, seats are distibuted among all parties receiving more than 10 percent of the votes in proportion to the number of votes won.

Most observers of Zimbabwe's electoral process in 1980 and 1985 have commented that in general the elections were open and fair.

The Party System

Origins of the Parties

The history of Zimbabwe's black political parties over the twenty years preceding independence was one of continually shifting alliances and party splits over the degree of cooperation with or opporition to the ruling white minority. The first organization founded to oppose white rule was the African National Congress organized by Joshua Nkomo before World War II. Banned, it briefly reemerged as the National Democratic Party in 1960. Banned again, it reformed as the Zimbabwe African People's Union (ZAPU) in 1961.

Banned again, ZAPU split in 1963, when Rev. Ndabaningi Sithole and others were expelled from the party for criticizing Nkomo's leadership and frequent absences from the country. The expelled nationalists (including Mugabe) then formed ZANU under Sithole's leadership. It was banned in 1964. Both ZANU and ZAPU went underground, and in the early 1970s, began to organize guerrilla armies. At the same time, several smaller parties sprang up which aimed at seeking a peaceful solution to the black-white conflict.

There are now thirteen parties in the country, most of them minor, recently created, personal followings of tribal leaders and opposed to the dominance of ZANU-PF and ZAPU (now PF). The exception is the UANC which has been in existence for a decade and had always sought a peaceful path to majority rule.

The Parties in Law

Political parties in Zimbabwe are recognized by the April 1980 constitution in that they have to register their party lists in order to participate in the elections.

Party Organization

Zimbabwe's parties vary greatly in the degree and style of their organization, representing almost every conceivable variety.

During the 1970s, the two main parties, ZANU and ZAPU, were the political wings of their guerrilla armies, ZANLA and ZIPRA, respectively. With the coming of black-majority rule in 1980, the two parties were faced with reorganizing for a peaceful political process. This created very different problems for the well-organized and governing ZANU-PF and for the PF which is a much less formally structured body. Both party organizations are in a state of flux.

Campaigning

The 1985 election campaign was opened to all parties that could meet the nominee deadline. The most difficult aspect of that campaign was the high incidence of violence between ZANU-PF and ZAPU-PF supporters. Because of this climate, with the attendant difficulty of registering voters, the election was postponed from June to August.

Patriotic Front (PF)

History

As part of its tactics in contesting the 1980 elections, ZAPU adopted the name of the Patriotic Front. The party was founded in 1961 in Salisbury. It is the oldest black party in the country, tracing its roots directly to the African National Union and National Democratic Party. It was banned from 1962 to 1979.

In the 1980 elections it won 23.6 percent of the vote and accepted a role in the Mugabe government. Nkomo and three other party members joined the cabinet. However, Nkomo's role was decreased in January 1981, and in February 1982 he and other PF cabinet members were ousted amid charges of plotting to overthrow the government, although some deputy ministers from the PF chose to stay in the government. In 1985 Zapo's decline continued. It won nineteen percent of the votes which translated into only fifteen seats in the senate.

Organization

To what extent the PF possesses any organization or infrastructure at all is unclear. It seems to be a mixture of Nkomo's personal following and the political wing of its former guerrilla movement, ZIPRA.

Policy

The primary aim of the PF since the end of the civil war has been to carve out a secure place for itself in the new political system. This has meant, primarily, defending itself against the pressures of the more dominant party. The PF was officially a Marxist party, but in the 1980 election it campaigned on a platform of national unity and moderate social reforms. It opposes what it sees as attempts by Mugabe to turn the country into a one-party state on the communist model. It is more pro-western than the ruling ZANU-PF.

Nkomo agreed to take part in a government of national unity after the elections to continue the guerrilla alliance that had defeated the RF government. However, Nkomo was dismissed from the cabinet and became the parliamentary opposition to the Mugabe government. Mugabe's landslide victory has encouraged Nkomo to engage in talks with the prime minister to explore a possible merger between the two parties.

Membership & Constituency

The party does not have a formal membership roll. In spite of Nkomo's attempts during the election campaign to broaden his party's base by stressing his record as a national rather than merely a Ndebele political leader, the party's major strength came from the Ndebele ethnic group (about 19 percent of the black population) in Matabeleland in the southwest of the country around Bulawayo. It won 73 percent of its national vote in the Matabeleland constituencies. Support for the PF is not confined to any particular class group.

Financing

The party relies heavily on personal contributions. During the guerrilla war, it relied also on assistance from the Zambian government.

Leadership

Since its beginning the party has been led by Joshua Mqabuko Nyongolo Nkomo (born 1917). Nkomo was born in Matabeleland; after working as a truck driver, he trained as a social worker in South Africa. From there he returned to Zimbabwe where he became a social worker for Rhodesian railways and a leading trade unionist. He graduated by correspondence from the University of South Africa. He has been a leading figure in the black nationalist movement ever since its revival in 1960.

Prospects

On the evidence of the 1985 vote, it is clear that the PF will never win an election; its only hope of influencing the government is by participating in it or using force against it. At first the latter course appeared to be quite probable since prior to the election, ZAPU-PF supporters and ZIPRA guerrillas were allegedly engaged in hostile activities against the government in Matabeleland. However, in face of the strong electoral victory of Mugabe and the ongoing negotiations between Mugabe and Nkomo, ZIPRA activities appear to have decreased considerably. It appears that Nkomo hopes to influence the government by participating in it.

Conservative Alliance of Zimbabwe (CAZ) (formerly the Rhodesian Front)

History

The CAZ was founded in 1962 as a white-supremacist party opposed to Rhodesia's membership in the 1953–63 Federation of Rhodesia and Nyasaland (now Malawi). Within a year, its total opposition to black-majority rule gained it a majority in Parliament under Winston Field. In the following election in 1965, the CAZ won all fifty seats in Parliament and then led the Nation to illegal independence under Ian Smith.

Guerrilla warfare and economic sanctions slowly forced the CAZ to modify its policies, but its brief attempt at a compromise arrangement in 1978–79 was ruined by the strength and determination of the guerrilla movements. In 1980, the party won all twenty white roll seats. In 1985, it retained fifteen of those seats.

Organization

The CAZ is a well-organized party with active branches throughout the country. It was the first mass party in Rhodesia. It is internally democratic and holds regular national party conventions. Local branches and committees play an active part in decision-making processes and in the selection of candidates for elections.

Policy

Policy is now limited to defending white interests against a govenment that is gradually moving blacks into senior positions in the armed forces, the police, the media, and civil service, and removing such symbols of the white heritage as English place-names and statues of colonial officials like Cecil Rhodes.

In 1981-82 about half the CAZ MPs left the party because of objections to Smith's intransigence. One, Andre Holland, established his own "Democratic Party" in April 1981. Early in 1982, nine MPs left the CAZ and decided to sit as independents in the House of Assembly. Both groups wanted to work more closely with the government rather than simply criticize all Mugabe's policies, as Smith has done.

Membership & Constituency

The CAZ still has tens of thousands of members. It finds support in all sections of the white population, among whom farmers and businessmen predominate.

Financing

The CAZ relied heavily on membership dues. Many of the foreign contributions it previously had received were, in 1980, directed towards the UANC, the black party to which the RF objects least.

Leadership

Ian Douglas Smith (born 1919) has been the leader of the CAZ since he ousted Field in 1964. After a distinguished record as a fighter pilot

for the British RAF in World War II, he turned
to cattle farming and then to politics.

Prospects

The massive white emigration—about 90,000
since majority rule—has, however, seriously
weakened the CAZ's position and is one reason
behind the recent splits in the party. The party
will continue as a point of focus for narrow
white interests for the time being, but its long-
term prospects are bleak.

United African National Council
(UANC)

History

The UANC was founded in 1971 by Bishop
Abel Muzorewa and the Rev. Canaan Banana
(now president of Zimbabwe) to seek a peaceful
path to majority rule. The peak of its influence
came in 1979 when it agreed to the internally
devised arrangement that led to elections in
April of that year. The UANC won a majority
(fifty-one) of the black seats in the House of Assembly. Bishop Muzorewa became prime minister and formed a "government of national
unity" with the Rhodesian Front and minority
black parties like ZANU-Sithole. The UANC
won only three seats in the 1980 elections, and
in the 1985 elections it won only one seat.

Organization

The UANC began life as a temporary pressure group in 1971 and since then has really
been little more than a collection of sympathetic groupings across the country backing
Bishop Muzorewa.

Policy

Muzorewa's party is the most right wing of
the major black parties and has never backed
the guerrillas. At the first election, it campaigned for traditional values and vigorously
opposed communism and Marxism. In spite of
this, the UANC platform differed from those of
the PF and ZANU more in degree than kind. All
three parties advocated free primary education,

improvements in the health service and housing, and some form of mixed economy.

Membership & Constituency

Support for UANC is not tribally or regionally based. The UANC's vote in 1980 varied
from 3 to 12 percent of the votes cast in each
province. It seems probable that its 1980 vote
relied more heavily on the black middle classes
than it did in 1979. Bishop Muzorewa's following is personal and ideological rather than ethnic.

Financing

Although the party does solicit individual
contributions, it is clear that most of its expensive 1980 and 1985 election campaigns were
funded by Western and South African business
interests who saw Muzorewa as the main bulwark against communism and terrorism.

Leadership

Bishop Abel Tendekayi Muzorewa (born
1925) was a cofounder of the UANC. He was
born in Umtali in Manicaland province and
studied theology there and in the United States.
He became a bishop and head of the United
Methodist church of Rhodesia in 1968. His involvement in politics dates from the foundation
of the UANC. After the party's poor showing in
1985, Bishop Muzorewa resigned from the party
and retired from politics.

Prospects

Given the strong electoral victory of Mugabe,
support for the moderate position of Bishop
Muzorewa appears to be on the decline, with little chance of revival.

Zimbabwe African National Union
-Patriotic Front (ZANU-PF)

History

ZANU was a splinter group from ZAPU. Ini-
tially led by the Rev. Ndabaningi Sithole, it left
ZAPU in 1963 because of its opposition to
Joshua Nkomo's leadership. From 1964 to 1979

it was banned, as was its guerrilla wing, ZANLA, in the early 1970s. Mugabe, who was originally leader of ZANLA, replaced the Rev. Sithole as leader, with the latter forming his own more moderate party in 1977. Thereafter ZANU and ZAPU agreed to unite as the Patriotic Front to pool their efforts to overthrow the government. This alliance lasted until the 1980 settlement when ZANU-PF fielded its candidates against ZAPU which now called itself the PF. In the 1980 elections Mugabe's ZANU-PF won fifty-seven of the eighty common-roll parliamentary seats.

Organization

ZANU-PF has a cellular structure with rural and urban cells electing higher committees up to the level of the Central Committee. Before he came to power, Mugabe normally referred all important decisions, including choosing lists of election candidates, to the Central Committee. However, most of the members of the Committee are not in Mugabe's cabinet. While the precise relationship between party and government remains unclear, the Central Committee is less powerful now than it was before Mugabe's accession to the prime ministry.

Policy

ZANU-PF is the most left wing of the black parties. Before the first elections it controlled the largest guerrilla army and was the party most committed to overthrowing the white government by force. It adheres to a form of Marxism-Leninism, although this was moderated in the 1980 elections. Mugabe then outlined only vague plans for state involvement in the economy and promised to preserve private enterprise. In power, ZANU-PF has not proved as radical as many of its opponents feared. It has not yet nationalized any major industry, although it has bought a controlling interest in a South African-owned bank and a newspaper group and has redistributed some land. The Mugabe government has also promoted blacks to many senior positions. Its main work to date has been to set up free primary education, a health service, minimum-wage laws, resettlement of refugees, and the establishment of a drought emergency fund.

In foreign policy, Mugabe looks toward his socialist neighbor Mozambique, but is by no means committed to the Soviet camp. There are, however, increasing signs of the influence on ZANU-PF of other communist powers such as China and North Korea (which helped to set up a party youth organization). As yet the party's policies are socialist and nationalist rather than communist.

Membership & Constituency

ZANU-PF has its main support among the Shona peoples who form three-quarters of the black population of Zimbabwe. However, the Shona are a collection of smaller tribes rather than a cohesive ethnic group. In the last elections ZANU-PF gained massive support in all areas except those with predominantly Ndebele populations; in five of the six non-Ndebele provinces, ZANU-PF won more than 70 percent of the vote. Even in the Ndebele provinces, ZANU-PF was the second-largest party. Mugabe's support is based on his guerrilla record as much as on his movement's ethnic base. Indeed, there have at times been quarrels within ZANU-PF among the different Shona tribes.

Financing

ZANU-PF spent so many years underground that details of its financial arrangements are unclear. Immediately following independence, it has received material support from the Mozambique government.

Leadership

The leader of ZANU-PF since 1976 has been Robert Gabriel Mugabe (born 1928 in Northern Mashonaland). He graduated from a South African college and taught in Zambia and Ghana before becoming a full-time politician in 1960. Subsequently, he was imprisoned several times until, in 1974, he went into exile and soon emerged as the leader of the ZANILA guerrillas and then of ZANU-PF itself.

Prospects

There is no doubt that ZANU-PF will remain the dominant party in Zimbabwe. Indeed, the primary issue in its future is whether and how quickly Mugabe can create a one-party state. ZANU-PF's landslide victory in 1985 has been seen by Mugabe as a mandate to consolidate his power and to move toward creation of a one-party state.

Minor Parties

Of the smaller parties, only ZANU-S won a seat in the 1985 elections.

Zimbabwe African National Union—Sithole (ZANU-S)

After many years in a leading role in the more radical black parties, the Rev. Ndabaningi Sithole founded this party as a splinter group from ZANU-PF in 1977. ZANU-S appears to consist mostly of his personal following. Sithole agreed to join Bishop Muzorewa's UANC in the multiracial transitional government of 1978, a move which owed something to personal ambition and lost Sithole much of his nationalist support. His party won only 36,000 votes in the 1985 election.

Zimbabwe Democratic Party (ZDP)

James Chikerema formed the ZDP in April 1979 when Bishop Muzorewa refused him a place in his cabinet. He left the UANC along with several other Zezuru MPs. The ZDP's support is concentrated among this Shona tribe who are centered around the capital, Harrare City (formerly Salisbury).

Democratic Party (DP)

The DP was established in 1981 by Andre Holland, a former RF MP, to work more closely with the black government in a spirit of "constructive criticism."

United National Federal Party (UNFP)

A black conservative party based on tribal interests, the UNFP advocates the creation of a federation giving a degree of autonomy to both Mashonaland and Matebeleland.

United People's Association of Matebeleland

Another rightist tribally based party, the Association was established in 1979.

Zimbabwe National Front (ZNF)

The ZNF is one of the new parties established in 1979 to challenge the domination of ZANU, the PF, and the UANC and to end the factionalism and tribal and personal rivalries among these black parties. It has had very little success in this respect.

Zimbabwe United People's Organization (ZUPO)

Founded in 1976 by Chief Jeremiah Chirau, ZUPO's aim has always been a reconciliation of tribal differences and the development of a united Zimbabwe. It supported the PF in the 1980 election.

Independent Zimbabwe Group

Started as a breakaway faction from CAZ in 1983, this group is led by Bill Irvine.

Other Political Forces

Military

The main political organizations outside of the parties are the former participants in the guerrilla war. These organizations, like the major ethnic groups, are closely linked to political parties.

The Zimbabwe African National Liberation Army (ZANLA) was the first ZAPU guerrilla organization. Since the splits within ZAPU, this name has usually been replaced by the Zimbabwe People's Army (ZPA) or the Zimbabwe Liberation Army (ZLA). At its peak it probably had more than 20,000 men led by Robert Mugabe, 16,000 of whom surrendered at official assembly points in 1980. Most of these are now members of Zimbabwe's new army, 70 percent of which is composed of former guerrillas. The PF's guerrilla movement, the Zimbabwe People's Revolutionary Army (ZIPRA), was less than 10,000 strong with 6,000 of these coming to assembly points before the elections. They operated in the northwest of the country while ZANLA was active in the northeast.

The third element in the new army is based on the former white-controlled Rhodesian Security Forces (RSF). In spite of their being on opposing sides in the civil war, these groups have managed to integrate in Zimbabwe's new army with remarkably few problems. Their experience in arranging the 1979–80 ceasefire together has helped in this. Most of the armed clashes since 1978 have been outside the army's ranks, between guerrillas who did not surrender their arms before the 1980 elections. In the future, armed opposition is more likely to come from former ZIPRA guerrillas.

Ethnic Groups

The major ethnic groups in Zimbabwe are the Shona and Ndebele tribes who together account for more than 95 percent of the population. The Shona tribes form 77 percent of the black population. There are seven major Shona tribes, the largest being the Karanga (22 percent of the population). These peoples have never formed a coherent political unit. They do not have a common religion and have begun to develop a common language (Chishona) only over the last century.

The Ndebele and the associated Kalanga tribe together account for 19 percent of the black population. Their common identity is based on the old Ndebele kingdom. Prior to the foundation of that kindgom in the early nineteenth century, the Shona and Ndebele groups were much more intermixed. The Ndebele share a common culture and religion. The Shona/Ndebele rivalry is based more on Ndebele solidarity and fear of being swamped than on the cohesiveness of the Shona. Successive white governments encouraged the rivalry.

The white minority that ruled Rhodesia for so many years used to be estimated at about 200,000. However, perhaps one half of them left after Mugabe was first elected, emigrating to South Africa or returning to Europe, but some of those have returned to Zimbabwe. Whites form about 3 percent of the population.

National Prospects

After seven years of civil war, Zimbabwe's transition to black-majority rule in February 1980 was surprisingly peaceful. Mugabe's clear majority in the elections allowed no arguments over who should form the government and his initial moves seemed calculated to reassure minority groups that their interests would be safeguarded in the now legally independent nation. Currently, Zimbabwe is recovering from a devastating African drought. Despite this problem, Zimbabwe is expecting another bumper crop of maize (an estimated 3 million tons). Furthermore, the 1985 electoral victory has encouraged renewed negotiations and discussions between Mugabe and Nkomo for a possible merger of their two organizations. If such a merger occurs, a one-party state in Zimbabwe would be quite likely. Also, now that the conservative white party headed by Ian Smith no longer monopolizes the white vote, it appears that the party may eventually lose its potential to disrupt the policies and aims of the Mugabe government. In summation, the economic and political climate in Zimbabwe can best be characterized as productive.

Further Reading

Bratton, Michael. "Development in Zimbabwe: Strategy and Tactics." *Journal of Modern African Studies*, Vol. 19, No. 3, September 1981.

Elliot, Hugh P. *Dawn in Zimbabwe*. London: Grosvenor, 1981.

Gregory, Martyn. *From Rhodesia to Zimbabwe*. Braamfontein: South African Institute of International Affairs, 1980.

Hills, Denis. *The Last Days of White Rhodesia*. London: Chatto and Windus, 1981.

———. *Rebel People*. London: Allen and Unwin, 1978.

Jones, W. H. Morris, ed. *From Rhodesia to Zimbabwe*. Studies in Commonwealth Politics and History, No. 9. London: Frank Cass, 1980.

Martin, David. *The Struggle for Zimbabwe*. London: Faber, 1981.

Meredith, M. *The Past is Another Country*. 2nd edition. London: Pan Books, 1980.

Nyangoni, C., and Nyandoro, G. *Zimbabwe Independence Movements: Select Documents*. London: Collings, 1979.

Rasmussen, R. Kent. *Historical Dictionary of Rhodesia/Zimbabwe*. Metuchen, N. J., & London: Sarecrow Press, Inc., 1979.

Rhodesia. Foreign and Commonwealth Office. *Rhodesia: Summary of the Independence Constitution*. London: HMSO, 1979.

Williams, R. Hodder. "Independent Zimbabwe." *African Insight*, Vol. 10, Nos. 3 and 4, 1980.

Smaller Countries and Microstates

PRINCIPALITY OF ANDORRA
(Principat d'Andorra [Catalan]);
(Principado de Andorra [Spanish]);
(Vallées d'Andorre [French])

by John Christian Laursen, Ph.D.

A tiny nation of 462 square kilometers, wedged between Spain and France in the Pyrenees Montains, Andorra is a co-principality. The two princes are the president of France and the bishop of Seu d'Urgell in Spain. This form of government dates back to 1278.

No written constitution exists for Andorra, although administrative statutes were written in 1748 and 1763, a Plan of Reform was passed in 1866, and, most recently, a Political Reform Law was passed in 1981. Political parties are prohibited, but much of the program of the Democratic Association of Andorra, a "quasi-party," calls for further democratic constitutional reforms.

The co-princes are charged with the conduct of foreign affairs, defense, and the judicial system. They are represented in Andorra by the *viguer episcopal* and the *viguier français*, and each prince names a Permanent Delegation for Andorran Affairs. The *viguer/viguier* each appoints two civil judges (*batlles*), and an appeals judge is appointed alternately by each prince. Final appeal is to the Supreme Court of Andorra at Perpignan, France, or to the Ecclesiastical Court of the bishop at Seu d'Urgell, Spain. The plaintiff may choose either system.

Criminal law is administered by *Corts* consisting of the *viguer* and *viguier*, the appeals judge, and two judges elected by the General Council. The attorney general is nominated on an alternate basis by the two princes for five-year terms.

Legislation is enacted by a General Council consisting of twenty-eight members, four from each of seven parishes, elected for concurrent four-year terms. Women were granted the right to vote in 1970, and a woman was elected to the council for the first time in 1984. In 1985 the voting age was reduced to 18. Legislative enactments are subject to the approval of the co-princes.

The 1981 reforms created an executive consisting of a prime minister appointed by the General Council, who in turn appoints an Executive Council of up to six members. Local government functions through elected parish councils.

Most recent elections to the General Council were held in December 1985. The elections confirmed support for conservative Prime Minister Josep Pintat Solans, who was first named to the post in 1984 upon the resignation of Oscar Ribas Reig after Ribas Reig failed to garner support for new taxes.

The population of Andorra escalated from just over 6,000 in 1954 to approximately 50,000 by 1985. In the process Andorra changed from a predominately pastoral, agricultural nation to an international ski and mountain resort, with the added attractions of low or nonexistent taxes on businesses and duty-free shops. Immigrants, especially from Spain, far outnumber the native Catalan-speaking population, and one contemporary issue is the proposed limitation of further immigration. Another issue of major importance is prospective integration into the European Economic Community following Spain's membership as of January 1, 1986.

Andorran stability derives from growth and prosperity. Seeds of unrest lie in native Andorran nationalism, necessary economic adjustments, and growing pressures for wider democratic reforms.

ANTIGUA AND BARBUDA

by Scott B. MacDonald, M.A. revised by Paget Henry, Ph.D.

On November 1, 1981, Antigua and Barbuda were granted independence from the United Kingdom. The new state, a parliamentary democracy on the British model, consists of three islands in the eastern Caribbean: Antigua (population, 74,000), Barbuda (1,200), and Redona (uninhabited). Although more than two political parties exist, the party system was clearly dominated by the Antigua Labour Party (ALP) and the Progressive Labour Movement (PLM). Between 1983 and 1985, the latter disintegrated and was followed by the emergence of the United People's Movement (UPM) and the National Democratic Party (NDP).

After a long period of colonial rule, Antigua and Barbuda became an Associated State of the United Kingdom on February 27, 1967. The islands' internal affairs were governed locally by a nationally elected legislature located at St. John's, Antigua. External affairs and defense remained the responsibility of the British. In 1980, the move for independence, initiated by the Antigua Labour Party and encouraged by the United Kingdom, became an important issue in the politics of the islands.

After the general elections of April 1980, the ALP government announced that the islands would seek independence. The move to independence, however, was not well taken in Barbuda where the inhabitants have consistently elected Eric Burton, an independent, as their man in Parliament, largely on a platform of secession for Barbuda. Negotiations for the establishment of the new state were held in London and included delegations from the Antiguan government, the PLM, representatives from the Barbuda Local Government Council, and the British government. The Barbudans, after being refused continued colonial rule by Britain, toned down their opposition. However, both the Barbudan and the PLM delegations refused to sign the final document produced at the London conference. Furthermore, the price of a united independence was that the ALP government, in April 1981, gave the Barbuda Local Government Council greater powers, making the island almost self-governing. There were also promises of increased economic programs for the smaller island.

The head of state is the British monarch represented by a governor-general. Executive power resides in the prime minister, the head of government, who presides over the Council of Ministers, which is responsible for the administration of the state. Parliament, the supreme lawmaking body of the state, is comprised of two legislative chambers: the House of Representatives, to which seventeen representatives are elected in single-member districts by simple pluralities every five years; and the Senate, composed of seventeen members appointed by the governor general on the advice of both the prime minister (eleven), the leader of the opposition (four), the Barbuda Council (one), and by the governor-general alone (one). The House of Representatives introduces all legislation, and the Senate reviews and gives assent to such legislation. The 1986 division of the House is sixteen Labour Party members, and one independent who has joined the opposition.

With its independence guaranteed under the constitution, Antigua and Barbuda's judiciary is completely autonomous. This independence is reinforced by the fact that the government of Antigua and Barbuda shares its judiciary with five other nations in the Eastern Caribbean; for example, the appointment or dismissal of judges has to be agreed to by six heads of state before it can be effected.

Along with these liberal democratic features, two other characteristics of the Antiguan and Barbudan state are important for an accurate portrait. The first is the tendency toward party splintering. This tendency is a major source of instability in the political system. The decline of the PLM is one example of this splintering tendency. This party emerged from a split within the ALP in 1967. The Antigua People's Party (APP) and the Antigua Caribbean Liberation Movement (ACLM) both had their origins in splits within the PLM in 1969. The APP, a conservative party, subsequently merged with the ALP. The ACLM is now a revolutionary socialist party, which is very vocal but has a small following.

The decline of the PLM started in 1983 with another internal split. This one gave birth to the UPM. In the elections of April 1984, the

ALP won 69.2 percent of the popular vote. The UPM was second with 23.5 percent, and the PLM third with 1.9 percent. The ACLM did not enter the contest. After the elections, there was a regrouping of elements of this splintered opposition which produced the NDP. It remains to be seen what the popular support for this party will be like.

Thus, between 1967 and the present, the ALP has been the most stable of the major parties. It has lost only one election since the introduction of universal suffrage in 1951. This, of course, was the 1971 election which was contested after it had been the victim of the split that gave birth to the victorious PLM. However, very definite factions have now emerged within the ALP, that could easily produce another split after the powerful leadership of V.C. Bird comes to an end. In short, the threat of party splintering remains very real.

The second important characteristic of the political system of Antigua and Barbuda is that, like most developing countries, it has well-developed entrepreneurial features. Thus, although it favors private enterprise, public sector investments have been averaging about 40 percent of total investments. These investments have been equally divided between directly productive activities, such as hotels and manufacturing, and basic infrastructures, such as ports and factory shells. This active state role in the economy makes it the primary local entrepreneur, given the small size of the Antiguan bourgeoisie.

However, despite these determined efforts by the state, the economic problems facing Antigua and Barbuda remain quite serious. Unemployment remains high (25 percent), and attempts to diversify the economy beyond tourism have met with only limited success. So, given this record of party splintering and only modest economic success, a certain amount of caution is necessary when considering the political future of Antigua and Barbuda.

Further Reading
Department of Information in the Ministry of Foreign Affairs. *Antigua and Barbuda, Independence.* Weybridge, Surrey, England: Goodyear Gibbs, Ltd., 1981.
Economic Development of Small States with Particular Reference to Antigua. St. John's, Antigua: University of West Indies Department of Extra-Mural Studies, 1981.
Paget Henry. *Peripheral Capitalism and Under-Development in Antigua.* New Brunswick, N.J.: Transaction Books, 1985.

BHUTAN
(Druk Yul)
by George E. Delury, revised by Leo Rose, Ph.D.

Bhutan, a nation of over one million people in the eastern Himalayas north of India, is a hereditary limited monarchy with considerable power residing in a representative assembly. With the exception of a brief period under Chinese suzerainty in the early eighteenth century, Bhutan seems to have been an independent, though often fragmented, political entity for many centuries. Bhutan is the English name for the country which the inhabitants call *Druk Yul,* Land of the Thunder Dragon, after the *Drukpa,* or Thunder Dragon, sect of Buddhism, which was introduced into the area from Tibet in the twelfth century. The *Drukpa* sect is a branch of the *Kargyupa* school of Lamaistic Buddhism whose most noted teacher was Milarepa.

The royal line was established in 1907, when the strongest provincial governor, with the help of the British, set himself up as the *Druk Gyalpo* (precious ruler). The present monarch, Jigme Singye Wangchuk (born 1955), is the fourth in the royal line. He ascended the throne in 1972, three years after the monarchy's power had been sharply curtailed and subjected to control of the national assembly, the *Tshongdu.*

The *Tshongdu* was established in 1953 and has slowly accumulated much of the real power of the state. In 1969 it was empowered to select and remove the monarch and to veto his legislation. The king can be removed by a two-thirds vote of the assembly and must submit to a vote of confidence every three years. In fact, most legislation now originates in the Royal Advisory Council (*Lodoi Tsokde*), which is responsible to the *Tshongdu*. The royal council was established in 1965 to advise the king and his ministers. It consists of a chairman appointed by the king, five representatives of the people, two of the monastic order, two southern Bhutanese, and a women's representative. All members serve five-year terms. The council is always in session.

The Council of Ministers, nominated by the king and approved by the *Tshongdu*, is responsible for administration. In 1985, a major reorganization program was introduced which was intended to "invigorate the administrative machinery" but may also have the effect of establishing a more classic cabinet form of government in Bhutan.

The *Tshongdu* has approximately 150 members, more than 100 of whom are chosen for three-year terms by public consensus in villages of the nation's seventeen districts. Ten representatives are chosen by regional monastic bodies, and forty are appointed by the king. The *Tshongdu* meets twice a year, but special sessions may be called by the speaker, who is elected by and from the assembly by secret ballot. Representatives have complete freedom of speech and legislation is approved by a simple majority. A secret ballot is used in matters deemed to be of national importance. Any Bhutanese over twenty-five years of age may be a candidate, but parties are banned and candidates must run as individuals. A small opposition Bhutan Congress Party operates out of India to little or no effect.

The population is relatively homogeneous, but divided into regionally isolated groups by ranges of mountains running north and south. About 25 percent of the population is Nepalese. The single most organized national group is probably the *Drukpa* monastic order led by the *Je Khempo*, whose social status is nearly equal to the king's. The *Je Khempo* is chosen by the central monastic body and must be formally approved by the king. The *Drukpa* order has some 6,000 monks and is involved in government at every level. It is apparently relatively free of factions.

The Bhutanese legal system is based on traditional Buddhist precepts with some modifications in recent times. Because of its religious base, it is relatively free of political influence, although the final court of appeal is the king.

Government policy has stressed rapid economic, political, and social development, while at the same time seeking to minimize as far as possible the damage to traditional and religious values. The nation's third monarch, Jigme Dorji Wangchuk (ruled 1953–72), abolished slavery and the caste system, carried through extensive land reforms, emancipated women, and initiated a secular school system.

China and India have competed for influence over Bhutan, and China laid claim to the territory in the 1950s. Bhutan accepts Indian guidance in its foreign affairs and has permitted India to build roads and other facilities for use by the Indian army in defense of Bhutan. India also provides the country with a small subsidy (less than $100,000 annually).

Bhutan's prospects for continuing political stability and economic security are bright.

SULTANATE OF BRUNEI
by George E. Delury revised by H. Monte Hill, Ph.D.

Brunei, a sultanate of about 215,000 people, consists of two enclaves within the Malaysian state of Sarawak on the northeast coast of the island of Borneo. Brunei chose not to join the Malaysian federation in 1963 and remained a protectorate of Great Britain until January 1985.

Sultan Hassanal Bolkiah ascended the throne in 1968 after his father resigned rather than agree to British demands for more representative government. In spite of a constitution promulgated by the sultan in 1959 and amended in 1965, he, his three brothers, and the Malay aristocracy of this essentially feudal country dominate the nation's politics. Opposition to the sultan's rule is not permitted, and some observers believe that as many as forty persons may be in prison on suspicion of such opposition.

He is assisted by the Council of Ministers appointed and chaired by the sultan. According to the constitution, the twenty-member Legislative Council is supposed to have ten popularly elected members, but since 1970 the sultan has appointed the entire Council. Members of the Council of Ministers fill most of the constitutionally appointive seats in the Legislative Council ex officio. The state's four districts and four municipalities are administered by appointees of the sultan.

The Supreme Court, consisting of the High Court and the Court of Appeal, was established in 1963. English common law and procedures predominate, except in matters concerning Islamic personal affairs, which come under the jurisdiction of special Islamic courts.

Although parties are banned, at least two political groups are reported to be operating in Brunei. The People's Independence Party (known by its Malay acronym, Baker) was formed in 1966. It is supposed to favor independence and more constitutional government. The People's United Party (Perkara) was formed in 1968 and appears to be a government party fully supporting the sultanate. A third party, the Brunei People's Party (*Parti Rakyat Brunei*), favored independence in 1962 and was crushed. One of its leaders, A. M. Azahari, a socialist, is reportedly living in Jakarta, Indonesia. Another of the party's leaders, Zaini Ahmad, a non-Marxist, escaped from prison in 1973 and lives in Malaysia. He reportedly favors closer ties to that country.

Nevertheless, there appears to be some relaxation by the government of the ban on political parties in what seems to be a second attempt at a "mild dose of democracy." As a result, in June 1985 a group of Bruneians announced—from the safety of Singapore city—that they had formed a new political party, the Brunei National Democratic Party (*Parti Kebangsaan Demokratik Brunei*), claiming that it had been registered by the Brunei government on May 30, 1985. The formation of the party obviously had the blessings of the government, and, in fact, some of its leaders are connected to the royal family and cabinet ministers. Its chairman, Pengiran Anak Hassannuddin, who runs a kindergarten in the capital, has a younger brother who is married to the sister of the sultan. The party president, Awang Haji Abdul Latifbin Awang Abdul Hamid, is a nephew of the minister of education and health, Pehin Abdul Azizs. On September 29, the government approved the official launching of the party at Bandar Seri Begawan.

The monarchy is obviously yielding to pressure from within the state, and possibly from outside, for some form of representative government. However, the extent of power actually and ultimately given to the people will be limited, and the government has hopes that the BNDP will strike a healthy balance between the demands of an absolute monarchy and total democracy.

It appears that the government has agreed to hold a general election in 1987, but the memorandum as a whole has still to be presented to the sultan, and even party leaders have not dared to speculate on his reaction. Considering its history, it is safe to conclude that the monarchy will stop short of giving even a simple majority to the people's representatives in the State Assembly.

Brunei has become a member of the Association of Southeast Asian Nations (ASEAN) to improve its relations with its neighbors, protect itself from external threats, and enhance its international image.

Brunei's population is approximately 52 percent Malay and Muslim; 28 percent Chinese and Buddhist; 15 percent indigenous tribes (mostly Dayak) and animist; and 5 percent others, including a sizable group of Dutch and British expatriates, many of whom are employed in the bureaucracy. The Chinese predominate in commerce and the oil industry, while the Malays are concentrated in agriculture and the bureaucracy. Most of the Chinese are not Brunei citizens; their rights are secured only by the British protectorate. Discriminated against in government employment and land ownership, the Chinese are reportedly emigrating in increasing numbers.

Brunei's economy is based on oil and natural gas extraction which provided the state with a $3 billion trade surplus in 1981. Brunei Shell, the concessionaire, is half owned by Royal Dutch Shell and half by the state. Oil and gas revenues provide free medical care, liberal pensions, and free education at home and abroad through the university level. There are no income taxes. In January 1985, a new five-year development plan was launched which stresses increasing food production and reducing dependence on oil and gas for income.

Brunei's prospects are cloudy. Corruption and inefficiency are commonplace in all areas not under direct British oversight and sagging oil prices have adversely affected its economy. Neither the sultan nor his brothers (Mohamed, Sufri, and Jefri, in that order of precedence), who will very likely hold all the reins of government, are considered responsible or competent managers. Difficulties in the past with Malaysia and Indonesia appear to have died down, but could again become problems in the future; Malaysia would still like Brunei to join the federation. The 800 Gurkha troops under British command, which are the basis of the state's defense, are paid by Brunei and are likely to remain after the British withdrawal, but whether they could deal effectively with a local uprising supported by a foreign nation is open to doubt.

REPUBLIC OF BURUNDI
(République de Burundi;
Republika y' Uburundi)
by Thomas Paul Ofcansky, Ph.D., revised by Peter 'Molotsi, Ph.D.

Burundi, a Central African nation of four and a half million people, has a highly centralized, one-party socialist system with nearly all power held by the president. The current president and leader of the official party is Lieutenant Colonel Jean-Baptiste Bagaza, who seized power in 1976 in a military coup. There have been three legislative elections: in 1961, 1965 and 1982. The National Assembly was dissolved in 1966 and re-formed in 1982.

Under the present military dictatorship, Bagaza is head of state, government, party, and the army. Despite the existence of an executive council, the president's authority is almost totally unrestricted, with most laws and legislation being enacted by decree. Bagaza also exerts tremendous influence over the appointment of civil servants and military officers. Although marginally aligned with the northern Tutsi of Rwanda, the southern Tutsi are the dominant ethnic group in Burundi and control the country's political system.

Burundi's judicial system and legal codes are patterned after the Belgian model. Nine judges, under a president, preside over the Supreme Court. Although Bagaza appoints superior court judges, the minister of justice—acting on the provincial governor's recommendation—assigns lower-court judges.

Burundi is divided into eight provinces, each administered by a military governor. The provinces are subdivided into eighteen *arrondissements*, each headed by a district commissioner. The *arrondissements* in turn are subdivided into communes, administered by a communal council under the direction of an appointed chief administrator.

Until independence in 1962 there were twenty-four political parties in Burundi. Only the National Progress and Unity Party (*Parti de L'Unité et du Progrès National*, UPRONA) and the Hutu-dominated *Parti du Peuple* (PP) survived the 1961 elections. Subsequently, the PP merged with the Hutu faction of UPRONA to form the moderate Monrovia Group, while the Tutsi wing of UPRONA established the radical Casablanca Group. After the 1966 coup, led by Michel Micombero, UPRONA became the sole legal party, and remained so until Bagaza seized power in 1976. Although the new government abolished all political parties, UPRONA eventually was revived, holding its first national congress in twenty years in 1979. After declaring Burundi to be a socialist state, the UPRONA Central Committee elected Bagaza party president and head of the Central Committee for a term of five years.

Burundi is one of the poorest nations in the world. Its economy is centered around the production of corn, sorghum, beans, coffee, bananas, and livestock.

According to 1982 World Bank estimates, Burundi's GNP per capita stood at $280. In 1985, 94 percent of Burundi's labor force was engaged in agriculture, mainly at subsistence level.

Economic development in Burundi will be spurred by the proposed construction of a railroad that will link the country with Uganda, Rwanda, and Tanzania. These plans were completed in 1984.

Foreign aid plays a vital role in Burundi's economy, providing much needed budgetary support and financing several capital projects. Most assistance is supplied by Belgium, France, and West Germany. Acting under the terms of the Lomé Convention, the EEC also gives substantial foreign aid to Burundi.

The most serious threat to Burundi's long-term stability is the Hutu–Tutsi ethnic rivalry. Until 1965, animosity between the two groups was primarily nonviolent, but in that year the conflict intensified as the Hutu majority attempted to seize power by force. The Tutsi brutally suppressed the revolt, killing at least 5,000 Hutu rebels. Tutsi extremists then proceeded to remove all Hutu from the armed forces and the government.

The conflict erupted again in 1972 in the vicinity of Bujumbura, the capital, and soon spread throughout the country. In the slaughter that followed, approximately 250,000 Hutu were killed, while more than 100,000 survivors fled Burundi. Although Bagaza has tried to promote national reconciliation through a limited land-reform program, it is by no means certain that ethnic unity has become a reality.

Since Bagaza took power in November 1976, relations between the Catholic church and the state have been difficult. The Tutsi minority (20 percent of the population), which controls power in Bujumbura, suspects the Catholic clergy, half of whom are foreign missionaries, of wanting to "export the revolution" that it supported in neighboring Rwanda and thus give the Hutu majority tribe (80 percent of the population), the bulk of political power. The Burundian leaders also accuse the missionaries (65 percent of the population is Catholic) of having fomented the "1972 tragedy" between the Tutsis and Hutus, and thereby obstructing the "march toward national unity."

The government is committed to fighting corruption. On June 26, 1980 an ordinance was enforced compelling public officials to declare their movable and immovable wealth, and to explain how it was obtained.

Following the elections, a revamped National Assembly was officially called into session on November 1, 1982. The government was reshuffled in 1983 to bring new personalities and a number of women into the cabinet.

Col. Jean-Baptiste Bagaza was named at the party congress on July 25-27, 1984 to a second five-year term as president of UPRONA. He was unopposed in popular reelection as president of the republic on August 31, 1984.

Further Reading

Lemarchand, Rene. *Genocide in Burundi.* London: Minority Rights Group, 1974.

———. *Rwanda and Burundi.* New York: Praeger, 1970.

Melady, T. P. *Burundi: The Tragic Years.* Maryknoll, N. Y.: Orbis Books, 1974.

Mpozagara, Gabriel. *Le République du Burundi.* Paris: Berger-Levrault, 1971.

Weinstein, Warren. *Historical Dictionary of Burundi.* Metuchen, N. J.: Scarecrow Press, 1976.

——— and Schire, Robert. *Political Conflict and Ethnic Strategies: A Case Study of Burundi.* Syracuse, N. Y.: Maxwell School of Citizenship and Public Affairs, 1976.

FEDERAL ISLAMIC REPUBLIC OF THE COMOROS

by Philip M. Allen, Ph.D.

Three of the four Comorian islands—Grand Comoro (Njazidja), Anjouan (Nzwami), and Moheli (Mwali) with a total population of 420,000—unilaterally declared themselves an independent republic in July 1975. Mayotte, the fourth island of this archipelago just northwest of Madagascar, resolutely remained a dependency of France. Less than a month after the declaration, the Comorian president, Abderramane Ahmed Abdallah, was overthrown in a coup by Ali Soilih, who led a secular, decentralizing, commando-enforced "cultural revolution" until May 1978, when Abdallah threw him out with the help of a fifty-man force of mercenaries. Required by France to offer concessions to Mayotte as part of a long-term reunification project, Abdallah agreed to a federal constitution, theoretically guaranteeing considerable autonomy to each island. In December 1978, the government prohibited political parties and in early 1982 established a one-party state.

The constitution, which gives considerable powers to the president, falls far short of its federal ideal. The electorate of each island chooses its own governor and legislative council, but there are no island constitutions; all their "autonomous" institutions are specified in the federal document. Island governors have responsibility for routine economic and police administration, but fiscal authority is centralized in the federal capital, Moroni, and only the federation government can implement the international (primarily French, South African, and Gulf Arab) assistance agreements on which the economy of the country depends. The thirty-eight member, unicameral Federal Assembly is elected at large; thus, particular island interests have little assurance of influence in federal decisions. Abdallah, whose home island is Anjouan, began his second six-year mandate in October 1984. He has persistently rearranged his cabinets—taking over the prime ministry himself in 1985—to balance island, clan, and ideological diversities.

The Union for Comorian Progress (*Union pour le Progrès Comorien;* UPC, or UDZIMA in its Comorian-Swahili acronym), the only legal party, was put together in early 1982 to stimulate participation in social and economic development on the part of a passive and skeptical population. The party helped organize new legislative elections in March 1982 and reconstituted the president (whose tool it remains) in October 1984.

Comorian society is just beginning to emerge from a semi-feudal system. Power and influence still tend to pass along personal, familial, ritual, and patron-client channels, rather than through formal institutional networks. A heritage of descent from the Prophet Mohammed gives the Arab elite the legitimacy to dispose of land; control the state administration; supervise the custom of the "grand marriage" (an elaborate and very costly marriage ceremony that must be undertaken by any man who wishes to gain entry to the social elite or to maintain and improve his political and eco-

nomic prospects); and entertain lucrative relations with the French concessionaires who dominate the archipelago's export production of cloves, vanilla, copra, and ylang oil used in perfumes. Many of the mercenaries who helped restore Abdallah to power established themselves in Comorian business and public affairs. Their conspicuous presence helps mobilize opposition to the regime, among Comorians at home and in exile and among French and other crucial foreign benefactors who find their inclusion in the wealthy president's entourage unsavory. Abdallah's reputation for profiteering in his rice-import business and through his commercial holdings on Anjouan, his deference to Islamic custom and use of the "politics of the mosque," and alleged mistreatment of political prisoners have alienated the French Socialists who have advocated the reintegration of Mayotte into the federation. Nevertheless, neither the Socialists from 1981 through 1985 nor the more conservative politicians who are expected to form the majority in Paris by March 1986 have discovered a more congenial alternative or satisfactory answer to their uncomfortable dilemma over Mayotte.

Well before the declaration of the one-party state, opposition groups began forming in exile. The strongest of these groups have developed a common front for the overthrow of the "tyrant Abdallah"—the only goal which could be agreed upon by the Comorian National Liberation Movement (MOLINACO or UNIKOM), the Comorian National Unification Front (FNUK), the Democratic Front (FD), and the more conservative National Union for Democratic Comoros (UNDC) and Committee for Public Safety (CNSP) of the aristocratic Said Ali Kemal. The first three groups represent radical elements who helped precipitate the declaration of independence and participated in Soilih's "cultural revolution." Shifting coalitions among these antagonists have been responsible since 1978 for an annual series of bungled coups d'état, but Abdallah, his ruling clans, and mercenary supporters remain in power.

The 56,000 Mahorais, the people of Mayotte, the southernmost island and the first to come under French sway (1841), have strongly indicated their preference to remain French in three referenda since 1974. Abdallah is personally abhorrent to Mahorais leaders who identify him with the potential mass migration to the fertile Mayotte of the inhabitants of overpopulated and deforested Anjouan.

While continuing to discuss eventual reintegration of Mayotte into the Comorian federation, France has so far deferred to what it regards as legitimate self-determination by the Mahorais. France finds itself under persistent, of relatively mild, criticism from Third World sources for this exception to normal decolonization procedures, but is unable to ignore the categoric repugnance of the Mahorais for reunification.

During the extended standoff, Mayotte enjoys direct French investment in its public works, education, banking, health, and other institutions. The French navy, gendarmerie, and Foreign Legion operate facilities at Mayotte's strategically situated and well-protected harbor in the Mozambique Channel. Granted these privileges and secure from "inundation" by hungry Anjouanais and Grand Comorians, the Mahorais leaders agitate to turn their provisional "Territorial Collectivity" into a permanent French asset, preferably as an overseas department. Meanwhile they watch the federation's social and economic miasma respond sluggishly, if at all, to modest doses of foreign aid and administrative stimulation. The economy (entirely dependent on export agriculture) turned stagnant once again in 1984 and in 1985, after a couple of hopeful annual performances stimulated by modest foreign investment and favorable vanilla and clove prices. Expressed through the Creole-dominated Mahorais Popular Movement (MPM), "Mayotte Française" retains an attentive audience among French conservatives, the conservative political leaders of Reunion island, and even more leftward-oriented Abdallah opponents.

Further Reading
Newitt, Marlyn. *The Comoro Islands.* Boulder, Colo.: Westview Press, 1982.

REPUBLIC OF DJIBOUTI

by Sally Healy, M.Sc., revised by Peter Schraeder, M.A.

The Republic of Djibouti is a very small one-party state at the southern entrance to the Red Sea. A 4,000-man French military contingent is garrisoned there. Until independence from France in 1977, it was known as the French Territory of the Afars and Issas (TFAI), these being the names of the two tribal groups between which its 250,000 population is almost equally divided. Since the Afars are a significant nationality within Ethiopia and the Issas are a Somali clan, Djibouti is inevitably caught up in the nationalist rivalries in the Horn of Africa. It attempts to steer a neutral course between them.

The present regime dates from May 1977 and resulted from a simultaneous referendum on independence and general election. The referendum result was 98.7 percent in favor of independence in a turnout of 77 percent of eligible voters, and ensured the achievement of independence on June 27, 1977.

For elections to the Chamber of Deputies, a sixty-five member unicameral body, a single list of sixty-five candidates had been drawn up at a "round table" conference on the future of Djibouti, held in Paris earlier that year. The participants at the conference represented four political groupings: two factions of the National Union for Independence (UNI) which was associated with the Afars and had been the ruling party in the TFAI Chamber of Deputies since 1967; the African People's League for Independence (LPAI), which was associated with the Issas and had been the official opposition party; and the Front for the Liberation of the Somali Coast (FLCS) which had been banned in the territory but had the backing of the government in Somalia. The Ethiopian-backed Djibouti Liberation Movement (MLD) and the Marxist-Leninist Djibouti Popular Liberation Movement (MPL) did not attend, although members of these organizations were included in the electoral list.

In the elections, with a turnout of 76 percent, 92 percent voted in favor of the single list which resulted in an assembly comprising thirty-three Issas, thirty Afars and two Arabs. Hassan Gouled, an Issa and leader of the LPAI, was acclaimed first president of the republic.

Hassan Gouled, as president, selects the government ministers (numbering between fourteen and seventeen) and has attempted to maintain a roughly equal balance between Afars and Issas. The prime minister has always been an

Afar, and since 1978 the post has been held by Barkad Gourad, who led the parliamentary opposition formed by dissatisfied members of UNI in the preindependence period.

In 1979 the previous parties were replaced by a new single party called the People's Rally for Progress (RPP), led by Hassan Gouled, who also appointed its Political Bureau. The RPP largely took over the organization of LPAI. Following the passage of a new electoral law by the National Assembly in February 1981, the president is now chosen by direct elections. The first presidential elections were held in June 1981, and Hassan Gouled, as the sole candidate of the single party, received 84 percent of the votes cast. He was elected for a six-year term.

During the summer of 1981, attempts were made to register a new party, the Popular Party of Djibouti (Partie populaire de Djibouti; PPD), but it was proscribed. In October 1981, the constitution was amended, making Djibouti a de jure one-party state. Legislative elections were held in May 1982, in which voters were asked to endorse the single (RPP) list. The 91 percent turnout in the election demonstrated a high level of support for Hassan Gouled's regime, and sixty-five deputies were installed for five-year terms. They included twenty-two new members.

An underground movement—the Democratic Front for the Liberation of Djibouti (FDLD)—opposes the present regime. It was formed in June 1979 and is led by Mohammed Kamil, an Afar. Kamil held the post of foreign minister in the first independent government as well as being prime minister from February to September 1978, when he was replaced by Gourad. The FDLD is a merger of two earlier Afar parties (MPL and UNI), which were banned at the end of 1977 following Afar disturbances in the town of Djibouti. It has rejected the presidential election results and calls for democracy and the release of political prisoners in Djibouti. It has a base in Addis Ababa and has received Ethiopian backing.

The presence of some four thousand French troops ensures the survival of Djibouti, but the tiny nation remains extremely vulnerable. Djibouti's raison d'etre is the port which contains 25 percent of its population and handles about 60 percent of Ethiopia's trade. The railway link to Addis Ababa is an obvious guerrilla target, and has been sabotaged both by Afar opponents of the present regime and by Somali insurgents fighting inside Ethiopia. Ethnic conflict currently is not very prevalent in Djibouti, a hallmark of the political acumen of Hassan Gouled.

By skillful diplomacy Hassan Gouled has succeeded in maintaining friendly relations with both Ethiopia and Somalia during and after the Ogaden war (1977–78), but relations between these two neighbors will continue to exert great pressure on the internal politics of Djibouti. Hassan Gouled's role as mediator is shown by his recent hosting in 1986 of a meeting between Siad Barre of Somalia and Haile Mariam Mengistu of Ethiopia.

Further Reading
Abdi, Said Yusuf. "Independence for the Afars and the Issas: Complex Background; Uncertain Future," *Africa Today*, Vol. 24, No. 1, January-March 1977.
Thompson, Virginia, and Adloff, Richard. *Djibouti and the Horn of Africa*. London: Oxford University Press, 1968.

REPUBLIC OF EQUATORIAL GUINEA
(República de Guinea Ecuatorial)
by Rolando Alum, Jr., M.A. revised by Mbella Mokeba, M.A.

Equatorial Guinea is a nonparty state with a resident population of about 380,000 in 1985 ruled by a military junta. It consists of the odds and ends of Spanish colonization in the Gulf of Guinea in west central Africa: a mainland enclave (Rio Muni) with 89 percent of the population; two major islands, Bioko (formerly Fernando Póo) and Annobon, about 350 miles apart; and several smaller islets. The capital, Malabo (formerly Santa Isabella), is on Bioko, which has a population of some 70,000.

The republic became independent on October 12, 1968, and held its first and only free elections shortly before independence. Francisco Macías Ngueme Biyogo Negúe, a coffee planter and colonial civil servant, was elected president and soon turned the country into a military-dominated police state with ties to Moscow and Havana. Macías's regime rivaled that of Idi Amin's in Uganda for its atrocities. An unknown number of people were killed (perhaps as many as 35,000) and an estimated 100,000 people fled into neighboring countries or to Europe, especially Spain. All political parties were prohibited except the Macías-established National Workers' Party (*Partido Único Nacional Trabajadores;* PUNT), which supplied forced labor to the cocoa and coffee plantations. Macías was overthrown in a military coup on August 3, 1979. He retreated to Rio Muni and held out there for several days with the aid of some 500 imported Cuban troops before he was captured, tried, and executed.

The country is now ruled by the Supreme Military Council (SMC) which has assumed full executive and legislative powers. The SMC is headed by the coup leader, Lt. Col. Teodoro Obiang Ngueme Mbasogo (born 1942), who is head of state and government. He is assisted by a cabinet of whom all but one are military officers. All, including Obiang, are from the dominant ethnic group, the Fang. Reports that Obiang is Macías's nephew are probably in error, in spite of the coincidence that they bear a common name, Ngueme. (It is Fang custom to call elders from one's home region "uncle" and "aunt.")

The SMC executed many of Macías's closest followers, expelled the Cuban troops, and repudiated the Macías treaties with the Soviet Union. The junta released political prisoners and began to return private property confiscated by Macías's statist regime.

Obiang received troop support from Morocco after he failed to convince the Spanish government to send replacements from its *Guardia Civil* for departed Cuban troops. Since 1980 Malabo has had a 600-man Moroccan presidential bodyguard, which is regularly rotated from Rabat.

The country's original constitution (1968) called for a bicameral legislature. Macías abolished the legislature in 1971 and replaced the constitution with new ones in 1972 and 1973. The SMC abrogated the Macías constitutions, and in August 1982 submitted a new democratic constitution to a national referendum which approved it overwhelmingly. The new constitution reserves the office of president for Obiang until 1989. The junta has approved legislation guaranteeing an independent judiciary under a Supreme Court.

The country's political divisions, in part, reflect ethnic divisions. The dominant ethnic group is the Bantu Fang, about 75 percent of the population and concentrated in Rio Muni. The country's social, economic, and cultural elite are the Fernandinos, numbering some 35,000 and concentrated on Bioko. They are of mixed racial descent—Europeans, Cubans, and Puerto Ricans—exiled to Fernando Póo by Spain in the nineteenth century, and blacks, including both native West Africans and freed slaves left on the island by the British in the nineteenth century. Despite their cultural status, the Fernandinos have never had a significant role in national government. The aboriginal population of Bioko and Annobon is called Bubis. About 6 percent of the population, they scored minor successes in the 1968 elections. A small Bantu group, the Ndowe (called *Playeros* or "coastals" by the Spanish) speaks Kombe and lives along the coast of Rio Muni. The smaller ethnic groups resent and fear the dominance of the Fang, but are also distrustful of each other.

During the Macías regime, military expenditures doubled and the number of men in arms rose from 1,000 to 5,000, a large proportion of them paramilitary. The army, called the National Guard—recruited almost exclusively from the Fang—was under the command of Obiang, who received his military training in Spain and continues as chief of the National Guard and vice minister of defense.

Popular opposition to the Macías regime was virtually destroyed inside the country, but many opposition organizations were founded in exile, mostly in Spain.

However, such exile opposition remains ideologically vague, disorganized, and sharply divided by past rivalries. In April 1983, five movements, including the dominant National Alliance for Democratic Restoration (ANRD), met to form the coordinating committee of the Opposition Forces (JCFOGE). A rival opposition group, the Democratic Group for the Liberation of Equatorial Guinea (RDGLE) formed its own government in exile. These exile groupings do not envisage a campaign to overthrow the government by force. The only real threat to the government would be a coup led by factions within it. Any reported coup attempts, so far, have been thwarted by the better-armed Moroccan guards.

The most noteworthy achievements of the Obiang regime have been in foreign affairs. In 1983 relations with Spain deteriorated over the "Miko Affair". Miko, who had been convicted of plotting to overthrow the Guinean government, escaped from prison, and was granted asylum in the Spanish embassy. Spain denied allegations it was behind the plot, but the two nations remained at odds until Miko was turned over to the Guineans with the provision that he be spared execution. During the controversy, aid from Spain was reduced. Equatorial Guinea found a way out of its political dependence on Spain by turning to France and its neighboring states. France had been the only Western power to maintain diplomatic relations throughout the 1968-1979 period, thereby increasing its influence and leading to a tremendous increase in its aid to Malabo. Also, Malabo's entry into UDEAC—the Central African Economic and Customs Union—as a full member, its role as a founding member in the ten-nation CEEAC—the Economic Community of Central African States—and its resultant change of currency from the Ekuele to the Franc CFA in 1984 were only possible with French blessings. Improved, friendly, and intensive relations characterize the country's ties with neighboring Nigeria, Gabon, and Cameroon. In addition, the United States established full diplomatic relations with Equatorial Guinea in 1983.

The present regime now has solid constitutional backing following the official inauguration of Col. Obiang Nguema Mbazogo as president in October 1982. The possibility of returning to democracy after 1989 will depend on his good faith and willingness to reintegrate exile groupings into the system. The country's economic growth depends on a revival of the cocoa and timber industries, as well as the exploration of on- and offshore oil for which French and American firms have been granted concessions.

FIJI

by Terence Wesley-Smith M.A.

The Dominion of Fiji is situated in the southwest Pacific Ocean about 1,500 miles due north of New Zealand and has a population of 691,000. Its territory consists of numerous islands, about 100 of which are inhabited. It gained independence from Great Britain on October 10, 1970, but remains within the Commonwealth. Fiji is a constitutional monarchy with a parliamentary form of government.

Queen Elizabeth II is the head of state, represented in Fiji by a governor-general. The governor-general's role is largely ceremonial, although his official functions include appointing the prime minister and the cabinet. Since the prime minister must command a majority in the House of Representatives, the government is answerable to the House rather than to the head of state. Similarly, although the governor-general appoints the twelve ministers and the attorney general comprising the cabinet from among members of Parliament, he does so upon the recommendation of the prime minister. Several ministers of state, who are not cabinet members, may also be appointed from among members of Parliament.

Over fifty percent of Fiji's population are the descendants of migrant workers from India and the structure of the legislature reflects the country's multiracial nature. It is bicameral, consisting of a twenty-two member Senate and a fifty-two member House of Representatives. The senators are appointed for six-year terms, half of them every three years, to represent the interests of various political groups and to ensure a role for traditional leaders. Eight senators are appointed by the Council of Chiefs, seven by the prime minister, six by the leader of the opposition, and one by the Council of Rotuma (a small island in the north of the Fiji archipelago, whose people are culturally distinct from other Fijians). Seats in the House of Representatives are allocated according to race, with twelve Fijians, twelve Indians, and three general members elected by voters on separate communal rolls. Those on the general roll are mostly Europeans and other non-Indian and non-Fijian citizens. In addition, ten Fijians, ten

Indians, and five general members are elected by voters on national rolls. Hence citizens vote separately for candidates of their own race and together for candidates of each race in turn. Elections for the House are held every five years.

The constitution reserves a special role for traditional Fijian institutions. In particular, the Great Council of Chiefs controls over a third of the membership of the senate. Legislation that affects Fijian land, custom, or customary rights cannot pass through the senate without their support. Furthermore, the Fijian Administration, under the control of the Fijian Affairs Board, is a comprehensive system of local government, affecting only the Fijian section of the population and acting to preserve traditional communal structures.

The independent judicial branch includes the Court of Appeals and the Supreme Court, which is presided over by a chief justice appointed by the governor general. Complaints concerning the actions of governmental authorities are investigated by an ombudsman.

There are two major political parties in Fiji. The Alliance Party is led by Prime Minister Ratu Sir Kamisese K.T. Mara and draws support from the ethnic Fijians, the European and Chinese communities, and about 25 percent of the Indian community. Parliamentary members of this party often have chiefly status and there are close ties between the party and other Fijian institutions, including the Great Council of Chiefs. Mara and the Alliance have governed Fiji since independence. The National Federation Party (NFP) receives almost all of its support from rural and urban Indian workers. The NFP has long been divided into two personalist factions, centered around Jai Ram Reddy and Saddiq Koya, and factionalism continues to frustrate its atttempts to win power. At present, Koya leads the parliamentary opposition, replacing Reddy who resigned his party leadership and parliamentary seat in April 1984 after a split over a parliamentary boycott. Other parties, such as the Fijian Nationalist Party, an extremist splinter of the Alliance Party, and the regionally based Western United Party, play minor roles in national politics. The Fiji Labour Party was formed in 1985 and may prove to be a significant new force in Fiji. Its appeal is to working people regardless of race, and it made an impressive debut when it won eight of the twenty seats in the Suva City Council in July 1985 elections. Although the Labour Party's candidate lost narrowly to a member of the Alliance in a parliamentary by-election in December 1985, it seems set to make a major impact in the 1987 general elections.

The main issues in Fijian politics stem from the multiracial nature of its population and the constitutional provisions that have helped the Fijians retain political control so far. Indians have long argued that the political system, particularly the composition of the upper house and the communal system of voting, discriminates against them. Furthermore, they argue that Fiji's land tenure system does not allow them the secure access to the land they need for farming sugar cane, citing the fact that over 80 percent of all land remains with Fijian owners. Fijians, on the other hand, resent the Indian domination of the economy and feel that their position is further threatened by Indian numerical superiority. Meanwhile, the economy remains among the healthiest in the Pacific Islands, although still dependent on sugar exports and tourism.

KIRIBATI

by Terence Wesley-Smith, M.A.

Kiribati, formerly the Gilbert Islands, is a republic in the central Pacific Ocean with a population of 61,000. It consists of 33 islands, all coral atolls except Banaba, spread over some two million square miles of ocean. It achieved independence from Great Britain on July 12, 1979, but remains within the Commonwealth.

The constitution establishes a form of government that is a mixture of parliamentary and presidential systems. The president, or *Bereti-tenti*, is both head of state and head of government. He is chosen by a national election in which there is a maximum of four candidates. The candidates are nominated by the House of

Assembly from among its members. The president selects a cabinet from among the members of the House of Assembly. The cabinet consists of a vice president, not more than eight other ministers, and an attorney general. The normal term of office for president is four years, and an individual can serve for a maximum of three terms. He can be removed from office by a vote of no confidence by the House of Assembly. In such cases, a Council of State is empowered to carry out the executive functions until a new president is elected.

The single-chamber House of Assembly, or *Maneaba-ni-Maungatabu*, consists of thirty-five elected members, a nominated representative of the Banaban community, and the attorney general, who is an ex officio member. The speaker is chosen by members of the *Maneaba* from among persons who are not members of the assembly. Elections for the *Maneaba* are held every four years in twenty-three single-member or multi-members constituencies. Each member must be elected by an overall majority of votes cast, and runoff elections are often necessary. All representatives, except ministers, can be recalled by a petition of a majority of registered voters in their electorates.

Kiribati has a Court of Appeal and a High Court, and each inhabited island has a Magistrates' Court. The High Court can hear civil or criminal cases and those involving constitutional matters. The ultimate right of appeal is to the British Privy Council. The jurisdiction of magistrates' courts is unlimited in land matters, but limited in civil and criminal cases.

Local government takes the form of statutory island councils with elected members and limited administrative and financial powers. However, groups of traditional leaders, or *Unimane*, are often the more effective local political force.

The constitution makes special provision for the Banaban community, whose home island of Banaba (Ocean Island) has been the site of extensive phosphate works since 1900. Most Banabans now live on Rabi island in the Fiji group, bought for them after the Pacific War. Their vigorous attempts to declare Banaba independent of Kiribati have proved unsuccessful, but the constitution reserves a seat for their representative in Parliament (which Banabans have declined to fill), provides for an island council, and safeguards land rights. A commission of inquiry into the Banaban issue was established in 1985, but the government has yet to respond to its recommendations.

Kiribati's new political institutions have demonstrated their viability in the postindependence period. National elections have been held successfully in 1978, 1982, and, after a vote of no confidence, in early 1983. Voter turnout has been very high in all cases. Fairly stable factions have emerged in the *Maneaba*, although no formal, mass-based political parties exist. Thirty-five year old Ieremia Tabai has led the government since 1978. His government has had to deal with several challenging issues, the most serious of which was the disruptive strike of urban wage workers in 1980. More recently, a 1985 agreement allowing boats from the Soviet Union to fish within Kiribati's 200-mile zone has occasioned strong reactions from Australia, New Zealand, and the United States. Internal opposition, especially from the churches, has also been strong and the Christian Democratic Party has been formed to pursue the issue. Since phosphate resources were exausted in 1979, Kiribati has faced severe economic problems. Future prospects are closely tied to the development of marine resources because few other exploitable resources exist. The Kiribati economy is likely to remain dependent on external aid funds for the foreseeable future.

PRINCIPALITY OF LIECHTENSTEIN
(Fürstentum Liechtenstein)
by John Christian Laursen, Ph.D.

Liechtenstein, a sixty-two square mile state between Switzerland and Austria with a population of about 28,000, is an hereditary constitutional monarchy. Constituted in 1719, it became fully independent in 1815; its present constitution dates to 1921.

The present prince and titular head of state is Franz Josef II (born 1906). In 1984 Franz Josef handed executive authority to his son and heir apparent, Hans Adam (born 1945).

The ruler must approve all legislation passed by the unicameral Diet (legislature), and he may dissolve it at any time. Its fifteen members are elected by direct suffrage to four-year terms on the basis of proportional representation. Women were granted the right to vote at the national level in 1984.

The highest executive authority is the five-member Collegial Board, appointed by the ruler after nomination by the Diet. The prime minister and head of government since 1978 has been Hans Brunhart. Since 1980 the deputy head of government, traditionally from the minority party, has been Hilmar Ospelt.

Liechtenstein's independent judiciary has three levels of courts for civil and criminal matters. An administrative court and a State Court determine constitutional matters.

The two significant political parties are the Progressive Citizens' Party (*Fortschrittliche Bürgerpartei*; FBP) and the Fatherland Union (*Väterlandische Union*; VU), which have governed together in coalition since 1938. Other parties have failed to win seats in the Diet.

The conservative FBP held the parliamentary majority from 1928 to 1970 and from 1974 to 1978. In the 1978 elections, the labor-oriented VU won a majority of the seats although the FBP won a majority of the popular vote. In 1982 the VU kept its seats and won the popular majority. Each party controls one of the two major newspapers.

Since 1919, Switzerland has handled routine diplomatic matters and defense for Liechtenstein, and in 1923 the two countries joined in a customs union. Liechtenstein uses the Swiss franc as currency. It is not a member of the EEC, but is a member of EFTA and the Council of Europe.

More than 80% of the population is Roman Catholic. Foreign workers outnumber the domestic work force. Per capita income is over $16,900 per annum, with a strong industrial base. Liberal tax and banking laws have made the principality a haven and nominal headquarters for over 30,000 foreign corporations, although some tightening of those laws has taken place in the 1980s.

Tradition and prosperity underwrite the nation's stability.

REPUBLIC OF MALDIVES

by Philip M. Allen, Ph.D., revised by Robert Griffiths, M.A.

An idiosyncratic blend of traditional patriarchy, customary Islamic law, and benign impoverished insularity keeps the 200 inhabited Maldive islands intact in a steamy, tropical micropolity stretching over a 500-mile range of the central Indian Ocean. Once an hereditary sultanate dating from the twelfth century, Maldives became a British protectorate in 1870, but was controlled only indirectly, via Sri Lanka, until independence on July 26, 1965.

Three years later, a referendum replaced the sultanate with a republic whose legislature (*Majlis*) of fifty-four members chooses the president for a five-year term. Eight of the *Majlis* seats are filled by presidential appointment. The remaining forty-six are elected to five-year terms, eight of them from the capital, Male, which has 36,593 of the country's 175,500 inhabitants. The eleven outlying groups of atolls are organized into nineteen districts with two seats each. The president appoints several vice presidents and a chief justice. He has veto power over legislation. The office of prime minister (head of government) had been left in an ambiguous power relationship to that of the president under the 1968 constitution. It was abolished in March 1975, after the incumbent, Ahmed Zaki, unsuccessfully sought to formalize his de facto position through a no-confidence vote in the *Majlis* against President Amir Ibrahim Nasir. The president (who had himself been prime minister under the sultanate from

1957 through 1968), thereupon resolved the constitutional issue by assuming immediate authority over the government. Nasir retired in 1978 in favor of Maumoon Abdul Gayoom, the current president. Gayoom released Zaki from confinement, sending him to the United Nations as ambassador. Gayoom was elected in his own right in November 1978 and subsequently (April 1980) defended his authority against a challenge from the Nasir family.

President Gayoom was reelected for a second five-year term on September 30, 1983. Earlier that month, Gayoom placed two Maldivian judges under house arrest on charges of plotting his overthrow, but rumors of a coup attempt were unsubstantiated.

The most recent Majlis elections took place in December 1984. All candidates for the Majlis ran as independents since Maldives has no political parties.

In 1982, President Gayoom announced that action on a new constitution would be forthcoming by the end of his first term. The revised constitution reportedly calls for more political participation, but is apparently still under consideration.

Clan loyalties determine political alignments and rewards on this preindustrial archipelago. Family solidarity assures job training, employment in traditional trades, and even social services normally provided by government. Each atoll has a relatively homogeneous mixture of Sinhalese, Vedda, Dravidian, Arab, and African ethnic influences, with the archipelago unified by the Divehi (Sinhalese) language, Sunni Islam, and eight centuries of common suzerainty under the Didi family sultanate. Vestigial Buddhist influence antedating the gradual triumph of Islam from the ninth to the twelfth centuries, has left a caste pattern of occupational distribution. The traditional elite clans assume the function of political parties, but without permanent coalitions or marked differentiation in ideology or program. Factional maneuvers among the clans and personal alliances express competing interests. The only distinct minority are the Bohra, a Shi'ite commercial caste once favored by the British. As a result of government intervention, domestic and foreign trade, once the province of the Bohra, now operates to the advantage of the political patriarchs.

Law in Maldives is based on the Islamic Shari'ah, with slight adaptations. Most issues of justice and internal security are regulated by custom and enforced through face-to-face relations. Sanctions are endorsed by communal precedent. Education reinforces the moral values that sustain social cohesion and resist what is elsewhere prized as "modernization." Women have enjoyed the vote since 1964, but are prohibited from holding office. Property transfer is essentially patrilineal, and families undertake responsibility for unemployed and otherwise needy relatives.

The archipelago is administratively divided into nineteen districts, each with an appointed atoll chief who supervises the island chiefs (kateeb). Centralized authority has produced a dramatic socioeconomic contrast between Male and the outlying atolls: only three islands outside the capital have electricity, and Male contains all administrative and educational institutions, as well as an airport and a satellite telecommunications station. Access to the capital is regulated by pass in order to discourage undue migration of labor.

British construction of a World War II air base on Gan island in southernmost Addu Atoll established an economic counterpole to Male, as wages became available to hundreds of Gan fishermen. The archipelago thereupon had two ports and two airfields. After Britain's occupation of the Gan base was formalized by an agreement with the sultanate, the southern atolls sought to secede as the Suvadivan Republic. The rebellion was suppressed in 1959 by the sultan's police force and militia; Suvadivan leaders were given state jobs. The Gan base was evacuated in 1976 and the facilities have subsequently been considered for a variety of purposes. A million-dollar Soviet offer to lease the port installations for fishing trawler support in 1978 was declined by Male in favor of development of recreation facilities for European tourists. Winter visitors began to arrive from Sweden and Western Europe as early as 1974, and Air France opened an inexpensive direct flight from Paris to Gan in the early 1980s, anticipating a volume of 20,000 passengers per year, largely at the expense of the better endowed but apparently less stable Seychelles.

While following a general policy of nonalignment and nonparticipation in international affairs, Maldives has joined the Colombo Plan, the Asian Development Bank, and several utilitarian United Nations agencies. The World Health Organization is particularly active among this tropical population beleaguered by poverty and endemic disease. With half its labor force occupied in fishing, Maldives has devoted much of its diplomacy to a search for modern technology in that industry. India has gradually replaced Sri Lanka as the primary center of support for the islands' economy, providing capital for public investment, educational and training opportunities, and banking, transportation, and communications facilities.

MAURITIUS

by Philip M. Allen, Ph.D. revised by Ram Mannick, Ph.D.

A densely populated, multi-ethnic island of almost one million people in the southwestern Indian Ocean, Mauritius has survived serious economic and social tribulations and sustained its British-style parliamentary system of government since it became independent on March 12, 1968. In 1982, its five main political parties managed a hard-fought, democratically conducted change of regime. The new leftist leadership has pledged to convert this Commonwealth state into a republic, replacing the formal sovereignty of the British monarch represented by a governor general with a nonexecutive president and a strong parliamentary prime minister.

Despite its overwhelming victory, the first of its kind in a Commonwealth country, the new MMM/PSM government held together for only nine months. Personality clashes, problems of ideology, caste, and ethnic loyalties began to surface. But perhaps the most unsurmountable problem confronting the new government was the magnitude of the economic problems inherited from the Ramgoolam regime—an economy entirely dependent on the International Monetary Fund for balance of payments support. Since then, an alliance government has ruled Mauritius.

The seventy-seat Legislative Assembly contains sixty-two members directly elected to five-year terms in multimember districts. The other eight members are appointed by the governor general in consultation with the judiciary on the basis of "best loser" results in the preceding elections. This device was intended to ensure representation for ethnic minorities—Africans and Creoles who, with Muslims, amount to 45 percent of the population, as well as smaller numbers of Chinese and white Franco-Mauritians. The majority of the population is Hindu.

The 1982 elections were the first to be held for national office since 1976 when the leftist opposition party, the Mauritian Militant Movement (MMM) won thirty of the elected seats, but was excluded from power by a coalition of the Mauritius Labour Party (MLP), led by the prime minister, Sir Seewoosagur Ramgoolam, and the conservative Mauritius Social Democratic Party (PMSD). Using various constitutional privileges, Ramgoolam managed to postpone elections until 1982, hoping that a major improvement in the country's economic fortunes would preserve his government. His fourteen-year-old regime could take credit for major advances in its early years: greater per capita income, thanks to buoyant sugar prices; an annual growth rate of 8 percent in the early 1970s; strong foreign investment and rapid technological and infrastructure development; and the reduction of population growth, perhaps the country's most threatening problem, from 3 percent to 1.3 percent a year, through emigration, effective family planning, and urbanization.

In the mid-1970s, however, declining income from the export of sugar, rising costs of imports, and chronic unemployment began to take their toll. Balance-of-payment deficits and inflation grew, the currency was devalued almost annually, new taxes proved difficult to raise, labor productivity declined, and emigration markets closed. Well-documented corruption and open bickering within the regime over the succession to the aged Ramgoolam all contributed to the MMM's complete sweep (with its partner, the new Socialist Party) of all elected seats in the Assembly.

The largely Hindu canefield labor force, first imported in the mid-1800s, grew rapidly into a slight majority of the entire population. Although itself divided into factions according to points of origin, religious allegiance, and caste structure, it was that majority, led by Hindu professionals and trade-union officials, which pressed successfully over three decades for self-rule. Its principal spokesman, the Mauritius Labour Party (MLP) of former prime minister Ramgoolam, began as an advocate of the rights of canefield workers in the mid-1930s. It has consistently struck formidable political alliances with the middle-class Muslim Action Committee (MAC) and with various ephemeral formations representing lower-caste Hindus.

Independence was vehemently resisted by the Franco-Mauritian aristocracy, whose ancestors had first settled the territory in the early eighteenth century. Francophone sensibility, Roman Catholicism, and apprehension over Hindu majority rule brought the Europeans into alliance with the island's large, variegated minority of African and Creole people, most of them descended from the former plantation slave population. (Slavery was abolished in 1835.) Many urban professionals and craftsmen among the Creoles joined Franco-Mauritians in emigrating during the late 1960s to destinations where their skills, capital, and ethnicity were welcome. Those who stayed to contest the independence movement tended to support (and still support) the Mauritius Social Democratic Party (*Parti Mauricien Social Démocratique;* PMSD), a conservative, market-oriented bloc. Under its mercurial Creole leader, Gaetan Duval, the PMSD thrice participated in Ramgoolam coalition governments after independence became an accomplished fact.

Younger generation voters from all ethnic groups have adhered in increasing numbers to the pragmatic Marxist program of the *Mouvement Militant Mauricien* (MMM) and its electoral ally, the Mauritius Socialist Party (*Parti Socialiste Mauricien;* PSM), both of them formed after 1968. While the PSM is a splinter formation of disillusioned Hindus from the MLP, the MMM emerged in the early 1970s as a response to the right-of-center drift of Ramgoolam's governments and, equally significantly, to the inability of the existing parties to transcend ethnic "community" interests.

Trade unions, organized with remarkable efficacy since the 1930s, play important roles in the political process. They represented the foundation of MLP power from the birth of popular suffrage after World War II until very recently. The MMM's success depended on gradually capturing that power base in the towns and countryside, subsequently knitting the various communal threads into a disciplined proletarian organization.

The August 1983 general election produced a political potpourri. Prime Minister Anerood Jugnauth formed his own party, the *Mouvement Socialiste Mauricien* (MSM) which in turn allied with the Hindu PSM. The new MSM could not oppose the MMM on its own and had to combine with Ramgoolam's LP and Duval's PMSD. After a bitter campaign, especially against the MMM, leader, Paul Berenger was defeated in his own constituency of Quatre Bornes/Belle Rose. The MMM held on to its urban seats, but a campaign based on communalism helped the MSM-led alliance to win forty-one seats with the remaining nineteen going to the MMM. It claimed 210,000 votes, 46 percent of the total compared with 239,000 votes or 52 percent of the total going to all the parties in the Alliance. Since then, factional strife in the LP has weakened the alliance government. The opposition MMM won the 1985 municipal elections. But it is not clear if this can be translated into larger national gains. The Jugnauth government appears to have been shaken by the defection of four ex-ministers and growing Hindu opposition. Mauritian politics tend to be fluid and the country's pluralistic society places pragmatism before ideology; Mauritius's political future is unpredictable.

The five major parties and a scattering of ephemeral groupings compete according to the rules of the British system in a relatively literate, technologically advanced society, but in a nation-state the size and virtual complexity of a large city. Patron-client relations traditionally determine loyalties, both in the Hindu-populated countryside of sugar plantations and smallholds and in the dozen highly politicized towns, including the capital city, Port Louis. Power consists in the manipulation of interest factions and the patronage attaching to elected office.

Despite the socialist ideals of the former MMM government, economic realities have dictated a more pragmatic, free-market approach by the Alliance government. Although the inflation rate has dropped from an all-time high of 25 percent to the present 6.5 percent, the problems of unemployment currently at 22 percent of the working population; debt servicing which consumes up to 40 percent of the country's foreign earnings; and the ever growing balance of payments deficit continue unabated. The Sugar Authority, established in May of 1984, imposed a degree of nationalization on the island's key industry, but left-wing critics complained that it did not go far enough. In all other respects, the government has been forced to dismantle its controls over the economy, and to place greater reliance on such sectors as the tourist trade, and the EPZ industries.

Further Reading

Mannick, A. R. *Mauritius: The Development of a Plural Society.* Nottingham, England: Spokesman, 1979.

Simmons, Adele Smith. *Modern Mauritius.* Bloomington, Ind.: Indiana University Press, 1982.

MONACO

by Charles R. Foster, Ph.D. revised by Kenneth E. Bauzon, Ph.D.

Monaco, a city-state of about 30,000 people, on the Mediterranean coast of France, is a constitutional monarchy headed by a prince. The prince assumes his title upon the death or abdication of the reigning prince, and must be a direct and legitimate descendant of the latter. He is chosen by order of primogeniture. The prince exercises sovereign authority in conjunction with the provisions of the revised constitution of 1962.

The executive branch consists of a minister of state, who is under the supervision of the prince, and three members of the Council of Government. The minister of state, who is the head of government, is a French citizen by agreement between France and Monaco. The minister of state is chosen by the prince from a list of several senior French civil servants nominated by the French government. Traditionally, he is appointed for a period of three years. His primary duty is the conduct of foreign relations, but he also directs the executive services, commands the public police, and presides over the Council of Government. The current minister is Jean Herly. The Council is a three-member body, each member of which is assigned distinct responsibilities: finance and national economy, public works and social affairs, and internal affairs. The member overseeing internal affairs, the minister of the interior, again by agreement between France and Monaco, must be chosen from the French administration; French nationals, therefore, occupy the two key posts in the Monegasque administration. Other departments whose management has been delegated to French administration include the postal service, customs, criminal investigation, and the port authority.

Under the 1962 constitution, the prince shares his power with the unicameral National Council. The eighteen members of this legislative body are elected for five-year terms by universal adult suffrage (over twenty-five years of age) from a list of names given to voters. If the prince decides to dissolve the National Council, new elections must be held within three months. Usually meeting twice annually, the Council votes on the budget and endorses laws proposed by the prince.

Ordinances passed by the National Council are debated in the Council of Government, as are the ministerial decrees signed by the minister of state. Once approved, the ordinances must be submitted to the prince within eighty days for his signature, which makes them legally enforceable. If he does not veto them within ten days of their submission, they become valid.

The executive branch exercises three forms of control over the legislative branch: it can require that every other session be dedicated to deliberation of bills proposed by the prince; the minister of state and the Council of Government have the right to be heard at all sessions; and the prince has the right to dissolve the National Council. The National Council is essentially a deliberative body only. Proposals of law originate in the executive branch, either with the prince or with the ministers. The National Council can only suggest legislation to the executive body.

Judicial power is controlled by the prince, but according to the constitution, he delegates full powers to the courts and to the Supreme Tribunal. Members of the Supreme Tribunal are named by the prince on the basis of nominations by the National Council.

The principality's local affairs are administered as one municipality (*commune*). The Communal Council is headed by a mayor, who is assisted by fifteen elected members. The prerogatives of the Communal Council are restricted to the administration of the four communal quarters: Monaco-Ville, La Condamine, Monte Carlo, and Fontvieille.

With an electorate of fewer than 3,000, politics in Monaco tend to be a matter of personal allegiance rather than ideology. The National and Democratic Union (*Union National et Démocratique;* UND), formed in 1962, is the only truly organized political party in Monaco. The UND captured all eighteen seats in the National Council in the 1983 elections.

NAURU

by Terence Wesley-Smith, M.A.

Nauru is an island republic of about 8,000 people in the western Pacific Ocean some 1,200 miles northeast of Papua New Guinea. Until it was granted self-government in 1966 and full independence on January 31, 1968, Nauru was a United Nations trust territory administered by Australia on behalf of its fellow trust powers, New Zealand and Great Britain. It is an associate member of the Commonwealth, belongs to some U.N. agencies, and maintains an extensive consular network. Phosphate-rich Nauru has one of the highest per capita incomes in the world.

Nauru's constitution—adopted on January 29, 1968, and amended on May 17, 1968 — established a republic with a parliamentary system of government.

The president is head of state as well as head of government. He is elected by the Parliament from among its members every three years. In his role as prime minister, he appoints four or five members of Parliament to join with him to form the cabinet. Cabinet ministers, including the president, take charge of the various government departments and are collectively responsible to Parliament.

The unicameral Parliament consists of eighteen members, who are elected every three years by resident Nauru citizens over the age of twenty. The Parliament chooses a speaker and a deputy speaker, as well as the president, from among its members.

A Supreme Court was established by the constitution and a District Court and a Family Court also operate. In most cases, the highest court of appeal is the High Court of Australia.

Nauru is divided into fourteen districts, which are grouped into eight electoral constituencies. Two representatives are elected in each constituency except Ubenide, which is composed of four of the smaller districts and has four representatives in Parliament.

The Nauru Local Government Council exercises important governmental functions. Charged with responsibility for Nauruan community affairs before independence, the council has retained certain powers within the republic. In particular, it owns and controls many of Nauru's economic enterprises and investments. The council has nine elected members. Its leader is known as the Head Chief and is elected by the council from among its members. It is common for individuals to hold seats in both Parliament and the council.

The political system—dominated by Hammer DeRoburt—has been stable. DeRoburt has served as president since independence, except for a fourteen–month period between December 1976 and May 1978 when he was replaced by Bernard Dowiyogo (Lagumont Harris served for three weeks in 1978). In the December 1983 presidential election, DeRoburt defeated Kinza Clodumar by ten votes to six. In addition, DeRoburt has been Head Chief continuously since 1955.

Electoral politics in Nauru has more to do with kin relationships than issues. Parliamentary factions form from time to time but, apart from the Nauru Party, which appeared briefly to oppose DeRoburt in 1976, there are no formal political parties.

Phosphate exports of about 1.75 million tons annually generate huge revenues for the Nauru government and allow it to levy no taxes and to provide free health and education services. Many of the material necessities of life, including water, are imported. At present rates of extraction, the phosphate will be worked out in the 1990s. However, a significant proportion of the phosphate revenue has been invested in commercial enterprises and overseas real estate developments, thereby assuring some future income for Nauru.

REPUBLIC OF RWANDA
(République Rwandaise;
Republika y'u Rwanda)
by Thomas Paul Ofcansky, Ph.D.

Rwanda, a nation of 5.1 million people in Central Africa, has a highly centralized, one-party political system with nearly all power held by the president. The president of the country and the official party is Major General Juvénal Habyarimana, who seized power in 1973 in a military coup that ended eleven years of parliamentary rule in Rwanda. The National Assembly elected in 1982 consists of suxty-four members.

Under the present military dictatorship, Habyarimana is head of state, government, party, and the army. Although assisted by the eleven-member Committee for National Peace and Unity, the president's power is practically unlimited. Rwanda is governed largely by executive decree rather than through legislation. Moreover, Habyarimana has the authority to appoint nearly all government officers, including members of the military-dominated cabinet and the Committee for National Peace and Unity.

Rwandan jurisprudence for the most part is codified and based largely on Belgian procedures and precedents. Uncodified customary law also is administered in certain rural jurisdictions. A supreme court with a president and five departments, each supervised by a vice president, heads the judicial structure. The six justices act as the constitutional court and the appellate court.

Rwanda is divided in to ten prefectures, each in turn divided into sub-prefectures and communes. Both prefectures and communes are headed by centrally appointed executives, respectively designated as prefects and burgomasters. Each of the 141 communes is managed by popularly elected communal councils. Prefects and burgomasters can be dismissed at will by the president of the Republic.

Elections in Rwanda are direct and universal, but there is no choice of candidates outside the ruling party. Active opposition to this limited electoral system is nonexistent.

Rwanda's first Parliament since Habyarimana seized power in 1973 was elected in 1982. All deputies are members of the National Revolutionary Development Movement (*Mouvement Révolutionnaire National pour le Développement*; MRND), which acts as the country's foremost instrument of social and political mobilization. Although Tutsi elements are virtually excluded from representation in Parliament (technically known as the National Development Council), the application of ethnic and regional quotas within the administration and the National University of Rwanda has meant that approximately 10 percent of the administrative cadres at the central and regional levels consist of Tutsi elements. Thus far this Rwandese version of affirmative action has been relatively successful in bringing about the integration the Tutsi minority, long considered by the central authorities as too closely identified with the old monarchy to be trusted fully.

As one of the forty-nine low-income countries, one of the twenty-nine least-developed countries, and one of the forty-five countries the United Nations considers to be the most seriously affected by the recent world-wide economic decline, Rwanda is one of the poorest countries on earth. Indeed, with approximately 75 percent of the country's population living in absolute poverty, it is essential for the Habayarimana regime to promote economic development. Otherwise, Rwanda could be plagued by widespread violence.

Foreign-aid grants have financed most post-independence public-sector investment. Belgium continues to be the major source of external assistance, furnishing about one-third of all foreign aid. Additional support is acquired from the European Economic Community (EEC) through its European Development Fund (FED). Other foreign aid contributors include the United States, the United Nations Development Fund, the Arab Fund, France, West Germany, Switzerland, Canada, and the People's Republic of China. It is unclear whether this assistance will have significant impact on Rwanda's agricultural or industrial evolution.

Though faced with one of the highest rates of population growth anywhere in Africa, Rwanda has coped remarkably well with problems of economic development. In part this is a reflection of the magnitude of externally funded development projects, and in part a commentary on the success of self-help schemes. The so-called *umuganda* system, which makes it mandatory for every adult male to work one morning a week on development-oriented projects, has greatly contributed to the country's impressive development record. The Rwanda way to development, overwhelmingly geared toward self-help and social mobilization, carries important lessons for anyone interested in the contribution of indigenous social institutions to issues of growth and development.

Further Reading

Kagame, Alexis. *Un Abrégé de l'Ethno-Histoire du Rwanda*. Butare, Rwanda: Editions Universitaires du Rwanda, 1972.
Lemarchand, Rene. *Rwanda and Burundi*. New York: Praeger, 1970.
Levesque, Albert. *Contribution to the National Bibliography of Rwanda*. Boston: G. K. Hall, 1979.
Linden, Ian. *Church and Revolution in Rwanda*. New York: Africana Publishing, 1977.

ST. CHRISTOPHER (ST. KITTS)–NEVIS
by A. Biorn H. Maybury-Lewis, M.A.

St. Christopher (known also as St. Kitts) and Nevis are among the northernmost islands in the Leeward Island Group in the Eastern Caribbean. Together, they constitute an independent nation with, in 1986, a population of approximately 49,000 people, primarily of African descent. The country's political system is essentially a constitutional monarchy within the British Commonwealth. St. Kitts became the first British possession in the Caribbean when Britishers settled there in 1623.

In 1816, the British decided to rule St. Christopher, Nevis, and neighboring Anguilla as a single colony. After 1871, the colony was expanded to a larger unit encompassing more islands and was called the Leewards Islands Federation. The early twentieth century saw the first stirrings of nationalism. In 1932, the socialist Labor Party (LP) was founded. It bore the mantle of the struggle for Anguillan–Kittian–Nevisian independence. The three-island colony joined the West Indian Federation during its brief 1958–1962 life. It gained the status of associated statehood on February 27, 1967: the English would continue to control external affairs and national defense while the islanders would manage internal affairs. During the 1970s, the Anguillans decided they would rather be an English colony than be subject to rule from the Kittian capital, Basseterre. The de facto separation of Anguilla from St. Christopher and Nevis was made formal on December 19, 1980. At the Constitutional Conference held in London in December 1982, it was decided that St. Christopher and Nevis should become independent. The Nevisians and Kittians formally gained independence on September 19, 1983.

The 1983 constitution dubbed St. Kitts–Nevis a "sovereign democratic federal state". The constitution requires that the reigning king or queen of England perform the ceremonial role of head-of-state, with a governor general of Kittian or Nevisian origin representing the English monarch. The governor general appoints as prime minister the person that commands a parliamentary majority. The remaining ministers are named by the prime minister. All ministers, with the exception of the attorney general, must be members of the legislature. The governor general also appoints, with the ruling coalition's approval, a deputy governor general for Nevis. Legislative affairs are entrusted to the unicameral National Assembly. Eleven of the representatives are elected through universal adult suffrage from single-member constituencies, eight of which are on St. Christopher and three on Nevis. Legislators may remain in office for a maximum of five years without being subject to new elections. The governor general may appoint additional members, known as senators, yet they may not number more than the two-thirds of the elected membership.

In federalist fashion, Nevis has its own island Assembly of five elected and three appointed members. The governor general appoints the Nevis Island Administration including a premier and two other members. A crucially important provision is that Nevis' Assembly has the right to order a political secession of Nevis from St. Kitts if two-thirds of the assemblymen approve such a move, and if in an island referendum two-thirds of the voters also endorse it.

The highest court is the West Indies Supreme Court (in St. Lucia), which is also comprised of the Court of Appeal and a High Court. A judge from the latter court resides on St. Kitts and has authority over a Court of Summary Jurisdiction, while district courts deal with petty offenses and minor civil actions. In rare cases, decisions may be appealed up to the Privy Council in London.

The central political issue remains the character of the relationship between the long dominant but now in opposition Labor Party (LP), and the presently preeminent People's Action Movement (PAM) and its ally the Nevis Reformation Party (NRP). It has recently been acrimonious. Anguilla and Nevis, during the last decades before independence, resented what they perceived as an "external" government of the St. Kitts-based LP that did not serve their best interests. The inter-island disputes revolved around differences in economic and social structures. The Anguillans opted for reestablishment of British colonialism. Alternatively, the Nevisians built a political party that, through an alliance with the PAM, was able to edge the LP in the 1980 elections and form a parliamentary majority.

Subsequently, the PAM/NRP coalition, led by Dr. Kennedy Alphonse Simmonds (born 1936), formulated an agenda for the 1982 Constitutional Conference in London that won the day. Nevis not only gained substantial governmental autonomy and the right to secede, it also won one of the two new seats in the post-independence National Assembly, the other seat going to the more populous St. Kitts. Thus Nevis has a disproportionately large representation in the newly independent nation's government. Prime Minister Simmonds and the PAM received in return a new political base. This base, coupled with a lowered voting age (to eighteen) that analysts agree most helped the PAM, catapulted the PAM to resounding victory in the June 21, 1984 general election. The PAM won six seats and the NRP three against the LP's two.

Despite this setback, organized labor remains closely tied to the recently defeated LP. Although youthful voters effected a change in leadership and marginalized the LP in 1984, a modus vivendi between the now-dominant coalition and the main St. Kitts–Nevis Trades and Labor Union needs to be forged to realize Prime Minister Simmonds left-of-center vision of economic growth based on tourism, transnational investment, and diversified agricultural production.

Suggested Further Reading

Barry, Tom, Beth Wood and Deb Preusch. *The Other Side of Paradise: Foreign Control in the Caribbean.* New York: Grove Press, 1984.

Midget, Douglas K. "St. Kitts–Nevis." In Jack W. Hopkins, Ed. *Latin American and Caribbean Contemporary Record, 1983–1984.* New York: Holmes and Meier, 1985.

MOST SERENE REPUBLIC OF SAN MARINO
(Serenissima Repubblica di San Marino)
by Martin Slater, Ph.D.

San Marino is a formally independent republic located entirely within the Italian region of Emilia-Romagna. Founded in 301 A.D., it is the world's oldest republic; and with a population of less than 22,206 living in 23.6 square miles, it is also one of the smallest. The present constitution dates from 1600 and shows its lineage by its resemblance to ancient Roman constitutions.

Unlike all other Italian states, San Marino never became part of Italy in the unification of 1861. Instead, its independent status was guaranteed in the 1862 Treaty of Friendship with the new Italian state. At the same time, a customs union was established. The Treaty with Italy has been periodically renewed and amended throughout the past 120 years.

Executive power is vested in the eleven-member Congress of State (*Congresso di Stato*) elected from and by the legislature. Two captain-regents (*Capitani Reggenti*), who are effectively joint heads of state, are chosen to head the Congress. They may only serve for six months and are not eligible to be reelected for a further three years. Formally, one regent represents the city of San Marino; the other, the rest of the country. Having two heads of state is convenient for the coalition governments of San Marino. One of the present officeholders comes from the Communist Party, the largest coalition partner; the other is drawn alternately from the two junior coalition partners, the Socialists and the Unitarian Socialists.

Legislative power is in the hands of the sixty-member Grand General Council (*Consiglio Grande e Generale*). The Council is elected by universal adult suffrage under a system of proportional representation. Only since 1960 have women been allowed to vote, and only since 1974 have they been able to stand for office. Women are still underprivileged in that, under the terms of a 1928 law, if they marry a foreigner they lose their rights of citizenship, including the right to vote, work and own property. The Council's normal term is five years. The only time premature elections have been held was in 1978, one year before they were due. The cause was serious policy disagreements among the parties of the governing coalition. Since World War II, the balance of power within the legislature has swung between the Christian Democrats and the Communists, with the Socialists playing a pivotal role. The present coalition, in power since 1978, with a bare majority of thirty-one seats, consists of the Communists and two Socialist parties. It was reelected to office in 1983, when it increased its majority by one.

Referendums may also be held to contest existing legislation. The most recent experience was in 1982, when there was an unsuccessful attempt to overturn the 1928 legislation discriminating against women's rights.

The highest judicial authority in San Marino is the Council of Twelve (*Consiglio de XII*), chosen by the legislature. The Council is the final court of review. The majority of cases, however, both civil and criminal, are dealt with by the Italian judicial system.

San Marino has a multiparty system in which six parties are represented in the Grand Central Council. To some extent, the system resembles that of Italy, most closely in the dominance of the Communist and Christian Democratic parties. There are also close organizational links between some of the San Marino parties and their Italian counterparts. All the parties, however, have formally independent organizational structures, with their headquarters in San Marino. Not all are related to Italian parties.

In the post–World War II era, no single party has been able to gain an absolute majority of seats in the Council. From 1945 to 1957, there was a left-wing coalition of Communists and Socialists; from 1957 to 1973, a center coalition of Christian Democrats and Social Democrats; from 1973 to 1977, a center-left coalition of Christian Democrats and Socialists, and finally, from 1978 to the present day, a three-party left-wing coalition of Communists, Socialists, and Unitarian Socialists. The Christian Democrats, Communists, and Socialists have remained an integral part of the party system during this period. Their levels of popular support have varied only marginally. The major changes have occurred with the demise of the old Social Democratic Party, which used to be San Marino's third-largest party, with approximately 15 percent of the popular vote. In 1975, this party split into two new socialist parties. Thus, San Marino now has three socialist parties.

The Christian Democratic Party of San Marino (*Partito Democratico Cristiano Sammarinese;* PDCS) is San Marino's largest political party, with twenty-six seats in the present legislature. Established in 1948, it was in opposition until 1957, when it formed a coalition with the Social Democrats. In 1973, it switched to a coalition with the Socialists. Despite gains in the 1978 elections, the defection of the Socialists in 1977 and the prior breakup of the old Social Democrats forced the PDCS into opposition. The party failed to increase its number of seats in the 1983 election, and has remained in opposition. It is ideologically conservative, vigorously opposing the introduction of income tax in 1984.

The Committee for the Defense of the Republic (*Comitato per la Difesa della Repubblica;* CDR) as its name implies, is a nationalist party on the right of the political spectrum. Founded in 1974, it has only one seat in the legislature and plays no role in government.

The Communist Party of San Marino (*Partito Comunista Sammarinese;* PCS) was established in 1941. Active in the Resistance movement against German occupation, the PCS is a moderate communist party by European standards, following closely the ideological line of the Italian party. With fifteen seats in the legislature, it is the republic's second largest party, and has been in and out of government. From 1945 to 1957, it formed a coalition with the Socialists. In opposition from 1957 to 1978, it is now the senior partner in a coalition of Socialists and Unitarian Socialists. Despite a slight decline in Communist support in the 1983 election, the coalition has endured through two legislatures.

The Social Democratic Party (*Partito di Democrazia Socialista;* PDS) was founded in 1975 as a result of a split in the old Independent Social Democratic Party of San Marino (*Partito Independente di Democrazia Socialista di San Marino;* PSDIS). It is the most right wing of the three socialist parties, and with only one seat in the legislature, it is also the weakest. It is currently in opposition.

The Socialist Party of San Marino (*Partito Socialista Sammarinese;* PSS) is the largest (with eight legislative seats) and oldest of San Marino's socialist parties. Traditionally proCommunist, it formed a governing coalition with the Communists from 1945 to 1957. In opposition from 1957 to 1973, it shifted ground in the 1970s and joined a Christian Democratic coalition in 1973. Withdrawing in 1977, it entered a left-wing coalition with the Communists and the Unified Socialists in 1978, increasing its legislative representation by one seat in the 1983 election.

The Socialist Unity Party (*Partito Socialista Unitario;* PSU) was established in 1975 by the more left-wing members of the old PSDIS. The PSU has been part of the left-wing governing coalition since 1978 and holds eight seats in the legislature. Like the PSS, it increased its representation by one seat in 1983.

DEMOCRATIC REPUBLIC OF SAO TOMÉ AND PRÍNCIPE
(República Democrática de Sao Tomé e Príncipe)
by Tony Hodges revised by Denise Jackson, M.A.

Two islands in the Gulf of Guinea with a combined population of about 110,000, São Tomé and Príncipe have been governed by the Movement for the Liberation of São Tomé and Príncipe (*Movimento para a Libertação de São Tomé e Príncipe;* MLSTP), under a one-party system of government, since their independence from Portugal in 1975. Manuel Pinto da Costa, who has been the MLSTP's secretary general since its founding in 1972 and the nation's president since independence, has established strong personal power.

The president is head of the government and commander of the armed forces. The country's legislature, which elects the president, is known as the National Assembly. Its deputies (eighteen in 1975) are elected indirectly and must be members of the MLSTP, according to the constitution adopted in December 1975. Elections were held in May 1978 and on August 16–20, 1985. In these elections, the District Popular Assemblies were elected by direct vote. The District Assemblies then elected the National Popular Assembly which reelected President Pinto da Costa for another five-year term.

The MLSTP was founded in exile in 1972 and set up its headquarters in Libreville, Gabon. After the downfall of the Marcello Caetano dictatorship in Portugal in April 1974, a pro-MLSTP "Civic Association" was formed in the islands to mobilize the population in support of independence. In November 1974, the Portuguese government set up a transitional government with MLSTP ministers to steer the country to independence in July 1975.

There has been a series of factional fights within the party since the days of the transitional government. In 1975, a conflict arose between some of the more left-wing former leaders of the home-grown Civic Association and the previously exiled MLSTP leadership. From 1975 to 1978, there was conflict between Pinto da Costa and a conservative faction headed by Carlos da Graça, the country's first postindependence health minister, who had established close relations with President Omar Bongo in Libreville before independence. Carlos da Graça went into exile again in Gabon and was accused in February 1978 of plotting a comeback with the aid of mercenaries. In 1979, there was a power struggle between Pinto da Costa and Miguel Trovoada, who had been one of the MLSTP's exiled founders. After losing the premiership to Pinto da Costa in April 1979, Trovoada was accused of fomenting antigovernment demonstrations in August 1979 and was arrested the following October. He was allowed to go into exile in July 1981. In January 1982, after riots on the island of Príncipe in December 1981, the powerful defense minister, Colonel Daniel Daio, was removed from the Council of Ministers and his portfolio taken on by the president. The major changes in government which have occured since the end of 1981 seem to indicate a certain move toward the West. In May 1984, Joaquim Rafael Branco was ousted from his post as minister of education because of his antiWest posture and the Ministry of Cooperation was created. The February 1985 dismissal of the foreign affairs minister, Mrs. Maria de Amorim, was also seen as part of a policy to better relations with the West. In March the president assumed the additional posts of minister of foreign affairs and of planning. A new government was announced in February, 1986. The changes are seen as an attempt to increase efficiency and the government's ability to carry out donor–assisted programs. Pinto da Costa has thus strengthened his hold on power and, since 1978, has enjoyed the protection of a force of some 1,000 to 1,500 Angolan troops and several dozen Cuban military advisors who together outnumber São Tomé's own tiny army of about 1,000 men.

The party's highest policymaking body is the congress, which met in 1978 and again in September 1985. The major change introduced by the last Party Congress was an enlargement of the Central Committee from thirty-five to fifty-one members with ten deputy members. Between congresses, policy is determined by the Coordinating Council, which the secretary general chairs. The government is assumed to be the main source of party funds.

The MLSTP defines itself as a "revolutionary front of democratic, anti-colonialist and anti-imperialist forces." It has taken several radical measures since independence—most notably the nationalization of the *roças*, the twenty-nine cocoa estates which occupied 80 percent of the cultivable land. However, the party is not Marxist; and, although military aid comes from Angola and Cuba, economic ties are primarily with the West. The party's foreign policy has been a highly pragmatic brand of nonalignment, designed to attract aid from governments of all political hues. It became a member of the IMF in 1977 and signed the Lome Convention, linking it to the EEC in 1978. Relations with Portugal remain very strong.

Manuel Pinto da Costa (born 1938) was educated in Portugal (University of Lisbon) and East Germany (University of Berlin) and joined the MLSTP's predecessor, the *Comité de Libertação de São Tomé e Príncipe* (CLSTP), in 1960. He was elected secretary general of the MLSTP in July 1972 and lived in Equatorial Guinea and Gabon between 1972 and July 1975, when he returned to São Tomé on the eve of independence.

The stability of the MLSTP regime may depend crucially on a factor completely beyond local control—the fluctuations in the world price of cocoa, on which São Tomé depends for about 90 percent of its export earnings. However, the continuing presence of Angolan and Cuban troops in the islands will tend to discourage bids for power by President Pinto da Costa's rivals or opponents.

Further Reading

Legum, Colin, ed. "São Tomé and Príncipe, Political Tranquility Despite Collapse of Cocoa." *Africa Contemporary Record*. Vol. 13, 1980–81. New York: Holmes and Meier, 1981.

Wisenberg, Laurie S., and Nelson, Gary F. "Mini-State with Maxi-Problems." *Africa Report,* March–April 1976.

REPUBLIC OF SEYCHELLES
(République des Seychelles)
by Philip M. Allen, Ph.D. revised by Ram Mannick, Ph.D.

A centralized, one-party presidential microstate in the western Indian Ocean, Seychelles has been independent from Great Britain since 1976. The ninety-two islands are spread out over more than 600 miles, running from northeast to southwest toward Madagascar. The granitic group of islands just south of the equator contains most of the 66,000 Seychellois (90 percent of them on Mahé, the largest island). A few coconut plantation workers and fishermen live on the flat atolls of the Amirantes and the southernmost Aldabra and Farquhar coralline archipelagos north of Madagascar. The islands were unpopulated until the eighteenth century. Descendants of original French plantation settlers and their African, Asian, and Malagasy slaves subsisted for two centuries in deep colonial obscurity. During much of that time, the islands were a dependency of Mauritius, a French and, later, a British colony.

Under British rule after 1814, the French aristocracy and its mode of life were allowed to dominate a largely Creole (mixed race) society. Britain was more eager to grant the territory independence than its indigenous leaders were to accept it. Political activity in the islands evolved sluggishly until the early 1960s, when it polarized between a conservative loyalist Seychelles Democratic Party (SDP) under James Mancham (born 1940) and a nationalist opposition favoring self-government, the Seychelles People's United Party (SPUP), led by France Albert René (born 1935). Mancham failed to persuade Britain to arrange for a relationship short of outright independence. He conceded the inevitable in 1974 and preempted SPUP's independence program. Two years later, he became first president of a new republic within the Commonwealth, governing through a broad coalition, with René as prime minister. While abroad in June 1977, the flamboyant, hedonistic president was deposed by his austere prime minister, who vowed as a socialist to take the job more seriously.

Within two years of René's *coup d'état* a new constitution was approved by referendum and was implemented on the coup's second anniversary, June 5, 1979. That same month, René was confirmed as president of the republic, chief of state, and commander-in-chief by 98 percent of the 26,931 voters, after running unopposed in the first elections to be held since before independence. A twenty-three-member Popular Assembly was also elected at that time. Having banned Mancham's SDP in March 1978, René governed through SPUP until the new constitution transformed that organization into the Seychelles People's Progressive Front (SPPF). Modeled to a degree on the Tanzanian experience, the SPPF's Executive Committee and twenty-three local chapters meet annually in congress with their affiliated National Workers Union, National Women's Organization, and National Youth Movement. Among other responsibilities, the congress nominates the president for a five-year term, subject to a plebiscite. The party also proposes nominees from party ranks to serve four-year terms in the Popular Assembly. In 1979, seventy candidates contested the twenty-three legislative seats in an election strictly controlled by the SPPF Executive Committee. Two additional Assembly members are appointed by the president to represent outlying islands with small, or seasonal, populations. The president's list of ministers is subject to approval by the Assembly. Minister of National Administration and Political Organization Guy Sinon serves as SPPF secretary general in a deliberately interlocking system.

Since seizing power, René has had to suppress several pro-Mancham countercoup attempts of foreign origin, including an aborted conspiracy in late 1979 which earned extended detention for seventy-eight local residents and the expulsion of several French military training advisers and one French government civilian. Two years later, on November 25, 1981, an invasion by forty-eight European mercenaries ended after a bloody airport skirmish. All but five of the intruders escaped on a commandeered Air India plane diverted from Mahé to Durban, South Africa, where they were subsequently convicted for hijacking. The other five and a woman accomplice were captured on Mahé and received heavy sentences for the conspiracy. High-level officials of both South Africa and Kenya were incriminated by testimony in both sets of trials. In addition to the pro-Mancham maneuvers, on August 17, 1982, army rank-and-file mutineers captured the radio station in Victoria, the capital, criticized certain government ministers, and appealed for improved treatment for military personnel. The mutiny was put down the following day.

Seychelles has calmed down after the coups and the activities of mercenaries and dissident groups in the early eighties virtually brought the country to its knees. President René's government appears to be making headway in socioeconomic areas. The provisions of its miniwelfare state are reducing the extreme inequalities that existed in the Seychellois society under the Mancham regime. Seychelles' now firmly established political stability has given it the opportunity to attract funds from friendly countries and to begin developing the infrastructure that will further increase its productive base and lead toward economic self-sufficiency. In the main, René's efforts to redistribute revenues through marketing and tax schemes and his education, housing, and health improvement programs are popular. But the country's tax burden and external debt costs are becoming serious problems. Tourist traffic, which had been somewhat affected by reports of social unrest and René's outspokenly nonaligned foreign policy, has now reached new heights. By 1986 over 75,000 tourists per year were expected, and the government set a limit on the number of visitors it would allow in future years.

Opposition to René has taken different forms since he took power. René was forced to change the rules of participation in his favorite Youth Training Corps from compulsory to voluntary service after vigorous demonstrations by students and parents in October 1979. This style of protest, exemplified in the 1982 army revolt as well, avoids direct challenge to René and the SPPF; it focuses instead on "misguided" advisers and unwise policy. Debates on policy have

taken place, including an ultimately crucial assessment of the priority to be given languages (French, English, and the Creole adaptation of French used as a lingua franca), but more serious conflicts may have been reflected in unconfirmed rumors of a coup attempt in 1985. René has hinted that the attempt was prompted either by people who had been threatened by recent reforms (including traders and large landowners) or those whose expectations from these changes have yet to be fulfilled (such as unemployed workers). Despite pressure from these groups, there are few signs that the government suffers a serious threat or that it is preparing to deviate from the course set out in its ambitious 1985–1989 National Development Plan.

The main political opposition remains outside of the country and centers around the exiled ex-president Mancham and his supporters in London, Paris, and some segments of the Middle East. The London-based group has been most vocal in challenging René to hold new and proper elections and to restore real democracy on the islands. The murder of the opposition leader, Gerard Hoareau, has given exiles in London a chance to make fresh demands and to draw the world's attention to problems in the young republic.

Despite the rumblings of discontent from both inside and outside the country, President René's government appears more secure now than at any time since the 1977 coup, and any repeat of the 1981 mercenary invasion would almost certainly meet stiff resistance following the 1985 build-up of the armed forces and the militia. But the increasing centralization of political and economic control is likely to create some strain and resistance to the economic restructuring the government is trying to impose.

While espousing rigorous "scientific socialism" and international nonalignment, dependence for foreign exchange on European tourists and on Western capital and technical assistance for the development of fisheries, energy sources, and a declining agriculture moderates Seychelles foreign policy. René tolerates foreign and private ownership of the most important hotel and recreation facilities, as well as the South African connection which helps fill them. He allows a benevolent French naval presence in Port Victoria and restoration of French military advice, partly to offset Soviet influence exerted through several of his ministers. Nonalignment for Seychelles entails preference for close relations with such "progressive" neighbors as Tanzania, Madagascar, India, and (since

June 1982) Mauritius, as well as participation in the regional Zone of Peace campaign against the military activity of the superpowers in the Indian Ocean. While Soviet naval deployment in that neighborhood draws some criticism, and the French presence is regarded as a benign anachronism, the United States base on Diego Garcia atoll to the east has been consistently denounced as a serious threat to regional and national stability.

Further Reading
Franda, Marcus. *The Seychelles, Unquiet Islands*. Boulder, Colo.: Westview Press, 1982.

SOLOMON ISLANDS
by Terence Wesley-Smith, M.A.

The Solomon Islands consist of a double chain of mainly volcanic islands lying to the east of Papua New Guinea in the southwest Pacific Ocean. More than 85 percent of the 252,000 people live in small, subsistence-based rural communities. Ethnic parochialism, reinforced by geographical fragmentation and the use of 87 vernacular languages, is a notable characteristic. Solomon Islands became internally self-governing in 1976 and achieved independence from Great Britain on July 7, 1978. The new state is a member of the United Nations and the Commonwealth. Its constitution established a modified Westminster form of government with the British monarch as head of state.

The head of state is represented by a governor general, whose discretionary power is deliberately kept to a minimum. The governor general is a Solomon Islands citizen appointed on the recommendation of the National Parliament (rather than of the prime minister as is usual elsewhere). He appoints a prime minister only after an election in Parliament, and can only dismiss him after a successful vote of no confidence there. Nor can he dissolve Parliament before its normal term expires unless Parliament favors this course of action by an absolute majority vote. The governor general's term of office is five years, with the possibility of reappointment for another five years.

Effective executive power is exercised by a cabinet consisting of the prime minister, elected by and from the members of the National Parliament, and no more than eleven other ministers, appointed from among the members of the National Parliament on the advice of the prime minister. The cabinet is collectively responsible to the National Parliament.

The thiry-eight-member unicameral National Parliament is directly elected for a four-year term from single-member constituencies on the basis of universal suffrage of adults over eighteen years of age. The Constituency Boundaries Commission reviews constituency boundaries at least once every ten years.

The High Court decides both criminal and civil matters, with a right of appeal to the Court of Appeal, established in 1982. The chief justice and the president of the Court of Appeal are appointed on the advice of the prime minister, in consultation with the Judicial Service Commission. The other judges of the High Court and the Court of Appeal are appointed on the advice of the Judicial Service Commission. Magistrates' and local courts also operate with limited jurisdictions.

There has been considerable debate in Solomon Islands regarding the suitability of a centralized form of government in such a fragmented polity. The constitution provides for provincial-level governments, but leaves Parliament to decide how many there should be, the form they should take, and the extent of their powers. Since independence, elected governments have been established in the eight provinces, but decentralization has proceeded slowly, despite calls in some circles for a quasi-federal government structure. A major review of the system was launched in early 1986.

There have been no constitutional crises in Solomon Islands since independence, but the fortunes of the various political actors have fluctuated wildly. National politics has had little impact at the village level, and electors tend to judge a candidate by his clan or religious affiliation, or by his perceived ability to deliver central government resources to the electorate.

Only about fifty percent of sitting members have been returned to office in the national elections to date (1976, 1980, 1984).

Political parties typically consist of loose parliamentary factions, centered around particular individuals, and lack coherent policy platforms or organizational structures. The result is government by fluid parliamentary coalition with regular defections and realignments. However, national politics has consistently revolved around two individuals: Sir Peter Keniloria (Chief Minister 1976–1978; Prime Minister 1978–1981, and since 1984), and Solomon Mamaloni (Chief Minister 1974–1976; Prime Minister 1981–1984). Relatively minor differences have been apparent in their respective governments' policy emphases, but there is a common commitment to the further development of Solomon Islands' oil, palm, logging, and fishing industries—often in joint ventures with foreign companies.

REPUBLIC OF SURINAME
(Republiek van Suriname)
by Edward Dew, Ph.D.

Upon independence from the Netherlands in 1975, Suriname, a nation of 392,347 (est. 1984) in northeast South America, became a parliamentary republic. Executive power belonged to the prime minister, while the president's role was largely titular and symbolic. On February 25, 1980, a military coup, led by sergeants, toppled the government of Henck Arron and installed Lt. Col. Desi Bouterse as the country's de facto ruler. Bouterse's National Military Council restored a semblance of civilian rule by organizing a moderately leftist civilian government, with Dr. Henk Chin A Sen taking the oath of prime minister from President Johan Ferrier in April 1980. Further changes occurred in August when Bouterse abolished the country's Parliament, ousted President Ferrier, and declared a state of emergency (effectively suspending the constitution). Chin A Sen became president, as well as prime minister. But this unification of roles could not disguise the fact that the military still was in control. Chin A Sen's efforts to have a new constitution prepared by a commission of legal experts ran afoul of the military's reluctance to leave power, and Chin A Sen was forced to resign in February 1982. He was replaced as acting president by L.F. Ramdat Misier, the acting president of the Supreme Court. At the same time, the military installed a new civilian cabinet headed by Prime Minister Henry Neijhorst.

Ethnic antagonisms have traditionally been the major source of Suriname's social cleavages. In the 1950s and 1960s, multiethnic alliances had been carefully crafted by the three principal parties—the East Indian Progressive Reform Party (VHP), the Creole Surinamese National Party (NPS), and the Indonesian Peasants Party (KTPI)—to transcend these divisions. But these arrangements broke down in the 1970s. Ethnic polarization subsequently led to tense, and at times, violent conflict as the NPS led a Creole and Indonesian bloc that pushed the country into independence over the resistance of East Indians together with smaller groups of Creole, Indonesian, and other dissidents. Democracy in the new nation-state was subsequently undermined by persistent parliamentary stalemates and spreading bureaucratic corruption. Emigration of skilled manpower to the Netherlands compounded economic problems caused by a decline in the price of bauxite and in agricultural productivity. Suriname's high per capita GNP ($2600 in 1981) masked conditions of widespread unemployment and underemployment that were alleviated principally by a substantial Dutch foreign aid program.

The February 1980 coup took Surinamese society by surprise. But it was received initially with enthusiasm. Parliamentary politics, because of the multiethnic nature of the society, had always involved costly, time-consuming tactics of log-rolling among the ethnic-based political parties. Elections involved appeals "to vote for your own kind" rather than programmatic policy discussions. Thus, the advent of a largely multiethnic team of development-minded young people caught the national fancy. The sergeants wisely abandoned long-range plans to develop the bauxite mining potential of West Suriname, plans that had been absorbing a great deal of the Dutch development aid. Instead, they redirected their efforts to improvements in housing and other social conditions.

The ruling military, however, has not acted as a unified, or unifying institution. Within the sergeants clique, two predominant factions emerged: one was interested in "cleaning things up," i.e., reestablishing priorities, improving standards, and then getting out; and the other favored radical structural reforms over a longer term of direct military rule. Each faction found supporters among small political parties perennially relegated to the sidelines by their major ethnic rivals. Bouterse played one group off against the other, purging pro-Cuban figures in the National Military Council on several occasions, and changing cabinets every year. While a few Dutch industries were nationalized, and enthusiastic contacts were made with Cuba, Nicaragua, Ghana, Libya, and, especially, Grenada, the Surinamese voting record at the United Nations has shown a measure of cautious nonalignment. At the time of the Grenadian invasion in 1983, Bouterse ousted the majority of Cubans working in the country, and an explicit choice was made to tie-in economically (if not politically) with Brazil.

Suriname's reputation for relaxed, Caribbean-style politics was shattered in 1982. In the summer of that year, pressures had risen for a return to democracy. Bouterse's promises of a new and better form of democracy (transcending the ethnic politics of the past) were coming back to plague him. A series of rallies, strikes, and other actions took place during the fall, and in December, a number of the most prominent leaders in the movement to restore democracy were arrested and murdered. The Neijhorst government resigned in protest, and the Dutch government immediately cut off its development aid (approximately $100 million per year).

Since 1982, Surinamese foreign exchange holdings have been virtually exhausted, a black market has emerged (abetted by the military police), and corruption has risen to unprece-

dented levels. Bouterse's efforts to stem the military's growing unpopularity has taken the form of patronage among the poor, but this has meant reckless monetary policies and huge budgetary deficits. The military have set up a 25 February Movement to try to woo this portion of the population away from the older, ethnic political parties, but its meetings and activities have not met with much popular response.

Condemnation by human rights commissions of the United Nations and Organization of American States dogged the military's efforts to find alternative sources of foreign aid. By the summer of 1985, Bouterse was engaged in serious negotiations with the leaders of the old political parties (Henck Arron of the NPS, Jaggernath Lachmon of the VHP, and Willy Soemita of the KTPI) to guide the country back toward democracy. An accord between these parties and the military leadership was announced on the tenth anniversary of Surinamese independence (November 25, 1985). Within seventeen months, a new constitution would be drafted, it would be submitted to a popular referendum, and general elections would be conducted. In the meantime, the three parties' leaders would take positions in the military-civilian executive body that coordinates government policy. The current (1986) Prime Minister is Wim Udenhout.

Further Reading

Dew, Edward. *The Difficult Flowering of Suriname: Ethnicity and Politics in a Plural Society.* The Hague: Martinus Nijhoff, 1978.

———. "The Year of the Sergeants: What Happened in Suriname." *Caribbean Review*, Vol. 9, No. 2, Spring 1980.

———. "Suriname Tar Baby: The Signature of Terror." *Caribbean Review*, Vol. 12, No. 1, Winter 1983.

———. "Did Suriname Switch? Dialectics a la Dante." *Caribbean Review*, Vol. 12, No. 4, Fall 1983.

Gastmann, Albert. *The Politics of Surinam and the Netherlands Antilles.* Rio Piedras, Puerto Rico: Institute of Caribbean Studies, 1968.

KINGDOM OF TONGA

by Terence Wesley-Smith, M.A.

Tonga is a constitutional monarchy of 169 small islands and about 100,000 people situated in the southwest Pacific Ocean some 1,200 miles northwest of New Zealand. The monarchy, which was established by a constitution in 1875, regained complete independence on June 4, 1970, with the abrogation of the Treaty of Friendship with Great Britain. Tonga is a member of the Commonwealth.

The executive branch of government comprises the king in the Privy Council and the cabinet. The king presides over the Privy Council which consists of the cabinet and the two governors of the Ha'apai and Vava'u administrative districts. The Privy Council is the highest executive body, acts as the final court of appeal in all except criminal cases, and can make laws, subject to parliamentary confirmation. The cabinet consists of ministers, who head the various government departments, and the two governors. It is presided over by a prime minister. The ministers and the governors are appointed by the king and remain in office until they reach the age of retirement, although there is provision for their impeachment by the Legislative Assembly if they act illegally.

The Legislative Assembly is unicameral with both appointed and elected members. The appointed members are the ministers and governors. Seven of the elected members are nobles who are chosen by the thirty-three hereditary nobles of Tonga, and one of these is appointed speaker by the king. A further seven are representatives of the commoners, elected by universal suffrage of all Tongans over the age of twenty-one. There are three electoral districts and elections are held every three years. The Assembly deliberates over bills which are introduced by the Privy Council. If there is agreement, the bills are approved by the king and become law.

The judicial branch of government consists of the Privy Council acting as the Court of Appeal, the Supreme Court, the Magistrate's Court, and the Land Court. Judges are appointed by the Privy Council and magistrates by the cabinet.

Local administration is conducted by the governors of Ha'apai and Vava'u and a small network of elected town and district officials.

Tonga's constitution reflects and reinforces the highly stratified nature of this Polynesian society. King Taufa'ahau Tupou IV exercises great power as do other members of the royal family. The king's younger brother, Prince Fatafehi Tu'ipelehake, has been prime minister since 1966, and his eldest son, Crown Prince Tupouto'a, is minister for foreign affairs and defense. Members of the noble class not only play an important role in government but often control access to Tonga's most important resource, its land. Commoners play only a small part in government, although education and personal ability do allow for some upward mobility. Five of the appointed ministers are now commoners. There are no political parties in Tonga.

Tonga is one of the poorest of the Pacific Island countries. Most Tongans remain dependent on subsistence farming and the production of coconut oil and bananas for export. Rapid rates of population growth and the unequal distribution of land create a growing number of landless farmers. Many Tongans emigrate in search of employment opportunities. The value of imports exceeds that of exports by a ratio of at least six to one and the balance is made up by remittances from expatriate Tongans and external aid. Attempts to diversify the economy are underway, but the immediate prospects are not bright. The political situation in Tonga remains remarkably stable although discontent is increasingly apparent among educated commoners.

TUVALU

by Terence Wesley-Smith, M.A.

Tuvalu is an independent constitutional monarchy in the southwest Pacific Ocean. Formerly known as the Ellice Islands, it separated from the Gilbert Islands after a referendum in 1975, and achieved independence from Great Britain on October 1, 1978. Its population of 8,400 lives on nine atolls with a total land area of less than 10 square miles. It is a member of the Commonwealth.

The British monarch is titular head of state and is represented by a Tuvaluan governor general. The governor general's functions are largely ceremonial and he is appointed on the advice of the prime minister in consultation with Parliament. Effective executive power rests in the cabinet which consists of the prime minister, who is elected by Parliament from among its members, and not more than four ministers, who are members of Parliament selected by the prime minister. The cabinet is collectively responsible to Parliament for its actions.

The unicameral Parliament has the power to make laws and consists of twelve members elected by universal suffrage of all citizens over eighteen years of age. It is presided over by a speaker elected by the members from their own ranks. Parliament can remove the prime minister from office by passing a no-confidence vote. Elections are held every four years, or sooner if Parliament is dissolved by the governor general in accordance with the constitution.

The constitution established a High Court and made provision for a Court of Appeal. There is also a Magistrate's Court and eight Island Courts. Appeals from the High Court can be heard in the Court of Appeal, which at present is the Fiji Court of Appeals, or finally in the British Privy Council. The Island Courts have limited powers to decide criminal and civil cases, with a right of appeal to the Magistrate's Court.

Local government consists of a Town Council on the main island of Funafuti and Island Councils, first established in 1965, on seven other islands. Each council provides local services and consists of six elected members, one of whom acts as president.

Tuvalu has proved politically stable. There has been some debate about the merits of declaring a republic, but a Select Committee of the Tuvalu Parliament is not expected to propose major constitutional changes when it reports in 1986. Tuvaluan politics are conducted in a low-key manner, and there are no political parties. However, members of Parliament have tended to align themselves with one or the other of the two prime ministers who have served since independence: Toaripi Lauti, who held office until after the 1981 election, and Doctor Tomasi Puapua, the present incumbent reelected in September 1985. The most contentious political issue since independence has been Lauti's entrustment in 1979, of a significant portion of Tuvalu's very limited funds to a California-based real estate dealer, which led to his ouster in 1981. Tuvalu's minute size and almost total lack of exploitable resources suggest that most of the population will remain dependent on subsistence activities for the foreseeable future. Tuvalu exports small quantities of copra, sells fishing licenses, and has a successful philatelic bureau. Otherwise, it must depend on remittances from expatriate Tuvaluans and external aid funds.

REPUBLIC OF VANUATU

by Terence Wesley-Smith, M.A.

The Republic of Vanuatu, formerly the Anglo-French condominium of the New Hebrides, consists of sixty-six islands situated in the southwest Pacific Ocean, about 1,200 miles northwest of Australia. Over 130 different languages are spoken among its 123,900 people.

After 1906, the British and French maintained parallel administrative systems and imposed their own linguistic, religious, and cultural divisions on an already fragmented society.

Vanuatu achieved independence on July 30, 1980, despite the opposition of secessionist movements, the French administration, French settlers, and francophone New Hebrideans. Vanuatu is a member of the United Nations and the Commonwealth.

Vanuatu's constitution establishes a parliamentary form of government with a president as head of state. The president's role is largely ceremonial. He is elected for a term of five years by an electoral college which includes the parliament and the Council of Chiefs. Executive power is vested in the Executive Council. It consists of the prime minister and up to nine ministers chosen by the prime minister from among the members of Parliament. The prime minister is elected by Parliament from among its members, and can be dismissed by their vote of no confidence.

The unicameral Representative Assembly is composed of thirty-nine members elected in fourteen constituencies for four-year terms. A system of proportional representation is employed and all citizens over the age of eighteen are eligible to vote. Parliament elects a speaker to lead the assembly and to act as president if the incumbent is absent from Vanuatu.

The constitution directs that the National Council of Chiefs be consulted about all matters concerning tradition and custom. The council consists of traditional chiefs elected by their peers. It plays a particularly important advisory role on land matters, since the constitution declares that all land, a significant proportion of which was alienated under colonial rule, belongs to the indigenous custom owners. The council also plays a part in making constitutional appointments.

Some constitutional provisions were designed to protect the rights of francophones in the face of an emerging anglophone dominance in the late 1970s. Thus, French was included as one of the national languages along with English and Bislama (Vanuatu pidgin) and the office of ombudsman was created. Francophone factions insisted on constitutional provisions for regional councils on the islands of Tanna and Santo in the hope that these would provide some counterweight to central government. However, when the 1979 elections brought anglophone parties to power in both these councils, riots ensued, the councils never met, and they were removed from the constitution in 1980. In their place, Vanuatu has established eleven elected local government councils with limited powers devolved to them by central government legislation.

Vanuatu has a Supreme Court, which deals inter alia with matters of constitutional interpretation, and a Court of Appeal. Village or island courts, dealing largely with the application of customary law, may also be established with a right of appeal to higher courts, including the Land Appeals Court.

The Vanua'aku Party (VP), led by the prime minister, Father Walter Lini, has been the dominant force in politics since its foundation (as the New Hebrides National Party) in 1971. It has a strong organizational network throughout the country, and a mass following among anglophone (often Protestant), citizens. It won a comfortable majority of the seats in Parliament in both the 1979 and 1983 elections (twenty-four seats in 1983), and Lini has survived several votes of no confidence with ease. Opposition political parties, currently organized into the Union of Moderate Parties (UMP), continue to find support among the francophone (usually Catholic) electorate, but are unable to mount a serious challenge to Lini's government. However, there are significant divisions emerging among the leadership of the VP which may serve to change the polarized nature of Vanuatu's politics in the future. Meanwhile, Lini espouses a foreign policy of non alignment and a domestic policy of "Melanesian socialism", while pragmatically attempting to revive his country's copra exports and stimulate the fledgling tourist and offshore banking industries.

VATICAN CITY STATE
(Stato Della Città del Vaticano)
by Martin Slater, Ph.D.

The Vatican is the world's smallest independent sovereign state. Though it has a population of less than 800 persons, it has great importance as the administrative and spiritual center of the Roman Catholic Church and as the principal residence of the pope.

The Vatican is the last remnant of the papal states. In the nineteenth century, the pope's sovereign territories stretched across central Italy, but were lost in the process of Italian unification. The Italian state which emerged as a result of this unification refused to recognize papal sovereignty, and instead issued the Law of Guarantees of 1871, which established certain rights and privileges of the Holy See. Denied a sovereign domain, Pius X refused to recognize the Guarantees. Pius XI eventually reached an accommodation in 1929 when he signed the Lateran Pacts with Mussolini's fascist government. The pacts consisted of a concordat establishing a privileged position for Catholicism in Italy and a treaty which gave the pope sovereign authority over the 108.5 acres of the Vatican. After the fall of fascism, fears that the Church would lose its privileges proved ill-founded. The status of the Vatican was reaffirmed in Italy's 1948 republican constitution. More recently, in 1984, following protracted negotiations on the role of the Church in an increasingly secular Italy, a new Concordat was signed. Under its terms, Roman Catholicism is no longer Italy's official religion, and the state has reduced its financial support of the Church. In return, however, the Church was assured a continuing special status regarding full freedom for Catholic schools, automatic recognition of Church marriages, and clerical exemption from military service.

Formally, it is important to distinguish the Vatican state from the Holy See, i.e., the ecclesiastical office of the pope. Even without a sovereign papal territory, the Holy See would continue to exist as a separate entity. In both cases, supreme authority is vested in the pope. He is, in effect, an absolute monarch, with supreme executive, legislative, and judicial authority (as well as spiritual authority).

The pope is elected for life by a conclave of members of the Sacred College of Cardinals. Within eighteen days of the pope's death, the College of Cardinals must assemble in the Sistine Chapel to elect a successor. Since 1268, when cardinals took two years to elect a pope, the tradition has been to lock the cardinals inside the chapel until a successor is found. The pope may be elected in one of three ways: by unanimous acclamation; by compromise in an elected committee; or by secret ballot with a two-thirds majority of the conclave. The last method has been the only one used in recent times. Though the proceedings are secret, there is, by all reports, a great deal of bargaining and discussion. Until 1903, a single negative vote could exclude a candidate. The present pope, Karol Wojtyla, formerly cardinal of Krakow, known as John Paul II and the first non-Italian pope since 1522, was elected in 1978.

The running of the Vatican state occupies little of the pope's time. He delegates authority to a Pontifical Commission of seven cardinals, whom he appoints for a period of five years. They pass on their decisions to a staff of laymen headed by a Special Delegate. Many of the executive decisions are concerned with such matters as the running of the post office and railway station. Controversy has occasionally flared. In the early 1980s, the Vatican was racked by the scandal of illegal share dealings carried out by its bank (*Istituto per le Opere Religiose*; IOR). The Vatican Bank had become involved in these dealings through its close association with the corrupt bankers Calvi and Sindona who later met violent deaths under mysterious circumstances. The Vatican emerged chastened and wiser from this experience. The Swiss Guard, remnant of the pope's once important temporal powers, now plays a largely ceremonial role. The Vatican is policed by the Italian state; and criminal cases are normally dealt with by the Italian courts, as was the pope's would-be assassin in 1980.

It is the administration of the Holy See—assisted by the College of Cardinals and the Curia—that occupies far more of the pope's time. Until the reign of John XXIII, the number of cardinals was limited to seventy; they now number about 130. All are appointed by the pope, hold titular offices in Rome, and are citizens of the Vatican state. As well as electing the pope, the College meets regularly in the Vatican to discuss important Church issues. The majority of the cardinals hold pastoral appointments in various parts of the world; other members live in Rome and are part of the Church administration, the Roman Curia.

The Curia, employing over 3,000 clerics and laymen, has legislative, executive, and judicial functions. The legislative function is carried out by committees of cardinals sitting as Sacred Congregations. There are nine congregations dealing with different aspects of Church business, each having a specialized staff and headed by a Prefect. The pope acts as prefect for three of the congregations. John XXIII showed his papal authority by disbanding old and creating new congregations. Since 1967, some democratization has taken place, allowing bishops with diocesan responsibility to attend plenary sessions of the congregations.

The executive functions of the Curia are carried out by various secretariats and commissions. By far the most important of these is the Secretariat of State, headed by Cardinal Casaroli. The Secretariat is the equivalent of a prime minister's office, coordinating and directing the work of the Curia. The deputy to the secretary of state is the substitute and secretary of the cipher, at the present time, Monsignor Somolo. He deals with the detailed policy of the Secretariat. A powerful substitute, such as Monsignor Benelli when Cardinal Villot was secretary of state, may sometimes emerge as the most powerful figure in the Curia. The next most important executive office after the Secretariat is the Council for Public Affairs, responsible for the Vatican's foreign policy. Its secretary is Monsignor Silvestrini. Other offices include those for financial administration and expenditure.

The judicial functions are carried out by the Tribunals, also headed by cardinals. They consist of the Apostolic Penitentiary, examining problems of conscience; the Sacred Roman Rota, dealing with annulments of marriages; and the Supreme Tribunal of Apostolic Signature, dealing with the formulation of petitions.

The Curia has changed very little in recent years. It is still dominated by Italians, despite the arrival of a Polish pope. Patronage continues to control promotions and social relations.

Though the Curia cannot be said to control the pope, who has the authority in appointments and the setting of agendas, it is not a body that any pope could choose to ignore, even if he wished. The only challenge to the authority of the Curia in recent years has been the Second Vatican Council of 1962 to 1965 and the International Synod of Bishops, which was established in the wake of the Council. The Council established the shared responsibility of bishops for governing the Church, under papal authority. The most recent Vatican Synod of December 1985 reaffirmed this role; but it did so in the midst of mounting concern over papal suppression of dissident views, particularly the views of the "liberation theologists," dominant in much of Latin America. Thus far, there is an uneasy compromise as both sides make concessions for the greater good of the Church.

WESTERN SAMOA

by Terence Wesley-Smith, M.A.

Western Samoa is an island nation of 158,000 people in the South Pacific about 2,300 miles southwest of Hawaii. Independence was achieved in January 1962 after Samoans exercised their right to self-determination in a plebiscite and the United Nations General Assembly voted to terminate New Zealand's trusteeship. Western Samoa joined the British Commonwealth in 1970 and the United Nations in 1976.

The constitution establishes a modified Westminster form of government. The position of head of state is largely ceremonial and was jointly occupied at independence by the holders of two of Samoa's four highest traditional titles. One of these title holders, Tupua Tamasese

Mea'ole, died in 1963. When the remaining incumbent, Malietoa Tanumafili II, dies, the constitution requires future heads of state to be elected by the Legislative Assembly for five-year terms. A Council of Deputies acts for the head of state in the event of his absence or incapacity. The prime minister is elected by Parliament from among its members. He, in turn, selects eight members of Parliament to be ministers in the cabinet over which he presides. The cabinet is collectively responsible to Parliament.

The head of state, together with the Legislative Assembly, compose the Parliament. The Assembly has forty-seven members, of which forty-five are traditional title holders, or *matai*, elected by their peers in forty-one one- and two-member constituencies. The *matai* titles are bestowed by extended family groups, or *aiga*, and there are about 12,000 people on the *matai* roll. The remaining members of the Assembly are elected by citizens who are part-Samoan, of other races, or otherwise not members of an *aiga*. All terms of office are for three years.

The judicial function is fulfilled by the Supreme Court, which is the superior court of record and has full jurisdiction in civil, criminal, and constitutional matters. A Court of Appeal and a Magistrate's Court have also been established and a Land and Titles Court is empowered to hear disputes over customary land and succession to *matai* titles.

Western Samoa's politics has been fairly stormy in recent years. The system of limiting suffrage to *matai* received its strongest challenge to date in 1982 when the Supreme Court decided that some aspects of the electoral system were unconstitutional. Although that decision was revoked on appeal, the controversy has continued. A three-month-long strike by public servants over wage rates in 1981 was also divisive and put much pressure on the government of Tupuola Efi, then in its second term of office. This marked the beginning of a period of unusual political instability as successive governments managed to hold office only for short periods. Efi was defeated by the leader of the Human Rights Protection Party, Va'ai Kolone, by one vote in the contest for prime minister after the elections of February 1982. However, Kolone's victory was soon soured when the Supreme Court upheld a petition alleging electoral irregularities and declared his election invalid. In one of a series of controversial decisions, the head of state did not call for fresh elections, but instead appointed Tupuola Efi to replace the unseated Kolone as prime minister. But Efi survived for only a few months before being forced to resign after his budget failed to win support. Tofilau Eti Alesana won the subsequent parliamentary vote for prime minister and was confirmed in office after the general election of February 1985. But, in December 1985, he resigned when ex-Prime Ministers and former opponents, Kolone and Efi, joined forces to command the majority in Parliament and the head of state refused Alesana's request to call an early election. The new coalition government, led by Kolone and with Efi as deputy prime minister, will have to deal not only with these factional gyrations, but with Western Samoa's poor economic circumstances and prospects.

INDEX

LIST OF ACRONYMS

Acronyms and Abbreviations

AAA —*see* Argentine Anti-Communist Alliance

ABVP —*see* All-India Students Organization

ACCTU —*see* All-Union Central Council of Trade Unions (Soviet Union),

ACLM —*see* Antigua Caribbean Liberation Movement

ACP —*see* Action Congress Party (Ghana)

ACOPI —*see* Colombian Association of Small Industrialists

ACTUS —*see* Chadian Action for Unity and Socialism

AD —*see* Australian Democrats

AD —*see* Democratic Action (El Salvador)

AD —*see* Democratic Action (Venezuela)

AD —*see* Democratic Alliance (Portugal)

ADF —*see* Arab Deterrent Force (Lebanon)

ADN —*see* Nationalist Democratic Action (Bolivia)

ADO —*see* Opposition Democratic Alliance (Panama)

ADO —*see* Workers Self-Defense Movement (Colombia)

AEG —*see* Gabonese Students Association

AESM —*see* All-Ethiopian Socialist Movement

AETU —*see* All-Ethiopian Trade Union

AFPFL —*see* Anti-Fascist People's Freedom League (Burma)

AFRC —*see* Armed Forces Revolutionary Council (Ghana)

AIADMK —*see* All-India Anna-Dravida Munnetra Kazhagam

AICC —*see* All-India Congress Committee

AIKS —*see* All-India Kisan Sammelan

AITUC —*see* All-India Trade Union Congress

AJ/MRDN —*see* AndJef: Revolutionary Movement for the New Democracy (Senegal)

AKEL —*see* Progressive Party of the Working People (Cyprus)

AKFM —*see* Congress Party for the Independence of Madagascar

AKP/ML —*see* Workers' Communist Party (Marxist-Leninist) (Norway)

AL —*see* Awami League (Bangladesh)

ALN —*see* National Liberation Army (Algeria)

ALÖ —*see* Alternative List of Austria

ALP —*see* Albanian Labor Party

ALP —*see* Antigua Labour Party

ALP —*see* Australian Labor Party

ANACH —*see* National Association of Honduras Peasants

ANAPO —*see* National Popular Alliance (Colombia)

ANC —*see* African National Congress (Mozambique)

ANDI —*see* National Federation of Industrialists (Colombia)

ANFER —*see* Revolutionary Feminine Association (Mexico)

ANP —*see* National People's Assembly (Madagascar)

ANRD —*see* National Alliance for Democratic Reorganization (Equatorial Guinea)

AP —*see* Alliance Party (Northern Ireland)

AP —*see* Popular Action Party (Peru)

AP —*see* Popular Alliance (Spain)

APC —*see* All People's Congress (Sierra Leone)

APK —*see* Worker Party Communists (Sweden)

APP —*see* Antigua People's Party

APRA —*see* American Popular Revolutionary Alliance (Peru)

APRD —*see* Alliance for Progress and Regional Development (Papua New Guinea)

APS —*see* Socialist Political Action (Peru)

APU —*see* United Popular Alliance (Portugal)

AREMA —*see* Advance Guard of the Malagasy Revolution (Madagascar)

ARENA —*see* National Renovating Alliance (Brazil)

ARENA —*see* National Republican Alliance (El Salvador)

ARP —*see* Anti-Revolutionary Party (the Netherlands)

ASDI —*see* Association of Independent Social Democrats (Portugal)

ASEAN —*see* Association of Southeast Asian Nations

ASI —*see* Federation of Labor (Iceland)

ASP —*see* Afro-Shirazi Party (Tanzania)

ASU —*see* Arab Socialist Union (Egypt)

ASU —*see* Arab Socialist Union (Libya)

AZAPO —*see* Anzianian People's Organization (South Africa)

BAMCEF —*see* All-India Backward and Minority Communities Employees Federation

BAU —*see* Bulgarian Agrarian Union

BCP —*see* Basutoland Congress Party (Lesotho)

BCP —*see* Bulgarian Communist Party

BCP —*see* Burma Communist Party

BDP —*see* Bahamian Democratic Party

BDP —*see* Botswana Democratic Party

BDG —*see* Gabonese Democratic Bloc

BDS —*see* Senegalese Democratic Bloc

BITU —*see* Bustamenk Industrial Trade Union (Jamaica)

BJP —*see* Bharatiya Janata Party (India)

BKD —*see* Bharatiya Kranti Dal (India)

BLP —*see* Barbados Labour Party

BNDP —*see* Brunei National Democratic Party

BNP —*see* Bangladesh Nationalist Party

BNP —*see* Basutoland National Party (Lesotho)

BP —*see* Farmers' Party (the Netherlands)

BPC —*see* Basic People's Congress (Libya)

BPR —*see* Popular Revolutionary Bloc (El Salvador)

BSP —*see* Belgium Socialist Party

BSPP —*see* Burma Socialist Program Party

CACIF —*see* Commercial, Industrial, and Financial Associations (Guatemala)

CAN —*see* Authentic Nationalist Center (Guatemala)

CAR —*see* Central African Republic

CASC —*see* Autonomous Confederation of Christian Syndicates (Dominican Rep.)

CCM —*see* Revolutionary Party (Tanzania)

CCP —*see* Confederation of Peruvian Peasants

CCP —*see* Communist Party of the Philippines

CD —*see* Center Democrats (Denmark)

CDA —*see* Christian Democratic Appeal (the Netherlands)

CDR —*see* Committee for the Defense of the Republic (San Marino)

CDR —*see* Committees for Defense of the Revolution (Cuba)

CDR —*see* Defense of the Revolution (Burkina Faso)

CDR —*see* Democratic Revolutionary Council (Chad)

CDS —*see* Center of Social Democrats (France)

CDS —*see* Social Democratic Center (Portugal)

CDS —*see* Social Democratic Center (Spain)

CDSP —*see* China Democratic Socialist Party

CDT —*see* Democratic Labor Confederation (Morocco)

CDU —*see* Christian Democratic Union (East Germany)

CDU —*see* Christian Democratic Union (West Germany)

CEFAC —*see* Economic Community of Central African States

CELU —*see* Confederation of Ethiopian Labor Unions

CENTO —*see* Central Treaty Organization

CERES —*see* Center of Socialist Studies, Research, and Education (France)

CERF —*see* Clara Elizabeth Ramirez Front (El Salvador)

CFDT —*see* Democratic French Confederation of Labor

CFP —*see* Concentration of Popular Forces (Ecuador)

CGEM —*see* General Economic Confederation of Morocco

CGIL —*see* Italian General Labor Confederation

CGS —*see* General Confederation of Trade Unions (Romania)

CGT —*see* General Confederation of Labor (Argentina)

CGT —*see* General Confederation of Labor (France)

CGT —*see* General Confederation of Work (Dominican Republic)

CGT —*see* General Central of Workers (Honduras)

CGTF —*see* General Confederation of French Workers–Senegal

CGTP —*see* General Confederation of Peruvian Workers

CHU —*see* Christian-Historical Union (the Netherlands)

CISL —*see* Italian Confederation of Workers' Unions

CISNAL —*see* Italian Confederation of National Workers' Unions

CITV —*see* Centre of Indian Trade Unions

CIV —*see* Convergence and Union Party (Spain)

CLA —*see* Czechoslovak People's Army

CLC —*see* Canadian Labour Congress

CLC —*see* Committee for the Liberation of the Congo (Zaire)

CMEA —*see* Council for Mutual Economic Assistance

CMLN —*see* Military Committee of National Liberation (Mali)

CMRN —*see* Military Committee of National Recovery (Central African Republic)

CMRN —*see* Military Committee of National Recovery (Guinea)

CMSN —*see* Military Committee for National Salvation (Mauritania)

CNA —*see* National Agrarian Confederation (Peru)

CNIP —*see* National Center of Independents and Peasants (France)

CNOP —*see* National Federation of Popular Organizations (Mexico)

CNT —*see* National Command of Workers (Chile)

CNT —*see* National Workers Convention (Uruguay)

CNT —*see* National Workers Federation (Mexico)

CNTP —*see* National Workers Central (Panama)

CNTV —*see* National Confederation of Voltaic Workers (Burkina Faso)

CNV —*see* Cameroon National Union

COB —*see* Bolivian Workers Central

CODE-IND —*see* Democratic Convergence Movement (Peru)

COMEON —*see* Council for Mutual Economic Assistance

CONADEP —*see* National Commission for the Disappearance of People

CONCAMIN —*see* Confederation of Industrial Chambers (Mexico)

CONCANACO —*see* National Chambers of Commerce (Mexico)

CONCP —*see* Conference of Nationalist Organization of the Portuguese Colonies

COPCON —*see* Continental Operations Command (Portugal)

COPIE —*see* Christian Social Party (Venezuela)

COPWE —*see* Commission for Organizing the Party of the Working People of Ethiopia

COSU —*see* Coordination of the United Senegalese Opposition

COSEP —*see* Superior Council of Private Enterprise (Nicaragua)

CP —*see* Communist Party of Great Britain

CP —*see* Conservative Party (Uganda)

CPA —*see* Communist Party of Australia

CPC —*see* Communist Party of Canada

CPDM —*see* Cameroon People's Democratic Movement

CPI —*see* Communist Party of India

CPM —*see* Communist Party of India (Marxist)

CPML —*see* Communist Party of India (Marxist-Leninist)

CPN —*see* Communist Party of the Netherlands

CPP —*see* Convention People's Party (Ghana)

CPS —*see* Communist Party of Sudan

CPSA —*see* Conservative Party of South Africa

CPSL —*see* Communist Party of Sri Lanka

CPSU —*see* Communist Party of the Soviet Union

CPT —*see* Communist Party of Thailand

CPT —*see* Paraguayan Workers Confederation

CROC —*see* Revolutionary Federation of Workers and Peasants (Mexico)

CRWP —*see* Confederation of Regions Western Party (Canada)

CSL —*see* Czechoslovak People's Party

CSS —*see* Czechoslovak Socialist Party

CSSR —*see* Czechoslovak Socialist Republic

CST —*see* Sandinista Workers Central (Nicaragua)

CSTC —*see* Trade Union Confederation of Workers of Colombia

CSU —*see* Christian Social Union (West Germany)

CSV —*see* Christian Social People's Party (Luxembourg)

CSV —*see* Voltaic Confederation of Unions (Burkina Faso)

CTC —*see* Confederation of Colombian Workers

CTC —*see* Confederation of Cuban Workers

CTH —*see* Confederation of Honduran Workers

CTM —*see* Mexican Federation of Labor

CTN —*see* Nicaraguan Confederation of Workers

CTP —*see* Republican Turkish Party (Cyprus)

CTP —*see* Workers Confederation of Peru

CTRP —*see* Confederation of Workers (Panama)

CTRP —*see* Confederation of Workers of the Peruvian Revolution

CTVY —*see* Confederation of Trade Unions of Yugoslavia

CUT —*see* United Central of Chilean Workers

CVP —*see* Christian Democratic People's Party of Switzerland

CVP —*see* Christian People's Party (Belgium)

CWP —*see* Correct Way Party (Turkey)

D'66 —*see* Democrats '66 (the Netherlands)

DAC —*see* Democratic Action Congress (Trinidad & Tobago)

DAP —*see* Democratic Action Party (Malaysia)

DBD —*see* Democratic Farmers' Party of Germany

DC —*see* Christian Democratic Party (Italy)

DCG —*see* Christian Democrats of Guatemala

DDLP —*see* Dominican Democratic Labour Party

DEMYC —*see* Democratic Youth Community of Europe

DFD —*see* Democratic Women's League of Germany

DFP —*see* Democratic Freedom Party (Dominica)

DFPE —*see* Democratic Front for Peace (Israel)

DFSS —*see* Democratic Front for the Salvation of Somalia

DIKO —*see* Democratic Party (Cyprus)

DISI —*see* Democratic Rally (Cyprus)

DISK —*see* Confederation of Revolutionary Labor Unions (Turkey)

DJP —*see* Democratic Justice Party (South Korea)

DKP —*see* Communist Party (Denmark)

DKP —*see* Democratic Korea Party (South Korea)

DKP —*see* German Communist Party (West Germany)

DLF —*see* Liberal People's Party (Norway)

DLP —*see* Democratic Labour Party (Barbados)

DLP —*see* Dominican Labour Party (Dominica)

DMC —*see* Democratic Movement for Change (Israel)

DMK —*see* Dravida Munnetra Kazhagam (India)

DNA —*see* Norwegian Labor Party

DP —*see* Democratic Party (Luxembourg)

DP —*see* Democratic Party (Turkey)

DP —*see* Democratic Party (Uganda)

DP —*see* Proletarian Democracy (Italy)

DRF —*see* Justice Party (Denmark)

DRP —*see* Democratic Republican Party (South Korea)

DS-70 —*see* Democratic Socialists (the Netherlands)

DSP —*see* Japan Democratic Socialist Party

DTA —*see* Democratic Turnhalle Alliance (Namibia)

DVP —*see* Democratic Unionist Party (Northern Ireland)

DVP —*see* Democratic Unionist Party (Sudan)

EAP —*see* European Labor Party

ECOWAS —*see* Economic Community of West African States

EDA —*see* United Democratic Left (Greece)

EDEK —*see* Unified Democratic Union of the Center (Cyprus)

EDU —*see* Ethiopian Democratic Union

EE —*see* Basque Left (Spain)

EEC —*see* European Economic Community

EFTA —*see* European Free Trade Association

EGP —*see* Guerrilla Army of the Poor (Guatemala)

EK —*see* Center Union (Cyprus)

ELF —*see* Eritrean Liberation Front (Ethiopia)

EPL —*see* The Popular Liberation Army (Colombia)

EPLF —*see* Eritrean People's Liberation Front (Ethiopia)

EPRP —*see* Ethiopian People's Revolutionary Party

EPS —*see* Sandinista Popular Army (Nicaragua)

ERC —*see* Republican Left (Spain)

ERP —*see* Revolutionary Army of the People (El Salvador)

ESA —*see* Secret Anti-Communist Army (Guatemala)

ETA —*see* Basque Nation and Liberty (Spain)

EVP —*see* Protestant People's Party of Switzerland

FAL —*see* Armed Forces for Liberation (El Salvador)

FALN —*see* Armed Forces for National Liberation (Puerto Rico)

FAN —*see* Northern Armed Forces (Chad)

FANLWVY —*see* Federation of Associations of National Liberation War Veterans of Yugoslavia

FAO —*see* Western Armed Forces (Chad)

FAP —*see* Popular Armed Forces (Chad

FAPU —*see* United People's Action Front (El Salvador)

FAR —*see* Armed Rebel Forces (Guatemala)

FAR —*see* Royal Armed Forces (Morocco)

FARC —*see* Revolutionary Armed Forces of Colombia

FARP —*see* People's Revolutionary Armed Forces (Cape Verde)

FAT —*see* Chadian Armed Forces

FAZ —*see* Armed Forces Union (Zaire)

FBP —*see* Progressive Citizens' Party (Liechtenstein)

FBSI —*see* All-Indonesian Labor Federation

FCD —*see* Congolese Front for the Restoration of Democracy (Zaire)

FD —*see* Democratic Front (Comoros)

FDC —*see* Forces Defense Committee (Ghana)

FDF —*see* Francophone Democratic Front (Belgium)

FDGB —*see* Free German Trade Union Federation (East Germany)

FDIC —*see* Front for the Defense of Constitutional Institutions (Morocco)

FDJ —*see* Free German Youth (East Germany)

FDLD —*see* Democratic Front for the Liberation of Djibouti

FDP —*see* Free Democratic Party (West Germany)

FDP —*see* Radical Democratic Party (Switzerland)

FDR —*see* Revolutionary Democratic Front (El Salvador)

FDT —*see* Chad Democratic Front

FED —*see* European Development Fund

FEDECAFE —*see* National Federation of Coffee Growers (Colombia)

FENALCO —*see* National Federation of Merchants (Colombia)

FESYGA —*see* Federation of Gabonese Unions

FICCI —*see* Federation of Indian Chambers of Commerce and Industry

FLCS —*see* Front for the Liberation of the Somali Coast (Djibouti)

FLEC —*see* Front for the National Liberation of Angola

FLING —*see* Front for the Liberation and National Independence of Guinea (Guinea-Bissau)

FLN —*see* National Liberation Front (Algeria)

FLNC —*see* Congo National Liberation Front (Zaire)

FLOSY —*see* Front for the Liberation of the Occupied South Yemen

FMC —*see* Federation of Cuban Women

FMLN —*see* Farabundo Marti National Liberation Front (El Salvador)

FNDR —*see* National Front for the Defense of the Revolution (Madagascar)

FNLA —*see* National Front for the Liberation of Angola

FNM —*see* Free National Movement (Bahamas)

FNRI —*see* National Federation of Independent Republicans (France)

FNUK —*see* Comorian National Unification Front

FP —*see* Progress Party (Denmark)

FPA —*see* Authentic Panamenista Party (Panama)

FPL —*see* Popular Liberation Forces (Chad)

FPL —*see* Popular Liberation Front (El Salvador)

FPMR —*see* Manuel Rodriguez Patriotic Front (Chile)

FPO —*see* Freedom Party of Austria

FPO-PT —*see* Ubangian Patriotic Front Workers' Party (Central African Republic)

FPV —*see* Voltaic Progressive Front (Burkina Faso)

FRAP —*see* Popular Revolutionary Action Front (Gabon)

FRAMPO —*see* Broad Popular Front (Panama)

FRELIMO —*see* Front for the Liberation of Mozambique

FRS —*see* Republican and Socialist Front (Portugal)

FSB —*see* Bolivian Socialist Falange

FSD —*see* Democratic Labor Front (Colombia)

FSLN —*see* Frente Sandinista de Liberacion Nacional (Nicaragua)

FSTMB —*see* Union Federation of Bolivian Miners

FSTRP —*see* Trade Union Federation of Workers (Panama)

FSTSE —*see* Federation of Unions of Workers in the Service of the State (Mexico)

FUDS —*see* Socialist Democracy and Unity Front (Romania)

FULRO —*see* United Front for the Struggle of Oppressed Races (Vietnam)

FUN —*see* United Front National (Guatemala)

FUNACAMH —*see* United National Front of Honduran Peasants

FUND —*see* Front for National Unity and Growth (Guinea-Bissau)

FUP —*see* Front for the Unity of the People (Colombia)

FUPI —*see* Pro-Independence University Federation (Puerto Rico)

FUR —*see* United Revolutionary Front (Guatemala)

GAL —*see* Anti-Terrorist Liberation Group (Spain)

GDF —*see* Guyana Defense Force

GDLP —*see* Grenada Democratic Labour Party

GDM —*see* Grenada Democratic Movement

GIM —*see* International Marxist Group (West Germany)

GMMLU —*see* Grenada Manual and Mental Labourers Union

GNP —*see* Grenada National Party

GPRA —*see* Provisional Government for the Republic of Algeria

GPV —*see* Reformed Political Union (the Netherlands)

GRAE —*see* Angolese Revolutionary Government in Exile

GSL —*see* Social and Liberal Generation (France)

GTUC —*see* Ghana Trade Union Congress

GULP —*see* Grenada United Labour Party

GUNT —*see* Transitional Government of National Unity (Chad)

HNP —*see* Herstigte National Party (South Africa)

HP —*see* Herri Batassna (Spain)

HSWP —*see* Hungarian Socialist Workers' Party

IBP —*see* Interim Batasang Pambansa (Philippines)

ICAP —*see* Cuban Institute of Friendship with Peoples

ICP —*see* Iraqi Communist Party

ID —*see* Democratic Left (Ecuador)

IDL —*see* Islamic Democratic League (Bangladesh)

IEPES —*see* Institute of Political, Economic, and Social Studies (Mexico)

IIP —*see* Irish Independence Party

ILO —*see* International Labor Organization

IMF —*see* International Monetary Fund

IN —*see* Nationalist left (Peru)

INLA —*see* Irish National Liberation Army

INNC —*see* Indian National Trade Union Congress

IP —*see* Independence Party (Iceland)

IRA —*see* Irish Republican Army

IRP —*see* Islamic Republic Party (Iran)

IRSP —*see* Irish Republican Socialist Party

JAAC —*see* Amilcar Cabral African Youth (Guinea-Bissau)

JCM —*see* Communist Youth of Mexico

JCP —see Japan Communist Party

JMPLA —see Youth for the Popular Movement for the Liberation of Angola

JMPR —see Youth Popular Movement of the Revolution (Zaire)

JP —see Justice Party (Turkey)

JSD —see National Socialist Party (Bangladesh)

JSP —see Japan Socialist Party

JUI —see Conference of Ulema of Islam (Pakistan)

JVP —see People's Liberation Front (Sri Lanka)

KADU —see Kenya African Democratic Union

KANU —see Kenya African National Union

KAU —see Kenya African Union

KB —see Cultural League (East Germany)

KBL —see New Society Movement (Philippines)

KCIA —see Korean Central Intelligence Agency (South Korea)

KDP —see Kurdish Democratic Party (Iraq)

KDS —see Christian Democratic Party (Sweden)

KF —see Conservative People's Party (Denmark)

KF —see The Cooperative Movement (Sweden)

KGB —see Committee of State Security (Soviet Union)

KKE —see Greek Communist Party

KMT —see Clean Government Party (Japan)

KMT —see Kuomintang (Republic of China)

KMT —see National People's Party (Taiwan)

KNDP —see Kamerun National Democratic Party (Cameroon)

KNP —see Korean National Party (South Korea)

KORPRI —see Officials' Corps of the Republic of Indonesia

KPB/PCB —see Communist Party of Belgium

KPD —see Communist Party (East Germany)

KPD —see Communist Party (pre-Nazi Communist Party) (West Germany)

KDP/ML —see Communist Party of Germany/Marxist-Leninist (West Germany)

KPNLF —see Khmer People's National Liberation Front (Kampuchea)

KPL —see Communist Party of Luxembourg

KPO —see Communist Party of Austria

KPRP —see Kampuchean People's Revolutionary Party

KPU —see Kenya People's Union

KRF —see Christian People's Party (Denmark)

KRF —see Christian People's Party (Norway)

KSC —see Communist Party of Czechoslovakia

KSS —see Communist Party of Slovakia

KTPI —see Indonesian Peasants' Party

KVP —see Catholic People's Party (the Netherlands)

KWP —see Korean Workers' Party (North Korea)

KY —see Kabaka Yekka (Uganda)

LAP —see Liberal Action Party (Liberia)

LCP —see Lebanese Communist Party

LCT —see Communist Workers' League (Senegal)

LCY —see League of Communists of Yugoslavia

LD/MPT —see Democratic League–Popular Labor Movement (Senegal)

LDP —see Liberal Democratic Party (Japan)

LDPD —see Liberal Democratic Party of Germany (East Germany)

LDU —see The Independent Alliance (Switzerland)

LESOMA —see Socialist League of Malawi

LINSU —see Liberian National Union of Students

LIPAD —see Patriotic Development League (Burkina Faso)

LMOI —see Liberation Movement of Iran

LNM —see Lebanese National Movement

LO —see Norwegian Trade Union Federation

LO —see Swedish Confederation of Trade Unions

LP —see Labour Party (St. Christopher)

LP —see Labor Party of South Africa

LP —see Liberal Party (Australia)

LPAI —see African People's League for Independence (Djibouti)

LPP —see Liberia People's Party

LPRP —see Lao People's Revolutionary Party

LRF —see National Farmers' Association (Sweden)

LSAP —see Socialist Workers' Party (Luxembourg)

LSSP —see Ceylon Equal Society Party

LSYY —see League of Socialist Youth of Yugoslavia

LUP —see Liberia Unification Party

MAC —see Muslim Action Committee (Mauritius)

MACHO —see Honduran Anti-Communist Movement

MAFREMO —see Malawi Freedom Movement

MANU —see Mozambican-Makunde Union

MAO —see Workers Self-Defense Movement (Colombia)

MAP/ML —see Marxist-Leninist Popular Action Movement (Nicaragua)

MARC —see Action Movement for the Resurrection of the Congo (Zaire)

MAS —see Movement Toward Socialism (Venezuela)

MBH —see Haya Grassroots Movement (Peru)

MBPM —see Maurice Bishop Patriotic Movement (Grenada)

MCA —see Malayan Chinese Association

MCLN —see Central African Movement for National Liberation (Central African Republic)

MCP —see Malawi Congress Party

MDB —see Brazilian Democratic Movement

MDN —see Nicaraguan Democratic Movement

MDP —see Democratic Popular Movement (Senegal)

MDS —see Movement of Social Democrats (Tunisia)

MEC —see Emergent Movement of Concord (Guatemala)

MFA —see Armed Forces Movement (Portugal)

MFM —see Militants for Power to the People (Madagascar)

MFP —see Marematlou Freedom Party (Lesotho)

MIC —see Malayan Indian Congress (Malaysia)

MID —see Integration and Developmentalist Movement (Argentina)

MIMD —see Independent Movement of Madre de Dios (Peru)

MIP —see Popular Interest Movement (Peru)

MIR —see Leftist Revolutionary Movement (Bolivia)

MIR —see Movement of the Revolutionary Left (Chile)

MISK —see Confederation of National Labor Unions (Turkey)

MKP —see Workers' and Peasants' Party (Pakistan)

MLD —see Djibouti Liberation Movement

MLN —see National Liberation Movement (Guatemala)

MLP —see Malta Labour Party

MLP —see Mauritius Labor Party

MLPC —see Central Africa People's Liberation Movement

MLSTP —see Movement for the Liberation of Sao Tome

MMM —see Mauritian Militant Movement

MN —see Movimiento Nacional (Costa Rica)

MNB —see National Barrientish Movement (Bolivia)

MNC —see Congolese National Movement (Zaire)

MNC/L —see Congolese National Movement–Lumumba (Zaire)

MND —see National Democratic Movement (Mauritania)

MNJR —see National Movement of Revolutionary Youth (Mexico)

MNR —see Mozambique's Movement for National Resistance

MNR —see National Revolutionary Movement (Bolivia)

MNR —see National Revolutionary Movement (El Salvador)

MNRH —see Historical National Revolutionary Movement (Bolivia)

MNRI —see Leftist Nationalist Revolutionary Movement (Bolivia)

MNRV —see Vanguard Nationalist Revolutionary Movement (Bolivia)

MNV —see Movement for National Unity (St. Vincent)

MNVR —see National Movement of the Union for Reconciliation (Zaire)

MOIR —see Independent Revolutionary Labor Movement (Colombia)

MOJA —see Movement for Justice in Africa (Liberia)

MOLINACO or UNIKOM —see Comorian National Liberation Movement

MOLIRENA —see Liberal Republican and Nationalist Movement (Panama)

MONIMA —see National Movement for the Independence of Madagascar

MOPOCO —see Popular Colorado Movement (Paraguay)

MORENA —see Movement for National Redress (Gabon)

MOULINAKA —see Kampuchean National Liberation Movement

MP —see Motherland Party (Turkey)

MP —see Popular Movement (Morocco)

MPC —see Popular Christian Movement (Bolivia)

MPDC —see Popular Democratic and Constitutional Movement (Morocco)

MPL —see Djibouti Popular Liberation Movement

MPLA-PT —see Popular Movement for the Liberation of Angola–Labor Party

MPM —see Mahorais Popular Movement (Comoros)

MPR —see Popular Movement of the Revolution (Zaire)

MPRP —see Mongolian People's Revolutionary Party

MPS —see Sandinista Popular Militia (Nicaragua)

MRD —see Movement for the Restoration of Democracy (Pakistan)

MRDN —see Revolutionary Movement for the New Democracy (Senegal)

MRG —see Left Radical Movement (France)

MRG —see Movement for the Renewal of Guinea (Guinea)

MRL —see Liberal Democracy Revolutionary Movement (Colombia)

MRDN —see National Revolutionary Development Movement (Rwanda)

MRP —see Popular Republican Movement (France)

MRP-IXIM —see Revolutionary Movement of the People (Guatemala)

MRS —see Senegalese Republican Movement

MRTK —see Revolutionary Movement Tupak Katary (Bolivia)

MSI —see Italian Social Movement

MSM —see Mauritius Socialist Movement

MTI —see Islamic Tendency Movement (Tunisia)

MTK —see Confederation of Agricultural Producers (Finland)

MTLD —see Movement for the Victory of Democratic Freedom (Algeria)

MUP —see Movement for Popular Unity (Tunisia)

MUZ —see Mine Workers Union of Zambia

NAF —see Norwegian Employers' Association

NAP —see National Action Party (Turkey)

NAP —see National Awami Party (Bangladesh)

NAP —see National Awami Party (Pakistan)

NAR —see National Alliance for Reconstruction (Trinidad & Tobago)

NATO —see North Atlantic Treaty Organization

NATT —see National Alliance for Trinidad and Tobago

NCP —see National Convention Party (Gambia)

NCR —see National Council of Resistance (Iran)

NDFLOAG —see National Democratic Front for the Liberation of the Occupied Arab Gulf (Oman)

NFDF —see National Democratic Front (Yemen Arab Republic)

NDP —see National Democracy Party (Turkey)

NDP —see National Democratic Party (Antigua & Barbuda)

NDP —see National Democratic Party (Austria)

NDP —see National Democratic Party (Egypt)

NDP —see National Democratic Party (Grenada)

NDP —see National Democratic Party (Pakistan)

NDP —see National Democratic Party (Thailand)

NDP —see New Democratic Party (Canada)

NDP —see New Democratic Party (St. Vincent)

NDP —see New Democratic Party (South Korea)

NDPD —see National-Democratic Party of Germany (East Germany)

NDPL —see National Democratic Party of Liberia

NEDIRPAC —see New Democratic Camp (Cyprus)

NF —see National Front (Malaysia)

NF —see National Front (United Kingdom)

NFP —see National Federation Party (Fiji)

NIA —see Northern Ireland Assembly

NJAC —see National Joint Action Committee (Trinidad)

NJM —see New JEWEL Movement (Grenada)

NKDP —see New Korea Democratic Party (South Korea)

NKP —see Communist Party of Norway

NLC —see New Liberal Club (Japan)

NLC —see Nigerian Labor Congress

NLF —see National Liberation Front (South Yemen)

NLF-B —see National Liberation Front-Bahrain

NLP —see National Liberal Party (Lebanon)

NNP —see New National Party (Grenada)

NOP —see National Order Party (Turkey)

NORAD —see North American Air Defense Command

NORAID —see Irish Northern Aid Committee

NP —see National Party (Australia)

NP —see National Party (South Africa)

NP —see Nationalist Party (Malta)

NPD —see National Democratic Party (West Germany)

NPF —see National Progressive Front (Iraq)

NPN —see National Party of Nigeria

NPP —see National People's Party (South Africa)

NPS —see Surinamese National Party

NRM —see National Resistance Movement (Uganda)

NRP —see Surinamese Religious Party (Israel)

NRP —see Nevis Reformation Party (St. Christopher)

NRP —see New Republic Party (South Africa)

NSC —see National Security Council (United States)

NSP —see National Salvation Party (Turkey)

NUC —see National Unity Committee (Turkey)

NUGS —see National Union of Ghananian Students

NUP —see National Unionist Party (Sudan)

NUPRG —see New Ulster Political Research Group (Northern Ireland)

NVA —see National People's Army (East Germany)

NVOI —see National Voice of Iran

NWU —see National Workers Union (Jamaica)

OADP —see Organization of Democratic and Popular Action (Morocco)

OAPEA —see Organization of Arab Petroleum Exporting Countries

OAS —see Organization of American States

OAU —see Organization for African Unity

OCA —see Organization for Communist Action (Lebanon)

OCED —see Organization for Economic Cooperation and Development

OGB —see Austrian Trade Union Federation

OIRA —see Official Irish Republican Army (Northern Ireland)

OLC —see Organization for the Liberation of the Congo (Zaire)

OMA —see Organization of Angolan Women

ONM —see National Organization of Veterans (Algeria)

ONR —see Organization for National Reconstruction (Trinidad & Tobago)

OPEC —see Organization of Petroleum Exporting Countries

OPM —see Military Political Organization (Paraguay)

ORPA —see Revolutionary Organization of the People in Arms (Guatemala)

OST —see Socialist Workers' Organization (Senegal)

OULG —see Unified Organization for the Liberation of Guinea

OUP —see Official Unionist Party (Northern Ireland)

OVP —see Austrian People's Party

OVSL —see Voltaic Organization of Free Unions (Burkina Faso)

OYAK —see Army Mutual Assistance Foundation (Turkey)

PA —see Action Party (Morocco)

PA —see People's Alliance (Iceland)

PAC —see Pan-African Congress

PACOREDO —see Communist Party of the Dominican Republic

PADIN —see National Integration Party (Peru)

PAF —see Peoples Armed Forces (Sudan)

PAI —see Marxist-Leninist African Independence Party (Senegal)

PAICV —see Africa Party for the Independence of Cape Verde

PAIGC —see African Party for the Independence of Guinea and Cape Verde (Cape Verde)

PAIM —see African Party for the Independence of the Masses (Senegal)

PAK —see Pan-Hellenic Liberation Movement (Greece)

PAL —see Progressive Alliance of Liberia

PALU —see Labor Party (Panama)

PAM —see People's Action Movement (St. Christopher)

PAME —see The Pan-Cyprian Renewal Front (Cyprus)

PAN —see National Action Party (Mexico)

PAP —see People's Action Party (Singapore)

PAP —see Peruvian Aprista Party (Peru)

PAPO —see Popular Action Party (Panama)

PAR —see Renovation Action Party (El Salvador)

PARM —see Authentic Party of the Mexican Revolution

PÅS —see Pan-Malaysian Islamic Party

PASOK —see Pan-Hellenic Socialist Movement (Greece)

PAVN —see People's Army of Vietnam

PBDS —see Savawak Dayak Party (Malaysia)

PC —see Progressive Conservative Party of Canada

PCB —see Brazilian Communist Party

PCC —see Colombian Communist Party (Colombia)

PCC —see Cuban Communist Party (Cuba)

PCD —see Democratic Conservative Party (Nicaragua)

PCD —see Dominican Communist Party (Dominican Republic)

PCDN —see Communist Party of Nicaragua

PCE —see Spanish Communist Party

PCELR —see Colorodo Party in Exile and Resistance (Paraguay)

PCF —see French Communist Party

PCI —see Italian Communist Party

PCM —see Communist Party of Mexico

PCN —see Party of National Reconciliation (El Salvador)

PCP —see Portugese Communist Party

PCR —see Communist Party of Reunion

PCR —see Romanian Communist Party

PCS —see Communist Party of San Marino

PCT —see Congolese Labor Party

PCT —see Tunisian Communist Party

PDA —see Democratic Party of Angola

PDB —see Party of German-speaking Belgians

PDC —see Christian Democratic Party (Brazil)

PDC —see Christian Democratic Party (Chile)

PDC —see Christian Democratic Party (El Salvador)

PDC —see Christian Democratic Party (Honduras)

PDC —see Christian Democratic Party (Panama)

PDC —see Christian Democratic Party (Paraguay)

PDC —see Christian Democratic Party (Peru)

PDCN —see Democratic Party of National Conciliation (Guatemala)

PDCS —see Christian Democratic Party of San Marino

PDG —see Democratic Party of Guinea

PDG —see Gabonese Democratic Party

PDI —see Democratic Independence Party (Morocco)

PDI —see Indonesian Democracy Party

PDIC —see Democratic Party of Ivory Coast

PDIUM —see Italian Democratic Party for United Monarchy

PDM —see Mauritanian People's Party

PDM —see Mexican Democratic Party

PDP —see Pakistan Democratic Party

PDP —see People's Democratic Party (Sudan)

PDP —see Popular Democratic Party (Spain)

PDPA —see People's Democratic Party of Afghanistan

PDS —see Democratic Social Party (Brazil)

PDS —see Senegalese Democratic Party

PDS —see Social Democratic Party (San Marino)

PDT —see Democratic Labor Party (Brazil)

PDUP —see Democratic Party of Proletarian Unity for Communism (Italy)

PDVA —see Party of Labor (Belgium)

PEKEMAS —see Malay National Organization of Singapore

PEPABRI —see Indonesian Armed Forces Veterans' Association

PFB —see Popular Front in Bahrain

PFL —see Liberal Front Party (Brazil)

PFLOAG —see Popular Front for the Liberation of Oman and the Arab Gulf

PFP —see Popular Front Party (Ghana)

PFP —see Progressive Federal Party (South Africa)

PGT —see Guatemalan Labor Party

PID —see Institutional Democratic Party (Guatemala)

PINU —see Party of Innovation and Unity (Honduras)

PIP —see Puerto Rican Independence Party

PIR —see Leftist Revolutionary Party (Bolivia)

PIRA —see Provisional Irish Republican Army (Northern Ireland)

PIT —see Independence and Labor Party (Senegal)

PKP —see Philippine Communist Party

PL —see Liberal Party (Honduras)

PL —see Liberal Party (Paraguay)

PL —see Liberation Party (Brazil)

PLAM —see People's Liberation Army of Malawi

PLAN —see People's Liberation Army of Namibia

PLD —see Dominican Liberation Party

PLI —see Independent Liberal Party (Nicaragua)

PLI —see Italian Liberal Party

PLM —see Progressive Labour Movement (Antigua & Barbuda)

PLN —see National Liberal Party (Panama)

PLN —see Partido Liberacion Nacional (Costa Rica)

PLO —see Palestine Liberation Organization

PLP —see People's Liberation Party (Senegal)

PLP —see Progressive Labour Party (Bahamas)

PLP —see Progressive Labour Party (St. Lucia)

PLP —see Progressive List for Peace (Israel)

PLR —see Liberal Radical Party (Paraguay)

PLRA —see Authentic Liberal Radical Party (Paraguay)

PLS —see Liberal Party of Switzerland

PLT —see Liberal Teeté Party (Paraguay)

PMDB —see Party of the Brazilian Democratic Movement

PMI —see Pro-Independence Movement (Puerto Rico)

PML —see Pakistan Muslim League (Pagara)

PMSD —see Mauritius Social Democratic Party

PMT —see Mexican Workers' Party

PN —see National Party (Honduras)

PNC —see People's National Congress (Guyana)

PND —see National Democratic Party (Morocco)

PNG —see National Gabonese Party

PNM —see People's National Movement (Trinidad & Tobago)

PNP —see National Pensiones' Party (Italy)

PNP —see National People's Party (Panama)

PNP —see New Progressive Party (Puerto Rico)

PNP —see Pakistan National Party

PNP —see People's National Party (Ghana)

PNP —see People's National Party (Jamaica)

PNQ —see Parti Nationaliste de Quebec (Canada)

PNR —see National Revolutionary Party (Mexico)

PNR —see National Renovator Party (Guatemala)

PNV —see Banque Nationalist Party (Spain)

PP —see Panamenista Party (Panama)

PP —see Party of People (Burundi)

PP —see Popular Party (Spain)

PP —see Populist Party (Turkey)

PP —see Progressive Party (Iceland)

PPA —see People's Political Alliance (Barbados)

PPBB —see United Bumiputra Party (Malaysia)

PPC —see Popular Christian Party (Peru)

PPD —see Popular Democratic Party (Puerto Rico)

PPD —see Popular Party of Djibouti

PPF —see Patriotic People's Front (Hungary)

PPM —see Popular Monarchist Party (Portugal)

PPN —see Niger Progressive Party

PPP —see Development Unity Party (Indonesia)

PPP —see Pakistan People's Party (Pakistan)

PPP —see People's Progress Party (Papua New Guinea)

PPP —see People's Progressive Party (Guyana)

PPP —see People's Progressive Party (St. Vincent)

PPP —see Perak Progressive Party (Malaysia)

PPP —see Progressive People's Party (Gambia)

PPR —see Radical Political Party (the Netherlands)

PPS —see Party of Progress and Socialism (Morocco)

PPS —see Popular Socialist Party (Mexico)

PPS —see Salvadoran Popular Party (El Salvador)

PPS —see Senegalese Popular Party

PPSC —see Popular Social Christian Party (Nicaragua)

PQ —see Parti Quebecois (Canada)

PQD —see Quisqueyan Democratic Party (Dominican Republic)

PR —see Radical Party (Italy)

PR —see Republican Party (France)

PR —see Republican Party (Panama)

PR —see Revolutionary Party (Guatemala)

PRA —see Authentic Revolutionary Party (Bolivia)

PRA —see Party of African Consolidation (Burkina Faso)

PRC —see People's Redemption Council (Liberia)

PRC —see People's Revolutionary Council (Kampuchea)

PRD —see Democratic Reformist Party (Spain)

PRD —see Democratic Renewal Party (Portugal)

PRD —see Democratic Revolutionary Party (Panama)

PRD —see Dominican Revolutionary Party (Dominican Republic)

PRF —see Revolutionary Febrerist Party (Paraguay)

PRI —see Institutional Revolutionary Party (Mexico)

PRI —see Italian Republican Party

PRIN —see Revolutionary Party of the Nationalist Left (Bolivia)

PRL —see Liberal Reform Party (Belgium)

PRN —see National Republican Party (Costa Rica)

PRON —see Patriotic Movement of National Rebirth (Poland)

PRP —see Popular Representation Party (Brazil)

PRP —see Popular Revolutionary Party (Zaire)

PRP —see Puerto Rico Renovation Party (Puerto Rico)

PRPB —see Popular Revolution Party of Benin

PRSC —see Christian Social Revolutionary Party (Dominican Republic)

PRT —see Republican Labor Party (Brazil)

PRT —see Revolutionary Party of Workers (Mexico)

PRT —see Workers' Revolutionary Party (Panama)

PRTC —see Central American Revolutionary Workers' Party (El Salvador)

PRVP —see Revolutionary Party of Democratic Unification (El Salvador)

PS —see Socialist Party (Senegal)

PS-1 —see Socialist Party-One (Bolivia)

PSA —see The Socialist Party of Andalucia (Spain)

PSB —see Belgium Socialist Party

PSB —see Brazilian Socialist Party

PSC —see Catalan Socialist Workers' Party (Spain)

PSC —see Christian Social Party (Belgium)

PSC —see Social Christian Party (Ecuador)

PSD —see Constitutional Socialist Party (Tunisia)

PSD —see Social Democratic Party (Bolivia)

PSD —see Social Democratic Party (Brazil)

PSD —see Social Democratic Party (Guatemala)

PSD —see Social Democratic Party (Portugal)

PSD —see Social Democratic Party (Madagascar)

PSd'A —see Sardinian Action Party (Italy)

PSDI —see Italian Social Democratic Party

PSDIS —see Independent Social Democratic Party of San Marino

PSF —see Provisional Sinn Fein (Northern Ireland)

PSI —see Italian Socialist Party

PSIUP —see Italian Socialist Party of Proletarian Unity

PSLI —see Workers' Socialist Party (Italy)

PSM —see Mauritius Socialist Party

PSN —see Nicaraguan Socialist Party

PSOE —see Spanish Socialist Workers' Party

PSP —see Pacifist Socialist Party (Netherlands)

PSP —see Portugese Socialist Party

PSP —see Progressive Socialist Party (Lebanon)

PSP —see Puerto Rican Socialist Party

PSP —see Sudanese Progressive Party

PSR —see Socialist Party of Reunion

PSS —see Senegalese Socialist Party

PSS —see Socialist Party of San Marino

PST —see Social Labor Party (Brazil)

PST —see Socialist Workers' Party (Mexico)

PST —see Socialist Workers' Party (Panama)

PSU —see Socialist Unity Party (San Marino)

PSU —see Unified Socialist Party (France)

PSUC —see Unified Socialist Party of Catalonia

PSUM —see Unified Socialist Party of Mexico

PT —see Party of the Workers (Brazil)

PTB —see Brazilian Labor Party

PTN —see National Labor Party (Brazil)

PUA —see Party of Anti-Communist Unification (Guatemala)

PUN —see Partido Union Nacional (Costa Rica)

PUNT —see National Workers' Party (Equatorial Guinea)

PUP —see People's United Party (Belize)

PURS —see United Party of the Socialist Revolution (Cuba)

PUSC —see Partido Union Social Cristiana (Costa Rica)

PVDA —see Labor Party (the Netherlands)

PVK —see Confederation of Small Farmers (Finland)

PVV —see Freedom and Progress Party (Belgium)

PWP —see Pakistan Workers' Party

PWP —see Peasants' and Workers' Party (India)

PZKO —see Polish Cultural and Adult Education Union

PZPR —see Polish United Workers Party

RDA —see African Democratic Rally (Ivory Coast)

RDCLE —see Democratic Group for the Liberation of Equatcrial Guinea

RDPP —see Social Democratic Populist Party (Turkey)

RENAMO —see Mozambique National Resistance

RI —see Independent Republicans (France)

RN —see National Resistance (El Salvador)

RND —see National Democratic Assembly (Senegal)

RNI —see National Grouping of Independents (Morocco)

ROC —see Reassembly of Communist Officers (Burkina Faso)

RPF —see Rally of the French People

RPF —see Reformatoric Political Federation (the Netherlands)

RPNP —see Republican Peasants' National Party (Turkey)

RPP —see People's Rally for Progress (Djibouti)

RPP —see Republican People's Party (Turkey)

RPR —see Gaullist Rally (Reunion)

RPT —see Assembly of Togolese People

RRP —see Reliance Party (Turkey)

RSDLP —see Russian Social Democratic Labor Party (Soviet Union)

RSS —see Rashtriya Swayamsevak Sangh (India)

RV —see Radical Liberals (Denmark)

RV —see Red Electoral Alliance (Norway)

RVC —see Royal Ulster Constabulary (Northern Ireland)

RW —see Walloon Rally (Belgium)

SAARC —see South Asian Association for Regional Cooperation

SAC —see Civic Action Service (France)

SACC —see South African Council of Churches

SADCC —see Southern African Development Coordination Conference

SADF —see South African Defense Force (Namibia)

SADR —see Saharan Arab Democratic Republic

SAF —see Federation of Swedish Employees

SAK —see Confederation of Finnish Trade Unions

SALA —see Afghan People's Liberation Organization

SALF —see Somali Abo Liberation Front (Ethiopia)

SAP —see Social Action Party (Thailand)

SAP —see Social Democratic Party (Sweden)

SAWPY —*see* Socialist Alliance of the Working People of Yugoslavia

SBPF —*see* Sind-Baluch-Palchtoon Front (Pakistan)

SD —*see* Democratic Party (Poland)

SD —*see* Social Democrats (Denmark)

SDA —*see* Social Democratic Alliance (Ireland)

SDF —*see* Social Democratic Front (Ghana)

SDI —*see* Strategic Defense Initiative

SDLP —*see* Social Democratic and Labour Party (Northern Ireland)

SDP —*see* Finnish Social Democratic Party (Finland)

SDP —*see* Seychelles Democratic Party

SDP —*see* Social Democratic Party (Bahamas)

SDP —*see* Social Democratic Party (Iceland)

SDP —*see* Social Democratic Party (Philippines)

SDP —*see* Social Democratic Party (United Kingdom)

SDPP —*see* Social Democrat Populist Party (Turkey)

SED —*see* Socialist Unity Party (East Germany)

SED —*see* Socialist Union Party (West Germany)

SEW —*see* Socialist Unity Party of West Berlin (West Germany)

SF —*see* Socialist People's Party (Denmark)

SFIO —*see* French Section of the Workers' International

SGP —*see* State Reform Party (the Netherlands)

SI —*see* Federation of Swedish Industry

SIAD —*see* Turkish Industrialists' and Businessmen's Association

SJO —*see* Austrian Socialist Youth

SKDL —*see* Finnish People's Democratic League

SKP —*see* Finnish Communist Party

SKP —*see* Social Democratic Party (Luxembourg)

SKP —*see* Swedish Communist Party

SLA —*see* South Lebanon Army

SLFP —*see* Sri Lanka Freedom Party

SLOMR —*see* Free Trade Union of the Working People of Romania

SLP —*see* St. Lucia Party

SLPP —*see* Sierra Leone People's Party

SNAP —*see* Sarawak National Party (Malaysia)

SNE —*see* National Education Union (Morocco)

SNM —*see* Somali National Movement

SNP —*see* Scottish National Party (United Kingdom)

SOBSI —*see* All-Indonesian Central of Labor Organizations

SODEP —*see* Social Democracy Party (Turkey)

SOK —*see* Central Association of Finnish Cooperatives

SOSAF —*see* Somali Salvation Front

SP —*see* Center Party (Norway)

SPD —*see* Social Democratic Party (West Germany)

SPD —*see* Socialist Party (East Germany)

SPLA —*see* Saharawi People's Liberation Army (SADR)

SPLA —*see* Sudan People's Liberation Army

SPLM —*see* Sudan People's Liberation Movement

SPO —*see* Socialist Party of Austria

SPPF —*see* Seychelles People's Progressive Front

SPS —*see* Social Democratic Party of Switzerland

SPUP —*see* Seychelles People's United Party

SSJ —*see* Confederation of Trade Unions (Yugoslavia)

SSL —*see* Party of Freedom (Czechoslovakia)

SSM —*see* Socialist Youth Union (Czechoslovakia)

SSNP —*see* Syrian Socialist Nationalistic Party

SSOJ —*see* League of Socialist Youth (Yugoslavia)

SSR —*see* Slovak Socialist Republic (Czechoslovakia)

SSRNJ —*see* Socialist Alliance (Yugoslavia)

SSRP —*see* Somali Socialist Revolutionary Party

SSU —*see* Sudan Socialist Union

STV —*see* Single Transferable Vote

SUBNOR —*see* Federation of Veterans' Associations (Yugoslavia)

SUDES —*see* Democratic Syndicate of Senegalese Teachers

SUPP —*see* Sarawak United People's Party (Malaysia)

SV —*see* Socialist Left Party (Norway)

SVLP —*see* St. Vincent Labour Party

SVP —*see* South Tyrol People's Party (Italy)

SVP —*see* Swiss People's Party

SWANN —*see* South West Africa National Union (Namibia)

SWAPO —*see* South West Africa People's Organization (Namibia)

TAA —*see* Tanganyikan African Association (Tanzania)

TAMI —*see* Movement for Jewish Tradition (Israel)

TANU —*see* Tanganyikan African National Union (Tanzania)

TCFS —*see* Turkish Cypriot Federated State (Cyprus)

TFCS —*see* Turkish Federated State of Cyprus

TFP —*see* Third Force Party (Ghana)

TKP —*see* Communal Liberation Party (Cyprus)

TLP —*see* Turkish Labor Party

TPA —*see* Tribunales Populares Anti-Somocistas (Nicaragua)

TPSL —*see* Social Democratic League of Workers and Small Farmers (Finland)

TVC —*see* Trade Union Congress (Bahamas)

TVC —*see* Trade Union Congress (Ghana)

TULF —*see* Tamil United Liberation Front (Sri Lanka)

TUP —*see* Turkish Unity Party

UAE —*see* United Arab Emirates

UAG —*see* Union Agricola Cartagenesa (Costa Rica)

UBP —*see* National Unity Party (Cyprus)

UBP —*see* United Bahamian Party

UC —*see* Cameroon Union

UC —*see* Constitutional Union (Morocco)

UCD —*see* Union of the Democratic Center (Spain)

UCN —*see* National Civic Union (Dominican Republic)

UCN —*see* Union of the National Center (Guatemala)

UCR —*see* Radical Civic Union (Argentina)

UCRI —*see* Intransigent Radical Civic Union (Argentina)

UCRP —*see* People's Radical Civic Union (Argentina)

UCS —*see* Union of Salvadoran Peasants

UDA —*see* Ulster Defense Association (Northern Ireland)

UDCV —*see* Democratic Union of Cape Verde

UDEAC —*see* Central African Economic and Customs Union

UDECMA —*see* Union of Christian Democrats (Madagascar)

UDENAMO —*see* National Democratic Union of Mozambique

UDF —*see* Giscardist Union for French Democracy (Reunion)

UDF —*see* Union for French Democracy

UDF —*see* United Democratic Front (South Africa)

UDLP —*see* United Dominica Labour Party

UDN —*see* National Democratic Union (Brazil)

UDN —*see* National Democratic Union (El Salvador)

UDP —*see* Democratic Union for Peace (Chad)

UDP —*see* Popular Democratic Union (Bolivia)

UDP —*see* Union for Popular Democracy (Senegal)

UDP —*see* United Democratic Party (Belize)

UDPM —*see* Democratic Union of the Malian People

UDPS —*see* Union for Democracy and Social Progress (Zaire)

UDR —*see* Ulster Defense Regiment (Northern Ireland)

UDRT/RAD —*see* Democratic Union for the Respect of Labor (Belgium)

UDSG —*see* Gabonese Democratic and Social Union

UDV/RDA —*see* Democratic Voltaic Union/Democratic African Rally (Burkina Faso)

UEDS —*see* Union of Democratic Socialist Left (Portugal)

UF —*see* United Force (Guyana)

UFPDG —*see* Women's Union of the Gabonese Democratic Party

UGEMA —*see* General Union of Algerian Muslim Students

UGESARIO —*see* General Union of Students of Sagvia el Hamra and Rio de Oro (SADR)

UGT —*see* General Union of Workers (Spain)

UGTA —*see* General Union of Algerian Workers

UGTD —*see* General Union of Dominican Workers

UGTS —*see* General Union of Saharawi Workers (SADR)

UGTT —*see* General Union of Tunisian Workers

UIL —*see* Italian Union of Labor

UJC —*see* Communist Youth Union (Cuba)

UJPDG —*see* Young People's Union of the Gabonese Democratic Party

UL —*see* Liberal Union (Spain)

ULC —*see* Union of the Communist Struggle (Burkina Faso)

ULF —*see* United Labour Front (Trinidad & Tobago)

ULL —*see* Union of Liberals and Leftists (Ireland)

UMNO —*see* United Malays National Organization

UMOA —*see* West African Monetary Union

UMP —*see* Union of Moderate Parties (Vanuatu)

UMT —*see* Moroccan Union of Labor

UN —*see* Union Nationale (Canada)

UNAG —*see* National Union of Farmers and Ranchers (Nicaragua)

UNAMI —*see* National African Union of Independent Mozambique

UNC —*see* National Union of Peasants (Honduras)

UNC —*see* Uganda National Congress

UNC —*see* United National Convention (Ghana)

UND —*see* National and Democratic Union (Monaco)

UND —*see* National Democratic Union (Chad)

UNDC —*see* National Union for Democratic Comoros

UNDD —*see* National Union for the Defense of Democracy (Burkina Faso)

UNED —*see* National Union of Democratic Students (Morocco)

UNEEM —*see* National Union of Students and Pupils (Mali)

UNEM —*see* National Union of Moroccan Students

UNFA —*see* National Union of Algerian Women

UNFP —*see* National Union of Popular Forces (Morocco)

UNI —*see* National Union for Independence (Djibouti)

UNIDO —*see* United Democratic Organization (Philippines)

UNIDO —*see* United Democratic Opposition (formerly) (Philippines)

UNIFIL —*see* United Nations Interim Force in Lebanon

UNIP —*see* United National Independence Party (Zambia)

UNIR —*see* National Union for Independence and Revolution (Chad)

UNITA —*see* National Union for the Total Independence of Angola

UNJM —*see* National Union of Mali Youth

UNMS —*see* National Union of Saharawi Women (SADR)

UNO —*see* National Opposition Union (Colombia)

UNO —*see* National Opposition Union (El Salvador)

UNP —*see* United National Party (Sri Lanka)

UNPA —*see* National Union of Algerian Peasants

UNS —*see* Sinarquista National Union (Mexico)

UNTA —*see* National Union of Angolan Workers

UNTG —*see* National Union of Workers of Guinea

UNTM —*see* National Union of Malian Workers

UNTS —*see* National Union of Senegalese Workers

UNTZA —*see* National Unions of Zairian Workers

UP —*see* United Party (Gambia)

UP —*see* United Party (Liberia)

UP —*see* United Party (South Africa)

UPA —*see* Union of the People of Angola

UPANG —*see* Patriotic Anti-Neocolonial Union of Guinea

UPC —*see* Union of Cameroon Populations

UPC —*see* Union for Commorian Progress

UPC —*see* Uganda People's Congress

UPD —*see* Popular Democratic Unity (El Salvador)

UPG —*see* Guinean People's Union

UPM —*see* Uganda Patriotic Movement

UPM —*see* United People's Movement (Antigua and Barbuda)

UPM —*see* United People's Movement (St. Vincent)

UPN —*see* Unity Party of Nigeria

UPNI —*see* Unionist Party of Northern Ireland

UPO-NP —*see* Unified Political Organization-National Front (South Yemen)

UPP —*see* United People's Party (Liberia)

UPP —*see* United Progressive Party (Zambia)

UPPE —*see* Union of the Spanish People

UPRONA —*see* National Progress and Unity Party (Burundi)

UPS —*see* Senegalese Progressive Union

UPU —*see* Uganda People's Union

UPUP —*see* Ulster Progressive Unionist Party (Northern Ireland)

UPV —*see* Voltaic Progressive Union (Burkina Faso)

USC —*see* Ulster Special Constabulary (Northern Ireland)

USFP —*see* Socialist Union of Popular Forces (Morocco)

USP —*see* United Socialist Party (Iceland)

US-RDA —*see* Sudanese Union-Democratic African Rally

UTC —*see* Union of Colombian Workers

UTC —*see* Union of Communist Youth (Romania)

UTLS —*see* Union of Free Senegalese Workers

UTM —*see* Mauritanian Workers' Union

UUP —*see* Ulster Unionist Party (Northern Ireland)

UUUC —*see* United Ulster Unionist Council (Northern Ireland)

UWP —*see* United Workers' Party (St. Lucia)

V —*see* Liberals (Denmark)

VCP —*see* Vietnam Communist Party

VHP —*see* Progressive Reform Party (Suriname)

VLBL —*see* Flemish Bloc (Belgium)

VP —*see* Vana'aku Pati (Vanuatu)

VPK —*see* Left Party Communists (Sweden)

VS —*see* Left Socialists (Denmark)

VSI —*see* Federation of Employers (Iceland)

VU —*see* Fatherland Union (Liechtenstein)

VVD —*see* People's Party for Freedom and Democracy (the Netherlands)

WA —*see* Women's Alliance (Iceland)

WCCP —*see* Western Canada Concept Party

WCPDM —*see* Women's Organization of the Cameroon People's Democratic Movement

WPA —*see* Working People's Alliance (Guyana)

WPE —*see* Workers' Party of Ethiopia

WPJ —*see* Workers' Party of Jamaica

WPRC —*see* Workers' Party Republican Clubs (Northern Ireland)

WSLF —*see* Western Somali Liberation Front (Ethiopia)

YCPDM —*see* Youth Organization of the Cameroon People's Democratic Movement

YSP —*see* Yemen Socialist Party

ZANC —*see* Zambian African National Congress

ZANU —*see* Zimbabwe African National Union

ZAPU —*see* Zimbabwe African People's Union

ZCTV —*see* Zambia Congress of Trade Unions

ZIMCO —*see* Government Holding Company (Zambia)

ZRC —*see* Zanzibar Revolutionary Council (Tanzania)

ZSL —*see* United Peasant Party (Poland)